The PC Multimedia & Web Handbook

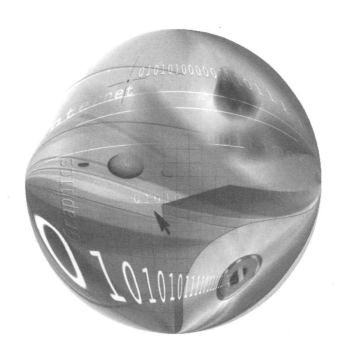

Technology

and

Techniques

By David Dick

Dumbreck Publishing

The P.C. Multimedia & Web Handbook
© 2004 by Dumbreck Publishing
ISBN 0-95417112-8

All brand names and product names mentioned in this book are trademarks or registered trademarks of their respective companies.

The book cover was designed by Kenny Cullen (kenny.cullen@virgin.net)

This publication is not covered by the CLA Licence.

Printed and bound in Great Britain by Antony Rowe Ltd., Chippenham, Wiltshire

Introduction

*M*ultimedia - where art meets technology

When multimedia was first beginning to become widely known, it was touted as the *"next big thing"* by most pundits. Unfortunately, despite the best efforts of Moore's Law, the technology was slow to catch up with the expectations of industry experts. For years, multimedia lay in the long grass, relegated to shovelware CD's full of sound, graphics and video clips loosely tied together by a hastily put together interface; or confined to between-levels video clips in computer games. Even then, of course, there was occasional use of multimedia in a meaningful sense; using graphics and sound clips as part of a presentation has long been common practice. But the predicted media revolution was slow to take place.

Recent years, though, have seen the home and office computer's capabilities reach the level where multimedia authoring is at last within reach of even the occasional computer user. Digital cameras are now as common as traditional style cameras, if not more so. Digital video, which had long been the cause of most of the bottlenecks, is now smooth enough for realistic use on even a modestly specified computer.

In short, the 'revolution' was a slow-burning one, and as such it may have passed by almost unnoticed by some. That fact does not, of course, detract from the importance of multimedia in today's computing and business worlds. They say a picture is worth a thousand words, and if that is true, then imagine how many words an interactive, moving picture is worth, when accompanied by sound effects, music, and animations.

We hope and believe that this book will help readers harness the potential of multimedia for whatever projects they may be undertaking. The revolution is not over yet, but it is certainly a good time for any computer user to learn how to unlock the potential of multimedia.

David Dick

Contents

Multimedia Basics

Multimedia - where art meets technology

There are many definitions of the term *'multimedia'*.   At its simplest it refers to using multiple forms of media.   In practice, it is the convergence of graphics, audio, video, animation, and programming skills with imaginative and creative skills.

Multimedia is different from all communication mediums that have gone before.   At a visit to the cinema, the material is watched as a continuous sequence; the film has a start and a finish and the viewer watches the material in the order that the filmmakers decided.   Watching television is similar.   Although the viewer can flick channels, the content of any one channel is fixed and the order of the material is printed in television schedules in newspapers.   Even interactive television provides only minor diversions from the main show.   Similarly, books and videotapes are designed for sequential use.   Audiocassettes, audio CDs and magazines are only slightly better, in that the user can jump between tracks or flick between pages, providing some control over the content.

Multimedia, on the other hand, is the combination of all of the above.   It contains audio, video, graphics, animations, video and text - and it is all under the control of the user.

Multimedia is not just the repackaging of existing material.   Early multimedia CD-ROMs made this mistake and used the large storage space of CD-ROM disks to store the entire text of books to CD, or place photographic albums on CD, and such.   While they undoubtedly help archive material, they were not true multimedia products.   They missed out on the true value of multimedia authoring.

A distinguishing feature of multimedia is the ability of the user to <u>interact</u> with the media.   This may be through choosing menu options or clicking the mouse on icons or areas of the screen.   The vast amounts of data are usually linked through hypertext systems or authoring packages. This is more correctly *'hypermedia'*, since it uses both multiple media elements <u>and</u> the ability to jump around the material. Of course, it is possible to create a multimedia production without any interactivity (e.g. a single TV advert probably contains video, audio, text and animation). However, the general term multimedia has come to replace the more accurate term hypermedia in most areas.

Multimedia should use the various types of screen output to more effectively communicate with the user or viewer. The kinds of facilities expected in a final multimedia package include:

- still graphic images
- animated graphics
- moving video images
- digitised sound/music
- synthesised sound/music
- plain text
- digitised photographs

This interaction is the key to the success of a multimedia product.   The experts vary slightly, but generally agree that we recall 10% of what we read, 20% of what we see and 30% of what we both see and hear.   However, because we learn more from taking part in active learning, we recall a massive 70% of what we see, hear and do.   Multimedia packages allow the user to control the viewing process and decide what they want to see/do, how long they want to see/do it and what they want to see/do next.

Applications for multimedia

New uses are constantly being found for multimedia.   The term 'REES' (Reference, Education, Entertainment Service) is occasionally used to group four of the most common multimedia applications, but these can be further refined into various subcategories.   There are also other uses that do not easily fall into the REES definition.   The main uses for multimedia are as follows:

Training

Training is concerned with the acquisition of specific skills, of the mind or the hand.   Examples are learning a foreign language or playing the guitar.   Boeing use multimedia material to train their ground personnel. CBT (Computer Based Training) means that the knowledge of lecturer/teacher/trainer/instructor can be embedded into a training package and used anywhere at any time.

Education

Education is *'knowledge based'*; specific skills may not flow from the absorption of this knowledge.   The theories of evolution, politics, religion, pure science, mathematics, etc. may be learned for their own sake rather than to be practised.   The Educational Software & CD-ROM Yearbook is an example of a Computer Aided Learning (CAL) package that is jam-packed with details of 1000 different educational CD-ROMs on subjects such as history, science, geography, art and architecture, economics and media studies, etc.

Distance learning

Distance learning assumes that the student is remote from the educational establishment. This could be for any of a variety of reasons, such as disability, family commitments, working overseas, shift working, etc.   Those undertaking study communicate via downloading material, uploading exercises and carrying on e-mail dialogues with support lecturers.   Students often use educational CDs where a teacher/lecturer is present to answer specific questions or to clear up any vagueness in the application's presentation.   This immediate help is less available with distance learning students and the multimedia material has to reflect this.   It must anticipate possible student problems, provide adequate help and guided support.   The package should have facilities for student self-assessment, to reinforce students in their learning.   Many establishments have, or are preparing, distance learning multimedia-based courses.

Edutainment

Edutainment combines elements of education and entertainment in a manner that imparts knowledge to a user while wrapping the material up as an entertaining experience.   Packages featuring the adventures of Peter Rabbit or Barney Bear provide children with animated stories.   The text of the story is displayed on screen and each word is highlighted as the story is read out.   Children can activate parts of the screen and can control the flow of the story by mouse clicks.   Serious learning is taking place in conjunction with the attractive activities.   Adult edutainment equivalents are CDs with conducted tours of *'The Louvre'*, investigating *'Great Artists'* and exploring *'The Ultimate Human Body'*.

Entertainment

These are solely aimed at providing fun with no attempt at any serious education, although in some packages a little general knowledge may be picked up along the way.   Applications include multimedia databases on films and music, interactive music CDs and the guide to *'Wines, Spirits and Beers'*.   Other well-known applications of multimedia are the effects produced in films such as *'Toy Story'*, *'Monsters Inc'* and the *'Jurassic Park'* series of films.   Although it may be stretching the definition slightly, almost all computer games today incorporate multimedia content.   In most cases these are non-interactive cut-scenes in between parts of the game, but there are a few whose gameplay centres around the video or other media found therein.

Simulation

Simulation provides a computer replica of a living or supposed situation and there are applications for use in both entertainment and industry.   Leisure applications cover both the real world (e.g. flight simulators) and the imagined world (e.g. fighting the aliens on the planet Zog).   Industry has many serious uses for simulations in situations where training staff can be hazardous both to the trainees and to real equipment.   Typical applications are training French train drivers using simulations of railway routes and British firefighters learning to handle dangerous situations.   Users can learn from their mistakes without any harm being done.

Marketing

Marketing covers the promotion of both opinions and products; it is aimed at altering the views and preferences of those who use the application.   After viewing the application, users are hoped to desire certain products, holiday at a particular location, study at a particular university, etc.   Example marketing applications are the *'virtual kitchens'* demonstrated by Matsushita, unattended public information displays (known as kiosks) promoting clothes or holidays, and CD-ROM travel guides covering from the *'AA Days Out in Britain and Ireland'* to *'Travel Mexico'* and *'Voyage in Spain'*.

Presentations

This is a specific form of marketing where the salesperson uses a multimedia presentation to enhance the effect of his/her delivery.   The material is projected on to screens or video walls.   Although these presentations may be interactive in the sense that the person delivering the presentation may control the course the presentation takes, these are not directly interactive with the audience.

Interactive Presentations

Although it borrows the name of a presentation, this type of multimedia product is actually more like a one-on-one demonstration.   This is due to the interactive element – it is very difficult to create multimedia presentations that interact with multiple users at the same time.

Home shopping

This also overlaps with marketing activities.   While marketing promotes the demand for the product, home shopping provides the convenience to place the order.   A growing number of product catalogues are provided on CD or many more are available on the World Wide Web.   Users can log into a company's web site and use the search facilities to bring up details of desired products.   The user can read the text descriptions and view the images.   The product range is huge covering from computers to books and clothes. The user can instantly place an order and can pay with a credit card.

Reference

Reference material is readily available in book format but multimedia versions provide many extra facilities such as very quick subject searching and cross-referencing, the use of animations to aid explanations and sound and video clips of famous people and events.   Examples of reference material are BOOKBANK (British books in print), specifications, dictionaries (e.g. the Oxford Compendium), the Guinness Book of Records and a range of impressive annually updated multimedia encyclopaedias (e.g. Compton's, Grolier, Hutchinson, Microsoft and Britannica).   Archiving of reference material is another popular use, where the ability to quickly move around material and have easy search facilities provides added value.   This allows for huge databases of material such as research results, specifications, legal documents, etc.   These may include diagrams, personal signatures, scanned documents and even voiceprints.   There is currently a huge growth in electronic publishing in the shape of news, books, technical manuals, public information, and promotional brochures.

Research

There have been database retrieval systems developed for aid in research in certain fields such as image processing and sound recognition. While these are specialised fields, they are nonetheless among the more cutting-edge applications of multimedia.

Delivery methods

The finished multimedia products are supplied to the user in a number of different formats. Multimedia is often spoken of in the same breath as CD-ROM or DVD. However the CD-ROM is not always used for multimedia purposes, and multimedia does not necessarily require the use of a CD-ROM or DVD.

It is true that projects that are rich in video and photographic content requires lots of storage space and these are often best met by the capacity offered by CD-ROM. However, much effort has been put into making multimedia suitable for Internet distribution and the relative merits of these and other methods are discussed below.

The delivery of multimedia products can be either offline or online. The offline version is usually self-contained. All the project's elements are included on the CD-ROM or within the kiosk's hard disk. The online version allows access to the material over local area networks, wide area networks or the Internet.

CD-ROM and DVD features

The CD (Compact Disk) and DVD (Digital Versatile Disk) are both optical technologies, explained fully in the *'CD Productions'* chapter, and as such they must be treated properly. Avoid touching the reflective surface(s) of the disk, and handle CDs or DVDs by the edges. Both CDs and DVDs are 4.5 inch disks, and although a DVD drive can read a CD, the reverse is not true.

- Works on any multimedia PC, with predictable results. Many users now also have DVD drives.
- Available to PC users who have no Internet connection.
- Stores large amounts of information in a variety of formats (i.e. text, video, sound, animation).
- Allows fast user access.
- No ongoing costs to the user, after purchase, to access the information.
- Expensive for the producer to update regularly, due to production costs.
- Contents are always available, undisturbed by telephone breakdown, busy periods, etc.

Internet features

- Can be potentially accessed by a huge audience.
- Provides two-way traffic (i.e. e-mail, form-filling, voting).
- The contents are dynamic - i.e. they are easily updated (daily, hourly, instantly as necessary).
- Poses potential problems of security. The site can be hacked into and the data can be altered.
- Slow for supplying large graphics and video to users, even though streaming techniques help to reduce the problem.
- A huge web site is required to store the same amount of data as a CD-ROM.
- Providers are charged by bandwidth usage. The more popular the site, the more the Internet provider charges the web site owner, (unless they have their own equally expensive web server).
- Many users will incur telephone charges or standing charges every time they access the material.
- Provides additional commercial opportunities (e.g. credit card transactions, auctions, gathering mailing lists, etc).

Some CD-ROM products now have web links, so that the viewer can get his/her modem to dial up a specific web site and fetch current data. This allows, for example, educational institutions to produce CD-ROMs that can be updated less regularly, since the users can fetch any new material via the institution's web site. Similarly, a manufacturer can create a CD-ROM catalogue of products and customers can click a hyperlink to fetch the current pricing and availability.

Intranet features

An intranet is a local area network serving a single organisation, with its own web server. The only computers connected to the intranet are the ones used by the company's employees and the multimedia content stored on the web server is only available to this limited set of users. There is no connection to the outside world and no one else can access the web server. It is like the Internet in miniature. Companies can use intranets to store and distribute company training and it also becoming more popular in educational establishments.

Kiosk features

These are standalone applications designed for stores, museums, trade fairs, information points, etc. The computer equipment is housed in a sealed unit and interacts with the public through its monitor and input device (usually a touch sensitive screen). The project is stored on hard disks and is potentially available 24-hours, 7 days a week.

Kiosks typically provide material in the form of an interactive presentation, although a few of the more basic types use simple loops of audio and video. Kiosk applications could be as simple as a PowerPoint demonstration, with simple choices presented to the user. It could be an in-depth system for locating information within a remote information source, such as an employment database; or it could even incorporate specialist hardware such as a card reader to enable shoppers to browse, order, or even buy products.   Thus, there is a degree of overlap between interactive information kiosk applications, and point-of-sale terminals.

Electronic presentations

The material is usually stored on a laptop computer and displayed via a projector on to a screen.   With large presentations, extra bright projectors, rear projectors or video walls may be used.

The origins of multimedia

Current multimedia systems have their roots in the development of interactive video, CBT (computer based training) and hypertext systems and this page examines these pioneering systems.

Interactive video

The system comprised a TV monitor and a videodisk player (usually the Philips laservision player which used larger versions of our current CD-ROM disks).   The player had a normal TV output and had a computer or microprocessor built in.   The disks were larger than modern CD disks and contained previously recorded video sequences that could be viewed by choosing options from the keyboard.   Commercial uses included training bank staff and creating staff training manuals on aircraft maintenance and repair.   Some used an actions/consequences approach, where a video displayed an activity and the play was suspended while the user (often in groups) considered and choose from a selection of responses. The chosen response ran another video clip that displayed the consequences resulting from the selection.   This method was also adopted for early arcade video games. These were radical applications in the early 1980's and the programs were very expensive to produce.   The user content was mostly video sequences linked together by text and user responses, reflecting the state of technology at that stage.   Nevertheless, these elements are in common use in modern multimedia applications.

CBT/CAL

With the growing popularity of desktop PCs, the drive towards interactive systems moved to centre round the computer and its programs.   This removed the requirement for specialist apparatus and early CAL/CBT was distributed on ordinary floppy disks. The system provided new levels of user support.   Computer Based Training (CBT) developed specific skills (e.g. typing tutors) while Computer Aided Learning (CAL) explored ideas (e.g. science and philosophy).   Both applications provided user options and stored user responses in variables.   In this way, a user's progress was monitored and appropriate advice given.   Users could be given assessments and told their scores.   Users could be given a certain number of attempts at a multi-choice question.   The support given for a wrong answer could depend on what incorrect choice was entered and the previous experience of the user as judged by previous responses.

CBT/CAL provided an *'intelligent'* system which users enjoyed as they had more control over the learning experience.   They could work at their own pace, reviewing a page, changing direction and stopping for a break. Early applications tended to have a linear format within each lesson and they lacked the visual impact of interactive video.   Again, most of the elements of CBT can be found in current multimedia systems and specially on the Internet.

Hypertext

Both interactive video and CBT tended to require the user to follow a fixed training pattern with clear end objectives.   Options were allowed but they were temporary detours from the main path to be treaded by the user. Although this had distinct advantages in certain situations, and is still implemented in some packages today, it did not follow the way humans think and approach issues.   Few people learn a subject by systematically working through a linear path of material.   Only fiction is read linearly.   People learn by association; having grasped a concept it leads them to one or more linked concepts.   For example, reading a car repair manual on fixing carburettors may inspire a reader to find out more about how the ignition systems works, what a catalytic converter is, or how to use a double-grommeted nut wrench.   Hypertext builds a system that supports that way of thinking.   Users can leave a particular subject area and explore something linked - or completely different; they can choose to return to the previous theme or can move onwards or sideways if they wish.   Each person will use the system in a different way.

Users move from one subject to another by selecting menu options or by clicking the mouse on a highlighted word (a hypertext link) or on a particular area of the screen (a hotspot).   Early systems were solely text based and graphical interfaces followed later.   The best definition of hypertext is that it:

> *"produces large, complex, richly connected and*
> *cross-referenced bodies of information"*

Hypertext is widely implemented in Windows applications' help systems and this *'navigation'* process is one of the cornerstones of multimedia packages.   The largest example of hypertext is, of course, the World Wide Web.

Hypertext's benefits include good browsing abilities, rapid navigation, the ability to annotate results and the ability to save results and queries for later use.

Reported problems with hypertext are disorientation (it is easier to get lost than when page-hopping with a printed book) and *'cognitive overhead'* (a large variety of options stuns the brain's ability to easily consider alternatives).

The multimedia machine

Most computers are capable of playing multimedia titles but the equipment for creating high-end multimedia products requires more power and more hardware.

The authoring computer

The requirements for computers that create multimedia products are more demanding than those used for simply playing multimedia. It is certainly possible to create basic multimedia projects with the simplest of computer systems, using little or no specialised hardware. A simple presentation involving text, graphics and limited animation, can be created on a basic computer without any extra hardware add-ons whatsoever. Of course, the more sophisticated presentations use sound clips, video sequences, complex animations, etc. and therefore require a high performance machine and special equipment to capture video, edit video, create multi-track sound, and so on.

The photograph shows the likely hardware requirements for a single computer used for producing multimedia products. In a large multimedia company, there will be many machines and they will share resources through networking. One computer may be equipped to carry out all the sound tasks of the project, while another is used for video editing, another for scanning and graphics creation, another for planning and managing the project, and so on.

Description of hardware components

Computer	The main processing chip (the CPU) should run as fast as possible, preferably at least 2GHz. This is the main engine of the whole process and a slow CPU will increase the time taken to complete processor-intensive tasks such as video editing and graphics rendering.
Monitor(s)	A large monitor size, 19" or preferably 21" or even greater, is required to get the best from some software packages. Programs such as Director, Premiere or PhotoShop use many pop-up windows and these will obscure some of the main working area (i.e. the main window where the objects and images are being worked on). Having more screen space allows an uncluttered layout. The photograph shows two monitors in use. The main monitor is often used for the main activities while the second monitor is used display the various toolbars. The second monitor could also be used to run a second application. The contents can then be cut from one application and pasted into the other application. Or the second application could be a word processor, so that the developer can write notes while working, or read test specifications while testing an application. This technique requires two graphics cards, one for each monitor, and this is easily set up in Windows 98 onwards.
Memory	The memory stores parts of the multimedia software, as well as the project being worked on. Increasing the amount of memory in the computer allows more application components and project elements to be instantly available from memory, thus speeding up processing. While 64MB is a tolerable amount, 256MB is a more realistic minimum and 512MB is preferable.
CD-ROM and/or DVD-ROM player	Required to install applications, copy over files from clip art collections, etc. Since the player is only being used for occasional file transfers, its specification need not be demanding.

CD writer or DVD writer	Used to *'burn'* (i.e. record) CD or DVD copies of the project on to Recordable CD or DVD disks. In a commercial setting, these may be copies for internal testing, or may be the master copy used for creating the glass master for mass production. Since these are generally one-offs, there is little real need for a particularly fast writing speed.
Hard Disks	Multimedia files are huge, with video clips requiring up to 2GB of storage each. There can never be too much disk storage space. A 40GB hard drive is realistically the minimum size and larger drives are preferable, with several drives providing more capacity and flexibility. For video work, in particular, the drives need to be fast and of consistent performance. UDMA-100 drives are a minimum, with SCSI or SATA types being preferable.
Video Capture System	The capture electronics usually fits inside the computer but may also use an external box that connects to the computer (e.g. to the USB port or to a special capture card). The output from a camcorder is connected to the system and it converts it into a video file for integration into a multimedia project. The poorest systems accept VHS connections, the middle range use S-VHS connections and the recommended cards use a digital interface (known as IEEE 1394 or *'FireWire'*). The first two connectors accept output from normal analogue camcorders and/or VCRs, while FireWire cards have to be fed by a digital source. The photograph shows a digital camcorder connected to the computer's FireWire socket.
Digital Camera Reader	Digital cameras capture photographs in computer format and have to be copied from the camera on to the computer's hard disk. Many methods are used. Some carry out the file transfers using the computer's serial port, while most connect to the USB port. Many cameras save their images on memory cards and these can be unplugged from the camera and inserted into a special card reader. The card reader connects to the computer or can be built in to the computer, as in the photograph.
Sound card/MIDI	The sound card allows a range of audio devices to be connected (e.g. microphone, output from a cassette player or VCR, etc.). The card converts these audio passages into computer files for use in multimedia projects. The card should also have a MIDI socket, for connecting an electronic keyboard. This allows electronic music to be composed, recorded and saved to disk. Some sound cards provide multiple audio inputs, so that multi-track recording can be carried out in real time. A high-quality card produces less background noise and improves the sound clip's quality.
MIDI keyboard	Connects to the sound card's MIDI connector and is used to record musical compositions. Requires additional music sequencer software.
Keyboard	This is the most basic input device. The computer keyboard consists of a normal typewriter layout with some additional keys, a group of function keys, a numeric pad on the right, and a group of direction keys also on the right side. The CTRL and ALT keys allow the same key to carry out several functions. For example, pressing the "L" key, the CTRL and "L" keys together and pressing the ALT and "L" keys together may provide three different results.
Mouse	The most common *'pointing device'* (a generic term for any device that is used to move a pointing cursor around the screen) is the mouse, a device that turns hand movement into pointer movement on the screen. They typically have three or more buttons, and may include a central *'scroll wheel'* for moving window scroll bars without having to click on them. Other pointing devices include the trackerball, digitising tablet, and touch-screen. These all perform basically the same task as a mouse, though they work in different ways, and some may provide additional functions (e.g. a trackerball is essentially an inverted mouse, such that the user simply rolls the ball directly.
Microphone	Connects to the sound card and is used to capture audio into the computer. The types and quality are discussed in detail in the chapter on digital audio.

Tablet	Used as a mouse replacement for graphics and photo-retouch activities, where the mouse does not provide accurate enough control. The tablet connects to the computer (usually through the USB port) and the pen or stylus is used in place of the mouse. The pen has buttons on the side of its body so that it can emulate the buttons on the mouse. The digitising tablet is intended to simulate using a pen and paper, by using a hand-held *'stylus'* as the pen, and drawing on the electronic tablet. The rectangular tablet corresponds to the screen area, so that drawing on any portion of the tablet equates to clicking and dragging the mouse on a particular part of the screen. Some types of tablet include a pressure sensitive stylus that can detect how hard the user is pressing it against the tablet. This is useful for graphics purposes, where increasing the pressure can indicate a thicker line, more opaque shape, or so on.
Video camcorder	Used to capture video sequences. Video is the most demanding of all elements in multimedia and poor equipment results in dropped frames (i.e. jerky video). The highest performers are FireWire camcorders and these should be used for serious work. The digital video camera takes much higher quality video clips, and some also take stills. Digital video cameras require much larger storage capacity, and so they use DV (Digital Video) cassettes instead of flash memory. Older analogue systems are still adequate for home and hobby use. The photograph also shows a webcam sitting on top of the computer. This is a low-quality device mostly used for video-conferencing.
Flatbed Scanner	Connects to the computer (usually through the USB or FireWire port) and scans in photographs, images signatures, etc. and converts them into computer graphic images. Since multimedia projects are designed for viewing on a screen (rather than the printed page) there is no need for a high-resolution scanner. However, the scanner should produce true colour representations of the image being scanned.
Royalty-free collections of graphics, clip art, photographs, music, and sound effects	Many CDs are available that supply collections of clip art or photographs. These can be inserted into multimedia projects and save a lot of time creating them from new. But commercial multimedia products have to avoid using any photographs, images, sound clips, etc. without permission of the owners of the copyright. This is got round by purchasing special collections where there are no restrictions on the use of the images or sounds.

Items not in picture

Modem	Used when the multimedia project is a web site. The web site pages are written and tested on the computer and then copied on to the web site. If the web site is one that is regularly updated, a fast modem should be used. The fastest current modem is a 56kbps model and consideration should be given to using the ISDN, or preferably ADSL system. Of course, the modem provides additional facilities such as conducting searches and research on the web, keeping in touch with clients via e-mail and joining user groups who have specialist knowledge in multimedia activities.
Headphones	Connects to the sound card and is used to monitor all audio output in the project. A home user may use a set of speakers but this is not suitable in an office where many computers are being used.
Touch-Sensitive Screen	The touch screen, as the name suggests, can detect the user pressing on the screen. Typically, this is used on public information terminals, where the computer displays a simple set of menu buttons, and the user may simply tap the screen to indicate which choice is to be selected. As such, touch screens are not a common form of input in home or office PCs, indeed they are almost never used except by such terminals or in their development. Its main use is in places where a keyboard is not practical, such as an unattended information point or other kiosk. They might also be used in training children and the handicapped - those who would find difficulty in using a keyboard.

Digital Camera	The term *'digital camera'* can refer to one of two devices – a digital stills camera, or a digital video camera, explained later. The still camera typically takes only still images, but some models can take short, low-quality video clips. In most cases these are stored on a memory card in the camera. The captured photographs or video is transferred later onto the computer. Like the scanner, high-resolution images are less important than the colour reproduction of the camera.
Voice-operated software	A useful tool where the user is physically handicapped or where a multimedia package expects the trainees to leave their hands free from the keyboard or mouse as much as possible, for use with other activities (e.g. a driving test simulation). It could also be used for teaching foreign languages.
Network card	If the computers in a multimedia company require access to a common pool of material, they could be connected via a local area network. There is a cost for fitting a network card in each computer, plus the cost of the main network server and cabling of the office.

Home users who have an older computer should not be discouraged. Most of the activities described in the book can still be carried out, although they may take a lot longer to complete.

Computer measurements

Computers use three measurements of volume and efficiency:

Measurement	Unit	Components	Explanation
Computer's Processing Speed	MHz	CPU chip	The computer's CPU clock speed is measured in *MegaHertz* (A MegaHertz, or MHz, being one million cycles per second). The clock speeds quoted for CPUs are their <u>actual</u> speeds - e.g. 500MHz means 500,000,000 pulses per second.
Capacity	Bytes, Kilobytes (KB) Megabytes (MB) Gigabytes (GB)	Memory, Disks	Measures how much data can be stored. A kilobyte is 1024 bytes, a megabyte is 1,0485,76 bytes and a gigabyte is 1,073,741,824 bytes.
Transfer rates	Bits per second, kilobits per second, megabits per second.	Modem, disk, scanner, capture card and network interfaces.	Measures how quickly data can be moved between components in the system. Usually shown as bps, kbps and mbps.

Although memory size and disk capacity are measured in bytes, other devices transmit data serially and are measured in bits per second. Some magazines, books, brochures, web sites, etc. use the terms Mb and MB, or MBps and Mbps as if they were the same measurement.

To avoid confusion, this book uses an upper-case *'B'* to denote Bytes and a lower-case *'b'* to denote bits.   So, for example, a card may transfer data in MBps while a modem may transmit data in Mbps.

The ins and outs

The diagram shows that some of the add-on devices are input devices (they bring data into the main computer) and others are output devices (they receive data from the main computer systems).

For example, the video capture card, CD drive, mouse, keyboard, tablet and touch screen are all input devices, while the CD writer and DVD writer are output devices (although they could be used as reading devices).

Other devices, such as memory, hard disks, modems and sound cards are both input and output devices.

At one moment they may be sending information to the computer, while at other times they may be receiving information from the computer.

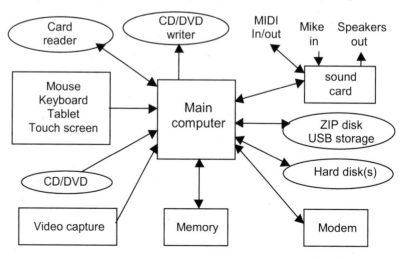

The playback computer

The Multimedia PC Marketing Council have produced standards for computer components that they think are required for the satisfactory playback of multimedia products.

Level 1 of the standard required a 386SX main processor chip and Level 2 required a 486SX main processor. Both of these chips are extinct, making the standards redundant. The Level 3 standard requires a Pentium processor running at 75MHz. Since it is difficult to buy a new computer with a Pentium chip slower than 2GHz or more, it follows that all modern computers can play back multimedia material to the Level 3 standard. Even the joint Intel/Microsoft PC 99 Guide (which predicts the specification for forthcoming computers) only specifies a 300MHz Pentium, 32MB of memory, AGP video card with 3D acceleration and hardware acceleration for video playback.

In other words, most users have computer systems that are easily capable of handling the minimum specifications for multimedia products.

Multimedia software

The hardware allows the multimedia components to be captured and saved.

These files usually require editing before being used (to shorten them, remove mistakes or to add effects).

Special software to edit sound, video and graphic files is available, as is a range of packages to create graphics, animations, etc. Most importantly, software is required to merge all these elements into a single multimedia project. The range of software to support the creation of multimedia products includes:

	Typical Examples	Purpose
Audio Editing	CoolEdit, Software Audio Workshop, Xing MP3 Encoder	Audio files can be manipulated in many ways to create the final clip to be included in a production. These include cut and paste, mixing, merging, filtering out frequencies, adding echo effects, looping, muting, reversing, pitch altering, volume altering, panning, fading and waveform editing. Other utilities convert audio files into compressed MP3 versions.
Video Editing, conversions and effects	Adobe Premiere, Avid Cinema, Adobe After Effects, Elastic Reality, Morph2, LSX-MPEG2 Encoder, DivX Encoder, Windows Media Encoder	Most packages use 'Non-Linear Editing' where the video clips are digitised and individual sections of the clip (right down to a single frame) are easily accessed for editing and the application of effects. Typical facilities are cut and paste, adding filters, transitions between scenes such as fades and wipes, titling, warping and morphing (gradually transforming one object into another object). The clips are organised into the correct running order and saved as the finished video clip. Other utilities convert video files into compressed MPEG versions.
Graphic Creation	PhotoShop, Paint Shop Pro, Paintbrush, Corel Draw, Freehand	These packages are used to create drawings, charts, cartoons, etc from graphic elements such as lines, boxes, circles and polygons. The line widths, styles (e.g. dotted, arrowed) and colour are alterable and a variety of fill patterns are provided. Text of various sizes, types styles and colours can be added. Packages such as Paintbrush produce bitmap files while upmarket products produce vector images (although these can be converted to bitmaps).
Animation Graphic Effects	3D Studio, Visual Reality, Ray Dream Studio	The most common effects are 3D objects using wireframes and rendered fills and animations. Many authoring packages provide animation facilities but these are not as sophisticated as dedicated animation packages.
Image Editing Photo Retouch	Photoshop, Picture Publisher, PhotoStudio	These packages are used to manipulate the contents of a photographic image. This includes altering the colours, altering contrast and brightness, and zooming, scaling and cropping of the image. It may also include special effects such as quantizing (producing an oil painting effect) and altering the data masks (producing a pop video effect). These packages are often used to alter the image's main contents (e.g. removing a blemish from someone's face, or removing the telegraph pole that seems to stick out of someone's head).

Authoring Packages	Director, Authorware, Icon Author, MasterClass, Toolbook	This is the key piece of software that integrates all the sound, video, graphic and text components into a meaningful order to achieve a prescribed effect.
Web Authoring	HTML editors, Dreamweaver, JavaScript, Flash	These packages are designed for creating web-based multimedia material. They may be the web equivalent of the authoring package (i.e. they integrate all the components into a set of interlinked web pages) or they provide animations and effects that are optimised for web use.
Music Software	Audio Architect, Cubase, Cakewalk, Steinberg B Box drum kit	These packages provide facilities to compose, record, edit and mix music tracks. The audio tracks can be real world audio, recording via microphones or can be synthesised MIDI tracks.

Multimedia Skills

The first two essential ingredients for creating multimedia have been covered. The third ingredient, the one that makes the hardware and software useful, is the skills of the individual or team producing the multimedia project.

At the end of the day, it is the skills of the designers, programmers, artists, etc. that decide whether a masterpiece or a monster is created.

This page attempts to outline the variety of skills that are involved. For convenience, it places skills in groups. This does not minimise the contribution of any group in the team. All the skills are required for a successful outcome. It is also readily acknowledged that there is some overlapping of skills, for example, a photographer may be told what scene to shoot but still uses his/her skills to get the best shot, or a video camera operator may spot an unusual activity and shoot it for later consideration). The aim is not to start a debate about the relative merits of individual jobs or their boundaries. The aim is to lay out the spread of skills employed by large multimedia companies and to consider the complex set of tasks and relationships involved in creating large multimedia titles.

Creative skills

This group of skills covers those who come up with the original ideas, or have the flair to advise on changes, additions and improvements.

Job Description	
Designer	There are two main design specialists: Instructional designer - ensures that the subject is clearly presented. Preferably an expert in the subject contained in the project. User interface designer - constructs the structure of screens that make up the project and the links between screens.
Copywriter	Also called content writers. They write all headings, body text, and the material for the voiceovers.
Graphic Artist	Deals with all that is visual in the project. This will involve creating original graphics and editing photographs supplied by the photographer.
Composer	Composes the music for the project.

Technical skills

This covers those who use their knowledge of their discipline and their equipment to achieve the tasks set for them.

Title	Job Description
Video Specialist	Captures the project's video sequences. May work on his/her own or may be in charge of a team of cameramen, lighting specialists, set designers, production assistants and actors.
Sound Specialist	Captures original audio clips and gathers existing available audio clips (from copyright free collections). May work on his/her own or may work with audio engineers, composers and musicians.
Video editor	Modifies video clips to fit allocated time, applies video effects, adds voiceovers, dubbing, background music, etc.

Photographer	Captures original photographs, often from a shooting list provided by the project manager. May be a permanent employee or may be a freelance brought in on a contract basis.
Animator	Creates animated sequences to the supplied specification.
Technical writer	Creates the installation instructions, user manual, database maintenance instructions, etc, as necessary.

Software skills

This covers all those who use their programming experience to implement the structures and screen contents that tie all the elements into a cohesive body of work.

Title	Job Description
Programmer	Usually creates projects using authoring packages such as Director, Flash, Authorware, Toolbook, or Icon Author. Builds up the project according to the specification.
Web Site Producer	Specialises in the production of multimedia for web sites. Usually has a wide knowledge of HTML, JavaScript, Perl, ASP, CGI, and can implement databases and e-commerce facilities such as shopping carts and secure transaction processing.
Tester	Subjects the project to exhaustive testing to discover errors and bugs before the project is shown to the wider world.

Management skills

This covers those who ensure that the multimedia project sticks true to its original aims and finishes on time and within budget.

Title	Job Description
Project manager	Also known as the team leader, this job controls overall design and management. The key figure in the day-to-day management of people and resources to complete the project on time, within budget and to the required quality.
Document manager	Keeps track of all the media files, authoring scripts and specification documents, to ensure that the most recent versions are the ones supplied to developers and that the previous versions are backed up for returning to in the event of a catastrophe. This is also sometimes referred to as version management.
Account Manager	Interfaces between the client and the production team. He/she sets up meetings with the client and maintains contact throughout the production schedule.
Researcher	Carries out additional research on behalf of the copywriter, artists and designers.

The above skills concentrate on those required for the successful completion of the final product. Other staff are obviously involved in a looser way - e.g. marketing staff, proofreaders, accounting staff, media distributors and so on. In a large company, a large number of staff will be employed to carry out these tasks listed above.

In a small company, many of the jobs will be rolled together - e.g. one person may both shoot and edit the video material, while another person may carry out all the design tasks.

For those working from home - you are the team!

Overview of production

A complex multimedia project is carried out in distinct phases.

- Work out the main aims of the project.
- Create an outline working prototype.
- Work out the project's technical requirements, navigation requirements, and screen layout specifications.
- Produce a storyboard.
- Produce a navigation map.
- Work out a project plan for handling people, time and resources.
- Assemble all the multimedia components (i.e. record all the sound and video clips, photograph all the pictures, draw all the graphics).

- Use an authoring package to tie all the elements together.
- Test the project and correct any errors.
- Distribute the project (i.e. put it on a web site, burn a CD-R, or create a CD master).

These are covered in more detail in other chapters.

Colour theory

This section is included here as it contains valuable insights into the working of the human eye and brain.   This is worth knowing in its own right.   From a multimedia perspective, it applies to graphics, photography, video, multimedia project design, web page design, etc.

It explains how we perceive colours and how digital cameras, camcorders, TV screens, and computer monitors work.

It also explains why certain colours work better than others and why certain colour combinations are more powerful than others.

How the eye works

Electromagnetic radiation has a wide spectrum that covers from radio signals to cosmic rays.   Within that spectrum lies a small frequency range known as the visible spectrum.

The visible spectrum is that portion of the spectrum that produces visual sensations.   The eye is sensitive to the energy from a broad band of wavelengths extending from around 350nM to 700nM.   Immediately below the visible spectrum is the infrared spectrum, which is used in television and camera remote controls, and for the transfer of digitised pictures from cameras to computers fitted with IrDa ports. Above the visible spectrum is ultraviolet, which can be damaging to the eyes and skin.

The diagram below shows a graph whose horizontal axis is measured in wavelength.   To avoid confusion, it is best to remember that as a wavelength gets longer, its frequency goes down, and vice versa.   So, the wavelength of 430nM has a higher frequency than the wavelength at 560nM.

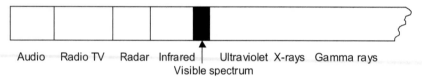

Audio   Radio TV   Radar   Infrared   Ultraviolet   X-rays   Gamma rays
Visible spectrum

The colours of the rainbow are simply the frequencies of the visible light spectrum, in ascending order.   These colours are red, orange, yellow, green, blue, indigo and violet.

The eyeball's interior, known as the 'retina', is lined with a collection of photoreceptors (i.e. photosensitive cells). Light enters the eye through the cornea (to achieve focus) and the iris (to control the amount of light) before being beamed on to the retina.

The retina contains two types of photosensitive cell, known as 'cones' and 'rods'.   When these are struck by light photons, they release electrical energy that is processed by the brain as visual information.
The rods are very light sensitive and contribute to the perception of movement and to the detection of objects at very low light levels (i.e. 'seeing in the dark').   They still detect light when the cones have stopped responding.
The cones are of three distinct types, each having their maximum sensitivity at different points on the visible spectrum, as shown in the diagram.

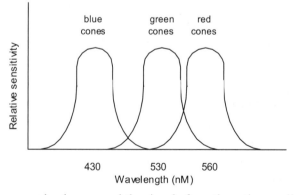

These are called the blue, green and red cones and the signals from these three collections of cones are mixed in the brain to arrive at the particular colour being perceived.   Although we often refer to 'seeing' colours, the perception of colour exists only within the brain.   Any possible colour is arrived at by evaluating the relative levels of signal coming from the different sets of cones.

Limitations of the eye

The ability to detect colours is known as *'photopic vision'*.   The inability to successfully process light of different wavelengths (particularly between the red and green areas of the spectrum) produces *'colour confusion'* which affects around 10% of the population.   The total inability to differentiate any colour differences is known as *'scotopic vision'* and results in a monochromatic view of the world. This is full colour-blindness.

So, the eye contains four different types of receptor - three for colour information and one for light levels.

Note

This is exactly how a colour television works. The TV station transmits four different pictures - one for the red components, one for the green components, one for the blue components and a monochrome picture to provide the light levels. These four streams of data are superimposed on each other on the TV screen to produce the television picture.

As the diagram above shows, the peak responses for the different cones are not evenly spaced.   The red and green cones are closer together in the spectrum.   The eye optimally focuses light from the upper-end of the visible spectrum on to the retina (somewhere around 560nM). This means that the blue cones produce a slightly more blurred image than the red and green cones. Therefore, they do not need the same spatial resolution as the other cones and this is reflected in the allocation of the number of cones on the retina of each type.   There are about 40 red cones and 20 green cones for every blue cone on the retina.

The rods and cones are not spread evenly over the retina.   The retina's central area, the *'fovea'*, is covered only in cones, with the surrounding areas being a mixture of cones and rods.   The cones are tightly packed in the fovea and these provide spatial resolution in normal light conditions (i.e. details and patterns).

Colour processing

Light from the sun and from fluorescent tubes is *'white light'* - it contains all the colours of the spectrum. Domestic light bulbs produce light with a slight yellow cast, while sodium street lamps produce light with an orange cast.

'White' light is the combination of all colours, while 'black' indicates the absence of all colour sources. Light that reaches the eye may be emitted directly by an object (such as the sun, a TV screen, computer monitor, torch, or light bulb) or may be light reflected off an object. When light is reflected, some wavelengths of the light may be absorbed. Therefore, there are two forms of colour perception. These are:

- Light reflected from an object (known as *'subtractive mixing'*)
- Light directly targeted at the eye (known as *'additive mixing'*).

Subtractive Mixing

Objects have no colour of their own; they only have abilities to absorb or reflect parts of the visible spectrum. We see what is reflected and don't see what is absorbed. Natural daylight reflecting off non light-absorbent paper (i.e. white) allows the full light spectrum to be reflected. These reflected wavelengths are mixed inside the eye and interpreted as white.   Adding ink or paint pigment to the paper surface results in the area affected selectively absorbing some of the wavelengths from the white light source. The viewer sees the resultant colour <u>reflection</u> from the mix. Since the introduction of the pigment has taken away some of the wavelengths, the process is termed *'subtractive mixing'*. An object is seen to be 'blue' because it reflects blue light and absorbs all other light.   For convenience, we refer to an object as being red, rather than saying that the object reflects wavelengths that are in the visible red spectrum. Similarly, we say that an object is cyan, rather than saying that it absorbs most red wavelengths and reflects most blue and green wavelengths. This shorthand makes life easier, as long as we know how light really works. White objects reflect all light, while black objects absorb all light.

Additive Mixing

The colour monitor exploits the fact that the three main colours, as detected by the eye, are red, green and blue.   In this case, the light is not reflected but is directly transmitted from the monitor screen to the eye.   Any other colour of light can be obtained from mixing the three primary colours of light - red, green and blue - in the appropriate ratios. For example, mixing red and green light produces yellow light, while mixing red, green and blue in the same full proportions produces white light.   Since the monitor's CRT (cathode ray tube) uses three different light <u>sources</u> to produce the colours, the process is termed *'additive mixing'*. If no light sources are added to the mix, no wavelengths reach the eye and the screen is perceived as being black.

The diagrams show the effects of colour mixing.

Additive mixing is shown in the left diagram.   Imagine three torches being shone into an eye, in a darkened room. If only the red torch is switched on, the eye sees a red pool of light. If only the green torch is switched on, the eye sees a green pool of light.   If the red and green torches are switched on together, the eye sees a red pool and a green pool of light. But, where these pools overlap, the user sees a yellow patch of light.

If the blue torch is now switched on, it will seen as a pool of blue light, with a cyan patch where it overlaps the green light and magenta patch where it overlaps the red light.   In the middle, where all the lights overlap, the eye sees a white patch of light. The monitor screen works in this way, replacing torches with illuminated coloured dots on the screen surface (see the chapter on technology for full details).

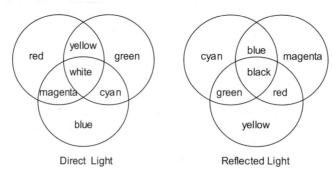

Direct Light   Reflected Light

Subtractive mixing is shown in the right diagram.   Imagine an eye looking at a white sheet of paper in bright sunlight.   All the light is being reflected and the eye sees a large white area.   Imagine the sheet of paper is now run through a printer so that a circular area is printed filled with cyan ink.   The cyan ink prevents light at that wavelength from being reflected and the eye sees a pool of cyan. If the paper were run through the printer a second time to print a magenta-coloured circle on the sheet, all light in the magenta areas of the spectrum would also be absorbed. The eye would now see a pool of cyan and a pool of magenta.   Where the two areas overlap, the eye would see a patch of blue. If the paper were run through the printer one more time, printing a yellow filled circle on the sheet, the yellow ink would absorb light in that part of the spectrum.   The eye would now see a yellow pool of light. Where the yellow pool overlapped the magenta pool, a patch of red would be seen. Where the yellow pool overlapped the cyan pool, a patch of green would be seen. Where all three inks overlap, all light in the spectrum is absorbed and the eye would see a patch of black.

A full-colour version of these diagrams is on our web site.

Colour range
Research shows that individuals can distinguish around 256 different levels for each colour.   This happily coincides with the range of values stored in a single byte of storage.   Therefore, a single byte can store 256 different levels of blue (or red, or green).

Since a monitor uses a light source for red, green and blue, and each colour need only be represented by 256 different levels, the maximum colours produced is

$$256 \times 256 \times 256 = 16,777,216$$

These 16.7 million colours are sufficient to provide all possible colours that can be perceived by the human eye.   For this reason, schemes using 16.7 million colours are known as *'true colour'*.

Each colour value is stored in a single byte, which is the equivalent of 8 bits.   Since there are three guns a total of 3 bytes or 24-bits stores all possible colours.   This explains why true colour systems are also described as having *'24-bit colour depth'*.

Intensity
The human eye, and digital cameras/camcorders, record information about objects by the wavelength of the reflected light (i.e. its colour) and the brightness of the light.

White objects reflect nearly all the light that shines upon them while darker objects reflect around 10% of the light.   So, a dark blue object and a dark green object both reflect different light wavelengths into the eye. However, they both reflect light at low levels.   When the general light conditions are poor, such as at dusk, there is even less light to reflect.   This is part of the explanation for the inability to distinguish between dark colours at night.   Witness statements at an evening crime scene often show confusion about the colour of the robber's jacket, the colour of the getaway car and so on.   This is because the colour-sensitive cones have ceased to respond to the low light levels, while the rods are still processing illumination information, with their maximum sensitivity being in the 510nM region (the green part of the spectrum).

Computer Technology

This chapter is in the book because the efficiency and reliability of the computer hardware, and the operating system, are as important to multimedia production as the efficiency of the multimedia software. This chapter looks at those aspects of computer technology that are important in the production of multimedia, including:

- The Central Processing Unit (CPU)
- Internal data storage (i.e. Computer memory)
- Long-term data storage (e.g. hard disks, CD-ROMs etc)
- Display technology
- Interfaces
- Peripherals
- The Operating System (O.S.)

Many everyday applications can be used on machines with fairly low specifications. Users can carry out word processing, web browsing, sending e-mail, and so on, with a computer with a slow processor, little memory and not much in the way of hard disk space. Multimedia systems are different. They require lots of power. They are asked to shift and store huge amounts of data. Sound and video files can be huge and this makes it difficult to move them around the system fast enough.

This is a key difference between multimedia files and other files. If a user finds that his/her Internet connection slows down, it just means that the web page takes longer to download. The web page is sitting on the web site and can be retrieved in small bursts until it is all fetched. This is not the case with, for example, capturing audio or video in real time. There is only one chance to capture the audio or video source. If the system is not up to the job, chunks of the source are left unrecorded and this appears as gaps in a sound clip or jerkiness in a video clip. The multimedia computer system is only as good as its weakest link. With multimedia, the concern is with the DTR (data transfer rate) of all the components in the chain.

Consider the diagram below. It shows how video data moves from the camera to storage on a hard disk.

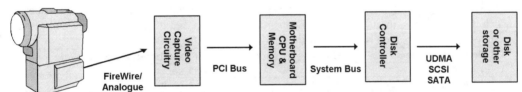

The following factors affect how efficiently a computer can handle multimedia data:

- Camcorders can have either analogue (eg VHS or S-VHS) outputs or digital (eg FireWire) outputs, with the latter requiring the fastest performance from the other components in the chain.
- The video capture card performance determines whether the data coming from the camcorder can be digitised fast enough, at a big enough resolution, in enough colours, without losing any of the data.
- The video capture card can connect into the main computer via a slower ISA slot, a faster PCI slot, or even a parallel port or USB port. All these have different rates of handling data.
- The computer's motherboard components, processor and memory all have different performances.
- The data, once it has been processed by the computer's CPU chip, has to be sent to a disk controller for writing away to the hard disk. The controller can be an older IDE type, a fast UDMA type or the most reliable SCSI or SATA type. Each has different abilities for shifting data to the disk.
- The last link in the chain is the hard disk. Even disks of the same type (i.e. UDMA or SCSI) have different specifications. For example, one disk may be manufactured to run at a faster speed than another. A disk may also provide a more reliable flow of data, free from sudden drops in data flow.

For all these reasons, the machine used for multimedia editing and authoring has to be chosen carefully.

Overview of computer systems

The main components in the computer system are:

CPU (Central Processing Unit)

The heart of any computer system is the Central Processing Unit. It is a silicon microchip and its function is to interpret and execute the program instructions. The speed and design of this chip largely determines the overall speed of the computer. Early PCs used a chip known as the 8088 and this was followed by a range of chips through to the present Pentium range. Early machines ran at a speed of 4.77MHz while the Pentium 4 can now run at several GigaHertz. Apart from improvements to their raw clock speeds, modern chips have other in-built improvements over earlier models.

The CPU is always attached to a '*motherboard*'. The motherboard contains a number of '*buses*' that allow the CPU to communicate with the memory, and with any external interfaces.

Memory

To work, the computer has to temporarily store the program and data in an area where it can be used by the computer's processor. This area is known as the computer's '*memory*'. Memory consists of computer chips that are capable of storing information. That information may be:

- The program that keeps the computer running (e.g. Windows).
- The instructions of the program that the user wants to run (e.g. an authoring or graphics program).
- The data that is used or created (e.g. multimedia scripts or graphic images).

Disks and other storage

These are used for the long-term storage of data. The bulk of the information (programs and data) used by computer applications is stored on disk and must be transferred to main memory before it can be processed by the CPU. Storage devices include magnetic disks (removable floppy disks and built-in hard disks), CD-ROM disks and magnetic tape.

Monitors

Programs send the output from their calculations to a screen via a graphics card. The screen is contained in a unit called the '*monitor*' - sometimes also called the VDU ('*visual display unit*') and these devices are covered later in this chapter.

Interfaces and Peripherals

Any computing device that is not part of the main unit of the computer is called a peripheral device. This category includes a diverse range of equipment; some people include the mouse and keyboard as peripherals, but it more typically refers to such items as printers, scanners, digital cameras, and so on.

Each peripheral needs to transfer data to and/or from the CPU at some point, and this is the function of various types of external interfaces available to the PC.

The Central Processing Unit

The power of a PC is usually indicated by the speed of the processor. The faster the speed of the chip, the more instructions it can process in any given time. The simplest measure of speed of a machine is the number of cycles per second at which it can operate – in other words, how many times per second it can process one unit of data. The unit of measurement of cycles per second is 'Hertz', as the following table illustrates:

Processor Speed	Cycles per second	Time between each cycle
1 Hertz	1	1 second
1 KiloHertz (1KHz)	1,000	1 millisecond (1ms)
1 MegaHertz (1MHz)	1,000,000	1 microsecond (1μs)
1 GigaHertz (1GHz)	1,000,000,000	1 nanosecond (1ns)

Different models of computer are designed to run at different speeds. Of course, the faster the machine, the greater the purchase price. The slowest PC was just under 5MHz. The fastest speed is always being improved upon and is currently over 3GHz, with even faster machines on the way.

The choice of machine depends very much upon its expected use. If the machine were used entirely for word processing, a lower speed machine is perfectly satisfactory. Since the slowest part of the process is the typist's thinking and typing time, there is little to be gained by having very fast processing in between long pauses at the keyboard. On the other hand, where there is going to be a great deal of machine processing, such as graphics calculations, video editing and other multimedia number crunching tasks, a faster machine becomes essential.

Of course, the raw speed of the CPU is not the only factor in determining the machine's overall speed. Other factors, such as the speed of the disk and video card, the amount of RAM available, whether the machine has an efficient caching system, etc., also determine the machine's performance.

Units of measurement

All computer data and program instructions (e.g. between the camcorder and the capture card, or between the CPU and memory) comprise movements of binary 0's and 1's. To make sense of the stream of 0's and 1's, the system must break the stream up into manageable groups and process data a group at a time. The standard ways of organising binary information are given below:

BIT - this is the single binary digit and stores only two conditions (ON or OFF). This is the basic unit on which the system works.

BYTE - this is a group of eight bits. It can store 256 different combinations (from 0 through to 255) and is the standard method of representing a single character.

WORD - A word is a group of bits that is treated by the computer as a single unit for retrieving, processing and storing. So, if a data bus happens to be 8 bits wide, it can process 8 bits at a time (i.e. the computer's word size is a single byte. If the data bus happened to be 16 bits wide, its word size would be 16 bits.

Measurement of capacity

When measuring data (either as disk capacity, memory, bus widths or as speed of transfer) it is always referred to in its binary state - e.g. One Bit, One Byte, One Kilobyte, One Megabyte, etc.

Memory or disk capacity describes the amount of data a device can hold at any one time and is measured in bytes. One byte can store a single character. A character can be a letter or a number, or any of the many special characters found on the keyboard. A byte may also store part of program instruction, part of a graphic image, part of an audio clip, etc.

In computing, where operations are often considered in units of 2, the Kilo or K actually means 1,024 characters with similar definitions for the larger numbers.

Kilo is 2 raised to the power of 10, or 2 x 2 x 2 x 2 x 2 x 2 x 2 x 2 x 2 x 2. Tera is 2 multiplied by itself 40 times, or exactly 1,099,511,627,776.

A rough measure of memory requirements is:

> 1 byte can store 1 character
> 1 KB can store a few paragraphs of text
> 1 MB can store the text of a reasonably sized book

The table shows the numbers that result from the binary numbering method. Since each number increases by a factor of two, no number can ever be an exact thousand or an exact million. In order to maintain the convenience of expressing size in thousands and millions, sizes have to be rounded to the binary number nearest to the wanted number.

Amount	Calculation (2 raised to the power of n)	Actual Amount
1 kilobyte (KB)	2^{10}	1,024 bytes
1 megabyte (MB)	2^{20}	1,048,576 bytes
1 gigabyte (GB)	2^{30}	1,073,741,824 bytes
1 terabyte (TB)	2^{40}	1,099,511,627,776 bytes

The range of Intel CPUs

From the beginning of the PC range of computers, the main CPU has been from the Intel range, supplemented by other manufacturers with 'clones' or improved versions of each chip in the series.

The most recent series consists of the following chips:

Pentium It replaced the 486 chip and had a 256-bit internal bus and a 64-bit external data bus. On most occasions, it allowed two instructions to be executed in parallel, greatly speeding up throughput. The chip also had the main mathematical operations (i.e. add, divide and multiply) hard-wired into the chip.

Pentium MMX This is a version of the Pentium with 57 additional instructions in the CPU instruction set. These are multimedia and communications extensions to the CPU giving them the title 'MMX' - multimedia extensions. The new instructions use a technique known as SIMD - Single Instruction, Multiple Data. One instruction can work on up to 8 bytes of data simultaneously. This provides very fast repetitive processing of data - ideal for video decompression, sound synthesis, multimedia, 3D rendering and other graphics-intensive activities. MMX aware programs - i.e. those using the new MMX instructions produce speed improvement in these areas. These facilities are now incorporated into current Pentium models.

Pentium II This was an improved Pentium Pro with MMX additions. It was released with a 100MHz processor/cache interface and a 66MHz system bus. The built in second level cache was taken out of CPU and was mounted, along with CPU, on a plug-in card. This card plugged into a special connection slot known as 'Slot One', which meant that the Pentium II needed a completely re-designed motherboard. The external second level cache only ran at half the CPU speed, which meant that the performance was diminished. However, the 32-bit performance, coupled with MMX capabilities, placed Pentium II machines in the lower multimedia and graphics workstations market. The newer Slot 1 Deschutes chip used the same slot as the standard Pentium II and operated at faster speeds. It also ran at system bus speeds of 100MHz (compared to 66MHz). A version aimed at the budget PC market, known as the Celeron, has a 66MHz bus.

Pentium III The Pentium III uses the Slot 1 connection with a bus speed of 100MHz, 133MHz or 200MHz. The internal second level cache is 512k but still runs at only half the CPU clock speed.

The Pentium III introduces 'KNI', Katmai New Instructions, comprising 70 new machine code instructions aimed at 3D graphics, MPEG2 video encoding/decoding, AC3 audio and image processing. These work on the same principle as the MMX (Single Instruction Multiple Data) moving large amounts of data with a single instruction. The PIII has a separate set of 128 registers for SIMD operations, thereby speeding up both SIMD and normal register activities. The Pentium III Xeon is essentially the Pentium II Xeon with the added KNI instructions.

Pentium 4 The Pentium 4 was introduced with a 100MHz Front Side Bus, with an internal multiplier of x13 to x22. This gave a processor speed of 1.3 to 2.2GHz, although speeds of over 3GHz are now available. However, it was at first only available with the Intel 850 chipset, which required RAMBUS memory. Later Pentium 4's became available with other chipsets, having a bus speed of 133MHz or 166MHz, and capable of using DDR memory. It uses a technique called *'quad pumping'* that quadruples the throughput of the Front Side Bus, essentially giving an 800MHz bus when clocked at 200MHz, for example. The instruction set includes Streaming SIMD Extensions 2 (SSE2) to improve Internet performance as part of Intel's *'NetBurst'* architecture. The Pentium 4's other main features include *'Hyper Pipelining'* based on larger instruction pipelines and deeper prediction techniques, and a *'Rapid Execution engine'* that consists of two clock-doubled Arithmetic and Logic Units.

Alternatives to Intel

The main challenge to the Intel line comes form AMD. The K7 chip uses its own proprietary slot connector, requiring a specially designed motherboard. It has a clock speed of 600MHz and a bus speed of 200MHz. Like the K6, it provides its own set of 21 SIMD instructions, known as 3DNow!. However, these are incompatible with KNI instructions.

Summary of P.C. Processors

	The first PC	Pentium	Pentium II	Pentium III	Pentium 4
Introduced	1978	1993	1997	1999	2001
Number of Pins	40	273	Slot 1	Slot 1	423, later 478
Transistors	29,000	3.1m	7.5m	9.5m	42m
Addressable Memory	1MB	4GB	64GB	64GB	64GB
Clock Speed (MHz)	4.77 / 8	60/233	166/450	450/1000	1.3 – 3.2GHz

Speeding up processing

If each new instruction was fetched from memory after the previous instruction has been fully executed, the only way to increase the computer's efficiency would be to increase the rate at which the CPU was clocked. Already, clock speeds have been raised from the original 4.77MHz to 3GHz and beyond. However, the laws of physics and the cost of manufacture restrict the ability to continually raise machine clock speeds. Very fast CPUs, for example, require very fast address buses and data buses to keep up with the demands of the CPU, adding to the cost of the motherboard. In practice, other methods are used to speed up the CPU's efficiency.

These include:

- Using two or more CPUs, so that several instructions can be processed simultaneously. Many Pentium motherboards have all the necessary logic on board to allow four CPUs to be connected for parallel running. This is known as *'symmetric multiprocessing'* and is ideal for heavy multimedia processing such as video handling, as the multiple CPUs even out the processing load and prevents time glitches that might result in dropped video frames.
- Clock multiplying - making the operations inside the CPU chip run faster while maintaining the existing speeds for the main buses and motherboard devices. All modern systems already employ this technique to some degree.
- Introducing efficient memory caching systems, either built in to the CPU chip and/or as external secondary cache. This is also standard on today's PCs.

CPU cache memory

Standard memory speeds have not progressed at the same rate as processor speeds. As a result, the CPU can process data faster than the data can be fetched from memory or placed in memory. Consider that a 3GHz CPU cycles every 0.33ns while the access time for main memory is usually 0.5ns or more. This could result in the CPU standing idle while the required location in memory is accessed for data to be transferred.

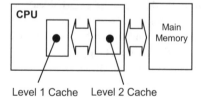

Level 1 Cache   Level 2 Cache

Rather than simply use faster, more expensive main memory, a favoured solution is to use a small block of very fast RAM inside the CPU known as *'cache memory'*. Any data held in the cache memory can be transferred to other parts of the CPU at much greater speeds, reducing or in some cases eliminating this delay. However, the cache memory is substantially smaller than the computer's main memory, so the cache memory can only hold a portion of the data that is resident in main memory. The aim is to ensure that only the data most likely to be required is stored in cache memory.

Cache memory in previous systems came in two 'levels' – Level 1 being internal cache and Level 2 being external to the CPU. However in most situations memory cache noticably improves the processor performance, and as a result both levels have become integrated into all PC processors. The table shows some common speeds:

	Pentium	Pentium Pro	Pentium II	Xeon	Pentium III	Pentium 4
CPU	233MHz	200MHz	450MHz	400MHz	550MHz	3GHz
L1 cache	4ns	5ns	2ns	2ns	2ns	0.3ns
L2 cache	15ns	5ns	4ns	2ns	4ns	0.3ns
Main Memory	60ns	60ns	10ns	10ns	10ns	1ns

PC bus architectures

To maximise the computer's efficiency, it is essential that data be transferred between the processor and memory (and vice versa) as quickly as possible. When a user wishes to use a slow speed card in the computer, this should not be allowed to slow down these CPU/memory transfers. The solution is to provide a separate high-speed bus linking the processor and memory. All the communication between CPU and memory is carried over this bus. The normal PCI bus remains to handle disk, video, expansion slots, etc.

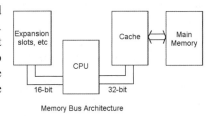

Memory Bus Architecture

Advantages:

- The memory chips run as fast as the CPU allows, while slower speed cards are catered for on the separate slower bus. The system runs at its maximum speed.
- Now that the memory has its own separate bus, a block of even faster memory (cache memory) can be introduced between the main memory and the CPU. The cache memory is used to handle pages of memory data at a time. (see previous notes on memory)

PCI Bus

Current computer systems use the Intel PCI ('_Peripheral Component Interconnect_') Bus. Initially designed as a 32-bit connection system for motherboard components, it developed into a full expansion bus system. The diagram shows a typical PCI configuration, although the details vary slightly with different CPUs and different memory

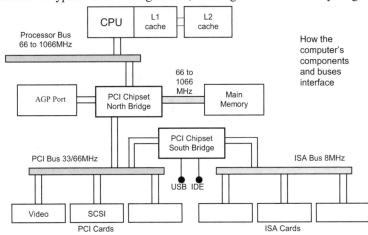

systems. The PCI bus exists as a local fast bus, separate from the slower ISA bus. A bridge controller (the _'South Bridge'_) may on older systems allow the use of legacy ISA cards on a normal ISA bus. However, the PCI bus system decouples the CPU clock and data path from the bus and interfaces to them through another chip in the PCI chipset (the _'North Bridge'_). The PCI bus is therefore independent of the machine's CPU. It works equally well with the 486, the Pentium or any future chips and is used with the DEC Alpha workstation and the PowerPC. All that is required is that each CPU has its own CPU-PCI chipset.

The chipset comprises two chips. The North Bridge handles the CPU, memory, cache and the PCI bus, while the South Bridge handles USB, IDE drives and the ISA bus.

Current PCI buses run at 33MHz or 66MHz, even though motherboards run at up to 1066MHz. The PCI bus is synchronised to the system bus but is reduced to a proportion of its speed. Early systems used a 66MHz front side bus, while current Pentium systems use between 100MHz and 1066MHz.

AGP is a port, rather than a bus, and is intended purely for graphics cards. As such, it is explained in the display section.

Comparison of Bus Systems		
Bus Type	**Clock Speed**	**Max Data Rate**
ISA	8MHz	7.629MB/s
PC Card	8MHz	20MB/s
CardBus	33MHz	133MB/s
PCI	33MHz	133MB/s
AGP	66MHz	266MB/s
AGP 2x	66MHz	533MB/s
AGP 4x	66MHz	1066MB/s

Plug and Play

Another major potential benefit of the PCI system is its _'Plug and Play'_ facility, known as _'PnP'_.

Plug and Play needs three key elements:

- The PC must support it (this is provided in all new computers).
- The adapter cards must support it (almost all new cards and devices have this feature).
- The operating system must support it (Windows does; NT, OS/2 and DOS don't).

PCI systems have a PnP-specific BIOS, which extends the normal BIOS POST operations to include device configuration. This auto-configuring of cards, makes alterations and additions to hardware a simpler process. With all other buses, the addition or swapping of cards involves ensuring that there is no clash of memory addresses, IRQs and DMA channels between the existing and the new devices.

These problems are intended to be eliminated with PCI since the BIOS will maintain a list of all memory addresses, IRQs and DMAs in use and provide non-conflicting allocations for new cards. Each of the new PCI plug-and-play cards has its own _'configuration space'_ - usually a set of memory registers that are solely devoted to storing configuration information. The Plug and Play BIOS chip interrogates these registers to determine the card manufacturer and type and the range of options it can handle. The cards are all capable of working with a range of different memory addresses, IRQs, etc. The BIOS determines the best settings for the cards and sends data to be stored in each card's configuration space detailing what the specific settings for the card are.

Windows, from version 95 onwards, has the additional Plug-and-Play services designed into the operating system. Plug and play is fully implemented when users have the required combination of PnP BIOS conforming to the PPA BIOS 1.0a specification, PCI motherboard, PnP operating system or BIOS extensions and all add-on cards being of the PnP variety. Additionally, some software still ignores best practice and bypasses some BIOS routines. True full PnP depends upon all the required features being present although partial benefits can be gained from a lesser specification although this will still involve some manual installation. PnP still functions when the computer has some older (non PnP) cards installed, as the PnP BIOS assigns the PnP cards' configurations around those of the existing non-PnP cards.

Interfaces

There are a variety of interfaces available for connecting devices to the motherboard. These can be divided into *internal* interfaces, and *external* interfaces. Internal interfaces are used to connect to devices inside the computer base unit, namely hard disks and other storage devices, memory modules, and expansion cards that attach directly to the bus on the motherboard.

External interfaces are found on the outside of the base unit, and attach to external peripherals via a cable. Some such interfaces are themselves provided by installing an expansion card. To facilitate the connection of external devices, PCs have a number of external ports at the rear of the machine. Normally, a PC will have at least a parallel port, serial port and USB ports, although some machines may also include a joystick port, FireWire, or other ports. All machines will have a keyboard interface and an outlet for attaching a monitor.

Interface techniques

All connections to the computer and its adapter cards use one of these interface methods:

Parallel

Data is sent with all the bits of the byte being transmitted simultaneously over a set of wires. Used by most printers, disk drives, etc.

Serial

The data is transmitted one bit at a time over a single connector wire. The basic serial interface (as opposed to modern serial technologies like USB or FireWire) is slower than parallel transmission but is much cheaper (particularly over long distances). Keyboards, monochrome monitors, some printers, the mouse, and LAN cabling use this method.

Analogue

Analogue signals have an infinite number of different states, as would be expected from real-world audio or video sources. They require special adapters to interface to the computer and examples are modems, microphones and video sources such as cameras and VCRs.

Parallel port

Also known as the '*Centronics*', '*LPT*' or '*Printer*' port. With the advent of improved ports, the conventional port is also now known as the SPP ('*Standard Parallel Port*'). By convention, the whole cable is described as a Centronics cable. Apart from its obvious use with printers, the parallel port is used as a means of connecting scanners and some video capture devices to the computer.

In parallel transmission, the data port has eight separate wires connecting the computer to the external device. There is a separate pin in the socket for each data wire, plus other pins for the control information.

Whereas the serial port has its own chip to carry out data transmission, the Standard Parallel Port requires these tasks to be carried out by the computer's CPU. Modern parallel ports are capable of running in ECP (Enhanced Communications Port) or EPP (Enhanced Parallel Port) mode as well as SPP, both of which provide some improvement in speed. Furthermore, all but the most basic transmission modes are '*bi-directional*' meaning data can be passed in or out via the parallel port.

Serial port

A serial transmission system is cheaper to provide, since it only requires a single channel between the PC and the external device. A byte of data is sent one bit at a time until the whole byte is transmitted. The PC often uses old 9-pin RS232 serial ports called '*COM*' ports, but the same serial system is also the basis for USB, FireWire and such ports.

Common devices to be found on a serial port are mice, modems, and card readers for digital cameras.

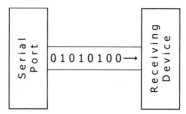

Although the above example shows data (i.e. the letter 'T') being transmitted <u>out</u> of the port to a device, it should be stressed that the RS232 port is essentially a bi-directional port. This means that data can also be passed <u>in</u> to the port from an external device.

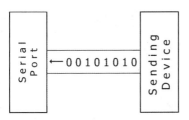

A good example of an input device is a serial mouse. Other examples are bar code readers, electronic tills and remote monitoring equipment.
In the case of a modem, the port will transfer data both <u>in</u> and <u>out</u> of the PC.

PC Cards (PCMCIA) & CardBus

Announced in 1990, the PCMCIA standard (<u>P</u>ersonal <u>C</u>omputer <u>M</u>emory <u>C</u>ard <u>I</u>nternational <u>A</u>ssociation) appeared as a standard interface for portable computer users. All major hardware and software suppliers support the standard. The standard aims to allow the easy connection of a range of add-ons. PCMCIA products are now referred to as 'PC Cards'.
The PCMCIA connection is the portable's equivalent of the ISA expansion slots on a desktop machine. Each add-on card is about the size of a credit card and the original intention was to provide the easy connection of additional memory chips.

Memory cards

The cards, some of which are also sometimes described as 'Flash memory', have a 68 pin plug at one end and connect to sockets inside palmtop/notebook computers and digital cameras. Once inserted, they act like a normal bank of memory configured as a RamDisk. When a card is withdrawn, it retains the data stored in its chips until it is required again. This also provides portability, as the card can be pulled out of one machine and inserted in another machine, just like a floppy disk. The cards mostly use static RAM as the storage medium with a small lithium battery maintaining the data contents. Flash RAM handles larger capacities but has some problems in ensuring that the programming voltages to set the memory contents are the same on all machines using the PCMCIA interface. Memory cards are available in sizes from 128kB to 64MB although they are very expensive at the high capacity sizes.

PCMCIA interface

PCMCIA is now used mainly as a hardware I/O standard, allowing the connection of a whole range of devices already associated with desktop PCs. These include disk drives, CD-ROMs, sound cards, digital cameras, video capture cards, data acquisition cards, modems, faxes, and LAN interface cards. These connect through the PCMCIA interface and ignore any ISA, MCA or EISA bus that might be on the machine. The system dynamically assigns I/O addresses and IRQs to the cards during the boot-up or when cards are inserted.

Advantages:

- Speed. Intel claims that flash RAM has an access time that is 10,000 times faster than a hard disk.
- Easy change of cards, while the computer is still running - known as 'hot plugging' or 'hot swapping'. The new card should be automatically detected and recognised by the interface, based on the information stored and supplied by the card. The functions of some of the pins on the interface are re-mapped according to the device detected. By default, the card is assumed to be a memory card. Since the process is automatic, there is no need to re-boot the computer each time a card is changed.

Disadvantage:

- The range of add-ons remains much more expensive then their desktop counterparts.

Physical versions

- Type 1 of the standard covers the use of the card as a memory storage device. This defines the physical thickness of the card as 3.3mm and size 54mm by 85mm.
- Type 2 announced in 1992, expanded the PCMCIA standard use to cover the connection between card and machine as the basis for designing a range of I/O (input/output) add-on cards for LAN adapters, SCSI controllers, modems, sound cards, video capture cards, etc. This card is 5mm thick and has a size of 48mm by 75mm. This is the type most commonly fitted to portable computers and digital cameras.
- Extended versions of Version 1 and Version 2 standards are available. These have the same width and thickness as the normal version but allow for extra long cards to be used. This allows even more complex circuitry to be mounted on the cards but means that the cards will protrude from the computer's casing by up to 135mm.
- Type 3 is 10.5mm thick to allow for the inclusion of larger peripherals and small hard disk drives such as the 170MB Maxtor drive, the 270MB SyQuest drive and the Hitachi MP-EG1A 260MB digital camcorder's drive.
- Type 4 is 16mm thick to allow for the inclusion of larger capacity hard disk drives. IBM, Western Digital and Hewlett Packard have already produced hard disks to this format, the first two being 1.8" and the HP being only 1.3". Other models are available from Maxtor and Conner.
- Type 5 is 18mm thick and was announced by Toshiba for its wireless network cards.

All types plug into the same 68-pin interface socket, arranged as two rows of 34 pins.   While cards can be inserted upside down, the interface ensures that this will not harm the card or the computer (although it will naturally prevent the card from working).

Data compression techniques can be used to store data on PC Cards, increasing their effective capacity.

Standards

The Personal Computer Memory Card International Association has evolved the following set of PCMCIA standards:

- PCMCIA 1.0 specified the minimum specification for early cards.
- PCMCIA 2.1 specified the interfaces used with the 16-bit cards.
- PCMCIA 3.0 is the new CardBus system and supports 32-bit working, DMA and 3.3volt working (older cards require 5 volts while newer portables work on 3.3volts).   It has a 32-bit address bus and a 32-bit data bus.   It supports bus mastering and runs at 33MHz, providing a throughput of 132MBps. Windows, from version 95 Release 2 onwards, has built-in CardBus card and socket services.

Universal Serial Bus

The Universal Serial Bus (USB) was developed by Intel as the new general-purpose PC port.   It could eventually replace serial ports, parallel ports and internal interface cards as the means of connecting slow to medium speed external devices such as keyboards, mice, modems, scanners, etc.

Unlike the large 9/25 pin serial connections and the 25/36 pin parallel connections, the USB requires only four wires in a light flex cable.   There is one wire for the common ground, two to identify data in each direction and a 5 volt power supply wire.

It has many distinct advantages:

- The bus is relatively fast with a maximum date transfer rate of 12Mbps and a lower rate of 1.5Mbps for slow devices such as keyboards and mice.
- USB is Plug and Play compliant. So, devices can be *'hot swapped'* - i.e. fitted and removed without rebooting or reconfiguring the machine. The configuration problems previously associated with adding and altering equipment is eliminated. If a new device is fitted while the computer is switched on, it is automatically configured.
- Since one entire USB system requires a single IRQ, problems of running out of machine IRQs will disappear.
- The bus provides its own power supply to any low-power devices that connect to it. There is no longer any need for each external device to have its own power unit.   This should make peripherals cheaper and eliminates the tangle of power connections at the rear of machines.   However, adding multiple devices may place a strain on the computer's own power supply.
- Devices were once designed to only work with their own manufacturer's interface cards (e.g. scanners, some mice). USB devices do not have this restriction.   This should make the new USB models of the devices cheaper and easier to connect.

USB allows a single port to connect many devices together in a daisy chain. Up to 127 devices can connect to a single USB port if hubs are used to expand the system.   A hub is a star-like connector that connects a group of devices to a single connection point.

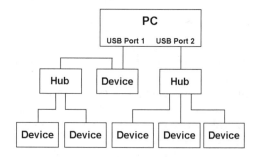

The diagram shows a PC with two USB ports.   Port 2 connects directly to a hub and this has three outlets connected to USB devices.   Typical USB hubs support four, five or seven port outlets.

Port 1 connects to two devices that are daisy chained to the port. One of these devices also acts as a hub and has two further devices connected to it.

A number of monitors are now available with multiple USB ports mounted on the base. So, a PC port may connect to a monitor with the speakers, headphones and microphones connecting directly to the monitor.   Or a keyboard could be designed as a hub, with a mouse, joystick and light pen attaching to a connection at the rear of the keyboard.

Many USB devices are now available (e.g. digital cameras, mice, joysticks, keyboards, video capture devices, sound cards, memory sticks).

USB is supported by all modern PCI chipsets but is not supported in early versions of Windows 95.

USB2

The current standard for Universal Serial Bus is USB 1.1.   This specifies the data rate of up to 12Mb/s, with low speed signalling at 1.5Mb/s, on the same interface as mentioned earlier. The consortium developing USB includes companies such as Intel, Microsoft, Hewlett Packard, Lucent and Philips.   It released a new standard (USB2) at the start of the year 2000. USB2 is entirely compatible with the existing cables and plugs, but runs at up to 480MHz. This frequency was chosen after calculations showed that it was as high as could be achieved on the existing cabling.

The consortium foresees USB2 co-existing with the IEEE 1394 FireWire (see below).

Generally, USB2 will connect computer peripherals like printers, scanners, and so on, while FireWire connects Audio/Visual and multimedia applications like digital camcorders, digital TV equipment etc. They hope to see USB2 sockets alongside FireWire sockets on future equipment. The first USB2 devices to be announced were purely of 'industrial' interest, being chipset extensions, protocol analysers etc. Mainstream USB2 equipment has recently started to appear, and because of the compatibility mentioned above, are easily integrated with existing USB systems.

FireWire

Another high-performance serial bus is IEEE-1394, commonly known as *'FireWire'*. This was developed from the Apple computer range and is also known as the *'Multimedia Connection'* since it allows camcorders, scanners, disk drives, DVD players, CD-ROMs and printers to share a common connecting bus. The common interface means that it is also suitable for the home networking of PCs.

Like the USB system, it supports up to 63 devices. However, FireWire does not require the use of hubs as each device has a common connection to all other devices - including the PC. The standard connecting cables are 6-wire; two for the power and four used to connect to consumer audio and video products (TV sets, VCRs, amplifiers, etc). The four bus wires are configured as two twisted pairs, crossed between ends to provide transmit and receive pairs. FireWire devices have several sockets and a 1394 cable plugs into the sockets of the devices to be connected. There are no cable length restrictions (as with LANS) and no need to set device ID numbers (as with SCSI). The only restriction is that the devices must not be cabled in a way that wires the system as a loop.

Sony uses a four-wire variant (known as *'I-link'*) for its products, using the IEEE-1394.1 standard.

Despite its simplicity, FireWire is an extremely fast interface that can move data at 100Mbps, 200Mbps or 400Mbps. 800Mbps, 1.6Gbps and even 3.2Gbps versions are being discussed. Even the slowest speed is capable of simultaneously delivering two full-motion video channels running at the high video rate of 30fps, accompanied by CD quality stereo sound. It multiplexes data such as compressed video and digitised audio along with device control commands on the common bus.

DVC (Digital Video Cassette) systems made by Sony already use FireWire on their camcorders. The other major players such as JVC, Hitachi and Philips will also have FireWire systems on their D-VHS (Digital VHS) recorders. Since DVC requires 3.5Mb per sec (i.e. 28Mbps), it cannot be handled by USB (12Mbps limit) but is well within FireWire's capabilities. On the other hand, a 90-minute video could require almost 19GB of hard disk space. This places this aspect of FireWire at the professional end of the video market.

FireWire devices, like USB devices, are hot swappable.

FireWire is fully supported from Windows 98 onwards and as an upgrade to Windows 95.

Relative uses

Both FireWire and USB are competing with Ultra SCSI and Fibre Channel for the high-speed bus market. The likely uses of USB and FireWire are complementary rather than competing.

- USB remains the option for input devices (mouse/keyboard/joystick), audio (sound/music/ telephone), printers, scanners, storage devices (floppy, tape) and slow speed communications (modems, ISDN)
- FireWire offers a higher performance for top-end devices such as DVD drives, DVC cameras, D-VHS recorders and wide-band networking.

Infrared

Sending data by infrared is widespread and is the method used in most TV and video remote control handsets. The beam of light is just below the visible part of the spectrum and data is transmitted by pulsing the light beam on and off. It is a very useful low-power short-range system.

It is now finding its way into the computing field and is being developed by a group of manufacturers known as the Infrared Data Association (IrDA).

Uses for IrDA include:

- Wireless keyboards and mice.
- Wireless printers.
- Wireless LAN adapters.
- Wireless peer-to-peer computer networks.

The initial IrDA implementation, introduced in 1994, was seen as a direct replacement for the serial port and had a data rate of 115kbps. It uses RZI (Return-to-Zero Invert) modulation. This means that a light pulse is transmitted for each logic *'zero'* in the data stream; a logic *'one'* will not produce a light pulse. By 1995, a faster 4Mbps version had been introduced. It uses PPM (Pulse Position Modulation) where a constant stream of light pulses is transmitted. The time between each pulse is not evenly spaced and the exact position in time for the pulse indicates one of four binary values from 00 to 11. The transmission of these 4-bits has named the system 4PPM.

115kbps systems are common in applications such as wireless printer connection whereas the 4Mbps system is commonly implemented in portable computers.

Bluetooth

Bluetooth is an open interconnection standard that has been available for some time but is yet to make significant impact. Bluetooth capable equipment offers short-range digital voice and data transmission by radio signals, for both point-to-point and multicast applications. Point-to-point transmission is useful for personal applications, where cables and infra red light links are currently used. Multicast will allow the use of networking, email, World Wide Web and no doubt other yet to be developed technologies. The use of radio links presents interesting problems. Higher frequencies only work between antennae that can see each other, so called "line of sight", whilst lower frequencies are subject to fading and interference. The Bluetooth standard overcomes these problems and incorporates encryption technology to ensure privacy where it is needed.

The current Bluetooth standard is capable of a 720kbps asymmetric data rate at a range of some 10m, or 100m with a booster. If symmetric data rates are required the data transfer rate drops to around 460kbps. By the year 2005, the consortium developing Bluetooth technology hopes to see 10Mbps, which is a data rate equivalent to that used in many mainstream office networks. As third generation mobile telephony drives technology development in the area, Bluetooth connections and the Wireless Application Protocol (WAP) are expected to become very popular.

Comparison of serial interface performances		
Interface	Cabling	Max Data Rate
Serial (RS232)	Twisted Pair	115kbps
Infrared (IrDA)	Optical Beam	4Mbps
USB	4-wire Cable	12Mbps
USB2	4 wire Cable	480Mbps
FireWire (IEEE 1394)	6 wire Cable	800Mbps
Bluetooth (now)	Wireless	720kbps
Bluetooth (full implementation)	Wireless	10Mbps

Computer Memory

When the user wishes to run a program (e.g. a sound editor), a copy of the program is loaded from the user's disk and placed in the computer memory. The program is then run from the computer memory.

This makes it possible for the computer to be a word processor, graphics package, Internet browser, video editor and many other functions. The computer, in fact, will run whatever program is currently in memory. If another program is loaded, that becomes the new function of the machine. This is what makes the computer so versatile - it is not tied to any one activity. The memory inside a computer stores a variety of information.

- A computer loads a program into its main memory, from where it can be run. A computer program is a list of instructions for the CPU, each instruction being stored as a numeric code.
- Computer programs exist to manipulate data. The data may be loaded from disk or CD, entered from the keyboard, downloaded via a modem - and a range of other input devices. The data may be in the form of video clips, audio data, etc. Whatever its format, the data will always be held in the form of numeric values.
- The computer stores some of its own system programs (such as Windows components) and its own system information (such as the nationality of the keyboard in use, screen display information, etc.).

All of these must share the same pool of memory held inside the computer. In addition, the machine stores much of the code it requires to handle its hardware in programs that are permanently blown on to chips. If the computer is to avoid getting into utter confusion, it must allocate these activities to separate areas, each with its own distinct boundaries within the machine's addressable memory.

The memory chips themselves consist of a large number of cells, each cell having a fixed capacity for storing data and each has a unique location or address. Memory comes in two types – RAM and ROM, which have different characteristics and functions.

RAM

The main type of memory is known as RAM (Random Access Memory) and its contents are 'volatile'. This means that the program and the data held in the memory is lost when the machine is switched off. This is not a problem for the program as it is only a copy - the original program is still stored on disk. However, any data created is only sitting in the memory and will be lost, unless it is saved to disk before the computer is switched off. The term 'random access' is used to distinguish it from serial access devices. With serial access devices, such as tapes, the data is read in with one item following the other. The last item takes longer to fetch than the first item. Random access means that any cell address in the entire memory area can be accessed with a uniform time overhead.

ROM

The other type of memory, known as ROM, 'Read Only Memory', chips are 'non-volatile' (i.e. the program code exists even when the machine has been switched off). These chips are used in a wide range of electronic control circuits, from industrial machine tools to domestic washing machines. They are also the ideal choice for computer control. A computer's control programs require to be non-volatile. The computer's basic functions are controlled by system software and there is a potential Catch-22 situation, in that

"the computer needs a program to be loaded, so that the computer can load a program"

By placing part of the operating system software into a ROM chip, the system BIOS, the basic machine control programs are available to be run as soon as the computer is switched on. The programs in the ROM provide the machine's basic input and output functions, to allow application programs to be loaded and run.   Unfortunately, if the system is to be updated, the BIOS chip has to be replaced with a new chip that contains the new program routines. This requires opening the computer case and is a job for experienced support staff or technicians.   As a result ROM BIOS chips have been replaced by EEPROM, or *'Flash ROM'* which allow BIOS updates to be carried out in software. This type of chip is used to store chunks of the system's own programs (e.g. to check for the user typing at the keyboard, or to handle disk activities. When the computer is powered up and running, some of the system programs are run directly from ROM.   Most system programs are loaded into the computer memory from the hard disk when the machine is first switched on.

Note

Confusingly, ROM chips are also random access devices. The difference between ROM and

RAM variants is not in their access methods, but in their volatility (or lack of it) and speed.

The operating system takes up some of the computer's available memory, so not all of the memory is actually available to the user.   Sophisticated software packages such as Macromedia Director and Microsoft Word take up large amounts of RAM and the user may create large projects and documents using these packages that can use up the rest of the available memory. This means that the more memory in a machine the more efficient the computer runs. Each year, machines are supplied with more memory and users can usually add extra memory to an existing computer.

Memory access

The machine has to separate one program instruction from the next. This is achieved by storing the machine instructions in different memory locations. This means having each consecutive instruction stored in its next consecutive memory address. It is important to differentiate between an address and its contents.   The address is a unique location in memory. The contents of this address may be part of an application program or system program, or may be data.

The CPU will fetch an instruction from the memory by placing the instruction's memory address on the Address Bus and a Read signal on one of the Control Lines.   The memory chip places the address's contents on to the Data Bus and this is picked up by the CPU.   The CPU then carries out the instruction.   If the instruction involves writing a piece of data to memory, the appropriate location is placed on the Address Bus, the value

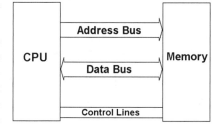

to be written is placed on the Data Bus and a Write signal is placed on one of the Control Lines. Once the instruction is completed, the CPU can fetch the next instruction, often stored in the next consecutive program memory address. The simplified diagram uses a single bus for both data and program instructions.   This is very common and is called the *'Von Neumann'* architecture.

Memory categories

A summary of the main memory definitions is given below; these are explained in greater detail later.

Type	Where used
DRAM (Dynamic Random Access Memory	Once was the only type used for main memory. It is dynamic, meaning that the contents need to be constantly refreshed, making it a slow but relatively cheap memory type in comparison to SRAM.
SRAM (Static RAM)	Fast access memory normally used for caching the CPU (see below).
SDRAM	Synchronous DRAM. Keeps the CPU and memory timed in step, thereby minimising the control signals between them and greatly increasing data transfer rates compared to both DRAM and EDO.
Double Data Rate (DDR)	A version of SDRAM that provides data on both edges of the signal, theoretically doubling its speed compared to normal Single Data Rate (SDR) SDRAM.
RDRAM	A serial memory chip type, also called Rambus available in speeds from 800MHz to 1.2GHz. RDRAM chips are held on a RIMM memory module.
Cache RAM (Level 1)	Memory built in to a CPU and sitting between the CPU and external memory to speed up data access. Access times are from 2ns to 10ns.
Cache RAM (Level 2)	Memory normally on the motherboard between the CPU and main memory to speed up data access. L2 cache is built in to the Xeon processor module.
CMOS RAM	Small block of additional memory is used to store information about the computer (e.g. type of drives in use, amount of memory in the machine, etc.).
ROM BIOS	The ROM chip fitted in every PC. When the machine is switched on, it tests the system and loads DOS.
BIOS Extensions	The ROM chips that are fitted to add-on cards to control their operations (e.g. video cards or disk controller cards).

Memory Characteristics

Computers use two types of RAM. These are termed Dynamic Ram and Static RAM and they have differing constructions and characteristics.   These characteristics include, speed, complexity and cost. Both types use arrays of transistor switches to store the binary data.   The main difference lies in how the transistors are switched and it is this that affects the chips' characteristics.

Modern chips measure their speed in '*bandwidth*' – the maximum number of bytes transferred per second, but the first SDRAM chips measured their speed by their bus frequency. Thus, a '*PC100*' chip operates at 100MHz, but a '*PC2100*' chip does not operate at 2100MHz. Instead, it is able to transfer up to 2100 megabytes per second.

Note

> Both types use different circuitry and are therefore <u>not</u> interchangeable. Static RAM
> cannot be plugged into sockets intended for Dynamic RAM and vice versa.

Memory Interfaces

Each memory chip has to transfer data to and/or from the CPU. The ROM chips are typically hardwired into the motherboard, so the exact interface used is of no concern to the average user. The RAM chips, however, are built to be easily removed and upgraded, and to facilitate this, each interface type has a distinctive connector into which the relevant memory module is placed. The following explains the memory interfaces used on PCs.

SIMMs

The '*Single In-line Memory Module*' is a now obsolete standard that is only encountered on very old machines and certainly should be avoided for multimedia authoring machines, though they may be used by client machines.

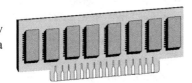

DIMMs

Standard now in most computers is the '*Dual In-line Memory Module*'.   It is a 168-pin module that has electrical

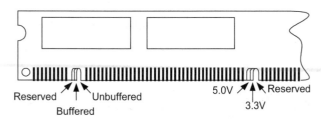

contacts on both side of the board. It has a greater reliability than SIMMs and is available as a non-parity 64 bit part or as a 72 bit parity device. Newer motherboards only support DIMMs, requiring less memory banks and providing a more compact layout. DIMM boards are available with both SDR and DDR SDRAM fitted. DIMMs are available in both rare 5v and common 3.3v versions.

The voltage of the component, along with whether or not it is buffered, can be ascertained by measuring the exact position of the keyway slots on the DIMM.

RIMMs

The '*Rambus In-line Memory Module*' is very similar to a DIMM connection. It is also a 168-pin module that has electrical contacts on both side of the board.   It is specifically designed for RDRAM so DIMMs and RIMMs are not interchangeable - a RIMM will not fit in a DIMM slot and vice versa.

RIMMs use RAMBUS technology. This is an extremely fast but essentially serial technology, as opposed to the more usual parallel arrangement. This is because it was originally developed to suit the setup of Nintendo games machines. The typical RIMM setup comprises 3 RIMM sockets. Each socket must contain either a RIMM module or a so-called RIMM continuity module. This continuity module is just a short circuit to allow serial memory signals to pass through. New motherboards that have RIMM sockets fitted come with RIMM continuity modules as part of the supplied hardware kit.

The table below compares the various types of memory.

Standard	Chip Type	Socket type	Physical bus Speed	Effective bus speed	Bus size	Max. Data throughput
PC100	SDR	DIMM	100MHz	100MHz	64 bits (8 bytes)	763MBps
PC133	SDR	DIMM	133MHz	133MHz	64 bits (8 bytes)	1014MBps
PC1600	DDR	DIMM	100 MHz	200MHz	64 bits (8 bytes)	1525MBps
PC2100	DDR	DIMM	133 MHz	266MHz	64 bits (8 bytes)	2029MBps
PC2700	DDR	DIMM	166 MHz	333MHz	64 bits (8 bytes)	2541MBps
PC3200	DDR	DIMM	200 MHz	400MHz	64 bits (8 bytes)	3200MBps
PC4200	DDR	DIMM	266 MHz	533MHz	64 bits (8 bytes)	4264MBps
PC5400	DDR	DIMM	333 MHz	667MHz	64 bits (8 bytes)	5088MBps
PC6400	DDR	DIMM	400 MHz	800MHz	64 bits (8 bytes)	6103MBps
PC800	RDRAM	RIMM	800MHz	800MHz	16 bits (2 bytes)	1525MBps
RIMM 3200	RDRAM	RIMM	800MHz	800MHz	32 bits (4 bytes)	3050MBps
RIMM 4200	RDRAM	RIMM	1066MHz	1066MHz	32 bits (4 bytes)	4264MBps
RIMM 4800	RDRAM	RIMM	1200MHz	1200MHz	32 bits (4 bytes)	4800MBps

Storage Devices

A computer needs somewhere to store its programs and data when they are not in the machine's memory. The most common storage medium is the disk system. The computer's disk systems are designed for the long-term storage of programs and user data. When the power is removed from a machine, the contents are lost from memory, so the hard disks are used for their preservation. In addition, almost all PCs allow data to be stored on removable disks such as *'floppies' or 'Zip disks'*. This allows data to be moved around by carrying disks from machine to machine, or sending a disk through the mail. Hard disks, on the other hand, are permanently built-in to the machine and are not normally accessible by the user. Floppy disks are not a suitable method of storing multimedia files and are not examined.

Hard disks

Hard disks hold an incredible amount of information, the first models held 10 Megabytes, but today 300Gbyte and larger models are commonplace. It is known as a *'hard disk'* because it is made from a solid sheet of aluminium. It is coated with ferric oxide or cobalt oxide and a number of such disks are stacked on top of each other and placed in an airtight casing. Each extra disk boosts the drive's storage capacity and each of these disks is known as a *'platter'*. The term covers both sides of that particular disk. So, if a drive had three platters, it would contain 6 sides. Areas of the hard disk's coating are magnetised and demagnetised to store the data. Modern drives can have many platters, depending on the capacity of the drive. For example, IBM's 32.8GB model uses ten platters.

The disks are mounted on a vertical shaft and are slightly separated from each other to provide space for the movement of read/write heads. The shaft revolves, spinning the disks. Data is stored as magnetised spots in concentric circles called *'tracks'* on each surface of the disks.

Each disk surface has its own read/write head and they are linked so that they will all move in unison.

The disks spin at a constant speed. The slowest models ran at 3600 rpm (12 times faster than a floppy disk) and current models range up to 10,000rpm. Apart from their large capacities, hard disks have a much better access time than a floppy disk. A hard disk's mechanism allows it to read in data, write a file and find files much faster than a floppy disk. Hard disk systems are composed of:

- A sealed drive unit.
- Disk controller electronics, either on a controller card or built in to the drive.
- Connecting cables between the drive and the computer motherboard.

Sectors

A hard disk holds from 30kB to over 50kB of data on a single track. To make the most economical use of tracks, they are divided into compartments known as *'sectors'*. Sectors number from 1 upwards and each sector normally holds 512 bytes, i.e. 1/2kB, of user data. Therefore, a 36-sector track on a hard disk stores 18k of data. The number of sides and the maximum number of tracks are determined by the hardware of the disk drive and are beyond the control of the user. However, the size and number of sectors are set under software control (hence the description *'soft-sectored'*)

Clusters

In practice, sectors are mostly grouped in a unit called a *'cluster'*. The cluster is the smallest area of disk that can be used to store an independent item of data. So, if a particular disk used 4 sectors to a cluster, a batch file of only a few hundred bytes would still consume 2k of disk space. If a program or a piece of data requires more than one cluster's worth of space, it can be stored in subsequent unused clusters.

Formatting

All disks, floppy or hard, have to be formatted. This lays down data on the disk that is never seen by users; it is solely used to distinguish between one track and another and between one sector and another. The read/write head is moved to the desired track and sector before reading or writing data in that sector. So, every block of data can be uniquely addressed by the read/write head used, the track used and the sector used to store it. Before any read or write operation is started, the system ensures that it has really arrived at the correct track and sector. A mechanical or electronic glitch may position the head over the wrong sector, resulting in either reading the wrong data or overwriting data. To overcome this, the data sections laid down on a disk are preceded by a Sector ID which contains the track number, the sector number and the sector size. If the information in the sector ID matches the desired location, the read or write operation proceeds normally. In the event of an incorrect head movement, the sector ID will not match the wanted location and the head is returned to track zero for another attempt.

Preparing a hard disk with sector IDs is known as *'low level formatting'*. A complimentary *'high level formatting'* process consists of preparing the disk for use by DOS. A low level format is carried out by the disk controller card and results in a disk that has its sectors identified and organised according to the required interleave. A high level format uses some of these sectors to set up the structures needed to store details of the fields and their whereabouts. Some hard disks allow a low-level format using a special utility and a high level format is carried out in Explorer by right-clicking on the drive and selecting *'Format'*. With floppy disks, the Format operation carries out both low and high level formatting.

Protecting hard disks

Hard disks require most of the safety precautions already mentioned concerning floppy disks to be observed. The need to keep the disk unit away from strong magnetic fields, avoiding smoke and dust, etc. apply as much to hard disks as floppy disks. On the one hand, the hard disk is in a sealed unit and therefore has a better chance of surviving a hostile climate. On the other hand, the repercussions of disk failure are much more serious. If a floppy disk is damaged, it can be thrown in the waste bin at little financial loss. If a hard disk is damaged, it is a very costly item to replace. In addition, a damaged floppy disk should have its backup copy immediately to hand and so productivity is not affected. With a hard disk failure, a new disk has to be ordered up, fitted and have all the backup files restored before the machine is ready for use.

Apart from the above environmental problems, hard disks are particularly vulnerable to knocks and jolts. If the case of the machine should be jolted while the machine is powered up, the head may make contact with the surface of the disk and scrape off some of the coating from the tracks. If this happens, the data in these sectors is lost and considerable permanent damage can be caused to the disk surface. This is termed a *'head crash'* and it takes out sectors from the system. If the head crash happens when the head is positioned over the system areas, the disk can be rendered unusable, since the system files cannot be relocated to any other sector, they must be found in specified tracks and sectors of the disk.

To minimise possible damage, modern drives have auto-park mechanics; that means that the read/write head is positioned out of the way of the data tracks when it is not involved in read or write operations.

Disk speed

The speed of a disk drive is based on
* The time to get to the required data (known as the *'access time'*)
* The time taken to read that data from the disk (known as the *'data transfer rate'*)

Access time

The time taken to reach the required data is based on two factors:
1. The time that the head takes to get to the wanted track (seek time) measured in milliseconds. Each track-to-track jump time may be different, since some head movements will wish to move across a larger amount of the disk than other movements. Due to the way that files are written, most track-to-track movements are not very distant. So, the average access time is calculated on the basis of 1/3rd of the tracks, instead of the expected half of the tracks. A poor seek time would be 25ms and a fast seek time would be 8ms. Drives with seek times lower than around 25ms are using voice coil actuators rather than stepper motor actuators.
2. The time taken to get to the wanted sector (latency period). This is the time spent waiting for the wanted sector to rotate to the position directly under the read/write head. On average, this is half a disk revolution. At 3600 rpm, this would be 8.33ms, at 4500 rpm this would be 6.67ms and at 10,000 rpm it would be 3ms.

The access time of modern drives range from about 16ms to under 8ms.

Data transfer rate

The rate at which a small amount of data (e.g. a single sector) is transferred is determined by the above factors and is a physical restriction that cannot be adjusted by the user. When a number of sectors require to be read, the most common case, the way that the disk is low-level formatted plays a large part in achieving the maximum data transfer rate. Low level formatting separates each sector with *'sector IDs'* that determine the sector boundaries. The maximum data transfer rate is reached when the head reads from a contiguous set of sectors, without having to move the head to another track. In such a case, the rate would be determined by the sector size, the number of sectors per track and the speed at which the data passes under the read head.

With a floppy drive, the disk rotates at 300 rpm and so the 18 sectors on a 1.44 MB floppy would be read in 0.2 secs. The transfer rate would be:

$$0.5k \times 18 / 0.2 = 45k \text{ bytes/second or } 360\text{Kbits/sec}$$

With a hard disk rotating at 4500 rpm the track reading time is 13.33 and the data transfer rate for a drive with 63 sectors/track would be:

$$0.5k \times 63 / 0.01333 = 17.3\text{MB/second or } 138\text{Mbits/sec}$$

So, reading a 1MB file from a large hard disk can be over four hundred times faster than reading from a floppy disk. Of course, the access time for both drives has to be included and this slightly reduces the overall performance of the drives. Most controllers also have to decode various timing pulses before sending the data to the computer. Dependent on the type of card used, this produces various levels of delay and affects the overall data transfer rate. The above figures are maximums, in that they assume that all the data is read in one contiguous read, with no additional track-to-track movements.

Another major factor in determining data transfer rate is the efficiency of the electronics in the disk controller card. A very fast disk requires that the controller be able to transfer the data to the motherboard at the same rate.

Disk Interfaces

The *'controller'* is the electronic circuitry used to control the operations of the drive mechanism and the head read/write activities. In most machines, this circuitry is built on to the machine's motherboard. In early systems, manufacturers produced their own interface arrangements and this meant that users had to always use the manufacturer's specific card and drive components. To overcome this, a number of standard interfaces have been arrived at, to allow the devices to communicate. The mechanics of drives mostly work in the same way but there are differences in the way that the drive communicates with the motherboard. The most common interfaces are described next.

EIDE

The rapid development of the other parts of the computer system has left the disk subsystem as the bottleneck for many activities. 1995 saw the more widespread use of an interface, known as EIDE (Enhanced IDE), capable of handling four devices. The devices are mostly disk drives but the interface easily handles CD- ROMs and ZIP drives. It is also cheaper than the other alternative fast interface - the SCSI interface. The EIDE interface offers significant improvement in speed over the previous IDE interface. An EIDE disk drive remains compatible with the older IDE system. Such a drive can be connected to an IDE controller and will work happily, although its transfer rate will slow down to that of the normal IDE performance. It is this compatibility that gives the Enhanced IDE its name.

This originated the current range of improved non-SCSI drive systems that remain backward compatible with older computers. Modern EIDE drives use Ultra-DMA to achieve high speeds. For example a UDMA/66 drive produces a full data transfer rate of 66.6MBps when connected to a motherboard and BIOS that are both compatible with UDMA/66. Faster systems use UDMA/100 or UDMA/133. However, its 40-pin plug still connects to an older motherboard IDE connection (the extra 40 wires in the cable are shields for the 40 pins) - although, of course, it would run at the reduced data transfer rate.

SCSI

The SCSI interface standard is the Small Computer Systems Interface (pronounced *'scuzzy'*). The SCSI drive has the controller circuitry built-in. The drive is connected via a 50-wire or 68-wire cable to an adapter card that connects to one of the computer's expansion slots. Since the controller circuitry is on the drive, the card is described as a *'host adapter'* rather than a controller card. Its only real job is to allow SCSI devices to connect to the computer bus. Since it is a simple device, it is able to connect up to seven or sixteen different devices. The connecting cable can have a number of connector plugs along its length, to connect to a number of internally fitted SCSI devices. External devices, such as DAT drives and external CD-ROMs, can connect to the bus via a D-shell connector on the SCSI adapter card.

When several devices are connected, the system is described as being *'daisy chained'*. The total length of the chain must not exceed 19 feet (reducing to 9 feet for Wide SCSI and only 5 feet for SCSI-3), to minimise transmission errors. Each end of the chain must also be fitted with terminating resistors. These terminate the cable and prevent signals being reflected back down the cable as noise. The terminators may consist of resistors built in to the device and activated by DIP switches, or they may be separate terminating plugs or *'blocks'*. Each external device has two connectors - one for connecting to the existing chain and one for either extending the chain or terminating the chain.

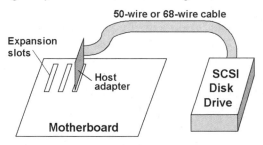

The intelligence built in to the host adapter is designed to relieve the machine's CPU from the tasks of organising the control of the various devices attached to it. The machine CPU can transfer these responsibilities to the circuitry of the host adapter card so that it can carry out other activities.

The generalised nature of this interface means that it is able to connect more than just disk drives to the motherboard. A range of devices, such as CD-ROMs, tape drives, scanners, etc. can be connected to the SCSI interface with ease. Each device must be given a different ID number. With SCSI-1 and SCSI-2, these range from 0 to 7 and the host adapter usually defaults to ID 7. Wide SCSI-2 and SCSI-3 support up to 16 devices. The ID number is set in each device with the DIP switches or jumpers on the cards.

SCSI versions

A range of different SCSI standards has evolved with the following data transfer rates from the device to the adapter card. These use different data bus widths and different electronic controls.

Bus widths are either 8-bit or 16-bit. This is the bus between the controller and the drive; the controller may well have a 32-bit interface via the PCI connector.

Fast SCSI doubles the transfer rate by using more stringent electronic parameters that allow timings to be altered and overheads reduced. Ultra SCSI's electronics run at double the normal clock frequency and this produces transfer rates that are double that of Fast SCSI.

Since the data transfer rate between the adapter and an ISA based computer works out at around 2Mb/sec; a SCSI adapter that connects to PCI bus produces far better results.

Type	Data Rate	Data Bus	Comments
SCSI-1/ SCSI-2	5MB/sec	8-bit	50-pin connector. Asynchronous
SCSI-2 Fast	10MB/sec	8-bit	50-pin connector. Synchronous
SCSI-2 Fast Wide	20MB/sec	16-bit	68-pin connector
SCSI-3 Ultra	20MB/sec	8-bit	50-pin connector. Also called Fast 20.
SCSI-3 Ultra-Wide	40MB/sec	16-bit	68-pin connector
Ultra-2	40MB/sec	8-bit	Also called Fast 40.
Ultra-2 Wide	80MB/sec	16-bit	68-pin connector
Ultra 80	80MB/sec	serial	Also called Fast 80
Ultra160 (or U160)	160MB/sec	8-bit	An implementation of Ultra-3
Ultra320	320MB/sec	16-bit	Also called SCSI-4

SCSI systems do not use the machine's BIOS, having placed a device driver in the CONFIG.SYS file to install the necessary control software.   This means that a SCSI drive can cohabit with an ST506 or an IDE system in the same machine without any conflicts.   In addition, since devices of different transfer rates can work with the same adapter, upgrading to a faster SCSI hard disk will involve no changes to the SCSI adapter.   Many CD-ROMs, scanners and Postscript printers now have SCSI-2 interfaces.

Notes

- The best UDMA performances compete with the middle/top SCSI performance but SCSI systems also have an edge on performance in multitasking environments. The CPU can send an instruction to a SCSI device and carry on with other tasks until the device responds. With EIDE, the CPU has to wait until the device responds before carrying out other tasks thereby slowing down throughput, particularly in situations of multiple I/O requests. This explains SCSI's popularity in multimedia systems.
- The performance of the interfaces has outstripped the speed of most current drives, which run at about a 10MB/sec sustained data transfer rate. Even the most modern and fastest drives (such as the 10,000 rpm Seagate Cheetah) can only provide a sustained transfer rate of up to 30Mb/sec.
- An ultra-wide controller card, such as the Adaptec 2940UW, has both 68-pin connectors (for ultra-wide devices) and 50-pin connectors (for SCSI-2 devices).

Disk cache

The speed of a computer's throughput is not solely determined by the raw speed of the CPU.   Many applications are disk based and large database applications are especially disk-intensive in their operations.   So, a large proportion of the time is spent in disk activities rather than processing activities.   Windows also makes heavy use of disk operations, particularly if machine memory is small and swap files are in operation.   Additionally, Windows uses many DLL (Dynamic Link Library) files.   These sub-programs are usable by various applications and function like overlay files.   However, this technique also increases the number of disk accesses required to run applications.

There has been continual progress in CPU development from the days of the 8088 processor.   Disk development, although making rapid progress of late, has remained the main bottleneck in the system as it is still largely limited by the mechanical nature of its operations.

Disk caching has proved a highly successful method of improving disk access times.   They work on the same principle as memory cache systems explained previously. Memory cache acts as a high-speed buffer between the fast CPU and slower memory.   With disk caching, memory chips are used as a high-speed buffer between the fast CPU and very much slower disk devices. It is also argued that the reduced need for disk accesses results in reduced disk wear, prolonging the disk's life

Full disk caching can be implemented in two ways:

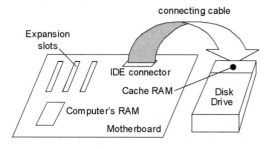

1. Using memory chips that are not part of the PC's normal memory map.   The cache memory chips are now located inside the disk drive case, as shown in the diagram. Modern drives have from 512k up to 16MB of this built-in cache memory.
2. Using a chunk of the computer's memory, under the control of the Windows disk caching subsystem.

In both cases, they provide extra memory that is dedicated to interfacing slow disk access with fast CPU access.

Both caching systems work in the same way.   The CPU demands data at a much faster rate than the disk mechanism can fetch it.   The cache memory in the disk drive - or in the computer memory - stores copies of the data that was previously read or written.   It also reads ahead - it reads in data from sectors beyond that requested.   If the machine wishes to read a file, there is a fair chance that the data is already stored in the cache memory. If so, then it can be transferred at a much faster rate than would be the case with reading directly from disk. If the data is found in cache, then it is described as a *'hit'*; if it has to be fetched from disk, then it is a *'miss'*. To improve the *'hit rate'*, the controller predicts the next data to be read (see notes on the principle of locality) and pre-loads this data into cache memory.

Windows caching

Windows uses a software system called VCACHE. This system is intelligent and is able to use the available system memory to best advantage. The amount of memory used depends on the demand on the systems resources and the application packages. Depending upon the amount of RAM available at any time, it allocates the amount it needs for cache at that time. If the system demands change, then VCACHE automatically reallocates the amount allocated to caching. Another benefit of VCACHE is that it caches CD-ROMs.

Fragmentation

Often, a file is stored as one contiguous block of disk space. However, files can end up occupying several non-contiguous areas of the disk when:

- An existing file is added to. Unless it is the last file in the FAT table (very unlikely), the extra data will have to be placed in the first free clusters.
- A new file is allocated the space of a smaller erased file. Again, the extra data is forced to overflow into a non-contiguous area of the hard disk.

The continual movement of the head from one area of the disk to another slows data retrieval by up to 25%. Fragmentation can be eliminated with utilities such as the DOS DEFRAG command, Windows *'Disk Defragmenter'*, or Norton's `Speed Disk'. These re-order the allocations to achieve contiguous space for files. The result of defragmenting is to have each file occupying consecutive disk clusters.

Using Disk Defragmenter

Windows has a built-in defragmenter, reached through Programs/ Accessories/ System Tools/ Disk Defragmenter. These offer a choice of disk to defragment, give a report on the current state of fragmentation and can show the details of the defragmenting process.

Windows 2000/XP disk defragmenter

The Windows 2000/XP version was totally re-written, to accommodate FAT, FAT32, FAT32X, and NTFS. Defragmentation is, as it has always been, a two-stage process. Firstly, the existing file system is analysed for fragmentation, then the fragmentation is removed by shuffling the contents of disk clusters to put fragments of the same file next to each other. In Windows 2000/XP, this two-stage process can be controlled. Analysis can take place

without defragmentation and an analysis report can be produced, detailing how much fragmentation has been discovered.

The report gives details of exactly which files are the most fragmented and how. This allows the user to decide whether to undertake the process of defragmentation.

Two *'spectrum'* style graphs are produced. One is from the analysis phase, which shows the state of the disk. The other is from the defragmentation phase, which initially looks just like the analysis display but which gradually changes with the defragmentation process, to show how much of the defragmentation process has been carried out.

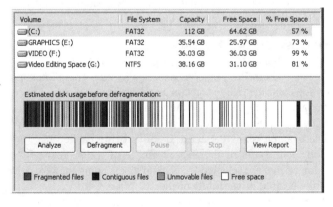

Disk problems

The user's data is always at risk of corruption through hardware, software or power problems.

Windows provides the SCANDISK utility as diagnostic aid for detecting problems with files and folders. When run, it compares the size of each file as given in the directory entry. It then checks whether there is the correct number of clusters in the file's chain to accommodate the file.

In making these checks, a number of problems are detected along the way. These problems are rarely hardware faults. They are usually software glitches that have made rogue writes to the FAT, or users switching off the power before a program has completed its disk housekeeping, or users pressing Alt-Ctrl-Del to escape from a problem they don't understand.

Protecting files

Computers are susceptible to temperature extremes, power cuts or fluctuations and magnetic fields. This can lead to a sudden machine breakdown and the collapse of the program it is running. Worse still, it can lead to the loss or corruption of important data. In most organisations, the data held in the machine is more important than the machine itself. If a hard disk crashes, it is a simple matter of purchasing and fitting another disk. However, if scores of Megabytes, or even Gigabytes, of data are lost, then countless amounts of person-hours are required to replace this data. In many cases, the data can be reconstituted from paperwork (e.g. customer forms, order forms, etc.). In other cases, the data has no paperwork equivalent (e.g. telephone orders or data that was automatically gathered in real time from remote stations) and can be lost forever.

Despite all efforts to achieve reliability, these losses remain a distinct possibility. The only defence is to ensure that important data is copied away at regular intervals, thus creating backup copies. In the event of machine failure and data loss, the user can reconstitute the data using the backup version. The user then only has to add the changes that have occurred to the data since the date and time of the backup.

Frequency of backups

The frequency of backups is a matter for the individual organisation and is decided by asking *"how much extra effort would be required to reconstitute lost data if backups were carried out weekly instead of daily?"* or *"is there any data that can afford to be lost at all?"*. If data changes slowly on a particular machine, there is less need to carry out frequent backups. Where the data on a machine regularly changes, the degree of change should be reflected in the frequency of backing up. There are occasions, however, when frequent backups are important even for slowly changing data. Where the data being added contains vital information, a more frequent backup ensures that this information is not lost.

Backup strategy

Organisations should conduct their backup activities in a way that minimises duplicated effort. When the disk is backed up for the first time, a full backup is carried out requiring much storage space to store the hard disk's data. With large amounts of data, tape streamer backup drives, ZIP drives or writeable CD-ROMs are used. In general, there is little need to back up application programs since they are readily available from the original installation disks or CDs. The only exception may be where an application is heavily customised at installation time and backing up would save these settings.

When the second backup is due, a great deal of time is saved if only new files and those files that have been altered are backed up to disk. This saves wasted time and disks backing up data that has not been changed since the last backup. This second, smaller, set is called an *'incremental'* backup. When the third backup is carried out, even fewer files are involved in the backup. The disks are grouped and labelled for an incremental restore, if required. Every so often, say monthly, a complete system backup would be instigated to freshen the set of backup disks, the older sets of disks being recycled.

Backup for Windows 95

The Windows 95 version is accessed through the
          Start/Programs/Accessories/System Tools/Backup
options and the main screen is as shown in the illustration. It offers an additional option to compare the files in the
backup set with the files on the hard disk. Entire drives, folders or individual files are selectable.

The example show the entire C: drive being backed up, along with parts of the *'export'* folder of the F: drive. Components are selected for backup by checking the box of the desired drive, folder or file.

When *'Next Step'* is clicked, the user can choose which device to copy the backup files to.

When the *'Start Backup'* option is clicked, the user is asked to enter a name for the backup set of files. The files are saved with this name and the *'QIC'* file extension (e.g. *'SALES.QIC'*)

If a particular set of files is regularly backed up, the settings for that set of files can be saved. This saves the trouble of selecting the same set of folders and files every time the backup needs to be carried out. Once the files and the backup destination are selected, the *'SaveAs'* option is selected from the *'File'* menu. The backup set name is entered and *'Save'* is selected.

Restoring

If the files ever need to be restored, the *'Restore'* tab of the *'Backup'* utility is selected.   From the left windowpane, select the drive that holds the backup file.   From the files displayed in the right pane, select the desired backup set (e.g. *'SALES.QIC'*).   Clicking the *'Next Step'* button provides the option to restore all or selected parts of the backup set.   Clicking the *'Start Restore'* button restores the selected files to the original drives and folders from which they were backed up.   Using the

Settings/Restore/Alternate Location

options allows the user to specify different destination folders for the restore process.

Backup for Windows 98/ME/2000/XP

The Windows 98/ME/2000/XP version is also accessed through the *'Start'* menu's

Programs/Accessories/System Tools/Backup

options.

The XP Backup Wizard

The XP Backup or Restore Wizard displays a left panel showing the computer's directory and file structure and the right panel displays the files that have been selected for backup.   Entire drives, folders or individual files are selectable.

The example shows that certain files in the *'zips'* folder of the C: drive have been selected, along with the entire contents of the *';shared'* folder.

Components are selected for backup by checking the box of the desired drive, folder or file.

Clicking the *'Advanced'* button produces a series of further dialog boxes as explained below.

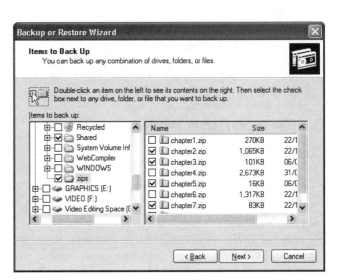

Type

The choices of backup type are:

Normal

This is a full backup of every file selected.

Copy

As above, except that the files are not marked as having been backed up.

Incremental backup

Backs up those files that have been modified since the last backup.   The archive bit is reset for each file that is backed up.   This means that a full restoration requires the files from the initial full backup and the files from every subsequent incremental backup.   This requires the storage of the set of all backups and is recommended where different files on a disk tend to be used and altered.

Differential backup

This also backs up of all files that have been modified since the previous full backup.   The difference with this method is that backups after the initial full backup do <u>not</u> result in archive bits being reset.   This option backs up all files that have been altered since the full backup, even if these files were backed up in a previous differential backup. Thus, the new differential backup supersedes all previous differential backup files.   This option only requires the storage of the full backup plus the last differential backup and is recommended where the same files are regularly being modified - e.g. budget files, price lists.

Daily

Only backs up those files that were created or modified on the day of the backup.

After selecting the files/folders for backup, clicking the *'Next'* button opens a further dialog box that allows the user to name the backup and decide which folder it should be stored in.

Clicking the *'Next'* button opens a further dialog box with three options. The first option, to verify that the backed up data

Clicking the *'Next'* button opens a further dialog box that allows the user to add the new backup to an existing backup, or replace the existing backups with the new backup.

Clicking the *'Next'* button opens a further dialog box that allows the user to backup immediately or schedule the backup for a later time.

Restoring

The Backup or Restore Wizard can be used for restoring backup files, by choosing *'Restore files and settings'* from the opening dialog box. This produces the screen shown in the illustration.

The set of files/folders to be restored is chosen by clicking the appropriate boxes.

Clicking any folder in the left panel results in its contents being displayed in the right panel. This way, individual files can be selected for backup, if desired.

Clicking the *'Advanced'* button opens a further dialog box, where the user can choose to restore the file to their original locations or to another folder.

Clicking the *'Next'* button opens a further dialog box that allows the user to replace any existing files, leave any existing files – or only replace existing files that that are older than the backed up version.

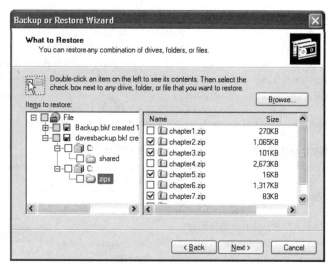

Note

The backup and restore utility can also be used to back up the user's My Documents folder along with the user's Favorites, desktop settings and any cookies. In addition, it can be used to create a system recovery disk that can be stored in case the computer has a system failure that corrupts parts of the operating system.

Other storage options

CD-ROM and DVD

These options are explained in more detail in the *'CD Production'* chapter. The basic CD is capable of storing 650MB of data, while a DVD can store 4.7GB. However, the CD-ROM and DVD-ROM are read only; special types of disk are required to record disks (CD-R and DVD-R) or to re-write to disks (CD-RW and DVD-RW).

Floptical Disks

A number of drives are available that make use of *'floptical'* disks. These disks are similar in principle to CD-ROMs, but are read/write capable. Making them more versatile. The most popular of these is the Iomega *'Zip'* disk, which comes in 100MB, 250MB and 750MB varieties. Like a floppy, the computer needs a Zip Drive to read Zip Disks. A 750MB drive can read 100MB disks, but not vice versa. Zip Drives can be internal to the PC, or can be removable devices that attach via the parallel port, or USB or FireWire port.

Other similar devices are also available. Iomega has a number of 'legacy' products that are no longer produced, such as the 2GB *'Jaz'* drive, and another drive that was popular is the 120MB Panasonic LS-120, which can also read standard floppy disks.

A relative newcomer is the DataPlay disk, a floptical cartridge that is just larger than a postage stamp but can store 250MB on either side of the disk. This has been in development for some time, and although it has great potential it has failed to catch on so far. It is intended for similar applications as ordinary CDs.

Tape drives

Although slowly declining in popularity, tape drives are still useful. Although there are many forms of tape drive available, the typical modern type system is a digital tape drive that can store large quantities of data (200GB or more on some tapes) but with a comparatively slow access time.

Tape drives, therefore, are excellent at archiving very large amounts of material, such as high-quality video files from a DV (Digital Video) camera. CD-Rs and floptical drives can be used for archiving, but CD-R's suffer from being read-only once created, and floptical drives tend to be either low-capacity or expensive. Tape drives offer a low-cost, high-capacity archive medium for those who need it.

Flash Memory

This type of storage medium is more normally used in digital cameras, and portable MP3 players. However, some of these devices incorporate additional functions to allow the memory to be used as temporary storage for other types of data, although the camera/player will not be able to make use of that data. Furthermore, there are small, convenient USB storage devices available. These are often called 'memory pens' because they are generally shaped like a thick pen. Flash memory is typically very small in comparison to other storage types, but they have reasonably good access speed, and are more convenient than most other forms of removable media.

Printer

The printer is used to produce a paper copy (often called a *'hard copy'*) of the letters, reports, graphs, etc. produced by the program. They have two connector cables; one for the mains supply and one to take the data from the computer to the printer. There are different printers for different jobs, but there are two main types in use for multimedia PCs, as explained below.

Ink Jet Printers

An inkjet printer is a *'non impact'* printer, preferring instead to spray dots of ink on to the paper. The ink is stored in a small plastic case about the size of a matchbox and this case also comprises the printing head. A small printed circuit board on the ink cartridge takes the signals from the computer right up to tiny holes in the ink reservoir. The ink is attracted through the holes and carries on to strike the paper. This produces an output that approaches the quality of the laser printer, at a fraction of the cost. It typically produces a resolution of about 600 dots per inch and is very quiet in operation. Colour inkjet models use four ink heads and mix their outputs to achieve an even greater range of colours. The inks used are the primary print colours (cyan, magenta and yellow) and black. These are known as CMYK printers.

Laser Printers

A laser printer works on a similar principle to the normal photocopier; in fact, a laser is like the second half of a photocopier. With a photocopier, the image from an inserted master is scanned and turned into a stream of digital information. This digital information is then used to modulate a laser beam on to a drum. The electrostatic charge thus built up attracts the toner powder, which is eventually transferred to the paper. With a laser printer, the stream of digital information is supplied directly by the computer, via the printer cable. So, the laser printer is like a cut down version of a photocopier.

The resolution of a laser printer is measured in the number of dots in an inch and is normally 600 dpi, with modern versions now at 1200 dpi or higher. They are thus capable of both high quality text and graphics.

A typical laser is capable of printing either 8 pages per minute or 12 pages per minute. These speed figures describe the number of pages that the printer can produce once the image is ready to print. In fact, the normal laser printer makes up a copy of the picture in its own internal memory, prior to starting the printing process. This time has to be added to the time for printing. So, for a single copy, the printing speed is fairly slow; if many copies are required, the image is still only built up once and the overall speed becomes closer to the printing speed.

The size of the printer's memory has an influence on the final quality of print that can be handled. If the printer has only a small internal memory, say 256k or 512k, then it will not be able to store a complete A4 page of graphics. To reduce retail prices, many manufacturers produce models with small internal memories. Of course, most printers can have their memory size upgraded by adding extra memory boards, although this is fairly expensive.

Due to their mechanics, laser printers are very quiet in operation. There is no impact noise, as the paper is not struck; there is only the sound of the motor and its roller mechanisms.

Colour Printers

Both laser and inkjet printers are available in colour versions. They are known as '*CMYK*' printers, because the inks required are in the colours Cyan, Yellow, Magenta, and black (known as 'Key'). Colour printers, of course, require colour cartridges, and are typically of lower quality than a professional colour print run. Unfortunately, the printers used for such jobs are very expensive and are not generally found on PCs.

Display Technology

The term *'Computer Video'* was used for many years to describe the techniques used to transfer computer images to the monitor. These images could be mainly static (as in the case of databases or word processing) or could be animated (as in the case of games, graphic simulations, etc). Now, computer video describes the specific technique of showing real-life video footage for multimedia presentations. This section examines the technology of monitors and other display devices, as well as computer graphics cards, and discusses the technical and operational factors to be considered when choosing - and using - such devices.

The monitor, and its hardware and software drivers, are becoming increasingly complex devices. There is a wide choice of specifications, techniques, performances and prices. There is no overall *'correct'* choice; there is only an appropriate choice for a particular use. For multimedia in particular, a large screen with high resolution and high colour depth is essential.

Picture Composition

In a TV receiver, the intensity of the beam can be varied continuously across the scan of the line, limited only by the quality of the controlling electronics. For computer monitors, each line is considered to have a certain amount of elements along its length. Each element can then be illuminated to any brightness level (from fully off to fully lit), to produce the picture intelligence. Each of the picture elements is known as a *'pixel'*. The number of picture lines and the number of pixels across each line are a measure of the *'resolution'* of the screen picture. A SVGA screen, for example, has a resolution of 800 x 600 - i.e. it has a matrix of 800 pixels across by 600 pixels down.

Frame refresh speeds

The screen produced by the above process has only a short life, as the glow from the phosphoresced areas will rapidly die away. The whole process has to be repeated regularly enough so that the persistence of vision of the human eye perceives the screen as a continuous display, with no detectable flicker. Where the picture has a dark background, any flicker is less noticeable.   Where there is a white background, the constant cycle of lighting a pixel, letting the pixel illumination dull, followed by again fully illuminating the pixel causes the most pronounced flicker.   This can be particularly noticeable with Windows, since most backgrounds are light-coloured.   40Hz is the rate at which most people can detect flicker.   Many people are capable of detecting and being bothered by flicker at up to 70Hz.   At 72Hz, flicker ceases to be a factor.

Over the years, the frame refresh speeds have gradually increased.   At the end of 1997, VESA recommended 85Hz as the refresh rate for 14" monitors. Modern monitors commonly have a top frame refresh speed exceeding 100Hz and some models have a top rate of 200Hz. The pace of improvement has been tempered by the fact that faster frame speeds increase the system bandwidth and thereby cost more to manufacture.

Aspect Ratio

his is the ratio of the screen's width to the screen's height.   Monitor CRTs, like conventional TV screens, are almost entirely built with a ratio of 4:3.   To maintain a uniform screen display, the screen must be driven at the same rate - i.e. there should be 4 pixels across the screen for each three pixels down the screen. Modern video adapters follow this standard for the majority of their video modes.

In terms of hardware, no CRTs are currently available in widescreen aspect ratio formats such as 16:9 or 2.23:1. However, LCD and plasma displays (see later in this chapter) are available in either aspect ratio, and an increasing number of video adapters have a '*TV out*' connector to allow display on a standard 4:3 or domestic 16:9 widescreen television.

If the screen is of a different aspect ratio from the pixel data, the output will be affected. Widescreen video, such as DVDs played in PC drives, or some computer games, will have to be shrunk to fit a standard 4:3 display. Conversely, a normal 4:3 ratio display will not fill a 16:9 screen. Fortunately, some recent video cards have display modes that better match the widescreen formats. See the DVD section of the '*CD Productions*' chapter for more details on aspect ratios other than 4:3.

CRT Monitors

In any modern display device, colour images are built up from just three colours: Red, Green, and Blue, as illustrated in the table opposite.

A CRT (Cathode Ray Tube) monitor generally comes in two types: the Shadow Mask Tube, and the Trinitron tube. Both types use three beams of electrons, each one corresponding to the Red, Green and Blue components of the pixel that is being created.

SIGNAL			COLOUR
R	G	B	
Low	Low	Low	Black
Low	Low	High	Blue
Low	High	Low	Green
Low	High	High	Cyan
High	Low	Low	Red
High	Low	High	Magenta
High	High	Low	Yellow
High	High	High	White

The difference between the two lies in their construction.   The screen area (the part seen by the user) of a shadow mask tube resembles part of the surface of a sphere. The screen is curved in both the vertical and horizontal directions. This system provides for easy focusing of the electron beams on to the phosphor inner coating. The screen area of a Trinitron tube looks like part of the rounded surface of a cylinder.

The vertical direction is flat although the horizontal direction remains curved in most models. Some monitors are flat in both planes.

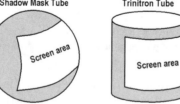

The Trinitron tube has the following mask variety:

- distortion of displayed lines is
- screen corners are sharper
- suffers less glare from lighting

advantages over the shadow

minimised

Resolution

The quality of a screen picture, in terms of its detail, can be defined by its '*resolution*'.

The screen resolution is measured by the number of pixels across the screen, by the number of pixels that can be displayed in the vertical direction. The table shows the most common display modes.

Even these high resolutions are unable to fully meet modern needs. Advertisers used to talk a lot about WYSIWYG (What You See Is What You Get). This meant that the screen would display the image in the exact size and detail as would be expected in the final printed output.   The higher resolutions of modern printers place an increasing demand on WYSIWYG DTP and graphics systems.

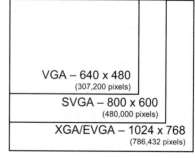

Comparison of common Display Modes

VGA – 640 x 480
(307,200 pixels)

SVGA – 800 x 600
(480,000 pixels)

XGA/EVGA – 1024 x 768
(786,432 pixels)

Consider that an A4 sheet is approximately 97 square inches - say 80 square inches printable area after taking borders into consideration. A typical laser printer or inkjet printer has an output at 600 dpi (dots per inch), or 360,000 dots per square inch. So, to display a full A4 sheet on screen - at printer resolution - would require 80 x 360,000, or a full 28,800,000 dots. Clearly, even the highest screen resolution is incapable of fully displaying detailed DTP and CAD work. With current printers having 1200dpi or higher capability, the problem is greatly worsened.

Mode	Resolution
Base VGA	640 x 480
SVGA	800 x 600
XGA	1024 x 768
EVGA/SVGA	1024 x 768
WXGA	1280 x 768
SXGA	1280 x 1024
SXGAW	1600x1024
UXGA	1600 x 1200
WUXGA	1920 x 1200
QXGA	2048 x 1536
QSXGA	2560 x 2048
QUXGA	3200 x 2400
QUXGA-W	3840 x 2400

These limitations are minimised by the *'zoom'* facility offered by many packages; this allows a close up view of a small area of the printed output. While zooming allows the fine detail to be inspected, it is no longer at the correct physical size. Many would argue that this is not a problem since users could not visually resolve 360,000 individual dots on a one inch square in any case.

Dot Pitch

In a shadow mask tube CRT, each pixel is made up a triad of phosphorous dots on the screen, one each for Red, Green and Blue. These dots are laid on the inner screen at a matching pitch. The distance between the centre of one triad to the centre of the next nearest triad is known as the *'dot pitch'*. The dot pitch, therefore, is a measure of the finest quality possible in the picture from that particular monitor. The dot pitch is measured in fractions of a millimetre. The lower the dot pitch value, the more closely spaced are the individual illuminated spots - hence the better picture detail. Since adjacent triangles are offset, the dot pitch value is usually a diagonal measurement.

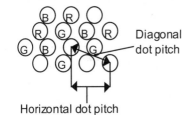

The importance of dot pitch is that on a smaller monitor, and/or a lower dot pitch monitor, higher resolution modes will not display properly since there are not enough triads to show each pixel independently.

The value of the horizontal *'dots per inch'* is therefore a more useful measure when deciding the quality of a monitor.

The table shows the <u>maximum</u> number of dots that can appear across different screen sizes.

Advertised screen size			14"	15"	17"	19"	21"
Theoretical width of screen			11.2"	12"	13.6"	15.2"	16.8"
Diagonal dot pitch	Horizontal pitch	Dots per inch	Maximum theoretical number of horizontal dots				
0.22mm	0.19mm	133	1492	1599	1812	2025	2238
0.25mm	0.22mm	117	1313	1407	1595	1782	1970
0.26mm	0.23mm	112	1263	1353	1533	1714	1894
0.28mm	0.24mm	104	1172	1256	1424	1591	1759
0.31mm	0.26mm	97	1094	1172	1329	1485	1641

The exact figures will vary by manufacturer and those in the table are working approximations. Manufacturers tend to err on the side of over-estimating the active image area of their screens. An inspection of a range of 17" monitors reveals that the actual screen diagonal size varies from 16.34" down to as little as 15.25". If the actual viewable area is less than the calculated area, then it follows that the actual number of viewable pixels is also likewise reduced. This means that the above table significantly overestimates the specification of the monitors. The real world performance is less than that shown. In the case of the 15.25" view from a 17" monitor, it means that the number of viewable pixels is less than 90% of the figure shown in the table.

As can be seen, there is a direct relationship between dot pitch, screen size and the maximum screen resolution. A .28mm dot pitch monitor has around 1424 dots per line on a 17" screen but has only around 1172 dots per line on a 14" screen. The 17" monitor in this case is capable of handling 1280 x 1024 mode with ease. The 14", on the other hand, has fewer dots on the screen than the number of individual pixels required by the 1280 x 1024 picture. The result is a marked loss of detail and the blurring of small characters. Since even the table shows idealised figures, the 14" monitor is best run at no more then 800 x 600.

Although the smallest dot pitch is more desirable, they are more costly to manufacture. .21mm and even .2mm dot pitch monitors are available but are expensive. Typical dot pitch sizes for colour SVGA monitors are 0.26mm and 0.28mm. VGA monitors and large-size SVGA monitors normally have up to 0.31mm dot pitch. Some manufacturers claim that a .28mm 14" monitor is a 1024 x 768 model and this is only true if an inferior picture is acceptable, since each individual pixel cannot possibly be separately displayed. For large-screen monitors, the dot pitch can be greater without any loss of detail. Alternatively, the dot pitch can be reduced to .26mm; in this case, more detail can be crammed on the screen.

Even where a screen's construction quality allows for the reproduction of high resolution, the higher resolution modes may not be realistically useable. A 14" monitor, for example, would display tiny icons and extra small text if it were driven at high resolutions. The table shows the most likely resolutions to be used with a particular screen size.

Resolution	Best Monitor Size
640 x 480	14"
800 x 600	15"
1024 x 768	17"
1280 x 1024	19"
1600 x1200	21"

Common Graphics Modes

Below is a brief description of the most popular graphics modes currently to be found in use. Earlier ranges, such as MDA, Hercules, CGA, EGA, 8514/A, EVGA and XGA, are no longer manufactured and are out of use.

VGA

Video Graphics Array. Introduced by IBM in 1987 and still accessible even on modern video cards. It introduced the first screen with square pixels, i.e. a 4:3 aspect ratio. It was also the first standard to dispense with TTL levels of screen drive and introduce varying levels of colour intensity. It handles a palette of 256 colours, with a resolution up to 640 x 480. It also supported refresh rates of 60Hz or 70 Hz. It has long since been superseded by more advanced video adapters.

SVGA

Super VGA. The original VESA SVGA specification was for a 16-colour 800x600 screen. A wide range of later VESA standards allowed for higher resolutions in a range of colour depths and refresh rates. Many of these standards are still in use, and have also provided the basis for many non-VESA modes. Common SVGA modes include 800x600, 1024x768, and 1280x1024 resolution at 16-bit, 24-bit or 32-bit colour.

High resolution colour modes

Although not a VESA standard or the name of a video adapter, the terms SXGA (Super XGA) and UXGA (Ultra XGA) have become commonplace to describe the 1280x1024 and 1600x1200 resolution modes, respectively. Note that UXGA has an aspect ratio of 5:4 instead of 4:3 like most other modes; using UXGA mode on a 4:3 screen will result in a very slightly squashed image. Conversely, using any of the 4:3 graphics modes on a 5:4 ratio screen (which is unusual even for portable computers) will result in a slightly stretched image.

QUXGA refers to 'Quad XGA', and as the name suggests this mode is four times the size of XGA, at 2048x1536. Similarly, QSXGA is Quad SXGA mode, and QUXGA is Quad UXGA. In addition, there are now a range of wide screen modes available, including WXGA (Wide XGA), SXGAW (SXGA Wide), WUXGA (Wide UXGA), and QUXGA-W (QUXGA Wide). These offer resolutions of 1280x768, 1600x1024, 1920x1200, and 3840x2400. Other, less common modes are also in use. Typically, a widescreen format is around 20% wider than a normal display mode, bringing it to an aspect ratio of 5:3, 25:16 or 8:5. None of these are exactly the same as a standard widescreen television at an aspect ratio of 16:9, so there will still be empty edges of the screen if this type of display is used.

Notes

- Specifications above the VGA standard have always suffered from a confusing mixture of names. Some manufacturers gave the name 'SVGA' to any product that was a better resolution or colour depth than standard VGA, for example, whether the screen mode was VESA-compliant or not. Also, the term XGA originally meant the specific video card of the same name by IBM, while it is now commonly used to describe one of the XGA card's resolution modes.
- A few older display adapters that state 'up to 32,767 colours' or '16 million colours' may only apply to a low resolution with higher resolutions only supporting 256 colours. The monitor, being analogue, is able to support any range of colours, and is limited only by resolution and refresh rate.
- The specification of a monitor should be checked, rather than relying on its title in an advertisement.

Screen Sizes

Higher resolution monitors allow more information to be simultaneously displayed on the screen - more of a worksheet, more of a database record, an entire A4 page of DTP.

Advantages

- Less time is spent on scrolling a window on the output.
- More data visible on screen at the same time means fewer errors.

Disadvantages

- Putting more information on the same size of screen means that text, icons and graphics are all smaller than before - and therefore more difficulty to read. A 14" model of SVGA monitor, for example, is only useful to those with gifted eyesight.
- To maintain the required readability requires a bigger, and therefore more expensive, monitor. The user is forced to move from a 14" model to a 17" or even 20" model.
- Bigger screens have problems maintaining an even resolution over the entire screen area. Some extreme areas become slightly fuzzy, due to convergence problems. An even quality can be maintained using 'dynamic beam focusing', but this involves extra, costly, construction complexities.

The average CRT monitor is a 15" to 19" model, with 20" and 21" models are typically used for DTP and CAD. For specialist work, multimedia and other presentations, monitors are available up to 43", at staggering prices.

Notes

- When a manufacturer's specification refers to the screen size, it is describing the measurement between any two diagonal corners.
- This measurement usually does not describe the <u>actual</u> screen area. It is common for the phosphor coating to only extend over a proportion of the front screen, resulting in a permanent, unlit border round the screen.
- The unused area of the screen does not result in any loss of resolution; it just means that the graphics detail is compressed into a smaller area than the screen dimension suggests.
- Although a small size monitor is capable of displaying a high-resolution screen, it is often not a practical situation, since the size of the text can be too small to be readable. This is being countered by the introduction of 'anti-aliasing', a technique in the video card that adds artificial shading to lines and letters, to give an appearance of added sharpness.

Screen Drives

Analogue

Early screen drives used discrete levels of intensity, with a limited colour range. These now obsolete modes were called 'RGB' drives, and have long been replaced by analogue drives that can display almost any shade or hue of colour. As such, the colour range is limited only by the video adapter's capabilities (see later). Some monitors call analogue video inputs 'D-SUB' due to the D-shaped connector used.

DVI

Flat panel displays are digital devices, while VGA is an analogue cable. Driving a flat panel display via a VGA cable results in unnecessary loss of detail during the conversion process, and the solution is a new digital cable – DVI. Although DVI interfaces have been around for some time, it is only relatively recently that a standard has been agreed upon. Despite the name, DVI comes in three flavours: DVI-d (digital only), DVI-a (analogue only) and DVI-i (integrated digital and analogue). The connector has three rows of pins for digital only and shared digital/analogue connections, and five pins for analogue only connections. Many graphics provide DVI output connectors.

DVI is also useful with CRT monitors that have DVI inputs, as it means the digital signal can be converted to analogue by the monitor rather than the display card, enabling the monitor to fine-tune the conversion process to suit the characteristics of the particular monitor.

TV-Out

Many display adapters now combine a conventional 15-PIN D-SUB video connector (or a modern DVI connector) with a 'TV-Out' facility. This uses one of several types of connectors to send video output to an ordinary or digital television, allowing these models to use some TVs as monitors, which can be useful. However, they suffer from poorer quality, as the extra signal processing circuitry introduces more noise and more signal distortion. The two connectors that may be available on a TV-Out capable video card are those of Composite or S-Video.

With the composite method, the output from the PC is a single signal that combines the three colour components and the synchronisation signals. The monitor has to separate these signals, before applying them to the monitor circuitry. The S-Video connector is a four-wire cable that transmits separate signals for chrominance (colouration) and luminance (brightness). This offers a slightly better quality of signal than the composite method.

Note however that not every television has composite or S-Video connectors. Many have only SCART connectors, for which a special converter adapter will be required.

Colour Management

One of the main problems in working with photographic images is ensuring colour consistency. The scanner, monitor, and printer in any given system are probably all manufactured by different companies, to different standards, and may even have their own colour model. The result is that colour shades may appear different on-screen from the scanned input, or may be different again when printed out. The user can minimise this effect by changing monitor brightness and contrast, or by editing the coloration of an image before printing, but this involves extra work and is never perfect.

To help combat this problem, a technology known as a Colour Management System (CMS) can be used. This software is used to control the output of colour to the monitor, so that it more closely matches the colour input from scanners and the colour output of printers. This ensures that the colours in the original image are accurately portrayed on the monitor screen and the colours seen on screen will be accurately reproduced by the printing process.

Characteristics of every colour device vary widely, and will change over time as the device wears. Therefore, the CMS settings have to be calibrated when the monitor is installed, and also if any significant changes are made – for example, if the brightness/contrast controls are altered in the monitor's On-Screen Display.

The CMS calibration consists of a series of colour matching steps, to ensure correct brightness levels are recorded for any given monitor. This includes a '*black level*' and a '*white level*' calibration, to make sure that areas intended to be pure black or white appear correctly on the monitor. The calibration details are then saved to an ICM (Image Colour Matching) file. ICM is supported by Windows operating systems and used by high-end photo editing packages such as Adobe PhotoShop. CMS systems are intended mainly to ensure correct colour output when printing, but multimedia creators may still find it useful when scanning images, to ensure correct colour display on any given output device.

Flat Display Panels

In the past couple of years, CRT replacements in the form of flat LCD / TFT panels have started to appear. Other technologies include Gas Plasma displays and IBM's HPA. The technology used in these displays has been perfected in laptop computers over the years and is based on individual pixels being addressed in an array. Such displays may either use a standard VGA card or may be based on the DVI digital video specification or a specialist proprietary digital card.

The principal differences between flat panel displays and CRTs are:

- As explained earlier, the actual viewing surface of a CRT is less than its quoted screen size. With flat displays, the entire viewing area is visible and exactly corresponds to the quoted screen size.
- CRT displays have to be constantly refreshed to avoid flicker effects, as explained earlier. Pixels on a flat panel display do not fade between refreshes, such that a frame rate of around 60Hz produces a flicker-free picture. Increasing the frame rate above about 60Hz produces no perceived improvement, while increasing the systems' bandwidth requirements.
- Because flat panels are built from a fixed matrix, they have a native resolution. Driving the display at a different resolution involves scaling (interpolation) of the incoming signal to either shrink it or expand it before using it to drive the display. Scaling up may cause pixellation making the image chunky and difficult to read. Alternatively, a signal of smaller resolution can be displayed as a small image in the centre of the screen. Scaling down may result in the loss of some important detail. CRT displays always use the entire screen area for display and cannot scale down.
- Some flat panels need a proprietary adapter card. Some use DVI interfaces, which are expensive and complex. Others are compatible with standard analogue SVGA outputs but require expensive internal electronics to digitise the signal.
- Viewing angles are smaller, and output brightness is usually less than the equivalent CRT display.
- There are only a very few manufacturing plants for large LCD "blanks" and the etched glass screens. Because of this, commercially available LCD screens over 19" are extremely expensive.
- Because of the low manufacturing yield and scarcity, flat panels tend to be expensive.

For general PC use, the benefits of a flat panel display may not outweigh the price tag. However, multimedia users may well find they are a worthwhile option, due to their flexibility.

The principle of operation of each of the major types of flat panel displays is explained below:

TFT / Liquid Crystal Displays

The Liquid Crystal Display is one of the most popular alternatives to cathode ray tube monitors and is particularly widely used in portable and notebook PCs.

Advantages of LCDs

- No electron beams, thereby eliminating problems with linearity, misconvergence, pincushion distortion, and sizing/positioning.
- Low power consumption and low voltages.
- Light weight - ideal for portables.
- No radiation or flicker problems, unlike CRTs.
- Flat displays - hang on wall / easy to locate in work area.

Disadvantages

- Restricted viewing angle.
- Poor contrast. Supertwist displays give more contrast but introduce a certain tinge. This is correctable with special film coatings and extra construction complexity. It is called '*triple supertwist*'. It is more expensive to manufacture and is used in the best LCD displays.
- Slow speed. When the liquid crystal structure has been pulled into a straight configuration, under the influence of the electric field, it takes a relatively long time to restore to its former state. This explains why LCD screens often 'smear' when scrolling or attempting other fast screen updating.
- Costly to manufacture, due to difficulties of quality control.

Passive Matrix

The cheaper of the versions, this screen is effectively a sandwich of three LCD screens, each screen emitting red, green or blue. All modern systems increase efficiency by using *'dual scan'* displays. These split the screen in two vertically and each half is simultaneously scanned and lit. So, a single screen is painted in half the time - i.e. the refresh rate is doubled and flicker is halved.

Active Matrix

Each colour triad comprises the necessary red, green and blue LCD elements and each is activated by its own switching transistor. In this way, the TFT mechanisms described above take place on light waves of pre-determined colour. Since each element is individually switched, the *'ghousting'* associated with older screens is eliminated. In addition, TFT elements are less sensitive to heat and brighter backlights can be used.

Unfortunately, these screens are expensive to produce, since even a VGA monitor would require almost a million transistors to be assembled on the one screen. A single non-working transistor means that a pixel has lost one of its colour elements. Too many defects means that the screen has to be scrapped. About a third of all units produced are unable to meet this very demanding quality control.

Plasma Displays

Gas plasma displays are produced by filling the space between two glass plates with neon /xenon gas and then exciting it with a suitable voltage, usually greater than 80V. The exciting electrode is etched onto the glass. The original gas plasma displays were orange and black and had high power consumption. Recently however various companies have resurrected the technology, extended it to full colour and are using it for display panels, High Definition Television (HDTV) displays and desktop monitors. Among the prime movers of this technology in Europe are Philips BV whose FlatTV is plasma based.

Large plasma displays are becoming more common for such locations as airports, hospitals, trains stations, and even domestic television. Many are capable of handling both computer and audio/video input. Models such as a 50" XGA compatible widescreen screen are available - at the price of a small car! The larger, static applications of multimedia might nevertheless require such an outlay.

Developments

Current developments include:
- Improved resolutions from plasma displays.
- Reflective LCDs. There is no backlighting source. Instead, a mirror is placed behind the display and this allows room light to be reflected back or blocked, dependent on the controlling electric field.
- Field Emissive Devices. FEDs promise to be as slim as LCD panels but are cheaper to produce and impose no restrictions in maximum screen size.

OLED Displays

The most recent display technology to be developed is Kodak's OLED (Organic Light Emitting Diode) technology. This consists of an 'electroluminescent' material coating on a plastic film. The material glows when electric current passes through, producing both colour and light, therefore eliminating the need for an additional light source. OLEDs are currently in development, and can potentially bring about low power consumption, extremely thin flat screens. They are already in use in cameras, and mobile phones using OLEDs are currently in development, with computer displays in the pipeline if the brightness level is acceptable on a large display.

Rear Projection Displays

Another recent innovation is the technique of using a small projector at the back of the display unit. The most notable form of RPD is the Digital Micro-Mirror Device, which works by passing light through a roughly one-inch square chip carrying thousands of tiny mirrors. Each mirror is mounted on an electrode, which allows it to be tilted 10 degrees to either side, thus either reflecting light toward the screen or away from it. These electrodes can switch so quickly that they can effectively present many shades of grey simply by switching quickly back and forward between blocking and reflecting light. This greyscale light is then passed through a spinning colour wheel which is co-ordinated with the electrodes, in order to produce a full colour image. RPDs can be roughly as large and thin as a plasma, and are of similar price, though this may change in

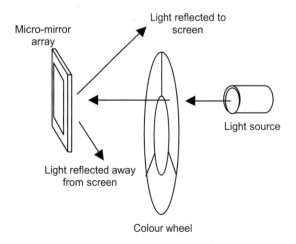

Micro-mirror array

Light reflected to screen

Light source

Light reflected away from screen

Colour wheel

the future. However, RPDs have none of the heat problems associated with plasma screens, though their viewing angle is considerably smaller.

Graphics Cards

The rapid development of computer applications such as video, animations, walkthroughs and photorealistic graphics has stretched both the demands on the computer monitor and the video card technology.   Graphics cards have undergone significant improvements from the early versions that only supported text and crude chunky graphics. The electronics to drive the monitor is mounted on a separate graphics card that slots into an expansion port on the computer's motherboard.   The monitor cable plugs into a socket on the video card.

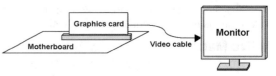

Graphic Card Performance

There are a number of factors to be considered when purchasing a graphics card.   Such a purchase might be as part of an entire system.   It is also possible to buy a matching graphics card and monitor, to upgrade the graphics facilities of an existing system.

The main considerations are:

- RAM size/Resolution/Colour Depth
- RAM type
- Internal bus size
- Chip Set used
- Extra facilities (e.g. video handling, 3D, TV)

- Bandwidth
- External bus type
- Refresh rates
- RAMDAC used

Graphics RAM Size

Display adapters typically have RAM memory of their own, for storing the screen image, and in some cases for applying special effects or storing 3D information.   At its simplest level, the minimum amount of RAM a display adapter needs is determined by the type of screen image the user wishes to be displayed.

Screen Memory

The number of colours that a monitor can produce is theoretically endless.   Tiny voltage changes to any of the monitor's guns will alter that colour and hence the mix perceived by the viewer. The limitation is in the ability of the computer graphics card to store all the possible colour permutations (in the form of a large range of numbers that represent colour brightness levels sent to the monitor) for each screen pixel.

All graphics standards use a *'memory mapped'* method of handling screen output.   An area of memory is reserved for holding the individual pixels that comprise the screen picture.   This screen memory is in most cases <u>additional</u> to the computer's main memory. Extra memory for storing the screen's composition is located on the graphics controller card, although AGP video cards systems lacking in memory can 'borrow' system RAM. The data in the video memory area is used to regularly update the picture.   The computer's CPU (or Graphics Processor on 3d cards) has the task of constantly updating the screen memory area.   The electronics on the graphics card reads this information and uses it to control the drive to the monitor.   For a simple, monochrome system the storage may only require a single bit per pixel.   If the bit is 0, the pixel is left unlit; if the bit is 1 then the pixel is illuminated.   In colour systems, extra pixels are required, to store the colour and hue of the pixel.

Thus, the RAM size required is determined by the maximum screen resolution and the maximum colour depth (i.e. how many colours to be displayed).

The formula to calculate the amount of memory required for a particular screen standard is:

HORIZONTAL RESOLUTION x VERTICAL RESOLUTION x COLOUR BITS / 8

The number of bits for each pixel depends on the number of colours that the pixel has to display.   For monochrome, only one bit per pixel is required (pixel is either lit or unlit).   For 4 colours, 2 bits per pixel are required, providing 2 to the power of 2 combinations.   For 16 colours, 4 bits are required, providing 2 to the power 4 combinations.   For 256 colours, 8 bits are required (i.e. 2 to the power 8 combinations).   A 16-bit system can provide 65,536 different colours for each pixel (called *'high colour'*), while a 24-bit system provides 16.7million colours (often termed *'true colour'*).   Some cards offer 30-bit depth producing 1,073,741,824 colours!   Other cards use 32-bits to handle true colour at faster rates.

The equation given produces a memory requirement specified in bytes.   Dividing the result by 1024 gives a requirement measured in Kilobytes (KB).   There are 1024 bytes to a kilobyte.   Dividing by a further 1024 produces a measurement in MB (MegaBytes).

It is argued that, for art and graphic work, a greater <u>variety</u> of colours on screen has a greater impact on the viewer than increased screen <u>resolution</u>.

If a video card runs the three colour drives at 64 different intensity levels, the possible colours produced are 64 to the power 3, which is 64x64x64 = 262,144 colours.   When the drives are 256 different levels, the result is 256x256x256= 16,777,216 different colours.

Examples

A 16-colour VGA screen would require

$$640 \times 480 \times 4 / 8 = 150 \text{ Kbytes}$$

A 256-colour 1024 x 768 screen would require

$$1024 \times 768 \times 8 / 8 = 768 \text{ KB (i.e. a 1MB card)}$$

A 16-bit, high colour 800 x 600 screen would require

$$800 \times 600 \times 16 / 8 = 937 \text{ KB (i.e. a 1MB card)}$$

A 16-bit, high colour 1280 x 1024 screen would require

$$1280 \times 1024 \times 16 / 8 = 2.5 \text{ MB (i.e. a 4MB card)}$$

A 24-bit, true colour 1024 x 768 screen with 16.7 million colours would require

$$1024 \times 768 \times 24 / 8 = 2.25\text{MB (i.e. a 4MB card)}$$

A 24-bit, true colour 1600 x 1200 screen with 16.7 million colours would require

$$1600 \times 1200 \times 24 / 8 = 5.5\text{MB (i.e. an 8MB card)}$$

Finally, a near top of the range system with true colour at 2048 x 1536 would require

$$2048 \times 1536 \times 24 / 8 = 9.00\text{MB (i.e. a 16MB card)}$$

Bits per pixel	Colours
4	16
8	256
16	65,536
24	16.7m

Notes

- If a board's design allows for future expansion, then extra memory can be fitted to the card to allow it to cope with greater resolutions. The pace of progress in the field of graphics has been so fast, however, that this design has become impractical in new video cards.
- Where the fitted RAM size is vastly greater than is currently required for a particular mode, the memory can be divided into *'pages'* - each page containing the data for a full graphics screen. This allows rapid switching between screens, since the second screen can have its pixel pattern built up in memory, while the first screen is being displayed. This is the basis of on-screen animation.
- The more basic video modes display a number of colours from a larger possible palette (e.g. 16 colours from 64 or 256 from 32,767). This is not suitable for multimedia, as colours which lie outside the palette will have to be '*dithered*' to use existing palette colours, which detracts from the quality of the project, especially if it contains digitised video or pictures.

Bandwidth

The term '*bandwidth*' describes both memory and display throughput, and there are important differences. The display bandwidth, measured in MegaHertz, of a video card measures the rate of data transfer to the monitor. Ultimately, this determines the refresh rates at various resolutions. However, the memory bandwidth, measured in MegaBytes per second, determines how many times the video memory allocated to any given resolution can be updated in the space of each second of time. This has a direct bearing on multimedia, as any high-quality video clips must fit within the bandwidth of the system to avoid dropping frames or stalling the video output.

This can be done by setting the frames per second, and the resolution of the video clip. The minimum bandwidth required to properly display a video clip can be calculated like so:

HORIZONTAL RESOLUTION x VERTICAL RESOLUTION x FRAME RATE x COLOUR DEPTH / 8

For example, to display thirty frames of 24-bit colour video per second, at a resolution of 800 x 600, the bandwidth must be at least 800 x 600 x 30 x 24 /8 = 43,200,000 bytes/sec, or 41.2 MB/s. If the graphics card's bandwidth is lower than this, then errors will occur such as dropped frames, marring the quality of the presentation.

For a system with a known bandwidth, a designer can therefore decide on an appropriate level of quality of video in the presentation. For example, a system with a given bandwidth can play a clip with high resolution and low frame rate, or one of low resolution and high frame rate.

RAM Type

At one stage all graphics cards used standard DRAM (Dynamic RAM) chips as a frame buffer to store the graphics information about that frame. Modern video adapters, with only a few rare exceptions, use either SDR (Single Data Rate) SDRAM (Synchronous DRAM), or DDR (Double Data Rate) SDRAM.

SDR SDRAM

The most common, and cheapest, form of memory found in video adapters on the market at the time of writing is SDR SDRAM (also simply called SDRAM). SDRAM is a form of DRAM that is synchronised to the data bus clock. In this case, however, the SDRAM is synchronised to the speed of the data bus on the card, not the data bus on the motherboard. Thus, the video card memory might run at odd speeds like 115MHz or 175MHz, and is not normally compatible with SDRAM designed for motherboards.

DDR SDRAM

A relatively recent innovation is Dual Data Rate or DDR SDRAM. Conventional SDRAM is synchronised with the bus, by carrying out transfers on the rising or falling edge of the bus's clock signal. DDR SDRAM is triggered by both the rising and falling edge of the bus clock. Thus it should optimally perform at twice the speed of conventional SDRAM. In practice, however, such extreme gains are never seen.

External bus type

Almost all graphics cards on sale today connect to the PC via the AGP port, with only a small minority still using the PCI bus. Although the AGP port is only a 32-bit port as compared to PCI's 64-bit bus, AGP is a high-speed connection that is specially designed for video adapters. As such, PCI cards should be avoided for multimedia applications where possible, although they might still be capable of running most projects.

Of course, multimedia projects for distribution to the public might need to take into account the possibility that older PCI (or perhaps even VESA or ISA cards!) may still be in use on older machines.

Internal bus size

The bus size in a graphics card's specification refers to its <u>internal</u> architecture, the path between the card's RAM and the card's graphics processor. The most critical element in graphics performance is not data flow into the graphics board; it is how the board organises and manages the frame buffer held in memory inside the graphics board. Having a 64-bit internal bus greatly speeds up throughput, enhancing the card's performance. The card's memory is organised into interleaved banks, allowing one bank to be written to while the other is being read. However, with increasing resolution, even 64-bit buses can act as a bottleneck and 128-bit versions are now common. Some cards are advertised as 256-bit models but are in fact just 128-bit cards using DDR memory which, theoretically, doubles the data transferred in any time period.

Refresh rates

Greater resolution and greater colour depth (i.e. bits per pixel) both mean that the card has to move more data for a single frame. This means that cards commonly have lower refresh rates at higher resolutions and at greater colour depths. For example, even a high performance card will have a wide variation in refresh rates. It might handle 200Hz at VGA and SVGA, 150Hz at 1024x768, 100Hz at 1280x1024 but only 85Hz at 1600x1200.

RAMDAC used

The graphics information is stored in memory in digital format and has to be converted into analogue values to drive the gun(s) of the monitor. A chip, known as a RAMDAC (RAM digital/analogue converter) carries out the conversion function. The frame buffer data for each pixel is read in the order that it is sent to the monitor for display. This data is passed to the RAMDAC for conversion. With 24-bit colour, the numbers stored in memory exactly relate to the intensity of the red, green and blue elements of each pixel. This makes the digital to analogue conversion simple.

However, this is not the method with lower colour depths. It is common that a card can only handle a subset of its full range of colours at any one time. For example, a card capable of 65,536 different colours may only be using 256 colours in a particular mode. This subset of colours is known as the *'palette'* and is stored in a look-up table in memory. During normal activities, the screen's pixel colour information is stored as a sequence of logical colour numbers. The colour number for each pixel is read from memory, translated into the values for each gun and these values are given to the RAMDAC to produce the actual colour that will appear on the monitor. Each Windows application package stores information about the palette it uses. When the application is run, Windows sets the RAMDAC to use that palette. When several applications are open at the same time, each application may have different sets of colour numbers in their required palettes. This can result in unexpected colour changes, as the range of colours supported by the card is less than the range of colours requested by the applications. RAMDAC performance is measured both in resolution (e.g. 24-bit) and conversion speed (up to 250MHz).

Chip set used

To reduce costs, all video graphics cards are based round a limited range of different VLSI chips, sometimes referred to as the *'graphics engine'*. These chips are dedicated to the one task and different manufacturers produce a range of chips with different performances. All these chips, and others, provide varying performances. It is best to compare the working speeds of the chipsets as used on various cards. This may use *'Wintach'* readings, measuring how cards cope with actual applications packages or general card tests may be used, measuring the bit manipulation features.

Method of screen writing

Every video adapter has a set of ROM chips containing program code to provide an interface to the video hardware. This is an extension to the BIOS routines that were originally used on the PC. The efficiency of this BIOS extension affects the screen writing speed. Some SVGA cards copy the extension software into an area of RAM to speed up screen handling. This technique is known as *'ROM shadowing'*.

Currently, there are three approaches to screen handling:

- Leave the computer's CPU to do all the screen handling. This is the simplest and cheapest method but can be the slowest. The problems worsen if the system is upgraded. Adding a 1600x1200 card, for example, means the CPU has to handle an even bigger amount of screen data - with no extra computing power to process it.
- Use a Co-Processor to take on the graphics work and relieve the CPU. This is fast but expensive and is usually found in CAD environments.
- Use a graphics accelerator card, which is fast and generally found in most modern high performance PCs.

When extra cards take over the graphics, the main machine has to have special software drivers installed, to allow communication to the cards. In Windows, these include the graphics adapter driver, and a graphical language driver such as DirectX or OpenGL.

3D Cards

Games and animations such as walkthroughs and flybys show a quick succession of frames with each frame showing the viewer a different viewpoint on the scene. As the viewpoint is moved, so the shading, shadowing and fine detail will alter.   Each scene comprises a range of objects (buildings, people, etc) and each object is made up from many individual graphics polygons, usually triangles.   Each triangle has its own colour and surface detail (e.g. grains of sand, bricks, leaves).   The scene will have one or more supposed sources of illumination; this could be the sun, streetlights, etc. As the viewpoint is moved the light source will illuminate the triangles differently.   To produce a 3D effect, the user is shown perspective (i.e. distant objects are made smaller than close objects) and defocussing (i.e. distant object are not as clear as close objects; they are usually dimmed or 'fogged').

The commonly implemented features in 3D cards are:

Facility	Explanation
Z-Buffering	Since x and y describe the horizontal and vertical co-ordinates, 'z' refers to depth. A Z-buffer stores the depth information of objects (e.g. the dog is behind the tree). This allows *'hidden surface removal'* - i.e. time is saved by not drawing parts of an object that are obscured by foreground objects.
Flat shading	The polygons are filled with a uniform colour, which is not as effective but is very quick. Flat shading can be implemented to improve frame rates.
Gouraud shading	Obscures the boundaries between polygons by drawing realistic colour gradients; produces smoother and more natural shapes.
Phong shading	Achieves better results than Gouraud shading but is more demanding of processing power.
Texture mapping	Filling polygons with the same graphics bitmap (e.g. woodgrain or feathers).
Anti-aliasing	Curved and diagonal edges produce a 'staircase' effect known as *'jaggies'*. If the colours of the boundary's surrounding edges are blended, the effect is minimised.
Perspective correction	If an object is receding into the distance, the bit maps used to texture should also gradually diminish. So, a brick wall bitmap would draw smaller and smaller bricks as the wall shrunk towards the horizon.
Mip mapping	Similar to the above, except that new patterns are rendered for distant polygons.
Bilinear/trilinear filtering	Large areas when rendered can appear like a patchwork quilt, with blocks of slightly differing colouring. Filtering determines a pixel's colour on the colour of the surrounding pixels thereby producing a more uniform transition.
Alpha blending	Controls an object's translucency, thereby providing water or glass effects. It is also used to mask out areas of the screen.
Logarithmic fogging	More distance objects are fogged to grey.

The routines to constantly calculate all of these objects and display them on the screen (typically at 20 pictures per second) require a great deal of computational power.   This is called *'rendering'* and it strains even the most powerful PC.   To overcome this problem, many of these computational routines are embedded in graphics card's chipset and called by special software drivers.   Initially these drivers, known as APIs (Application Programming Interface), were written by graphics card manufacturers for their own range of cards.   The routines for a Matrox card would not work with a VideoLogic card, and so on.   As a consequence, games supplied with one card would not work with another graphics card, as the games were specially written to use the card manufacturer's APIs.   Games bundled with the Diamond Stealth 3D 200, for example, are specially written for the card's VIRGE chipset.

There was a need for standard interfaces and this has been met by Silicon Graphic's OpenGL and Microsoft's Direct 3D.   OpenGL is not designed for the games market but for high-end graphical workstations.   With the rise of comparatively cheap PC 3D cards this market is shrinking. Windows 95 Release 2 and later Windows operating systems provide DirectX facilities, which includes Direct3D.   Card manufacturers only have to write drivers to interface their cards to the Direct3D API's functions.

Microsoft's DirectX

Microsoft has produced a number of APIs under the title DirectX.   These are:

Direct 3D	Provides a standard interface for 3D object display and rendering.
Direct Draw	Reduces CPU time by allowing software direct access to alter video memory.
Direct Sound	Reduces CPU time by allowing software direct access to sound hardware. Also provides synchronisation of video and sound data.
Direct Play	Aids running applications over networks or communications lines.
Direct Input	Speeds up mouse and joystick responses.

Monitor Interface

The output from the graphics card appears on a socket at the rear of the computer case.

The diagram shows the VGA connector used with PCs.

The chart shows the use of the pins.

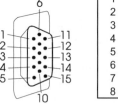

Pin	VGA/SVGA/XGA	Pin	VGA/SVGA/XGA
1	Red	9	No Pin (used as key)
2	Green	10	Ground
3	Blue	11	Not Used
4	Not Used	12	Not Used
5	Not Used	13	Horizontal Synch
6	Red Return	14	Vertical Synch
7	Green Return	15	Not Used
8	Blue Return		

Many cards also offer other connections to extension devices. The range of connections includes:

VESA Feature Connector	This is a set of 26 pins on the graphics board that allows the connection of other video add-on cards e.g. video capture facilities. Unfortunately, the connection only supports VGA and 256 colours.
VAFC	The VESA Advanced Feature Connector is an 80-pin connector that overcomes the limitation of the standard VESA connector. It works up to 1024x768 and has a throughput of 150Mb per second.
VMC	The VESA Media Channel (VMC) is an edge connector on the graphics card. It is designed to handle up to fifteen different audio and video sources on a single channel, allowing a great flexibility in connecting together sound cards, video capture cards, MPEG systems, video conferencing systems and anything that the future may throw at it. Its first appearance is in the Video Logic 928Movie and PCIMovie cards.
Video Input	The ability to display input from live video sources such as VCRs and camcorders, as provided in the Media Vision 1024 card. An extra daughterboard may have to be fitted for this.
TV Aerial Input	A number of graphics cards, such as the ATI Wonder Pro, now have a built-in TV tuner, allowing both viewing of television programmes on the monitor and the capture of television programmes to hard disk.
TV Output	Some graphics cards are capable not only of TV input but output as well. The user may decide whether to output the display to TV or monitor, or possibly both.
RGB output	Used for connecting to high-quality monitors and other video devices that use RGB connectors.

AGP

The Accelerated Graphics Port was developed in response to the huge memory and consequent data transfer overheads required for 3D graphics. A large number of texture maps require to be stored in memory. This allows rapid access to the texture data for the rapid rendering of 3D objects. Fetching directly from disk would be far too slow to maintain the frame refresh rates. However, 3D rendering produces two main problems:

- The memory requirements of these maps can exceed the actual amount of memory fitted in the graphics card.
- Very large amounts of data need to be transferred to produce rendered screens at up to 30 frames per second.

The solution is twofold - use some of the computer's existing memory and access it at far faster data rates. This requires a motherboard with an Accelerated Graphics Port.

The Accelerated Graphics Port is used on all new systems and very few systems in use are so old as to have no AGP port. The AGP port is separate from the 33Mhz PCI bus. As the diagram shows, the card is plugged directly into the separate AGP 66MHz bus that connects, via the chipset, to the CPU and memory. This is called 'x1 mode' and provides a maximum throughput of 264MBps - double that of the PCI bus. This data rate is still half of that travelling over the 64-bit connection between the CPU and memory. To compensate, the 'x2 mode' was developed. This transfers data on both the rising and falling edge of the clock pulse, which doubles the theoretical throughput to 528MBps. The computer's memory is shared between the application program's usage and the graphics card usage.

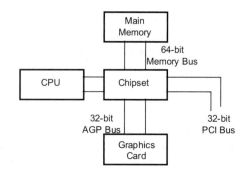

Systems using the 100MHz bus system push the data rate up to 800MBps and the new AGP4x standard is included in the Intel i8X0 chipsets, where the AGP function is wholly integrated into the chipsets. The AGP 8x standard is in development but currently no system is fast enough to utilise the entire bandwidth it would provide.

Normal 2D graphics do not require this extra performance and normal applications will not particularly benefit from this new technique. Since support for AGP did not appear until a new DirectDraw in Windows 98, the shared memory usage ability of AGP cards were inactive until then. In the short-term, AGP provides a faster data transfer rate. In the long term, it offers a cheap and fast video system.

Other facilities

The preceding pages outline some of the more important features of graphics cards. However, many more factors may prove important for a particular user or for a particular activity.

These might include:

- Support for DPMS power saving. The ability of the graphics card to control the power usage of the monitor at times when there is no user activity.
- Virtual Screen or virtual desktop. A user may wish to display a great deal of detail on the screen (e.g. many Windows groups or many Windows applications open at the same time). This would normally require a large screen monitor otherwise each window would be too small for comfortable viewing. An alternative is to use a normal monitor screen size and only view a part of the full screen at any one time. Moving the mouse to an edge of the screen scrolls the display in that direction. Thus a 640x480 screen can act as a window on a larger 1280x1024 display held in screen memory.
- Zoom. The virtual desktop provides a scrolling window on a larger screen. The zoom facility allows the user to magnify any portion of the screen, usually to allow detailed editing of graphics or DTP. There is no scrolling in this case. The Number 9 GXE64 Pro card, for example, magnifies the screen up to 5 times normal size.
- Support for the connection of multiple monitors - either through installing multiple graphics cards or fitting the new graphics cards that have twin video outputs. This allows separate multitasking programs to be run on separate monitors.
- Drivers to allow the user to switch resolutions without having to reboot the machine to activate the new screen mode.
- Drivers for a wide range of monitors, applications and operating systems such as Windows 98, Windows ME, Windows NT, Windows 2000 and Windows XP.
- MPEG-2 players, to handle DVD drives.

Video handling

Many graphics cards support a range of full motion video options, including MPEG, QuickTime, Video for Windows and Intel Indeo formats. Video playback is often achieved by fitting an extra daughter board or using additional video handling software. Video for Windows (AVI) is the most common PC video format although MPEG systems are becoming very popular. MPEG initially required special hardware to decode the compressed files, although with the advance of CPU power software methods have overtaken more expensive dedicated hardware decoders in many instances. The popularity of DVD players has led to a resurgence of dedicated hardware decoder cards, as these also provide 'theatre quality' audio output.

Modern cards should be capable of supporting both AVI and MPEG video standards. Since video playback places the greatest strain on CPU resources, CPU usage tests are a valuable indication of a card's performance. A low CPU percentage usage is desired and large variations can be measured between cards.

Co-processor cards

Co-processor cards use a second processor to carry out the graphics tasks. The computer CPU passes brief instructions to the CPU on the co-processor graphics board and the co-processor carries out the graphics calculations and board memory updates. Typical functions given to a co-processor would be text display, line drawing, rectangles, ellipses and area colour fills. The 8514/A boards and the VESA XGA boards initiated this method and other co-processor systems are based on the Texas TI-34000 series.

Accelerator cards

Like co-processor boards, the accelerator board is designed to relieve the computer's main CPU of valuable graphics processing time. In a co-processor system, a second processor chip is employed for the graphics tasks. In an accelerator system, the main graphics tasks are implemented in hardware. These main tasks are line and box drawing and 'bitblitting' (bit-to-block transfers - i.e. memory flooding). Since these operations are implemented in hardware, there is no need for a processor to determine what needs to be done - the tasks are pre-defined. This results in the graphics functions being carried out more quickly. Most graphics cards on sale currently use some form of graphics acceleration. A number of hardware-based 3D accelerator cards are produced. The trend, however, seems to be towards producing combined 2D/3D chipsets.

Note

There can be significant variations in the efficiency of each card's method of handling graphics functions. For example, one particular card may need less information passed to it, in order to carry out a particular graphics function, compared to another card. Some cards will carry out a smaller range of graphics functions, the remaining functions being left for the computer's main CPU to process.

Card performance

There is no doubt that graphics accelerator cards substantially improve a system's performance. However, manufacturers' claims should be put in perspective:

- The claims only consider the graphics functions being tested in isolation.
- When considered as <u>part</u> of the overall activities of an application program, the performance is nowhere near as spectacular.

The majority of multimedia projects use video and graphics, but relatively few of them make use of 3D real-time rendered animations. As a result, many of the 3D-specific performance claims are often irrelevant to multimedia.

Assembling the system

A multimedia professional is not expected to act as a computer technician, but it certainly helps to be able to connect to peripherals, since this kind of activity happens regularly in multimedia work; and to rectify simple faults when they occur. When a computer is first purchased, it arrives in several boxes. The monitor is in one box, while the system unit, keyboard, mouse, manuals and disks are usually packed separately. The monitor has its own power cable and video cable permanently connected to it in most cases, while the system unit comes as an independent component with separate cables.

The steps for assembling the system are:

- Choose a suitable location for the computer. Avoid situations of excessive heat, cold, damp, dust or vibration. Also avoid locations close to magnetic disturbance such as lift motors, power trans-formers, etc. A good location would be one with a flat, stable surface and good air circulation.
- Carefully unpack the components from the boxes. The contents of the boxes should then be checked against the system checklist, to see that all components have been delivered.
- Read the assembly instructions carefully to ensure that you understand the necessary steps and that any special precautions are understood.
- Gather any tools that you may require. Normally, the only tool is a Philips screwdriver to secure connections to the system unit. Some connections use thumbscrews to make a secure connection and do not require a screwdriver - read the manual.
- Carefully connect the components together, in the order directed by the computer manual. Do not force any connections; if a plug will not easily connect to a socket, it may mean that a connector pin has become bent. It might also mean that the wrong socket is being chosen, or the plug is being inserted upside down!

A typical order of assembly is:

- Place the system unit on the surface to be used.
- Place the monitor on top of the system unit.
- Attach the video cable from the monitor to the video out socket of the system unit. Ensure that the plug and the socket are of compatible types. A modern monitor has a 15-pin plug, as shown. Note that the edges of the plugs are shaped so that they only connect one way round. On some connectors, the plug is secured to the system unit with metal screws and a screwdriver is required to tighten the screws. With other connectors, the plug has plastic thumbscrews that are tightened by hand.
- Connect the mains lead to the system unit. This cable has a normal 3-pin plug on one end and a connector similar to those used in electric kettles on the other end. Do not connect the mains plug to the mains at this time; simply plug the other end of the cable into the system unit mains inlet socket.
- Connect the monitor to the mains supply. Some monitor mains cables have a 'kettle' plug that attaches to the PC power supply so that no extra 3-pin plug sockets are required. Many users consider this useful, since switching on the system unit also supplies power to the monitor. So, if the monitor power switch is left on, both units can be powered up from the system on/off switch.
- Connect the keyboard and mouse to the system unit. The modern PC and mouse both have a 6-pin 'PS/2' plug connector, though some use USB and on laptop computers, infra-red connectors are not unknown. The PS/2 connector has a matching socket on the system unit and can only be connected one way since the socket has a key to guide the plug. Care should be taken to plug the keyboard and mouse into the correct sockets. The system unit should either clearly label them as *'KBD'* and *'Mouse'*, use pictures depicting the correct connection, and/or colour code the sockets and plugs.
- Check that the monitor is at an angle that affords easy and comfortable viewing and adjust this if necessary; the monitor rests on a plinth that allows the monitor angle to be altered.

- Connect the loudspeakers to the *'line out'* socket on the sound card (the socket is marked with the engraving shown on the left). If the card has two line out sockets, the first is used for the main speakers while the second is used for rear speakers. If greater volume is required, cables can connect the card's line out to another system such as a domestic audio system.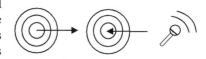
- If the computer is to be used to record audio, a microphone can be connected to the 'microphone' socket (engraved with the diagram shown on the right. Additionally, the output of an audio device such as a cassette deck or audio CD player can be connected to the sound card's 'line in' socket (the engraving shown in the middle). Windows has a utility that allows the volume levels of each device to be individually set.

Attaching Peripheral Devices

A multimedia user may need to attach and detach a range of devices. The device must be physically attached, but also a driver must be installed, to allow Windows to communicate with the device.

In some cases, this is as simple as clicking on the *'Add New Hardware'* option in the Control Panel, and installing the driver suggested by Windows. However, many devices do not have drivers built in to Windows, and in any case installing the software provided with the device is often useful. Typically, the driver will be provided on a CD-ROM that will automatically load up the installation procedure, which will be different for each device.

If not, then the driver can be installed from the *'Add New Hardware'* option, and selecting the appropriate type of hardware, and clicking on *'Have Disk'*. The user can then locate the driver on the CD manually and install it.

Attaching a Printer

Connect the printer to the system unit. The most common cable was the *'parallel'* or *'Centronics'* type, with its 25-pin cable. The cable at the system unit side terminates in a 25-pin plug that connects to the socket marked *'Parallel'* or *'LPT1'*. The other end of the cable connects to the socket on the printer. Many printers now have USB cable that connects to one of the computer's USB sockets. Next, connect the printer to the mains supply and ensure that it is supplied with paper and is on-line.

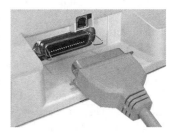

Basic Troubleshooting

This section is not intended to be a full faultfinding guide. However, the following are a few causes of common faults on multimedia systems:

- Adapters improperly connected. Loose or unplugged cables will, of course, not allow the computer to communicate with the device.
- Incorrect device selection. With certain types of peripheral, it is necessary to select the correct one before use. For example, a system could have access to a network printer, fax, and also have a driver to print to PDF documents. If the user forgets to change the printing device to the one that he or she wishes to use, it will print to the default device instead. Other examples include making sure the correct TWAIN device is selected, or selecting the correct video capture device.
- Unpowered devices. As simple as it sounds, it is a common error to attach a device to the PC, but forget to attach its power cable. Obviously, this will prevent it from operating.
- Correct drivers not installed. Although modern equipment makes full use of plug-and-play technology to try to reduce these problems, older equipment or user error can result in drivers failing to be installed, or the wrong driver set to be installed. For the device to work properly, the correct drivers must be installed. In some cases, the driver files may become corrupted, so removing and reinstalling the drivers can help in some cases.

The Operating System

The Operating System (OS) is the lowest level of software on a computer, and applications or utilities such as word processors or anti-virus programs run 'on top' of the operating system. The OS automatically loads when the computer boots up, and must finish loading before any applications or utilities can be loaded and run. As a result, the type of operating system must take into account the way, or ways, in which that system is used.

There is a wide range of OS platforms available today, and careful consideration should be taken before deciding on which to use.

The following are common systems in use today:

- Windows 9x: This is a general term for Windows 95, Windows 98, and Windows Millennium Edition. While Windows 95 was vastly superior to its predecessor, Microsoft DOS, all Windows 9x systems are now superseded by Windows XP. However, they are still in use in a number of organisations. All Windows systems in general operate on similar basic principles.

- Windows NT: Although Windows NT is not widely used in comparison to other operating systems, it provides the basis for various other systems, including Windows 2000 and Windows XP. Providing a wider range of network-capable functions than Windows 9x systems, Windows NT-based systems also use the NTFS filing system for the hard disks, making it less prone to errors.
- Mac: The operating systems used by Macintosh computers, of which OS-X is the current model, are not available for PCs. However, Macs are widely used in multimedia, making compatibility with Mac operating systems desirable.
- Unix: Although Unix itself is largely reserved for major networks, there are numerous offshoots of Unix that are available to PCs, the most popular of which is the Linux range.

Many PC manufacturers simply supply the most up to date version of Windows on their PCs. In many cases, this may be perfectly acceptable. However, if the system is to be used alongside other computers, such as an existing computer network, or a client who uses Macs, then it is important that products from one platform are capable of being used on another platform.

This 'inter-platform operability' can be provided by using a standard form of media, for example creating PDF documents or MPEG video files which can be displayed on any major system. Alternatively, a 'platform-independent' system can be used, such as Java, to develop the multimedia application.

Health & Safety

EC directive 90/270/EEC was passed in May 1990. It took effect from 1st January 1993, with all new and modified workstations coming under its terms. All workstations, both existing stations and new sales, were covered by 1st January 1996.

The directive ensures that workers using VDUs are:
- given full information on the use of office equipment
- provided with monitors to required standards on ergonomics and emissions.

In the UK, the Health and Safety at Work Act, through the Health and Safety (Display Screen Equipment) Regulations, embodies the EC directive and the British Health and Safety Executive will provide guidelines on the directive. The directive sets out minimum requirements in a range of areas such as VDU, keyboard, desk, chair, lighting, noise, heat and humidity, along with employer obligations to train employees, reduce employee VDU time, protect employees' eyesight and enact worker consultation and participation. The standards of the directive are contained in its annexe and this is largely based on the ISO standard 9241 *"Ergonomic requirements for office work with visual display terminals"*. Of course, the HSE and employers' organisations such as the CBI have differences with the trade unions on the interpretation of individual items of the directive. The aim should be the creation of a safe, functional and productive working environment for the benefit of all.

The legislation ensures that employers will provide VDU operators with a free eyesight test when requested by an operator. If necessary, the employer will also provide *"corrective appliances"* (spectacles). The definition of a VDU operator is one who uses a VDU for between 3 and 5 hours per day. The HSE provide a pamphlet entitled *"Display Screen Equipment Work"* that explains definitions for different types of VDU user. Legislation also covers the hardware design. As a result of EC action, from 1st Jan 1997, monitors, like other goods, will carry the 'CE' mark - an EC safety mark. This covers limits of EMI (electromagnetic interference) and EMS (electromagnetic susceptibility).

Risk assessment

Other issues such as hazardous materials, operating plant and machinery, unsafe employer practices and unsafe employee practices threaten the safety of people and equipment.

Organisations should have agreed health and safety procedures to examine all possible hazards and risks in the workplace. A 'hazard' is something that has the potential to cause harm, while a 'risk' is an assessment of the likelihood of the hazard actually causing harm. All activities should be subjected to risk assessment, to see what hazards exist, what risk they may cause and what steps can be taken to eliminate or minimise them. For example, it is easy to identify some hazards, such as spilled chemicals, while other hazards (such as RSI or eyestrain) are not immediately noticeable. Similarly, some can be immediately eliminated (like the spilled chemicals) while others (such as lifting objects or typing at a keyboard) are necessary parts of the job. In these cases, the aim is to specify procedures (such as staff training on lifting or regular breaks for typists) that minimise the risk to staff or the public.

Using monitors

The layout of keyboard, monitor and documents in relation to the user's vision and easy physical reach is of great importance. Prolonged periods of body inactivity, particularly in bad seating, can itself result in backache and neckache. Add uncomfortable seats and badly laid out desks and the situation is worsened. Bad desk layouts not only contribute to back problems - they are also a source of eye problems, as users strain to read monitors and documents in adverse conditions. In a normal day, the human eye experiences a variety of muscle movements. The eye normally moves rapidly from one object to another, with the vertical, horizontal and focusing changes that are entailed. In contrast, prolonged viewing of a VDU involves prolonged muscle tension, to maintain concentration on a relatively small flickering viewing area. VDU users complain of a range of symptoms from redness, watering and ache through to focusing difficulties, loss of clarity and double vision.

A range of measures to improve user conditions includes:

- Size of desk. An inadequate desk surface usually results in an unmanageable clutter, loss of productivity and user stress. Consider placing the CPU unit under the desk, or using mini-tower CPU units. Most desks are about 70cm high, which satisfies the average user.
- Seating position. The seat should be comfortable and be of the swivel type, preferably on castors. The seat height and backrest should be adjustable. Certain users may require footrests to maintain adequate posture.
- Size and type of monitor screen. The screen size should be adequate for the job being carried out. Detailed graphic or DTP work on a small screen is a sure way to cause eyestrain and lost working days.
- Position of monitor. The monitor should be moved to suit the user and not the other way round. EU regulations require that monitors have positional adjustment (e.g. a tilt and swivel base or adjustable monitor arm). The VDU user should be able to rotate the display from side to side as well as tilt the screen up and down. Many users prefer to stand the monitor directly on the desk surface, rather than on top of the computer case. Some desks have glass top so that the VDU can be situated under the glass. This frees the desk space but may introduce extra reflections from office lighting. A preferred position would involve the user being stationed about 30" from the monitor and looking down on it from a small angle. Flickering first affects the edges of a user's vision. If a user sits close to a monitor, the effects of flicker is more pronounced.
- Regular breaks - necks suffer most when forced to maintain a fixed position for long periods; eyes suffer from maintaining a fixed focal distance. Those employees on permanent screen operations - data entry workers, database operators, program coders, etc. - should have scheduled breaks in their working day.
- Use of document holders - these can be adjusted for the most comfortable reading position. This avoids the continual refocusing involved when reading documents that are left on the desk.

Screen Glare

The aim is to minimise the amount of office light that reflects from the screen surface of the monitor. Screen glare makes reading the screen data extremely difficult and is very tiring to user eyes. The aim is to have as little contrast as possible between the screen and its surroundings. Preventative measures include both lighting and environment changes and choice of monitors.

- Fluorescent lighting should be completely avoided and the room lighting should be diffused. Both the Lighting Industry Federation and the Chartered Institute of Building Service Engineers provide booklets that cover the problems of poor lighting and the lighting required for areas where VDUs are in use.
- Don't place a monitor in front of windows or other bright light sources. If there is no alternative to having a monitor face a window, use blinds or curtains.
- The room walls and furnishings should have matt surfaces with neutral colouring.
- Use monitors with FST tubes, as they suffer less glare than conventional tubes.
- Use monitors whose screens have anti-glare silica coatings. The screen can also be etched to refract the light. A smooth panel can be bonded to the surface of the screen. This lets light out, but minimises glare by breaking up light that strikes the screen. By preventing light entering the tube, the picture contrast is improved - as in Trinitron tubes.
- Use monitors with fast refresh rates as this minimises flicker effects. Some monitor tubes use long-persistence phosphors to minimise flicker, but they also tend to blur movement.
- Fit a non-glare filter in front of the monitor screen. These are mostly made from glass, although some are plastic. But beware, the Association of Optometrists believe that filters reduce glare - at the expense of making the screen more difficult to read. Keep the screen clean, with an anti-static cleaning compound.
- Use VDU spectacles when working at screens; these are specially tinted and can include prescription lenses.
- Where the application allows user-defined screen colours, choose screen colours carefully. There is evidence that dark lettering on a light background aids readability. It is more protective to the eyes when using handling text as there is no need for the user to constantly adapt to differing contrasts. On the other hand, dark backgrounds suffer less from the effects of flicker.

Radiation

The harmful effect of electromagnetic radiation from monitors has been an issue that is controversial and still not satisfactorily resolved. Some reports, mainly from Sweden, Finland and Denmark, suggest that monitor radiation can induce leukaemia and brain cancer. Others, including the UK Health and Safety Executive, dispute the reports and there are claims that the reports are under-researched and discredited. Still others accept that there is a cancer danger from monitor radiation - but small in comparison to cancer dangers from smoking and diet. Computer monitors produce high magnetic fields. These are essential to the running of the monitor, as high currents are required for the beam deflection circuitry. They are no different from the magnetic fields that are emanated from all 50Hz mains electrical equipment and wiring. It is the effects of sustained exposure that causes concern. After all, a user would not normally sit in front of an electric kettle for 8 hours a day but a computer user could easily spend 8 hours a day less than two feet from a monitor. In this respect, it is similar to the claims of harmful effects of living under high-voltage power lines.

Radiation from monitors occurs mostly from the rear, although an appreciable amount also occurs from the front. The fields diminish sharply with distance.

For increased safety, the following steps can be taken:

- Use an LCD screen, or other non-CRT display, if this is acceptable.
- Use a monochrome monitor, if possible. These have lower radiation levels.
- Purchase a low radiation monitor (usually tagged as 'LR'). Note that if a monitor has a special screen coating to reduce radiation, this coating also reduces the screen brightness.
- Position the monitor about 30" from the user.
- Ensure that no other workers are seated less than 4' from the rear of the monitor.

The EC Directive 90/270 talks of radiation levels being reduced to *'negligible levels'*. Radiation is categorised as both ELF (Extremely Low Frequency - i.e. 5Hz to 2KHz) and VLF (Very Low Frequency - i.e. 2KHz to 400KHz). The Swedish MPR-II standard (also called MPR 1990) has become an international standard, because it specifies actual radiation levels.

However, the Health and Safety (Display Screen Equipment) Regulations exempt the UK from the requirements of MPR-II. Nevertheless, almost all monitors on the market are at least MPR-II standard. The Swedish regulatory body NTUEK, in contrast to the UK, works on the assumption of a link between radiation and cancer and has mandatory minimum radiation levels.

Furthermore, various TCO standards, of which TCO-03 is the most recent, requires equipment such as monitors to meet certain ergonomics and other requirements.

Selecting a Multimedia System

While a major organisation is likely to have a selection process, involving evaluation and purchasing policy amongst other things, multimedia systems have more stringent requirements than the typical office machine. The technology needed for a multimedia development system depend largely on its intended uses.

The technology needed for the computer system should be specified according to the needs of the user. In other words, a high-end system should not be bought simply for its own sake – it should match the specification required of it. A high-end video editor, for example, needs a computer with plenty of RAM and disk space, a fast processor, and a good video card, not to mention the requisite video capture and editing software. However, the system used to develop simple web pages would require only a basic system with rudimentary HTML editing software.

A process known as *'requirements analysis'* can be used to document the technical and user needs of the system to be acquired. The *'Project Design'* chapter explains the general concept of requirements analysis; however, it is applied to system specification rather differently than to producing a multimedia project:

- Often, the software to be used is already known. Most software has a minimum technical specification for memory, processor speed, and so on. These must be followed if the software is to work properly.
- There may be specific requirements for special functions, such as TV-out, or dual-monitor support. These should be determined before looking into the system to be purchased.
- For any organisation, there are specific standards that should be followed. Monitors have specific ergonomic and safety standards, as detailed earlier in this chapter. Also, there are a wide range of other European standards; these are encapsulated in the 'CE' (Certified European standard) mark. If a component does not bear a CE mark then it may not be suitable for use.
- Although over-specifying the system can be a waste of money, many users wish to incorporate a degree of *'future-proofing'*. In other words, it can be useful to include at least the capability to incorporate software or hardware that may be needed in the future. This would entail keeping up to date with current standards and equipment, as well as expected future developments.

Once the system requirements are determined, the buyer can select the precise hardware and software. Compatibility with existing systems or data may require the use of a certain version of software – for example if a client wishes to give presentations in the current version of PowerPoint then this software must be specified. This rarely applies to hardware, however, so the requirements specification can be used to determine the precise model of each part of the system.

Where new software or hardware is to be used, the user must of course be trained in its use. In some cases training can be provided either in-house or by external training companies. However, if this is not financially viable, or if the change is simply an upgrade from one version to another, then training manuals, videos, or other media may suffice.

Project Design

This chapter and the next chapter are all about design. This chapter concentrates on the overall project design, while the next chapter looks at navigation design and screen design.

Those planning to create large projects, whether for college/university or for real-world clients, should read the two chapters in their entirety. Those planning a small home-grown project can be selective in the parts of this chapter that is read, with the following chapter covering more immediate issues. Nevertheless, all readers should consider the design approaches and project structure described in this chapter.

The design chapters cover all design aspects - for kiosks, CDs/DVDs, web sites, etc. In these chapters, the overall work is termed the *'project'* and this is intended to cover all distribution formats. Similarly, all independent user views are termed *'screens'*. When the chapters are being read with a view to creating web content, the *'screen'* refers to an individual web page and the *'project'* refers to the collection of pages that make up the web site. The chapters on web site creation look at the additional special factors that apply to design for that medium. The term *'home screen'* is used to describe the main screen of any project.

Introduction to design

Projects are undertaken to satisfy a particular educational, promotional or leisure need. The design and content support this primary need. Poorly designed and badly laid out content will spoil an otherwise worthy project. On the other hand, clever and innovative use of graphics, video, etc will not save a project whose content was flawed from the start.

The best projects are *'user-centred'*. That means that the project, from beginning to end, is focussed on the needs of the end users. Matters such as screen design and layout should mainly serve to make the project easy to use, easy to understand and enjoyable. It is a case of function over form.

There are many approaches to project design and layout. There are many heavy books that examine the human mind in detail and advise on design approaches. Their work is very important and has produced studies on how humans learn and interact with their environment. The lessons for designers are covered in the concepts of HCI (Human-Computer Interaction) and the many observations are embodied in all design guides. Ultimately, designers are concerned with results - design is what works. That is not to say that extremely valuable lessons cannot be learned from the theoretical work and practical examples of others. It's just that there are added ingredients, such as flair and imagination, which use these principles and practices to better effect than using a simple checklist approach to design. The bottom line is that design is what is effective, efficient, easy to use, and solves problems.

An effective project is the result of effective design and this is characterised by three factors.
- Content   - what the project will contain and how it its pitched.
- Structure   - how the contents are organised and accessed.
- Presentation   - how the contents will be displayed and interacted with.

These headings over-simplify the process and they are looked at separately in this chapter and the next.

Comparing print design and screen design

Readers who have taken an advanced course on word-processing or DTP will take for granted the ease by which material can be laid out – in columns, in frames, dropping in images and diagrams at any spot.

However, readers cannot simply apply all existing knowledge of print production to web and CD/DVD projects. There are many similarities - but there are also substantial differences.

The table below compares designing for print with designing for screen (i.e. web sites, CDs, DVDs and kiosks).

Document detail	
Print	Printed to many thousands of dpi (dots per inch). Provides highly-detailed illustrations, photographs, maps, drawings, etc.
Screen	Displayed at around 72dpi or 96dpi. Large and high-quality images can be stored on a CD/DVD but the viewer would need to scroll vertically and horizontally to see a portion of the image at any one time. Additionally, it would take a long time to download such a large image over the Internet.

Document size	
Print	A typical broadsheet newspaper is huge and all the content of two large pages is always visible.
Screen	CD/DVD material is usually displayed on monitors whose sizes vary from 15" to 24", a difference in screen area of a factor of 2.56. Web material may be displayed on the tiny screens of hand-held devices and cellphones, up to 24" high-performance workstation monitors – a difference in screen area of up to 15,000%. Again, screen content will probably need to be scrolled to be viewed.

Reader focus

Print	A single document (e.g. a page) is considered as a whole, with the reader focussing on a particular set of information. A huge amount of different material fits on one double-page spread. Readers can see many different articles at once, can see how long each article is, which have accompanying diagrams, photographs, etc.
Screen	Since the screen is a small display area, it is unlikely that all the content of a subject will be fitted on a single screen. Users can't judge how large the document is and how much more has still be viewed.

Reading ease

Print	Page content is easily scanned.
Screen	Users' reading speeds can be up to 25 percent slower on monitor screens compared to reading printed copy. However, usability tests suggest that users remember twice as much material read from a screen compared to read from a printed document.

Interactivity

Print	Limited abilities, usually just filling in a crossword or completing an application form.
Screen	Users continually control the flow of information through making choices (e.g. through navigation, searching databases, controlling games, etc.).

Speed

Print	Readers can quickly scan or jump from one topic to another.
Screen	Material is stored over multiple screens, requiring more operations to recover all the segments of the material (i.e. more clicks on a CD/DVD menu, more hypertext jumps on the web). It also takes a long time to download a high resolution image that is easily reproduced in a magazine.

Media elements

Print	Reproduces text, line art, images (i.e. static images), with the final presentation detail decided before printing. Most magazines are in colour but most other printed material is black and white (due to additional printing costs involved in colour printing).
Screen	Can also reproduce audio and moving images such as video clips and animations. What media elements the user sees/hears depends on what the user initiates. All screens can be in colour at no extra cost.

Currency

Print	Newspapers are produced on a daily or weekly basis, with magazines being fortnightly, monthly or quarterly. Readers have to wait a long time for their next edition.
Screen	With projects committed to CD or DVD, users have to wait for the next release to access fresh material. However, with many websites, fresh information is constantly being added on a 24/7/365 basis.

Layout

Print	All readers see the material in the exact same way. All the layout rules such as leading, kerning, white space, etc. can be applied and elements can be placed exactly where and how the designer wants the reader to view them. A huge variety of fonts can be used.
Screen	Projects will be read by viewers with different settings (e.g. font sizes) or different hardware (e.g. different screen resolutions, screen readers for the blind). This is less of a problem with multimedia projects, as designers can control the layout, down to the placing of individual pixels. With web sites, however, the screen layout can often not be controlled, as browsers can dictate the final look of the material (even between different browser versions). As long as a project has its fonts built in, as in most multimedia products, their reproduction is assured. This is a real problem for web-based projects, as there is no guarantee that the user has the required fonts installed

User attitude

Print	In general, readers are prepared to read more material, are more patient, and material is usually read from start to finish.
Screen	Reading from screen places a greater strain on the eye than reading from print. So, users tend to spend less time in each area (especially on the web). Long download times mean that users' attention span will be exhausted and they will move on without seeing some material.

Diversity

Print	Most printed material (magazines, newspapers, and catalogues) promotes a single point of view. To find another viewpoint, the reader has to obtain another printed item.
Screen	The Internet allows instant access to many viewpoints, providing plenty of choice.

Funding

Print	Requires considerable initial funding which can be recovered from consumers (through sales or subscriptions) or advertisers.
Screen	Can have low startup costs, which can be recovered from consumers (through CD/DVD sales, e-commerce or membership subscriptions), advertisers or site owners - depending on the nature of project.

Interconnections

Print	It is rare for an article to have a connection to another article in the same document (although there are occasionally a set of articles on one major news story).
Screen	It is common to have large numbers of interlinked pages of material, both within a project and to other external sources. The navigational abilities are what enhance a user's experience compared to reading print.

Portability

Print	Printed documents can easily be carried around, even where they have a large size (e.g. a folded map) or contain a large amount of information (e.g. a book or Sunday newspaper).
Screen	Most screen-based devices are too large to be truly portable although a new range of hand-held devices (e.g. mobile phones, portable DVD players, e-book readers) are available.

Conclusions

While print and screen share similar design approaches on issues such as layout, fonts, colours and so on, screen design has some limitations compared to printed copy. However, it also provides many extra opportunities for presenting information.

When technology develops to the stage where every user has a high resolution screen the size of a newspaper, downloading from fast mass storage devices or ultra-fast Internet links, some of the present hardware constraints on screen design will be removed.   Perhaps, one day everyone will use exactly the same screen resolution, the same operating system and the same browser software – lifting the present software constraints on designers.

Even then design for screen will still require additional skills – how to chop up content into small, meaningful chunks (information architecture) – how to write copy to suit screen use, understanding how interact with technology, etc.

These issues are addressed in this and the next chapter.

Overview of the design process

Like most design processes, there is no 'right way' to design a project. Experts on the subject disagree, just as painters, sculptors, musicians and other creative artists have different views on their art.

That is not to say that project design is left to individual discretion. Common practices have emerged and there are some standards (e.g. ISO13407, ISO 9241, ISO 18529, and also standards for accessibility for the visually or physically disabled). Many common practices are common sense but others stand accused of being dogmatic in a creative environment.

The short version

Here is a quick look at the main steps in designing a project.

What is to be done	Finding out what the client wants and who the project is for.
How to do it	Working out how to organise the project information for easy access.
	Deciding on how the project and its individual pages will look.
Doing it	Implementing the design; creating the graphics, text, audio, etc; writing any code.
Checking its been done correctly	Testing; checking that the final project is easily accessible and usable by the people that it was created for.

Each step is considered separately in the coming pages.

Video production analogy

Some approaches are based on techniques used for video production and the terms used are those expected in film studios.   This includes concepts such as:

'the pitch'	The basic summary of the idea, production costs and timescales are used to attract financial support/approval for the project.
'the proposal'	A production overview including themes, elements or characters, and activities.
'the treatment'	The development of the proposal to include style and plot development.
'the script'	The comprehensive guide to the entire production, in written form. This includes the breakdown of the script into sub-sections, which include all details such as spoken content, setting and mood. The draft script is later refined into the final script.
'the storyboard'	The visual description, with a set of sketches and notes that show the location and movement of elements within each scene, camera angles, lighting and edits.

These terms are included for reference purposes, as they sometimes appear in some other texts.

Development Techniques

Just as in developing any software products, there are many techniques that can be used to assist in the development of multimedia projects. Many of the experiences of software designers and programmers are used in creating robust and cost-efficient projects.

Waterfall method

This is a tried and tested technique in software development, although now going out of favour with many developers. As the diagram shows, it is a sequential process, outlining the main stages of the development process.

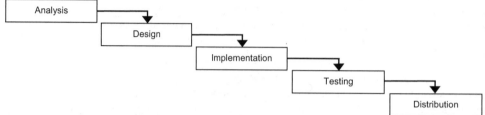

It assumes a step-by-step approach, with progress to the next stage only being permitted when the current stage is satisfactorily completed and signed off. There is no returning to a previous stage. This means that this model makes planning, staffing and testing simpler. However, any mistakes or inadequacies in an earlier stage may not become apparent until the testing stage. Since these defects have not been detected at an earlier stage, they are more expensive to correct.

As a result, the pure waterfall method is used mostly with simple projects where the requirements are easily identified.

Exploratory programming

This *'build and fix'* method is similar to the way that many individual users develop projects. An outline specification is used as a guide to the implementation of the project. When the project is completed, it is tested and any flaws or inadequacies are addressed at that stage. This usually requires much iteration, as there are often many alterations required.

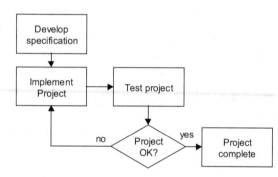

In a commercial environment, it is really only suitable for small projects or for projects where it is difficult to define the specification requirement in detail. It also requires software that supports rapid system alterations.

Re-usable components

This technique builds projects from modules and components that have already been designed - for stock use or more usually for previous projects. The aim is to use a 'building block' approach to a project, selecting the required components and making the minimum of alterations.

Clearly, this is of limited use, as most projects are quite different from each other. Of course, there are exceptions; such as creating a series of tutorials that all use the same basic interface and navigation. An example might be a set of CDs covering car maintenance. Although each CD will cover a different vehicle, all projects will have the same basic structure and menus (e.g. they will all have sections on *'changing spark plugs'* or *'changing tyres'*). A new CD can be quickly assembled from the existing material, with changes to the photographs, diagrams and text where appropriate.

Iterative design

The exploratory programming technique produces a completed project for evaluation, with changes being made after user evaluation. This is not suitable for large projects, as a mistake at an early stage of the development process results in errors all the way through the rest of the project work. And, while the quote of the famous author Ernest Hemingway that *"the first draft of everything is sh**"* may slightly overstate the case, it is certainly true that no design is correct at its first attempt. Unlike the pure waterfall method, the exploratory method has no rigorous set of design stages. The project has no structure and therefore there are no ways to effectively managing time scales, costs, and quality.

Many large projects are now designed using iterative methods, which combine the waterfall idea of thoroughly planned development stages with the idea of returning to improve previous work. Iteration allows individual earlier stages to be returned to so that changes and additions can be made, without waiting until the project is completed. This requires testing at all stages and is widely regarded as the best approach in maximising a project's final effectiveness. However, it is not without problems. In particular, where the client is involved in the continued evaluation and testing process, it provides endless opportunities for the client to redefine needs and query previous decisions. While a mutually agreed comprehensive project specification and design document will minimise disputes and clarify who is financially responsible for the costs of the changes, it will still introduce delays in completing the final project. Most of all, iterative design requires a user-centred approach at every stage.

User-centred design

Projects are designed for use by the target audience. The primary purpose of the project is not to satisfy the client and it is not to provide a showcase of the skills of the designer. A project design should primarily allow the users to carry out their tasks in the easiest and most efficient way possible, meeting client's and designer's objectives as a result.

A user-centred approach must flow through the whole development process, reflecting the target group, their real-world tasks and their working environment. The drive to develop a project must not divert the designer from focussing on the way that the final project will be used.

Task Analysis and Usability Testing are both necessary steps and their effectiveness can be tested. Task Analysis concentrates on how users interface with the project (e.g. what tasks do they want to carry out, did they achieve their tasks). Usability includes these factors but also includes what the user gained from the project (e.g. did they enjoy using the system, was their activity efficient).

ISO 13407

User evaluation that is only carried out at the end of the project's creation is of limited use. By that time, the necessary changes and amendments that are uncovered are expensive and time-consuming to implement. Much better to avoid the problems in the first instance. Problems are minimised by having user-based evaluation at all stages of the design process (i.e. from the first prototypes right through to the pre-release product).

ISO 13407 is the international standard for user-centred development. It can be used with different development environments (such as the waterfall method explained earlier), although it is most effective when used in an iterative way. A copy of the standard is available from BSI (www.bsi.org.uk or 0208-996-7858).

ISO 13407 outlines four principles of human-centred design:
- Active involvement of users, or those who qualified to speak for them.
- Appropriate allocation of function, ensuring skills are used properly.
- Iteration of design solutions.
- Multi-disciplinary design.

It also outlines four human-centred design activities required at the earliest stages of a project:
- Understand and specify the context of use.
- Specify user and organisational requirements.
- Produce design solutions.
- Evaluate designs against requirements.

The diagram shows the method used with this model.

Four of the stages are in a loop. The process iterates around the loop until all the project's requirements are met. The first time round the loop should produce the most results (e.g. the detection of unanswered requirements, mistakes and misunderstandings). Subsequent excursions round the sequence should generate fewer and fewer changes, until the design meets all requirements.

The process could be applied to the waterfall method but, since that would result in only one visit to each stage, there would be greater emphasis on each stage. The greatest benefits, therefore, are found in using the process iteratively.

The stages of the process are explained next and a stage should not be entered until all the activities of the previous stage have been thoroughly carried out.

Plan the human centred process

This stage ensures that all those involved in the design understand the importance of user involvement at all stages. It also ensures that the development plan includes enough time to carry out adequate user involvement in the requirements analysis and user testing (e.g. inclusion of these activities into project management plans). It may also create a 'validation plan' to review the progress and results of each user involvement.

Specify the context of use

This stage ensures that the design incorporates important issues such as the target audience, the task analysis and the physical and social requirements. These issues are covered fully later. This stage may result in the creation of a *'Context of Use'* document that covers these issues. Alternatively, they may be produced as separate documents on target audience, etc.

Specify the user and organisational requirements

This stage is like creating an extended version of the traditional Functional Requirements document. It covers issues such as HCI (human-computer interface), the quality and content of user tasks, and the performance of the project measured against operational (and possibly financial) objectives. This stage should produce usability criteria for future testing. This may be in the form of a *'Specification of User and Organisational Requirements'* document.

Produce design solutions

This stage creates the design that will be tested against the user requirements. In the first iteration, the design will be a result of the designer's craft and the initial input from the users. In further iterations, it will bring in the results of the feedback from user evaluations. The initial design may incorporate standards, existing modules, existing knowledge and experience, examples from other projects, etc. It may be in the form of a paper prototype, a software prototype, a simulation, a mock-up, a storyboard, or any form that produces a credible representation of the design. It is common to begin with a simple paper prototype that shows content and navigation layout, with later iterations using software prototypes that bring in greater functionality and content.

Evaluate designs against user requirements

This stage ensures that the design meets the originally-stated requirements. It may involve comparing the design against the document checklists that have been developed along the way. It will certainly involve user evaluations. User evaluations should be carried out in as realistic an environment as possible.

This approach does not demand any particular practices. It does not seek to prescribe screen resolutions, use of tables or frames, use of Flash, use of colours, or any other presentation consideration. It simply stresses the need for user involvement in the design evaluation process.

Stages in a multimedia project

Software designers learned a long time ago that starting a project without proper planning was hugely wasteful of time and resources. The main steps in designing projects for multimedia or the web are similar to those for any software project, although there are extra considerations.
The main phases are:

Project brief	This states the main aims of the project and is supplied by the organisation commissioning the work.
Requirements analysis (client needs)	This clarifies the brief and provides the specification of the project requirements in terms of content, purpose, function, style, etc.
Target audience	This defines the type of users targeted by the project, their requirements, abilities and expectations.
User requirements	Task analysis, Usability testing.
Design constraints	This clarifies any content, hardware, operating system, browser, or other factor that will influence how the project is designed.
Create/test prototype	This is a skeletal version of the project and is used to clear up any misunderstandings regarding user needs. The lessons from this stage are used to create the requirements specification.
Requirements specification	This states the project's content requirements, technical requirements, and functional requirements.
Design document	This provides a detailed plan, showing the project structure, all navigational paths and sketches of screen content (showing media components, user interactions and screen layout). This should also include the creation of storyboards, flow diagrams, navigation maps, style guides and asset lists.
Project plan	This states the financial and operational tasks in producing the project. It allocates individual responsibilities and creates the running order for events (e.g. shooting lists). Often a Gantt chart is used to plan the sequence of activities and milestones (dates for the completion of significant stages).
Test document	This includes the test specification, which in turn includes tests for usability and functionality, fitness for purpose and consistency. After testing, the test results are added, for comparison with the expected results.
Implementation	This is the main phase of the project, covering the capture/creation/editing of material and their integration into a complete piece of work.

Project testing	This checks the project, to ensure that it passes all the tests specified in the test document, including usability evaluation checks.
Development report	This records the approach taken to the project, any assumptions made, any problems encountered, and any suggestions for future improvements.
Project assessment	This is a critical analysis of the project, noting its strengths and weaknesses and making comparisons between it and any other similar applications.
Maintenance & development	This is the ongoing changes to projects to reflect changes in content, additional features, and changes in technology.

Although these chapters explain these issues separately, they are linked in many respects. For example, the page content and page design might depend upon screen size, which in turn depend upon hardware constraints. The implementation of projects is covered in other chapters, as are issues of testing, uploading, CD/DVD creation and marketing.

Major issues

Before examining the stages of design in detail, first consider two over-riding issues that should be in your mind throughout the process.

Accessibility

This specifies that the project content should be equally accessible by all users, regardless of any physical impairment. This might mean considering, for example, providing high-contrast screens with large fonts or text-only alternatives for electronic readers for the blind.

Usability

Accessibility ensures that all users can access the project material. Usability ensures that the project is designed so that users can fully understand what is available, can easily access the material and get the results that they wanted.

These issues are looked at in detail in the chapter on *'Project Testing'*.

Clients' needs

It is vital that a clear understanding of the project is achieved before any major work is undertaken. This prevents many wasted hours and potential disputes with the client commissioning the project.

The client should be asked to provide a project brief, which is a short summary of the aims of the project. The task of analysis is to convert the project brief into a project plan that can be implemented. Clarification of the aims, and agreement on the project's scope, minimises any misunderstandings and helps avoid mistakes.

Creating complex CD/DVD projects and web sites can be very expensive. For web sites, the maintenance (e.g. new prices) and development (e.g. new products or services, site new features such as chat rooms) mean a further on-going expense for the client. The client, therefore, needs to have a clear idea of the benefits expected from the project.

The analysis phase should end in the production of a written statement that is agreed by both parties. This prevents *'feature creep'*, the addition of facilities not originally mentioned by the client but *"assumed"* to be included in the project. The statement should incorporate an agreement that any features or facilities not specifically included can only be added at extra cost.

A written agreement is useful for both parties and is an essential in all commercial negotiations. The client can hold you to account for anything missing from the specification, but equally cannot demand anything beyond the specification. This approach normally identifies additional areas of work required in the project and clearly defines the project's purpose and strategy.

The initial meeting with the client

The initial meeting with the client sets the tone for future relations and communications. Therefore, time spent planning for the meeting will prove invaluable. Do some research on the client and its products and/or services. This knowledge inspires confidence in the client and allows for more productive questioning during the analysis stage.

Remember that it's the designer's responsibility to clarify all aspects of the problem with the client. It is best to begin by explaining how the project will be created – from pre-production right through to the post-production phase. This should detail where the points where the client's input may be required. This lays down the boundaries of the client's participation in the design process, overcoming any tendency of the client wish to manage every stage of the process.

The meeting should take as long as is required to get a thorough understanding of the client and the proposed project. Listening is an important element of the meeting, as is taking notes. However, it is helpful if you focus the discussion on the particular goals of the project. The use of pre-prepared charts (see examples later) helps direct the discussion and ensures that all the necessary important areas are covered. Remember, what the client thinks they *want* may not necessarily be what they actually *need*. An open, frank, and persistent approach is essential to draw out all the client's needs and expectations. Always be courteous and professional, and explain the reasoning behind your opinions and suggestions.

A client often concentrates on the look and presentation of a project and may need to be persuaded to start by looking at its content, purpose and accessibility. A client will respond better to a business case for this approach (e.g. it will maximise sales or contacts), rather than any design reason.

The following pages outline approaches that support the definition of the client's project.

Requirements analysis

Analysing the client's needs should begin with studying the client's brief. In addition, most companies and organisations have some form *of 'mission statement'*, which outlines their core activities along with statements about their intended direction. These documents can form part of the research prior to the initial meeting with the client.

The requirements analysis examines:

- The purpose of the project
- The content of the project
- The intended audience that will use the finished product
- The functional requirements of the project
- The technical requirements and any technical restraints.

The aim of the analysis phase is to produce precise statements that can act as a checklist in the later testing phase. This requires specific questions to get answers that can be added to the checklist.

The client may have a good general idea of what he/she wants. On the other hand, the client may only have the vaguest notion. Either way, you must end up a clear idea of what the client needs.

Project content

A designer does not create a site's content and purpose. These are things that only the client really knows. Our job is to aid the client in clearly expressing them, then transforming them into a project that meets the client's requirements. Typical questions to ask regarding the subject or topic are:

- What is the nature of your organisation?
- Which aspects of the organisation should be included in the project?
- Which aspects should be most prominent in the project?
- Who is your target audience? This is very important and is covered fully later.
- If the project is a website, will it be linked to any other websites?
- How much information should the project provide? Clearly identify the breadth of information and the level of detail that should be included (e.g. is the project simply an introduction, inviting telephone or written follow-up, or should it include a full database, searchable contents, specifications, etc.).
- Are there specific items that you want to include (e.g. existing brochures, photographs, logos, articles, etc.)?

For example, a teaching application may begin by listing the expected learning outcomes from using the package and may include self-test questions at the end of each section.   The package may supplement the learning of those doing badly in the self-assessments by supplying additional material and references for the subject areas in which the user scored less well.   Educational packages may also include a glossary of terms or explanations of acronyms.

Project Purpose

The content specifies *what* goes in the project, while the purpose specifies *why* the project is needed. Some clients have a vague notion of *"having a web presence"* or similar unrefined attitude. So, questions here are designed to focus the client on a project that supports and extends their existing operations. This minimises wasted effort and maximises the project's impact.

Typical questions to asking regarding the goals of the project are:

- Why do you want this project?
- What specifically do you expect to gain from it, in the short term and in the longer term?
- How will you measure the success of your project?
- If you currently have a web site or CD-ROM project, why do you need to commission a new one? How does the current project fail your needs?
- How should your organisation differentiate itself from others?

Since there are so many possibilities, including some that the client may not offer without prompting, it may be useful to provide the client with a chart that outlines typical goals. The client can then tick the features that apply to the organisation. If too many boxes are ticked, the client may be asked to enter priorities, by placing a "1" for the most important feature, "2" for the next most important feature, and so on.

The next page shows example charts of project goals, although the precise sets of goals will depend upon the nature of the client.

For CD/DVDs/kiosks

	Training	To provide training CD/DVDs for staff
	Databases	To provide information / support to staff over an intranet
	Catalogues	To demonstrate our product range
	Educational	To produce educational material for use in schools, colleges or universities
	Entertainment	To produce entertainment materials
	Simulations	To provide simulations for industry or games
	Reference	To produce reference libraries, encyclopaedias, etc.
	Promotion	To aid shoppers in evaluating and selecting goods (for kiosk projects)
	Revenue model	Tick if the product is to be sold, otherwise you are fully funding its creation.

For web sites

	Raising your profile	To explain what your organisation does. To portray your organisation in the best light. To strengthen your brand image.
	On-line brochures	To provide detailed information on products, for use by distributors, retailers and the general public. To direct readers to retailers who stock your products.
	Generating contacts	To develop a list of prospective customers, members, subscribers. To develop a mailing list or e-mailing list.
	Off-line sales	To generate sales through customers contacting us by phone, fax, mail or e-mail.
	E-commerce (national)	To sell products directly to the public, through taking credit card information over the Internet. To provide a full product range catalogue, with an online ordering system, including automated replies to customers. To provide on-line tracking of customers orders, by customers.
	E-commerce (international)	To sell as above, with the added complications of currency exchange, customs regulations, carrier requirements, etc.
	On-line delivery	To sell products that can be purchased and delivered over the Internet (e.g. music, stock art images, subscriber-only areas for news or information).
	Customer support	To provide online FAQs (Frequently Asked Questions), troubleshooting guides and knowledge bases. To provide a channel for technical support queries from customers.
	Revenue model	Tick if site is to recover its costs through revenue raising such as e-commerce, advertising or user subscription, otherwise you are fully funding its creation.

It may be a good idea to send a copy of the questionnaire in advance, so that the client has time to consider the issues before meeting you.

The client should be made aware of the financial implications of some of the decisions.
For example, a project that requires the creation of high-quality images, animation or video, or a web site that provides comprehensive e-commerce operations will cost substantially more than a project that uses a simple structure with simple content.
On the other hand, the client may make substantial savings by introducing the new project. For example, the use of FAQs and troubleshooting guides will reduce the demands on customer support staff, while producing on-line catalogues, specifications and price lists reduces printing and distribution costs.

Smaller organisations may wish to consider raising revenue through selling advertising on their sites, although this should not form the basis of their revenue models; there are already too many sites chasing too few advertisers. Another income source is through affiliate marketing. A link is placed on a client's site that advertises a particular product or service. If a viewer clicks on that link, he/she is directed to the website of the company that sells that product or service. If the viewer makes a purchase, a commission is paid for providing the lead. Again, this is not a stable revenue source and both income methods should be seen as a possible additional income, rather than the main financial support. Larger organisations, or organisations that wish to project a professional image tend not to use these methods. Instead, they may wish to set other targets such as the number of site visitors, site commercial turnover, etc.

Functional requirements

The discussion should move into specific tasks that the client wishes to incorporate into the project. Since the client may not have much experience in this field, some options, or examples from existing projects, should be presented.
The biggest decision is choosing between static or dynamic content. With static content, each page of the project is pre-formatted in advance. So, a typical project may have 1,000 ready-made pages that can be viewed. The user simply calls up individual pages by clicking on a link such as a button, hypertext link or image map. With dynamic content, the elements of many of the pages are assembled *on-the-fly* from the contents of a database that included in

the project. If a project was trying to sell cars, then the database would store all the details of each model. Any user might wish to view only models of a particular engine size or seating arrangement, colour and so on. When the user requests information, he/she is required to fill in an on-screen form or click a choice from a menu. That data is fed into the project's database engine and a page is made up that includes the information requested. The page is then formatted and displayed on the screen. This provides a much more flexible system with a huge range of possible page results. Since the data is centralised in the database, updates are carried out there, rather than having to update the contents of hundreds of individual pages.

Another flexible facility is the provision of a search capability, where the user can enter a word, the entire contents of the project are searched, and areas that contain the match are listed. The user can then choose which matches to display on the screen.

Other possible functional requirements include questionnaires, multi-choice assessments, chat rooms and forums. Questionnaires can be used to gather user information, polls on various topics, surveys on various products and other valuable information. Multi-choice assessments can be used for educational projects, quizzes, health checks, etc. Chat rooms and forums provide a mechanism for users to share problems and ideas, although this can have a hefty overhead as someone has to moderate their content to prevent possible libellous or other illegal content.

Style, look and feel

If the project content is described as the *'what'* and the site purpose as the *'why'*, then the site presentation must be described as the *'how'*. How a site looks and what impression it conveys is often seen as the main priority by a client. Certainly, this must be defined in the early discussions with the client.

The content style is dependent on the intended audience. Projects won't all have music/video/ graphics on every screen just because the technology exists. An estate agent, for example, will have many properties and require many screens, each containing graphics. A project reporting law court proceedings, on the other hand, is likely to require large screens with lots of text.

The style has to reflect the knowledge, experience and tastes of the target viewer. A project for teenagers has an entirely different approach to a project aimed at young schoolchildren. Again, if the project was targeted at a mature/elderly audience, it would use yet another approach. Consider how a project on alcohol abuse would differ if written for each of these age groups.

Sometimes, the content is determined by user expectations (e.g. primary colours for children, clean line art for diagrams, rendered graphics for objects, digital photographs for real estate, etc.).

The project *'style'* describes the slant of the material - e.g. sober, trendy, or outrageous.

There is also the *'look and feel'* of the project. A project can be given the correct style and still not work because of the implementation of the elements. All the elements used in the project (e.g. logos, buttons, colour schemes, headlines, body text, etc.) should look like they belong as a family. A project is often spoiled by using different buttons or different colour schemes on different pages. This can be prevented by fully fleshing out screen layout details in the Requirements Specification document.

To a large extent, the mood of a project is set by the nature of the organisation. Moods that could be suggested to a client include:

- Cutting edge (e.g. selling computers, audio/video equipment)
- Funky and feminine (e.g. selling women's magazines, cosmetics, clothes, some cars)
- Homey (e.g. providing medical advice)
- Comfortable (e.g. selling soft furnishings, life insurance)
- Corporate (e.g. pushing brand identity)
- Family business (e.g. selling local products, hand-crafted products)
- Professional (e.g. providing legal or consultancy services)
- Ethical (e.g. selling non-GM products, free-range products, renewable resources)
- Supportive (e.g. providing sympathetic advice on drugs, pregnancy, divorce, bereavement)
- Practical (e.g. no-nonsense advice on home repairs)
- Agitational (e.g. strongly promoting a cause or idea)
- Fun (e.g. light-hearted approach to events, cartoons, games, competitions)

In some cases, a project can combine several elements. For example, a project may combine an ethical and a practical approach. In other cases, mixing would be disastrous. Rock music and flashing colours, for example, would hardly be appropriate for a funeral undertaker's business.

The client may already have a strong brand identity and wish this to be reflected in the project. This would mean the organisation's logos, fonts, colour schemes, etc. being incorporated into the project. However, the client might take the opportunity to break from the existing image. For example a company that is identified with an older, more affluent, age group may want to use a web site to attract a new clientele from a younger age group. This would need a fresh approach and a new image.

Follow-up investigations
After the initial meeting, it is often important to carry out further information gathering. After all, the head of an organisation may overlook features that can easily be provided by staff in the various departments. With the approval of the client, some shorter meetings can be set up with such individuals. This might reveal what kind of information a department would like a website to capture from its readers, how often the department's information (e.g. prices) change, and the technical considerations involved in running the department.

It may also involve market research, to confirm that the project assumptions are correct (e.g. is there really a market for a Westlife CD game any more? Just how many small companies would be prepared to buy an interactive tutorial on completing VAT returns? and so on).

Checking out the competition
To maximise impact, the client must know its competitors, or similar organisations in the case of non-commercial clients. This helps provide an understanding of its own relative strengths and weaknesses. This is best achieved by examining the products (e.g. CD-ROMs, web sites, etc.) of others in the same field. The client should already know who they are and should be able to supply details of their products/services. If not, use a keyword search to find sites that market similar products or services. Clients are always impressed that you take an active interest in ensuring that their projects equals or betters those of others.

These projects should be studied from the following standpoints:
- What are the content, design, look, feel, and navigation capabilities of these projects?
- What are the good/bad features (e.g. do they load quickly, do they focus on their target audience, are they useful and relevant)?
- Are there are features that you might want to suggest be added to the client's project (e.g. a users discussion forum for a web site)?
- What is the competitors' main strengths in this area?
- What do the competitors offer that is unique (e.g. different products, better support, bulk discounts, etc)?

Where possible, it may be desirable to have these checks made by a representative sample of the client's own target audience.

The aim is not to copy these projects but to use them as a benchmark for designing the client's project to surpass them. Of course, they will also be upgrading their CD-ROMs, web sites, etc. on a regular basis and the aim is to design something that will be even better than their next offering.

Also, the client's project may well be competing with material that is not computer-based (e.g. radio, television, printed matter). Where possible, identify any features that a computer-based project can offer that improves the client's impact compared to these other media.

Note
Be aware that the client may redefine the content and/or purpose of the project once a thorough discussion clarifies issues in his/her mind. That is to be welcomed, as long as these changes appear in the agreed joint statement.

Target Audience
A project is designed to be used by one or more sets of users, known as the 'target audience'. This is probably not the same thing as those who are commissioning the project. The clients may be a group of venture capitalists, or a group of boardroom members who have little appreciation of the skills and experience of those at whom the project is targeted. So, the content, presentation and usability of the project must take into account the knowledge, abilities and interests of this target group. For example, a tutorial on 'computers for beginners' makes different assumptions from a tutorial on 'advanced networking techniques'. In the first case, the users may not even know how to use mouse, while the other set of users will understand even advanced terminology used in the text.   The project has to take into account the likely abilities and limitations of the users, understanding what they will want to do and what problems they may encounter using the package.

Of course, users other than the intended group may access the material (especially on the web) but the main target group(s) must be specifically designated, to maximise the impact of the project.

Often, the target audience is not a single homogenous mass, but comprises a range of different groups with their own goals and expectations. There will even be differences within a group (e.g. a group of users may share the same interests but have different levels of expertise).

Defining the users
The client should know what sort of audience a project is intended for. Typical questions to ask the client are:
- Who is project aimed at? Who will use this project?
- What will users gain from it?
- What delivery system will they be using?
- How do these factors affect the design?
- How do they affect the content, usability and accessibility?

A project may have a specialist audience   – e.g. camera enthusiasts, stamp collectors, trainspotters.
It may have a general audience   – e.g. film reviews, football fanzines.
It may also have more than one audience   – e.g. consumer information and suppliers.

Here are some likely user groups that can be used to help clarify the client's view of its target audience.

Age	Toddlers, teenagers, middle-aged, pensioners?
Gender	Women? Men? Everybody, but mostly women? Adults of both genders? Teenage girls?
Lifestyle preferences	Gay? Straight? Couples? Singles? Hippy? Alternative lifestyles? Religious?
Social Group	Specific groups of workers by trade or profession? Specific groups of people by income? Specific groups of people by social class?
Ethnic background	Specific ethnic groups? Multi-ethnic?
Location	Local audience? National audience? International audience?
IT skills	Beginners? Average? Experts? Technophobes?
Literacy level	Illiterate? Semi-literate? Average Literacy? High Literacy?
Sociological factors	Project used alone / used in pairs / by a group? Used as a presenter or lecturer's aid? Does target group exhibit any factors that might inhibit usage (e.g. cultural, reading right to left, language, social exclusion due to poverty, location, age or sex)? Is target group more inclined to prefer variety or to prefer pattern and routines?
Physical needs	Any vision, mobility, hearing or cognitive impairments?
Workplace needs	Training? Support? Team building? Intranet newsletters? Databases?
Environment needs	Poor lighting? Noisy environment?
Specialist consumers	Consumers of specialist goods/services (e.g. undertakers, diamonds, yachts)?
Special interests	Hobbies? DIY? Dating? Politics? etc.
Frequency of use	Daily users? Regular users? Irregular users? Chance users?

A discussion on these group categories helps focus the attention of the client on the real purpose of the project, as well as providing the essential information for the design. Clearly, there can be big differences between the needs and expectations of different groups.

Selecting a narrow group of target users allows for a finely tuned design.   However, this may restrict the user base. Alternatively, selecting too wide a target audience makes it more difficult to cater for all their requirements in a single project.

In addition, the client has to decide which user groups the organisation can serve.   For example, a local builder will only seek work in the immediate area, while a small manufacturer of arts and crafts may seek international sales.

User requirements

While the client may have a very good idea of who the project is aimed at, it is much less likely that he/she will be as knowledgeable about the way that the target group(s) will view and use the project. Indeed, even the designer is unlikely to fully appreciate these factors without a detailed examination.

The user requirements of a project are largely determined by the target audience, the task analysis of that particular target audience, and the initial usability testing with a representative group of target users.

Task Analysis

Task analysis is the close examination of the tasks that the users would carry out while using the project.   It looks at the following questions:

- Who are the users (see the report on Target Audience)
- What do they want from the project (not what the client *thinks* they want)
- What are their goals when using the project
- What specific tasks do they want to perform
- How will users interface with the project (e.g. with JavaScript enabled? with graphics enabled? with a Braille reader? with an old operating system? with an old version of a browser? with modern video codecs?). See more in the section on hardware and software requirements.

The aim of task analysis is to:

- Understand the user's requirements, to ensure that all project content and functionality is covered
- Ensure that the content, structure, navigation and presentation serve these requirements

The analysis is approached from the point of view of the user. For example, a car dealer may think customers want a single screen dedicated to each car model, whereas task analysis shows that they may prefer to view screens that compare models.   The client thinks data should be grouped in one way but analysis may show that users prefer to view data grouped in a different presentation. Indeed the user may expect differing content from the client. While the client may want to highlight car performance data, users may wish data on car safety or exhaust pollution. The only way to find out is to talk to members of the target audience about the project's content and functionality.

Task analysis research

Designers may be asked to create a project that is not in their current knowledge. Although the client and the target audience may be experts in flyfishing, nuclear physics, or whatever, the designer has to be sufficiently knowledgeable about what information such users want to view and manipulate. Before sensible discussion can be had with the target audience, the designer has to carry out some basic research into that topic. This does not mean that the designer has to become an expert in that field, since the project content is going to be provided by the client. It does mean that the designer should find out how other projects and other media handle and present this information. This knowledge can be gained from electronic data such as websites and competitor's CDs/DVDs, publications (e.g. magazines, books), literature (e.g. company brochures) and journals (e.g. medical, scientific). This knowledge provides the basis for the preliminary material that is placed before the target audience.

Task analysis methods

There are many methods that can be used to conduct meaningful task analysis, including:
- Focus groups
- Observation
- Surveys and questionnaires
- Interviews

Focus Groups

This method is commonly used by market researchers and political researchers to gather feedback.

This approach is *'qualitative'*, not *'quantitative'*. This means that it is preferable to have small group that truly represents the target audience, than a larger group that is not representative.   It is not how many take part, it is the reliability of the feedback that is important.   A later, quantitative, analysis can be carried out to confirm the findings with a larger group of users.

A focus group can often identify trends, attitudes or issues that may not have been included in the designer's pre-prepared questionnaires and surveys. New insights into the client's products, branding, marketing, pricing, support and more can be revealed in this process.   That is why focus groups should be used at the beginning of the development process.

The results of the focus group can form the basis for composing questions for quantitative surveys.

The group is usually up to 10 users, depending on the nature of the project and the nature of the group.

Show users various ideas, other products, outlines, etc. This may be verbal, paper-based, or based on actual working software (e.g. prototypes, existing systems or methods, previous projects, competitors' projects, other similar systems, etc).   The users should be asked to use software products, either to provide feedback on how they perceived certain tasks, to comment on missing facilities, or just to comment on their overall impression regarding the *'look and feel'* of the products. If possible, avoid pinpointing the client's project as this may influence users' reactions (i.e. telling the designers what they want to hear).

Ask users to comment on various topics and various sample screens.   Users should be encouraged to participate in a *'brainstorming'* session, where first impressions, contrary views, and fresh ideas on features and functionality are often generated.

Where the topic may be considered embarrassing by some (e.g. questions of sex, politics, religion, morality) the users can be provided with additional facilities to comment anonymously (e.g. using comment forms, e-mail, on-screen comments boxes, etc).

Observation

While focus groups are very useful in obtaining feedback, they are based on users being able to accurately report on their own needs, tasks, activities and behaviour.   This may be a particular problem where a focus group is out of its normal environment (e.g. sitting in an interview room, instead of at an office desk, a bedroom computer, or a school desk).

The analysis process can be augmented by the use of observation.   In many cases, the users are told that they are being observed. In some cases, tests are conducted with observers watching users through one-way mirrors. Users should be asked to follow a specific set of tasks identified in earlier research.

The activities of users, especially with prototypes, are watched and logged. This catalogues the tasks that the users carried out, whether they were successful, what difficulties they encountered - not forgetting tasks that they attempted where the software did not provide the required functionality, attempts to enrol on-line help, and so on. Observation also notes how users carried out their tasks and in which order tasks were performed, along with any special techniques used by participants.   It also notes which tasks were used most frequently and any facilities that were left unused.

Observation provides valuable information on how users interact with the project information in an active environment instead of on paper. The results should lead to design improvements, such as providing alternative navigational paths or multiple paths.

Questionnaires and surveys

Once a qualitative analysis has been conducted, the material that was produced by the users can be validated by presenting it to a wider body of user opinion. This gives a quantitative revue of the earlier findings and confirms whether the focus group's results are well-founded.

For projects with specialist content or usage, the survey must target people from the same target audience group. This could be employees from the same firm, fans of the same football team, members of the same support group or members of an on-line discussion group.

For projects with a wide target group, a more general approach can be adopted for surveys. This could take the form of telephone polling, street surveys, and/or online forms.

The survey can take important information items and operational tasks and ask participants to rate their importance (perhaps on a scale of 1 to 5 or 1 to 10). It should also provide comments boxes to pick up on any new aspects that were missed by the focus group.

Of course, the nature of the questions depends on the nature of the project and the feedback from the focus group.

Interviews

Focus groups benefit from the interaction between participants to bring out reactions, while surveys contain mostly pre-defined questions for participants. Another free-flow technique is individual interviewing. This can be used as a standalone technique, or can be used to extract further detail from participants in focus groups or surveys. Interviews can be on-site or off-site.

As a standalone technique, it is similar to focus groups in that it outlines the project's first draft and seeks comments on the content, approach, etc., and seeks suggestions for alterations and additions.

As a follow-up technique, it allows the designer to get a deeper understanding of why users react in a certain way, make certain choices or have certain attitudes. For example, users at a focus may have agreed that they wanted *"more searching options"*. During interviews, this statement may be found to be satisfied by adding a few more database fields into the search facility – or it may require comprehensive changes to the project's search facility, such as finding and displaying screens of comparisons between similar products (e.g. *"display a list of all saloon cars, over 2litres and costing under £15,000"*). The interview could also find out exactly what tasks the user expected to carry out to obtain such a result.

Task analysis produces the User Requirements and also the test data for later usability studies.
Examples of typical feedback from task analysis are:

"Lots of help"   (specially from new users)
"Fewer images, multiple reference navigation" (specially for reference project such as legal cases)
"Lots of feedback"   (specially from inexperienced users)
"Order tracking"   (the ability to see the current shipping status of an online purchase)
"Order customisation"   (the ability to place online orders after choosing additional options
                              e.g. to car or computer systems)
"Importance of privacy" (e.g. only being prepared to give personal information where it is really
                              required, such as online transactions or requesting subscriptions)

Human-Computer Interaction

Human-Computer Interaction (HCI) is the study of how computers and people communicate with each other and how the computer interface can be improved. In this context, the *'interface'* does not just mean the look and feel of the screens. It also covers how tasks are performed, how information is presented, what kind of questions are asked, etc. In other words, computer programs (including multimedia applications) have to be modelled around the physical and psychological characteristics of the human beings that use them. The programs must adapt to the users, and not the other way round.

HCI takes into account how people learn, including what aids learning and what inhibits learning. HCI is applied to all computer programs, since they all have some degree of user control. Multimedia titles, in particular, are created so that users have a high degree of control over what is seen and what is done. This makes HCI an even more important discipline for multimedia designers and developers.

Some HCI issues revolve round the physical world (e.g. don't use dark green letters on a black background because the eye will not sufficiently distinguish the text).

Most HCI questions examine how the human brain functions, how we understand external stimuli, how we store experiences, how we recall and use knowledge, and so on. An understanding of these processes allows software programs to adapt to these general rules of behaviour. This chapter adopts many of the lessons from these studies and these are embodied in the many suggestions in the chapter.

Human Memory

As the diagram shows, the memory process occurs in stages. Short term memory helps the user understand how to navigate or make informed choices, while long term memory is used to educate, etc.

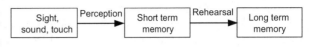

Perception

The human senses are continually receiving information from the outside world. Sight, sound, touch, taste and smell all process information that has to be categorised by the brain.   For example, walking down the street may produce sights (other pedestrians, cars, shops), sounds (mobile phone ringing, police siren), touch (rain on face) and smells (hamburger stand). The brain constantly filters out less important information.   Of course, what is regarded as important is dependent on the human's condition at the time.   If the person is hungry, the smell of hamburgers may predominate, whereas the sound of a phone is only meaningful if the person owns a mobile phone. The process of filtering unwanted information and identifying required information is shown as *'perception'* in the diagram. Important HCI issues arising are:

- Any movement, such as flying text or pop-up windows, attracts attention - also alerts peripheral vision.
- Temporal media (video, animation, sound) dominates over static media (text, graphics, tables).

The designer has to prevent *'sensory overload'*, where there are too many screen stimuli competing for the viewer's attention. The main points here are:

- A user can look and listen at the same time (i.e. can easily process both visual and aural incoming information).
- A user can't look and look at the same time (i.e. can't easily read text and watch video/graphic simultaneously).
- In multiple windows, only have activity in one window at a time.
- Don't show multiple graphics, videos, and photographs all at the same time.
- Don't overdo strong stimuli. Excessive bright colours and sound warnings/feedback cause stress/fatigue.
- Minimise distractions during memorisation tasks (no pop-up *'well done'* messages/fanfares).

Short Term Memory

Short-term memory acts as the temporary store for information.   If the information is really significant, it will be processed into long-term memory. Examples of short-term memory are:

- Someone consults a telephone directory and recalls the number just long enough to dial it.
- Someone carries out a mathematical calculation in their head, memorising interim calculations just long enough to complete the calculation.
- Someone is introduced to twenty people at a party, and each name is stored long enough to say *"Hello Kris"*, *"Hello Danielle"*, etc.

Once the information has been used, it is quickly forgotten.
The working memory can be easily overloaded. For instance, a person will recall a local telephone number long enough to dial it, but will have great difficulty in memorising a number that includes a long international code. Important HCI issues arising are:

- Don't expect users to store a great deal of information.
- Users can handle around seven items at any one time (known as the *'seven-plus-or-minus-two'* rule).
- The number of options in a menu should not exceed seven (see above).
- Don't ask multiple questions in the same screen.
- Images are best remembered if accompanied by text.
- Don't expect users to carry over much information from one task to the next.
- Structuring information, known as *'chunking'*, helps memorisation. For example, breaking a telephone number into the area code, the exchange code and the local number (e.g. 0141-775-2889 is easier to remember than 01417752889).
- Lower the task complexity by dividing a task into a sequence of smaller tasks (e.g. most software installation routines have separate screens for inputting user details, information on which folder to store the application, software serial number and site key, etc).

Long Term Memory

When an item is regarded as being significant, it will be committed to long-term memory. All our experience, knowledge and attitudes are stored in long-term memory.

Getting it in

If an item is considered to be of great importance, it is quickly processed into long-term memory. For example, if a patient is told that he/she has 143 days to live, the number is not forgotten!   Similarly, if one person stands out in a crowd, that person's name is usually recalled from all the others.

The aim of most multimedia titles is to impart information and knowledge to the users. The information may be in the form of significant knowledge (e.g. quantum physics, mathematics, and electronics) or it may even be entertainment (e.g. trivia questions, holiday information or the rules for playing chess).

In many cases, the information is processed and stored because the user wants to retain the information. In other cases, such as preparation for examinations or learning a programming language, the user may lack motivation and has to force himself/herself to absorb the information. This is usually achieved through a process of 'rehearsal'. If a piece of information is repeatedly spoken, written down, read over, practiced, then the information is likely to be stored in the long-term memory.

Getting it out

Unfortunately, humans are better at recognition than recall. They may not remember what Mr Jones the butcher looks like but they will know him when they meet him. The user's ability to recall information is improved by the user employing reasoning and understanding during learning. In other words, if the user is presented with a list of facts, they have less chance of being recalled than information obtained through on-screen activity (e.g. virtual experiments, exploration, searches, and other user tasks).

Important HCI issues arising are:

- Provide aids to user recall. These may be keywords or spatial memorisation (items are better remembered in groups).
- The use of analogies bases itself on the user's previous knowledge or experience to attach fresh memory links. Users learn by using previous knowledge. For example, everyone is familiar with the address on a letter containing a name, address, town and country. Similarly, an e-mail address has a name, host name, domain name and country. Making the comparison aids the appreciation of the concept.
- Consistency of associations creates better contexts for memorisation and recall
- Structuring information helps categorical memory by creating extra links for retrieval.
- Recall of video material can be poor if the content is too detailed or too much. The brain is forced to filter out most of the detail in the short time it has to process the material. Even the main points can be lost if complex material is presented over a short time. This also applies to audio material. Providing controls for the user to pause or rewind the material, although helpful, do not fully solve this problem. The real answer lies in adjusting the pace of the presentation and in chunking the material into separate items.
- Long continuous tasks should introduce a mental break (e.g. display a summary, quiz, etc.).

Design Constraints

The designer does not have a free hand in creating a project. The needs of the client and the needs of the user will place limitations on the design. These constraints may be:

Content related   Is the project for children, users with learning difficulties, etc.?
Hardware related   Is the user's computer system able to handle all aspects of the project?
Software related   Is the user's computer software able to handle all aspects of the project?

The questions of content should be settled in discussions with both the client and the target audience, although these may also have hardware or software implications. For example, a project for children, a fanzine, or a website for an estate agent would all require lots of images. The children's project may require additional features such as animations and the fanzine may want to feature interviews with the rich and famous.

The ability to add the latest bells and whistles to a project depends upon the delivery platform of the users. So, for example, a project with very large resolution, high-quality video clips is inappropriate for use on older computers, while web-based projects should only use technologies that the users are liable to have installed on their computers. Designers need to identify any possible constraints at an early stage, before too much fruitless work is carried out.

Hardware implications

In some cases, the hardware in use by the target audience can be clearly defined. For instance, where a company or organisation uses an intranet (an internal network) the computer equipment that runs the project is known. This simplifies the design process and testing process, as the computer speeds, processor types, monitor sizes, peripheral types, etc. are known.

Resolution:

Unknown	74(0%)
640x480	287(2%)
800x600	3460(35%)
1024x768	5307(54%)
1152x864	246(2%)
1280x1024	304(3%)
1600x1200	31(0%)

In other cases, a project is designed for a specific group of users who require certain hardware features to run the project. For example, a simulation project may require specific input, output devices such as joysticks, sensors, dual screens, etc.

Projects with a more general target audience still need to take into account the likely hardware configuration employed by users. For example, should a project expect that users would have monitors with a minimum resolution of 1024x768, or 800x600, or even 640x480?

The illustration shows the statistics on screen resolution gathered by a typical web site log. Of a sample of about 10,000 viewers, almost everyone is using SVGA or above. However, there are hundreds of users viewing with the older VGA resolution, probably comprising the poorer sector of the audience. A web site selling new Mercedes Benz cars might be happy to ignore such an audience, while a web site set up to inform people of welfare rights might specially want to reach that group. The constraints on screen design will follow from such decisions.

Other possible hardware constraints are:
- Should users be assumed to have computers that are capable of satisfactory playback of video content? If so, to which image size and frame rate?
- Should users be assumed to have the latest drivers and codecs installed?
- Should users be assumed to have audio output? If so, stereo or surround sound?
- Should website pages be written so that they are capable of being loaded quickly by even the slowest modem or slowest CD/DVD player?
- Should websites include streamed content, assuming users have ADSL or other high-speed links?

There are also hardware implications for users with special needs. The project has to be compatible with the use of specialist devices such as touch screens, Braille readers, or a Braille output keyboard. Project code may need to be added or modified to provide these extra facilities.

Software implications

The designer has to take into account the software on which the project will be run by the target audience. This includes issues such as:
- Operating system
- Browser
- Plugins

A project for use on an organisation's Intranet (internal network) benefits from the designer knowing exactly what operating system, browser, plugins, codecs, etc. are installed on users' computers. This allows the design to obtain the maximum benefit from any existing technologies available on the user's system. It also makes testing much simpler, as there is no need to test the project with different operating systems, different browsers, etc.

For other target audiences, the designer has to know if the user's client software will be able to support all of the project's functionality. This includes deciding whether to use facilities provided in the latest versions of Explorer, Flash, ActiveX, JavaScript and so on. Specialist sites may be designed knowing that the target audience will download any new facilities needed to access the project information. For projects aimed at the broad mass of people, expecting them to go to another site and download a piece of software, then install it, just to view the project contents, is likely to drive away potential viewers. In this case, the design has to be able to work with the oldest expected software, with all the limitations that may entail.

Identify and document potential operating system issues

Different operating systems (e.g. Windows, Unix, Mac) and different versions of the same operating system may produce different results for your project. This is because they may:
- Handle visual interfaces differently.
- Provide different support for facilities such as JavaScript, cookies, etc.

Their screen rendering, data transfer and processing function differences may result in the project being viewed in a different way than intended – or it may even prevent some users from using all the project's facilities.

It follows that the likely operating system used by the target audience should be discovered. If the client has an existing website, this information can be easily accessed where the ISP (Internet Service Provider) or third-party agent provide visitor logging statistics. The illustration shows the kind of report produced by www.thecounter.com.

The figures must not be taken as typical, as certain sites are more likely to attract users with certain operating systems. For example Apple Mac users are generally found among graphic artists, video and multimedia workers, etc. while Unix users are found in educational and more specialist circles.

Where the project is aimed at a more all-purpose audience, general statistics can be found at www.statmarket.com. Where there is no existing site, the information will have to be gathered during the questionnaires and surveys stage.

Operating systems (OS):

OS	Count (Percentage)
Win 98	4511 (44%)
Windows XP	2581 (25%)
Win 2000	1249 (12%)
Win NT	914 (8%)
Win 95	637 (6%)
Unknown	231 (2%)
Mac	58 (0%)
Win 3.x	23 (0%)
Linux	17 (0%)
Unix	7 (0%)
Windows ME	2 (0%)
Amiga	2 (0%)
WebTV	1 (0%)

Armed with this knowledge, the project can be designed to work on the operating systems found to be the most popular with the target audience. In the example above, the target audience is clearly made up of Windows users. In other cases, the results may show a greater number of Mac or Unix users, and the designer would have to ensure that the project would run satisfactorily in these environments. This means the project being tested on computers running these operating systems.

Identify and document potential browser issues

Different website browsers (e.g. Internet Explorer, Netscape, Opera) and different versions of the same operating system may produce different results for your project. This is because they may:

- Render page content differently (browsers parse and render HTML according to their own set of rules).
- Provide different support for feature sets and HTML versions.
- Provide different support for facilities such as JavaScript, cookies, etc.
- Inhibit project functionality because the user has turned off support for a feature (i.e. displaying graphics, disabling JavaScript, etc.)

Once again, these differences may result in the project being viewed in a different way than intended – or it may even prevent some users from using all the project's facilities.

This problem is diminishing due to the stranglehold that Internet Explorer has taken on the browser market, although there is some activity using WebTV (mostly American), and browsers that run on palm-top computing platforms like Windows CE. More likely issues concern how to handle security (e.g. will the website use SSL or 128 bit encryption?) and user functionality (will the website still be effective if cookies, JavaScript or graphics display are turned off?).

Cross-platform issues

While most users are running Windows on a PC system, some the target audience may be using other hardware systems and operating systems. This raises potential problems, with a product running according to the designer's wishes on one platform but not another. These problems can be overcome, as long as the designer identifies them before proceeding with the project implementation.

Examples of possible cross-platform problems are:

- The typical screen resolution for a PC is 96dpi, while a Mac is 72dpi and Unix xWindows is either 75dpi or 100dpi.
- Different platforms use different fonts. If a project specifies a particular font that is not on the user's computer, a default font is substituted. Courier is the default font on a Macintosh and Arial on a PC, so a serifed font might be displayed instead of a sans serif font, or vice versa.
- Windows fonts are larger than Mac fonts at the same point size.
- The default gamma correction is different on a PC from that on a Mac, so that the reproduction of a photographic image will vary depending on the platform viewing the project. An image that is fine on a PC may appear washed out on a Mac, while Mac images may appear to have excessive contrast on a PC.
- PCs and Macs display different representation of some special ISO characters.
- Specialist file formats for one computer system may be unreadable by another computer system.

Producing a design rationale

By this stage, there should be a good appreciation of the client's and the users' needs for a particular project. Before starting to create the detailed specifications for the project, time should be spent preparing a rationale for the project. This provides the foundation and motivation for the next stages.

The rationale should summarise

Why   This outlines the expected benefits of the project and is the most important part of the rationale
What   This outlines the project content
How   This outlines the project medium and the project navigation

A document containing these points can be regarded as a statement of intent to show a client. In other words, if you were asked to send a short e-mail explaining the project, the rationale is what you would send. The strategy contained in the rationale must reflect the client's purpose, the needs of the target audience, the state of the competition and the design team's own resources and abilities.

It may contain a purpose statement such as

"To promote our company's computer products"

and it may also contain specific objectives for the project such as:

- To provide images, descriptions and prices of our product range.
- To provide facilities for searching the product range.
- To provide facilities for purchasing goods.
- To provide support FAQs.
- To provide buyer assistance (e.g. explaining different standards and acronyms).

and so on.

The rationale can be constructed from:

- The client's requirements analysis.
- The users' task analysis.
- The background research on competitor's products, market analysis and current trends.
- Brainstorming sessions in the design team.

Brainstorming is a powerful technique that draws out the best ideas from a team. Sessions are carried out in a comfortable atmosphere designed to promote communication. All members are encouraged to maintain a flow of thoughts, no matter how unlikely or fanciful they seem.   Ideas that are generated by one team member are often developed and added to by other members. Although most of the ideas are eventually discarded, the central themes are used as an inspiration for the design rationale.

Design evaluation methods (principles)

Design principles are general principles that require interpretation for a particular project, to take into account the nature of the content and its intended audience. They are independent of any existing technology and seek to stress the principles upon which the project is based.   Understanding these principles helps designers adopt a more user-centred approach and produce a more usable product.

Examples of design principles are that the system is:

Recognisable	The user can easily recognise the current state of the system and can clearly identify the alternative possible actions (e.g. the user is informed about his/her location in the project and the navigation choices are easily understood).
Predictable	The user knows the result of a future action based on experience of previous actions (e.g. clicking the backwards arrow always returns to the previous screen; users who are familiar with Windows already understand how pull-down menus work).
Traceable	The user can assess the effect of past operations on the current state (e.g. the user has passed five self-assessment tests and knows that he/she is on the final test that moves him/her to the next learning outcome).
Familiar	The user can employ knowledge and experience from the real world (e.g. an icon of a dustbin symbolises deletions, while an icon of an open door symbolises entry to another area of the project).
Consistent	The user is comfortable with a consistent look to screens/buttons/backgrounds, and consistent feedback (e.g. buttons may always have rollovers or may click when depressed).
Controllable	The user controls the system and not the other way round. (e.g. the user controls the pace of events, the user can by-pass animation/videos, the user may be provided with video playback controls/volume control/etc.)
Adaptive	The system assesses user understanding and adapts to that level. The content and/or the interface is altered to suit the capabilities of the user. (e.g. the user may choose from beginner/average/expert level when entering the project, or may be provided with specially chosen content that accords with his/her answer to previous questions).
Responsive	The user is provided with full and continuous feedback. All responses are given in context (e.g. unhelpful *'incorrect response'* messages should be replaced by messages giving help on what the user is doing wrong.
Supportive	The system should anticipate user problems in knowledge and in navigation (e.g. it may provide wizards or pop-up help)

These are principles. That means that they are applied to real situations and will result in differing design requirements for different projects. For example, some training packages may provide less user control than others. An employer may decide that the employee must review all parts of the training course and specify that users will not have the ability to skip sections of the project. Or a college/university package may prevent a user from moving out of a section until it is successfully completed. On the other hand, this approach would be unworkable in, say, an encyclopaedia.

Applying design principles to the project should lead to the production of a set of design requirements.

Prototypes and mock-ups

When the design rationale has been completed, the detailed project design and implementation could be started. However, there are still risks that the client and/or users may have different conceptions and expectations of the project from the designers. The way to avoid this is to present a small-scale representation of the project to them, based on the established structure and style guide, for their reactions and comments.

This representation could be:

Horizontal	The entire front-end interface is simulated, with no depth to the representation.
Vertical	There are in-depth implementations of a few example features.
Mixed	A horizontal representation, with a few key features developed more fully.

The mixed model is a commonly used one, as it demonstrates both the key structural and layout details.   It has the structure, navigational controls and front end implemented. In addition, one or two other sections are completed, to show how the finished project would look.

This is an excellent, although time-consuming, way to sharpen up the definition of needs and to develop an understanding and a client agreement on a project. Misunderstandings and extra features can be picked up and settled at this stage, before a great deal of expensive and possibly wasted effort has been expended.

Used properly, mock-ups and prototypes play an important role in the design process. The initial time and cost of prototyping should result in much greater savings in time and cost in the overall development process. The final project will be implemented from the information collected from the prototype model.

Mock-ups and paper prototypes

A mock-up is a representation that is presented in a different medium from the final intended project, because mock-ups are usually much quicker to create than using multimedia or web-building tools.

Various methods are used to create mock-ups, the most common being:

- Paper prototypes (hand-drawn screen layouts, storyboards
- PowerPoint presentations.
- Example screens created using graphics packages such as PhotoShop or Paint Shop Pro.
- Interface building software such Visual Basic or Delphi.

Their intention is to display the project's concepts, branding, screen layouts, typefaces, colour schemes, navigation buttons, menus and scrollbars, etc.   They may use existing images or logos and often fill screen text areas with dummy text (to show the screen effect). The pages should be laid out exactly as they are intended to appear on the screen of the completed project.

Flow charts and navigation maps may be hand drawn or may be created using a charting program such as Visio.

In addition, interfaces built with Delphi or Visual Basic might demonstrate some elementary user interaction.

Approaches to prototyping

Unlike a mock-up, a prototype is created using the same medium as the final project. In other words, a multimedia project would be created using Macromedia Director (or other authoring tool) while a website would be created using Dreamweaver (or other website creation tool).

It is only partly developed but provides enough content, layout and interaction to give a good representation of the final product. Nevertheless, at this stage it is only providing a simulation of the features of the intended system.

Since it uses the medium it is destined for, and since it provides greater functionality, it is a superior model to mock-ups and paper prototypes. However, it takes longer to prepare.

Types of prototype

There are two commonly used prototyping methods:

Throw-away   The initial model is only used to sharpen up client and user needs and is then discarded. Mainly used where critical features need clarification.

Evolutionary   The initial model is improved in incremental steps until it becomes the finished product. Mainly used where needs are well understood.

Throwaway prototypes

Throwaway prototypes (also known as rapid prototypes) are developed quickly, to explore and clear up confusion or shortcomings in the client or user needs specification. This approach uses an iterative technique, allowing the developer to clarify the project requirements. The cycle is repeated, until the client and target users are satisfied with all the specifications. Once these problems are cleared up, the prototype model is discarded and the true development process begins with the new fully worked out design specification.

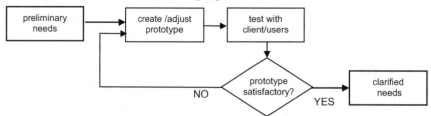

Although the disposal of the prototype seems like wasted effort, it has achieved its purpose – the delivery of an improved set of requirements.

As the diagram shows, the input to the process is a presentation model using the designer's initial appreciation of the project client and user needs. The output from the process is a final set of needs that can be used to create requirements specification documents, structure charts, storyboards, flow charts and project plans. This technique is not used where the needs are well developed, since the process will uncover little of extra value.

Since they are built quickly, with little regard to quality or functionality, these models are often described as *"quick and dirty"*.

A throw-away prototype has the following advantages:
- The model does not have to be perfect.
- It can use whatever software produces the model in the shortest time.
- It requires no initial documentation, as the writing of the detailed specifications occurs after the process is complete.
- It can be used to evaluate an existing system.
- Several prototypes can be created, to present different approaches for evaluation.
- Several prototypes can be created, to examine different parts of the project.

It also has the following disadvantages:
- It increases development costs.
- The initial prototype may simply be accepted by the client as the final project (defeating the feedback process). This is known as 'premature concretisation'.
- The prototype may proceed in a direction that may ultimately prove to be ineffective, unwelcome and very costly to correct.
- Since this approach concentrates on the screen design and navigation, it may ignore other important aspects such as download times.
- Clients and users will tend to regard the prototype as a "nearly finished" product, instead of being the beginning of the development. This can raise over-optimistic expectations for delivery dates.
- Developers who are under time pressures may be tempted to use parts of the prototype in the final product. This is dangerous, since the prototype was based on an inadequate understanding of needs, and is not properly documented. This will create later problems of content, functionality and testing.

Incremental prototypes (Evolutionary Prototypes)

With the conventional software development cycle, user involvement occurs at the requirements definition stage and again later at the alpha testing stage. There is no user involvement in the main development of the project. Throwaway prototypes elicit the requirements that *begin* the development process. This development could proceed without further user involvement, although continued user involvement is desirable. Continued client and user involvement, however, is guaranteed with evolutionary prototypes. This is because the prototype will evolve into the final system in a series of incremental stages. Each stage is subject to scrutiny and approval, before a further stage is commenced. The prototype is not discarded; instead, the final project is built from this original prototype.

An initial model provides the outline of the system, as with other methods. The prototype begins by developing those critical requirements that are most understood. Since it converges towards a final working project, real-world data is used during prototyping.

Each discrete part of the prototype, where the requirements are fully understood, is developed according to proper engineering life cycle standards - one stage at a time. Each stage is then subjected to client/user review and approval. This allows any modification or redirection to be implemented before too much effort is expended. If necessary, this stage will be reworked until it meets client/user needs. When one feature is fully developed and accepted, another discrete area of the project is begun. The experience of using the prototype is expected to prompt the users to better express their needs for the less understood features of the project.

With each iteration in the development phase, further functionality is added, until the project has evolved into a finished system.

An evolutionary prototype has the following advantages:
- It produces the most needed functionality first. The client and users do not have to wait until the end of the development process to see working sections of the project.
- Early delivery of stages means reduced delays if any problems arise in the requirements.
- Due to their involvement throughout the process, the final project is more likely to satisfy the client and user requirements.
- The project can be used, albeit partially, from an early stage (e.g. a website can have basic promotional material up and running, with later phases adding search, ordering and support facilities, etc.)
- As each stage is documented during its development, the project documentation accumulates naturally during the development.

It also has the following disadvantages:
- It requires that the project's design be sufficiently understood at an early stage, to allow the project to be decomposed into discrete parts. This is sometimes overcome by employing throw-away prototypes

before embarking on an evolutionary prototype. While this combines the benefits of both methods, it also combines their disadvantages.

- It requires frequent feedback from the user, which is very time-consuming.
- It can inflate the original project's scope, as client and users progressively realise the project's possibilities and demand extra functionality.
- It is especially problematic in situations where the project may be subject to significant and/or rapid changes, where previously completed stages may become invalid.
- It requires a break from the traditional management of projects, producing new problems of organising properly skilled development teams, defining contract obligations, predicting development and maintenance costs, keeping on top of change and configuration management, etc.
- Constant changes make the system structure difficult to define and maintain, with resultant extra costs during maintenance activities.

Requirements and specifications

There are so many documents that can be generated by a major project that a single document that gathers together all the essential material is required. This is called a *'requirements specification'* or a *'system requirements'* document. In practice, requirements and specifications address different issues but, since they are closely linked, they are often produced as a single document.

This document contains two main elements:

- The objectives (i.e. the *what*) of the final project, (defined in the project requirements).
- The rules (i.e. the *how*) for creating the project (defined in the project specifications).

When complete, the document is presented to the client to be *'signed off'*. This way, both sides agree that the document specifies what the final project will provide for the price and delivery date.

Requirements

A requirement is an objective that has to be satisfied by the final project. Requirements are not wish lists or possibilities – they are necessities. As such, requirements can be used a measure of the success of the project and be included in the testing and evaluation of the final project.

Requirements are usually described in functional terms – what objectives will be met, what functions will be provided, what performance and reliability will be provided,

Specifications

Specifications detail *how* the project's requirements will be created and implemented, so that the objectives are met. So, for example, they may define the fine detail of how a particular activity is carried out, the order of events in each activity, how the system will react to user errors, how a database table is organised and displayed, how the content will be laid out, how the navigation will be carried out, any required system software or hardware configuration, etc.

All these can be expressed in specific terms and this is a ready-made checklist for future testing and evaluation. In many respects the specifications are a more accurate way to test a project, as it is possible to meet all the project requirements without the project meeting all its intended quality targets. For example, a project might carry out all its functions and still not meet the required expectations of end-users. On the other hand, a specifications checklist is easily understood and applied.

The requirements specification document

This document covers the content requirements, functional requirements and technical requirements and must be as factual as possible.

It is an extremely important document as is embodies much of the contractual work to be undertaken. Therefore, before presenting this document to the client, it has to be examined to ensure that all aspects are correct, complete, able to be tested, and are realistically achievable in the time allocated. This examination must take into account the time, money, skills and equipment that is available for completing the project.

Refer to the sections on *'Design principles'* and *'Design requirements'* in the next chapter for further details.

The main elements in the requirements specification document are:

Functional requirements

These were made known and listed during the requirements analysis stage with the client. They are re-presented to the client after removing any unworkable or unrealistic requirements. The document may also include additional functions not specified by the client but necessary for the project's success (e.g. the ability to create or read cookies, content-sensitive navigation, special error-handling mechanisms, etc.). The document must also ensure that all accessibility legislation requirements are addressed in the project's functionality.

While these requirements may have implications regarding user interface design, these issues are addressed in a separate design document.

Technical requirements

This specifies all hardware and software requirements, including the specification of the computer and all peripherals. This is dependent upon the delivery method (CD/DVD, web, intranet, or kiosk). For example, projects designed for standalone kiosks can have a specific set of requirements- such as the need for a touch screen or large screen monitor. Other possible factors are a sound card, and a particular amount of memory or hard disk space.   The specification may also lay down performance requirements such as the speed of computer, the access time of a CD/DVD drive or a hard disk, the screen resolution, the colour depth and frame handling rates of graphics cards, or the lowest acceptable version of the operating system.

The software requirements must list the range of operating systems that the project will work on and the range of browsers that can access the project (if it is a website). It must also list any plug-ins that must be present in the computers that will run the project. Demanding that particular video/audio CODECs, add-ons (e.g. QuickTime or Divx), or specialist drivers be installed may enhance the project's abilities but has to be balanced against the possible reduction in the size of the target audience (since not every user will have the latest technologies, or wish to specially install them).

Content requirements

Much of the information is contained in the content inventory and the results of the information architecture analysis. The document should specify exactly what content the client has to provide, what provisions for content accumulation are required (e.g. access to the client's site, access to the client's staff, shooting video footage in exotic locations, etc).

Design and navigation requirements

This deals with the specifics of how the user negotiates the project.   The methods may be different for each project. Some may use a web-style interface with hyperlinks, while others may use a windows-style interface with pull-down menus and dialogue boxes.   Others may use image maps or other navigation methods. It also specifies the position of all the project's main elements and may include menus, buttons, active screen areas, video display areas, etc.
A few examples of these requirements are:

- Always place forward/backward/home/quit buttons in the same place.
- Always issue a warning message before changing or deleting any data.
- Always display a site map in the lower left corner of the screen.
- All icons should have a caption under them.
- Access to all main project sections is from a set of pull-down menus/ side menu of buttons.
- The main menu bar/ side menu will appear in all screens.
- Access to all navigation options is by mouse click.
- A single mouse click will activate any option.
- The menu bar will include a *'help'* facility.
- The menu bar will include a *'quit'* option (not required for web sites).
- Within each section, the user should be able to navigate backwards and forwards through the screens.
- The cursor will change shape/colour when it is over an active area.
- The shape/colour of an active area will alter when the cursor is over it.

This example list provides some key features such as allowing the user to control the pace of the project material, allowing the user to access any main section at any time, and allowing the user to seek help or to quit at any time. This is not a shopping list or a checklist. It is NOT a list of recommendations. It presents examples that may act as a guide to constructing a list that is appropriate to a particular project.

As always, these requirements must focus upon <u>users</u> and their <u>tasks</u> and the requirements may be clarified by encouraging client and user participation.

The appearance of the screens, in terms of colour schemes, etc., is not considered at this stage. That is because aesthetic appeal is not an end in itself. It is more important at this stage to get the logical visual design correct, with screen design issues coming later.

Developers make use of *'paradigms'*. These are extensions from earlier successful examples and may provide experience and expertise in both design requirements and the creative use of technology.

It is important, however, that developers don't design for the computer or the technology - they design for the user. They should only add features when they are required - not because it can be done.

Deciding the design requirements may be time-consuming but shortcuts should be avoided.   If the design requirements are not fully developed, the whole project may be flawed as a result. Never attempt to fix problems in the project documentation. Don't tell users how to get round your problem - fix the problem at this stage.   Equally, don't decide to fix problems in the next release. If this project is poor, there won't be a next release!

Notes

Some of these sections are inter-related.   For example, if the technical requirements specify the use of a touch screen, then the screen layout specification will have to reflect this by stating that menu buttons have to be spaced slightly further apart. Similarly, designing the project for use on an intranet may mean that the project is designed to set and assess student performance in examinations or training exercises.

Unlike design principles, design requirements are unambiguous. They require no interpretation by the programmer. The items can be evaluated with a checklist. That is the whole idea. The designer creates a set of requirements that are so specific that there is little room for errors or ambiguities during the implementation stage. The larger the team working on the project, the more scope there is for errors between members.

Even the multi-billion dollar big boys get it seriously wrong from time to time. The 1999 Mars Climate Orbiter crashed on the back side of Mars because one NASA team was using imperial measurements while the other was using metric units. The result was that the spacecraft was put into too low an orbit and crashed!

Design document

Agreement on the requirements specification leads the project into the last main design stage - the creation of the Design Document. This document fills in all the important details and is used as the set of tasks that face the team. The tasks are then worked into a Project Plan for implementation.

The design phase lays out how the project will work in detail. A number of methods are used by different developers, but a top-down approach (where the main functions are outlined followed by subsidiary functions, continuing to the end of the outline) and flowcharts (showing the links between screen pages and the flow of activities) are common development methods. The design phase produces all the content details. This will cover all internal resources (i.e. the company's own talent, hardware and raw material) and requirements for buying in skills (e.g. commissioning photographers, video camera teams, sound studios, graphics artists, animators, voice-over artists, etc). Details of copyright would also be addressed at this stage.

Design standards

These are the rules that the developers (content writers, code writers, etc.) must use when building the project. Some standards are general (e.g. legal standards on accessibility and ergonomics) while others are specific to a project (e.g. style guides, performance benchmarks, etc.).

A standard may be physical (e.g. no web page should be larger than 60k), operational (e.g. must work with a specific maximum download speed from the web or a CD/DVD), logical (e.g. there must be no broken links or orphaned pages) or presentational (e.g. must use a style guide to present a consistent *'look and feel'* throughout the pages).

These rules are documented for use during the building phase. So, no matter who is working on what part of the project, there is a single set of rules that can be referred to.

Output from design phase

The main documents that are produced from the design phase are:

Design standards   - the rules and checklists developers must follow.
Navigation map   - the map showing how individual screens are connected by buttons or hyperlinks.
Storyboard   - the drawings and descriptions of screen contents.
Screen design   - the specification of screen elements (e.g. fonts, point sizes, colours, etc.).

Structure and Navigation

A project's content and functions have been the main focus up to now. However, the way that the content is organised and the way that it is accessed and used have a huge impact on the project's usability. The larger the project, the greater this challenge becomes. If a large project has its content contained in thousands of individual screens, poor organisation of the content will make the project hard to use – particularly if the navigation aids are also poorly set up.

On the other hand, if that same project has its content organised logically and has plenty of navigational aids, the usability is much improved.

Users are intolerant of poor organisation and poor access. This is particularly true on the WWW, where viewers may only access as few as three pages before leaving a poorly organised site.

A good starting point is the attitude of Albert Einstein who said - *"Things should be made as simple as possible, but no simpler".*

Simplicity has many advantages, as a simple structure and navigation system is:

- Easier to create.
- Less prone to errors.
- Easier to test.
- Easier for users to use.
- Simpler is more compatible.
- Easier to maintain.

Ideally, a user should be able to visualise a project's structure, understand how different pages and elements relate to each other, and how to move around the project.

This approach does not look at visual style, which is a separate issue.

Structure and navigation are covered separately in the following pages, although they are interlinked.

Structure

Information architecture

Information architecture is the technique of ordering a project's content in such a way that it develops the project's structure, along with the routes that users will travel in exploring and retrieving the information.

The identification of the client and the users' needs for a particular project should result in a list of the content that should be included in a project – and a plan for the corresponding navigation requirements.

Most content in a project, particularly web sites, is placed in short pages that are designed to be read non-sequentially. This technique, known as *'chunking'*, as mentioned earlier, has borrowed and adapted from the publishing world. Chunking provides small pieces of information that can easily located and understood. So, for example, this book contains hundreds of thousands of words covering a range of topics.   The words are divided into main chunks (i.e. chapters) and sub-chunks (i.e. headings and sub-headings).   Tables and bulleted lists provide even further chunking. The book's table of contents provides a quick look up of main chunk and sub-chunk contents.   The reader can read the entire book's contents sequentially, or can jump in and read sections of particular interest.   The table of contents acts as the user's navigation system.

This technique is carried over into multimedia and web projects – with the addition of hyperlinks as the navigation system.   Just as with a book, a project's table of contents can act both as a navigation system and as an overview of the entire project's structure.   However, unlike a book, users do not enjoy reading long passages of text off a monitor screen, as they are forced to scroll long distances and also to remember information that has moved off the screen. Faced with this, they are likely to print the screen contents for reading from paper.

Organising the content is not a problem for a small project. For example, a family website might simply contain a few photographs and a few details about family members. However, consider the content required for a website for a large retail organisation.   The site may wish to sell hundreds of thousands of products, perhaps grouped by product type, by price, by manufacturer's name, and so on. The process of listing the project content and grouping the content into meaningful chunks is known *as 'information architecture'*.   Of course, it is closely linked with the physical structure of the project and the methods of navigating through the content, and these issues are covered later. Information architecture determines much of the navigation.

The input to the process is the data that was identified during the needs analysis and task analysis stages, the functional requirements, the review of competitor's products, and the feedback from mock-ups and throw-away prototypes.

The output from the process is Content Inventory (list of contents), content grouping, functional requirements, navigation tasks.   Listing content minimises later problems with identifying content requirements (gathering too much, forgetting others).   These findings are added to the requirements document.

The steps in the process are:

Gather the contents

This first stage ensures that all necessary material is available for inclusion in the process. Adding material at a later date, either through omission during this stage or through the appearance of new material at a late stage, can totally upset a seemingly settled structure.

Gather lists of the project's contents, including include both static and dynamic content. Content elements may include text (such as descriptions, specifications, prices, etc.), images, animations, graphics and video clips.   Entire screens can also be regarded as content.   So, for example, a conditions of use statement, a privacy statement, a copyright notice, a user form, a login screen, etc. can be regarded as content elements. Some elements, such as the login screen or user form, can also be regarded as functional elements.

Chunk the contents

This stage divides the content into meaningful portions that can accessed and viewed either individually, or as a set or related items. The general approach is:

- Split over-general topics into sub-topics.
- Merge small topics into a single topic. This avoids having too many screens with little content.
- Don't split a single topic over several screens. This causes confusion (particularly on web sites, where a user may jump from another site straight into the second screen of a series of linked pages). If the content is too large for a single screen, consider reorganising content to create sub-topics, rather than having scrolling screens.

Creating too few screens results in redundant data (see the later section on linear structure) and long download times (for websites), while too many screens result in the user spending more time jumping around than reading.

As always, there are exceptions to the rule. Consider a website that provides advice on repairing a punctured tyre. The user is unlikely to read a page, run out to the car, carry out the single task, and then return to the house to read the next instruction. It is much more likely that the user will print out the set of instructions. This user would much prefer to print out a long single page of text, than print out a set of instructions spread over many pages.

Similarly, long scrolling pages may be acceptable for projects that provide legal rulings, technical specifications, medical descriptions and other areas where users might be more prepared to absorb material in a linear fashion. Where this technique is used, it is common to place important material *'above the fold'* (i.e. in the part of the page that is viewed without scrolling). This area often displays abstracts and summaries of the entire content, perhaps with links to lower areas of the page.

Create categories

When all the material is gathered, their order is determined using the following criteria:

- Not all the project's content can be on the front page.
- Some content is more important than the rest.
- Many chunks of content are related.
- The structure should conform to the *'seven-plus-or-minus-two'* rule.

First, chunks of information should be ranked in importance. From this, create main categories with group headings. The main categories are determined by the site's purpose and the expected tasks of the users. Each category may have sub-categories under them. A common structure uses a starting page (the 'Home Page') that provides an overview of the project and outlines the main categories with links to sub-categories.

For example, a category called *'Products'* may have sub-categories for *'Furniture'*, *'Lighting'*, *Carpets'*, etc. The *'Furniture'* category might be further categorised as *'Bedroom'*, *'Sitting Room'*, etc. Not every category need have sub-categories. A category called *'Our Privacy Policy'*, for example, may only store a single page of material with no further sub-material.

This process is often referred to as creating a *'hierarchy'*, where the more general information is placed high in the structure while the detailed information is held at lower levels. In the example, *'Products'* is a category that is high in the hierarchy, *'Furniture'* is lower, *'Bedroom'* is lower still, while details of individual products will be even lower in the hierarchy.

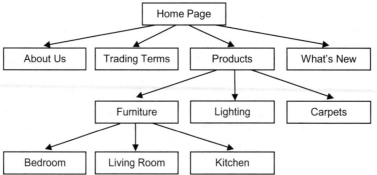

The above diagram shows part of a project but it demonstrates that at each lower level of the hierarchy, the information becomes more and more specific. This structure prevents users wasting time navigating through categories that have no interest to them.

There are different types of hierarchy, as described below.

Deep and narrow hierarchy   A project with a deep hierarchy uses many levels. At each level, the user choices become more and more focussed until the required page is accessed. This structure is often used for large projects where many pages of information have to be included. The disadvantage of this structure is the large number of user clicks required to access the required detailed pages. Some designers advocate a *'three clicks rule'*, which says that users will abandon a project if it takes more than three clicks to reach their required pages. However, a deep hierarchy will not deter users who are using the project to access specific information, but may deter users who are casual browsers. It is also easier for the user to get lost in this structure, although this can be minimised by ensuring that the sub-categories take the user to their desired page(s) in a logical and smooth progression.

Wide and shallow hierarchy   A project with a shallow hierarchy uses fewer levels, so that every page in the project is accessible with a few clicks. This would not be suitable for a large project, since it would need to have many category options at each level, too many links on each page, and individual pages containing too much material (resulting in unwelcome scrolling). However, it is ideal for smaller projects that contain less information.

The aim is to create a structure that has no more than five to seven categories, as usability studies suggest that users stop reading options after they have absorbed four or five different choices.

The categories must reflect the evidence from the requirements stages. Unnecessary categories obscure the user's view of the site and inhibit usability. It also helps to group like categories together in the order of the structure. For instance, categories relating to product information should appear adjacent to each other, as should categories relating to company policy (e.g. ordering, returns, FAQs).

If a project such as a website is always growing or changing, it is a continual struggle to maintain the balance between the structure and the content.

Label the categories

This stage provides meaningful labels for each main category and each sub category. Simple labels are sufficient as users are accustomed to seeing labels such as *'Contact Us', 'Our Company', 'What's New'*, etc.

Assemble content lists

This stage assembles the lists of content elements under the category headings. Some designers use a word processing package, so that elements can be easily cut and pasted. Others use cards, each card with a content element written on it; cards are then stacked in piles of related interest. Still others use graphic illustration software. Some web authoring packages have in-built site structure facilities, so that a project's structure can be linked with pages of content as they are constructed.

Check the structure consistency

This stage ensures that the structure matches the information order preferences identified earlier in the user observations. It ensures that important content is not stored down too many levels of depth and what information should always be available on screen (e.g. copyright notice, search facility, site map). If necessary, the structure may have to be altered.

It also checks how the information groups relate to the users' preferred access methods (e.g. do they want a table of contents, multi-level menus, search facilities).

This stage also ensures that all content requirements are met in the functional requirements. For example, a search page must be accompanied by the ability to carry out the search (i.e. the necessary database and search coding). Note any functional implications for inclusion in the project's functional requirements section of the requirement specification.

If more than one designer is working on a project, it is a good idea that they carry out the information architecture phase separately, then compare results.

The results of the information architecture construction should be documented as this provides the structure plan for those who will implement the project.

The Opening Page

When a user opens a multimedia package or accesses a web site, they are presented with an initial opening screen which is the gateway to the entire project.

This may be the project's *'main page'*, it may be a *'splash page'* or it may be a *'doorway page'*.

Home page

Every project has a home page. It has two main functions:

- To inform the user of the main purpose of the project, sometimes called the USP –Unique Selling Proposition. This might be a statement of an organisation's aims or it might be an introduction to the products of a company. The user should be left in no doubt what the project is about after looking at the home page; there should be no need to 'explore' to discover the project's purpose.
- To provide the main index to the project by providing the links to the main project content categories. This would include a menu (displaying the major categories) and perhaps a site map (also displaying all the sub-categories).

The home page is usually designed for quick retrieval, to prevent users from wandering off. This means avoiding large graphics, video and animations and ensuring that any graphics images that are used are optimised.

Splash page

A splash page is a page that might be presented to the user *before* displaying the home page.

It is so named because it hopes to make a *'splash'* through using lots of graphics, animations and the latest technology to capture the user's attention. In many cases, it is simply used as a brand exposure and is intended to impress. It often requires the user to wait while a large animation file is loaded and run, without providing any additional functionality to the project. So, a user with a slow dial-up modem may wait for minutes just to see a pretty animation and an *'Enter our Site Here'* button. Some may not even allow the user to by-pass the introductory animation sequence, failing to provide a *'skip intro'* button.

In other cases, a splash page warns the viewer that a particular minimum version of a browser is required, a certain screen resolution is required, certain plugins or codecs are required, JavaScript must be turned on, or other similar requirements must be met to view the project properly. Of course, a project that places such limitations on its viewing audience probably has just lost some of its potential viewers who are not inclined to install plugins or adjust hardware or settings just to view a project.

One possible use for a splash page is to provide information that only needed to be viewed once (e.g. a copyright warning). After viewing the splash page, it is no longer accessible without re-running the project; the home page effectively becomes the top-level page, saving the user from repeatedly viewing the once-only information.

Some splash pages run through their animation then automatically jump to the project's home page. Others require the user to click a button or text link to continue. Designers might reflect on the fact that most successful websites do not use splash pages. Some websites may be set up to display a company's expertise in graphics design or animation. In these cases, they may use a splash screen as a demonstration of their skills, to impress potential customers. Even here, there should be control over the splash page. This may take the form of user choice (e.g. selecting between a Flash or non-Flash version) or placing a cookie on the visitor's computer so that the splash page is not displayed on subsequent visits to the site.

Notes

Make sure that a splash page also provides a text link to the home page, in case the technology prevents visitors (e.g. those with older systems (no Flash player, no new codecs, older browser versions) or those with JavaScript disabled) from entering the project.

Make sure that the splash page clearly defines what content is to be expected within (at least one large institution has an impressive graphics-rich splash page that even forgets to tell the viewers who they are).

Make sure that the home page and not the splash page is submitted to search engines. Since most *'unsavoury'* websites use redirect code, search engines often ignore pages that contain this code. Alternatively, ensure that the splash screen does not contain redirect code.

Doorway Pages

Like a splash page, a doorway page is the first page seen by a user, before being taken to a web site's home page. Like a splash page, after it is viewed it plays no further part in the site's navigation. No other page has a link to the doorway page.

Like a splash page, a doorway page is sometimes used to inform the user of any special requirements needed to view the project. It may also be the page that offers users the choice of a frames or non-frames version, or a text-based or Flash-based version. Mostly, however, they are used as a way to improve a web site's position in a search engine.

Unlike the splash page, a doorway does not contain anything that might impede the indexing of the page. So, it contains no frames, tables or scripts. It rarely contains graphics beyond a simple logo and rarely displays animations or video content.

Since this is the first page that is looked at for search engine placement, it is the one that is given the most weighting for position ranking. This is exploited by packing the page with rich descriptive content, keywords and META tags. If an image is included, even the ALT tag is used to squeeze in some more key words. Some even advocate creating multiple doorway pages, with a separate page for each main category of the project. This allows each category to have more distinctive keywords, thereby improving the ranking of the whole web site.

This is all aimed at achieving a high rating but this now often fails because many search engines now penalise such behaviour by reducing the site's ranking, or even ignoring the site.

Like splash pages, very few large successful sites use doorway pages.

Other pages

Although the main categories should have been identified during the analysis stage, there are some items that may have been overlooked for inclusion in the project's structure.

While the organisation's products, services or views will have been examined in great detail, it is worth ensuring that the project has an *'About Us'* category. For a large company, this might be an opportunity to strengthen the brand image. For an emerging company or organisation, this might provide details of its history, its staff, its ethos and other features designed to build the users' trust. These pages may also include a map of where the office(s) are situated.

Another overlooked feature is an *'Archives'* section. While this does not directly promote the organisation's current products or interests, it is useful for many viewers. For example, users can look up a specification for a product that they own that is no longer produced, they can read FAQs on older technology, they can read reviews for holiday destinations, etc. In other words, old information can still be useful information – and can be used to attract users to the project. For web, sites it has the added advantage of maintaining pages that might be in users' *'favorites'*, allowing them to still access the site and navigate from there to the home page and the newer contents.

Some projects use an *'exit page'*. This is displayed to the user prior to him/her exiting the project. It my display a message thanking the user for using the project, it may provide suggested reading, it may provide useful links to other projects, it may remind users of any special offers, or any other closing material that helps the user or leaves a good impression of the organisation that sponsors the project.

Note

A *'site map'* is one that is placed on the user's screen and shows the project structure and links to other pages. This is different from a *'navigation map'* or a *'flow diagram'* which are for the developer's use, as explained later.

Structure design

The previous pages looked in detail at information architecture – the process of determining and prioritising chunks of the project content.   It used a hierarchical example to structure the information.   While this is the most common approach, other structures are also used.

The structure of the project is dependent upon the size and nature of the project.   Larger projects will have more individual screens than smaller projects and some projects are better implemented with a particular structure.   For example, a free-running presentation for an exhibition may simply cycle through a series of screens in an entirely linear fashion, while a CD/DVD for a travel agent may require direct entry to any topic from anywhere in the structure.

The Information Architecture document contains the results of analysing and organising the sites content in the most logical and easily used fashion.   This document is the model for creating the project structure.   The structure design reflects how chunks of information relate to each other and how they are navigated.

Designers often talk of the need for users to access information in no more than three clicks.   This should not be regarded as an iron rule but as a reminder to keep the structure and navigation as simple as possible.

Thought has to be given on how screens are linked, which screens are linked and how the user is likely to view and use the project. Above all, navigation must be obvious and intuitive. For example if the project is an electronic book, screens could use a page metaphor.   Individual screens would be displayed like book pages, with page turning arrows.

The most likely structures to be implemented are:

Hierarchical structure

The project content is broken down into different sections and each section, in turn, sub-divides its information into more detailed options.   Generally, moving down provides more specific information while moving upwards provides more generalised information. The diagram shows links moving <u>down</u> the structure.   When the user clicks the link (i.e. menu button, hyperlink, etc) the screen pointed to by the link is displayed.   In practice, there will be links allowing the user to move back <u>up</u> to a previous screen and probably move straight back to the home screen.

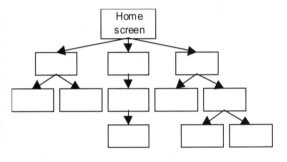

Linear structure

Some projects benefit from a linear structure where the user is prevented from jumping around the project. This is known *as 'directed learning'*. These projects present ideas in a progressive fashion (i.e. the user must acquire one piece of information before the next piece makes any sense).   Example projects

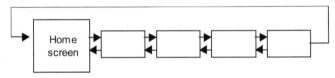

are those where order is important (e.g. step-by step cookery or car maintenance instructions) or where ideas build on previous ideas (e.g. telling a story or developing certain training programmes). A linear structure only provides links that step the user forwards or backwards through the project to allow the user to review information.   The project will also provide a link in the last screen to return the user to the home screen.

A web site variation on linear structures is a single large web page with links pointing to sections within that page. This is common on pages with large text content.   The advantage for the site designer is that one large file is easier to update than a collection of files.   It also allows existing text documents to be quickly converted into hypertext pages.

From the user's point of view, a single large web page is easier to print out than a collection of smaller files.

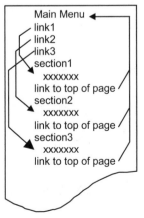

There are also a number of disadvantages for users in this method.   The file is large and takes a long time to download.   The user spends time and telephone costs downloading whole chunks of the page that may be of no particular interest, just to get to the one required item.   Once the page is downloaded, it can be difficult to navigate.

In the example shown, the top of the page provides all the links to the sections of the document.   But once a user jumps halfway down a long document, there is no further navigation apart from links to return to the top of the page.   Adding links to point to other sections of the document is impractical in a document with lots of sections. Imagine if the example document had 50 sections instead of three.   While it may just be acceptable to have 50 links in the top menu, repeating the 50 links after every section makes the page extremely cumbersome.

However, this method is commonly used in reference works, where users are expected to be more patient and diligent.

Web structure

This web, or *'network'*, structure has an opening home screen with some initial links. The user is encouraged to wander round the screen without any particular order. This is useful for projects where there is no evident strong link between one screen and another and there is no hierarchy of information. An example of this type of project is one promoting a particular holiday resort. The project may have many screens with information on travel, climate, currency, historical sites, restaurants, entertainment and so on. Each screen can be read without having any special relevance to any other screen.

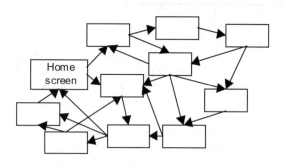

Hybrid structures

An entirely hierarchical structure is cumbersome to use, since the user has to go all the way back up the structure to navigate down another path. It is more user-friendly to provide links that allow the user to move <u>across</u> the structure as well as up and down. Since this combines elements of linear and hierarchical structures, it is call a hybrid or composite structure.

In the case of a linear structure, an element of choice can be built into the serial links. For example, a tutorial on

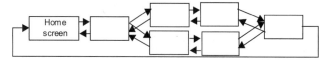

upgrading a computer's hard disk has many logical steps. However, there are different steps for fitting an IDE drive compared to fitting a SCSI drive. The user chooses which path to follow. After the steps for that choice are navigated through, the user joins the main common linear path again.

A further variant is the *'menu structure'*. This is a simplification of the hierarchical structure, with linear elements.

A number of routes are displayed in an opening menu. Each route consists of a linear set of screens. When the set of screens is completed, the user is automatically returned to the opening menu. This is different from the hierarchical structure, which allows further sub-routes at each lower level. While the hierarchical structure is useful for further detailed information at each lower level, the menu structure is useful for taking a user through a collection of tasks. For example, a project on financial investments may have an opening menu's opening screen that offer options on different investment schemes (ISAs, Bonds, etc.). Choosing a particular menu option results in the user being taken through a linear presentation on that subject.

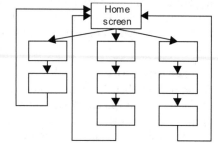

Physical structure

It is worth pointing out at this stage that the project may consist of many hundreds or even many thousands of individual elements (pages, images, video clips, audio clips, animations, script, etc.). If these were all held in a single folder on the storage disk, maintaining them would be a nightmare. Therefore, the way that they are physically stored should be logical and reflect the project structure. The project elements may be stored in multiple folders and sub-folders, each clearly labelled. Some folders may be labelled to match the project categories, while other may be labelled as *'Images, 'Video', 'Audio'* etc. It is common to place the supporting materials within each category folder. For example, a folder called *'Car Accessories'* might contain a sub-folder called *'Images'* and the sub-folder would contain all the images that relate to the *'Car Accessories'* folder. Similarly, each other category folder might contain its own *'Images'* sub-folder.

Setting up a physical structure in this way makes the whole project easier to organise and maintain. As each category is developed, the folders should be filled with the appropriate material. Later alterations to a category's contents need only be carried out within that part of the physical structure. It is also easier to check whether old images, etc have been left behind in the structure when alterations are made.

Storyboards

At first, it may seem odd to include material on storyboards at this point in the chapter, as they are often used for describing video action. However, a storyboard can be much more than that. It is what is says – it is a board that tells a story. The user navigates round the project and - in doing so - is told a story. In other words, it is concerned with flow. This could be the flow of an action (e.g. an animation) but could also be the flow of user activity (e.g. navigation). Although a storyboard can be used as a simple design draft, it can be usefully employed to demonstrate a path through the project, or more usually parts of the project. They derive their name from the fact that a project is interactive.

Storyboards, then, are used for:
- Outlining what navigation is required for sections of the project.
- Specifying the content and presentation of video clips.
- Specifying what result animators have to achieve.
- Specifying the visual design of screens.

A project consists of many separate, but linked, screens. The navigation map describes how each screen is linked and the storyboard describes what happens inside each screen, or across a set of screens.

A single storyboard might be enough to describe a small project whose screens are made up of static, or largely static material. Its purpose here is to document the layout and features of each screen (fonts, colours, navigation buttons, etc.). Most often, though, there is a collection of storyboards, with some storyboards describing a particular set of screens, while others describe animations or video clip contents. In addition, individual screens may contain their own dynamic content, such as video clips and animations. Since the use of a project is a dynamic activity, the storyboard has to chart this movement.

The essential features of a storyboard are:
- It is a set of sketches and notes.
- It can be a rough sketch or can be finely detailed (see below).
- It can convey the main points or can be thoroughly documented (see below).
- It shows the interface at different points in the interaction.
- It provides snapshots of the intended sequence to convey the impression of the final result.
- It provides key frames to show clients.
- It provides a useful tool in user-centred design.
- It describes the mood to be set.
- It can be hand-drawn or can be created using storyboard software.
- It combines with the navigation maps to define the entire project.
- It is not a static set of documents. It may require redrafting several times before agreement and understanding is reached between the client, the designer and those who will implement the project.
- Used correctly, it shortens the time taken to agree the project with the client, and also speeds up production time.

There are many systems that have been developed for creating storyboards and there are two main approaches:

Schematic approach

This is basically just a rough sketch or outline of the project. The entire storyboard could be drawn and hand-written. The aim is to get over the essential elements of the project. This takes less preparation time than the detailed method, but the savings may be lost again because of additional changes and additions at a later stage.

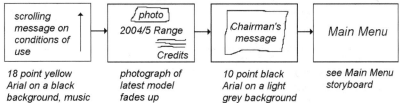

scrolling message on conditions of use	photo 2004/5 Range Credits	Chairman's message	Main Menu
18 point yellow Arial on a black background, music	photograph of latest model fades up	10 point black Arial on a light grey background	see Main Menu storyboard

Consider the rough sketch in the illustration. Its aim is to illustrate the way that the opening screens will unfold.

However, without the detail under the boxes, there would be considerable scope for wasted time and wasted resources, as the output from the programmers is found not to match the expectations of the client. Storyboards that are more of a rough guide sometimes require more versions to be produced to even adequately define the overall parameters of the project. This technique is useful to demonstrate the flow of a user process. For example, it could be used to show the stages of a customer ordering process, or how a user would navigate to finding specific information on a particular topic.

Animation example

The above example works fine with screens that are static or have simple moving elements.

The storyboards for animations and video clips are more complex, in that they have to show the positions of objects at different points in time.

The example on the right shows the steps for an animation that shows one way that numbers can be sorted into ascending order.

It shows movements and the resulting states for each stage of the animation.

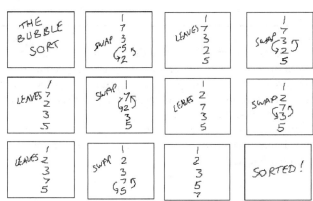

A hand-drawn representation is perfectly sufficient for this.   There is no need to spend extra time producing perfect images. The aim is to show the <u>order</u> that events take place and the <u>movements</u> in the animation.

This animation would likely run in a window of the main screen.   The main screen details (background, buttons, colours, etc.) would already have been described in a separate document.   This sketch would therefore be accompanied with details of the animation's timing, along with the colour/content of the background and the size, font style and colour of the numeric elements.

It is helpful if a template is created containing the empty boxes that will contain the animation. The small amount of time spent on preparing a master template is repaid later. The result is a cleaner presentation where the elements inside the boxes become the focus of attention.

Video Storyboard example

Project .... Clip Number ....

Clip Description..

View	Shot No.	Description	Audio, Effects, Other Information
	89	Over the shoulder shot Time: length of dialogue.	"I'm glad you could come over. It's nice to see a new neighbour. I notice that you look a bit anaemic".
	90	Medium Close Up Time: length of dialogue.	"Can I get you a drink?"
	91	Extreme Close Up of teeth. Time: length of dialogue.	"I'll just help myself, thanks"
	92	Extreme Close Up on eyes. Time: 3 seconds	"Gulp"
	93	Mid Shot of vampire slowly closing in on victim. Time: 3 seconds	Dramatic music.
	94	Extreme Close Up of hand producing a crucifix. Time: 4 seconds	Fanfare. "Arghh"
	95	Long Shot of vampire retreating out of frame. Time: 6 seconds	"I'll be back"

Rough drawings are all that is necessary for this storyboard. Note that the storyboard includes details of all main movements, camera angles, sounds and music and any audio or video effects. The screen sketches and the screen descriptions are adequate for all but the largest productions - those with huge detail and a cast of thousands. This is probably not the shooting order or production order of the final project.   This is taken care of with project management tools, which may result in more efficient shooting lists and lists that maintain continuity (see the notes in the chapter on digital video).

Creating a template similar to that above speeds up future storyboards, as the blank template can be printed and copied for future use, although organisations may have their own internal systems and standards and may use storyboarding software.

User Interface Design

This chapter looks at User Interface design, a term that encompasses:
- How the user interacts with the project content (i.e. navigation).
- How the user interacts with individual pages (i.e. screen design).

Navigation

The structure specifies how the project content is arranged. However, even the best content and most rational structure can be let down if the navigation system is poor. The navigation system ties all the content together and determines how the content is accessed. It looks at ways of mapping the user's flow through the structure (e.g. a navigation map) and the methods used to achieve the navigation (e.g. buttons, image maps, etc.). The *'user interface'* is the term used to describe the layout of the screen content and navigation links. When users experience difficulty in using an interface, the interface is usually the problem. Project navigation allows a user to make best use of the content. In so doing, it addresses questions such as:

- Can the user always work out where they are in the project structure? Is this also true when the project is a web site (where the user can access a page directly, without coming via the home page)?
- Can the user always work out how to get a particular destination, or access a specific item of information?
- Can the user easily get back to where he/she was, or to the home page?
- Can the user work out when they have seen all they wanted to see?
- Can the user recover from being 'lost' in the structure?
- Can the user be assisted when he/she makes an error?

This is really about two key issues.

A sense of place	A user knowing where he/she is in the structure at any stage and understanding how to use the interface to achieve their goals. A major complaint from usability tests is that users cannot easily find the information that they need, even though that content is present in the project. This is overcome by a consistent design across the projects' pages, and aids to navigation such as clear menus, project content maps, meaningful page titles, breadcrumb trails, etc.
A sense of procedure	A user knowing what steps are required at any stage. This is achieved by clear navigation flow and lots of task support. For example, if a web site has a product ordering system, it could start by saying there are four steps in the ordering process and use a sentence to describe each step (e.g. entering product details and quantities, entering customer details, entering delivery details, entering credit card details). The page for the first step would be headed *'Step 1 of 4 – Products details'*, the page for the second step would be head *'Step 2 of 4 – Customer Details'* and so on. Alternatively, each page could repeat the descriptions of all four steps on a separate line and the current page could be highlighted. So, if the user were on step 4, the line saying step 4 would be highlighted in the list.

User Interaction Design

The user interaction design is that part of the design requirements that deals with the specifics of how the user interfaces with the project. The aim is to make the system as usable as possible and to achieve the project's goals safely, effectively, efficiently and enjoyably.

Early computer programs only provided *'command line interfaces'*. Every command had to be typed at the keyboard. The development of WIMP (Windows, Icons, Menus, Pointers) environments opened up new abilities for *'direct manipulation'*. So, instead of typing in a command to delete a file, a user can simply drag the file and drop it into an icon for a garbage can. Similarly, navigation can be as simple a clicking on a button or an image map.

This following section on interaction design is broken down into sub-headings for ease of reference. In practice, there is some overlap between these sections and with other parts of the design requirements document.

Usability

- The project's pages must be accessible to users with disabilities, including blind users.
- The project must be able to be used without an instruction manual (either printed or on-line).
- The project must be able to be used without special training. The only exceptions are where users are prepared to invest their time in learning new rules in order to obtain special results (e.g. an online banking system or an ordering system).

- Dialogue should not need to be remembered from one screen to another.
- The project must use familiar terms. There should be no jargon, no irrelevant information, and no rarely needed information.
- Where unfamiliar terms are essential to the project, their meaning must be explained.
- The project must not use symbols that users have to learn or look up in a guide. Test with users that all symbols used are recognised.
- The interface must be consistent (e.g. a button should not do different things in different screens; the controls should be in the same place on every screen).
- If a screen uses image maps, indicate it. Their use must be obvious. Text links must be provided as alternative navigation system.
- There must be no hidden links. All navigation control must be easily distinguished. Users must not have to click on all screen objects, searching for links.
- Screens must not use graphic images that look like link buttons but aren't.
- Screens must not use buttons that don't look like link buttons.
- Still frames can be used as links to video clips.

See the chapter on *'Project Testing'* for greater coverage of usability issues.

Navigability

- Task complexity should be reduced, by breaking the task into a sequence of smaller tasks.
- The purpose of each link should be clearly understandable by the user.
- No user should be served a page that offers no way out of that page. Every page in the project must have at least one link, the one that takes the user to the home page or to another navigational aid such as a site map or a table of contents.
- A page link must not load the same page as the user is already viewing (a common problem where every page has a link to every other page). Such a link should not appear on menus and navigation bars, or should be disabled (i.e. unclickable) and greyed out. The exception is where a link takes the user to a named anchor within a long page.
- Provide shortcuts for experienced users.
- Provide support for mouse and keyboard navigation.
- For websites, users should be able to navigate using links within the site, rather than navigating using the browser's Back and Forward buttons.

Feedback

- The user must receive immediate feedback from mouse activities (e.g. 'key click' sound on clicking the mouse button, or button rollovers when the cursor hovers over them).
- The user must be given appropriate error messages, in context, when an illegal operation is attempted.
- Where the system has a long response time (e.g. database activities or loading a large video clip), the user should be given update messages or a progress indicator (e.g. a bar that grows from 0% to 100%).
- The novice user should be given the option to enable information windows that automatically pop up when tackling complex options or tasks.
- The user should be informed of his/her position within the structure at all times, using navigation beacons (e.g. displaying an annotated site map or displaying the path already taken).

User support

- The user should have access to built-in help facilities.
- The novice user should have access to wizards, where appropriate.
- Further material should be available for those needing more learning support.
- Where appropriate, the user should be able to choose the difficulty level (e.g. beginner/average/expert) when entering a project.
- Slow learners should be easily able to repeat sections of the project.
- Menus should include shortcuts for experienced users, where appropriate.
- The user must be warned about options that may modify or delete data, and choices must be offered and clearly explained.

User control

- No action should take place without user initiation (see below).
- The user should be able to switch off the sound or adjust the volume control.
- The user should be able to replay videos/animations, or switch them off.
- The user should be able to by-pass opening introductions (e.g. long Flash splash pages).
- The user should be able to by-pass parts of a sequence.

These suggestions will not all apply to every project. For example, although most projects are based on user-initiated actions, there is some need for computer-initiated activities. Any form filling or question-and-answer tasks in a project are computer-initiated and the user often has to complete the tasks before being allowed to proceed.

Navigation and the user interface

User interaction design leads directly to the creation of the project's navigation map. Before this, some thought should be given on the best method to support users. They need the maximum navigational support to know where they are in the project, and to know how to get to other pages. This mean providing navigation links that are clearly described and explicit.

Two common techniques are:

Multiple navigation   The user is provided with multiple ways to access the same piece of information, perhaps through menus, search facilities, etc. So, for example, a web site may provide two routes for product ordering – one for new customers and a quicker route for existing customers whose delivery and payment details are already saved. Equally, a project may provide both a simple search facility and a separate advanced query system. The first provides more possible matches that the user can browse through, while the advanced user can narrow the search with more informed criteria. Additionally a particular item may be located through different links in the project. For example, a jacket may be accessed through links such as *'Men's Wear'*, *'Sports Wear'*, *'Special Offers'*, and so on.

Cross-navigation   Each page of the project provides the same menu bar or navigation bar, in the same place, providing the same link options. Wherever the user is in the project structure, there is a clear path to all other parts of the project.

Every project has a main menu system. This can be as simple as a single set of links, often located down the left-hand side of the page. Alternative menu systems are located along the top of the page or along the bottom of the page.

Other common interface features that may be considered include shopping carts, search facilities, site maps, accessing help, providing Q&A facilities, chats rooms, and links to *'Special Offers'*, *'What's New'*, *'The 10 Most Common Purchases'*, etc. These should be considered before compiling the navigation chart. Also, since some of these involve extensive scripting, early identification of these needs is helpful for the project management.

Finally, remember that in addition to aiding the user, a project that is easy to navigate will also be easier to maintain.

Navigation maps

These are required for all but the very simplest of projects. They detail every connection between one part of the project and another. Users navigate (i.e. move round) the application by choosing menu options, clicking on icons, buttons or hypertext entries, or clicking on *'hotspots'* (active areas of the screen - e.g. a country on a map).   A navigation map shows where the user is taken on activating one of the navigation tools.

Maps should also mark any grouping of pages, which pages are generated dynamically, which pages are used to receive user data, and which parts of project carry out specific functions (e.g. data collection and verification, e-commerce, etc.).

For large projects, a number of navigation maps will be required, starting with top-level categories and creating separate maps for large sub-categories.

Navigation maps can be hand-drawn, or they can be created using drafting packages such as Visio, or even using Word's Flowchart AutoShapes.   Ideally, the method should allow quick and easy alterations and additions to the structure and this would favour a dedicated drafting package.

There is no preferred method or layout for creating navigation maps (unless an organisation has set its own internal standards). The over-riding requirement is that the map be legible and complete.

The diagram on the next page illustrates part of a navigation map for a tutorial on data communications.

Notes

Each screen has a direct link back to the main menu.

Each screen has a direct link to quit.

The *'Summary'* screen has a link back to the *'OSI'* sub-menu.

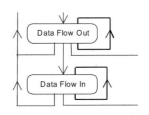

Some screens show internal loops as shown on the right.   These screens contain animations and the user can opt to re-run the animations as often as required, before moving on.

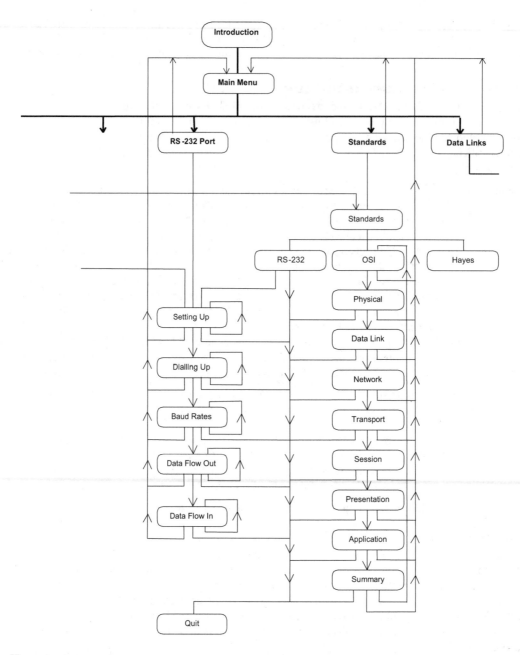

Flow diagram

For a small simple project, a flow diagram (also known as a logic diagram) is essentially the same thing as a navigation map.

However, for larger and more complex projects, a separate flow diagram may be desirable. As its name suggests, it is less concerned with the overall project links and it concentrates on the flow through certain sections of the project – and any logic decisions made as a consequence.

An example of this is a project that allows users to enter their personal details and works out their general health prospects. The user is escorted through a series of pages that gather the relevant facts (age, weight, height, drinking habits, smoking habits, etc.) In this way, the flow is largely pre-determined and users have only two options – carry on through the sequence or jump to another part of the project. However, within this process, there is scope for user errors (e.g. the user enters his/her age as 999, his/her height as 20 metres, or leaves a question blank). A logic diagram describes how any such errors would be detected and how the flow would be altered as a consequence (e.g. jumping to a page that provides an error message and helpful advice, before returning to the earlier page for a second chance at user input).

Other examples of processes requiring flow and logic diagrams are e-commerce operations (e.g. checking for valid credit cards, checking for valid email addresses, allowing users to customise their own computer or other purchases) and database search queries.

Flow diagrams should ensure that the designer understands and plans for maintaining the user's flow through the process.

This should include the following approaches:

Maintaining the user's concentration	Some projects have key sequences of user activities. These may be the steps in completing an on-line purchase, subscribing to a newsletter, or following steps in an educational tour. These types of page should only display content that relates to the task at hand. If these pages had links to non-related areas, they may entice the user away from completing the current task. Therefore, these pages should only provide a link to the home page or other key pages.
Validating user's data at an early stage	Data validation and logic checks should be carried out at the earliest possible point in a process. Consider an online ordering system that asks for order details, personal details, credit card details, etc. over five or six pages. Now consider the reaction of a user who spends time completing all these stages, only to be told that the order is invalid because a product code was incorrectly entered on the first page or an item such as a post code was left empty on the second page. Such negative user reaction is avoidable by checking the user's data on each page, before proceeding to the next page.
Assisting the flow	In the above example, consider the user's reaction on being told that an error occurred on the third page, and that all the details need to be re-entered from the beginning. If an error occurs on one page of data, the user's data from previous pages should be stored for re-use. Additionally, an e-commerce site should not ask the user to enter all name, address, post code, phone number, etc details as the purchaser – and then demand that all the exact same details be entered in a page for delivery details. The delivery details should be able to be entered, where appropriate, by the user clicking and option called *"delivery address same as customer address?"*.

Navigation charts and flow diagrams can be presented to clients to help them visualise the final project. They are also very useful in giving direction to the developers and providing a framework for final testing.

Interaction Styles

Users can interact with a project on two levels
- To navigate round the project.
- To communicate with the project (e.g. running video clips, entering data).

User interaction design was examined earlier in this chapter. We will now look at interaction styles – the developer's options for conducting this interaction between the user and the project content.

Many project designers come from a purely arts background and produce visually stunning pages. However, in this context, *'style'* is not mainly measured by the attractiveness of the page, although this is also a desirable aim. Interaction style mainly aims to allow the user to focus on the tasks he/she wants to perform. It aims to provide the ways to make the project easier to use and the content easier to find.

The navigation tools used for a project will vary depending upon the particular project. For example, a website for a boy band may make extensive use of graphic images as links *('click on the picture of your favourite band member for the latest gossip')* while a project dedicated to legal case law may make extensive use of search engines with complicated criteria.

In all cases, each page should clearly explain its purpose, perhaps with a short heading at the top of the page, and each link should clearly portray what the user can expect if it is clicked.

Possible navigation tools include:
- A navigation bar on the left side of the page. This is a very popular method, with the bar being a different background colour from the main screen content. However, it can be wasteful of screen space, since this area plus the area used by the browser controls can consume a large proportion of the available screen space. This leaves less for the actual project content.
- A navigation bar on the top of the page. This can provide standard hyperlinks, drop-down menus or file-folder style tabs (like flicking through a set of files in a filing cabinet).
- A navigation bar at the bottom of the page, using text hyperlinks, to ensure accessibility.
- A navigation bar repeated at the foot of a long scrolling page. Users will tolerate scrolling pages where the text length is a complete document (e.g. the minutes of a meeting). It is best to display the important links *'above the fold'* (i.e. in the screen area that is visible without scrolling).
- A site map that is displayed upon request. It is a page that clearly displays the site structure, with links to all the major categories, and maybe some sub-categories.
- A table of contents or index at the top of the page, usually displaying the sub-headings of a long scrollable page, or of a long document that is spread over a set pages.

- A search engine which can be permanently displayed (for single word searches) or called up upon request (usually for complex searches). This becomes more important as the project becomes larger and/or more complex.
- *'Next'* and *'Previous'* links to provide a logical flow to a series of linked pages. For a web site, note that these may not necessarily carry out the same function as a browser's *'Back'* and *'Forward'* buttons.
- *'Home Page'* and *'Start of Section'* links, so that users can easily return to the start of a category or return to the home page, if they get lost.

Menus

Since all navigation systems use some kind of menu, here is some advice on setting them up.

- Each menu should have a clearly marked title (e.g. *'Orders Menu'*, *'Repairs menu'*, etc).
- Menu options should have names that are meaningful to the user (e.g. an option called *'Romford'* is only useful if you expect all your users to already know that you have a factory or a showroom in Romford).
- The labels should clearly distinguish between options on the same menu (e.g. what is the difference between two links called *'About Us'* and *'What We Do'*?).
- Menu items should be grouped logically into menu blocks or even separate menu screens. Related buttons should be grouped together, with different groups located slightly apart or separated by a line.
- Menu options should be placed in logical order (e.g. operational sequence, frequency of use, importance).
- Every menu should include a clearly marked exit option.
- Menus should include the ability to return to the main menu or to return to a previous sub-menu.
- Menus should contain no more than seven items, to avoid information overload.
- If a menu item is not active on a particular screen (e.g. the *'home'* button on the *'home'* screen), it should be disabled and greyed out - rather than ignoring the user's clicks or giving error messages. Alternatively, it may be made much brighter, so that it stands out and provides the user with a sense of position.
- Always provide alternative text hyperlinks when the navigation system uses mouseovers, JavaScript menus, Flash, etc.

Specific navigation methods

The forms of navigation include:

Structure links   The links are part of a menu system and are chosen from that list
Associative links   The links are embedded in a piece of the page text content (e.g. "I use a <u>Sony XYZ</u> camcorder") and are chosen by clicking on the underlined word in the text. In some cases, the link may be a graphic image.

In both cases, the hyperlink can be either *'inter-page'* (jumping between pages) or *'intra-page'* (jumping from one section of a long page to another section of the same page).

The most common implementations of navigation are:

- Text link navigation
- Button navigation
- Graphic image navigation, including image maps
- Tab key navigation
- Rollovers
- Pulldown menus
- Frames navigation
- Script-based navigation
- Search navigation

Text links

Text hyperlinks were the earliest forms of navigation link and are still the most commonly used technique. Words in plain text are used to describe the purpose of the link.

Advantages

- Easily identified as links (assuming they are underlined and blue).
- Easily understood (no trying to interpret what a particular icon means).
- Quick to load, as they only consume a few bytes.
- Easier to change compared to graphic image links.
- Easily understood by assistive technology (e.g. screen readers for blind).

Disadvantages

- Not so pretty as graphic buttons.
- Not so 'high-tech' as drop-down menus.

Link colours and underlining

Users are accustomed to web pages having blue underlined text to represent unvisited links, and purple underlined text to represent visited links. This widely used custom provides users with a perception of where they have already been and where they have still to visit. We also know that underlined hyperlinks aid users in scanning a page and quickly identifying links.

Therefore, it is unwise to change the links from this well-recognised default colour coding. Although other colours can be selected, they will only confuse users for the dubious benefit of being *'different'*. In this case, being different is a disadvantage, as users will lower the project's usability, with users revisiting pages they have already seen and omitting to navigate sections of the project. It also follows that normal text in the body of page should not be coloured blue and underlined, as users may assume that they are hyperlinks.

A contrary argument is that altering the default colour and underling provides other advantages.
For example, link colours could be different for different sections of a project (e.g. if the links are green, you must be in the category about gardening). Also, the removal of underlining could produce cleaner links such as
        < Previous Page>   and   < Next Page>
It is also suggested that the links that are obviously enclosed in a navigation bar will be understood to be links by users, without needing special colouring or underlining.

Some web developers even provide links whose colour is the same as the surrounding and have no underline. This provides a *'secret'* link that is hidden within a sentence or paragraph. This allows a developer to upload some new pages to a website for testing without being spotted by the average user.

The designer has to decide whether the provision of non-default links is justified by any extra benefits – and whether the target audience will be able to understand any new link system.
Whatever scheme is adopted, there is agreement that the scheme should be applied consistently across the entire project. There is also room in both schemes for having a link change colour while the user hovers that link (this is covered in the section on using Cascading Style Sheets).

Button navigation

This uses graphic images as the links between project pages. The image contains the text label within its graphic design. This technique is very popular on multimedia applications and web pages because the links are so attractive. Buttons are usually rectangular with bevelled edges and are usually grouped together on the page. As with text links, the text in the image describes the purpose of the link.

Text buttons are mostly designed to display two or more states. The normal state is the image that is seen when the button is inactive. The button's active state is the one that is displayed when the button is clicked. This is usually a representation of the inactive button as if it had been depressed. This may be accompanied by an audible click as additional feedback. A possible third state is the rollover state, where the button changes in some way when the user hovers it. The button may change size or change colour to show that it is the current clickable option.

Advantages
- Look nicer than text links.
- Can use graphic icons (see later).
- Can use fancy or exotic fonts that are not present on a user's computer, as the font is embedded as part of the image.

Disadvantages
- Slower to load than text links, as some image files are very large indeed, and all images are greater in size than their text link equivalents. In addition, each button may require three separate image files (one representing each state).
- Harder to alter than text links.
- Possibly less usability than text links. Text buttons can be a problem on websites as they will not be visible if users turn off their graphics, or the site has to be read by a text reader. This can be minimised by ensuring that all text buttons use their ALT tags to describe the link.
- Provide poor accessibility, as most screen readers can't read text that is stored as a graphic.

Icon navigation

Like text buttons, icon navigation uses graphic images as links. Unlike buttons, they do not contain any text. Instead, they rely on images that represent links or functions. So, for example, a project that offers its text in multiple languages can display a set of national flags. A Spanish-speaking country would click on the Spanish flag, while English-speaking country would click on a Union Jack. Thereafter, users would be presented with content in their own native tongue. The use of icons allowed a single interface to be presented on the opening page.

Other common examples of icons are dustbins representing deletions, envelopes representing e-mail, an hourglass representing a waiting period and binoculars or a magnifying glass representing a search function.

Projects can also create their own icons, based on readily identifiable objects. For example, the menu for a travel agent's website could have icons for a ship, an aeroplane and a coach to represent their various modes of travel.
Advantages
- Icons provide improved usability, as they are based on the user's existing knowledge of real-world objects. This also aids users with cognitive impairments.
- An interface can be international in nature, serving most languages and cultures.
- Icons are prettier than text links or text buttons.

Disadvantages
- The purpose of each icon must be clear to every possible user. No one should have to guess what an icon might represent.
- There is a danger that users may think that an icon is just a piece of clip art or *'eye candy'* and not treat it as a link.
- Icon graphics are slower to load than text links.
- Icons should have clear outlines for easy identification. Since many icons are small, it can be difficult to design such icons. Some of the usability problems with icons could be overcome by providing a text label next to the icon, although this may be seen as negating the whole point of having icons in the first place.

Metaphors
An icon is always a graphic representation. A metaphor is also often visual but can also be more abstract. An icon always bases itself on well-recognised objects (e.g. a Stars and Stripes flag represents the USA). A metaphor, on the other hand, takes the user's understanding of one object, process or concept and uses it to help understand *another* object, process or concept (usually one that is new to the user). Metaphors can be literal (e.g. using a collection of icons of national flags) or they can be abstract (e.g. the functional concepts of user tasks such as *'cut and paste'* and *'drag and drop'*).

Importantly, metaphors can provide users with mental shortcuts to concepts. It is even possible to sum up an entire design by a statement such as *"the project for xxx will be presented using a ship as the metaphor"*. Here, the single word *"ship"* has been used to evoke a structure and purpose that is easily understood.   So, if the menu uses links such as *'crew'*, *'captain'* and *'ports of call'*, the user knows what to expect in each category.

Research suggests that the strength of a metaphor lies in the choice of language and terminology (e.g. the names of links) rather than the graphic image.   The labels used to describe the overall metaphor and its component parts provide the greatest effect for users.   Graphics are used as a powerful way to support the metaphor, whereas icons rely solely on their visual impact.

A metaphor can be applied to the entire project structure, or to just part of it.

Examples of metaphors applied to an entire project are:
- A project for an instruction manual, where the screen resembles the pages of a book that can be *'turned'* by the user.
- A project for a company, where the opening screen displays a picture of a corridor with a number of doors. Each door has a brass nameplate marked *'Sales Dept'*, *'Finance Dept'*, and so on. Pressing the buzzer on the door opens the door, taking the user to the appropriate category.
- A science project has a screen showing a shelf with a collection of jars. The jars are labelled and hovering over a jar results in a pop-up window displaying information about the its contents.

Examples of metaphors applying to parts of a project are:
- The *'Play'*, *'Pause'* and *'Stop'* buttons as used in Windows Media Player (mimicking the icons found on CD players).
- The *'paint bucket'* representing flood filling colours, as used in PhotoShop and Paint Shop Pro.
- The *'Razor'* tool representing cutting video footage, as used in Adobe Premiere.
- The use of switches, knobs, sliders, VU meters, etc. in audio editing software.

The advantages of using metaphors are:
- They can provide a central and unified theme to a project.
- They can provide added interest to a project.
- They can help users in understanding new functions or concepts.
- They can improve the project's usability.

The disadvantages are:
- Not every project is appropriate for using metaphors.
- Inappropriate or confusing metaphors do more harm than good.
- Using too many metaphors in a single project confuses users.
- An over-elaborate metaphor can make a project appear gimmicky and cheap.

Used carefully, metaphors are a useful design tool. If the metaphor applies to the entire project, it should be considered at the stage of designing the site structure. Even if metaphors cannot be applied to an entire project, parts of the project (such as the navigation system) might still benefit from their use.

Image maps

An image map is a single graphic image that has a number of spots that are used as links to other pages of the project. Clicking one of these *'hotspots'* takes the user to the linked page.

Advantages
- It can look visually appealing.
- Hotspots can be any shape, no matter how irregular.
- In some cases, an image map is seen as a *'natural'* way to navigate. So, for example, if a user wished to know the population of Orlando, he/she is presented with a map of the world and clicks on the USA. A map of the USA is then displayed and the user clicks on the state of Florida. This, in turn, displays a map of Florida.   When the user clicks on the city of Orlando, the population numbers for that city is displayed.

Disadvantages
- If they are not carefully constructed, they may not even be understood to be a navigation tool. Some projects even have to tell users that the page is an image map and has to be clicked upon!
- They are often very large.
- They are time consuming to construct.
- Individual hotspots be difficult to place when representing some real-world image. For example, on a map of the UK, many towns and cities are very close to each other, making accurate selection difficult.
- They are more difficult to alter than either text or button menus.
- They do not provide feedback to users (e.g. hotspots do not change colour after its link has been visited.
- Search engines cannot easily spider an image map. That is why many image maps are employed after the opening page.
- If an image map is over-fussy, users will not know which parts are links and which parts are just decorative.
- Users will not necessarily recognise individual parts of the map (e.g. will all users be able to identify Rutland on a UK map?). Of course, parts can be labelled, but this negates some of the purpose of using a graphical representation.
- Poor usability and accessibility, as they are a problem on web sites if users turn off their graphics, or if the project has to be read by a text reader.

In practice, image maps are not often used without text labelling or an accompanying text menu bar.

Image tables

Image table, or pseudo-image maps, are sometimes used as a simpler alternative to full image maps.
A graphic image is cut into rectangular pieces and each piece is located in a cell of a table. The resultant image looks and functions like an image map but is really made up from many separate images, each with its own hyperlink.

Advantages
- The image that is hovered over can change colour, or even change image content.
- Greater usability and accessibility than image maps, as each individual image can be provided with text support through its ALT tag.
- Easier to alter than image maps.
- Each image can be optimised separately. This improves the overall compression for the total collection of images, making their total size smaller than an equivalent image map.

Disadvantages
- Slower to construct than a single image map.
- Less easy to set up irregularly shaped areas. This can be partly overcome by using a collection of the rectangular images to approximate to a shape, with each of the images in the collection pointing to the same target page.

Frames navigation

Used for web sites, frames divide a page into a set of horizontal and vertical regions. Each region can be filled with the contents of different HTML files and regions can be made scrollable or non-scrollable. The content of one frame can be altered without changing the contents of any other frame on the page.

Advantages
- A menu, especially one rich in graphics, can be loaded into a region (on the left or on top) and can remain there for the rest of the user's session on the site. The page does not need to be refreshed and reloading time is saved.
- Usability is good, as the main navigation menu is always on the screen.
- Hyperlinks in the menu region can be used to alter the contents of any of the other regions.
- Individual region's contents can be scrolled without the rest of the screen being scrolled.
- Users can be provided with specific help information in one frame, while carrying out that specific activity in another frame.

Disadvantages
- Printing a screen is difficult.
- Bookmarking is difficult, as the screen represents a number of different URLs.
- May result in low placing in search engines.
- Very old or vary basic browsers do not support frames, requiring the possible creation of an entirely separate site version for non-frame users.
- May be considered less visually attractive than other techniques, as scroll bars can be ugly and fixed-width menu regions can reduce the available screen size for users with low-resolution monitors.
- Can be more difficult to code and to maintain.

Frames-based web sites remain popular despite some of their shortcomings.

Script based navigation

This covers any navigation technique that requires the use of a scripting language to create it.

At its simplest, it could produce a *'hover'* effect on text links, changing their colour, or could produce a *'mouseover'* effect on buttons, displaying alternative images. At the other end, a script might analyse user input and make certain navigational decisions. For example, an educational project might look at a certain set of user data in a Q&A dialogue, update the student's score, and take the student to a different level of learning depending on the nature of the student's answers. In this case, the navigation is temporarily taken out of the hands of the user. A variation on this technique is form-filling, where the user inputs control data which determines the navigation. For example, if a user inputs data on car prices and performance, he/she will be taken to a page that displays models that match that request. The script can check that all parts of the form have been completed and that data is verified (e.g. a user does not enter a price as -£3000).

Although scripting can be used for flow control in navigation, it is mostly used to provide direct user-controlled navigation methods such as:

Pop-up menus	The menu appears when the mouse is hovered over a link.
Drop-down menus	A menu is displayed along the top of the screen. When one of the categories is clicked, a menu of the corresponding sub-categories is displayed below that link.

Advantages
- Provides presentational features that are not provided for otherwise (e.g. where normal HTML or authoring software cannot provide them).
- Provides logic and flow control that would not otherwise be possible (e.g. data validation, error checking, decision making).
- Can be used with frames navigation, to allow a click in a link in one frame to update the contents of several other frames, something not allowed in normal HTML.
- Drop-down menus can save a lot of screen space, as they are only visible during the time taken to select and click on a link from the menu.

Disadvantages
- Requires developers to learn one or more scripting languages, such as Java, JavaScript, ActionScript or Lingo.
- Web users may not have their browser set to allow scripting, disabling much of the functionality.

Web sites can use scripting to achieve these effects, although the need to learn languages can be reduced by using software tools to create pull-down menus, etc. Multimedia authoring tools also have similar facilities built in to their software. For example, both Flash and QuickTime movies can have in-built scripts for controlling navigation.

It should be borne in mind that these features are only visual enhancements. They cannot improve on a navigation system design that is flawed.

Search navigation

This is useful for quickly getting to specific content in a project. Casual browsing of the project may eventually take a user to that content, but a project's in-built search engine can quickly identify those pages that contain the keywords entered by the user.

With a multimedia project, committed to CD or DVD, this function may be met by providing a full project index, with all keywords listed and with links to relevant pages.

With a web site project, the developer's search engine scans the web site and sets up an index entry for every page in the site. When users enter their keywords, the engine returns a list of matches that the user can click on.

Advantages
- Welcomed by experienced users.
- Useful on large projects with lots of data.
- Handles web sites that have ever-changing content.
- No need to learn a language, as search engine applications are easily available in commercial, shareware and freeware, versions.

Disadvantages
- Requires knowledge to set up.
- For web sites, setting up can be a long process, as each page has to have its own META tag with its own page description.
- The index is essentially a static page and has to be refreshed when the site contents change. For large sites this may mean daily index updates.

User interaction

User interaction is not confined to navigational decisions and can enhance the user's experience with the project. Users can also interact with projects by controlling the flow of audio or video clips, customising their environments, conducting database searches, completing surveys, entering competitions, purchasing through shopping carts, requesting help, joining chat rooms, etc.

Advantages
- Provides additional user control over the project.
- Provides greater involvement of the user.

Disadvantages
- Expensive and time-consuming to include.
- Some facilities can be seen as *'gimmicky'* and can lower the tone of an otherwise professional site.

Orientation problems

It is important that the user feels comfortable using the project. That involves the user knowing where he/she is in the project and being able to take logical decisions to move round the structure.

Users often *'live in the moment'* – i.e. they know where they are at any point, but don't recall how they got there or how they get back again.

Loss of control or loss of orientation is a desired feature in some web structures, for special effects. For all other projects, it is to be avoided.

Loss of orientation is caused by:

- Poorly designed structures, resulting from:
    - Creating confusing web structures through lack of preparation.
    - Mixing hierarchical and linear structures. This practice is fine in some instances (e.g. it is widely used for FAQ (Frequently Asked Questions) and similar text-based web sites). However, care has to be taken in the provision of links. If a user goes down a level, across a linear path and comes back up a level they are not returned to their original point in the site, causing confusion.
    - Poorly worded links.
    - Using links titled *'Forward'* and *'Back'*, other than in linear structures where the user understands their meaning.
    - Links called *'Up'* and *'Down'* being used in a meaningless way in projects with mixed hierarchical and linear structures.

There are a number of ways to ensure that the user is in control:
- Avoid bad design (e.g. sending a viewer away, mid-thought, to another screen or another web site).
- Avoid unnecessary mixing of hierarchies.
- Provide logical links (e.g. *'Return to Home Screen'*).
- Provide understandable link titles (e.g. *'Disk Specifications'*).
- Provide a project map. This is not usually a graphical map but a list of the main screens on the project. This could simply be a set of links placed along the bottom of the screen. Better still is placing them in the map in a *'frame'* that is continually displayed as the user navigates the project. Even better, provide information about where the user is on the map. This can be achieved by titling each screen.
- Provide a *'breadcrumb trail'* (see below).

For web sites, each web page should be able to stand on its own because:
- Another site may provide a link to your site, not by pointing to your home page but by pointing to any page in your site.
- A user's search may take him/her into any page on your site.

The project should attract users to look at the other screens. It is important that each screen makes sense on its own - even when it constitutes part of a linear series of screens. References to the contents of other screens should be kept to a minimum. Above all, ensure that each screen has a link to the rest of the project, even if only to the home screen. Best of all, place a site map on each screen.

In the example web page shown, the hierarchical menu on the left links to a lower set of pages in the hierarchy. In some cases, such as the '*Contact Us*' and '*Useful Links*' options, the lower web page has no lower level.   In the case of the '*Support Handbook*' and '*Multimedia handbook*' options the pages have links to multiple lower-level web pages - one for each book chapter.   In each case, there is an '*Index*' option that has 26 lower-level web pages - one for each letter of the alphabet.   There are no orientation problems, since the left panel displays a map of the site layout at all times.

Breadcrumb trail

In a hierarchical project structure, users navigate by moving up and down the levels of the structure. One method of informing users of their position in the structure is to provide a '*breadcrumb trail*'.   This is an information bar that displays the categories and sub-categories visited.

The example shows that the user began in the home page and clicked on the '*Desktop & Stationery Items*' category, followed by clicking on the '*Adhesives*' and '*Office Tape*' sub-categories.

This approach is becoming more popular because:
- Users know exactly where they are.
- It provides a clear indication of the route already taken.
- Each item in the trail is also a hyperlink, so a user can move up several levels of the structure with a single click.

The example uses a graphic image of an arrowhead to indicate the navigation steps. Other sites use a > symbol, a colon, or a slash.

Where a section of material is spread over several pages in serial order, it is advisable that the user be kept informed regarding which page in the series is currently being displayed. This can be carried out by displaying a numbered list at the top or bottom of the page, as shown in these examples:

1 | **2** | 3 | 4 | 5

<u>1</u> | 2 | <u>3</u> | <u>4</u> | <u>5</u>

The current page is highlighted, either by emboldening the page number or by removing the underscore.

Navigation and search engines

Most design effort goes into creating the most visually stunning and most usable form of project. However, for websites, they are not the only considerations.   Most websites want to attract new users and this usually means attempting to get listed in search engines. The search engine spiders, as used by Google, Webcrawler, AltaVista, Lycos, etc., can follow hypertext links and navigation images that are accessed through a hypertext link. However, they have problems dealing with frames, image maps and drop-down menus.

So, a navigation system that uses graphical links (i.e. image maps or buttons) must supplement them with hypertext links. The most common way is to have a bottom bar on the page, displaying a set of links like those below:

Home Page | About Us | Products | Services | Email Us

This preserves the look of the interface, while possibly improving the site's standing in search engine lists.

Pop-up windows

There are two types of pop-up windows:

- Ones you asked for.
- Ones you didn't ask for.

The first type can be useful. For example, it allows users to be in an e-commerce site and have a look at the detailed specification of a product, while the main page is still on screen. After reading the product information, the user closes the pop-up and reverts back to the original page of the e-commerce site.

The second type of pop-up windows are the ones users find infuriating. They display unasked for content, perhaps disabling the browser's recent history and making the *'Back'* button useless.

Even when users try to jump to another site, that site is presented inside an additional window, thus keeping the user in the original site. It is a pointless attempt by the site to prevent users from leaving. Users react very unfavourably to this attempted coercion and usually do not return to that site again.

Screen design

Information architecture compartmentalised the content into meaningful categories and easily handled chunks. Navigation maps show how the content is linked and how pages are accessed.

Screen design concentrates on <u>how</u> the content is presented to the user.   A well-structured project, with efficient navigation, can easily be spoiled if the content is not displayed in a way that the user finds pleasant to the eye and easy to comprehend.

The key screen design issues are covered next.

Cultural issues

There is no such thing as a cultureless, or cross-culture, product.   Every designer carries his/her own background/preferences/prejudices.   Laying aside stereotypes, there are huge cultural differences, even between nations with apparently similar cultures.   American and UK citizens have very similar cultures. They speak a common language, have similar dress codes, eat similar foods and follow similar religious and political beliefs.   Yet, the American fervour for the right to carry arms sends shivers down the spines of most UK citizens.   On the other hand, they overwhelmingly respect speed restrictions, while the British treat speeding as their second national sport.

The differences between other countries are even more marked.   There are different political cultures, different geographic cultures and different social cultures.   There are co-existing cultures within any one country or market. These, for example, may be ethnic or religious.   There are even different cultures <u>within</u> cultures. These may be differences of social class, of religion or of age.

The project's use of words and images should take into account cultural differences throughout the world.

It is relatively easy to identify areas that might offend people from other cultures, but it is a lot more difficult to identify grey areas and to avoid the transmission of confusing messages.

Some words and phrases (e.g. *'using a rubber'*) have different meanings in different countries while certain images (e.g. nudity, alcohol, etc.) have differing levels of acceptability. When Chevrolet launched their *'Nova'* range of cars in Spain, they were at first unaware that the Spanish translation of *'Nova'* means *'Does not go'*.   Even colours have different symbolic meanings in different countries and this is covered later.

Of course, some projects are consciously designed to attract a particular culture (e.g. teenage fanzines or ethnic material).

Layout issues

The eye is drawn to temporal (moving) object before static objects.   This means that a video clip or animation will dominate a screen.   The designer must ensure that any textual material on the same screen is not swamped by these images.

Less overpowering is the use of animated text. This has the benefit of drawing attention to itself without distracting from the screen message, as long as it is used sensibly. Indeed, the fact that the text dissolves/fades to introduce new text draws greater attention to the message.

With totally static screens, the eye is first drawn to photographic images, clip art and diagrams, etc.

There are preferred positions on the screen for placing information.   Corners and edges are regarded as areas of peripheral vision - the eye concentrates on the central area of the screen.   Screen layout should follow reading conventions.

Most cultures read text from left to right and from top to bottom.

What's good	What's bad
The use of contrasts (big/small, heavy/light, bright/dark, thick/thin, etc.).	Ugly colour clashes.
Lots of white space.	Using colours schemes that hinder viewing by users with colour confusion.
An uncluttered screen.	Busy, fussy screens.
Eye grabbers (e.g. a single brightly coloured object on a grey scale background, or a single photograph and elegant script text on a light embossed background),	Buttons that produce melodies, voices, bells, klaxons, drum rolls when pressed.
Shadows.	Frilly borders.
Gradients.	Too much text, too many numbers.
Shaded text.	Flashing images (consider potential epilepsy problems).
Projects that establish their presence quickly on startup, with a display title window.	Lame humour, regional humour, in-jokes.

Serious consideration should be given to the effective use of *'white space'*.   This term originated from the printed page and indicated those areas of the page that were not printed on. In multimedia terms, it indicates those areas of the screen on which there is no text, graphic or other object.   Some large web portals, such as Yahoo and AltaVista, completely cover the screen with text hyperlinks.   The text is usually well organised and is acceptable as a quick way to access other resources.   However, the screens are very crammed and this would not be effective on another type of web site or project.   White space allows the eye to rest a little and helps focus the eye on what is important on the page.   The key headings are not submerged in a morass of text and other objects.

The uses of text and of colour are covered in their own sections later.

Layout grids
The requirements for a proficient interface include:
- Easy on the eye
- Easy to use
- Easy to remember

All of these can be met with a disciplined approach to screen layout. This uses a *'layout grid'* approach, where the screen area is divided on a grid to create a defined area that will each hold specific content. The resulting layout is designed for use in a consistent manner throughout the project's pages.   Using a template approach means that users are not faced with different layouts on different pages, each placing their text, logos, menus, etc. in different places. Of course, some individual page layouts will vary from the template, depending upon their nature, but using templates unifies the overall feel of the project.

The panels that are created by the layout grid may contain text content (static or scrollable), static or dynamic content, user input areas (e.g. forms), graphics, videos, animations, etc. Importantly, it also specifies the positioning of the project's navigation controls. The panels ensure alignment of page contents and should be set up to direct the user's eyes to the most significant of the screen. Not all elements on the grid are of equal importance. For example, a copyright notice may be required but it is much less important than the main selling point of the page. The relative significance of the page elements should be reflected in the amount of screen space devoted to them – and the relative positions on the screen.

The illustration shows an example of a page produced by a layout grid.   The layout is independent of the software method used to create it.   The example specifies that the video controls occupy two-fifths of the bottom panel, which itself occupies one fifth of the screen area.   This specification is independent of the screen size or resolution used to view the project.

For programmers producing scaleable screens (e.g. as with Flash), the layout grid may be measured in percentages of the screen area, or may be measured in screen pixels. Web programmers may also decide to use implementations using tables or frames to create the layout of panels.   Where measurements are in screen pixels, designers have to take into account the likely resolution of the users' monitors and any loss of screen area (e.g. that used by browser software).

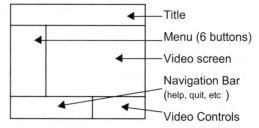

Backgrounds
Backgrounds are <u>back</u>grounds; they are intended as a backdrop for the main screen content. They must not dominate the screen.   For example, a piece of text with a small font size and grey or white colour is almost invisible with a background that is a brightly coloured, highly detailed photograph.

The backgrounds supplied with some applications are very elaborate and, although effective for an introductory screen that will have large bold headings, they obscure the text message when used for all the subsequent screens.   It is best to use plainer backgrounds with the main project screens.

Graduated tints also make effective backgrounds. If a gradient fill is being used, the fill should be light at bottom and dark at top.

Using dark text and objects with a light background produces lower user errors and increased user completion times, compared to light objects on a dark background. Using black on a white background is universally acceptable, if not the most visually stunning. Users with low vision often use yellow text on a black background.

Whatever backgrounds are chosen, there must be a large contrast between the text colour and the background colour, for maximum readability.

A constant background should be used in most projects.   This provides consistency, a feeling of completeness/unity, and perhaps a corporate identity.

Occasionally, changing backgrounds can be used to good effect.   Consider a project for a travel agent or an estate agent.   Here, a different background could be used for each section of the project.

Also, subtle alterations to the <u>shade</u> of the background are effective in notifying viewers that they have entered a new area of the project.

Designing with colour

Before reading this section, it would be advisable to re-read the section on colour theory in the chapter on *'Multimedia Basics'*. It explains how light and colour is processed by the eye and by the brain.

Colour has an instinctive appeal.   Indeed, it has become so widespread that advertisers now use monochrome photographs in advertising so that they appear distinctive.

People respond to the colours on a screen before they respond to the actual visual elements on the screen.
Colour can be used to convey mood and to convey information.

Colour associations

The eye operates according to strict physical properties but the brain's processing of the information imposes <u>meaning</u> upon the information.   The cultural and personal experience of colours means that they may be perceived as being happy, sad, threatening, etc.   Some interpretations may be cultural (e.g. black representing death) or may be personal (e.g. if all tax bills were printed on green paper, every green document would be viewed with suspicion by that person).   Colours have been given subjective properties.   For example, some colours are described as *'warm'* while others are *'cold'*.   Colours have also entered our language to describe emotions.   For example, being caught *'red-handed'* or telling *' little white lies'*.   In the first case, red indicates negative attitudes, while the white in the second example indicates something harmless.

Some common colour associations are:

Colour	British Associations	Some Alternative Associations
Red	Anger, danger, heat, negative values	In China - festivity and joy
Green	Environment	In Muslim culture - holy
Blue	Cold, sea, sky	
White	Purity	In China, Japan and India - death, funerals, mourning
Black	Death, mourning, evil	
Purple	Luxury	In Latin America - death
Yellow	Sun, happiness	In Egypt - prosperity. In America - caution

In the real world, objects do not have a consistent colour, since they only reflect the light that illuminates them at the time.   For instance, brightly adorned streets may appear drab and grey in the twilight, just before the streetlights are switched on.   Also, the blue of the sky changes with the time of day.   This trait can be exploited by project designers and graphic artists, who can alter the colouring for objects to convey the time of day or the mood (e.g. New York's Central Park at night has a different mood from Central Park in the bright sunlight).

Colour coding

Colour has long been used to categorise information and this technique can be employed in multimedia projects.   It is called *'colour coding'* and there are two types:

Ordinal Coding	The depth of a colour or set of colours is used to indicate relative values of a piece of information. For example, a map may use increasingly dark shades of blue to indicate the increasing depth of the seabed, while using ever-lighter shades of green to indicate ever-higher heights of land. Similarly, a scale from pink to deep red might indicate rising temperatures. There is no need to consult a chart, unless exact readings are required; a glance at the colours is sufficient to discover the relative height, depth, speed, temperature, sales, age, etc. of an object.
Nominal Coding	In this system, colours have been picked on an arbitrary basis to indicate an object. For example, the various lines on the London Underground are colour coded for ease of use. Similarly, maps use one colour for motorways and other colours for minor roads, rivers, etc.

Colour coding only works when the user is aware of the purpose of each code.   The meanings of colour codes have been learned over years (everyone understands that a red traffic light means stop).

In a multimedia project, care should be taken if the colour codes used are different from those that are commonly recognised.   Users will not be prepared to learn elaborate colour systems just to navigate the system or categorise information - unless they perceive that it is absolutely necessary and that the package is worth persevering with.   In other words, colour coding can be an advantage or a disincentive, depending upon how it is used.

Colour and learning

Learners prefer colour screens to black and white screens.   Their preference is for dark foreground objects on a light background.   In reality, the learner's immediate performance in using a package is similar with black and white or colour.   However, there is evidence that the use of colour can lead to greater retention and recall of information, as coloured material is recalled more accurately than black and white material.

- Colour is a useful way to emphasise learning cues.   However, used indiscriminately, it distracts from the important learning cues.
- Also, viewers will tolerate more text on a screen if colour is used to highlight important sections of the text.
- Colour highlighting is more effective than shape highlighting, except for users who suffer from colour confusion.
- Projects aimed at children should use primary colours, as children only learn to distinguish between shades later.
- The number of colours used on a screen also impacts on the learning experience.
- Using up to seven different colours increases viewer interest, while increasing the number of colours beyond seven makes identifying information more difficult.   People's short-term memory can only handle a limit of between five and nine colours.   Using more than seven colours may actually reduce the amount of material accessed in a project.
- Projects should therefore use this limited set of colours for screens (excluding colours in photographs, of course).
- Finally, since colours have associative properties, the same colour should always be used for the same function.

Using Colour

The point should be repeated that colour should be used as an additive feature.

Projects should not rely on colour unless it is an integral part of the project.   For this reason, it is commonly advised that a project be initially designed in black & white.   The slogan to *'get it right in black and white'* before considering colour slightly overstates the case but provides the correct emphasis.   Of course, there are exceptions to this rule. Some projects may rely heavily on the use of colour in order to make the project's message effective.   For example, detailed animations of chemical, electrical or mechanical processes may rely on the use of different colours to make the process legible.

Colour perceptions

As previously explained different colours produce different reactions.   This is partly physical (how the eye processes) and partly psychological (how the brain translates colour).

- The yellow and red ends of the spectrum increase eye fatigue.
- Red produces the most fatigue, but is also the most stimulating.
- Blue produces the least fatigue, and is perceived as being the most cheerful.
- Green is perceived as the most restful to the eye.
- Yellow is said to have a calming effect.
- Brighter or larger areas of colour attract attention.
- Intense hues and light colours are perceived as foreground elements, while dull hues and dark colours are perceived as background elements.   This mirrors the user's perceptions of the real world.
- Areas of high contrast between colours appear in the foreground.
- Areas of low contrast recede into the background.
- Viewers are attracted to bright colours.
- Bright colours quickly tire viewers' eyes.

Colour usage

- Save the brightest colours for the objects that viewers should look at first.
- Overusing bright coloured objects confuses the viewer, who doesn't know which objects are meant to be the most important.
- Use the minimum number of colours on one screen. Some designers use as little as four colours on a page, including black and white.   Too many colours, particularly bright colours, make the project look

gaudy and cheap. Users tolerate grey scale colours and these can be used without counting as additional colours.

- A headline or caption that uses different colours for each letter almost always fails to impress and usually irks users.
- Basic colours (black, white, yellow, red, blue, green and grey) work best for text colours.
- Cluttered screens can handle fewer colours.
- Screens with relatively few items can handle more colours.
- Colour is more attention-grabbing than blinking or *'inverse video'* (white text on a black background).

Colour combinations

Colours always appear along with other colours and care must be taken that the colours used work with each other, and that they maximise the screen impact for the greatest number of viewers.

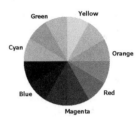

The colour wheel is used when selecting colour combinations. Colour schemes can either be analogous or complementary. Analogous schemes use colours that are close to each other on the colour wheel (e.g. blue and cyan) and use the similar hues to provide a calmer screen. Of course, this scheme is not intended for displaying text as the contrast is too low. Complementary schemes use colours that are on opposite sides of the colour wheel (e.g. green and magenta) to provide a high contrasting scheme.

Some guidelines are:
- Use appropriate combinations.
- Avoid clashing colour schemes such as green/blue and red/blue.
- Avoid a red/green colour scheme, as around 10% of the population suffer from colour confusion.
- Colours look darker and smaller against a white background.
- Colours look brighter and larger against a black background.
- Use a consistent colour scheme - for text, hyperlinks, buttons (e.g. don't use red for exit on one screen and then green for exit on another screen).
- Colour schemes can be dependent upon the era. For example, house-decorating colours in the conservative 50's or the psychedelic 60's are at odds with current house paint colours.   Certain colours are more popular at certain times and their use can set the intended mood for an era.
- Insufficient contrast between background and text colours increases eye fatigue.
- Over contrast (e.g. white text on black background) is also tiring. Use light grey on a black background.
- Select colours with text links in mind. The background colour of a menu box should not be the same colour as a visited or unvisited link.

While the correct use of colour can be highly effective, it should not be used as the sole way to colour code, express mood, etc. (see the chapter on *'Project Testing'* for details).

Web site issues

Web pages could contain other useful information, apart from the main project content - e.g. the date the page was last updated.

Pages could also provide a link that allows the user to contact the site creator.   This is a courtesy to allow user feedback to the designer and is also a marketing tool that encourages users to contact the site promoter.

Text

A picture may be worth a thousand words, but certain ideas can only be expressed or summarised in text format.   For example, a scientific formula or a table of figures is difficult to represent in any other media.   The bandwidth restrictions on web sites also often push designs towards an emphasis on text content. A web site that describes a holiday resort rather than showing multiple photographs and video clips may be less exciting but is a lot smaller to store and a lot quicker to download.

There is little difference between user comprehension of words read on a screen and words read from a printed page. However, users read around 25% slower from a monitor screen.

All multimedia applications employ text and their attributes used should reflect the nature of the application. The later section on fonts discusses typefaces and their attributes.

Text layout issues

Too much text on the screen repels viewers and the screen layout seeks to make the viewing experience both easier and more enjoyable. Of course, some projects of necessity use a great deal of text and the users know what to expect when they open such screens.   Viewers who wish to examine historical records, court transcripts, scientific papers, component lists, price lists, etc. expect to see a great deal of text on a screen. In fact, spreading the text over many separate pages makes the researcher's task more difficult.

For all other projects, however, the viewer may have much less motivation and the layout should be an invitation to browse and not a barrier.

Some recommendations for text layout are:

- Do not place all the text centred on the screen.
- Do not use text that is too small or too large, as it makes the viewer uncomfortable.
- Headings, subheadings and main points in a screen should be highlighted, to draw the audience's attention to the importance of that particular item.   This may be achieved by formatting the text to be bold, italicised or displayed in a prominent colour, or the text may be placed in a filled box.
- Don't use underlines on headings; instead, use a bold heading to summarise the screen.
- Avoid having more than 12 words on a line; 8 to 10 words is a more practical limit.
- Use the same point size for the body font throughout the project.
- Use the same point size for all headings and sub-headings in the project.
- Never rescale text to make it fit the screen.
- Screen text should be left justified and ragged on the right edge.   Block justified text may look better but is harder to read.
- Apart from necessary blocks of text, each line should make a single point. Each new concept should appear on its own new line/block/bullet.
- Avoid using all upper case letters, as lower case letters are easier to read. A mix of upper and lower case is acceptable.
- Using text that is all capitals makes reading more difficult for those who speed-read, as they use word shapes to help identify words (see the illustration).
- Use underlining sparingly, as underlining words obscures their shape, making reading more difficult.
- Use serifed typefaces for quotes.

Text Effects

Designers are always looking for ways to make their projects more distinctive.   Some text effects work, while others make things worse.

- Avoid having text of many different colours on any one screen.
- Using colours to highlight titles or hypertext links is effective.
- Wipes and transitions can attract viewers' attention, if not overplayed.
- Users prefer fixed screens to scrolling screens.
- Scrolling is only suitable as an aid for browsing lists. It should not be used as a method of reading body text. If it's big enough to requiring scrolling, break it up into logical chunks on separate screens.
- Be careful of typestyle choices for web sites. If an uncommon font is used, it will not be recognised by other's browsers and they will substitute their own choice of font, losing the graphic effect intended by the designer. The only sure way to ensure viewers see the pages as they were intended is to create a graphic image of the text. Unfortunately, this results in large file sizes for the text graphics.
- Reversing letters is an eye-catching technique.
- Inverting letters is an eye-catching technique.
- Using letters sizes and shapes to produce the outline of an object such as a car, a house, etc. can be effective in some situations but requires a little imagination and a lot of patience.
- Initial capital letters at the start of a paragraph, known as *'drop caps'* can enhance text and draw the readers' attention. The first two words are generally capitalised, to prevent the drop cap effect being too overpowering.

> MULTIMEDIA AUTHORING packages do not generally have spell-checking or grammar-checking features and the author has to be very careful that misspelled words do not slip through and mar an otherwise professional project.   All packages allow

Language issues

The language used also develops a mood.   The words used to review current youth music would not be very effective on a government project or a project for the over-70's.   Similarly the choice of words used in the text is important; the grammar should suit the intended audience.   Young children should not be bamboozled with complex words and older users should not be patronised.

Jargon, abbreviations and acronyms should also be avoided, although some 'foreign' words or phrases are eye-catching and add glamour or mystery to the screen (just think of how many perfumes are given French names).

Grammar/punctuation checks

A well thought out presentation is spoiled if it contains typing errors, grammatical errors or other inconsistencies that detract from a professional feel.

Points to bear in mind are:

- Always spell check the text. Bear in mind that a sentence will pass a spell check as long as the words exist. They might still be the wrong word for the sentence (e.g. compliment mixed up for complement). If in any doubt, consult a dictionary.
- Always grammar check sentences, preferably using both software and manual checking.
- Use active verbs.
- Always use the same tense within screens and between different screens.
- Avoid prepositions, adverbs and adjectives.
- Punctuation marks should be in the same format as the word it follows. For example, if words are in italics any commas, colons, semi-colons and full stops should also be in italics. Similarly, words in bold should be followed by bold punctuation marks.
- An ellipsis is a row of full stops and is used to effect in a number of ways. Each full stop in an ellipsis must have a space before and after it.

Text importation

Multimedia authoring packages do not generally have spell-checking or grammar-checking features and the author has to be very careful that misspelled words do not slip through and mar an otherwise professional project. All packages allow text to be imported into the project and this is the safest way to protect against typing or grammatical errors. Text can be entered into a word-processed file, which can be checked before being imported into the authoring package's project. The file types allowed by the authoring package should be checked and the text file should be saved in one of the acceptable formats. For example, this may mean converting a modern Word file into an older Word format.

Lists and Tables

Bullet points and numbered lists aid readability. Users, particularly those with reading difficulties, can be intimidated by the thought of tackling a large chunk of text. Breaking down information into smaller chunks allows the user to read as much or as little as they want. Lists are a convenient way to summarise a set of facts or arguments. It is best to use an odd total when numbering lists. When viewers see a heading such as *'10 reasons to buy our product'*, they assume the list has been padded to bring it to an even number. A heading such as *'9 reasons to buy our product'* is more acceptable.

Tables, on the other hand, are difficult to comprehend and large tables are only fully read by the dedicated viewer. Naturally, small charts are easier to read than large ones. There may be scope to reduce the table's content to show only the essential data (perhaps about four columns and four or five rows).

Where a lot of data has to be displayed, the key facts may be picked out in a different colour from the rest of the table entries. In addition, making each row a different colour aids scanning along the rows.

Consideration should be given to exposing one row of the table at a time, so that the information is explained as it is built up. This works where the table is a central part of the screen presentation.

Also, be careful that sans serif types are not confused in tables. The figure 1 and the capital I are almost identical. This is an even bigger problem when used in displaying formulae.

Lastly, if trends in numeric data are being displayed, it may be best to use a graph rather than a table.

Fonts

In the world of Windows and Windows applications, fonts are understood to be collections of alphabetic, numeric, punctuation and symbol characters as seen on the computer monitor or printed to paper. Windows fonts have four main characteristics:

TYPEFACE -	the actual *shape* of the characters, such as Arial, Times Roman and Univers.
TYPE FAMILY -	the collection of *variations* on the basic typeface, such as weight (e.g. bold, light, black), slant (e.g. italic or oblique), width (e.g. expanded, condensed, narrow), or combinations (e.g. bold-italic or normal-italic).
TYPE SIZE -	the *height* of the characters as measured in points, there being 72 points to an inch.
TYPE STYLE -	such as bold, italics or underlined.

From a printer's point of view, a font is a collection of the characters of one typeface, at one point size. So characters at 18 point Arial bold, regular and italic are all part of the same font, while these same Arial characters at 20 point make up another font. Equally, a set of 18 point characters in Times New Roman would make up yet another font. Since most multimedia applications handle fonts using the Microsoft definition rather than the printer's definition, designers are advised to adopt this approach.

Typeface definitions

The illustration shows the descriptions that are given to the different dimensions of a typeface.

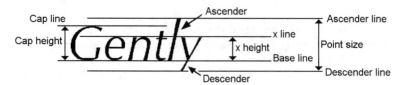

The *'base line'* is the line on which the main body of a character sits.   The *'x height'* is the height occupied by main body of each lower-case character.   The *'cap height'* is the height occupied by the main body of upper case characters.   Many lower-case characters, and even upper-case characters in certain faces, have extensions to their main body.   An *'ascender'* is an upward stroke, as in an *'l' 'd', 't'*, while a *'descender'* is a downward stroke as used in *'g'* and *'y'*.   Note that the font in the example has an ascender line that is significantly above the cap line (i.e. some lower-case letters are taller than capital letters).   In many cases, the ascender rises no further than the cap line and the full height is not used (see below).   A *'counter'* is the curved bowl of a character, such as in a 'b' or 'p'.

Point size

The height of text is measured in points.   There are 72 points to one inch and a 36-point headline might therefore be expected to be half an inch in height.   However, the point size is measured from the ascender line to the descender line and is not the same as the cap height.   If the text is entered in upper case, or a font contains only upper case characters, the space from the base line to the descender line is lost.   There are normally no typefaces with a single character that touches both the ascender line and descender line.

Additionally, the typefaces rarely use the full height given to them and the displayed or printed text is less than expected.   The illustration shows the upper-case letter 'I' being displayed in a range of different typefaces.   It can be clearly seen that there are large differences in the cap height of each character - even though they are all formatted to the same type size!   There are also large variations in the x-height of different typefaces.

Bitmapped vs scaleable

The chapter on *'Computer Graphics'* examined the difference between bitmap graphics and vector graphics.   The same principles apply to text fonts.   Bitmap fonts contain the actual images of each character (i.e. the actual dot pattern that makes up the character's outline).   This requires a separate file for each point size, as rescaling a small type size to a larger size results in ugly *'jaggies'*, just as with other rescaled bitmap images.   Bitmapped fonts are now largely ignored in favour of TrueType fonts.

TrueType fonts contain the vector information for drawing each character at display time.   These instructions are used to create the rasterised version.   As each face has the same shape at all sizes, the same instructions are merely given different dimensions to create the face at any given point size.   They are *'scaleable'*.   Since TrueType fonts only contain descriptions, they have small file sizes - and they only require one description for each variation (i.e. there is a file containing a normal description, one containing an italic description, one containing a bold description, and so on).

Serif vs sans serif

A serifed font, such as Times Roman, has small details and strokes added at the top and bottom of characters.   The added detail aids readability.   They keep individual letters apart while keeping words linked as a group. They also make letters more distinctive (i.e. the lower-case letter 'l' is distinctly different from the upper-case letter 'I').   The serifs at the top of characters are used by readers to speed their recognition of words (to test this, cover the bottom of a line of text and see how readable the words are in serif and sans serif fonts).   Serifed faces are used in almost all printed publications.

A sans serif font has a plain outline with no feet or twirls, the word *'sans'* being the French for *'without'*. It has a cleaner outline and is commonly used for titles, captions, labelling items in diagrams, and displaying scientific formulae.   It provides a good screen contrast with the main serifed body text, but its suitability for formatting large areas of body text is a matter of debate.

Proportional vs non-proportional

The output from typewriters is of fixed width.   Every character occupies the same amount of space along the horizontal line.   So, narrow characters like i, l, f, 1, etc take up the same space as wide characters such as w and m.   This makes the text much harder to read.   That is why typewritten notes always look inferior to book and newspaper print, which use proportional spacing of characters.

This is an example of proportional spacing
`This is standard width printing`

With proportional spacing, a character only occupies as much of the screen width as it actually needs.   So, the letter *'m'* uses more space than the letter *'i'.*   As a result, proportional spacing results in more professional output, similar to typeset documents as seen in books.

However, one problem with proportional spacing is lining up data into columns as seen in this example.   Since each digit occupies a different screen width (e.g. an eight is wider than a one), figures do not line up in neat columns.   In this situation, a fixed-width character set produces more readable results.

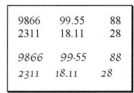

9866	99.55	88
2311	18.11	28
9866	*99.55*	*88*
2311	*18.11*	*28*

Leading

Leading (pronounced as *'ledding'*), is the term used to describe the spacing between individual lines of text.   In the early days of printers, thin slices of lead were inserted between lines of typeset characters, hence the name.   The technique is also termed *'line spacing'* or *'interlinear spacing'* and is a a feature available with web sites using Cascading Style Sheets.

Generally, the leading is about 20% greater than the text size.   So, for example, a 20 point text would have a 24 point leading between lines of text.

Increasing the leading can be used to space out the lines of a screen quote. It can also be used to increase the space between scrolling lines of text, allowing the viewer more time to read the lines as they scroll.

It is never a good idea to decrease line spacing as the lines start to merge, making the text unreadable.

Kerning

Proportional spacing ensures that each character does not occupy excessive screen width.   Nevertheless, each character occupies its own space; there is a distinct boundary between each character.

Kerning allows certain character combinations to overlap their boundaries, for a more snug fit and a more readable text.   For example, a lower case letter may partially sit under the previous letter's overhang, as in the example below.

Two WAV files   These words are unkerned. Notice the gaps between the letters.

Two WAV files   These words are kerned. Notice how the 'w' fits under the top of the 'T' and how the
                    extremities of the 'W', 'A' and 'V' overlap each other's space.

Kerning facilities are common in DTP and word-processing packages such as Microsoft Word.

If the graphics/authoring package does not provide kerning facilities, this effect may have to be manually created in the graphics package (i.e. letters are cut and paste so that they kern).

Hinting

When typefaces are displayed at very small point sizes, it is difficult to define the character shapes accurately. For example, the stem (the vertical part of a character) may be displayed as one pixel wide on one character and two pixels wide on another character, or the pixels of a curve might merge into a single blob.   Hinting uses instructions that ensure consistent displays at these lower point sizes.

Body text vs display text

Windows applications have a large range of typestyle savailable to them.

Some are designed to be used as the main text of screens and printed pages.   These types are known as *'body'* typefaces.   Other typestyles are designed for their decorative or descriptive effect and these are known as *'display'* typestyles.

Examples of display faces: **Bodoni Poster**   Chicago   Taffy   Space Toaster
Examples of body faces: Bookman Old Style   Times New Roman   Book Antiqua

Display faces are usually difficult to read at smaller point sizes and are rarely used as a body text. Display typefaces are designed for headings and sub-headings and should normally be displayed no smaller than about 14 point.

Displaying web/screen fonts

At one time, font design was concentrated on achieving the most readable printed output.   To achieve WYSIWYG (What You See Is What You Get) results, the font destined for the printer was faithfully reproduced on the monitor screen.   This did not pay any regard to how readable the font might be on the screen, as the emphasis was on printed reproduction.

With the huge growth in reading information directly from the screen, printed output is a secondary issue. Indeed, for most multimedia work, the end user will not require printed output.

The aim is now to achieve the most readable <u>screen</u> output.   Fonts should be readable for longish periods without causing eyestrain.

The point was made earlier that most typefaces do not use the total allocated height.   In particular, a small x-height means that the main body of the text is using up a small proportion of the screen allocation.   The font size cannot be increased, as this makes the line width longer, resulting in fitting fewer words to a screen.

The answer lies in using typefaces with x-heights that make up a larger proportion of the height allocated by the point size.   Well-known typefaces that use this technique are Rockwell and Lucida.

V V	G G	Microsoft has produced two typefaces that are designed primarily for screen display. The serif version is called Georgia and the sans serif version is called Verdana.
e e	e e	If these are not already on the computer, they can be downloaded free from the Microsoft site (www.microsoft.com/truetype/) and installed.
r r	o o	The leftmost column displays the Verdana typeface, while the column next to it shows the same word displayed in Arial, at the same point size.
d d	r r	The third column displays the Georgia typeface while the last column displays the same word in Times New Roman, at the same point size.
a a	g g	
n n	i i	In both cases, the x-height of the new Microsoft screen fonts is substantially larger than the other fonts, making them look like a larger point size.
a a	a a	The trick is to avoid increasing the x-height to the point where it is difficult to spot the difference between upper and lower case characters.

They are also designed so that the characters never touch, even at tiny point sizes (as low as 4 point).

In the longer term, higher-resolution screens will provide more screen pixels for each screen character.   This will allow anti-aliasing techniques that result in clearer text displays at smaller point sizes.

Specifying web fonts

When designing web sites, there is no way of knowing what computer or browser is being used to read and interpret the web site's scripts.   If simple serifed and non-serifed body fonts are used in the design, there is a good chance that the site will be displayed at the receiving end in the same way, or a broadly similar way, as the designer intended.   The HTML code can, for example, instruct the computer to use Arial (for PCs), Helvetica (for Macs) or any other sans serif typeface.

When rare and exotic typestyles are required to be used for a web site, this raises serious problems.   It is highly unlikely that the site visitors will have the same fonts installed on their computers and they will not see the screen effect that was planned.

There are a number of ways that this problem is tackled and these are examined in the chapter on web site creation.

Using body fonts

The purpose of type is to make the text easy to read.   Fonts are a medium.   Therefore, body fonts should not draw attention to themselves.   The aim is to have the viewer read the text, not marvel at the fonts.

Most users do not like having to do a lot of reading from the monitor screen and anything that gets in the way of smooth and easy reading will deter the user from delving into the main text; instead he/she is more likely to skim over the screen headings and sub-headings.

The following advice is offered for using body text.
- Use the same font face and size on all body text throughout the project.
- Avoid using serifed fonts at small point sizes.
- Where the script specifies the font size, do not use less than 12 point for serifed fonts and 10 point for sans serif fonts.
- Bold typefaces at small point sizes tend to be difficult to read.
- Do not overuse capitals, bold face or italics in the text, as they tend to obscure the message.
- Bear in mind that underlined text can be used to provide emphasis - but is also used for text hyperlinks.
- Avoid using large fonts to emphasise parts of the main text.
- Use italics to emphasise a word in the text.
- Use a small graphic next to a block of text, or place the text between lines, to bring emphasis to the text.

Using decorative fonts

Decorative fonts are a different issue altogether.   They can be used very effectively to convey a mood
Consider these examples:

ACE Builders Merchants   Wick childrens Nursery

Chizzel & Robbem Accountants   Brenda's Hair Salon

Crossroads Coffee Shop   Bargain SuperStore

HENRY'S PICTURE GALLERY   HONG KONG RESTAURANT

Family Laywers   Ajax Computer Repairs

Tradition and advertising have conditioned the public into certain visual expectations. For example, many Chinese/ Cantonese restaurants use fonts like that shown above for their shop signs and printed menus. And a *'trendy'* or *'whimsical'* font would not look too good on a project for funeral undertakers, while *'traditional'* and *'formal'* fonts would never be used on a teenage magazine or fanzine.

There is no formal categorisation of fonts and an examination of the surrounding environment quickly reveals current practice. Magazines, advertising, catalogues, promotional leaflets, etc. are full of examples of the selection of fonts for different effects.

General descriptions of common fonts styles include:

- Traditional fonts use small x-heights and long ascenders and descenders.
- Elegant fonts use small x-heights, long ascenders and descenders, and have angled counters and hairline accents.
- Contemporary fonts use high x-heights and short ascenders and descenders.

Additional advice

- The aim of headings and sub-headings is to organise text information and present it in meaningful and readable chunks.
- Lots of subheadings help the viewer find information quickly and prevent the screen being one intimidating mass of text.
- Use larger spacing above a heading than below a heading.
- The importance of a piece of text can be indicated to the viewer by increasing its size and/or weight.
- Any typeface can be used as a heading, if the point size is big enough.
- A project should use a limited number of font styles.
- Do not use two different sans serif fonts in the same project.
- Do not use two different serifed fonts together in the same project.
- Many fonts will have similar outlines, but will have different typestyle names. This is because typeface names can be legally protected, while the designs of typefaces are much harder to protect (after all, the letters of the alphabet are not copyrighted).
- It is OK to use a serifed and sans serif font in the same screen.

Media Requirements

Graphics

Graphics tend to dominate the screen's text content, because viewers scan images much more quickly than text. This means that the use of graphics has to be carefully planned. The designer has to justify the use of every graphic used in a project. The purpose may be defined as decorative, educational, informational, or whatever - but they should not simply be inserted to fill a space.

The designer has to be aware that photographs and images are subject to misinterpretation. People use their own experience and knowledge to interpret a vague photograph or drawing. Users may be unintentionally offended by some material or be misled by taking the wrong meaning from it.

The purpose, type, colouring, use and positioning of graphics can all affect how well the project is received. These issues are dealt with below.

Graphics and learning

- Illustrations should be there for a distinct purpose.
- Using pictures generally is of more benefit to poor readers than good readers, who are more prone to appreciate concepts in written format.
- Using pictures displaying analogies is particularly helpful for slower learners. (e.g. using diagrams of shopping baskets and wallets to illustrate material on world economics).
- Viewers prefer illustrated text to viewing text on its own.
- Viewers are more drawn to a realistic drawing than to a basic sketch.
- Coloured pictures are recalled more accurately than black and white pictures.
- An organised layout of photographs is better understood and retained than a collage of photographs.
- Complex diagrams and illustrations may not produce the optimum results unless the text directs the reader's attention (e.g. in a series of steps relating to diagram annotations). The text must aid the reader, not hinder their absorption of the graphic information (e.g. if the text is too confusing, the diagram is largely ignored).
- Adding detail to an element on a drawing can improve comprehension, while adding too much detail can be counter-productive, as the essentials get lost in the detail.
- Pictures on their own (i.e. not linked to text) do little to aid learning, although they may be decorative.
- Relevant pictures aid learning and recall.

- Diagrams are only useful if they are carefully constructed to ensure that they contain relevant and useful information.
- Although a picture can sometimes substitute for text, generally graphics do not replace text.
- A photograph or image should be placed close to the text that it relates to.
- A graphic in one part of the screen only helps the text it relates to - any other text is not improved on.
- Consider the cultural implications of including each image.

Graphics layout

- Take advantage of white space - don't fill every available space with the image.
- Do not place a border round the entire screen. Use borders above and below, or left and right, but not on all sides.
- Similarly, graphic images can be placed on two sides of a block of text, but there should not be images surrounding the entire text.
- Placing too many images on one screen is often a waste.   Generally, there should be no more than three images per screen, excluding image maps and navigation buttons.
- Where many images are necessary on a screen (e.g. a project displaying the facilities of a hotel), small images should be used as links to larger images, rather than cramming the screen.
- Use a high contrast between graphics image and the background, as this maximises legibility.
- Use white, grey or earth tone backgrounds for pages that display high quality images. Avoid dark or heavily textured backgrounds.
- The shadows on buttons should not be too heavy (perhaps just one pixel wide) or they will be too overbearing.
- Captions should be positioned underneath or to the right of the graphic.
- For web sites, stick to traditional hyperlink colours. Although they can be set to whatever the designer decides, new colours schemes will confuse the user.

Finally, ensure that the source of all images is legal.   This may mean purchasing royalty-free clip art libraries or royalty-free photographic collections. Alternatively, images can be created in-house or can be commissioned to freelance artists and photographers.

Video

The human eye is adapted to perceive movement better than uniform prolonged information.   This means that moving material such as animations and video will predominate on a screen. The eye will roam around the screen if there is no movement to observe but will immediately detect and lock on to any screen movement.

Motion video can do what all the other media can't - provide realism to a project.   Static photographs are very useful and are small in size, but video can convey mood much better than photographs. For example, the New Orleans Mardi Gras viewed on video and viewed as photographs are entirely different experiences.   Unfortunately, video clips consume large amounts of disk space and have to be used in moderation. Therefore, the designer has to choose where they can be used to best effect. The question has to be asked whether the same learning or the same impact can be achieved by audio or graphic means.

Typical uses of video are demonstrating processes, interviewing well-known or colourful personalities, promoting products, and revealing destinations (e.g. a drive through a town, a walk through a factory).

There is a huge source of video material available.   This may be original material (such as old videotapes, old cine film) or may be purchased or licenced from commercial sources.   Alternatively new material can be shot or commissioned.

The designer must decide how a video is introduced into a screen.   A clip may:

- play as soon as the screen is entered.
- only appear when the viewer opts to see the clip.

Video clips must be controllable. Viewers must not be forced to watch a long introductory video clip; there should be an option to by-pass the opening screen.   Similarly, viewers should not be forced to watch other video clips. The screen should allow user controls to start the clip, stop the clip, replay the clip, freeze the action, play in slow motion, and play in a frame-by-frame mode.

The controls provided should have a familiar and intuitive appearance.   They should be simple and look like typical VCR controls.   Inventing new control symbols just confuses viewers.

Animations

Animations are a common and effective way to aid learning. They can display actions that cannot normally be viewed (e.g. the working of the heart or of the combustion engine) or are too small to see (e.g. the working of a watch mechanism).

Animations are often seen as being significant parts of a project and should be used for explaining key points. A long animation (e.g. showing the 25 steps involved in carrying out a particular task) is better broken into a set of shorter animations.

The trick is to structure the set of sub-tasks so that the viewer does not stop after looking at the first few elements. Animations often have a verbal narration, as this is more effective than just using accompanying text.
Since they are large files and make the page load more slowly, they should only be used where they serve a purpose. In particular, avoid those little animated cartoons that constantly repeat, distracting the user and becoming more and more annoying.

Some packages, such as RoboHelp, allow the designer to capture a computer session as a file that can be replayed later. This is ideal for teaching viewers how to use a particular software package. They also allow a voiceover to be added to the screen action, so that the entire animation can be used as a *'talk you through'* utility.
As with video, animations should be provided with user controls to stop, start, pause the animation and these controls should use the familiar VCR button icons.
Lastly, the designer must be aware of the dangers of flashing animation sequences. Photo-sensitive epilepsy affects 1 in 200 people between 3 and 18 years. The problems normally occur at around 10-20 flashes per second, but no more than 3 flashes per second is allowed on television. The dangers are worsened with high contrast black and white flashes. In 1997, almost 700 Japanese children were hospitalised with convulsions, vomiting and irritated eyes, after watching *'Pocket Monsters'* - a children's cartoon. The cartoon included a three-second scene of a bright flashing explosion.

Sound

Sound is an additive feature and must complement the screen content and not distract from it. The careful selection and inclusion of voice, music and sound effects add to the experience of using the project.
Typical uses of audio are:

- Verbal introductions (e.g. *"Welcome to the planet Zogg . . . . ."*. Can get tedious after repetition).
- Musical introductions. Don't have a long musical introduction that the user cannot bypass. Keep it short, or let the user by-pass the introduction.
- Aural warning (e.g. if the time limit for a self-assessed test is due to expire).
- Aural feedback (e.g. if correct/if wrong, clicking sound when the mouse key is pressed). Avoid having annoying fanfares, etc. every time a button is pressed.
- Verbal instructions.
- Reinforcement - encouraging words from the computer intended to *'humanise'* the project.
- Provide atmosphere, with sound effects, appropriate music and background vocals.
- Background music - intended to pass time or create an overall atmosphere. Remember, the user may have to listen to this music for hours. The designer has to decide whether background music is necessary, is atmospheric, or is just downright annoying.   Particularly annoying are the MIDI clips that play throughout the browsing time of some web sites.
- Music in context - clips that are played at specific points in the project.

The designer should try to use sound in a way that the user would expect to experience it in real life situations. For example, clicking on a screen button should result in an *'click'* sound response – not the sound of a car horn or a voice saying *'Thank you Dave'*. The unexpected use of sound can disturb users.
As with video and animations, sound should be controllable by the user. The user should be able to listen, pause, stop, rewind and alter the volume.
There is an even bigger source of audio material available than video. This may be original material (sound removed from old cine film or old videotapes) that is owned or may be used with permission.   Alternatively, new material can be recorded or commissioned.   There are royalty-free collections of sounds covering a wide range of real world and synthesised sounds and music.   These will not cover all situations and specially recorded material will usually need to be gathered.

Sound and learning

Most audio content is not easily remembered.   Sound is therefore not very effective at conveying detailed information and should only be used as a voiceover (a background commentary) for video, graphics or animation. Similarly, sound should not be used as the only method of communication, as users may be deaf, hard of hearing, or viewing in a noisy environment.
Sound should only be added to a project where it is relevant and enhances the page's presentation.   The indiscriminate use of sound can actually impede usability by distracting users from their intended tasks.
Natural sounds (e.g. baby crying, water running, traffic noise) have more impact than artificial sounds (e.g. alien sounds, zaps and pings).

Style Guides

All the issues of screen style were covered earlier. After deciding on the best approaches for a particular project, the choices should be incorporated into a *'style guide'*. Style guides are important documents that specify exactly how pages are laid out.   The guides may provide general specifications that apply to all pages in the project, or may provide specific details for individual pages.

Content style guides

These define the 'house style', providing a checklist approach.

Examples of some possible general style questions are:

Use of abbreviations	Some abbreviations are widely recognised and can be used in most situations. Examples are mph (miles per hour), mm (millimetre) and cm (centimetre). Less well-known abbreviations should be spelled out in full. For example *'frames per second'* instead of *'fps'*, or *'pages per minute'* instead of *'ppm'*.
Use of capitalisation	Avoid unnecessary capitalisation. Do not use all-caps for company names (e.g. DUMBRECK PUBLISHING) unless the name is an acronym (e.g. BMA).
Displaying dates and times	Use the local conventions for specifying dates (e.g. 28th January 2006) or the international standard date notation, yyyy-mm-dd. (e.g. 2006-01-28). Use the 24-hour clock to specify times (e.g. 19:53) or use a.m. and p.m. (e.g. 7:53 p.m.). Where appropriate, use time zone abbreviations, such as GMT (Greenwich Mean Time), CET (Central Europe Time) EST (Eastern Standard Time in the USA).
Displaying quantities	Always display a zero before decimals that are less than zero (e.g. 0.53) Use decimals (e.g. 0.75) instead of fractions (e.g. three-quarters). Spell out numbers between zero and nine. Use digits for numbers between 10 and 999,999. For higher numbers, spell out the words million, billion, etc. Where a sentence begins with a number, spell the number out unless it is a year. Examples are: *"2005 saw over 2 million homeless and 750,000 dead when six rivers burst their banks in China"* *Seven is the maximum number of items in most menus, although we have seen as many as 45 in the worst examples"* Always use numerals for measured quantities (e.g. 3.2GHz, 100mph). Do not use " for inches or ' for feet (e.g. 32" TV or 12' bridge) instead of spelling out the words (e.g. 32-inch TV or 12-foot bridge).
Accreditation	Credit contributors for use of images, quotes, etc. Any major facts should be accompanied by the source of the information (e.g. *"As the Financial Times leader said in 21st Jan 2005......"* Clearly indicate when a statement is an opinion instead of a fact (e.g. *"We think..."*, *"We believe...").*
Names and titles	Company names are described in neutral terms (e.g. *"IBM claims it has discovered...").* In general, drop the 'www' when mentioning web sites (e.g. *'there is a faultfinding guide at pchandbooks.com'.* When referring to a specific web page, provide the full address (e.g. *"http://www.scotlandgolf.com/tourism/travel-tips.htm").* Avoid the use of Mr, Mrs, and Ms, unless they are being used to differentiate between sexes (e.g. *"Mr J Jones and Mrs M Smith decided to....")* or status (some women will want to be described as Mrs while others prefer to use Ms). In most cases, simply use the person's name (e.g. *"Jack Jones of Leeds ...").*

The list does not specifically include the more obvious questions such as spell checking, grammar checking, and avoiding jargon. These should be taken for granted as applying to all projects, anywhere and at any time.

Important Notes

These are only six examples of general content styles. They are not to be taken as a definitive list. They cannot even be taken as the correct approach for all projects. There is no one definite list – there is only the list that the design team creates for its own use, in its own environment. However, when a design team constructs its own style guide, the points in it can then be regarded as a checklist for future testing.

The guide points can also be altered for specific projects that have differing requirements (e.g. a project aimed at computer technicians can happily use terms that are common within the industry (e.g. dpi, ppi, MHz, Kbps, etc).

Visual style guides

Previous pages have covered approaches to determining the look and feel of a project, the options for fonts, graphics, video, etc. The pages also covered layout issues and layout grids.

The purpose of the visual style guide is to document the layout and interface options that are selected for a particular project. The document should be treated as if it was going to be passed to a group of developers who have not been involved in any of the early design stages. The document has to be very detailed, so that the developers understand exactly how the pages should be created.

The document should include:

Naming conventions	This lists the names that are going to be used to describe different parts of the screen and different objects, to prevent any possibility of misunderstandings. Examples are "logo area, left navigation bar, content area, page title area, footer bar, bread-crumb bar", etc.
Layout grid	This gives the exact screen proportions to be devoted to different screen content. It may also sub-divide the content area into text area, image areas, video playback area, etc. provides balance between screen components.
Look and feel	This specifies the visual style (e.g. corporate, homely, fanzine, etc.) and the highlighting techniques to be used.
Navigation method	This specifies whether buttons, text links, image maps, etc. are to be used.
Visual feedback	This specifies whether rollovers, error message windows, help windows, etc. are to be used.
Text	This specifies the typestyles, point sizes, colours, orientation, drop shadows, etc. and specifies the maximum lines per page to be used.
Colour scheme	This specifies the colour sets and background colours.
Images	This specifies the maximum size of images, any compression used, their contrast with the page background and any icons and metaphors to be used.
Video	This specifies the image size, compression ratio, frame rate and codec required for playback.

This approach provides full details of every screen, including descriptions of the text, fonts, graphics, images, sounds, animations, videos, button shapes and sizes, user responses, etc.

While this takes a long time to prepare, it eliminates most ambiguities at an early stage. It leaves less margin for error at the implementation stage and less scope for client misunderstanding.

Media asset lists

When all the project's documentation is pulled together, the grand plan for the project is ready. Before proceeding to the implementation stage, the team has to ensure that there is a detailed list of all the media requirements for the project.   Some, such as product specifications, may be readily available. Other, such as voiceovers, video clips and animations, will have to be created.   The client usually provides the text content for the individual pages.   The developers can offer advice and can proof read the contents, but the client decides the final text content.   Text content, then, is treated as another item of media.

An asset list is essentially an inventory that specifies every individual item that will be included in the project. This list can be complied as the design process develops. When the structure and page contents are decided, the media requirements can be added to the asset list. The resulting checklist shows, at a glance, the scope of the project's resources and the tasks involved in acquiring these resources.   It is also useful for project management task assignment and for budgeting and scheduling.

The two main issues are source and format.

Source

The main sources of project assets are:

Client material	When the client has accepted the project's site map, the list of the resources to be supplied by the client can be agreed. This should include the copy text along with the appropriate logos, product photographs or illustrations, brochures, catalogues, price lists, product/ service descriptions or specifications. These will need to be examined for their suitability and to ensure all copyright regulations are observed.
Purchased material	e.g. royalty-free images, video clips, clip art.
Produced in-house	e.g. animations, images, font design.
Commissioned material	e.g. voiceovers from professional actors, music, video material.

Format

All material used as project assets should conform to an agreed standard (e.g. JPEG for images, WAV for sound, MOV for video, SWF for animation). The standard will depend on the nature of the project and the hardware of the intended audience. For example, lossless images and uncompressed video can be used for kiosk-based projects where quality is more important than project size.

All new material that is created or commissioned for the project should be produced to the agreed standard.

Material given over by the client is often a little more difficult, as it is probably not in the acceptable format. The client can be requested to provide the material in the desired format or, more likely, the client can be charged for converting the material into the required format.

The conversion of material sometimes is via hardware.   Examples are:

- Scanning the text of brochures, product details, etc. using OCR (Optical Character Recognition) software – producing text files.
- Scanning photographs, maps, diagrams, etc. using a flatbed scanner – producing image files.
- Processing audiotapes through a sound card – producing sound files.
- Processing analogue videotapes through a video capture device – producing video files.
- Processing digital camcorder footage through a FireWire port – producing video files.

Sometimes the conversion is carried out in software. Examples are:

- Using applications such as Adobe Premiere to convert DV files into compressed video formats.
- Using applications such as Sound Edit Pro to convert audio files.
- Using applications such as PhotoShop or Paint Shop Pro to convert graphic image files.

In these ways, the asset list can be compiled with all assets in the correct format.

Of course, conversion only puts assets into their required format. There may still be additional work needing carried out on files (e.g. editing video files, touching up photographs, etc.).

Each asset should be given a meaningful filename that quickly identifies it later. Filenames could include:

- The category area of the project (e.g. by using a front portion such as 'menu')
- The purpose of that asset (e.g. by using a middle portion such as 'help')
- The screen position (by using a description such as 'left', 'footer' or 'bottom')
- The navigation function (e.g. by using a final portion such as 'up' for 'mouseup', 'ov' for 'mouseover').

Examples:

salesbg.gif	The background image that is used in all the project's sales pages.
splashanim.swf	The animation used on the splash page.
menuhelpdown.gif	The help button on the menu; the image that is displayed when the button is in the *'mousedown'* state.
aboutmain.txt	The text that will fill the main area of the *'About Us'* page.
salesleftline.gif	The image of a decorative line that appears on the left of the sales pages.

The design document can specify how files should be identified. This means that all developers will work to that coding and produce files that are usefully named and easily identified by other developers. For example, all assets, whether text, images, or whatever that relate to the sales pages begin with 'sales'.

Incidentally, make sure that filenames do not include any spaces.

The final asset list

The final asset list is a table that contains all the important information about each asset. Like all good reports, it must contain the vital elements of who, what, why, when, where and how.

Typical entries in an asset list table are:

- The web site page or section where the asset is to be used.
- A description of the asset (e.g. a video clip, an interview, a specification).
- The source of the asset (e.g. purchased stock images, supplied by client, commissioned works, produced in-house).
- The format of the asset (e.g. video format, audio format, format of word processed documents).
- The production tasks associated with the asset (e.g. procuring a design house, hiring a camera crew, creating an in-house animation team).
- The person responsible for gathering the asset and ensuring its compliance with all relevant laws (e.g. copyright, decency, privacy).
- The date the asset has to be produced.

The completed table is used in conjunction with project management tools to ensure their timely production and efficient document management.

Copyright

There are two copyright issues to be considered when creating multimedia projects:

- The elements that are included in the project must be fairly and legally used.
- Original work created for the project must be protected against abuse by other parties.

Copyright law relates to a whole range of multimedia and web material, such as the use of text (books, user manuals, newspaper and magazine articles), audio (musical and sound recordings), video, images (photographs, diagrams, illustrations, maps) and computer programs.   Incidentally, it also covers films, television programs, paintings, sculptures, dance routines, and other original works.

Copyright law exists to provide the creators of original work with the credit and the financial rewards for their efforts. The original work that is created can be regarded as property – the intellectual property of the creators. Like all other property, laws exist to protect copyright from theft or abuse.

Copyright rests with the owner, who can decide whether or not to grant permission for reproduction, what conditions are placed on the reproduction, what price should be paid, and what steps to take to enforce any infringements.

With only a few exceptions, unauthorised reproduction of copyright material is an offence. However, for minor infringements, the offender and the copyright owner often come to a mutual agreement on use and/or payment. Where this fails, action can be taken at a civil level, where court penalties for infringement include:

- Injunctions to prevent the offenders from using the material and/or from repeating the infringements.
- Court orders that the offenders deliver up infringing material to the copyright owners.
- Awards of damages to the copyright owners from the offenders.

For serious infringements, usually involving large-scale piracy and counterfeiting, criminal prosecution can be initiated by the police or by Trading Standards offices.   If the offending material is imported from outwith the European Economic Area, Customs and Excise can also take action.

Copyright law does not protect names and titles, as these may come under trademark registration procedures. Patents and trademarks are different issues entirely.   Copyright cannot be applied to ideas, only to the way that the idea is expressed. For example, if someone wrote an article describing a great idea for a project, someone else is entirely free to adopt the idea and turn it into a commercial work.   However, if he/she writes another article repeating the idea, it is an infringement of the idea's copyright. So, the idea itself is not protected, but the way that the idea is documented is protected.

Using other material

The purchase of a copyrighted work, such as a book, CD, video, or image, does not provide any permission for the use or reproduction of its contents, unless this is specifically allowed for in the purchase (e.g. a CD of royalty-free images).   Even where certain permissions are granted, any use beyond that already authorised requires extra permission.

While professionals rarely react to their work being adopted for personal use, they will certainly take action when their photographs, film clips, audio tracks, etc are re-used in a commercial product.

What you can't do
- Direct copying, such as photocopying, scanning, OCR, saving web pages, saving images from the web, saving an image from a CD to disk, requires permission from the copyright holder.
- Indirect copying, such as typing in an article verbatim from a printed copy or a web page, is treated in the same way as direct copying.
- Changing the presentation medium, such as reproducing an article in a magazine in a web page or in a multimedia project, does not get round the law. Copyright law protects original works, regardless of their presentation medium.
- Converting a program script from one language into another language does not get round the law, as this is regarded as 'adapting' the original work.
- Downloading an image or an item of clip art and altering some colours or adding on an extra piece here or there does not get round copyright.   The original work remains and is the copyright of the person who created it. Altering someone else's work does not free it from copyright.
- Making an exact copy of another piece of work, starting from scratch, does not make the piece free from copyright. The original work is the intellectual property of its creator.
- Providing a credit for the source of an original work does not provide an escape from copyright protection.

Copyright confers 'moral rights' on the creators of certain original material, allowing them to object to the distortion or mutilation of the original.

What you can do
- Contact the copyright holder for the desired material and agree a contract that allows its use. This often involves accepting conditions and/or making a payment. In some cases, they may be happy to give written unconditional permission, if it is deemed to provide free publicity to their products, services or views.
- Contact one of the organisations that act on behalf of groups of copyright owners. If the copyright holder is represented by that organisation, it will negotiate for the owners. Copyright law does not specify what constitutes acceptable terms but other laws, such as competition laws, might be applicable in some cases. If the terms or charges are deemed to be excessive, they can be referred to the Copyright Tribunal (an independent body appointed by Government ministers).
- Use works in quantities or situations where they do not require the approval of the copyright owners. This can include research, private study, teaching and some not-for-profit activities.
- However, copying large amounts of material, or making multiple copies of specific sections of material, would almost certainly require the owner's permission.

- Take advantage of the *'fair use'* provisions that allow, for example, a few lines from a publication to be used without permission. The material should be cleared displayed as a quote and the source of the material should be correctly attributed to the copyright owner. This can become a grey area (how much is too much?) and permission should be sought if at all possible.

Another grey area is the programming scripts used on web sites and in multimedia products (HTML, JavaScript, ActionScript, Lingo, etc). A complete copy of a piece of source code, including the same commenting and the same errors and typos, may well constitute a copyright infringement. On the other hand, some simpler tasks such as displaying an error message cannot be written in a wide variety of ways and cannot reasonably be regarded as copyright material.

An alternative in some areas is the use of copyright-free sound, pictures and clip-art collections that can be purchased on CDs, DVDs and as Internet downloads. The original purchase price of the media should include a licence to reproduce it in any projects thereafter, without any further payments being required. There are many stock photographs that can be purchased in this way, although getting the appropriate image may not always be so easy.

Of course, self-created material is generally copyright-free, with the following conditions:
- Audio/video recordings and photographs must be made after obtaining any necessary permissions.
- General photographs, such as crowd scenes or country villages, present no problems.
- Rock concerts have strict bans on recordings the live performance of their artists.
- Photographs and recordings of individuals, without permission, raise questions of invasion of privacy, if not legal repercussions.
- The rich and famous have the financial/political muscle to deter unapproved recording.
- While media representations of objects are strictly controlled, there is less of a problem with creating images of the original objects. For example, there is not a problem with taking a photograph of the Eiffel Tower, or creating an original drawing of a particular brand of car.

In all cases, it is best to adopt a policy of *"better safe than sorry"* and seek permission if there is the slightest doubt over copyright ownership. The last thing that a client wants is a legal wrangle over the final product.

Obtaining copyright

Once the project is completed, the entire work and its individual elements (i.e. the written words, drawing, animations, photographs, video clips, etc) are committed to some medium such as CD-ROM or a web site. At this stage, the 1998 Copyright, Designs and Patents Act provides legal protection for computer material, as it is considered to be a *'literary'* work. This happens automatically, without any documentation being required by the creators of original works. The project does not have to be specially registered with any public body, there is no filling in of forms, paying fees, etc. In the UK, as in most of the world, copyright exists from the moment the work is produced.

The work should contain the word *'copyright'*, followed by the name of the person or organisation and the date of origin.   The use of the international copyright symbol © is not compulsory or legally required in the UK but is recommended, as it is required in some other countries. It is also useful in any future infringement proceedings, as it clearly shows the offender knew that the material was copyrighted. If certain use is permitted, this should be clearly stated in the opening pages of the project.

Of course, putting a date on a document does not prove that the date stated is genuine. The traditional method is to post a copy of the work to one's self, using registered post (to get a dated receipt). The package remains sealed until it needs to be publicly opened to prove the date of originality. For very expensive projects, the work should be deposited with a solicitor. Bear in mind that this procedure proves that the material was someone's possession at a certain time. It does not in itself provide proof of *'originality'*. However, if there is a dispute over who first produced a particular image, photograph, video clip, or whatever, the judgement goes in favour of the individual who has the earliest proof of owning/using the material.

In general, the owner of the copyright is the person who created the original material. The Copyright Licensing Association point out a distinction between those who create material in their own right and those who create material for their employer. For example, if a lecturer writes student notes in college time, the material is commissioned, paid and owned by the college. Similarly, if a multimedia designer creates material during the working day, it belongs to the company. However, any work carried out in an employee's own time, using his/her own resources, is probably the property of the individual (unless the organisation's contract with the individual explicitly states otherwise).

Copyright is regarded in the same way as any other more physical property. This means that copyright can be sold, given away, passed on to family members in a will, etc. The new owner of the copyright inherits all the rights inherent in that work. The moral rights, however, remain with the creator of the work, even where the copyright for the work has been sold or given away. The moral rights can be passed on to the creator's heirs.

Protecting copyright

For all works created from 1st January 1996 onwards, copyright law was harmonised within the European Economic Area, therefore UK law protects the copyright on different material for different timespans as below:

Published editions	– 25 years
Sound recordings	– 50 years
Literary works	– 70 years
Photographs	– 70 years
Film	– 75 years

These periods usually commence from the date of the death of the creator of the works and refer to works originating in the UK or other parts of the EEA. Where the material comes from outside the EEA, UK law provides protection for the period specified by the country of origin.

Copyright allows owners to control how the material is used. This includes

- Copying works (e.g. copying DVDs, photocopying documents, scanning photographs, tape-recording music),
- Adapting works (e.g. altering a photograph or image, translating a document/script into another language,)
- Renting or lending works (public libraries are excluded from lending restrictions)
- Displaying the work in public (e.g. through broadcasting, plays, using material on VDUs or OHPs in training sessions, quoting material during lectures or speeches).

If any of the above activities are carried out without the copyright owners permission, an infringement has occurred. The Copyright Licensing Agency run a *'Copywatch'* scheme to detect illegal copying and advice can be sought from them at 90 Tottenham Court Rd, London W1T 4LP (www.copywatch.org).

Original work created in the UK has its copyright automatically protected throughout most of the world. The UK is a member of four major international conventions on copyright and most countries of the world belong to at least one of them.

Berne Convention	The Berne Convention for the Protection of Literary and Artistic Works is administered by the World Intellectual Property Organisation (WIPO – www.wipo.org)
Rome Convention	The Rome Convention for the Protection of Performers, Producers of Phonograms and Broadcasting Organisations is also administered by WIPO (www.wipo.org).
UCC	The Universal Copyright Convention is administered by the United Nations Educational, Scientific and Cultural Organisation - (UNESCO - www.unesco.org/culture/laws/copyright/html_eng/page1.shtml). This body requires the use of the international copyright © symbol.
TRIPS	The Trade Related Aspects of Intellectual Property Rights (TRIPS), is a part of the World Trade Organisation (WTO – www.wto.org) Agreement.

Original works created in the UK are automatically copyright protected by the national laws of the countries participating in these agreements and conventions. Most countries, including Western Europe, USA and Russia, are lined up with at least one of the conventions, usually the Berne Convention or the UCC. Full details of conventions and their members are available from the Copyright Directorate (www.patent.gov.uk/copy/).

All these bodies provide some measure of international copyright protection, although the legal and financial implications of copyright action deter many individuals and small organisations.

Legal issues

Apart from copyright, which is covered later, there are a number of other important content issues:

- All the contents (text, video, graphics) must be legal.   Care must be taken over laws on Copyright, Pornography, Official Secrets, Privacy, etc.
- Contents must be accurate. Apart from the project losing credibility, the owners may fall foul of the laws of Libel, Trades Description, etc.
- While projects destined for web sites are viewed by an international audience, there would be great difficulty in another country trying to make the content subject to their laws. Nevertheless, respect for other cultures should be taken into account.   Even at its most base level, the thought of losing sales in that country should guide the decisions on screen content.

Credit should be given to all works or references used on the screen. This can be a verbal acknowledgement or, on web sites, by the provision of a link to the other's site.

Computer Graphics

By computer graphics, we mean all images that are artificially created, in contrast to images of the real world as captured by a camera (see the next chapter).

The image content may include drawings, text, and imported clip art. It may also be a hybrid image, combining drawn elements with real-world pictures imported from scanned photographs, pictures from digital cameras or still photographs captured from video sequences.

The use of images

Humankind has always used drawings and paintings to communicate - from the early cave paintings to the latest brand logo. We see graphic symbols every day and understand their meaning without thinking about them. Examples of everyday graphics include:

- Road signs (Stop, No Entry, etc.).
- Toilet signs (male and female outlines).
- *'No Smoking'* signs (a cigarette with a bar across it).
- The CND peace symbol.
- The nazi swastika.
- The communist hammer and sickle.

The list is endless, once it is given a little thought. No words have been used and sometimes the graphic is not particularly obvious - yet we are accustomed to responding to the symbolism of the graphic.

In other situations, graphics play an important informational or educational role:

- Street maps.
- The London underground map.
- Diagrams on how to assemble a model or kit furniture.
- Flowcharts for deciding on benefit entitlement.
- Car wiring diagrams.
- Cartoons demonstrating safer sex methods.

Other uses of graphics include making multimedia screens more readable (by breaking up large chunks of text) and providing brand identification (such as the McDonalds logo).

For all the reasons given above, graphics are a very important element in all multimedia productions. Some of the above examples use only black and white, while others use colour to add extra vitality to their message.

Sources of images

Before editing and making use of digital images, a source of these images must be obtained. There are several ways to acquire digital images:

- Clip art and stock images. Various web sites and software CDs maintain a wide range of simple but effective images. As always, the copyright on an image should be checked before that image is used in a product.
- Scanned images. Hand-drawn pictures can be scanned at a pinch, and if the copyright allows it, professional quality illustrations can be scanned in to the computer at a high resolution. Other items that can be scanned include photographs slides, overhead transparencies, and even some real-world 3D items.
- Digital Still Photographs. Digital cameras are covered in more detail in other chapters.
- Stop Motion captured images. In an analogue camera, pausing the tape and taking a snapshot will rarely produce an effective image. However, digital video cameras provide much more effective still images when taken as *'stop motion'*. This simply means that a single frame of the video is converted into an image for use.
- Drawn images. Relatively few users are sufficiently skilled with the mouse to draw effectively, but a stylus and graphics tablet can be very effective at drawing illustrations and such. This can also provide an authentic *'sketch'* feel to the image. Alternatively, the stylus can be used to trace existing paper images where scanning would be too slow or impractical.

Image Properties

Although the content of images may vary widely, they all have some basic properties that describe them. Firstly, every image has resolution and colour depth. Resolution describes the size of the image while colour depth describes how many colours are in the image. An image can be quite large and have few colours, or even be in black and white, while a small image may contain many colours. They are only related in the effect that they have on the final file size. Larger images mean larger file sizes, with more colours also usually resulting in larger file sizes.

An image may also have other properties such as animation or transparency.

Resolution

As the chapter on technology explained, the screen display surface can be depicted as a grid of separate picture elements (pixels). At any one moment, each element is individually controlled to display a particular colour and intensity.   Early monitor screens were constructed to display a smallish grid of a few hundred elements in each direction.   Modern monitor screens can easily handle a grid size of at least a thousand elements in each direction. The monitor's resolution is a measure of its size when measured in pixels (i.e. how many pixels in the horizontal and vertical directions).

Similarly, the resolution of a graphic image is measured in terms of the number of pixels used for the image's width and height.

A VGA monitor screen has a resolution of 640 pixels x 480 pixels.   Displaying an image of 640x480 would fill the screen.   Similarly, an 800x600 image would fill an SVGA screen.

It is generally accepted that most monitor screens display around 70 to 90 pixels per inch, so all graphic images intended to be displayed on computer monitors (i.e. web sites, kiosks, multimedia CDs) should be created to this standard.   Creating files to a larger resolution results in them being too large to be fully viewed on the screen and large resolution graphics should only be produced for printed output.

Colour Depth

The *'palette'* is the range of colours that the system is capable of displaying.   In the past, graphics cards were unable to handle large screen resolutions and large palettes at the same time - due to the slow speed of the hardware and the lack of sufficient video memory.   Even today, with faster cards and large amounts of memory on video cards, the user has to sometimes decide between having the high screen resolution screen (but only 16-bit colour) or having full colour (with less than the highest possible resolution).   Most cards can cope with both demands at a reasonable frame refresh rate, but force the user to choose a lower specification when a faster refresh rate is selected.

The table shows the most common colour depths used with graphic images.

Typical working colour schemes	
Bit Depth	Number of Colours
1-bit	2 colours (usually black and white)
2-bit	4 colours
4-bit	16 colours
8-bit greyscale	256 shades of grey
8-bit colour	256 colours
16-bit	65,536 colours
24-bit	16.7 million colours
32-bit	16.7m plus greyscale mask (alpha channel)
48-bit	4.3 billion colours
64-bit	4.3bn plus greyscale mask (alpha channel)

The 8-bit colour depth is commonly used for web graphics, while 16-bit and 24-bit depths are used for photo-realistic images. The 16-bit system is often described as *'high colour'* while the 24-bit system is described as *'true colour'*.

All graphics packages provide facilities for reducing the colour depth of an image.

Examples of reducing colour depth are:

- Reducing a true colour image to 256 colours for placing on the Internet,
- Reducing a 256-colour image to 16 colours, where the image only contains a simple logo or cartoon.

The reduction in colour depth will shrink the final file size.   In the first case, there will also be a reduction in quality. In the second case there is no loss of quality, since the image uses less colours than the range provided in the 256-colour palette.   If the image, for example, was a web button or logo with seven different colours it could be reduced to a 4-bit scheme.

The 24-bit colour system handles the screen output in a straightforward manner. A 24-bit graphics card can vary the intensity of each primary colour (red, green and blue) to 256 different levels.   Every pixel in the image requires three bytes (i.e. 24 bits), one for the intensity level of each primary colour.   Each byte stores a value from 0 to 255, representing the 256 different intensity values. The monitor screen is displayed by three guns and each gun's intensity is controlled at any one moment by the value held in the corresponding byte. Therefore, if all three values are 255, each gun's intensity is at maximum and the pixel is perceived as being white.   If all values are at zero, the guns are switched off and the pixel is perceived as being black. The setting of different values for each gun produces the 16.7 million colours (i.e. 256 x 256 x 256).   This is known as the *'RGB colour'* system and is used by JPEG files and other 24-bit file formats.

The 16-bit colour system only has 16 bits to store colour information on each pixel. Most commonly, it allocates 5 bits for red levels, 6 bits for green levels and 5 bits for blue levels.   So the range of levels used to drive each monitor gun is less than with 24-bit systems and results in a set of 65,536 different colour combinations (i.e. 32 x 64 x 32).

The 48-bit and 64-bit colour depths use 16 bits per channel for red, green, blue and alpha.   Although these colours depths are supported by the PNG format, they are still very rarely found in use.

CLUTs

The GIF format has a maximum colour depth of 256 colours and 256 different levels fit in a single byte (a third of the size of the 24-bit formats). This means that the image data cannot be directly used to control the monitor guns.

Header
Pallette
Bitmap data

The solution used by GIF and other low colour range images, is to use a pre-defined set of colour values, stored in a *'palette'* table. Each colour has a colour number or *'index'*. This table is called a *'CLUT'* (Colour Look-Up Table) and it stores a maximum of 256 values. The diagram shows the contents of a bitmap file. The header contains information about the image size, compression, etc.

The bitmap data is usually compressed, although BMP files are either uncompressed or use the lossless RLE compression system.

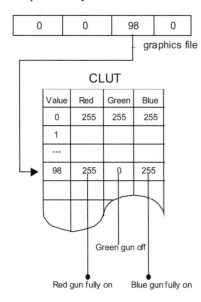

The palette values stored in the file are used to set the proportions of red, green and blue to be used in each colour in that particular image. Typically, zero would store white, while 255 would store black, 35 red, 210 blue and 185 for green. Since each colour is represented by a number, these numbers can be stored in the graphic file, along with a table that matches each colour to a table number. 256 values (ie 0 to 255) can be stored in a single byte, hence the name *'8-bit'*.

The diagram shows the process when the graphics file is read. Firstly, the lookup table is read from the file and stored in the computer's memory. Then each byte of the file (i.e. each pixel value) is read from the file and compared to the table. The corresponding red, green and blue values are used to control the monitor guns.

In the example, the third byte stores a value of 98. The values in the table switch the red and blue guns fully on, while the green gun is switched off. The result is that the pixel is displayed as a magenta colour. The two earlier pixels had a value of zero and these resulted in all the guns being switched on. This produced three white screen pixels. The limit of 256 colours to a CLUT means that its smaller file size is gained at the expense of the colour range that it supports.

Notes

- For simplicity, the example concentrates on how the lookup table works and does not show the effects of compression or of dithering.
- The range of colours currently stored in the table is called the *'palette'*.
- An image may not use all of the colours provided in the table. A CLUT may provide a palette of 256 colours but the image may only be designed using a few colours.
- Each image may use a different set of colour combinations. An image of a burning building may have a palette containing many shades of red, while an image of a gloomy dungeon may have a palette that contains mostly shades of brown and grey.
- If the hardware or software handles less colours than an image's palette, the colours not included in the palette are obtained by *'dithering'* (see below).
- Squeezing a 16.7 million colour image into a 256 colour version (e.g. converting a JPEG to a GIF) results in many colours being outside the palette's range and the colours not included in the palette may also be displayed through dithering (see below).

Compression

Often, file sizes are too big for practical use on web sites or in multimedia productions. Compression techniques. attempt to store and convey the same image information using less bytes. In some cases, a little of the image quality is sacrificed to achieve this smaller file size. Files that degrade their quality are known as *'lossy'* systems. Compression techniques include:

Run-Length Encoded	RLE is the simplest, and most limited form of compression, and works by replacing multiple occurrences ('runs') of an identical same pixel colour with a single symbol. It is great for compressing images with a limited number of colours and sharply defined lines and shapes. However, it is sometimes worse than useless when faced with a complex full-colour image.
String-table	Also called a dictionary based method, the string table compression system looks for repetitions of small patterns ('strings') of identical colours, and replaces each string with a single symbol. This makes it most suited for medium-complexity images, where minor changes in colour tone are common but there are still patterns of colour changes to be found. Lempel-Ziv-Welch (LZW) is the most widely known type of string-table compression.
Colour space	It is possible to discard a certain amount of colour information, with little or no perceived loss in quality, since the human eye is more perceptive of changes in brightness than in coloration. This method requires that the image be, at least transitorily, in a colour space that

separates colour and brightness information, such as YUV. Colour space compression is of course a lossy method of compression.

Discrete Cosine Transform	This compression system breaks the image up into blocks and transforming the data into frequencies. Then, a *'quantization'* process is performed, which removes high frequencies. This results in a lossy compression system, but one that is excellent at compressing images with a large range of subtle colour gradations.
Huffman	Also called CCITT encoding, the Huffman method uses a binary tree algorithm that results in the more commonly-occurring strings of pixels being represented by short symbols, and the more scarce strings of pixels being represented by long symbols.
Fractal	This method of compression is a complex mathematical method based on repeating patterns that manifest themselves in both larger and smaller scale within the image. This makes it a lossy compression method, and perhaps the slowest to encode decode, but results in good compression ratios.

Image format features

Although some image formats are simply ways to store and retrieve graphics data, most provide some additional functions, including but not limited to the following:

Interlacing	This technique does not store lines of raster images in sequence. Instead, it stores, perhaps, every fifth line, then fills in the gaps step by step. This allows web browsers to approximate the final image and display it before it is fully downloaded, and still display the full image once it is fully downloaded.
Animation	Some formats store multiple images, and use some method to display one of these after another. This provides a simplistic method of animation, though it is no match for a proper animation format such as Flash.
Transparency	This effect allows one colour to be used as a transparent area. The transparent area is fully transparent, and the software should clearly show whatever is 'behind' the image. This is most useful on web pages where the image can be placed seamlessly on top of a general background.
Alpha	The next logical step on from a transparency effect, is an *'alpha'*, or a graduated transparency. In other words, the background shows through parts of the image which have an alpha level, but the alpha level of each pixel determines how transparent that pixel is, i.e. how strongly the background shows through.
Gamma Correction	It is possible to include gamma correction information along with the image data itself. This makes colour matching for professional printing a slightly less tedious process.
Progressive or preview images	Many image formats include a *'preview'* image, which is a low-resolution version of the full image contained within. Some formats go further, having two or more such images at varying resolutions. This allows web users to download progressively, i.e. viewing the lowest resolution image while the second-lowest resolution image is loaded, then showing that image while the next is loaded, and so on.

Dithering

When a palette of 16.7 million colours is used, all possible colours are catered for. When that same image is reduced to a lower colour depth (e.g. down to 256 colours for web use), it cannot contain the same range of colours as previously. Dithering is a method of representing other colours that are not included in the palette, so that the image appears to contain more colours than those allowed by the range stored in the palette. A colour not in the palette is displayed as mix of pixels of other colours that are included in the palette. Consider the case of pink not being included in the image's colour palette.   Any pink areas could be represented by a checkerboard of white and red pixels. When viewed from a distance, these screen areas appear pink.

Note

Since the colour is obtained from mixing pixel colours, a single pixel cannot be dithered; only an area can be dithered.

The problem with dithering arises when a colour requires several other colours to be included in the mix. This can easily result in a *'grainy'*, *'hatched'* or other patterned effect being evident in the dithered area.

The *'Bayer'* algorithm is fast but does not produce great results and most software packages use an *'error diffusion'* method of dithering. These use the Floyd-Steinberg, Burkes, or Stucki method of dithering. The method recognises that the colours used to mix will not produce an ideal match for the colour being dithered. Therefore, it uses an error-adjusting method, where any deviation from the desired colour in a pixel is compensated for by a deviation in the opposite direction in the next pixel. This brings the dithered area closer to the desired colour and results in improved image quality.

'Screen dithering' is another form of dithering that is produced when the application package, or more commonly the hardware, is unable to handle the image's colour range.   So, for example, if a 24-bit image were viewed with a graphics card that only supported 256 colours, the additional colours are dithered.

Colour schemes

The colour scheme of an image is sometimes referred to as *'colour mode'* or *'colour space'*. The colour space used by an image tells the software how to create the colours within that image. For example, RGB colour space (the standard for nearly all screen-based image types), specifies that each pixel should have its colour determined by a set of Red Green and Blue values. Colour space should not be confused with colour depth.

From a hardware point of view, there is only one method of obtaining different colours on a monitor screen -and that is controlling the amount of emissions from the monitor tube's red, green and blue guns. From an artist or designer's point of view, other methods of controlling colour are preferable and more natural and the range of common colour schemes is outlined below.

Greyscale

Although this is not technically a colour scheme, it is a common mode of representing pixels. Each pixel simply has one byte (although some systems can use two) to represent the brightness of each pixel. No colour information is stored. This makes it one of the simplest modes

RGB

The RGB model is based on setting the values that will directly drive the red, green and blue guns. Adjusting the value of one of the guns alters that gun's brightness and changes the pixel's colour. The RGB model is also sometimes called the *'additive primary model'* as it matches the way that the human eye perceives colour, and is the method used by scanners, digital cameras, camcorders and monitors.

The data in a file that is used to store RGB information is sometimes referred to as the Red, Green and Blue *'colour channels'*. The colour space known as 'RGBA' is an extension of RGB colour, using an additional *'alpha channel'*. The alpha level of each pixel determines how transparent that pixel is.

HSL/HSB/HSV

Although the RGB model is easy to understand, it is quite difficult to make small colour adjustments with it. If the shade of a particular colour needs to be slightly altered, it might need the values of all three guns to be changed, and this can be a tricky process.

The HSL (Hue/Saturation/Lightness or Luminance or Value) model is also sometimes known as the HSB (Hue/Saturation /Brightness) model. As the name implies, it adjusts colours from three different standpoints:

Hue	the pure base colour (red, orange, yellow, green, blue and purple)
Saturation	the strength of the colour
Lightness	the brightness of the colour

There is sometimes confusion over the relationship between these factors. Each hue operates at a particular light wavelength. If the wavelength is altered, the hue changes. If light at all other wavelengths are added, the original wavelength is less dominant - i.e. its saturation level has been lowered. So, for example, pink is a red hue at a low saturation - not red at a high lightness level.

Software packages allow the user to control the image's HSB components, as an alternative to setting the RGB values. The value of the hue is often expressed (e.g. as in PhotoShop) in degrees on a colour wheel. The outer rim of the wheel starts at red, runs through to green, to blue, and back to red. Red sits at 0°, yellow at 60°, green at 120°, blue at 240° and magenta at 270°.

The values for saturation and lightness are expressed in percentages. A colour with 100% saturation is bright and vivid. The vividness diminishes as the saturation is lowered, until it appears as a shade of grey at 0% saturation. A colour with a lightness of 100% is pure white, while a 0% lightness is pure black. Intermediate values set the overall brightness of the image.

CMYK

This colour scheme is used for creating printed output, as commercial printers make a colour print based on plates that store the Cyan, Magenta, Yellow and Black (described as *'Key'*) components of an image. This colour model is not used in computer multimedia, but is important when dealing with print-based formats, since this is the method used by colour printers.

YUV

This format is also known as YCC or YCbCr. It is used in the PAL video format, but is also of use in static images. For example lossy JPEG compression uses YUV colour space to separate luminance and chrominance information before compressing.

Pantone

This is a colour catalogue used by the printing industry. As such, only print-based image formats need be concerned with Pantone colours. The actual Pantone standard uses a series of numbered coloured cards; the computer version is intended to produce identical output on the printed page to the colour viewed on the monitor. Due to hardware constraints, though, Pantone is notoriously difficult to convert accurately into printed form.

CIE

Also called 'Lab' colour, this method stores three channels of data: Red/Green; Blue/Yellow; and Luminance. This makes for a much broader range of colour; in fact pixels stored as Lab colour pixels may well be out of the range of a printer and/or monitor, and will simply be displayed as the nearest equivalent colour. This wider range of colour makes picture retouching more flexible.

Graphic Images

A graphic can be stored as a bitmap, or as a vector image. Bitmaps are pixel-based, while vector images are description-based. For multimedia purposes, the majority of uses are filled by bitmap images, although Flash is a popular medium for vector animations on the web.

Bitmaps

A bitmapped image is one in which every pixel on the screen or in the image is *mapped* to a *bit* of data. With a monochrome image, there is a direct correlation between the number of screen pixels and the number of bits to store the picture. Each bit only stores whether the pixel is white or black. With colour pictures, each pixel is represented by a group of bits that determine the pixel's colour (more accurately described as *'pixel mapped'*). Either way, the image file contains information on every pixel in the image. Bitmap formats are used to store and manipulate photographic images, either scanned or imported from digital cameras.

Vectors

A vector image is one where the data represents not pixels, but *objects*. These objects could be text, circles, squares or such. The image file does not contain data on every single image pixel.   Instead, it contains a list of drawing instructions along the lines of

'go to 50 pixels in and 60 pixels down and draw a line to the point that is 120 pixels in and 200 pixels down'.

Of course, the instructions are more complex than that, as they may contain instructions to draw a curved line, a dotted line, a thick line, and so on.   Vector formats are popular with freehand drawings, maps, diagrams, logos and cartoons, where the lines and filled areas are clearly defined.

Picture Scaling

The benefit of vector files lie in their *'scalability'*.   The user may wish to expand or shrink a picture so that it fits into a particular space in a document. This should be achieved with no loss of detail or picture distortion. The top diagram shows the result of scaling up a bitmap picture that contains a straight line to twice its height and width.   Where there was a single pixel there is now a group of four pixels.   Scaling the picture to four times its original size results in a group of 16 pixels for every original single pixel.   The result is a very *'blocky'* image and the effect is known as *'pixellation'*.   The vector file on the other hand represents

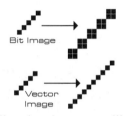

the line as *'draw a row of pixels between point A and point B'.*   Scaling the picture up still produces a single row of pixels, maintaining the fine detail.   The illustration shows a magnification of a curve produced by a bitmap, compared to one created by a vector image.

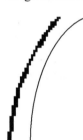

Resizing a bitmap image to twice its height and twice its width results in four times as many pixels to describe the new contents. If the file is saved, it is now four times larger. With a vector image, resizing simply means changing the vector values, not adding in any extra data. This means that the new vector file displays a much larger image, without increasing its own file size.   The vector file size will only increase if extra details are added to the picture, requiring extra data to be stored.   Vector images are described as being *'resolution independent'*.

Depending on the image, either form could be more efficient. Bitmapping is far easier to use on complex coloured images such as digitised pictures, whereas a simple piece of computer-drawn clip-art would be much more efficiently stored as a vector oriented image.

However, if a large bitmapped graphic could be easily converted to a vector image without loss of quality (which is not often the case) then the vector image would most likely be smaller in size.

Graphics software

Application packages described as *'Paint'* software usually create and manipulate bitmap images, while those described as *'Draw'* packages usually work with vector images.

Corel Draw, Adobe Illustrator, Macromedia Freehand, and Serif Draw Plus are examples of high-quality vector packages. Adobe PhotoShop, Photo-Paint, Paint Shop Pro and Picture Publisher are examples of high-quality bitmap packages. The *'Paint'* utility supplied with Windows is a typical lower-end basic facility, while many freeware and shareware packages sit between these in terms of facilities. Paint Shop Pro 6 can work with both vectors and bitmaps and most quality vector packages can *'rasterize'* (export their files in bitmap formats).   However, due to the complexity of many bitmap images, particularly photographic images, it is unusual to effectively *'trace'* (convert a bitmap image into a vector format).

Aliasing

Software packages recognise the problem with scaling edges on bitmap images. It is not noticed on vertical and horizontal edges but can be very unpleasant on diagonal and circular edges. This applies to all objects including text.

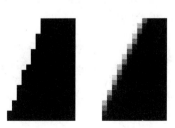

The effect is minimised by a technique known as *'anti-aliasing'*.   The diagram shows two drawings of the same diagonal edge. The one on the left was drawn without using any anti-aliasing method and has crude steps along its edge, while the other looks much smoother. The anti-aliasing technique adds intermediate pixels of shades that merge between the two main colours. If the background was white and the object was black, anti-aliasing produces pixels of varying shades of grey, to remove the hard stepped edge. If the background was blue and the object was red, it would produce additional pixels of varying shades of magenta.

Using anti-aliasing to place objects or text into images with a large colour depth presents no problems and improves the overall image quality. However, it will present problems with file size with images of low colour depth. For instance, a simple two-colour title only requires a 1-bit colour depth (with the bit set on for the foreground colour and set to off for the background colour). Since anti-aliasing introduces extra pixels with intermediate colours, the range of colours used has been increased. A simple 2-colour text may now use, for example, 32 different colours. This increase in colour depth results in a larger file size. Another problem with anti-aliasing is its effect on transparent GIFs used for the web (see the chapter on web site creation).

File sizes

The final storage requirement for a bitmap image depends on its resolution and colour depth. The size of an uncompressed file is calculated thus:

File Size = Bit Depth x Screen Resolution / 1024

Dividing by 1024 converts the answer into kilobytes. For very large files, the answer can be divided by a further 1024 to get the answer in megabytes.

Some example file sizes are:

An 8-bit image that fills a VGA screen would require
1 x 640 x 480 = 307,200 bytes
An uncompressed true colour image at 800x600 requires
3 x 800 x 600 /1024/1024 = 1.373MB
An uncompressed 1280 x 960 true colour image requires
3 x 1280 x 960 = 3,686,400 bytes or 3.515MB

Since files sizes can be very large, they are usually stored in a file format that provides compression.

File Formats

As for bitmapped images, the only difference between one file format and another is the way the data is compressed, and how much extra information is needed, such as height and width of the picture, number of colours, etc. This information is normally stored in a portion of the file called a 'header'.

The most common graphic file formats on a PC are:

GIF : The acronym 'GIF' is meant to be pronounced as 'jiff', but is usually pronounced 'giff'. GIF was designed by Compuserve for fast transfer of graphics data over modems, and stands for Graphics Interchange Format. It uses LZW compression on graphic images, making them smaller for faster transfer over the Internet. Now a very common file format, GIF files can be found on web sites and graphics packages everywhere.

GIF files can have a colour range of any power of 2 - up to 2 to the power of 8. This means it could have 2, 4, 8, 16, etc. up to 256 colours. This does not mean that all those colours must be used, however. The 256 colour limitation limits its ability to store photographic images with any realism, although GIFs containing photographic images are often used satisfactorily on the web.

There are two GIF formats - GIF87a and GIF89a. The GIF87a format is the most common and it supports transparency (of a single colour) and interlacing. In addition, the GIF89a format supports animation.

The type of compression used by GIF files is lossless, making it an ideal format for storing plain images such as logos, cartoons, etc. On the other hand, photo-realistic images lose a lot of quality from being converted from 24-bit format to 8-bit format and JPEG is usually the better option in this case (see below).

GIF files use a CLUT (colour lookup table) as explained earlier.

Interlaced GIFs and Transparent GIFs are covered in the chapter on web site creation.

PNG : Unisys owns the patent for the LZW compression used in GIF files and this produced a demand for royalties for the use of GIF files. In response, the Portable Network Graphics standard was produced for transferring bitmap graphics files over CompuServe and the Internet. It improves on GIFs a wider range of colour depths and has its own 'zlib' lossless compression system. Although a modern format, it surprisingly does not support animation.

PCX : Nobody seems to know what PCX stands for, other than that the first two letters are for 'Personal Computer'. PCX files use run-length encoding (RLE), which means that simple computer-generated pictures are stored fairly efficiently. It is comparatively inefficient at storing digitised or complicated pictures. Nonetheless, it has been around for some time and is now fairly common. PCX pictures may be found in monochrome (2 colours), 16 colours, 256 colours, 24-bit true colour, or even, rarely, in 4 colours. PCC files are PCX files by another name though they are usually smaller, intended for clipart.

TIFF : The Tagged Image File Format originated on the Mac computer, and was designed for use with desktop publishing. It is a complicated standard, so much so that some alleged TIFF-using packages may not import TIFFs from other packages. It can use a variety of compression schemes, and can have any number of colours, as well as a huge array of options, used by putting 'tags' in the file header. The more exotic 'tags' cause TIFF readers to occasionally *'screw up'* on TIFF files. TIFF files tend to be used more for DTP than multimedia.

BMP : BMP stands for Bit-Mapped Picture and is the Windows standard bitmap graphics file.   BMP files are used for the background wallpaper in Windows. It is uncompressed, meaning that simple pictures will occupy much more file space than is necessary. It also means that complicated, true colour pictures do not require a sophisticated decoder to display them. A damaged BMP file means image distortion may occur, while corruption to most compressed files means complete unusability. There is also another format called the RLE format, which is a compressed version of BMP, but this is little used. Finally, a BMP file may be found with the extension DIB, for Device Independent Bitmap, but is basically the same as a BMP file.

JPEG : When the Joint Photographic Experts Group was appointed by the CCITT to design a graphic compression and storage scheme, the JPEG (pronounced *'jay-peg'*) file format was eventually created. It uses *'lossy'* compression, which means that slight detail is lost during compression. The level of detail loss is controllable, and a substantial space saving can be made even with very little detail loss. The JPEG compression standard is a complicated process involving several levels, and at first specialised hardware was needed to perform the process. There is a lossless version of JPEG, but this may require the extra hardware. JPEG files are stored in true 24-bit colour, and the JPEG scheme is much less efficient in storing images of any lower colour range. Although the system is lossy, it is better at storing photographic images than the GIF format, as the losses are small in comparison to the loss of quality in reducing the colour depth of photographs to fit the GIF 8-bit depth.

JPEG files are 24-bit, with a byte allocated to each of the three primary colours. This drops the need for a CLUT, as the red, green and blue monitor guns have a direct feed each of 256 different levels.

WMF : The Windows Meta-File format is a comparatively simple vector oriented format born through the Windows interface. It is very effective for DTP. Like most vector formats, it is little used for multimedia.

EPS : Encapsulated PostScript. This file format uses the standard PostScript language to talk to PostScript printers and is used for high-quality output.   It is independent of the make of printer as all Postscript printers produce exactly the same text and graphic images when given the same PostScript commands. Most video cards are not equipped to display files in the PostScript language and it is common to embed pre-prepared EPS images into other applications such as DTP documents.

CDR : The vector file saved by the Corel Draw application package with a .CDR extension. Corel Draw is also capable of saving its files in a variety of formats such as EPS, PCX, etc.

CLP : The file saved in the Windows Clipboard when the user uses cut and paste operations or presses the PrintScreen button.   The Windows Clipboard viewer allows the image to be saved away as a .CLP file. This file can be recovered from disk and placed back in the clipboard at any time.

TGA : The bit-mapped file format used by Fantavision's Targa systems. It is mostly used for 24-bit colour, though it may also be 8-bit colour, or even monochrome. Targa files can be run-length compressed, which works well with monochrome and some 8-bit files, or uncompressed, which is most useful with 24-bit files.

HPGL : The Hewlett Packard Graphics Language is most common format for use with plotters.

JSP/SVG : The JSP (Java Server Page) technology is Sun's answer to Microsoft's ASP system. Using JSP, it is possible to dynamically create SVG (Scalable Vector Graphics) files. This can be done relatively easily since the SVG format is basically a text file containing XML tags describing an image, in similar manner to an HTML file. This is useful in creating dynamic content, such as maps, graphs, and charts, as they can be generated according to any parameters specified by the user. However, it requires that the browser has a plug-in installed to handle SVG files. Since SVG is a vector graphics format, it is not suitable for photographs or similarly complex images, despite being able to include effects such as embossing, lighting, gaussian blur and so on.

EXE : Some packages are able to create actual executable files from graphic images. In order for these to work, the package must incorporate some executable code, and integrated graphics data. These were most common in the days of DOS, when the user could not simply double-click a graphic file to load up the appropriate viewing program. The main problems with EXE graphics is that they cannot be used on non-PC computers, and cannot easily be imported into other applications. Some presentation packages can create EXE files for Windows, which integrate multiple images and other media as well.

MNG : The Multiple Image Network Graphics format is based on the PNG format, but as the name suggests it is based around the concept of multiple images in one file. MNG takes this further than the animated GIF format, but stops short of being suitable for video files. For example, it includes delta compression techniques as well as being able to use lossy or lossless compression, but does not have the motion compression used by MPEG files.   It can include loops, delays between frames, moving sprites, transparency, CRCs to detect corrupt files, and other features. This makes it excellent for viewing by users on relatively slow modem connections, although it is not expected to replace Flash animations except for the smallest animations.

PICT : The PICT format originates from Apple Mac computers. It can be either raster or vector, although the majority of PICT files are of the raster variety. Only limited number of packages on the PC can make use of PICT images, so it may be advisable to convert them into a more compatible format.

PSD : This is just one example of a proprietary file format that is used by a specific program. PhotoShop is the package that uses PSD files, but Paint Shop Pro uses a similar format called PSP. Both formats are pre-production formats, intended for use during creation and editing of graphics. However, PSD files are also sometimes used by professional print companies. PSD files include a wide range of features, the most important of which is the layering capability which allows multiple image or effect layers which all add up to create a final image.

File type	Type	Print or Screen	Colours	Compression	Features
GIF	Raster	Screen	1 to 8 bit	String-table	Interlacing, animation, transparency
PNG	Raster	Screen	1 to 64 bit	String-table	Alpha channels, gamma correction, interlacing
PCX	Raster	Screen	1 to 24 bit	Run-Length	
TIFF	Raster with tags	Print	1 to 32 bit	Various	Tiling, alpha channel, proprietary tags, CMYK and other colour spaces, etc
BMP	Raster	Both	1 to 24 bit	None or RLE	
JPEG	Raster	Screen	1 to 24 bit	Chromatic, DCT & Huffman	Progressive
WMF	Vector	Print	16/24 bit	None	
EPS	Vector	Print	24 bit	None	Preview image
CDR	Vector	Print	24 bit	None	
CLP	Raster or Vector	Screen	1 to 32 bit	None	
TGA	Raster	Screen	1 to 32 bit	None or RLE	
HPGL	Vector	Print	24 bit	None	
SVG	Vector	Screen	24 bit	None	
EXE	Raster or Vector	Screen	Variable	Variable	
PICT	Raster or Vector	Screen	24/32 bit	None, RLE, or JPEG	Alpha
PSD	Raster or Vector	Both	1 to 24 bit	None	Layers, alpha, effects, watermarks, preview image, etc
MNG	Raster	Screen	1 to 64 bit	String-table	Alpha channels, gamma correction, interlacing

Image applications

Different image file formats are better suited for different purposes. For this reason, it is wise to look at the final output of the project, as well as the methods that will be used in producing the final product, in determining which file formats to make use of.

Some of the more common areas using digital images are:

Screen based image applications

Web pages These make use of various types of graphics. All browsers recognise GIF and JPEG images (suitable for low and high colour images, respectively), but depending on the plugins installed they may also make use of PNG, MNG, SVG or other image types. The SVG format is generally only used with server-based dynamic web pages, and anything other than GIF and JPEG will rely on the user installing the appropriate plugin.

Intranet pages These are generally similar to web pages. However, on an Intranet, it is much easier to ensure that image files will have the appropriate browser support, making file types such as PNG or SVG a more attractive proposition.

Presentations The most common presentation format is the Powerpoint PPT format, which can import a variety of image formats for use in the presentation.

Software Applications Some computer programs make use of graphics in their interfaces. On a Windows PC, the obvious choice for these images is its native BMP format, which is supported by most programming APIs.

Digital Newsletter Some digital newsletters are published as web pages, in which case they should be treated as such with regard to file types to use. However, others may be provided as PDF files, which make best use of imported TIFF files; or as EXE files containing images.

Print based image applications

Advertisements Small adverts are best created in a high-end graphics package such as PhotoShop, using the PSD file format. Some print companies will accept these PSD files, while others may require that they are converted to TIFF, PDF or other format first. Some may even require a high-quality printed master copy. Large adverts, such as full-page or mult-page spreads, should be designed in a more appropriate package such as Corel Draw.

Magazine covers These are intended to be eye-catching, and therefore they should have accurate colour representation and high-quality images, with additional printing information such as 'bleed' (the paper edges which are discarded during cropping of the pages). This can be provided by a professional graphics package such as PhotoShop.

Posters These are larger scale than almost any other printed format. As such they require the highest quality of image, and should have accurate colour matching. This indicates that a high-end graphics package should be used; even PhotoShop will struggle with huge, high-quality, high-colour images, so specialised software might be required.

Books The majority of book data is text, but most books contain at least a few images. The type of text file used (e.g. Word DOC) will determine which image formats can be imported. However, TIFF is the most reliable format to use in this respect, since it contains dpi information that will determine the image size exactly within the page.

Printed newsletters If the newsletter is printed in-house, then the page images should be converted into a printer-based format such as PostScript or HPGL for the printer to deal with. For outside printing, again the most likely candidates are PSD, PDF or TIFF images, though this will vary from printer to printer.

Print and Screen optimisation

Although Alpha transparency, layers and such effects can be useful in the development of an image, the final image displayed on a monitor or printed to the page has no such information in it, so it is largely irrelevant.

Other details, however, are more important.

- Gamma correction, by its nature, is intended for screen-based images, and should be optimised for the particular display device in use. The Adobe Gamma software can create a gamma profile that will allow the gamma level to be set so that the actual image on screen is shown as it was intended.

- Dithering will be necessary to display colour images on a low-colour display, or to print colour or grayscale images to a black-and-white printer. This can be left to the printer driver, but if the designer wants more control over the process then the image can be dithered to black and white, using whichever algorithm and settings are available in the editing package.

- Interlacing and progressive download features might be desirable in any media that is to be used on the web, due to their greater accessibility to those with slow connections.

Resolution Concerns

As explained earlier in this chapter, the resolution of an image intended for screen-based applications should take into account the expected resolution of the screen on which it is to be displayed. Image resolution when stored on a disk is measured in pixels per inch (ppi), and this corresponds to either the pixel resolution on screen, or the dot resolution (dpi) on paper when printed.

As explained in the *'Computer Technology'* chapter, printers have a vastly higher resolution than a monitor. When working with images for print, the developer must consider at which resolution to create his work. This must take into account the following:

- The resolution of the output device. There is no point designing images at an equivalent to 600dpi if it is to be printed on a 300dpi printer. Note, also, that some older commercial printing systems work in 'lines per inch' (lpi) instead of dpi. Such a printing device may have greater horizontal resolution than vertical resolution, and this may need to be taken into account to avoid images looking 'stretched'.

- The colour or greyscale capacity of the output device. If a colour or greyscale image is to be printed on a black-and-white printer, it must use dithering (as explained earlier). Since this will replace colours with patterns of black and white, a colour photographic quality image will lose much of its detail unless the image's resolution is considerably poorer than the output device's resolution.

- Storage and manipulation concerns. Consider that a 600dpi image of size 8"x11" (roughly an A4 page) will have over 31 million dots. If each dot is to correspond to a single pixel in a colour image file, then this would mean a file of 93 megabytes before compression. At 1200dpi this increases to nearly 400MB per page. Although most modern computers could store several such images, an entire magazine would quickly fill an entire hard disk, and such images would be very slow to work with.

Graphics Creation

This chapter does not attempt to be a tutorial for graphic artists. The issues of imagination, construction, perspective, etc are the subjects of another book - or a college course. This chapter, however, looks at the main technical and practical issues involved in creating graphic images.

The main considerations when creating graphics are:

Format type

Bitmaps can store photographic images while vector graphics consist of many drawn components. Bitmaps provide a range of manipulation options that are not available to vector images but lose much of their quality when scaled (see below). Vector images are scaleable with no loss of quality and would be the likely choice for creating symbols, line drawings and logos.

Elements
Unless the image is from a real-world source (i.e. scanned photograph, picture from a digital camera, or other bit image), it is constructed from a collection of squares, rectangles, circles, polygons, lines, arcs or bezier curves.

Content
The elements have certain properties that can be altered for the maximum impact. These are element size (i.e. circle diameter, line width, rectangle dimensions) and appearance (e.g. box or circle, colour, line type -plain, dotted).

Location
Where the graphics appear on the screen and what proportion of the screen they occupy will depend on the nature of the final application. Large graphics are suitable where they have a crucial role in the presentation (e.g. a car repair program would use large and clear diagrams). Small graphics should be used where they should not distract the viewer from the main presentation. Similarly, graphics backgrounds should not overpower the foreground message.

Perspective
The monitor screen is two-dimensional; all screen content has only width and height. To provide the illusion of depth, images can be made to appear as if they recede into the background. The left box in the diagram has a front panel and rear panel of the same size. The rear panel in the right-hand box is smaller, which is perceived by the viewer as depth.

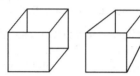

Layer
Graphics layering allows one item to partially obscure another. In the boxes above, the front square is layered over the other lines and partially hides them from view.

Graphics importation

Multimedia authoring packages do not generally provide more than elementary painting features that are sufficient for basic boxes and lines. For all other purposes, images are created in dedicated fully featured graphics packages and the finished item is imported into the authoring project. The file types allowed by the authoring package should be checked, as it is unlikely that every file format is supported by the authoring package. This may require, for example, exporting a Corel Draw image as a BMP file to be acceptable by the authoring package.

Graphics manipulation

The facilities offered by graphics packages vary and the most common manipulations are:

Scaling
The sides of the image can be pulled or squeezed so that it shrinks or expands to fill a given area. While this poses no problems for vector images, bitmaps will lose detail on shrinking and will become *'blocky'* when expanded.

Filling
The diagram shows a number of squares that have been filled with either a plain solid colour, a fountain fill (e.g. linear, radial or conical gradations) or a pre-determined pattern (e.g. bricks, curtains, granite).

Transitions
As with text transitions, the graphic can be written to the screen in a pre-defined way such as being drawn form the left or filling in from the centre outwards.

Clipping/cropping
Images often contain more detail than is required. This distracts the viewer from the essential detail and occupies more disk space than is necessary. The image can be clipped or cropped. This brings the picture in from the top or bottom, or left and right borders. The example shows the continent of Africa being taken from a map of the globe.

Rotating
The text can be rotated from its normal horizontal axis to any degree and in any direction. This can be used for visual effect or can be used to align the text along the outline of an object.

Reflections
A mirror image of an object can be in either the vertical plane, as in the example, or in the horizontal plane. It is used for visual effect, or to save drawing time by drawing half of a symmetrical shape and creating an identical mirror image of the other half.

Reflections
Ｒeflections

Morphing
This takes two images and creates a set of intermediate images, showing the stages of transformation from one to the other. Morphing can be applied to objects (e.g. swords are turned into ploughshares) or photographs (e.g. Tony Blair turns into Margaret Thatcher).

Getting started with Computer Graphics

The creation of computer graphics requires a certain level of hardware as well as the correct software.

Graphics hardware

Obviously, certain image-related equipment such as scanners, digital cameras and so on, will be desirable if not essential. However, the PC itself must also be of sufficient specification. This is explained in better detail in the *'Computer Basics'* chapter, however it is worth mentioning that working with extremely high resolution images for printing, can take up a surprising amount of hard disk space and memory. Of course, this is not a problem for designing graphics intended for the computer screen. As always, consult the manual of the software in use for minimum specifications, but keep in mind the type of image you will be dealing with.

Furthermore, for print-based formats, the final image will have to be printed. If this is done by a third party, then no extra equipment is strictly necessary, although at least a basic printer is recommended to preview the work quickly without having to send it to the print company. There are a number of colour technologies available:

- Colour dot matrix printers are really only suitable for draft copies, and even at that they are outdated.
- A simple colour inkjet is sufficient for some of the lower end computer graphics, such as one-offs for entertainment value, letterheads or so on. Special paper types can make some of the higher end inkjets almost as good as the more professional types, at much lower cost.
- For any serious design work, a more powerful printer is essential. Colour lasers and solid ink printers are expensive, but can print good quality relatively fast, for larger print runs such as pamphlets.
- At the top end of the scale, however, some serious hardware becomes necessary. Dye sublimation uses vaporised ink to create *'continuous tone'* colour, rather than dots, so that the colours can blend more subtly. There are inkjets which employ similar technologies, and these can be a good halfway between the two technologies both in terms of cost and quality. Dye sublimation is slow to print, however, and is not suitable for high-volume printing.

Graphics software

The most widely used professional graphics packages are Adobe PhotoShop and JASC Paint Shop Pro. Both of these packages are capable of producing high quality images in a wide variety of screen-based and print-based formats. However, there is other software on the market, specifically aimed at certain computer graphics areas.

For example, web graphics such as buttons and bars tend to be smaller, with fewer colours, crisper, and simpler. Packages such as Adobe ImageReady and Macromedia Fireworks are specifically intended for the creation of web graphics, and there are plenty of small, simple packages to create '3d effect' web buttons from text.

At the other end of the spectrum, there are packages specifically for print based media. Some of these are almost an entire DTP package in themselves. For example CorelDraw is a graphics suite based mainly on vector images, which makes it excellent for creating whole pages of print media, including plain or stylised text. There are also specialist graphics packages such as Visio, Corel Designer, and so on, which are intended for a specific purpose such as technical graphics or plans.

The reason for the popularity of PhotoShop and Paint Shop Pro, perhaps, is its relatively low price tag, wide range of functionality, and general purpose ability that allows it to be used, with varying degrees of practicality, in almost any area of computer graphics.

The examples in this section use Adobe PhotoShop version 6, although the techniques used are common to virtually all major graphics packages. PhotoShop is a high-end graphics package aimed at professional graphic artists, and a cut-down and simplified version called PhotoShop Elements is available for the lower end of the market. Elements has easier access to some functions and effects, as well as a more user-friendly interface, but at the cost of the more advanced publishing related functions such as CMYK, Proofing, Gamut and so on.

Paint Shop Pro uses a different interface to PhotoShop, but as its main competitor there are a number of similarities. Where Elements or Paint Shop Pro differs largely from the text it will be explained.

Using PhotoShop

PhotoShop's interface is as shown in the illustration. There are numerous versions of PhotoShop in use, but they all follow the same basic principles, with each successive edition simply introducing new features.

Like all Windows applications, the top of the PhotoShop window consists of the window bar, containing the Maximise, Minimise, and Close buttons; and the menu bar. Underneath the menu bar is the PhotoShop *'Options bar'*, which contains various options relating to the tool currently selected at any time.

The main working area in PhotoShop can contain one or more graphic image windows, as well as extra tool or information windows, called *'palette windows'*. The example shows a single image window containing the file 'OWL.JPG', accompanied by the Layers palette, the History palette, the Color palette and the Navigator palette windows. The column of icons on the left is the *'toolbox'*. There is also an optional *'status bar'* at the bottom of the window, which is shown in this example. In fact, all of the windows are optional and can be hidden if desired.

PhotoShop Elements also has a toolbar alongside the options bar, and will start up with a dialog box allowing a variety of options to begin editing. These include creating a new image, open an existing image, pasting in an image from clipboard, and acquiring an image from scanner.

Paint Shop Pro has a toolbar in place of the PhotoShop options bar, which contains the most common commands such as load, save, and print. Paint Shop Pro also has a different toolbox and palette windows.

Creating a new image

Choosing the *'New'* option from the *'File'* drop-down menu opens the dialog box shown in the illustration. The Image Size is usually entered as pixel values and the example shows a size that is a normal 1024x768 super-VGA screen. The Resolution value is usually set to 28.346 pixels per cm (72 pixels per inch), this being the most common

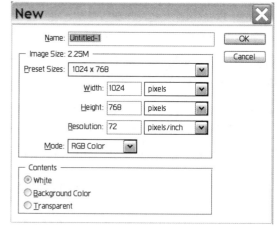

monitor resolution. Higher figures are only necessary for obtaining more detailed graphics intended for printed output.

The *'Mode'* setting decides the image's colour depth. Paletted colour modes such as 256-colour are called '*Indexed Color*' in PhotoShop, but a new image cannot be created in this mode. RGB color, as shown here, is the standard and refers to 24-bit colour. Note that a number of PhotoShop's tools and effects only work with 24-bit images. If necessary, the file can be created at this depth and reduced to 256 colours before saving.

Clicking the *'OK'* button creates an image window within the main work area. In the main window shown earlier, the image "VENICE.JPG" is sitting in the main work area, displayed at full size. This image area becomes the default background layer of an image (see next).

Using layers

Before discussing all the objects and shapes that can be placed in the image editing area, it is best to understand some of the practical limitations of working with bitmaps.

Consider the image displayed here. It has a background photograph, a foreground photograph and some text.

To create this image in a traditional (non-layered) paint package, the background image is loaded and the text is laid on top. As the text is fixed in position in the work frame, it permanently obscures the content underneath it. The data for the final picture only stores one colour value for each pixel. The white pixels of the text replace all previous values stored for those pixels. The user can move the text around, to find the best position but, once the text position is set, the user cannot go back and move it again.   Similarly, if the font size needs to be increased or decreased or the type style needs to be changed, this can cause major adjustments.   If the need for an adjustment is immediately spotted, the user can use the 'Undo' facility, to revert to the layout before the text was fixed in position, and a second attempt at adding text can be made.   However, the need for the alteration may only become apparent after a further series of additions to the image, such as the example of adding a face to the image.   Now, the text can only be altered by initiating multiple undos, but these remove all the other additions.

Clearly, then, this is not satisfactory except for the simplest of graphics.

Major applications such as PhotoShop and Paint Shop Pro solve this problem by allowing the user to place different objects on separate layers.   This is similar to the technique used in the early cartoons, where the background was painted on one sheet of transparent plastic, midground scenes were painted on another transparent sheet and yet another transparent sheet had the foreground figures painted on it.   When the sheets were laid on top of each other, the entire picture was visible.   Now, if one scene was altered, it had no effect on the other layers.   Extra layers could be added, layers could be removed and layers could be modified - all independently of each other.   The top-most layer will still obscure some of the contents of the lower layers, but the layer contents remain intact nonetheless.

The computer application equivalent is to store the various layers of the picture as if they are separate pictures.   Each layer can be viewed on its own, or along with one or more other layers.   Now, each layer has its own values for every pixel and these can be changed within any one layer at any one time.   When the entire design is finished, the layers can be amalgamated to produce a single raster such as a JPEG file.   This is known as 'flattening' the image and it is only at this stage that the final decision is made on the value of each pixel in the final image.   Where two layers have content in the same area of the screen, the values for the pixels at the upper layer are used in the final image.

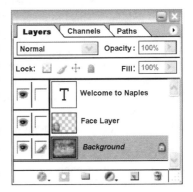

The illustration shows the Layer Palette with three layers being worked on.   Note the chequered area in the middle layer - this represents a transparent area, allowing the background to show through in those parts of the image.

The layer palette in Paint Shop Pro looks different, for example it has no layer preview, but it performs much the same job.

Creating new layers

When a new file is opened, the software will create the first layer automatically.   To add an extra layer, choose *New / Layer* from the *'Layers'* menu or click the *'Create a New Layer'* icon in the Layers palette. Always name the layers when using multi-layered images, as this helps the user recognise individual layers.

Layers can be named by right-clicking on the layer in the palette and selecting '*Layer Properties*'.   The layers Palette can be displayed at any time, by choosing the *'Layers'* option from the *'Window'* menu.   Any layer except the background layer can be dragged and dropped into a new position in the order of layers, so that is contents take a higher precedence in the final flattening process.

The other main benefit of layers is the ability to blend the contents of the layers for added effects.   Note how the first letter of *'Naples'* and a section of the face blend in the same space.   This is a very powerful tool and is covered later.

Layers are essential for complex images but the user should get into the habit of always using them for all but the most simple of compositions.

Layer Styles

Any layer, whether vector or raster, may have a Layer style applied to it.   A layer style consists of a number of '*Blending Options*' that determine how the layer is displayed in the image.   By default, none of the blending options are selected.

However, the user may set any number of layer options, or select a Layer Style from the Style palette, which will apply one of a number of pre-defined sets of blending options.   Right clicking on a layer and selecting '*Blending Options*', or double-clicking on a vector layer, will bring up the Layer Style dialog box, as shown.

The example shows the settings for a layer that has had the predefined style '*Striped Cone*' applied to it.

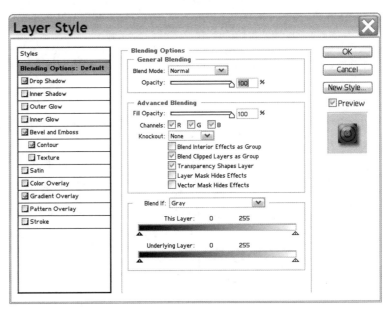

The Blending Options include:

- Default Options. The layer may be blended using any of the paint modes, explained later in this chapter, such as Dissolve, Lighten, Darken, Dodge or Burn.
- Drop Shadow and Inner Shadow. The Drop Shadow option, as the name suggests, has the effect of rendering a 'shadow' of the layer below it. Inner shadow is the opposite, placing a shadow inside the layer. This makes it appear as if the layer contents are dug out of the image.
- Outer Glow and Inner Glow. These options have the effect of slightly lightening a small area around the layer edges, either inside or outside of the actual layer contents.
- Bevel and Emboss. This option add shadows and highlights around the edges of the layer in such ways as to make the layer contents look bevelled, or embossed. This option has sub-options called '*Contour*' and '*Texture*', which are used to add a profile to the bevelling, or to use texture-based embossing.
- Satin. A colour is applied to the inside edges of the layer contents, with certain edges receiving more colour than others. Used properly, this can make a layer look like ruffled material.
- Color Overlay, Gradient Overlay, and Pattern Overlay. These options are all used to replace the layer contents with a colour, a colour gradient, or a pattern. However, all of these can be semi-opaque, allowing the original content to appear through the colour, gradient or pattern.
- Stroke. This option is used to place a border round the edges of the layer contents. This border can be on the outside or inside of the layer contents, and can be a colour, gradient or pattern.

A combination of these options, with various settings for each, produces a wide variety of effects. Some of the more useful combinations have been saved as Layer Styles that can be accessed through the Styles palette. These are split into several groups of styles, for buttons, image layers, text layers and so on.

PhotoShop Elements only allows its own built-in styles, with no user editing of blending properties. Paint Shop Pro has no direct equivalent to Layer Styles, but it does allow layers to be displayed in different Blending Modes such as Darken, Lighten, Hue, Saturation, Dodge, Burn and so on.

The Shortcuts bar

Unlike many other applications, including Paint Shop Pro, PhotoShop has no toolbar. Instead, all commonly used options such as saving or Undo are accessed by the menu bar or by keyboard shortcut. PhotoShop Elements is a cut-down and simplified version of PhotoShop aimed at the lower end of the graphics market. It has a '*Shortcuts bar*' as shown below, that contains buttons for easy access to common functions.

The first icon is a link to Adobe's web site, with the next three options providing the usual functions – create a new image, load an existing image, or save an image (either a newly created image or one that was loaded and modified).

The fifth icon is '*Save for Web*' and brings up a window showing how the image will look in a web browser.

The next two icons are used to print the image, and to display a print preview. The following set of icons are used to cut, copy, and paste, and to step forward and back in the edit History (see below).

The last two buttons are show/hide rulers, and open the help pages.

Finally, palettes such as the File Browser, History and Effects are included in the Shortcuts bar in Elements, while in PhotoShop they are shown as floating palettes inside the main window. The earlier illustration of the PhotoShop main window showed three palettes - Layers, History and Colors.

Palettes are useful, but can obscure the image window. Palettes can be made visible or invisible in Photoshop by selecting the appropriate palette from the '*Window*' menu. Note that some palettes share a window with other palettes and only one can be displayed at a time. In Elements, because the palettes are on the Shortcut bar, they are accessed simply by clicking on the palette name.

Other aids

Before beginning to create graphics, there are two more points of support.

The '*Help*' facilities are extensive and have a comprehensive Index.

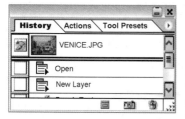

The other, indispensable, tool is the '*Undo*' facility. This can be used for all kinds of purposes such as correcting mistakes and, when used in conjunction with the '*redo*' facility, switching back and forward to compare the effect of a particular modification (i.e. looking at the '*before*' and '*after*').

PhotoShop (but not Paint Shop Pro) also provides a '*History*' palette that allows the user to jump back and forward through various states of editing. The History can also be used by the '*History Brush*' tool in PhotoShop to restore only some portions of the image to the previous state.

The Toolbox

PhotoShop has a number of paint tools, which are displayed in a 'toolbox' that is normally along the side of the window. A brief summary of these tools is given below.

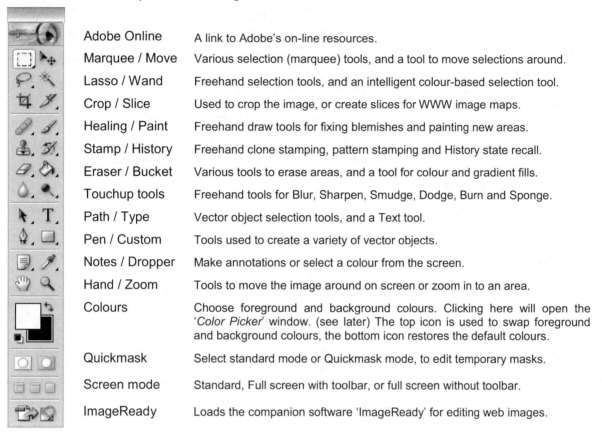

	Adobe Online	A link to Adobe's on-line resources.
	Marquee / Move	Various selection (marquee) tools, and a tool to move selections around.
	Lasso / Wand	Freehand selection tools, and an intelligent colour-based selection tool.
	Crop / Slice	Used to crop the image, or create slices for WWW image maps.
	Healing / Paint	Freehand draw tools for fixing blemishes and painting new areas.
	Stamp / History	Freehand clone stamping, pattern stamping and History state recall.
	Eraser / Bucket	Various tools to erase areas, and a tool for colour and gradient fills.
	Touchup tools	Freehand tools for Blur, Sharpen, Smudge, Dodge, Burn and Sponge.
	Path / Type	Vector object selection tools, and a Text tool.
	Pen / Custom	Tools used to create a variety of vector objects.
	Notes / Dropper	Make annotations or select a colour from the screen.
	Hand / Zoom	Tools to move the image around on screen or zoom in to an area.
	Colours	Choose foreground and background colours. Clicking here will open the 'Color Picker' window. (see later) The top icon is used to swap foreground and background colours, the bottom icon restores the default colours.
	Quickmask	Select standard mode or Quickmask mode, to edit temporary masks.
	Screen mode	Standard, Full screen with toolbar, or full screen without toolbar.
	ImageReady	Loads the companion software 'ImageReady' for editing web images.

PhotoShop Elements has a similar toolbox, but some of the more advanced options are removed while there are additional buttons for quick access to typical effects. For example, Elements' toolbox includes a Vertical Type tool, an Impressionist Brush, and a Red Eye removal brush; but removes the Slice tools, Stamp and History brushes, Path and Pen tools, Notes, Quickmask, Screen mode and ImageReady link.

The Paint Shop Pro toolbox also contains several similar tools, which all perform in a similar manner although the interface differs from that of PhotoShop. For example, Paint Shop Pro's Flood Fill tool performs the same function as both the Paint Bucket and Gradient fill tools in PhotoShop. There are some different tools, and these are explained later in the chapter.

The Options Bar

Every tool in the PhotoShop Toolbox can perform its function in a range of subtly different ways. In order to control the exact behaviour of any given tool, there is an 'Options Bar', normally located immediately below the menu bar, which will display the options available for any given tool. For example, the following shows the left hand side of the Options bar when the Paintbrush tool is selected.

This shows various Paintbrush options, such as the brush style selected, the paint mode, the opaque level and whether to use Wet Edges. Other tools will have other options dependent on the operation of the particular tool.

On the right hand side of the Options bar is a 'Palette Well', a small grey box into which can be dragged any of the palettes, such as the Layer, Color or History palettes. Depending on the tool selected, there may also be a 'Brush Palette' icon on the right hand side of the Options bar. This will open a popup menu with a varying number of options to control how the brush-like tools are used. See the paintbrush tool, later in this chapter, for more details.

Paint Shop Pro does not use an Options bar; instead, popup dialog boxes appear when the user selects a tool. These dialog boxes control generally the same kind of options that are available in PhotoShop's Options Bar.

Mode selection

One drop down menu that is available for most tools in PhotoShop is the '*Mode*' option. This determines how the selected tool operates on the canvas. There is a wide variety of options, the following is just a sample of their effects:

Mode	Effect
Normal	The tool operates as normal. Usually this means painting in the foreground colour.
Behind	Paints onto any transparent areas only.
Multiply / Screen	The colour values (expressed in CMYK) are multiplied together. This is similar to mixing paints. Screen is the opposite effect.
Color Dodge / Color Burn	Color Dodge mode brightens those areas which are already light, accenting highlights. Burn does the opposite, darkening already dim areas.
Darken / Lighten	These modes make the painted areas darker or lighter by an amount equal to the lightness or darkness of the foreground colour.
Hue / Saturation / Color	These modes change the HSV values of pixels in the area painted, to match the level of the foreground colour. Using '*Hue*' is akin to tinting the canvas; '*Saturation*' will make all colours as vibrant or grey as the foreground colour is; '*Color*' makes the painted area into a shade of the foreground colour.

The equivalent in Paint Shop Pro is the '*Retouch*' tool, which provides many similar options. Layers can also be blended using any such modes.

Adding shapes

This is the easiest way to get started with PhotoShop, and many images employ basic shapes. The toolbox gives access to a number of shape tools including Rectangle, Rounded Rectangle, Ellipse, Line, Polygon, and Custom Shape. Once a tool is selected, simply drag and drop the shape inside the draw window to create a new Shape layer. Shape layers can contain any number of shapes of the same colour; to use shapes with more than one colour, additional layers will be required.

The shapes created are vector objects; as such they cannot be edited in the same way as raster images. For beginners, vector Shapes can be difficult to work with, and the alternative is to change an option on the Options bar from '*Create new shape layer*' to '*Create filled region*'. This means that the Shape is drawn as a filled raster rather than an object layer. For those more familiar with PhotoShop, the preferable method is to create the shapes as vectors until some operation (such as gradient fill or pattern stamp) that requires rasterisation is to be carried out. The layer is then turned into a raster and edited as desired.

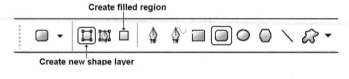

Create filled region

Create new shape layer

In PhotoShop Elements, there is no '*Create Filled Region*' option, but the vector layer is easily rasterised by clicking the '*Simplify*' button.

Selecting the '*Custom Shapes*' tool in the Toolbox will allow the user to draw using a set of pre-defined shapes. The Options bar will then contain, amongst other things, a drop-down '*Custom Shape Picker*' that will display the current set of custom shapes available. The default set contains stars, arrows and other symbols, but there are a number of other sets of shapes that can be loaded in to replace or supplement the basic set.

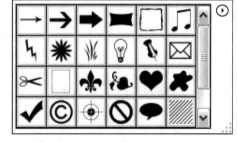

The user can create his or her own custom shapes in PhotoShop, by creating a layer that contains shapes and/or Pen drawn objects, and *clicking Edit / Define Custom Shape*. This is not supported in Elements.

Paint Shop Pro has a range of predefined elements for the Preset Shape tool, but cannot store user-defined shapes. If the user wishes to create a shape, they can do so using vector tools, but cannot save it as a Preset Shape.

Paths and Shapes

Vector objects in PhotoShop come in two forms: *Paths* and *Shapes*. There are also two special types of Paths: *Work Paths* and *Layer Clipping Paths*. A Shape is, in fact, composed of two elements : a 'Fill' layer filled with a colour, gradient or pattern; and a Layer Clipping Path that defines the areas of the layer that should be used. The Clipping Path can be edited using the vector object editing tools in PhotoShop, but Elements does not support viewing or editing Layer Clipping Paths.

A Layer Clipping Path can also be rasterised – it is then referred to as a Layer Mask, and can be edited using bitmap tools such as the Eraser or Paintbrush. This gives great flexibility to Shapes in PhotoShop.

Ordinary Paths and a temporary Work Path can be created with the vector tools. They can be '*stroked*' various ways to turn them into raster content, or filled with colour onto the currently selected raster layer. They can also be turned into a selection area.

Paint Shop Pro does not work with Paths and Shapes. Instead, it uses a predefined set of vector shapes within a layer, each of which can be individually modified. This arrangement is simpler but less flexible.

Selecting colours

The drawing and painting tools will draw in whatever colour is selected as the current foreground or background colour.   The Colour Palette is displayed in a floating window in PhotoShop and in any colour mode it will appear as shown. In Greyscale or bitmap mode, the RGB channels will be replaced with a single grey level channel. The foreground or background colour can be set either by picking a colour from the sample colours at the bottom, or by setting the exact RGB (or greyscale) values. If the colour is '*out of gamut*' (in an unprintable colour) it will display a warning.

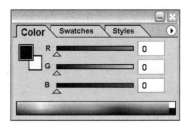

If more precision is required, clicking on the foreground or background colour boxes in either the Toolbox or the Color Palette will open the '*Color Picker*' dialog box.

The Color Picker dialog box allows the user to select a colour through a variety of means. It displays a colour grid that can be based on any of the three components of the RGB, HSB and Lab colour models.

The example shows the default colour grid based on the Hue component of HSB colour. The user can pick a colour from the grid, or alter the hue by dragging the slider to the side of the grid. Alternatively the user can enter the exact

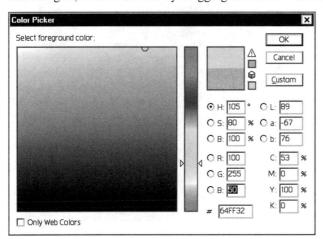

values for HSB or RGB. The screen also shows the CMYK values for the colour, and the corresponding code to use for that colour in HTML documents.

Once the desired colour is found, click '*OK*' and the foreground or background colour will be changed, whichever was clicked on to bring up the Color Picker in the first place.

PhotoShop Elements also uses a slightly reduced Color Picker, but instead of a Color Palette it uses the '*Swatches*' palette that can contain user-defined colour selections.   Paint Shop Pro does not use the Lab or CMYK colour models.   Also, the colour palette is a vertical window with similar contents, but the dialog box used to select colours has a '*color wheel*' that is intended to make colour selection easier.

An alternative method for selecting colours is to use the '*Dropper*' tool. This tool changes the mouse pointer into something that looks like an eye dropper. The user can then click the dropper on any individual pixel in the image, and the colour of that pixel will be selected for the foreground colour.

Browser-safe colours

Internet Explorer and Netscape Navigator use the same set of 216 colours in their palette, with all other colours being dithered. If the final image is intended for web use, the image colours must be '*browser-safe*' - i.e. be made up from these 216 colours.   The safe colours are those made up from multiples of 51 and therefore suitable values for the Red, Green and Blue entry boxes are 0, 51, 102, 153, 204 and 255. The '*Only Web Colours*' tick box in the colour picker will reduce the colour grid so that only browser-safe colours are displayed.

Using Colour and Gradient Fills

At this stage, the image consists solely of bold, solid shapes against a solid colour background.   Users often experiment with different colour options, deciding that the background colour or one of the object's colours should be changed.   The Paint Bucket tool, the one that looks a pot of paint being poured, is used to change an entire area of one colour to another colour.   The area need not be painted with a single, uniform colour - the Gradient Fill tool allows the user to select a fill that varies in colour.

The steps for creating flood fills are:

- Set the foreground colour to the desired fill colour.
- Click the Paint Bucket icon; the Options bar will now show the options for flood filling.
- Change the Paint Bucket options if necessary and click on the colour (making sure you are in the appropriate layer) that is to be changed.

The Paint Bucket can fill in all the modes available, and can also fill with a pattern that is selected from a '*Pattern Picker*'.

The Paint Bucket can be used to replace all occurrences of a colour by unticking the '*Contiguous*' checkbox, and can also operate across all layers. In order to perform a gradient fill, however, the separate '*Gradient Tool*' must be selected.

The Gradient Tool in PhotoShop differs from the Paint Bucket in that the Gradient tool will fill the whole of the selected area, or the entire window if no area is selected, so it should be used with care. In contrast, the Fill Tool in Paint Shop Pro will fill only one colour, regardless of whether it is filling with a colour or a gradient.

The steps for a gradient fill in PhotoShop are:

- Click the Gradient Tool icon; the Options bar will now show the options for flood filling.
- Select the gradient colours to use. This can be done through the '*Gradient Picker*' if necessary, although the default is normally to use the current background and foreground colours.
- Select the gradient type – Linear, Radial, Angle, Reflected or Diamond, and any other options.
- Click and drag anywhere in the paint window. The gradient will start from one end of the line created by dragging the mouse, and end at the other. Areas past each end of the gradient will simply be filled with the colours at either end of the gradient.

The illustration below shows just a few of the effects that can be achieved with fill styles.

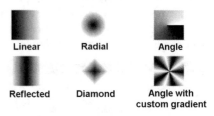

It should be noted that the effects vary with the paint package used; for example in Paint Shop Pro the fill called '*Radial*' has the same effect as the '*angle with custom gradient*' shown, while the fill called '*sunburst*' is closer to the '*radial*' fill shown for PhotoShop.

Solid colour fills are useful for logos, cartoons, diagrams, etc, while gradient or pattern fills are useful for backgrounds, web buttons and special effects.

For a solid fill, simply click the left mouse button in the area that is to be

filled. This will fill the area with the selected foreground colour. For a gradient fill, click and drag with the left mouse button. The start and end of the drag operation define the distance over which the pattern will be applied.

The examples show a angle fill and a radial fill being used as a background.

Note

The colour will flood into adjacent pixels whose colour is close to that of the colour of the current pixel. This '*flooding*' will continue until it meets a pixel that is sufficiently different to stop the process. The level of difference required is called the '*Tolerance*' and can be set by the user via the Options bar.

This means that if two adjoining areas of similar colour overlap, the new colour fills both objects. For example, if a filled circle and a filled triangle of the same colour overlap, or even touch, both are changed to the new colour.

Of course, if the objects are placed in different layers, they are treated separately.   In this case, they can only both be changed by flooding them individually in their own layers, or by checking the '*all layers*' tickbox in the Options bar.

Care must also be taken to avoid flooding areas that were not intended for alteration.   For example, if an area to be filled is surrounded by the outline of a box or other shape, clicking inside the shape will only flood that area. However, if the boundaries of the shape are incomplete, the fill will leak out the gap and fill the entire area.

Flooding a selection.

PhotoShop and Paint Shop Pro both have facilities to make a '*selection*' (see later) which defines a shape on the screen. This shape is usually a part of the area of another object. The selection area can be defined and subjected to its own flood fill. The image of the cruise liner was obtained from IMSI's Master Photo Collection, (1895 Francisco Blvd. East, San Rafael, CA, USA). The right-hand image shows the effect of defining some extra selections and filling them to represent the shadow of the hills, the

reflection of the ship, etc. This technique is examined again in the chapter *on 'Digital Photography'*, as its opacity and tolerance settings provide an ideal method for remodelling photographic images.

Drawing lines

There are several ways to draw lines, each of which is suited to different effects., In PhotoShop, the Pencil, Shape or Pen tools can be used to create different types of lines. In PhotoShop Elements, there are no Pen tools. In Paint Shop Pro, the Draw tool is used to create all forms of lines.

The types of lines that can be drawn are:

Single Line

The Shape tools, which were used earlier to place boxes and other shapes onto the image, include a '*Line*' option. This is the simplest way to draw lines on the screen, and when in Line mode the Options bar will include a Weight for the line to define its width. Clicking on the drop-down box in the Options bar will allow the user to define arrowheads that will be attached to the ends of the line. The user then simply clicks and drags in the window to create a line from one point to another. As explained earlier, the line thus created can be either a vector (shape layer) or raster (filled region).

Freeform Lines

A freehand line is drawn by clicking the mouse and dragging it over the screen. Unlike the Single Line above, however, freehand lines follow the mouse movements, creating curves and angles as the user dictates. It can be used to create hand-written effects, signatures and artist sketches.

There are two ways to do this in PhotoShop. The *Pencil* tool is a simple way to create (non-filled) freehand lines within a raster layer. The *Freeform Pen* tool, available in PhotoShop only, is used in a similar way to create a vector shape, but lines created in this way will turn into an unfilled Path or a filled Shape once the freehand drawing is finished. When creating a Shape, the area bounded by the lines is filled in the foreground colour. If the last point laid down does not meet the first point, a line is automatically added between these points. Given the difficulty in maintaining accurate control with a mouse, this option is used most effectively with a graphics tablet.

Point-to-Point Lines

The *Pen* tool (as opposed to the *Freeform Pen* tool) in PhotoShop draws a set of joined-up lines between nodes, called *anchor points*, designated by the user by a mouse click. The lines may be straight or curved, and these may be combined within the same Path or Shape. To start a path, simply click where the first anchor point is to be placed. The two types of line can be created as follows:

Straight lines

When the next point is clicked, a line is drawn between the two anchor points. This is continued until the shape is completed. To complete the shape, either hold down '*Ctrl*' and click with the left mouse button to create an ordinary line, or click on the starting anchor point to create a shape outline.

Curved lines

To add a curve, click the left button and drag it slightly. The direction and length the mouse is dragged while the button is held down will define the curve created.

While dragging the mouse a '*direction line*' will appear, showing the direction the line will curve to point in, as illustrated in the diagram. These lines, and the squares around the anchor points, will not appear in the picture. The line is completed in the same way as a straight line.

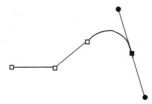

Editing lines and curves

If a line or curve is created with one of the Pen tools in PhotoShop, it can be edited using the *Direct Selection* tool. This tool will allow the user to select a line or curve, and drag the direction lines to change the shape of the curves. The same tool can be used to move individual anchor points, and the right-click menu allows the user to add or delete anchor points along the path.

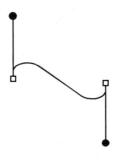

The editing of curves can take a bit of getting used to. The principle is that a curve moves from one anchor point to the other, such that at each anchor point the line has curved to 'point' in the direction indicated by the direction line.

If the direction lines point in opposite directions, the line has to curve right round and back again in order to point in the correct direction, as shown.

Paintbrush

The Pen and Pencil facilities are useful for creating outlines shapes and adding detail to charts, diagrams and illustrations. The Paintbrush is a more artistic tool that can be used with a mouse, but works better with a graphics tablet, where the tablet pen can be used almost like a paintbrush. The Paintbrush tool paints in the active raster layer, using a larger range of effects than the draw tools.

Like flood fills, the paintbrush can be used to paint inside selections. An area can be outlined as a selection (see later) and the painting will only affect the area. Any movements of the paint brush that stray outside of the selection are ignored. And of course, like all tools, the paintbrush only affects the currently selected layer.

Clicking on the Paintbrush tool will change the Options bar to that shown. As usual, the Tool Options window is where such options can be found in Paint Shop Pro.

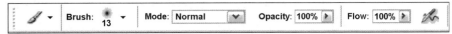

The options provided are:

Brush

This drop-down picker menu offers a selection of different brush tip shapes. There are a variety of brush sets providing square brushes, calligraphic styled brushes and others. The illustration shows just a few round brushes of varying sizes.

The calligraphic brushes are useful in emulating handwriting, where the user may have a heavier vertical stroke than horizontal stroke.

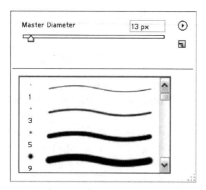

The numbers beside the brushes indicate the brush size in pixels if the brush is too large to be depicted in the box. Finally, the user can create custom brushes by clicking on the dropdown menu icon, and clicking the '*New*' icon. This is explained more fully later in this section.

Mode

This setting dictates the effect the brush strokes have on the active layer, as explained earlier in this chapter. For example, the brush can be used in normal mode, or used to lighten, darken, dodge, burn, or paint on the background.

Opacity

This sets the degree to which the paint is transparent, with 100% covering everything beneath it. As the percentage is lowered, the image from below shows through increasingly. For example, painting over a pale-looking face with a light brown colour at low opacity can make it healthier looking.

Flow

This sliding bar option specifies how quickly the 'ink' should flow onto the 'page'. Higher levels mean that the colour is painted more strongly on the image.

Airbrush

The last button on the Options bar activates '*airbrush mode*' which, as the name suggests, simulates the use of an airbrush.

Brush Dynamics

As mentioned earlier, the effect of certain tools can be modified by the '*Brush Palette*' popup menu. The Brush Palette contains tabs for '*Shape Dynamics*', '*scattering*', '*texture*', and other settings. All of these represent brush settings that can be set to change *while the brush is being used to paint.*

Most of these options default to '*Off*'. In order for any one to be used, the user must set that option to '*Fade*', '*Pen Pressure*', or one of the other options. The Pen Pressure option allows a graphic tablet to vary the strength of the setting, while the Fade setting allows the effect to be stepped. '*Pen Tilt*' and '*Stylus Wheel*' are options that allow these features of certain stylus boards to be used.

Some of the more commonly used dynamic controls include:

Size

This setting alters the brush size. If it is faded out, then it will shrink the brush until eventually it disappears. If it is stylus controlled, then the pressure of the stylus dictates the size of the brush stroke.

Angle

This is most useful when set to either '*Direction*' (meaning the angle of the brush will change to match the direction of the brush stroke) or '*Initial Direction*' (meaning that the first brush stroke determines the direction until the mouse or stylus button is released.

Color

The third setting allows the user to control the colour saturation of the brush. If it is set to fade, then the brush will gradually step towards the background colour. If it is stylus controlled, then the pressure controls the colour as it varies between the foreground and background colours.

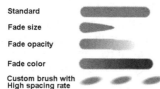

Opacity

The user can fade the opacity of the brush, making it gradually more transparent as the step size is approached. If this is controlled by stylus, then stylus pressure will vary the transparency of the brush.

The '*Brush Tip Shape*' tab is of particular importance, but it has no dynamics settings.

Brush Tip Shape

This tab contains several options: a selection box containing numerous brush shapes; and settings for diameter, angle, roundness, hardness and spacing.

Diameter:

This determines the size of the brush. If a non-standard brush type (such as a star, or leaf) is used, the diameter is still used to determine its size.

Angle:

This is used to rotate the brush shape. The example shows the brush being rotated 72 degrees to the left.

Roundness:

A low roundness indicates a 'squashed' brush. Roundness may not be greater than 100%.

Hardness:

This indicates how 'soft' the edges of the brush will be.

Spacing:

This means that the effect of the setting takes place gradually over a series of brush marks on the canvas. For example, a spacing of 1% is indistinguishable from a continuous stroke; while a spacing of 100% would typically appear as a linked chain of brush dabs. Spacing of over 100% will appear as separate dabs of the brush in the line drawn with the mouse.

Custom Brushes

To create a custom brush, the user should first use the brush palette to set the options as desired. Then drop down the brush picker (not the brush palette), then the dropdown menu, and select '*New Brush*' and give the brush a name.

The Custom Brush facility is not available in PhotoShop Elements. In Paint Shop Pro, the Paintbrush dialog box itself contains settings for the brush shape, size, hardness, opacity, step and density.

Airbrushing and Scattering

The Airbrush tool no longer exists as a separate tool in Photoshop since version 7, when it became part of the paintbrush tool. However, a more realistic approximation of an airbrush can be obtained by using the '*Scattering*' Dynamics. This allows the user to control how widely the brush scatters, and also provides a few other options. One of these is '*count*', which controls how many scattered brush spots are used, and the other is '*count jitter*' which is used to dynamically change the count level, providing a less uniform feel to the brush stroke.

Zooming and navigating the image

When PhotoShop loads or creates an image, it will try to display the image on the monitor at a 1:1 (or 100%) ratio. In other words, if the new file has been set to 320x240 pixels, that's how much space it will occupy on the workspace. If the image will not fit into the window at this ratio, it will 'zoom in' on the image until it fits.

The user can also zoom in on parts of the image, to view or edit parts of the image in more detail. Zooming in enlarges the view of an image or area of an image, but it does not affect the *actual size* of the image. In other words, a 320x240 image zoomed in to 200%, will take up 640x480 pixels on the screen, but is still only 320x240 pixels for editing purposes.

It is possible to zoom in so far that it is no longer possible to see the entire image on the screen. When this happens, simply zoom back out, or use one of the navigation tools to move around the image.

The user may also zoom out. For example, after close-up editing, the user may wish to view the whole image again. If the user is working with several images, cutting and pasting to create a montage, then the user may wish to zoom out below 100% in order to fit several images in the window at once.

Zooming in and out and navigating can be carried out in a number of ways:
- The View menu includes several zoom options. Zoom in and zoom out will cycle the zoom level between pre-set zoom levels; '*Fit on screen*' will zoom to an appropriate level to fit the whole image on screen; '*Actual pixels*' will zoom to 100%; and '*Print size*' will zoom to attempt to display a WYSIWYG image.
- By using the zoom tool. With the zoom tool selected, a left mouse click will zoom in to the next pre-set level. Using Alt-click will zoom out to the next pre-set level. When the zoom tool is selected the Options bar also displays three buttons, which perform the same function as the menu options. Double-clicking the zoom tool will set the zoom to 100%, while double-clicking the 'Hand' tool will set the zoom to fit to screen. Finally, clicking and dragging the zoom tool over an area will zoom in on that area.
- By using the hand tool. Selecting the hand tool allows the user to click and drag, moving the image around as if he/she were using hi/hers own hand to move a sheet of paper. The hand tool can also be accessed without clicking on the toolbar, by holding down the space bar on the keyboard and then clicking and dragging.
- Using the Navigation palette. This palette allows the user to enter a zoom percentage, or set it using a sliding bar. It also allows the user to move around within the image, by showing a thumbnail of the image, and a red box showing which portion of that image is currently being displayed. The red box can be dragged around the thumbnail to navigate the image.
- By hitting Control-Plus (Ctrl +) on the numeric keypad to zoom in, and hitting Control-Minus (Ctrl -) to zoom out.
- By rolling the mouse wheel (if the mouse has a wheel) back and forward.
- If the Status bar is displayed at the bottom of the window, entering a zoom percentage into the bottom left hand box will zoom to that level.

The zoom out will reduce the image up to a two-thousandth of its normal size, a zoom level that is more than enough to reduce even the very largest of images to a manageable size.

The zoom can enlarge the image up to 16 times its normal size.   As the zoom in becomes greater, the individual pixels that make up the image become visible. This allows the user to carry out *'pixel editing'*.
Zooming in Paint Shop Pro can be done by using the '+' and '-' keys, or the Zoom icon.

Note that if the picture does not fit entirely within the window, it can be moved around, either by using the scrollbars or by using the '*Hand*' tool (or '*Arrow*' tool in Paint Shop Pro) to 'push' the image around.

Pixel editing

The illustration shows the effect of zooming in on a picture of the Empire State Building.   When fully enlarged, as shown on the right, the individual pixels are easily identified and, more importantly, can be easily painted individually.

This allows the fine detail in drawings, maps, logos, etc. to be painted with the paintbrush.   It also allows photographic images to be cleaned up or doctored, and this is covered in the chapter on *'Digital Photography'*.
The width of the paintbrush can be set to a size of a single pixel, so that the brush only accesses a single pixel at a time.

Eraser

The Eraser tools are used to remove content from a bitmap layer. There are, in fact, three types of Eraser tool in PhotoShop - the standard Eraser; the Background Eraser and the Magic Eraser.

- The basic Eraser tool is used to remove all content in the current bitmap layer. If the current layer is the background layer, the eraser will replace areas with the selected background colour. Otherwise, it will effectively 'paint' areas transparent. It can be used in four modes – Paintbrush, Airbrush, Pencil or Block, each of which performs the erasure in a slightly different fashion. All modes except Block use the selected brush.
- The Background Eraser removes detail from the background, leaving foreground items intact. It is only available in Paintbrush mode, but the *'Limits'* option is available to alter the way the eraser performs. Although there is no such tool in Paint Shop Pro, the *'Color Replacer'* tool can be used to replace individual colours.
- The Magic Eraser is essentially a flood-fill eraser. It is used in an identical manner to the Paint Bucket, but floods an area with transparency instead of the foreground colour.
- Paint Shop Pro only has the standard Eraser.

Decreasing colour depth

The colour depth of an image, as explained earlier, can be reduced to decrease the final file size. With PhotoShop, the '*Image*' menu includes a '*Mode*' submenu with a variety of options. These include Bitmap (single colour), Greyscale, Indexed (Paletted), RGB (true colour), and other colour modes primarily concerned with publishing methods. PhotoShop will only convert between certain colour modes. For example, to turn an RGB image into a monochrome bitmap, it must first be turned into a greyscale image.

When converting into Indexed or Bitmap mode, there are a variety of options concerning how the colour reduction is carried out. In both cases, the user has to select a Dithering method. This will determine how colours outside the reduced colour range are represented in the new image. For Indexed colour mode, the user can also determine how many colours will be in the resulting image, from 0 to 256.

Note that some actions in PhotoShop can only be performed in RGB colour mode, as they require each pixel to have individual values for separate colour channels.

In Paint Shop Pro the '*Decrease Color Depth'* option from the '*Colors*' menu is used to reduce the colour depth of an image, and includes options to select dithering methods.

Increasing colour depth

While decreasing the colour depth is commonly used, there are occasions when it is necessary to increase the colour depth of an image. This will not alter the colours used in the existing image.   However, it will increase the number of colours in the available palette.   This allows extra colours to be added to the image. Examples of this are adding coloured captions to monochrome images and adding a true-colour photograph into an image that was previously 256 colours.

PhotoShop uses the same Image Mode options to increase colour depth.   For example a 256-colour GIF could be changed into RGB for editing, then reduced back to Indexed colour before being used in a web page. In Paint Shop Pro, colour reduction is achieved via the *'Increase Color Depth'* option of the *'Colors'* drop-down menu.

Adding text

Many graphic images will have text embedded in the image.   For example, this may be used to add annotations to a diagram or to have a graphic background to a text message.

The text tool in PhotoShop is the icon of a capital '*T*', and selecting it will place the text tool options in the Options bar, as shown below. Most of the same options in Paint Shop Pro appear in a dialog box that pops up on selection of the text tool. On selecting the Text tool, the user can drag a box on the screen into which to create text. The user must then type (or cut and paste) in the text which is to appear in the image.

There are four different text tools. Horizontal Type and Vertical Type are used to create text that flows horizontally or vertically, into a new text layer. The Horizontal Type Mask and Vertical Type Mask tools are used to turn the area that would be created by the text into a selection instead.

Text layers are treated as objects; they can have styles applied to them but if precise editing is required it may be necessary to convert the layer to a bitmap. PhotoShop and Paint Shop pro both call this process '*flattening*'. In Elements it is referred to as '*Simplifying*'.

From left to right, the options on the Options Bar are as follows:

- Horizontal or Vertical orientation. This allows the text to flow in either axis.
- Font face, style and size. The example shows 12-point Courier, in Medium style. Any TTF font can be selected, many including bold and italic ('oblique') styles.
- Anti-aliasing. This menu includes options to determine how the edges of the font are smoothed.
- Alignment. The text can be left-aligned, centred, or right-aligned using these options.
- Text colour. This is the colour the text will be created in. It may not have any effect if a layer style is applied to the text layer.
- Warped text. This option brings up a dialog box that allows the text to be 'warped'. Users of WordArt may find this familiar, as it allows the text to flow in various patterns such as waves or arches.
- Palettes button. This button displays the text palettes, '*Character*' and '*Paragraph*'. These palettes can be used to control the display of individual portions of text.

The Character palette (not available in Elements) can be used to set the font, style, size, leading, kerning, tracking, scale, baseline shift, and colour. '*Leading*' and '*Tracking*' dictate the amount of space between lines and characters respectively.

'*Kerning*' is the level to which two individual characters may overlap into each other's space – the example shows both a kerned and an unkerned piece of text. Paint Shop Pro can perform kerning automatically by selecting the '*Auto Kern*' checkbox. In PhotoShop it is called '*Metrics*' in the Kerning drop-down menu.

WAV
WAV

The vertical and horizontal scale options allow the user to stretch the text in either direction, as a percentage of the standard font for that point size. '*Baseline shift*' allows characters to be above or below the baseline for that paragraph. In this way subscripts or superscripts can be created.

The Paragraph palette includes control over alignment, justification, indentation, spacing and hyphenation. The justification options allow text to be justified, with the final line either right, left, centred or fully justified. Indentation allows the user to select left and right margins as well as the indentation of the initial line in each paragraph. The spacing option allows individual paragraphs to be separated from each other by a user-selected amount.

Text Effects

Plain text is required for the body text of web sites, for annotating diagrams, etc.

The Headline text and web buttons are usually created with added effects for extra appeal. In PhotoShop, the simplest way to create text effects is to apply a Layer Style to the text layer. PhotoShop supplies a variety of Layer Styles in different categories, including a '*Text effects*' category. These are accessed by selecting the text layer, and then in the Styles palette using the drop-down menu to load the text effects styles. Then select a style and it will be applied to the layer. Alternatively, the user can use their own Blending Options, as explained earlier in this chapter. Paint Shop Pro however, uses the '*Effects'* option of the *'Image*' drop-down menu for similar effects.

Frosted Glass

Black Stroke

Overspray

Polished Chrome

Pixel Selection

A useful feature of any graphics package is the ability to select areas of pixels. When an area is selected, any editing is carried out only in the selected area. The selection can be flood-filled, painted, transformed, and subjected to many other image manipulations. Once outlined, the selection can be dragged to any part of the active image area. The selection can also be cut from the frame and pasted into a new layer or as a new image. The selected area is always indicated by '*crawling dots*' around the selected area.

Some pixels may be partially selected, meaning that any tools or effects will only be partially applied to pixels in such a state. If any pixels are only partially selected, then PhotoShop will only show the crawling dots around those pixels which are more than 50% selected.

Selections create a boundary around an object and that selection can then be manipulated. There are occasions when the area <u>outside</u> the selection is the part to be processed. This can be achieved by choosing the *'Inverse'* option from the *'Select'* menu. The outer area is now treated as the selection and can be dragged, copied, deformed, etc.

Once a selection is made, the selection area itself can be modified through various options in the '*Select*' menu, or by using the selection tools in add, subtract or intersect mode. These modes are chosen in the Options bar, and allow multiple selections at one time. Selections can also be '*Feathered*', which basically involves a sort of selection gradient. A feathered rectangular marquee might fully select pixels in the center of the rectangle, while only partially selecting pixels near the edges.

There are a variety of ways to create a selection in PhotoShop, including Marquee, Lasso, Magic Wand, and Quickmask, although Quickmask is not available in Elements. Paint Shop Pro uses Selection instead of Marquee, Freehand instead of Lasso, and has no Quickmask mode.

The example shows an image created using selections. A picture was loaded, and an Elliptical Marquee was selected. A second Elliptical Marquee was added to the selection, and then the selection was inverted. The resulting selection was turned to black, to create the 'binocular' style effect.

Marquee

The Marquee tools are used to select an area of the current layer. In Paint Shop Pro the similar set of tools are called Selection tools. The basic Marquee tool is a Rectangular Marquee, which allows the user to select a rectangular area of pixels by clicking and dragging the mouse to create a rectangular shape. Holding the mouse button down over the Marquee tool will bring up a menu allowing the user to select the Elliptical (oval) Marquee, and single row and column Marquee tools, which select individual rows or columns of pixels.

Lasso

The Lasso tools are also used to select an area, either in a freehand form, an irregular polygon selection, or '*Magnetic Lasso*', which tries to intelligently select an area based on mouse movement around colour edges. In Paint Shop Pro the Freehand, Point-to-Point and Smart Edge tools perform the same functions.

The basic freehand Lasso was the tool used in creating the example, earlier in this chapter, of a cruise liner. Areas of the picture were freehand selected, and then flood filled to create the smoke effect. Simply click the mouse down and move it around to create a freehand selection.

When the button is released, a straight line is added to join the point where the cursor currently sits to the first point of the selection. So, unless a straight edge is wanted, ensure that the mouse is moved as close as possible to the starting point before releasing the mouse button.

With Polygon Lasso, the first mouse click designates the start of the lasso, with each successive click adding a new line in the polygon. When finished, the user can either click near the start of the lasso, or double click the last point in the lasso to let PhotoShop complete the lasso with a line back to the start.

Freehand   Polygonal   Magnetic
Lasso   Lasso   Lasso

The Magnetic Lasso is more useful when an individual object is to be selected from a photographic picture, as in the example . This would be difficult to achieve in freehand mode, and polygon lasso would have too many unnatural-looking straight lines. Magnetic Lasso is used by clicking the mouse near an edge of the object, and then moving the mouse around the edges until the shape is complete. The Magnetic Lasso tries to intelligently sense the outline of the object and select appropriately, using curved lines if necessary.

Other selection methods

The '*Magic Wand*' tool will select all pixels that are of a similar colour to the pixel clicked on. The Options Bar for this tool has similar Tolerance, Anti-aliased, Contiguous and Use All Layers options as those that appear for the Flood Fill tool. Also, as mentioned earlier, the text tool can be used to select a text-shaped area in PhotoShop.

'*QuickMask*' mode can be used to select an area. When in Quickmask mode, any tool can be used to define an area for selection. For example, the user could use the paintbrush to paint a selection, or the airbrush to partially select an area, and then the eraser to unselect some portions, then add a custom shape to the selection.

The picture shown uses two layers. The background is a pattern fill. A new layer was created, and Quickmask mode was selected. After drawing and editing two custom shapes, the user returned to standard editing mode, inverted the selection, and removed the selected area.

As noted earlier, paths can also be turned into selection areas. Another options is the '*Colour Range*' option in the '*Select*' menu.

This allows the user to select all pixels that fall within a certain range of colours, which is particularly useful in selecting areas in photographic images. Using this method, the user chooses a colour, and a *'fuzziness'* level that allows a range of nearby shades of colour to be selected.

Working with selections

Areas of pixels are not the only things that can be selected. The user may select text, layers, paths and so on. Each of these can be cut, copied, pasted, deleted, moved around with the *'move'* tool, and so on. However, the tools which may be used on selections depends on the type of object selected. For example, pixel selections may be painted over; text may be transformed; or shapes may have their anchor points edited.

Transformation

The illustration shows a piece of text, followed by examples of rotation, skewing, distortion and perspective. Other transformations available include flipping and scaling. Transformations can be applied to text, clip art, photographic images or a selection, but to distort or apply perspective to text it must first be rasterised. Also, like many tools, most transformations cannot be applied in bitmap colour mode, but must first be converted into RGB colour mode.

To apply a transformation, the user must select a layer or area of a layer, and either press Ctrl-T for freeform transform mode, or select an option from the *'Transform'* submenu of the *'Edit'* menu.

To transform a selection or layer, the user can either press Ctrl-T for free transform mode, or select an option from the *'Transform'* submenu of the *'Edit'* menu.

In free transform mode the selected object is surrounded by a transform box, which has eight tags as shown in the diagram.   Another tag appears at the centre of the object, used as the centre point for rotation.

Resizing

If one of the tags on the vertical edge (i.e. between the corners) is dragged, the horizontal size of the image is shrunk or expanded, while dragging the tags on the horizontal edges changes the vertical size.   Dragging a corner tag changes the size in the horizontal and vertical directions in a single operation. If the Shift key is held down while dragging a corner box, it will maintain the selection's aspect ratio, ie. the object's size will change by the same degree both vertically and horizontally.

Rotating

If the user clicks and drags the mouse outside of the transform box, it will rotate the selection in the direction of movement from the initial point where the mouse was pressed down. If the *'centre'* tag is moved away from the centre of the selection itself, then the object will be rotated around the new centre location. This is useful when wishing to rotate an object in relation to another object.

Skewing

If the user holds down the Ctrl and Alt keys while dragging a corner box, the selection will be skewed. The direction in which the image is skewed is decided by the direction in which the mouse is dragged. Skewing can be useful in making text look more dynamic.

Deformations

Holding down the Ctrl key while dragging a box will apply a deformation to the selection. To distort the transformation relative to the centre tag, hold down the Alt key. Deformation is used to make the corners of an object distort in any direction necessary, while keeping all other corners in place.

Perspective

Holding down Ctrl-Alt-Shift while dragging a corner will give perspective to the selection. The perspective applied will be relative to the corner chosen and the direction the mouse is moved. This option will make the object look as if it is sloping toward or away from the viewer.

These transformations can be used in combination, and in conjunction with other effects, to produce greater control over how objects are displayed.

Paint Shop Pro has a separate *'Deformation'* tool that performs the same functions, though with a slightly different interface. For example, in Paint Shop Pro, rotation is achieved by clicking and dragging a 'handle' that protrudes from the centre tag.

Image Adjustment

PhotoShop also contains a number of adjustment tools that change the entire image's appearance. These are collectively found under the *'Image'* menu, and the *'Adjust'* submenu.

Some of the most widely used adjustment tools include:

Levels

The *'levels'* tool allows the user to modify the tonal range of the image. An image is composed of a range of colours or tones, and these can be 'remapped' to varying levels to improve contrast, brightness, colour casts and other problems all in one dialog box. That dialog box looks like the one on the right.

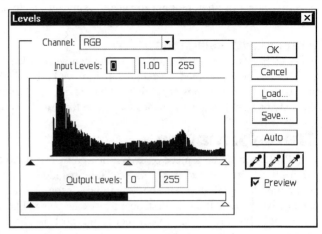

This dialog box shows a *'histogram'* graph representing the spread of colour tones in the image. As can be seen, there are few or no pixels in the lowest part of the range, which indicates black pixels as denoted by the black arrow. This particular image came from a scanner that had its brightness settings incorrectly adjusted. To fix the brightness of the image, simply drag the black arrow until it is near or touching the start of the data on the histogram. The tone of each pixel in the image will then be adjusted so that they fit into a new histogram where the lower part of the range is used.

Note also that, unused black pixels aside, the histogram shows quite a heavy reliance on the darker end of the scale. Dragging the middle, grey arrow slightly to the right could produce an image with a greater diversity of colour, rather than the image being quite dark, but without sacrificing the lighter pixels.

The slider at the bottom represents the output levels. If the output levels are adjusted, then it will shift all the pixels' colour tones toward one end of the histogram, making it paler, or shadier.

All of the above applies to colour images and greyscale images. However, colour images can also have individual colour channels adjusted, by selecting the appropriate channel from the drop-down box. This can be used to eliminate colour casts, or introduce a pastel effect.

Auto Levels

This adjustment tries to estimate the best levels adjustments for your image and applies them. In images where the tonal range is already quite well spread out, the auto levels function will have little or no effect.

Curves

Similar to the *'levels'* tool, the *'Curves'* tool allows the user to modify the tonal range of the image. This tool simple allows the action to be performed through a different interface.
The curves interface allows the user to adjust from 2 up to 15 points on the curve, or a freehand drawn curve, instead of just three arrows on the levels dialog box.
The example shown uses five such points, to perform a similar cleaning operation to the image shown in the *'levels'* example. The straight portion on the bottom left has been added to make the darker pixels completely black, while the slightly upturned curve on the left hand side will lighten the darker end of the scale. The right hand side, which was bright enough, is left as it is.
Like the levels dialog, the curves dialog can also be used on individual channels.

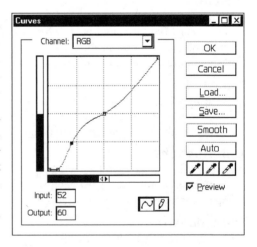

Cropping

Where the required final image is smaller than the existing overall image size, the wanted section can be extracted by cropping. This removes the unwanted section round the image, resulting in a more balanced image content - and a smaller file size.
The steps for cropping an image are:
- Click the *'Crop'* icon in the Tool palette.
- Move to one corner of the image to be retained and click the left mouse button.
- Hold down the button, while dragging the cursor diagonally to other opposite corner.
- Release the mouse button (the crop area is outlined).
- Choose the 'Crop' option from the 'Image' drop-down menu, or click the 'tick' button in the Options bar. Alternatively, just select a new tool from the toolbox.

This results in a smaller rectangular image. The image can also be cropped to any selected area, by simply choosing the 'Crop' option from the 'Image' drop-down menu.

Retouching tools

Both PhotoShop and Paint Shop Pro provide a variety of ways to touch up photographic images. In Paint Shop Pro, they are accessed as tool options for the Retouch tool. In PhotoShop, there are several tools specifically for providing these functions. In every case, the retouching is done in a similar manner to using the Paintbrush tool. The functions available include:

- Blur: This retouch tool is used to create a hazy, out of focus effect.
- Sharpen: This is the opposite of blur, used to pick out detail.
- Smudge: The user can smear colours around the image using this tool.
- Dodge: This tool is similar to the Paintbrush tool used in Dodge mode, but can be more precise because it can be used individually on highlights, midtones or shadows.
- Burn: Again, like the Paintbrush tool in Burn mode, but with more precision.
- Sponge: This tool 'soaks up' colour, leaving images slightly more drab and pale.

Photo retouching is covered in more detail in the chapter on *'Digital Photography'*.

Other Edit facilities

Apart from the options that are provided on the Tool palette, major paint packages provide other editing facilities that are accessed from the drop-down menus and some of these are covered below.

Flip

This facility does what it says - the object is flipped head over heels; what was the top of the picture is now the bottom, and vice versa. The effect can be applied to a layer or to a selection.

Canvas size

There are times when the image area is full of graphic objects and there is a need to add yet more to the image – for example, to add a caption or a title.   The *'Canvas Size'* option from the *'Image'* pull-down menu provides an opportunity to increase the overall dimensions of the image without disturbing the existing image pixels.   The dialog box reports on the current file dimensions and the user can enter new dimensions. If the new dimensions are greater than the existing dimensions, extra pixels are added around the existing image and the original image can be placed in any spot within the enlarged area.

If the new dimensions are less than the existing dimensions, the image is cropped to the new size. This is not shrinking the image (see the Resize option next) but removing some of the existing image information.

Image Size

Cropping removes part of the image to produce a reduced image area, while Canvas Size adds extra pixels to enlarge the image area.   In both cases, the remaining image details are represented by the same number of pixels as before.

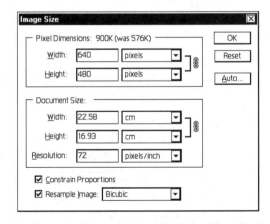

The purpose of the Image Size facility is to alter the resolution of the image, so that each detail is represented by less (or more) pixels than previously.

If the image is resized downwards, there are less pixels used to represent the same image.   This produces a smaller file but has lost some detail consequently.   This is a common method of reducing file sizes for use on web sites.

If the image is resized upwards, the image is enlarged and the extra pixels are interpolated (estimated).

The facility is reached by choosing the *'Image Size'* option (in PhotoShop) or the *'Resize'* option (in Paint Shop Pro) from the *'Image'* drop-down menu. The dialog box shown is for the PhotoShop Image Size menu option.

There are several options for resizing an image:

The *'Pixel Dimensions'* option has entry boxes for specifying the final pixel width and pixel height for the image.   It can also be specified in percentages of the current image size, by changing the 'pixels' box to 'percent'.

The '*Document Size*' area allows the user to specify the image size in centimetres, inches, points, picas or columns. In order to do this the resolution in pixels per inch or pixels per centimetre must also be specified.

Checking the '*Constrain Proportions*' option box (called *'Maintain aspect ratio of'* in Paint Shop Pro) ensures that a change to a *'width'* or '*height*' entries will result in an automatic change in the other entry box, to maintain the same ratio between vertical and horizontal size.   If the box is unchecked, the aspect ratio can be altered to any value, although care should be taken to ensure that the graphic content does not look elongated or squashed.

The '*Resample Image*' option specified a method for increasing pixel size. Where extra pixels have to be inserted to resize an image, the computer must decide which colours those pixels should be – simply copying a pixel will result in a blocky appearance. The options are:

Nearest Neighbor	This is a simple copy of the nearest pixel's colour, which results in blockiness in the image, but may be best for images that contain boxes, cartoons, etc.
Bilinear Resample	Uses interpolation techniques to reduce the jagged edges that often result from expanding a bitmap image.
Bicubic Resample	Another resampling option, slower but more precise. It is the best choice for enlarging photo-realistic images and images that are irregular or complex.

Saving the image

Layers, alpha channels and other information attached to an image can be extremely useful in the development or editing of that image. However, when it comes time to save the image, a file format must be decided upon.

Saving in PhotoShop or Paint Shop Pro's own format (the PSD or PSP format respectively) saves the image and all its properties. This allows a piece of unfinished work to be saved, complete with all its separate layers, channels, etc. If the work is saved to a general format such as GIF, PCX, JPG, etc, the layers are flattened and lost.

It is common practice for graphic artists to save their work in the native, layered format (e.g. PSD or PSP) while work is ongoing. However, when the image is to be used, it will be saved as an appropriate file type, as explained elsewhere. This typically means that the layer information will be lost. For this reason most artists keep a copy of the final image in a layered file format in case alterations need to be made, or part of the image can be reused later.

Font Design

There are a staggering variety of fonts available for use. Like software and other media, there are some fonts that are free to use, and others that cost money. Fonts are typically quite small files, however, and there are many web sites distributing fonts illegally, many of them without even realising it. Furthermore, some projects require rather specific outlines, such as a pictorial font or a foreign alphabet which is not currently available in a font.

One way to solve both of these problems is to design your own font. This requires an amount of craftsmanship, but the result is copyrighted to the author, and therefore is definitely legal to use, and the font will (hopefully) look exactly the way the user wants it to look.

TrueType Fonts

Other chapters explain in detail how to use TrueType Fonts (TTFs), which are the most common type of font for the PC. However, before creating or editing fonts yourself, it is necessary to learn a little about the internal workings of TrueType Fonts. The TTF consists of a series of images, called '*glyphs*', one for each character in the font face. Each glyph is defined by two pieces of data: the '*outline*' and the '*hints*'.

Font Outline

As the name suggests, this data relates to the outline of the font. This forms the backbone of the font, indeed it is possible to have a font with only an outline and no hints, although such a font would not be rendered well at low resolution.

The font outline is, in essence, a small vector-based graphic, which typically consists of straight and curved lines. Each line is considered to go in one particular direction, and several lines are joined together in a loop, to form a solid shape. This is the '*outline*' of the font.

However, this is rarely sufficient – characters such as 'A' and 'B' are not solids: they have white areas within the outline. The TTF specification resolves this by examining the directional flow of the lines in the font. Those that travel clockwise are considered to be the '*outer*' area, and therefore anything within is to be painted black. Those lines which travel anti-clockwise are considered to be an '*inner*' area, and therefore anything within is to be painted white. The example on the right shows a very basic font face of the upper-case character 'A'.

Font Hints

The main benefit of vector-based images is their scalability. However, fonts demand a high level of consistency, which a low point size can make difficult. For example, the rasteriser that turns the vectors into raster output on the screen could easily make the leftmost stem of the upper case letter 'M' two pixels wide, while the rightmost stem might be only one pixel wide. Such irregularities make fonts hard to read, and so some font types, including TrueType, include a form of '*hinting*'.

The name '*hinting*' is based on the fact that the hints are used by the font rendering software, to 'tweak' the outline by at most one pixel in any direction, in order to make it more readable. Such a small change makes little difference to high resolution displays, and is completely unnoticeable in professional quality printing. However, with small font resolutions such as those commonly used in computer displays, a single pixel can make all the difference to the font's readability.

Technically, hinting is in fact a programming language, capable of including loops and decisions like any other high level language. This makes it extremely versatile, but also complicated, and it takes some time to learn. The full extent of hinting is well beyond the scope of this book. Fortunately, most font design programs implement hinting at a more basic level, as more vectors.

Furthermore, the most popular font design programs also incorporate automated hinting. Although this is never anything like as good quality as a well-hinted font prepared by hand, it is often enough for those who don't have the time to learn hinting thoroughly.

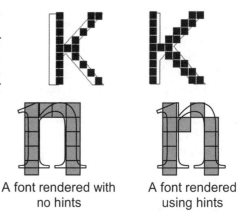

A font rendered with no hints

A font rendered using hints

Font Design Programs

There are a number of font design programs available. Unfortunately, due to the complexity of TrueType hinting, every program that creates TrueType fonts has slightly different capabilities. Some ignore hinting entirely, and these packages are to be avoided. Others expect the user to have in-depth knowledge of the hinting system, and these provide the best final result but are by far the hardest to learn. The most popular font design programs incorporate auto-hinting for ease of use, but allow the user to create his own hints, or tweak the existing ones, where necessary.

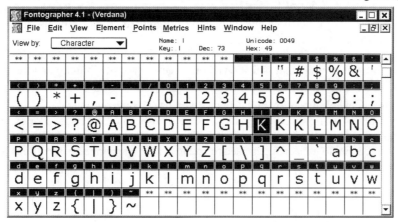

One popular font design program is Macromedia's Fontographer. This application is able to load TTF font files or create new fonts from scratch. Fontographer uses its own proprietary .FOG file format, but can create TTF fonts or PostScript fonts. The illustration opposite shows the Fontographer main Font Window, upon loading the 'Verdana' font.

As can be seen, the glyphs are shown in a grid, and each glyph that is present in the font file is highlighted in black, while missing glyphs are in white. Double-clicking any glyph will create a new glyph if that character does not yet have one, or it will edit the existing glyph if there is one.

The glyph editing consists of three parts: the Outline Window, the Bitmap Window, and the Metrics Window. When a glyph is edited it is the Outline Window that will load up first. The other windows can be accessed though the Window menu on the toolbar.

Outline Editing

The Outline editor resembles a vector paint package, because that is essentially what it is. The toolbar along the left hand side contains various tools, many of which have additional options if they are double-clicked. The tools are as follows, from left to right and top to bottom:

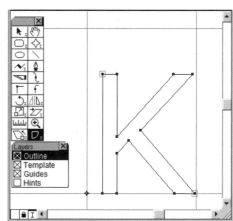

Selection Tool: For selecting points in the glyph, and moving them. Double clicking this icon accesses the Transformation dialog box.

Hand: For moving the screen view of the glyph around.

Rectangle: For drawing rectangles. Double-clicking this icon allows the user to create rectangles with rounded corners.

Multigon: For drawing polygons and stars. Double-clicking this icon gives access to the settings for this tool, so that it can be switched between polygon/star mode, and the number of sides can be changed.

Ellipse: This tool draws ellipses, although they are in fact simply four curved points joined together.

Line: This is one of the most basic tools in the editor, creating two points and linking them together.

Freehand / Calligraphy Pen: Allows the designer to draw parts of the font freehand, using the mouse. Double-clicking brings up a dialog that allows the user to change the freehand pen style, for example to make wider strokes or angled strokes.

Pen: This tool creates a single point, not linked to any other point.

Knife: The designer can use this tool to *'cut'* existing lines. When the knife is pulled across an existing line or multiple lines, each of those lines has a new point added where the knife tool passes through. This is useful to insert new parts into an existing glyph.

Curve point: This tool is used to insert points one by one with each mouse click, joining each point to the last by a curved line.

Corner point: Like the curve point, this adds points one by one, but this time each point is linked to the last by a straight line.

Tangent point: This inserts a tangent point, which is a point that is used to smoothly connect straight and curved lines. The user can switch between curve points, corner points and tangent points, and Fontographer will still link to the last point added.

Rotate, Flip, Scale and Skew: These are simple shortcuts to the respective transformations, just as in any image editor. Double-clicking any one will bring up the Transform dialog box.

Ruler: This tool is used to measure the distance between any two points.

Zoom: As the name suggests, this is used to zoom in on parts of the glyph.

Perspective: This is another transformation tool.

Arc Tool: This tool is used to create an arc. Again, this is simply three points linked together, by one horizontal line, one vertical line, and one curve. Double-clicking allows different arc types to be used, such as convex or open (no vertical or horizontal line) arcs.

In addition, there is a Layers Palette. This box contains four items: the Outline, the Template, Guides, and Hints. By checking each box the user can control what is displayed on screen. Also, the highlighted item is the layer which is currently being edited, and it can be changed simply by clicking on another layer.

Outline: This layer contains the outline of the font. Each glyph has its own outline.

Template: This layer contains user-defined images to aid in the creation of the fonts. For example, bitmaps can be imported into the Template to be traced into vector fonts. This is not a function of the TrueType specification, but a part of Fontographer. Once a Fontographer file is used to create a TTF, the templates are discarded.

Guides: This layer contains, by default, four lines that delineate the bounds of the glyph. However, users can add their own guides, and there is only one set of guides for the whole font, so these guides can be used to facilitate the standardisation of glyphs.

Hints: This layer contains the hinting information on each glyph. Fontographer uses a graphical method of hinting rather than using the full flexibility of the hinting mechanism. The hint layer can be used as a graphical method of changing the Vertical Alignment Zones, as well as changing the direction of any hints.

Hint Editing

Editing hints is done in the Outline window. For simple fonts, turning on auto-hinting might be sufficient.

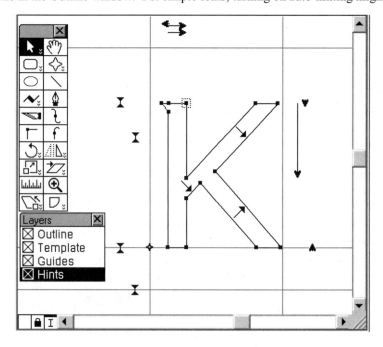

However, if the fonts are likely to be used at low point sizes or on low-resolution devices, it may be worthwhile to do some or all of the hinting by hand.

Hints may be added by selecting one or more lines, and using one of the *'Make ...'* options from the *Hint* menu.

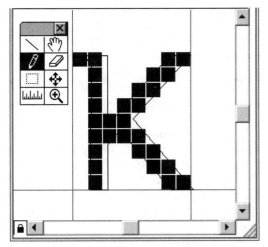

The types of hints provided in this way include:
- Vertical Stems: This can be added after selecting the horizontal line at the top or bottom of a vertical stem.
- Horizontal Stems: This can be added after selecting any vertical line at the left or right of a horizontal stem.
- Vertical Serifs: This can be added after selecting the top or bottom of a vertical stem, as well as the two lines that make up the serif off the stem.
- Horizontal Serifs: This can be added after selecting the left or right of a horizontal stem, as well as the two lines that make up the serif off the stem.
- Diagonal Hints: This can be added after selecting any <u>two</u> diagonal lines. It is used to specify an area that is intended to run diagonally at low resolutions.

The illustration above shows Fontographer's Outline Window while editing the letter 'K'. The glyph has been given a serif hint, which constitute the top two arrows. The next arrow is the vertical stem hint that indicates the stem to which the serif is attached. To the right of the glyph is a downward arrow, which indicates that the upward diagonal part of the 'K' has been specified as a horizontal stem. The three arrows within the glyph itself indicate the presence of three Diagonal Hints.

Bitmap Editing

The Bitmap Window provides a simplistic bitmap editor to enable the designer to edit individual glyphs at certain font sizes by hand for optimum results. It is not recommended that the Bitmap Window is used too often, as this partly defeats the purpose of TrueType fonts. Indeed, some fonts can be quite useable without any bitmap editing whatsoever.

Before entering the Bitmap Window, the current set of bitmaps must be calculated. Fontographer does not keep a bitmap of every glyph at every point size, so only a few point sizes are normally generated. Clicking *Element -> Bitmap Info* will allow the user to specify which point sizes to calculate bitmaps for; the default is point sizes 10 and 12.

Once the point sizes are selected, the bitmaps can be generated by selecting *Element -> Recalc Bitmaps*. Then, going to the Bitmap Window will show a screen similar to the shown. Fontographer will render each glyph at the specified point sizes, as it would be rendered in any program that uses the final font. Here, the designer can make any final modifications to the glyph's appearance at that point size.

This window is essentially a basic bitmap graphics editing program, and the tool set reflects this:
- Straight Line Tool. This tool is used to draw a line of pixels. If the first pixel in the line is white, it will draw a black line, and vice versa.
- Hand Tool. This tool moves the displayed area around on the screen.
- Pencil. Used to add pixels freehand to the output bitmap, making them black. If the first pixel in the freehand drawing is white, it will draw in black, and vice versa.
- Eraser. Used to remove pixels from the output bitmap, making them white.
- Marquee. This tool selects, and moves, a square section of pixels.
- Move. This tool moves the entire bitmap.
- Measuring Tool. This is used to measure distances from one pixel to another.
- Magnifier. This is used to zoom in (or, more likely, zoom out, by using the Alt key and clicking).

Metric Editing

This window is used by typing characters into the text box at the top of the window. This will cause Fontographer to display the same phrase, in the font being designed, in very large point size, with metric details such as kerning, character widths, and so on. The designer can edit these values to provide better kerned fonts.

Copyright of graphics

Like any other media, computer graphics are subject to copyright laws. These are explained in detail in the *'Interface Design'* chapter. However, it should be pointed out that there may be certain additional complications with computer graphics regarding copyright.

Particularly, a graphic image that depicts a well-known person, place, or product can easily run foul of the law. Care should be taken that 'impressions' of such images are clearly more than just reproductions, and of course a digital photograph or scan of a picture by another artist is completely out of the question without his or her permission.

As has already been made clear, simply altering a copyrighted graphic image does not get around the law, but copying is nonetheless rife on the Internet and elsewhere. The chapter on *'Interface Design'* explains how to produce a simple copyright statement. Such a copyright notice can be physically inserted on top of a graphic image, but that can always be removed by someone with a little graphics skill, and reduces the quality of the image. Some file formats include a text tag or text area, where a copyright statement can be inserted, but this is easily removed or ignored. So, to help protect copyrighted images, *'watermarks'* can be inserted into them.

Digital Watermarks

The digital watermark has been given this name as it mimics the way a watermark is embedded into paper currency notes.   The watermark on a pound note is not visible, unless the note is viewed in a certain light.   Then the underlying pattern embedded in the paper becomes visible.

Digital watermarks are similar in concept to the physical kind – they are intended to cause as little irritation to a casual user as possible, yet can be detected by authorised personnel to discover the true owner of the copyright on the material.

The concept is that a code is digitally 'hidden' inside an image. If a potential copyright challenge arises, that code can be extracted from the image, and used as a reference to a database containing copyright information. This entails the use of a third party watermarking company, and there is debate over how robust the watermark must be to avoid losing the code if the image is manipulated to any great extent. Also, since the watermark is hidden within the image data, it must be subtle enough that it does not alter the image to a noticeable degree.

Some watermark users think that the watermark should be displayed any time the image is accessed, for example when it is opened in an image editor or when it is displayed in an image reading and displaying package (called a 'rastering device'). Others feel that the code should remain a secret so that abusers of copyright can be identified.

PhotoShop makes use of a Digital Watermarking technology known as *'PictureMarc'* (or *'ImageBridge'*) by the DigiMarc corporation. To make use of it, the user must first register with DigiMarc, and receive a *'creator ID'* that can be embedded into PhotoShop images. Once pictures have been watermarked, the user can also use DigiMarc's *"MarcSpider"* to automatically check a variety of web pages for digitally watermarked files used illegally.

The DigiMarc facility can be accessed from the *'Filter'* drop-down menu by choosing *'Digimarc'* followed by *'Embed Watermark'*.   The dialog box allows details such as the unique Creator ID, image attributes (e.g. permission to copy, adult content. etc.) and watermark durability.

The technology is constantly developing and there is some debate about how durable the watermark is.   Proponents of watermarking claim that the image can be scaled, cropped, rotated, requantized, compressed, etc - and still maintain the watermark content.   Other claim that the watermark can be detected and removed. In many respects, it mirrors the virus race - someone invents a virus and someone else invents the virus detector.   In this case, someone invents a watermarking system and someone else works out how to remove it.   However, just as with viruses, the system with all its imperfections is better than no system at all.

Digital Photography

The power of the photograph

"A picture is worth a thousand words"

Like all clichés, it contains some truth.   A photograph can often sum up a mood or a situation far better than even the best advertising slogan, sound bite, or explanatory text. Like all photography, digital images can be used to accurately record details (e.g. pictures of machinery, accidents, etc) or to create or capture a mood (e.g. sunsets, weddings, goal-scoring, etc).

Digital processing offers the addition of easy picture manipulation and editing (e.g. removing red-eye, making the sunset warmer, removing drunken old uncle Bert from the wedding photographs, etc.).

Photojournalism

Photojournalism has produced many famous photographs recording significant events in history, or the state of a nation or technology throughout history.

Some classic photographs are:

- Youth standing in front of tank in Tiananman Square, China 1989 (Charlie Cole).
- President Kennedy slumped over in his open-top car after being assassinated in Dallas, Texas.
- Man chips at the Berlin Wall. 1989 (Anthony Suau).
- Starving Child in Sudan 1993 (Kevin Carter)
- The Loch Ness Monster.
- Winston Churchill giving his *'V for Victory'* hand sign.
- Pictures of the holocaust.
- Pictures of troops in First World War trenches.
- The execution of Ruth Snyder in New York State 1928 (the only known photograph of anyone dying in an electric chair).

Some pictures graphically report on events (photojournalism) and some have significantly altered public opinion. One such photograph was of Vietnamese children running along a road, flesh melting, after a US napalm bombing run. The revulsion against the US action helped shorten the Vietnam War. The lesson was well learned by governments when, in later conflicts, they sought to control information by replacing free-wandering reporters/photographers with *'embedded reporters'* and selected military briefings to chosen journalists.

Advertising & promotion

The power of photographs for advertising is also well known, with many examples such as:

- The Che Guevara portrait that appeared on millions of bedroom posters, tee-shirts, etc.
- Government road safety campaign posters.
- The desperate pictures of starving children used by aid agencies to raise funds.
- The Benetton advertising billboards.
- The cover of the Beatles' *'Abbey Road'* album.

Advertising executives, sport and media personalities and politicians used to work to the old adage that says, *"there is no such thing as bad publicity"*.   Now they are less sure, as photographs of mad cows, the live exporting of livestock, brawling footballers and drunken personalities have harmed individuals and even entire industries.

Nevertheless, *'photo opportunities'* are regularly engineered to promote individuals, as in the following examples:

- The Royal Family, politicians and personalities parading their offspring.
- Government ministers kissing babies, visiting hospitals, opening prestigious events, and so on.
- Marilyn Munroe, with her dress blown up by a rush of air from a street vent.

Education & information

While the above examples may be well known or dramatic, the use of photographs in explaining issues is a long-established practice.   Consider how useful a manual on car repairs or a mail order catalogue would be without the photographs.

Getting the picture

There are four ways that real-world pictures can be captured for use in multimedia projects:

- Using a scanner to transfer copies of any photograph (either newly developed or old pictures).
- A 35mm or APS scanner, to digitise slides, negative strips or an APS (Advanced Photo System) adapter.

- Using a digital camera to capture directly as a computer file.
- Extracting a still image from a video clip.

The first three techniques are covered in this chapter and the chapter on digital video covers extracting stills from a video clip.

A quick guide to digital photographs

With a normal film camera, the light reflected from the subject being photographed is focussed on to a film that is covered in multiple coatings of a silver halide emulsion.   Tiny particles of silver are created on the film in correspondence to the light intensity hitting different parts of the film surface.   After processing, this forms the film negative from which the final prints are made.

With a digital camera, the light still passes through the lens but is shone on a complex digital device known as a CCD (see later).   The CCD contains hundreds of thousands, or millions, of light sensitive sensors.   The electrical charge in each sensor is proportional to the amount of light hitting it.

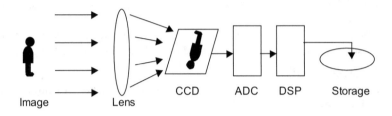

These analogue values are passed through an ADC (analogue to digital converter). This converts the picture information into a digital equivalent.   The signal is then passed through a DSP (digital signal processor). This adjusts the signal for the optimum contrast range and can also compress the signal if desired. The signal is then saved to some storage medium as a computer file. This file can be loaded into any graphics editing package at any later date, optimised or edited, and integrated into multimedia projects.

Comparison of digital images and 35mm film

Inevitably, comparisons are made between conventional film quality and the quality from digital photographs.   It is true that early models of digital cameras had very low resolutions and were totally unable to compete with emulsion film in terms of quality.

However, even the early digital cameras had some benefits over film cameras:

- The results of a photographic session can be reviewed immediately.   The photographer can leave the location, knowing that the required images have been successfully captured.
- There are no time delays, waiting for the film to be processed, possibly to find that not all the images were usable.
- There are no ongoing costs in purchasing fresh rolls of film.   The images can be downloaded into the computer and the memory can be re-used for other photographic sessions.
- There are no film processing costs (of course, the camera is much more expensive to buy initially).
- There is no wastage.   Unwanted images can be deleted from the camera's memory and the memory capacity can be re-used to store other photographs.

The best current digital cameras rival the quality of conventional film.   The silver halide coating on 35mm film has over 86 billion crystals per negative.   These are contained in multiple (up to 17) layers of emulsion, each layer with different sensitivities. After removing the effects of lens error and focus error, it is roughly equivalent to a 4 million pixel CCD.   Conventional 35mm film quality is the equivalent of 2400 lines per inch, which can be achieved with a digital camera using a 4 megapixel CCD.

Of course, the emulsion of a 35-mm print is evenly distributed over the film surface, while the sensors on CCD are regularly laid out in even lines and columns (due to the way they are produced). This subtle symmetry in the final output is noticeable to professional photographers. This effect is minimised in the Fujitsu Super CCD which uses hexagonal elements arranged in a honeycomb pattern, to break up the regular lines and columns.

Scitex are developing a CMOS (Complementary Metal Oxide Semiconductor) sensor that is designed to fit into the back of a professional film camera, in place of the spool of film.   This allows the existing professional photographer to get into digital photography without replacing all the camera equipment.   The sensor has a claimed resolution of 6.6 megapixels.

How digital cameras work

Many of the principles, such as the operation of the lens, focal length, filters, etc apply to all cameras, whether they are digital or take standard rolls of film.

The Lens

Lenses are seen in many everyday objects such as spectacles, monocles, binoculars, telescopes and magnifying glasses.   They are made from a glass or transparent plastic material.

In a camera, its job is to focus the image of objects in the real world into the camera for processing and capture.   The larger the diameter of the lens, the more light it is capable of gathering.

Light from the image is gathered at the front of the lens and the light beams are concentrated on an area at the rear of the lens. With a film camera, the area focussed upon is the film; with a digital camera, it is a light-sensitive electronic device known as a CCD (see later).

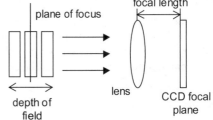

Depending upon the exact dimensions of the lens used in a camera, there is a point at which the image is sharply formed (i.e. in focus). This distance is known as the *'focal length'* and is the measurement from the centre of the lens to the spot at the back of the camera (i.e. the camera film or the CCD) where the image is sharply focussed.   For cameras with a fixed focal length, the measurement is taken when viewing a distant object.   The spot where the incoming light hits the sensors is termed the *'focal plane'*.   The small size of CCDs means that they have a shorter focal length than those in 35mm film cameras.   It is typically about 8mm (somewhere between 6mm and 10mm).   This is equivalent to the 40mm to 55mm focal length found on a film camera, as the CCD area is much smaller than the frame of a 35mm film.   By convention, the specification of a digital camera's focal length is usually given as the equivalent figure for a film camera (presumably on the basis that most purchasers are ex-film camera users).

Optical zoom

When a camera has an optical zoom, the zoom lens can be physically moved in relation to the back plane.

Altering the focal length alters the distance an object has to be from the lens to be in focus and alters the amount of the scene that enters the lens. The zoom lens has a variable focal length so that its field of view can be varied from wide angle, through normal to telephoto. Increasing the focal length is *'zooming in'* or taking a *'telephoto'* shot, while decreasing the focal length is *'zooming out'* or taking a *'wide-angle'* shot.

The range of focal length of a camera is measured in millimetres, while the range of a digital zoom is measured in multiplication factors.   Most models offer 2X or 3X, with the some models offering 5X and a few offering up to 14X optical zoom.

Notes

The zoom factor measures the amount of <u>area</u> that is included in the captured image, not the vertical and horizontal dimensions.   So, if a camera was currently set to capture an image from an area that was 9m wide by 6m high, it would capture an area of 54 square meters.   If the zoom is then set to a factor of 3X, it will now capture an area that is one third of the previous size (i.e. 54/3 = 18 square metres).   It does not divide the dimensions down to 3m x 2m.   This would give an area of six square metres, which is a ninth of the original size, not a third of the size.

Typical figures for a digital camera's range are 28mm up to 115mm (expressed as 35mm film equivalents).

A camera with a stated focal length of 35-70mm has a zoom range of 2X.

Digital camcorders usually have a superior optical system to digital cameras.   A digital camcorder usually offers a zoom range of 10X or even 15X, while a typical digital camera has a 3X zoom.

Digital zoom

Some cameras also provide a further digital zoom factor. There is a great difference in how optical and digital zooms operate.   The optical zoom is used to fill the CCD area with light from a smaller or greater object area.   So, if the camcorder zooms in on an object, only the light reflected from that smaller area enters the lens and the full CCD area is used to capture the new image information.   This maintains high quality pictures at all zoom settings.   Digital zoom, on the other hand, reads in the entire image information into the CCD and only uses the centre portion of the data, discarding the rest.   The data in the centre portion is then expanded to make it fill the camcorder's screen resolution.   The greater the digital zoom is advanced, the blockier the picture and high zoom settings result in unusable content.   The optical zoom should be used at all times, unless a deliberately blocky effect is required.

Add-on lenses

If the camera's existing zoom range does meet all the photographer's needs, additional converter lenses are available. These screw into the front of the existing lens and range from a .45x wide-angle converter to a 5x telephoto converter. These ratios are applied to the existing zoom range.   Therefore, a 3x optical zoom on a camera is extended to a 15x optical zoom when the 5x converter is fitted.   As the lens is zoomed in, less and less of the scene enters the lens.

From the opposite point of view, the wide-angle converter allows more of the scene to enter the camera lens. A 0.5X converter, for example, would double the area that is captured as an image. Wide-angle shots are particularly useful when the camera operator cannot get far enough back from the scene to be shot (e.g. filming in a small room, or wide panoramic scenes).   Wide-angle settings also exaggerate perspective.   This is sometimes used to achieve special effects (e.g. using a wide angle to shoot someone's head close up results in their nose and mouth being extra-prominent).

Aperture

The aperture of a lens controls the amount of light entering the camera.   The maximum aperture for a lens is set by the physical diameter of the lens.

The aperture is adjusted to suit the subject being shot and the prevailing light conditions.   In very bright sunlight, a lower aperture is required, while the aperture would be much greater for low-light conditions.

The setting of aperture sizes is on a scale of *'f numbers'*, such that each step on the f number scale lets in half the amount of light of the previous f number. This is not a linear scale so, for example, settings may be f2.8, f4, f5.6, f8, f11, f16 and f22 for a film camera. Digital cameras usually have only a five-stop range.

Moving from a setting f8 to f11 halves the amount of light, while moving from f5.6 to f4 doubles the amount of light. This scale is not a set of absolute values, since different cameras have different lens diameters and hence allow different amounts of light in at their maximum setting. Consequently, it is a relative scale that measures the ratio of the focal length to the diameter of the aperture. So, a 50mm lens with a 12.5mm aperture = f4.

Depth of field

A camera is focussed on a particular subject, so that it is clearly captured within the camera. The spot that produces the clear image is known as the *'plane of focus'*. Another object in the same focal plane will also be clearly focussed in the camera. Objects that are positioned closer or further from the plane of focus distance may not be clearly focussed in the camera's image.

The *'depth of field'* describes the distance in front and behind the focal plane in which objects will still be sharply focussed. For a camcorder, it is also the amount of distance that an object can travel during a recording and remain clearly focussed.

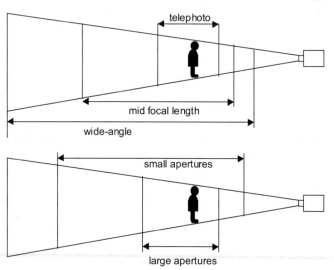

The scope of the depth of field is determined by the camera's focal length, the lens aperture setting and the distance between the lens and the plane of focus. A shorter focal length and a smaller aperture (i.e. higher f-stop number) increases the depth of field.

The diagrams give some indication of the relationship between the various factors. It shows, for example, that the depth of field is much smaller when shooting with a focal length set at telephoto, compared to shooting with a focal length set at wide angle.

It also shows the greater depth of field that is achieved with smaller aperture settings.

This limitation can be a problem in some situations. At other times, the photographer takes advantage of this to deliberately have a defocused background (e.g. to concentrate on the foreground subject or to hide an unsightly background).

CCDs

Digital cameras do not use a roll of film. The images are captured on to a magnetic storage medium. The camera's electronics carry out the conversion from light intensity to digital computer file.

Light passes through the camera lens and is converted into electrical signals by a CCD (charge-coupled device). The CCD is a solid-state chip as small as 1/3" or 1/4" that contains a matrix of light sensors. Each sensor is a tiny photodiode that produces a value of electrical charge that varies according to the amount of light that hits it. Each row and column of sensors corresponds to the picture's horizontal and vertical resolution.

The number of pixel sensors has a bearing on the final picture quality, with greater resolution being achieved by CCDs with a greater number of pixels. This is not the only factor that determines picture quality as the quality of the lens, method of writing to tape, etc also have a significant impact.

When the user presses the button, a microchip reads the amount of charge in each cell. The values from each row are read off and make up the serial image output stream. The electronics uses analogue shift registers to move the image data off the CCD and through the ADC.

The CCD specification fitted to different models varies and typical examples are:

Under 2 million pixels

Covers all *'budget'* models. Their specification is well beyond the needs for creating photographic images for web sites and for domestic photo-reproductions (printing 8in x 6in images on an inkjet with adequate results).

Over 2 million pixels

Covers all *'mid-range'* models. Aimed at quality images on CDs, presentations and printed material. A 3 megapixel camera will provide good results on an A4 sheet (i.e. 10in x 8in) while a 4 megapixel image will print a 11in x 9in image.

Film quality CCDs

Priced more at the *'professional'* market, these cameras provide at least 5 megapixel resolution and are increasingly being used as alternatives to emulsion film models. They often come with added features such as SLR (see later) viewing, more comprehensive user controls and better quality lenses.

Colour

As described, the camera would only produce a monochrome output, with the output signal varying purely in sympathy with the intensity of the incoming light.   The production of a colour camera is a little more complex.   Firstly, there are three sensors for each pixel, sitting next to each other in the horizontal row.   Each sensor is dedicated to producing an output that corresponds with the intensity of the red, green and blue components of the incoming light.   Colour filters are placed in front of the CCD to break down the incoming light into its components.   In this way, only the varying intensity of the red component reaches the sensors set aside for the red signal.   Similarly, only the blue component of the light reaches the blue sensors and the green component of the light only reaches the sensors on the CCD set aside for handling green.

The camera has three colour outputs, one each for the red, green and blue components of the picture and their relative values are combined to produce the final colours stored for each pixel in the image.

Triple-CCD systems

Using three CCDs has been common in professional equipment for some time and is now being provided in some top-end consumer cameras and camcorders.   A separate CCD is dedicated to converting each colour component and a prism separates the incoming light from the lens into its red, green and blue components.   The prisms direct each of these to a separate CCD.   This provides improved sensitivity and colour reproduction, compared to single-CCD models.

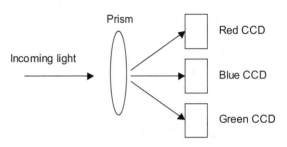

Some triple-CCD systems use a technique known as *'pixel shift'*.   One of the CCDs is fixed slightly out of alignment with the others.   The summing of the three signals will produce a monochrome signal that has the same resolution as a system that is not using pixel shift.   However, the overall effect is to improve low-light sensitivity.

Filters

Although photo-editing software can enhance the final graphic file contents, it cannot replace areas that have been completely darkened or washed out at the capture stage.   Therefore, digital cameras often require the use of filters.   Filters are additional optical devices that look like ordinary lenses.   Cameras that provide for filters have a fine thread machined in the barrel of the lens housing.   The filter screws in this thread and fits over the lens.   This means that all light entering the camera has to pass through the filter and it can therefore affect the light in some way.   The filters themselves are threaded, allowing more than one filter to be fitted to a camera.

UV filter

This filter absorbs ultra-violet rays, preventing haziness and fogginess in distant landscapes.   Many owners keep this filter permanently attached to the camera as it is neutral in most situations and acts as a protector for the lens.   The lens fitted to a camera could be very expensive to replace if it became scratched or cracked, while a UV filter is a very cheap component.

Polarising filter

This is probably the most common filter that is used.   Light from the sun, a flashgun or a studio lamp are all unpolarised - the light travels in several different planes.   Sometimes, the light can reflect from a particular surface, such as water, glass or shiny surfaces apart from metal.   The reflection is at a shallow angle (around 30°) such that the light waves then all travel in the same plane. This makes it very difficult to shoot without interference from these reflections.   A good example is trying to shoot through a shop window; the reflections from the glass spoil the image. Similarly, water scenes can be spoiled by reflections from the sky. The polarising filter is fitted in front of the lens and rotated in its mount until the unwanted reflections are minimised or eliminated.   Note, however, that some cameras rotate their barrel during auto-focus altering the setting of the polarising filter.

The polarising filter also increases the final colour saturation (the richness of the colours).   For example, the blue of the sky is deepened and the clouds are displayed more strongly.

Star filter

Sometimes called a *'cross screen filter'* it is available in 4-point, 6-point and 8-point versions.   A bright light in the picture is extended across the screen area in the shape of a star.   This is mostly used for night-time filming, where a sunset, traffic lights, car headlights, hotel neon sign, etc. are enhanced.

Soft focus filter

It removes any harshness from the lighting and gives a *'misty'* look to the scene.   It is often used for nostalgic or romantic photographs (e.g. the virginal heroine, the sleepy valley, etc)

Graduated filters

One end of the filter is clear, with a progressive tint towards the other end. It is used to overcome the extremes of contrast in sunny locations.   Normally, the camera's automatic exposure system averages out the incoming light.

This might leave the bright sky washed out and the foreground too dark. Moving to manual exposure allows the foreground to be given more exposure, but this results in the sky becoming even further washed out. The filter is fitted with the darker end at the top. This reduces the amount of light from the bright sky, lowering the contrast ratio and preventing the scene contents from being driven into the extremes of darkness or washout. These filters are effective with both automatic and manual exposure. Graduated filters are produced with varying properties.

| Graduated Filters and their uses ||
Filter type	Description
Graduated blue filter	Minimises extreme light difference between sky and landscape. Does not affect the colour content of the scene.
Graduated grey filter	Minimises extreme light difference between different areas of a landscape. Does not affect the colour content of the scene.
Graduated tobacco filter	Used to enhance shots of sunsets and sunrises.

Other filters
Many filters that are available for film cameras fit on digital camera lens. This allows a whole range of special effect filters to be used.   In addition to the filters mentioned above, other filter types include:
- Multi-image filters (multiple copies of the image are captured in a prism-like effect)
- Warm filters (have a slight orange tint to overcome some cold effects from harsh light. People look sun-tanned and locations appear to be bathed in an evening sunlight).

Storage problems
As digital cameras have developed, their CCDs have included more and more pixels. While this provides a great boost to the image's resolution, it also means that there is a greatly increased file size.
There is always a trade-off between the amount of storage, the resolution at which the image is captured and the number of pictures that can be stored. Early digital cameras were sold with a fixed amount of built-in storage. This meant that the user had top either settle for low resolution image, or take less photographs. The arrival of removable storage eases the situation, but purchasing a collection of memory cards is expensive.

Colours
Photorealistic images are much larger than cartoons and clip art. Clip art only uses a small number of different colours, while a real-world image is made up of millions of different colours and shades. The amount of storage space for a photograph is therefore much higher than simple graphics. Cartoons, logos, etc. use up to 256 different colours, while photographs use 16.7 million different colours. Cartoons only requires eight bits (i.e. a byte) to represent any individual pixel, while the digitised photograph uses 24 bits (i.e. three bytes). This means that photorealistic images will always be three times larger than a 256-colour graphic. It may be possible, in some circumstances, to reduce a photographic image to 256 colours. This reduction in colour depth (i.e. bit depth) may be used to create special effects. Alternatively, it may be used to further shrink the storage needs of a small web image, where a reduction in colours may not be so noticeable.

Resolution and file size
The largest possible file size, for a single image, for a particular camera is produced by storing its highest resolution setting, at full 24-bit colour, without any compression.
The storage requirement of an uncompressed photo-realistic file is calculated thus:
    File Size = Bit Depth x Screen Resolution / 1024
The bit depth for a photograph is always 16.7 million colours which requires 3 bytes of storage for each pixel in the picture (i.e. 24-bit colour divided by 8 to convert the figure to bytes). Dividing by 1024 converts the answer into kilobytes. For very large files, the answer can be divided by a further 1024 to get the answer in megabytes.

Some example uncompressed file sizes are:
- A photograph intended to fill a VGA screen would require
    3 x 640 x 480 = 921,600 bytes
- A 1280 x 960 image requires
    3 x 1280 x 960 = 3,686,400 bytes or 3.515MB.
- A 1792x1200 image requires a huge
    3 x 1792 1200 / 1024 / 1024 = 6.152MB
- The Nikon D1x has a maximum resolution of 3040x2016, requiring a massive
    3 x 3040 x 2016 /1024 / 1024 = over 17.5MB of storage for each uncompressed image.

An alternative way to calculate the largest file size is to take a camera's CCD, multiply it by three and convert it into binary numbering.
So, if a camera states that it has 2.1 megapixels, the calculation is
    2,100,000 x 3 /1024 /1024 = 6MB

Compression

It is currently impractical to store many images of 6MB and 13MB on a removable storage system, although the supply of digital cameras with miniature hard disks will ease the problem. Even then, the huge files will take a little time to download from the camera into the computer.

The current solution lies in compressing the image files down to a much smaller storage size. This is usually some form of JPEG algorithm and files are saved with the .jpg extension. More details on compression techniques are given in other chapters.

Since JPEG compression is a *'lossy'* system, some degradation of the image results from this squashing of the file size. The greater the file compression, the greater the file degradation. Most cameras offer both a choice of resolution (e.g. standard, high) and level of compression (e.g. good, better or best).

For example, a 8MB storage card may hold 36 images at high compression, 18 images at medium compression and only two uncompressed images.

Storage media

Early models had permanent, built-in memory chips (of around 4MB or 8MB) and there was no means of adding extra storage. A few models still provide built-in memory but also allow the use of add-on memory cards.

Most cameras use memory cards that are slotted into the camera. When the card is full, it is removed from the camera and another card is inserted. All forms of removable media have to be small, to match the small size of the cameras. Most are solid state devices, offering non-volatile flash memory. This means that they do not lose contents when the camera is switched off.. The full range of devices used to store digital images is explained below.

SmartMedia

This storage medium is as thin as a credit card and shaped something like a small floppy disk, although a lot smaller at 45mm x 37mm x 0.78mm. It has a row of 22-pins for its connection. Its popularity has waned with the introduction of even smaller memory cards with greater capacities (see xD below).

CompactFlash

This card is roughly the same size but at 43mm x 36mm x 3.3mm it is about the size of a book of matches. It is available in capacities up to 8GbMB. It has a 50-pin connection that fits a PCMCIA type II 68-pin card adapter.

Sony Memory Stick

This is a technology developed by Sony. At 50mm x 21.5mm, it looks like half a stick of chewing gum. It is available in capacities up to 2GbMB and has a write-protect switch like a floppy disk. It is used in some digital cameras and is also used to store still images in some digital camcorders. Note that the newer Memory Stick Pro is not compatible with standard Memory Stick devices.

SD (Secure Digital)/MMC

Developed by Matsushita, SanDisk and Toshiba, the card is only 24cm x 18cm and has capacities up to 8Gb, although 1Gb is more typical.

The SD and MMC devices are the same physical layout and dimensions, allowing some devices to use either type. However, the SD is capable of storing copyrighted data and this means that some devices will only accept SD cards.

XD

Developed by FujiFilm and Olympus, this is essentially an advanced version of the SmartMedia card. It measures only 20cm x 25cm. Since it is the newest of the technologies, it has not yet caught up with the others in terms of large capacity versions.

Storage disks

The idea of removable disks for image storage began with the Sony Mavica range of cameras. These cameras used standard 1.44MB floppy disks to store the images. Since the images were stored as standard JPEG files, the floppy could be placed in the floppy drive of any computer and immediately copied or imported into an application. This avoided the need for a separate hardware device or software driver to transfer files between the camera and computer. While it is convenient, the size of the floppy meant that the cameras were large and the storage on any one floppy disk was very limited.

Iomega Clik! produce a miniature 40MB disk drive that appeared on a few cameras The disks have much larger storage capacity than a floppy disk and can be inserted into any computer that has a Clik! drive.

Even greater storage capacity is provided by cameras that fit the tiny Microdrive hard disk. The drives have capacities ranging from 340MB to 4GB and use a PC Card slot.

Some other models stores their images on a 730MB magneto-optical disk and download images using its FireWire connector. Models that write to a mini CD-R or CD-RW create disks that are readable on all CD and DVD players.

Videocassette

A growing number of camcorders provide facilities for capturing still pictures. The data from a single frame is taken from the CCDs and recorded as a still onto the videotape as a short video clip (of perhaps seven seconds), normally allowing a voiceover to accompany the still.

Connections to the computer

Once the images are stored to the camera's storage medium, the files need to be transferred or copied from the camera into the computer.   There are a number of ways that the camera can connect with a computer, to transfer the images to the computer's hard disk.

Serial cable

Older digital cameras connected to the computer via its serial port. Since every computer has a serial port socket, there is no need to provide special hardware.   The cable plugs into the camera at one end and the other end plugs into the computer's serial port.   Providing that the software exists for the transfer (see the notes below on TWAIN) the files can be transferred at the relatively slow peak transfer rate of 115.2kbits per second.   While this is fast enough for small files, the transfer of an entire microdrive's 1GB contents would be far too slow.   All other transfer methods improve on this transfer rate, sometimes by a very large margin. Fortunately, only a very few cameras still offer a serial connection method.

USB cable

This is by far the most common method of connecting cameras to computers. A cable connects the camera to an unused USB port on the computer.   Again, no other hardware is necessary, although the file transfer software has to be installed on the computer. The data transfer rate for USB peaks at 12Mbits per second, which is far faster than serial transfers. Of course, this method can only be used with newer computers, as older computers did not have USB connections.   To overcome this, an add-on card is available that provides USB facilities for older computers, as long as they have at least Windows 98 installed.

Media readers

A media reader is a dedicated piece of hardware that connects to the computer's USB port. The CompactFlash card, Smartmedia card or Memory Stick module is removed from the camera and placed in the reader's card slot.
As above, the computer must have a USB port or an add-on USB port adapter. Some readers offer faster download times than reading from the card while it is still in the camera.

Parallel adapter

The parallel adapter is a dedicated piece of hardware that connects to the computer's parallel port.   The CompactFlash or Smartmedia card is removed from the camera and placed in the reader's card slot. These are faster than serial connections but slower than USB transfers. Examples are the CardPort Swift P/Port range of adapters for SmartMedia and CompactFlash cards and the Pico PC PhotoReader.

Floppy disk

As mentioned above, the early Sony Mavica range of cameras used standard 1.44MB floppy disks as the storage medium. No special hardware or drivers was needed. The images were stored in normal file format were read in the same way as any other file on a normal floppy disk.

Floppy adapter

The SmartMedia card is removed from the camera and inserted in an adaptor which is designed to fit in a computer's floppy drive. As long as the software driver is installed, the images on the card can be read and copied onto the hard drive. An example is the FujiFilm FlashPath adaptor FD-A1.   At a transfer rate of 250KB per second, it is over twice as fast than serial connection transfers. Sony also produces a floppy adaptor for its own Memory Sticks modules.

PC Card adapter

Most portable computers are fitted with PC card slots (also called PCMCIA slots).   These allow a range of add-on devices such as modems, drives and CD-ROMs to be added to the system by plugging them into spare PC Card slots.   Adapters are available for SmartMedia and CompactFlash cards and Sony Memory Sticks.   The cards are inserted in the adapter and the adapter plugs into the PC Card slot.

Infrared

A few cameras use infrared waves to transfer images between the camera and any computer with an infrared (IrDA) receiver.   There is no physical connection between the units and the medium is not removed from the camera.

FireWire

The more expensive Kodak, Nikon and Sanyo models provide FireWire connections.

TWAIN drivers

At one time, all manufacturers produced their own driver software for downloading files into the computer. The files were then brought into the graphics editing package as a separate operation. TWAIN is now an accepted standard used in data acquisition (e.g. cameras and scanners).   It defines the major operations that are required for image capture.   If all capture devices and all software used the same operations, then every piece of software could communicate with every device. This allows TWAIN-compatible software, such as PhotoShop and Paint Shop Pro, to directly import images from any hardware device that is also TWAIN-compliant. TWAIN supports serial, USB and PC Card transfers. It allows photographs to be downloaded from the camera directly into the editing application. It also allows the application programs to import images straight from a scanner, without leaving the application.
Some cameras are not TWAIN-compatible and the images still have to be downloaded into the computer using the supplied software, then brought into the editing application.

Other camera features

Additional features to consider when buying a digital camera include:

TV output

Many digital cameras provide a video output.   This does mean that they record video clips.   It just means that the photographic images can be shown on a television screen by connecting a cable to the television's *'video in'* sockets. This is mainly a facility for camera owners to displays images to a group of people, without the need for a computer.   If the LCD viewing screen is not showing enough detail, this facility provides a useful way to examine photographs while on location.   For the UK, the video output should be in PAL format.   Some cameras have both PAL and NTSC outputs and this allows photographs to be displayed on televisions while on holiday in the USA, etc.   The video output of cameras can often be fed into a video capture card and used as a video camera to capture movie clips.   This is a cheap alternative to purchasing a digital camcorder but, since the camera has to remain attached to the computer, it is not only suitable for studio recording.   A separate camcorder should be purchased, if possible, as it usually has a superior lens system, has built-in audio recording and other refinements.

Batteries

Digital camcorders are notorious for the heavy drain on their batteries.   Much of this is caused by illuminating the LCD viewing panel.   Some models use standard AA type NiCad batteries (Nickel Cadmium), whose regular replacement is a costly business.   Some models use proprietary rechargeable batteries, which are also expensive to replace after their useful life.   The most flexible choices are cameras that use normal rechargeable lithium ion or nickel metal hydride batteries.

Flash

Many cameras have a built-in flash.   This must be under the control of the operator.   Flash must be able to be turned on and off by the user, as the automatic setting is not always suitable.   There are occasions, for example, when it would be used in bright daylight to fill in shadows on a face or object.   At other times, it would be turned off even during light conditions that are poor.   This would include situations when a flash would be intrusive e.g. a church service, shooting wildlife, surveillance, etc.   On the other hand, an underexposed photograph might be required, for artistic effect.

LCD panel/optical viewfinder

Most cameras provide a rear LCD panel, to allow the camera operator to see exactly what image will be captured. It also allows previous photographs to be recalled and examined or deleted.   As an alternative, or as an addition, it may provide an internal optical or electronic viewfinder.   The disadvantage of the LCD panel is that the screen is washed out when viewed in bright sunlight.   It also consumes a fair amount of power from the battery pack.   The optical viewfinder saves on battery consumption and is much easier to view in brightly lit conditions.   On the other hand, an LCD panel is useful for viewing awkward angles, where looking though an eyepiece is not practical. Examples are recording a passing parade, where the camera is being held above the heads of the crowd, or turning the camera round so that the camera operator can photograph himself/herself.

The best film cameras use an SLR (single lens reflex) optical system that allows the operator to see exactly what will appear in the captured image.   This is rarely found in digital cameras.   Some top-end manufacturers produce models provide an SLR optical system. This has the advantages of not having to use the LCD viewing panel (hence saving on battery drain) and always being able to see the content of the scene under the brightest light conditions.

Writing time

When taking posed or still-life photographs, the time taken to write the captured scene to the media does not pose any problems.   However, in capturing real-world events, the time delay makes the difference between capturing enough of the event - or spending more time waiting than shooting.   The writing time of digital cameras depends upon the medium.   Writing to a mechanical medium is slower than writing to memory chips.   The delay ranges from a few seconds up to 10 seconds or more.

Some models have a time lapse mode.   The user can set intervals of 1 minute up to 24 hours between taking photographs.   These images can be grouped together (using a package such as GIF animator or Animation Shop in Paint Shop Pro) into a time-lapse video sequence showing a flower opening, the movement of clouds, etc.

Video capture option

Newer models now offer the facility to capture miniature video clips.   These are all of small resolution and short duration, due to the even greater storage demands of video recording.   This facility is not a serious alternative to recordings from a digital camcorder.   For hobbyists on a low budget, it is the ideal way of capturing web-sized video clips as clips can recorded without the need to purchase a camcorder.

Those digital cameras that provide the video capture facility only offer screen resolutions ranging from 160x120 to 320x240.   The amount of video captured varies from about 10 seconds to over a minute and the formats offered include AVI, MPEG-1, MJPEG and QuickTime.   The frame rates are also pretty low – around 5 fps to 15fps.

A related facility is the ability to use *'continuous capture'*.   This captures a set of individual images in rapid succession.   The result is not a movie clip but a sequence of separate files.   A typical use is capturing the sequence of a racehorse crossing the finishing line.   Some models can capture many images at slow capture rates (e.g. 2.5fps) while others capture at faster rates (e.g. 5fps) but have a limit to the number of images captures.   So, for example, a single press of a button may record a sequence of forty images over a period of eight seconds.

Automatic/Manual Controls

Cameras usually automatically adjust their focus and exposure settings in response to the nature of the incoming light. While this is satisfactory for *'point and shoot'* situations, the operator will often require more control than the default automatic settings. For example, the camcorder's auto focus allows the subject to remain in focus whether at close range or at long distance. The operator, however, may wish to have the foreground subject out of focus, with the background being in focus. The camera should allow the manual override of exposure, focussing and other settings.

Voice annotations

Some cameras provide a built-in microphone. This allows a brief audio description to be attached to an image file. This could be a useful aid for cataloguing shots.

DPOF support

DPOF (digital print order format) has no particular benefits for multimedia use. It is supported by Kodak, FujiFilm, Canon and others. It allows normal prints to be created from the memory card, from shops supporting this scheme.

Capturing digital images

The techniques involved in taking digital photographs differ little from using standard film cameras. With standard cameras, the steps are plan, prepare, shoot, develop and hope for the best.

The steps for capturing photographic images are:
- Plan the photographic session.
- Prepare all necessary resources.
- Shoot the pictures.
- Examine the captured images and reshoot if necessary.
- Download the images into the computer.

Digital photography provides more control over the process, as the results can be viewed as the shoot proceeds. Of course, the camera's results are determined by its operator's skill and experience.   Like video recording, digital photography is a creative process as well as a technical process. This section does not provide all the knowledge and experience necessary for professional results.   Readers interested in this area are invited to join a camera club or take an evening course at a local college.

This section, along with a section in the chapter on digital video, contains useful information on picture composition, lighting the subject, camera positioning, use of zoom, etc.   These pages reflect the conventional wisdom on the subject but, as in all creative work, breaking the rules can achieve special effects.

Orientation

Digital cameras usually have an aspect ratio of 4:3 (e.g. the image may be 640x480 or 800x 600) to match the aspect ratio of computer monitors.   This means that the camera takes a rectangular picture that can be shot in *'Portrait'* or *Landscape'* mode. The default orientation of the captured image is landscape format.

The camera has to be physically rotated 90° and held this way, to capture images in portrait format. With the camera in this position, it can sometimes be awkward to reach the camera controls.

The example pictures illustrate images captured in both formats. The picture on the left was taken in normal landscape format and there is a lot of wasted space in the image.   The second picture shows the same picture captured in portrait format.

Of course, the first picture can be cropped and resized to produce exactly the same result - except that many of the pixels in the image would be discarded and the image quality would suffer.

The second set of pictures shows a view of the city of San Francisco, taken from a boat in the Bay, with a camera fitted with a wide-angle lens adaptor.

In this case, the default landscape view shown on the right is much more efficient, as it includes a wider content than that captured in portrait mode. It is also more natural, since the flow of content is in a horizontal plane.

Large sections of the panoramic view are lost in portrait format and, since the camera cannot be moved further back, there is no way to encompass the entire panorama in this format.

For photographs of groups (families, workmates, football team, etc) the landscape format uses the capture area to best advantage. It is also best for panoramic scenes.

The portrait format is best used for photographing individual portraits and tall objects such as full-body shots, high-rise buildings, etc.

Note

When an image is captured in portrait mode and transferred to the computer, it is stored on its side. Fortunately, all image editing software has a *'rotate'* facility that will rotate the image through 90° so that it can be saved in the correct orientation for use in projects.

Composition

Composition is the term used to describe the two essential ingredients of a successful photograph - subject and context. Since the images are for use in a multimedia project of some description, these are even more important questions than photographs taken for the family album (although the rules can be applied to good use in all photographic situations).

Each photograph should have a purpose and a list of shots might have been prepared by a storyboard or a shooting list drawn up from a web site plan. Each shot in the list should specify the main content of the photograph. This should not be listed in terms of *'picture of school'* or *'picture of footballer'*. The photograph is intended to play a particular part of the final project and the context describes the location, activity, surroundings, or any other element that conveys the mood or meaning of the photograph.

Examples of shot descriptions may be *'picture of school with students playing'* or *'picture of school from a majestic angle'*. The first picture conveys a *'feel good'* mood, while the second is more formal.

Similarly *'picture of footballer tackling an opponent'* and *'picture of footballer in pinstripe suit'* convey entirely different moods.

Most photographs can be improved by correctly balancing the subject and context. For example, a photographer of a watchmaker or a miner at work conveys more meaning than pictures of them standing next to their tools or machinery. This means that the main subject is rarely positioned in the middle of the photograph, a common mistake among beginners. The exception may be portraits of the bank manager or college principal.

Centres of Interest

Artists and photographers often use the *'Rule of Thirds'*. This divides the picture area into thirds, both horizontally and vertically. The four points where the lines intersect are regarded as the *'centres of interest'* (i.e. the main spots where the eye is attracted in a scene). Centres of interest are also known as *'hot spots'*. Many photographs are improved by avoiding having the main subject in the centre of the area. The landscape picture of San Francisco placed the dark skyscraper in upper left hot spot.

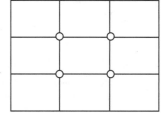

The main subject is often placed on a vertical axis, with a subsidiary object occupying the other axis. An example is a Member of Parliament positioned on the right axis of the screen, while Big Ben is visible in the background on the left axis. This is a good example of using context in a photograph. The viewer may not recognise the individual but he/she is immediately identified with Parliament because of the background context.

Other useful composition points to note are:

- Secondary objects should be smaller than the subject or be placed well in the background.
- The primary subject should be the most prominent in the composition. This may be achieved using the relative size of the subject compared to subordinate objects, or the main subject may be the most brightly coloured picture element.

Horizons and Lines

We generally think of horizons as being the area where the sea or land meets the sky, some way off in the distance. From a photographer's point of view, the horizon is any horizontal object that meets the sky to create separate picture areas. Therefore, the roofline, a wall or rows of trees are all examples of horizons. The horizon should not divide the picture exactly in half. Dividing a picture into three-thirds is generally accepted (e.g. the beach, the sea and the sky). The earlier San Francisco landscape photograph cut the picture into sea, cityscape and sky. The rule can be relaxed to achieve particular effects. For example, a low horizon emphasises the expanse of sky and suggests spaciousness, while a high horizon draws the viewer into a more intimate foreground scene.

If possible, avoid major vertical or horizontal objects in the picture. For example, a river or road is best shot running diagonally across the frame.

Professionals regularly use *'lines and paths'* within the compositions. These may be real or inferred lines that lead the viewer's eyes into and around the picture content. These may be objects such as roads, rivers, fences, railway lines, overhead cables, etc. that meander naturally. Alternatively, they may be the outlines of furniture, equipment, human limbs, etc., which lead or point around the picture.

Many photographs look flat and uninteresting. In some cases, this is due to a lack of perspective in the picture. Viewers cannot grasp the relative dimensions of objects, as there are no reference points in image. This is

traditionally overcome by using *'vanishing points'*.   These are real
or inferred lines that provide perspective to a composition. The lines
are parallel but run for such a long distance that they appear as if they
will merge at some distant point.   The diagrams show two examples.
The first shows two symmetrical lines.   This would be achieved
when the camera is placed looking down a street, airport runway, railway line, telephone lines, etc.   The second
diagram shows that the camera can be offset from the lines and still achieve the same effect.   In both cases, depth
has been added to the picture and the relative size of objects is easier to comprehend.

Framing

The framing technique is exactly what it sounds like. The main subject is in the centre of the image and a foreground
object, or objects, provides a graphic frame around the image.   The chapter on computer graphics (*'Welcome to
Naples'*) shows an image of a pool viewed through an archway. All sorts of objects can be used for frames (e.g. trees
or bushes). Shooting the subject through a doorway or window is another more obvious framing technique. Frames
add depth and interest to a picture and focus the viewer's attention on the subject being framed.

Use a sharp focussed foreground for photographing scenic images, as an out-of focus foreground distracts the viewer.
An out of focus foreground is acceptable, and desirable, for most portrait work.

Backgrounds

The photographer has to have an eye for the background content of an image and not just concentrate on the main
subject being shot.   The following points should be considered:

- A relatively uncluttered background helps concentrate the viewers' attention on the main subject.
- Avoid stark lines in the background. These attract the viewers' attention away from main subject.
- Avoid shooting a subject against a dark background.   The camera adjusts to the overall level of
  incoming light (i.e. dark) and overexposes any lighter objects.   In human subjects, this is seen as
  'burnouts' of the highlighted areas of the face such as cheeks and forehead.
- If a dark background is unavoidable, zoom further in on the subject. This reduces the ratio of dark in
  the overall picture.   Alternatively, use lighting to illuminate the background and/or the subject.
- Be watchful of poles or trees sticking out of people's heads.

Camera height

Not all photographs are taken from a normal standing height.   A kneeling position provides an alternative camera
height and is ideal for photographing children, dogs, people who are seated and objects that are close to the ground.
Filming at their own eye level produces a much more natural result than pointing the camera down at them.

For really low camera positions, even a mini-tripod is too tall. On other occasions, a normal tripod may be too small
(e.g. trying to photograph a passing parade). Use a beanbag, small pillow or folded blanket. This can be sat on the
ground for low shots.   It can also be sat on a wall or bus shelter for recording high shots.   This is preferable to the
operator holding the camera above his/her head.

Importantly, the height of the camera in relation to the subject can be used to convey mood or status.   Shooting
upwards makes the subject tower over the frame and appear larger than life.   Shooting down on the subject makes the
subject appear smaller and less significant.

Portraits

Portraits of individuals is a common use for photographs and these appear in everything from family albums to
company reports.   Portraits range from formal (picture of the company chairperson, police mugshot, etc) to informal
(holiday pictures).

These often have no broader context and are capturing the personality of the subject.   There are exceptions, such as
wedding pictures, graduations, and so on.   One useful approach is to try to capture the person's personality through
extending the formal setting of portraits.   This might involve taking a portrait of the person at work, at play, or
working on a hobby.   Although a portrait only covers the person's head and shoulders, the image can still include
elements that encapsulate the individual's personal traits.   Examples are subjects holding a phone, listening to a
Walkman, wearing a party hat, wearing their uniform, holding a fishing rod, and so on. These are all much better than
the subject sitting on a chair, wearing new clothes and grimacing the word *"Cheese"*.

It is important to relax the subject. It is also best to avoid posing the subject. If they settle naturally, they usually
strike a better pose.   It is often best to photograph the subject with the camera slightly above eye level.   Subjects
often stare into some point in the distance when being photographed.   However, a photograph where there is eye
contact draws the viewer into the picture.

Composition issues with portraits include:

- Filling the frame with the subject is acceptable with portraits.
- Always use plain, or out of focus, backgrounds. Using a telephoto setting and a large aperture
  setting makes the background out of focus.
- Set the camera focus on the subject's eyes.
- Avoid wide-angle settings with portraits as they creates *'big nose'* facial distortions.

Lighting issues include:
- The lighting for portraits varies a little compared to scenic shots. While scenic shots benefit greatly from bright sunlight, this creates problems for outdoor portraits, as it makes the subject squint. Placing the subject with his/her back to the sun prevents squints but means that the camera is now shooting into the sun. It also means that the subject's face is hidden in deep shadows.
- If possible, shoot when the sky is overcast as this produces a much more even light.
- Otherwise, look for a shaded area.
- Always use the camera lens hood to minimise stray light from entering the lens.
- Use reflected light or a flash fill, to lighten the darkened shadow areas of the subject's face.
- Consider using a soft focus filter on the camera.

Red-eye

The curse of flash photography is the appearance of 'red-eye'. This is caused by light reflecting from the retinas at the back of the subject's eyes. The effect seems to be more common among people with blue eyes and is mainly a problem in low light environments. In dark conditions, the pupil of the eye dilates to allow in more light, thereby exposing more of the retina. Some cameras provide red-eye reduction systems. They all work based on presenting light to the subject, just before taking the photograph. This is either by illuminating a small lamp or by emitting one or more low-power bursts from the flashlight. These cause the pupil to contract just before the main flash goes off and the photograph is taken. Alternatively, the red-eye can be eliminated at the editing stage.

Close-ups

Majestic panoramas, crowd scenes and human portraits are all large-scale images that make up the bulk of the images used in projects. However, the miniature world can be captured for interest or impact. An image of a single tear running down a cheek conveys an immense message. Similarly, other close-up shots such as a bead of sweat, the petal of a flower, a train ticket, etc. can be used to convey mood or intent.
At an even more miniature level, the macro shot provides an unusual view of the world. Examples of such shots are a bent paper clip, the mechanics of a watch, an insect's head, or the wording on a stamp or coin.

Capturing action

A still photograph can capture a moving subject and still display the sense of the original movement. There are two basic types of action shot - the 'freeze frame' and the 'blurred motion' shots.
The stop action shot, also known as a 'freeze frame' shot, aims to capture a clear image of the moving subject, either through using a fast shutter speed or using flash.
Alternatively, an action can often be captured at a peak moment. In many activities, there is an action, followed by a period when motion is almost suspended, followed by further action. The photograph can be captured during the moment of suspended animation. Examples of this are children on swings or with skipping ropes, carpenters sawing, athletics hurdling and pole vaulters.
Blur is also minimised if the action is shot from a distance rather than close up, as the closer the camera is to the action, the quicker the subject passes across the lens. If possible, capture the subject moving diagonally or towards camera, rather than across camera view.
With freeze frame shots, the subject and the background are photographed free from any motion blur.
Blur, however, can be used to provide the feeling of moment. Some element of blur is not only acceptable, but is desirable. If the photograph is taken while the camera is panned to follow the subject's movement, the subject is captured clearly but the background is blurred. This is a commonly used effect. Slow shutter speeds increase the background blur, making the action appear even faster.
Of course, motion blur can be introduced in an image at the editing stage.

Camera positioning

Before considering positioning, consideration should be given to ensuring that the camera is as stationary as possible during the taking of a photograph. It is difficult to hold a camera steady while pressing its shutter button. Pressing too hard can move the camera and blur the shot or capture a shot whose content is not placed as expected. When a telephoto setting is used, the slight movement is even more exaggerated. The solution lies in mounting the camera on a tripod.
The tripod has a ¼" bolt that screws into the base of the camcorder. When the tripod's legs are spread, the camcorder is held in a very stable grip. Of course, it is not always possible or practical to use a tripod, particularly when the camera has to move around a location quickly. An alternative for these situations is the mini-tripod. It provides many of benefits of the large tripod, but is small, easy to carry round and can be sat on wall or table to provide stability for the camera.
If all else fails, the camera operator can stabilise the camera by resting against a wall, a tree, a car or a lamppost. The ideal shooting stance is legs apart, knees slightly bent, arms tucked into the sides of the body so that wrists are straight when holding the camera.

Lighting

Lighting is an extremely important factor in photography. Please read the chapter on digital video for full details.

Scanners

The operation of a scanner is similar to that of the digital camera described earlier.

Consider the operation of a photocopier. It has two separate phases. The first phase is capturing the image from the document that is placed on the glass. The second phase is writing a copy of the image on to a sheet of paper. These operations can be also be carried out by two well-known computer peripherals - the scanner and the printer. Indeed, software is available to use them as a photocopier.

The scanner can be used to bring all kinds of images into the computer. Although this chapter is concerned with photographic images, the scanner can be used to capture line art, logos, hand-written signatures, diagrams and other flat objects such as a driving licence or bus pass. However, many flatbed scanners are not limited to flat objects and can provide a useable image from objects placed on the glass bed. This allows pages from books and magazines to be scanned, as well as 3-D objects such as a human hand, coins, and so on. Anything that is scanned on a photocopier at the office party is capable of being scanned on a flatbed scanner.

How a scanner works

The quality of the final image depends on the quality of the scanner components - and on the resolution of the scanning mechanism. The scan resolution is measured in dpi (dots per inch). Since many measurements are metric, conversions have to be done into inches to calculate file sizes (see below). The most common type of scanner is the flatbed model and the description for this type follows, although the general principles apply to all scanner types.

The photograph (or other object) is placed face down on the scanner glass bed and the capture software is started. This can be a dedicated capture application, or can be any graphics package that has a capture facility through a TWAIN interface. A bright cold cathode light and a scanning head are mounted on a frame that is slowly moved down the photograph by a stepper motor. The light is shone on the surface to be scanned and the reflected light is focussed on to the scanning head. The scanning head consists of a CCD (see the earlier explanation of CCDs). The head only contains a single row of sensors, compared to the megapixel arrays of camera CCDs. The camera captures all the image data at the one time, while the scanner captures the photograph's detail one line at a time. This much simpler CCD assembly makes the scanner a very much cheaper device than a digital camera.

Since most flatbed scanners handle an A4 sheet, the width of the scanned area is a minimum of 8.27", with most models having an 8.5" scanning width. If a scanner supports a maximum scanning resolution of 600dpi, the CCD in the scanning head will contain 8.5 x 600 = 5,100 sensors. Even a top-quality 2,400dpi optical resolution requires just over 20,000 sensors. Current digital cameras now mostly contain CCDs with millions of sensors. Older scanners made three separate scanning passes, to gather the red, green and blue information in the photograph. Current mainstream models use a single-pass method, with colour filters in front of the sensors (as used in digital cameras).

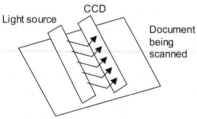

Some models are *'dual scan'* which means that they have one with a highly-dense CCD to scan small images such as film transparencies, while a larger, less dense CCD is used for scanning larger images.

Alternatives

Some scanners now use a CIS (Contact Image Sensor) system. This replaces the cold cathode light source with a single array of red, green and blue LEDs to produce white light. This replaces the mirrors and lenses of CCD models and allows the light, the source image and the sensor to be very close together. This produces a thinner and lighter scanner that is thinner, lighter and cheaper to manufacture than a CCD model. The CIS system has still to catch up with the quality of CCD models.

The scanners used by the top end of the market, such as colour prepress companies, use PMT (photo-multiplier tube) technology. The image to be scanned is mounted on a drum that is then spun at high speed. The drum is then moved across the sensing system that comprises a light source and a sensor. The reflected light is split into three beams that pass through filters (red, green and blue) and are detected by the photo-multiplier tubes. This system is more sensitive and has lower noise levels than CCD systems. However, they are expensive and complicated to operate and are now only used in specialist areas.

With each system, the scanner gathers the image data as a series of pixel data and this is sent to the computer via the cable interface.

Controlling the scan

The scanner can record the entire area of the scanning bed. However, the user often only requires scanning a smaller photograph area, or even a part of a photograph. In addition, there may be some adjustment to be made to the resolution or colour settings for the scan.

The steps for scanning a photograph are:

- Run the scanner capture software, perhaps through a TWAIN-compliant application.
- Run the initial scan, to acquire a preview of the entire image placed on the glass.
- Set final desired area to be scanned.
- Set the desired resolution.

- Set the desired colour depth (including colour, greyscale, line art).
- Set any brightness, contrast, gamma correction, or sharpen settings.
- Perform a final scan
- Save the image - usually as a compressed JPEG file or perhaps as a BMP, PCX, TIFF or GIF file.

Twain interface

See earlier in this chapter for a general description.   The interface controls how capture operations are carried out. It does not specify what piece of software is required to interface with it.   A scanner manufacturer may supply its own software for operating the scanner and this software would communicate with the hardware through the Twain driver. Alternatively, the user may access the scanner through his/her existing application packages.   For example, in PhotoShop, the scanner is accessed through the 'File' drop-down menu.   Choosing 'Import', followed by 'TWAIN' displays a list of the TWAIN devices connected to the computer (e.g. a camera and a scanner).

There are more Twain interface controls for scanners than for cameras, as there are more factors to control in the capture process. The Twain interface gives instructions to the scanner, under the control of the user. In fact, the range is large enough for Agfa to distribute two versions of their Twain driver with their scanners. FotoSnap has a simple set of controls for beginners while FotoLook has more advanced controls for more experienced users.

Optical resolution

As explained above, the construction of the CCD determines the maximum scanning resolution. This is called the 'optical resolution' and is usually 300dpi, 600dpi or 1200dpi in the horizontal plane.   The stepper motor moves the head in amounts set by the user. If the user chooses 600dpi for the vertical resolution, the head is moved 1/600th of an inch for each vertical scan. If the scanning head is moved down the bed in movements that are equal to the CCD sensor spacing, the final resolution is equal in both planes (e.g. 300dpi x 300dpi or 600dpi x 600dpi).   If the head assembly is moved in smaller steps, the vertical resolution becomes greater than the horizontal resolution (e.g. 600dpi x 1200dpi, 600dpi x 2400dpi or 1200dpi x 2400dpi).

Interpolated resolution

Most manufacturers also quote a figure for their scanner's 'interpolated resolution'.   This is a much higher figure, up to 9600dpi, to make the specification appear more impressive.   Since the scanner cannot actually detect any more data than its number of CCD sensors, the 'extra' data for the higher resolution is interpolated (i.e. estimated).   If, for example, a scanner has an optical resolution of 600dpi and an interpolated scan of 1200dpi is chosen, there is four times as much data to be stored in the file than is being physically scanned.   The scanner software looks at the actual readings on adjacent CCD sensors and works out the likely values of colour and contrast that would appear in between.   If the two sensors both detected the same colour, then the intermediate pixels would be saved as being the same colour.   If a colour value of 222 was detected in one sensor and 218 in the next sensor, the software saves 220 as the intermediate value.   The process would be applied to horizontal and vertical image data.   The image file contains twice as many pixels values in both the horizontal and vertical planes.   No extra original information has been extracted from the photograph, but the file size is four times larger. In addition, since the process averages out the values at edges, the final scanned image is slightly softened.

Improved techniques include 'bicubic interpolation' (which uses all the values around the new pixel to estimate the pixel contents) or 'colour curve interpolation' (which takes into account the rate of change of a colour along a run and fits in a new value which need not be a linear fit between the existing pixel values).   At the end of the day, however, an estimate is still an estimate.

Since interpolation can also be carried out within a graphics editing package (e.g. when using a 'resize' option), there is little benefit in choosing an interpolated scan.   The extra time required to resize an image is a price worth paying compared to storing all images in a huge size.

Interpolation is generally more successful when used with line art scans, as they have clean outlines, sharp edges and are only black and white.

If a photograph is to be scanned at less than a scanner's maximum resolution, it is best to set the resolution to whole fractions of the maximum resolution. For example, if a scanner maximum optical resolution is 1200dpi, it has 1200 sensors in its CCD reader.   If a document is scanned at 600dpi, it only uses the reading from every second sensor, while a setting of 400dpi reads from every third sensor, and so on.   Setting to, for example, 500dpi, involves unnecessary interpolation of values, with a possible loss in quality.

Colour depth

The values from the scanner's CCD are read off into the electronics, where the ADC (analogue to digital converter) digitises the scanned red, green and blue values. Most scanners work in a final 24-bit colour depth. This provides 8 bits (i.e. one byte) to describe the amplitude of the image for each of the three (red, green and blue) sensors of each pixel. Since a byte can store 256 different levels (from zero to 255), the total number of colours that can be displayed is

$$256 \times 256 \times 256 = 16777216 = 16.78 \text{ millions colours}$$

This is the standard amount of colours used to represent all the colour shades necessary to reproduce a photo-realistic image. Darker areas of the photograph will reflect less light and are given lower values in the light level scale.

Oversampling

Some scanners are marketed as 30-bit or 36-bit models.   Most are sold as 42-bit and some even as 48-bit models, although these scanners do not actually save the image file at this colour depth.   They are used to provide *'oversampling'*.   This is used to compensate for image noise that may be generated during the scanning process. Increasing the dynamic range of a signal improves its signal-to-noise ratio.   With 36-bit sampling, the photograph is scanned at a greater colour depth than is required.   Each colour has a range of 4,096 possible values compared to only 256 values with 24-bit working.

The theoretical colour depth of the scanned image is now

4096 x 4096 x 4096 = 68,719,476,736 different colours

However, this would result in vastly more colours than the eye is capable of discerning, not to mention impossibly large storage requirements (see later).

Therefore, the image data is subsequently converted to a 24-bit colour depth.   This reduces the total bits allocated to the image and reduces the noise proportionately.   The result is a cleaner sharper image than a normal 24-bit scan.

Although oversampling provides an improved image, the difference is often so slight as to be unnoticeable, especially with small, highly-compressed images for the web.

Line art

Line art describes all images where there is only black and white used in the composition.   This may be a cartoon, a diagram, a map or a hand-written signature.   With colour images, each pixel used 24 bits to store the information for each individual pixel.   With line art images, each pixel requires a single bit to describe it.   It is either black or white, it is either digital 'off' or digital 'on'.   Since a single bit can only have two values - zero or one, this corresponds to the two colours states.   So, the information about each pixel in a line art image can be stored in a single bit.   This means that a line art image only requires one twenty-fourth of the storage size of a full-colour image of the same size.   It would not make sense, therefore, to use a colour scan setting for monochrome image.   Of course, the images that are used as the scanning source can be in colour and the line art setting will ensure that the scanned copy of the image is in black and white.

Greyscale images

Not all photographic images are in colour.   All old photographs are in shades of grey and even contemporary photographers use monochrome film for special effects.

The scanner has a setting for scanning in greyscale.   Since there is not a separate red, green and blue component to the image, a single byte is sufficient to store 256 levels of greyscale (from black to white). If a colour photograph is scanned with a greyscale setting, the scanned image will be in greyscale and be one-third the size of its colour equivalent.

The illustrations show the effect of scanning a colour photograph in greyscale and in line art settings.   The 256-greyscale image retains much of its clarity, while the line art settings has forced all pixels down to black level or up to white level.   This effect is often used in pop-art and advertising images.

256-greyscale   line art

Scanning printed images

There is a huge resource of existing graphic material in magazines, books, etc. and these can be scanned for use in multimedia projects (subject to obtaining permission, of course).   The printed material is made up of millions of tiny dots.   The scanner, in turn, wants to scan at a set rate of pixels.   Since these will not neatly correspond, an interference pattern can be created between the two layouts - known as a Moiré pattern.   Most modern scanners provide a *'descreen'* option to minimise this effect.   Alternatively, the photograph can be scanned at a resolution that is higher than required, and the scanned image can be run through a blur filter in a graphics editing package.   The image resolution is then reduced to the final size required, and run through the sharpen filter.

File sizes

The number of pixels in a scanned image is calculated by taking the screen area to be scanned and multiplying it by the number of dots per inch.   The file size in bytes for storing a greyscale image is the same figure as this number of pixels.   Dividing this figure by eight gives the file size for a monochrome scan and a 24-bit colour scan is three times the size of a grey scale scan.

An A4 sheet of paper is the size of this book and many magazines.   The dimensions are 210mm x 297mm, or 11.69" x 8.27", when converted to inches.

If the entire page were to be scanned in colour, the file size for a range of different scanning resolutions is given in the table.

Take the example of scanning at 600dpi.   The page is 8.27" wide, so this requires 8.27 x 600 = 4962 dots of horizontal resolution.   The page is 11.69" long, requiring 11.69 x 600 = 7014 dots of vertical resolution.   The number of dots to

| File sizes for various scanning resolutions (from an A4 sheet at 24-bit colour) ||
Scanning resolution	Uncompressed File Size
300dpi	25MB
600dpi	100MB
1200dpi	398MB
2400dpi	1.56GB
4800dpi	6.22GB
9600dpi	24.89GB

represent the entire A4 sheet is then 4962 x 7014 = 34,803,468 dots. This represents the size for a monochrome image, each dot being either black or white. To store a colour image, each dot is represented by varying amounts of red, green or blue. A byte is required to store each of these colour values. The file size has then to be multiplied by three to get the final size in bytes. In the example, a staggering 100MB of storage space is required for an A4 image at a respectable 600dpi.

Since a photograph in a magazine can expect to be printed at a minimum of 4800dpi, a scanned A4 image would not even fit on an entire DVD disk.

If the 36-bit sampling mode discussed earlier was actually stored in that format, the files sizes shown in the table would have to be multiplied by a factor of 36/24 = 1.5. This would make the 9600dpi scan require a staggering 37.34GB of storage - greater than the capacity of many hard drives!

Scanning for multimedia use

Fortunately, photograph images for multimedia are much less of a problem. This is for a number of reasons.

Most importantly, a monitor has a much poorer resolution than the range offered by scanners. A typical monitor only displays around 72 pixels per inch of screen. This means that the scanning resolution can be turned down to this lower figure and massive savings can be made on file size.

Consider a full monitor screen of 1024 x 768 pixels, on a 17" monitor. The 1024 pixels are spread across a theoretical horizontal dimension of 12". In practice, only about 90% of the actual screen area is visible. The 1024 pixels are contained in a horizontal row of about 11.5". This equates to about 72 pixels for each inch and this is a common resolution to use for scanning images that are required for display on computer monitors.

To fill the screen at the full resolution of the monitor, only 1024 different pixels need to be scanned. If more pixels are scanned, the extra details cannot be physically displayed on the screen. The file is extra large, without providing any greater viewable information. If less pixels are scanned than the amount physically supported by the monitor, either the content of the unused pixels are interpolated (estimated) so that the full screen is still occupied - or the photograph is displayed at less than full screen size.

Source sizes for various scanning resolutions (to fill a 1024x768 screen)	
Scanning resolution	Size of original
90dpi	11.38" x 8.53"
100dpi	10.24" x 7.68"
150dpi	6.83" x 5.12"
300dpi	3.41" x 2.56"
600dpi	1.71" x 1.28"
1200dpi	0.85" x 0.64"
2400dpi	0.43" x 0.32"
4800dpi	0.21" x 0.16"

The table shows the size of photograph area that would be scanned to fill a 1024x768 screen, at various scanning resolution settings. At 90 dpi, an A4 photograph, taken in landscape, would almost match the monitor's full screen. It can also be seen that high scanning resolutions are useful when a small area of a photograph is required to fill the screen. For example, scanning at 1200dpi allows a postage stamp to fill the monitor screen. In multimedia, a photograph is rarely used to fill a full monitor screen. While a background may sometimes require using an entire photograph, photographic images normally only occupy a part of the screen area.

The scanning resolution for a particular purpose can be calculated with the following formula:

Scanning Resolution = Screen Resolution (in dpi) x Width of display / width of original image

So, for example, if the image was to occupy 5 inches on the screen and the original was only 2 inches wide, the resolution calculation would be

72 x 5 / 2 = 180 dpi

In most cases, the screen resolution can be assumed to be 72 dpi.

Optical Character Recognition

This is not particularly applicable to photographic scanning but is included for completeness. It may be useful in other areas of multimedia, such as storyboarding, planning, correspondence, and other areas where text plays a part in the process.

If a source document contains text, it can be scanned and converted to a plain text file that can be read with any word-processing package. This is carried out in several steps by the OCR software. Firstly, it scans the document, detects where the individual lines are (by looking for the white space between lines). It then scans each line, breaking it into individual characters (by looking for the spaces between the characters). At this stage, the software has a collection of little graphic images - one for each character in the text. The software stores a set of known font descriptions and compares these with the characters that have been scanned. It starts with the first scanned image and compares it to the font descriptions. When a match is found, that letter is added to the text output file.

While OCR software packages talk of achieving 98% accuracy, it is the few percent of errors that cause all the problems. While a package may include a spell-checker, other techniques are applied to improve the accuracy. The interpretation of the scanned images are often made using neural network techniques. These learn from successful recognition and apply them to text has different fonts from the standard sets. They may also use POWR (Predictive Optical Word Recognition) which attempts to recognise whole words at a time. With older techniques, there may be a problem knowing whether a letter is an 'e' or an 'o', for example. This can lead to the word 'bite' being read as 'bato'. With POWR, placing all possible interpretations of an unknown letter in its context reduces any ambiguity. There is no such word as 'bato' in the recognised list, while 'bite' is a recognised word.

Scanner interfaces

Scanners are supplied with differing ways for connecting it to a computer, some offering a choice of connection:

Parallel

There is a parallel port fitted on every computer and this is usually used for connecting a printer. Where a scanner has a parallel plug connector, the user can unplug the printer from the computer's parallel port and insert the scanner plug, or he/she can fit a parallel *'pass-through'* connector. This connector allows two parallel port devices to be connected at the same time and saves plugging and unplugging each time the scanner is to be used.

Care has to be taken with parallel systems, however, as most new scanners assume that the computer has a parallel port that operates to the EPP (Enhanced Parallel Port) standard.   This allows faster transfers than the standard parallel port, but is only fitter on newer computers.   If the scanner transfer system is EPP only, it will not work with an older, non-EPP, computer.

This interface has now almost been fully replaced with the faster USB, SCSI and FireWire connections.

SCSI

This provides faster data transfers than the parallel port system and is useful where lots of photographs need to be scanned.   The SCSI interface card usually supplied with the scanner.   With the introduction of fast USB scanner interfaces, SCSI scanners have become much less popular.

USB

This is now the most common way to connect a new scanner to a computer. It is easily connected - there is no special adapter card to fit, as with SCSI, or pass-through adapter, as with parallel. The cable from the scanner is simply plugged into the computer's USB socket, the scanner software is installed and the scanner is recognised when the computer is restarted.

FireWire

This interface is now available on a few scanner types, as an alternative, fast, interface.

Scanner types

Although flatbed scanners are by far the most popular models, other scanner types are marketed and these are explained below.

Handheld

This type of scanner looks like a large mouse and its small size was a selling point. There is no mechanism to move the scanning head or the image.   The user has to roll the scanner over the surface of the object to be scanned, at a steady pace. If the hand movement is not steady and at a constant speed, the image is distorted.   Unfortunately, as with a mouse, these scanners are difficult to push in a straight line. They never really caught on as they only covered a small width (3" to 4") and larger areas had to be constructed from patching together several smaller scans.   It is difficult to scan objects smaller than the scanning head. For example, to scan a postage stamp or a small photograph, they would have to be glued or taped to a larger surface.   It was used mainly for scanning small items for clip art, signatures and other small images.

As flatbed scanners became ever cheaper, there was no financial reason to choose a handheld.   They were then marketed on the basis of their flexibility. The HP CapShare 910 is a modern version of this device.   It is a self-powered device and does not connect to the computer while scanning.   Instead, it stores its scanned data in 4MB of internal memory.   This means that the scanner can carried around and used anywhere, independently of the computer.   Images can then be sent to the computer later, using its serial port or an infrared port (if one exists).   The supplied software carries out the stitching of sections into a complete document.

Sheetfed

This type, also described as a page scanner or document scanner, looks and works in a similar way to a fax machine. It usually has a small footprint (i.e. it does not take up much desk space).   It uses a roller to move the paper past the head and can be fitted with an automatic sheet feeder to hold multiple sheets. It is designed for handling A4 sheets, and some are unable to handle smaller sizes. It is commonly used with OCR software (see earlier) for archiving correspondence and documents.

A major drawback is its inability to scan books and real-world objects, as they will not pass through the rollers.   The flatbed scanner is the only type that allows the scanning of thick documents or objects. Some scanners combine the traditional flatbed system with a sheetfed system, providing the maximum flexibility. The sheets are placed in an ADF (automatic document feeder) where they are automatically fed through the scanner, one at a time.

Drum scanner

These types are used for high-resolution scanning of large original documents.   With flatbed scanners, the image remains stationary, while the scanning head moves across it.   The drum scanner takes the opposite approach. The document is attached to a glass drum that is then slowly spun past a scanning head. They provide excellent colour reproduction.   However, they are expensive and are used mainly in high-end professional publishing and reprographic markets.   They are able to scan very large sheets - up to A0 (an area that is sixteen times greater than an A4 sheet).

Slide scanner

These types are dedicated to scanning mounted slide transparencies or strips of negatives.   Some also handle APS (Advanced Photo System) cartridges and others may supply adaptors to handle APS cartridges.   Since they are used to digitise transparencies, they don't work on reflected light.   The light is shone thorough the transparency.   The method is said to be *'transmissive'* rather than *'reflective'*. They still use CCDs as their method of detecting light patterns and some provide an automatic slide feeder for batch work.   Since the area being scanned is much smaller than that of an A4 flatbed scanner, the scanner requires a much higher scanning resolution, to produce a reasonably-sized digital image.   Figures up to 4000dpi are typical.

Some flatbed scanner manufacturers sell an optional add-on to convert them to slide scanners.   This is a replacement lid with a built-in light source, to shine through the transparency.   These are much cheaper than buying a dedicated slide scanner, but the resolution is not good enough for many professional purposes. Their poorer performance is caused by the physical layout of the flatbed scanner's light sensors.   The CCD sensors are spread over an 8.5" wide strip, while the slide is about 1" wide.   Since only one-eight of the sensors scan the slide, the effective resolution is lowered by this ratio (e.g. a 1200dpi scanner only uses 150 sensors to scan the 1" slide are - producing a 150dpi resolution).   This is still sufficient for multimedia use, where the image is displayed on a television screen, web site or television monitor.   A publishing house would have to invest in a higher quality dedicated film scanner.   If this is not an affordable solution, the film can be developed and printed on A4 photographic paper, for scanning in the normal manner.

Photo-editing

Most digitised pictures, whether scanned or captured by camera, gain from editing.
Typical editing activities are:

- Removing scratches and dust marks from old film photographs.
- Compensating for problems with brightness and contrast in all types of photographs.
- Retouching images (e.g. removing scars or moles from a face, swapping one background for another).
- Creating photographic effects.

Before starting, read the section on PhotoShop's tools in the chapter on *'Computer Graphics'*.   The rest of this chapter introduces other PhotoShop tools, although the principles (and many of the names) are identical in other packages.

Some general advice

There are many different adjustments and effects that can be applied to images and these often provide control over their attributes.   Many of these activities can be carried out on the same image (e.g. an image can have its colours adjusted, have its dimensions distorted, have several filters applied to it, and so on).   This provides a vast range of different potential configurations.   Some adjustments and effects have to be tried to test their effectiveness on a particular image.   Although PhotoShop uses a history palette, once the file is saved the original contents are lost forever.   It is strongly recommended that all editing work should be carried out on a <u>copy</u> of the original image.   In that way, if it all goes horribly wrong, the original is still there to start all over again.   For the same reason, if a file is being worked on over several sessions, it is best to save copies of the edited work as it progresses.   However, it should be noted that when a image is saved to a standard graphic format, such as JPEG or GIF, the layers and other elements of the composition are flattened into a single layered image.

For this reason, the best policy for ongoing work is saving in PhotoShop's own PSD format.   This is not a format intended for distribution.   Its importance lies in its ability to save all the layers and other information for future editing.   When the file is re-opened later, all the layers are available for manipulation.   So, when the editing is finally complete, it makes sense to save one copy with a PSD extension as well as one in the required final format of GIF or JPEG, etc.   This allows the image to be returned to for any future alterations.

Incidentally, it is best to view the image at the actual size it will be displayed before saving, to ensure that the details appear as good in small size as they did when edited full-screen.

Editing tools

The main tools for editing digital photographs are:

Crop tool	Used to remove unwanted areas and borders from an image.
Marquee tool	Used to select a particular part of an image for separate processing.
Lasso tool	As above but works with irregular shapes.
Magic Wand	Used to select an area from an image, based on its colour.
Clone Stamp	Used to retouch photographic images
Touchup tools	Used to retouch photographic images

These tools, when used in conjunction with layers and with the many extra utilities provided on the pull-down menus, provide a rich variety of editing and effects options.

Examples of utilities provided from the drop-down menus are colour adjustments, and special effects filters such as embossing, glowing edges, crystallizing, etc.

Rejuvenating old monochrome photographs

There are huge stocks of photographic images that encapsulate times past.   These may be of historical or family interest.   They are monochrome images that show the signs of their age.   They may have faded, browned, been scratched or folded, and may contain flaws from the photographic process (e.g. poor lighting, dust spots, etc).   The techniques for restoring old monochrome images can be put to good use with colour photographs, although colour images provide extra problems as covered later.

The first task is to remove any tiny dust spots from the image by using the *'Despeckle'* tool from the *'Noise'* sub-menu of the *'Filter'* drop-down menu.   It creates a mild blurring of the image, except for edges and areas of good contrast. This has the effect of neutralising dust spots.   The *'Median'* filter that is also available from the *'Noise'* sub-menu has a different approach.   It examines each pixel in relation to the pixels surrounding it and alters the pixel's colour accordingly.   This has the effect of softening the image and any rogue pixels (e.g. a white dust spot in a dark area) are replaced by the median colour for the area.

Any larger blemishes, such as scratches, are tackled using the Dropper and Paint Brush tools.
The steps are:

- Zoom in on the affected area.
- Use the Dropper to pick up the shade from the surrounding pixels.
- Use the Paint Brush tool, with a small soft brush, and opacity set to around 50%.
- Paint over the affected pixels.

If it is a large blemish, do not paint out the whole area with the one shade, as it will look obvious. Keep using the Dropper to sample afresh from the surrounding area, so that a mix of the subtle shades is painted over the blemish. Of course, if the blemish happens to appear on a solid shaded area, the painting is much easier.   For larger blemishes, particularly on areas with complex content, the Clone tool should be used, as detailed later.

Adjusting colour photographs

A digitised photograph may require having its colour components adjusted.   This may be due to imperfections in the camera or scanner, or imperfections in the camera operators' settings.   It may also be due to a colour cast on the subject, caused by light reflecting from a large brightly-coloured object (wall, side of a van, etc.).
There are different tools for tackling these problems.

To assist in deciding where the problems lie, PhotoShop provides a Histogram option that shows the levels of each RGB component in the image.   This is accessed by selecting '*Histogram*' from the '*Image*' menu. If the graph data gathers at the left of the horizontal scale, the image has a general low brightness, with less vivid colours.   If the data gathers at the top of the scale, it indicates that either a certain colour is over-saturated or the entire image is too light.

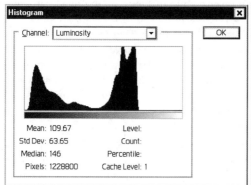 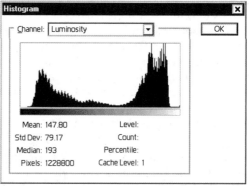

The histograms illustrated above show the effect of adjusting an underexposed photograph.   The left illustration shows the original image with a high proportion of its content at the bottom of the scale. The right histogram is of the same image after having its brightness and contrast levels increased.   The image is generally brighter and the colours are now more vivid.

The *'Image'* drop-down menu has an *'Adjust'* option whose sub-menu provides a range of tools. These tools provide dialog boxes to make the adjustments and most have a '*preview*' option that will apply changes to the image as adjustments are made. Most of these options are accessed in Elements via the '*Enhancements*' menu.

The *'Brightness/Contrast'* option opens a dialog box with two sliders to set the levels of brightness and contrast. The *'Hue/saturation'* option opens a dialog box with three sliders to set the percentage levels of the hue, saturation and lightness in the image.

Many users find these utilities fiddly and hard to master and often rely on the *'Color Balance'* utility. Selecting this option will bring up the dialog box shown. It provides sliders to set the red, green and blue levels, for areas of shadow, midtones or highlights. Using this dialog, the user can fine-tune the colours of the image, if for example the image has a slight colour cast due to a reflection from a brightly coloured object.

If the '*Preserve Luminosity*' checkbox is ticked, the sliders will set the colour levels but not the overall lightness of the image will be unchanged.

The Color Balance utility can be used to help make a colour image look like an old photograph. The steps are:
- Load the image.
- Choose the *'Add Noise'* option from the *'Noise'* sub-menu produced by the *'Filter'* drop-down menu.
- Check the *'Uniform'* box, to apply noise uniformly across the image.
- Select a low percentage of noise.
- Draw a few white or grey lines to simulate scratches and folds.
- Convert the image to grey scale, to remove all colour components.
- Convert the image back to 24-bit colour.
- Open the *'Color Balance'* dialog box.
- Adjust the Blue value to zero or a small value.
- Adjust the Red and Green values to achieve the sepia colour of old photographs.

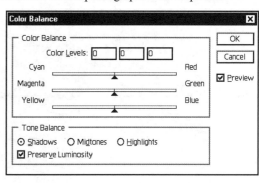

In PhotoShop Elements, there is no Color Balance utility; instead, colour casts can be removed by using the '*Color Cast'* option.

Working with selections

The chapter on computer graphics explained that a selection was an area that can be defined and can then be treated separately from the rest of the image. The selection can be flood-filled, painted, deformed, and subjected to many other image manipulations. Once outlined, the selection can be dragged to any part of the active image area. The selection can also be cut from the frame and pasted into a new layer or as a new image. This facility is probably the most important editing tool.   It can be used equally effectively on large or small areas of the image. Its most common uses are in adjusting colour and brightness levels, and as a tool for retouching images.

Many photographs have areas that require to be treated separately.   Consider a photograph with one area darker than the rest.   If the entire image has its brightness raised, the excessively dark is lightened - but so is all the rest of the image.   This will probably result in some areas becoming washed out.   The solution lies in only adjusting the brightness of the excessively dark area and ignoring the rest of the image.

Consider, for example, wishing to lighten both the sea and the sky in this image. Fortunately, the sea area is a perfect rectangle. To brighten this area, it is first selected using the rectangular marquee tool. The *'Brightness/Contrast'* utility in the *'Image'* drop-down menu is then adjusted for the desired effect.

The skyline poses a more difficult problem.   It has a very irregular outline that would be slow to trace using the freehand lasso or even the magnetic lasso selection tool.

For this area, the Magic Wand tool in the Tool Palette is used. As the sky is not a single block of colour, the tolerance level is increased to a point where it selects the entire sky area, without starting to include the buildings in the selection. The selection can then be adjusted independently of the rest of the image.

This technique has many uses in compensating for inadequate lighting or poor contrast in photographs.   As long as the contrast was not so high as to push dark objects down to black level (and light objects up to white level), they can be at least partially recovered. If, however, an entire area was reduced to a single blob of black or white, the details are irrecoverable.

Another use for selections is in cutting, pasting and copying parts of an image. Once outlined, the selection can be dragged, or copied, to any part of the active image area. The selection can also be cut from the frame and pasted into a new layer or as a new image. This provides huge opportunities for doctoring photographs.   This technique is sometimes used for comic effect (e.g. placing Cousin Bill's head on the body of Arnold Schwarzenneger). However, it is most commonly used to repair blemishes or make cosmetic improvements in an image.

A portrait can be improved by removing blemishes such as a wart, a tattoo or perhaps facial jewellery.
The procedure for such a task is as follows:
- Look at the skin tone around the blemish and find another skin area with the same tone.
- Use the freehand selection tool, set to a small amount of feather.
- Select an area of the blemish-free skin, using an irregular shape. Do not draw a regular shape such as a rectangle or circle as it is more easily detected.
- Use the *'Copy'* option from the *'Edit'* menu (or use Ctrl-C).
- Use the *'Paste'* option from the *'Edit'* menu (or use Ctrl-V). The copied area appears as a new layer.
- Position the new selection over the blemish. Unless other effects are desired the new layer can be merged into the existing layer.

Example using selections

The photographs of this house front illustrate the use of various selections.

The first task was to replace the dull sky for a brighter version with some clouds, to add interest.

The house image was opened and an improved sky image was extracted from another photograph and placed on a separate layer of the house image. The order of the layers was swapped, to make the sky the background layer. The house image was made the active layer and the areas of sky were selected using the Magic Wand and deleted from the image.

The Eraser was used to delete the telephone pole and wires from the left of the image and the top of the street lighting pole in the centre of the image.   The sky is now visible through all the deleted areas.

The following steps removed the figure and the street lighting pole.

- The bricks on the garden wall and the house facing brick were built to a regular pattern. This allowed the selection of brick areas to be copied on the areas obscured by the figure and the bottom of the pole.
- A small section of the pavement surface was selected with the freehand tool and copied over the area obscured by the figure's foot.
- A polygon selection of a section of the wooden roofline fascia was used to cover the section obscured by the street lighting pole.
- The obscured area of the wooden seat was recovered using the Clone Stamp (see below) although polygon selections would have achieved the same result.
- The remaining wall area obscured by the human torso was recovered using a combination of the Clone Stamp (see below) and the copying of freehand selections from the pebbledash wall surface.

Another example

A common technique, beloved by advertisers, is to create an image where the subject is in full colour while the background is in grey scale. Adobe Premiere provides a tool for achieving video sequences like these.   The PhotoShop method for still images is to create a selection around the figure or object. This can be a freehand lasso or a magnetic lasso selection, depending on the complexity of the outline.   The *'Invert'* option is then chosen in the *'Selection'* drop-down menu.   This results in everything except the subject being selected. The *'Desaturate'* option is then chosen from the *'Adjust'* submenu of the *'Image'* drop-down menu. This removes all colour from the selection while leaving the unselected area in full colour.

Working with Channels

Of particular use in editing digital photographs in PhotoShop, is the ability to edit channels. In a standard RGB image, there are four channels: one for red, green and blue; and a composite RGB channel. Similarly, CMYK images have a channel for Cyan, Magenta, Yellow, Key, and a composite CMYK, while LAB colour has Lightness, A, B, and composite LAB channels. Monochrome bitmaps, duotone images, and greyscale images have just one channel. However, the user may add additional *'alpha'* (transparent colour), *'QuickMask'* (explained in the *'Computer Graphics'* chapter), or *'spot colour'* (used in professional colour printing) channels.

The user, through the *'Channels'* palette, can select any channel in the image and use any of the usual editing tools to change its contents. Most of the effects that can be obtained by editing channels (changing colour casts, removing redeye, etc) can be obtained using other methods, and in this respect channel editing merely provides one other way to edit the image.

However, as pointed out earlier, the QuickMask function essentially creates a channel which the user edits in order to select an area of the image. When changing into QuickMask mode, a new channel is created, and when changing back to standard mode, the channel is removed and the appropriate area selected. This allows the user to change back and forth between the modes, adding and removing selected areas using both the selection tools (in Standard mode) and the painting tools (in QuickMask mode).

Editing Images using Layers

Layers in PhotoShop are explained in the *'Computer Graphics'* chapter. However, there are further functions which are of particular use in retouching photographic images. For example:

Adjustment layers

By selecting one of the options under *'New Adjustment Layer'* in the *'Layers'* menu, the user can create one of these layers. Each adjustment layer has a different function, identical to using the same adjustment from the *'Adjustments'* submenu of the *'Image'* menu. However, an adjustment layer can be hidden or removed, or the order of adjustment layers can be changed, without affecting the underlying content. The same is not true of adjustments on the layer contents themselves. This allows the user to experiment more easily with various adjustments, and how they interact with one another to affect the image. For example, a Brightness/Contrast adjustment layer and a Levels adjustment layer might be used, and the user might find that the interaction of the two layers together is too strong, producing a *'washed out'* image. It would be simple to edit the layers so that they produce a less strong effect. If adjustments had been performed without layers, the user would have to go back through the history, undoing the adjustments and any other changes made in-between, to try a new set of adjustment values.

Layer Masks

Any layer, except the background layer, may have a *'Layer mask'* added to it. This layer mask is essentially a new channel which is applied to the contents of one layer only. The mask's basic function is to temporarily cut portions of the layer from view. These portions are defined by the content of the mask channel.

This facility is particularly useful in transposing part of one image on top of the other. This can of course be done in other ways, but using a layer mask leaves the original layer content intact in case future editing should require it, for example to include a little more of the 'top' layers contents.

Calculations

PhotoShop also includes a *'Calculations'* command in the *'Image'* menu. This takes two channels of the same size (typically two channels from one or more layers within the same image) and applies one of the Blending options to result in another channel being created, or a new area being selected.

This is useful for combining two photographic images. It can be used to present a *'ghostly'* image of one picture over another, for example. Even using calculations between two channels of the same image, however, can be useful. It can be used to make certain coloured parts of the image stand out, for example, or it can blur everything that is not of one colour to give it a sort of *'background'* effect.

The Clone Stamp

The clone tool, as its name suggests, paints on an area of the image, using pixel information from another part of the image (or even from part of another image). The area being chosen for copying is called the *'source point'* and the area being painted over is called the *'target point'*. The content of the clone target is overwritten with the content picked up from the clone source. If required, the cloning can be confined to a defined area by creating a selection before cloning, or an area can be cloned into a newly created layer.

Cloning is used for painting over dust marks, scratches and other imperfections in a photograph. If the imperfection is in an otherwise plain image area, it can easily be remedied by picking up the surrounding colour with the dropper and painting over the blemish. However, if the blemish sits in an area of varying shades or intricate detail, this is not a satisfactory method. This is where cloning comes in.

Consider the photographs of the house front. The pole for the streetlights obscured part of the house. However, the house has an uneven pebbledash surface with many shades. Painting over the pole, using the dropper and paintbrush, would leave an obvious vertical block of uniform colour. With the clone brush, an area of the pebbledash texture is selected as the source and this texture is used to paint over the pole. Similarly, the wooden seat under the window is obscured by the seated figure. The Clone tool was used to extend the slats of the chair to cover the obscured part of the seat. This approach is useful for copying any complex area, such as brickwork, clouds, foliage, skin, fur, scales, clothing, and so on. The cloning is used for covering over blemishes, or for creating duplicates (adding extra clouds in the sky or turning someone's baby into twins).

The Clone tool is accessed by clicking its icon, the one with two paintbrushes, in the Tool Palette. This brings up a dialog box that sets the brush size, density, opacity, etc.

The steps for cloning an area are:
- Select the area to be copied, the source area, by Alt-clicking on it.
- Select the image, layer or selection to be used as the target.
- Hold down the left mouse button and paint over the area to be changed. The crosshairs on the image indicate which pixels are being copied at any particular moment.

For best results, avoid painting in straight strokes, as this tends to leave noticeable edges. It is also often best to keep changing the spot being used as the source.

Finally, ensure that the source area has the same texture and shades as the potential target area. For example, the texture on a jacket will vary depending upon whether it is a flat area or a curved area, flooded by light or in a darkened crease, and so on. The characteristics of section chosen as the source should match those of the target area.

Photo Retouching

The tools mentioned above are applied to an entire image or to an entire selection. Many users want more precise control - even down to pixel level. Users with graphics tablets would also value the ability to use their pen in freehand mode to carry out fine adjustments in images.

The Touchup tools in the Tool Palette provides a paint brush that applies effects to the image, rather than applying paint to the image.

The Options bar provides settings for the brush size, mode, and pressure or exposure.

The effects of the touchup tools are explained in the chapter on *'Computer Graphics'*.

Colour Replacement

Paint Shop Pro provides a Color Replacer tool to paint over all occurrences of one colour with another. PhotoShop, however, performs this function through the options in the *'Adjust'* submenu of the *'Image'* menu.

The *'Hue/Saturation'* option can be used to change the hue of a selected area, or the *'Replace Color'* option can be used to change the hue of individual colours in the image.

Consider a user who wishes to alter the sky colour behind the tree area of the house front image. As can be seen, there are many isolated pockets of sky, in between the branches of the tree. While it is easy to flood fill the large area to the right, the small areas present a problem.

The user may use the Replace Color option to change all light blue areas to, for example, shades of orange. However, if other objects have the same colour as the sky, this will change those objects as well. Fortunately, the user can select an area before using this option, to make sure certain objects are not altered.

Elements also has a Replace Color option, under the *'Enhancements'* menu.

Filters

Filters apply a process to all the pixels in an image, or in a selection. Earlier use was made of the *'Despeckle'* and *'Add Noise'* filters. In PhotoShop 6, all filters are accessed by the *'Filter'* menu.   The drop-down menu show sub-menus for various effects. Some filters are used quite often, to subtly edit the image. Others provide special effects that should not be over-used.

The *'Blur'* filters smooth out the pixel contents and are used for removing blemishes and compensating for any patterns imposed on the image during filming or scanning. There are six different varieties of Blur. The *'Blur'* and *'Blur More'* filters reduce the contrast between pixels to soften the image.   The *'Gaussian Blur'* filter is the first variety to provide user control over its strength.

The *'Motion Blur'* filter is used to add a sense of movement to an image by emulating the picture blur often resulting from photographing a fast car, a sprinter, a child on a swing, etc.   The user can set the angle of the blur movement and the intensity of the effect.

'Radial Blur' is used to produce special blurring effects such as to make the image appear as if it is zooming in or out, or spinning round. Finally, the *'Smart Blur'* option tries to blur the background while maintaining the foreground information.

The *'Sharpen'* filters produce the opposite effect of the Blur filters, as they seek to accentuate the contrast between individual pixels. Where a dark area meets a light area, the dark edge is further darkened, while the light edge is further lightened. This highlights the image's edges providing the illusion of a sharper all-round picture.

There are four varieties of Sharpen. The *'Sharpen'* and *'Sharpen More'* filters provide fixed levels of effect, while the *'Unsharp Mask'* filter provides user control over the intensity of the effect.   Remember, however, that since it highlights existing edges, it will make dust marks more prominent - so use Despeckle, etc to remove dust marks before applying this filter.   Anyway, in most cases this is the last tool to be used before the image is finally saved.

Special Effects Filters

PhotoShop, like many other image editing packages, provides extensive special effects that can be applied to images. Add-on filters from third parties, such as Kai's Power Tools, can be added to those supplied with PhotoShop. Some of these effects are more useful than others and they should all be used sparingly.   A special effect should remain special as the repeated use of these effects in a production will quickly annoy the viewer.

Nevertheless, used carefully and moderately, photographs that have had special effects applied to them can be very eye-catching and effective.

The first image was created using the *'Pointillize'* effect, which seeks to make an image look as if it was painted in the Pointillist style.

The steps are:
- Crop the image to the desired size.
- Invoke the magnetic lasso tool and trace round the desired object.
- Choose the *'Invert'* option from the *'Selection'* drop-down menu. This selects all of the image, apart from the eyes are.
- Hit the *'Delete'* key to remove the outer area of the image.
- Choose the *'Pointillize'* option from the *'Artistic'* submenu of the *'Filters'* menu.

The *'Lens Flare'* effect seeks to emulate the effect that bright sunlight has on a traditional camera. The steps for this are:
- Load the image.
- Select the *'Lens Flare'* option from the *'Render'* submenu of the *'Filters'* menu.
- Set the area in which the flare is to appear, and set the brightness to a high enough value.
- Select the type of camera to be emulated. This example is trying to look like the result of a 105mm camera.
- In this example, a second, less bright flare was added slightly offset from the first for added effect.

Obtaining the best results may require that the image brightness and contrast be adjusted before the effect is applied. In many cases, the final flattened image is improved by using the *'Auto Levels'* option, which automatically adjusts the levels of red, green and blue in the image.

These are only two of the effects that are in the Effects menu.   Others, such as Emboss and Distort are useful and its worth spending a little time trying out various effects.

Digital Watermarks
Piracy is common on the Internet. Computer software, games and music albums are all copied and placed on pirate web sites.   Huge efforts are made by the software publishers and the record industry to combat this growing trend. Photographers and graphic artists are not immune from this piracy and their work is easily downloaded from a web site and re-used in another production.   Most creative people wish to protect their intellectual property and one response has been the introduction of *'watermarks'* into image files.   See the *'Computer Graphics'* chapter for more detail on watermarks.

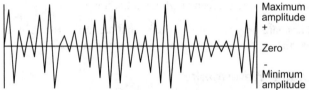

The Nature of Sound

Sound is produced and carried by the rapid variation of the pressure of the air surrounding the object that is creating the sound.

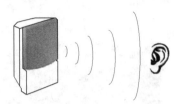

Consider listening to the sound from a computer's speaker system. The audio card's output drives the cone inside the speaker. The speaker cone vibrates in sympathy with the audio card signal. As the cone vibrates, the air next to it is alternately compressed and rarefied. This constant change of air pressure sets up sound pressure waves, which travel through the air until they reach the listener's eardrum. The sound waves then vibrate the eardrum, stimulating the auditory nerves and producing the sensation of sound.

The air does not actually travel between the speaker and the ear.   As the air next to the speaker cone moves back and forth, it passes on this movement to the air next to it - and so on. It is similar to the water in a pool when a stone is dropped in it. The waves move outwards but the water does not travel outwards. The knock-on effects of the variations diminish as the waves travel outwards, resulting in sound becoming quieter the further away the listener is from the source.

The air is alternating between a compressed and a rarefied state- i.e. at one point it is more compressed than its normal state, while it is more rarefied than normal at another point.

This constant alteration of the state of the air is converted into the alteration of electrical signals within audio equipment, where the signal alternates between being above and below a quiescent figure. Often, the quiescent figure is at electrical potential zero, with the voltage swing positive and negative from this value.   These varying signals can be directly replayed through an amplifier or can be recorded to audiotape. In the case of computer audio, the varying signal is digitised and saved to hard disk as an audio file.

The Hearing Process

The normal hearing process is described as being *'binaural'* - i.e. the listener hears with the use of two ears that point in different directions and are a distance apart. The brain processes the information received at these two receptors to identify the type of sound (e.g. car, voice, musical instrument) and its location within the surrounding three-dimensional space (e.g. to the left or right, in front or behind, above or below).   In the real world, sounds are heard from all around the listener - often all at the same time.

This is a complex process and the output from the computer's sound card has to match these natural conditions as much as possible.

Sound Systems

Sound cards and audio reproduction software has developed greatly from the early editions. They have followed much of technology used in hi-fi equipment, digital TV and in the movie industry. The three most commonly used audio formats are:

Mono

The most basic audio signal is *'monophonic'*. The sound sample is captured into a single audio channel, often using a single microphone to record the sound. The resultant audio waveform stores the essential information that allows the listener to identify the sample as a particular voice or musical instrument. It also provides some information regarding the volume of individual objects within the same (e.g. the drum is loud while the piccolo is quiet).

Stereo

Stereophonic samples record the audio on to two separate channels, using a separate microphone for each channel. If the microphones are spaced apart, then sound from objects on the left will record at greater amplitude on the left channel. Similarly, sounds from the right hand side will record at greater amplitude on the right channel. Sounds that situated in between the microphones will record with equal amplitude on each channel. When the sample is replayed through two speakers, the relative volumes from each speaker reproduce the relative positions of the original sound sources along a left-to-right plane (e.g. the bass guitar is on the left, the drums are on the right and the vocalist is in the middle).

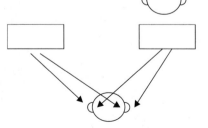

Since the microphones pick up reflected sound along with the direct sound, some *'depth of image'* is also captured.

Surround sound

Basic Surround Sound, such as the Dolby Surround Pro Logic, uses four speakers (two in front of the listener and two behind), which creates a circle of sound around the listener. The most commonly used surround sound speaker layout is the 5:1 system provided by both Dolby Digital and the MPEG-2 systems. This process is explained in more detail later.

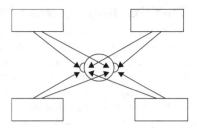

The Components of Sound

Sound has three essential elements:

- Frequency.
- Amplitude (the sound's volume).
- Harmonic content (the richness and uniqueness of the sound).

Frequency

This describes how often the amplitude of the signal changes over a given time period and is measured in complete cycles per second. The unit of measurement is the Hertz (Hz), where 1Hz equals one complete cycle per second. In the first example, two complete cycles of the audio signal have been completed within a one-second period, so the diagram shows a 2Hz signal.

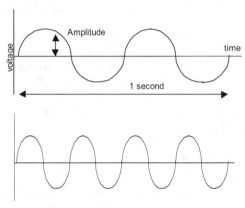

The second example shows four cycles being completed in the same time, so it is a 4Hz signal.

The UK mains supply varies at 50Hz and the US mains supply runs at 60Hz.

The human ear often detects sounds down to about 100Hz, although some can detect lower frequencies (e.g. the hum from the fluctuating 50Hz power mains or even as low as 20Hz). At the other extreme, the ear can detect frequencies as high as 20kHz, with the average person's upper limit being around 17kHz. These values steadily reduce with old age, to 15KHz or lower. The human ear does not detect ultrasonic sounds but such sounds are audible to many animals.

Most of the useful audible range is between 300Hz and 3000Hz (i.e. 3 kHz), a fact that is exploited in many telecommunications systems to reduce bandwidth and minimise costs. The human voice can produce frequencies in the range 40Hz to 4kHz, with vowels producing low frequencies and consonant producing higher frequencies.

Notes

Computers measure capacity or speed in bits or bytes. A byte is made of a collection of eight bits. The upper case 'B' usually denotes bytes while the lower-case 'b' usually denotes bits, although there is sometimes confusion in the use of these suffixes. A modem may transfer data at 56kbps. The computer may have 512MB of memory installed. A hard disk may store 300GB of data.

In these examples, all values are in binary denominations. So, a Kilo is 1,024, a Mega is 1024 kilos and a Giga is 1024 Mega. Therefore, a 1MB memory chip stores 1024 x 1024 = 1,048,576 bytes, while the 56kbps modem is processing 57,344 bits (i.e. 56x1024 bits) every second.

With waveforms, a Kilo is 1000, a Mega is 1,000,000 and a Giga is 1,000,000,000. Therefore, a 3GHz CPU runs at 3,000,000,000 Hz.

Frequency and pitch

The terms 'pitch' and 'frequency' are often used interchangeably but they have slightly different meanings. Frequency is a measurable quantity and is the one most used in electronics and computing (e.g. the operating frequency of a CPU or a modem). Pitch, on the other hand, is a more subjective quality based on how the brain perceives a note and this term is mostly used in music.

The relationship of frequency to pitch is almost exponential. A note changing from 100Hz to 300Hz is perceived by a listener as a significant change, while a change from 10KHz to 10.2KHz is much less noticeable.

In electronics, frequency is measured in Hertz, KiloHertz, MegaHertz, GigaHertz, and so on. In music, pitch is measured on a musical scale with the doubling of a note's frequency being defined as raising it by one 'octave'. In the West, an octave is divided into 12 notes, or 'half steps', and these could each be further divided into 100 smaller steps known as 'cents'. The human ear can detect a change of pitch down to about 5 cents. Since frequency and pitch is relative, the international standard is to have the A above middle C on the piano set to 440Hz (often known as 'A-440').

The Frequency Spectrum

Information is received through our sense of sight, sound, touch, taste and smell. Much of the information is conveyed in the form of waves - sound waves, light waves and heat waves. In addition, waveforms such as ultrasonics, radio waves and microwaves are used as a vehicle to carry information.

We do not actually hear the radio waves, just the picture or sound information that was previously imposed on them. The table shows the frequency spectrum for the common carriers of information. There are other frequencies exist, such as heat and X-rays but they are not used as information carriers.

Description	Range	Typical Use
Sub-Audio	Up to 20Hz	Below the hearing threshold
Audio	20Hz to 20kHz	The entire range of sounds, speech and music
Ultrasonic devices	20kHz to 30kHz	'Silent' dog whistles, some remote control devices
Long wave	30kHz to 300kHz	Radio
Medium wave	300kHz to 3MHz	Radio
Short wave	3MHz to to 30MHz	Radio
VHF	30Mhz to 300MHz	Radio
UHF	300MHz to 3GHz	Television, aircraft landing systems
Microwaves	3GHz and above	Radar, satellites, TV and communication links

The audio spectrum is not equally used by all objects and living things. The male voice spans a lower range of frequencies than a female voice, while a bass tuba's fundamental range is much lower than that of a clarinet.

The table shows where some of the objects lie on the audio spectrum.

Source	Fundamental	Total range including harmonics
Bass Tuba	40Hz to 375Hz	40Hz to 7kHz
Trombone	80Hz to 500 Hz	80Hz to 8kHz
Cello	70Hz to 900Hz	70Hz to 14kHz
Speech (male)	---	100Hz to 8kHz
Speech (female)	---	180Hz to 10kHz
Soprano Clarinet	150Hz to 1.7kHz	150Hz to 14kHz
Violin	190Hz to 3kHz	190Hz to 15kHz
14" Cymbal	----	300Hz to 17kHz
Room Noise	----	30Hz to 18kHz

Amplitude

There are two measures of amplitude:

- The 'volume' or 'intensity' of a sound as heard by the human ear.
- The changing signal levels in equipment such as sound cards and amplifiers.

The intensity of sound is measured in decibels (dB). This is not a linear scale, as the human ear does not perceive volume changes in a linear way. Doubling the sound energy arriving at the human ear is not perceived as being twice as loud. The sound energy has to be increased tenfold before it is perceived as being twice as loud. The ear's response to sound changes is logarithmic and therefore audio volume controls are similarly logarithmic. Turning up the audio volume results in logarithmic increases in output and not linear increases. Doubling the volume is a 3dB increase, while quadrupling the volume is a 6dB increase. Increasing the volume by eight times is a 9dB increase and a 30dB increase turns up the volume to 1,000 times its previous amplitude.

Absolute sound intensity decibel levels are calculated thus:

intensity in dB = 10 log (measured value/reference value)

where the measured value is expressed in watts per square metre and the reference value is 10^{-12} watts per square metre. In practice, noise levels readouts are obtained from meters that are calibrated in decibels.

Examples of everyday audio levels, expressed in decibels are shown in the table.

Prolonged exposure to excessive noise results in permanent hearing impairment. For example, daily exposure to 110dB for as little as 3 minutes per day presents a likely damage risk, while a level of 85dB risks damage at a daily rate of 4 hours per day. The source of the excessive levels may be work-related (such as factory machinery or working on building sites or airports) or may be social (such as the over-zealous use of ghettoblasters, or attendance at loud concerts). The first problem is a matter for Health & Safety procedures, while the latter is more difficult to resolve. The damage is always permanent and losses are not restored with time.

DB Level	Example
160	Jet engine
130	Large orchestra at full blast
120	Start of pain threshold
110	Power tools
100	Loud rock music
90	Subway
80	Car/Truck
70	Normal conversation
60	Background noise in busy store
50	Background noise in house or office
40	Quiet conversation
30	Whisper
20	Quiet living room
10	Background noise in recording studio
0	Hearing threshold

In addition, increasing age results in declining hearing ability, particularly of the higher frequencies. Elderly people commonly are unable to detect frequencies above 10kHz, no matter how high the volume is set. Hearing loss commences at age 25 and declines steadily until aged about 60. Thereafter, the decline in women's hearing tends to tail off, while men's hearing continues to decline. A male aged 60 may have a typical hearing loss of 7db for frequencies around 500Hz while the loss at 5000Hz might be around 35dB. The corresponding figures for women may be 9dB and 18dB.

At low sound pressure levels, the human ear is less sensitive to the higher and lower end of the audible range (i.e. less than 1KHz and above 6KHz). This is known as the *'equal loudness contour'* and explains why some hi-fi units have a *'loudness'* button to boost the upper and lower ends of the audible signal.

The decibel is also used to measure the voltage changes that an amplifier can achieve. In this case, the decibel is not an actual value - it measures the <u>ratio</u> between a reference point on a logarithmic scale and the value that is actually measured. It measures how far the signal deviates in any one direction (i.e. how high or how low).   Different electrical and electronic devices make use of the mean or average value of the signal, while others are concerned with the RMS (root-mean-square) value.

For audio digitisation, the maximum or peak value expresses the greatest range that the signal covers and determines the scale to be covered by the equipment handling the signal.

Harmonics

If a number of people were to sing exactly the same musical note, their voices would remain unique and identifiable. This is known as the *'sonic signature'* and is caused by the harmonic content of each person's voice. Apart from sounding the basic frequency of the note, the human voice will introduce an individual collection of other sounds that are mixed with the basic frequency. These other sounds are multiples of the original frequency and are known as *'harmonics'*. It is the quantity and relative volumes of each of these harmonics that makes each person's voice different. In the same way, a piano is very rich in harmonics while a tin flute is devoid of harmonics. The extra components give the piano its *'richness'* of tone in comparison to the purer sound of the flute. A sound that is rich in

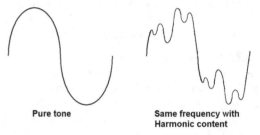

Pure tone   Same frequency with Harmonic content

harmonics contains much more detailed information than a purer simpler sound and this causes problems for their storage on computer, as explained later.

The diagrams show three waveforms.
The first diagram shows a basic waveform that carries out two complete cycles within a one-millisecond period. It represents a pure sine wave with a frequency of 2kHz. If this is the basic component of a particular sound, it is described as the *'fundamental'* frequency or first harmonic.

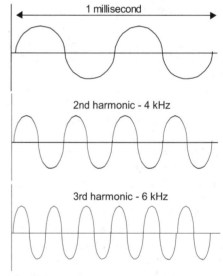

The second diagram shows the second harmonic, or *'first overtone'*, of the sound. It occurs at twice the frequency of the fundamental. The third diagram shows the third harmonic, or second overtone, which occurs at three times the fundamental frequency.

The fundamental frequency provides the sound's pitch, while the harmonics provide the sound's tone (often called *'timbre'*).

Different musical instruments produce different mixes of harmonics. They also produce harmonics at different amplitudes.   To further complicate the issue, they often produce different harmonic mixes/amplitudes dependent upon how high the fundamental frequency is or how hard the instrument is plucked/struck/blown. These intricacies give instruments their uniqueness and explain why real-world sampling produces more realistic results than synthesised sounds. An instrument that produces strong higher harmonics is described as having extra *'brightness'*.

Harmonics also impose demands on the overall system, if true audio reproduction is to be achieved.   Consider a sound with a basic frequency of 4,500Hz and a 9,000Hz second harmonic and a 13,500Hz third harmonic (there is no *'first harmonic'* as this is the basic or *'fundamental'* frequency). If the sound passes through a component that has a top handling frequency of say, 10,000Hz, then only the basic frequency and second harmonic will pass through. The waveform will have been changed and the sound, although having the same pitch as before, will no longer sound the same. Sources that may cause this loss of clarity include:
- Digitising the sound at too low a sample rate (see later).
- Using poor quality sound systems (e.g. playing tapes through an old tape deck) as the source for audio capture.
- Using cheap microphones with a limited frequency range.
- Playing the finished sound through poor quality loudspeakers or headphones.

Timbre

Two musical instruments may play the same note at the same level of loudness and still sound completely different. The distinctive quality of a particular instrument is known as its timbre (pronounced *'tamber'*).

Timbre is dependent on:
- The sound's spectral distribution (the mix of harmonics and their relative strengths).
- The way that the sound radiates from the instrument over time.

An instrument's sound is often described in terms of its *'envelope'* and this encompasses four different features - often called the ADSR.

ATTACK	The speed at which the note's initial volume increases.	
DECAY	The speed at which the volume fades away.	
SUSTAIN	The main amplitude that is maintained	
	during the note (e.g. if a synthesiser keyboard key is held down).	
RELEASE	The time it takes for the sound to completely stop.	

Acoustics

Sounds rarely travel from their source to the human ear without being affected in some way by their surroundings. Acoustics is the science that examines the production and distribution of sound through different mediums. Knowledge of simple acoustics will help improve the quality of sound recordings. This includes the effects of reflection, absorption and resonance and how they alter the original sound wave.

Reflection

Just like light, sound can 'bounce' off a surface and this sound reaches the ear at a later time than the original source, as it has longer to travel. This may combine with the original sound in a way that produces reverberation effects, or it may combine to produce distortion through phase cancellations.

Echoes are perceived individually (e.g. shouting in an empty hall or a deep valley). In a deep valley, the time taken for the sound to travel outwards and return to the ear is long (perhaps a full second). This means that the sound is heard after a distinctly different delay.

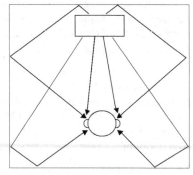

With a smaller space, the return time is less (measurable in milliseconds) and the reflected sound tends to merge with the original sound – producing an effect known as *'reverberation'*. Often, there are several echoes that are added to the final reverberation. The original sound may reflect off several surfaces (e.g. all four walls of a room as in the diagram). The sound may only bounce once or may bounce several times before reaching the listener.

Hard surfaces, such as glass, tile and concrete are very reflective and are usually avoided during sound recording, as explained later.

Absorption

With reflection, most of the energy of the sound wave is returned into the air. With absorption, most of the acoustic energy arriving at the material is turned into heat energy and little is reflected.   The amount of absorption is dependent on the size of the surface area and the shape of the absorbent material, and the degree to which it is absorbent (its absorption coefficient).   Other factors include the type of material (the absorption coefficient of each particular material is frequency dependant), its location and even how it is mounted.

The degree of reverberation and the resulting sound patterns are dependent upon the absorbent qualities of the room where the recording is being made (or the sound is being played).   A room with highly reflective surfaces is described as being *'reverberant'*, while a room with few reflected surfaces is described as being *'anechoic'*.

Of course, the properties of a room also depend on other factors. An empty room is more reverberant, than a room full of people. This explains why a band that sets up their audio equipment and practices in an empty hall finds that the sound is different on the night of the performance. The audience dampens the reverberation and alters the sound.

Where a material does not completely absorb a sound, some of the sound is refracted on the other side of the material. Examples of this are the muffled sounds that are heard through a wall or the effect of placing a pillow over your head.

Resonance

Resonance describes the tendency of an object to vibrate at a particular frequency. Examples of resonance are an opera singer sustaining a note and vibrating or shattering a wine glass, or feeling your ribs vibrate with the bass notes at a concert.   Objects tend to vibrate at a frequency that depends on their mass and their stiffness.   Resonance can cause physical problems. For example, a troop of soldiers cannot march in step over a bridge in case they set up a resonance that will damage the bridge.   In an audio environment, the vibration of a resonant object creates unwanted additional sound waves.

Tackling acoustic problems is covered later in this chapter.

Sources of audio

Multimedia and web productions employ audio files that are stored in digital format.
Some audio files are created or supplied in digital format.

This includes:
- Files that are created on the computer, without coming from a real-world audio source. These range from MIDI files that are created by sequencing software, to synthesised sound effects. These files did not have their origin in an analogue sound file.
- Files that are purchased from digital libraries. These include CD collections of digital music and sound effects, usually royalty-free.

This chapter mainly concentrates on audio files that are recorded and/or digitised by the user. The audio source is a real-world analogue source that is converted into a digital version for use in computer-based projects. This includes:
- Files that are purchased in analogue format and converted to digital format (e.g. CD collections of analogue royalty-free music and sound effects.
- Files that are produced by recording via microphones.

In either case, the nature and properties of a digital audio file need to be understood.

Using sound in applications

Before examining the technology behind digital audio sampling and the process of capturing and editing audio, consideration must be given to the creative use to which sound is used in multimedia applications.

We are so accustomed to letting audio inform us that we only notice it when it is absent. If in any doubt, simply turn down the volume on the television set to see just how much mood and information is conveyed by sound.

Purpose of sound

Sound plays a variety of important roles in everyday life and this is also true in multimedia and web projects.

Among the many intentions of using sound are:

To inform users	Providing the user with essential information – facts, figures.
To influence attitudes, emotions and perceptions	Using selected audio sources designed to establish a frame of mind that can persuade or motivate the user (e.g. child's voice, elderly statesman, class issues, tone of voice).
To establish atmosphere/mood	Using background sounds and/or music to indicate that the screen content is intended to be sad/happy, serious/light-hearted, etc., or is set in a particular location or era. (See later)
To aid usability/accessibility	Using audible prompts, audible feedback, warning sounds, text readers, etc. to make the project easier to understand and manipulate, and to direct the focus of attention. In addition, many users prefer learning by listening rather than reading (e.g. the visually challenged, poor readers and dyslexics).

The ability of sounds to produced desired results like those above are referred to as their *'efficacy'* and applied correctly can have remarkable results (as can be seen in many TV commercials and blockbuster movies).

Sound types

There are many ways to categorise types of sounds.

One method defines sounds as being either literal or abstract. Literal sounds include speeches from actors, music from on-stage band, and the sounds of moving objects. These sounds are regarded as being essential to the content of the production. Abstract sounds, on the other hand, are not essential but generally help convey the mood of the production (e.g. melancholy music, eerie music, quirky bright music, footsteps fading into the distance, etc.).

Another method lists sounds by whether they user can see their origin on the screen and defines two sound categories:

On-screen	These are often literal (typically dialogue), and can include some narration.
Off-screen	These are mostly all abstract, with some literal and some narration (think wildlife documentaries). Common off-screen sounds are for mood setting or changes of pace (e.g. explosions, screeching tyres, blood-curdling screams).

Yet another method categorises sounds by their content, as in the table below.

Sound Types	Examples
Narration	The audible description of the project content as it unfolds (see below).
Music	Sampled music to create a mood.
Synthesised	Computer-created effects such as laser guns, sci-fi feel, and rocket ships.
Natural	Non man-made sounds such as water running in a stream, thunder, rain
Ambient/ Environmental/ Atmospheric	A combination of sounds that remains relatively constant. Examples are traffic, office hubbub, birds, insects, wild animals, machinery, a pianist in a club, a fairground, the stock exchange, the theatre, a football stadium, party conversation, a restaurant's clatter of plates and cutlery, etc.
Incidental	One-off sounds that contribute to the plot or the general background. Examples are a single gunshot, the sound of a foghorn, announcements such as *"the train leaving on platform …"*.

Narration

A short definition of the word is:

> *"That part of a discourse which recites the time, manner or consequences of an action, or simply states the facts connected with the subject"*

while a shorter version states:

> *"Anything told or recounted"*

In both cases, the audio content is provided by an individual telling a form of story. That story could be a simple advertising claim that *"Brand X washes whiter than Brand Y"* for various reasons, or might be a full-blown documentary where the voice is off-screen for the entire programme.

Narrative styles

The way that a narrative is delivered alters the user's attitude towards the presentation. For example, there are certain connotations in the use of national or regional dialects. People tend to regard a Scottish accent as representing honesty, while a French accent is usually associated with romance. A refined accent is associated with the upper classes, while regional accents are associated with lower classes.

Similarly, different speaking methods are used to establish the tone of the content in the user's mind. So, for example, powerful voices are used to punch home a message and dominant or assured voices are used to imply the correctness of what is being said in a less aggressive way. A husky female voice is used to imply a sexy tone, while a hesitant child's voice implies innocence. In some cases, the narrative may be in the form of a poem or even a song.

Narrative delivery

The way that a narrative is delivered also affects its impact on the user. These factors include:

Speed	The time taken to deliver each individual word. For example, the user impact is different for a fast-talking Scotsman or Italian, compared to the slow delivery of a person from the southern states of America.
Rhythm	The pattern made by the words of a spoken statement. This can vary from an absence of any rhythm, through a melodic delivery, to a poetic delivery. A well-delivered rhythm can be very effective, while overuse can make the delivery sound *'hammy'*.
Tone	The inflection in the voice of the narrator can impart a huge range of attitudes or emotions. Some, like anger, joy or questioning, are easily detected by the user. Others, such as sarcasm or irony, are often better detected in the spoken word compared to a textual equivalent.
Volume	The amplitude of the spoken word can be used to imply situations or emotions. For example, certain words or certain passages can be emphasised by speaking them more loudly. On the other hand, a wildlife documentary may use a softly-spoken or whispered narrative to imply that the narrator does not want to disturb the birds or animals (even though the narration may have been added on after the video footage was shot).
Pace	The time taken to deliver sections of the spoken statement. Varying the pace can suggest changes in action or urgency.

Varying tone and pace are common ways to motivate users, or to highlight points. Positive attributes in narration are being candid, sincere, straightforward and amiable. Negative attributes include being arrogant, sarcastic, disrespectful, flippant, pompous and pretentious.

Narrative genres

The word *'genre'* is derived from the French for *'class'* or *'kind'* and is used in narration to specify a common content type. To some extent, narrative genres are shaped by actual experience, while others are learned conventions. For example, a comedy genre uses a narrative that is common to every person who makes a joke. The tone and the pace used mirror the everyday approach to humour in the real world. On the other hand, on hearing a warbling voice, users associate it with an alien, even though no one knows what aliens actually sounds like (assuming they exist). In this case, it is a learned response.

So, users have an expectation of how a narrative will be presented in any given context. The tone set in a romantic narrative, for example, would be deemed inappropriate for a science documentary. In practice, there are a range of different narrative genres including romance, documentary, horror, sci-fi, comedy, war, adventure, period pieces, and education.

Users draw their own connotations regarding a production, taking clues from the genre used in the narrative. So, for example, a listener to a radio broadcast responds to the genre in the narrative. This may well include the use of language; consider the words used in a production of Oliver Twist or My Fair Lady, compared to the words used in Star Trek or in a teenage music channel.

While the narrative used in a production normally follows the expectations of users, there are times when a special effect can be achieved by contradicting these expectations. Producers may create a road safety film for adults using a documentary genre, while using a comedy genre for the same material slanted at young schoolchildren. Similarly, spoof horror movies use normal horror genre narrative, accompanied by comic screen content.

The selection of narrative genre depends on the effect to be achieved. In most cases, professionals would be used to provide off-screen narratives, with on-screen parts being played by trained actors. However, to obtain an authentic flavour, professionals would be replaced by subject experts, staff, customers, and vox pop, where appropriate.

Using audio
Composition and interplay
A few productions, such as vox pop interviews, news reports and some documentaries use only the audio that was recorded along with the video. Most other productions use audio from different sources to create the final audio effect. The addition of music, voiceovers and additional sound effects are often used to engineer an improved audio content. These audio components may be chosen to create a mood or atmosphere and may be further manipulated in terms of their volume and spatial context.

Combining several sounds
Perhaps the most common audio enhancement is the combination of several audio sources. This may be used to create an audio background to an animation or other computer-generated screen content. It may also be used to improve on the audio soundtrack of a video recording from a real-world source.   The clip may contain the actor or commentator's voice but lack any useful background sounds. Adding them in later improves the finished effect.

For example, a home movie clip may be of a reporter from a supposed war zone. Various audio clips of tanks, guns, explosions and screams can be added in at the editing stage to provide the expected background noises. More peaceful audio combinations may be Hawaiian music and the lapping of waves, or whistling kettles accompanied by the popping of toasters and the chatter of children.

The nature of the sources that are combined will produce different effects. For example the sound of monkey plus children suggests a zoo, while the sounds of monkeys plus birds plus insects suggests a jungle.

Logic and form
The finished audio content should meet the expectations of the users. This means that certain audio elements are logically in the same mix. For example, a fairground needs more than just the sound of the barrel organs; it needs the sounds of crowds and of laughter.   Similarly, the sound of a fireworks display is incomplete without accompanying 'oohs' and 'ahs' from a crowd.

When mixing sounds, their relative volumes in the final mix must be correct to obtain a successful result.

Particular problems that might be experienced during mixing are:

Masking	Care must be taken to ensure that a louder sound does not drown out a softer sound. This usually masks the harmonics of the softer sound, making it more muddy and less clear.
Beating	Where two audio signals are close in frequency, the difference between the two frequencies appears as a separate audible tone. This phenomenon is useful when tuning an instrument to a tone of a reference frequency but is a problem when an orchestra has instruments that are slightly out of tune with each other (e.g. a choir of multiple violins).
Clipping	Where a signal's amplitude is set too high, the peaks of the signal overdrive the sound circuitry causing distortion (see later).

Another issue is the approach to narrative in a multimedia or web project. The narrative form will be different from that used in a written project and also different from that used in normal conversations or interviews. Presenting both text and audio information to a user can improve the usability of the project, as it reduces the natural losses and errors that occur in the brain when processing information.

This introduces an element of 'channel redundancy' - presenting the same or closely related information through both visual and audible channels. The use of audio reduces the amount of text that has to be displayed on screen, which is a good thing (see 'coherence' below). To work successfully, the information in both channels must be similar and must not be not be contradictory. Using exactly the same words in both sound and text also leads to poorer results than words that reinforce the text content.

Coherence
The coherence principle rests on the maxim that 'less is more' – i.e. adding too many unnecessary visuals, texts and sounds impedes the user's appreciation of the content. Such material:
- Distracts users from the key content.
- Gets in the way of the user processing the essential information.
- Activates irrelevant knowledge previously stored by users, further impeding the assimilation of the essential new information.

Such issues were examined in the chapters on design and should be borne in mind when designing the audio content of a presentation.

Spatial context
This looks at how the various audio elements are placed on the audio tracks.   A simple monophonic track does not have to take this issue into account, as all the audio sources are replayed from the same single source. However, most user systems are either stereo or 5:1 (or even 7:1) systems, where the sounds reach the listener from multiple directions.   This allows the designer to place each individual audio element in the most appropriate setting for the best overall effect, a technique known as 'spatial placement'.   Its uses both the amplitude and the stereo field of

individual audio elements, so that the listener perceives them to come from the left/right/front/behind in position and close or far away in distance.

It also allows the designer to provide the illusion of movement through a technique known as 'panning' (see 'Surround Sound' later). Objects, or people, can be presented as if they are moving around the listener. Footsteps, a train, a car, or an aeroplane can be projected as moving from left to right, right to left, towards the listener or away from the listener. However, most sounds don't pan in the real world and the technique should not be overused.

In addition to the physical placement of sounds, there is the issue of *'frequency placement'*, which looks at how audio sources should be placed in the spatial placement with regard to their frequency. A common use of this technique is to ensure that instruments with similar frequencies should be placed on to separate left and right channels. This minimises the risk of masking that was explained earlier.

The art of mixing is the key to balancing out all the factors mentioned above.

Some techniques are well known. For example, a narrator, a lead vocalist or a lead instrument is almost always placed in the centre of the stereo field. Also, as people's heads turn towards the source of sounds, dialogue should always be placed left and right in the field.

The volume and augmentation effects (e.g. echo, etc) set for each audio element should ensure that they complement each other. It is the interplay between different audio sources that helps establish the overall scene. So, for example, if a father calls to a child that is some distance away, the spatial placement should ensure that the two voices are set in the correct audible planes, while the volume of the father's voice should be much greater than that of the distant child. If the father then walks over to the child, his volume of his voice should gradually subside, to provide the illusion of movement.

The original audio element has sometimes to be modified or augmented before being used in the mix. Consider, for example, a recording of an organ that was made in a studio. This would be free from any of the alterations that would be expected in the real world. If the organ was meant to be played in a church or another echoey environment, the audio clip would require to have some reverberation added to it before it was added to the final audio tracks.

Creating moods

The use of audio elements including music, which is considered separately next, plays a substantial role in influencing the user's perceptions. Most people can sit with their eyes closed and still follow most of a television programme. Indeed, the government only allows registered blind people to claim a 50% discount on their television licence! Even further, people need only hear a snatch of a programme's sound to identify what the scene is about. The murmur of people and the clinking of glasses is identified as a pub scene, the revving of engines and squealing of tyres is identified as a car chase … and so on.

Some key points of using sounds in this way are:

Priming atmospheres	Using audio to set the scene. This could be through mood music or the use of sound effects. The listener uses these to paint a mental picture of the scene. For example, the screen may only show a man standing at a bar, but the continual honking of taxi horns might indicate the bar was in Manhattan, while the sound of sophisticated piano playing might indicate the bar was in an up-market night club. This technique can even be used with no screen image. The sounds are used to prime the user's expectations, prior to fading the image into view.
Anticipation of events	Using sounds to raise the listeners' expectations. Examples are notes rising in pitch, approaching footsteps, a creaking door, or a rifle being cocked. The listener, based on previous experiences, knows what might happen next.
Evoking responses	Using sounds to manipulate the listeners' reactions. So, a ticking clock suggests time and a forthcoming important activity, while different types of music can shape user reactions (see later). A response of surprise can also be made very effectively (an unexpected scream, a sudden explosion, the crack of a twig in a dark wood).
Smoothing transitions	Using audio to move the user from one page content to another. The most famous is the use of *'dream'* music e.g. (the strumming of harps) to take an actor back to an earlier time. Transitions can also be made using narrative (*"meanwhile back at the police station…"*).
Mood transition	Using audio to change the user's mood between scenes or within a scene. A common technique is the change of background music (the subdued background music suddenly builds to a crescendo as the lovers embrace, the idle chatter in the castle dies away as the clock strikes midnight, etc.).
Juxtaposition of moods or atmosphere	Using two sets of audio to emphasise the contrast in the content of two different scenes. For example, the screen content may switch from showing the front of one to showing the front of another almost identical house. If the first house is accompanied by riotous party sounds and the other is accompanied by silence, or the sound of snoring, users get two entirely different experiences from looking at almost identical screen content.

Hit points and timing	Using music, speech or effects to accurately match the screen content. This is concerned with where an element is inserted in a sound track and how long that elements plays.
	Hit points are specific points in the video content where an item of audio must be introduced. This applies to both computer-generated animations and to real world video and may be a piece of music or a sound effect. The timing is often essential. For example, the sound of a gunshot must be synchronised to the on-screen action.
	The length of the audio element must also be considered. A piece of music, for example, may have to be edited so that it fits the on-screen action without being too short or too long. For large productions, an orchestra can be presented with a musical score that is specially written for the occasion. However, the selection/creation and editing of music remains an issue for all scales of production.
Reinforcing actions	Using audio to reassure users that their mouse or keyboard activities have been recognised and acted upon. This could be a simple reassuring *'beep'* when a menu choice is selected. Better still, is to use sounds from the real world that match the user's activities. Examples are camera clicks, switch clicks and the sound of page turnovers. These match the listener's expectations if they carried out similar activities in the real world and provide reassurance that the project is being used properly and that progress is being made.
Qualifying sounds	Using sound to warn the user about some screen content or event. For navigation purposes, this might mean issuing a warning beep if the user tries to perform an illegal operation or enters invalid information. In an educational package, it might mean providing audio feedback, explaining what was wrong with the user's choice of answer.
	For mood setting purposes, it might mean using sound to paint a different picture from the one presented by the screen content. For example, the beach scene in the film *'Jaws'* presents a happy user response – until the sinister music is introduced to indicate the presence of the shark. The user is being warned that the screen content is not what it seems.

Setting and altering moods, then, utilises the listeners expectations from audio sounds to shape moods.

The audio track expected from a funeral parlour is expected to be different from that of a children's' party.

In many cases, this means working with the user expectations to engineer the required overall effect.

Although the audio content normally works with user expectations, there are occasions when the audio can be used to work against these expectations. For example, the old classic *'Rocky Horror Picture Show'* showed great innovation by using rock music in a horror setting.

Use of music

Earlier in this chapter narrative genres were described as using the expected connotations of words and phrases in particular situations. This is also valid when looking at music as an audio element in a project.

People are accustomed to associating different musical genres with different situations, places, etc.

This allows designers to use music clips or backgrounds to set the mood.   Music can also be used to provide continuity, to set pace, or to signal a turn in events.

Since most people find music pleasant, it can be used both as an attraction or a distraction, depending on the needs of the project at any point in time.

There are many music types, such as classical, pop, folk, rock, hillbilly, jazz, blues, rap and many more – all with their own ability to establish a mood.

Music and emotion

Users are quick to associate music with mood and there are many options to choose from. For example, classical music is associated with elegance or class, while rock music is associated with fast paced excitement. Similarly, light jazz is associated with sophistication, while circus music is associated with comical or ludicrous situations.

The choice of music tempo also conveys emotions. A slow tempo is associated with romance or casualness, or sadness, while a fast tempo is associated with action and fervour. If the tempo is overdone at either end, the result is usually one of humour, whether intended or not..

In addition, personality or mood can be conveyed through the choice of instrument used to play the music. A tuba is recognised as being fat or sluggish, while a clarinet is thought to be playful. Similarly, a piccolo suggests tinyness while a trumpet suggests bold or brassy.   So, a clip of a sparrow might have a piccolo backing, while a clip of a hippopotamus might have a tuba backing.

Even the same tune, played with a different instrument, produces different results (think of a long haunting violin or fast banjo, an acoustic guitar or a Stratocaster).

Music and era

Music is also commonly used to establish the era in which the video is set.   Consider screen content displaying a scene of rolling hills.   If the background music is a minuet, the setting is in distant past, while traditional jazz, 60's rock, big band, or rap all conjure up different time periods.   Without seeing an actor dressed in period costume, the listener knows what era of the clip about to be watched.

Music and location

Music can easily establish the location of a scene.   Some obvious examples are rhythmic drums (Africa), castanets (Spain), Sitar (India), oompah band (Germany), bagpipes (Scotland) and many others.   While many are based on stereotypes, they are nevertheless effective.

Sound and image

Filmmakers and professional advertisers have long used carefully blended combinations of audible and visual information to make the maximum impact.   Filmmakers often have the luxury of time to build up a mood or rise to a climax.   Television advertisers, on the other hand, only have a minute or less to get their message across.   As a result, they use both image and sound to complement each other and achieve their maximum effect in the shortest time.   This often involves the clever, and unexpected, use of words and images to grab the attention of the public who are easily able to click a button on their TV remote to avoid an advertising break.   Concepts are reduced to their essentials and the number words is minimised to get across the essential message and slogan.   Images are designed to sell themselves (e.g. cars) or are used to hold the viewer while the message is imparted audibly.

The frantic pace of television adverts is also employed in videos of concerts, particularly rock concerts. The attention span of the viewer is low, especially when staring at a screen that displays the concert stage for long periods.   So, the attention of the viewer is maintained by regularly (and usually rapidly) changing the screen content.   Although the sound may be continuous, the screen content may present different views of the band (e.g. long shots, close ups, etc.) or shots of the audience or the venue.

Although the audio and image are mostly combined in projects, there are times when one will play a greater role than another.   In some cases, the screen content is of prime importance and the audio is for supporting background only (e.g. when a travel programme shows the spectacular views of the district).   In other cases, the audio content is the most important (e.g. when the screen displays a hospital ward while the voiceover explains the latest health figures).

There are also times when only the image or only the audio is presented, so that a particular result is achieved.   There are some situations, for example, where the images are so powerful or so heart wrenching that words would get in the way.   Examples are the silent display of starving children or war atrocities.   On a less frightening level, silence can be used to impart a mood of emptiness or hopelessness (e.g. displaying derelict factories or empty streets).   If a picture is genuinely worth a thousand words, only the picture should be displayed and words should be omitted altogether.

There are other times when it is best to present the sound with no screen image.   This leaves much to the user's imagination and is a positive use of silence.   Examples are a scream in the dark, or a single shot being heard (who died?).   This technique can also be used for preparing or priming for the display of an image (e.g. *"its behind that door"*, *"turn away now if ...."*).

The decision as to when to combine and when not to combine depends on the overall effect to be achieved, as outlined above.

The ultimate test of a combined piece is whether or not it was successful in its effect.   There are some people who have *'synesthesia'*.   This means *'joined feelings'* (just as anaesthesia is the lack of feeling).   There is an overlap between different senses and feelings, such that they can 'hear' colours or 'see' musical notes.   The purpose of combining image and audio is to achieve a similar link between sight and feelings or sound and feelings.   After all, mood is just the psychological association of images and sounds with user experiences.

Digitised Sound

Audio in the real world is analogue; it contains infinite variations in amplitude.   However, the computer only stores data in digital format. Therefore, the circuitry on the sound card has to convert analogue sounds into a digital equivalent. These digital files can then be incorporated into web sites or into multimedia CD-ROMs.

Analogue-to-Digital Conversion

Sound is fed into a sound card in analogue format, usually from a microphone or other audio source.

The conversion is carried out by a chip in the sound card called the *'ADC'* - the *'Analogue-to-Digital-Converter'*.   The ADC processes a sample of sound and generates a series of numbers that can be stored to disk for later replay. The numbers store the amplitude of the sound waveform at progressive points in time during the duration of the sound sample.

The diagram shows a waveform whose amplitude is varying with time.

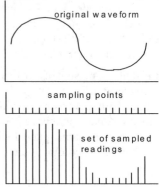

The amplitude of the waveform is measured at regular time intervals and the value read at each time interval is stored. The set of sampled readings represents the changes in the waveform and can be used to recreate the original sound using a DAC.

The DAC ('*Digital-to-Analogue Convertor*') works in the reverse manner to an ADC. It accepts a digital input and uses the values to build a varying audio signal output. In most formats, the waveform swings above and below a reference point of zero. This means that low amplitude levels have a negative integer representing them while positive integer numbers represents high amplitude levels.

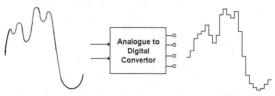

The diagram shows an ADC being fed with a sound source. The output shows the effects of digitisation.

The ADC circuitry looks at the amplitude of the audio input at regular time intervals and converts the value that it finds at each moment into its nearest binary value. Since the input has an infinite number of possible amplitude levels, the ADC chooses the nearest binary level that the chip offers. This is known as '*quantisation*'. The chip carrying out the conversion has a binary output system. In this example, there are four output pins. This allows values from 0000 (i.e. decimal zero) to 1111 (decimal 16). If the chip had eight output pins (as in 8-bit sound cards), it would provide 256 different output levels. The DAC in a 16-bit sound card has 16 output pins, allowing output resolution down to 65,536 different values.

The conversion process is called PCM (Pulse Code Modulation) and the raw data with no compression (e.g. a RAW or WAV file) is described as an LPCM (Linear PCM) file.

Two factors determine the quality of digitised sound:

- The dynamic range (i.e. the accuracy in terms of absolute amplitudes).
  The larger the range of values stored, the greater the accuracy of the sound's reproduction.
- The sampling rate (i.e. the accuracy of the amplitude at any one instant).
  The more samples taken in a time period, the greater the sound's fidelity.

Dynamic Range

The more complex the waveform to be stored, the greater total of different numbers required to store the sound. The span from the lowest amplitude to the greatest amplitude is known as the '*dynamic range*'.

This is sometimes also described as '*resolution*' or '*bit-range*'.

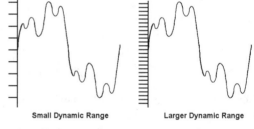

Small Dynamic Range   Larger Dynamic Range

In the left diagram, only a small number of bits are allocated to store the waveform, so it is incapable of handling the small amplitude variations in the waveform and these details are averaged away.

In this case, the ADC produces a series of numbers that approximate to the overall waveform but the harmonics that make a piano sound different from a guitar are lost as are the harmonics that differentiate between different human voices. The right-hand diagram shows a greater dynamic range allowing the same analogue signal to be converted into a greater number of digital levels. This allows for a greater clarity of reproduction, as the replayed sound is closer to the original sound.

The early 8-bit sound card used 8 data bits to store each sound sample. Eight bits allows a range of 256 different levels. This is still sufficient for some purposes (e.g. voice samples and digital telephony) but does not provide a high quality sound sample. Current 16-bit sound cards handle a range of 65,536 different sound levels, giving the quality expected from a domestic audio CD system. This is not a fully professional quality, since each of the 65,536 levels is a linear step while the human ear responds to amplitude variations in a logarithmic way. This means that many of the discrete stored levels do not store changes that can be detected by the ear and so are wasted. Even with these limitations, 16-bit sound recordings have obvious quality advantages over 8-bit recordings. They do, of course, require twice as much disk storage space as their equivalent 8-bit sound samples.

The maximum dynamic range of a digital signal is the ratio between the smallest and the largest value that can be stored, with 0dB as the threshold of human hearing. A 16-bit resolution card has a maximum range of 96dB, while an 8-bit resolution card has only a 48dB maximum range. Since a 96dB range is the approximate range perceived by the human ear, it was the natural choice for CD audio and music.

While uniform PCM uses linear steps in its sampling range, mu-law files have a dynamic range that uses logarithmic steps for quantisation. With logarithmic quantisation, an 8-bit file represents the same range of values that would require 14 bits with uniform quantisation. This produces a compression ratio of 1.75 to 1, with the lower amplitudes being more accurately encoded than higher amplitudes. This is particularly suitable for speech processing, where most of the voice information is low levels.

Cards are now available with 18-bit, 20-bit and 32-bit resolution, to provide greater quality output.

Sampling Rate

The dynamic range determines the accuracy of the amplitude reading at any one point in time. Of equal importance is the frequency of taking these readings. If the readings are too infrequent, an amplitude change will pass undetected. If the readings are too frequent, the conversion will produce a giant series of amplitude readings. The timing of the conversions is known as the *'sampling rate'* and is measured in kilohertz (i.e. how many thousand amplitude conversions are carried out each second).

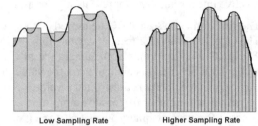

The left diagram shows the effects of a low sampling rate. The sound sample is converted into six samples with varying amplitude levels. When the sample is replayed, the sound card's DAC (Digital-to-Analogue Converter) uses the six levels to reconstruct the sound wave. This sound wave is then amplified and sent to the loudspeakers. As the diagram shows, the final output is an approximation of the original sound with a considerable loss of detail. The inertia in the loudspeaker cones acts to smooth the transitions between different output voltage levels from the DAC. The right-hand diagram shows the same sound sample with twice the sampling rate. The audio is now stored in twelve different samples and this is much more representative of the original sound source.

Quality signal processing is based on the *'Nyquist Theorem'* which states that the sampling rate must be at least double the frequency of the highest frequency to be sampled. If, for example, the sampling rate was exactly the same as the input frequency of a sine wave, the input source would be sampled at the exact same spot on the wave for every sample - the source would appear to be a constant value.

Since the average human ear can only hear frequencies up to about 20kHz, a sampling rate of 44kHz is adequate for most uses. Indeed, the human voice itself does not produce useful sound information above much more than 3kHz.

The original Sound Blaster card was first introduced with a sampling rate of 11kHz. Sound cards now usually operate up to 48kHz (the same rate as audio CD operates at 44.1kHz) and sampling rates are adjustable down to as low as 4kHz. DAT (Digital Audio Tape) for domestic use samples at 48kHz while professional studios use sampling rates up to 96kHz.

Noise

Noise is unwanted electrical signals that exist in the signal along with the original signal. As long as the noise stays at a low level there is no serious problem - but when the noise increases to the point where it is becomes noticeable, it detracts from the final sound.

The measure of sound quality is the *'signal-to-noise ratio'*. This compares the level of noise present in a signal to the amplitude of the wanted signal. This is measured as a ratio and expressed in decibels.

$$\text{S/N ratio} = \frac{\text{average signal power}}{\text{average noise power}}$$

This ratio is a better measure of quality than simply measuring the noise level. The noise cannot be drowned out by turning up the volume level, as the amplifier will increase both the noise and the wanted signal by the same amount. The sources of noise have to be minimised, so that the signal has little noise content. Noise from poor installation can be corrected but all sound cards introduce some background noise.

The quality of the output from the budget sound cards is limited and higher quality cards have a much better performance. For example, a professional card has a signal to noise ratio of 120dB compared to the average of 90dB for most cards (and only around 60dB for older cards).

The main sources of noise are:

Quantisation Noise - caused by the nature of the sampling process, although much more pronounced with low bit-resolution. The smooth analogue input waveform is converted into a squared off, stepped version as shown. Signals with steep sides are rich in harmonics. This way, extra unwanted signals have been introduced in the digitised waveform. These are high in frequency and are heard as background noise. Increasing the bit range results in more digital levels and reduces the larger steps. For example, using 4-bit resolution results in a signal-to-noise ratio (SNR) of around 24dB, while 8-bit and 16-bit resolutions provide SNRs of around 48dB and 96dB. In practice, the introduction of other noise reduces the system's overall SNR figure. The worst effects can also be minimised by using filters to smooth the transition between each step.

Component Noise - caused by random or unwanted electron fluctuations within both inactive devices (such as resistors) and active devices (such as integrated circuits). Professional and high-quality equipment uses gold-plated plugs and sockets for all audio and video connections to minimise bad and dirty connections.

External Interference - caused by everything from natural sources (such as cosmic radiation and electric thunderstorms) to manmade sources (such as radiation from electrical appliances). This can be minimised by ensuring that all audio cables are adequately screened and ensuring that electrical apparatus is kept at a distance from the audio and PC equipment.

Crosstalk - caused by signals from one cable being picked up on another cable. This occurs due to the effects of capacitive and inductive coupling between lines that run adjacently. This can be minimised by ensuring that audio cables use screened cable and are not run alongside power cables, loudspeaker cables, etc.

Underdriving - caused by feeding a very low level of signal into an input that expects to be driven by a signal of greater amplitude. The input signal level may be hardly any greater than the general noise level present in the amplifier. In such a case, increasing the gain of the amplifier increases the noise by the same amount as the wanted signal. This can be minimised by matching the output of the driving device (e.g. the output voltage from a CD player) to the range required to sufficiently drive the input device.

Hum loops - caused by inadequate earthing (grounding) arrangements. Power supply cables to the various devices should be fed from the same mains socket, through a multiple outlet strip if necessary. If not, a ground loop may exist between the PC and the other equipment. This is caused by the devices' own earths not being at exactly the same potential. The resulting voltage difference produces a small current to flow in the shielding of the audio cable and this can introduce a hum or buzz into the audio signal.

Distortion

The digitised version of the analogue signal would only never be accurate if the ADC was able to convert the signal to an infinite number of digital values. This would require an infinite number of samples taken every second and an infinite number of binary values to store the reading. This is unlikely to be achieved in the near future and the digitising process tolerates the present compromise between quality and practicality. Nevertheless, the current sampling rates and bit resolutions inevitably lead to distortion of the sound quality.

Another source of distortion is the mismatch between signal levels when devices are connected.

A sound card has two main audio inputs:

- The *'Microphone'* input, designed for the connection of low voltage drives up to around 100mV (i.e. one tenth of a volt).
- The *'Line In'* input, designed to be fed voltages up to around 1 volt from CD players, etc.

The diagrams show the effects of connecting a 200mV input signal to both types of input connector. In the first case, the input signal is applied to the *'Line In'* socket. The input swing is within its operating range and it successfully handles the signal. It is passed on to the digitising circuits. In the second case, the signal is connected to the 'Microphone' socket. This signal greatly overdrives the sound card amplifier circuitry. The signal is amplified to such an extent that it exceeds the maximum output signal swings of the amplifier. This effect is known as *'Clipping'* and introduces a great deal of distortion into the signal prior to digitising.

Input signal   Amplified signal   Overdriven signal

Sound cards often employ *'AGC'* (Automatic Gain Control) circuitry to minimise clipping problems. The AGC components detect large input signals and reduce the gain of the amplifier to prevent it being overdriven. Of course, the incoming signal should be fed from a high-quality source. Playing a high quality tape through an old tape recorder, for example, is certain to introduce distortion into the signal before it even arrives at the sound card.

Distortion can also arise within the sound card's circuitry. Even a good quality amplifier will introduce some distortion of the signal, as it is very difficult to design amplifiers that produce the same amount of amplification of the signal at every possible frequency and at every amplitude level. The output amplifiers that are built into the sound card - the one that drives the loudspeakers - are commonly of lesser quality than those found in stereo systems. Users often the *'Line Out'* socket of the sound card to connect to the domestic stereo system for better quality reproduction.

Storage Overheads

Current sound cards have stereo channels, allowing each channel to process independent contents. This improves the character of the reproduced sound but requires double the storage space.

The table shows the amount of disk space required for even short digitised samples, when sampled at 44.1kHz. The storage figures in the table can be halved if the sampling rate is dropped to

	bytes per sec	bytes per min
8-bit mono	44,100	2,646,000
8-bit stereo	88,200	5,292,000
16-bit mono	88,200	5,292,000
16-bit stereo	176,400	10,584,000

22.05kHz and can be halved again if an 11.025kHz sampling rate is used.

From the table, it can be seen that a four minute song in CD-quality stereo occupies over 40MB of disk space. A more detailed table is displayed later in this chapter.

A professional 24-bit multitrack system, using only eight tracks, and sampling at 96kHz, stores 2,304,000 bytes per second and requires over 500MB to store the same song!

The storage requirements of an uncompressed audio sample can be calculated thus:

Storage   = sampling rate   x sample duration   x   bit resolution   x number of channels   / 8
               (in samples per sec)   (in secs)   (i.e. mono/stereo)   (to convert to bytes)

Therefore, the calculation for a 1 minute stereo sample at 16-bit resolution and CD-quality is:
Storage =   44,100 X 60 X 16 X 2 / 8   = 10,584,000 bytes

This calculates the raw data, known as *'Linear PCM'*, as used by Red Book (i.e. audio) CDs.
Dividing the answer by 1024 will produce the value expressed in kilobytes.

Format Considerations

The table shows the generally accepted descriptions for some commonly used recording formats.   Of course, many more permutations are available.   Another common standard for speech is 8-bit mono at an 8kHz sampling rate.

Dynamic Range	Number of Channels	Sampling Rate	Quality Description
8-bit	mono	11,025	Telephone Quality
8-bit	mono	22,050	Radio Quality
16-bit	stereo	22,050	Most Home Audio
16-bit	stereo	44,100	CD/MiniDisc Quality
16-bit	Up to six (Dolby 5.1)	48,000 or 96,000	DVD Quality
24-bit	multi	96,000	Recording Studio

There is a trade between the file's quality and the file size.   These are vital considerations for recording audio files intended for use on a web site, as the person browsing the site is unlikely to wait for a long period just to listen to the site's opening jingle or the site author's words of welcome.   Audio files are more easily accommodated on a CD-ROM, with its 650MB of capacity but even productions here can get tight for space.   DVD disks have even greater capacity and can accommodate many large files.

The table shows the rate at which data would have to be supplied to the user playing back an audio file.   While CD-ROMs can handle these data rates, the higher quality clips could not be sent in real time - even with current top-quality 56k modems.

Dynamic Range	Number of Channels	Sampling Rate	Data Rate per second
8-bit	mono	11,025	10.7kB
8-bit	mono	22,050	21.5kB
16-bit	stereo	44,100	172.3kB

Designers wishing to minimise the storage and data transfer rate problems have to consider the following options:

Dynamic Range

8-bit recordings are noisier than 16-bit recordings, as they introduce signal levels that were not present in the original audio signal.   In addition, as described earlier, the poorer approximations in the final recording lose much of the fine harmonic detail.   This results in *'flatter'* reproduction.   Nevertheless, 8-bit recordings are adequate for reproducing speech, feedback noises and low-quality music (particularly basic synthesised sounds).   For quality recordings of music, 16-bit recording is necessary.   Professional studios require 24-bit or greater working.

Number of Channels

Stereo requires twice as much storage space on a CD-ROM, or twice the download time over the Internet.   Stereo should be used where it is necessary, such as with high-quality sound or where stereo sound effects are required (e.g. a passing train or plane).   Mono is perfectly satisfactory in some situations, such as speech, proving user feedback sounds (e.g. 'bleeps' or 'clicks') and most uses of music, particularly on the web.

Sampling Rate

As the sampling rate is reduced, the sound becomes more *'muddy'* as detail is filtered out.   This is more pronounced at the lower end of the range of sampling rates.   The difference between dropping from 44.1kHz to 22.05kHz is less noticeable than dropping from 22.05kHz down to 11.025kHz.

The best quality to be expected from domestic audio equipment, such as tape decks, is the equivalent of a 16-bit, 22.05kHz recording.   Sampling such signals at higher than 22.05kHz increases the file size without producing any noticeable improvement in quality.

Audio File Formats

One of the first things a user notices is the bewildering array of file formats and acronyms.   All elements of multimedia, even simple text, have several different formats, each with its own benefits and restrictions.   Dredging through the morass of standards to find the one that is best suited may seem a huge task, but many of the file formats are either very specialised or just too old and inefficient to be of use.   For instance, sound samples may come with extensions like WAV, MP3, WMA, AU, IFF, SAM, RAW, ULW; some may even have no extension at all.   There are also many samples out there that are *'raw'* samples, and have completely arbitrarily extension names, such that they may appear to be separate file formats.   However, there are only really a few ways to store digitised sound, and the rest is just dressing.

All the file formats below may be used to store the same audio content; only the manner of storage is different.
All audio file types, apart from RAW files, are called *'self-describing'* and comprise two information sections.

Header   Also known as the *'wrapper'* or *'Format Chunk'*.   The
header information of different formats vary but
generally contain: Name of the clip, size, duration,
number of channels (e.g. mono/stereo), resolution, sample size (in bits), sampling rate (in kHz) and type of
compression used.

Header	Audio Data

The header of a WAV, for instance, provides the option for the inclusion of a whole range of additional
information, such as:

Artist	the name of the artist appearing on the clip
Source	the source of the recording
Genre	the category of the sound (e.g. rock or classical)
Medium	the medium on which the original recording was made
Comments	general comments on the sound clip

If this information is added to a file, it can be viewed by carrying out these steps:
- Open Windows Explorer.
- Highlight the wanted WAV file.
- Click the right mouse button.
- Choose the *'Detail'* tab from the dialog box that is displayed.
- Choose the *'Other Information'* option.

Data   Also known as the *'Data Chunk'*, this stores the audio information in binary format. This is the actual audio
data stream that is used to reconstruct the original sound.

RAW files contain no header information.

The most important sound file formats are:

RAW : This extension indicates that the file's contents consist solely of the string of numeric data, with no
special processing or headers. Its uses PCM (Pulse Code Modulation) to store the data and is the format
used for audio CDs. Although raw sound samples may be stored on a PC with the extension .RAW, more
often they have a less obvious name or sometimes no extension at all. .SOU, .PCM and some .SND files
are raw files with a short header to tell the playback software information on what sampling speed to use
for the playback. If the raw sample has no header storing the frequency of the sample, then the user has to
calculate, or estimate, the sampling frequency (number of samples per second of digitised sound).   It
should be obvious when the user hears the sound whether the frequency selected is correct.

WAV : Introduced along with Windows, the basic uncompressed WAV file is a linearly encoded sound sample
with a short file header. The benefit of WAV files is that many Windows programs can play them using
the same common Windows sound driver. Of course, the Windows sound driver is not limited to WAV
files, but Windows programs themselves tend to prefer WAV files since they are the native format for
Windows sound.   The WAV format offers a variety of encoding methods, with ADPCM being the most
common, although encoded WAV files may not play on some non-PC systems and some older software.

MP3 : The most popular way of storing audio files in a compressed format. Used with portable players, web
sites, etc.   Is available in a number of formats.   MP3 is either the popular MPEG-1 Audio Layer 3 format
or the emergent MP3Pro format, while mp2 files are MPEG-1 Audio Layer 2.

WMA : This is the Microsoft compressed format released in the summer of 1999.   Produces CD-quality
reproduction in files that are smaller then MP3 files. Commercial tracks may *'package'* the contents to
provide file encryption, so that the user requires a decryption key (supplied with user licence) to play the
file.

RM : This is a format, produced by RealNetworks, designed for streaming audio (and video) over the internet,
although the files can be stored and played from disk.

ASF : This is the Microsoft streaming format, covering both audio and video content . These files can also be
stored and played directly from disk.

IFF : The Amiga's IFF format is used for many other things apart from sound samples. The Interchange File
Format stores 8-bit sound samples in unsigned format - i.e. the wave is sampled from zero upwards, rather
than from zero in either direction. Can be identified by its .iff file extension. Some other digitised
samples, with the extension .SMP or .SAM, use the unsigned format but are not IFF files,.

AIFF : The Audio Interchange File Format from Apple uses the .aif file extension and is most commonly found
on Macintosh computers.   Although it offers a range of sampling rates and channels, it is most commonly
used for CD-quality samples.   Apple also produced a compressed format known as AIFF-C or AIFC
which compresses files up to a 6:1 ratio, with some loss of sound quality.

VOC : A digitised sound format that was created for the Sound Blaster card. Other than the sampled data itself,
a VOC file can contain other 'blocks', such as a loop, end-of-loop, or silence block. A silence block allows
any length of silence in a sound sample without the comparatively data-hungry sampling of that silence.
VOC files also allow compression of the sound sample, albeit usually with some noticeable loss of quality.

Compression

The large files required to store audio files, and the long times taken to download them over the web, encouraged the development of a range of storage methods that involved compressing the file on saving and decompressing again on

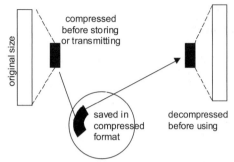

playback.   This means that the processed file is smaller and therefore requires less space to store, less time to load from hard disk or CD and less time to transmit over the Internet. This can be achieved without any loss in the quality of the audio sample.

If desired, the file can be made even smaller although this amount of compression results in some loss of quality.

Some systems offer a range of possible compression ratios, ranging from low-compression lossless samples to high-compression samples with loss of some detail.

Lossless compression may only reduce an audio clip to half its original size. *'Lossy compression'*, on the other hand, can reduce a clip to one tenth or one twentieth of its original size.   Additional software can be installed (see MP3 later) that provides compression ratios of up to almost 100:1.

CODECS

The utility that carries out these transformations is known as a CODEC (compressor/decompressor).

The compression stage uses an algorithm (i.e. a certain set of rules) to shrink the file size. This means that when the file has to be enlarged again for use, it must use the same type of algorithm (in reverse!) to recover the file.

Most of the audio CODECs are implemented as software routines, although top-end equipment may use built-in hardware CODEC chips.

Carrying out the tasks in hardware speeds the process. Implementing the system in software used to be a problem, as the higher sampling rates required a very fast response from the processing software (which explains why some boards could only compress while recording at low sampling frequencies).

Windows installs a number of software CODECs and others may be installed as part of the installation of other hardware or software.   The CODECs present on a computer can be examined by selecting

Start/Settings/Control Panel/Sounds and Multimedia

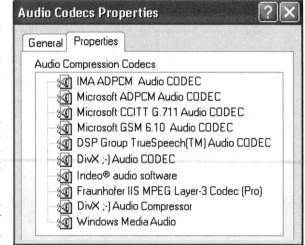

Clicking the *'Advanced'* tab (in Windows 95), the *'Devices'* tab (in Windows 98/ME) or the *'Hardware'* tab (in Windows 2000/XP) and opening the *'Audio Compression Codecs'* folder displays a list of the CODECs installed on that computer.

The most significant CODECs supplied with Windows are:

Codec Name	File Extension	Description of Best Use
IMA ADPCM	.wav	4:1 compression of 16-bit 22.05kHz audio is used in QuickTime and the Sony MiniDisc recorder/player. Also supports 8kHz, 11.025kHz and 44.1kHz.
Microsoft ADPCM	.wav	4:1 compression of 22.05kHz mono or 11.025kHz stereo. See more below. Also supports 8kHz and 44.1kHz.
GSM 6.10	.gsm	10:1 compression of mono at 8kHz was originally developed for digital cellular telephones and is now used for Internet phone applications. Also supports 11.025kHz, 22.05kHz and 44.1kHz.
CCITT G.711	.au	2:1 compression of 16-bit audio is the standard for international telephony. Known as A-law in Europe and µ-law (pronounced mew-law) in the USA. Now also used for videoconferencing. Supports 8kHz, 11.025kHz, 22.05kHz and 44.1kHz.
DSP TrueSpeech	.wav	8:1 compression of 8-bit 8kHz mono only. Adopted by the ITU as the G.723 audio standard for videoconferencing.
MPEG Layer 3	.mp3	See later.

The table shows the top performance of each CODEC.   Each CODEC is able to provide user choice of a range of sampling rates and dynamic ranges and this is covered later. WMA (Windows Media Audio) format was supplied with ME onwards (or with a Media Player upgrade on 98) and is also covered later.

ADPCM

The ADPCM CODEC shown is one of a range of standards based on the *'Adaptive Delta Pulse Code Modulation'* system. This takes standard audio that has been encoded into its normal PCM values and compresses the data so that it requires less space than its raw .WAV equivalent. By only storing the deltas (i.e. changes between samples), it requires about a quarter of the normal disk space. Since a sample size does not vary greatly from the previous sample, its difference value can be stored in only four bits compared to the 16 bits required for storing the absolute value. This method appears the in ITU (International Telecommunications Union) standards such as G.722 (for video phones/ videoconferencing) and G.726 (for noisy industrial / military environments). Variations and sub-sets of ADPCM appear in manufacturers' own proprietary CODECs. It is also used with CD-I disks.

ADPCM is supported in Windows and the IMA variation is used by Sony for its Mini Disc recorders/players.

Speech Encoding

Particularly good compression rates are available for speech-only encoding. These codecs are optimised for speech compression and are not suitable for other audio processing. These systems (known as *'vocoders'*) are designed for uses such as cellular telephones although they are also used for Internet phone applications. They are not used with multimedia applications. These methods are called LPC (Linear Predictive Coding) and CELP (Code Excited Linear Prediction) and they use an analytic model of the human vocal tract to optimise the encoding/compression process. GSM 6.10 is a variation of the LPC system.

AC-3

This compression system is produced by Dolby Laboratories and produces high quality *'Surround Sound'* audio for DVD, cinema and HDTV.

Like most compression systems, AC-3 is *'lossy'*. It divides the audio spectrum into narrow frequency bands that closely match the audio selectivity of human hearing. A vigorous policy of noise reduction is applied to these bands, allowing bands with little or no information to be coded with fewer bits, thereby releasing the extra bits for bands with greater frequency content.

The AC-3 *'shared bitpool'* also allows bits to dynamically shared among various channels, allowing channels with greater frequency content to use more bits than channels with less content. The result is that AC-3 coding provides multichannel audio surround sound while still requiring a much lower bit rate than that required by an ordinary stereo channel on an audio CD. More details on surround sound systems are given later.

Playback CODECs

Many different audio files are available and these will have been saved using different compression methods. Sometimes, the type of file compression is obvious from its extension. For example, the .ra extension is used with RealAudio files. However, as the earlier table shows, the .wav extension is used for ADPCM, the IMA variation and True Speech and others. In addition, each compression type supports a range of different sampling rates and dynamic ranges. The playback process must be automatic. When an audio file is played, the correct CODEC and the correct playback parameters must be chosen without user involvement.

There are three ways that a CODEC can be brought into use to decompress a file:

File Associations

In Windows, a file's extension can be linked to a corresponding application package. As new applications are added to the computer, the file extensions used by the new application is added to the added to the database of associations.

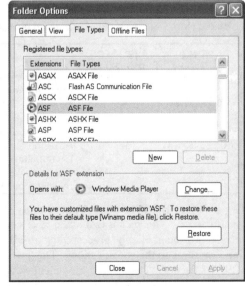

Clicking on an audio file in Windows Explorer loads and runs the application that is associated with file, then the application loads the audio file. If the file association has been configured correctly, the application uses the CODEC that is appropriate to the audio file compression method.

Where more than one application can process a file with a particular extension, only one application can be the default association - i.e. the one activated when the file is double-clicked in Explorer.

These default associations can be viewed and altered within Windows Explorer by pulling down either the *'View'* menu (Win 95, 98, ME) or the *'Tools'* menu (Win 2000, XP).

In Windows 95, the *'Options'* choice and in Windows 98/ME/2000/XP, the *'Folder Options'* choice both provide a *'File Types'* tab as shown in the illustration.

In the example, files with the *'AU'* and *'SND'* extension are played using the *'MPLAYER2'* application.

The *'Edit'* option allows the default application to be altered.

Application-invoked

Many applications will automatically use existing CODECs when required. Examples include Internet browsers, multimedia authoring packages and videoconferencing software.

Standalone Players

An application may be dedicated to handling a particular CODEC. The best known of these is the range of applications to handle the MP3 format (see later). These include software players that can be invoked from DOS or Windows (such as Winamp) and hardware players (such as the portable *'Diamond RIO'* player).

Playback Rates

Files must be played back using the same parameters as were used to compress the file during recording. If a file saved using a low sampling rate is played back at a high sampling rate, the audio playback will cease much earlier; the result is that the audio clip is heard at higher frequencies.

When a file is opened by a CODEC, it examines the information in the file's header (see the section on File Formats). Embedded in the header is data on dynamic range and sampling rate.

Transmission Rates

Reference is often made to the *'Bit Rate'* of various compression systems. Users have two conflicting demands. On the one hand, they want audio files of the highest quality. On the other hand, they want to be able to send these files over transmissions lines (e.g. telephone links, ISDN links) as quickly as possible - preferably in real time.

The final audio may be mono, stereo, or multi-channel (such as surround sound 5.1). The designer is concerned with the <u>total</u> information that has to be sent in a given time. Increasing the number of audio tracks increases the number of bits to be sent. Providing greater compression reduces the number of bits to be sent.

As a result, the final demands are expressed in the bit rate. This is usually the number of data bits that need to be sent in a single second.

So, for example, the stereo audio from a CD would require a data rate of 1378kbps while an equivalent MP3 file would require a bit rate of 384kbps and a Dolby Digital Surround Sound AC-3 file (with six audio channels) would require a bit rate of 448kbps.

MPEG Audio

On of the most significant recent audio compression systems is MPEG audio. It is used in a wide range of applications in communications, broadcasting (e.g. BSkyB), DVD and web music.

The Moving Picture Experts Group is directed by the ISO (International Standards Organisation) and IEC (International Electro-Technical Commission). Despite its title, the group develops standards for both audio and video.

The chapter in this book on video discusses the MPEG video standards but it is important to distinguish between video and audio standards.

The MPEG video standards are MPEG-1, MPEG-2 and MPEG-4.

The audio standards are sub-sets of the MPEG-1 and MPEG-2 standards.

For MPEG-1, it is part three of the specification (IS-11172-3). For MPEG-2, it is parts 3 and 7 of the specification (IS-13818-3 and IS13818-7).

Although this compression system is widely used, its Layer 3 variety, usually shortened to *'MP3'*, has produced the biggest impact on multimedia and web music.

The table shows the main standards and their capabilities.

MPEG Standard	ISO/IEC Reference	Capabilities
MPEG-1	11172-3	Mono and stereo compression at 32kHz, 44.1kHz and 48kHz.
MPEG-2 BC	13818-3	As above, plus: • Sampling rates of 16kHz, 22.05kHz and 24kHz • Support for 5.1 surround sound
MPEG-2 AAC	13818-7	Advanced Audio Coding. Also known as MPEG-2 NBC (Non Backward Compatible) as files are not interchangeable with the other standards. Supports 48 main audio channels plus 16 low frequency ('woofer') channels, 16 multilingual channels and 16 data streams.

The MPEG-2 BC (Backward Compatibility) audio specification allows for compatibility with the MPEG-1 audio specification. This means that audio files sampled at any of 32kHz, 44.1kHz or 48kHz and encoded by an MPEG-2 encoder will be able to be processed by an MPEG-1 decoder, and vice versa. However, it also includes a *'low sample rate extension'* to the specification. This provides for additional sampling rates of 16kHz, 22.05kHz and 24kHz, and MPEG-1 decoders cannot read files encoded this way.

These standards all support the same three main compression levels (known as Layers 1, 2 and 3). Each higher Layer number denotes a compression algorithm of increased complexity and an increased sound quality per bit rate.

The MPEG-1 and MPEG-2 BC Audio Layers are:

Layer	Allowable Bit Rates	Typical Compression ratio	Typical Bit Rate	Typical Use
1	32kbps to 448kbps	4:1	384kbps	Digital Cassette
2	32kbps to 384kbps	6:1 up to 8:1	256kbps to 192kbps	Broadcasting
3	32kbps to 320kbps	10:1 up to 12:1	128kbps to 112kbps	DVD, portable music players, Web music

The 'Typical' figures in the table are those that maintain CD stereo quality.   The highest layer number has the most complex algorithms but provide the best quality for the sample rate.

Layer-3 decoders can handle all layer types, while the Layer-2 decoder can handle files compressed in Layers 1 and 2. A Layer-1 decoder can only handle Layer-1 files.

These standards are public and, although generally not promoted or supported by commercial music interests, it is very popular among music and Internet enthusiasts.   This is because many applications such as MP3 encoders and players are freeware or shareware and anyone is free to write their own code for their own applications without incurring any licence fees or restrictions.

MPEG-2 AAC looks like being more business oriented and is already the means used by a2bmusic.com for playing its downloadable music.   It has a more complex compression algorithm and achieves a ratio of 20:1, resulting in a bit rate of only 64kbps per channel.

MP2
Layer 2, commonly known as MP2, is used in professional applications such as broadcasting and film.
It has less loss than Layer 3 and provides a more dynamic sound as a result.   The lower compression means that the files are larger than their Layer 3 equivalents and consequently have a higher bit rate.

MP3
The most popular standard for general use is MP3, officially known as MPEG-1/2 Layer-3.

As the table shows, a file can be compressed to a bit rates of 128kbps. This means that a user with an ISDN link to the network, can combine the two 64kbps channels to carry full CD quality transmissions in real time.   This has been used by radio stations for high-quality links to other sites, without incurring the much higher costs of renting noise-free dedicated broadcast links.   The encoding and decoding is carried out in this instance by studio equipment. Layer 3 encoders/decoders for PCs are available as hardware (add-on PC cards) or as software (e.g. L3ENC, and AudioCatalyst from Xing).

Layer-3 can also compress using lossy algorithms, to achieve even smaller files at the expense of some quality.   The choice of compression ratio will depend upon the type of audio source being recorded.

Typical compression ratios are:

Sound Quality	Typical Compression ratio	Bit Rate	Bandwidth
CD Quality	Up to 12:1	128kbps or greater	20kHz or greater
Almost CD Quality	12:1 to 16:1	96kbps to 128kbps	15kHz or greater
FM Radio Quality	24:1	64kbps	11kHz
AM Radio Quality	48:1	16kbps	4.5kHz
Telephone Quality	96:1	8kbps	2.5kHz

Even at compression ratios of 24:1 and above, the finished product is still of much better quality than trying to reduce file size by reducing the sampling rate or the dynamic range.

MPEG audio compression uses 'perceptual audio coding' to reduce file sizes.   The amplitude and harmonic relationship between frequencies in the sample, along with the set of frequencies present in the sample at any one moment results in parts of the signal not being heard by the human ear.   If a particular frequency is very loud at one point, the ear does not distinguish any nearby frequencies of lower amplitude.   These lower frequencies can be filtered out without any loss of perceived quality. It is also common to filter out frequencies that are likely to be above the threshold of human hearing.   Since the signal contains less detail, it occupies less space. A typical audio track may occupy around 50MB when stored as a WAV file and just over 4MB when stored as an MP3 file.

The MP3 format is now being supported by many software applications including Microsoft's Media Player, Flash, Director Multimedia Studio, and SoundEdit.   It is also supported by Internet Explorer (i.e. MP3 files can be called within HTML pages - see the chapter on web site creation).

MP3Pro
The problem with the standard MP3 format is that it requires a high bitrate to produce CD-quality or better reproduction. Therefore, many MP3 tracks are encoded at 128kbps or higher.

Smaller file sizes are only obtained by reducing the bandwidth of the signal being encoded (e.g. only extending to around 10kHz, while the audible range extends up to around 20kHz). The higher frequency parts of the signal are not encoded and the resulting digitised audio lacks life. Alternatively, the encoder can attempt to cover the entire spectrum but this spreads the bit allocation more thinly resulting in audio artifacts.   The loss of these higher frequencies can be seen by using a player that has a frequency spectrum display. The original file would show output above 10kHz, while files compressed at 64kHz would display little or no output at the higher end of the spectrum.

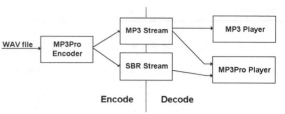

MP3Pro offers an improvement on the MP3 format, whereby the same bitrate produces higher quality audio – or the same quality can be produced with a lower bitrate.

MP3Pro processes a WAV file and produces two streams – the normal MP3 component and the SBR (Spectral Band Replication) component.

The file is saved with the normal MP3 extension (e.g. *"songbird.mp3"*).

The MP3 stream encodes the WAV file up to about 8kHz or 10kHz. This normal stream plays through any standard MP3 player. This makes the file backward compatible – new files still play on MP3 players as the high frequency material is ignored. The SBR stream is not actually a complete encoding of the higher frequency components of the audio file. Instead it stores information regarding where in the new file the higher components reside and the amplitude of these components.

Most of this format's effort comes at the decoding stage. The decoder generates the higher frequencies, based on analysing the MP3 stream and using the information supplied by the SBR stream.

The decoder requires more computer processing power than conventional MP3 files, as it has to deal with extra SBR processing in addition to the MP3 stream processing.

An MP3Pro file encoded at a 64kbps bitrate has the equivalent quality to an MP3 file of 100kbps or more. The format supports mono bitrates at 24kbps, 32kbps, 40kbps and 48kbps and stereo bitrates at 32kbps, 40kbps, 48kbps, 56kbps, 64kbps, 80kbps and 96kbps. The lower bitrates are used for improved speech encoding and Internet radio.

MP3Pro encoding is built into modern burning software, such as Nero, or is available as a plug-in. The conversion of MP3 files to MP3Pro format is also available in Nero. It is also possible to convert MP3 files back to WAV format and then encode them as MP3Pro files. Bear in mind, though, that converting MP3 to WAV to MP3Pro introduces losses (known as *"tandem coding losses"*). Some quality was lost in the original encoding and further losses occur when the file is encoded into MP3Pro format. It is best to always use the original WAV file as the source wherever possible.

Playback of MP3Pro files can be achieved through Winamp using the MP3Pro plug-in.

MP3 Players

A huge range of MP3 players has appeared on the market, using PC-based software players or dedicated players (both portable and non-portable).

Software players

The most popular players are Winamp (available from www.Winamp.com), FreeAmp (from www.freeamp.org) and Sonique (available from www.sonique.com). These are all freeware products. Microsoft's Media Player handles all the major audio formats, but does not provide all the additional facilities that are available from dedicated MP3 players. Players such as Winamp can be enhanced by additional software. These are known as *'skins'* and *'plugins'*. Skins improve the appearance of the interface while plugins add extra functionality such as audio effects, track mixing, screen animations, light shows and the display of the track's frequency spectrum.

WINAMP

The diagram shows the main screen for Winamp, the most popular freeware MP3 player. Clicking on the *'PL'* button opens a dialog box for creating and modifying the *'playlist'*. The user can browse through a disk's folders and select a number of tracks to be played, or the list can be saved into a .PLS or .M3U, so that it can be easily fetched for playing again in the future.

Clicking the *'EQ'* button displays a graphics equaliser, to setting the output at different frequency bands to individual taste (e.g. being heavy on the bass). Hitting the Ctrl and P keys on the keyboard brings up a dialog box for setting the current skins, plugins and many other options.

Hardware players

Most players are portable and are designed to be carried in a pocket. Most are based on storing MP3 files in memory. These models have no moving parts.

Other models use a portable CD player that handles both normal audio CDs and CDs containing MP3 tracks. A few models use a miniature hard disk to store the tracks.

Some devices are designed for fitting as a replacement for a car cassette player, while others are built in to cameras and even watches.

To augment the built-in memory, most players use SmartMedia cards for extra file storage, with some products using CompactFlash, SD (Secure Digital) memory, or the Sony Memory Stick flash RAM.

MP3 and the Music Industry

The Good...

The MPEG format was originally designed as a means of compressing video files, including both the video and audio components of the file.   It soon became apparent that the audio compression offered by MPEG Layer 3 had uses other than with video files.   It was soon used to compress audio files, particularly with music tracks.

MP3 has provided an ideal medium for up and coming bands to advertise their abilities.   They record their own material, convert the songs into MP3 format and place the files on their web site.   Since they are greatly compressed, a band can provide a good selection of their work on a moderately sized web site.   With files in WAV format, they would have to decide between having fewer files on the site or renting out extra web site space and extra bandwidth from their Internet provider.   Many web sites now provide audio MP3 files of this type and even some major bands provide tracks for these sites.   Check out www.mp3.com, which is a web site with over 10 million downloadable tracks, mostly of unsigned bands.   All of this is absolutely legal and is a great example of the Net being used for most people's benefit.   The only potential losers in this are the few giant music corporations that currently control the market through the traditional distribution of music media.

The Bad ...

However, MP3 has also become the chosen format for the distribution of pirate audio CDs.   The ability to store the contents of up to 12 normal commercial music CD's on a single disk has led to a mushrooming of this illegal industry.

And the ....

The potential breaking of the distribution monopoly - combined with piracy of existing artists - has produced widespread fear throughout the recording industry.   The turnover in the US music industry is immense and the UK music industry turnover is around £3 billion.   Five giant music corporations, along with their many subsidiary labels, dominate the generation and distribution of the music media.

Critics point to the excessive amount of money floating round the industry, with high CD prices subsidising overpaid megabands and recording industry fat cats.   They also point to the UK pricing policy (it is cheaper to buy a UK band's CD in the *'foreign import'* section of a US store than it is it buy it in a UK store).   These factors are used as the explanation for the rise in pirate copies.

Music industry spokespeople defend the status quo on the basis of the amount of people employed and the export gains provided to the country; they also point out that the law is on their side.   With vast amounts of money at stake, all the major music agencies have taken steps to limit the damage from pirate MP3 CDs.   The RIAA (Recording Industry Association of America) has pursued vigorous legal action, closing down web sites that offered free music that had not been authorised by the artist or the recording label.   The RIAA, along with the BPI (British Phonographic Industry) and the IFPI (International Federation of Phonographic Industries) made an unsuccessful legal bid to prevent Diamond Multimedia from marketing the Rio portable MP3 player. The UK copyright watchdog for music is the Mechanical Copyright Protection Society (see www.mcps.co.uk).

In fact, the industry would dearly love to have killed the entire MP3 distribution method, even for legally produced music, as it threatens the existing production, distribution, and control of music.   Having failed to kill the medium, the major players are now exploiting MP3 and other compressed format for marketing and distribution on the Internet.   Vivendi Universal has joined with Sony to buy up mp3.com.   BMG has partnered with EMI, Warner Music and RealNetworks to create MusicNet.. Napster is now back online and ITunes has proven very popular.

While the music manufacturers have nightmares over MP3, the artists themselves are less troubled by the medium. They are much more concerned that their work is heard and is properly paid for.   This is the attitude adopted by the Musician's Union in the UK.   From the artists' point of view, a combination of MP3 compression and file encryption would protect the performers' rights.   Fears that MP3 distribution will kill the music industry are not treated seriously as similar claims were made that the invention of cassette recorders and VCRs would kill the video industry.

SDMI

Recognising that they are fighting a losing battle, manufacturers are coming round to the view that they have to embrace and control this medium.   SDMI (Secure Digital Music Initiative) is an attempt by the music, computer and consumer electronics industries to take control of the distribution and playback of commercial MP3 audio.   It proposes to encrypt MP3 files so that they cannot be played on the existing software decoders, both freeware and shareware.   The encrypted files will have to be played through dedicated hardware or commercial software players that will be sold through the normal retail outlets.   The players will be able to decrypt and play the MP3 files - if the encryption code that is embedded in the audio file matches that expected by the players.   This means that future audio media will be sold with unique codes for each purchaser, who can only play the material through their own matching players.   The media is no longer truly portable; the music probably cannot be played at a friend's house, for instance.   While this system is intended to prevent illegal copying, it will probably also build up resentment against the restrictive nature of the media.   In the end, this may push even more users into piracy, as hackers will inevitably find ways to get round this protection system.

AT&T have developed *'PolicyMaker'* which provides a variety of playback arrangements.   The code embedded in an audio file can be sold with in-built restrictions such as the number of times the track can be played, the expiry date for the track, whether a set number of copies is allowed, etc.

MP3 and the Law

The law in the copyright area is generally based on common sense and fair play. For example, nobody calls for the abolition of VCRs because they can be used to illegally record films.   As with videotape and audiotape, a distinction has to be made between the medium and the content.   In the case of MP3, the medium is the CODEC and the content is the file that is compressed.

What's legal

MP3 software decoders are legal.   They play back MP3 files.

MP3 hardware players are legal. These are the many standalone devices such as the iPod.

MP3 encoders are legal.   They create compressed MP3 files from WAV files.

MP3 rippers are legal. They grab the digital audio stream off a normal audio CD and convert the audio tracks into WAV or MP3 files.   This, of course, assumes that the manufacturer of the CD allows such copying (as in the case of royalty-free samples).

Most MP3 files from legal sites can be downloaded and stored for personal use.   Such sites, at the time of writing, include:

www.mp3.com	www.burbs.org.uk	www.peoplesound.com
www.mp3.lycos.com	www.vitaminic.co.uk	

Many sites allow downloading of individual music tracks for a payment.   These include www.emusic.com, www.itunes.com and www.napster.com

What's illegal

The manufacture and distribution of copyright material without permission is illegal.   However, this is true of all media, not just MP3 files.   Copying copyright material onto tape or uncompressed audio CD is equally illegal. In the UK, this includes copying a purchased CD onto a tape for personal use in a car.

The use of MP3 files for public performances (e.g. playing them at a public function or playing them on the radio/TV) is prohibited without the permission of the artist(s).

Most artists have copyright agreements with the record producers.   This means that both would have to agree that tracks be placed on the Internet.   While the artist or band might be happy to place material on the Net, record producers would almost certainly prevent this.   Exceptionally, they may allow a snatch of a song to be released as a marketing tactic.

Where there is any doubt about the copyright on material, the project manager must either clarify the material's status or capture a fresh sample (capturing with consent, of course).

ATRAC3

ATRAC3 is Sony's own proprietary format primarily designed for storing audio files on portable players using their Memory Stick storage.   Their ATRAC3 products include the MiniClip player and the Sony Memory Stick Walkman. ATRAC3 is a development of the ATRAC system already widely used on MiniDisc players and achieves twice the compression of the MiniDisc format. It is now used on MDLP (MiniDisc Long Play) devices.

The saving of files to a user's CD is prohibited, although the use of the system for distributing (i.e. downloading and purchasing) tracks over the Internet is being developed.

Sony produce their own software, OpenMG Jukebox, that rips CDs, downloads files from the Internet plays files and converts WAV and MP3 files intro ATRAC3 format.   Files are stored with OMG extension (e.g. *"songbird.omg"*)

Copyright protected OMG files have restrictions on their use. For example, a file copied from a PC to Memory Stick Walkman can only be downloaded back to that same PC. This means, of course, that OMG files cannot be exchanged between PCs.   Also, the number of times that files can be transferred back and forth between the PC and Walkman is limited to three.   While this provides maximum security for the commercial interests of music distributors, it has also limited the uptake of this format.

The ATRAC3 system uses *"Adaptive Transform Acoustic Coding"*. This reduces the file size of a WAV file to about a tenth of its size with little loss in quality. Compression is achieved by splitting the audio signal into four frequency bands and applying the compression to each band individually before amalgamating them again. This optimises the compression process.

Audiograbber and RealProducer can create ATRAC3 files, once the ATRAC3 codec is installed.

WMA

This is the compressed format developed by Microsoft to compete with MP3.   It uses the WMA extension (e.g. *"songbird.wma"*) and produces files that are smaller than MP3 files at the same quality.

WMA files can be played through many software players, led by Microsoft's Media Player and by a range of portable players such as those by Rio.

The format supports sampling rates of 8kHz to 48kHz, mono or stereo, 8-bit or 16-bit, with bitrates between 5kbps and 192kbps.

MP3 and WAV files can be converted to WMA format using Windows Media Encoder (downloadable from the Microsoft web site), or with shareware packages such as Advanced WMA Workshop.

OGG

Manufacturers of MP3 players (both MP3 and MP3Pro) have to pay a royalty for each device produced that uses the MP3 codec, whether they are hardware or software implementations.

In response, Ogg Vorbis has produced a compressed audio format that is open source (i.e. it is royalty free). The audio format is part of a plan to produce a multimedia system based entirely on open and free standards.

The files have the OGG extension (e.g. *"songbird.ogg"*) and produce files that are about 60% of the size of an MP3 file for the same quality. The format is supported by Winamp, Sonique, GoldWave and Sonic Foundry. Winamp can both play and create OGG files.

The format currently supports bitrates of 18kbps to 128kbps per channel but can be expanded to cover a much wider range of bitrates.

MPEG-4

MPEG-4 Audio is set to find its way into mainstream applications.

It provides even lower bit rates and uses a range of different compression methods including CELP and an extended version of MPEG-2 AAC called MPEG-4 AAC (although MPEG-4 players will still be able to handle MPEG-2 AAC files).

Its bite rate of 2 to 24kbps at 8kHz sampling and 14 to 24kbps for 16kHz sampling compare very favourably to existing communications CODECs such as G.721 (32kbps), G.722 (48/56/64kbps), G.723 (5.3/6.3kbps), G.728 (16kbps) and G.729 (8kbps). In particular, its *'communications quality'* rate of 2kbps has become the lowest international bit rate standard. It is an ideal vehicle for communications systems, Internet telephony, video conferencing and a range of multimedia applications.

Streaming Audio

Files with a *'streaming'* format provide low bitrate encoding for transmitting in real time over the Internet. This allows the transmission of radio programs, etc in real time. For example, users in the UK can listen to US baseball match commentaries as they happen. The disadvantage is generally poorer audio quality. The main formats are Real Audio, and Microsoft's ASF (Advanced Streaming Format) which includes MS Audio. Most of these files need their own special decompression software to play back the content, although ASF files can be played through Windows Media Player (older versions will need a codec that can be downloaded from Microsoft's web site).

More information on streaming audio formats is provided in later chapters on web site creation.

Sound Hardware Standards

Sound standards are intended as a guide for computer purchasers and as a spur for software developers.

The audio specifications contained in the two currently accepted guides are:

MPC3

The MPC specifications set the expected performance levels of the individual components of the multimedia computer system. This included the CPU speed, memory capacity, hard disk size, CD performance, etc.

The audio specification for MPC Level 3 was:

- 16-bit DAC and 16-bit ADC.
- Linear PCM encoding with a CODEC capable of 11.025kHz, 22.05kHz and 44.1kHz sampling rates.
- Multi-voice, multi-timbral wavetable synthesiser capable of 16 simultaneous melody voices plus 6 simultaneous percussive voices. Multi-voice, multi-timbral FM synthesiser capable of 6 simultaneous melody voices plus 2 simultaneous percussive voices.
- Internal mixing capability for three (preferably four) audio sources. The sources being Red Book CD (i.e. audio CD), synthesiser, DAC (waveform) and preferably also an auxiliary input source.

This is now an old standard and is effectively replaced by PC99 below.

PC99

Intel and Microsoft jointly publish their views on PC specifications and these have a great influence on PC manufacturers. The audio requirements for PC99 are not greatly upgraded from PC98, with 3-D Audio being removed from an earlier draft. The main changes are that future sound cards have PCI interfaces instead of ISA, and the inclusion of three USB connections on computer motherboards. These improvements pave the way for the inclusion of surround sound using USB distribution.

Sound cards

Early PCs used the internal speaker to provide a limited audio facility. This is still used to *'beep'* for a user's attention (e.g. to signal a hardware failure) but the size of the single internal speaker restricts the quality of the sound generated. The solution rests in add-on cards dedicated to providing high quality stereo sound from a PC. All machines are now supplied equipped with at least a basic sound card.

Sound card functions

The leader in the field of PC sound was the range of Sound Blaster cards from Creative Labs. It was not the first sound card on the market, but it balanced quality and effectiveness with a reasonable price tag. It handled input from many sources, through a variety of physical connections and competitors were forced to create 'SoundBlaster Compatible' models. There are now a range of cards, from budget to professional, offering various functions and levels of quality.

The basic sound card

The basic sound card performs the following elementary functions:

- Recording of audio. An audio source, such a human speech or music is processed into digitised data for later re-processing.
- Playback of digitised audio. The audio file is translated from digital data into audio.
- Playback of audio CDs.
- FM synthesis. The sound card contains synthesiser chips that are capable of generating a sound that is broadly similar to that produced in the real world. For example, the chips can produce the sound of a piano or guitar even although no musical instrument was involved in its creation. The chips can also produce sounds that are intended to have no human equivalent - e.g. the electronic organ. The sound card uses dedicated chips employing frequency modulation techniques (i.e. using one sine wave to modulate the amplitude of another sine wave) to produce a sound with the desired harmonic mix. Each different synthetic sound is known as a 'voice'.

Synthesisers also have the following qualities:

POLYPHONIC
The card is capable of outputting many different notes at the same time, allowing the playing of musical chords.

MULTITIMBRAL
The card is capable of outputting several different voices at the same time, allowing the playing of multitrack music. The Midi Manufacturers Association defines a multitimbral device as one that can play at least two different instruments and at least five different music notes simultaneously. In practice, sound cards offer between 32 and 128 simultaneous voices.

Although most audio cards still provide FM synthesis for compatibility with older software and games, newer software uses wavetable synthesis as explained below.

- MIDI equipment interfacing. The sound card is able to communicate with an external MIDI device, such as a musician's electronic keyboard. The sound card carries out the processing of the musical score but the MIDI device produces the actual sound from its own synthesiser chips.
- Wavetable Synthesis. Synthesised sound output is not comparable with a natural sound. The richer the sound source is in harmonics, the more difficult it is to reproduce synthetically. That is why even expensive electronic keyboards have had difficulty in emulating the humble piano. The solution lies in converting an actual sound into a set of digitised data and storing the sample in ROM on the sound card. This is called Wave Table Synthesis and produces greatly improved sound quality. Wavetable cards normally also provide on-board RAM so that users can use their own captured samples. PCI cards take advantage of the fast speed of data transfers between card and the computer's own system memory to store samples in system RAM. This results in less memory on the sound card and lowers the card's price. A typical sound card has 64 voices stored in , with the ability to store up to another 1024 voices in the computer memory. Sets of SoundFont banks of samples can be pre-loaded into RAM for instant access. To store a sample for every possible musical note for every possible instrument played in every possible way would require massive amounts of storage. The card stores a set of samples for each instrument (called 'multisampling') and slows or speeds the playing of a sample to generate lower or higher musical notes. This involves complex processing as some instruments have different harmonic content at different pitches or at different playing volumes.
- Digital in/out. This produces higher quality audio transfers, as the losses involved in the conversions between analogue and digital (and vice versa) are eliminated.
- Surround Sound, using up to eight separate speakers.
- Environmental effects to simulate sounds in a concert hall or under water, for example.
- Full-duplex working. This allows simultaneous recording and playback. This is used for multi-track music recording and the provision of Internet telephony and videoconferencing.

All sound boards use ADCs and DACs. The ADC (Analogue-to-Digital Converter), as explained earlier, converts an incoming audio sample into its digital equivalent. The DAC (Digital-to-Analogue Converter) circuitry converts the stream of digital audio data into a varying analogue signal that is fed out through the sound card's 'Line Out' socket.

Most cards have a DSP ('Digital Signal Processing') chip to carry out audio signal enhancements such as reverberation and chorus effects, as well as handling MIDI and sound file compression /decompression.

Sound card connections

The diagram shows the essential connections of a basic sound card.

Input Connections
MICROPHONE IN

The *'Microphone Input'* connects live real world sounds to the sound card for digital storage. The maximum voltage drive to this socket is typically 100mV (100 millivolts = one tenth of a volt). Most microphones, in fact, produce a drive level much lower than the maximum input.

```
                                    ┌─
 Audio In from CD ▥      Line In ▮  │
                    Microphone In ▮ │
                        Line Out ▮  │
                      Digital Out ▮ │
                   MIDI/Gameport ▮  │
    PCI Interface                   │
   └─────┐ ┌───────────────────────┘
         └─┘
```

LINE IN

The *'Line Input'* connects other audio sources such as that from the
'audio out' sockets of a cassette player, an audio CD player or a domestic video recorder. The maximum voltage drive to this socket is typically 1v rms.

The *'Audio In'* connection (pins mounted on the sound card) allows the internal connection of an audio source into the card. This is most commonly connected to the *'Audio Out'* socket on a CD-ROM, allowing normal audio CDs to be played on the computer's CD player (with the appropriate software).

GAMES PORT/MIDI

The 15-pin *'Games Port'* allows the connection of a joystick or of a MIDI interface.
The MIDI input allows the real-time capture of a musician's work, for example from an electronic music keyboard. This is stored in the MIDI format as explained later. The MIDI interface is also an output connection, as the computer can control any MIDI device that is attached to the MIDI port, with appropriate software.

BUS CONNECTION

Of course, audio cards can also receive input via the normal bus connections to the computer (i.e. where the card plugs into the motherboard slot). This allows programs to directly send data to the sound card through the data bus.

Output Connections
AUDIO OUT

Most older ISA cards had an inbuilt amplifier capable of around 4 Watts of audio output power, usually with a volume control mounted on the card's plate. Most PCI cards abandoned the use of internal amplifiers, as they were low power devices and users now demand higher wattage outputs.

LINE OUT

The *'Line Out'* socket connects the card's analogue audio output to external amplifiers, headphones or computer speakers. Manufacturers produce sets of external speakers for sound cards. These are generally mains-powered with some providing a battery option. One of these speaker cases usually houses an in-built amplifier and volume/tone/balance controls. Alternatively, the *'Line Out'* connection can be taken to the input of another amplifier to achieve greater output wattage. Connecting to a domestic hi-fi will boost the audio output to the maximum provided by the hi-fi amplifier. The maximum voltage output from this socket is typically 1v rms. The dropping of internal amplifiers also improves the quality of sound cards, as the amplifiers were generally built to a low budget and introduced unwanted noise. Removing the amplifier improved the cards' signal-to-noise ratio.

The MIDI output connects to a MIDI-compatible device such as an electronic music keyboard, synthesiser or drum machine.

Older sound cards were capable of directly interfacing with a CD-ROM. The cable between the card and the CD-ROM took the control signals to the CD-ROM that carried out the usual drive functions such as moving the head, etc. This was in addition to the normal data cable that carries the digital audio data on the CD into the sound card for translation into an analogue audio signal.

Modern interfaces

The two major possible additions to modern cards' connections are:

DIGITAL I/O

Better sound cards provide an auxiliary external input/output known as SPDIF (Sony/Philips Digital Interface). It is a digital output for direct connection to other digital recording devices such as DAT (Digital Audio Tape - a common standard for music professionals), Mini-Disc machines and some CD players. Direct digital connections maintain the sample in digital format and avoid the distortions introduced by digital/analogue/digital conversions. DAT, MiniDisc and CD systems should be connected to a 44.1kHz SPDIF connection. SPDIF connection types include RCA/coaxial and optical cable.

CONNECTIONS FOR DVD AUDIO

Allows the audio output of a DVD player to be reproduced in full Dolby Digital Surround (see later).

Software interfaces

Sound cards are connected physically through plugging into the motherboard's ISA or PCI bus.

The computer's programs need to communicate with the sound card, passing on the information to be processed.   The basic information is the digital waveform data that is to be converted back into an audio waveform.

Early computer games (and even some current games) were DOS-based and communicated directly with the sound card through DOS.   The games software had to be able to work with a variety of software drivers that were specific to a manufacturer's own sound card. With the arrival of Windows, it became possible for any Windows application to utilise a sound card's basic benefits using a single sound driver.   As long as the correct driver for the sound card was installed, all Windows programs could communicate with the sound card.

However, modern sound cards can now handle a variety of enhanced audio activities such as waveform synthesis, wavetable handling and 3D effects using multiple speakers.   In addition, most card manufacturers still have their own hardware interface methods using their own brand's sound card device driver.

This would cause nightmares for the writers of applications and games if it were not for the use of APIs.

The API (Application Programmable Interface) is a piece of the application code that passes advanced audio instructions to the sound card.   As long as the sound card's hardware or software is compatible with the API, it can understand and implement the instructions.   In this way, the same program is able to work with a range of sounds cards, despite their different internal workings and different drivers.

In most cases, the sound card implements these API instructions through dedicated circuitry on the card.

Effects APIs

Almost all new cards provide some form of three-dimensional effects.

Microsoft provides DirectSound and DirectSound3D (DS3D) as part of its DirectX APIs. Although DS3D can be implemented by the computer's own CPU, most cards handle DirectSound instructions through hardware.

Aureal Semiconductors introduced the A3D standard in 1997 and then A3D2.   Some cards handle these instructions through their hardware (using Aureal's own Vortex II chipset), while others use slower software emulations.   Many do not yet support this API at all.

Creative Audio introduced the EAX (Environmental Audio Extensions) and EAX2 API standards.   Support for these standards is still very patchy with most cards not yet able to handle them.   However, since the system comes from the manufacturers of the famous SoundBlaster range, compatible software drivers are continually being developed for other cards. EAX is now incorporated into Microsoft's DirectSound, making any software developer's job simpler.   Similarly, the Sensaura standard can be accessed via Microsoft's API, although some effects currently remain proprietary.

Where a card cannot handle an optimised standard, it will usually revert to handling sound samples at the basic DirectSound3D standard (with some loss of quality).

Surround Sound

The human brain and auditory system perceive their audio surroundings in terms of its frequency, harmonic content, amplitude, direction and time.   The early sound cards adequately handled frequency, harmonics and amplitude.   Mono audio samples gave the listener reasonable reproduction of the original sound but did not reproduce the normal listening process.   Although an improvement, even stereo samples do not provide the listener with a normal listening experience.

In the real world, the listener's brain processes a range of audio factors.

Consider listening to the sound of an orchestra.   The instruments are situated from left to right and from back to front.   In addition, the acoustics of the hall in which the music is played affects the final sound.   The listener will hear most sounds directly from the instruments. However, sound will also be reflected from the hall's walls, roof, etc. The listener will hear sounds from many different directions - from behind, above and from the side.   The shape of the human external ear canal receptors results in a slightly different frequency response to sounds picked up from the rear

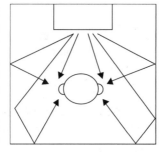

A mono sample stores the sounds of all the instruments but provides little positional information.   If a particular instrument is louder than another, the brain will generally consider it to be closer than a quieter instrument.   However, it does not indicate whether the instrument is to the left or the right of the listener.   A stereo sample provides further information. This requires the listener to be situated in a defined listening area, with the speakers placed to the listener's front-left and front-right. This effective listening area is smallish and is known as the *'sweet spot'*.   Now, if one of the instruments were only recorded on to the left channel of the sample, its sound would reach the listener's left ear before if reached the right ear. The brain detects this small time delay (the *'inter-aural delay'*) and interprets it as a sound coming from the left.   If the audio sample recorded the instrument equally on both channels, the sound would reach each ear at the same time and be interpreted as coming from directly in front of the listener. Adjusting the relative volumes of the instrument on each channel can therefore place the sound in any part of the left-to-right plane.

In addition, of course, a sound could be initially recorded at high amplitude on the left channel and low amplitude on the right channel to make it appear to be positioned to the listener's left.   Then the volumes could be gradually reversed, lowering the amplitude in the left channel while raising the amplitude in the right channel.   This way, the sound would appear to move across in front of the listener. This technique is known as *'panning'*.

Although stereo techniques provide additional positional information, the listener requires further *'depth of image'* information.

Sound cards normally implement three-dimensional sound effects by providing for the connection of four speakers. The traditional stereo speaker layout has a speaker at the front-left and front-right of the listener.   Improved 3D effects are achieved by also having a rear-left and rear-right speaker.   The listener is then placed within a defined listening area, which is significantly larger than the stereo sweet spot. By adjusting the amplitude of the audio signal sent to each speaker, the sound is perceived to be anywhere within that listening area.   In this way, listeners can hear a door opening behind them or can hear a bird or a plane circling around them (using panning).   This technique is not new and was employed for the film *'Fantasia'* as early as 1940.   It was further developed by Dolby in its four speaker *'Pro Logic'* systems.

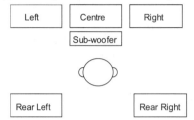

The surround sound system used with DVD videos has a 5.1 speaker layout (i.e. 5 speakers and 1 sub-woofer).   This is associated with the Dolby Digital system and the MPEG-2 audio system.

The four-speaker system has an additional speaker located directly in front of the listener.   Since much of the sound from a DVD movie is in front of the viewer, a separate centre audio channel is used to feed a centrally positioned speaker.   This provides more effective *'localisation'* than using the left and right speakers to place sound in this central area.   The sub-woofer handles the lower audio frequencies (about 20Hz to 120Hz) and is particularly effective in reproducing bass guitars and low frequency effects such as thunder and explosions in movies and games.   The sub-woofer speaker needs no special positioning, as the human ear is poor at detecting the direction of lower frequencies.

Full 3D effects

But, it is not only the relative volumes that provide positional information, since a quiet sound nearby can still be drowned out by a distant loud noise.   Amplitude levels alone are insufficient to reproduce the normal listening experience.   A listener also distinguishes local and distant sounds by the amount of reflected sound from that object. A quiet sound that is close to the listener has less reflected sound than that from a loud distant noise.   The brain processes the ratio of reflected sound to the original sound to help estimate how far away the original sound source is. In the acoustically dead recording studio, multi-track recordings are made with each channel independently recording each instrument.   Since this loses all reflected information, it has to be re-inserted artificially, by adding reverberation effects.

While Surround Sound provides realism in two planes (i.e. left to right and front to back), the real world is three-dimensional; sounds also have a third plane (i.e. up and down).   For example, the sound of a plane should appear to be above the head of the listener.   The sound of someone climbing stairs should not only pan from left to right but should also be perceived as moving from a low level to a higher level.

Most 3D audio techniques use HRTFs (Head-Related Transfer Functions) which can employ up to a dozen audio filters mimic the effect of normal listening.   The human outer ear acts as a filter that processes sound from different directions differently.   Most sound arrives directly at the ear but some is also reflected from the listener's face, shoulders and ears. This information is used by the brain to help the listener pinpoint the direction that a sound comes from.   Sound samples that have been rendered with HRTFs mimic the filtering of the ear and fool the brain into placing a sound in any position in a three-dimensional area surrounding the listener.

Aureal's A3D system uses this method to imitate the effect of multiple speakers positioned above, below and behind the listener - with only two speakers connected.   The 3D2 system uses HRTF positional audio on a front pair of speakers and stereo panning on a rear pair of speakers.   Sensaura uses HRTF on all four speakers.

Other effects

The APIs are capable of transforming the basic sound sample by adding echo, reverberation, ring modulation, flanging, distortion, vocal morphing and pitch-shifting effects.   They also provide a range of *'environmental'* effects, where the sound sample is processed differently according to the scene in which it is played.   For example, a sound sample of a footstep would be given added echo when placed in the setting of a large hall or empty rooms; the same sound would be muffled if the rooms were heavily carpeted.   Similarly, the sound of music, gunshots, etc sound differently when heard underwater.

The listener is also able to detect *'Doppler'* effects with some sounds.   For example, the frequency of the sound of a passing train lowers as it moves past the listener.   Of course, this effect cannot be reproduced using simple panning techniques.

Sound on a DVD-Video

A DVD video is capable of storing up to eight separate audio streams along with the video data.   The audio can be compressed or uncompressed.   Each audio stream can contain from one (i.e. mono) up to six (i.e. surround sound) channels.   The number of available audio streams will depend upon the number of channels placed in each stream, the audio encoding method used, and the video bit rate required.

The audio encoding methods for adding sound to a DVD video depend upon the television system in use in a particular country (e.g. the UK uses the PAL system while the USA uses the NTSC system) and are:

Disc Type	Required Provision
NTSC	Linear PCM or Dolby AC-3
PAL/SECAM	Linear PCM, MPEG-1, MPEG-2 or Dolby-3

Therefore, a DVD disk designed for the US market must have either LPCM tracks or Dolby AC-3 tracks (see below) but may also provide MPEG tracks.   So, it may have LPCM and Dolby, it may have LPCM and MPEG, it may have Dolby and MPEG - or it may carry all three audio tracks.

Although LPCM provides the highest quality sound tracks, it requires a much higher data rate than compressed audio streams and most DVD disks use a compressed encoding method such as AC-3.

A typical DVD disk (DVD-5 type single sided) will hold 133 minutes of MPEG-2 video and three surround sound channels and four subtitle channels.   The audio is currently sampled at 20-bit resolution, with a 48kHz sampling rate, although 24-bit, 96kHz sampling will become more common.

The possible options are:

Bit resolution	Sampling rate	Number of channels
16	48kHz	8
20	48kHz	6
24	48kHz	5
16	96kHz	4
20	96kHz	3
24	96kHz	2

Dolby Digital

This system is also known as Dolby Surround Digital or Dolby Surround AC-3 and is to be found in a growing number of applications.   These include multichannel digital cinema sound, HDTV (High Definition TV), satellite broadcasts, digital cable TV and DVD.

It is a 5.1 system using Dolby's **AC-3** (Audio Coding version 3) compression.

AC-3 is a very efficient compression system, resulting in very low bite rate as can be seen in the comparison table below.

System	Bit resolution	Sampling rate	Number of channels	Maximum Bit Rate
AC-3	20	48kHz	6	448kbps
MPEG-1	20	48kHz	2	384kbps
MPEG-2	20	48kHz	8	912kbps
LPCM	20	48kHz	6	5.76Mbps
Audio CD	16	44.1kHz	2	1378kbps

AC-3 encoding provides a six channel stream of audio at 20-bit resolution and yet only requires about one-third of the bit rate of a normal 16-bit stereo channel.   However, the provision of additional language streams will increase the required bit rate, or may require a reduction in the quality of some streams down to only stereo or mono.   For example, a disk aimed at the English-speaking market may provide full 5:1 surround sound in English, while only providing Spanish, French and German streams in stereo.

DVD-Audio

Current music CDs can store a maximum amount of 74 minutes of audio.   This is due to the use of the Red Book CD standard (uncompressed 44.1kHz, 16-bit encoding).   This limitation is being tackled with the introduction of the DVD Forum's new 'DVD-Audio' specification.   The greatly increased storage capacity of DVD disks offers extended playing times, higher audio quality, multiple audio channels and additional features such as optional text and still pictures - along with some limited user interaction such as menu selection.

The DVD-Audio Specification (Book C) provides for a range of encoding methods such as LPCM, AC-3, MPEG-1, MPEG-2, etc and a range of sampling frequencies (44.1, 48, 88.2, 96, 176.4, 192kHz). It also allows the bit resolution to be 16, 20 or 24-bit.   The playing times of DVD-Audio disks will range from 43 minutes (6 channel, 96kHz, 24 bit unpacked on a single layer disk) to 622 minutes (2 channel, 48kHz, 24 bit on a dual layer disk using Meridian Lossless Packing).

Music CDs will be encrypted and watermarked so that they only run on licensed players.

Sony and Philips are producing a rival standard known as the *"Super Audio CD"*.

Capturing audio

A wide range of digitised sound samples exists, covering music, sound effects and real world sounds (e.g. dogs barking, gun shots, etc.).   While these are very useful, there are many occasions when a specific sound or message is required.

Examples of this include:

- Voiceovers to accompany video clips, animations or photographs, explaining how something works or how useful an object is.
- Interviews with significant people (e.g. a products technical designer, a company's chairperson or a sports personality). The content of such an interview is unique to the production and will not exist as an off the shelf clip.
- Specific background music, perhaps specially written to match the multimedia production.
- Sampling of specific sounds that would not be found on royalty-free disks of audio clips. This might include the sound of the company's new product, the crowd noise at a sports event or public demonstration, or an unusual sound effect.

The stages in sound production are:

- Preproduction (deciding on goals, deciding on timing, writing the material, auditioning, budgeting, securing the location, obtaining permissions, securing facilities). The chapter on computer video contains material on planning considerations and a recording checklist that is also relevant to audio recordings.
- Recording (preparing the computer, connecting up the audio source(s), capturing the audio, keeping records, acting professionally).
- Mixing (editing, sweetening, volume adjustment, levelling, panning, spatial setting, filtering, fading, etc.).
- Postproduction (compressing, storing, distribution).

Almost all computers now have sound cards fitted and although these are mostly used to output audio, they are all capable of digitising an audio source.   The quality of the sound depends largely on the quality of the audio source (mike, audiotape, videotape, etc.) and the sound card, while the added features (e.g. editing facilities, adding echo, etc) depend on the software that is used to capture and manipulate the audio clip.

The steps for making a recording are:

- Connect the audio source to the sound card.
- Configure the computer for recording
- Make tests to adjust the incoming sound levels.
- Make the final recording.

Connecting the audio source

The first step is to check that all the necessary components are present. This will include ensuring that all source devices have a suitable output socket and that all the necessary cables for connecting the sound source to the sound card are available.

The diagram shows the most common types of plugs used in audio connections.

Most sound cards use 3.5mm stereo sockets on the rear panel, although some also provide RCA phono sockets and/or digital connections.   RCA phono sockets are often found on consumer electronics, TVs, VCRs, etc.   Both 3.5mm and RCA sockets use the outer shield as the return wire for the audio signal, being described as an *'unbalanced'* line. This reduces the cost of constructing cables but makes them more prone to outside interference.

3.5mm Mono   3.5mm Stereo   Phono (RCA)   XLR

XLR plugs are often found on microphones and PA equipment and are *'balanced'* lines. This means that each audio channel has two separately wires and the outer shield is used purely for preventing interference reaching the lines carrying the audio signal.   Balanced lines have the added advantage of being able to run over greater distances, specially with low impedance devices. Adaptors are available for connecting balanced and unbalanced lines together.

Where to connect

The audio input can come from a microphone connected to the computer's *'Microphone'* socket, or the *'Line In'* socket of sound card can be connected by cable to the output socket of an audio player such as an audio CD player, cassette player, video recorder, etc.   This allows the sampling of music or voice from a variety of sources, although the provisions of copyright will apply to such samples.

Load matching

It is important that the load matching of the audio source and the sound card is correct, to ensure the transfer of the audio signal without any losses, distortion, or introduction of noise.   This means that the impedances of the devices should be similar, and both should operate over a similar voltage range.   The output voltage from a microphone can be around 1mV, while the output from a device's line level socket can be between 300mV and 1.23V. The higher semi-pro voltage levels are generally found in devices such as drum machines and synthesisers. Accordingly, the sound's card's *'Line In'* socket can handle larger voltage input swings than the microphone socket and should be used for all high input sources. The output from a device is best taken from the *'Aux'* or *'Audio Out'* socket of the device, as this output is designed to be at the same line level as the sound card's *'Line In'* socket. Do not use the headphones socket of a player as the audio source as this does not properly match the sound card's inputs and will produce disappointing results. The headphone socket is sometimes used as a last resort, when the player has no other audio output socket. Much better, however, is using another audio source with a proper audio output socket. Do not connect an audio player's *'Aux'* output to the sound card's microphone input, as it will almost certainly produce distortion or even damage. If the output level of a device is insufficient to fully drive the *'Line In'* socket, the device can be connected to the socket through a pre-amplifier. Pre-amplifiers, known simply as *'pre-amps'*, raise the voltage amplitude level to that required.

Connect digitally where possible

It is always best to connect digitally, where at all possible. For example, an audio track can be copied in digital format from the surface of a CD in to a file on the hard disk (see *'rippers'* later). The CD is placed in the computer's CD caddy. The same CD could be placed in an audio CD player and connected to the sound card's line input. However, this would involve converting the audio track from digital into analogue format, then sending it to the sound card where it would be converted back to digital format. This method introduces all sorts of possible noise and quantisation errors. Even worse would be to record the track by placing a microphone next to the CD player's loudspeaker.

The SPDIF connector discussed earlier provides an ideal format for audio transfers. For example, an interview that was carried out on location might be recorded on a DAT recorder that has recorded and digitised the conversation onto digital tape. The DAT recorder's digital output can be connected directly to the sound card's SPDIF socket, allowing the transfers to be carried on in digital format.

Minimising interference

Always use shielded cables for connection between the audio source and the sound card, to minimise any stray electrical pickup. Keep the mains cables and the audio cables apart. Cables are available with gold-plated plugs to reduce contact resistance and the better soundcards also use gold-plated sockets.

When an audio source such as a cassette or CD player is used, the player and the computer should share the same mains wall socket. This prevents a ground loop from being set up, which might result in a hum or buzz being added to the recording. If necessary, connect the audio source and computer to the same trailing mains socket and connect this to the wall supply.

Configuring the computer

Before making recordings, the computer should be configured for the best performance. This involves optimising the hard disk used for storage and ensuring that the operating system and recording software are working together.

Check for free disk space

As mentioned before, although nowhere near as hungry as video, audio still consumes large amounts of disk space. The table shows the amount of disk space required for storing a single second of digitised, but uncompressed, audio.

At the top of the range, a five-minute audio clip requires over 53MB of disk space.

Before recording, a check on the available disk space should be made. The free space left on a hard disk can be checked with the following steps:

	5.5kHz	11.025kHz	22.05kHz	44.1kHz	48kHz
8-bit mono	5.38kB	10.77kB	21.53kB	43.07kB	46.88kB
8-bit stereo	10.77kB	21.53kB	43.07kB	86.13kB	93.75kB
16-bit mono	10.77kB	21.53kB	43.07kB	86.13kB	93.75kB
16-bit stereo	21.53kB	43.07kB	86.13kB	172.27kB	183.11kB

- Run Windows Explorer.
- Click on *'My Computer'* in the left pane.
- Look at the wanted drive letter in the right pane.
- Read the amount listed under *'Free Space'*.

Enable the input devices

The next step is to ensure that the chosen input device is enabled (i.e. not muted) and this uses Microsoft's *'Volume Control'* panel. With Windows 95, the *'Volume Control'* option is found in the *'Multimedia'* option of the *'Accessories'* menu within the *'Programs'* menu. In Windows 98/ME/2000/XP, it is found in the *'Entertainment'* option within *'Accessories'*.

Each device has a *'Mute'* check box. If the box is checked, the input from that source is not passed through to the sound card's digitising circuitry. All unchecked boxes are treated as valid inputs and any incoming level can be adjusted by moving the slider on the corresponding volume control.

Using Sound Recorder

Many sound cards provide their own software to create audio samples and these recording applications have various advanced features. However, Microsoft's *'Sound Recorder'* is supplied with Windows and, although simple, is adequate for many purposes. In Windows 98/ME/2000/XP, Sound Recorder can be found in the *'Entertainment'* option of the *'Accessories'* menu.

The interface is as shown in the diagram. The right hand button has a red circle and clicking on this icon starts the recording process that creates a digitised sample from the signals received at the currently active inputs.   The time of the sample is shown on screen as the recording is made. The middle window displays a real time oscilloscope representation of the incoming signal.

When the recording is finished, the user clicks on the button to the left of the record button (the button with the square on it).   The final sample length is displayed. Clicking the middle button causes the newly recorded sample to be replayed.

The recommended sequence is:
- Make tests to adjust the incoming sound levels for optimum recording (see below).
- Make the final recording.
- Replay the clip to check its content and quality.
- Save the clip as digitised audio file, with meaningful file names being used.
- Enter the details of the new clip into a database of the sound files used for the project.

Note: There is a default limit of 60 seconds recording time.   This can be overcome by creating a large empty file, which can then be used for recording.   First, a 60 second blank recording is made.   When the 60 seconds recording is finished, click the record button again to add another 60 seconds to the file.   Repeat this until there is enough time available for the required recording. If required the blank recording can be saved for later re-use.   Drag the bar back to the 0 seconds mark and begin the actual recording.

Settings levels

The aim is to record at the highest possible level without affecting quality.   Two variable controls affect the recording level. The first is the output control of the source and this is normally the source's own manual volume control.   The second control is the input level control of the recording software (e.g. the microphone or line level control in Microsoft's *'Volume Control'*).

Recording at too low a level introduces noise into the sample, as the signal to noise ratio is lowered.   Although the editing software can increase the sample's amplitude, it also increases the noise.   It is also a mistake to set the output level from the source to a low level and try to compensate with a high recording level at the recording software.

Recording at too high a level produces clipping (see the earlier section on distortion).   If flattening of the higher amplitude signals is seen, this is a sure sign that the system is being overdriven.   The only cure is to lower the drive to the card, or lower the level controls in the software, whichever is the culprit.   Bear in mind, however, that the sample may be perfect and that the problem may be the audio amplifier overdriving the loudspeaker. If, for example, a 5-Watt amplifier is connected to 1-Watt speakers, the speakers are overdriven and the distortion is taking place at that spot.   Similarly, cheap loudspeakers systems are easily driven into distortion when their volume control is turned fully up. If the distortion disappears when the audio amplifier's volume is reduced, the problem is with the hardware.   Alternatively, if the recording software allows examination of the waveform during recording, then the clipping can be confirmed as an overdriven sample or an overdriven loudspeaker system.

The level controls are adjusted while observing the effects on the display on the recording software.

With most applications, apart from *'Sound Recorder'*, the incoming signal is shown by the levels on VU meters that appear on the applications window.   The incoming level is adjusted until the bars in the bar graph are at their highest amplitude without entering the red *'overload'* area.   This test should be carried at the loudest level expected from the audio source.   Better software will have a *'Record Pause'* facility.   This allows the levels to be set without having to actually record a sample. Note, however, that the level meters in some applications may not be entirely accurate and it is best to confirm the settings by listening to a test recording.   Since Sound Recorder does not have VU meters, a recording sample is created while watching for signs of clipping in the oscilloscope window - and adjusting the controls accordingly.

Mixers, pre-amps and recording software may all provide a meter that allows the amplification of the incoming signal to be monitored.

The meter's scale is in *'volume units'* (hence the name *'VU Meter'*), with 0VU marking the signal that the system can accept without producing distortion. The meter may use a needle pointer or may simply use LED lights, with a software implementation displaying a graphical image of either type.   LED systems are usually better as they do not suffer from the delay of physically moving a needle.

Settings formats

In many recording software applications, the quality of the sample is set before making the recording. With Microsoft's Sound Recorder, the sample is recorded and the sample's attributes are decided just before saving the file. The steps are:

- Make the recording.
- Click on *'File'* in the top menu.
- Click on *'Save As'* in the drop-down menu.
- If the reported Format is not suitable, click on the *'Change'* button and select a new CODEC.
- Enter the name of the file in the *'File name'* dialog box.
- Click the *'Save'* button.

Windows also allows the properties to be set before making the recording.

- Click on *'File'* in the top menu.
- Click on *'Properties'* in the drop-down menu.
- Select *'Recording Formats'* from the *'Choose from'* menu.
- Click the *'Convert Now'* button to bring up the *'Sound Selection'* dialog box.

There are two ways to select the settings for a recording:

1. Choosing from a named list.
2. Setting each parameter individually.

The named list

The 'Name' drop-down menu allows a choice from a well-known set of attributes (e.g. radio quality or telephone quality). The example shows CD Quality being selected. This displays the attributes for that choice at the top of the *'Attributes'* list.

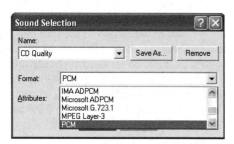

The attributes

Names, such as CD quality and radio quality, only apply to the most well known sets of attributes. There is not a name for every possible combination. Other sets of attributes can be selected from the list and the resulting data rate for each option is displayed. So, for example, CD quality will record at 172kB per sec. The attributes are made up of three elements:

- Sampling rate
- Dynamic Range
- Number of channels

The expected quality and storage overhead for each choice was discussed earlier in this chapter.

The Format

The *'Format'* describes the way that the file is stored - either in uncompressed format or compressed by a CODEC.

The drop-down list of options includes all the CODECs that are installed on the computer and will vary between users. All computers with Windows will have the standard set, such as plain PCM, ADPCM and so on. In the example, the computer has additional CODECs installed and this allows the capture of sounds directly into MP3 format.

The desired CODEC is selected from the list.

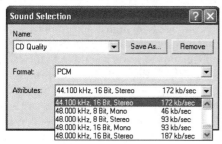

Best practice

It is best to record a sample at a reasonable quality, even where that level of quality might not be the expected final quality. The audio editing software can convert a sample to lower sample rates and lower bit resolution, if the file is to be shrunk later. Although, the software can also increase the clip's sample rate and bit resolution, this produces no extra quality, although the file size has been considerably increased. It is not possible to add improved quality into a sample and so the sample should be saved at the best quality that can be achieved, with decisions on its final quality/size being taken later.

Microphones

All recordings of real world sounds, such as interviews, birds sounds, traffic noise, etc are captured using a microphone, also known as a *'mike'*. A microphone is a pressure transducer. That means that it aids the conversion of air pressure changes into changes in voltage. A variety of types are available and they have different uses.

There are two basic microphone transducer methods:

- Those that generate their own electrical signal, such as moving-coil, ribbon or crystal microphones. These are known as dynamic microphones.
- Those that vary an existing voltage signal, such as capacitor and carbon microphones.

They are available in the following formats:

HAND MIKES

> These are the most common types and are designed to be held by the user. They can also be mounted on a mike stand or on a boom.

TIE CLIP MIKES

> Also known as *'Lavalier'* mikes, these attach to someone's tie, lapel or other part of clothing. They are used by commentators for live filming, and for attachment to musical instruments.

RADIO MIKES

> Radio mikes attach a mike to a transmitter and the modulated radio signal is picked up by a matching receiver and the demodulated audio is fed to the audio equipment (e.g. audio mixers, a camcorder's mike socket or a sound card's line input). They are widely used in TV studios and live concerts. The mike used can be a hand mike, a tie clip or a headset.

Microphone characteristics

Microphones are designed to pick up sound in different ways. Some are best for up close recording while others are best for distance recording. Some are best for quiet interviews while others are best for capturing the ambience of a concert.

The way mikes respond to the sounds around them is described as their *'polar diagram'*. Polar diagrams - also known as *'polar patterns'*, *'polar plots'* or *'directional patterns'* display the response of the microphone to audio signals coming from the front (*'on axis'*) and the comparable response from other directions (*'off axis'*).

A polar diagram shows a line that joins all points around the microphone that will produce the same microphone output from a given audio source.

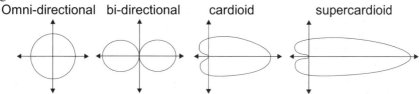

Omni-directional   bi-directional   cardioid   supercardioid

Omni-directional

> The output from the microphone is equal from sound all round the microphone. Any sound of a particular amplitude will produce the same mike output when picked up from any point at the same distance from the mike. So, for instance, if a dog runs round the microphone barking, it will produce the same output whether it is in front of the mike, behind the mike, to the side of the mike, etc.

Bi-directional

> The bi-directional microphone is constructed so that its corrugated ribbon diaphragm responds equally to air pressure changes from the front and from the rear.

Unidirectional

> While some occasions require the benefits of omni-directional pickup (e.g. recording the crowd at a football match), the user will often require a more selective pickup. This requires a greater pickup at the front of the microphone compared to sounds at the sides or rear. The mike picks up sounds mostly from the direction in which it is pointed. The three varieties are:
>
> Cardioid   This has the basic cardioid (i.e. heart-shaped) directional characteristic as shown.
>
> Supercardioid,   Also known as *'shotgun'* mikes, these have a narrower pickup response area
>   (i.e. more directional).
>   They are usually bought to replace the camcorder's integral mike.
>
> Hypercardioid   These have an even narrower pickup response area and are used in specialised areas.

Microphone types

In each case, the changes in air pressure vibrate a thin plate called the *'diaphragm'*. The diaphragm in turns varies either an inductive or capacitive value in the mike's circuitry and this varying value changes in sympathy with the audio being picked up. The varying signal is fed to the amplifier or the microphone input socket of the sound card.

Condenser

All electronic circuits use condensers (known in the UK as *'capacitors'*).

These components can be found in radios, televisions, computers, hi-fis, etc.

A condenser is made up of two metal plates that are separated by air or some insulating material. They are capable of storing an electrical charge. The capacitance (i.e. amount they can store) is determined by the size of the plates, the nature of the dialectric (i.e. the material between the plates) and the thickness of the dialectric. The condenser microphone uses a moveable diaphragm as one of the two plates. Changes in sound pressure move the

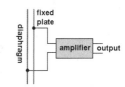

diaphragm closer and further away from the fixed plate.   As the capacitance alters, the voltage stored alters and this change is in proportion to the audio being picked up.

Professional versions use an electrostatically charged plate that is is powered by a separate 48 volt power supply or a voltage feed from a mixing desk or from a pro-level camera.   A more down-market version uses a permanently charged plate powered by its own internal 1.5 volt battery. This is called an *'electret'* microphone and is the most common type used with camcorders. Capacitor mikes are usually unidirectional or omni-directional and are popular with professional users, due to their flat frequency response and tolerance of varying operating conditions.

Moving coil

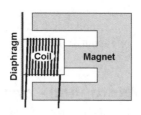

The moving coil mike works like a loudspeaker in reverse.   In a loudspeaker voltage changes are applied to a coil that moves and vibrates the surrounding air.   With a moving coil mike, the air fluctuations move the coil and induce a voltage change. As the diagram shows, a diaphragm is attached to a coil of wire. As the diaphragm fluctuates, it pushes and pulls the coil within a magnetic field provided by a permanent magnet.   The moving coil has a voltage induced into it. The faster the movement of the coil, the greater the voltage.   Hence, the mike's voltage output is proportional to the amplitude of the audio signal.   The faster the coil vibrates the quicker the voltage changes and thus the frequency of the audio is detected. This construction is commonly used for omni-directional mikes.   These are commonly found used on stage and are used by announcers and vocalists.

Ribbon

The bi-directional microphone is constructed so that its corrugated ribbon diaphragm responds to air pressure changes from the front and from the rear.   The ribbon sits in a magnetic field and the ribbon's movement through the field induces a voltage across it in sympathy with the changes in air pressure.

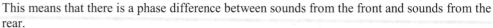

It works on the *'pressure gradient'* principle.   There is a pressure difference between the front and the rear of the ribbon.   Loud sounds from the front push the ribbon towards the rear, while loud rear sounds push the ribbon towards the front.   The mike responds equally to sounds from its front or rear. Since sounds at the sides of the ribbon do not create differences in air pressure between the front and rear, the mike does not detect these sounds.   This gives the ribbon mike it characteristic polar diagram, often referred to as a *'figure of eight'*.
This means that there is a phase difference between sounds from the front and sounds from the rear.

Others

Other types, such as crystal mikes and carbon mikes are no longer found in audio recording work.
The carbon microphone was widely used for telephone handsets and was a low quality device.   The vibrating diaphragm altered the pressure on a cup of carbon granules. Increasing air pressure compressed the granules together and lowered the resistance of the microphone.   This altering resistance was used to alter the current through the device.   The crystal microphone works on the *'piezoelectric'* effect.   The microphone contains a slice of crystal. Altering air pressure slightly bends the crystal and this causes an electric charge to be developed across the faces of the crystal.   This altering charge is then amplified.

Impedance

Microphones are categorised into two impedance bands:
- Low impedance, typically between 600 ohms and 10,000 ohms.
- High impedance, typically 50,000 ohms and over. These are not normally used with sound cards.

Some degree of mismatch is acceptable and a device with a low input impedance usually accepts any low impedance mike. However, large variations from the manual's stated input impedance causes loss of power transfer and lowers the level of the incoming signal (resulting in a poor signal-to-noise ratio).

Summary of microphone types and their characteristics

Mike Type	Polar Diagram	Quality	Likely Use	Comments
Crystal	Omni-directional	Low	Speech, background sounds, sound effects	Fallen out of use.
Moving Coil	Omni-directional and Cardioid	Good	Speech, Vocals Music (drums, bass)	Can be used outdoors.
Ribbon	Figure of Eight	High	Speech Music (woodwind, strings)	For indoor use.
Condenser	Omni-directional and Cardioid	High	Speech Music (piano, brass)	Can be used outdoors (use with wind gag)

Use of mikes

Although most microphones can be used for all purposes at a pinch, the results will not be adequate for professional use.   The characteristics of different microphones result in their use for specific purposes.

Omni-directional

These are often used as a general purpose hand mike, as the speaker does not need to be on-axis at all times.   It is still common, and annoying, to see TV interviewers conducting street interviews with unidirectional mikes.   They ask a question into the mike and are too slow in pointing the mike towards the interviewee.   The result is that only parts of the conversation are intelligible.   This problem is avoided with an omni-directional mike.

Another popular use is to record the proceedings at a meeting.   The mike is placed on the table and is able to pick up each participant equally.   It is also useful for capturing ambient sounds.   It is not for situations where public address systems are in use, as it will pick up the sound from the P.A. loudspeakers and create howl round feedback.

Bi-directional

While the cardioid mike reduces off-axis sounds, it also eliminates the echoes and reverberations that provide the characteristics of a recording (e.g. from a church or a sports stadium).   The figure of eight pattern of a bi-directional mike provide the compromise, allowing both the presenter and the background ambience to be picked up.

Cardioid

This is the type fitted in most camcorders.   Its selective pickup pattern makes it ideal for picking out one sound from a noisy environment.   For example, it can be is used in an auditorium or other large gathering to record one speaker in an audience.   While one member of the audience is being recorded, the coughs, sneezes and other unwanted sounds are minimised.

Hypercardiod mikes are often used when it is difficult to get close to the audio source.   They are also useful in locations that produce lots of echo, as they will not pick up most of the reflected sounds.

Similarly, they are helpful in a commentating situation where there is lots of unwanted noise.

The more directional the mike, the more difficult it is to control the recording.   So, for example, it is difficult to record an audio source that moves, since the source might easily move out of the angle over which the mike receives.   Also, the more directional the mike the harder it is to maintain stereo.

Popping

A mike is often held close to the presenter's mouth to help minimise background noises.   During some sessions, the speaker's voice will project a quick puff of moist air into the mike aperture.   Words with the letter *'p'* or *'b'*, such as *'Pepper'* or *'Bobby'* are the worst offenders.   This causes a *'popping'* noise to be introduced to the recording.   Ribbon mikes are the most affected by this problem.

The effect is minimised by:

- Speaking further away from the mike
- Fitting a windshield or *'pop shield'* to the mike.

Wind noise

When strong winds are present during an outdoor recording session, it is picked up by the mike as a roaring noise. This noise can be reduced at the post production stage.   The computer's audio software can apply a low pass filter to the audio file.   This reduces the roaring sound but it also removes some of the wanted signal.   Prevention is better than cure and the best approach is to minimise the effect of wind on the mike. This is achieved by using a windshield, or wind gag.   This is a *'furry sock'* that covers the microphone.   The material is *'acoustically transparent'* and therefore does not impede the capture of audio.   However, the fur reduces the air velocity around the mike.   The cheaper sponge wind gags are only partially effective.   In an emergency, any piece of sponge, or a woolly sock, is better then nothing.

Sibilance

Sibilance is the word used to describe the distortion that affects certain letters such as *'s'* and *'c'* .   For example, the word *'yes'* is recorded as *'yesh'* or *'yessss'*.   This is usually caused by talking too closely into a microphone and producing too high a signal amplitude at certain frequencies.

There are three solutions to the problem:

- Talking over the microphone rather than directly into it.
- Using a hardware de-esser processor (only an option for a studio)
- Using a software application or plug-in that can process the audio file.

Microphone techniques

Positioning mikes

A little thought and a little preparation can make a big difference to the quality of the final recording.

Position the mike as close to the source as is practical, as this minimises the pickup of unwanted surrounding noises. It does tend, however, to also accentuate the bass component of the sound (known as the *'proximity effect'*).

If the session is being taped with a camcorder, do not use the camcorder's internal mike.   These are generally unsuitable for all but the closest of work.   More often, they are too far back from source and even a cardioid mike will

pick up sounds from the sides in these circumstances.   Camcorder mikes are also notorious for picking up the sound of their own motors.   In almost every situation, it is preferable to use an external mike and most camcorders have sockets for external connection.   When recording a conversation or interview, the microphone should be located as close to the subjects as possible, without the mike being seen by the camera.
This is usually achieved by:

- Using a boom mike. A mike is held on a long pole that is mounted on a stand. The boom is adjusted so that it is close to the subjects but is above their heads and out of camera view.
- Using a hidden mike.   A mike hidden within a bunch of flowers, behind an object on the table, etc, so that it is close to the subjects without being obtrusive.

In general, it is preferable to use the mike on a stand, to avoid handling noise. For voiceovers, this prevents handling noise and leaves the speaker free to turn pages of notes.
For recording a meeting or a discussion panel, it is best to use multiple mikes where possible.   This provides better results and more control than a single omni-directional mike.
Lastly, the public is generally scared of using a mike.   They tend to either shy away from it, or shout into it from a very short distance.   It pays to spend a few moments training someone in the handling of mikes.   It is also useful to make a few test recordings to ensure that they are being used properly.

Tackling acoustic problems

The location and environment for an audio recording should be considered for minimising any harmful acoustic effects.   Parallel surfaces, such as walls, floors, ceilings and large pieces of furniture cause room resonance and standing waves.   In a studio, this is tackled by having the walls at different angles, the ceiling not being parallel with the floor, the glass window of the control room glass set an angle, etc.   In addition, 3D wall surfaces are used to break up continuous flat surface areas.   These often consist of acoustic tiles. It is also difficult to prevent low frequency sounds from penetrating in or out of a room and some studios use 'float' rooms to minimise this.   These are rooms within a room, with no fixtures between them that might allow sounds to be transmitted between them.   Studios use such an isolation booth to record each performer individually, with the multiple audio tracks being merged during the mixing stage.

Outside a studio environment, recordings sessions should normally avoid large empty rooms, tiled areas, areas near large windows, etc. Where recordings are made within a building, there is more control over the recording process.   Often, there is time to prepare the location where the recording will take place.   This includes mike placement and the spotting of any possible recording interruptions (e.g. does a train pass the window every two minutes, is the air conditioning noisy, has the switchboard been told to bar any incoming calls, are noisy computers and tape decks positioned away from the mikes, etc).

The biggest room problem is usually unwanted echoes from large unfurnished areas, such as large tiled areas and large window spaces. If possible, hang blankets or heavy curtains around the problem areas and cover large smooth tabletops with a cloth.   Even better, create a temporary isolation booth using any absorbent materials such as foam, carpets, etc.

Monitoring the recording

Listen while recording, to prevent unwanted sounds slipping through undetected.   Camcorders often have a headphone socket.   If possible, a second person should listen to the recording, allowing the camera operator to concentrate on the filming. Even better, use noise cancelling headphones.   These greatly reduce the external surrounding noise allowing what is actually being recorded to be clearly heard.   Bear in mind that camcorders also have automatic gain control - they adjust their amplifiers to match the incoming audio volume.   A sudden unwanted local noise could result in the amplifier reducing its gain and the wanted signal being lost for a while.

Sound mixing

With sound mixing, two or more audio sources are combined in proportions that produce the desired balanced output.   The sources can be speech, music, and sound effects and can be obtained via microphones, CDs, cassette tape, or pre-digitised computer files in WAV or other format.   The amplitude of each input signal can be independently adjusted.

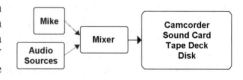

There are three types of mixing:

Live mixing

The live audio from the microphone is mixed in at recording time.   The other audio sources can be live (e.g. a second mike) or pre-recorded (e.g. from a tape).   This is most useful for situations where the background sound is a one-off; for example, an interview with a promoter while the band plays live in the background.   This involves some careful setting of the levels before making the recording and can be tricky and prone to errors.

Studio mixing

Where resources allow, it is much better to record a separate audio track for each audio component and mix them later. Mixing desks provide electronic filters and tone controls to adjust, correct and augment individual signals. They also allow additional processing such as fade, panning, echo, etc. Unlike live mixing, all the sources are individually accessible at any time. So, for example, an adjustment or effect can be can be applied to a single component, leaving the others untouched. As a minimum, the foreground sound, the background ambience (such as crowd noise and sound effects) and background music should be stored separately. For music recordings, there may be many separate channels for different instruments, backing vocals, lead singer and so on.

The tracks are still being mixed in analogue format, although this is being replaced by digital processing.

Computer mixing

For those with more limited resources, similar facilities are provided by most respectable audio editing software packages. The audio components are copied from the storage device, such as tape deck or camcorder audio output, and are digitised into sound clips. These sound clips are then processed and mixed in digital format. For professional results, it pays to invest in a good multitrack sound editor. This provides separate tracks for speech, effects, music, etc and the software can cross-fade between the tracks. CoolEdit Pro is an example of a standalone audio editor that supports 64 tracks. Of course, multitrack facilities are already available in video editing software such as Adobe Premiere and Media Studio Pro.

Mixing can be a repetitive task, playing sections over and over again to evaluate the effect of small changes that were applied to the audio signals. This introduces the possibility of *'ear fatigue'*, where the constant playing of audio sections makes the person carrying out the mixing lose objectivity. To prevent this, the people working the mixing desk should take regular breaks, so that they bring fresh minds to each mixing session.

Other dangers lie in the mixing process. If all sources have their amplitudes boosted by the same amount, the components in the final output still have the same relative amplitudes as before – but the danger of clipping may arise. In addition, increasing one channel may result in unintended masking of another channel, requiring attention to frequency placement as well as stereo placement.

The audio trail

Over time, a large collection of audio clips will accumulate. While this is very useful for incorporation into future projects, it raises the possibility of inadvertently breaching user permissions or copyrights.

This can be prevented if all audio clips are properly documented from their initial recording or acquisition.

When a clip is first recorded or acquired, its main features should be logged. This should include details such as source of origin, copyright, permissions, format, clip length, etc. When a clip is altered, any changes such as editing, enhancements, added effects, compression details, changes of format, change of file name, where stored, etc. should be noted. This documentation should also note what audio files were used in particular projects.

Editing audio

A user-created sound sample is rarely immediately usable. It may contain unwanted pauses or noises, or require augmenting by special effects before it is used.

Editing software packages provide a variety of facilities and these may involve different steps in different packages. For example, one package may require the user to understand how to use of a set of tools to eliminate hiss, while another may have automated the process by having a *'Hiss Removal'* feature. Dart Pro, for example, has range of features such as *'DeClick'*, *'DeNoise'* and *'DeHiss'*.

Sample Re-ordering

These tools do not alter the quality of the audio sample. They are used to change the length and order of parts of the sample.

Cropping

Also known as *'Top and Tail'*, this removes periods of silence from the start and end of the wanted sound.

Cut/paste

A section can be cut from one point in the clip and placed in another point in the same clip - or in another clip. For example, a gunshot can be extracted and placed in a more appropriate point. It can also be used to delete unwanted sections, such as someone's coughing fit during interview. It can also be used to delete a pop or click that occurs during a period of silence.

Copying

Used to extract a sample from one part of the clip and insert it in another part as a duplicate sound. For example, the sound of a taxi horn could be repeated in various parts of a clip.

Looping

Used to repeat a section of the sound several times in succession. Commonly used to create music loops and to make a background atmosphere clip last longer.

Sample restoration

These facilities attempt to bring the quality of the sample back as close to the original sound as possible.
This involves removing any blemishes that may have occurred during recording or digitising.

DC Offset

The signal should vary above and below a value of zero, where zero represents no output voltage and hence no audible signal. Zero represents silence and if the quiescent value of an audio clip sits above or below the zero line, then the signal is said to contain a *'DC Offset'*. This is often caused by equipment that is not properly earthed. It may introduce noise into the output and the DC Offset (or DC Bias) control exists to adjusts the signal so that it varies around the zero value.

Noise gate

The noise gate is used to remove background hiss from the quiet sections of a clip. The signal has to exceed the value set as the threshold before it is included in the output signal. This eliminates the smaller value signals from the clip. The usual controls are:

Threshold

Sets the amplitude level at which the gate opens and allows the sound to pass through. This value can be gradually increased until the hiss is removed from quiet sections of the clip. Increasing the threshold to too high a level results in parts of the wanted signal being lost. This is the reason that the noise gate cannot be used to remove background hiss from louder sections of the clip (see Noise Elimination below).

Decay time

Sets the time, in milliseconds, before the noise gate fully closes and prevents any sound from passing through. A very small value results in a sudden cut-off of the signal and the value should be set so that the signal quietens more naturally.

Noise Elimination

This is useful for eliminating broadband noise (noise that covers a wide frequency spectrum) as conventional filters cannot remove this noise without lowering the amplitude of the wanted signal. It is also useful for eliminating hiss where the noise gate cannot operate (see above). The technique is to highlight a section of noise, usually in a section where the main audio is silent or quiet. The application uses it as the sample for eliminating this noise throughout the file. A new profile should be sampled for each file, as the noise composition in a file is different for each clip.
CoolEdit also allows a sample of the inherent noise in the system to be tested before a recording is made. This noise profile is then applied to recorded signal in real time and carries out noise elimination before it is saved.

Interpolate

This facility uses linear interpolation to smooth out the content of a part of a clip marked by the user. So, for example, if the selected section had a starting value of 18 and a finishing value of 30, interpolation would replace all existing values within the marked area by values that rose from 18 up to 30. This is very useful when used on a small area that contains a pop or click, as their sudden amplitude increases are removed. It cannot be applied over a large area, as too much of the original signal would also be removed. The area to be marked should be selected after using zoom to view the section at close quarters.

Silence

This reduces the level of the marked section of the clip down to zero. This is a simple way to eliminate clicks, pops and hiss during quiet periods in the clip.

Low Pass

High frequencies are described as *'treble'* and low frequencies are described as *'bass'*. Many pieces of domestic hi-fi equipment are fitted with treble and bass controls. The application's high and low pass filters are the equivalent of these controls.
The low pass filter allows low frequencies (bass) to pass filters but progressively attenuate high frequencies (treble) above the assigned cut-off frequency. They are used to reduce high-end hiss noise or other unwanted high frequency sounds. Setting the cut-off frequency too low removes too much of the wanted signal, leaving the remaining signal sounding too deep and muffled.

High Pass

High pass filters progressively attenuate low frequencies below the assigned cut-off frequency, while allowing high frequencies to pass. They are used to remove deep rumbling noises (such as some motor noise and wind roar) or other unwanted low frequency sounds. Setting the cut-off frequency too high removes too much of the wanted signal, leaving the remaining signal sounding tinny and hollow.

Bandpass

A bandpass filter blocks all frequencies outside the specified range, and only allows frequencies within the specified range to pass. This can be used to pick out a particular sound from a clip, where the main content of the sound lies within an identifiable range. In addition, blocking the lower and upper ranges of a signal narrows the audible band to the mid frequencies and produces an effect similar to that of listening on a telephone.

Bandstop

A bandstop filter has the opposite effect to a bandpass filter.   It blocks all frequencies within the specified range, and only allows frequencies outwith the specified range to pass.   This can be used to suppress narrow band noise, such as a hum, within a clip.

Parametric EQ

Equalisation boosts or cuts the amplitude of certain frequency ranges within a signal.   It was first introduced to compensate for losses in analogue signals that were sent long distances over a line.   The aim was to restore all the frequency elements back to their original levels (hence the name *'equalisation'*).   It now appears in hi-systems as *'graphic equalisers'* consisting of a panel of sliders used to adjust for room acoustics or for personal taste (e.g. turning up the bass).

Equalisation is now available with most computer audio software players (e.g. Winamp), where it acts on digital signals.   It is now more often used to accentuate a particular frequency range, so that a particular feature of the audio clip (such as the speaker's voice or a particular musical instrument) is brought to the fore.   It is also used to compensate for the inadequate bass response of most users' systems.   For example, radio stations boost low frequencies to compensate for the bass frequency response of most portable radios and car radios.   It is good practice to monitor a project's audio signals using the quality of speakers likely to be found in typical user installations (rather than relying on the superior speakers to be found in most development labs).

With standard equalisation, there is a set of filters, each covering a fixed band of the frequency spectrum.   Since hearing is logarithmic, the bands' allocations are not linear but are spaced in octaves.   The gain of each filter can be adjusted to boost or attenuate the amplitude of that band.

With parametric equalisation, the user can not only set the amplitude of each band, but also has control over the centre frequency of each band and the bandwidth of each band.

It is generally preferable to lower the gain in the unwanted bands, rather than boosting the wanted bands, to avoid boosting unwanted noise.   So, for example, to improve the voice part of a clip, the frequencies that lie outside the main voice band (i.e. under 300Hz and above 3kHz) should be attenuated.   It is very useful to correct the loss of treble that is common with streamed audio clips.

Equalisers are also widely used to *'restore'* a recording.   For example, acoustic instruments are best recorded in a voluminous location with a mike situated some distance from the instrument so that the full timbre of the instrument is captured.   Where the recording is made in a more confined location with a mike closely positioned to the instrument, some of the original timbre is lost.   Equalisers are used to try to recover the original sound.

Normalise

This facility is used to improve the clip's quality by increasing its dynamic range.   This is used where a signal has been recorded at a low level, such that its peaks never reach the maximum swing allowed by the dynamic range of the system (usually the sound card).   The entire clip (or the section that is selected from a clip) is examined and the highest peaks of the signal are found.   The clip's volume is then increased to the maximum percent possible without producing distortion through clipping.   This is a useful tool for bringing up the level of all clips in a project to the same level, ironing out any differences in recording levels of clips.   It is often the last process to be applied to a clip.

Changing amplitude levels

Normalising maintains the ratio between different sound components.

However, there are occasions when individual sections of the clip will require having their amplitude increased (e.g. where one person on a discussion is quieter than the rest).   The section of the clip can be highlighted and have its volume increased relative to the rest of the clip's contents.

Compressing

Compression reduces the difference between the highest and lowest amplitudes in a signal.   It should not be confused with file compression such as MP3s, which is covered later.   The effect of compression is to raise the level of all sounds within the clip.   This is useful where some of the components of the sound were recorded at too low a level.   For example, it can bring up the voice of a member of an audience at a meeting.   It is also used to even out a commentator's voice, where the amplitude has varied during the recording.   Also, making a recording with the microphone placed too close to a musical instrument artificially increases the dynamic range of the sound, requiring the use of compression to bring out a more natural sound.   However, over-compressing will make a clip sound flat.

De-essing

If an audio clip suffers from sibilance problems (see earlier) the effect can be greatly reduced by tackling the frequencies that are causing the effect.   The trick is to attenuate the sibilant portion of the signal without affecting the rest of audio.   One technique, called *'frequency conscious compression'* relies on adjusting the graphic equaliser's to boost the sibilant portion, adjust its attack and release time to ensure that no other components get affected, then relying on the compression system to reduce the amplitude of the sibilant portion.   This is a fiddly business and most users prefer to use automated software to achieve the same effect.   Applications such as Diamond Cut Audio Restoration Software and plugins for Cubase are used to de-ess audio track.

Sample augmentation

These alter the content of the sound, to improve on the original – a process known as *'sweetening'*.

Fade in

This facility gradually increases the volume of the highlighted section of the clip, from a prescribed percentage starting value (i.e. 0% fades up from complete silence, while 50% fades up from half volume).

Fade out

This facility gradually decreases the volume of the highlighted section of the clip, to a prescribed percentage value (i.e. 100% fades to silence, while 50% fades to half volume).

Cross-fade

A simple butting together of two audio clips usually causes a click at the point where they joint, unless clip 1 ends with a silence and clip 2 begins with a silence.   On any other occasion, the content of both clips are at different voltage levels at the point of butting and the sudden change of voltage causes a clicking sound.

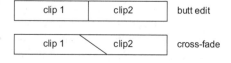

When butting two audio files together, it is possible to fade out clip 1 and then fade in clip 2.   However, this introduces a quiet section in the middle.

The cross-fade fades out clip 1 while simultaneously fading in clip 2.   Initially clip 1 is at full volume and clip 2 is zero volume.   By the end of the cross-fade, clip 2 is at full volume with clip 1 at zero - with a seamless join.

Envelope shaping.

You are presented with Shape Controls. With these controls, you can define the amplitude envelope of a sound. The shape line is initially horizontal at 100. By bending/moving the line, you can dynamically change the volume of the selection.

Combining

This facility allows the addition of extra content to that already present in the clip.

It is common to create sub-masters (e.g. music, dialogue, effects) that are individually processed for maximum quality and effect, with the intention of combining these sub-masters later.   This allows, for example, for recording separate drum tracks for bass drum, snare drum, cymbals, etc., with each track being adjusted before being combined into a single drum mix track.

Panning

This facility controls the balance between the volumes in the left and right channels of a stereo sample.

With panning, the volume of the sound in the left channel is decreased while the volume in the right channel is increased. Panning allows a mono signal to be positioned, or moved, anywhere within the stereo plane.

In multitracks, panning is used to position sounds in the stereo plane of the final file. With interviews, it may require placing the interviewer's sound to the left channel while the interviewee's sound is directed to the right channel.   With music tracks, it may be used to position the vocals in the middle and position the instruments (e.g. bass guitar to the left, lead guitar to the right).

Panning is more of a problem with stereo samples.

When the source has been recorded in mid-position between the stereo mikes, the Balance control is used to between channels with stereo. However, if the sound source was positioned closer to one mike than the other during recording, then changing the balance does not provide a panning effect; it simply reduces the overall volume of the source.   For example, if the source is closer to the left mike, there is little signal recorded on the right channel.   So, fading the left channel reduces the audio output while increasing the right channel does not produce any appreciable increase in output.

If a panning effect is anticipated, then the source should be recorded in mono, or with the source in the middle of stereo mikes.

Adding in extra audio

It is common to add to the original sound, to augment the effect. Often, an interview will take place in the absence of the sounds that normally provide the correct ambience for that setting. This is corrected by adding the extra material later. This may be music, background environment sounds (e.g. car traffic or pub sounds) or sounds off (e.g. gunshots or doors creaking open).   These are secondary sounds to the foreground content and must partially fade (known as *'dipping'*) during foreground speech.   This prevents a sudden drop during speech. A likely setting is to fade for about half a second, then overlap the speech content by about quarter of a second.

Sounds can also be added to suggest a time of day. For example, a toaster/alarm clock/coffee percolator suggest early morning while crickets and owls suggest evening.

Adding in effects

These alter the basic audio signal to create unusual or distinctive sounds, or to radically alter the way that the sound is presented.

Echo

This facility produces an echo to the source, to provide the effect of large acoustic spaces.   So, for example, the effect of a sound being played in a football stadium or a church can be imposed on any audio being reproduced.

The sound should always be initially recorded without any echo; the echo can always be added later whereas the echo cannot be removed from a clip pre-recorded with an echo.   As the amount of echo is increased, the source appears to fade more into the background, so the effect should not be over-applied as it will eventually destroy the clarity of the original.

Strictly speaking, echo is a single repetition. In other words, if the speaker says *'Hello'* the word is repeated slightly later for a single time. With reverberation, the word is repeated a number of times, getting fainter with each repetition.

The basic settings for echo are:

Delay - The time taken for the echo to bounce back. Long delays suggest larger locations.
Typical delays are 0.5 to 1 second for voice signals, up to 1.5 seconds for a small
group and up to 2.5 seconds for a full orchestra.

Volume - The volume of the echoed content. Use low levels, unless the effect of standing in
a large cavern is required.

Reverb - Whether a single or repeating echo is to be used.

Other controls are provided by some applications including reflection, diffusion, decay and pre-delay. The provided preset values are a good way to get into using reverberation, until the controls are mastered.

Echo/Reverb is a very useful tool to brighten vocals but should not be overdone or applied to all clips. It tends to be used less on the lower frequencies.

Reverse

Reverses the order of the data in the clip, so that it will play backwards.   The facility is of little practical use, apart from a few novelty effects.

Playback rate

This facility alters the rate at which the clip is played.   The sound will play faster (or slower) and its pitch will be higher (or lower).

Transpose

This facility changes the musical pitch of the highlighted sound by resampling it at a different sampling rate. For example, take a one second recording that is sampled at 44.1KHz and resample it at 88.2KHz. When the sample is played back at the normal 44.1KHz speed, the clip lasts for two seconds. Since the same waveform takes twice the time to play, the pitch that is heard is half the frequency. This *'pitch shifting'* is often used to convert a note recorded from a musical instrument into a set of samples covering the musical scales.

Resample/Time stretching

This facility alters the sampling rate of the entire clip, so that it plays for different length of time without altering the pitch of the final sound. It re-calculates and interpolates all the clip's digital values, so that the pitch remains unchanged within the new time slot.   This is only effective with minor time alterations, as any large changes affect the quality of the final output.   Commonly used to stretch the time taken to play the sound of an explosion, to enhance its impact.

Resampling is also useful for converting files down for use on the web. It makes file sizes considerably smaller and therefore speeds up the transfer of the files over the Internet.

Chorusing

If an orchestra has ten violins, the sound they make is not just louder; it is much richer and fuller. This is because all the instruments have slightly different acoustic properties, are not exactly in perfect tune with each other and the musicians do not play the note starting at exactly the same time and lasting for exactly the same time.   The combination of the slight differences in these instruments and they way they are played combine to give the rich sound made by a chorus.   The same effect is achieved by a chorus of singers.   The same effect can be created electronically using just one audio source. If the signal is slightly time delayed or detuned and then mixed back with the original, this creates changes in the relative strengths and phase relationships of the two signals. The process is known as *'chorusing'*.

A similar technique called *'flanging'*, mixes the original sound with delayed sound and feedback for a distinctive new sound.

Other effects

Other special effects can be created by deliberately distorting the original sound.

For example, a *'ring modulator'* can be used to create sounds such as the Daleks from Dr Who, Cher singing *'Believe'* and various special guitar effects.   It uses amplitude modulation and uses two audio inputs, one is the main source and the other is often a simple plain tone, although more complex waveforms can be used. The ring modulator uses the two signals to produce an output that contains the sum and the difference of the two signals (these are known as *'sidebands'*). The original two signals do not appear in the output and the results, although the ring modulator's output can be mixed back in with the original main audio source, to create a fuller sound.

Another technique is to deliberately introduce distortion into a signal. This is used, for example, to overdrive an amplifier with a guitar input to produce a much harsher sound.

Editing Software

Many competent applications packages are dedicated to the editing and processing of audio samples.   These include Goldwave, SoundEdit and CoolEdit. The manufacturers of sound cards often bundle commercial editing packages with their products, or supply their own editing software.   The *'Sound Recorder'* utility provided with Windows provides some basic tools such as Top and Tail, echo, sample reversal and basic mixing. Sound Recorder is limited but is a useful starting point.   Industry standard recording and editing software such as Sound Forge, Black Diamond and WaveLab provide a full suite of facilities. Apart from the editing, restoration, augmentation and special effects tools already mentioned, a useful additional facility is the ability to batch process - e.g. converting all sound clips to mono, resampling all files to the same sampling rate, etc.

File Compression/Conversion

The advantages and growing popularity of saving and distributing audio files in MP3 format were discussed earlier in this chapter. New versions of software have support for MP3 included.   This includes authoring packages, CD-burners (such as CD Creator 4) and Windows itself (from 98 onwards).   However, all older software requires add-on software to enable MP3 to be handled.   In addition, MP3 is not always the automatic choice of format.   This means that there is a need to convert audio files between formats. The following notes cover file conversion - and the conversion from CD audio into computer audio files.

MP3 Encoders

There are two basic operations that a user may wish to perform:
*   Encoding from a WAV file to an MP3 file.
*   Ripping tracks from an audio CD.

Ripping

Ripping is the term used for extracting the audio content from a CD track and saving it as a computer audio file, such as a WAV file.   It is useful for converting samples from royalty-free CDs, which contain background music or sound effects, into compressed clips.   Although it is also widely used for reading off commercial audio CDs, this practice is illegal without permission.   There is some argument about whether anyone would be prosecuted for creating compilations from their own legally purchased music CDs, but these remain prohibited under the law.
Ripping requires the appropriate hardware and software.

Many very old CD-ROM drives were unable to read from audio CDs, as the drive has to support the reading of RAW data.   In some cases, older CD-ROMs were capable of reading RAW data but the supplied drivers were incapable of providing the *'Read_Long'* service.   Most ripper software will report on the suitability of the CD-ROM installed on the computer. As a last resort, the audio source can be fed into the sound card and converted into a WAV file by Sound Recorder.   This is not satisfactory, as distortions are introduced by the extra digital/analogue and analogue/digital conversions carried out by the CD player and the sound card..

Rippers maintain the sample in digital format and at the same quality as the original (assuming no downsampling). Many utilities are available that rip and encode in a single operation.   The track is copied straight from the CD and saved directly as an MP3 file, without first being converted to a WAV file.   Examples of combined rippers/encoders are Xing's AudioCatalyst, CDEX, MusicMatch Jukebox, and RealJukebox Plus.   Examples of simple rippers (i.e. audio to WAV only) are CDDA for use in MSDOS and plugins for Winamp.   Other rippers can be found on www.mp3.com

The illustration shows the screen layout of the CDEX freeware ripper/encoder.

When the audio CD is placed in the CDROM drive, the information on each track is displayed in the main panel.   This includes information on file size and playing time. The user selects the files to be ripped by highlighting them.   In the example, tracks four to seven have been chosen for processing, but all tracks on the CD can be highlighted if desired.

The buttons on the right side offers the option of ripping to WAV format or ripping directly to MP3 format.   The *'Configure'* button provides control over the encoding options.

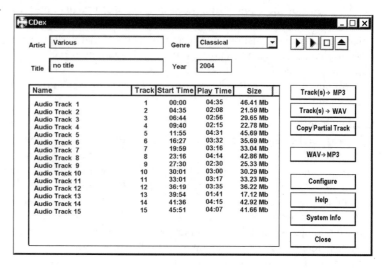

Encoding

MP3 encoding can be built in to a ripper, as mentioned above, or can be provided by a dedicated piece of encoder software. An example of a standalone encoder is the freeware BladeEnc encoder. In either case, control over the encoding settings is provided.

The main decisions are:

Bit Rate Selection

Selection of bit rate. This is normally set to 128kbps, although it can be lowered (to say 16kbps for Internet files) or raised (to say 320kbps for high-quality file archives). BladeEnc supports up to 256kbps, while MusicMatch Jukebox and AudioCatalyst support up to 320kbps.

CBR/VBR Selection

By default, all encoding is carried out at CBR (constant bit rate). If the usual bit rate of 128kbps is used, then 128kbits is used to encode a second of audio, 12.8kbits for a tenth of a second and 1.28kbits for a hundredth of a second, and so on. The same amount of bits is allocated to encode a period of silence as is allocated to encode another equal period of time when there may be a great amount of audio detail in the recording. An orchestra playing a dramatic background to a piece of dialogue, with included sound effects is a very complex piece of audio and requires more bits to encode it. Since CBR runs at a constant rate, bits are wasted during quiet times and are in short supply during complex passages. The result is a loss of quality during the complex passages and a consequent variation of quality throughout the clip.
The only solution is to use a bit rate that is high enough to cope with the most detailed audio passage. This would greatly enlarge the size of the audio file, to cope with a small proportion of the clip time. This is only currently a viable option for broadcast systems.

VBR (variable bit rate) encoding tackles the problem by allocating the same average bit rate dynamically. This means that a VBR setting of 128kbps would pass an <u>average</u> of 128kbits of data per second, and would allocate the bits as required - allocating less bits for quiet passages and more bits for complex passages. The overall effect is to provide a fixed quality throughout the sample.
MusicMatch Jukebox and AudioCatalyst, for example, both allow the selection of VBR. The OGG Vorbis format only uses VBR.

Speed vs Quality

The encoding *'algorithm'* is the program's method of achieving the compression. When many files are being processed in batch mode, the speed of encoding is an important factor. But, even more important at the professional end of the market, is the quality of the completed file.
The record for the fastest encoding speed is currently held by AudioCatalyst. However, AudioCatalyst is faster because it uses the *'Xing'* algorithm and this ignores all audio above 16kHz. Most applications, such as MusicMatch Jukebox and MP3 Producer, use the *'Fraunhofer'* algorithm. This is slightly slower because it processes up to 20kHz. The trade between audio quality and encoding speed is a matter of preference. If the files are destined for web sites, they may already have had their sampling rate and dynamic range reduced to reduce file size and any small reduction in quality may be of no significance. If the files are destined for professional use, or for playing over high quality amplifiers, then the quality of the encoding algorithm is more important than final file size.

The illustration shows the Thomson encoder converting a WAV file into a 64kbps MP3Pro file. This is a combined player and encoder and can also convert MP3 or MP3Pro files to WAV format.

Other facilities

- The extra facilities offered by different packages vary and may include options to:
- Play each track while compressing in real time.
- Convert between audio file formats, particularly WAV, MP3, WMA.
- Add lyrics to song files.
- Fetch song titles from the on-line database of CDs and their track details (CDDB at www.cddb.com).
- Encode audio direct from the computer's soundcard (e.g. as with AudioCatalyst).

Converting MP3s to WAVs

With the growth in the number of files that are now available in MP3 format, there is also a need to be able to convert them into other formats.   Likely reasons for the conversion are:

- To integrate into multimedia packages that do not support MP3 files.
- To write to CD-R as CD audio tracks that can be read on any domestic or car CD player.   Most CD writing software uses WAV files as the source for creating audio CDs, although CD Creator 4 can convert MP3 files directly into CD audio tracks for burning.

Most modern applications now provide facilities to convert between formats.

Using Winamp

The freeware Winamp MP3 player package can also be used to convert MP3 files into WAV files.   The exact steps vary with the Winamp version, but the general steps are:

- Open Winamp's Playlist Editor.
- Load in the MP3 files to be converted.
- Select the *'Options'* from the main menu.
- Select the *'Preferences'* option and click on its *'Output'* tab, as shown..
- Set the *'Output Device'* to WAV (sometimes marked as *'Nullsoft Disk Writer'*).
- Select a destination folder for the new files.
- Click *'OK'* to return to the main screen.
- Click on the play control to convert the files.

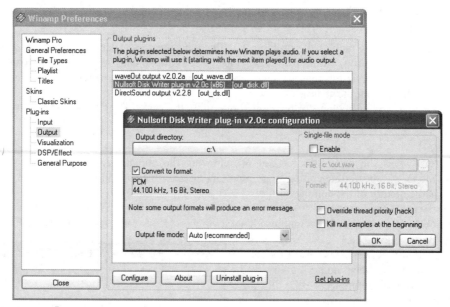

Other Conversions

Sound Recorder is capable of carrying out a range of file conversions.   After a file is loaded, choose the *'Properties'* option from the *'File'* menu.   Choose *'Recording Formats'* from the *'Format Conversion'* dialogue box.   Click *'Convert Now'* and choose the new format from the drop-down list.   Click *'OK'*, play the converted sound and save it if is satisfactory.

The illustration below shows the Windows Media Encoder converting a WAV file into a WMA file.

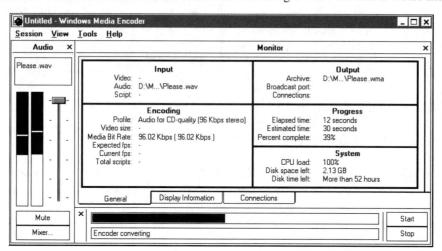

This software also converts Audio CDs, MP3 and OGG files to WMA format.

This illustration shows RealProducer creating a Real Audio file from a WAV file.

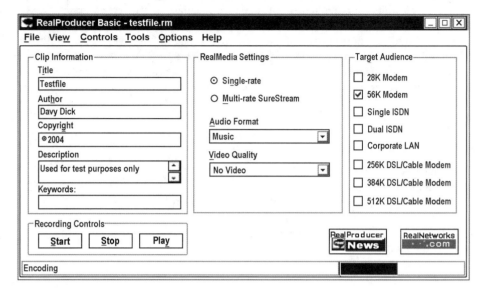

Music

There are two distinct categories of music reproduction with the PC:

- Replaying pre-recorded music to liven up a presentation, impart information, or for personal pleasure.
- The creation of musical pieces.

The first category requires no knowledge of music theory as the *'artistic'* work has already been done. The user only requires to connect the correct equipment and to install and use the correct software. The creation of new musical pieces is not considered here.

A basic musical piece will, in general, contain a table of musical notes, played in sequence much like a musical score. Each note has a number of characteristics:

Frequency

Note	Frequency	Note	Frequency	Note	Frequency	Note	Frequency
C	65.41	C	130.81	C	261.63	C	523.25
C#	69.30	C#	138.59	C#	277.18	C#	554.37
D	73.42	D	146.83	D	293.66	D	587.33
D#	77.78	D#	155.56	D#	311.13	D#	622.25
E	82.41	E	164.81	E	329.63	E	659.26
F	87.31	F	174.61	F	349.23	F	698.46
F#	92.50	F#	185.00	F#	369.99	F#	739.99
G	98.00	G	196.00	G	392.00	G	783.99
G#	103.83	G#	207.65	G#	415.30	G#	830.61
A	110.00	A	220.00	A	440.00	A	880.00
A#	116.54	A#	233.08	A#	466.16	A#	932.33
B	123.47	B	246.94	B	493.88	B	987.77

The table shows a range of musical notes and their corresponding frequencies.

All instruments would produce the same frequency for a given note, even though the sound of the notes may be widely different.   A saxophone and a piano, for example, would both produce exactly the same frequency for Middle C on the musical scale.
 The notes are often referred to as having *'pitch'* rather than frequency.   A note may have a *'vibrato'* effect superimposed upon it, with the note being swung above and below the original frequency.   In such a case the frequency is always slightly altering but there remains a base frequency - the pitch.

Timbre

The difference between musical instruments lies in their different harmonic mixes, as explained earlier. The mix of harmonics and their relative strengths is referred to as the instrument's timbre (pronounced *'tamber'*).   Sound cards may refer to the *'voices'* they support.   These are usually the number of different instruments that the card's synthesiser is capable of playing concurrently.   Each of these voices will correspond to an instrument timbre but it is likely that the card will handle more instruments (timbres) than it is capable of playing concurrently.

Duration

Each note's length is considered relative to the other notes in the musical piece, since a musical work can be played at differing paces.   The diagram shows the relative lengths of the commonly used durations.   So, a Semi-Breve lasts 32 longer than a Demi-Semi-Quaver, regardless of the tempo of the piece being played.   The note lengths would be supplemented by 'rests' of various durations.   These are short periods of silence.   A rest may be used as part of the overall composition or may be inserted between notes to make note distinct to the listener.   This is more important where there is a long run of notes of the same frequency, as the listener must discern different notes rather than hear a continuous longer note.

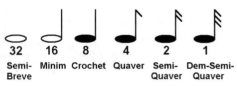

Other attributes

The sound is often described in terms of its *'envelope'* and this encompasses four different features - often called the ADSR.

ATTACK   The speed at which the note's initial
                volume increases.
DECAY   The speed at which the volume fades away.
SUSTAIN   The main amplitude that is maintained during the
                note (e.g. if a synthesiser keyboard key is
                held down).
RELEASE   The time it takes for the sound to completely stop.

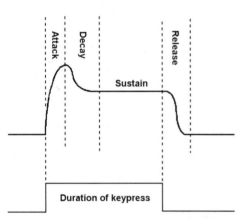

Music formats

Music formats vary with the following being the most common:

CMF : The Creative Music Format was introduced with the Sound Blaster card. It uses instruments defined in the file, or in .SBI Sound Blaster Instrument files, along with a note sequence, to play the music. CMF music is generally not as good as some other formats, but produces compact files.

ROL : Similar in basic idea to the CMF file, the ROL musical format was introduced with the Roland sound card. Again, it generally means small files, but slightly lesser quality.

MOD : Designed on the Amiga, the MODule format uses digitised instruments played at different sampling frequencies. Since each instrument is digitised, MOD files have a much more convincing, realistic feel, but are usually slightly larger files. MOD files are prolific on BBS services, and other than MIDI, it is probably the most used music format on PCs.

WAV : Introduced along with Windows, the WAV file format is a simple sound sample with a short file header. It is used for music as well as speech, sound effects, etc. The benefit of WAV files is that many Windows programs can use them with a single Windows sound driver.   Of course, the Windows sound driver is not limited to WAV files, but Windows programs themselves tend to prefer WAV files since they are the native format for Windows sound.

MP3 : Uses a compression ratio of up to 12:1 to produce compact audio files for playing from a computer, or from a dedicated portable MP3 player. See earlier in the chapter for more details.

MIDI

The *'Musical Instrument Digital Interface'* was developed as a standard interface between different pieces of musical apparatus such as electronic keyboards, synthesisers, sequencers, drum machines, etc. These were initially produced by different manufacturers with different interfaces and were notoriously difficult to connect together.   As a response, the first MIDI standard was introduced in 1983 as an agreement between manufacturers.   This standard (The MIDI 1.0 Specification) specifically mentioned the use of home computers but MIDI-compatible items can be connected and used together without the need for a computer.   However, there are many benefits from using a computer in a MIDI music system.   When music is played directly at a music keyboard, the keystrokes can be saved and manipulated.   The computer can be used to synchronise the notes more accurately, allow cut and paste of passages of music, etc.   The completed piece can be saved for later playing through a MIDI music device.   MIDI music can be played through computer sound cards, but is much better when used in conjunction with MIDI connected instruments such as keyboards. This allows the computer to read a .MID file and thereby tell the MIDI instrument which notes to play. The result is that the sound comes from a dedicated musical instrument rather than a simple wave modulator.   This usually provides a superior and more versatile result.   However, sound cards are available which incorporate the quality waveforms associated with external instruments.   GM (General MIDI) compatibility allows the playing of commercially produced MIDI music files.   It is an extension of the MIDI specification, such that specific channels and voices are linked to specific pre-defined sounds (e.g. 26 is always an electric guitar).

The MIDI interface

External connections to MIDI instruments require a dedicated MIDI port on the computer. This is either directly available from a sound card or is supplied as an add-on to a sound card. The MIDI standard specifies both the hardware and software requirements for the interface.

Hardware

The computer's MIDI connection will have both an input and an output socket. The input connector (marked as 'MIDI IN') can be used to receive input from an electronic keyboard. The output connector (marked as 'MIDI OUT') takes the messages from the computer to the external synthesisers, etc. Many MIDI devices also support a MIDI THRU connector and this reproduces whatever appears on the device's MIDI IN socket. This allows multiple MIDI devices to be connected together.

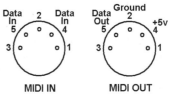

The connectors are of 180-degree 5-pin DIN type and pins 1 and 3 are not used and have no wired connections. The connecting cable is twisted-pair wires with a protective shielding to prevent electrical interference to the signal. It is important that this shield is only connected at the one end, to provide interference protection while maintaining the electrical isolation of both devices.

The messages are passed in serial format comprising byte-sized packets as shown in the diagram. The signal is very similar to that used in the RS232 serial interface. The signals are asynchronous and have a start bit, eight data bits and a stop bit. The start and stop bits are used to ensure the proper synchronisation of the data (i.e. the receiving device is able to properly decode the status of each data bit at any

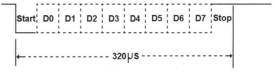

one point in time. No parity bit is used. The ten bits require a time of 320 microseconds. This means that the MIDI messaging system runs at a 31.25Kbaud rate. This is a relatively slow interface but it is a simple serial device saving the use of multicore cable or multi-wire ribbon cable to connect devices. Cables must be a maximum of 50ft in length.

Messages

Note that the MIDI message does not contain any actual sounds embedded in it. The message contains a <u>description</u> of each note in terms of its frequency, timing and timbre (which musical instrument). Each message is spread over several bytes and typical information includes:

Message	Meaning		
Note on	indicates the start of information on a note.		
Channel number	indicates which of the 16 available channels to use. This is allocated to a particular instrument and acts like a single recording track on a conventional recording studio system. However, different devices may use a particular channel number for different instruments. So, a note intended for a guitar may be reproduced as a piccolo. Windows includes a *'MIDI Mapper'* utility to map the correct instruments for particular MIDI devices.		
Key	indicates the pitch of the note.	Duration	indicates the note's length.
Volume	indicates the note's amplitude.	Velocity	indicates how hard a key was struck.
Note off	indicates the end of the note information.		

These explanations simplify the process and interested readers are advised to read up on the more detailed issues of Omni Mode, Poly Mode, Channel and System Messages and the detailed content of the Data Bytes. The use of sophisticated software for music score writing and printing is also beyond the scope of this chapter.

Digital Video

VIDEO - an introduction

Of all the multimedia components, video has the greatest impact. The message for the viewer may be adequately contained in the project's text but a picture commands more instant attention. A moving picture has yet even more appeal, where "seeing is believing". It provides an immediate perception and can convey feeling and influence attitudes. The viewer can see the effects of natural disasters or the plight of refugees, making the point much more vividly than words alone. This is well recognised and news reports and charities make good use of video to create the desired impression.

Video is also an important tool to further understanding of a situation or a process. A simple video clip, demonstrating how a car's spark plug is changed, is worth thousands of words of explanation.

For these reasons, video is now found in many applications - in information kiosks, on CD-R, on web sites, etc.

Video is a sequence of individual pictures which, when displayed on the screen at a fast enough rate, provide the illusion of movement. This technique is used to project movies in cinema theatres and transmit television pictures. It also used by camcorders to capture moving sequences.

Each picture is called a 'Frame' and the more frames that are displayed in each second, the smoother is the perceived motion. The 'frame rate' describes the number of individual frames that are displayed each second and is measured in frames per second (fps).

The chart shows the number of frames displayed per second in various systems, to maintain the illusion of continuous movement.

Computer video is the term used to describe the set of pictures taken out of the camcorder and stored as a computer file on the hard disk. The audio that is recorded along with the video is included within the video file. It is not saved as a separate audio WAV file.

Typical frame rates and their uses	
0fps	Still frame
10fps	Web video
15fps	Minimum acceptable for motion
24fps	Motion pictures
25fps	British television (PAL)
30fps	American television (NTSC)

The early days

Video remained a specialist area for many years. Traditional cine cameras used rolls of film that had to be processed before they could be viewed or edited. Since film processing took time, there was no way of knowing that the scene had been properly recorded. Multiple takes had to be made to ensure that one clip would be usable. The editing of developed cine film was largely a job for experts. Apart from the simple cutting and splicing of pieces of filmstrip, all other editing tasks required studio facilities.

The introduction of analogue video cameras changed all that. The scene was recorded on to videotape and the tape could be instantly rewound and played back, to examine the scene. However the editing process was analogue based and very expensive. Editing consoles were cumbersome and used a process known as 'Linear Editing'. The editing equipment was based on the mechanical movement of videotape, with multiple players and recorders being used to copy clips back and forth. Putting special effects on a project required special electronic devices.

Benefits of digital editing

The breakthrough came with the arrival of the computer video capture card. Video footage taken from VCRs and camcorders could now be converted into computer files and these files could be edited within the computer. Transition effects and special effects were easily applied to provide professional results at a fraction of the price of previous methods. It uses 'Non-Linear Editing', where all the video content is stored digitally and processed digitally. Once the clips are taken off the tape, the camera equipment plays no further role in the editing process.

Like analogue, there is no reel of film, no processing and no waiting time. However, the computer software has the distinct advantage of easily manipulating the digital clips. Individual scenes can be deleted, cropped, optimised, re-ordered and have effects added. Every individual frame of the video clip can be cleaned up, sharpened, tinted, and so on, with all the work being carried out by the computer program. The computer's CPU is used to figure out all the changes necessary to achieve the special effects. This allows a whole range of special effects that were previously impossible or very expensive to achieve.

Current PC video editing software can quite easily provide such facilities as:

- Titles (fixed titles, scrolling credits, sub-titles, etc)
- Chroma key (a foreground object is superimposed on a different background scene)
- Fades (one scene is faded down as the next scene becomes visible)
- Dissolves (one scene merges into the next scene)
- Wipes (one scene moves on to the screen as another is pushed off)

These are discussed further in the chapter on video editing.

The initial limitation with NLE (non-linear editing) was the specification of computers. They did not have the processing power, data transfer rates or storage capacity required to handle large video files. Modern computers have fast processors, loads of spare memory and large fast hard disks and these have begun to alleviate the problem.

However, there is still a long way to go before all users have computers that are capable of displaying full-screen, high resolution, fast-moving video.

Overview of the process

As the illustration shows, many different video sources may require to be incorporated into a multimedia project. The computer system has to be capable of dealing with some, or all, of these different sources.

A summary of the entire video process is:

Camcorder ⇒ link to computer ⇒ computer file ⇒ editing software ⇒ final output media.

The above stages are:

- The camcorder records the video scenes.
- The camcorder's output is fed to the computer's video capture device (usually a plug-in capture card or interface card).
- The computer hardware/software turn the video signal into a computer file that is saved to hard drive as a disk file.   This is known as *'digitising'* and the file may also be compressed at this stage.
- The computer's editing software uses this file, along with others, to compose a complete video/audio/animation sequence.
- The completed project is output to one or more media formats. This could include outputting to video tape, uploading to a web site, or recording on a CD or DVD.

The block diagram below highlights the main features of creating digital video and each feature is briefly explained below.

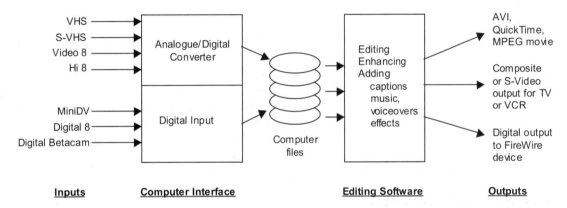

| Inputs | Computer Interface | Editing Software | Outputs |

Inputs

The diagram shows the range of possible connections to a video capture card or interface card. Of course, not all are used at the same time.

There are two basic type of video input:

| Analogue | These may be of different qualities (VHS, S-VHS, Video 8, Hi8) and may use different signal processing methods (composite, S-Video) |
| Digital | These may use different digital formats (MiniDV, Digital 8, Digital Betacam) |

Computer Interface

The purpose of the computer interface is to get a copy of the video clip content held on the videotape into the computer as a disk file.   Most older camcorders record on to the videotape in analogue format, while newer camcorders record the video content on to the tape as digital data.

As a result, there are two different types of interface, as shown in the diagram on the previous page.

| Analogue | The electronics inside the video capture card converts the incoming analogue video clips to digital files (i.e. the Analogue to Digital Converter shown in the diagram). |
| Digital | Some camcorders record in digital format on to tape and the video data is transferred directly to computer in digital format.   They do not need to be converted from analogue format to digital format and so do not use the analogue/digital conversion system.   This digital interface is known as an IEEE 1394, or *'FireWire'*, connection. |

Some interface cards provide both analogue and digital connections. In this case, the analogue signal is digitised while the digital connections bypass that circuitry.

Editing Software

The editing software is used to prepare the content.   This involves activities such as trimming the clips, placing them in the required playing order and adding effects, transitions, titles, overlays and audio dubbing (see the chapter on video editing).

Outputs

The finished project consists of one or more video clips, stored on the computer's hard disk.   If the interface card has composite or S-Video output sockets, the disk files can be converted back into a television format, for feeding directly to a television set or to the inputs of a VCR.   This tape output would be in PAL format for UK VCRs or televisions. (See the video editing chapter for details of TV standards).

FireWire cards have *'digital out'* connections that allow the video files to be sent to other digital devices such as a camcorder's DV-in socket or a Sony MiniDisc recording input.   The content remains digital throughout these data transfers, avoiding the losses and distortion associated with analogue/digital conversions.

More commonly, the files are held on disk in a file format that is easily integrated into larger multimedia productions. Likely file types are AVI, QuickTime movie and MPEG (versions 1, 2 and 4).

Before saving the file, a number of decisions have to be made about the clips' characteristics.
These are:

- Choose the final desired screen resolution.
- Choose the file's data rate.
- Choose the compression method.
- Choosing a frame rate for the clip.

These characteristics and their effects are explained in this chapter and in the chapter on video editing.

Creating a project

The steps for creating a video project are:
Plan the shoot.

- Prepare all necessary resources.
- Shoot the clips.
- Digitise and store the clips.
- Edit and compose the project
- Review the final project.

The steps surrounding the recording are often divided into two categories - pre-production and post production.   The pre-production phase includes issues such as research, scripting, storyboarding, scheduling, and logging.   They are all designed to save shooting time (the expensive bit) and wasted editing time (the other expensive bit).   This stage might also include resource gathering such as purchasing royalty free CDs, recording voiceovers and background music, etc.

The post-production phase covers the tasks of digitising, editing, formatting and outputting the project.

Recording Technology

The basic principle of the camcorder is simple.   The light reflected from the subject being recorded is converted from light variations into electrical variations.   These electrical variations are then recorded on to a cassette tape.   For domestic use, the recorded video is played through a television set.   For multimedia use, the changing electrical content is converted into digital information on hard disk.

Light passes through the camcorder lens and is converted into electrical signals by one or more CCDs (charge-coupled devices).   See the chapter on digital photography for more details. The CCD specification fitted to different camcorder models varies and typical examples range from under 500,000 to over one and a half million pixels.   A typical CCD size is ↓" to ¼", with a professional model being around ½".

Each row and column of the CCD's sensors corresponds to the picture's horizontal and vertical resolution.   The values from each row are read off and make up the serial video output stream.   The lines are read off in an *'interlaced'* manner.   First, all the odd lines are read followed by all the even lines being read.   Each set of alternate lines is known as a *'field'* and the two fields are combined to compose the complete picture, known as the *'frame'*. Each field is read off in 1/50th of a second and a complete frame is built up every 1/25th of a second.   This provides the 25fps (frames per second) associated with UK video.   This speed was chosen to match the frame rate of UK television systems.   In the USA, the frame rate is 30fps and so the lines are read 60 times per second.   Interlacing is only used for television reproduction and the capture card converts the picture into a non-interlaced version for computer use (See the chapter on technology for more information).

The camera has three colour outputs, one each for the red, green and blue components of the picture.   It also has an output that carries synchronisation information, so that the device receiving the signal knows when to start a new scan line or to return to the top of the screen.

Camera signal processing

Every camera works in the ways described above. With analogue systems, such as Composite Video, S-Video and Component Video, the output is kept in an analogue state while it is stored to a VCR or transmitted as a television picture.   With digital systems, such as MiniDV camcorders and digital television, the signals are digitised before being stored or transmitted.

S-Video

The three colour signals store all the information about the picture's colour.   They also, in total, store all the information about the brightness of the picture.

The brightness (known as *'Luminance'* and represented by the letter *'Y'*) can be separately extracted to supply, along with the synchronisation information, a monochrome picture.   The remainder, the colour picture with the luminance removed, is known as the *'Chrominance'*.

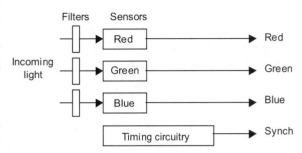

Put another way, chrominance information is the extra information that is required to turn a monochrome picture into a colour picture. This system is used to provide the *'S-Video'* output that is available on most decent camcorders. S-Video stands for Separate Video and it can be used with both PAL and NTSC systems.

The diagram shows the layout of the female S-Video connector.   It is the same size as a PS/2 mini-DIN socket and has four pins.   Pin 3 carries the luminance information and pin 4 carries the chrominance information. The other two pins are at ground potential.   Although better quality than composite video, the picture is sometimes degraded due to *'chroma crosstalk'* which is the leakage of chrominance information into the luminance channel. This produces some moiré effects on the final picture.

Composite Video

When all the signals are mixed together on to a single output socket, it is described as *'composite video'*.   This is the most common form of analogue output to be found on camcorders.   Having a single output cable is convenient and the receiving device (the television set or the video capture card) is left to unscramble this information back into C and Y signals and from there back into RGB signals.   However, there is a certain amount of mutual interference between signals when they are composited and this reduces the final picture quality.   The most common artifact is the colour strobing that appears on moving patterns such as a presenter's tweed jacket.   Highly saturated vertical edges can also result in dots crawling along the edge.

RGB

When all four signals are separately output, it is described as *'RGB'* output.   This method does not create luminance and chrominance channels.   It simply outputs the relative intensities of the red, green and blue components of the incoming picture at any point in time. This produces the highest quality output, as there are no processing losses associated with the other methods.   Resolution is a direct function of the bandwidth of each channel. This type of output requires four sockets and four separate connecting leads.   The

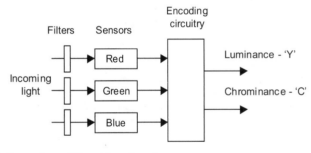

fourth connection carries the timing and synchronisation information of the video signal.

Digital Video

The technique used with digital video is to convert the signal into luminance and two chroma channels.   This is known as *'component video'*.

The DV circuitry records the picture as three separate components:

- The Luminance (the basic monochrome picture information) and the synchronisation pulses - known together as the *'Y'* signal.
- The Chrominance signal, which is broken into two component signals known as *'R-Y'* and *'B-Y'*.   These are described as the *'colour difference'* signals, and the three analogue values are described as *'YUV'* signals. Once the colour difference signals are digitised, they are called the *'Cr'* and *'Cb'* components and the overall signal is described as *'YCbCr'*.

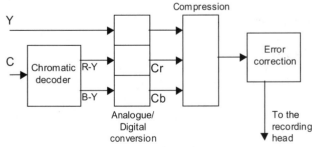

This is similar to the method used for television broadcasting, as the transmission of two colour difference signals requires less bandwidth than the three original red, green and blue channels.

The amplitude of each of the three component signals is represented by an 8-bit value.

All three analogue components have to be sampled to digitise them and the *'sampling rate'* of the various components is expressed as a ratio. DV uses a 4:1:1 ratio for NTSC and 4:0:0 for PAL systems. This means that the luminance signal is sampled four times more often than the two colour components. Professional formats, such as Digital Betacam (DB), use the ITU-R 601 standard of 4:2:2 as a sampling ratio to ensure higher resolution. The chrominance information is sampled less often, as the human eye does resolve chrominance information as effectively as luminance information, allowing for bandwidth savings.

The actual data rate for DV, excluding audio is:

Horizontal resolution x vertical resolution x 1.5 samples/pixel

For DV PAL formats, the data rate is

720 x 576 x 25 x 1.5 x 8 = 15,552,000 samples per sec

The three signals are then passed through compression circuitry in the camera, known as DV25, which achieves around 5:1 compression. The video is compressed, frame at a time, using the same DCT (Discrete Cosine Transform) method that is used with JPEG stills compression. The signal is then passed through very effective error correction circuitry before being sent through the camcorder's recording circuitry to the recording head.

Adding in the audio stream, etc. brings the data rate of DV to around 3.6MB/sec.

Unlike other formats, DV is a fixed data rate. The compression, screen size and data rate are all fixed.

Progressive scan

Many digital camcorders now provide the ability to take still pictures. Having still and video capture in a single camera is a useful bonus and the facilities of the camcorder are usually better than those provided on digital cameras. For example, the lens on a camcorder is often of higher quality and the zoom range is greatly superior (usually around 10x compared to a still camera's 3x zoom).

The great problem with capturing stills from a camcorder is the way that the picture is constituted from two separate fields. It takes a 1/50th of a second to complete the scan of the odd fields of an interlaced picture. So, by the time the start of the even fields is started the adjacent lines are always separated in time by 1/50th of a second. If the subject is moving, this will cause blurring of the combined picture. The solution rests in progressive scanning, where the entire picture is scanned as a single frame. The frame is then broken up into single fields for recording in interlaced mode as normal. When a still is required, the information is taken from the complete frame version that was captured before being split into fields. To the video world, a progressive scan system has an identical output to an interlaced scan model. But, for the still pictures, the best possible picture is saved, with minimum blurring.

Camcorder Specifications

A camcorder's specification is viewed in terms of its quality of recording and its variety of recording features. The intrinsic quality of the construction reflects in the condition of the final recording. Construction issues include the quality of the lens, the quality of the electronic components, and the stability of the drive mechanism. The optical and light gathering system in better camcorders results in sharper pictures and improved colours. The better quality components result in less unwanted picture noise. The better mechanism results in smoother sequences, with lessened jerkiness of the recorded clip.

The ingenuity and skills of the camera operator or the video editor cannot adequately compensate for deficiencies in the camcorder equipment's components. Camcorder manufacturers often emphasise the additional features that are supported by their models. Some features, such as image stabilisation add to the quality of the recording. Other features, such as built-in titlers, fades and effects, are aimed at hobbyists, as more control over such effects can be exerted during the editing process. Within limits, it is always best to obtain the highest-quality equipment that can be afforded.

Analogue and digital features

The following features and characteristics are available in models that are based on analogue recording or digital recording. The additional features found on digital camcorders are covered separately.

Lens/Filters

These features are covered in the chapter on digital photography.

Zoom Range

The lens has a variable focal length so that can be varied from wide angle, through normal to telephoto. This is covered more fully in the chapter on digital photography. The optical zoom range of a camcorder is typically up to 10X or 15X. Most camcorders also provide a further digital zoom factor (e.g. some models provide up to 180X digital zoom). The optical zoom should be used at all times, unless a deliberately blocky effect is required (see chapter on digital photography).

Some camcorders also provide a *'Macro'* facility. This allows the camcorder to remain in focus while up close to very small objects, some positioned right up to the lens. In this way, small objects such as insects, watch mechanisms, etc. can be shot. In this mode, the depth of field is small and the subject is difficult to illuminate as the camcorder blocks the light.

Most camcorders provide a motorised zoom. While a manual zoom is perfectly useful for framing a scene before shooting, it is less suitable for zooming while a recording is taking place. The power zoom provides a smoother control.

Number of CCDs

Triple-chip CCDs produce improved light sensitivity and colour reproduction compared to single-chip CCDs, although the camcorder is significantly more expensive.

Image Stabilisation

The image stabiliser system keeps the image steady when using the telephoto zoom setting and prevents jitters from minor camera movements. Optical stabilisation mechanically alters the lens to maintain a stable picture as the camera shakes. This is the most expensive option. Electronic stabilisation is cheaper but less effective. It does not allocate all the available sensors in its CCD array. Some are only used when the camera shakes and are not counted in the overall picture resolution. When the camera shakes, the electronics uses the light from these extra rows or columns to replace the rows or columns displaced by the camera movement. The result is that a picture area identical to the previous area is sent for storage.

Viewfinder

A camcorder may provide a foldout LCD panel, to allow the camera operator to see exactly what is being recorded. As an alternative, or as an addition, it may provide an internal optical or electronic viewfinder. The advantages of each method are discussed in the chapter on digital photography.

Remote Control

This is a handheld infrared remote control, similar to the type used to control a VCR. This allows control of the camera without the operator being close to the equipment. This is useful for the recording where the operator's presence is

- Obtrusive (e.g. recording wildlife). The camcorder is hidden in a bush or under branches and is operated from a distance.
- Dangerous (e.g. recording car racing). The camcorder is mounted on a tripod next to the track and operated from a safe distance.
- Impossible (e.g. recording in a small crevice, over a cliff edge). The camcorder is fixed to a pole that can be mounted where required and operated with the remote control.

Since the remote control also has playback buttons, it can be used with the camcorder connected to a television's video input sockets. In this mode, the camcorder acts like a VCR and the user operates the start, stop, rewind, fast forward and pause buttons in the same way as operating a TV remote control.

Time Code

This feature is mostly found in digital camcorders but is also available on top end analogue systems.

Every frame of the video clip includes a value that denotes how far into the tape the frame appears. It is measured in hours, minutes, seconds and number of frames. So, for example, a time code of 01:22:07:19 indicates that the frame appears 1 hour, 22 minutes, 7 seconds and 19 frames into the tape. A PAL camcorder counts frames from zero up to 23. Then the seconds figure is incremented by 1 and the frame count resets to zero. This is very useful later for accurate video editing, as the editing software can control the camcorder's tape mechanism to capture a specific range of frames, or a particular batch of clips from a tape. A new tape does not have a timecode and this is only written when the tape is first recorded on. New tapes should be *"blacked"* before use. This involves recording on the tape, usually with the lens cap on, to record a continuous timecode series along the tape. Otherwise, a gap in the timecode can be created, upsetting the automated capture process from the tape. A gap can be created by viewing a recording and stopping the tape slightly beyond the last recorded frame on the tape. When recording the next shot, the timecode is not contiguous (possibly reset to zero). Blacking prevents any possible break in the tape's continuous timecode.

Automatic/Manual Controls

Camcorders usually automatically adjust their focus and exposure settings in response to the nature of the incoming light. While this is satisfactory for *'point and shoot'* situations, the operator will often require more control than the default automatic settings. For example, the camcorder's auto focus allows the subject to remain in focus whether at close range or at long distance. The operator, however, may wish to have the foreground subject out of focus, with the background being in focus. Similarly, special effects can be obtained by setting the white balance to a value other than the default.

The camcorder should provide a manual override on exposure, focussing and other settings.

Low Light Filming

There will be times when filming is carried out in less than ideal lighting conditions. If an event takes place in overcast weather conditions or at dusk, the camcorder should still be able to capture the scene with some degree of usefulness. Camcorders have varying abilities in this regard. Models with low *'lux'* values can record in lesser light conditions than models that demand a higher illumination. Typical current values range from 0 lux to 11 lux, with some models offering 0 lux for nightshots. This issue is covered later.

Shutter Speeds

The camera allows light in as a series of snapshots. The frequency of these snapshots is called the *'field rate'*, while the time that the lens is opened for each shot is termed the *'shutter speed'*. Variable shutter speeds range from slow values (1/3, 1/6, 1/12 sec) for filming in low light conditions, to high values (1/50 to 1/10,000 sec) for filming fast moving objects. With fast shutter speeds, the camcorder still samples at 50 times per sec, but the sensor is exposed to the light source for a shorter time.   Since the object moves less in the shorter time, there is less blur.   The shortened exposure time means that high shutter speeds only work in good lighting.

Audio Features

The chapter on digital audio covers the types and uses of microphones. Nearly all camcorders provide some sort of built-in microphone. This is only of use for quick point and shoot recordings, where there is no time to set up a superior audio system. The microphone should at least face the direction that the lens is being pointed.   Some microphones point towards the sky and some actually face *away* from the subject being recorded.   The camcorder should have provision for the connection of an external mike, usually a microphone socket and shoe mount.   The external mike is necessary to prevent the pickup of camera motor noise, the operator's breathing and to get closer to the source that actually needs to be recorded.   The camcorder should also provide a headphone socket, so that a set of headphones can be connected to monitor the quality of the incoming sound.

Digital only features:

The features mentioned above are all applicable to digital camcorders and the list below covers the additional features that would only be expected with a digital camcorder.

Digital Interface

Every digital camcorder has a DVi link, also known as an IEEE1394 or FireWire output. This enables the digital recording to be transferred to the computer via its FireWire connection.   Older and cheaper models only provide a digital out connection.   The camcorder should also have a connection that allows the digital output from the computer to be recorded back to the camcorder.   This is a separate FireWire connection and is marketed as *'DV-in'*.

Digital Stills

A growing number of camcorders now provide facilities for capturing still pictures. The data from a single frame is taken from the CCDs and handled as a digital file that can be stored separately.   Most record a still onto the videotape as a short video clip (of perhaps seven seconds), normally allowing a voiceover to accompany the still.   Some Sony camcorders use a separate *'Sony Memory Stick'* to store still images.

Progressive Scan

Progressive scan CCD provides the best quality stills. These camcorders process images by the frame rather than the field (see earlier in this chapter).   Their output is not so good if it is going back to a television screen, but it is better for computer applications as the picture is improved (it contains no artifacts caused by the interlacing process).

Special Effects

Digital camcorders can easily incorporate special effects and scene transitions (wipes, dissolves, fades, titler, sepia, strobe, monochrome, mosaic, negative, pastel, etc) as the movie is being shot.   This is useful for amateur moviemakers but is mostly left unused by operators shooting for multimedia (as these effects and more can be added at the editing stage.   If the effects are applied at the editing stage, they can be removed or altered.   Effects embedded during video recording can not be removed later, to recover the original footage underneath.

Chroma Key

A digital still picture is stored in memory to fill a blue background of a live image (e.g. Sony use their Memory Stick for this purpose).

Typical camera connections	
Connection	**Description**
Power	Used to recharge batteries, or to run the camcorder directly.
Composite video	Used to connect to a video capture card, domestic VCR or television with composite input (usually RCA sockets). The yellow socket carries the video information while the stereo audio is carried by white (for left channel) and red (for right channel) sockets. The television sometimes only has a SCART socket (the standard European 21-pin connection) and a composite/SCART adapter would then be required
S-Video	Used to connect to a video capture card, S-Video recorder or a television that accepts S-Video in.
DV out	Used to connect to a FireWire card, digital recorder or another DV camcorder with a DV-in connection.
DV in	Used to connect to the output of the digital devices mentioned above.
External microphone in	Used to connect an external mike, in place of the camcorder's own internal mike.
Headphone socket	Used to connect a mike for monitoring the sound recording.
Edit control socket LAN-C	Used to connect to control circuitry for the automatic command of the camcorder functions such as play, fast forward and rewind.

Camcorder Video formats

While digital video is regarded as the future of all video recording and processing, there are a very large number of camcorders in use that still use analogue formats. The sheer size of the user base, and the vast amount of material that is already available in these formats, means that these formats have to be understood and given serious consideration.

Analogue Formats

The analogue camcorders are grouped into two quality bands:

Low-band types - VHS, VHS-C, 8mm

High-band types - S-VHS, SVHS-C and Hi8

The main characteristics of each type are considered below.

VHS

This was an early runner and is still the most popular format. It is the format used by almost all VCRs and is the distribution format for UK videotapes. It uses ½" tape (12.65mm) in a large cassette and each frame stores 250 lines of video. There is a huge existing base of source tapes, either commercial or from home taping.

VHS has been overtaken by formats with smaller cassettes, higher quality and higher resolution. In many cases, these higher formats are used for the captured, editing and storing of video. However, the popularity of VHS VCRs means that VHS format remains the most likely choice for distribution of a project in cassette form. After editing, a video project is recorded back to tape for distribution.

VHS-C

This format uses the same type of ½" tape as VHS but stores it in a smaller cassette. An adapter is used, so that the cassette can be played on a standard VHS VCR. It also stores 250 lines per picture.

S-VHS

Super-VHS is a superior format to VHS and manages to store 400 lines per picture. However, it never took off as a distribution medium, due to its large ½" tape cassette size and the fact that S-VHS tapes could not be played on existing VHS VCRs. Although it used the same cassette, it needs a S-VHS video player and these are very expensive. It remains a popular choice for the capture of analogue material.

Video 8 (8mm)

This is the most popular of the low-band types for domestic use. Its cassette is small and its tape is only 8mm wide. Although it only stores 250 lines per picture, it has an improved audio system.

The cassette will not play on a VHS player but the camera's output can be linked through composite leads.

Hi8

This is a better quality than both the 8mm and S-VHS formats. It uses metal evaporated tape and stores 400 lines per picture. It has the best audio system of the high-band types, with AFM and PCM tracks.

It uses a small cassette, which will not play on VHS VCRs.

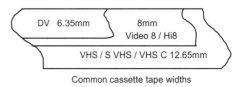

Common cassette tape widths

Digital Formats

The predominant digital format is known as *'MiniDV'*, although a new Sony format called *'Digital 8'* has been released.

DVC/ MiniDV

This format first appeared in 1995 as a standard developed by 55 manufacturers of consumer digital equipment, such as camcorders and VCRs.

All the formats discussed above record their information on to tape in analogue format (i.e. the amount that the tape is magnetised reflects the analogue level being recorded). Digital systems still record to tape but the information that is stored on the tape is purely digital (i.e. a series of '0's and '1's). This system is less prone to signal noise and level fluctuation.

Currently, MiniDV is primarily an acquisition system, not a distribution system. There are no domestic DV players and few DV decks are available. The Digital Video Cassette will not play on VHS players. Of course, the camcorder can be connected to a television's composite input, allowing the cassettes to be played (although this does not make the best use of the system's 500 line per picture capability).

MiniDV is designed for the serious amateur/semi-professional market and is the ideal format for computer and multimedia use.

It uses 6.35mm (1/4") metal evaporated tape, which is available in two cassette sizes:

Digital Video cassette sizes		
Type	Cassette Size	Description
Standard	125mm x 78mm x 14.6mm	Slightly larger than an audio cassette. Almost no models use this size. It is intended for long recordings of up to 4.5 hours.
MiniDV	66mm x 48mm x 12.4mm	This 3" x 2" cassette opened the way to a whole series of pocket-sized camcorders, with high specifications.

Digital camcorders also provide analogue outputs, so their composite or S-video outputs can be fed into an analogue video capture card, as already discussed.

The full benefit of digital camcorders is gained when the camcorder's FireWire output is connected to a computer's FireWire interface card.   This allows the data to be transferred in full 500-line digital format, without any signal degradation associated with analogue transfers. All analogue systems suffer from degradation when copying due to the losses, especially when copying from copies.   There is likely to be a loss of up to 15% of the quality each generation (i.e. each time the tape is copied). Digital systems make perfect replicas time after time.

The video signal requires a bandwidth of around 3MHz to handle the 500 horizontal lines at a PAL resolution and 25fps. The system also supports a time-code capability.

The sound track is also recorded digitally, with either two pairs of 12-bit stereo tracks or one pair of 16-bit PCM stereo tracks.

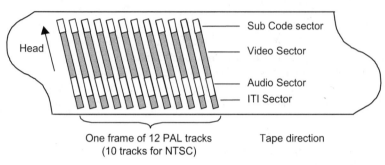

One frame of 12 PAL tracks
(10 tracks for NTSC)   Tape direction

As the diagram shows, the signal is recorded on to the tape as a set of diagonal tracks. A VHS tape would only require two tracks for each frame but DV requires much more because it contains much greater detail and requires greater bandwidth. An NTSC tape, as used in the USA, requires 10 tracks to record a full frame.   In the UK and other countries using PAL, each frame requires 12 tracks per frame.

Each track is written as four separate areas of data.   The main areas store the video and audio data, while the Sub Code sector stores data such as the time code, and the ITI sector stores tracking information for later audio dubbing and editing.

Digital 8

The Digital 8 format was introduced by Sony in 1999.   It records digital video and audio on the analogue Hi8 tapes. Digital 8 camcorders can play Digital 8, Hi8 and Video 8 recordings.   These camcorders can then digitise analogue tapes by sending the digitised version out through the *'digital out'* socket to a computer or DV edit deck.   American models also have analogue inputs and this allows analogue in/digital out conversion from VHS VCRs.   The claimed performance of 500 lines is equal to MiniDV.

MPEG

Most digital camcorders, like analogue models, record on to conventional videotapes.   The difference is that the recording format is digital instead of analogue.

However, camcorders are produced that record and compress the video in real time.   The compressed MPEG video is stored using a variety of methods, other than videotape:

- A PC Card Type III hard disk. A miniature hard disk with typically 260MB or more of storage.
- SmartMedia cards. This is typically capable of storing 10 minutes of video at 320x240, or 60 minutes at 160x120, on a 32MB card.
- A 650MB MiniDisc.
- A CD-R mini-disks (3" disks that store 190MB of data).

The video data is read later from the camcorder using a USB cable, a FireWire cable, or a SmartMedia card reader. In the case of CD-R storage, the disk is simply removed from the camcorder and placed into a computer's CD drive or DVD drive.

Professional formats

If regular high-quality shooting work is anticipated, consideration should be given to buying, or hiring, a BetaCam SP camera.   This is a professional analogue format and requires subsequent digitising with a suitable capture card.   It records between 600 and 850 lines and is the choice of broadcasters.

Other options are Pro DV systems, such as DVCAM and DVPRO, which are used for low end broadcast work.   They use the same tape as standard MiniDV (i.e. the larger of the two DV cassette sizes) but record between 500 and 850 lines.   They use a wider track pitch on the tape. This results in less recording time per DV tape, while allowing more accurate editing with editing decks.   They also produce better results for chroma-key (also known as Bluescreen) effects. DVCPRO 50, or DV50, run at double the data rate of normal DV and record at 750 to 1000 lines.   JVC produce their own standard - Digital S - it records on 750 lines on a tape that is the same size as a S-VHS cassette.   Its data rata is 50Mb/sec, compared to DV's

Performance of different video standards		
Standard	Compression	Data Rate
VHS	9:1	2MB/sec
S-VHS	6:1	3MB/sec
DV	5:1	3.6MB/sec
BetaCam	3:1	6MB/sec

25Mb/sec, the track pitch is greater, the tape speed is faster and it samples at 4:2:2 compared to DV's 4:1:1. It is by far the best digital video format. Along with the Sony BetaCam, it has received the approval of EBU for use for mainstream broadcast use.

Shooting Video

There are many excellent books that adequately cover the creative side of video filming and they are full of hints and tips on the art of scriptwriting, scouting, screen composition, direction and other related issues. This section covers the technical and practical considerations for video filming.

The first consideration is to understand the limits of the team's capabilities. Some jobs have special video demands (such as filming someone rock climbing or skydiving) or special audio knowledge (such as recording in a church or auditorium). If the job demands it, and there is any doubt over the ability to deliver, call in the professionals. The cost of hiring a team may be expensive but this should be compared to hiring a famous personality to promote a product or service then finding out that the recording was useless - after everyone has gone home. Apart from camera expertise, there are professionals who specialise in lighting or in audio capture. Bear in mind, however, there are differences between the video shot for eventual use on web sites, video streaming or any other situation where small file sizes are important. Normal video recordings remain on videotape, where there are no considerations of clip size and distribution.

Technical Considerations

Many questions on camera use are covered in the section of digital photography and that section should be read before carrying on. The following notes consider the additional factors that have to be considered for video filming compared to capturing still images.

Lighting

Precise lighting and camera settings are the key to video filming and this raises several related issues:

Colour Balancing

The *'colour temperature'* of a light source depends upon its wavelength and is measured in degrees Kelvin. Typical colour temperature readings are shown in the table. The daylight values will vary with time of day and weather conditions, from around 4000°K to 8000°K.

Typical Colour Temperatures	
6500°K	Arc light
5500°K	Average daylight
4500°K	Fluorescent lamp
3200°K	Studio floodlight
2000°K	Domestic light bulb

The camera has to be adjusted to match the *'colour temperature'* of the scene being recorded. Artificial light is warmer than daylight, while an overcast day produces light that is colder than direct sunlight. The human eye normally adjusts for these changing conditions, but the camera faithfully records what it sees. The resulting clip can have a perceived unnatural colour tinting. High colour temperatures produce a bluish tint, while lower colour temperatures produce an orange or reddish tint. This effect is seen most clearly on a white colour subject. Colour balancing is the task of adjusting the camera so that a white object is recorded as neutral white - without a cold or warm tint. Most cameras carry out this task automatically, but can be overridden for manual setting. Most cameras provide an Indoor/Outdoor option from their menus or, for older cameras, from a press button or switch.

Try to avoid mixing natural and artificial light, as the camera cannot adjust for both tints simultaneously.

Light Levels

While degrees Kelvin measures the *wavelength* of the light, it does not measure the *amount* of available light. The measurement of light illuminating a specified object is in *'lux'*. A well-lit office might be lit to around 200 lux, while domestic lighting is always substantially lower. Natural daylight can vary from a few hundred lux up to over 10,000 lux in very sunny conditions. Despite improvement in camcorder technology, the quality of footage still deteriorates as the light level drops.

The automatic exposure system in the camera adjusts the opening of the iris of the lens in response to the *average* level of incoming light. This means that the predominant level controls the iris. If the average level is high, the iris closes more to allow less light into the camera. In scenes that have mostly low light levels, the iris is opened further and the gain of the camera's internal video amplifier is turned up in an attempt to maintain the picture detail. Leaving the exposure setting on automatic can result in a number of practical problems that are covered below.

The exposure can be manually set by the operator for greater control, but the following factors have to be taken into consideration:

- Over-exposure - Allowing too much light into the camera drives up the video content levels, with all the bright details of the scene ending up at white level. Details washed out this way are irrecoverable.
- Under-exposure - Allowing too little light into the camera reduces all video content low (towards black level). The darker details end up at black level and are also irrecoverable. Since the entire video signal has a lower contrast ratio of lightest to darkest, the compression CODEC is examining a smaller dynamic range and outputs a lower range of video values. This results in excessive video noise.

Any details lost and any noise introduced during recording cannot be adequately dealt with during editing. Lighting levels of 1000 lux to 2000 lux for the foreground subject and roughly half these levels for the background will result in a lens that is stopped down and a signal that is lifted out of noise.

Low Light Level Filming

Of course, there are times when low level lighting is an integral part of the shoot (e.g. Shooting a night scene or inside a dark castle).   Viewers expect to view murky pictures; that's all part of the atmosphere and is perfectly acceptable. Manufacturer's specifications quote camcorders as recording at very low lux levels (e.g. the Sony PC100 works at only 7 lux).   These are the *minimum* figures for achieving any kind of video signal and do not indicate the level for normal satisfactory recording.   Nevertheless, there are advantages to cameras that work at low lux levels, as they allow recording of wildlife, surveillance recording, etc.

Some cameras offer *'NightShot'* facilities and these record scenes as low as zero lux.   Since this level is complete darkness, the camera uses infra-red transmitters and filters to records these scenes.   The output from these recordings is lacking in all colours, apart from a slight tinge of green (similar to that the monochrome display expected from using nightlights).   The transmitters may be built round the front of the camera or may be sold as an infra-red spotlight attachment.

Backlighting

The camcorder's automatic exposure control adjusts itself to compensate for changes in incoming light.   This causes problems where there is backlighting. For example, a person may be filmed in a seated position, with darks trees as a background. As the person stands up, he/she is gone from the dark background and now is silhouetted on a sunny sky as a background. Other examples are people walking in front of a window or patio doors, or sitting down next to a table light or candles. Other sources of backlighting are car headlights, street lamps, domestic lamps and office fluorescent strips.

When these situations occur, the camera adjusts to the increased average light by allowing less light into the lens. This dims the foreground subject.

It is best to either avoid these situations, provide additional front lighting, or switch to manual over-ride (some cameras provide a *'Back Light'* button). The aim is to sacrifice the background, which may be washed, so that the subject is adequately exposed. Sometimes backlighting is used for effect. A person standing against the sun has a halo effect around them, or a church, castle, hills or other objects can be silhouetted against the sky.

Outdoor Lighting

Filming outdoors is much easier than filming indoors, as there is usually an abundance of natural lighting, hitting the subject from all angles.   Therefore, it's best to interview people outside, if possible.

The exception is bright sunlight, which can introduce deep unwanted shadows to a scene (e.g. around the human face).

These unwanted shadows can be filled in with reflectors (see below) or artificial lights (as a last resort).

Indoor Lighting

While outdoor shooting can often rely on plenty of light around a subject, indoor shooting requires more attention to providing adequate lighting.   If possible the subject should be shot with natural lighting. This may involve locating a subject next to a window, an open door or patio doors.   Larger scenes will almost certainly require supplementary lighting.   The benefit of understanding and owning artificial lights is that they can be used in any situation, or at any time of day or night.

Light sources

These vary from small lights that attach to the camcorder, to large studio lights.   Full descriptions are available in the product catalogues.

The simplest and cheapest option is a halogen-quartz video light that fits on to the camcorder. These are usually 10W to 30W, and can be mounted so that they point straight at the subject. This produces poor results compared to lighting a subject from a side angle.   For improved results, they should be used detached from the camcorder, or at least used with a diffuser. An alternative is to purchase a light that has an adjustable mount, so that the light can be pointed at the walls or ceiling for a deflected, more even lighting.

The next stage upwards is a photoflood bulb mounted on a tripod.   Again the light mount should be adjustable and the tripod's height is already adjustable.   This provides a variety of positions to achieve general even light fills.   For more serious work, halogen-quartz tubular with rectangular reflectors, or halogen-quartz bulbs in cans with *'barn doors'* can be purchased.   These can be mounted on canopies and the *'barn doors'* are hinged flaps that shape the beam and screen the camcorder from its direct light.

Light Diffusers/Filters

Direct sunlight or indoor lighting results in *'hard'* lighting, with high contrast, pronounced shadows and a feeling of depth. It picks out the outlines on features, making them stand out (including facial wrinkles).

Hazy or cloudy conditions result in *'soft'* lighting. Light is striking the object from many angles and this reduces the contrast around edges.   Wrinkles are minimised and the picture has a smoother warmer look. This can be achieved indoors by fitting translucent diffusers (known as *'scrims'* or *'gauzes'*) over the lighting units. These scatter the light to achieve an effect similar to outdoor lighting.

In addition, lamp filters can be fitted to change the colour from the lights. These are most often used to change artificial light for mixing with natural light. They are specially made to withstand the high temperatures of the lamps.

Placing Lights

Although the lighting demands of each location will vary, artificial lighting setups normally use three separate light sources - known as the keylight, the fill-light and the backlight.

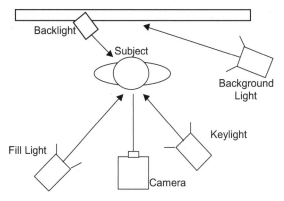

The keylight is used as the main illumination source. It is placed to the side of the subject (by about 45° from the camera) and directed down on the subject (by about 20°). The keylight is a hard light and provides depth to the picture. It also creates pronounced shadows - both on the contours of the subject and also on the background.

The fill-light is about quarter or half the wattage of the keylight and is placed about 45° from the camera in the opposite direction from the keylight. It reduces the dark shadow on the subject and a soft light is best for this purpose. The backlight provides separation of the subject from the background and to provide any additional subject enhancement, such as providing highlights to the subject's hair or providing a halo effect).

The background light is used to illuminate the background by little more than half the level of the subject. It can be used to bring a darkened background into the focus of the main picture, or it can be used to soften the shadows cast on a wall from the keylight and fill-light.

Notes

- The viewer has certain expectations in terms of lighting. A modern office, hotel or kitchen is expected to be brightly lit, while drab surroundings are expected to be dimly lit.
- Scenes will not always require the use of all of these lights. For example, an interviewee in a large workshop or auditorium may be standing 100 feet away from any background surface, removing the need for a background light. On the other hand, for close up work, a reflector may prove more useful than a fill-light. These lighting rules may be broken to achieve special effects. Brightly lit and evenly lit scenes suggest normality, while light subjects shot against a dark background is perceived as being sinister, builds tension, and suggests danger. Hard lighting on a face suggests an austere or menacing character while soft lighting suggests softness of character.

Reflected Light

A useful way to achieve soft lighting is to use *'Bounce lighting'*. This involves illuminating the subject with light that is reflected off walls and ceilings. While this is less efficient than direct lighting, it provides a much more even and soft source of light and interviewees much prefer this to the direct glare of frontal lighting. Walls can used as natural reflectors or a range of additional reflectors can be used. These can be professional reflector umbrellas, or can be improvised when required. For example, white sheets, aluminium foil that has been crumpled and straightened out again, cine-projector screens, and even foam ceiling tiles all make good reflectors.

Other scene considerations

The chapter looks later at the role of storyboarding in planning the content and nature of individual video scenes. This tries to anticipate all likely problems. In practice, certain decisions have to be made upon arrival at the location. These concern the positioning of the main subject to avoid recording problems and to optimise the video content for future editing.

Backgrounds

Where the recording is planned to be distributed on videotape, there is no concern about how the video content affects computer file sizes. However, since most video clips will be used in conventional multimedia use, a little planning can ensure that the scene is adequately recorded, while the clip does not become too large for distribution.

The key consideration is that scenes that have a lot of detail, or are constantly changing, create larger file sizes when they are finally compressed for distribution.

The following guidelines are useful:

- Keep the detail in the recorded picture to a minimum, to achieve best compression.
- Use plain backgrounds if possible, to maximise spatial compression.
- Avoid backgrounds that are constantly altering (crowd scenes, trees blowing in the wind, etc.) to maximise temporal compression.
- If a constantly altering background is unavoidable, make the background out of focus, to avoid distracting the viewer's eye and to improve future compression. This helps with both spatial and temporal compression.

At the end of the day, however, the above considerations must not outweigh the artistic needs for the screen content to adequately convey the required mood or information.

Avoiding moiré

A moiré pattern is seen as a shimmering or the appearance of unwanted colours in certain areas of the screen. It is caused by the inability to handle fine detail in some picture elements such as some men's suits and ties with fine stripes. This effect was noticed in early television broadcasts and now the clothes worn by newscasters are chosen to avoid this effect. This effect will not be seen through the viewfinder. They are artifacts produced during the processing of the signal. The results cannot be removed from the picture. If in doubt, make a quick test recording and view the results.

Subject Positioning

Depending upon the final intended media for the footage, consideration should be given to the degree to which the subject fills the screen. The diagram shows the display screen with two inner areas marked off. The outer area is the total screen size but this is not always visible on all screens, depending on the adjustment of the screen controls. This means that some content positioned at the edges may not be visible on some screens.

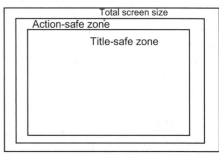

To ensure that all of the subject content is always visible, the area known as the 'action-safe zone' should be considered as the main screen area for all subject recording.

Likewise, the inner area, known as the 'title-safe zone' should be used as the area in which all title text should be placed. The camcorder operator should bear these zones in mind during filming. Objects filmed outside these areas may not be visible on some screens, or suffer from the distortion that some screens have at the edges of the picture.

This problem mostly affects television screens and it only applies to full-screen footage. If video is being shot for display on a small area of the screen, these zones do not apply as the clip can be positioned on a safe area of the screen before being sent to videotape. If the footage is being used on a known system, such as a kiosk, the safe boundaries can quickly be confirmed by creating a test video clip.

Shot Sizes/Uses

The subject positioning discussed above was to avoid technical problems. Subject positioning also plays a major role in the artistic composition of a shot. Shot size describes how fully an object fills the frame. It is usually applied to the human figure and the common shot sizes are shown in the table.

Shot sizes should reflect the use of the scene. A tutorial on jewellery repairs would require a close-up shot, while a tutorial on constructing a bridge would require a medium long shot or long shot. In practice, a clip would switch between shot sizes, as the content unfolds.

In some cases, viewers take their psychological cue from the positioning of people on screen. If two people are having a heated argument, a mid shot or medium long shot indicates that the viewer is an observer of the argument. If the participants are shown in close-up, the viewer is being drawn into the scene and this can disturb the viewer (of course, that might be the dramatic intention of the scene!). Similarly, if two lovers are having an intimate conversation, a long shot appears to be too aloof a setting.

Common Shot Sizes		
ECU/XCU	Extreme Close-Uo	Part of face
CU	Close-up	Head, maybe shoulders
MCU	Medium Close-up	Head and shoulders, maybe chest
MS	Mid-Shot	Head to waist
MLS	Medium Long Shot	Head to knees
LS	Long shot	Full body

Watch television programmes and notice that the subject is not always in the centre of the frame, especially if there is an interesting background. If the person on screen is looking to the left, leave some screen space on the left. When a single head and shoulders is to appear on screen, do not leave too much free space above the head. It is better to move the camera closer or zoom in slightly.

Using the Camcorder

The operator's control of the camcorder contributes greatly to the effectiveness of the final recorded clip.
Largely, it is a question of practice, although the following guidance should prove useful.

Camcorder Positioning

As with the still camera, a tripod is a great aid in video filming. The added stability greatly enhances the recording. There is nothing worse than viewing a recording that has obviously been made with a hand-held camcorder, complete with shakes, wobbles and jolts. In addition, small camcorder movements when recording at a fully zoomed setting result in large changes in the picture content. The greater the zoom, the more obvious the wobble.

If the camcorder has to be moved during the recording, some form of image stabilisation should be used. This could either be within the camera (optical or electronic stabilisation), or be a physical device, such as a motion stabiliser (e.g. a Steadi-Cam or a Steadymate). However, walking while filming is an art that has to be practised.

There remain few occasions when the more 'natural' effect of hand held recording is desirable. It gives an 'amateur' or 'documentary' feel. (as in "The Blair Witch Project").

Focusing

The theory and problems with depth of focus are covered in the chapter on digital photography. It is best not bypass the automatic focus, wherever possible. The automatic system uses the centre of the image as its focus point and this need not always be where the centre of attention is in the picture. The result is that the wrong object is in focus. A recent example involved filming the flight of a microlight aircraft, with the camera filming the scene from inside a screened porch. The camcorder auto-focus decided to focus on the mesh of the screen and the aircraft was completely out of focus. The automatic focus can be left in operation in situations where there is likely to be rapid changes in focus (e.g. filming a football match or a street demonstration).

Zooming

The zoom lens is a very useful tool, when used in the correct way. On most occasions, the zoom facility is used to frame the shot, but is can also be used while filming.

Zoom then shoot

The camera's zoom control alters the focal length of the lens and thereby alters the amount by which the subject is magnified. This also affects the depth of focus. Therefore, the best way to fill the frame is to move the camcorder closer to the subject, rather fill the frame using the zoom.

Its main use is to allow a subject to dominate the frame without the camera being moved where moving closer to the subject is not practical. This could include dangerous situations (e.g. filming a burning building, or passing trains) or to avoid disturbing a natural situation (e.g. children at play, birds feeding, etc).

Another problem with recording scenes when zoomed in is the difficulty in keeping a moving object in focus if it moves towards or away from the camera. The telephoto setting reduces the depth of field, so that the subject can easily move out of focus.

Zoom while shooting

Zooming can help place an object in its surroundings. For example, zooming out on a car might show that it is one of thousands sitting in a car park. While this can be pretty dramatic, it is an effect that can quickly be overused. Zooming in and out while shooting should be used very sparingly and only when the effect is planned in advance.

The manual zoom on camcorders is less smooth than the operation of the motorised zoom. Better cameras have progressive zoom. Pushing the zoom button slightly produces a slow zoom, while pushing the button further produces a faster zoom. This produces a very smooth gradual slow zoom.

When the camcorder is set to manual focus, the zoom in operation can leave the subject out of focus. To prevent this, carry out the following steps:

- Zoom in on the subject.
- Adjust the manual focus, to get the subject in focus.
- Zoom out to the required starting zoom setting.
- Start recording the scene.
- Zoom in on the subject, while recording.

By ensuring that the subject is in focus at the end of the zoom, the zoom effect is successful.

Panning/Tilting

Some shots involve a stationary camcorder recording a fixed scene. All the subject's movement or content are contained within the area being recorded by the camcorder. Other shots require the camera to be moved. This could be to follow a moving subject, or to bring into view another part of a scene that is too large to be fitted in a single frame.

'Panning' is the movement of the camera in a horizontal direction, while 'tilting' describes moving the camera in a vertical direction. If panning or tilting, use a tripod with a smooth fluid head, so that camera movement is smooth.

Panning involves the camera being rotated (preferably on a tripod's pan head) to follow the movement of the subject in a scene. Examples are following someone walking along a street, following a bird in flight, or following a horse at a racetrack. It is always useful to stop panning towards the end of the clip, so that the subject exits off the end of the frame. Panning is also used to record a scene that will not fit into the frame, even using wide-angle attachments (e.g. wide panoramic scenes).

Poor panning results in jerky picture sequences. These look bad and result in poorer compression ratios. If no tripod is available, the camcorder should be held firmly against the body, elbows against the sides of the body, with the hips being swivelled to follow the movement.

A panning sequence should start and end with a stationary shot. This aids the audience in placing the background and prevents travel sickness! If used with a telephoto converter, the rapid panning of a panoramic view produces a dramatic effect in the direction of the panning.

Tilting is used to follow vertical movement (e.g. a rocket taking off, a kite being launched, someone climbing a rock face). It can also be used to scan a large vertical object (e.g. scanning the Empire State Building from ground level to the tip of the top tower).

Care has to be taken as the tilt may result in the lens being pointed directly at the sky, with the resulting problems with the camera's automatic exposure system as mentioned under 'Lighting'.

Tracking/Crabbing

Zooming is carried out with the camcorder remaining stationary, while it is rotated in a horizontal or vertical direction. Tracking involves physically moving the camera during the recording. Similarly, a crab is a movement of the camera to the left or right during a recording. These are regularly seen in movies and are powerful effects when carried out successfully.

Planning Considerations

The script for a multimedia video shoot is largely determined by the overall specification of the project. That does not mean that the content of the video shoot should not be planned in detail. The check list later in this chapter provides some suggestions for those planning a shoot at an external location. Some of the points are mundane, such as checking equipment, organising transport and checking that the people to be filmed will be present at the agreed time. However, consider the consequences if any of these checks failed. The checklist looks at the mechanical and technical factors in preparing for a recording, but even more important is planning the content of the session. The storyboard is there to help prevent errors and to ensure that the final video content matches the needs of the larger project.

Storyboard

This subject is covered in the chapter on design, but some aspects also apply for video shooting. A simple recording of a two-minute interview seems straightforward enough. But, consider having to visit a factory hundreds of miles away, to shoot clips of their production process for an educational or promotional production. The visit has been specially arranged, so that a supervised visit with the safety officer and production manager is present. The visit involves general and close up shots of the equipment and structured interviews with the key operators and controllers. A storyboard is an essential part of the video shoot, as returning to shoot an overlooked piece of equipment or a forgotten question in an interview cannot easily be returned to.

The storyboard would also tell the camera operator details of the individual clips (e.g. factory in wide angle, drilling machine in close-up, finished product in macro, etc). Even smaller shoots benefit from a little planning. Even a two-minute interview with a rock star after a concert can go badly wrong, if you forget to ask the big question. As in other aspects of multimedia, it is not only about planning the look. The content is vital and may well involve some research before shooting. Other events, such as a birthday party or a wedding would benefit from having its video coverage planned. The contribution of the storyboard to the technical performance of the file compression systems is covered later.

Software packages, such as *'Script Werx'* and *'Story Board Artist'* are designed for script and storyboard creation, while *'The Executive Producer'* also provides scene logging facilities.

Continuity

Continuity is ensuring that the finished product appears as a single cohesive piece of work. Everyone loves to spot the deliberate mistake in films and television plays. For example, the ones where the pirate has a patch over his left eye in one scene and over his right eye in the next scene.

This is an obvious continuity error and large productions hire staff to do nothing other than check for such possible errors. This may also be an issue for shooting video for multimedia, when the video recordings are spaced out over several days. Taking notes and digital photographs at the end of a shooting session minimises errors in the next session.

Again, viewer expectations shape the filming continuity. If a plane is leaving London for Boston, it should fly off the left of the screen and not the right, as Boston is to the west of London.

A common mistake to avoid is *'crossing the line'*. If a person or object is moving from left to right in one clip, it should not move from right to left in the next clip. So, for example, if a train is filmed moving leftwards leaving a station, subsequent clips should also show the train moving leftwards, otherwise the train is perceived as returning to the station.

Similar care should be taken when filming an interview or conversation between to people. If one person is filmed talking towards the left of the screen, the other person should be filmed talking towards the right of the screen, otherwise the viewer perceives that the two people are talking to a third participant. This is often avoided by using an *'over the shoulder'* technique so that the main person is viewed over the shoulder of the listener. This ensures that both participants remain in the shot.

Continuity is also an issue at the editing stage, to maintain a smooth logical flow of clips. For example, it would be wrong to insert an interview with the company sales director in the middle of a set of clips detailing how a product is manufactured.

Scene content

- The mood of a movie can be set by recording clips in a particular weather condition (e.g. sunny, snowy, windy, raining) or at a particular time of day (e.g. dawn, noon, twilight, moonlight).
- The mood can also be set by the environment in which the clips are recorded (e.g. busy rush hour, empty street, noisy crowd scene).
- The clothes that the actors wear also sets the tone of the movie (e.g. an audience assumes that a girl in a

bikini means a warm setting – even if the clip was recorded on a sunny January day!).

- The use of simple props can immediately establish the actor's role (e.g. if the man is carrying flowers he is a lover; the same man carrying a gun is an action figure).

Pace

- Bearing in mind the short attention span of many viewers, ensure that a scene is captured in an appropriate time scale. The lengths of most individual scenes are about 2 to 3 seconds up to around 7 or 10 seconds. Short movie clips provide a sense of fast action, while longer clips portray a more leisurely pace (e.g. in a love scene or a travel advert). Most movies employ a mix of shot lengths.
- The rapid switching between two movie clips is often used to heighten excitement (e.g. man runs towards woman, woman runs towards man). A similar technique is the rapid display of short clips with a similar theme (e.g. a football match or rock concert).
- If the camcorder can capture at a lower frame rate, it can be used to achieve a time lapse effect or a *"Keystone Cops"* effect.
- Continuing filming after the main subject has gone from view is often used for poignant effect. For example, a man looks dejected, lowers his head and slowly walk out of view. The camera does not pan to follow him and the viewer is left looking at the spot where he once stood. This provides a mood of emptiness, misery, or a time for reflection.
- Set the camcorder to widescreen mode to capture panoramic views. This provides the feeling of epic movies.

Shooting to edit.

In the early days of camcorders, there was no easy way to get the footage out of the camcorder, edit it and store it. Recorded footage was kept on videotape. So, amateur users used to *'edit in camera'*, which meant that the clips were recorded in the sequence that they would be displayed.

With the current easy access to video capture hardware and editing software, users no longer have to work in this restrictive way. Now, camcorders users work to a *'shoot to edit'* approach. This recognises that the recording process should be carried out with editing in mind, producing good quality clips with sufficient options at the editing stage. The final video depends on the quality of the video recordings, as even great editing cannot overcome all the problems of poor footage.

Shooting to edit is not about just recording everything and anybody; its about consciously recording video clips that may add to the final edited clip. It can be planned before the shoot, at the script or storyboard stage, and must also be carried out during shooting.

The chapter on video editing shows that the editor's creativity can heighten the movie's impact. Of course, the editor can only work with the material that is provided. Much thought is given to producing professional movies before a single scene is recorded. The storyboard as a creative tool is covered in other chapters and can dictate how movie clips are shot (from what angle, what distance, etc.). It also dictates what scenes are recorded. The motto of filmmakers is *"think in terms of shots"*. Every piece of pre-planned video footage has a purpose for the project and this determines its length, content, etc.

Of course, there are often unplanned sequences that are worth recording. Indeed, these may prove useful precisely because they are spontaneous.

Non-linear editing means that:

- Clips can be recorded out of sequence and re-ordered at the editing stage.
- Several copies of the same clip can be recorded and the best clip chosen at the editing stage.
- Clips can be recorded from different angles and with different shot sizes for selection at the editing stage.
- Clips that were not originally planned for shooting can be captured for possible use.
- Clips that are known to have some defect or error can be left on the tape for removal during editing.
- In-camera effects such as fade to black or adding titles can be ignored, with such effects being carried out at the editing stage, once the exact required length of each clip is known.
- Similarly, automatic time and date features can be ignored, although some notes on each scene should be taken down for future reference.

Shooting to edit implements the shooting plan by capturing the essential elements that tell the story, with a beginning, a middle, and an end. It also adds to the plan by capturing relevant clips such as local environments, audience reactions, etc.

Composition

The chapter on digital photography looked at issues such as centres of interest (i.e. the *'rule of thirds'*), horizons, etc. The earlier part of this chapter looked at issues such as colour balancing, lighting, shot sizes, zooming, panning, etc. Composition considers how shots should be set up for filming, to provide the variety, the interest and to meet the expectations of the viewers.

Using different shots

As mentioned before, a long video production should consist of a sequence of short clips of varying duration and content. Even a televised football match, where all the real action takes place within the confined area of the pitch, uses a variety of shots to enrich the programme. This includes different views of the match from different cameras, wide views of the pitch, close-ups of the action, and a variety of off-the-pitch clips such as crowd reactions, club manager antics, and even shots of the commentators. This mix makes for a more interesting programme for the viewer and maintains their attention for longer.

It is common to use long shots to establish the location, while using mid shots and close-ups of the same scene to record the detail. Complex scenes, such as a busy beach or street, need a longer clip duration to allow viewers to register the information, while reaction shots and other close-ups are usually of a shorter duration.

Bearing in mind that most video footage will be viewed on a small screen, large scenes, such as fairgrounds, rallies, etc., should supplement wide shots with mid shots and close-ups, so that the viewer can greater appreciate the overall content. Real close-ups, where a person's face fills the screen, should be reserved for showing emotion.

Remember, if at all possible, shoot the same clips from different angles. Usually, this applies to fixed sequences, such as filming manufacturing processes, carrying out DIY jobs, engaging in arts and crafts, and so on. Unfortunately, wedding services or sports fixtures cannot be re-run for the sake of some extra shots. However, rehearsal of some clips such as interviews, training clips, etc. are possible and desirable.

Establishing shots

An establishing shot is one that informs the viewer of the location of the scene. They are usually only shown for a short time and can be a wide view of an area (e.g. Bondi Beach), a street sign (e.g. "Wall Street") or a famous landmark (e.g. Buckingham Palace). Notice that episodes of 'Friends' show the street front of the coffee house before showing midshots of the actors seated inside.

Another type of establishing shot shows footage of an object (e.g. a tree with fairy lights indicates Xmas while viewers will soon understand the meaning of a birthday cake, a set of golf clubs or a packed suitcase.

Cutaway shots

As the name suggests, these shots cut away from the main action to some supplementary content. Cutaways are used for:

- Shortening a sequence without the viewers realising that some of the action has been cut. For example. a player scores a goal, a shot of the crowd going wild is then shown before continuing with more of the match. Cutaways have distracted the viewers from realising that boring sections of the game have been removed.
- Smoothing the flow from a clip taken from one camera position to another clip with a different camera position, by inserting a suitable transition clip. This avoids the effect known as *'jump cuts'*.
- Breaking up long clips. For example, someone makes a long speech at a wedding so the viewer's interest is maintained by inserting clips of the guests, the wedding cake, a bottle of champagne, etc.
- Generating extra mood (e.g. flowers at a wedding, toys at a party, shots of an audience and general local ambience shots such as broken windows, graffiti, local skyline, passing traffic, commuters, etc).
- Suggesting the passage of time (e.g. a candle burning down, a clock ticking).
- Showing what a person is talking about (e.g. a director discussing his products or a travel presenter describing a location).

Some of the clips have to be recorded at the time of the shoot (e.g. the football crowd or the wedding guests). Other cutaways, such as a burning candle or a champagne bottle can be recorded later. In fact, is it is quite common to record clips of an interviewer after an interview is over. Such clips can include the interviewer nodding wisely (a *'noddy'* shot) or giving a smile of encouragement. Cutaways filmed after the main recording are particularly helpful for providing the sense of variety and perspective when filming is carried out with a single camcorder.

Aids to editing

All videotapes should be *'blacked'*, as mentioned earlier, to lay down timecode information on the tape. When one of these otherwise empty tapes is inserted in the camcorder, the lens cap should be left on and about ten seconds of blank recording should be made. This ensures that any noise or effects of tape stretching are not introduced to the first clip to be recorded.

It is also good practice to record about 5 seconds of black between each major shooting session. This leaves a safe margin between each clip and also provides easy to locate boundaries between clips during editing.

Always start the recording a few seconds earlier than you might think necessary, and leave the camera recording for a few seconds after you feel the recording is complete. This provides a margin for editing that can often lead to the extra footage being included in the finished work.

Smaller projects record video with a single camcorder but larger productions might use two or more cameras to ensure that the action is captured simultaneously from all angles and shot sizes. At editing time, there can be a problem of lining up the clips from different video cameras in the timeframe. If a natural event occurs, these can be used as references for alignment. The marker may be audible (e.g. the champagne bottle popping, the referee's whistle, or a single gunshot) or may be may be visual (e.g. lightning or a flashgun). Such an event will appear on all clips and they can be quickly identified and synchronised in the editing software's timeline. Where practicable, such events can be artificially introduced into the session, using a bleeper, whistle or flashgun; of course, this technique is not suitable in many circumstances.

Subject positioning

There are a number of everyday techniques used by camera operators that can be easily copied:

- Avoid always placing every subject in the centre of the screen, a problem known as *'headhunting'*. Use the *'rule of thirds'* to make for more interesting composition.
- Avoid shooting into the sun. The strong light plays havoc with the camcorder's automatic exposure system and makes all the subjects appear in silhouette.
- When indoors, take care when shooting near windows. In bright conditions, it poses the same problems as above. When it is dark outside, the camera equipment and operators may be visible in the glass.
- Set up the situation so that the subject is not inclined to talk directly to the camcorder. This may involve one person interviewing the subject while another records the discussion. If only one person is available, then the camcorder should be set up (e.g. on a tripod) so that the subject looks at the interviewer and not the camera.
- Consider recording the subject by filming over the shoulder of the interviewer so that only back of the head of the interviewer is seen in the shot. This allows for flexibility during editing, as the interviewer's words can be overdubbed later (e.g. if the interviewer fluffs a question).
- Try to blend into the background as much as possible. This prevents subjects feeling conspicuous or playing to the camera and results in more natural recordings.

Camera positioning

Imaginative positioning of the camcorder can enhance a project, while misuse of the camera's features can spoil the video content. Some general rules are:

- Avoid filming the entire movie from one fixed spot, a problem known as *'rooting'*. It is better to have a set of clips, with the camcorder position, angle and zoom settings altered between clips. If necessary, the changes between clips can be anchored by cutaways.
- Avoid panning back and forward across a scene, a problem known as *'firehosing'*. Panning is sometimes used to capture panoramic scenes, but only when the panning movement is low and smooth. Panning is best kept to follow a person or object moving across the main scene. This still allows the panorama to be viewed while still following some screen activity.
- Experiment with capturing video with the camcorder at different heights from the ground. Not all clips are best viewed from a standing height.   For example, a clip of some indoor sports might be best captured from a balcony looking down on the action. On the other hand, using a camcorder at waist level gives a view as seen by children or by a seated audience.
- Only move the camcorder around during filming if a *'documentary'* feel is required. Otherwise, leave it to the people or the objects to move around the screen. Viewers find it more natural for subjects to move inwards from the edges of the screen, rather than moving from the centre towards the edges (unless the subject is meant to leaving the picture).

Timing

Some tips on timing are:

- If conducting an interview, carry out changes of camera position, frame size, zooming, etc. during the asking of the question. Any footage lost during this time can be overdubbed later (see the last tip in the section on subject positioning).
- Always find a natural point to stop filming (e.g. when the person finishes a sentence, when a car finally comes to a halt, when the cheerleader actually catches the baton).
- Never stop recording a shot while panning, zooming or moving the camera around.

Zooming

An earlier part of this chapter recommended a policy of *'zoom then shoot'*, so that the zoom facility was used as a means of properly framing the screen contents, particularly in awkward filming environments.   It is best to avoid zooming while recording (specially if moving the camera at the same time), as the effects can be nauseating and are mostly seen as being amateurish. Where zooming is an essential part of a shot, it is usually carried out slowly and smoothly. However, zooming out can sometimes be used for dramatic effect (e.g. a close-up of a girl is zoomed out to reveal that she is standing in a long empty street in a derelict area). Many cameras have an overfast zoom facility and the user should spend some time practising before using it in an important recording.

Other shooting tips

- Always white balance before shooting. If necessary, carry around a piece of white card to assist in the process. If you change location, or sometimes the angle of a shot, carry out white balancing again.
- For special effects, experiment with using tinted cards while balancing, to achieve warmer or colder colours in the clip.

- For other functions, learn how to use the manual setting, rather than relying on automatic settings. This allows more control and provides better results.
- Where possible, use a tripod for professional results. This is particularly true where a shot requires a high degree of zoom, as even small camera movements mean huge changes in screen content at these settings.
- Where a camcorder has to be handheld, use an image stabiliser.

Sound

The chapter on digital audio looked at microphone techniques and all the points covered are relevant in video recording. Indeed, they should be read carefully, as the audio picked up from most microphones built into camcorders can be of poor quality. This is mostly due to their being positioned too far away from the source of the audio to be recorded (and often too near the motor of the camera).

Tips for best audio capture during video recording are:

- Don't zoom in on a person when the camera could simply be taken closer. This brings the microphone closer to the audio source and improves the recording through greater pickup from the wanted source and minimising pickup from background sources.
- Where it is impossible to take the camera operator closer (e.g. dangerous machinery or dangerous environment) use an extension microphone or a wireless mike, positioned near the subject.
- Where it is impossible to take the microphone closer (e.g. crowded area, security fence) use a shotgun microphone.
- Beware of background noise (the video may be recorded adequately, but the audio may have picked up a car horn, an aeroplane overhead, or simply someone coughing.
- Use headphones to monitor the audio during the recording, to minimise the risk of overlooking unwanted noises, disconnected cables, flat batteries, etc.
- Try to get a connection to the PA system (e.g. at a conference, a wedding disco, etc.), to obtain the best quality audio source, free of all external background noise. In background sounds are required, record them separately, allowing for the two sources to be balanced during the editing stage.
- For important interviews, play back the recording before leaving the interview, in case it has to be re-shot.

Recording Check List

This is a suggestion list. Not all points need to be carried out and they need not necessarily be implemented in the order given.

Checks before the shoot

Permission to shoot at the location (if required).	
Permission to shoot the subject(s), if appropriate.	
Confirmation that any person(s) appearing in a shoot will be present at the agreed time/date.	
Confirmation that the location is safe for the subject, camera operator and any equipment.	
Location identified of electrical wall outlets for lighting, camera and other equipment.	
Check that all the equipment works, including power extension cables, power strips, lighting, light meter, microphones and headphones work.	
Carry a mobile phone, for unforeseen emergencies.	
Confirm that all camera accessories are packed (spare tapes, all lenses and filters, spare batteries, AC charger, lens brush, cleaning cloth and fluid, tripods).	
Confirm that all audio apparatus is packed (microphones, microphone batteries, headphones, audio cables, stands, booms, wind socks)	
Confirm that likely ancillary materials (electric cables and adapters,, electrical tape, Duct tape, clamps, spring clips, basic tools, stands, reflectors, diffusers, cables, and spare bulbs) are packed.	
Clean the cameras (use air brush cleaner to blow away dust and fibres, use anti-static cleaning cloth or lint free tissues to clean the lens, in worst cases use lens cleaning fluid)	

Check that the camcorder batteries are charged including the spares.	
With new cassettes, record on the entire tape with the lens cap still fitted, to ensure that the timecode is written to the tape before use. If the tapes lies unused for a period, fast forward to the end of the tape and then rewind to loosen any sections of tape that may cling together and cause jerky tape movements during recording.	
Provisions are made for keeping people and equipment dry in poor weather conditions.	
Transport for people and equipment is organised.	

On site activities

Check location for unexpected problems (crowds, weather, etc.)	
Screw camera to tripod and locate at best viewing point.	
If capturing direct to disk, connect the camera to the computer capture card and run capture software.	
Frame the subject according the specified storyboard shot size.	
Check the lighting. Set up any additional lighting required.	
Focus on the subject. Check if auto or manual focus will be required.	
Record the clips, according the storyboard instructions.	
Log each shot.	
When a cassette is full, rewind it, remove it, label it, and write protect it (DV cassettes have a write-protect lever).	
Store cassettes on their side or end, to minimise the risk of the tape slipping off the spools.	
Store tapes in dust-free container in a condensation-free area.	

Digitising Video

The video source material has to be converted into computer files that can be stored and manipulated. The video source will usually be a camera source (such as a camcorder or webcam) or a VCR.   Their video outputs can sometimes be connected directly to the computer's parallel port or USB port, but all professional results are obtained by feeding their output into a special card designed for the purpose. This is called a *'video capture card'* and is an add-on card that is fitted into one the computer's expansion slots (ISA for older cards and PCI or AGP slots for newer cards).   Some have analogue connections for use with composite and S-Video inputs, while others use digital connections to a FireWire source.

Video Sources

There are two sources of video material:

Live Capture

The video data is captured live from the camcorder or webcam to the computer, for storage to hard disk. The material does not require to be first recorded to cassette tape. The advantage of this method for analogue capture is improved quality, as the cassette recording is always inferior to the direct output from the camera. Live capture is at its best in controlled situations, where the recording can be repeated until the desired effect is obtained. Examples are studio footage and location footage where planning time and human resources are available.   Since the computer equipment has to be set up on location, live capture has serious practical limitations.

Digitising Pre-recorded material

Most material will come in the form of pre-recorded camcorder cassette tape. This is essential for uncontrolled situations where a second take is impossible, or where it is impossible to set up computer equipment.   Examples include sports events, concerts, holiday footage and vox pop interviews.

There is often a need to use previous footage that was recorded on older equipment and copied to VHS tape. Although digital video is becoming very popular, there will still be a sizeable source of material being recorded for the foreseeable future in S-Video and BetacamSP format.

Capture Methods

There is a range of hardware/software options when capturing video:

Capture raw video without any compression

No compression is used and therefore the resulting files are very large but the data is of the highest quality. This is an ideal format for quality archives and provides the best material for further processing and editing, with the decision on the compression method being decided later. Indeed, the same source material may be required at different quality levels - perhaps one version for web site use and another version for CD distribution. Storing the uncompressed version allows flexibility in the later use of the clip. The down side, of course, is the amount of storage required even for short video clips. The falling price of large hard disks, CD-R, tape drives and DVD-RAM make this less of a problem than it once was.

Use this method for analogue systems, wherever possible.

Two-Step Digitisers

This was an older system where the video input was saved directly to disk in uncompressed form. The package's CODEC (compression/decompression) system then created a smaller version by compressing the saved file. The CODEC was implemented by a dedicated chip or by a software program. This two-step system was useful for less-powerful computers that could not cope with simultaneous reading and compression of data. It was a more laborious method and required more free disk space than single-step digitisers, as it had to store both the uncompressed version and the newly created compressed version.

Capture and compress in real-time, using software compression.

Single-step digitisers convert the video input into a digitised form, compress it and save it - all in a single stage. There is no need to first store it in uncompressed form. Single-step compression is also known as 'On-the-Fly' compression since it occurs in real time.

Using software compression means that the process is heavily dependent on the speed of the computer's CPU and the efficiency of the other system components such as the hard disk. If the computer cannot keep up with the amount of data coming from the capture card, some of the data is discarded and this results in dropped frames.

Capture and compress in real-time, using hardware compression.

An even more efficient system results from using hardware for single-step compression. The chip on the capture board does all the compression processing and relieves the computer's CPU of that work. These always produce better results than software implementations. Most capture cards provide hardware facilities for compression and examples are given later. The most common hardware capture compression systems are the M-JPEG and MPEG formats.

Capture in all-digital format

A growing number of digital video cameras are providing FireWire outputs (see the chapter on computer technology). These cameras carry out the analogue to digital conversion internally and pass on the digital information directly to the PC. This conversion occurs in real time and removes a previous bandwidth bottleneck. The stored video can remain in DV format or can be compressed. Manufacturers are working on high-performance VCRs that have FireWire connections, allowing them to record high-resolution material. This will be a future source of pre-recorded material.

Use this digital system, if it can be afforded.

Stop motion

The beginning of this chapter defined video as:

"a sequence of individual pictures which, when displayed on the screen
at a fast enough rate, provide the illusion of movement".

The camera in a television studio or a camcorder work on this principle, converting live action into a sequence of digital images.

This principle, however, is not confined to capturing action in the real world. The first Mickey Mouse cartoon was produced in the Walt Disney Studios in the 1928 and used a sequence of hand-drawn images to create a moving cartoon sequence. Even earlier, in 1925, a film called *"The Lost World"* used animated models and this was followed in 1933 by the famous *"King Kong"* movie. The technique was employed in movies throughout the years, including *"Clash of the Titans"* and *"Dragonslayer"*. It was recently used in famous videos such as *"Wallace and Gromit"*, *"Chicken Run"* and *"Bob the Builder"*.

The stop motion technique uses a camera that is capable of capturing a single frame at a time. With cartoons, an image is drawn and photographed. The contents of the image are slightly altered and are re-photographed, slowly building up a sequence. When the sequence is played back the illusion of movement is produced. With models, the objects are slightly altered between each frame being captured (e.g. an arm or a leg might be slightly moved). Stop motion animation is a very slow process as even a short video clip of one minute requires 1500 different poses to be set and captured (i.e. 60 seconds at 25 frames per second).

Much of the work that was carried out by stop motion techniques has been replaced by software techniques to create computer generated sequences.

Capture connections

There has been an expanding market in devices to interface computers to camcorders.   They are of varying quality, power, features and price but are broadly of three interface designs.

Through the parallel port

The camcorder was connected to the device and the device was plugged into the computer's parallel port.   The software supplied with the device allowed it to read in the video data via the parallel port lines for digitisation.   This method was commonly used with analogue cameras and older webcams.   The rate of data transfer across a parallel port meant that the system was too slow for serious use.

Through the USB port

The camcorder is connected to the device and the device connects to one of the computer's USB ports.
Newer webcams use this method, as do some of the video capture systems.

Through Capture Cards

Initially, capture cards were add-ons to the graphics card that fed the monitor. The two were usually connected by a ribbon cable through the *'feature connector'*

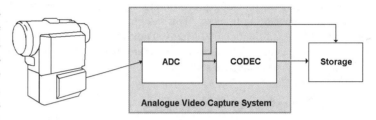

extension port on many graphics cards. This was a pin-out on the internal circuitry of the card called the *'feature'* connector, which could be attached by a ribbon cable to other cards such as video capture cards, full-motion video cards and genlocking equipment.   Currently, some cards function both as a normal graphics card and as a player/recorder of full-motion video.   These capture cards combine the capture facility with the normal 2D and 3D acceleration expected from a graphics card. The more professional end of the market uses a separate card for the capture process.

There are three basic capture types - analogue only, digital only, and analogue + digital.

Analogue cards

The diagram shows the process of capturing via an analogue capture card.

The analogue signal is taken from the camcorder's composite or S-video output socket and fed into the capture card. The ADC (Analogue to Digital Converter) converts the varying analogue signal into a corresponding set of digital values. These values can then be stored directly to disk in uncompressed format.   Alternatively, the digital signal can be fed through a CODEC where it is compressed before saving to disk.

Until the coming of digital camcorders, this was the dominant method of capture video footage.   This system will be around for some time, due to the number of analogue camcorders in use and the amount of footage already available in analogue format.

FireWire digital connections

These cards can only be used with digital camcorders using FireWire (also known as *'iLink'* or *'IEEE1394'*) connectors.   For simplicity and cheapness, many FireWire cards only provide FireWire inputs, while some provide in and out. Since the data is always shifted round in digital format between the camcorder and card (and possibly back again), the card has no ADC chip.   This vastly improves signal quality as explained earlier (see the section on camcorder formats).

Like the analogue cards, there is the option to save the video data in uncompressed or compressed format.

FireWire adapters are available with a wide range of features and prices, almost all being PCI cards (PCMCIA adaptor cards by Belkin, DViCO and Western Digital are available for use with laptop computers). All cards provide the same basic feature of transferring video data from the camcorder into the computer.

Cheaper cards are provided with basic capture/editing software, although a user can also capture using a more professional software package such as Adobe Premiere. Depending upon the bundled software, these cards can save movie clips in AVI, ASF, MPEG, QuickTime or RealVideo formats.

Some cards also provide internal FireWire connectors, for connecting to future FireWire devices such as FireWire hard disks. The Adaptec Ultra HotConnect 8945 has an Ultra-Wide SCSI connection on its card, so that SCSI hard drives can be connected directly to the capture card.

More expensive cards are available with additional hardware facilities (e.g. for compression or real-time rendering) and comprehensive software for capture, editing, titling, etc.

Digital/Analogue

Most cards are FireWire only or analogue only, while the more expensive models handle both types of input. This supports the highest quality for new digital recordings, while maintaining the ability to digitise old VHS and S-Video footage. These cards provide composite video, S-Video, audio and FireWire inputs. The DV output connects to a camcorder's digital input or to a FireWire digital VCR (there are currently very few in circulation). The cards have analogue to digital converters, but they are only used when an analogue signal is being processed.

Breakout Boxes

The problem with all add-on cards is that their sockets are located at the rear of the computer case. This is not a problem for connecting a mouse or a keyboard that is not removed or replaced very often. However, it is a big headache for users of capture cards, as they wish to plug and unplug various devices (camcorders, VCRs, video decks, audio equipment, etc) on a fairly regular basis. They do not wish to haul their computer out of its corner to access these rear sockets.

The solution lies in providing a breakout box. This is a box with a cable that connects to a socket on the capture card. The box is then brought round to the front of the computer where its sockets can handle the range of audio and video connections that it supports. The swapping of devices to the breakout box becomes an easy task.

Dual Stream

Until now, transition effects and titling were usually rendered in the editing process (see next chapter).

The new Dual Stream capture cards have two hardware CODEC streams and this allows:

- A bitmap in one stream and the video in the other - real-time static titles.
- Video in both streams - blending two clips for real-time transitions, such as wipes and dissolves.
- Video in Video.

Since this merging is taking place during the digitising process, there are no long waits as occurs with rendering during the later editing process. This system was available a few years ago in the DPS Perception RT, at a cost of around £9,000 and the £10,000 Matrox DigiSuite. This facility now appears in some more reasonably priced cards. For reliable results, dual stream cards are best used with RAID disk systems, since they have can handle reading/writing simultaneous streams.

The Capture Process

When a video clip is being captured for use on the web, no great pressure is put upon the computer components. The video clip will be of small resolution and will have a low frame rate. This means that the amount of data being transferred around the computer is comparatively small.

Over time, users constantly demand improvements in multimedia performance -including bigger and smoother video clips. The space required to store one minute of video is becoming ever larger. However, buying a larger disk drive does not solve the problem. The recording system still has only one minute to move around this larger set of data. This places greater demands on all components in the system. The recording process involves a series of data transfers - from the camcorder to the capture card, to the computer's memory, through the CPU to the disk controller and finally to the disk. The system is only as powerful as its weakest link. The *'data transfer rate'* of each component must be high enough to cope with the fastest demands placed upon it. Temporary slowdowns in the data transfer rate, anywhere in this chain, would result in lost frames while recording

The selection of components for a multimedia computer system was covered in the first chapter.

There are two problem areas for video recording:

- The hardware may not be capable of handling the highest data rate.
- The software may not be optimised for recording.

Check the hardware

Check that the hard disk is fast enough to handle video transfers, especially with older hard disks. SCSI drives tend to have fewer problems with data rates, but UDMA disks are improving all the time. The disk controller interface also has to be high performance, with IDE being replaced by UltraDMA and SATA. The computer's processor should be spending most of its time controlling the capture process. Any unnecessary interruptions to this process could result in dropped frames.

The following steps should minimise unwanted interruptions:

- Use Scandisk to check and isolate any disk surface errors. Once the disc surface has been checked, and any possible faulty sectors isolated, the Recycle Bin should be emptied.
- Defragment the disk, to minimise the number of head movements occurring inside the drive.
- If possible, the captured data should be saved to an empty drive or partition.
- Put a disk, any disk, in the computer's floppy, CD-ROM and ZIP drives. This saves the computer checking the drives at regular intervals.
- Turn off the printer.
- Disable a network card, if one exists.

Use a sound card with a good SNR (see the chapter on audio). Avoid using sound facilities that are built in to computer motherboards, as they generally have inferior performances to add-on cards. Some video capture cards include audio capture on the card to aid the synchronisation of audio and video data.

When the hardware has been tested, the video source should be connected to the capture card. This may be a camcorder, VCR, or MiniDisc player, as required.

Prepare the software

There are other software steps that can be taken to avoid unwanted computer activities that might interfere with the smooth flow of data during the capture process.

- Ensure that all devices are using the latest drivers.
    These can be downloaded from the manufacturer's web site on the Internet, if necessary.
- Close all applications, apart from those required for the capture process.
- Turn off screen saver.
- Enable write caching on the drive, and disable read-ahead optimisation
- Disable write-behind caching for all drives.

Run the capture software

The exact steps for capturing video clips depend upon the hardware and software in use. It is possible to capture through the utility supplied with the capture card, or through a video editing package such Avid Cinema or Adobe Premiere. The capture format available depends upon the choices offered by the system but might include native DV, uncompressed video, M-JPEG, MPEG-1, MPEG-2, etc. Where the content is being used in the later editing process, an uncompressed option should be chosen. Where a clip is being taken from a VCR, the content may already be in satisfactory condition and the capture process can chosen to digitise and store in a compressed format.

Batch capture

A videocassette will probably contain a collection of video clips and it is a common practice to keep back winding, looking for the start of a particular clip. The constant play and rewind gradually scratches the tape surface and degrades the signal. It also produces excessive wear on the heads.

Some capture software supports a batch capture facility where the software recognises the start and finish points of each clip and saves all the clips to hard drive in a continuous operation, without further operator intervention. This is a great time saver, but it assumes that there is plenty of disk drive space to store all the clips. Since disk drives are now cheap, this is an efficient way to carry out mundane tasks. The clips are easily deleted or clipped after they are saved as disk files. For more control, some software supports edit decision lists, where the operator can choose which clips to capture and only those are saved to disk.

With camcorders that have "device control", the movie can be started, stopped, paused, fast forwarded, rewound, moved back or forward a single frame – all from within the capture software (e.g. within Premiere) without any need to touch any of the buttons on the camcorder. This uses the tape's timecode discussed previously.

Capture at highest resolution

The user has control over the resolution that the incoming video will be digitised to. The highest resolution should be chosen, as the final output resolution can be chosen after editing. The disadvantage of this choice is the larger file size. This results in greater storage needs and slower editing, as there is more data to be moved around. The advantage is greater quality. The high quality clip can be archived for future use at any resolution. A high-resolution clip can always be converted to a lower-resolution clip for web or other use. In fact, the scaling down process averages out adjacent pixels reducing video noise and improving the compression ratio. Most video clips suffer from 'overscan' (sometimes referred to as 'edge blanking'). These video clips have to be cropped before use. If the clip were captured at the desired final size, the cropping would result in the clip being smaller than required. Scaling up to the desired size would introduce unnecessary picture degradation. Capturing at the higher resolution allows for cropping before scaling to the desired resolution, maintaining picture quality.

Capture at greatest frame rate

It is always best to capture at a high frame rate, even where the clip is intended for use on the web. It is easy to lower the frame rate in the final output. However, frames cannot be easily inserted into a file with a low frame rate. In addition, footage with high frame rates can be archived and used for other projects.

Capture at low, or no, compression

The capture software often provides user control over the capture settings. One control allows the compression ratio to be set. Often, there is a single 'Quality' control slider that sets up the file resolution, frame rate and compression ratio in a single operation. There is often control over individual elements. The example shown is the compression control for typical capture software.

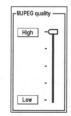

The highest quality possible should be selected, even if the final destination for the file is only the web. If possible, capture in uncompressed mode. Like the resolution mentioned above, the compression CODEC and compression ratio can always be decided after editing.

If a file is captured with an AVI CODEC, it introduces artifacts into the file. Subsequent MPEG compression is therefore less effective, resulting in larger file sizes and extra noise. So, always capture video uncompressed, if the intention is to have MPEG as the final destination.

Applications often provide preset combinations (see the Premiere section of the 'Video Editing' chapter). These can be useful for beginners or for those who know the final destination of their clips (e.g. to a DVD). Those intending to edit their material should ensure that no compressed preset options are chosen.

The Data Rate

The *'Quality'* slider of a CODEC produces a range of options:

- The *'High'* end of scale produces low compression, high image quality and high data rates.
- The *'Low'* end of the scale produces highly compressed, poorer quality images at a lower data rate.
- Intermediate settings on the slider produce files with values between these extremes.

If the slider is set to, say, a compression value of 20:1, it will compress all parts of the video stream by that same amount. However, not all parts of the clip may require compression. Some scenes contain simple content detail while others contain complex content.

The illustration shows the varying rate of a typical AVI file, displayed using a facility provided in Adobe Premiere. A fixed compression ratio could easily result in one part of the clip being compressed unnecessarily, while other parts are not sufficiently compressed. This degrades the picture in the sections with simple content and introduces artifacts in the sections with complex content. Both parts of the clip are being treated inefficiently and producing a poorer quality final result than is possible.

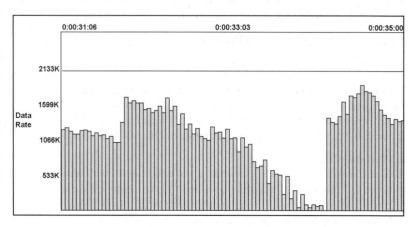

A better approach is to set the maximum data rate for the clip. All parts of the clip with content that would fit within that limit are left untouched, while the other sections are compressed. This improves the quality of the simple sections and minimises the introduction of artifacts in complex sections. If the chosen CODEC cannot compress to required data rate, the complex content sections will produce data rates in excess of the maximum set by the user. The solution in that case, is to use another CODEC with a higher maximum compression ratio. The alternative is to set a lower maximum and accept a lower quality than was originally anticipated.

DV AVI Files

The camcorder stores the movie as a single continual data stream containing both the video and audio tracks. When the data is transferred by a FireWire card, the data entering the computer is unchanged. However, the capturing software then packages the data in a way that can be understood by other applications. In fact, there are two variations on how the data is stored.

Type-1

The data is left untouched but has an AVI header attached to the start of the file. This makes the file simple and quick to create. Saving a Type-1 file back to a camcorder only requires that the header be stripped off, leaving the original data for transfer. However, although the header is in AVI format, the actual content is not in the normal AVI format. Many applications expect to see AVI files as a header followed by multiple data streams, with a minimum of one video stream and one audio stream. This makes Type-1 the less compatible of the two types, as the files can only be handled through Direct X and DirectShow. Premiere 5.1, for example, cannot handle Type-1 files, while Premiere 6 can (with a bit of manipulation).

Type-2

To ensure compatibility with most applications, Type-2 files take a copy of the audio content from the DV stream and create an additional AVI format audio stream. In this way, compatibility is ensured at the cost of a slightly larger file size (since the audio is being stored twice). The capture process also requires a more powerful processor in the computer, as it has to create the extra stream. In this case, if the file is to be saved back to a camcorder, both the header and the AVI audio stream have to be removed to recover the raw DV file before transfer. Type-2 files are compatible with Premiere, Video-for-Windows, QuickTime, etc.

Since they differ mainly on how the data is packaged, both types contain the same quality of video and audio reproduction.

The existence of two types of DV AVI file explains why some captured material will not be read by some application packages. Fortunately, software is available to convert between the two types. EditStudio, for example, has such a utility (it is available from www.puremotion.com).

2GB File Limit on AVI

One of the great obstacles to video editors is the limit of 2GB that is placed on saving AVI files. This limit was initially due to the 16-bit FAT file system used by DOS. It was carried over into early versions of Windows. Although Windows 95 onwards used a 32-bit FAT system and could handle beyond 2GB, the code for Video-for-Windows was not re-written to suit. Therefore, the 2Gbyte file limit for AVIs is imposed by Video-for-Windows and does not apply to a non-AVI format such as native DV.

This is not a regular problem, as a project is often composed from a collection of smaller files, for ease of edit and assembly. However, there are occasions when no editing is required, such as the simple copying of a videotape format to digital file format.

Various attempts have been made to get around this problem.

Some editing software can daisy chain lots of AVIs into an apparently seamless production when output to a VCR. The Pinnacle card, for example, includes a Premiere plug-in that plays a seamless list of clips to screen or to DV out (for a DV recorder).

The software supplied with some cards allows the batch capture of a long videotape into a set of sub-2GB files and a scene list is automatically built for referencing individual file clips.

As a more permanent solution, the Open Digital Media Consortium produced a new OpenDML format, sometimes called the 1.1 format. This is a 64-bit hierarchical indexing AVI file format extension that removes the 2GB limit, allowing video clips of any size to be stored – limited only by the operating system in use and the size of the hard disk.

FAT32 as used by Windows 95 onwards, does not support file sizes larger than 4GB, while the NTFS filing system of Windows 2000, NT and XP have no such limit.

These calculations assume, of course, that the video software and the drivers support OpenDML. Modern capture cards (e.g. Pinnacle) and capture software (e.g. Premiere) support the OpenDML format.

OpenDML is supported by the Windows Media Player and by QuickTime.

Test Captures

It is best to make a small test recording before committing to a long capture session. This checks the efficiency of the system and ensures that the capture settings are not greater than the ability of the computer. Problems are shown up as dropped frames. Most capture software will produce reports on the number of frames captured during a session and will report on any dropped frames. Playing back files with dropped frames shows up as jerks in the smooth playback. The test also shows if the equipment is of sufficient quality (no algorithm artifacts, no excessive camera/capture card noise).

Backup

The chapter on Windows stressed the importance of backups. This is true of all media but some are more important than others. It may be possible to reconstruct correspondence, meeting notes, scripts, and even Director scripts. But, material that is time sensitive (e.g. a football match, an interview with an American personality while in the UK, etc) cannot be replaced. Backups are even more important in these cases. If possible, the original videocassette should be retained, labelled and stored. The video files can be archived to tape drives, CD-R, or Zip drives. See the chapter on Windows for more details.

Video Storage

Digitised full-motion video can easily occupy huge amounts of hard disk space. The chapter on technology covered the storage requirements for a single picture frame at different resolutions. Video clips are stored (i.e. saved to disk) and played back between 15 and 30 individual screens per second.

The storage capacity per second of uncompressed video can be calculated thus:

File Size = Bit Depth x Screen Resolution x Frames/Sec

This is divided by 8 to get the answer in bytes, divided by 1024 to get the answer in KBs and divided again by 1024 to get the answer in MBs.

So, one second at full-colour (i.e. 24 bits) MPEG-1 (i.e. 352x288) at a 25fps screen update would require

352 x 288 x 24 x 30 / 8 / 1024 / 1024 = 7.25MB

The chart shows the storage requirements for a range of popular video modes.

Note that the table describes the storage requirements and this is not the same as the actual screen data that will be processed. So, for example, a graphics card that drives a monitor at 1600x1200 will have to either:

- Display the video in a part of the monitor screen.
- Interpolate the video data so that it fills the entire screen.

Most common use	Screen resolution	Frame rate	Storage/sec before compression
PAL MPEG-1	352 x 288	25	7.25MB
PAL MPEG-2	720 x 576	25	29.66MB
PAL MPEG-2 widescreen	1280 x 576	25	52.73MB
NTSC MPEG-1	352 x 240	30	7.25MB
NTSC MPEG-2	720 x 480	30	29.66MB
NTSC MPEG-2 widescreen	1013 x 480	30	41.73MB

The smallest figure for an MPEG-1 image is 7.25MB, while a PAL widescreen storage figure is around 53MB per second! Even a large hard disk or a CD/DVD can soon become full.

But the problems of large files are not confined to storage. These large files have to be delivered to the user's screen at a fast enough rate to reproduce the original video footage. Transferring such huge amounts of data will strain even the fastest of computers, those with fast hard disks, fast CD/DVD drives, fast CPUs and fast video systems.

For Internet use, they cause even greater problems. File sizes are measured in megabytes, while Internet traffic is measured in megabits per second.

Since there are eight bits to one byte, an uncompressed widescreen PAL video clip would need to be transmitted at over 400 megabits per second (i.e. 42.73MB x 8).   Since a modem only works at 56kbps and a typical ADSL line usually only runs at a theoretical maximum of 512mbps, there is no prospect of delivering high-quality uncompressed video to the majority of users.   In most cases, large video files means huge download delays and high bandwidth charges.

So, these storage figures are not practical and a number of methods are introduced to reduce this size:
- Using only a portion of the screen to display the video.   If the video occupies a quarter of the screen area, it only needs a quarter of the storage space.
- Reducing the colour palette to 256 colours may mean a barely noticeable loss of colour gradation, but would result in a video clip that is a third of the size of a 16.78m colour clip.
- Lowering the frame rate at which the picture is displayed. This makes savings but the picture is jerkier.
- Compressing the files for storage and decompressing them when they are to be played.   Unlike the other three methods, compression need not produce any deterioration in picture quality.   The user also has the option to make even bigger savings at the expense of some picture quality.

While reducing the video screen size is a common option, most designers use one of the many compression options that are available.

Note

As explained earlier, the circuitry in a camcorder digitises the analogue signal and then compresses it to a data rate of 3.6MB/sec. So, the digital video that is transferred to the computer via the FireWire port is already DV compressed. When people talk about *'uncompressed DV'* they really mean the digital signal that is transferred between the camcorder and the computer and has not yet been subjected to any *further* compression.

The transfer of the data between the camcorder and the computer is not a digitising process – it is really just a file transfer.

File Architectures

When discussing compressed file formats there are two separate issues:

The CODEC	This describes the way that the data is compressed and decompressed. Indeo and Cinepak are examples of video CODECs. The way a CODEC works is explained in the chapter on digital audio.
The Architecture	This describes the way that the file is packaged for delivery. This includes file format, CODEC used, playback format and packaging details for multiple tracks. Video for Windows (AVI) and QuickTime are examples of architectures.

Confusion sometimes arises because the AVI architecture can encompass many different CODECs.   The type of CODEC used to compress the file is embedded in the AVI or QuickTime file's header, to indicate the type of CODEC required to decompress the file.

So, if a user attempts to activate a file called *'test.mpg'*, the file's architecture header informs the computer that the file's data has been compressed using a particular MPEG compression type.   The computer then has to use another piece of software, the CODEC, to actually convert the compressed version into a version that the computer can use. Similarly a file with a .fla extension will tell the computer to view the contents using the Flash player.

AVI and QuickTime are architectures designed for CD, kiosk, web and general use, while RealVideo is an architecture specifically designed for web video use. Microsoft decided to phase out AVI in favour of ASF (Advanced Streaming Format) which supports both streaming and non-streaming files, then to WMV and WMA for video and audio content.

Although the above examples relate to video files, the distinction between file architecture and CODECs can apply to animation, audio and graphics files.

Compression

This section looks at the general principles involved in file compression. Specific techniques are considered at the end of the chapter.   Compression involves the restructuring and possible elimination of data to achieve a smaller file size.   This restructuring is carried out by a CODEC (compressor/decompressor). This is an engine that compresses (shrinks) the files on saving and decompresses (expands) them again when they are to be used. CODECs can be implemented in either hardware or software.   Hardware CODECs are more expensive but, because they use dedicated chips instead of the computer's CPU time, they can be significantly more efficient.   CODECs are designed to minimise the time taken to decompress the material, so that files play smoothly.   This often means that the compression stage is complex and time-consuming.

CODEC selection and configuration is based on three factors:
- Compression level.
- Compression quality.
- Compression/Decompression speed

With the current level of technology, the designer has to decide which factors are more important. For example, higher levels of compression usually mean that the resultant file suffers greater loss of quality. Compressors that produce both high quality files along with high compression usually need a fast computer to decompress the files in real time, which may not be suitable for many projects.

At its best, compression may result in a smaller file size with no loss in picture quality. If a file saved in a compressed format can be uncompressed to produce a picture that is identical bit-by-bit with the original, it is described as *'lossless compression'*. The GIF format for graphic files and the GIF89a format for animated GIFs are examples of lossless compression. Lossless compressed files are used for high-quality images or for archiving of quality original images.

Files can be compressed to a greater degree if some loss of detail is acceptable. Since the human eye cannot detect small detail changes, *'lossy compression'* techniques are the types found in most compression systems.
If the degree of compression is not too great, the loss of quality will not be noticed. This is termed *'perceptually lossless compression'*. The human eye is used to viewing objects from a variety of distances, from the side of the eye and through adverse conditions such as rain, fog and darkness. The human brain adjusts to cope with these degraded images. So, if the compressed video results in images that correspond to the brain's ability to compensate, the losses are not perceived by the viewer. Indeed, sometimes a small degree of detail loss is perceived as an improvement in the picture. The picture is perceived as being *'cleaned up'* with some of the *'grain'* being removed.

Increasing the compression and lowering the image quality will eventually result in visual artifacts (e.g. blockiness, the removal of edges to objects, the creation of spurious edges, etc.) that will be identified by the viewer as a poor quality picture.

The degree of compression can be altered to suit the purpose of the final product. For example, a video file destined for placing on the web will be compressed further than a video for use on a CD. The poorer quality is traded for faster Internet transfer.

Noise and compression
Noise is the result of unwanted elements in the video signal; elements that were not part of original image that was captured. Noise is often produced by the electronics of the hardware. These are usually unwanted electrical signals, signals introduced by the electronic components in the camera or the video capture board. Their position in the picture is more random than algorithm artifacts and appear as *'snow'* in the picture in worst cases.
Video clips can also suffer from 'quantisation noise'. Digitising the continuously varying analogue signal into a fixed number of digital levels results in quantisation noise. This is particularly significant when the digitisation process forces the analogue signal into lower than a 24-bit colour resolution.
Noise is also worsened when the camcorder is unable to properly resolve a picture shot in low light conditions. Since there are fewer differences in light levels in the scene, the quantisation process converts the analogue signal into a lower range of digital values, resulting in more noise and less compression.
Similarly, if the video signal is overloaded, either at the recording stage or the processing stage, the analogue signal is quantised into the range of higher digital values only. Often, the upper ranges of the signal are all converted to white level. This produces a bleached effect and greatly lowers the dynamic range of the digitised signal.

The software cannot tell the difference between fine picture details and general unwanted video noise. It will process both through its compression algorithm. Any fine picture detail lowers the compression ratio and this is often a price worth paying for picture quality. However, noise in the signal lowers the compression ratio, without adding anything to the picture quality. If test recordings produce significant levels of noise, the camcorder, cables, and capture card should be individually tested, usually with a temporary replacement. The higher the quality of the original clip, the greater the compression, because there is less noise in the signal. BetaCam SP is best, followed by DV, then the high band analogues, the low band analogues and finally the webcams.

Problems with Artifacts
Artifacts are unwanted visual elements that appear on the picture and are the result of applying the CODEC algorithm. Some algorithms produce more artifacts than others, in given situations. The inability to maintain picture quality under all picture content conditions shows itself as:
- Problems around the edges of objects, particularly large plain geometric shapes. This is known as the *'Gibb Effect'* and produces a blurring or hazing effect around the object's boundaries. It also produces a shiimering effect in the background around a person or object that moves.
- Blockiness of diagonal surfaces. Since MPEG compression operates on blocks of 8x8 pixels, they can become noticeable in scenes involving the fast movement of objects.

A big advantage of storing video in digital format is its capability of being reproduced many times over without any degradation of quality. This is greatly superior to tape storage, where there is a loss of quality with each copy made.
On the other hand, when a digital copy suffers any loss of quality, it may affect a large chunk of the clip. Even an error in a single bit in the video stream can affect a large block of the screen content. This effect can be seen from time to time on digital television channels.

Storyboards and compression

The camera operator can ensure that the video is shot in sufficient light to reduce noise and improve compression. Where a particularly small video file is required, extra care has to be taken at the storyboard stage to prevent camera operations that result in poorer compression.   Compression algorithms work less efficiently with scenes that contain a lot of detail or a lot of movement.   Careful attention should be paid to the amount of unnecessary detail that will appear in a scene. This may result in removing a very leafy plant from an office scene, or changing the heavily patterned curtains for a plainer set.   Shooting the subject in front of a plain backdrop such as a matt painted wall is recommended. Alternatively, the camera can be adjusted to make the background out of focus. Similarly, prevent the subject wearing fussy clothes, such as a herringbone jacket, paisley pattern blouse, or striped suit.

The question of movement is a little more difficult.   The less movement in the scene, the higher is the compression ratio.   The movement may come from the camera (panning, zooming) or from the subject. However, a clip with little or no movement soon becomes uninteresting.   A balance has to be struck that reflects the nature of the clip.   A busy factory shop floor may make an interesting background for an interview with the company manager, but if the interview is being conducted in the factory car park, avoid a background of moving cars, people walking, trees blowing in the wind, etc. If a particularly animated object is to be filmed, shoot from further back if possible, as this reduces overall scene movement in the frame.

Using 'hard cuts' during editing in place of fades, wipes, pans and dissolves will also improve compression.   These effects produce constantly changing frame contents (that's their purpose!).

Keeping the exposure control on manual reduces the problems of people moving in front of/away from windows and changing the automatic exposure.   The camcorder operator should stay on manual, or plan to avoid these light changes which reduce compression.

At the end of the day, these technical considerations have to be balanced with the dynamism created by fast moving video clips.

Compression and editing

Since compression systems almost always introduce artifacts, all handling and editing of DV material should be in DV format until the delivery stage. Only then should the footage be subjected to compression. This minimises the likelihood of introducing too many artifacts.

When deciding which compression method to use, remember the following:

- Uncompressed AVIs can be played on all systems – but are huge.
- All Windows PCs can play AVIs that are created using a CODEC that is supplied with Windows Media Player – but this limits the designer's possibilities.
- All PCs can play any video file, as long as it has an add-on CODEC installed – but this requires the end user to find and install the CODEC just to view the project's video clips.

Since is very unlikely that Microsoft is ever going to bundle its competitors' CODECs with its Media Player, the project has to consider the context in which the project will be used.

AVI CODEC types

The AVI (Audio Video Interleave) format is the original Windows standard and is so-called because it stored the audio and video information as a single file, with the video data and audio being divided into blocks and interleaved in the file.   Since both streams of data were stored next to each other in time, it aided the synchronisation process. Where video and audio files are held separately, the delays in reading both sets of data from disk and interpreting the separate streams leads to severe problems of keep the sound synchronised to the picture.

AVI files can be in compressed or uncompressed format depending whether one of the compression algorithms (see below) has been applied them.

All modern versions of Windows (i.e. after version 3.1) include software CODECs.

These all result in files with 'AVI' extension and are:

Cinepak

Developed by Apple for their SuperMac computers and then licensed to Microsoft, it was a popular Video for Windows CODEC.   It is also supplied with Apple's QuickTime. It handles 8-bit colour (for animations and cartoons) and 24-bit (for everything else).   This was a good general software purpose CODEC for CD ROM distribution but has been replaced by more efficient CODECs. Its ability to produce good quality compressed video has been matched by newer CODECS that produce much smaller file sizes.

Indeo

This system was initially developed by Intel then purchased by the Ligos Corporation. Indeo 3.x had a slightly better compression ratio and shorter compression time than Cinepak but introduced more artifacts. Indeo 4.x, then renamed Video Interactive 4, took advantage of the new improvements in Pentium technology to improve performance and quality.   It also introduced transparency masks for their clips. This is the same technique as 'chroma key' (see chapter on video editing).   Version 5.0 is aimed at web video by including progressive download (see QuickTime for details).

Like, Cinepak, Indeo has been overtaken by other more efficient CODECs.

MSVC

The Microsoft Video Compressor, also known as Video 1.   It was developed to use algorithms that placed less pressure on the CPU. It has not found a place in general use. It only supports 256 or 32k colours and there is no control over the data rate.

RLE

Run Length Encoding takes a horizontal area of a colour and stores the length of the band rather than the individual pixels. This is very effective in animations where backgrounds are plain but produces poor results as a video CODEC. Its 8-bit colour depth is satisfactory for animations but is not good enough for real life video.

AVI CODECs are simply CODECs that produce files with the .avi extension.   They cover a range of compression methods that are provided with Windows or are installed as add-ons. Popular AVI CODECs that are not provided along with Windows include:

M-JPEG

Motion-JPEG, called M-JPEG, is similar in basis to the JPEG graphic format.   Each individual frame is compressed using JPEG techniques and each frame is stored individually and separately. By concentrating on individual frame compression, it produces less spectacular compression ratios (around 8:1) but provides 24-bit depth, higher quality and easier manipulation and editing.   Its larger file size and subsequent increased data rate needs meant that it could not be supported by the slow speeds of early CD players and no mass-market M-JPEG players were produced. It is a storage and editing medium but is not used as a distribution medium. A M-JPEG clip would be converted into another format such as MPEG for distribution. It has the normal *'AVI'* file extension, e.g. *'wedding.avi'*.

This CODEC is not supplied with Windows but is usually bundled with a capture card that has M-JPEG compression, since is essentially an analogue capture CODEC.

Microsoft MPEG-4 v2

Versions 1 and 2 of this CODEC encoded AVI files. Version 3 did not produce AVI files and the CODEC was later renamed Windows Media (see later).

Despite its original name, it is not the same as the standard MPEG-4 CODEC. The Microsoft version is based on the Working Group specification but uses its own compression system. While its quality is slightly poorer than Windows Media CODECs, the file sizes are very small.   It does not require a licence and is available for free download from the Microsoft web site.

DivX 3.xx

In their bid to move users towards the ASF format (see later), Microsoft's MPEG-4 version 3 CODEC would only encode ASF files and would not support the AVI format. So, a French teenager hacked Microsoft's version 3 so that it could encode AVI files, adding other features such as larger frame sizes and different audio CODECs. This was called DivX3, also known as Divx ;-) (the smiley face is not my comment, it is part of the CODEC description).

So, DivX 3.xx is totally illegal and should not be used. It can cause real legal problems if used, especially with commercial projects. The CODEC is best left to those who use it to distribute pirate movies and porn, where it is a very popular CODEC. It is also used to further compress movies on DVDs so that they fit on standards CDs.

DivX 3.xx comes in two varieties, Low-Motion and Fast-Motion, both being separate hacks of the Microsoft product. The Low-Motion version is the most popular and is used for video that does not contain a great deal of screen motion. The Fast-Motion version produces better results for video footage that contains very fast moving action sequences.

Users who wish to view DivX3.xx encoded files have to find this CODEC on the Internet and install it. This also makes it unsuitable for commercial applications.

DivX 4.xx

The DivX4.xx is CODEC that was written from the bottom up, is fully compliant with the MPEG-4 standard, and is not based on Microsoft's product (making it fully legal).

It was initially called OpenDivx, before being developed into the commercial versions DivX4.xx and DivX5.xx.

The *'Pro'* version is commercial but a search of the Internet will find adware-supported versions (i.e. free) and possibly free versions without adware.

The DivX 4.xx CODEC can play videos that have been encoded with the DivX3.xx CODEC but the DivX3.xx version cannot handle DivX 4.xx files.

DivX 4.xx uses two-pass VBR encoding for better quality.

DivX 5.xx

The DivX 4.xx version did not provide all the benefits that were expected and was replaced by DivX 5.xx which provided real improvements over both DivX 3.xx and DivX 4.xx. Like DivX 4.xx, it is fully legal.

DivX 5.xx is particularly effective at low bit rates, where the quality of the encoded files are regarded as superior to other DivX versions, including the Microsoft version. Often, however, its compression ratio is not as good as other CODECs. Although most DivX encoded files use the AVI extension, DivX 5.xx can also produce files with a .divx extension.

XviD

This MPEG-4-compliant CODEC remains an open-source product, which adds to its popularity.

Its two pass encoding results in picture quality that is comparable with other MPEG-4 CODECs, except at lower bit rates. However, its compression ratio is much better than DivX 5.xx.

Its main problem is its erratic behaviour with different players, which makes it unsuitable for commercial products.

Microsoft is trying to get users to switch to using their Windows Media format system. For the moment, the popularity of the AVI format and the many varieties of compression that it encompasses means that AVI files will be around for a long time yet.

Non-AVI Codecs

Apart from the standard CODECs supplied with Windows, there are some other very significant and popular CODECs that can be installed, such as MPEG, QuickTime, Windows Media and RealVideo.

MPEG

Many compression systems tie the user to a particular CODEC. So, if a particular CODEC is used to compress a file, the exact same CODEC must be used to decompress that file. MPEG is more flexible, as you don't need to use the same CODEC for encoding and for playback.

The Moving Pictures Experts Group was set up in 1988 as an ISO (International Standards Organisation) working group. It developed a series of internationally recognised standards for compressing audio and video files. Each standard was designed to produce the best bit rate for a specific application.

The MPEG format uses a complicated set of compression methods including spatial compression, Huffman coding and predictive compression - based on only saving the differences (or 'deltas') between successive frames. Depending on the quality and speed required, it may sometimes require expensive hardware, but can achieve surprising compression rates. Compression ratios up to 50:1 can be achieved before the picture quality deteriorates noticeably. The MPEG standards are:

MPEG-1

This first standard was brought out in 1992 and was initially designed for the compression of non-video sources. However, it was found to handle video as long as it was converted from its original interlaced mode into a progressively scanned format.

Most systems were initially designed around MPEG-1 with data rates of around 1.4Mbps and frame rates up to 30fps. Its maximum bit rate is 1.856Mbits/sec.

It provides the lowest common format as it can produce 352x288 at 25fps for European PAL TV (or 352x240 at 30fps for American NTSC TV) from a standard CD-ROM player.   This is sometimes referred to as SIF - the Standard Interchange Format. It is also a common multimedia format. It produces a result similar to television's VHS quality.

Although a few programs were transmitted in MPEG-1 format by satellite, it is mainly used for placing video on CDs, using CD-I or VideoCD format. It is also commonly used for video on the web.

Many video clips found on CDs use this format, to ensure that the largest possible audience can view them. Of course, modern PCs have significant hardware improvements that allow them to handle larger (i.e. better quality) files and so the use of MPEG-1 has declined. Nevertheless, it remains a good general choice, as these files can be played on PCs, Macs and Unix systems.

MPEG-1 files use an 'mpg' extension. VCDs (Video CDs) use the DAT extension to name MPEG-1 files. DAT files can be renamed to the MPG extension, if required, before being played in an MPEG-1 player. Level 3 of MPEG-1 is widely also used for compressing audio files and these have an 'mp3' extension.

MPEG-2

In 1994, the committee brought out a standard aimed specifically for compression of interlaced video. MPEG-2 is a higher quality standard, with a consequent increase in data rates.   It delivers a screen resolution of 720x576, at 25fps, for PAL and 720x480, at 30fps, for NTSC.

Although it can handle SIF formats, it is mostly used for broadcast quality video as it supports a wide range of bit rates and also supports multi-channel surround sound. Encoding files is complex (especially when the files need to conform to strict DVD standards) but the resulting files are of high quality.

The table shows some typical MPEG-2 applications.

Level	Size	Bit-rate	Application
Low	352 x 288	4Mbits/sec	Consumer (e.g. CD White Book films, video games, SIF clips in CDs
Medium	720 x 576	4Mbits/sec	DVD
Main	720 x 576	15-20Mbits/sec	Studio TV
High 1440	1440 x 1152	60-80Mbits/sec	HDTV
High	1920 x 1152	80-100Mbits/sec	Film production

Other applications include DBS (Direct Broadcast Satellite), DVD video, Tivo digital recorders, and VOD (Video on Demand). In the UK, it is used by Sky, On Digital and digital cable companies.

Any manufacturer of MPEG-2 hardware or software devices must pay a licence fee, which explains why software DVD players are only installed on computers as an extra add-on.

M2V files contain MPEG-2 encoded video and M2S files contain both video and audio streams. .VOB files are MPEG-2 files that are encoded for use on DVDs and they cannot simply be renamed to view them on MPEG-2 players; they have to be run through converter software.

MPEG-3

MPEG-3 was planned for HDTV and other very high quality video applications. Since MPEG-2 was found to easily scale up to HDTV resolution and bit rates, the MPEG-3 standard was dropped. Its provisions have been merged into MPEG-2.

MPEG-4

This standard was primarily targeted at web, video conferencing, telephone and cellular phone markets, where very low bit rates are required. For example, audio-on-demand over the Internet is transmitted at only 16kbps. The UMTS mobile radio standard is also based on MPEG-4 compression.

In fact, MPEG-4 compression is not confined to low bit rate applications. It is increasingly used for video compression of relatively high quality, as it can handle a range of bit rates from as low as 5kbps up to a very respectable 10mbps. This allows videos to be created for a range of purposes, from small low-quality clips for web purposes up to the distribution of commercial movies.

MPEG-4 provides the basis of DivX movies, where the video bit rate can be set for high quality (least compression) through to maximum compression (poorest quality). In practice, MPEG-4 can deliver greater compression ratios than MPEG-2 for comparable video quality.

Although MPEG-4 is a CODEC, it is also referred to as a 'container'. This is because the specification allows for the inclusion of multiple media types and for interactivity, although these parts of the specification have not been widely implemented. Like MPEG-2, this standard requires manufacturers to pay licence fees.

The Windows Media CODECs are now considered to have overtaken the MPEG-4 specification, although it remains in widespread use.

Typical MPEG-4 file extensions are MP4, AVI (e.g. using DivX) or MOV.

Other versions

MPEG-1, MPEG-2 and MPEG-4 all describe how a video file is compressed. The committee has produced another standard, known as MPEG-7 and this describes the actual content of the video. It is intended as a complement to MPEG-4 and not a replacement. This is aimed at the content management of multimedia assets and is known as the 'Multimedia Content Description Interface'. It provides a standardised scheme for describing media content, down to such details as colour histograms and textures. This provides new opportunities to index and retrieve media content, with uses such as search engines, broadcasting, streaming, news distribution and digital libraries. The MPEG-7 Consortium describe how individual users can search for media files by sketching an object's shape or humming part of a melody. Mobile applications have already begun to combine MPEG-4 and MPEG-7 techniques.

Another standard is in development. This is MPEG-21, also known as the 'Multimedia Framework'. Like MPEG-7, it is not a compression standard. It defines an open framework for the creation and delivery of multimedia over various devices and networks.

QuickTime

Apple originally produced the QuickTime architecture for their range of Macintosh machines but it is now 'multi-platform' - versions are also produced for PC and Unix systems. As one of the early pioneers, it has a large following. Its files have the extension 'MOV', e.g. 'racing.mov', and are referred to as QuickTime movies. MOV files are 'cross platform' - if, for example, a MOV file is placed on a web site, it can be downloaded and played by any hardware system that has a QuickTime player. If the file is a streamed version, it can start playing as soon as it starts to download. Alternate extensions for QuickTime files are .QT and .MP4.

Starting with version 6, QuickTime can encode files to the MPEG-4 standard. These have the MP4 extension and are playable on any MPEG-4-compliant player, as well as through QuickTime.

Like AVIs, QuickTime is a container that stores files that have been encoded by any one of a number of compatible CODECs. Many AVI CODECs have to be downloaded as third-party add-ons. QuickTime, however, provides a range of useful CODECs along with the player. QuickTime Standard, the free download, produces regular start-up messages suggesting upgrading to the commercial QuickTime Pro version.

Sorenson Video 3

This is the CODEC most chosen by professionals for creating QuickTime files. Version three produced significant improvements in picture quality at the same bit rate, compared to earlier versions.

There are two versions. The Standard Edition is included with the Quicktime installer. It provides basic controls over data rate, keyframe rate, and frame rate. The Professional Edition is a commercial product that provides even better quality through two-pass VBR (Variable Bit Rate) encoding, along with new features such as support for alpha channel/chroma keying.

Its quality is good, even at low data rates, and is up with the best of other CODECs. Unfortunately, its compression ratio is not as competitive.

Since it is bundled with the QuickTime player, any computer that has the player installed is able to play the video. For those machines that do not have the QuickTime player installed, it would have to be downloaded and installed.

MPEG-4 Video

This was first incorporated into QuickTime 6, but it is not as good as other MPEG-4 or Sorenson CODECs. Its picture quality is poorer and it produces larger file sizes, mainly because it uses a CBR (Constant Bit Rate) encoding system. However, it is fully complies with the MPEG-4 standard, providing some degree of compatibility.

H.263

Although strictly a standard for videoconferencing, this CODEC has been used for video encoding, since the encoded files can be played back in all MPEG-4 standard players, not just through QuickTime. Its highest resolution is 352x288, with any higher resolutions being scaled down. Although motion is encoded smoothly, including low data rates, the edges of objects exhibit *'jaggies'* (i.e. blockiness). It provides a higher degree of compression than Sorenson, specially at high data rates.

Others CODECs

Like AVI, QuickTime has some older CODECs like M-JPEG and Cinepack. See the earlier section on AVI CODECs for general descriptions.

QuickTime uses an open architecture that allows it to support many different formats. These include DV, MPEG1 to MPEG-4, H261, QuickTime VR and web streaming systems.

QuickTime Player

The QuickTime Player is free and can be downloaded from www.apple.com/quicktime/

It is a software based application and therefore requires some of the computer's CPU time.   The player handles a wide variety of media, being able to display or reproduce AVIs, MPEGs, WAVs, MP3s, Audio CDs, Flash, FLC/FLI animations, GIFs, JPEGs, MIDI, text and much more (over 60 different file types).   The MOV file contains a header that informs the computer about the format of the contents.

However, it is its ability to package a wide range of multimedia objects within a MOV file that has resulted in its adoption as the first choice for most multimedia developers.   It soon became the most common plug-in for the Netscape and Windows Explorer web browsers and has the major share of use on CD and kiosk projects.   It provides a comprehensive set of commands for embedding in HTML files.   These allow control over the playback of MOV file from the web (see the chapters on design).

MOV files also support multiple tracks, where each track can contain a different media type.   So, for example a MIDI track can play while a video file is being displayed, or a URL can be placed in a text track so that a web site is automatically opened at a certain point in the file.

QuickTime Pro

QuickTime Pro is the authoring version of the application and is not provided free.   It has much superior facilities to Video for Windows.   It provides tools to capture, edit, compress and package video. It can also be used as file converter, as it can import and export a wide range of common file formats.

Streaming

QuickTime Pro provides facilities to create files for the web that accommodate both *'Progressive Download'* and *'True Streaming'*.   Like all streaming files, the web site server has to be capable of handling the format.   Normal, non-streamed, files have to be downloaded then played.   Streaming allows the movie to be watched while the file is being downloaded.

With progressive download, the user is provided with a file at a pre-determined level of speed/quality (see *'Scalability'* below). There may be a slight delay before playing, but thereafter the movie is played in real time.

With true streaming, the video is delivered in real time by the server. This is often used for live interviews, concerts, etc but can equally be used to transmit pre-recorded material.

If the effective transfer speed of the user's connection is reduced, through noise or congestion, the real time playback is maintained by dropping frames (reducing the playback quality of the video).

Scalability

QuickTime Pro is used by web site developers to create a number of different versions of the same video file for placing on a web site. Each version has a different compression/quality level.   The Internet user can set the computer's connection speed within the QuickTime settings, as shown.   When a video clip is selected for viewing, the clip that matches the user's Internet speed is selected.   This produces the best possible results for each user. Those with slow modems are given the smaller, poorer quality, file; those with fast connections are given the larger, higher quality version. The new Microsoft Advanced Streaming Format provides a similar facility although it is limited to handling just two (high bandwidth and low bandwidth) versions of files.

Editing

Although most editing of QuickTime movies will be carried using well-known editors such as Adobe Premiere or Macromedia Director, QuickTime Pro offers some basic editing facilities such as cut and paste. A range of video effects such as emboss, blur, lens flare and edge detection are also provided through the package's built-in filters.

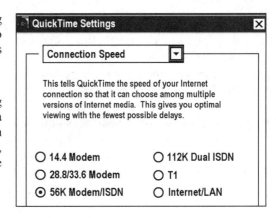

Windows Media

Originally titled *'MS MPEG-4 version 3'*, the name was changed to *'Windows Media'* after the Moving Pictures Experts Group adopted an MPEG-4 standard that was not compatible with Microsoft's CODEC.

Like AVI and QuickTime, Windows Media is also a file container, enabling the production of compressed files for normal storage or for streaming over a network.

Microsoft has targeted the CODEC for web delivery purposes and its use is now widespread. This is due to the high quality of the encoded video and the small size of the files (about half the size of an MPEG-4 file at the same data rate).

The file extension for Windows Media encoded files was .asf and this covered both compressed audio and compressed video files. Many of these files are still around but later CODECs saved video files with the .wmv extension and audio files with the .wma extension. These extensions are used both for downloading and streaming purposes.

The purpose and technique of streaming is explained in detail in the *"Developing Web Sites"* chapter. The Windows Media metafiles (i.e. pointer files) are

.wax	For files with the .asf or .wma file extensions.
.wvx	For files with the .wma or .wmv file extensions.
.asx	For files with the .wma, .wmv, . or .asf, file extensions.

These are text files that contain instructions on how to handle the data files.

A typical call in an HTML document is:

<A href="filename.asx">link description goes here </a>

When the user clicks on the link, the browser downloads the metafile and its instructions launch the Windows Media Player and begin the streaming of the data file (i.e. the wmv, wma or asf file). ASX files can contain playlists, so that a number of different files can be played in succession.

A free Windows Media Encoder is available from the Microsoft web site and this includes a plug-in for Adobe Premiere.

RealVideo

This is marketed by RealNetworks. It does not offer the wide range of facilities provided by QuickTime, as it is primarily aimed at Internet use. Its CODEC applies Fractal Image Compression, which provides high compression, resulting in very small file sizes (half the size of an MPEG-4 file at the same quality and quarter the size of an MPEG-2 file at the same quality).

It provides both progressive download and true streaming and files can be viewed with a *'RealOne'* player that is available free from the RealNetwork web site. An expanded commercial version is also available. RealNetworks also supply the CODECs for creating RealVideo and RealAudio files.

Videoconferencing CODECs

A number of CODECs have been developed for use in videoconferencing systems. Since these systems have lower bandwidths the CODECs generally work with smaller screen resolutions. These are known as CIF (Common Intermediate Format). The standard CIF resolution, known as FCIF (Full CIF), is 352x288 and even smaller variations are the QCIF (Quarter CIF) at 176x144 and the SQCIF (Sub Quarter CIF) at 128x96. Larger formats are the 4CIF at 704x576 and the 16CIF at 1408x1152.

The basic videoconferencing CODEC is H.261, which was developed to transmit CIF and QCIF over ISDN links at 64kbs or its multiples. It encodes at a constant bite rate, instead of using a constant quality, variable bit rate approach. This means that the quality of the image is maximised when there is little movement in the picture, while a picture that rapidly changes produces a poorer quality image. The CODEC uses DCT, along with intraframe and interframe compression (see later). It is implemented either in hardware or software.

H.263 is an improved version of H.261 for use with modems. It also supports CIF and QCIF but can also handle SQCIF, 4CIF and 16CIF.

Determining the CODECs installed

Over time, different CODECs will be added to the default set provided with Windows.   To see the list of CODECs on a particular computer, the following steps should be carried out:

- Click the *'Start'* button on the main menu bar.
- Choose *'Settings'* from the pop-up menu.
- Choose *'Control Panel'* from the sub-menu.
- Choose *'Multimedia'* or *'Sound, Speech & Audio'*.
- In Windows 95, click on the *'Advanced'* tab.
- In Windows 98/ME, click on the *'Devices'* tab.
- In Windows 2000/XP, click on the *"Hardware"* tab.
- Click on *'Video Compression Codecs'* in the displayed list of devices.

The list of CODECs that are installed on the computer are then displayed, as shown.

If a CODEC is highlighted and the *'Properties'* button is clicked, extra information on the codec may be displayed.   If the *'Settings'* button is not greyed out, it can be clicked and individual CODEC features may be enabled.

Determining the CODEC used on an AVI File

Since an AVI file may have been encoded using one of a variety of CODECS, Windows provides a method to get a report on a file's configuration. If an AVI file is highlighted in *'Windows Explorer'* and the mouse right-hand button is clicked, the *'Properties'* option of the resulting menu produces the screen shown (with slight variations between different Windows versions).

The options include:

- The *'General'* option shows file dates, size, etc.
- The *'Preview'* option (not available in XP) runs the clip in a miniature window.
- The *'Details'* or *'Summary'* option shows that the file called *'testfile1'* is designed to be run in a quarter of a VGA screen at 15fps using a Cinepak CODEC.   Its data rate is only 146kbps, allowing it to be run directly from even the slowest CD-ROM drive.   This is a good example of how early AVI files were produced to match the lowest possible hardware performance.

Since even compressed video clips tend to be enormous, most clips found in the public domain are low resolution with a low frame rate. The result is below TV quality, but gets the message across effectively, which is the intention of multimedia in the first place.   The clips that are found in many magazines' *'free'* CDs are of larger size but they still have to be tailored to the lowest standards, to be compatible with the largest numbers of user machines.

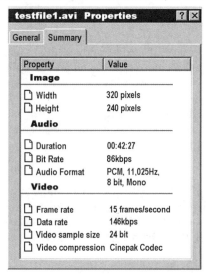

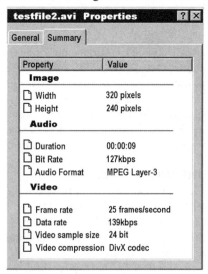

Compare this with the second example.   Both are using approximately the same bit rate.

Despite this, the second clip has a significantly higher frame rate (25fps compared to 15fps), has much higher quality audio and has higher quality video.

This is because the second clip has been encoded with a DivX CODEC which has a much better compression ratio (and better picture quality) than the Cinepak CODEC.

Playback Systems

All compressed video files require to be played back using some type of CODEC.

In the early implementations, hardware CODECs were often used, as older computers could not process the video decompression sufficiently fast to maintain the video display without jerkiness and loss of screens.   The hardware was mounted on graphics-processing cards and the processing chips relieved the computer's CPU from the CODEC tasks. Now that computers are much faster, they usually have the capacity to carry out the CODEC tasks in software. Hardware CODECs are still available, although they are now usually confined to videoconferencing and other real-time encoding/decoding tasks.

The point was made earlier in this chapter that the decoding time should be as short as possible for maximum usability, even if this requires more effort at the encoding stage. Most software CODECs carry out encoding in less than real time. For example, a 10-minute video clip may take 15 or 20 minutes to encode. Since the decode time is shorter than the encoding time, this is called *'asymmetrical processing'*. This is not a problem when files are encoded and then placed on a CD/DVD or web site for future retrieval.

However, this method is not acceptable in real-time situations such as real-time broadcast streaming, videoconferencing and dialogue mode applications. Ideally, both encoding and decoding should take place in real-time. This is known as *'symmetrical compression'*. As a minimum, the encoding should occur in real-time.

Compression theory

Before looking at the various techniques used for compression, consider how compression is possible. If all the information in a file is necessary, how can the file be compressed? The answer is that not all the file's information is required to provide a reproduction of the original content.

Digital files, audio, video or images, contain some redundancy. Examples of redundancy are:

- In many images, the colour of a pixel is the same as the previous pixel.
- In a video clip, a newsreader sits motionless, apart from her mouth moving.   Almost all of the image content in a frame of that clip is the same as the previous frame, and the same as the next frame.

These are examples of *'redundancy'* – the same data is stored more than once. In the first example, there is *'spatial redundancy'*, while the second example shows *'temporal redundancy'*.

Spatial redundancy describes identical data being stored in the same *space* (e.g. on a single image or movie frame), while *temporal* redundancy describes identical data being stored over *time* (e.g. the identical content of successive movie frames).

In addition, compression can be achieved by taking advantage of human perception factors. For example, the human eye is less sensitive to higher spatial frequencies than to lower spatial frequencies. It is also less sensitive to the chrominance (colour) component of the picture than the luminance (brightness) component, allowing the chrominance component to be compressed without perceived loss of quality.   The eye is also less sensitive to quantising distortion at higher luminance levels. Equally, the human ear can perceive intelligence from a restricted range of audio frequencies compared to the original (e.g. a telephone conversation transmits only a part of each participant's voice frequency range and yet both parties recognise each others voices).   This means that the compressed file need not store an exact replica of the original information to be clearly recognised and understood by the user.

So, the content of an original piece of material has two parts:

- The useful information, known as the *'entropy'*, which should all ideally be retained in the compressed file.
- The redundant information, which can be removed from the compressed version, with no ill effects whatsoever.

Lossless compression retains all of the entropy, while removing all of the redundant information.

Lossy compression removes the redundant information, along with some of the entropy. The lossier the compression, the greater the amount of the entropy that is lost.

Data compression schemes can employ the following techniques:

INTRAFRAME (Spatial Compression)	This considers each individual frame and discards any redundant data. This is the method used by RLE, DCT, VQ, JPEG and M-JPEG compression systems.
INTERFRAME (Temporal Compression)	This considers the differences between successive frames, removes the unchanged parts of the information and applies JPEG type compression on what is left. This is also called *'difference compression'* or *'delta compression'* and is used by the MPEG system.

A range of techniques is employed to achieve file compression. CODECs will often employ more than one of these methods in its algorithm.

Classification of Compression Techniques

There are two approaches to compression:

Entropy encoding

This is a lossless compression method, which retains all the entropy (essential information) while removing or reducing all the redundant information from a file.

This method ignores the actual purpose of the file. It does not care whether it is an audio file, a video file, or even a word-processed document, for instance. It processes the file's digital sequence regardless of what the individual bits represent.

It examines the bit stream, looking for ways to remove common or repetitive sequences.

Methods using these techniques include RLE (run length encoding), zero/blank replacement, codebooks, CLUTs (colour look up tables) pattern substitution, Huffman coding, statistical coding.

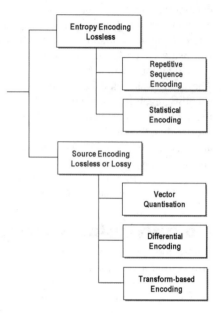

Entropy encoding techniques are used where the file's contents must remain entirely lossless. Examples are computer programs, fingerprints, legal, scientific and medical documents, and high-quality photographs, video and audio. In these examples, every detail is significant and must be preserved.

The decoding process recreates the original in every detail, making the encoding process completely reversible.

Source encoding

This could produce a lossless file but is most usually a lossy system. Some of the entropy is sacrificed to achieve even greater compression ratios than entropy encoding.

Source encoding makes use of both data redundancy and the human perception factors mentioned earlier. It considers the semantics (i.e. the meaning) of the data and considers strings of bits in relation to other strings of bits. For example, it knows that a video file is a sequence of individual frames where each frame's contents may only vary slightly from the previous frame. The degree of compression can then be made dependent on the data being examined. It knows that users will tolerate losses or even errors, particularly in ever changing content such as audio or video streams.

Source encoding produces the highest compression ratios and is routinely applied to audio and video files.

Methods using these techniques include vector quantisation, content prediction, delta modulation and transform based encoding.

Hybrid encoding

Multimedia systems generally use a mix of entropy and source encoding, to achieve the maximum compression possible. For example, JPEG, MPEG and H.263 use combine both entropy and source encoding techniques.

Compression Methods

Simple Compression Techniques

There are three simple compression techniques that, while not providing high levels of compression, produce simple encoding and decoding. These are truncation, CLUTs and RLE.

Truncation

This is a lossy method that can be applied to images. It reduces the file size by reducing the number of bits per pixel. So, for example, using PhotoShop or Paint Shop Pro to alter an image from true colour to high colour changes the colour depth from 24bpp to 16bpp. This makes a saving on file size of about one-third. As the number of bits per pixel is reduced, the image resolution deteriorates. If overdone, the image becomes cartoon-like in appearance.

CLUTs

The chapter on computer graphics explains how a Colour Look Up Table works.

It is used with 256-colour images and each colour in the image is represented by a number between 0 and 255.

So, for example, using PhotoShop or Paint Shop Pro to convert an uncompressed true colour (i.e. 24-bit) image into a GIF (i.e. 8-bit) image produces a file that is around one third its original size (the table has to be stored in the file along with the bitmap of the image). This saving is achieved by reducing the number of colours in the image from a possible maximum of 16.7m colours down to only 256 colours. A further saving is made by GIF's own compression system. So, CLUTs are a lossy techinque.

Run Length Encoding

This is a simple example of entropy encoding, as lossless compression is achieved.

Run Length Encoding (RLE) is available as a Windows CODEC and as a standalone video CODEC. The techniques are also incorporated into the Discrete Cosine Transform method (see later).

A single video frame consists of a long series of pixels that are displayed as a set of rows on the screen. Often, adjacent pixels will have identical colours. For example, part of a background may consist of a horizontal run of 20 identical pixel colours. RLE stores the length of the band rather than the individual pixels. If the colour of the pixel was represented by the number 19 then the uncompressed file would have to store the same pixel colour value 20 times as below:

19 19 19 19 19 19 19 19 19 19 19 19 19 19 19 19 19 19 19 19

An RLE file would store it as:

19 20 (i.e. the colour 19 repeated for 20 pixels).

In practice, a run is represented by three characters, with an initial character, such as @ or ~, being used to tell the decompression algorithm to treat what follows as a run. So the above example would be stored as @ 19 20

This technique works best with images that use relatively few colours and have little detail (such as cartoons and animations). The solid blocks of colour allow significant compression to be achieved. 24-bit real-world images contain lots of detail and many colours. The constant change of colours means that a long run of the same colour rarely appears - and the compression is poor as a result. For this reason, it would not be suitable to be used on its own for video compression, except for cartoons and animations.

Variations on RLE are zero replacement, blank replacement, text compression and Diatomic coding. Unlike standard RLE which seeks to replace and run of bytes with a byte+count, these only seek to replace zeros, blanks, whole words or parts of words.

A further variation is zero compression. All the other methods work by detecting strings of bytes. But every file is really a long string of 1s and 0s. Zero compression looks for sequences of zeros in between ones and replaces these with a repetition value.

Statistical encoding

Covers a range of entropy coding techniques.
They use the following method:

- The file to be encoded is examined, looking for patterns of bits or bytes that appear over and over again in the file content.
- Common patterns are then linked to smaller code words, each longer pattern and its corresponding code word being stored in a table (known as a 'code-book').
- The encoded file is written with the code words replacing the longer patterns, achieving compression.
- The file is saved along with the code book.
- The code book is used to decode the file, by replacing the code words with the original patterns, achieving lossless decoding.

Pattern substitution

The simplest implementation of statistical coding is *'pattern substitution'*, which is mainly used for compressing text information. Consider the following sentence:

I think that Dumbreck Publishing is commendable

If the words *'Dumbreck'*, *'Publishing'* and *'commendable'* were found to occur frequently, they would be placed in a table as below:

Words found in regular use	Code words for replacement
Dumbreck	~D
Publishing	~P
commendable	~c

As with RLE, a pre-determined prefix (~ in the example) is used to indicate that what follows is code word. The encoded sentence would now be saved as:

I think that ~D ~P is ~c

Huffman encoding

The problem with pattern substitution is that large files will probably contain many frequently occurring patterns. This means that the table will contain many code words, which will soon exhaust the available character set. So, code words will require two characters, then three characters, and so on. Since pattern substitution makes no attempt to prioritise code words, long code words may be used to replace frequently occurring patterns, while small code words may be allocated to less frequently used patterns. Alternatively, each code word may be allocated the same larger size. Both of these obviously reduce the efficiency of the compression.

Huffman coding addresses this problem by using variable length coding; some code words are shorter than others. As before, the input file is examined for frequently occurring patterns. This time, however, the most frequently occurring patterns are allocated the shortest code words, while those with the lowest probability of occurrence are allocated the longest code words. In this way, the maximum possible compression is achieved, while still maintaining completely lossfree compression. Like pattern substitution, the code book has to sent along with the encoded material.

Source encoding

Previously discussed compression methods were applied to streams of data, regardless of the purpose of the file. Source encoding, however, also takes into account the *nature* of the content. So, for example, a graphic file is stored as a continuous stream but is actually displayed as set of horizontal lines. Similarly, a video clip is stored as a continuous data stream but is actually displayed as a sequence of frames, each frame being made up of sets of lines.

This means that encoding can take into account content that is related to the surrounding data in extra ways. So, for example, a pixel in an image does not only relate to the pixels before and after it, but also to the pixels above and below it. Similarly, a frame from a video can be compared to the content of the previous frame or the following frame. This provides more powerful compression techniques as explained next.

Vector quantisation

Consider a SVGA screen image that is is made up of a grid of 800x600 pixels. The image is divided into small blocks (known as vectors) of 2x2 or 4x4 (as used Cinepak and Indeo). If 4x4 blocks are used, the image will be divided into 200 blocks in the horizontal direction and 150 blocks in the vertical direction, a total of 30,000 blocks. Some of these blocks will contain pixels with identical colours (e.g. 16 blue pixels or 16 yellow pixels), while others will contain a mix of colours that are laid out in different patterns. Within these 30,000 blocks, some are identical while others are similar.

Vector quantisation looks for blocks that appear most frequently and creates a table (i.e. the code book) of these patterns, each one being given a different lookup value. Once the code book is created the encoder starts to create the output file. As it does so, each block in the sequence is examined and assigned a lookup value that most matches those available in the code book. In some cases, there will be an exact match and these areas will be lossless. Where an exact match is not found, the block is allocated a lookup value of the pattern that most closely resembles the block. In these instance there is some loss, as the decoded image will not exactly match the original.

Compression is achieved by saving the image as a series of lookup values, along with the code book. During decompression, the image that is constructed will be made up of areas that are exactly replicas of the original, and areas that approximate to the original.

The level of compression is altered by deciding how many different code words will be placed in the code book. Greater compression is achieved by having fewer entries in the code book. However, as the number of code book entries is reduced, there will be fewer and fewer exact (or even close) matches and the decoded image will become more lossy.

Due to its intensive number crunching, this method is slow at encoding, but the decode algorithm is efficient and results in fast decompression.

Fractal based encoding

This is a form of vector quantisation that looks for patterns (e.g. stars or squares) in the image instead of examining square blocks of pixels. If a sample of a pattern is able to be recursively displayed to generate the larger area of the image, it can be stored in a codebook along with its details. The decoder uses each small piece of fractal information to recreate each larger area of the screen image. Consider a simple example of an image that includes a chess board with a pattern of 8 squares by eight squares. If the pattern that covers the four squares in the top-left hand corner is repeated 15 times (in the correct places) the pattern has generated an area 16 times bigger than itself. Similarly, patterns can be used generate areas representing surfaces such as human skin, human hair, grass, cloth, etc.

Large areas are called domain blocks and smaller areas are called range blocks. Every pixel in the original image must belong to at least one of the range blocks. The pattern of the image's domain blocks is called the image partition. All this information is stored in the encoded file.

One big benefit of fractal compression is its scalability. Since the encoded file is stored with equations that control the reconstruction of the display, the image need have no fixed size and can be made to fill a low resolution 15" monitor or a high resolution 21" monitor screen. As the image resolution is increased, the algorithm does not actually provide any greater detail. It carries out an advanced form of interpolation – i.e. it estimates what the extra pixels should look like. If it is an area of skin, for example, it simply displays even more of the skin pattern; it cannot add in extra detail such as stubble or pores.

Overall, it is a lossy compression system that provides comparable results with JPEG for most graphic images.

It is not widely used, although Softvideo use this method for their video CODEC.

It is a very asymmetric CODEC, since it requires large amounts of computing time to encode the file, but takes little time to decode.

Discrete Cosine Transform

The Discrete Cosine Transform (DCT) is the most common type of *'transform based encoding'*. A *'transform'* is a process that converts data to a form represented by less data than the original. An inverse transform is then used to decompress the data during replay. It is the most common video compression method and is used in JPEG, M-JPEG, MPEG-1, MPEG-2, MPEG-4 and video conferencing standards such as H.261 and H.263.

DCT works on 8x8 blocks of pixels. These 64 pixels are given 64 output values, known as the DCT coefficients. Each value is calculated by comparing it to the pixels adjacent to it in the two-dimensional plane. If a pixel's colour is identical to those around it (e.g. in a solid block of colour such as a blue sky or other plain background) its value will be zero. The coefficient is said to have a zero spatial frequency and this is called the DC coefficient.

The other values, known as the AC coefficients, are used to store values that represent the increasing difference between a pixel and its neighbours.

The highest value means that a particular pixel is unlike all the pixels adjacent to it in the block (e.g. a single cyan dot in a block of blue pixels). Since these small details are often missed by the human eye, the compression system can ignore such small changes (e.g. the block is regard as a single block of blue pixels).   This produces greater compression at the expense of some loss of detail. The degree to which such differences are removed determines both the picture quality and the file size.

RLE (Run Length Encoding – see earlier) is then applied to the set of coefficients to further compress its size.

Discrete Wavelet Transform

This is another transform technique, used in Intel Indeo versions 5.x and in the VDOWave CODECs.

The image from each frame of the video clip is passed through a high pass and a low pass filter.

The low pass filter outputs a coarse, low-resolution image (i.e. the low frequency components), while the high pass filter outputs the added image detail (i.e. the high frequency components). These are sometimes called the '*base layer*' and the '*enhancement layer*'. In some implementations, the enhancement layer is passed through one or more extra sets of filters. The final enhancement layer then has vector quantisation applied to it to achieve compression, before being recombined with the base layer.

Although a lossy system, DWT is often regarded as having superior quality to DCT systems, at the same compression ratio.   In addition, is relatively free from the '*blocking'* or '*tiling'* artefacts experienced with DCT systems.   As the compression ratio is increased, DWT (like DCT) encoded video starts to display blurring and ringing artefacts at sharp edges.   The ringing artefacts are also described as '*contouring'* or displaying the '*Gibbs Effect'*.

Interpolative Techniques

Strictly, this is not really a compression system. Compression works by reducing the amount of data required to represent *all* the pixels in a frame image.

This technique reduces file sizes by not processing every pixel in a video frame.   Instead, a subset of the pixels is stored and the CODEC reconstructs each video frame by replacing the missing pixels by '*interpolation'*. This uses a '*best guess'* approach. So, for example, a missing pixel in the middle of a set of blue pixels is expected to be another blue pixel. Also, a missing amplitude value in the series 72, 73, …, 75, 76 is expected to be 74. Of course, this is not always a correct assumption and hence the method is lossy.

This technique is used for converting a video output from RGB format to component video format as described earlier in this chapter. Compression is achieved by reducing the amount of detail in the U and V signals. The human eye has a poor colour resolution anyway, so the losses in colour detail are compensated for by the human eye and the human brain. Using this method, the video stream can be reduced from 24 bits per pixel (bpp) to only 9bpp.

Interpolation techniques are also used in MPEG video compression, where certain frames are compressed as if they were still images and interpolation techniques are used to help construct the frames between these key frames.

Differential/predictive encoding

This is an '*intraframe'* compression technique. This means that it examines the *changes* between one frame of the video and the previous frame.

Consider a video clip that displays a static opening title page for 20 seconds. At 25fps, five hundred frames are at the start of the video stream, with 499 of them being exactly the same as the first frame. Consider also the earlier example of a video clip of a newsreader sitting motionless, apart from moving her mouth – a very small part of the total screen area.

In both these examples, all, or almost all, of the image content in a frame of a clip is the same as the previous frame, and the same as the next frame. This is described as having '*temporal redundancy'* between the frames. Predictive techniques ignore this common (redundant) information and concentrate on identifying and savings the changes between successive frames in a video clip. The unchanging areas and their values are not included in the frame being saved.   When an area's content is altered, this is detected and only the changes are included in the frame being saved. Since these changes represent a small part of each frame, they take up less space to store and hence compression is achieved. Of course, the full contents of the first frame have to be stored as the basis for the sequence of later frame alterations.

DPCM (Differential Pulse Code Modulation) and ADPCM (Adaptive DPCM) are examples of predictive techniques that are mainly used for audio compression. A variation on this is the '*motion compensation'* technique that is used with QuickTime's '*Sorenson Video'* CODEC and the more well known the MPEG format.

MPEG

The Moving Pictures Experts Group was founded in 1988 by the International Standards organisation. Their remit was the production of standards covering the transmission of digital video and audio.

The MPEG-1 standard was published in 1990, the MPEG-2 standard was published in 1995 and MPEG-4 appeared in 1997. The MPEG-3 standard was never adopted.

The two key techniques used in an MPEG CODEC are intra-frame Discrete Cosine Transform (DCT) and motion-compensated inter-frame prediction.

With MPEG compression, the frames that make up the video picture are made up from three differently coded types:

I-Frames

The Key frame, or I-frame (Intracoded Frame), is always the first frame of a video clip. As such, it has to store the entire picture information for the frame. The only compression on the frame is spatial compression (using a form of DCT JPEG compression). It is coded without reference to any other frame contents. I-Frames also provide access points for MPEG playback.

P-Frames

The Delta Frame, or P-Frame (Predictive-coded Frame) follows the first frame of the clip. Its contents are dependent on the content of the previous frame. It employs a combination of temporal and spatial redundancy, along with motion vectors that chart the movement of groups of pixels in a scene (e.g. a bouncing ball or a bird's flight). Motion vectors work on the basis that a frame is often composed of the same elements as the previous frame, expect in slightly different positions. The frame contents are examined for motion prediction as macroblocks of 16 x16 pixels in the luminance channel.

The distance that an element has travelled, horizontally and vertically, is estimated and stored as vector information. The total information is used to construct the new frame from the changes or *'deltas'* in the frame compared to the previous frame's contents.

The P-Frame does not store the detail of an entire picture - it stores the instructions that allow a frame to be constructed; the P-Frame uses the information stored in the previous frame to build a new frame.

The second frame of a clip will be a P-Frame that uses the data from the first (I-Frame) frame to construct the frame to be displayed. The third frame will also be a P-Frame and it will alter the picture constructed by the previous P-Frame, and so on.

Since the P-Frames contain only data on the changed areas (and even this is compressed), the I-Frames are much smaller than P-Frames. DCT techniques are applied to the P-Frame in macroblocks of 8x8 pixels in the chrominance channels.

Maintaining Quality

Ideally, a video file should contain only one large I-Frame, with all other frames being the much smaller P-Frames. This would produce the greatest amount of compression possible under this system.

However, as the predictive element in each P-Frame introduces some small error, the effect is accumulative. To maintain picture quality, it is necessary to include extra I-Frames in the video stream. This introduces a freshly sampled complete picture at regular intervals as below:

I P P P P P I P P P P P I P P P P P I

Increasing the number of I-Frames in a file increases the file size but also improves its quality. In practice, the repetition rate for I-Frames can be set by the user and is often around every 12 to 15 frames.

B-Frames

B frames (bi-directional frame) are frames that search for data from both past and future frames. As such, they contain fewer instructions than P-Frames and are even smaller, providing even better compression. Not every MPEG-2 system makes use of B-Frames.

A typical sequence, known as *'IPB encoding'* might be:

I B B P B B P B B P B B P B B P B B I

GOP (Group of Pictures)

The total sequence of frames from one I-Frame to the next is known as a GOP (Group of Pictures).

The video encoding is carried out on a Group of Pictures at a time. First the I-Frames are encoded, followed by the intermediate P-Frames, and finally the B-Frames are constructed using the B-Frame data.

Motion compression provides the best compression when there is little change in the video scene. Since there is less change, there is less error drift, requiring fewer I-Frames (i.e. the GOP becomes longer). Clips with little movement, can have key frames inserted every 30 frames.

Conversely, if the clip has rapid scene changes and other major changes to the image (e.g. a recording of a Formula One race), extra I-Frames are required to maintain picture quality.

The repetition rate for key frames can be set during MPEG encoding. Also, extra I-frames can be added to fast-moving scenes during MPEG encoding.

Therefore, as can be seen, MPEG-2 does not insist on a regular GOP structure. This means that the CODEC outputs a variable bit rate, depending on the complexity (and predictability) of the video stream and the effectiveness of the motion-compensated prediction.

Video Editing

Much of the mood of a movie is determined at the shooting stage, through the use of weather, lighting, clothes, props, dialogue, etc. Nevertheless, the editing process is often argued to be the most important stage in the creation of a movie. While bad editing can spoil a movie, creative editing can enhance the video content and even give it new pace and meaning.

Editing involves the selection, arrangement, timing and presentation of video footage.

In the film world, the individual video footage elements are called *'shots'* while computer users tend to simply describe them as *'clips'*. The post-production phase involves the selection of clips, the editing of clips, the addition of special effects, audio dubbing and mixing.

Video editing is very much a creative as well as technical process.   The techniques for manipulating content can be learned as a mechanical process.   However, the ability to create a single, cohesive project requires a completely different range of skills.

This chapter has two main sections:

> **Why** – the creative process. The approach to editing for gaining maximum effect.
> **How** – the technical process. The use of application packages to carry out the editing.

The chapter concentrates on computer-based editing.

In a large organisation, there will be two type of editor:
- The creative editor, who makes the decisions on what is used and how it is presented.
- The technical editor, who assembles the finished product and applies any processing.

Hobbyists, amateurs and those working in smaller organisations roll the two jobs into one.

Creative editing

The producer is presented with a large selection of video clips, spread over many tapes and containing a variety of angles and shot sizes (close-ups, long shots, etc.). The art is choosing the correct selection of clips that best get over the required story or message. The chosen clips then have to be assembled in the most appropriate order and edited to provide the optimum timing and impact. The transitions between clips also have to be considered. These issues are covered more fully later.

The way that these tasks are tackled can produce entirely different effects from the same footage.

Editing can:
- Advance the story or message.
- Influence the viewer's emotions, by providing humour, romance, suspense, etc.
- Ensure continuity of the whole production.
- Ensure that the viewer's interest is focussed on the main centre of interest.
- Influence the pace of the production, to maintain interest or to alter the mood from the same content)..
- Manipulate time (e.g. a viewer is comfortable seeing a weeks events occurring over a period of one hour).
- Manipulate space (e.g. the viewer is instantly transported from one country to another).

Apart from dynamic editing (covered later), the overall production should appear seamless to the viewer, with smooth natural flows between clips and scenes.   The viewer should not even notice that an edit has taken place. The production should unfold in a way that mirrors how the human brain absorbs and processes information. Everyone already creates their own edited version of reality (e.g. seeing policemen in riot gear produces a specific reaction with connotations of what is happening or about to happen). Editing plays with the mind through the presentation of the sound and video clips.   Individual techniques are covered in this chapter but the starting point is to strive for the finished production to be true to the concept that *"The whole is greater than the sum of the parts"*. No one approach or activity will produce the finished effect – it is the skilful blending of them that matters.

That is why this chapter examines the creative process before turning to the technical process. Fancy transitions and effects cannot compensate for poorly shot source video material. Equally, some of the classic movies of all time used simple editing techniques.

There are two basic editing techniques:
- Continuity editing
- Dynamic editing

Continuity editing

Continuity editing advances the story or message without any discordant jumps in time or space. It establishes the direction of view and maintains continuity in the direction of action. It also maintains continuity between the video content, audio content, scene lighting, etc. Its aim is to obscure rather than highlight the changes between clips.

Its pace is usually slower than dynamic editing and it uses the video clips in a sequence that projects a logical sequence of ideas or events. It shows a variety of shot angles, cuts and transitions to bridge between individual clips and scenes.

The choice of sequence for displaying clips can project different moods or scenarios, even using the same set of clips. Consider, for example, a clip showing a woman looking up in horror and a clip of a man firing a gun. If shown in that order, the viewer thinks the woman has been shot. Reverse the showing of the two clips and the woman is obviously reacting to the gunfire. When choosing from many hundred clips, there is great scope for controlling the flow of the material so that it projects the desired effect.

Techniques of continuity editing

A variety of techniques can be employed to ensure a continuous sequence in the minds of the viewer and these include:

Flashback

The viewer is temporarily taken back in time to an earlier event or period and flashbacks are used in several ways:

- To explain the background to the current screen material (e.g. why the people are homeless)
- To reveal a part of the story not previously shown (*"here's what really happened that night"*).
- To show different viewpoints of the same event (often used in murder mystery movies).

Examples of this technique are found in movies such as *'The Fugitive'*, *"DOA"* and *'Ghosts of Mars'*.

While this allows the director to manipulate time, its overuse (with too many flashbacks from too many people or too many angles) will make the production overly complicated for the viewer. Flashbacks, used carefully, play a valuable role in providing a smooth control over events and their timing.

Flash Forward

This is the opposite of flashbacks, with the viewer being taken forward in time. This might be a return from a flashback, or might take the viewer into the future.

It can be used in several ways:

- To display someone's hopes or dreams (e.g. dreaming of a luxury holiday).
- To be a premonition of the future (e.g. worrying about dying alone).
- To show the consequences of a current action (e.g. current deforestation and future climate change).

Movies using this technique include *'They Shoot Horses, Don't They?'* and the ghost of Xmas Future in *'Scrooge'* or *'Scrooged'*.

Morphing

This allows the producer to alter an object from one shape or form to another and can be used for:

- Simulating the passage of time (e.g. a boy becomes a man).
- Demonstrating progress (e.g. showing a particular car and how it has changed between different models).
- Creating special effects (e.g. a man turns into a vampire or a werewolf).

Movies using this technique include *'The Mask'*, *'The Nutty Professor'* and countless horror movies.

Incomplete continuity

In movies, the script can present material that leavers the viewers guessing or placing their own interpretation on what they see. For example, the final scene of a movie shows a couple walking away from the camera. They have had a love/hate relationship during the movie and they are still arguing as the film ends. Some viewers will infer that the couple will end up living together, others will infer that they will part – while others will infer that the couple will carry on arguing like this for the rest of their lives. The viewers are taking part in the production by inventing their own ending. Similarly, a murder mystery might show the various suspects exchanging knowing glances or smirking. Viewers draw their own conclusions as to the significance of each action.

This approach, however, is not acceptable in educational and documentary material. The user must be presented with material that leaves no scope for misunderstanding. The sequence of clips must be as clear and explicit as possible. For example, if a commentator talks about a new product, the viewer expects to be shown a close-up view of the product.

Cause and effect

This technique seeks to explain *why* a clip is being displayed. It works on the principle that actions cause reactions and relates the two on screen. In most cases, the cause is shown before the effect. In other words, a clip showing a man opening a door should follow a clip where the doorbell is rung – and not the other way round.

The cause can sometimes be omitted and will be inferred by the viewer. For example, if a clip shows a man lying on a hospital bed with his leg in plaster, everyone knows that he has had an accident. There is no need to show how it was caused, unless it is central to the story.

Movie editing should also seek to challenge the viewer. Although most movies show cause before effect, this can be successfully reversed. For example, a clip may show a boy looking glum, pulling back to show his scooter is broken. The viewer is shown the effect, wonders what happened, and is then shown the cause.

The clips showing cause and effect do not necessarily have to immediately follow one another. Indeed, the essence of a good murder mystery is not revealing the cause until the end of the movie.

Another element in cause/effect is motivation. This might be explicit or left to the viewer to infer. A clip may show a boyhood rivalry (cause) and a later clip may show the unsuccessful man robbing and murdering the successful man. The viewer might be told that the motive was purely money or the viewer might be left to work out their own motive (greed, jealousy, hatred, etc).

Other continuity problems
A sequence will use clips of varying size and these should be used to ensure that the viewer understands the setting in which the action is taking place.

The recognised approach is:
- Display a wide shot, or *'establishing shot'*, to show the overall setting of the action.
- Display a medium shot to show the immediate location where the action is taking place.
- Display close-ups of the faces of those taking part.

Consider an example of an interview with a company director on the factory floor. The establishing shot would let the viewer see the kind of business that the interview is about. The medium shot would show the director and the interviewer standing next to the most important machine in the process. The close-ups would then show the faces of the two participants in the interview. This provides a smooth continuous flow to the viewer. Jumping straight from a wide shot to the head of the interviewer, for example, might be too great a change for comfortable viewing.

If the interview lasts a long time, further insertions of the medium shot, or even the establishing shot, should be displayed to remind the viewer of the overall setting. IN some cases, the interview might end by reversing the shot sequence. The interview says the closing lines in close-up, the medium shot of the two participants are then displayed, closing with the wide shot.

As always, there are exceptions to this sequence, usually for dramatic effect. A scene might begin with a close-up of a person's face or an object (a gun, a hypodermic needle, a *"Danger:Radiation'* sign, etc.). This grabs the attention of the viewer before being shown medium and wide shots.

Another continuity issue is that of the angles used to display successive clips of the same subject. It is common practice to ensure that there is a minimum of 30 degrees difference in the angle of shots, to prevent a *'jump cut'* (see later) that leaves the viewer uncomfortable.

Technical Continuity
Apart from ensuring the smooth flow of action and events, the project has to ensure that the video clips used match each other in terms of:
- Light levels and exposures.
- Colour balance and picture sharpness.
- Audio levels and quality of sound.

Even though the clip contents may produce smooth transitions, the overall project would be marred by sudden changes in volume or picture quality, for example. Such changes are quickly noticed by viewers. Some of these can be addressed in the editing stage by processing the video or audio content, so that successive clips match each other. Many of these are preventable at the recording stage if care is taken to colour balance cameras, make optimum use of lighting, set up microphones, etc. Despite this, some adjustments may be still required at the editing stage.

Dynamic editing
While continuity editing concentrates on the smooth unfolding of the story or message, dynamic editing is mainly concerned with maximising the visual impact of the material. This is achieved by playing a large number of small clips in a short time, described as *'flash cutting'*. The rapid changes of clip inserts pace and excitement into the material and is widely used in television commercials and pop music videos. Movies using this technique include *'Braveheart'* and the beach assault sequence in *'Saving Private Ryan'*. Here, rapid succession of short action clips is referred to as an *'action montage'*.

The technique can also be used to create a time montage, where the rapid display of clips shows the rapid passage of time (as in the movie *'The Time Machine'*).

The mood montage, also described as *'thematic editing'*, does not rely on the clips being in a particular time sequence. Instead, it rapidly plays a set of clips with a common theme, intended to create a general mood. Individual clips may be less than a second in duration and might even include *'flash frames'*, where a clip may only occupy a frame or two of the final sequence. Since the viewer does not have time to fully absorb each image, an impression is created instead.

Clearly, these effects are achieved at the editing stage and not during filming. The choice of material and the speed of the montage dictate the mood that will be created. The rapid display of dead bodies produces a reaction of horror. On the other hand, a less frantic montage of characters is used at the beginning of some television series (e.g. 'Friends') and soaps.

Editing methods

A variety of editing methods exists. The simplest is in-camera editing and this technique is still used by amateurs who do not wish to buy and learn more complex systems. It is also quick and easy for short and simple video projects.

Post-production editing uses either linear or non-linear editing equipment. Although more complex, these systems provide a more flexible and more precise control of the finished product. The ready availability of cheap software-based video editing systems has moved the editing market towards NLE (non-linear editing) systems.

In Camera editing

An old technique was to 'edit in camera'. The series of clips for the project was pre-planned and shot in the correct order. The camera's own titling, fading and other effects were applied during the recording. The videotape was removed from the camera as a finished product. These facilities still exist in camcorders and the synchronisation of digital camcorders means that the clip transitions are smooth (older cameras tend to exhibit a picture roll or picture break-up at the junction of two separately recorded clips). Compared to editing in the computer, this is a much less flexible approach and one that is less tolerant to errors. For example, when played back, an effect may look less effective than anticipated. Even worse, consider a wedding shot of the happy couple, with the in-camera titler being used to add the wrong spelling of the bride or groom's name. The problem would not be discovered until it is too late to reshoot the scene.

Some camcorders provide limited facilities for overwriting existing sound or video with new material. For example, if a recording of an outdoor wedding reception is spoiled by constant traffic noise or aeroplanes passing overhead, the audio section could be replaced with a piece of suitable music. On the other hand, if a section of the video was spoiled (e.g. by someone standing in front of the camera), the audio track could be left untouched while a video clip of the wedding cake or similar can be inserted in place of the affected video footage.

Replacing a section of the video content, while leaving the audio track intact is known as a 'video insert edit'. Replacing a section of audio, while leaving the video track undisturbed is known as 'audio dubbing'.

Linear editing

The ability to remove clips, change the order of clips, etc., provides far more creative flexibility to the editing process. Unfortunately, simply cutting and splicing (gluing together) footage, as used for many years in film studios, cannot be applied to videotape.

With linear editing, the video clips stored on the camcorder's tape are transferred to another tape. This may use the camcorder in conjunction with a VCR, or may involve using multiple VCRs. This approach involves a lot of playing, fast forwarding, rewinding, replaying - to identify the clips to be used in the final project.

Simple assemble editing

The steps for a simple camcorder to VCR system are:

- The VCR is set to record and left on pause.
- The camcorder is rewound to the start of the first clip.
- The camcorder is set to play and the VCR is taken off pause.
- At the end of the wanted clip, the VCR is put back on pause.
- The camcorder is moved to the start of the second clip and the process is repeated.

This is known as an 'assemble edit' since the clips are assembled in the correct order on the destination tape 'on-the-fly'. Of course, any editing process assumes that the desired clips have already been chosen and this is covered later. This method is described as being 'cuts only', since it cannot provide transition effects between clips.

A/B Roll Editing

The 'A/B Roll' is a description that separates main material from supporting material. The 'A' roll is the videotape that contains the main screen scenes, while the 'B' roll contains additional supporting material such as inserts and cutaways.

An 'A/B Roll Edit' is another analogue tape-to-tape technique and was the only comprehensive system until the introduction of computer-based NLE (Non Linear Editing) systems.

A/B Roll editing uses two playback decks (one for the A roll and one for the B roll) that feed a single record deck used to store the finished product. An 'edit controller' is used to decide the operation of all the decks.

Initially, this was a dedicated suite of equipment, until analogue editing controllers became available for PCs. The suite provides facilities for AV mixing, superimposing titles and audio dubbing, along with the ability to provide a range of transition effects between clips (e.g. fades, wipes and dissolves).

The edit controller handles all the operations of the decks, such as play, pause and wind forward or backward to a given point. The record deck stays in record mode during the whole process.

The most basic tape to tape editor system uses only a single camcorder and a VCR. The hardware controller connects to the camcorder via its LAN-C socket, with an infrared controller to operate a VCR. The hardware connects to a PC and the process is automated using the computer software. One such package is *'Video Director'*.

The final requirement is a method of telling the edit controller what clips are required, from which roll and in which order of recording. This is carried out using tapelogs and an EDL (Edit Decision List).

Tapelogs

In the ideal world, the collection of tapes sitting on the video mixing desk will all be well documented as to their content and length of each clip. This approach should certainly be encouraged, as it focuses the mind of those making the recording and minimises the risk of shots being omitted. It also speeds up the editing process. In many situations, however, the contents have to be viewed and documented after the event. Logging a tape records the clips as they appear on the tape and does not necessarily reflect their suitability or order in any final production.

As the chapter on *'Digital Video'* explained, digital videotapes have a track that contains SMPTE (Society of Motion Picture and Television Engineers) time codes. The time increments in hours, minutes, seconds and frames and starts at zero for all values. Every frame on the tape has its own time code value and every separate clip on a videotape, therefore has a starting time code value and a finishing time value. These are known as the *'start codes'* and *'end codes'*, or *the 'cue in'* and *'cue out'* codes. When using multiple tapes, the number of each tape must be included in the tapelog, as tapes for the same production will have identical timecode information and will need the tape number to provide unique identifiers.

This table shows the minimum information that would be found in a tapelog:

Tape No.	Start Code	End Code	Duration	Scene Description
	: : :	: : :	: : :	
	: : :	: : :	: : :	
	: : :	: : :	: : :	
	: : :	: : :	: : :	

Each tape is rewound and played from the beginning. Each clip's timings and contents are entered in the table in the order that they are stored on the tape. Other likely details to appear on a tapelog are linked sequence information (e.g. clips from a love scene or a bar brawl), date and time of the recording, location of shot, word-for-word transcriptions of the dialogue used in each clip, and any links to script pages.

Tape logging has another useful function. Since the producer/editor has to look at every clip that was recorded, he/she ends up with a very detailed appreciation of what clips are available. This is useful for the clip selection stage (see later).

Computer programs are available to help with creating tapelogs.

Tapelogs are useful for all video editing methods, as the same initial appraisal of tape contents is necessary and useful. After logging the tapes, the clips could fall into three categories:

- Those that will never be used on any project, due to errors in filming, etc.
- Those that will not be used for the current project but should be archived for possible future projects (e.g. general country scenes, seascapes, skylines, church bells, etc.).
- Those that will be required for the current project.

The last category is known as the EDL (Edit Decision List).

Edit Decision List

This is a list of all the clips that will appear in the final production. As a minimum, it will list the clips in the order in which they will be assembled on the final output tape. It may be a written list or it can be a computer-generated list. Where a tapelog is created on the recording site, clips that are candidates for the EDL can be noted at the time, saving time at the editing stage. Many laptop computers allow the direct connection of a camcorder and, with suitable software, details of start codes and end codes and other information can easily be documented on the recording site or soon thereafter (e.g. travelling back from a shoot on the train or plane).

The contents of an EDL are similar to a tapelog, with details of the source tape, the cue in and cue out timecodes, clip durations and clip descriptions. While the tapelog lists all clips on each tape, the EDL table only lists the clips for use in the final project. The EDL table will also list additional information such as which transitions are to be applied between various clips. It may also list the cue in points for the record deck (i.e. specifying exactly where on the master tape to start recording the clip).

In a written EDL, the clip information from the tapelog can be transferred into the EDL table. The time for the total number of clips entered in the table can be added to determine the total running time of the production. If the production is too long, clips or sequences can be removed from the EDL until the required time is obtained. In a simple tape to tape system, the software uses the LAN-C control of a camcorder to output the video clips named in the EDL to the VCR for recording the final master tape. With A/B Roll editing, the EDL is used to control the operations of the two playback decks and the record deck.

With a computer-generated EDL, the table is created off-site, in the editing room and is saved as a computer file for use during the creation of the master tape. The process of creating the EDL is known as *'offline editing'*, as the final destination tape is not created during this stage. The software allows the operator to view clips and mark the in-points and out-points of the required clips. These in and out markers are stored in the EDL.

Using the EDL

When the EDL is completed, it can be used immediately or can be saved for running later.

The *'online editing'* process creates an output tape from the source clips listed in the EDL. Each entry in the EDL is processed in the order that it appears in the list. The playback deck containing that clip is wound on or backwards to reach the cue in marker and the tape is played until the cue out marker is reached. The next entry in the list is then similarly processed. If the list shows a transition effect between two clips, it is applied at the boundaries between the two clips, before carrying on.

The mechanical delays involved in winding and rewinding tapes means that A/B Roll editing can be a slow process.

Outputting to storage medium

It is important to note that this can be a purely 'analogue' technique – the video content need not convert to digital files at any time in the process. The sources are videotapes and the destination is also videotape.

If the finished product needs amending, the destination tape should not be used as a new source tape in a further editing process, as the quality will deteriorate with each copy made. Instead the EDL should be amended and used with the original source tapes to create a new output tape. This involves going through the entire slow process all over again, in order to include the amendments.

To minimise the risk of such lengthy re-runs, it is common to create a *'rough cut'*. This quickly assembles the clips in the correct order and uses only straight cuts between clips. This eliminates the time taken to apply transitions and effects and gives the operator/director a good overview of the finished product in a shorter time.

Non-linear editing

The development of computers and computer software allow video editing to take place on a reasonably specified personal computer. Turnkey systems are available and these are just computers that have their disks, memory and video cards optimised for video editing. Modern PCs are now sufficiently powerful to support video editing using appropriate editing software (and a FireWire port or video capture card).

With non-linear editing, all the required video clips are stored digitally and processed digitally. Once digitised from the tape, the source tape plays no further part in the editing process. This means that any mistakes in the editing process can be undone without affecting the content of the original footage. The individual scenes are stored as separate computer video files that can be easily accessed, deleted, re-ordered, enhanced, modified and have effects added. This can be carried out with individual frame accuracy using a software package. Access to each element of the project is quickly accessible.

Computer-based NLE (Non-Linear Editing) systems have many added advantages:

- Multiple video and audio tracks can be handled (e.g. one audio track can carry the commentary while another provides background music or sound effects).
- The order and length of clips can be quickly and easily altered.
- Transitions, titling and effects are easily applied (including complex processes such as picture in picture and chromakeying).
- Sound levels, colour properties, etc. are easily managed.
- The production, or parts of the production, can be easily previewed.
- There is almost no degradation of the original signal.
- A range of output packaging is available – to videotape, to kiosk, to CD or DVD, or to the web.

Although there is some requirement to learn how to use the editing software, NLE systems are easier and quicker to use than A/B Roll editing systems.

The steps in using a NLE package are:

- Select and digitise the chosen clips.
- Arrange the clips in the required sequence.
- Specify any video transitions, effects and other signal processing needs, such as colour correction.
- Add in any audio effects or specify any processing needs.
- Add any titles, credits or other graphic additions.
- Save the project specification (i.e. the EDL, even if it is not called that by name).
- Output to the chosen media format.

When the production is output, the EDL entries are used to fetch each video clip in turn and bind them into a continuous AV stream for packaging.

Some editing software applications use a flowchart or other view of the production, but most use a timeline view.

Timeline editing

Consider this analogy of editing cinema film. The processed cine film contains each frame that was shot and holds them in a long sequence, as one long continuous strip,. The filmstrip is chopped up into a set of separate scenes and is assembled in the required order. Imagine all the pieces lying on a large table. The individual strips are placed in a row to create the new running order, with unwanted strips going in the bin, or to archive. The remaining strips are positioned in the order that they are displayed in the final movie. This collection is ordered with respect to time. When the collection of end-to-end strips is joined together, they form the new film and the individual clips are viewed as a continuous movie. This same approach is used with computerised editing. Clips are digitised and the wanted clips are placed on the editing table (e.g. Premiere's Project Window). The clips are then placed in the required order as a continuous sequence (e.g. Premiere's Timeline Window). Since all the clips are stored on the hard disk, editing tasks are simpler and quicker. Titles may be altered, the order of scenes altered and different effects can be tried and discarded. This all takes place within the computer and only the chosen clips, titles and effects are composited into the finished product.

Rendering

The editing software can handle multiple video tracks and audio tracks at the same time. Additional effects, such as transitions, filters and titling may be added at this stage. When the project is completed, it is saved as a single computer file (AVI, MPEG, etc) or sent back to a video recorder. The editing software has to take all the clips and effects and merge them into a single video and audio stream, applying all the alterations to the frame contents. This process is known as *'rendering'* and can be time-consuming if complicated transitions and effects have been used.

In a home or small production environment, the operator waits to see the effect of a rendered production. In a larger production environment, the tasks of titling, captioning, adding effects, etc. are handed to the technical staff to carry out. The next morning, before the next shoot, the results of the previous evening's work, known as a *'digital rush'* are viewed by the producer/director.

The editing process

At the initial stage, the editor is armed with the storyboard, script and tapelogs detailing each clip.
The editing process goes through the following stages:
- Clip selection and capture.
- Clip ordering.
- Clip length, timing and pace.
- Creating a rough cut.
- Choosing transitions, video and audio effects, and titles.

Clip selection

For the hobbyist, video editing may be simply making the best use of the existing footage to create a wedding or holiday video. The individual clips may have been recorded almost at random and the editing process involves selecting the shots and ordering them in a way that conveys the mood of the event. For the multimedia editor, the footage was shot to meet the needs of the production. The camcorder operator may have been given a list of required shots, arising from the development of the storyboard. Even here, the operator may notice angles, views or content that would enhance the final project that would not have been known by the storyboard creators. The team on location often uses its initiative to capture extra material.

As a result, even the best professionals shoot many times more hours of footage than is ever used. The editor reviews the clips and will discard material for a number of reasons:
- Shots that are redundant (e.g. multiple clips of crowd scenes may be recorded, so that the best clips can be selected).
- Shots that are unusable due to poor recording (poor sound, wind noise, bad lighting, being out of focus, etc), although the ability of the operator to review footage on location and reshoot minimises the wasted footage reaching the editor.
- Shots with unusable content (e.g. footage of the operator's feet, *'outtakes'*, swearing, sneezing, forgetting to turn the camera off, etc.).
- Shots where only part of the clip is used (e.g. extracting a 20-second clip from a five-minute speech).
- Shots from multiple different angles (e.g. a close-up shot may be passed over in favour of mid-shot).
- Multiple cutaways that are not all required (see later).

While some clips are obvious candidates for rejection, others will require more consideration. Involving others in looking at the footage can be useful, as their reactions can help shape the choices.

When selecting clips to match the storyboard and script, it is not sufficient that the individual clips match the required list. Other factors come into play such as the need for pace and supportive footage such as cutaways from the B roll. The selection process must look at the needs of the production as a whole. In many instances, a collection of clips are selected to satisfy a particular video sequence (e.g. an interview or a practical demonstration).

The selection process must also take into consideration the creative issues discussed earlier. This requires the appropriate mixture of camera angles, shot sizes, cutaways, etc.

Lastly, only add clips if they contribute to the main presentation.   A scene of a beautiful beach, a sunset or a fairground may look great but should only be used if in context with the main theme.   Adding extra material, just because it looks good, can distract viewers from the central message of the production. Remember that most amateur productions run much longer than required, to the stage of boredom in many cases.

Clip capture

Once the likely clips are selected, they should be copied from tape and transferred to hard disk files. In most cases, this will involve the identification of the clips followed by their capture, perhaps on a batch capture basis. Other software packages run through an entire videotape, detecting scene changes and converting the total content into a series of separately named video files. There is also the opportunity to connect a camcorder to a portable hard disk, ignoring the videotape and saving the footage directly to disk. In the last two cases, the effort in converting individual clips is saved, but there will be many unwanted clips saved to disk. It is good practice to store groups of similar clips in separate folders, having folders for different captured sequences, captured inserts and cutaways, imported footage (from previous archives or from royalty-free stock footage), additional audio and graphics elements. In these circumstances, the main footage folders and the folders of supporting material provide a similar resource to the A rolls and B rolls in linear editing. In this respect, the A/B Roll remains a useful concept for NLE.

Clip order

The captured clips are likely to be stored on disk with file names that are either in a numeric series such as File0001, File002, etc. (if the content has been captured automatically in a batch process) or have been given meaningful names (if clips have been individually captured and saved by the operator). In either case, there will be no direct link between file names and the order that they will appear in the final production.

The traditional story-telling approach uses a sequence of *'beginning, middle, end'* in terms of content. However, the flow of material will have already have been previously determined by the storyboard and script. The task is to place the clips in an order that meets the storyboard and also provides the greatest impact. First, the sequences that match the storyboard have to be identified and ordered. A sequence is a set of clips that make up a complete scene or segment of the production. So, for example, a scene displaying how to change a car tyre may be require ten different clips.

Within a sequence, there may be scope for ordering the clips to maximise their effect. In particular, clips at the end of a sequence should attempt to flow smoothly into the beginning of the next sequence (including the shot angles, shot sizes, cutaways, cause and effect issues, and technical continuity issues mentioned earlier).

Clip length

There are three reasons why clips may need to be trimmed in size:
- To remove unwanted footage at the beginning and/or the end of a clip.
- To make the clip length reflect the mood of the sequence.
- To make the clip length match the expectations and understanding of the viewers.

The material at the start and finish of each clip is often too long, as this is a deliberate policy during recording to provide some latitude to the editors. Trimming the ends speeds up the editing process, reduces clip storage needs, and makes the final project more crisp.

Trimming is also used as a creative technique to control the pace of a sequence.   Viewers like to see changes in pace in a production. A constant frantic pace tires an audience, while a constant slow paces bores an audience. Sequences that display a conversation or a rural panorama may use longer clips, while car chases and other action sequences may use much shorter clips. Trimming clips allows the editor to inject pace into a sequence.

The length of a shot also depends upon the target audience. For example, if the production was intended for a mature audience, only a short clip of the Eiffel Tower need be displayed for it to be instantly recognised. If the production was for a young audience, the clip would play for longer, as it is a sight that most viewers will not have seen before. In both cases, the shot is displayed for the length of time necessary for the audience to appreciate its significance.

Similarly, the clip length is determined by the content of the clip. Viewers need time to absorb the contents of a chart or table, or the details of a map. The clip is cut at the stage where viewers understand the content and want to move on.

The rough cut

As explained earlier, before embarking on a full editing and compiling operation, it is advisable to create a *"rough cut"*. This is simply the compilation of the clips in the expected final running order – but with no titles, transitions, video effects, sounds effects, etc.

Viewing the rough cut provides the overall sense of feel and pace of the movie and is used by the editor to decide what clips to remove or change the running order. In most cases, it shows that the movie is too long and requires the removal of unnecessary footage.   It also exposes differences in sound levels between clips, any need for audio dubbing, and any need for colour correction (to compensate for situations where shots, which have to be viewed in a certain order, were actually recorded separately and in different light conditions).

As always, it is preferable if others are invited to view and comment on the rough cut, as their comments can prove very valuable as to what works and what does not work.

Cuts and when to use them

A *'cut'* is simply the boundary between separate shots in a video. Productions mostly use *'straight cuts'* between clips. This means that the video content of one clip ends and another clip instantly begins, with no effects being used to ease the transition. Viewers are accustomed to viewing straight cuts and can easily handle the change of screen content, if the changes are not too abrupt or too contrasting. As long as the content seems to flow naturally, viewers will hardly notice that cuts are taking place.

A *'transition'* is an effect that is applied between video clips. This may be used to smooth the flow of video content, or may be for special effects.

Every cut and transition has to be justified. There must be a reason why the clip was cut at a particular point or why a particular transition was applied.

Jump cuts

A jump cut is a cut that disturbs the viewer's continuous absorption of the message or story and makes the viewer focus on the movie's editing characteristics rather than its content. Examples of mismatched editing that cause jump cuts are:

- Unexplained gaps in time in an apparently continuous shot (e.g. to remove an interviewee's swearing or because the camcorder was inadvertently paused for a few second during someone's speech).
- Unexplained changes in a person or object's position (e.g. the angle of shot in the second clip is slightly different from the angle in the first shot, making the person or object appear to 'jump').
- Unnatural movements between clips (e.g. in one clip the woman runs from left to right, while in the next clip she is running from right to left).
- Unexplained changes from one scene to another (e.g. a clip of the factory canteen is inserted in the middle of a sequence showing how plastic goods are manufactured).
- Continuity errors (e.g. the main character wears a red tie in one clip in the sequence, has a blue tie in the next clip – and reverts to wearing a red tie in the third clip).

Most such problems are preventable in the recording stage, with a little forethought by the director and camera operator. If there are not alternative clips to work with, the editor can use other cutting methods to overcome the shortcomings listed above.

Alternative cuts

Cutaways

A *'cutaway'* is a clip that temporarily diverts from the main action of the sequence, to show footage that is relevant and supportive to the main sequence. The content of the added clip contains material that is not seen in the main sequence (i.e. it is a cut 'away' from the main content).

Cutaways are regularly used by editors to:
- Enhance the story.
- Overcome jump cuts.

These uses can be complementary and typical examples of cutaways are:
- Breaking up a long continuous clip, to ensure that each sequence shows some action. Even travel movies that show exotic locations introduce movement (e.g. birds flying, holidaymakers surfboarding, or even just the presenter walking along the beach).
- Showing reaction shots such as spectators at a football match, guests at a wedding listening to the speeches, and interviewers *'noddy'* shots.
- Bridging a time lapse between clips (e.g. pages peeling away from a calendar).
- Removing material from a clip without it being noticeable (e.g. deleting a portion of an interview by replacing a large chunk of footage with a short cutaway).
- Adding drama (e.g. close-ups of a ticking bomb or a ticking clock).
- Providing extra detail (e.g. close-ups of machinery or processes).
- Providing unspoken comment (e.g. an MP sleeping during speech, knowing glances in a drama, huge crowd at a rally).
- Providing symbolic alternatives, for example, to sexual scenes (e.g. waves breaking on beach) or car crashes (e.g. an egg being crushed).

Where a jump cut looks inevitable, because there is no alternative footage, a cutaway can be used to bridge the gap. For example, it can cover over continuity problems such as abrupt changes in shot angles. The viewer is shown cutaway material before returning to the clip with the offending angle. The cutaway diverts attention from the angle changes in the clips.

In most cases, the audio content of the main clip is left unaltered during a cutaway. For example, the football commentary and the crowd noise would continue when a cutaway of spectators is shown. This provides continuity while still maintaining viewer interest in a long scene.

Cut-ins or inserts

The cutaway shot contained material that was not visible in the main scene. The insert shot, or cut-in, contains a closer view of a person or object that is already visible in the main clip. This is used for emphasis (e.g. a close-up of a gun), to provide more detail (e.g. a close-up of a map, an antique or a craftsman at work) or to break up a long clip. In many cases, the insert content is essential to the main message. As with cutaways, the audio track should continue uninterrupted during an insert.

Cutting on action

This technique ends a clip while the subject is still in motion. For example, if a subject were exiting the screen area, the clip would be cut before that subject fully exits the screen. This adds pace and prevents the movie action slowing down (the audience is not left looking at an empty and inactive scene).

In many cases, two clips contain the same subject, at different stages of an action (e.g. a subject leaving one scene and entering a different scene). Cutting on action results in viewers concentrating on the action and being less inclined to notice changes in the scene background. Since viewers see both clips as a single action, the subject should move at the same speed and the same direction in both clips and the second shot should be filmed from a different angle. Cutting on action, therefore, is often employed to avoid jump cuts.

Remember, viewers do not need to see an entire action to understand that it has taken place. So, for example, an ambulance can be shown leaving the scene of an accident. The next clip can show the ambulance arriving at the hospital. Everybody understands that the trip was made between the two places, without being shown the actual journey. This also applies to a single clip. Viewers can be shown a barman beginning to fill a beer glass and viewers will accept that he completed the job, without seeing it all happen.

Cutting on action also recognises that an action or movement by a subject may initiate a cut. If someone opens a box, the viewers expect a clip showing its contents. When an interviewer stops asking a question, the viewers expect to see a clip of the interviewee's answer. If someone throws an object to another person who is off-screen, viewers expect a shot of that person catching the object. If someone even throws a glance off-screen, viewers expect a clip exposing what was being looked at. In each case, the on-screen action motivated a change of scene.

Cutting at rest

In this case, the edit occurs at a moment after the on-screen action has stopped and can be used to create a mood. For example, a lingering shot of a sleeping child after being laid in bed conveys the mood of a happy family. Similarly, when a clip shows a man walking off-screen looking dejected, the empty screen provides a mood of emptiness, misery, or a time for reflection.

Another advantage of a clip that uses cutting at rest is that most types of clip can follow without any jump cut effects.

Parallel cutting

Parallel action shows two or more stories at the same time, by interspersing them in the video sequence. This is more interesting for viewers, compared to a single continuous story line.

'Cross cutting' is the simplest implementation of this technique. It alternates between events that are occurring at the same time, and usually at the same place, to keep the viewers up to date with all the action. So, for example, if the sequence was located in a casino, the clips would jump between displaying the cards of each player during a card game. There is also the overused scene of man runs towards woman, woman runs towards man, man runs towards woman …

Cross cutting is also regularly used in chase scenes, where the video content keeps switching between the escaping bad guy and the pursuing cop. This technique, coupled with ever decreasing clip lengths, can raise the pace and tension in a sequence.

'Parallel cutting' is similar to cross cutting. The technique matches clips that contain similar content, although these may be separated by time or space. Examples of parallel cutting are the feverish activities on board the space ship and simultaneously at Mission Control in the movie 'Apollo 13' and the opening car and motorcycle sequences at the start of the movie 'Speed 2'. There are also numerous examples in war movies, include presenting the view of a battle as seen from the soldiers and generals of both sides;

The technique can also be used to associate two dissimilar activities that are separated in time. Consider a sequence of a man dressing and placing an object in a suitcase. If the sequence is broken up into several smaller clips and interspersed with scenes from a birthday party, the viewers draw the conclusion that he took along a present to the party. If, however, the same sub-clips were interspersed with scenes of carnage, the viewers draw the conclusion that the man is a terrorist! Two different interpretations from the same initial footage, simply by parallel cutting with other suggestive material. Indeed, the original sequence might just have been of a man preparing for a day at the office!

Parallel cutting, therefore is a powerful editing tool and is often used in productions.

Parallel cutting is a very useful way to manipulate the viewers' appreciation of time. Editing can both expand or condense time, although shortening time is the most useful tool for productions.

Maintaining continuity

Jumps cuts are caused in part by butting together clips that make the subject appear to 'jump' in position or suddenly change direction of movement. These should be prevented during recording but the editor often has to select clips to overcome thoughtless filming techniques.

Smooth clip changes are achieved if consideration is given to:

- The Line of Action
- The Line of Interest

Line of action

From a writer's point of view the *'line of action'* is the central theme to a production. While some parallel actions and sub-plots may take place, the storyboard must constantly progress through the main story.

From an editor's point of view, it is an approach to filming/editing that maintains a continuity of direction when a sequence of clips shows action or movement. The line of action is an invisible line that a person or object is travelling along, The *'180 degree rule'* states that all filming should be shot from one side of this line.

Consider the television coverage of a football match. If the camera is mounted along the side of the football pitch, it can pan between the two goalposts.   Team A is trying to move the ball rightwards down the pitch, while team B is trying to move leftwards. As long as this single camera records all the action, all the clips will show the same directions of movement.   Adding a second camera on the *same* side of the pitch produces extra clips that are fully compatible with the first camera (e.g. all team A drive is to the right). However, if the second camera were placed on the *other* side of the pitch, it would record team A as moving the ball *leftwards* and team B moving *rightwards*. Mixing the clips from the two cameras into a single sequence would totally disorientate viewers. At one time, team A are moving leftwards, while at another time they are moving rightwards. This problem is known as *'crossing the line'*.

The problem is also apparent when one shot shows a person facing leftwards in one shot and rightwards in the very next shot.

The solution is to always use clips that were shot on the same side of the line of action. And, of course, ensure that the camera operator only shoots footage that way in the future. If there are no enough clips available for a scene and clips have to be used that cross the line of action, cutaways should be inserted between the clips that clash. For example, the clip shows a man walking leftwards, cutting to a close-up of a street sign, followed by a clip of the man walking rightwards.   The cutaway helps to deflect the viewers attention from the clash.

Line of interest

The line of action looks at maintaining continuity in moving subjects.   However, there can also be continuity problems with more static scenes.   Similar problems can also affect dialogue or communication between two characters, or between a person and a prop.

The line of action is the line along which subjects are *travelling*. The line of interest is the line along which subjects are *looking*. Most commonly, it is the line of sight that connects the eyes of the subjects in the scene.

Consider a scene with two men standing at opposite sides of the screen, as viewed from a camera in front of the two men. The script would have the man on the left (e.g. an interviewer) speak, the man on the right (e.g. an interviewee) reply, the man on the left speak …. and so on.   The conversation would take turns in coming from the left side and right side of the screen. If a camera recorded the scene from behind the two men, this would also work quite happily. The problem arises when clips from both cameras are mixed. Now, a man on the *left* speaks – and a man on the *left* replies (since the man on the left is no longer the interviewer but the interviewee!). The effect of the participants constantly changing sides is very disturbing and jars on viewers, who are constantly trying to adjust to who is speaking from where.

Again, the best solution is to avoid crossing the line and only use the clips from the one side of the line of interest.   If mixed clips have to be used, cutaways should be inserted between the offending clips. For example, a clip of the interviewer asking a question could be followed by a cutaway of the interviewers hands or notes. When the next clip shows the interviewee on the same side of the screen, the jarring effect has been dulled by the cutaway.

In a scene, the line of interest may change many times and the editor has to take this into account. For example, a domestic argument might have man and wife arguing, parents questioning son, son arguing with his sister, etc. Despite all the hubbub, there is still a distinct line of interest at each point in the sequence.

Finally, sight lines need not only be between on-screen subjects. Consider a scene of a woman being rescued from a fire. If the first clip shows the woman leaning from a window and shouting downwards and leftwards, the clip of the fireman should show him looking upwards and rightwards.

Video effects

Special effects can be created by manipulating the video stream, as described below:

Freeze frame

> A single frame is repeated over a entire clip and the screen action appears to freeze. This can be used to highlight some detail (e.g. the clock has reached midnight) or to create a powerful dramatic effect (e.g. a football player punching the air after scoring a goal).

Slow motion

Introducing slow motion playback of a section of a movie is another effective technique to heighten tension (e.g. the last few yards before the runner hits the finishing tape). All the frames of the movie are used but each frame is repeated several times. For example, each frame in a sequence of frames 12345 is copied and pasted to produce a timeline with the frames 111222333444555. When played back at the normal frames-per-second rate, the clip lasts three times longer than previously.

Strobe effect

A similar technique is used to produce a strobe effect, with its feeling of frenzy, chaos, or surrealism. The effect can be heightened by combining it with jerking the camera around during recording. It is often accompanied by loud voices, laughing, shouting, or music. This time, not all the frames of the sequence are used. The timeline shows samples of the movie clips contents at pre-determined regular intervals. It is achieved by placing two or more frames of the same image in the timeline, then missing out two or more successive frames. So, instead of the timeline showing frames 123456789 and so on, it would hold the frames in a sequence of 111444777 and so on. The clip plays back at the normal pace but appears very jerky due to the missing content.

Reverse action

The frames in a video clip are stored in reverse order. When played back, the action runs in reverse.

This can be used for comic effect (e.g. a dart leaps out of the dartboard and flies into the hand of the player) or for educational purposes, especially when used in conjunction with slow motion.

Another favourite use is to stage difficult or dangerous activities safely. For example, a car can be positioned facing a tree and just touching the tree trunk. The car is then filmed reversing away from the tree. When played in reverse, the car appears to crash into the tree. Similarly, a sword can be held close to an opponent's chest and filmed being jerked away quickly. When played back, it appears that the man has been run through (the clip should be cut just before the end of the sequence, so that the viewers finish off the activity in their minds).

All these effects are valuable for special purposes but if they are overused, they soon become very tiresome and obscure the main story or message.

Other processing

The editing tasks covered so far have affected how the content is ordered in the production. Editing can also alter the actual content of the video itself, usually on a group of frames, a whole clip or on the entire video content.

Editing software allows a range of video processing tasks to be undertaken. Some tools are used to correct flaws in the original footage (e.g. image stabilisation, image sharpening, correction of geometric distortion, cropping), some are used to provide special effects (e.g. blurring, posterising, colour replacement) and some are used to provide transitions between clips.

Transitions

Transitions alter the way the video content at the end of one clip changes into the beginning of the next clip. Some of these, such as fades, dissolves and wipes, are covered later in the chapter. Many editing application packages provide a huge range of transitions. In practice, only a few of these will be regularly used. In particular, those that provide unusual and spectacular effects should be avoided as they almost always get in the way of the continuity of the sequence. Like cuts, the best transitions are the ones that people hardly notice, as they fit in with the overall flow. Attention should also be paid to the time specified for a transition. For example, fades are normally fairly short but if the scene is of a dying man, then a longish fade is interpreted as his final demise.

Colour alterations

Software is able to process the colour information in the video content, while leaving the basic video information (e.g. monochrome information, frame rate, etc.) untouched. This is sometimes used to correct imperfections in the colour content produced during filming (e.g. through colour castes in the recording environment, the incorrect use of camera filters, etc.). This facility is also used to create special effects.

A number of significant movies (e.g. 'Schindler's List') create the final output in monochrome to produce a documentary effect. Similarly, the "Brothers in Arms" television series used washed out colours during battle scenes. Converting a movie clip to monochrome produces documentary, flashback, or stylised results, while converting to sepia (brownish) replicates the feeling of very old footage.

For the effect of a very old film, the jerky action should also be replicated, as older films were shot at lower frame rates. Don't forget, of course, that the audio for the sequence should be monophonic as stereo would spoil the impression.

Titling

Consideration should be given to how much tilting, if any, is required in a movie. A title called "Our Holiday in Blackpool" may be replaced by a clip of the Blackpool Tower, for example. Many movies use an 'establishment shot' that sets the initial scene. This may be a town name sign, a close-up of a golf ball being struck or whatever and this is often followed by a medium shot then a close-up.

If titling is being used, then use vertical scrolling titles, as they are on the screen longer than horizontally scrolling titles. Credits traditionally either scroll upwards or simply appear one after the other.

Handling sound

During the recording stage, the audio and the video information are stored separately on the recording tape.

When the tape is digitised, the two are still kept separate, allowing one to be altered without affecting the other. When a clip is brought into an editing package, the audio and the video are placed in separate, editable, tracks. In most cases, the software allows other video and audio material to be placed in further, independent, editable tracks (see the example in the Adobe Premiere interface later). The multiple video tracks can be merged, superimposed, faded into each other, etc. Similar effects can be applied to the audio tracks. When editing, the audio content can be processed along with the video content (e.g. in cuts) or can be processed separately (e.g. in audio dubbing).

The creative use of sound is covered in the chapter on *'Digital Audio'*. Nevertheless there are problems, and opportunities, with sound when video editing.

The sound issues when editing video include:

- Ensuring that the audio and video content remains synchronised, especially during speech.
- Maintaining audio continuity when video cuts are performed.
- Maintaining consistent sound levels and sound quality across clips.
- Providing voiceovers and audio dubbing.
- Providing background music that complements the mood and pace of the screen action.
- Providing sound effects at appropriate points in the clips.
- Controlling sound levels for fade effects and mixing of different audio tracks.

Clearly, the editing process has to fully consider the relationship between the audio and video content, so that the sound maximises the overall impact.

Continuity of Sound

A video production is made up from many separate video clips. This could easily result in a disjointed experience for the viewer. Audio, both spoken and musical, plays a big role in keeping the material flowing smoothly. Consequently, it is best if the audio track is considered as a continuous whole, even though the video comprises multiple segments.

Problems in achieving sound continuity while editing include:

Changes in speech levels

Different clips may have used different microphones with differing sensitivity or directionality, or the subjects may have stood at differing distances from the microphones. The result is that the speech amplitude jumps up and down between clips. This can be overcome by adjusting the volume of specific sections of the audio track.

Changes in background levels or content

These changes may be between clips (e.g. one clip is recorded closer to machinery or traffic than another clip) or may be within the one clip (e.g. a plane flies overhead or a dog barks). In the first case, the amplitudes of the audio in the clips can be adjusted. The second case is a little trickier. In most recording situations, the camera operator is asked to record some local ambient sounds (traffic, crowds, running water, etc.). If the main audio track does not contain any significant speech content, that section of the track can be replaced with a piece of the ambient sound. If there is no ambient sound recording, music could be substituted. If the clip contains speech, some adjustment of graphic equalisers might minimise the offending noise without affecting the speech too greatly; otherwise consideration should be given to using cutaways or voiceovers.

Cutting on a background sound

This can occur when the main video content of a clip suggests that a cut is required but a troublesome background sound is present. Continual background sounds such as restaurant sounds or traffic sounds can be cut at the same time as the video. The problem arises with a one-off sound in the audio stream. For example, cutting off a clip in the middle of a hooter sounding or a drum roll is readily noticed as a jump cut. If possible, it is best to avoid cutting on a prominent background sound, even if the video goes on for a little longer. Alternatively, consider fading the sound down at the end of the clip.

Matching music to video

This occurs when a music track that is being used as a background lasts longer than the video clip. The background music is ended abruptly in mid-tune instead of at a natural point. This is because editors tend to start playing the music at the beginning and it therefore does not finish at the same time as the video content. The answer is simple:

- Determine the running time of the video clip (e.g. 3 minutes).
- Determine the running time of the music clip (e.g. 4.5 minutes).
- Calculate the difference in their running times (e.g. 4.5-3 = 1.5 minutes).
- Trim this amount from the beginning of the music clip (e.g. leave only the last 3 minutes of the clip).
- Align the shortened audio clip with the start of the video clip in the software timelines.

Now both clips will end at the same time. Since the beginning of the shortened music clip is unlikely to start at a convenient time in the music, it may have to be faded up so that this shortcoming is not noticed.

Audio Split Editing

Since the audio and video tracks are placed in separate tracks in the software timeline, they can be edited separately. A *'split edit'* occurs when the audio content of a clip is allowed to carry on longer than the video content, or vice versa.

The top diagram shows a typical straight cut, with the audio and video content of clip 1 both ending at the same time, and the audio and video content of clip 2 both starting at the same time. The sound and video cuts are simultaneous.

The middle diagram shows a split edit, with the audio content being allowed to carry on to its normal completion. However, the video content has been trimmed to finish earlier and new content has been inserted to fill the missing section. The audio and video content of clip 2 both start together as normal. The new video content may be an insert (e.g. to show a close-up), a cutaway (e.g. to bridge a jump cut) or even an early start to the video of clip 2. Since the original content of clip 1 carries on through the time of the inserted video, there is a continuity of flow in the production.

The lower diagram is of a split edit where the video carries on to completion but the audio being trimmed back. The new audio content may be replacing a section of poor quality audio, or may be a piece that acts as a *'sound bridge'*. A sound bridge lets the viewer hear the sound before its source is displayed on screen. For example, the sound of bells is played, followed by clip 2 showing a church, or viewers hear a screech of tyres before a racing car is displayed. Using audio to introduce video content is a common technique to lead viewers' expectations and overcome sudden jump cuts. In fact, it is so common that most viewers don't even notice it is happening (checking out movies, television plays, etc. will reveal just how common this transitional approach is used).

Using separate audio and video cue-in points provides the editor with an easy means of editing background sounds, music and sound effects, as well as fading, dubbing, mixing and other audio manipulations. These tasks are easily carried out on the timelines of editing packages such as Adobe Premiere.

The Editing Suite

The essentials for a post-production suite depends upon the intended output.

Minimum equipment for editing

- A camcorder, preferably with a FireWire digital output.
- A VCR for digitising older VHS footage (needs an analogue capture card).
- A computer with a FireWire port (or a video capture card) and ample fast disk storage.
- As much computer memory as possible. Premiere uses three image buffers to store the file at different stages. So the total memory required is three times the file size + the amount of memory to hold Windows and the editing software. For example, a computer with a reasonable 256MB of RAM can only directly handle a file of around 84MB. Larger files can be handled, but are slower to process as they cannot all fit into memory at the same time.
- Video capture software (usually supplied with the capture card or can use Adobe Premiere, etc.).
- Video editing software (e.g. QuickTime Pro, Movie Maker, Adobe Premiere).
- A microphone, for voiceovers.
- The CODEC to be used for processing the final output (e.g. MPEG, Sorenson, RealVideo).

Useful additions

- A dual-monitor card to allow two monitors to be connected to the computer. The work area and application toolbars can then be displayed over the two windows. This allows more tools (even from different applications) to be seen at the one time, and leaves an uncluttered main work space.
- LAN-C connections, to allow control of the camcorder from the computer keyboard. This sends timecode information to the camcorder, informing it where to start playing a clip and for what duration.
- Animation software (3D Studio Max, Poser, True Space).
- Image Manipulation software (e.g. PhotoShop, Paint Shop Pro).
- Royalty-free audio and music clips.
- Batch processing software such as Debabilizer and SmartCapture.
- Video enhancement software such as Adobe After Effects and Media Cleaner Pro.

Using Microsoft Movie Maker

What it is
Movie Maker is Microsoft's small but useful video editing program. Although its facilities are limited, it is bundled along with Windows ME/XP and is therefore available to a large user group of hobbyists at no extra charge.

What it can do
The diagram shows the basic capabilities of the package.
It can combine video clips, audio clips, digital photographs and clipart, to produce a finished movie project. The video format is .wmv by default, although it can also be set to produce .asf files.

The interface
The package is opened by choosing the
        Start/Programs/Accessories/Movie Maker
options.
The illustration below shows the main working screen.

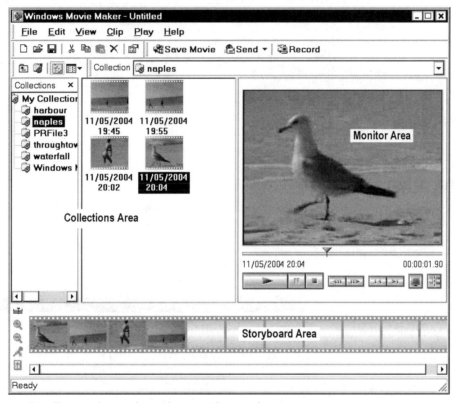

Apart from the usual toolbars and menu bars, there are three main screen areas:

The Collections Area
The source material for a project may be stored in different folders, over several disks – and some may even still be in the camcorder!
The files do not need to be copied into a common folder on the hard disk. Movie Maker simply needs to know what clips you regard as being the set for the project. It does this by having a *"Collections"* area. The user decides what clips will be included in a particular collection and Movie Maker creates the list and knows all the clips' actual locations.
The example shows a collection called *"naples"* and it contains four video clips. The first frame of each clip is displayed for easy recognition.

The Monitor Area
This allows a clip from a Collection to be previewed, either by playing the entire clip or by moving through the clip frame at a time. The *"Split File"* button allows clips to be trimmed (see later).

The Storyboard Area

This area allows the clips from the Collections to be assembled in the order in which they will appear in the final video. The example shows that the four clips from the Collections area have been assembled in the Storyboard in a different order from the order that they were captured.

Options

Before using the application, the user should select the options for working. These are obtained from the *"Options"* selection from the *"View"* drop-down menu. This produces the dialog box shown.

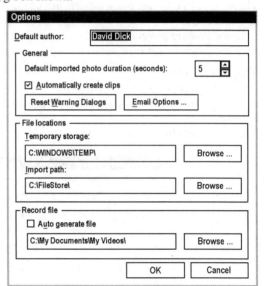

Default Author	Name of project author.
Default imported photo duration	Sets the time that a graphic image will play in a video.
Automatically create clips	When checked, Movie Maker will detect changes in the scene and create a set of clips from a single video stream.
Temporary storage	Where files are held during the record and editing session.
Import path	Where source files are imported from and to where movies are saved.
Auto generate file	When checked, works with the Record dialog settings to automatically save files when the specified time limit for a file is reached.

The folders used for these options should be on disks that have plenty of free storage space, as files are likely to require Gigabytes of storage.

Recording video

Clicking the *"Record"* button on the toolbar brings up the dialog box shown.

The type of recording device currently in use is displayed. In the example, a Sony PC100E digital video camcorder is connected to the computer through a FireWire card.

The first dialog box allows the recording of:

Video and Audio

The most common choice.

Audio Only

Only records the audio from the camera's microphone (e.g. for recording background sounds for providing atmosphere).

Video Only

Only records the video content (e.g. in a situation where the audio track is to be added later).

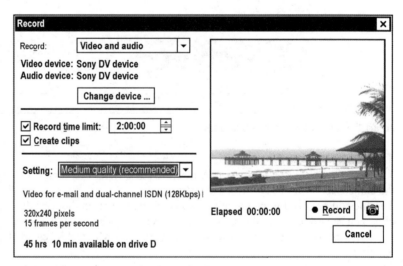

The *"Change Device"* button opens a menu that allows the user to select which device to use, if there is more than one device connected. For example, a computer may have a camcorder attached to a FireWire card or a webcam attached to a USB port. The menu also allows the selection of different audio and video devices (e.g. the video from the camcorder and the audio from a CD).

The *"Record Time Limit"* option sets the maximum time that a video can be recorded. When this limit is reached, recording is stopped. However, if the *"Auto generate file"* box is checked in the Options, the software will carry on recording and will save a new file at the end of each expiry period (with names such as Tape 1.wmv, Tape 2.wmv, Tape 3.wmv, etc.).

The *"Settings"* menu allows for the clips to be saved in one of a variety of formats, to allow for a choice between quality and file size/data transfer rate.

The options are:

Setting name	Video size	Frames per second	Suggested Use
Low Quality	176 x 144	15	Web use at 56kbps
Medium Quality	320 x 240	15	Web use on ISDN (128kbps)
High Quality	320 x 240	30	Web use on broadband (256kbps)

The *"Other"* option provides additional choices:

Video size	Frames per second	Suggested Use
160 x 120	15	Web use at 28kbps
240 x 176	15	Web use on ISDN (64kbps)
320 x 240	30	Web use on broadband (384kbps)
320 x 240	30	Web use on broadband (768kbps)

There are three options of 320x240 at 30fps. The difference lies in the bitrate used for the clip. This is covered later but basically the options provide different levels of compression and therefore different levels of picture quality.

Recording live video

When the settings are selected, clicking the *"Record"* button starts the recording process, the logo on the Record button changes to *"Stop"* and clicking this button stops the recording. When recording is stopped, the user is prompted for a filename and the file is stored in a Collection that is given that name. If the screen content changes dramatically during recording (e.g. exuberant camera movements or large object entering or leaving the view), the session may result in a set of clips being created in the Collection.

Capturing video from the camcorder

If the camcorder is set to its playback mode, the *"Record"* window will then include a set of camera controls as shown in the illustration.

These allow the camera to be controlled via the FireWire port.

The controls can be used to find and set the starting point of the clip. The recording is then carried out as for live video.

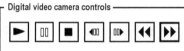

Digital video camera controls

Practical considerations

Movie Maker compresses video files on-the-fly – the video material is saved directly in the compressed .wmv or .asf format; there is no AVI file produced. Since this compression is carried out during the recording process, it relies heavily on the processing power of the CPU. An older computer may not be able to keep up with the processing power required and this would result in the completed file having dropped frames and/or chopped audio.

The advantage of this system is that the storage requirements are minimised, as there is no intermediate or uncompressed version of the video. In fact, the compression into .wmv format is very impressive compared to MPEG.

Capturing still images

While in *"Record"* mode, the camcorder can be used to capture still images. Clicking the camera icon next to the *"Record"* button will capture the current image viewed by the camcorder. The user is then prompted for a filename and this is given a .jpg extension and is saved in the current Collection.

Recording audio

Setting the *"Record"* dialog box to *"Audio Only"* allows an audio clip to be recorded. Using the *"Change Device"* button, the choice of audio device can be selected (e.g. from the camcorder mike, from the sound card's line or microphone socket, from an audio CD, etc.).

The *"Settings"* allow for a wide range of quality settings, ranging from 6.5Kbps up to 128Kbps.

When the settings are selected, clicking the *"Record"* button starts the recording process, the logo on the Record button changes to *"Stop"* and clicking this button stops the recording. The user is then prompted for a filename and the audio file is stored as a .wma file in the chosen Collection.

Importing clips

Where the video file already exists, on hard disk or CD-ROM, the files can be included in Movie Maker projects by *"importing"* them. Using the *"File"* option from the menu bar, the *"Import"* option opens a dialog box where the file can be found and selected. When the *"Open"* button is clicked, the video clip is placed in a new Collection that is given the same name as the file. If the *"Create Clips"* box is checked, the video file will be broken into separate clips for each scene in the file.

Importing audio and graphics files

These files are imported into an existing Collection. Before selecting, the user decides which collection the file is to be included in, by clicking on it in the Collections Area. Selecting the *"Import"* option from the menu bar's *"File"* menu allows a file to be found and selected. When the *"Open"* button is clicked, the file is included in the chosen Collection.

Trimming clips

Movie Maker allows the user to trim his/her video and audio clips.

The steps for trimming a video clip are:

- Click on the desired clip from the Collections Area. The clip appears in the Monitor window.
- Use the *"Next Frame"* and *"Previous Frame"* buttons to position the clip at the point for cutting.
- Click on the *"Split Clip"* button.

The clip appears to be split into two separate clips. For example, if Clip 3 were being cut, there would now be a Clip 3 and a Clip 3(1) in the Collection.

Note

This process does not affect the original source files.

Movie Maker has simply kept a note of the starting points and end points of each clip, for later use – and shows them to the user as if they were now separate files.

To trim an audio clip:

- Click on the desired clip from the Collections Area. The clip appears in the Monitor window.
- Click the *"Play"* button and listen to the audio.
- Click the *"Pause"* button when the point of the split is reached.
- Click on the *"Split Clip"* button.

Clips can also be trimmed while sitting in the Timeline (see later).

A video or audio clip can be renamed by right-clicking on it and changing the clip name in the resulting *"Properties"* dialog box. This is useful because the actual content of each clip can be easily confused when they are only given numbers as clip titles. A text description of each clip is much more useful and well worth the small amount of time needed to title each clip. It is also possible to add a description to each clip at this stage.

Creating a project

The clips are assembled into a project using the Storyboard. The Storyboard is traditionally the method of planning the order, style, content, etc. of clips in a project. In Movie Maker, it is simply a location for setting the order of clips. A clip is dragged and dropped onto the Storyboard. A clip can be dropped in between two clips that are already sitting in the Storyboard. The clip is dropped at the join of the two existing clips and is inserted between them, the other clips being shuffled along to accommodate it.

To delete a clip from the Storyboard, click on the clip and then click the right mouse button. Choosing *"Delete"* from the menu appears to remove the clip from the Storyboard. The clip is only removed from the project; the actual clip still remains untouched in its original location on the disk.

The order of clips can be easily altered by dragging and dropping a clip from its place in the Storyboard to a new position. As with insertion, the other clips shuffle along to allow the clip to be positioned.

The Timeline

The Storyboard area of the screen can be replaced by a Timeline area. This is achieved by clicking on the Timeline icon, or by choosing the *"Timeline"* option from the *"View"* menu. The Timeline is used to edit clips, re-arrange clips and apply transitions and audio dubbing.

The example below shows two clips sitting in the Timeline. The first frame of each clip is displayed and the user can zoom in and out using the magnifying glass icons. A sound icon in corner of a clip indicates that the clip contains audio content.

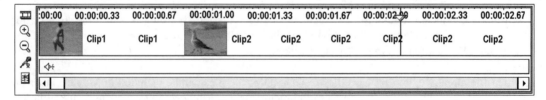

The vertical cursor (known as the *"Play Indicator"*) can be dragged to any part of the Timeline and the Monitor window displays the frame that the cursor is sitting on.

The user can return to the Storyboard by clicking on the icon above the magnifying glasses.

Trimming clips in the Timeline

Clips can be trimmed while they are sitting in the Monitor area and this is a popular method. They can also be trimmed within the Timeline, using *"Start Trim"* and *"End Trim"* points. The Start Trim removes frames from the beginning of clip, while the End Trim removes frames from the end of a clip.

The steps for using a Start Trim are:
- Click on the clip to be trimmed (the clip should now have a blue border round it and a triangle should appear in the first frame of the clip).
- Use the magnifying glass to zoom, so that individual frames can be accessed.
- Move the mouse pointer over the triangle and a double-headed arrow should appear.
- Click the left mouse button, hold it down and drag the mouse rightwards. The Monitor window will show the current frame as the mouse is moved.
- When the desired point is reached, release the mouse button. This removes the leading section of the clip and shuffles all clips along the Timeline.
- If you drag too far into the clip and cut off some of the clip that you want to keep, click and drag the triangle leftwards until the correct point is reached. Releasing the mouse button restores the section previously removed.

The steps for using an End Trim are similar:
- Click on the clip to be trimmed (the clip should now have a blue border round it and a triangle should appear in the last frame of the clip).
- Use the magnifying glass to zoom, so that individual frames can be accessed.
- Move the mouse pointer over the triangle and a double-headed arrow should appear.
- Click the left mouse button, hold it down and drag the mouse leftwards. The Monitor window will show the current frame as the mouse is moved.
- When the desired point is reached, release the mouse button. This removes the trailing section of the clip and shuffles all clips along the Timeline.
- If you drag too far into the clip and cut off some of the clip that you want to keep, click and drag the triangle rightwards until the correct point is reached. Releasing the mouse button restores the section previously removed. However, this restored section will overlap the following clip.   Movie Maker does not shuffle clips correctly on this occasion.   This made right by dragging the following clip rightwards until the two clips butt up to each other.

Adding transitions

When Movie Maker adds clips to the Timeline, they should be butted up to each other. So, when one scene ends, the next scene is immediately displayed. This is known as a *"Straight Cut"*, commonly called a *"Hard Cut"*, and is the most-used method of moving between scenes (watch some film and TV footage).

Movie Maker also offers one other transition, known as a *"Cross-Fade"*, commonly called a *"Dissolve"*. With a cross-fade, the fade in and fade out happen at the same time. Scene one is getting darker as scene two becomes brighter, maintaining screen brightness throughout the transition.

Adding titles

Movie Maker can add text titles to a project. This can be used for a variety of purposes:
- Opening titles.
- Closing credits.
- Adding opening titles to individual scenes (e.g. "Washington DC 4th July").
- Adding content for the hard of hearing.
- Adding content in a second language.
- Using titles in conjunction with a set of graphic images, to produce a slideshow similar to PowerPoint.

The steps for adding titles are:
- Create a graphic image of 320x240. Since Movie Maker does not have its own drawing package, the image will have to be created with a package such as Microsoft's Paint, Paint Shop Pro, or one of the many other similar packages.
- Save the finished graphic and import it into the project's Collection.
- Drag and drop the title image onto the Storyboard.

Movie Maker is very limited in its handling of titles. The title can only be inserted between video clips and/or graphic images. It is unable to overlay a title on to a clip, so there is no way that a title and a video clip can be viewed at the same time. This rules out the creation of sub-titles or captions.

A title can only be overlaid on a graphic image by editing the image in some other drawing package to include the desired text. The amended graphic, complete with title, is then imported into a Collection.

Even the limited titling facilities can be used for added effects. For example, the creation of a solid black image, without any text, can be inserted between scenes to produce a feeling of time passing. It can also be used with cross-fade transitions to fade the scene away to black and fade up the new scene.

Another effect uses two graphic images – one is completely black and the other has title text on a black background. The solid black image is placed at the start of the Timeline, followed by the graphic containing the text. Applying a cross-fade transition between the two results in the title gradually materialising.

Audio Dubbing

There are many times when the audio track recorded on the camcorder is unsuitable for use. This may be due to wind noise, or unwanted sounds on the audio track (whirring from the camcorder's motor, traffic noise, children crying, etc.). It may simply be that the user's narration was poor (forgetting his/her lines, hesitating, coughing, etc.). Additionally, a user may wish to add a musical background or sound effects to a project.

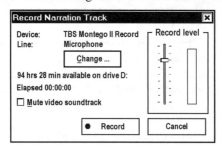

To add new audio to a project:
- Check the Collection in which the new recording will be saved
- Ensure that the Timeline mode is enabled.
- Click on the microphone button (known as the *"Record Narration"* button). This results in the display of the dialog box shown.
- Use the *"Change"* button to select the type of audio to be recorded (e.g. microphone, line, CD-ROM).
- If the new audio is to completely overwrite the existing audio track, check the *"Mute video soundtrack"* box.
- Set the required record level (i.e. do a test run without clicking the *"Record"* button).
- When the audio level is set, click the *"Record"* button.
- When finished, click the *"Stop"* button.
- At the prompt, enter the name that the file should be given.

Audio levels

Movie Maker is not sufficiently sophisticated to provide detailed control over the audio content. For example, it only has a single audio track and cannot provide fades for audio clips.

It does, however, have a single control that allows the user to set the relative levels of any audio already existing on a video track and the new added audio content.

Choosing the *"Audio Levels"* option from the *"Edit"* menu produces the audio levels slider shown in the illustration.

This can be set so that only the existing audio is heard, through varying levels of mix, up to only hearing the new audio. This setting then applies to all occasions where there is added audio sitting along with audio from the original video. There is no opportunity to set the different levels for different audio clips.

Getting started in Adobe Premiere

Adobe Premiere is the most common professional choice of video editing software.   It has a great many features and has provisions for add-ons from other software houses, to enhance its abilities.

Many excellent books go into detail on the subject of video editing in general and using Premiere in particular.   This section of the book covers the general techniques and looks at the most common editing activities.   The material is based on Premiere Pro, although most of activities covered can be carried out in earlier versions.

Using Premiere – an overview

Here are the main steps in creating a project with Premiere:
- Select the input settings.
- Gather files for the project (capturing video from a camcorder or using existing clips).
- Carry out any processing (e.g. clipping)
- Select the running order for the final sequence.
- Place the elements on the timeline.
- Apply any transitions.
- Export the finished project.

The Interface for Premiere

The main Premiere window contains a collection of sub-windows, each dedicated to a part of the editing process. Together, they offer a wide range of tools to edit digital video.   Each window can be displayed or hidden by clicking on its name in the *'Window'* drop-down menu.

The main purposes of the windows are outlined briefly below:

Project Window

The source items to be used in constructing the final project are first imported into the project window. These may be video clips, audio clips or graphic files.   From here, they are dragged and dropped into the timeline, where they may be chopped, altered or added to in many different ways.

When a file is highlighted in the Project window, the window displays the most important information about the clip. This includes the clip's duration, video frame rate and resolution, and audio sampling rate and dynamic range.

It is also possible to right-click on a file in Project window and choose *'Properties'*. This provides additional information, such as the file size, aspect ratio, colour depth and compression CODEC used.

Timeline window

The Timeline window has a number of horizontal containers.   The illustration shows three containers that are capable of holding video streams, three containers capable of holding audio streams and a separate stream for storing the master audio track.   At the start of a project, these containers are empty.   The files are added to the timeline in their chronological running order, as the playback of the content is from left to right.   Video clips are dropped into the video containers on the timeline.

If the video clip contains an audio track, as in the example, the audio component of the file is automatically dropped into the audio container.   Separate audio files, such as background music, effects and voiceovers can also be dropped into the audio containers.

These containers are usually simply referred to as *'tracks'* (i.e. Audio 1 track or Video 1A track).   Track 1A and 1B are used to store movie clips and still-images.   Track 2 and higher are known as *'superimpose'* tracks.   Their contents can be superimposed on any video that may be contained in the other tracks.   These tracks have several other uses, as shown later.   Extra video and audio tracks can be added to the window, as Premiere supports up to 99 audio and 99 video tracks.

Along the top of the window is a ruler that marks out the timecode. A cursor drops down from the ruler and this can be dragged along the timeline. As the cursor moves, the screen contents in the time slot under the cursor are displayed on the Monitor's sequence window.

Monitor window

The Monitor window allows the video to be viewed during the editing process, without first having to render a complete movie. It contains two viewing screens. The *'Source'* screen (the one on the left) shows the video clip currently being worked on and allows it to be edited. The *'Sequence'* window allows the content of the entire timeline to be displayed and edited.

They also show the timecode value of each frame as it is displayed. In the example shown above, the project consists of five separate clips that make up a sequence that lasts for 3 minutes, 10 seconds and 19 frames in length. The player is currently displaying the frame that is 42 seconds and 8 frames in from the start of the project. The monitor screen shows the first clip of the sequence and it is 1 minute, 45 seconds and 7 frames long. It is best to reduce these windows to the smallest size that is still viewable, as the software creates a special file that is just used for displaying previews. The preview file allows the effects of transitions, fades, etc to be seen. A smaller preview window reduces the rendering time and disc space required for the preview file, allowing the editing process to run faster.

Tools menu

The vertical bar to the left of the Timeline is the Tools menu, providing tools to select, edit and manipulate elements.

Input settings

When a new project is initiated, a pop-up window appears. It allows users to load a preset from a given list. This includes NTSC options (for US footage) and PAL options (for UK footage). The presets also offer standard or widescreen resolutions and different audio sampling rates. For most operation, the PAL, standard, 48KHz preset is satisfactory. Where a non-standard source is being used, the options in the *'Custom Settings'* tab allow control over the video frame rate, frame resolution, aspect ratio, etc. The user must ensure that the input settings match the video and audio characteristics of the input source (e.g. the audio rate of 32KHz or 48KHz must match that of the original recording). In both cases, the input boxes at the bottom of the window are used to name the project and to decide where the project files will be stored.

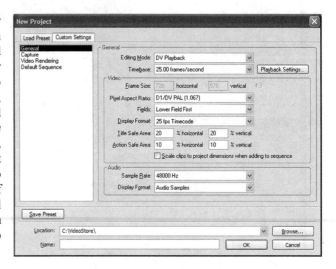

Gathering project clips

Developers will use both imported clips (i.e. existing footage) and captured video (i.e. footage specially recorded for the project).

Importing files

Premiere can import a range of different file formats, such as:
- Video (e.g. AVI, MPG, MOV, WMV)
- Audio (e.g. WAV, WMA, MP3)
- Graphic images (e.g. JPEG, GIF, PCX, PNG, TIFF)
- Animations (e.g. animated GIFs)

There may be a need to rename some of the media files before they are imported. It is much easier to identify a file later if it is called *"interview.avi"* rather than *"file17a.avi"*. The ability to use long file names makes choosing meaningful file names easier (although it is best to check that this causes no conflicts with any other software that is being used). The steps for importing a file into the Project window are:
- Choose *'File'* from the main menu.
- Choose *'Import'* from the drop-down menu.
- Navigate through the hard disc's folders to find the desired file.
- Highlight the desired file.
- Click the *'Open'* button, to add the file to the list in the Project window.

To delete a clip from the Project window, highlight the file and press the Delete key. If the clip is being used in the Timeline, this is reported and confirmation of the deletion is requested.

Capturing video

The steps for capturing video are:
- Connect the camcorder to the computer's FireWire socket.
- Open Premiere and Open/Create a project.
- Choose *'File'* from the main menu.

- Choose *'Capture'* from the drop-down menu.
- Choose the required capture settings in the Capture window (see below).
- Record and name the clip.

Capture settings

The illustration shows the Capture window.

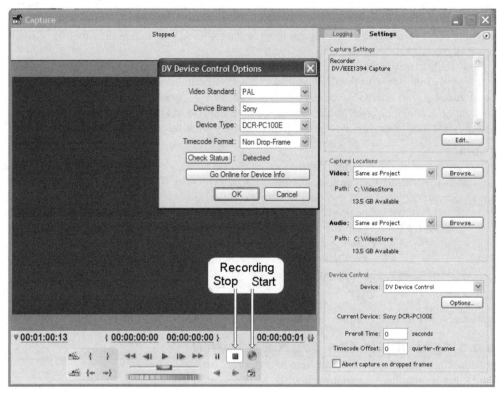

Clicking the *'Settings'* tab allows the user to decide where video and audio content is stored.

It also allows *'Device Control'* to operate, where a FireWire camcorder or video deck is connected. Device Control means that the Play, Stop, Pause and other tape transport operations are controlled from the bottom panel of the Capture window, instead of from the controls on the camcorder. This is more convenient as well as providing greater precision.

Clicking the *'Options'* button in the Device Control section produces the pop-up window shown. In the example, PAL (the UK video standard) has been selected and a Sony DCR-PC100E camcorder has been connected.

Capturing

With the camcorder connected to the FireWire socket, the video from the camcorder is displayed on the Capture screen. If required, the live content being picked up from the camcorder can be used as the source, or the transport controls of the capture window can be used to find the start of the desired clip on the tape.

When the required source appears in the capture window, clicking on the *'Record'* button starts the capture process. Clicking the stop button ends the capture session and the clip is then named before being saved as a video file, and added into the Project window. As mentioned in the last chapter, always leave a little extra material at each end of the clip, to provide flexibility in editing.

Adding files to the Timeline

When all the project's resources are assembled in the Project window, the running order of the material is decided and the clips are placed in the timeline in the required order. Note that the material does not have to be imported into the Project window in any particular order. For example, the earlier example of the Premiere interface shows that the clips have been placed in the timeline in a different order from the way they are presented in the Project window.

In the bottom left corner of the Project window, there are two icons, as shown in this illustration.
Clicking the left icon produces a *'List View'*, with the files in the Project window displayed as a list (see earlier example). Clicking the right icon produces an *'Icon View'*, which displays an image for each graphic or video clip. This allows a *'Storyboard'* approach to be adopted, which many find an aid to assembling clips in an effective running order.

Files are added to the timeline by clicking on them in the Project window and dragging them into the timeline window. A video clip is dropped into one of the timeline's video streams (stream 1 if there is only one video channel being used), while audio clips are dropped into an audio stream. Where a video clip has an audio track, dropping the video into video track 1 automatically drops the audio component into audio track 1.

In many cases, video clips will be dragged from the Project Window into the Source monitor window, have unwanted footage trimmed from them (see later) and will then be dragged from Source monitor window into the timeline. Graphic images are also dragged into a video channel.

The default for Premiere is *'Snap to Edges'* which means that the new file will butt directly behind an existing file, without the need for any accurate positioning by the user. If a gap is required between clips, the clip can be dragged along the timeline until the left-hand edge of the clip aligns with the required point on the time ruler.   If a clip is required to overlap an existing clip (e.g. for creating a transition), the new file would not be placed in the same video track as the existing file.   It would then be dragged to sit at the required position on the timeline, using the time ruler for accurate positioning.

It is important to note that any changes made to a file within Premiere will not change the contents of the original file. The changes only apply to the *copy* of the file that is stored within Premiere and displayed on the timeline.

A file can be included in the timeline as many times as required.   Any changes to one instance of the file (e.g. trimming or adding effects) applies only to that instance of the file and has no effect on the other copies of the file in the timeline.   They are treated as entirely separate files once they are brought into the timeline.

Saving a project

Once all the files are added to the timeline, the project should be saved, as this is effectively the Edit Decision List. The Timeline stores a list of all the resources being used, which order they appear in the project, and how they interact with each other (e.g. fades, dubbing, etc.). There are various save options:

File/Save	The project details are saved and the user continues working with that project.
File/Save As	The project details, at that point, are saved as a *new* copy with a *new* name chosen by the user, and the *new* project is the one that is worked on. All subsequent changes affect only the *new* version.
File/Save a Copy	The project details, at that point, are saved with a *new* name. The user continues working with the *original* project, with its *original* name. All subsequent changes affect only the *original* project.
Edit/Preferences/Auto Save	The project is saved at regular intervals, as set by the user.

Viewing a single clip in the Source window

Drag a video clip from the Project window into the Source window. Click the Play button on the Source window controls, to view the video clip. Each playback window has its own set of controls for play as shown in the illustration. There is a slider bar above the time code. This can be

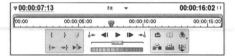

grabbed by the mouse and moved to any part of the clip. Clicking the left or right Nudge buttons moves the view one frame back or forward, giving control down to frame level.

Viewing any part of the project

If the vertical cursor in the Timeline window is grabbed by the mouse and dragged along a section of the time ruler, the video contained during that section of time is displayed in the Sequence window.   This process is known as *'scrubbing'* and the section that is scrubbed could be part of a single file, or could encompass several adjacent files, or even be the set of files for the entire project. The cursor can be dragged to the left or the right and the video is played backwards or forwards. This is a quick way to get an appreciation of the running order and content of the clips.

However, it does not give a feeling for the pace of the project, as the user's control of the mouse is not identical to the actual real-time playing speed of the clip.

To view a part of the project in real time, the start of the section to be viewed should be identified by either positioning the cursor on the time ruler, or by moving the slider bar.

Viewing the entire project

Highlight the Sequence window in the Monitor window. Click the Play button on the Sequence window's controls to view the set of video clips that are present on the timeline.   As a clip is played from the timeline, a vertical pointer, the *'cursor'*, moves along the time ruler, to indicate the progress through the playback.

Previewing the project

The above two methods display the project's timeline contents, displaying each clip in their correct running order but ignoring the results of any effects or transitions that have been applied.

To view transitions and other effects, the material has to be rendered and previewed. Users can preview the entire project, but this can take some time to render. More often users preview a selected *part* of the timeline (e.g. to see the effect of a transition). There is no point in rendering whole areas that are not being examined.

The Work Area Bar controls how much of the timeline content is rendered as a Preview or as the final movie output. The bar is situated just below the Time Ruler, as shown in this illustration. The markers at each end of the bar can be dragged along the time line, to denote the area to be previewed. The entire bar can be moved along the timeline by grabbing the centre marker.

Once the work area has been set to each side of the area that to be viewed (e.g. to see the effects of a fade or transition), the user simply hits the *'Enter'* key. This renders the material in the work area and displays the output in the Sequence window.

A Rough Cut

Before beginning the time-consuming and detailed editing work, there is often a need to view the general run and feel of the project.   This allows the editor to see how the various clips fit into their sequence, whether the overall general effect has been achieved and what specific tasks need carried out that may not have been included in the storyboard.   The viewing of the sequence of clip, before any editing or application of filters, transitions and effects is called a *'rough cut'*.   The editor can view a rough cut at any time during the editing process.   Premiere's output options allow for a project to be created that ignores all these time-consuming processes.   It does not act on these modifications and the raw footage can be examined.   The settings are then altered prior to the final project output being created.

Viewing in greater detail

The timeline is measured horizontally in units that were selected for *'Time Display'* and *'Timebase'* when choosing the *'General Settings'* at the start of the project.   For the UK's PAL video, this is 25fps, requiring 25 separate time markings on the timeline for each second.   If, for example, a set of clips totalled 30 minutes of shooting, there would be 30 x 60 x 25 = 45,000 separate time markings on the timeline.   It is impossible to see them all in the window at any one time and so the user must control the amount of detail seen at any time.   The user may wish to view the entire project in the window, so that an appreciation of the size and location of each file is quickly achieved.   On the other hand, for accurate editing, the user has to work at individual frame level.

The controls for expanding and contracting the timeline, as shown in the illustration, are found at the bottom left corner of the timeline window.   The left icon is a *'Zoom Out'* control.   It shrinks the timeline so that more of the content is visible in the timeline window.   This is used to get an overview of the timeline contents.   The right icon is a *'Zoom In'* control.   It expands the timeline, to provide a more detailed examination of the contents.   Fewer elements are visible in the window but clips can be examined down to an individual frame.   The middle control is a zoom slider that can be quickly dragged to the left or the right to contract or expand the timeline that is visible in the window.

The timeline can display video content in several ways. Clicking the icon below Video track 1 displays a pop-up menu as illustrated. When the option for displaying frames is used in conjunction with the maximum zoom in, this allows great accuracy in editing and applying transitions.

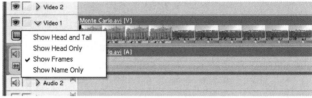

Editing clips

Camera operators usually shoot with spare footage at both ends of the usable material and these unwanted sections will both need to be removed. In many cases, this is carried out in the Source monitor window, before the clip is added into the timeline.   Clips can also be trimmed when they are in the timeline, when required.

Trimming in the source window

The clip is dragged from the Project window into the Source monitor window. The monitor window displays the total duration of the clip.

The new clip length is determined by the *'in point'* and the *'out point'*.   Initially, these points are the first frame and the

last frame of the clip.   To trim from the front of the clip, move the cursor along the timecode up to the desired new start for the clip.   When the *'In Point'* icon is clicked (see the illustration), the clip in the Project window is shortened.   If required, the end of the clip can also be trimmed by moving to the last wanted frame and clicking the *'Out Point'* icon.

An alternative method is to drag the in and out markers that appear at each end of the clip.

Trimming clips in the timeline

The three methods of trimming clips that are already in the timeline are:

Dragging the clip

A clip can be shortened by clicking on an edge of the clip and dragging it inwards.   The frames that have been removed from the timeline will not appear in any preview or in any final rendered output.   During the editing process, however, they remain available, so that the clip can be dragged back to restore some or all of the hidden frames if required.   This method shortens the clip, leaving a gap in the timeline; the total project duration remains unchanged.

Using the ripple edit tool

The Tool bar includes a *'Ripple Edit'* icon that should be chosen. The edge of the clip can now be
dragged to shorten the clip, as before.

This option shortens the clip and moves other clips along the timeline so that there is no gap. The total project
duration is shortened by the amount of time removed from the clip. Like the previous method, the removed
frames are available for any subsequent stretching of the clip. In both cases, the clip cannot be dragged to a
duration that is larger than its original duration.

Using razor cuts

Select the *'Razor'* from the Tool bar and click on the frame at which the clip should be shortened. This
splits the clip into two smaller clips. Return to the *'Select'* tool, the one that is shaped like an arrow. Use
the Select tool to select the portion of the clip that is to be discarded. Once the sub-clip is highlighted, right-click
the mouse and choose *'Ripple Delete'* from the menu that appears. This option removes the unwanted sub-clip
and moves other clips along the timeline so that there is no time gap left. The total project duration is shortened
by the amount of time used by the sub-clip. Unlike the other methods, the removed frames are no longer
available for any subsequent stretching of the clip.

This method is also very useful for removing sections in the middle of a clip. In this case, the start and end frames
for the cut should be marked with the Razor tool. This produces three sub-clips and the middle section can then
be removed (i.e. ripple deleted).

Cropping

The composite and S-Video outputs from a camcorder are designed for displaying on a television screen. However,
televisions leave an area of the screen picture that is unseen. Only 576 out of the transmitted 625 lines are displayed
on the screen.   Likewise, a little of the screen edges are unseen. This is termed *'overscan'* or *'edge blanking'*.
Television transmitters use the unseen lines to send Teletext and other signals.   On some poorly set up televisions,
the Teletext data is seen as a row of white dots at the top of the screen.

Since overscan techniques are not used with computer video, these extra borders are visible and produce ugly borders
to the clip. They also consume file capacity.

Another popular use for cropping is removing unwanted material from a scene. For example, a video clip may have
an unwanted spectator at the side of the picture, or the boom mike may be visible at the top of the picture.

Premiere provides a utility for overcoming overscan and removing distractions at the edges of clips.

The steps for cropping a video clip are:

- Highlight the selected video clip in the Timeline.
- Click the *'Effect Controls'* tab in the Monitor window.
- Click the *'Effects'* tab in the Project window.
- Select the *'Video Effects'* option.
- Select the *'Transform'* option.
- Select the *'Crop'* option.
- Drag the *'Crop'* icon into the *'Effect Controls'* area.
- Enter each value for the amount of clipping required (the values are in percentages).
- Check that the image in the Sequence window matches the requirements and re-adjust if necessary.

The screen should look similar to that below.

The *'Zoom'* box can be checked (for cropping) or left unchecked (for clipping), with the results being:

Checked   This utility removes the edges from the video clip and resizes the clip to fill the original resolution of the clip. It results in the same size of file size, without the ugly borders.

Unchecked   This utility removes the edges but does not resize the clip. The results in a smaller file size, but it may not fit in with other material recorded at the original resolution. This is not a problem for a standalone clip, or for a set of clips from the same source that are all similarly clipped. It may also cause difficulties when it is output to videotape which expects a fixed resolution.

Bear in mind that altering one edge by a large margin will alter the scene's horizontal and vertical ratios. For example, setting the left slider to a high value, while leaving the rest untouched, results in a picture that is too tall compared to its width.

Splitting Files

A file may require to be split into two sections. This may be required for various reasons:
- So that one of the sections may be copied elsewhere.
- So that an effect can be applied to one section of the clip but not the other section.

Move the cursor to the desired place on the timeline and use the Razor tool as described earlier. The clip will be split into two smaller clips that can be processed independently of each other.

Deleting from the timeline

To delete a clip and move the other clips to fill the gap, use *'Ripple Delete'* method explained in the earlier section on razor cuts.   A clip can also be deleted by highlighting the clip and pressing the Delete key.   This deletes the clip but leaves a gap in the timeline.

When a clip is removed from the timeline it remains in the list in the Project window.

Altering a clip's speed/duration

Altering a clip's speed/duration can produce special effects, or (within limits) can make a clip fit a particular time slot.

Premiere allows the speed of an individual clip to be altered.

This is achieved through the *'Speed/Duration'* option on the *'Clip'* drop-down menu. A dialog box is opened as shown in the illustration.   It reports on the current duration of the clip and the clip speed, which is always initially 100%.

If the New Rate is set to 200%, the clip runs twice as fast, as every alternate frame is dropped. The clip's duration is halved and the clip has a jerky, high-speed appearance. Setting the New Rate to the maximum value drops most of the frames and provides a time-lapse photography effect that can be used to demonstrate how a slow moving process operates (e.g. a clock's mechanical movement, the construction of a building, etc).

If the New Rate is set to less than 100%, extra frames are inserted and the clip duration is lengthened. For example, a setting of 50% results in the repetition of each frame, doubling the clip duration.   This can be used to create a slow-motion effect for dramatic effect (e.g. lovers running along a station platform to embrace) or to demonstrate fast-moving processes (e.g. to show the limb movements of a galloping horse or a ballerina).

An alternative method is to alter the duration of the file by entering a new value for *'Duration'*. The value in the box is edited to enter the new value and the number of frames in the clip are increased or decreased to provide the new duration.   This provides more precise control over the clip's final duration, but large variations will produce the slow-motion or speeded-up effects mentioned above.

If precise settings are not required, users can employ the *'Rate Stretch'* tool in the tool bar.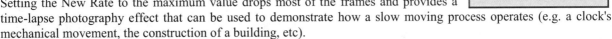

The tool is selected from the Tool bar, is placed on an edge of the clip, and is then used to drag the sides of the clip to lengthen or shorten the clip's duration.

Capturing a still from the video clip

A still picture can be captured from a video clip by placing the clip in the Source window.   The tab should be slid and/or the nudge buttons clicked, until the desired frame is displayed in the Source window.   The *'Export'* option should be chosen from the *'File'* drop-down menu and choosing the *'Frame'* option from the sub-menu opens a dialog box to name and save the frame as a still image.

Capturing from a stationary or slow-moving clip will obviously produce better results than extracting from a fast-moving clip (unless a blurred image is required for effect - a speeding car or a sprint runner).

Adding a graphic to the timeline

Designers may occasionally wish to include a static picture into their projects for purposes such as:
- To display a helpline number, while a voiceover reads out the details.
- To display an oil painting, while its merits are discussed.
- To display the static end credits with background music.
- To allow video players to get up to speed (see below).

If the end of the movie has a particularly dramatic feature, it is common that the action be frozen while the credits roll. This maintains an impact even after the moving footage has ended. It is wasteful of precious disc space and transmission time, to have a ten-second shot of video while the music or voices play over a static display. It is much more economical to take a graphic file and make it stretch over the ten-second period. The graphic can be a digitised picture, a file created in a drawing package or a frame extracted from the video clip.   The graphic file is first imported into the Project window, and then dropped on to the video track. Premiere will display the graphic for a default duration.

This time can be extended by either:

- Dragging the file size wider.
- Right-clicking the file, choosing the *'Speed/Duration'* option to open the duration dialog box, where a precise value can be entered.

If it is found that a video player, or Macromedia Director, jerks the content at the start of a video, extract a frame from the start of the video clip and place it in front of the video clip in the timeline. Extend the still frame to cover the time needed for the player to operate smoothly (adjust the length of time by trial and error the first time it is used).

Applying transitions

A *'hard cut'* describes the way that two files are butted together in the playback, such that the content of the first file ends abruptly and the content of the second file is displayed immediately afterwards.

An examination of footage in the cinema and on television reveals that many cuts are of this kind. A *'transition'* is a description of the way that the first clip changes over time into the second clip.

Some transitions can be used to convey a comic effect, while fades and dissolves can be used to indicate the passage of time, *'flashbacks'* in time, or simply provide an effective pause in the project flow.

Transitions, fades and dissolves should not be overused. Too many detract from the video, require excessive rendering time and lower the compression ratio. Transitions should not just be used because they exist - they should be used where they add to the project (e.g. by pacing the project or by conveying extra meaning (see the table below). Most transitions should last between half a second and about two seconds. Excessively long transitions aggravate the viewer.

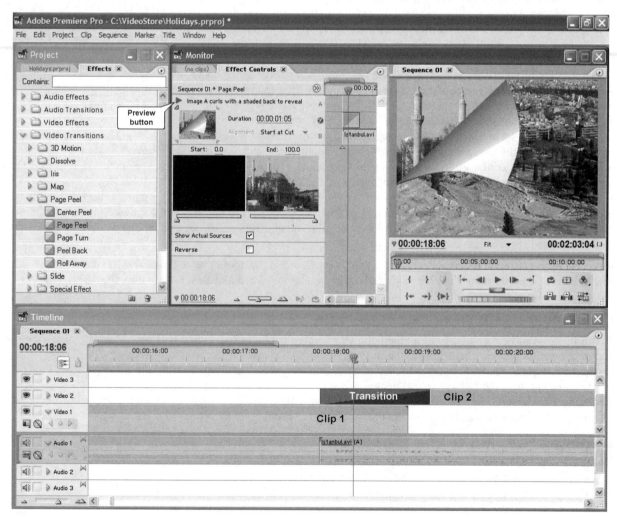

Note

Earlier versions of Premiere placed clips in separate video tracks and used a separate transitions track to store transitions. Premiere Pro does not use a separate transitions track and video clips can be placed in separate video tracks, butted together in the same track, or even have a gap between clips on the same track. The transition is placed on one of the video tracks, at the point where the transition is to take place.

The steps for applying a transition are:

- Place clips in the video track(s). The illustration above shows overlapping clips on separate tracks (the beginning of Clip 2 includes the transition).
- Expand the timeline, if necessary, to adequately view the transition area.
- Click the Projects window's *'Effects'* tab.
- Expand *'Video Transitions'*.
- Expand the required transition group (e.g. the *'Page Peel'* group).
- Choose a transition from that group (e.g. *'Page Turn'* or *'Page Peel'*).
- Drag the transition to the junction of the two clips on the timeline.
- Click on the transition effect block on the timeline. The *'Effect Controls'* in the Monitor window will display the effect and show the options that are available for that effect.
- Enter the duration of the transition.
- Select any other effects (e.g. in the illustration the page peels from the left and checking the *'Reverse'* box makes the page peel from the right).
- Click the Preview button to view the effect of the transition, in the small window below the button. This provides a quick view of the transition.
- Alternatively, press the 'Enter' key to render the transition and the transition can be viewed in the larger Sequence window.
- Adjust, if necessary, until the required effect is achieved.

The Video Transitions list includes some of the more common transition types and these are explained in the following table.

Type	Action	Typical Purpose
Fade in	Displays a black screen, which gradually lightens to reveal the content of the clip.	Commonly used to open a project.
Fade out	Gradually darkens the screen content, until the last frame is completely black.	Commonly used at the end of a project.
Fade out / fade in	Two fades happening one after the other. The first scene fades completely to black, followed by the second scene lightening up from complete black. The two fades are separated in time. The fade in does not start until the fade out has completed.	Used to mark some significant break in the project flow. The darkened pause provides time for reflection on the contents of the previous scene, or marks a change in time, location or general subject content.
Dissolve	The fade in and fade out happen at the same time. The picture never becomes black. Scene one is getting darker as scene two becomes brighter, maintaining screen brightness throughout the transition.	Used to mark scene changes or the passage of time when the location in the two scenes does not change. Hard cuts are preferable where a more dynamic feel is required.
Wipe	The screen is divided into two sections by a line that can be horizontal, vertical or diagonal. At the beginning of the wipe, 100% of scene one is visible on one side of the line, while scene two occupies 0% of the screen. As the line moves, a smaller percentage of scene one is displayed, while more of scene two is visible. Eventually, scene one occupies 0% of the screen, while 100% of scene two is visible.	Horizontal wipes have a slow, deliberate, majestic effect that can control pacing of the project. Other wipes are used to indicate scene changes, such as a new subject content or a new location.
Ripple	The frame content appears as if it is a reflection on water.	Used at the start and end of a 'flashback' in time.
Page turn, also known as a peel	One corner of the first clip is progressively turned over, revealing the contents of the second clip.	This is used where a 'story' is being told, as it is an analogy of turning pages in a book.
Displacements	The second clip is brought into the picture as an animated object that pushes the first clip out of the picture and gradually replaces it. The second clip's path can be chosen from Push, Swap, Cross Stitch and Cube Spin. Unlike the other effects above, both clips are moved across the screen.	Attention grabbing method for scene changes.

Notes

Hard cuts are by far the easiest transition to compress.   A simple vertical or horizontal wipe is also relatively easily compressed.   Complex transitions such as page turns or rotary transitions produce the poorest compression and often result in unwanted artifacts.

Premiere provides its own system for achieving fades and these are covered later.   There is no fade transition effect listed as an option in the Project *'Effects'* window.

Creating a dissolve

The steps for creating a dissolve between video files are:

*   Place the video clips in the timeline. In this example, the clips are butted together on the same video track.
*   Drag the *'Cross Dissolve'* transition to the junction of the two clips on the timeline.
*   Click on the transition effect block on the timeline.
*   Enter the duration of the dissolve in the *'Effect Controls'* in the Monitor window.
*   Preview the results.
*   Adjust the settings, if necessary, to achieve the desired effect.

In the example, the video and audio content at the end of Clip 1 is gradually reduced, while the content of Clip 2 is gradually increased.

Creating a fade out

This can use the above technique but, since there is no following clip, the screen contents fade to black.

Creating a fade in

Similar to above but, since there is no preceding clip, the screen contents fades up from black.

Creating a fade out/fade in

A fade in/fade out is similar but there may be a gap in time between the clips, instead of them overlapping each other. During the gap time, there is no video output and the screen is black. (also see the use of keyframes below).

The steps for creating a fade out/fade in between video clips are:

*   Place both clips in the video track. Note the gap between the clips in the timeline.
*   Drag a dissolve transition to the end of Clip 1.
*   Drag a dissolve transition to the beginning of Clip 2.
*   Enter the duration of the dissolves in the *'Effect Controls'* in the Monitor window.
*   Preview the results.
*   Adjust the settings, if necessary, to achieve the desired effect.

Using the 'Opacity' control

The fade effect is not provided as a separate transition that appears in the Project's Effects window. That is because it automatically provided for each clip. If a clip in the timeline is highlighted, the *'Effect Controls'* panel displays an *'Opacity'* control as shown in the illustration.

Dragging the slider fades the video by different amounts.
This provides a simpler method of controlling fades.
It can also be used for special effects. Consider placing a clip of a castle into Video track 1 and a clip of a woman walking across the screen into Video track 2 – both clips being in the same portion of the timeline. By adjusting the opacity of track 1, the contents of track 2 become partially visible – the woman appears to be a ghost that walks about the castle!

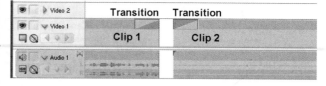

Using keyframes

Premiere allows effects such as opacity and other filters and transitions to be varied within a clip. So, for example a clip with the *'Lens Distortion'* filter applied to it may begin with a low level of distortion, have more distortion in the middle of the clip and have no distortion at the end of the clip.   This would require the setting of three *'keyframes'*.

A keyframe is a handle that appears on the clip's keyframe timeline, as shown in the illustration above.   A keyframe contains all the information of the clip's filter settings that apply at that point in time. If multiple keyframes are added to the keyframe timeline, each can have different settings. Premiere then uses linear interpolation to work out the contents of each frame between the keyframes. This means that the filter's effect on the clip can be increased or decreased over different areas of the clip.

Keyframes can be added by moving the cursor in the timeline to the required position and clicking on the icon that adds a keyframe (see the illustration). Keyframes can be deleted by right-clicking on them and choosing the *'Clear'* option. The positions of keyframes can be altered by dragging them along the timeline.

Creating a fade out using keyframes

The steps for creating a fade out are:

- Highlight the video clip in the timeline.
- In the *'Effect Controls'* panel, move the cursor along the timeline to the point where the fade is to start.
- Click the icon that adds a keyframe (see the illustration above).
- Ensure that the opacity slider value is set to 100%.
- Move the cursor along the timeline to the point where the fade is to end (i.e. the end of the clip).
- Add another keyframe.
- Drag the opacity slider to a value of 0%.
- Preview the results.
- Adjust the opacity settings and/or keyframe positions, if necessary, to achieve the desired effect.

A fade in is similar to the above, except that the first keyframe is at the beginning of the clip and is set to 0%

Creating a mid-fade

A mid-fade is applied to a single video clip. It is not a transition between clips, but a fade down/fade up within a clip. The video scene is faded but the audio track continues to play over that period. This might be used to simulate a power cut affecting lights, or may be a temporary fade while a voice from the audio track ponders a situation.

The steps for creating a mid-fade are as above, except that four keyframes are used, one at 100% (the start of the fade down), one at 0% (the end of the fade down), another at 0% (the start of the fade in) and one at 100% (the end of the fade in).

Filters

Video filters, called *'Effects'* in Premiere, are used to alter the content of each frame as it is rendered. Unlike fades and other transitions, which only apply to a section of a clip, a filter is often applied to all of the frames in a clip.

There are two types of filter - those are used to enhance a clip's overall quality, and those impose special effects on the clip contents. Any filter, like transition rendering, requires extra processing time. Most filters offer user control over the filter settings, to adjust the effect for the required purpose. Premiere provides a good selection of filters and additional filters are sold as plug-ins to the Premiere application.

Filters for frame enhancement

The higher-quality construction of a computer monitor means that it can reproduce a greater colour range than is available from a television screen. Since videotape has been recorded with television in mind, it is designed to cater for the range handled by the TV screen.

Filters can be applied, before compression, to improve the colours in the movie. A small increase in contrast can produce significant improvements to the vividness of colours, as well as improving the black to white contrast. The clip should be scrubbed through, to ensure that the changed settings have not adversely affected any part of the movie. It is important to ensure that changes to contrast and brightness leave the blacks at true black level; otherwise it introduces noise and lowers compression.

Filters are commonly used to brighten up an under-exposed clip or to adjust colours to compensate for an incorrect white balance.

The filters supplied with Premiere include:

Brightness & Contrast, Color Balance, Color Offset, Hue Lightness & Saturation, and Gamma Correction

The Gamma Correction filter lightens or darkens a clip by changing the brightness levels of the midtones (the middle-grey levels) while leaving the dark and light areas unaffected.

The Levels filter manipulates the brightness and contrast of a clip. It combines the functions of the Color Balance, Gamma Correction, Brightness & Contrast, and Invert filters into one filter.

Effects Filters

Fancy effects filters can be very effective in the right situation. However, they tend to introduce noise and artifacts and should only be used when necessary.

The filters supplied with Premiere include:

Alpha Glow, Anti-alias, Backwards (Video), Blend, Better Gaussian Blur, Blur and Blur More , Camera Blur, Camera View, Color Replace, Crystallize, Emboss, Gaussian Blur, Gaussian Sharpen, Horizontal Flip, Horizontal Hold, Invert, Lens Distortion, Lens Flare, Median, Mirror, Mosaic, Pinch, Pointillize, Polar, Posterize, Posterize Time, Radial Blur, Ripple, Roll, Sharpen and Sharpen More, Sharpen Edges, Shear, Solarize, Spherize, Twirl, Vertical Flip, Vertical Hold, Video Noise, Wave , Wind, Zig Zag.

Applying a Filter

Filters can be applied to a portion of a clip, an entire clip, or to a collection of clips.

The alteration of filter settings during a clip is mostly used for special effects, while video enhancement filters are usually applied evenly to the entire clip.

The steps for applying a filter to a video clip are identical to those for applying a transition.

The steps for applying filter effects with keyframes are:

- Highlight the video clip in the Timeline window.
- Select the desired filter from the Project Effects list and drag it into the *'Effect Controls'* panel.

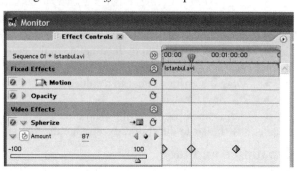

- Choose the filter settings in the dialog box that is displayed. These settings apply to the entire clip unless other keyframes are added, or the end keyframe settings are altered.
- Move the timeline pointer to where the effect should begin and click just below the effect name (the one just to the left of the word *'Amount'* in the illustration). This adds a keyframe at that point on the timeline.
- Enter the required value for the effect (or use the slider if one is displayed) at that point.
- Add further keyframes with their values, as required.
- Keyframes can be dragged along the timeline to reposition them.   As a keyframe moved, the *'Time'* reading below the timeline indicates the exact position of that keyframe along the timeline.
- To remove a keyframe, highlight it and click the *'Delete'* button. The first and last keyframes cannot be removed.

If the keyframe timeline only contains the start and end keyframes, they can be set to different settings, for a gradual change of filter over the entire clip.

Applying multiple Filters

More than one filter can be added to a clip, if more complex effects are required.   The filters are applied in the order that they appear in the *'Effect Controls'* window and changing the order can change the final effect.   The first effect is applied to the clip, then the second effect is applied to the result from the first filter, and so on.   Each filter retains its own keyframe timeline and its own set of keyframes.   Alterations to one filter's settings have no effect on the settings of another filter. The order of filters in the *'Effect Controls'* window can be changed by highlighting a filter and dragging it up or down the list.

The effects of a filter can be increased by adding it to the *'Effect Controls'* list more than once, although applying multiple filters will result in much longer rendering times.

Black & White filter

This very simple filter converts a clip to greyscale.   There is no settings dialog box and the effect has to be applied to the entire clip, as no addition keyframes can be added.   For more control, see the Color Pass filter discussed next.

Color Pass filter

The Color Pass filter, like the *'Black & White'* filter, converts the content of each frame in a video clip to a greyscale.   However, this filter is adjusted to allow a specified colour to escape the greyscale conversion.   There are many examples of this technique in television adverts, where the entire world is grey is except for someone's bright red dress or lipstick.   The filter does not attach itself to the object, just to the colour.   The planning of the project can take this into account and ensure that as much as possible of the object to be filmed for this treatment is in a colour that is not likely to be found in the surrounding area of the shot.   Examples are purple (e.g. someone wearing a purple dress), red (e.g. playing football with a bright red ball) and canary yellow (e.g. driving a yellow car).

The steps for applying this filter to a video clip are:

- Highlight the video clip in the timeline.
- Select *'Color Pass'* from the Project Effects list and drag it into the *'Effect Controls'* panel.
- Use the eyedropper to select the required colour in the *'Clip Sample'* window.
- Entering a value for *'Similarity'* sets the range of colours that allowed through the filter. So, for example, a blue sky will not be evenly blue across a frame or throughout a clip.   Increasing the similarity range ensures that more shades of blue are accepted to maintain the effect.   A range of 100% means that all colours in the scene are passed through the filter.

Ghosting

The Ghosting filter overlays transparencies of the immediately preceding frames on the current frame. This effect can be useful, for example, when you want to show the motion path of a moving object, such as a bouncing ball;

the effect is best used with uncluttered scenes.   The effect can also be used to simulate the view of someone who is drunk, drugged or dazed from the effect of a punch or loss of memory. There is no settings dialog box and the effect has to be applied to the entire clip, as no addition keyframes can be added.

Replicate

The Replicate filter divides the screen into tiles and displays the whole image in miniature in each tile. The number of tiles is set by dragging the slider in the Replicate settings dialog box.   This filter supports additional keyframes.

Tiles

The 'Tiles' filter divides the entire frame equally into a set of tiles, with each tile displaying a part of the frame content. The number of tiles is set by entering a value in the settings dialog box.   This filter supports additional keyframes.

Resize

The Resize filter resizes the clip to the output frame size using interpolated scaling. This provides better scaling than QuickTime or Video for Windows can achieve, adjusting the size when you export the final video project. There is no settings dialog box and the effect has to be applied to the entire clip, as no additional keyframes can be added.

Strobe

The Strobe filter is used to suggest a mood of hyperactivity or chaos (e.g. dance scenes or crowd scenes). The filter simulates a stroboscopic effect, or strobe light, by hiding frames at a regular rate as the clip plays. The regularity of the effect is set by specifying the number of visible and hidden frames in the settings dialog box. When the clip content is hidden, the frame is filled with a user-selectable colour.

Tint

The Tint filter applies a tint to the frame content.   The dialog box allows the tint colour and percentage of tint to be set.   This filter supports additional keyframes. It can be used along with the Black and White filter to simulate the sepia tones found in old films.

Picture in Picture

A basic 'picture in picture' is deemed a high tech effect but is simple to achieve.
It can be used for a number of purposes, including:

- Displaying the commentator's head and shoulder in a corner of the frame, while the rest of the frame displays the content being discussed.
- Displaying a close-up of a process, while the main frame content displays the wider view.
- Displaying a set of sub-features of the main display (e.g. the main display shows a holiday resort, while the insert shows clips of the pool, the restaurants, the bedrooms, etc).
- Displaying special effects such as placing the insert in the area occupied by the main clip's television screen, computer monitor, videophone, etc.

The steps for achieving a picture in picture effect are:

- Place main video clip in Video track 1.
- Place the clip to be inset in Video track 2, in the same timeslot as the other clip.
- Select the 'Zoom' transition from the Project Effects list and drag it into Video track 1.
- Extend the transitions until they cover the duration of the clips being inserted.
- Click on the transition in track 1.
- Set the start and end points to 100%.
- Click on the transition in track 2.
- Set both the start and end points to size of the inset (25% in the illustration).
- Drag the clip to the desired screen position (the top left corner in the illustration). This is achieved by dragging the box that contains the letter 'B'.
- Set the colour and thickness of any border to be placed round the insert.

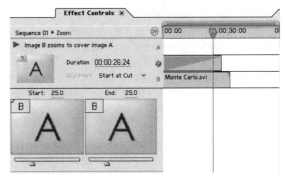

Thought should be given at the storyboard stage to the use of picture in picture.   For example, if a scene involves two people having a conversation via a videophone, both clips should be recorded to reflect the eyelines of the participants. Both people should be positioned for recording such that they appear to be looking at each other in the final video.   In addition, the quality of the inserted clip may be deliberately be downgraded, to give the impression of losses to the signal through travelling great distances.

Split Screen

A common effect is to split the screen into two horizontal sections, with a different video playing in each section.   It has the same uses as mentioned in picture-in-picture above and is also used for *'before and after'* situations (e.g. the garden before and after the makeover, the model's hair before and after using a particular brand of hair conditioner, etc).   The steps to achieve a split screen effect are:

- Place the 'left' video clip in Video track 1.
- Place the 'right' video in Video track 2, in the same timeline slot as the first clip.
- Select the *'Wipe'* transition from the Project Effects list and drag it into Video track 2.
- Extend the transition until it covers the duration of the clips being used.
- Click on the transition in the timeline to bring up the Wipe settings dialog box.
- Drag the left-hand slider to the proportion of the screen to be occupied by the left clip (e.g. 30%).
- Drag the right-hand slider to the value of 100% minus the size of the left screen (e.g. 70%).

Chromakey

This is one of 15 transparency effects provided by Premiere. It provides the effect of the weather forecaster or holiday presenter in a studio, yet with all kinds of maps and exotic locations in the background.   Chromakey uses two clips.   The foreground clip (e.g. the presenter) is recorded against a background of a certain colour, generally blue (ensuring that no blue clothes are worn).   Then the blue area of the clip is made transparent.   The content of the second clip is now visible in all parts of the previously blue area.   Of course, both clips need to sit in the same timeline slot.   This effect is accessed through the *'Video Effects'* options of the Project window (in the *'Keying'* group).   The effect is dropped into the main clip.   The dialog in the *'Effect Controls'* allows the selection of the transparent colour and the similarity and threshold levels to be set.   These can be tweaked, and the results, viewed, until optimum results are achieved.   However, the compression on digital video may make the edges of objects appear more harsh, making effective chromakeying a difficult and tricky operation.

Handling audio tracks

Most video clips are recorded with a sound track and the *'Audio 1'* track will hold the audio track of the main video clip.   The second video track will use the *'Audio 2'* track, if it contains audio information.   Additional audio is often added to a project.   This may consist of background music (for creating a mood), background effects (to provide atmosphere for the scene) or a voiceover (to explain a process, sell a product, etc).

Audio clips can be separately recorded.   Many unusual sounds (e.g. a laughing hyena) or sounds that are difficult to record (e.g. the flight of a low-flying aircraft), can be purchased as royalty-free samples.

The clips are added to the Project window and are dragged and dropped into the *'Audio 3'* track.

If a further audio track is required, it has to be added to the Timeline window. With the Timeline window active, selecting *'Add Tracks'* from the *'Sequence'* menu displays a dialog box that allow extra audio and/or video tracks to be added to the timeline.

The effect can be tested by highlighting the Timeline window and pressing the spacebar.   The audio from both tracks is mixed together and played.   Additional audio tracks should be at slightly less volume than might first be thought, as there is a tendency to set background tracks to excessive volumes.

Controlling audio levels

It is important to recognise that when separate audio clips appear in different tracks of the timeline, their volumes are additive.   This means that at certain times, the combined peak volume is greater than can be accommodated by the range of the software, resulting in distortion.   If distortion is detected during the preview stage, the volume of individual audio tracks will need to be reduced.

The gain of an entire track can be adjusted by the following steps:

- Highlight the audio clip in the timeline.
- Choose *'Clip'* from the main top menu.
- Choose *'Audio Options'* from the drop-down menu.
- Choose *'Gain'* from the sub-menu.
- Alter the percentage value in the *'Gain Value'* box (between 0% and 200%) and click the *'OK'* button.

There are also ways to lower the volume of a *section* of an audio clip. This allows, for example, a background music track to be faded during a voiceover, or allows the cross-fading of two music clips.   The music should be faded slightly before the voiceover begins, so that the fade becomes less obvious.   The voiceover should start about half way through the fade down and finish about half way through the fade up.   This technique is also used to link two video clips with different background sound levels.

The steps for altering a section of an audio clip's volume are identical to those listed earlier on *'Creating a fade out using keyframes'*.   The audio track is highlighted and the *'Audio Effects'* is selected in the *'Effect Controls'* panel, instead of *'Video Effects'*.   The *'Level'* slider is used to set the volume at the various keyframes.

Audio Mixer

Premiere Pro provides a comprehensive mixing and balancing utility called the *'Audio Mixer'*. It is accessed from the *'Window'* menu and is shown in the illustration.

Each audio track in the timeline has its VU meter, gain control and stereo balance control.

When the timeline is played, the levels of each audio track are displayed in real time on the VU meters. This allows the user to check whether any track is overdriving the system or is running at too low a level.

The sliders can be dragged, in real time, to increase or decrease the gain of each individual track. While it is effective to lower the gain of a loud track, it should be remembered that increasing the gain of a quiet track will also increase the noise level in that track.

Clicking on the loudspeaker icon above a track slider toggles muting of the track off/on.

Clicking on the microphone icon above a track slider enables the recording controls that are along the bottom of the panel.

Audio Filters

Ideally, the audio clip should have its quality optimised before bringing it into the Project window. This may involve increasing a quiet audio passage, removing unwanted noise, adding echo and so on, as explained in the chapter on *'Digital Audio'*. However, many audio processing facilities are provided by Premiere.

The steps for applying an audio effect are:

- Highlight the audio clip in the Timeline window.
- Select the desired filter from the Project's *'Audio Effects'* list and drag it into the *'Effect Controls'* panel.
- Choose the settings that are required (some may be entered by the keyboard and some may provide sliders).
- Preview the results.
- Adjust the settings, if necessary, to achieve the desired effect.

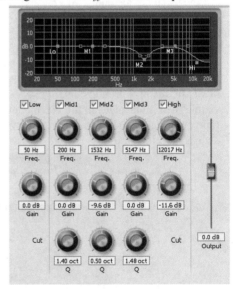

Audio quality filters

Some filters enhance or correct a clip's characteristics. These include Balance, Bandpass, Bass & Treble, Denoiser, Dynamics, Parametric Equalization, High Pass and Low Pass, and Notch,

The illustration shows the EQ tool, which provides the same facilities as a parametric equaliser in a hi-fi system.. The audio bandwidth can be split into specific frequency bands (using the *'Freq'* controls) and the level of each band can be individually set (using the *'Gain'* controls). This tool can be used to compensate for poor audio recordings providing extra bass boost, removing a hum or a noise at a particular frequency, etc.

Audio effects filters

Some filters add special effects, such as the Delay, Pitchshifter, and Reverb filters.

The illustration shows the *'PitchShifter'* utility. As the name suggests, it is used to change the pitch of an audio track. For example, it can lower the pitch of a particularly shrill voice, or increase the pitch of a particularly deep voice.

The left control alters the pitch in steps of one semi-tone, while the right control alters the pitch in steps that are less than a single semi-tone. Overuse of this tool can lead to comic or cartoon-like voices.

Premiere Pro 1.5 onwards add De-Hummer (removes background hum) and De-Esser (removes sibilance) filters.

Other audio considerations

The audio is often recorded along with the video track. This is particularly important for ensuring proper synchronisation between the audio and video content. Other audio recordings can be made to add to the effect. An interview with a plant manager, for instance, may be recorded during a lunch break to ensure quiet recording conditions. A separate recording of the factory machinery is made after the lunch break and the two sounds are mixed later. This allows the relative levels to be controlled during the editing stage and provides a much better result. The second recording can be made with a separate tape recorder, such as a DAT recorder or MiniDisc recorder, or with the camcorder.   If the camcorder is used for audio recording, the video component is ignored during the editing process.   It is also common to repeat the playing of a clip of background atmosphere (e.g. street noise or office sounds).   A single clip can be inserted several times to appear as a longer clip.   For this to work smoothly, the edges where the clips butt must be at levels, and have content, that makes the join unnoticeable.

Titling

For most web and CD-ROM use, video clips will not require titles, as they are played by clicking a hyperlink or menu option.   Other projects benefit from titling and examples are:
- Projects designed to be output to videotape.
- Projects for the deaf, where sub-titles are of great benefit.
- Projects where a foreign language sub-title is displayed.
- Projects where a voiceover is not viable (e.g. a voiceover would spoil a video of a band and the additional information would be in written form as sub-titles).

The title text should be left on the screen long enough for it to be read twice.

The steps for creating a title are:
- Design the content.
- Create the title, using Premiere.
- Save the title.
- Import the title file into the Project window.
- Place the title clip in a video track above any other occupied video tracks.

Design

The user should plan what should be included in the title.   Care should be taken to achieve a balance in terms of content and of time.   A title that flashes up for a second is too fast while nobody wants to watch screens of text slowly crawl up the screen for five minutes.   The amount of necessary text should be included and the pace at which any moving text is animated should be considered before editing the title.

All the usual advice on use of type styles, font sizes and colours apply here (e.g. use larger and bolder fonts for titles on smaller clips such as those for use on web sites).   The title may also include drawings made with the Titler's drawing tools or items of clip art.

Colour balance

There is an additional consideration for titling on a video clip.   The title may be opaque or transparent. With a transparent title, the title content is displayed over any video content that may be present in the main video track.   In this case, the background content may be constantly changing.   Care should be taken that the title contents remains visible over all changes in the video content.   For example, black text would disappear if the video scene showed a train entering a tunnel, while blue text would become unreadable if the video content showed a plane taking off into a clear morning sky.

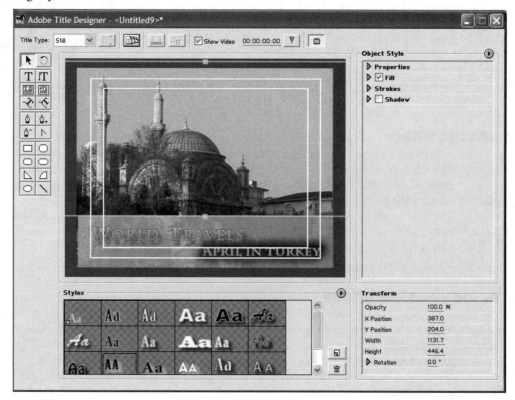

Creation

The title editing utility is accessed by clicking on the *'File'* menu, choosing *'New'* from the drop-down menu and *'Title'* from the sub-menu. This opens a Title window, where the title content can be added.

The inner white rectangle marks out the *'title safe zone'* - the area that is visible on all viewing screens. Objects outside this may not be visible on some screens, or suffer from the distortion that some screens have at the edges of the picture. The two zone markers do not appear in the final title.

Clicking the second button to the left of the *'Title Type'* box produces a pop-up menu that offers a wide range of ready made title templates, where the user need only change the default text.

The set of tools at the left of the window provides the facilities for adding and modifying the title contents.

Titles can incorporate both static text and scrolling text. Text can be scrolled upwards for opening and closing captions, while rightward scrolling text is useful for sub-titles.

With scrolling text, consideration should be given to the spacing of the lines of text. Adding extra carriage returns before the opening line of text produces a pause before the title text lines scroll into view. Adding carriage returns after the last line of text results in all the title text scrolling out of sight. Adding carriage returns between lines of text produces a time delay between individual lines in the title.

Saving

When the title is completed, Click the *'Save As'* option from the *'File'* menu. The file is named with a .ptl extension.

Using

The title should be dragged from the Project window and dropped into a video track above any other occupied video tracks.unused superimpose track. As the title is designed to superimpose on all other video content, it should be in the highest video track.

The effect of merging the title with other screen content can be viewed by carrying out a Preview. If the animated content of the title is moving too fast, the clip's duration can be lengthened by dragging the right edge of the title clip along the timeline.

Another attractive effect is to play the title sequence over a static background that uses a graphic file or digitised picture. The graphic is added to the Project window and brought into the timeline. It is then stretched to cover the same time duration as the title sequence.

A digitised picture could usefully be the first frame of the video, or it could be another picture entirely. See the earlier section on *'Adding a Graphic'* for details.

Working with multiple layers

On occasion, a very large project may require the inclusion of more video or audio tracks than is the maximum provided by Premiere. This requires the project to be built up in stages. The existing tracks are filled and the edited and the clip is saved to disc. It is then reloaded into the Video 1 track and additional tracks can then be added and the process repeated.

Test, test, test!!

Large projects using multiple clips and many effects and transitions take a long time to render. As the project is built up and added to, the time to render a full preview becomes ever longer. There may be a temptation to cut corners by assuming that each change and each alteration has produced the required effect. This could prove a costly mistake, as errors or unexpected results are only spotted after distribution. Like all software and authoring projects, the video editing process should be subject to continuous review. In a larger project, the completed video output may have to vetted by the rest of the authoring team or the project clients.

Rough cuts can be created using the *'Ignore Filters'* options in the output rendering options (see later). This will produce an output that is quick to create, since it does not render the transitions that have added during editing. While rough cuts are very useful in confirming the timing and order of the project's clips, they do not display the results of applying filters, transitions, etc - the processes that may also make or break a project.

The following points may prove useful for creating larger projects:

- Build up the project in stages.
- Use the Work Area Bar, so that only the area encompassing the effect, filter or transition is previewed. This will save a lot of wasted rendering time.
- Save each stage. That way, if a major blunder is made, the earlier version can be easily retrieved. This can be a time saver but supposes that the user has plenty of storage or backup capacity.
- Don't compress the material each time it is saved. Each time a clip is compressed, its quality is reduced and continued re-compression will further degrade the clip. If possible, always work with uncompressed clips up the moment when the final output is being rendered.
- Save project sections at hard cuts, as this makes them easier to re-integrate later.

Other Packages

VidEdit, Personal AVI Editor, Avid Cinema and Adobe Premiere are among the many video editors that are available.   Other editing packages are Media Studio Pro, MGI VideoWave and SpeedRazor.   They have varying degrees of sophistication and features but they their main reason for existence is the amalgamation of video clips into a single production.   They are primarily time-oriented - getting clips trimmed to the correct length, assembling in the correct time sequence, aligning the content in separate layers for the correct synchronisation, and so on.   Although some of these packages also provide a large range of transitions and effects, they are not optimised for these purposes.   Consequently, other software products are available for handling the video footage after it has been edited.   Some of the most popular packages are covered below.

Adobe After Effects

This package is aimed at the top end of the market (it costs as much as some PCs).   Adobe advertises the product as designed for the broadcast, film, video, multimedia and on-line production markets.

It can incorporate video clips, audio clips and graphics files that were produced in other packages.   Each is allocated to a separate layer and each can have effects applied to it.   The effects include animation, morphing, warping, masking, zooms, filters and flying layers.   It has a flowchart view to visualise complex projects, as it displays the relationship between the various objects (e.g. video clips, audio clips, graphics files) and the multiple effects that are being applied to them.

It can use other effects via extra plug-ins, such as the *'Eye Candy'* effects produced by Alien Skin Software.   It also supports *'network rendering'* - the package is installed on a number of computers on a local area network and they then share the rendering tasks so that they complete much earlier.   This is an example of *'parallel distributed processing'*.

Media Cleaner Pro

This package has more intelligent compression algorithms than those available with Premiere, providing better compression ratios.   For example, it has algorithms that selectively blur the frame contents.   Object edges are kept distinct, unlike when using Premiere's normal Blur filter. It also has a Black/White Restore function that ensures that black areas, such as backgrounds and shadows, are reduced to a more solid black.   This reduces noise and further improves compression.   So, many edit their clips in Premiere, then compress using Media Cleaner Pro.

Other Media Cleaner Pro facilities include batch processing and multiple conversions.   Multiple conversions, for example, converts a QuickTime move into a CD version and a variety of smaller and/or streamed versions in one activity (instead of the multiple separate conversions required with Premiere).

Others

Since Premiere imports any kind of AVI file, the output of 3D modelling and rendering packages can be directly included on the Premiere timeline.   Packages that produce such AVI files include 3D Studio Max, TrueSpace and Lightwave.   DeBabilizer is another useful tool for batch processing of graphics files and video clips.   It can carry out file format conversions and convert AVIs to sets of still images.

Exporting the project

When the project is finally completed its editing stage, the material is output in an appropriate distribution format, a process known as *'exporting'*.

Types of output

Premiere can output the timeline content in a variety of formats, depending on the needs of the user. These include:

- DVD and CD-ROM.
- Videotape (both analogue and digital).
- Web (including streaming and animated GIFs).
- Kiosk.
- Video files for integration into other programs.

Two methods

The range of possible output formats is covered by two general output methods in Premiere Pro.

Using Media Encoder presets.

This is useful for beginners, who do not need to understand the meaning of all the video and audio settings. The presets also cover most of the output formats that most users would need. The presets are accessed from the Adobe Media Encoder tool.

Exporting as a file, with user-controlled settings.

This provides detailed user control over compression, frame size, frame rate, etc.

How much video

Generally, a videotape can store hours of footage and is therefore not subject to any physical restriction on the amount and length of video that appears in the final project.   The restriction is rather one of design and user reaction (does the audience really want to watch four hours of a wedding?).

Most output is designed for later computer use, through a kiosk, CD-ROM or web site and there are obviously much more restrictions in the amount of video that is included in these media.

The amount of video that is included in any multimedia project is largely determined by the purpose of the material. A rock video must have full video content by definition, while a web site may still be very effective even with a video clip dropped in favour of an animated GIF or a Flash sequence.

Most CD-ROM and kiosk projects will mix live video with still photographs, graphics and animations. A CD advertising holiday homes in Florida may look impressive with a large amount of video clips but would soon run out of disc space. In many situations, a still photograph (perhaps with music, audio or a voiceover) would be sufficient. This balance should already have been addressed at the storyboard stage.

Exporting with Media Encoder

Media Encoder provides the settings for encoding to many popular delivery methods, including DVD, VCD and web streaming.

The steps for using Media Encoder are:

- Choose *'Export'* from the *'File'* menu.
- Choose *'Media Encoder'* from the *'Export'* menu. This produces a dialog box as shown in the illustration.
- Choose the required output format from the *'Format'* drop-down menu.
- Choose the required option from the *'Preset'* menu. The options and sub-options that are offered depend on the format chosen.
- Click the *'OK'* button'.
- Name the file that is being exported and click the *'Save'* button.

The default settings are optimised for each project purpose. However, users can alter the settings, if required and can save them for re-use later. It is also possible to import, export and delete presets.

Exporting as a file

Premiere offers a wide range of output options and these are grouped in dialog boxes that are accessed via the *'File'* menu.

Choosing *'Export'* from the drop-down menu, followed by choosing *'Movie'* from the sub-menu, followed by clicking the *'Settings'* button opens the dialog screen shown in the illustration.

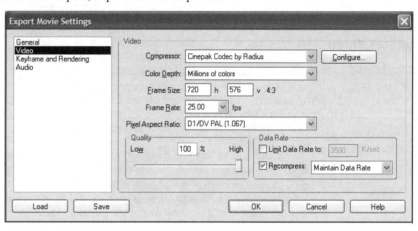

General settings

The first option is for *'General'* Settings and it provides the main controls as described in the following table.

Option	Description
File Type	Decides whether Video for Windows or QuickTime CODECs are offered in the *'Video Settings'* panel, or whether the video is exported as an Animated GIF, FLC file, etc.
Range	Decides how much of timeline content appears in the final output.
	Choosing *'Entire Project'* includes all material that appears on the timeline.
	Choosing *'Work Area'* only includes material that sits under the Work Area bar.
Export Audio/ Export Video	Checking the *'Export Video'* box ensures that the video content appears in the final output.
	Checking the *'Export Audio'* box ensures that the audio content appears in the final output.
	Checking both options ensures that the entire recording content appears in the final output.
	Checking only one option allows the audio or video component to be stripped from a recording.
Add to Project when finished	When the material in the timeline is exported, it is also placed in the Project window as a separate item. This allows large projects to be built in stages.
Beep when finished	When the export process is completed, the computer informs the user by issuing a beep sound.

If the *'Compile Settings'* button is greyed out, there are no further options open for that file format. If exporting to an animated GIF, this button opens up options over looping, transparency, etc.

Export Audio Settings

Option	Description
Compressor	Decides what audio CODEC should be applied to the project's audio output. Read the chapter on audio for details of audio CODECs.
Sample Rate	Decides which sampling rate to use for the audio output. The range of options offered depends upon the compressor chosen in the 'Compressor' selection. For example, the 'TrueSpeech' compressor only offers a 8000Hz rate, while 'Uncompressed' offers a choice from 5KHz to 48KHz plus the option to type in any other sampling rate from the keyboard. This facility can be used to reduce the size of audio files recorded at 44K.1Hz by outputting at a lower rate. This lowers the audio quality but produces files that are more efficient for web use. Also, resampling adds to the time for export processing.
Sample Type	Decides the bit depth of channels for the final audio output. The options offered are controlled by the choice of audio compressor. The G.723.1 compressor, for example, only operates at 16-bit mono. ADPCM offers 16-bit mono or 16-bit stereo, while the uncompressed option offers a choice of both 8-bit or 16-bit in either mono or stereo. An 8-bit depth halves the storage size of a 16-bit clip but lowers the quality.
Channels	Decides the number of channels for the final audio output. A mono sample requires half the storage space of a stereo sample. It maintains the audio quality but loses the stereo effect.
Interleave	Decides how audio content is merged with video content. The options are to insert audio data between every video frame or to have larger amounts of audio inserted between groups of video frames (up to two seconds worth of frames). The audio data is read into the computer's memory and played until the next section of audio data is read. If the computer has to process the audio data too often, the audio does not run smoothly and breaks up. Higher interleave values prevent this but require more memory to store the large audio chunks. The value chosen should reflect the expected specification of the computer playing the material.

The 'Advanced Settings' button will be greyed out unless the chosen compression format allows further tweaking.

Export Video Settings

Option	Description
Compressor	Decides which CODECs to use for compressing the final output. The selections offered depend on the Editing Mode selected. With QuickTime as the editing mode, compressors such as Cinepak and Sorenson appear on the list. With Video for Windows as the chosen editing mode, the compressors offered include RLE, and Video 1. There is a 'None' option that results in no compression to the output. This is useful to retain a high-quality archive copy, or to obtain intermediate files for re-insertion into the timeline. Some compressors (e.g. the Matrox MJPEG and the MPEG-4) also provide options to configure their data rates or compression ratios. In these cases the 'Configure' button is not greyed out and can be clicked to access these controls.
Depth	Decides the colour depth of the final output. Sometimes this option is greyed out, while other CODECs allow the user choice of 256, thousands or millions of colours. Choosing 'None' or 'Video 1' for the compressor and 256 for Depth is a good way to reduce a clip to 256 colours for web use
Frame Size	Decides the final resolution of the video output and is input as pixels amounts. The values chosen will depend on the final destination of the file (e.g. set to 352x288 for an intended MPEG-1 file, smaller for web use and larger for CD and kiosk use).
Frame Rate	Decides the number of frames per second that are used in the final output. If the value chosen is different from the rate used for clips in the timeline, Premiere compensates by dropping or inserting frames. Premiere offers a choice of rates between 1fps and 30fps.
Pixel Aspect Ratio	If the footage has been recorded on a camcorder, it normally records at a 4:3 aspect ratio. In this case, the '4:3 Aspect' box should be checked, to ensure that the correct vertical to horizontal relationship is maintained. Some camcorders can record in a widescreen 16:9 ratio and the vertical and horizontal values chosen in this case should maintain the ratio and avoid picture distortion.
Quality	Decides how lossy the compression is. More loss means greater compression but lower quality output. Some CODECs are tweaked via the 'Compressor' option mentioned above. Most CODECs use the 'Quality' slider to control the compression ratio. As expected, the 'None' option does not provide compression controls. This control is used to reduce quality and decrease file size. Trying to increase quality beyond that of the original recording produces larger file sizes without any increase in quality.
Data Rate	Decides the maximum amount of data that is included in each second of the output. This is required to ensure that the amount of data does not overwhelm the system that it is intended to be used on. The 'Limit Data Rate' box is checked and the maximum rate is entered. This is

	useful when outputting to videotape from the timeline, since the many of output options discussed only apply to outputting to disk files. A clip's average data rate can be determined by right-clicking on the clip in the Project window and choosing *'Properties'*.
Recompress	Decides how clips are processed, to ensure that the final project is outputted within the above user specified maximum data rate. When the box remains unchecked, no compression is applied to clips (even previously compressed clips that have been imported) that have not been altered during editing. In practice, the editing process often results in significant alterations to frames through the use of filters and transitions, or the alteration of frame rates, CODEC options, etc. These alterations may significantly change the final data rate, thus requiring recompression of the final project. When the *'Recompress'* box is checked, there are two options. The *'Always'* option compresses every frame during the output processing, even if the contents have not been changed or the maximum date rate is not being exceeded. Since most compression systems are lossy, the recompression of previously compressed clips will reduce the picture quality. The *'Maintain Data Rate'* option only compresses frames when it is necessary to bring the output within the maximum data rate. This ensures a higher quality of output. If all files used in the project were imported as uncompressed clips, then they are all compressed at the output stage

Keyframe and rendering options

Option	Description
Fields	Decides on the way that the video content is packaged. There are three options: • No Fields - provides a progressive scan as used by computers and motion-picture film. • Upper Field First or Lower Field First - provides an interlaced output as used by video recorders and television. See the chapter on technology for an explanation of interlacing.
Deinterlace Video Footage	Decides what piece of software carries out any deinterlacing. If the box is left unchecked, these activities are carried out by the CODEC selected earlier. If the box is checked, the activities are carried out by Premiere at a better quality.
Optimize Stills	Decides whether long displays of still frames are processed as a series of frames. Checking the box results, for example, in a four-second display of a still being stored as a single frame being displayed for four seconds. Unchecking the box results in, for example, a four-second display of a still being stored as 100 separate frames (i.e. four seconds at 25fps). The optimised option saves storage space but may not replay properly on all systems. The non-optimised is a safer choice if there is any doubt about the capabilities of the computer that the final project may be used on.
Keyframes Every _ Frames	The first box can be checked to allow a value to be inserted in to the adjacent box. The user enters the frequency of inserting keyframes. This value is the size of the Group of Pictures. For example, setting the value to 12 results in a keyframe being inserted after every 12 frames. When the CODEC exports the clip it inserts keyframes at the chosen rate.
Add Keyframes At Markers	Checking this box results in an output file that has a keyframe inserted at each marker on the Timeline.
Add Keyframes At Edits	Checking this box results in an output file that has a keyframe inserted at each edit point in the Timeline.

The chapter on *'Digital Video'* discussed the use of keyframes during temporal compression. Some CODECs use keyframes and the user can maximise the picture quality and compression ratio by controlling where keyframes are inserted in the final video clip. If the chosen CODEC does not support keyframes, keyframe options will not be able to be accessed. In Premiere, the user can mark points on the timeline where keyframes should be inserted. These can be additional to the set of keyframes inserted at regular intervals by Premiere, or the final clip can use only the keyframes inserted by the user.

Exporting a sequence as a file
When all the settings have been selected, the sequence is rendered to that specification when the *'OK'* button is clicked and the file is named.

Choosing the output CODEC

The types of CODEC and their operation was covered in the chapter on *'Digital Video'*. The CODEC chosen for a particular project's output will depend upon the intended final use of the media. Apart from dedicated systems, such as kiosks, it is best to use software-based CODECs, as there is no guarantee that the end user has the appropriate hardware CODEC on his/her computer. The remainder of this chapter considers the factors that influence the choice of CODEC and their settings.

Media Type

CD

If the material is for general circulation on CD, a decision has to be made on the balance between the speed of CD players and the video quality. The clip size and frame rate could be sacrificed, so that the file will play on even the oldest CD ROM drive.   Alternatively, the better quality clips could be used, in the knowledge that older computers will not be able to reproduce them very effectively.   For reference, an old double-speed CD-ROM drive has a maximum data transfer rate of 300 KB per second, while a current 50x CD ROM drive has a maximum data rate of 7,500 KB/sec. Practical rates are a little less than these values.   A decision must also be made on how much of the disc space is allocated for video.   Usually an AVI or QuickTime CODEC is used on CD.

DVD-ROM

The main development in video is the increased storage capacities offered by the DVD, which can store 4.7GB on a single surface.   The future promises both double sided and multi-layer versions with ever-greater capacity.   This provides around eight times as much storage space than CD discs and there is a growing base of users with DVD players. This media allows high-quality full-screen MPEG-2 videos of about an hour's duration.   Future larger size DVD discs will provide an opportunity for even greater video storage.   Many multimedia products will not require that the video clip occupy the entire screen and this means that even more footage can be stored on the disc.

The output can be in any popular CODEC format and can include MPEG-2, since all DVD players are supplied with either hardware or software MPEG-2 CODECs.

Kiosk

The computer used for controlling kiosk presentations is known before the project is commenced. It is usually a high performance machine and can have as much fast hard drive storage space as is required.   This imposes far fewer restrictions and output can be chosen for quality rather than file size. The output can even have no compression applied, for maximum quality.

Intranet

Universities, colleges and companies may run internal networks (intranets), where training or reference material is instantly available over the local cabling. Although local area networks may run at 10MHz or 100MHz (or even faster), this bandwidth is shared among large numbers of users. Generally, the faster networks are there because there are more users requiring services. Consequently, most systems do not have great spare capacity for each individual user. The best that can be expected is 20KB up to around 100KB per second. Of course, this is still much faster than normal Internet speeds. The data rate of the intranet should be determined (the network supervisor should be able to supply this information) and the CODEC's video data rate should be matched to it.

Web site

This is the slowest medium for carrying video.   Although many UK users have access to ADSL or other fast connections to the Internet, the vast majority of users are still connecting via a 56k modem.   The speed of modem controls the effective transfer rate of the files.   A 56 kilobits per second modem has an effective maximum data transfer rate of around 5 Kilobytes per second (the Internet communications signals consume a chunk of the bits). While scalability facilities (see earlier) cater for a range of sizes, even the best case is a large file. Consideration should be given to:

- Reducing the clip resolution.
- Reducing the frame clip frame rate.
- Lowering the CODEC data rate.
- Converting a piece of video footage into an animated GIF.
- Converting the clip to a streamed file.

Back to tape

The only data rate restrictions are those imposed by the computer's hardware.   The computer system disk's, CPU, etc., should be capable of outputting the file to videotape without dropping any frames.

Frame Rate

PAL video runs at 25 fps.   NTSC videos run at 30fps.   These are high rates for some systems and it is common to package video for much smaller frame rates.   For example, a video clip at 5fps contains only a fifth of the video information of a PAL clip.   Therefore, it is only one fifth of the size and is suitable for low-end applications such as Internet video-conferencing.

At the other end of the quality scale, a video clip might require to run at the full PAL rate.
The frame rate trades file size for quality.   15fps is the minimum used to maintain any illusion of constant movement and is often found on videos clips supplied on CD-ROM with books and magazines.   Sometimes, the jerkiness of a low frame rate is deliberately chosen for effect, such as simulating a security camera or an old movie.

Resolution

Video intended for videotape should be created at the frame rate and resolution of the intended tape format. Video for CD-ROM, kiosk and web use does not suffer from these restrictions and can be a resolution that best fits the requirements.
In general, the highest resolution for video pictures is the first choice, where possible.   In practice, many compromises are forced on the designer by hardware and software restrictions.
High-resolution clips require more storage space and require fast transfer mechanisms. When a clip has both high resolution and high frame rates, it requires a high-performance software CODEC (such as Sorenson Video) running on a fast computer, or a hardware CODEC implementation such as an MPEG card.   In a multimedia product, there may not be so many requirements for full-screen video. The nature of the content may require a smaller resolution to allow screen space for navigation buttons, menus, explanatory text, company logo, etc.   The hardware specification that can be expected from the end users' computers is rising all the time.   A screen of 240 x 180 was once a typical size, but much larger sizes are now be supported by most systems.

I-Frame Setting

When a file is to be compressed with an MPEG CODEC, the user should control the size of the GOP (Group of Pictures).   In practice, this means setting the frequency of the key frames in the clip.   Generally, an insertion frequency of every twelfth or fifteenth frame is used, with more insertions for clips with rapidly changing screen content.
If users have control over the playback, they wish to access the clip at random points.   If too few key frames are used, random access results in a delay while the CODEC reconstructs the current frame from a larger amount of P-frames.
If a clip is prepared to be played through uninterrupted, the number of key frames can be reduced, thereby achieving higher compression rates without sacrificing quality.

Target computer

The video must run on the minimum target computer that will be used to play the clips.   The CPU on older computers may not be fast enough to decode the video stream without dropping frames; the hard disk or CD player may be too slow to transfer the data in real time.   It can be decided that the user base must have a high minimum specification.   This ensures adequate performance but lowers the market for the product. This could also be a problem in an environment (e.g. college or university) where there is a mix of old and new computers.
The project should always be tested on the lowest target computer before it is finally packaged for distribution.
Typical considerations are:
- Does the target computer have the necessary CODEC installed?
- Should a well-known CODEC be used such as Cinepak be used in the knowledge that it is installed on all computers using Microsoft Windows?
- Can the video be packaged with its own software CODEC? Does this raise legal or licensing problems?
- Can a user be reasonably expected to install a CODEC to watch the video?

Exporting to DVD

Where a computer has a DVD writer attached, Premiere can write the timeline contents to a DVD. It creates a DVD that plays automatically when inserted in a DVD player. This is a useful but basic facility. For example, it cannot create menus and chapters. For more complex DVD disks, a full DVD authoring program is needed.
Premiere Pro will attempt to make all the timeline content compatible with DVD specifications. For guaranteed best results, the source files in the timeline should already be in DVD format.
The specifications for DVD sources are:

Frame size –   720x576. If not, Premiere scales them automatically.
Frame rate –   25fps (All clips must have same frame rate).
Aspect ratio –   4:3 or 16:9
Audio bit depth   16 bits, with a sampling rate of 48KHz

The steps for creating a self-running DVD presentation from the timeline are:
- Select the *'Export'* option from the *'File'* menu.
- Select the *'Export to DVD'* option from the *'Export'* menu.
- Select the required settings in the *'General'* panel.
- Select the required settings in the *'Encoding'* panel.
- Select the required settings in the *'DVD Burner'* panel.
- Inset a blank DVD disk in the writer and click the *'Record'* button.

Note

Premiere Pro provides the MainConcept MPEG codec which can create MPEg1 and MPEG-2 files. Earlier versions of Premiere did not have direct MPEG encoding facilities, although additional plug-ins could be added to carry out the task. For example, *'AVI2MPG1'* and *'AVI2MPEG2'* are freeware programs that can be used as a standalone converter or as a Premiere plug-in.

Alternatively, video files can be compressed perior to bringing them into a Premiere Project. Typical standalone compressor programs are *'MPEG Kit'* and *'ConvMP3'*, *'Xing MPEG Encoder'* and *'Ulead MPEG Converter'*. VirtualDub is a freely distributable capture and processing program that can convert MPEGs into AVIs. It is available at www.geocities.com/virtualdub/

Exporting to an animated GIF

Web sites commonly use animated GIFs as a means of adding animation or video content to a site. This is an economic measure, as an animated GIF is much smaller than a comparative video clip.

This reduction in size is achieved because animated GIFs can:

- Use lower frame rates.
- Use loops.
- Use a clip in both forwards and backwards actions.

Consider creating a web site home page with an animation of the author waving to the viewer. The author's hand is moved up and down in a waving action and this is recorded as a video clip of relatively low resolution (say one eighth of a screen size). This smaller size is perfectly acceptable in an animation and has already made a very substantial saving in size compared to a video clip.

An examination of the clip shows that the downward movement of the arm is simply a reverse of the upward movement. This is a waste of footage and only one of these actions need remain in the clip. The section showing the arm being lowered is cut and the video footage has been reduced by a half. The remaining section of the clip is copied and butted up itself. There are now two clips of an arm being raised. The second clip is now reversed, using the *'Backwards'* filter. When played back, the arm is raised and lowered and the clip is the same duration as before it was edited. However, since the exported version uses the same frames for both movements, the size of the clip is halved.

The frame rate for the clip can also be reduced substantially compared to the original footage. A frame rate of 6fps or 9fps is perfectly acceptable for an animated GIF and this reduces the file size by another factor compared to an original frame rate of 25fps.

The animated GIF option from the *'Export Movie'* settings provides an option to have the clip with a transparent background and an option to continuously loop the animation. Choosing the looping option provides an animation that continuously repeats - which would be very large if implemented as a video clip. The Premiere controls for handling GIF animation are limited and the exported GIF can be brought into the *'Animation Shop'* in Paint Shop Pro, where greater control is available. Animation Shop also has a very handy *'Resize Animation'* utility that reduces the frame size for creating smaller movies for web sites. This also allows an AVI video clip to be loaded, shrunk and saved back as an AVI file.

Exporting to videotape

There are three methods of transferring a project to videotape :

- Using the computer's FireWire connection to record material from Premiere's timeline into a DV camcorder. Since all material is transferred and stored in digital format, this provides the best quality output.
- Using a computer that has a graphics card with a composite output. The card contains a scan convertor that takes the video signal and ensures that the television scan rates and signal encoding are added to the output. The material from premiere's timeline is sent out the video card's composite sockets and fed to a domestic VHS video recorder or an analogue camcorder. This produces domestic quality output.
- Recording the timeline on a digital camcorder, followed by playing back the newly-recorded tape and taking the camcorder's composite output into a VHS recorder. This saves having to purchase a computer graphics card with a composite output. The quality of the VHS product is identical to the method above.

After the movie is compiled and saved, the steps for exporting a project to videotape are:

Using a composite connection

- Connect the computers' composite output to the VHS recorder composite input.
- Place videotape in the recorder and ensure that it is rewound to the start, or other desired tape position.
- Ensure that the timeline cursor is positioned at the start of the project sequence.
- Press the *'Record'* button on VHS recorder.
- Click the *'Play'* button in the Monitor window.
- At the end of the export, click the *'Stop'* button in the Monitor window,, followed by pressing the recorder's *'Stop'* button.

Using a FireWire connection

- Connect the computer's FireWire connection to the camcorder's FireWire connection.
- Insert the videotape cassette into the camcorder.
- Place the camcorder in VTR (sometimes called VCR) mode.
- If the export is to be added onto existing material on the tape, play the tape, locate the required position and note the timecode at that position.
- Choose *'File'* from the main menu.
- Choose *'Export'* from the drop-down menu.
- Choose *'Export to Tape'* from the sub-menu.
- Check the *'Activate Recording Device'* box, to allow Premiere Pro to use Device Control (i.e. control the camcorder).
- Leave the *'Assemble at timecode'* box unchecked, if recording is to begin at the current tape position..
- Otherwise, check the *'Assemble at timecode'* box and enter the timecode where the recording should start.
- If required, check the *'Delay Movie Start'* and enter the number of quarter-frames of delay. This allows some devices to properly synchronise the camcorder circuitry and the movie output.
- If required, check the 'Preroll' box and enter a value next to it (Premiere recommends a value of around 150 frames for many decks). This delay allows time for the recording deck motor to get up to a constant tape speed, before starting the recording.
- When ready, click on the *'Record'* button.

TV/VCR Video Standards

If a project is output to a videocassette, it should be in the format used by the intended country in which it will be distributed. Different countries have different standards and they are not interchangeable - even when the cassette holding the tape might be the same size for some countries. It is the way that the video is recorded and the quality of the recording (resolution, etc) that creates the difference. For example, UK and US tapes are not interchangeable, although they are both described as VHS. Special video players are available that allow the playback of both types of recording - but normal VCRs cannot handle both types.

The terms NTSC, PAL and SECAM refer to the method of colour coding, but they are often referred to in terms of the expected resolution from each system. It is technically possible to make a 525 lines system using PAL or a 625 line system using NTSC. It's just that all the countries of the world have decided on a standard for their own transmissions and they are grouped around the three different specifications discussed.

The nature of colour analogue television signals was determined by the move from monochrome transmissions. When colour televisions were introduced, there was a huge base of black and white televisions in use. As there was not enough bandwidth available, a single transmission had to be used by both monochrome and colour television receivers.

As a result, even to this day, the analogue television signal is basically a monochrome (luminance) signal, with colour (chrominance) added as separate information (this part is ignored by mono TVs).

PAL

The PAL system (Phase Alternate Line) is used throughout the UK, most of Europe, Australia, China, most of Middle East and Africa.

It embodies 625 lines, with a 24-bit colour picture using a 50Hz interlaced field system (i.e. 50 fields per second), to produce a 25fps picture.

Books and magazines tend to give different resolutions for PAL including 736 x 560, 520 x 380, and 768 x 576. ITU-R 601 is the international standard for digitising component video for television. It defines the active area as 720 x 576. This is the standard used by most video software, such as Adobe Premiere.

Note that although a UK television system works on 625 lines with a visible 576 lines, the domestic VHS recorder only records and plays back at 250 lines.

NTSC

The NTSC system (National Television Standards Committee) was introduced in the USA in 1952.

It is used in the US, Canada, most of Latin America, and Japan.

It embodies 525 lines, with a 24-bit colour picture using a 60Hz interlaced field system (i.e. 60 fields per second), to produce a 30fps picture. The VGA computer resolution of 640 x 480 is based on the visible screen area of an American television picture tube.

SECAM

The SECAM system (Sequential Colour and Memory) is a 625 line, 50Hz system that is used throughout France, Russia, ex-French colonies in Africa, parts of Eastern Europe.

Authoring Systems

Having gathered the graphics, sound and music for the presentation, the developer's task is to integrate them and link them in the way laid down in the implementation plan. While it is possible to write simple applications directly at the keyboard, larger and more complex projects require a careful plan to be developed, including navigation maps and screen layouts. These issues are covered in the chapters on design.

The authoring software required depends upon the complexity of the project, the level of interactivity provided for the user, and the provision of additional facilities (such as linking to databases, animation, web tools, etc).

Multimedia development software is generally of two types:

Linear

The user watches a sequence that has already been determined by the designers and he/she has no influence over the presentation. This approach is best suited to exhibitions, point of sale and other information providing situations. Linear presentations can be achieved with simple software and there are many freeware and shareware packages to provide these development tools. Although they use multiple forms of media, the finished projects are not full multimedia products as there is no real interaction with the user. Simple multimedia presentations can also be easily constructed using a programming language such as Delphi or Visual Basic.

Interactive

The user controls the flow of the presentation, to explore particular areas, ignoring others and even returning to a particular area of the presentation. The package may have built-in intelligence to know where a user keeps going wrong and giving targeted advice. This is suited to the learning environment where the user controls the pace and the content of the presentation. Computer Based Training programmes use this method, as each run of the presentation can be different, changing with the needs of the student. CD-ROMs for the domestic market, such as encyclopaedias, use interactive techniques. Interactive presentations require more sophisticated, and more expensive, software. While some useful shareware packages can handle some interactivity, the top-end products provide the extra tools such as animations, layering, scripting and flexible packaging options that make the final project into an altogether different level of product.

All multimedia products can be written using conventional programming languages such as Pascal or C++, although they are time-consuming. Using GUI-oriented (graphical user interface) programming languages such as Delphi and Visual Basic provide pre-written routines for buttons, user input, etc., saving programming time. Best of all, multimedia authoring packages provide comprehensive facilities that greatly speed up the development process. Although programming and authoring methods both require analysis and design skill, some authoring packages can produce very useful results with no coding skills whatsoever. Most packages are able to produce run-time versions - executable files that do not require the use of the original package to display them. Packages range from hobbyist products to those with full-blown commercial aspirations.

Approaches to authoring

An authoring system is an application that provides pre-programmed elements to speed the development of multimedia applications (e.g. ready-made buttons, etc). They create multimedia applications in a fraction of the time that would be required by script programming tools. Buttons, dialog boxes, etc. can be brought onto the screen, positioned and linked to functions - without writing any code. Interface design and screen editing are made much easier and quicker. Animations can be complex and detailed and yet created in a relatively short time.

Of course, there is still the same amount of time required to plan, design and create the content. The designer still needs to know how programs work and have an appreciation of heuristic thinking and algorithm design. Knowledge of module construction and basic screen construction skills are also still required. Nevertheless, these packages are learned much more quickly than programming languages, especially for simpler projects.

Authoring methods

Designers and software engineers have developed a number of approaches to multimedia authoring. These are aimed at reducing the development time through the provision of design systems that are easily understood, coupled with a variety of useful tools.

Their methods are designed around 'metaphors'. A metaphor is a figure of speech where the description of one object is used to describe another object. For example, the designer can readily understand an authoring package that uses a 'page turning' metaphor, even although there are no physical pages that are turned.

The main systems are:

System	Typical products
Linear, frame-by-frame	PowerPoint, Illuminatus, Neobook, and many freeware/shareware products.
Scripting language	GLpro or programming languages such as Pascal or C++, with Visual Basic and Delphi supplying improved interface tools.
Iconic/flow control	Authorware, IconAuthor, Masterclass
Card/scripting	Toolbook, ClickWorks
Cast/score/scripting	Director, Emblaze, Flash
Hypermedia Linkage	Any HTML editor, with packages such as Dreamweaver supplying increased functionality and requiring less scripting knowledge.

Linear, frame-by-frame metaphor

This is the simplest metaphor of all. The project is designed to run in a linear fashion. That means that it has a beginning and an end and the viewer is intended to watch the project's contents unfold a page at a time. There is little or no user control of the project, apart from perhaps pausing or exiting. This method is best suited to unattended presentations at exhibitions and in supermarkets and for some product promotions. Since the flow material is determined for the viewer, there is only a single route to be followed and every piece of screen activity follows from the previous one in an orderly fashion.

Since the method is simple, the products are quickly assembled using basic authoring tools. There are a large number of freeware and shareware packages available for producing these kinds of projects and PowerPoint is the most common commercial product used for linear productions (although it can also offer some limited interactivity).

Programming

Programming requires scripts of code to be written by the developer. Early languages required complex scripts just to draw a box on the screen, while modern programming languages such as Delphi, Visual Basic and Visual C are blurring the boundaries between conventional programming and multimedia authoring. GUI-based development tools, such as Delphi and Visual Basic can bring in buttons, display graphics, and call up video and sound clips, etc. without resorting to heavy scripting.

Visual Basic, for example, uses a screen form (which can have a graphic image as a background), on which can be placed objects and controls. The developer then sets the properties that should apply to the controls. This is an 'event-driven' system. Code is attached to a screen object and is only run when the object is activated. This allows some practical projects to be created without any coding. The package creates a compiled (i.e. self-running) product and provides comprehensive error checking and debugging facilities.

In all, there are three types of scripting:

Scripting type	Example
Scripts to create the entire project.	GLPro is an authoring package that is entirely script-based, with no on-screen authoring.
Scripts that supplement authoring packages.	Director's Lingo script, Flash's ActionScript.
Internet advanced scripts.	JavaScript, Perl, etc.

Hypermedia linkage

This method covers the linking of any number of separate resources that allow user access. The most common implementation is a web site, although CD's can use hyperlinks for navigation and for linking to wider resources through the Internet. This system produces the widest possible navigation facilities and the most likely methods for implementing these systems are HTML scripts, JavaScript, CGI scripts, Perl scripts, etc.

Card/scripting

These are also sometimes called 'page-based' systems. The project data is organised to simulate pages of a book, or a stack of cards. Each page has its own individual set of objects and its own layout. It can display graphics or play sounds, animations and video clips on any page.

It uses a book metaphor as its presentation format. Using navigation buttons, viewers can flick through the pages of the book in any order. This presentation method is best used when a number of page sequences of pages are used, although viewers can also jump between pages. Toolbook, Mediator and Illuminatus used this method.

Iconic/flow control

This method makes the project's structure and links highly visible to the developer, as the main screens and user choices are represented on a flow chart.

These flow diagrams display the navigational links and flow of ideas. This aids the development of projects with complicated structures, as a top-down approach starts from the higher-level tasks and breaks them into lower levels tasks.

A flow chart plots the possible routes between activities; this is the *'navigation map'*. An activity is represented by an icon which could be a decision to be made, a user entry to be requested, a new screen of graphics to be shown, a video or sound clip to be run, and so on. At the design and implementation stages, groups of icons can be grouped together under a single icon - implementing a top-down design of sub-modules. Major points can be added to the flow line, and these can be returned to later to flesh out their sub-units and contents.

The example shows the second level of a package that displays a top menu with four choices (e.g. Memory Types, Organisation). Each choice produces a drop-down menu with other choices (e.g. Error Detection, Cache Memory).

Authorware and IconAuthor used this method.

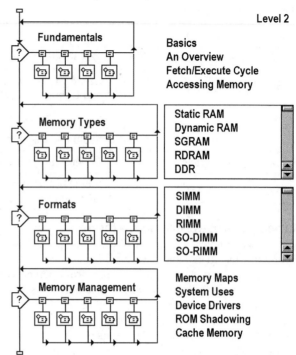

Cast/score/scripting

These packages often use the terminology of the film producer or theatrical producer, with a *'stage'*, a *'cast'* and a *'score'*. Little wonder, then, that one the most used package of this type is called *'Director'*, the other being *'Flash'*. The package uses a cast (i.e. the elements such as text, graphics, sound clips, video clips, user entry buttons or dialog boxes, screen effects, etc.) and a score (e.g. a chart of all events and when they will occur in time).

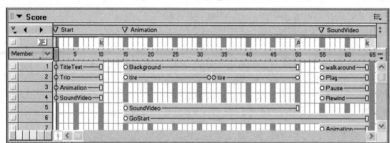

It is based on a *'timeline'* as in the example, where each vertical frame stores all the objects that are used during that particular timeslot.

Each object can therefore be controlled down to the precision of a single frame (for a 25fps production, this means control down to $1/25^{th}$ of a second). This allows animations to be set to precise durations, sound clips to be played at precise times that synchronise with other events, and so on.

The entire project is laid out as a long chart of possible events (i.e. the timeline), navigation controls allowing the user to jump to any point in the timeline.

There is no concept of individual pages; just what will be displayed on the screen at any one time.

Other considerations

Apart from the design method, there are many other considerations when choosing an authoring package:

- The range of drawing, animation, text manipulation facilities.
- The range of transitions and special effects.
- The range of packaging options (standalone executable, HTML file, Shockwave file, video clip, etc).
- Whether the package allows royalty-free distribution of the final project, or applies charges or conditions on the distribution. This may apply to a runtime module (a miniature version of the package used to create the project, with the development tools removed, leaving only the play functions).
- Whether the package can create cross-platform projects (e.g. can compile for PC and a Mac).

Scripting facilities

Some packages provide very simple navigation links but for greater control of navigation, and to support internal logic decisions, the author has to learn the programming language behind the package.

The examples show the minimum scripts used by the leading *'Director'* and *'Toolbook'* packages.

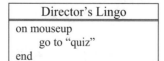

Director's Lingo	Toolbook

on mouseup
      go to "quiz"
end
	TO HANDLE buttonClick
	      go to next page
	END buttonClick

Some authoring tools have no in-built scripting facilities (e.g. Illuminatus and Multimedia Fusion), some have very little (e.g. Mediator) and some have comprehensive facilities (e.g. Director, Flash and Toolbook).

Control facilities

In all multimedia presentations, the user approaches the application in an interactive way, expecting to be given control over the package. The three most important elements are:

Buttons

The user has to control the flow of information in a package. Normally this is achieved by the user clicking the mouse on on-screen *'buttons'* that represent a particular choice. The choice may be from a selection of menu options (i.e. where to go next) or might be from a selection of possible data entries (e.g. choosing a correct answer or saving or loading a set of data). Buttons can be the default grey variety provided in most authoring packages or can be user-defined such as pictures or shapes.

Alternatives to buttons are dialog boxes, where the user is asked to enter data (e.g. user name or age) and *'hot spots'* where areas of the screen act as equivalents of large buttons. Clicking a hot spot has the same effect as clicking a button but a hot spot can be an irregular shape. For example, this allows the user to click anywhere on the Isle of Wight in a screen map of the UK to see more information about that island.

Other on-screen system controls are:

- Radio buttons (i.e. only one option can be active at a time).
- Check boxes (i.e. more than option can be active at the same time).
- Scroll bars.
- File/directory selection.

Events

Normal conventional programs are written to be mainly sequential. The program starts at the beginning of the code and finishes at the end of the code. Multimedia products are explored in a different manner. With event-driven systems, code is attached to objects and remains inactive until it is called. Calls can be initiated by the user (e.g. clicking a mouse) or by the system (e.g. a timeout). The clicking of the button or hot spot is tied to a particular action. So clicking the *'Show Interview'* button always plays the same video clip. Clicking a *'More Details'* button may produce an entirely new screen with more information and a further set of buttons. Clicking the *'Quit'* button should exit the user from the package. The navigation activities are called *'simple branching'*.

Control structures

For more control, *'conditional branching'* can be carried out. So, a user when presented with six buttons representing six levels of difficulty may only be allowed to pursue a higher level if the lower level has been successfully completed. The program has kept the user's previous performance in a set of variables and the branching allowed is a combination of what button the user pressed and what information is already stored. In a multi-choice question, the user may only be allowed three attempts.

Control can be passed to internal code using constructs such as:

IF ...   e.g. if a user score is less than 50% ....
REPEAT ...   e.g. repeat the question until the user chooses the correct answer.

Getting started in Director

The Macromedia Director package is one of the most powerful multimedia applications and is regularly used to produce the interfaces for the CDs that are given way with computer magazines, as well as creating countless commercial and educational products. Director provides many facilities within the one application. For example, it can create vector graphics, bitmap graphics, and animations. It also provides sound editing facilities and the final project can be packaged as a standalone program, or a Shockwave or Java-enclosed file for using on the web. Since all these facilities are built into the program, they can all be used without leaving the application to run lots of separate packages to do parts of the job. Of course, the professional user may still wish to use a full-blown graphics tool, such as PhotoShop, to create graphics images for use in Director. That is catered for, as Director can import a wide range of file formats such as Flash, animated GIFs, MP3s, PowerPoint presentations, etc, that will have been created on other packages.

The following pages look at Director MX, but the material covered applies to most versions of this package.

The quick tour

- Director uses a list of resources (the cast) from which the developer chooses those elements that are used or seen on the screen.
- These are placed on a timeline (the score) at the points in time that they should be visible or active on the screen (the stage).
- These components (the sprites) can be animated to move around the screen, or can be text or static images.
- The Control Panel allows the developer to view the overall project, while the mouse can be used to place the playback head on any time slot on the timeline to display the screen contents at that moment.
- When the playback head sits on any one time slot, its screen contents are viewed in the stage window and the screen elements are viewed in the channels that have contents in that particular time slot.

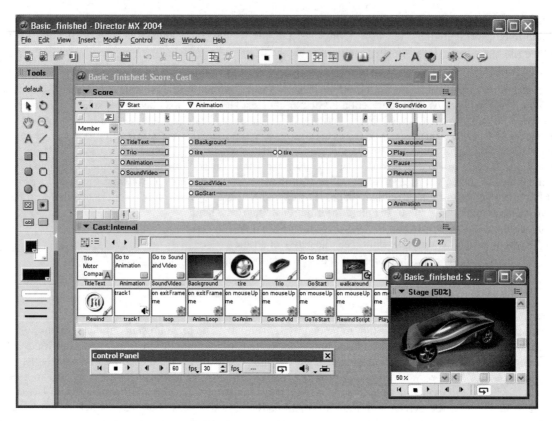

Movies

The projects created by Director are called *'movies'* and are given the file extension .DIR (e.g. *'swimming.dir'*). During development, the project should be saved as a .DIR file, as this stores all the project's components in a format that can be individually accessed later for subsequent alterations, amendments and maintenance.   This also allows the project to be developed by another person. When complete, the project can be packaged for distribution in a variety of ways (e.g. standalone programs, web material, video clips, etc) and these are covered later.

Cast

The Cast is simply the list of resources (*'Cast members'*) that can be used in the multimedia project.
Director can import a wide range of file formats into the cast database:

- Animations (Flash movie, animated GIF, FLC, FLI).
- Text (ASCII, RTF, HTML).
- Graphic images (BMP, GIF, JPEG, TIFF).
- PowerPoint presentations.
- Video movies (QuickTime, AVI).
- Sound files (WAV, MP3, AU).

When a new project is started, the Cast window is empty and the resources are added by using the *'Import'* option from the *'File'* drop-down menu. This produces the dialog box shown in the illustration.

When a file, or set of files, is selected from the list, clicking the *'Import'* button adds the file to the cast list.

These files are treated as *'internal'*. That means that they are bundled into the final product and will not be seen as separate files. This creates a tidier final product and helps prevent the elements from being re-used without permission.

As the illustration shows, the *'Media'* menu default option is *'Standard Import'*, which is the internal option. Choosing the *'Link to External File'* option does not embed the elements into the project. Instead it provides links to them and these links fetch the file contents as the project runs.   The external files obviously have to be supplied separately, along with the project that uses them. This allows the same components to be used in

different projects. It also allows any one file to be updated or amended without altering the main project. This is useful for business (just change prices, photos) and different language versions (just change text files, audio files).

Adding cast members does not automatically include them in the project. They are equivalent to the crowd of hopeful actors waiting to be chosen to appear in a play. In both cases, they take no part in the production until they are brought onto the stage and told where to stand, what to do, etc. In Director, a cast member is brought into use by dragging it from the cast window into the timeline or the stage. For example, if a graphic file were dropped into time slot 10, it would only appear on screen during that one time period. If the project runs at 15fps, the graphic appears 0.6 seconds (9 slots of 1/15secs) into the playback and lasts for 0.0666 seconds, while a project running at 25fps would show the graphic for 0.04 seconds.

Director provides for the creation of multiple cast lists. For large projects, this organises separate casts for storing different resources, particularly if they are external. So, all video clips can be stored in one cast, all graphic images in another cast, Lingo scripts in another, and so on. Alternatively, all the resources for each section of a project could be stored in separate cast lists. A single cast window is automatically provided when a new project is begun.
The steps for creating a new cast are:

- Choose the *'New'* option from the *'File'* drop-down menu.
- Choose *'Cast'* from the sub-menu.
- Enter the name for the cast list in the *'Name'* entry box.
- Decide whether the cast list should contain internal or external components and check the appropriate radio button.
- Click on the *'Create'* button.

Sprites

When a cast member is dragged on to the stage or the score (the timeline), it is called a *'sprite'*.
Sprites follow these simple rules:

- A sprite is a single instance, a copy, of the cast member.
- There can be more than one instance of a cast member (i.e. there can be two or more sprites based on the same cast member).
- Each sprite has its own properties and actions.
- Altering (or even deleting) a sprite does not alter the original cast member, or any other sprite based on that cast member.
- Altering the cast member alters all sprites based on that cast member.
- Removing a cast member from the cast list makes all sprite instances of the cast member unusable.

Many sprites are a single instance of a cast member. For example, a heading, a piece of text or a video clip may only appear once in a project.
But sprites also allow multiple appearances of a cast member on the stage at the same time. So, for instance, a single drawing of a bird can become a flock of birds, or an image of a single person can be used to construct a crowd scene. Moreover, each bird or person can be moved independent of the rest. So, changing the movement, speed or size of one of these sprite images has no effect on any other sprite, or on the original cast member.

Score

The score is the most important tool of Director. It is the main construction window and it describes the movie frame by frame and shows the changes in the movie with time. The score is used to position sprites, add sounds and transitions, set timings and create the required navigation controls.
The score looks like a spreadsheet, with a grid of rows and columns. Each column is a time slot. The value of the time slot depends upon the playback rate set (e.g. 15fps or 25fps). For example, a movie set to 25fps allocates one twenty-fifth of a second to each time slot in the score's timeline.
Each row is known as a *'channel'* and modern versions of Director support up to 1000 sprite channels. This allows a huge numbers of elements to be included in a project. In practice, however, developers strive to minimise the number of channels used as this improves performance and makes the development process easier to handle.
An icon of two arrows sits in the top right-hand corner of the Score window. This is the *'Hide/Show Effects Channels'* icon and can display two separate areas of the score, known as the *'Members Channels'* and the *'Effects Channels'*.

Members channels

The lower set displays the *'members'* channels and each one holds a sprite. If a graphic image sprite is placed in a single *'cell'* (i.e. in one channel in a single time slot), it will fappear on the screen for the short period that the playback head is over that time slot. If the sprite is copied across a range of cells in the channel, it will display for the amount of time that the playback head is over these cells.
Objects in higher channel numbers appear at the front of the stage and objects in lower channels are towards the rear of the stage. For example, if channel 1 holds the image of clouds and channels 2 holds a sprites of an aeroplane, animating the sprite in channel 2 makes the plane pass in front of the clouds, since it has a higher channel number.
When there are multiple sprites on the stage, altering channel numbers makes sprites pass in front or behind objects as required.

Effects channels

The upper set of six channels are the *'effects'* channels. These are, from the top:

- A Tempo channel (insert pauses, waits for sound or video to finish before moving on, etc)
- A Palette channel (controls the colour palette in use - Windows, Mac, Grayscale, Metallic, etc).
- A Transitions channel (creates smooth fades and other transition effects between scenes).
- Two Sound channels.
- A Script channel (stores scripts for navigation, loops, and all other Lingo scripts).

Note

Although the Director Score sets out all its activities in sequential time slots, users may jump around the timeline, to use different parts of the project as they see fit (see the section on navigation).

Stage

The Score is vital for setting out the objects in relation to time, but provides no help in positioning the objects on the screen.

The Stage therefore has two tasks:

- To allow the developer to place objects in their correct positions on the screen.
- To allow the developer to view the movie, or part of the movie.

The steps for setting up the Stage properties are:

- Select *'Movie'* from the *'Modify'* pull-down menu.
- Select *'Properties'* from the sub-menu. This will display the dialog box shown in the illustration.
- Set the stage size, background colour palette, number of sprite channels to be used for the project, etc.

Note

If developing a project for use on the Internet, the colour palette should be set to *'Web216'*, as this is the set of *'browser-safe'* colours that is recognised by all computers using the web, whether PC-based, Mac-based or other.

Control Panel

The Control Panel is the tool the developer uses to switch between frames, to preview changes, to see the results of applying special effects, etc.

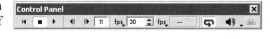

The explanations of each of the parts of the Control Panel are:

A	Rewind - move the playback head to the first frame in the project.
B	Stop playback. Leave the playback head at the current frame.
C	Play forward from the current frame.
D	Steps backward one frame. The stage displays the previous frame's contents.
E	Steps forward one frame. The stage displays the next frame's contents.
F	Displays the number of the current frame being displayed on the stage (e.g. second frame, seventieth frame).
G	Sets the number of frames allocated to each second of time.
H	Sets the manner of a project playback. The setting shown above is *'single play'* and this plays the movie on the Stage, starting at frame 1 and ending on the last frame in the movie. If the setting is changed to *'loop'* (see the earlier illustration accompanying *'The Quick Tour'*), the playback head returns to frame 1 and plays the movie again and again until the stop control is pressed.
I	Set the volume for playback (from mute to loud). This value is used in the final movie or projector version. This means that if it is set to mute or a low setting for a more peaceful development environment, it must be returned to a higher setting before outputting the project. The maximum setting is usually best, as it leaves the volume control setting to the user at their end.

J	Only plays back the section of the timeline between selected frames. Frames are selected by highlighting a set of time slots. This is very useful, as the developer will not want to sit through a long project just to preview a change in a small section. This button can be used in conjunction with looping to allow the developer to continuously replay a selected section of the project, so that it can be thoroughly analysed.

There is no *'Fast Forward'* button. To play from a frame that is later on the timeline, the playback head can be dragged to that new position and play started from that point.

Adding sprites

A sprite is added to a project in one of two ways:
- By dragging a cast member from the cast list into a channel and dropping it at the required time slot.
- By moving the playback head to the required time slot and dragging the cast member from the cast list and dropping it into the stage.

In both methods, the sprite has to be placed in the correct timeslot(s) and, for visual information (i.e. text, graphics, animations, video), has to be placed in the correct screen position.

To assist in accurately placing sprites, the Stage can have a grid superimposed upon it. The grid will not appear in the final output and only acts as an alignment aid. The grid is turned on from the *'Guides and Grid'* option of the *'View'* drop-down menu, by checking the *'Show Grid'* option in the sub-menu. The same sub-menu has a *'Snap to Grid'* option. When this option is checked, it aligns any object placed on the Stage to the nearest grid line. The distance between grid lines, and therefore the amount of positioning control, is determined by the number of pixels entered in the *'Settings'* dialog box, accessed from the *'Guides and Grid'* sub-menu.

Another method of aligning sprites is to highlight a group of sprites in the Score. The sprites may be in the same frame or may cover a range of frames. Clicking the *'Align'* option from the *'Window'* drop-down menu provides the dialog box shown in the illustration. The developer can choose from a range of alignments in both the vertical and horizontal axis. The illustration shows the option to align the tops of a set of objects. When the desired option is chosen, the *'Align'* button is pressed. This is a quick way to line up a set of navigation buttons, along the top or bottom of the screen or down the side of the screen.

There are some occasions when a sprite may only appear on the Score in a single cell. Examples are:
- When an introduction screen is displayed to the viewer and appears for a set amount of time (under the control of the Tempo channel - see later).
- When a set of instructions is displayed on the screen until the viewer clicks a mouse button to move on (see the Tempo channel later).
- When a menu is displayed on the screen until the viewer clicks on a menu choice button (see the MP3 player example later).

In many other instances, a sprite will have to appear many times across a channel. Examples are:
- A background image may have to be displayed throughout the project.
- A foreground image (e.g. a tree or a lamppost) may have to remain static during a scene, while other objects are moved around it.

Director allows a text or graphic sprite to be easily copied across many cells in a channel. The steps are:
- Highlight the cell in the Score containing the cell to be copied.
- Right-click the mouse on the cell.
- Choose *'Properties'* from the menu that appears and click on the *'Sprite'* tab in the resulting dialog box.
- Enter the number of the time slot when the object will start being displayed, into the left box, marked as *'Start Frame'*.
- Enter the number of the time slot when the object will stop being displayed, into the right box, marked as *'End'*.

Alternatively, simply drag an end of a group of cells and pull to extend its range.

Sprites can also be easily moved from one position on the Score to a new position. The cell(s) are highlighted and dragged from their position and dropped in the new position. Care must be taken to ensure that the cells are not dropped over existing required sprites, as the new contents will replace what was there before.

Finally, it is good practice to colour code sections of the Score (e.g. part of a channel, or part of a group of channels) that carry out a distinct function in the project. This helps identify these sections later. For example, all help pages may be marked in yellow, all menus in cyan, and so on).

Colour coding is carried out by highlighting the required section of cells in the Score and clicking on one of the colour shading boxes that are displayed below the list of *'Members'* (i.e. sprites).

Text

Text can be imported, as previously explained, or can be directly added to the Stage, using the following steps:
- Move the playback head to the frame where the text is to appear.
- Click on the text icon (the one that looks a capital 'A') in the toolbar.
- Click the left mouse button on the place on the screen where the text is to sit.
- Enter the text into the text frame that appears.
- Re-position the text if necessary.

The above method is ideal for quickly adding headings and subheadings, whereas large amounts of text are best produced in a word processing package where the content can be spell checked and grammar checked before being imported into the cast window.

Any text sprites can have their properties altered at any point in the development of the project. The developer can decide to change the typeface, font size, etc. at any time and this is best carried out with the tools in the Text Inspector. This utility is activated by choosing the *'Text Inspector'* option from the *'Window'* menu. It produces the floating window shown in the illustration. Highlighting a text sprite in the Score displays its properties in this utility and these can be viewed and altered by the developer. It provides formatting functions such as choice of typeface, font size, alignment, kerning and line spacing.

The Property Inspector provides control over the anti-aliasing of text. If a text sprite is highlighted in the Score and is right-clicked, a drop-down menu appears. Choosing *'Properties'* displays the Property Inspector. Clicking the *'Text'* tab provides the developer with the choice of anti-aliasing text, since small font sizes look better without anti-aliasing.

Where many text sprites are going to be edited or formatted, Director provides a Text Window, as shown in the illustration. It is activated by choosing the *'Text'* option from the *'Window'* pull-down menu.

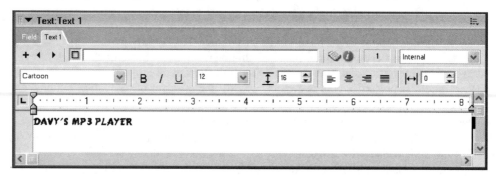

Its facilities are similar to the Text Inspector but provides additional facilities such as:
- The text can be entered or modified directly in the lower window, without touching the Stage window. Any amendments made within the Text Window are immediately seen on the Stage, if the playback head is sitting in the time slot storing the text sprite.
- New text cast members can be added within this utility (see the '+' button in the illustration).
- The arrow buttons in the top left corner are used to cycle through all the text sprites, to examine them or amend them.

Notes

Since text is regarded as a sprite, any text can be animated, rotated, etc. This allows flying headings, bullet points that move round obstacles, etc. This is in addition to any text effects that may be set up using the Transitions facility (see later).

Director's scripting language, Lingo, can be used to control text as the application runs. This provides personalised facilities. For example, the user may enter his/her name at the beginning of the program and this is used to display personal messages (e.g. *"Well Done, Dave"*). It can also be used to display a user's status in the application (e.g. *"Your score so far is 50"*). Lingo can also alter the typestyle or font size of a piece of text.

Fonts

Developers design projects with an overall look and feel. This includes the typefaces used, as they help to convey mood. This subject is covered in greater detail in the chapters on design.

The developer, therefore, wishes to ensure that the typefaces used in the creation of the application are the ones seen by the viewer, regardless of what fonts are installed on the user's computer. If no steps are taken, the finished application will use the viewer's own default system fonts at runtime.

The solution is to embed fonts in a movie, to ensure that the text appears in the specific typefaces intended. This is achieved by storing the fonts either in bitmap or vector format.

Bitmap Fonts

A bitmapped font is simply a vector font that was used for formatting a piece of text - converted into a bitmap graphic file.   Since it is now a graphics file, it is totally independent of any font technology and is guaranteed to display correctly on every viewer's computer.   Since the text is now a graphic file, it can be edited in Director's Paint Window.

The steps for the conversion are:

- Highlight the text cast member in the Cast Window.
- Choose the *'Convert to Bitmap'* option from the *'Modify'* drop-down menu.

Once the text is converted to a bitmap, it cannot be reversed; there is no *'bitmap to text'* utility'.

Although this method is quick and easy, it is not very versatile. For example, bitmaps don't rescale well and result in ugly ragged edges known as *'jaggies'* when magnified (see the computer graphics chapter).

Embedding fonts

Director allows fonts on the developer's computer to be embedded within the movie.   The font information is stored inside the movie and the font is only rendered (and anti-aliased) at playback time. This means that even the most obscure of fonts, or homemade fonts, can be included and will reproduce faithfully on the viewer's computer.

Embedded fonts are compressed and take up about 14KB to 25KB of extra file size and, because they are not separately accessible, there are no copyright problems with distributing fonts in this way.

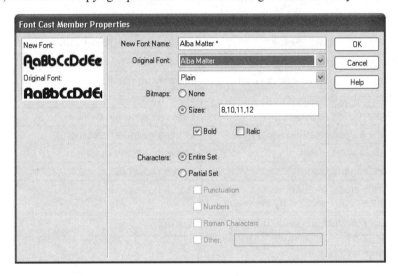

The steps for embedding a font are:

- Choose the *'Media Element'* option from the *'Insert'* drop-down menu.
- Choose the *'Font'* option from the sub-menu.
- Use the *'Original Font'* menu to choose the required font from the computer's installed list.
- Choose whether to include any bitmapped font sizes, by checking *'None'* or *'Sizes'*.
- If *'Sizes'* is checked, enter the specific font sizes required for bitmapping, with a space or comma between each size.
- Check the *'Bold'* and/or *'Italics'* check boxes, if the bitmapped sizes are to include these variations. This option produces an improved outline but increases the final file size.
- Choose to embed the entire font (i.e. every letter, number, symbol and punctuation mark) by checking the *'Entire Set'* button, or choose to embed only the characters required for the project, by checking the *'Partial Set'* button.
- If the *'Partial Set'* button is checked, choose the sub-set of characters to be embedded. The *'Other'* option allows each individual character for embedding to be listed and provides the maximum optimisation.

At smaller font sizes (up to about 12 point), bitmapped fonts are usually clearer than anti-aliased vector fonts. This is why Director offers embedding of bitmap fonts, even though they take up extra file space.

Many developers decide on the fonts to be used in the project and embed them before any text is added to the project. This is good practice, but Director allows files to be embedded at any time during development.

When a font is chosen from the list in the *'Original Font'* box, the font name is also displayed in the *'New Name'* box above it, with an asterisk added at the end.   This is now an additional font choice for developers.   In the example on the previous page, the *'Architecture'* font was embedded.   Any text that was previously added to the project with that font will now automatically use the embedded version instead, without the developer having to go back over every instance and amend it. Every new piece of text can also be formatted to use the embedded text. 'Architecture*' will appear on the Director font list and can be used just like any other font.

Embedded fonts are seen by Director as cast members and appear in the Cast Window.

Adding graphics

There are three ways to add a new piece of graphics to the cast:

- Import a graphic file.
- Draw a bitmap image in Director's Paint window (with very similar tools to Paint Shop Pro).
- Draw a vector image, using Director's Vector Shape tool.

Both drawing tools are available from the *'Window'* drop-down menu.

The import option is regularly used for bringing photographic images, stock clip art, previous drawings, etc. into a project, while the drawing options are best for creating new images.

Vector drawings are smaller, more scaleable and easier to alter at a later date, compared to bitmap images.

The Vector Shape tool is shown in the illustration and provides a reasonable set of vector drawing tools. The illustration shows an object with handles that can be manipulated to provide endless variations of a shape.

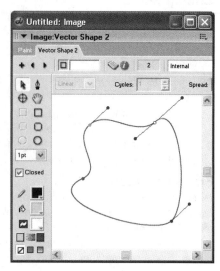

The Tool Palette

The tool Palette is activated by checking the *'Tool Palette'* option in the *'Window'* drop-down menu. It provides the following facilities:

Left choice	Right choice
Selection tool.	Rotate and Skew.
Hand tool to move image around.	Magnifying glass.
Add text to the screen.	Draw a line.
Draw a filled rectangle.	Draw a rectangle outline.
Draw a filled rounded rectangle.	Draw a rounded rectangle.
Draw a filled ellipse.	Draw an ellipse outline.
Add a check box.	Add a radio button.
Add a piece of editable text (e.g. to capture data entered by the user).	Add a button.
Select the foreground and background colours.	
Select a fill pattern.	
Select a line width.	

The buttons are very basic and are frequently used to quickly assemble a working prototype of the project, replacing them with crafted graphic buttons later.

Transparent backgrounds

Most graphic files are intended to be laid on top of other objects on the screen. This can often lead to ugly superimpositions, with the background of an image obscuring other images. Consider the example below. The main screen is blue and a graphic file with a red circle on a yellow background is placed on the screen. The left picture shows the result. If this is the wanted result then that's fine. However, it is more likely that the

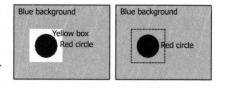

yellow background is undesirable and the effect on the right screen is the actual wanted result (the dotted line does not appear on the screen; it is only included to show the image's boundaries). In the right picture, the yellow background of the image has been declared transparent. This means that Director will not display this part of the image and all underlying content is visible. Only the red ball will obscure part of the background.

Consider the example of moving shooting stars across a skyline. The skyline is black and the buildings are white. If the comet is drawn with a black background, it can cross the sky without a problem. When the comet wishes to pass in front of a building, however, it is seen as a moving black square with a comet in the middle. Drawing the comet with a white background simply reverses the problem. The image can cross the buildings happily but shows up as a moving white square against the skyline.

The only solution is to ensure that the background to the comet image is rendered invisible. Director will import a graphic file that already has its background colour set as transparent. For example, if the image of the comet had been drawn in Paint Shop Pro as a GIF image, its background colour could be made transparent before it is saved. It would then be imported with a transparent background straight into the cast list.

Director can also make the background of a vector or bitmap image drawn within Director be stored as transparent. If an image is right-clicked, it produces a menu from which *'Properties'* can be selected. This displays the Property

Inspector as shown in the illustration. The illustration shows the inkpot with the *'ink'* option selected from the *'Display'* options. If the ink option is changed to *'Background Transparent'*, the background colour chosen for that image is ignored when the image is displayed. All other instances of that colour in other objects are still displayed. Similarly, many images may use different background colours and the act of making the background transparent only applies to the display of that colour for that image only.

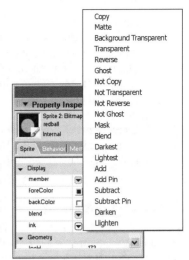

Alpha channels

Director also supports the use of alpha channels. These are 32-bit bitmap images, with 24 bits used for storing the colour depth information and an 8-bit greyscale bitmap that acts like a filter to control how much of the graphic is displayed. The black areas of the alpha channel prevent any of the picture from showing through, while the white areas allow all the picture content to show through. This means that an alpha channel with a graded fill from white at the top to black at the bottom results in a graphic display that gradually fades away towards the bottom of the screen.

Director provides transparency effects through the *'Ink'* option of Property Inspector shown above. To apply ink effects to a sprite, a copy of the sprite is placed in the next position in that cast list (i.e. if the original is cast member 5, the copy is cast member 6). This places the mask in front of the graphic image. The copy is then painted with black and white only and the *'Ink'* properties of the copy are set via the Property Inspector.

Sprite depth

Graphics in higher channel numbers appear at the front of the stage and may appear in front of graphic images with lower numbers. The order of layers can be altered to send an image further back or bring an image forward to a more prominent layer. The steps are:
- Highlight the sprite to be moved.
- Choose the *'Arrange'* option from the *'Modify'* drop-down menu.
- Choose the *'Bring to front'*, *'Send to back'*, *'Bring forward'* or *'Move backward'* option, as required.
- Alternatively, use the Ctrl-Up arrow, Ctrl-Down arrow key combinations to move the sprite's order.

Moving the sprite on the Stage also changes its member number in the Score.

Adding video

A video clip can be imported into a cast list. QuickTime movies and AVI files are directly supported by Director and MPEG movies can be imported using an *'Extras'* add-on utility. A movie is added as a cast member that can be placed as a sprite on to the Score where required, in a sprite channel. As a sprite, it can be manipulated and controlled within the Score or by Lingo commands. It can even be animated, although the demand for a flying video clip may be a little limited!

A video clip starts to play when the playback head reaches the time slot where the video clip sprite is stored. If the sprite sits in a single time slot, the clip will only play for that amount of time before the playback head moves on. So, for example, if the Director movie is set to 25fps, then the video clip will only play for one twenty-fifth of a second. There are three ways to ensure that the video clip plays to the end before the project moves on:
- Go to the timeslot where the video clip is stored, right-click and choose *'Tempo'*. The *'Wait for Cue Point'* and *''End'* options in the Tempo dialog box should be chosen (see the section Tempo later, for more details). This option prevents the playback head from moving to the next frame until the video clip is fully played.
- Use a Lingo script to prevent the playback head from moving on until the video clip is fully played.
- Extend (drag) the video clip sprite across enough timeslots on the Score, to give the video clip sufficient time to finish playing. This method is particularly useful if there is to be any other activity going on (e.g. fresh text being displayed, animation, etc.) during the playing of the video clip. This requires the *'Direct to Stage'* option to be unchecked (see below).

Setting a video clip's properties

Director provides a range of controls over how the video clip is displayed. The following steps set up the controls:
- Right-click on a video clip and choose the *'Cast Member Properties'* from the menu. This displays the dialog box shown in the illustration.
- Click the *'AVI'* tab of the Property Inspector.

The options are:
- Checking the *'Direct to Stage'* option allows the QuickTime and AVI drivers installed on the viewing computer to control the video clip's playback. This is the most efficient option but has the potential disadvantage that the video clip always plays at the forefront of the stage, preventing other sprites from being overlaid on the video (e.g. captions, language translations).
- Checking the *' Video'* option ensures that the video content of the clip is displayed.
- Checking the *'Audio'* option ensures that the audio content of the clip is to be included.

- Checking the *'Preload'* option loads the video clip into memory when the movie starts, so that it is immediately available when the clip is to be played. If the viewer's computer does not have sufficient memory to load the entire movie, Director loads as much as will fit in the existing memory. If this option is left unchecked, the video clip is played from the disk resulting in poorer video performance, as each frame has to be retrieved from the disk before being played.

- Checking the *'Paused'* option stops the video clip when it first appears on the Stage (while playing the Director movie).
- Checking the *'Loop'* option sets the video clip to play continuously. This is useful for displaying a welcoming video message until a key or mouse is pressed (e.g. for presentations at exhibitions).

Adding sound

A sound clip can be imported into the cast window as a new cast member and from there it can then be dropped into a time slot on the Score, in one of the audio channels.

Like the video clip discussed earlier, the audio clip will start to play when the playback head reaches the time slot where the audio sprite is stored. If the audio sprite is placed in a single time slot, then the clip will only play for that small single segment of time before the playback head moves on.

As with video clips, there are three ways to ensure that the audio clip plays to the end before the project moves on:

- Go to the timeslot where the audio clip is stored and add an entry into the Tempo channel. The *'Wait for Cue Point'* and *''End''* options in the Tempo dialog box should be chosen (see the section Tempo later, for more details). This option prevents the playback head from moving to the next frame until the audio clip is fully played.
- Use a Lingo script to prevent the playback head from moving on until the audio clip is fully played.
- Extend (drag) the audio clip sprite across enough timeslots on the Score's audio channel, to give the audio clip sufficient time to finish playing.

The Property Inspector for a sound clip provides a *'Loop'* option that makes the audio clip play continuously.

Director's scripting language, Lingo, provides much more control for playing audio clips, with facilities such as:

- Controlling the clip's volume.
- Turning the sound off and on.
- Preloading the audio clip into the memory of the viewer's computer.
- Queuing multiple sounds.
- Creating accurate sound loops.
- Synchronising audio clips to animations.

The later section on navigation shows an example of audio clips being controlled by user buttons.

Animations

One of the most powerful utilities in Director is its set of animation tools. Animations are powerful in their ability to attract attention, focus attention and enrich the learning process. Animations can be as simple as a flying banner to a complex animation demonstrating mechanical or scientific processes. Director provides four methods for creating animations.

Cel Animation

Director describes this as *'frame-by-frame animation'* and *'multiple cast member animation'*, both describing the general process. At its simplest, this technique works exactly like an animated GIF. Each frame in the animated sequence is created as a separate graphic file and imported into the cast list. When these are placed into consecutive time slots, they play back as a continuous animation. For a 25fps movie, fifty separate graphic images would be required to be imported for a two second animation (assuming that no two frames were identical). This process consumes a lot of space but can achieve results that the other methods cannot. This is the only method that can use photographic image as the basis for the <u>content's</u> animation (as opposed to simply moving an image around). A photographic image may be used, with changes made to the image on successive frames. For example, a picture of a human head could be displayed with an eye winking, something that the other methods cannot handle.

Tweening

This term is taken from the language of the early film animators. The head animator would create a key drawing showing a cartoon character or an object in a certain position. He/she would then create another drawing indicating the next key position for that person or object. The animation assistants would then draw the cels that were required to take the animation from one key stage to the next, by breaking the movement into a set of frames that gradually altered the positions in the drawing. The process of creating the in-between frames is called *'tweening'*.

Tweening is a key utility for computer animators, as the computer is used to calculate and draw all the intermediate frames between key action frames. In Director, tweening can involve moving a sprite, resizing a sprite, rotating a sprite, altering colours in a sprite - or a combination of any, or all, of these effects. Since they commonly use vector-drawn sprites, they are also very economical in size.

The steps for animating a sprite are:

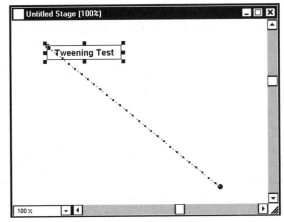

- Place the sprite in the first time slot on the Score.
- Extend the sprite across as many cells in the channel as required.
- Select the sprite's last cell on the Score.
- Right-click the mouse and choose *'Insert Keyframe'* from the drop-down menu that is displayed.
- Drag the sprite across the Stage to the final resting place of the animation.   This will produce a Stage similar to that in the illustration.   The circle in the bottom right corner is the position of the sprite in the first time slot and the upper-left corner shows the final position of the sprite (i.e. as stored in the last time slot).   The marks between these two points represent the time slot between the start and finish cells. If there were 20 time slots between the start and finish cells, there would be 20 marks along the line.
- Selecting any of the sequence's other time slots on the Score, right-clicking and selecting *'Insert Keyframe'* provides extra key points where the object can be dragged to new positions on the stage.

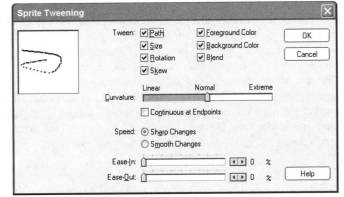

- Continue until the required path is created. The illustration shows a text sprite entering from the top-left of the screen and looping the loop before stopping in the middle of the screen.
- Run the animation and go back to make alterations, if required. Highlighting any cell along the row of animation cells displays the path on the Score and places the sprite on the position in the path that corresponds to the time slot being examined (e.g. if the seventh cell in the animation is highlighted, the sprite is shown on the seventh mark along the path).

The illustration shows the Tweening dialog box, accessed from the *'Tweening'* sub-menu choice of the *'Sprite'* drop-down menu of *'Modify'*. The lower set of controls alters the animation path.

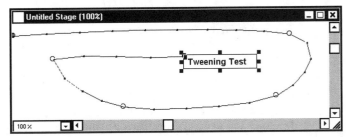

Checking the *'Continuous at Endpoints'* box ensures that there is a smooth transition between the start and end positions of the sprite and is used with continuous loops.

The *'Curvature'* slider moves from *'Linear'* (with straight movements between points on the path), through *'Normal'* (with a curved path between the keyframes) to *'Extreme'* (with extended curves between keyframes).

The *'Speed'* options are *'Sharp'* or *'Smooth'* changes and they determine how abruptly the sprite changes direction (e.g. over a few frames or over many frames).

The *'Ease In'* and *'Ease Out'* sliders control the acceleration and deceleration of the sprites movement. Each slider is scaled to 100%, but the totals for the two must add up to 100% (e.g. the sprite cannot be accelerating 80% of the time and decelerating 60% of the time). Increasing one slider too high will reduce the other's value, to maintain 100% overall.

Of course, tweening is not restricted to changes in position of a sprite. For example, a sprite can be rotated (or even be rotated while being moved) and the Tweening utility will calculate and store the intermediate frames in the process.

Step Recording

Also known as Step Frame Recording, this technique builds up an animation one frame at a time.   It provides better control for irregular animation paths.

The steps for creating a step-record animation are:

- Drag the cast member from the Cast window and place it as a sprite in the time slot in the Score that is the beginning of the animation.
- Position the sprite on the Stage to the starting position of the animation sequence.
- Highlight the starting cell in the Score.

- Choose the *'Step Recording'* option from the *'Control'* drop-down menu. A red arrow appears next to the channel, to indicate that recording is in operation.
- Click the *'Step Forward One Frame'* button on the Control Panel. This moves the animation forward to the next frame.
- Drag the sprite to the next position on the Stage.
- Repeat the above two steps until the animation sequence is complete.
- Choose the *'Step Recording'* option once more, to end the recording.

The animation can be returned to for alterations or fine-tuning. Clicking on any cell in the animation displays the entire path on the Stage and individual points on the path can be dragged to new positions.

Although the steps refer to a single sprite, the technique can also be used to animate multiple sprites at the same time.

Real-time recording

This technique involves the developer dragging a sprite on the stage while recording its motion. The software then creates the set of frames that comprise the animation. Since the recording is being made in real-time, the number of frames used for the animation depends upon:

- The speed at which the developer traces the movement.
- The frame rate of the recording.

So, for example, if the developer ran a recording at 25fps and took 2 seconds to trace the animation, the sequence would occupy 50 cells across the channel.

The steps for creating a real-time animation are:

- Highlight the cell containing the sprite to be animated.
- Choose the *'Real-Time Recording'* option from the *'Control'* drop-down menu. A red circle appears next to the channel in which the animation frames will be created, and a red and white *'selection frame'* is displayed round the sprite.
- Drag the red and white selection frame to start recording the animation path.
- Release the mouse button to end the recording. The channel fills with the additional cells that make up the completed animation. These extra cells extend from the initial starting sprite along the same channel, so the developer has to ensure that there are sufficient free cells in the channel before starting the animation.

Many developers prefer to record at a slow tempo (i.e. reduce the number of frames per second), as this slow-motion recording gives them more control over the animation. The playback of the animation sequence is then speeded up to the normal tempo during playback. So, for example, if a developer requires a four second animation, he/she might half the tempo, recording the animation over eight seconds. When played back at the normal tempo, the animation takes four seconds to play. The required time span has been achieved but the longer tracing time provides more control of the mouse and hence a smoother animation path.

If a specific time is allocated for an allocation, that will equate to a specific number of frames (multiply the number of seconds by the tempo). Before the animation is recorded, the *'Selected Frames Only'* option on the Control Panel should be checked. This ensures that the animation completes within the allotted time span and prevents the possible overwriting of other sprites further along the channel.

This recording technique is useful for simulating the movement of a pointer (e.g. a pointing finger graphic is used as a moving sprite to point to key features in a piece of software, while a voiceover discusses their use). It is also used for quickly tracing a complex motion that can be tweaked later. Another use is to check the *'Trails'* option in the sprite's Property Inspector. This can provide special effects with photographic images or can be used to simulate handwriting.

Transitions

Director provides a range of transition effects that can be applied to a sprite when it is first due to appear in a frame. An abrupt change of image can be avoided by gradually blending the content of one frame into the next frame. It can also be used to reveal text, one line at a time.

The steps for creating a transition are:

- Go to the time slot where the transition is to take place.
- Choose the *'Frame'* option from the *'Modify'* drop-down menu.
- Choose *'Transitions'* from the sub-menu. This brings up the transitions dialog box shown in the illustration.
- Choose the desired transition and click the *'OK'* button. The transition becomes a cast member.

An alternative method is to double-click on the appropriate cell on the transition channel.

Tempo

Tempo is the number of frames per second at which the movie is set to play back. It only controls the sprites in the frames. It cannot be used to make videos or audio clips play faster or slower and the settings have no effect on the time taken for transitions.

The tempo can be altered along the timeline. It will run at one tempo until it meets another setting in the Tempo channel and will then run at the new tempo.

The steps for setting the tempo are:

- Select the cell in the score's Tempo channel time slot where the setting is to be inserted.
- Right-click on the cell, to display a drop-down menu.
- Choose *'Tempo'* from the drop-down menu, to display the dialog box shown in the illustration.
- Choose the setting required.
- Click the *'OK'* button.

The four settings are:

Choice	Activity	Example use
Tempo	Adjusts the maximum playback rate.	Controlling recording speed for the recording and playback of animations.
Wait	Keeps the playback head in the selected time slot for the amount of time set on the slider, before moving on.	Make a heading appear for a set time (e.g. opening credits, splash screens, etc).
Wait for Mouse Click, etc	Keeps the playback head in the selected time slot until the mouse is clicked or a key is pressed.	As above, except the user decides when to move on (e.g. providing a *'click anywhere to start'* message).
Wait for Cue Point	Keeps the playback head in the selected time slot, until the system tells it to move on.	Wait until a sound clip or video clip finishes, or wait until a cue point embedded in a video clip.

Note

The fps value set for Tempo is the maximum playback speed. The actual playback speed may be slower, depending upon the efficiency of the computer playing the project or the complexity of the sprites and animations used in the project.

Lingo

Lingo is Director's scripting language. This means that the developer moves away from using the mouse as the only means of controlling the project flow and activities and starts to use the keyboard to write *'scripts'*. Director Scripts are programs that are written in a language that Director understands and the developer has to learn the scripting language to write these scripts. Scripts add much greater functionality to a project but may have a steep learning curve for many developers.

A project may have many scripts scattered throughout the project. Some may be attached to objects on the screen (e.g. a script for a button sprite) and some may be embedded in a frame of the Score (e.g. for looping back to a certain time slot) or even attach to the entire movie.

A script may be very small (e.g. a script attached to a 'Quit' button may simply require the developer to enter a single line saying *"go to exit"*) while others may be very complex (e.g. scripts for database handling).

Lingo is not like any other language and even those with some previous programming experience have to start from the beginning. Their knowledge of constructing logic, decision-making and mathematical calculations is very useful but they will still have to learn Lingo commands.

The structure of a Lingo script is

```
on event
    do something
end
```

Each script is known as a *'handler'*, as it is designed to respond to an event. The event might be a user activity (e.g. pressing a key or clicking on a button) or might be time-related (e.g. stop after 30 seconds) or logic-related (e.g. stop after five attempts).

The script for the project's quit button might be:

```
on mouseDown
    go to exit
end
```

In this case, the event is mouseDown, one of the special events built into the Director language. Other examples of events are mouseUp, keyDown, keyUp, RightMouseDown and RightMouseUp.

The instructions to be followed are contained between the event and the word 'end'. In this example, there is only a single command - to move the playback head to a specific point in the Score labelled as 'exit'. Many scripts will use a list of commands, with each command appearing on a different line. When the handler is run, the commands are executed in sequential order (e.g. the first command is carried out first, the second command second, and so on).

Director provides a 'Lingo Dictionary', which is accessed from the 'Help' pull-down menu. This lists all the Lingo commands and explains their purpose and their syntax (the order and manner in which they are written). Lingo is not case-sensitive, so scripts can be written using upper and lower-case letters.

Variables

The Lingo language contains many commands but the developer will need to extend these commands by tweaking them to meet specific demands in the projects. Examples include:

- Using the viewer's name in the project (e.g. 'First Aid Test for Jim Smith').
- Making an animation repeat a set number of times.
- Keeping the score for a viewer's self-test.
- Providing messages that depend on the user's input (e.g. 'Too Old' or 'Too Young').

There are many other examples of such tasks, but they all have the same requirement to have a temporary store to hold a value (i.e. a name, the number of times round the animation loop so far, the running total, or an age). Each variable has a name (e.g 'name', 'loopcount', 'score', 'age', etc).

This temporary store is called a variable and there are two types in Lingo.

Global variables	The values stored in these variables can be accessed and altered from anywhere within the movie. If the finished projector contains multiple movies, then the values are available across all the movies. So, for example, the viewer's total score in a test or in a game can be updated as the viewer tackles different parts of the project.
Local variables	The values stored in these variables are only accessible within the handler. This is useful for the temporary storage of values that will not be required by any other part of the project. Examples are loop counters and temporary storage for mathematical calculations.

Navigation

A major use for Lingo scripts is in allowing the viewer to navigate through the project.

A simple project, such as a standalone exhibition presentation can be created as a sequential set of events, with text appearing and disappearing, graphics flashing up, videos and sound playing, etc. All this can be very effective and is achieved without any scripting (apart from getting the playback head back to the beginning to repeat looping).

For all other projects, there is a need for user interactivity. This means that the user controls where to go in the project and this requires two things:

- Navigation controls (buttons, menu choices, etc).
- Scripts attached to the controls.

The controls are the parts that the viewer sees and the scripts control what happens when the viewer presses a button or menu choice.

Navigation scripts are usually quite straightforward and mainly jump the playback to another frame on the Score or to another frame in another project. Occasionally, navigation scripts can be more complex, using logic as part of the navigation choice. So, for example, an educational project may have a button to move the viewer on to the next lesson but the section jumped to may depend on the score achieved by the user in the previous section.

An 'Iconic/Flow Control' authoring system has the advantage of dividing up a project into manageable modules and these are easily recognised and the links between them are readily understood.

Since Director uses a 'Cast/Score/Script' technique, the entire project spreads across the Score window and can be a bit awkward to create, visualise and amend. This is why Director is often the choice for creating linear projects, or projects that contain long linear sequences.

To aid recognition and to allow navigation, markers can be added to the Score. Each marker has a name to describe the contents of the following frames and this marker name is also used as a reference for navigation. A marker is added to the Score by left-clicking the mouse in the bar above the six effects channels and entering a name for the marker. A marker can be removed by dragging it out of the Score.

MP3 player example

This following simple example shows a cast list of twelve items made up of 5 items that appear on the screen (one heading and four buttons), four scripts (one for each button and one to create a loop) and three MP3 sound files.

The first frame has a marker that names the time slot 'begin' and there is another marker titled 'exit'.

The script channel has a script in the first, as shown in the illustration, with the contents

```
go to "begin"
```

At the end of the frame, the script is run and this returns the playback head to the start of the frame, creating a tiny endless loop that simply displays the text and the buttons.

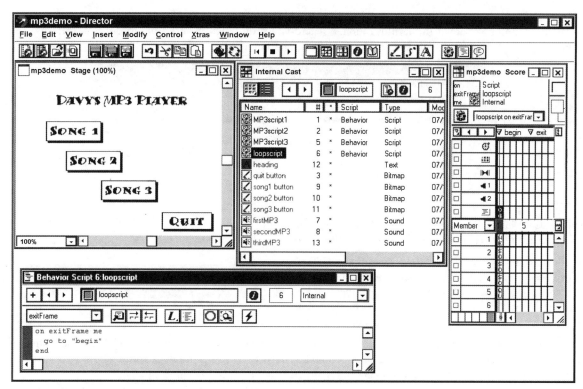

Each button has a script attached to it, which plays one of the MP3 files. For example, the script attached to the 'Song 1' button uses the Lingo 'PuppetSound' command:

```
PuppetSound "firstMP3"
```

When a song button is pressed, the script plays the MP3 file, and this will play to the end if no further buttons are pressed.   If another song button is pressed the new script is run and this plays the new MP3 file instead of the previous file.   The *'Quit'* button has the following script attached to it:

```
go to "exit"
```

When the *'Quit'* button is pressed, the script moves the playback head to the time slot marked as *'exit'* and this jumps the program out of the loop and terminates the application.

Creating sub-modules

The simple menu system in the MP3 player only required a single frame in the Score. For larger projects, clicking a menu option would result in a set of actions being carried out rather than a single activity. Each menu option would wish to run a different section of the Score contents before returning to the main menu.

The illustration shows a miniature menu system. The first time slot contains four cast members. One is a screen background image and the other three are menu buttons.

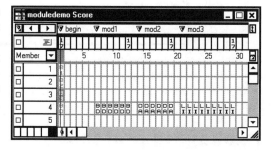

The first button has a script attached that contains the command

```
go to "mod1"
```

This moves the playback head to the *'mod1'* marker (i.e. to the seventh frame) and the playback would continue stepping through frames from that point.   When the playback head reaches the end of the section (i.e. the twelfth frame in the example), it runs the script in the script channel and this contains the command

```
go to "begin"
```

This takes the playback head back to the first frame where it displays the menu again and waits once more for user input.

A similar process occurs when the viewer clicks the other menu buttons. Of course, there is no reason why a sub-module should not contain another level of menu, which takes the playback head to yet another range of sub-modules. The illustration shows the very minimum necessary to explain the technique. In practice, a sub-module will make use of sprites in many channels. For example, the *'mod1'* section of the Score could have animations, text, graphics, sounds, and so on, as part of its playback - as long as these components were stored between frames 7 and 12.

Behaviors

To simplify scripting, Director provides *'behaviors'*. These are pre-written scripts that reside in a Director library and can be selected and attached to a sprite or frame by dragging the behavior on to it.

The behavior library is accessed through the *'Library Palette'* option on the *'Window'* drop-down menu. This produces the dialog box shown in the illustration. There is a drop-down menu at the top of box, offering sets of behavior scripts covering areas such as animation, controls, internet, etc.

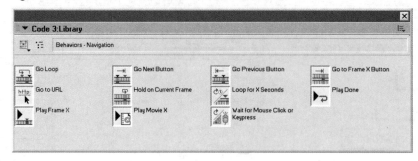

The illustration shows the scripts available in the navigation section of the library.
Some of the behavior scripts require parameters (information need to complete the process).

This illustration shows the dialog box that is produced when the *'Play Movie X'* script is dropped onto a sprite. The developer enters the parameter (i.e. the name of the video clip) and that particular video will play when the button sprite is clicked.

The behavior script is included as a new cast member in the project and the script attached to the button is an *'instance'* of that script. This is exactly the same method as used with, say, a graphics sprite. This, of course, means that the same script can be dropped on another button and a different video file name entered.

Parameters are also required for some navigation scripts. For instance, the *'Go To Frame X Button'* will ask the developer to enter the frame number to be jumped to. This behavior script can be attached to as many sprites as required, using different parameters for each instance of the behavior script.

Although Director supplies ready-made behaviors, these can be amended by the developer, or completely new behaviour scripts can be written by the developer.

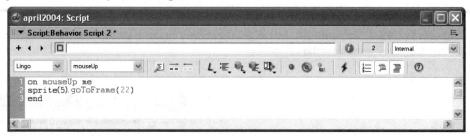

Right-clicking on a sprite brings up a menu and choosing the *'Script'* option displays the dialog box shown in the illustration. It shows the script attached to that sprite and allows alterations to be entered. The '+' button in the top-left corner of the window allows the developer to add a new behaviour script, while the arrow buttons are used to cycle through all the scripts to examine them or amend them.

Packaging projects

Projects created by Director are called *'movies'* and are given the file extension .DIR (e.g. *'firstaid.dir'*). Projects are stored in this format during development, as this format keeps all the elements used in the project fully accessible and alterable by the developer. Projects should also be stored in this format to allow later access for maintenance. Movies in .DIR format are not suitable for distribution, as they allow anyone with Director to edit them.

When the finished movie is ready for distribution, there are a number of ways that the movie can be packaged.

- They may be compiled into standalone applications - called *'projectors'*. This method is designed for CD and kiosk uses.
- All, or parts, of the movie may be converted into a set of graphic images.
- They may be saved as Shockwave files, with the extension .DCR (e.g. *'firstaid.dcr'*), for playing on the web. The person viewing the Shockwave file needs a Shockwave plug-in with older browsers (this is already supplied in newer browsers).
- They may be exported as AVI or QuickTime MOV files (e.g. *'firstaid.avi'* or *'firstaid.mov'*). The finished video clips can be used in other applications, or imported into a Director movie.

Many of these options are chosen from the *'Publish Settings'* dialog box, accessed from the *'File'* drop-down menu. It displays a dialog box as shown in the following illustration.

The settings are divided into six main categories:

- Formats
- Files
- HTML
- Projector
- Shockwave
- Image

Standalone projectors

A projector is designed for use on CDs and kiosks. It contains all the project's internal and external components, packaged as a stand-alone application (e.g. *'firstaid.exe'*). The components include external files, external casts, any Xtras, and a player (called the Standard player). It can also include several different movies, played one after the other, or linked by Lingo commands. If all the project's resources are internal, a single self-sufficient application file is created. Since the projector is self-contained, all the components are secure from tampering and the file will play on any PC, without any special adjustments or add-ons.

If the project contains external components, such as linked music files, these will not be embedded in the final projector file and have to be distributed along with the projector. When a projector is played, it will expect to access all external linked files in the same way it accessed them during authoring. This means that all linked media must be stored on a distribution CD, or kiosk hard disk, in the same relative locations as during authoring. These problems can be minimised, if all external files are stored in a single folder - and this folder is also used to store the final projector. This may not be convenient for very large projects, in which case great care must be taken over the way that external files are located on the final distribution media.

Another option, the Shockwave projector, is to have a standalone projector file that uses the Shockwave player installed on the viewer's computer. Since this does not require any player code inside the projector, the finished file is smaller. Of course, if the viewer does not have a Shockwave player he/she will have to download and install a copy to view the projector. This is recommended for web distribution, with the actual playback ignoring the browser software and using the Shockwave player directly.

Creating a projector

Clicking the *'Projector'* tab of *'Publish Settings'* displays the dialog box shown in the illustration.

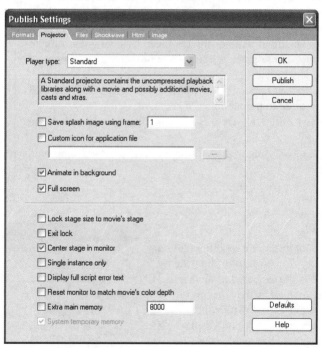

The options are:

- Choosing *'Standard'* as the Player Type, is includes the player code with the movie, to create a standalone projector. This starts the movie fastest, but creates the largest projector file. If the *'Shockwave'* option is chosen, it does not include any player code in the final projector, expecting the projector to be viewed with a Shockwave player already installed in the viewer's computer.
- Checking the *'Animate in Background'* box means that the movie continues to play in the background when the user switches to another application. If unchecked, the movie pauses when the user runs to another application and resumes when the user switches back to the projector application.
- Checking the *'Full Screen'* box displays the movie over the entire monitor screen. Otherwise, the movie is displayed in a normal window.
- Checking the *'Centre stage in monitor'* box centres the displayed Stage on the screen. In Windows, projectors are always centred.

Within the *'Files'* tab, there is a *'Play every movie in list'* box. If the *'Play Every Movie'* box is checked, the projector plays all its movies in order. If this is unchecked, the projector only plays the first movie, unless Lingo commands in the first movie call other movies.

When all the projector options are set, clicking the *'Publish'* button creates a standalone projector file with the name and folder location specified by the developer within the *'Formats'* tab options.   The *'Preview after publishing'* option displays the Shockwave file in the developer's browser, on completion of the file's creation.

Macromedia make no charge for the distribution of compiled applications and movies, but require that a *'Made with Macromedia'* credit be placed on the products.

Creating a Shockwave movie

Shockwave is Macromedia's own playback system for the Internet and these movies are intended for viewing in a web browser that has a Shockwave player installed as a plug-in.   Consequently, it does not have its own player code built in and this makes the final file size much smaller. The movie data is also compressed, further shrinking the final file size.

Choosing a Shockwave version of the project creates two files:

- The Shockwave movie, stored as a .DCR file.
- The HTML code containing all the tags necessary to run the .DCR file.

Where there are external casts, these are stored as a .CTT file.

Therefore, creating a Shockwave movie usually involves altering settings under both the *'Shockwave'* and *'HTML'* tabs.

The 'Shockwave' tab options

Clicking the *'Shockwave'* tab of *'Publish Settings'* displays the dialog box shown in the illustration. The options are:

- The *'Image Compression'* option offers two compression methods. Checking the *'Standard'* radio button produces a fixed compression level and is best suited for graphics that contain relatively few colours. Checking the *'JPEG'* radio button allows the developer to set the level of compression using the slider. Higher figures mean less compression and greater image quality. These settings control the bitmap compression for all cast members in the movie.
- The *'Audio Compression'* options allow the audio data rate to be set and the audio to be converted to monophonic, if required,
- The *'Volume Control'* option allows viewer's to adjust the volume of the movie's audio.
- The *'Transport Control'* option allows the viewer to start, stop and rewind the movie.

The 'HTML' tab options

The options here are:

- The *'Page Background'* option specifies the background colour for insertion in the HTML code. This is the colour that appears in the rectangular area in which the movie will play, while the movie is downloading.
- The *'Display Progress Bar'* option displays the download progress bar while the file downloads.
- The *'Display Logo'* option displays the logo while the file downloads.

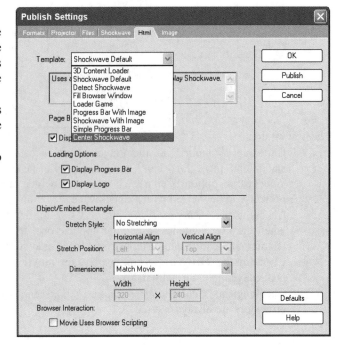

The *'Template'* menu has the following options:

Option	Result
3D Content Loader	Used for movies with 3D content.
Shockwave Default	Uses OBJECT and EMBED parameters in the HTML file to display the Shockwave file.
Detect Shockwave	JavaScript and VB Script determines whether the correct version of the Shockwave plug-in or ActiveX is on the viewer's computer and advises on an update if necessary.
Fill Browser Window	Expands the Shockwave file to fill the browser window.
Loader Game	Displays a game with a progress bar while the Shockwave file loads.
Progress Bar with Image	Displays a progress bar and image while the Shockwave file downloads.
Shockwave with Image	Automatically detects and uses the Shockwave player or Active X control on the viewer's browser. If Shockwave is not on the viewer's computer, and the viewer is using Internet Explorer, the browser automatically installs the Active X control. Otherwise, the image specified in the *'Image'* tab is displayed..
Simple Progress Bar	Display a progress bar while the Shockwave file downloads.
Center Shockwave	Centres the Shockwave movie in the browser window.

The *'Dimensions'* options provide three ways to specify the Shockwave movie screen size.

Option	Result
Match Movie	Makes the Shockwave movie the same size as the DIR movie. The width and height values of the movie are included in the OBJECT and EMBED tags in the HTML file.
Pixels	Allows the developer to specify the Shockwave movie's dimensions by entering values in the *'height'* and *'width'* boxes below the menu.
Percent of Browser Window	Allows the developer to specify the movie's dimensions in terms of the browser window size (e.g. 90% or 100% of the browser window).

The *'Stretch Style'* options determine how the movie displays when the *'width'* and *'height'* values in the HTML file are different from the movie's size.

Option	Result
No Stretching	Displays the movie plays at its original size.
Preserve Proportions	Maintains the movie's aspect ratio when the viewer changes the size of the browser window.
Stretch to Fill	Stretches the movie to fill the height and width values specified in the HTML file, even if this produces some distortion.
Expand Stage Size	Expands the Stage size to the size of the height and width values in the HTML file, while leaving all stage sprites at their original size.

The *'Stretch Position'* settings specify how the movie is positioned within the OBJECT or EMBED values in the HTML file (i.e. Top/Bottom, Left/Right, Centred).

The 'Image' tab options

These settings choose the image to be displayed on the user's screen when the user does not have a Shockwave player installed. The JPEG image of the screen content is displayed instead of the movie.

The frame number to be used is entered in the *'Poster Frame'* box and the slider is used to set the compression ratio. The image can also be set to be progressive, so that it displays first at low quality and increases in quality as it downloads.

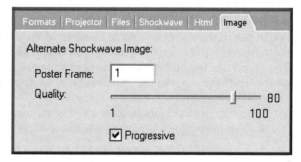

Shockwave streaming

A Shockwave movie can be configured for streamed playback over the Internet. When the viewer chooses to look at a Shockwave movie, the browser's Shockwave player loads the components required to display a screen. While the viewer is examining the first screen, the following frames are being loaded. This means that the viewer does not wait until the entire file is downloaded before beginning to watch the movie. This results in much reduced time before the viewer sees results and this increases the viewer's satisfaction with the project.

The dialog box for setting the options is accessed from the *'Playback'* option of the *'Movie'* sub-menu that is reached from the *'Modify'* drop-down menu. This displays the dialog box shown in the following illustration.

Checking the *'Lock Frame Durations'* box locks the Shockwave movie speed to the project's tempo settings.

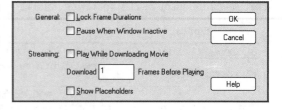

Checking the *'Pause When Windows Inactive'* box pauses the movie when another window is opened in the foreground.

Checking the *'Streaming'* box turns on the streaming facility.

The *'Download __ Frames Before Playing'* box should be set to match the needs of the project. The default setting is to begin playback as soon as the first frame is downloaded. However, sometimes there are a lot of cast members, or a number of linked elements, appearing early in the playback. In this situation, it may be better to wait until these are all loaded before beginning playback. The value entered should reflect the time needed to load these elements.

Checking the *'Show Placeholders'* box results in the movie displaying placeholders, in the shape of rectangles, for those media elements that have not yet been downloaded.

Notes
- These settings are used in conjunction with the settings available in the *'Publish Settings'* dialog box.
- When played, Shockwave movies loop by default. To make the movie play only once, the last frame of the movie should have the *'Hold on Current Frame'* behavior added to it.

Streaming audio

Director can also create streamed audio over the Internet. The files have the extension .SWA (ShockWave Audio).

The file cannot be transmitted on its own. It is not intended as a competitor to audio streaming formats such as RealAudio. It is intended as a compressed audio file that is bundled with a Shockwave movie. As such, it is a cast member in the movie's score.

The first step is to compress the file. A WAV file is imported as a cast member. Then the conversion utility is accessed from the *'Convert WAV to SWA'* option in the *'Xtras'* drop-down menu. This displays the dialog box shown in the illustration.

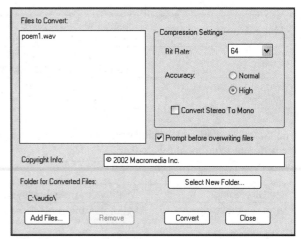

The dialog box allows control over the bit rate of the audio, with 16kbps being the recommended rate for normal modem transmission and higher rates being achievable with ADSL links. The more the file is compressed, the lower is its bit rate and the quicker it is streamed. Of course, higher compression also results in lower quality. Stereo audio clips with bit rates below 48kbps are automatically converted by the utility into mono clips.

The utility can compress internal audio cast members as long as they are in WAV format, while MP3 files or files already compressed into SWA format cannot be compressed further.

A Shockwave Audio Player is included in the final compiled Shockwave file.

Exporting as digital video

All, or part of a Director movie can be exported as a digital video file. This file can be used with other applications or it can be imported back into a project as a single video clip.

The export functions allow the movie to be exported in AVI format, or in QuickTime format if QuickTime is installed on the developer's computer. Alternatively, each frame of the Score can be converted into a bitmap image of the Stage, thus building up the video sequence.

There are serious limitations to these conversions that have to considered:
- All interactivity in the movie is lost.
- Sprites that are solely animated by a Lingo script are ignored.
- When exporting to an AVI file, the audio content is ignored.

To export a movie, first choose the *'Export'* option from the *'File'* drop-down menu. This displays the dialog box shown in the illustration.

The *'Format'* menu allows the developer to choose to export as:
- An AVI file.
- A QuickTime file.
- A series of BMP graphic images.

The *'Options'* button allows the AVI options (simply setting the frame rate for the exported video) and the QuickTime options (type of compression, compression quality, etc.) to be set.

Clicking the *'Export'* button produces a small dialog box where the developer enters the name to be given to the exported movie. When the file is named, clicking the *'Save'* button creates the exported file. Exporting to an AVI or QuickTime file produces a single video clip.

Exporting as a set of bitmap graphic files produces a numbered set of files. For example, if the name of the exported file is given as *'Davy'*, the first frame is saved as *'Davy0001'*, the second frame as *'Davy0002'* and so on.

The options in the dialog box for creating one or more still images (as BMP graphic files) are:

- Checking the *'Current Frame'* radio button exports the current frame on the Stage as a BMP file.
- Checking the *'Selected Frames'* radio button exports the frames that have been selected in the Score, as a set of BMP files.
- Checking the *'All Frames'* radio button exports all the frames in the movie.
- Checking the *'Frame Range'* radio button exports only the range of frames entered in the *'Begin'* and *'End'* boxes.
- Checking the *'Every Frame'* radio button exports all the frames in the range chosen above.
- Checking the *'One in Every __ Frames'* radio button exports frames at the interval set in the data entry box (e.g. entering 5 in the box results in every fifth frame being used in the exported video clip).
- Checking the *'Frames with Markers'* radio button exports those frames that have a marker in the Score.
- Checking the *'Frames with Artwork Changes in Channel ___'* radio button exports only those frames where has been a change in cast member in the channel number entered in the data entry box.

CD/DVD Production

Multimedia productions including images and sound can easily run into several megabytes. When digital video or very high-resolution images are included, it can reach into the hundreds of megabytes, even after compression. This is not a problem for productions intended for a kiosk, or a presentation using the same computer on which it was created.

However, if the product is to be used by other systems, distribution of such a large amount of material becomes an important consideration. There are several methods of distributing material, including the Internet, floppy disks, and removable drives. Each of these is suitable for distributing certain types of data.

Distribution media

The Internet is a powerful tool for distributing up-to-date information. E-mail and web pages are excellent ways of providing fast, frequent updates. However, bandwidth is limited, and a large data file will take a long time to download. With streaming audio and video, the problem is eased, but the average modem can only download at most 5KB of streaming data per second, seriously limiting the quality of such material. In the UK, many Internet users also pay by the minute for Internet access, which could cause potential consumers to avoid downloading or streaming large files. CDs and DVDs are not as convenient as Internet downloads, but they are capable of storing a large amount of high-quality video, sound and graphics that would take many hours to download from an Internet site.

Floppy disks are used less and less in distribution, to such a degree that virtually nothing is distributed on floppy any more except device drivers and operating system startup disks. Floppy disks simply don't have the storage capacity distributors require, and also have extremely slow access times. CD-ROMs do not suffer from either of these problems. However, CD-ROMs, unlike floppies, require that the system is already able to access a CD drive. Hence the reason for distributing drivers and boot disks on floppy.

Removable drives, such as the Iomega Zip disk or Jaz drive, vary greatly in their capabilities. In general, they store between 100MB and 2GB, and access speeds vary even further. Some of these drives are noticeably superior to CD-ROMs, and offer read/write access instead of read-only. This makes for an excellent backup facility or in-house data transfer system. However, as a distribution media they are less useful – the cartridges are generally expensive, and not all end users can be assumed to have access to a drive capable of reading the media.

Even the humble VHS tape is no longer the most efficient method of distributing video. Video CD and DVD provide digital quality and additional functionality. If the video can fit on a single CD, then Video CD is also the cheaper option; VHS duplication is normally from £1-£2 per unit, while a blank CD-R costs well under £1, and if large numbers of stamped CDs are printed the cost drops to just a few pence each.

In the audio market, CD already dominates. Magnetic Cassettes are still available but suffer from degradation after time, something that is much less of a problem with digital media. The MiniDisc from Sony is an impressive technology, but currently it has nowhere near the market penetration that CD can claim.

Advantages of using CDs

- Large storage capacity. CD-ROMs can potentially store up to 650MB of computer data, or 741MB of digital video. At the time of writing, only extremely large or video-intensive products need more capacity than a single CD-ROM can provide.
- Widely supported. With the exception of floppy disks, no other computer media has such a large user base. Productions on CD-ROM can be used by virtually all PCs – anywhere in the world (unlike VHS tapes). Because of their popularity, DVD drives also support the reading of CD-ROMs, further extending their life into the foreseeable future.
- Low cost. Due to the sharp rise in sales of CD writers for PCs, their prices have fallen greatly since their first appearance, both for the CD writer and the blank CDs themselves.
- Long storage life. CD-ROMs are digital media, and as long as the disc is kept safe, a recordable disc will have a shelf life of 50 to 100 years. Manufactured CDs have a shorter lifespan of 10 to 15 years.
- Compact. While an individual CD might not seem particularly compact in comparison to an audio cassette, it is lighter and more easily stacked for distribution. When CDs are used for data or video, the space savings are even more marked.
- Convenience. A modern CD writer can be used to 'burn' a disc in under an hour, using only a standard desktop PC equipped with a CD-R drive.

Disadvantages of using CDs

- Slow access times. CD-ROM drives have become much faster since they first appeared, but they are still very slow compared to hard disks and even some other removable media. Data that requires fast data transfer, such as high-quality digital video, may not run at an acceptable speed on some CD drives.

- Slow to create. Building a master disc to press large quantities of CDs makes CD production faster by an order of magnitude, but unless many hundreds of CDs are to be pressed it will prove to be an expensive proposition. If fewer CDs are to be created, the most cost-effective method is to use a CD writer to 'burn' copies of discs. Even with the most up-to-date 16 speed and even 24 speed writers, the process takes several minutes. This is due to the overheads of testing the writer, building an image, fixing the disc and so on. While this is quite acceptable for occasional convenient use, it is less useful for mass production.
- Large number of standards. An audio CD is playable on any CD unit, and a basic Yellow Book Mode 1 CD-ROM is readable on any computer CD drive. Beyond that, however, there are a large and often confusing number of standards, any one of which might not work on some of the systems of the target audience. A producer must consider the options carefully before deciding on which standard to use.
- Static. CD-ROMs cannot be updated once created; if a new version of the CD is designed, then the old CD can only be discarded. Furthermore, if the CD is to be distributed widely, it means that consumers have to be kept abreast of updates by other means or by additional CD updates.

How CD-ROM works

The simplified diagram shows the basic layout of a side view of a section of a CD ROM disc.   The plastic disc has an embossed surface consisting of areas of normal thickness ('lands' or 'hills') and sunken areas ('pits'). The discs are stamped out from a master disc. After the high initial costs of creating the master disc, individual CDs can be stamped out very cheaply as can be seen by the number of computer magazines that include free CDs of shareware and program demonstrations.

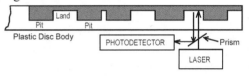

The changes of height along the track represent the data on the disc, although the coding method is more complex than the simple storage of the data's 1's and 0's.   The top surface of the disc is coated with a layer of reflective aluminium (the shaded area of the diagram) and this is covered with a protective plastic layer; the total disc thickness is 1.2mm. Pressed CD-ROMs are known as 'silver discs' due to the colour of the aluminium used.

The disc is read from its underside by firing a laser beam at the revolving surface.   The beam reflects from the aluminium coating and is diverted to a photo sensor by a prism.   The normal depth areas - the 'lands' - reflect back most of the laser beam while the 'pitted' areas scatter the beam as shown in the diagram.   So, the photo sensor will detect different reflected strengths from the two different surface areas.   The laser beam passes through focusing lenses so that the beam is a tiny spot at the point of contact with the disc surface.

The spot is only 1 micron in size - one millionth of a metre. This means that much more data can be packed on to the disc surface compared to standard magnetising methods.   This explains the ability to pack up to 650MB of data on to a single disc. Since the head does not require being close to the disc surface, it does not suffer the risk of head crashes associated with normal floppy and hard discs.

Light scattered   Light reflected

The disc contains only a single track, organised as single spiral similar to a long-playing record, except that the disc is read from the centre outwards.   The laser, prism, lenses and photodetector are all enclosed in a single unit that is moved between the inner and outer parts of the spiral. It is the equivalent of the ordinary read/write head of a hard disc. Reaching a wanted sector requires the head to be moved to the approximate location on the spiral track.   The head then follows the track until it reaches a sector header; this header information is then used to locate the wanted sector.

Although CDs use a number of error detection and correction techniques, they should still be handled with care. Grease from a fingerprint diffuses the laser beam while surface scratches deflect the beam.

Disc organisation

The disc is 120mm in diameter with a 15mm hole is punched in the centre. A 6mm area of the surface, next to the hole, is used by the drive mechanism to clamp the disc while rotating.   The next 4mm area is used to store information regarding the disc's contents; this is known as the VTOC (volume table of contents). The data area width is 33mm and comprises a single track spiralling outward about 20,000 times and totalling around 3 miles in length. The outer area of 3mm is used for handling the disc.

Centre hole
Table of contents
Handling area
Data area
Clamping area

A single-speed drive reads 75 of these sectors per second, giving a transfer rate of 150kb/s.   A double-speed drive reads 150 sectors/sec while a 32x drive reads 2400 sectors/sec, giving transfer rates of 300kb/s and 4,800kb/s respectively.   The original single speed model spins at 300rpm and other models are multiples of this - i.e. a quad speed rotates at 1,200 rpm and a 32x rotates at 9,600rpm.

Most CDs have a 2352 byte sector size of which 2k or over is used for data and the remaining bytes for error-detection and synchronisation information.

Hard discs specify a particular disc area in terms of track and sector. CD ROMs, showing their origins as audio discs, specify areas in terms of minutes, seconds, and sectors within each second. Thus, a 74 minute CD has a capacity of: 74 x 60(secs) x 75(sectors) x 2k = 650MB of user data area.

A standard CD stores a maximum total of 333,000 sectors. These sectors are evenly spread throughout the spiral on the disc.

There are several methods of reading the data on the disc:

CLV - Constant Linear Velocity.

Using this method, the disc is rotated faster when reading the inner spirals than when reading the outer spirals. This ensures a constant data rate, but requires a more expensive drive motor.

CAV - Constant Angular Velocity - also known as Full CAV.

With this method, the disc is rotated at the same speed throughout, meaning cheaper manufacture. However, since the spiral is smaller near the centre of the CD, the data rate is slower there than near the edge of the CD. Thus, a CAV CD-ROM drive might be described as being '14/32x' speed: it reads at 14 speed near the centre but 32 speed near the edge. Since CDs only use the outermost spirals if they are completely filled, CAV drives may not even reach the full speed on many CDs.

PCAV - Partial Constant Angular Velocity.

Many CD drives are now a CLV/CAV hybrid, using CLV (i.e. changing speeds) on the outer tracks and CAV (i.e. constant speeds) on the inner tracks.

CD-ROM performance

The performance of a CD-ROM is determined by the following factors:

- The access time of the drive.

  These times vary from 65ms to 100ms for newer models and 350ms to 900ms for older models. Compared to hard disc speeds, these are very slow times. That is because there is one single continuous spiral track. The read head cannot first go to the exact track and wait for the wanted sector to come round. It has to make an approximation to the correct distance in then wait for the first sector header to tell the system where the head is positioned. It then makes a second seek to get to the correct position. This slows down the sector access times.

- The data transfer rate of the drive.

  The most common rates are:

Data Rate	Description	Data Rate	Description
150kbs	single-speed	2400kbs	16x
300kbs	double-speed or 2x	3600kbs	24x
450kbs	triple-speed or 3x	4800kbs	32x
600kbs	quad speed or 4x	6000kbs	40x
1200kbs	8x	7200kbps	48x
1500kbs	10x	8400kbps	56x

These figures do not give a complete picture - a 48x drive will not provide double the throughput of a 24x drive, for example.

This is for a number of reasons:

- The higher transfer rates only apply to long sequential reads. If the head has to make a number of random access seeks, the faster transfers are offset by the substantial individual access times. The result is an average figure somewhat less than the performance suggested by the speed multiplier ratings.
- With CLV models, there is an additional time delay while the motor changes speed when moving between inner and outer tracks.
- For the same reasons above, the sustained data rate shows up better with bigger files.
- AVI video files are sometimes designed for double or quad speed and drives with faster rates have to work at the slower rate to be compatible with the data being presented.

- The detection and elimination of read errors.

  Errors occur due to slight imperfections in the boundaries of cells or from fingerprints or scratches obscuring the data read. For small data losses, the error detection system also has an error correction system that alters the read data to the original information. This is an improvement on normal discs and provides a more secure storage medium.

- The size of the drive's buffers.

  The current drive cache sizes vary from 16k to 1024k, mostly available in 128k or 256k. The cache size can have a significant influence on the smooth performance of multimedia presentations. SmartDrive can be used to gain a reasonably useful improvement in CD-ROM performance and utilities such as CD-Speed copy the CD's most commonly used files to the hard disc to speed up their access.

CD Standards

Many of the standards are named after the colour of cover used to report on the new standard. So, the standard for audio on CD became known as the Red Book standard because it had a red cover.

Broadly speaking, standards for CDs can be separated into two categories: physical standards and logical standards. In other words, standards such as Red Book and Yellow Book define how information is physically stored on the CD, while data standards such as ISO 9660 and Joliet define how that information is logically organised into a computer readable format.

Standard	Purpose
Red / Scarlet Book	Audio CDs
Yellow Book	Computer data (e.g. application installation CDs)
Green Book	CD-Interactive applications, games and, entertainment
White Book	Video CDs
Blue Book	Music CDs with text
Orange Book	Recordable CDs
Purple Book	Double Density CD
Photo CD	Kodak's multi-session picture storage

ISO 9660

Often known as *'High Sierra'*, since it was first discussed in the High Sierra Hotel in Nevada in 1985. By 1987, a superset of High Sierra, known as ISO 9600, was agreed as the common standard for computer CD ROMs. ISO 9660 is a logical standard, defining the way files may be stored on a disc. ISO 9660 is designed for use with a variety of computer systems including DOS, Unix and Macintosh, and thus has to cater to the lowest common denominator.

It comes in three *'levels'*, but only level 1 is used to any real extent, and the other levels may not even be catered for by all systems. In level 1, filenames are very similar to DOS filenames, with an eight-character name and three-character extension. However, filenames are further restricted in their choice of characters, allowing only upper case letters, numerals, and the underscore character. Directory names are restricted to eight characters with no extension, and any CD is allowed a maximum of eight levels of directories. These restrictions must be taken into consideration when creating an ISO 9660 CD-ROM.

All computer CD systems are capable of dealing with this logical standard for handling files and directories. The PC version is implemented with the MSCDEX or CDFS driver software. If the CD itself is to be truly cross-platform, then any executable or other machine-specific data should be stored in separate directories for different computer systems. For example many CD-ROMs have a directory on the root of the CD called 'DOS', one called 'MAC' and one called 'UNIX', each containing executable code for that system.

The ISO 9660 standard is built upon by most other CD file standards, such as Joliet.

JOLIET

From Windows 95 onwards, PC users have access to filenames longer than the previous 8+3 specification, something that was already available to Mac and Unix users. The ISO 9660 standard became very restrictive for PC users, and so the newer Joliet standard was introduced to provide more flexibility. It allows up to 64 characters in a filename (which is however still less than Windows can handle), and is less restricted in the choice of characters, since it uses the international *'Unicode'* character set and allows the use of spaces.

However, Joliet discs cannot be read by any non-Windows system. For that reason, the Joliet specification states that discs should also contain an ISO 9660 file system that points to the same data.

Filenames longer than the normal 8.3 standard are truncated in the same way as Windows truncates files for DOS. For example *'Staff Memo 99.Doc'* would be stored on the ISO 9660 section as *'STAFFM~1.DOC'*.

ROMEO

The Romeo standard, like Joliet, is a logical standard that allows for long filenames, this time of up to 128 characters. However, Romeo does not use the Unicode character set, and all filenames are converted to upper case to increase backwards compatibility. Romeo filenames are also stored in a truncated format for ISO 9660 readers, but the truncation is much simpler. For example *'Staff Memo 99.Doc'* would be stored on the ISO 9660 section as *'STAFFMEM.DOC'*. This can potentially cause problems if several similar filenames are used, which are truncated to the same ISO 9660 filename. Further complications arise when the disc is used in a Macintosh, where the disc is readable only if all filenames are of 31 characters or less.

Due at least in part to these complications, Romeo has not seen as widespread use as Joliet.

Macintosh HFS

The Hierarchical File System used on Macintosh computers can also be used as the filing system on a CD-ROM. PC users cannot access Mac HFS discs, though, so a number of CD-ROMs have been produced as *'Hybrids'*, combining a Mac HFS filing system and an ISO 9660 filing system on the same disc. This works by having an HFS volume in the first 17 blocks, which are ignored by ISO 9660 CD readers.

Rock Ridge Extensions

This system is another logical format that, like Joliet, encompasses ISO 9660 for backwards compatibility but also provides further functions. In this case, the Rock Ridge extensions provide for more detailed file handling as demanded by UNIX systems.

Red Book

Established in 1980, this physical standard is also known as CD-DA (Digital Audio). The *'Red Book'* standard was the first of the series and defined the specification for the audio CD currently in use. It specified that the audio would be stored in digital format and be subject to error detection and correction. All CD drives are capable of reading Red Book audio CDs.

The Red Book standard specifies that an audio CD should contain up to 74 minutes of audio. It also specifies that this audio should be stored uncompressed in Pulse Code Modulated (PCM) format in stereo, 16-bit samples at a sampling rate of 44.1KHz. Thus, each sample consists of two channels of two bytes each, or four bytes per sample. At 44.1KHz (i.e. 44,100 samples per second), that means 176,400 bytes of data per second of audio.

The standard also specifies that audio data is to be stored in sectors each containing 1/75th of a second of digitised audio. Therefore, each sector (also sometimes called a *'large frame'*) contains 1/75th of 176,400 bytes, or 2532 bytes. This is further split into 98 frames of 24 bytes each. Since each sector stores 1/75th of a second, a full 74-minute CD stores 783,216,000 bytes of audio, or nearly 747MB.   Finally, the Red Book standard allows for 99 audio tracks per CD, with the disc's TOC (Table Of Contents) containing the starting point of each track.

Since Red Book is an audio standard, measurements are normally expressed in terms of minutes, seconds and sectors. Nearly all common CD standards are built upon the Red Book as a basis, and it is therefore not uncommon for other standards to refer to minutes or seconds of storage space rather than kilobytes or megabytes.

One sector (2353 bytes)

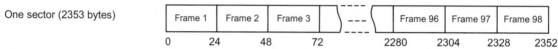

The Red Book audio specification includes a number of error detection and correction techniques. One form of error detection is called *Cross-Interleaved Reed-Solomon Code* (CIRC), and is often able to fix several bad frames in any sector. A method of error correction involves the insertion of sound values interpolated between surrounding values or repeated from the previous value. A single error corrected this way will not be noticed because individual frames contain less than a thousandth of a second of sound each.

In addition to the normal audio data in a Red Book CD, there are additional bits that normally remain hidden to the user, and which are only available in Red Book CDs. Most of these contain the error detection and correction data mentioned above, but there are also 8 bits per frame that can sometimes be accessed for use. These are called *'subchannels'* and are assigned letters from P through W.

- The 'P' subchannel is used to indicate the beginning of each track.
- The 'Q' subchannel is where the Table Of Contents is stored during the Lead-in, and gives time information during the music tracks. In addition to being available only to Red Book CDs, the 'P' and 'Q' subchannels are only available to the CD producer when the disc is created in Disc-At-Once mode.
- The 'R through W' subchannel (The remaining 6 subchannels are combined because they are used for the same data) can store additional information such as graphics or MIDI information. These discs are sometimes referred to as CD+G (Graphics) and CD+MIDI discs, but are uncommon.

Philips and Sony introduced the "Scarlet Book" format in 1999 as a range of alternatives to the standard Red Book format. Red Book stores audio data in uncompressed format while Scarlet Book uses lossless compression to reduce the file size and therefore allow six channel sound. The format envisages single layer and multi-layer disks.

Yellow Book

The *'Yellow Book'* standard of 1985 defined the computer data CD specification that is now commonly described simply as CD-ROM.   This standard is based on the Red Book format, but uses the 2352 byte sector for other purposes than pure audio.

It has three modes:

Mode 1 is used to store computer data. If a few bytes of audio data are corrupted, it will make next to no difference to the overall sound. However, if a single data bit is incorrect in a computer program, it could cause it to crash. To reduce such errors, Mode 1 uses just 2k (2048 bytes) of each sector for data, with 16 bytes used for synchronisation and 288 bytes used for Error Detection Codes (EDC) and Error Correction Codes (ECC). This is in addition to some of the error correction techniques provided by the Red Book standard.

Mode 2 was the original attempt at CD-I and provided for compression of audio and graphic information. It offered a 741MB maximum capacity since it dropped the 288 error correction bytes, allowing each sector to store 2336 bytes of data.   Since the disc was spinning at the same speed, its data transfer rate was also greater - 170kb/s instead of the normal 150kb/s. Mode 2, however, was unable to access computer data and audio/visual data at the same time, since they were stored on different tracks of the disc (only one mode is allowed per track).   This limited its usefulness and Mode 2 was never especially popular for the role for which it was intended.

Mode 3 was termed Mixed Mode as it allowed computer data tracks and audio tracks to be placed on the same disc. Usually, the first track contains the computer data with the remaining tracks containing audio data. The audio tracks could be played through a domestic audio CD player in which case the player would require to be manually stepped over the data track.   A CD ROM drive would recognise the computer data tracks and would be able to play the audio through its audio output. However, it could not do both at the same time.

Some references to Mixed Mode refer to a drive that can handle both Mode 1 and Mode 2.

CD XA

It is possible for audio and graphic information to be stored in different CD tracks.   When each of these data items is used separately there is no problem but multimedia demands that both audio and graphic information be presented in a synchronised manner and this is not easily achieved.   The Extended Architecture (XA) specification allows both audio, video and computer data to be stored in the same track in an interleaved fashion, thus allowing greatly improved synchronisation.

CD XA is based on the Yellow Book Mode 2, but specifies two *'Forms'* of storing data. Form 1 is for computer data, and Form 2 for audio or video data. Since they are both based on Yellow Book Mode 2, they both require 16 bytes for synchronisation, and both Form 1 and Form 2 allocate an additional 8 bytes for the same purpose. Form 1, being for computer data, required extensive error detection and correction, for which 280 bytes are allocated. This leaves 2k (2048 bytes) for user data per sector. Form 2 does not require such rigorous checking, allocating just 4 bytes to error detection and none for error correction. This leaves 2324 bytes for audio or video data per sector.

Since Form 1 and Form 2 work under the same XA Mode, they can both be placed on the same track. This allows Form 1 sectors containing computer data to be interleaved seamlessly with Form 2 video or audio data sectors. CD drives can then read these sequentially, ensuring proper synchronisation of data, audio and video.   XA also saved space in the storage of audio by using a method called ADPCM (Adaptive Delta Pulse Code Modulation).   This stores the difference between sound samples rather than the values themselves and results in smaller values being produced and saved.

Green Book

This is also an extension of the Mode 2 of the Yellow Book, and this is designed for playing CD-I interactive applications.   It stores files compressed to the MPEG format and interleaves the picture and sound elements. All CD-I tracks are in Mode 2 XA format, and as such can use Form 1 data (such as foreign language text) and Form 2 video and audio.

Unlike White Book, it does not provide the standard ISO 9660 access and requires a special CD-I player, a PC upgrade such as ReelMagic, or a special device driver, since a normal CD ROM drive cannot handle the format. Dedicated CD-I players are available with their own CPU and video memory and these connect to a monitor or television.

One other capability provided by Green Book is the ability to write data into the gap before the TOC. Since audio CD players never try to access this area, it can be safely used for data, without any possibility of the track being accidentally played as audio, which could potentially damage the sound output device.

CD-Bridge

As the name implies, this standard allows a drive to handle CDs that were both XA and CD-I compatible.   This special bridge CD disc is really a CD-I disc with extra XA information added to it.   The Photo CD disc explained below is an example of a bridge disc.   The disc has more than one disc label and this allows the same disc to be played in a CD-I player or an XA capable CD drive.

White Book

Used for Video CD - i.e. the storing of full-motion MPEG-1 video. The disk output cannot be taken directly to any ordinary video card. It has to be decompressed through special hardware or software to restore MPEG files to their original size. MPEG-1 compression results in a CD with up to 74 minutes of VHS-quality video and stereo sound track. Videos that are longer than 74 minutes have to be split up over two discs. MPEG-1 handling now appears on many video cards, with software or hardware decompression. Video CD is now overshadowed by DVD, but there are a far larger number of CD-R drives available in comparison to DVD-RAM, and the price of DVDs is high compared to CDs.

White Book has seen a number of versions, of which the most widely supported have been version 1.1 and version 2.0. A disc created in White Book version 2.0 consists of a CD XA Form 1 track for computer data such as the program used to play back the video, and a CD XA Form 2 track containing the video data itself.

Blue Book

Also known as CD Plus, Enhanced CD or CD Extra, this is designed to provide multiple sessions on a disc. The first session contains Red Book audio tracks and the second session contains computer data. The main TOC (table of contents) contains information on audio tracks and points to a further TOC storing data tracks. If the disc is used in a normal hi-fi CD audio player, it will not attempt to play the data tracks as it will not recognise the second TOC. A blue book drive will recognise and use both TOCs. The most likely use for Blue Book systems appears to be in the music industry where a CD can be played both in a standard audio CD player and in a computer CD drive. In the latter, photographs, text and even video about the performers can be supplied with the music. This, along with White Book covers most manufacturers' approaches to multimedia CDs.

Orange Book

Also known as CD-R (CD-Recordable), this describes the <u>writing</u> of CD discs, instead of the physical layout of sectors on the disc.

The three parts to the standard are:

I.   The use of Magneto Optical (CD-MO) drives which allow data to be written, then erased or overwritten.

II. The use of the *'Write Once'* (called CD-WO, essentially the same as CD-R) format, where the data is written in a single session or multiple sessions but cannot be altered after it is written.

III. The Rewritable format (CD-RW) which allows the disc to be re-written up to 1,000 times. This requires a Multi-Read CD drive or a DVD drive to read discs written by a CD-RW writer.

CD Writers can produce discs in CD-ROM, CD-DA, Mixed Mode, XA and CD-I format and an eight-speed drive will record an entire disc in about 9mins. However, this bare recording speed does not take into account fixing the disc, creating an image, or gathering the material for the disc in the first place. See the *'Recordable CD'* section below for further details.

Purple Book

Developed by Philips and Sony as a double density CD (DDCD) format. The disks use a narrower track pitch and shorter pit lengths, so that they can store 1.3GB per disk. They also offer a faster scanning velocity and an improved error correction system – but they cannot be played on existing CD-ROM or DVD-ROM drives.

Kodak Photo CD

The Kodak Photo CD system allows photographs taken with an ordinary camera to be placed on CD discs.   When the film is taken to the developer, the images can be reproduced in both standard photographic print format and in CD format. A Photo CD can store 100 photographs and these may be built up over a period of time with additional photographs being added at later dates by Kodak.   However, an older CD is not capable of reading any added data since each new additional group has its own unique storage key and this cannot be accessed by the old technology. A *'Multi-session'* CD-ROM (i.e. all models currently on the market) is capable of reading any subsequent additions. CD-I players or CD drives that support XA Mode 2/Form 1 are also capable of reading these files.

Universal Disc Format

Universal Disc Format, or UDF, is a format designed to allow easier and more efficient recording of CD-ROMs. It was developed by the Optical Storage Technology Association (OSTA), which is a group of hardware and software vendors, and its current version is 1.50. UDF supports a technology called *'incremental packet writing'*, (see *'CD Recording technologies'* below) which means that data can be written to CD-Rs in packets without having to create a disc image. Using UDF, a CD-R can be formatted, at which point any system equipped with a CD-R drive and UDF compliant CD writing software can send packets to record on the disc. Drivers using UDF can allow a CD-R disc to appear as a drive letter, which can be read from and written to in a similar fashion to hard disks or floppies.
UDF, however, is not compatible with ISO 9660. In order for other systems to read a UDF disc, there are two options. The reading system can have a UDF driver installed – note that any system which is capable of writing UDF discs can also read them. Alternatively, a UDF disc can be *'finalised'* by writing an ISO 9660 readable volume, which consumes approximately 20MB of CD space. Even when the disc is finalised, a CD-R drive can still write to the disc. However, further changes will require to be finalised once again, consuming another 20MB, if they are to be ISO 9660 compatible.

Standards Hierarchy

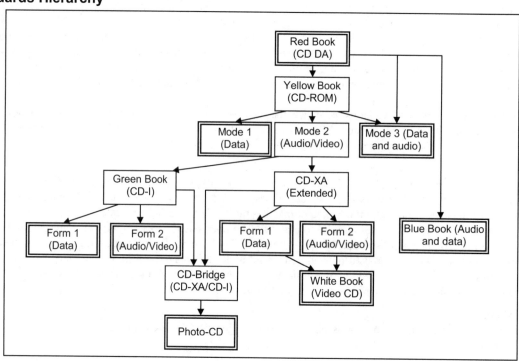

The diagram shows how the various physical standards described previously relate to each other.

Those standards with a double box around them are fully writable CD formats; the others are standards used as a basis for other formats and cannot be used on their own to create CDs. The diagram does not include Orange Book, as this standard simply defines how to create Recordable CDs of any type.

Re-writable CDs

The Orange Book specification defines three CD recording methods. Of these, two methods involve re-writable CD media. These are MO (Magneto-Optical) and CD-RW (CD Read/Write).

Magneto-Optical disks operate differently from conventional CDs. The laser beam heats the alloy on the CD surface, to such a temperature that its magnetic properties are lost. Then, an electromagnet on the other side of the write head is able to change the area's magnetic polarity before it cools. Later, when a low power laser beam is used to read the data back, the light in the laser beam is influenced by the magnetic field of the alloy, allowing the reader to detect these changes and interpret them as data. Obviously, conventional CD drives do not have the circuitry to do this, and so cannot read MO disks.

The Sony MiniDisc operates on a magneto-optical basis, but it does not follow any of the standards defined in this chapter, not even the MO section of the Orange Book. It is not as yet used as a computer data storage medium, being almost entirely restricted to audio.

CD-RW systems are more correctly called CD-E (CD Erasable) drives. They operate using a phase change technology, but there are a number of compatibility problems between CD-RW writers and conventional CD-ROM drives.

Firstly, the original PCR (Phase Change Recordable) disks were larger than normal CDs. Later, Panasonic's PD disks were introduced, which were physically similar to CD size but were logically incompatible due to a much smaller sector size on the PD disk.

When Orange Book was introduced, it defined a CD-RW standard for phase change disks, which could potentially be used by conventional CD-ROM drives with a little modification. Normal CD disks reflect 65 to 70 percent of light, while CD-RW disks only reflect 15 to 25 percent. This means that the read head on a normal CD drive requires additional circuitry (called *'automatic gain control'*) in order to detect the reflected light.

This is one major problem for distribution of CD-RW. While modern CD-ROM drives generally have the gain control built in now, not everybody can be expected to have a modern CD-ROM drive. Furthermore, because CD-RW is not created using sessions, it makes use of the UDF system. The disks need to undergo a process called *'freezing'*, similar to closing a CD-R disk, which makes it readable in a standard CD drive. CD-RW disks are also expensive compared to CD-Rs, and have even more limited space than CD-R disks due to the specification of 14KB of slack space after each 64KB block. This leaves just 530MB useable space on a CD-RW disk.

All of these problems may well make DVD distribution a more attractive option.

Future technology

A range of techniques is being developed to improve both the capacity and speed of CD ROMs. The main areas are:

Creating multiple levels of disk.
IBM is developing a sandwich of ten CD-R disks. By changing the beam's point of focus, different disks in the sandwich are used.

Using higher frequency lasers.
Blue violet lasers have a higher frequency (i.e. shorter wavelength) than red lasers and so smaller pits can be cut. This results in more data per spiral - up to 10GB per disk.

Reading multiple bits simultaneously.
Data from a normal CD drive is read sequentially, one data bit at a time. Several manufacturers are looking at the possibility of having multiple read heads, potentially increasing the throughput of the drive by a noticeable factor but not affecting its total storage capacity. This technique could even be applied to existing CD-ROM disks.

More speculative technologies that could potentially succeed the CD-ROM and DVD include:

- MFD (Multi-layered Fluorescent Disk), a disk that allows laser light to travel right through in a similar manner to a prism, and the varying wavelengths received at the other end can represent several bits at a time instead of the single bit of a CD-ROM.

- AFM (Atomic Force Microscopy), a technology that is reminiscent in operation to phonograph recordings. A microscopic 'needle' touches the track as it passes by, sensing minute changes in height and interpreting them as data.

- HD-ROM (High Density ROM), which uses a very narrow beam of gallium particles to write data onto almost any surface, including metal. This could store up to 165GB on a CD-sized disc.

Recordable CD

For large quantity production of CDs, a master copy is laser cut into a glass master copy, which in turn is utilised to create metallic *'stampers'* that are used to stamp out the lands and pits on the reflective layers of each blank CD. The master copy costs around £500 to produce but subsequent stamped CDs are extremely cheap by comparison, at just a few pence (which is why they are given away with computer magazines and audio magazines). For small quantities, this is an expensive option. CD-R (CD-Recordable) systems utilise a CD writer that uses disks of a different construction from the standard pressed disks. Recordable CD blanks have a layer of dye that can be spot heated by a laser beam to create the 'pits' (technically, they create small mounds, but because the end result is identical to a pit, the terminology remains the same). The blank disks, known as *'gold disks'*, are supplied with a

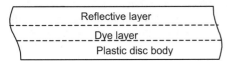

'pre-groove' moulded on its surface, into which these pits are burned. The groove provides tracking information for the drive's head servo and provides a cheap way to ensure quality tracking. The individual blank disk is more expensive than a pressed disk but there is no expensive master to create. CD-R disks read normally on any normal CD drive, and CD Writers are also capable of reading normal CDs. The dramatic fall in the price of CD writers has led to their widespread use as a backup device. Current models can record at up to eight-speed, although depending on the manufacturing quality of the blank disks it might be advisable to use slower speeds than the drive is capable of using.

Preparing to write a CD-ROM

Before the CD-ROM writing software is even loaded up, a CD designer must prepare their material thoroughly. Ordinary CD-R or pressed CDs are not erasable, so any important mistakes will require the whole production process to be restarted.

The process of gathering material for a CD involves a number of activities:

- Deciding on material for the CD.
- Selecting the system on which the material should be available.
- Designing and testing the material.
- Creating an installation method for users.
- Writing, packaging and distributing the disks.

Deciding on material for the CD

Generally, the CD producer will already have at least a basic concept of what the CD should contain. In many cases, by the time it is decided to create a CD, the contents may already be largely or even completely decided. This especially applies to bespoke productions, audio CDs, video CDs or *'shovelware'* CD-ROMs.

However, that is not always the case. A producer who believes there is a niche in the market for, say, a surgical procedures CD-ROM including video footage of how to perform certain procedures, may have a concept but no material. At the other end of the scale, there may be a large amount of acquired material but no cohesive structure for collecting it onto a CD.

Although many CD and DVD writing software packages include tools for recording and editing audio and video, these tasks are much better done in a dedicated editing package. See the appropriate chapters of this book on how to acquire and edit audio and video for the project. On the other hand, the *format* the audio and video is in can be vitally important, as explained below.

Storage concerns can play a large part in deciding what material to include on a CD. Some literature quotes inflated storage capacities for CD-ROMs such as 765MB. These numbers do not take into account such things as lead-ins, track gaps, the TOC, error correction codes, synchronisation and so on. A more reasonable limit for storage capacity on a data CD is around 630MB, and this should be borne in mind when designing material. There is nothing wrong with supplying material on multiple CDs, but to require a second CD for just a few megabytes of material that didn't fit into the first disk hints at poor project management. For more information on CD storage space, see *'Storage Concerns'* below.

Selecting the system on which the material should be available

There are a number of options for consideration when it comes to selecting system availability of a CD to be produced, unless a plain audio CD is the target. These are technical or marketing considerations, rather than design issues.

Target System

First of all, the target computer system should be selected. If the project involves a lot of machine-specific executable code (for example a computer game, or a complex interactive multimedia CD on a highly technical subject) then it is highly likely that development time and space considerations will limit the project to one type of computer. For example an .EXE program for a PC cannot normally run on a Macintosh or UNIX system.

However, if the disk comprises mainly machine-nonspecific data such as images, sound, and/or video, then a cross-platform CD could be considered. For example, a CD containing scanned historical documents could be written as a CD-ROM full of TIFF images. In this case, a directory could be included for DOS, Windows, Mac and UNIX, each containing programs able to view, catalogue and export such images on that system.

However, PCs are not the only systems that use CDs. Audio disks are generally compatible with all CD players. CD-I disks run on some computer systems, but otherwise require special CD-I players. Photo-CD disks are also readable by computer systems with appropriate software, but are also useable by consumers without computers at all, via computer-equipped photographic developers.

Furthermore, the Video CD (VCD) and Super Video CD (SVCD) standards will be compatible with any modern PC, Mac, or UNIX box, as well as running on the majority of home DVD players.

As for DVD itself, there are still a few legacy systems in use that are not equipped to read DVD disks, but it is unlikely that any multimedia project will be targeting users with obsolescent equipment. However, DVD-Rs are expensive in comparison to CD-R, so it could well be economical to use multiple CD-Rs, especially if the data takes up just two discs.

Also, if DVD is to be used as the project's supplied media, it must be borne in mind that the vast array of standards makes it impossible to guarantee that the media will be compatible with any given DVD drive. Older DVD drives, in particular, do not support all standards and any given drive may not be able to read from some of the cheaper DVD media at all.

Target Specification

However, even once the system is selected, the selection of target specification may not be complete. For CD-ROMs that are designed for computer use, the producer must also decide on a minimum specification of computer to design for. For most other types this is not be a problem; for example Photo-CDs, VCDs and video DVDs have no executable code and any system capable of reading these disks will be able to access the material store on it.

Even basic disks containing little more than, say, a catalog of images, will require some means of accessing that data, however. Expecting the end user to already own software capable of dealing with the files is bad practice and could limit the product's appeal. Even the most basic of file viewers has some form of minimum specification, although most have a minimum specification so low that no modern PC would fail it. The specification should set a 'target' for hardware as a minimum, including such things as display capabilities, system memory, CD-ROM speed, audio capabilities and any hard disk storage requirements if the CD installs to disk.

CD Standard

The physical and logical standard that the CD is to follow must then be selected. In many cases it is immediately obvious which type of CD to create. For example a CD of Beethoven's symphony is definitely best printed as a Red Book audio disk, unless it is to contain additional video footage or other multimedia information on the life and times of the composer.

In some cases it may not be so obvious which standard to use. For example, a virtual product demonstration that occupies 200MB of a disk has ample room for a standard CD audio score as background music. Alternatively, the music can be stored in the same data track as the program (as compressed MP3 files) to make space for more detailed graphics and video.

If the CD is to contain computer data, then the logical standard that the data is to conform to must be chosen. For maximum cross-platform readability, ISO 9660 is the best option. However, if the target audience is PC users running Windows, as many projects are, then Joliet provides better functionality while its drawbacks are not a concern in this case. Other standards might also be considered depending on the circumstances.

Designing and testing the material

- The chapter on 'Project Design' goes into detail about the kind of considerations that must be dealt with when designing and testing multimedia material. Similar guidelines apply to creating software for CD-ROM. However, there are additional factors to consider for CD production.
- File formats. CD-ROM, with its large storage capacity, often makes use of large amounts of media files. It is a good idea to decide on a common file format wherever possible. Supplying a catalog of images with various images in GIF, TIFF, JPEG and PCX format is not terribly impressive. Additionally, some CD types require specific file formats – for example SVCD and DVD both use MPEG-2 video files.
- Hard disk installation. Although it is often quite possible to run multimedia files or even executable code directly from CD-ROM, many manufacturers implement a hard disk installation routine (See 'Creating an installation method for users', below). Some users resent having to give up hard disk space to something that is already stored elsewhere, so careful thought should be given to just how much of the project should be installed on the local hard drive, and how much remains on the CD.
- Data Rates. It is a temptation to go for high-quality video in multimedia projects due to the capacities offered by CD-ROM. This is not a problem if the target specification is high enough, but if the target CD drive is slow then this limits the use of video, or indeed any files that require fast throughput. An option is to cache the video files to hard disk, but this can be messy and/or use up a lot of hard disk space unnecessarily.
- Updates. CD-ROM is a static media – ROM means 'Read Only Memory' and as such ordinary CD-ROMs cannot be changed at a later date, though they may be replaced. Replacing CD-ROMs may or may not be an expensive option, but it is likely that much of that update is duplicated material, and the logistics of the whole operation can sometimes be infuriating. Another option is to include a utility on the CD that will access a web site on the Internet to download updates to the local hard drive.

Creating an installation method for users

CD-ROMs that run fully from the disk without installation are the exception rather than the rule. Nearly all products provide some kind of installation feature. This is to facilitate future updates, as well as providing writeable configuration files on the hard disk.

The IMA (Interactive Multimedia Association) has produced a set of standards concerning installation procedures, known as the IMA Recommended Practices for Developers. It is a good idea to follow these guidelines, to provide a more recognisable installation method for users. It recommends the following:

- Perform system checks to ensure that the target system is capable of running the software <u>before</u> beginning the installation. This means checking that there is sufficient hard disk space for the installation, as well as checking that the system is capable of running the project adequately.

- Installation paths and drives should be able to be customised. In particular, the user should be able to specify the CD-ROM drive letter for cases where it differs from that expected by the software.

- When writing files to the hard disk, existing files should not be over-written without the permission of the user. If possible the option should be offered of backing up existing files. For safer installation, IMA recommends installing as many files as possible in an entirely new folder. Again, the user should be able to change the path of this folder, and it should not be created without the user's knowledge and consent. This is a particular problem with Windows DLLs (Dynamic Link Library files, which contain snippets of reusable program code). Microsoft recommends that DLLs are written to the C:\WINDOWS\SYSTEM directory, but this can cause serious problems if one package's DLL overwrites another package's DLL, and the new DLL does not perform the same functions as the previous version. The IMA recommendation would have DLL's in an entirely separate folder, which is non-standard but safer.

- Avoid making changes to the target system where possible. If the software absolutely must make changes, then display a dialog box explaining the changes and asking the user for approval before committing those changes. Any changes might require the installer to reboot, or at the very least ask the user to manually reboot, in order for the changes to take effect. All such changes made should be tracked and stored in a file in case of later uninstallation.

- An uninstall procedure should also be supplied that is capable of removing all files created by the application, and removing any modifications made to system files by the installation. However, any files that might be shared with other applications (such as DLL files) should not be deleted until and unless the user has agreed to do so. In Windows machines, this criterion is fulfilled by complying with the *'Add/Remove Programs'* utility found in Control Panel. When uninstalling, any changes made to system files should be undone.

Additional features that are desirable in an installer include:

- A splash screen, to display the company or software logo.
- The ability to abort the installation at any point.
- Options for a minimum installation, full installation, or custom installation. This will vary the amount of files copied to the hard disk, but also might affect functionality and/or speed.
- Looking for existing versions of the software, and offering to update them, over-write them, or back them up before continuing.
- Checking that the user has a valid license, for example by asking for a serial number and checking its validity.
- Licensing requirements. Many packages now include a licensing screen as part of the installation procedure, thus theoretically ensuring that the user has read and understood the terms of the license.
- Tutorials and help. If the install procedure takes a long time, it is common to display minor hints and tips during the install procedure. Also, the last thing many installers do is to load up a document explaining the basics of the program, any changes from the previous version, troubleshooting information and so on.
- Supplementary software and files. Some products might include, for example, PDF documentation, which will require the installation of Adobe Acrobat Reader to display the files. Another example might require new fonts to be installed, which the package will use when it runs.
- Compression. While CDs can hold a large amount of data, developers tend to squeeze as much performance out of their product as possible. Compression of data allows in some cases over 1GB of data on a single disk. The installer has to be able to uncompress files directly to hard disk in this case.

While it is possible to write an in-house installation tool for all products, or even a separate tool for each product, this takes time and provides an interface to the user that he or she is likely to be unfamiliar with. To help provide a more intuitive, familiar interface, several installer packages are available commercially. For Windows, the most common installation product is the *'Installshield'* program.

Using Installshield

This package provides all of the above functions, and provides a common interface that users will be able to instantly recognise. There is now a version of Installshield designed specifically for the enhanced installation tracking used by Windows 2000, although the more conventional Windows 95/98 installation routines can still be used.

Installshield includes a wizard to aid in the creation of installation routines, but creating a proper installation routine can still be a difficult task for large, complex programs, and even simpler routines can appear daunting to the uninitiated.

At its heart, Installshield uses a script, usually named SETUP.RUL, which appears very similar to a source code file for the C++ programming language. Despite this, it is entirely possible to create reliable setup routines for small software packages without even touching this code (which can be difficult to understand to those who have never done programming).

The install script is basically a set of rules governing how the finished SETUP.EXE program supplied with the finished CD product will go about the installation procedure. It performs a number of functions, such as telling the finished installer which screens are displayed in what order, which files are part of the installation types, and how to deal with user interaction and even error checking. The SETUP.RUL file can be very complex, and its precise structure is beyond the scope of this book.

However, the wizard can be used to create a basic script file from scratch, after asking the user a number of questions about the desired

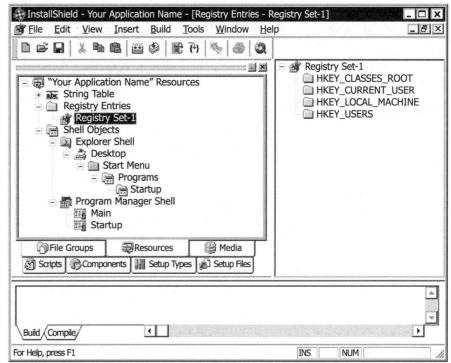

setup routine. This way, the user can manage the setup files and resources with a minimum of programming knowledge.

In addition to the script file, there is one or more *'setup types'*. This allows, for example, the commonly provided option in install procedures whereby the user is given a choice of Minimum, Typical, or Custom installations. At this point, each setup type should be associated with one or more *'components'*, describing which features should be installed as part of each installation type.

For example, the *'Minimum'* installation could install only the *'Program Files'* component and the *'Shared DLLs'* component, while the *'Full'* installation will also install the *'Sample files'* and *'Help files'* components. It is possible to specify that a certain component can only be installed if another component is also installed. For example, the user may specify that the email component should only be allowed if the communications component is also selected.

Each of these components is further divided into 'File groups'. Each component can specify one or more file groups, and two components may specify any of the same file groups as another component. However, the file groups in a component should be chosen to accurately describe what that type of install includes. For example the *'Program Files'* component could include the *'Program DLLs'* file group and the *'Program Executable files'* file group.

The file groups themselves contain *'links'*, which basically specify which individual files fall into that file group. Again, each file group is allowed to specify files that overlap with the files in any other file group.

Besides these, there are a few other files associated with each installation routine. These include splash screens, (which can be dependent on language just like string tables), licensing information text files which are displayed during the install, and 'README' notes. These should be edited to provide new versions for the individual project, as the standard files provided with the wizard do not project a professional feel to the install procedure

Installshield also deals with *'Resources'*, which is a general heading for anything other than files that are installed on the system by the installation routine being created. In other words, this includes registry entries, links to be added to the start menu, desktop, or program manager shell, and string tables. String tables are collections of short messages that are used by the installation procedure (such as error messages, product keys, and version names), and they are grouped together by language so that multiple language installations can be created.

Once all the resources are gathered in an appropriate manner, the installation media can be generated using the *'Media Build Wizard'*. This allows various installation sets to be created including several forms of floppy disk, web install, and of course CD-ROM.

Creating an Autorun CD

Finally, there is the option of autorunning the disk on target machines. In Windows 95 and later, the operating system includes the ability to detect the insertion of a CD, and run software if it is specified on that CD. This is done through a file called AUTORUN.INF, which is located in the root folder on an individual CD-ROM disk. At its simplest, it consists of a header, and a line to tell the operating system which program or data file to load up. The only other setting that is particularly frequently used is a setting that assigns an icon (located in a file on the CD) to the CD when it appears in Explorer. An example file might look like the one shown in the illustration.

```
[autorun]
OPEN=INSTALL.EXE
ICON=MEDIA.ICO
```

A CD with this AUTORUN.INF file in its root folder will, upon insertion into the CD drive, tell the Windows operating system to run the INSTALL.EXE program, beginning the install procedure automatically. The filename here need not be a program. Autorun can be configured to load up the default HTML browser by specifying a .HTM file instead, for example. The 'ICON' setting lets Windows Explorer know which .ICO file to use when displaying an icon for the CD-ROM drive while it contains that CD. In this case, both the INSTALL.EXE and MEDIA.ICO files are also located in the root folder of the CD-ROM disk.

Storage Concerns

Depending on the recording software, the system may already take into account all recording overheads and simply present the user with a simplified drag-and-drop interface. However, if not, then the user must be aware of several factors affecting storage capacity of CDs.

As stated earlier, CD-ROMs do not use their full capacity for storing user data. A large portion of CD storage space is used in low-level error detection and correction, as well as data modulation. However, these cannot be removed under any circumstances and so they are of no concern to CD producers.

After these, the CD is left with 74 minutes of audio, or nearly 747MB of data as explained under the *'Red Book'* explanation. Red Book is the only standard that can use all 747MB of storage space for user data. All other standards use at least some of that space for synchronisation and additional error correction codes.

The table below shows how the storage space in each sector is divided up under each standard.

2352 bytes total available sector size

Red Book (CD Audio)	2353 bytes uncompressed digital audio data

Yellow Book Mode 1 (CD-ROM)	Sync (12)	Header (4)	2048 bytes user data	EDC (4)	Unused (8)	ECC (276)

Yellow Book Mode 2 (Audio/Video)	Sync (12)	Header (4)	2336 bytes user data

(This mode is only used as a basis for other standards)

CD-XA Form 1, and CD-I Form 1 (Data)	Sync (12)	Header (4)	Sub head (8)	2048 bytes user data	EDC (4)	ECC (276)

CD-XA Form 2, and CD-I Form 2 (Audio/Video)	Sync (12)	Header (4)	Sub head (8)	2324 bytes user data	EDC (4)

CDs are normally manufactured with a maximum of 74 minutes capacity, giving a total of 333,000 sectors. Some manufacturers are capable of producing CDs of up to 81 minutes length by compressing the spiral greater than normally. However, these are not standard CDs and do not follow the Red Book format. As such they are not guaranteed to work on all CD players, and are best avoided where possible.

On the other hand, shorter CDs can be played in any standard CD player – 60 minute CDs are not uncommon, and there is a special *'mini'* CD just over 3 inches wide. These smaller disks can still be played in almost all CD players, because data is recorded from the inner spiral outwards.

From a standard CD with up to 333 thousand sectors, the following <u>theoretical maximum</u> storage capacities can be calculated:

Red Book	333,000 sectors x 2352 bytes = 783,216,000 bytes (approx 747MB)
Yellow Book Mode 1	333,000 sectors x 2048 bytes = 681,984,000 bytes (approx 650MB)
Yellow Book Mode 2	333,000 sectors x 2336 bytes = 777,888,000 bytes (approx 742MB)
XA or CD-I Form 1	333,000 sectors x 2048 bytes = 681,984,000 bytes (approx 650MB)
XA or CD-I Form 2	333,000 sectors x 2324 bytes = 773,892,000 bytes (approx 738MB)

Unfortunately, storage on a CD is not just a simple matter of just writing sectors away to disk. CD has its roots in audio, and so each disk is split up into *'tracks'*. In an audio disk, each track normally does represent one musical piece, and the Volume Table Of Contents lists up to 99 track locations. If a basic computer CD-ROM is produced, without additional music or video tracks, then the entire CD-ROM will comprise a single data track, either in Yellow Book Mode 1 or CD XA Form 1.

Things get more complicated, however, when other types of disks are produced. Generally, all data within a track must be of the same mode. However, a CD-XA or CD-I track will allow each sector to be either Form 1 or Form 2, so that data of both types can be interleaved to improve synchronisation. That means that, for example, a CD-XA video and data track could have 25 sectors of computer data and 25 sectors of video data, then back to computer data and so on. The storage capacity can only be calculated then by understanding just how many sectors will be Form 1 and how many will be Form 2.

Then there is the case of multiple tracks. Red Book CDs containing nothing but audio, and written in a single session, are the only type that can have tracks back to back. Every other type of CD must have a gap between each track. That gap is 2 seconds before audio tracks, and 3 seconds before every other type of track. Three seconds is 225 sectors, or 450KB in Yellow Book Mode 1, which is no longer available for recording data.

Finally, there is the consideration of multiple sessions. CDs written in a single session have an area called a 'lead-in' before the tracks, and a 'lead-out' area after the tracks in that session. If the CD is recorded in more than one session (see 'Tracks and sessions' below) then each individual session must have its own lead-in and lead-out.

Each lead-in area occupies 4500 sectors, while the lead-out area occupies 6750 sectors for the first session and 2250 for each subsequent session. These overheads can seriously eat into the storage capacity of a CD, so for any distributable CD it may be wise to have as few sessions as possible.

For example, an often-used CD format is to have a single Red Book session of audio, followed by a second session of CD-ROM data. This format allows most computers to access the data, while normal audio units will only recognise the audio session. The audio in the Red Book session can be written back to back, and if it takes up say 45 minutes, then that corresponds to 202,500 sectors. Add to this the 4500 sector lead-in and the 6750 sector lead-out. The Red Book session would therefore consume 213,750 sectors, leaving 119,250 sectors for the second session. With the lead-in of 4500 sectors and lead-out of 2250 sectors, the data session has a maximum useable data area of 112,500 sectors, or approximately 219MB.

For computer data, the storage considerations do not end there, unfortunately. While audio or video data can be stored 'as-is', computer data requires a logical format in order to access the data. This might be an ISO 9660 format, Joliet, or some similar standard. In all cases, the logical standard requires some data on folders, filenames, and so on. ISO 9660 also stores a path table, and a root folder record. Furthermore, each folder will require disk space, and there is additional wastage when storage of a file leaves the last sector less than fully utilised. It is impossible to give hard and fast figures on the amount of space this will consume, but CD images should always be created with these additional overheads very much in mind, in order to avoid last minute trimming of files.

CDs written using packets in UDF have the added burden of a table that has to keep track of all packets and the files they belong to. This means a UDF packet written CD-R is reduced to around 600MB of space. CD-RWs written using UDF also use 'sparing' techniques to prevent over-using areas of the disk, which further reduces available space to about 500MB.

CD and DVD manufacture

Once the content of the disc is finalised, it has to be shipped out to the consumers of the product. This involves producing copies of the disc, packaging them, and finally distributing them. While small production runs might make it feasible to record each disc using CD-R, this is not effective if large quantities of discs are to be produced. Larger numbers should either be created using a special duplication machine, or be stamped using the process explained previously.

To complicate matters, there are numerous copy protection schemes in use on CDs as well, such as SecuRom and SafeDisk, and DVD uses a protection scheme called CSS. Many CD protection methods use hardware 'hacks' to provide their protection – in other words, the discs are altered from the standard CD format. In many cases this makes them impossible to create in a standard CDR, and even some duplicating machines are not able to replicate these discs. For this reason, many PC software providers use an algorithm to create serial numbers as a response to piracy, a method which is usually slightly less effective but is generally cheaper to implement.

A duplicator is essentially a simple PC with up to eight CD-R or DVD-R drives attached, making the production of discs much faster. At the low end, there are still some types of disks that cannot be replicated, mainly those discs that use copy protection. However, the top end of duplicating machines (at over twenty thousand pounds) use high-speed data streaming that dramatically improve throughput even further, as well as allowing for specialised recording techniques that facilitate CD protection schemes.

Since stamping is done from a specially cut master disc, a simple CD-R burned in the normal fashion is not sufficient for this type of duplication. However, most CD production companies are happy to take a CD-R and copy the data there directly onto the glass master. This method makes the replication process a relatively simple one of locating a reputable mastering and stamping company. However, be careful to ensure that the CD-R master is finalised – it is unprofessional, and could cause problems, if open multi-session discs are sent to be turned into masters.

If the mastering and stamping is to be done in-house, then specialised, and expensive, equipment will be required, not to mention the need for specially trained duplication engineers. Creating a professional stamping is not to be undertaken lightly. Even third-party stamped CD runs are expensive, and recommended only for high volume runs.

With DVDs, the mastering process is a little more complex, since DVD-Rs can only run to 4.7GB while stamped DVDs can contain over 9GB. Furthermore, commercial DVDs use the CSS encryption scheme for copy protection.

This is commonly resolved by having one or two DVDs of authoring material, which are created using a specialised DVD-Authoring drive, which is considerably more expensive than a DVD-R drive, and uses a 635nm laser instead of the 650nm laser found in a General Use (GU) DVD-R drive.

CD and DVD Packaging

This consists of the CD artwork, the case, and the case artwork. These come in various forms:

- Silkscreen CD artwork. This is the professional method, and is typically provided by the same company that creates the glass master and stamps the discs. It is rare for companies to provide silkscreen printing without stamping.
- Adhesive CD artwork. Be careful if 'sticky' artwork is to be applied to the CD-R or DVD-R. Not only is it possible that a logo on the media might be visible through the sticker; there are also some low-quality stickers that use adhesive which can slowly degrade the CD or DVD.
- Printed CD artwork. Some CD burners are now able to 'burn' an image straight onto the CD media. Currently, this is only available in a two-tone form, but is safe from causing damage to the CD's contents and involves no third party costs.
- Jewel case. The most common packaging for commercial CDs is a plastic case often referred to as a 'jewel case'. They are available in single-disc and multiple-disc forms.
- Slimline case. A somewhat cheaper, and more space-efficient, alternative to the jewel case is the slimline, which is similar but thinner. It is not often used for commercial products but is common for home-made CD-Rs.
- Wallets. Simple paper wallets and card wallets are some of the cheapest forms of packaging and some applications are sold in this type of package to cut costs. Plastic wallets are rarely used however in commercial products, being seen as tacky.
- Digipak. This form of packaging is most common on 'limited edition' music CDs, and is a folding card and plastic container with a sleeve for inserts, sometimes seen in multiple-disc forms.
- Amaray case. This is the most widely used form of packaging for DVDs. Being larger than a jewel case, and opaque, it is also available in single-disc and multiple-disc forms. Many similar types of case are sometimes called 'Amaray' cases even though they may be from a different manufacturer.
- Prestige cases. A wide range of other types of cases are available, from tin boxes and plastic snap cases to wooden craft boxes and exotic packaging. Obviously, these are the most expensive but are also the most impressive.

The case artwork is usually simply a printed paper insert of the correct size for the case. However, Digipaks, card wallets, and most prestige cases have their artwork printed directly onto the case, and this must be discussed with the packaging supplier.

Finally, many products that are provided on CD come in a larger cardboard box along with the manual and any other equipment that comes with the product. In some cases this is done simply to make the product more noticeable on shop shelves.

CD recording technology

As mentioned previously, a CD has one or more sessions, with each session being further divided into tracks. Each session's lead-in contains the TOC for that session, listing up to 99 tracks in the session. If the recording has not been finalised then the TOC also contains the location where the next session recording can begin.

Each track can be of any mode. For example *'mixed mode'* CDs often have CD-ROM computer data in track 1 and up to 98 audio tracks following it. A Video CD might have up to 99 different MPEG clips, each in a separate track. For CD-ROM however, there is almost never more than one CD-ROM track per session.

Disk Images

Generally, CD creation software allows for the user to make *'CD images'*. This makes use of one large, and preferably contiguous, file located on a hard disk. The file is used as an exact replica of the data that is to be written to the CD. Since the reading of the file can be done easily and quickly in serial, this makes for good data throughput. Also, a disk image is useful when recording an entire disk in one go. (see *'disc-at-once recording'*, below)

Alternatively, most packages also provide for *'virtual images'*. Like a normal CD image, the virtual image is used to provide data for writing to CD. However, virtual

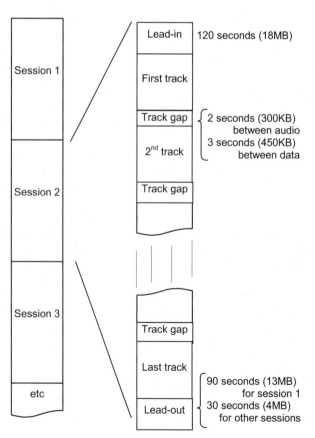

images do not store an exact replica of the data to put on CD. Instead, they store a database of filenames and information on them such as their size, and where to put them on the CD. The software must then look through this database when writing CDs, and load the files into memory before sending them to the recording device. This method is sometimes called *'on-the-fly'* CD writing.

Virtual images have one major benefit, which is their convenience. This method does not require the slow and disk-hungry creation of a full CD image. However, care must be taken to ensure that the data is available on time to be written to CD. (See *'Preparing a system for writing'*, below)

A disk image is described as a *'raw'* file, because it stores the raw data that is to be placed on the CD. Audio tracks that contain basic 16-bit stereo PCM wave samples are also raw files, because they contain the exact data that can constitute a single audio track on a CD.

Disc-at-once and track-at-once recording

Both of these methods of CD creation use only a single session. Disc-at-once recording involves writing the entire CD from start to finish in one go, while track-at-once recording involves writing individual tracks separately, generally with a pause in between to assemble the next track. Some CD recorders do not support disc-at-once, while some others do not support track-at-once recording.

Using Disc-at-once recording means that the entire CD has to be assembled before writing, so that the Table Of Contents can be written at the start of the disk, and also so that the recording process is not interrupted. However, Disc-at-once allows the gap between tracks to be of any length, including zero. It also allows access to the 'P' and 'Q' subchannels. Disc-at-once recorded CDs may be used as masters to create batches of pressed CDs, but require careful planning to ensure that a buffer underrun does not ruin the disk during recording.

Track-at-once recording, on the other hand, creates the TOC after all the tracks have been written, meaning that it has to go back to write the lead-in after all the tracks have been created. Furthermore, because the system is paused between writing tracks, a track gap is required, as explained earlier. This gap is of two or three seconds depending on the type of track, or equivalent to 300 to 450KB of CD-ROM data. The gap creates an audible clicking sound when played on audio CD players, and as such is unsuitable to be used as a master to press CDs. However, under some circumstances a track-at-once recorder can partially recover from buffer underrun errors and write the rest of the tracks successfully. It can then leave the affected track(s) out of the TOC when it writes the lead-in.

Track-at-once allows other processing to be carried out between tracks, for example reading in another track from a source CD to copy into the new CD.

When creating a Yellow Book CD-ROM or CD-XA without audio, there is essentially no difference between disc-at-once and track-at-once recording. Barring the track gaps, which are an almost insignificant 300KB out of 650MB, the CD-ROM will appear identical to the end user when recorded in either method.

Multi-session recording

There are various circumstances where it is not desirable or not possible to write an entire CD is one go. Multi-session recording was introduced in the Orange Book, and allows users to write data to CD in one session, and come back to add more sessions at a later date. In order to use multi-session recording, every session must be recorded in multisession mode, even the first session.

Care should be taken when considering multisession recording. Audio CD players can only read the first session, and some older CD drives do not support reading of multi-session disks. There is also more than one implementation of multisession recording, and so there may be compatibility issues with disks recorded as multisession disks. Finally, reading of multi-session disks is even more problematic if the disk is still open for new sessions to be added. Until the last session is added, there is no TOC and only drivers that are written to handle open multisession disks can read them.

On the other hand, multiple sessions are instrumental in certain other situations. Kodak's Photo-CD system relies heavily on multisessions, for example. Since one set of photographs will not take up the full space on the CD, the CD session is written in multisession mode and left open. That way, when the user wishes to add new photos, the developer simply continues to append new sessions until the CD no longer has room, at which point the disk can be finalised.

Another standard which requires multisession mode is CD Extra, which relies on the added session to prevent accidental playing of computer data on CD players.

CD-ROM data can also be written in multiple sessions. For example, if company finance spreadsheets are to be archived at the end of each month, a new session could be created every time the archiving is to take place. This works by having the directory structure in the most recently written session point to both new files, and files in previous sessions. Drives which can read multisession disks will use the most up-to-date volume data. In this way, data can actually be 'deleted' from a CD-ROM – the file is not removed from the disk but the most up-to-date volume descriptor contains no reference to the file and so it does not show up for users to access.

Once the last session has been written, the disk must be *'fixed'* (also called *'fixating'* or *'closing'* the disk). Fixation of a disk involves writing a lead-in, including a Table of Contents, so that normal CD drives may access it. Another benefit of multisessions is that an individual session can be written in Disc-At-Once mode, with the benefits that this entails (See below).

Alternatives to multisession recording have been created to reduce the space overheads taken up by session lead-ins and lead-outs. These include recording data track-by-track (i.e. track-at-once), or sector-by sector (also called 'incremental packet writing').

Incremental Packet Writing

This is a useful alternative to multisession disks. Data is written to the CD in 'packets'. Depending on the implementation, these packets might be one or more sectors long. At best, then, the minimum size of data that can be written to CD-R at one time is 2048 bytes. This is significantly smaller than the multi-megabyte overheads required by each session of a multi-session CD.

Incremental Packet Writing is normally used with UDF (see above), and so can provide convenient drive-letter access to the device, but needs to be 'closed' before it can work in a normal CD-ROM system. Like multisession disks, files can be 'deleted' from CD-Rs, though no space will be freed in doing so. Packet writing can also prevent buffer underruns, because of the much smaller amount of data that the software needs to access in order to write to the CD.

Bootable CDs

For specialised purposes, a CD-ROM can be made 'bootable'. That is, a computer whose BIOS allows it to boot up from CD-ROM instead of hard disk or floppy, can boot up, loading its operating system entirely from such a CD. Of course, the target machine's BIOS must support booting from CD-Drives for this to be useful. Some versions of Windows CDs are bootable, allowing that operating system to be installed with less fuss. However, in order to maximise the target audience, producers should take into consideration the option of supplying a boot floppy for users whose machine does not support this capability.

The standard which defines the operation of bootable CDs is, like the High Sierra standard, named after the place where it was drafted - the El Torito Grill. The 'El Torito' standard is supported by nearly all modern BIOS systems.

When creating a bootable CD, it should be borne in mind that the media on which the program resides is read-only. For example, the Windows 95 operating system needs to read and write to and from the media that it is boots from, and so it is unsuitable for a bootable CD. In general, virtually the only use to date for bootable CDs is in the installation of operating systems.

An El Torito CD-ROM contains a standard ISO9660 area, but also a separate boot image. The boot image is a direct copy of the system files from an existing bootable media, which can be a floppy or hard disk. A bit image is made of these system files, which is then written to the CD-ROM.

Recording a CD

Once the material for a CD is available, and has been appropriately tested, preparations can be made to begin recording. For an existing setup that is already known to work sufficiently, there may be little or no preparation involved. However, every system has to be set up the first time, and CD writing requires fast access in order to make sure the writer is kept supplied with data to place on the CD as it spins by.

Preparing a system for writing

Many of the same factors are involved in ensuring steady data rates for CD recording, as with video capturing.

Most users select a list of files for recording to a CD-R. This list is stored in a database that is set up by the writing software. When the program is instructed to write the CD, the database is examined for each file in turn, a copy of the file is fetched from the hard disk and the data is sent to the CD writer. This database is known as the "virtual image" and the technique is known as "on the fly" recording.

The recording hardware maintains a 'buffer' area of memory, which is used to load data from disk and store it until it is needed by the recorder. If there were no buffer, or if the buffer is empty when data is required (known as an 'underrun'), then the recorder will want to write data when there is none there. During this period the CD will still be spinning and the laser is still turned on, and so an area on the finished CD will not be storing readable data. This will, under normal circumstances, ruin an entire CD.

If the user is only saving a few very large files (e.g. video files), the flow of data is fairly smooth after the file has been located. However, if a large number of small files are being recorded on the CD, a great deal of time is spent simply consulting the database and accessing the file on the hard disk. This is all time when no data is being sent to the writer and substantially lowers the overall data rate between the hard disk and the writer.

The data rate required by the recording hardware varies depending on its recording speed, and the amount of data per sector (sector size). A single speed drive needs to write 75 sectors per second, which equates to 150KB of computer data per second, or 172KB of audio data, for example. Thus, due to the larger sector size, audio and video CD writing requires even higher data rates than CD-ROM writing. Writing at double speed or higher will increase the required data rate even more.

Most CD-R drives have between 512KB and 2MB of buffer space. If this is filled up before the recording begins, then it gives some capability to recover from periods of interruption. This 'interruption time' is based on the buffer size and writer speed. For example if a 1MB buffer is full, and the CD-R drive is writing a CD-ROM at double speed when an interruption occurs, it can continue to write for just over three seconds before an underrun occurs. (1024KB buffer / 300KB required data rate = 3.41 seconds).

BURNproof writers were introduced by Sanyo to reduce the number of ruined CD-R disks. These are *"Buffer Underrun Proof"* systems which means that the amount of data in the buffer is monitored. If the level drops too low, the laser beam is switched off and there is no further writing to the CD-R. Once the buffer is refreshed, the writing process starts up again , with only a tiny loss (a few milliseconds).

The components that are relied upon to keep things going smoothly include the hard disk, the processor, the writer itself and the recording software. Some of these are covered in more detail in the *'Digital Video'* chapter.

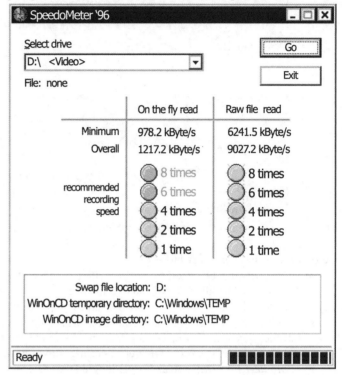

Hard disk speed. The software needs fast access to the disk image, to pass the data on to the drive. For slower requirements, a UDMA IDE hard disk will suffice but for higher data rates a SCSI-2 or SCSI-UW might be required and an AV classification disk would be preferable.

Many CD recording packages include a hard disk speed tester, which will check that the system's hard disks are suitable. The illustration shows the *'SpeedoMeter'* software supplied with WinOnCD. It can be used on any hard drive, and indicates suitable CD recording speeds using either a raw or virtual (on-the-fly) image on that disk.

Furthermore, defragmenting the hard disk before writing CDs may improve its performance.

Processor availability. While the speed of the processor is rarely an issue except in older PCs, the recording software must have the processor's full attention. It is the processor that must supply the recorder with data, and if it is busy servicing another application it cannot do this. To this end, all other packages should be shut down, including any software in the system tray that could affect performance. Examples are virus checking, screen savers, alarms and reminders, and network sharing.

The CD Recording hardware and software. Modern CD-R units are capable of writing CDs at eight-speed or even faster. However, less modern units will not record so fast. In either case, the CD producer has to make sure that the recording speed set in the recording software matches the speed the drive is capable of handling.

Testing recording speed
Before writing CDs, most recording software has a facility whereby the writing of CDs can be simulated. Data is passed to the CD-R drive as if a CD is to be created, and the CD spins in exactly the manner it would if creating the CD. However, the laser is not fully powered and so no data is actually written to the CD. At slower speeds, this is a lengthy process, but it is well worth checking if more than one CD is to be created.

If the system is not capable of recording at anything but the slowest recording speeds, the solutions lie in:
- Upgrade the hard disk system, if that is the bottleneck.
- Upgrade to a newer, faster CD writer, if that is the bottleneck.

Where affordable, they are the answer for those who intend to create many CD-R projects.

For those on a more modest budget, the solutions lie in:
- Selecting a slower writing speed.
- Using a full CD image rather than a virtual image. The files for the final compilation are selected and the software creates a giant ISO image combining all the files into a single block. This means that when the CD is written, there is only a single file to be located and the data can be smoothly read from that file.

Using Nero burning software
There is a variety of CD Recording software available, but the basic functions are generally very similar. These examples show how to create a CD using Nero Burning Software.

Apart from the main application, Nero provides utilities for testing the computer's performance and for designing the artwork for CD covers.

When the Nero authoring/burning application is opened, it displays a wizard that provides simple steps to getting a recording project completed. However, it provides no detailed control over the process and experienced users will by-pass the wizard to see the following window displayed.

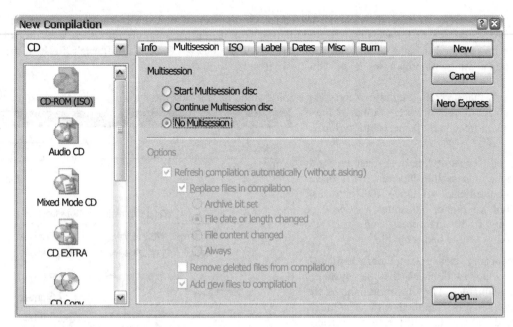

The type of project is selected from the list on the left, which includes other options such as creating an SVCD and a bootable CD.

Nero provides these main options:

- *"CD-ROM ISO"* creates a project with a single CD-XA Form 1 track. This track can form either a single session CD, or the first session of a multisession CD. As its names suggests, this option creates a CD-ROM track in the Joliet format, with backwards compatibility for ISO 9660 only systems.

- *"CD-Copy"*, as should be obvious, performs a direct copy of a CD or a drive image held on the hard drive. If the user has a CD or DVD player in addition to the CD writer, the program copies directly from the CD reader to the CD writer. Of course, normal copyright laws apply.

- *"Audio-CD"* creates an audio CD in Red Book format.

- *"CD EXTRA"* creates a Blue Book CD made up of one or more Red Book audio tracks, and a CD-XA Form 1 track in Joliet format.

- *"Video-CD"* projects consist of a CD-I portion not normally visible to PCs, a Joliet-based CD-XA Form 1 track containing the Video CD runtime files, and one or more CD-XA Form 2 tracks for the video data.

Once a project type has been selected, the main screen displays the opens for that format.

Recording a CD-ROM

In the example, a CD-ROM ISO project has been chosen and the user controls the recording parameters via seven tabs. So, clicking the *"Multisession"* tab displays options to create a new multisession CD, add to an existing multisession CD or create a CD and immediately close the disk making it single session. Depending on the amount of data written to the disk, the user may wish to keep the disk open in order to make use of the remaining space at a later date. However, open disks may not be read by many normal CD-ROM drives.

The other tabs allow the user to add information such as the CD volume's label, the name of the author, the date it was published, etc.

When the user has completed the selection of parameters for the project, clicking the *"New"* button displays the main authoring environment for that project. The options for that project type chosen can be returned to at any time before burning, by choosing *"Compilation Info"* from the *"File"* menu.

The main screen displays four panels.

The third panel displays all the folders on the user's hard drives, while the fourth panels displays all the files in any highlighted folder. This allows the user to find and select the files to be used on the new CD.

The first and second panels display the files and folders that will be written to the new CD. This is known as the *"compilation window"* and will initially be blank except for a volume label in the first panel.

At its simplest, the required files can be selected from the fourth panel and dropped into the second panel and the software is ready to burn the CD-R.

The example shows that, if required, a structure of folders can be created for the project. These folders are created in exactly the same way that they are within Windows Explorer. The user highlights the volume label in the first panel (*"PROJ0902"* in the illustration) and right click the mouse. The *"Create Folder"* option is chosen from the drop-down menu and the user enters a name for the new folder. Files can then be dropped into any folder as well as the root level.

In addition, an entire folder and its contents can be dragged and dropped into the compilation window.

As files are added to the compilation window, a bar at the bottom of the application displays how much space the selected files will occupy on the new disk. A dotted vertical marker bar indicates the maximum amount that can be stored on the CD. The software keeps track of the amount of all data put into the project, so the user need only glance at this bar to see how much space is left in their CD project.

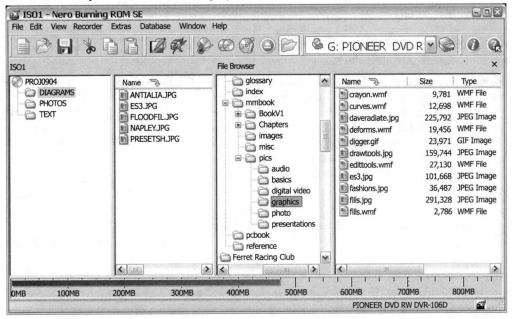

A file can be removed from the compilation window by right-clicking on it and choosing the *"Delete"* option from the drop-down menu.

Once all the files for the CD-ROM are in the project, the CD-R disk can be recorded. Choosing *"Write CD"* from the *"File"* menu brings back the seven tab window shown earlier.

If the CD writer or the hard drive is being used for the first time, it is best to uncheck the *"Write"* and *"Finalise"* boxes and check the *"Simulate"* and *"Determine maximum speed"* boxes. Clicking the *"Simulate"* button simulates writing to the CD. This checks whether the hard disk system and interface can supply the CD writer with a sufficiently constant supply of data to maintain a continuous write without any loss of data. There is no actual writing to the CD during this test. If the test is passed, the user can write the CD. Otherwise, the writer's writing speed can be lowered and the test can be re-run.

When the user is satisfied that the hardware is up to the writing task, the *"Write"* and *"Finalise"* boxes can be the boxes that are checked. In this case, clicking the *"Write"* button starts the writing process.

A window appears, containing a progress bar and a *'Used read buffer'* status bar. The buffer goes from empty up to full as the CDR's buffer is filled, and then the writing begins. The progress bar shows how much of the complete CD has been written.

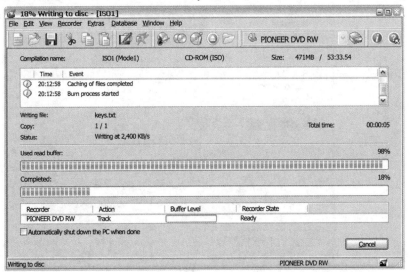

When all the files have been written to the disk, the software writes the disk's the lead-in and lead-out. As this occurs, the last remaining data is drawn from the buffer and the bar in the buffer window will reduce until the bar is empty.

CD Writing in XP

Windows XP has its own built-in CD-writing capability. The steps for writing data to a CD-R are:

- Go to a folder and select the file(s) to be written to the CD-R
- Select '*File & Folder Tasks*' from the left-hand panel.
- Select the '*Copy the selected items*' option.
- In the dialog box that opens, choose the CD-writer from the drives displayed.
- Click the '*Copy*' button. This adds the files to a temporary copy store.

- Repeat the above steps until all the files are selected.
- Click on the CD-writer in the drives list. This will display all the files that will be written.
- Select 'CD Writing Tasks' from the left-hand panel.
- Select the 'Write files to CD' option. This opens the CD writing wizard.

Recording an audio CD

Choosing "Audio-CD" from the "New Compilation" window allows the user to create an audio CD that can be played in a standard domestic audio CD player or hi-fi system. The conversion of the user's audio files into Red Book format are carried out by the software.

When this option is chosen, it displays a main screen with three panels instead of the four panels shown when creating a CD-ROM. The two panels on the right, as before, display the folders and files on the user's hard drives. In this case, there is only one panel on the left. That is because an Audio CD stores all its files in the root folder and there are no-sub folders on an audio CD. The first panel, therefore, displays all the audio tracks that will be written to the CD.

When first opened, the first panel is empty. As before, files are selected from the right-hand panel and dropped into the first panel.   Nero supports the selection of WAV, MP3 and WMA files. All types can be dropped into the compilation window.

Nero provides two extra buttons on the compilation panel.
Highlighting an audio file in the first panel and clicking the "Play" button plays that file.
Highlighting an audio file in the first panel and clicking the "Edit" button opens up a new window that displays Nero's audio editing application. The file can then be edited (cut, paste, delete, crop, etc.) and can have effects added to it (chorus, reverberation, etc.).

A further range of processing can be carried out on any file in the compilation window by right-clicking on it, selecting "Properties" from the drop-down menu and clicking the "Filters" tab on the window that opens up. This displays the options shown in the illustration.

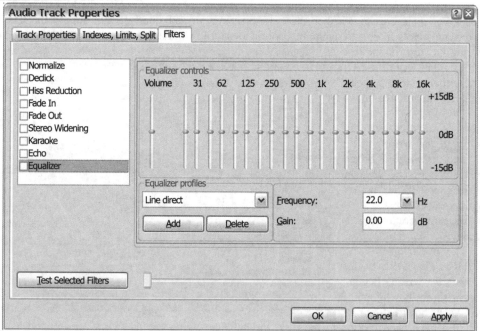

Any changes made only alter the contents of the file that is selected.
The main tools offered are:

- The "Equalizer" tool will be familiar to most users, as will the concept of fading in or fading out on an audio track.
- The "DeClick" option removes transient noise from audio tracks that were taken from old vinyl disks (LPs, EPs and singles).
- The "Hiss Reduction" option is useful where the audio file was taken from an old cassette tape recording that has deteriorated with time.
- The "Karaoke" option attempts to remove the vocal content of a track by eliminating any content that has equal volume in both stereo channels. This is meant to leave behind only the instrumental content.

There is a noticeable difference between disc-at-once and track-at-once CD writing. Track-at-once usually inserts a two-second gap between tracks, and only disc-at-once CDs can contain track limit marks.

Track limit marks are used to split one audio track into several audio tracks. This is useful when a single recording has been made, instead of each track being recorded separately. For example, a live recording of a concert would require track limit marks to indicate where each song ends and a new song begins. Nero can load in a single waveform and use track limit marks to separate tracks, but it still sees them as a single continuous waveform.

File splitting can be carried out on any file in the compilation window by right-clicking on it, selecting *"Properties"* from the drop-down menu and clicking the *"Indexes, Limits, Split"*.

When finished, the user clicks the *"Write CD"* option from the *"File"* menu and then clicks the *"Write"* button.

Using CD images

Nero allows the collection of files assembled for writing to be saved to the hard disk as an image file. This means that all the system files, menus and user files are all saved as one large file. This offers two benefits:

- It allows computers with slow drives to burn CDs (as explained earlier).
- The image file can be backed up for later re-use, or it can be e-mailed to another location for immediate burning.

The steps for creating an image file are:

- Drop all the required files into the compilation window.
- Select *"CD Recorder"* from the main menu.
- Select *"Choose Recorder"* from the drop-down menu.
- Select *"Image Recorder"* as the device and click the *"OK"* button.
- Select *"Write CD"* from the *"File"* menu.
- Click the "Burn" button and, when prompted, enter a filename for the image.

This creates an image file with an NRG extension (e.g. HOLIDAYS.NRG). However, when burning an image file, Nero is able to use one of several image formats, including .ISO and .CUE/.BIN files. While .ISO files are a simple image of the ISO data, the .CUE file is a text file containing data on the exact format of the raw image data held in a .BIN file. In this way the .BIN file can contain the entire sector data, rather than just the 2048 bytes of user data in an ISO disc.

The steps for burning from an image file are as follows:

- Select *"Choose Recorder"* from the drop-down menu.
- Select *your CD writer* as the device and click the *"OK"* button.
- Select *"Burn Image"* from the *"File"* menu.
- Browse and find the image file.
- Highlight it and click the *"Open"* button.
- Click the *"Burn"* button to start writing the CD.

Recording a video CD

At its simplest, video files can be stored on a CD as a set of files and each file can be double-clicked in Windows Explorer to view it. There are a number of ways of storing video on disk so that the video files can be automatically played, or chosen from an on-screen menu. These range from low-resolution formats intended for CD use to high-quality formats on DVD.

Bit Rates

The amount of detail in video sequences varies dramatically. Similarly, the amount of motion in various sequences varies greatly, with some sequences being almost static while other have fast-moving action.

Most software allows the user to control the bitrate during compression. This is the amount of data that is allocated to any segment a video clip and is usually measured in Kbps – how many kilobits of data are used to store one second of video. There is a trade between file size and file quality. High compression produces a low bitrate, smaller files and lower quality, while high compression results in high bitrates, larger files but better quality.   There are two approaches to compression – the CBR and VBR systems.

CBR

Constant bit rate. Used with MPEG-1 and thus with VCD.   Each sequence of frames in a video is compressed to the exact same degree as any other sequence in the video, regardless of the complexity of individual segments of the clip. This results in a varying quality but a constant data rate (useful for guaranteeing successful data transfer with devices with limited bandwidth).

VBR

Variable bit rate.   Used by SVCD, DivX, DVD and MiniDVD. The user sets the average bitrate required for the sequence but the degree of compression at any one time depends upon the complexity of the scene being handled. This results in a varying data rate but ensures that the quality of the clip is maintained throughout.

Most VBR encoders can also be configured to produce CBR output, but CBR encoders are generally single purpose (i.e. produce CBR output only).

VBR compression can be set to any size of bit rate over a large range. However, most software players are optimised for displaying VBR output at the more common levels (e.g. 1,374Kbps for VCD).

Format comparisons

Each format has benefits and drawbacks and some of the considerations for choosing a format are:
- What will be the distribution medium (a CD limits the amount of quality video that can be stored).
- How much picture detail will be lost during compression for each format.
- How well does each compressor handle fast-moving action scenes and low motion scenes.
- Will the finished product of a particular format overtax the user's playback systems. This is not a factor when the project is designed for kiosk use, but could be a problem for CD distribution to computers with poor specifications)
- Must the finished product be able to run on a standalone player (this rules out using the DivX format, and might also rule out MiniDVD and SVCD).

The table provides an overview of the capabilities and restrictions of each format.

	Media	Video	Resolution	Audio	Audio compression	Normal playing time
VCD (Video CD)	CD	MPEG-1	352x288 (PAL) 352x240 (NTSC)	Stereo	MPEG-1, layer II	74 mins
SVCD (Super Video CD)	CD	MPEG-2	480x576 (PAL) 480x480 (NTSC)	Stereo or 5:1	MPEG-1, layer II or MPEG-2	37 mins
DivX	CD/DVD	MPEG-4	variable	Stereo	MP3 or other	variable
MiniDVD	CD	MPEG-2	720x576	5:1	MPEG-2	17 mins
DVD	DVD	MPEG-2	720x576 (PAL) 720x480 (NTSC)	5:1	MPEG-2	33 to 133 mins

The figures for VCD and SVCD are for the UK/European PAL format – the resolution is different for the American NTSC and other video formats. A fuller explanation of each system follows.

VCD

The Video CD specification was brought out in 1993 by Philips and JVC. It became the *"White Book"* format and the current VCD 2.0 specification included input from Sony, Matsushita, Pioneer, Technics and others. It is particularly popular in China and in Asia.

VCD version 1.1 was designed for linear playing (the video content was displayed from start to finish) with the option of selecting a particular track for display. VCD 2.0 allows further interactivity, with the ability to jump from any one track to any other.

A VCD movie can be played on a computer CD-ROM drive, a computer DVD drive, most standalone DVD players, portable players (those, such as the NAPA player, that play audio CDs, MP3s and VCDs) and a Playstation or Dreamcast with a VCD add-on. Windows plays VCDs using the Windows Media Player.

It is commonly used to store a full-length movie on two CDs.

Most authoring programs can create a playing sequence, such that the video clips are played one after the other in a continual play. The format allows for the handling of up to 98 AV tracks.

The VCD format works with an MPEG-1 file (ISO standard IEC 11172) with a fixed 1,150Kbps bit rate, providing around 74 minutes of video on a CD. The audio bitrate is fixed at 224Kbps, using 16 bit stereo at a 44.1KHz sampling rate. The total bitrate, for both audio and video, is 1,374Kbps.

Although video conversion software can create video streams at a wide range of bitrates, the standard players are designed for playing clips at the White Book specification. It is usually easier, therefore, to use a software package that knows the requirements and converts AVIs to MPEG-1 White Book specification. Examples of such software are listed later.

A little-used variation on VCD is the XVCD (Extended VCD) format. This allows an additional option to take the video up to 720x576 with a bit rate up to 3.5Mbps.

SVCD

The Super VCD standard was originally developed in 1998 by the Chinese government, Chinese manufacturers and the VCD Consortium. An SVCD movie can be played on a CD-ROM drive, a portable VCD player, or a DVD drive, including many standalone players.

Since a CD can only store a limited amount of MPEG-2 video, SVCD is commonly used for high-quality presentations on a CD (e.g. promotional or training material).

SVCD uses MPEG-2 (ISO standard 13818 standard) compression with a variable video bit rate up to a recommended 2600Kbps. The SVCD standard has an odd 480x576 aspect ratio and is encoded by squashing the image in the horizontal direction (e.g. people look taller). This is corrected during playback, where the image is expanded to fill the screen to the usual 4:3 aspect ratio.

SVCD also supports 16:9 anamorphic widescreen mode (see explanation later).
It can use simple menus or a multi-level hierarchical menu structure can be set up, with the videos indexed into multiple chapters. HTML-type hyperlinks can be used to index locations throughout the disk.
It supports having four different subtitles. Since these are overlaid on the image at runtime, they can be turned off by the user.

SVCD audio uses MPEG-2 Layer II with a variable bit rate between 32-384 Kbps. It uses a 44.1KHz sampling rate.
It can store two stereo tracks or 4 mono tracks and also supports 5:1 surround sound. The audio bitrates are:
- Single stereo – 32 to 192Kbps
- Dual stereo – 64 to 384Kbps

Although the video specification is 2,600Kbps, it is best to keep the combined video and audio bitrate to a maximum of 2600Kbps. By reducing the video bit rate, a CD can hold up to 74 minutes of video, the same as VCD. This provides a larger screen resolution, at the expense of greater compression and the resulting picture degradation.

Many applications (see the table that appears later) are capable of converting normal AVI files to this format.
A little-used variation is the XSVCD (Extended SVCD) which takes the video up to 720x576 with a bit rate up to 9.8Mbps.

DivX

Originally designed for the distribution of commercial movies, this format has been adopted by non-cinema video users (although it is often used to store a movie on 1 or 2 CDs).
It is now used for low quality net streaming applications up to better-than-DVD quality displays.
A DivX disk only plays on a computer with a CD-ROM or DVD-ROM drive. It won't work on a standalone DVD player and standalone DivX players are virtually nonexistant. The computer must have a DivX codec installed to play a DivX video.
DivX encoders and decoders are available and these allow users to create and play their own DivX movies, without the restrictions inherent in commercial versions.
The format has the benefit of using MPEG-4 compression, allowing a variable bit rate to be set for both the video and audio streams. Since the format has not been adopted by leading hardware and software producers, there is no recommended resolution or bitrate level. The player simply uses the DivX codec to display the video stream at the settings used during encoding. The DivX codec is freely available and can be used with Adobe Premiere and other video editing packages.

MiniDVD

MiniDVD has all the benefits of DVD (same video quality, same menus, subtitles, surround sound) but is stored on a CD. It provides fully interactive video on a CD but does not normally play on a standalone player because it is mistaken for VCD data when it is in fact DVD data on a CD. Although the content is in DVD format, the player sees it as a CD-R and looks for CD-ROM files or VCD files.

DVD

This format is covered in full later in this chapter.

Creating a VCD

Choosing *"Video-CD"* from the *"New Compilation"* window allows the user to create a VCD.
The main window has two vertical panels on the right-hand side. As before, they display the folders and files stored on the user's hard drives.

In this case, there are two horizontal panels on the left-hand side, as shown in the illustration.

All the folders and files shown in the top panel are automatically created by the application. Video CDs use the White Book version 2.0 standard. So, the first track must be a CD-XA Form 1 track containing video CD application files, as well as an ISO 9660 / Joliet file system that can contain any additional user files. These are created and updated by the software and require no user intervention. They inform the player on the location of the user's files and instruct on how to play them.
All other tracks on that disk must be CD-XA form 2 tracks containing MPEG-1 video. The file must be a multiplexed MPEG-1 file, and the video data must be at a bit rate of 1.152Mbit/s, while the audio must have a bit rate of 224 kBit/s.

Just as with other CD creations, the desired files are dragged in to the compilation window – the bottom panel. The files are stored in the MPEGAV folder and are renamed aveseq01.dat, avseq02.dat, etc.

The files used can be in uncompressed AVI or MPEG-1 format. Others, such as MPEG-2, QuickTime movies and DivX movies, have to be converted before use in Nero. If an AVI file is dropped into the compilation window, Nero converts it into a Video CD 2.0 compliant MPEG-1 file – <u>after</u> the choice has been made to burn the CD (this potentially saves wasted time if files may be removed prior to burning).   If an MPEG-1 file with the wrong format (e.g. wrong resolution, wrong frame rate, etc.) is dropped into the compilation window, Nero will report on the problem and provide options to cancel the file from the play list or to re-encode the file to the required MPEG format. Older writing software expects video files to be in Video CD 2.0 format prior to being placed in the compilation window. In these cases, there is a need to convert the file format before opening the writing application. Adobe Premiere, AVI2VCD, etc. can be used for this purpose (see later).

When all the clips are placed in the compilation window, the project can be written away to a CD-R by clicking on the *"Write CD"* option in the *"File"* menu.

When the VCD is played back in a player, the video clips are played in sequence, from beginning to end.

VCD Menus

Nero 5.5 onwards, like most modern pieces of writing software, is able to create menus for VCDs (and SVCDs). When used in a player, the PC keyboard or the standalone player remote controls select an option from the displayed menu, and a different MPEG track is played for each option.

The steps for creating a menu system are:

- Drop all the video clips for the project into the compilation window.
- Rename the files in the compilation, by right-clicking them and choosing *"Properties"* from the drop-down menu. The filenames will appear on the menu screen, so changing *"clip17a"* to *"Our House"* makes sense.
- Choose the *"Compilation Info"* option from the *"File"* menu. This opens up an *"Info"* window.
- Click the *"Menu"* tab to produce the display shown in the illustration on the following page.
- Check the *"Enable menu"* box.
- Check the *"Preview first page"* to bring up a pop-up window that shows the screen that will be displayed when the completed VCD is run in a player.
- Select the menu layout from the option offered in the *"Layout"* menu. The options are mainly on how the menu text descriptions are displayed (e.g. centred, left-aligned, in columns). If desired, the text descriptions can be replaced with a thumbnail graphic of the first frame in each video clip.
- Choose a picture to act as a background to the menu, if desired. This can be a still from a digital camera, a still removed from one of the video clips, or can be a graphic specially designed in PhotoShop or other drawing package. Use the *"Browse"* option to find the file.
- If no background picture is chosen (i.e. the box is left empty), the menu will display a plain background of the colour selected in the colour picker (click on the box to the right of the *"Browse"* button).
- Enter descriptions in the *"Header text"* and *"Footer"* text, if required.

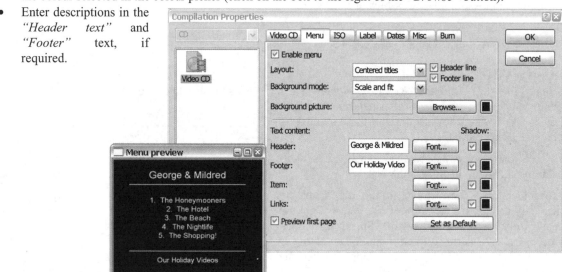

When the menu is completed to the satisfaction of the user, the VCD can be written by clicking on the *"Write CD"* option in the *"File"* menu.

Creating an SVCD

The procedure is identical to creating a VCD, except that the SVCD option is selected.   Thereafter, the same steps are taken to add files, create menus, etc. The current version of Nero only converts AVIs if it has its MPEG-2 plug-in installed. This is purchased separately.

Alternatively, the files can be converted with other software such as Premiere, AVI2MPG2, etc. (see next page)

Creating a DivX disk

Since a DivX disk is intended to be played from beginning to end, the disk has no menus or playing options. After conversion, the file still retains the AVI extension.   It can therefore be played through any Windows player that has a DivX codec installed (e.g. the later versions of Windows Media Player).

The files can be created using Premiere, Virtual Dub, or Windows Media Encoder – as long as the application has a DivX codec installed, usually in a separately installed package.

The illustration shows VirtualDub being used to create a DivX move from an AVI file.

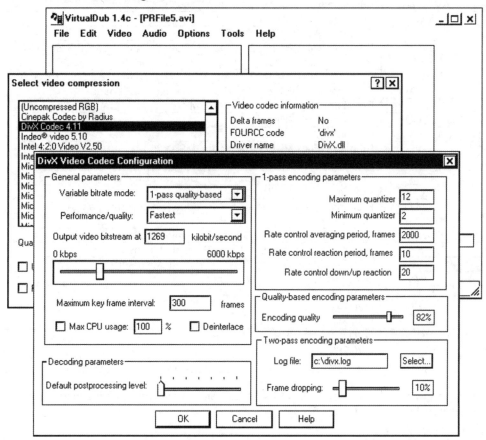

After selecting the file for conversion, the user has selected 'DivX' from the list of codecs.   Highlighting the codec and right-clicking brings up a dialog box where the setting for the DivX conversion can be tweaked. A slider allows the user to set the bitrate for the conversion, so that the maximum quality can be used for a given file.

Many freeware bitrate calculators, like the one shown, are available on the Internet and these allow the user to enter the file's length and resolution, the CD-R's capacity, etc. The utility then displays the maximum bitrate that can be used to encode the file so that it fills the CD-R.

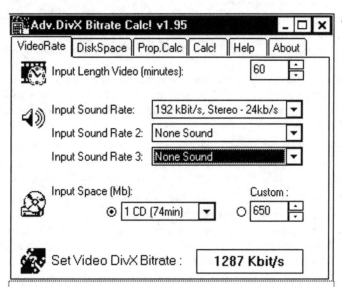

File conversions

The chart shows the many format conversions that a user may wish to carry out.
While many of them can be carried out using Adobe Premiere, the table shows shareware and freeware alternatives.

From	To	Packages that can be used
AVI Type 1	AVI Type 2	Edit Studio
AVI Type 2	AVI Type 1	Edit Studio
AVI	MOV	Premiere, SmartVid, Switch
AVI	VCD	Premiere, AVI2VCD, FlyVCD
AVI	SVCD	Premiere with BBMpeg2 codec, TMPGenc, Tsunami MPEG Encoder
AVI	MPEG-1	Premiere with BBMpeg codec, AVI2VCD, TMPGEnc, AVI2MPEG
AVI	MPEG-2	Premiere with BBMpeg2 codec, MPEG2i, AVI2MPG2, LSX MPEG Encoder
AVI	DivX AVI	Premiere with DivX codec, Virtual Dub with DivX codec
MOV	AVI	Premiere, MOV2AVI, SmartVid, Switch
MOV	SVCD	Premiere, TMPGEnc
MPEG-1	MPEG-2	Premiere
MPEG-1	AVI	Premiere, FlaskMPEG, eXstream, MPAV100
MPEG-2	MPEG-1	Premiere, FlaskMPEG, eXstream, MPEG2AVI
MPEG-1	DivX	Premiere with DivX codec, Virtual Dub with DivX codec
MPEG-1	VCD	Premiere, Nero (while burning a VCD)
MPEG-2	SVCD	Premiere, Nero with its MPEG-2 codec (while burning an SVCD)
VCD	MPEG-1	VCD Gear
VCD	DivX AVI	FlaskMPEG, Advanced Bitrate Calculator is also desirable
AVI	ASF	Windows Media Tools, VIDTOASF (both Microsoft)
MOV	ASF	Windows Media Tools, VIDTOASF (both Microsoft)
AVI	WMV	Windows Media Encoder (Microsoft)
MPEG-1	WMV	Windows Media Encoder 7(Microsoft)
DVD	AVI	DVD2AVI
DVD	MPEG-2	DVD2MPG
DVD	VCD	DVD2VCD, DeCSS
DVD	SVCD	DVD2SVCD
DVD	DivX	FlaskMPEG, Advanced Bitrate Calculator is also desirable

The shareware and freeware applications, and the DivX codec, can be found by searching on the Internet.
Microsoft provides free downloads of their encoding products:
- Windows Media Tools
- Windows Media 8 Encoder (runs from command prompt)
- Windows Media 7 encoder (runs within Windows)

The Media Tools bundle includes a Premiere plug-in, so that it can output in ASF format, along with other conversion and publishing tools.

DVD

Current CDs have the following capacity limitations:
- Most hard disks are now much larger than the 650MB storage of a CD.   So, backing up drives involves writing to multiple CDs per drive.
- A full-length movie, even in MPEG-1 format, stores on two CDs and requires the disk to be changed during viewing.

The response is the high-capacity *'Digital Versatile Disk'*.   It was mainly viewed as a mechanism for distributing films and the first DVD disks are of this type.   It also provides an ideal medium for a wide variety of applications ranging from training material to encyclopaedias.   Their large storage capacity makes the writeable versions a good choice of backup medium.

The disk retains the conventional CD diameter of 120mm but can be double sided and can have two separate layers capable of storing data.   The largest capacity types have a sandwich of two layers (i.e. four storage surfaces).   With double-sided versions, the disk must be flipped over to allow the player to read the other side.

Single layer disks, both single and double sided, are manufactured in a very similar way to current CD-ROMs.   Like CDs, the DVD uses an aluminium disk with pits and lands (see earlier). However, with double-layered disks, an extra layer is placed over the disk. The second layer comprises a resin layer with partially transmissive qualities.   The reflections from both layers vary only slightly in intensity requiring a particularly sensitive detection system. Because the extra layer has a lower reflectivity, it uses a slightly longer pit length. As a result, it is only capable of storing 3.8GB instead of the normal 4.7GB.   This explains why the table on the next page shows the capacity of a DVD9 double layered disk as 8.5GB (4.7GB + 3.7GB) instead of 9.4GB (4.7GB + 4.7GB).

To create even higher capacity disks, two disks can be bonded together back to back.   Note that such a disk, the DVD10 is now twice the capacity of the DVD5.

The DVD specifications are known as *'books'* and are shown in the table. Type A is a general storage medium for storing data, archiving files and distributing applications. Any video content is played through the computer. Type B is a DVD-ROM tailored to the interactive display of high-quality video. It is the main method of distributing DVD movies and is also used in training and point-of-sale systems.   Primarily intended for playing on a DVD player connected to a television set.

Book	Specification
A	DVD-ROM
B	DVD-Video
C	DVD-Audio
D	DVD-R (Write Once)
E	DVD-RAM
F	DVD-Rewritable

Type C is a DVD that acts as an improved version of the older CD-I and CD-G systems. It *stores 'better than CD'* audio, along with graphics or video.
Type D is the type of writable DVD that can be produced on home or office computer systems, without being sent away for pressing at a manufacturing plant. It is a *'write once'* medium.
Type E is the type of DVD whose contents can be re-recorded many times over, like CD-RAM.
Type F stores the data on the disk surface in a non-permanent manner.   The contents can be later erased or written over. The options include DVD-RW and DVD+RW.

The range of DVD products is shown in the table.   A 4.7GB disk stores the equivalent of around 133 minutes of video with three audio streams.

Product	Capacity	No of layers	No of sides	Mode	Comments
DVD5	4.7GB	1	1	Playback	Pressed or created with a DVD writer
DVD9	8.5GB	2	1	Playback	Pressed or created with a DVD writer
DVD10	9.4GB	1	2	Playback	Pressed by a manufacturer
DVD18	17GB	2	2	Playback	Pressed by a manufacturer
Version 1.0 DVD-R	3.95GB or 7.9GB	2	1 or 2	Record-once	Created with a DVD writer
Version 2.0 DVD-R	4.7GB or 9.4GB	2	1 or 2	Record-once	Mostly DVD-ROM compatible
Type 1 DVD-RAM	2.6GB or 5.4GB	1	1 or 2	Record-many	Created with a DVD writer Cartridge based.
Type 2 DVD-RAM	4.7GB or 9.4GB	1	1 or 2	Record-many	Not generally DVD-ROM compatible
DVD-RW	4.7GB or 9.4GB	1	1 or 2	Record-many	Created with a DVD writer
DVD+RW	4.7GB or 9.4GB	1	1 or 2	Record-many	Created with a DVD writer

While DVD5 and DVD9 disks can be pressed by a manufacturer, CD writers can achieve the same result for smaller quantities and DVD5 drives are the models that are currently produced as standard DVD players.

How DVD stores 4.7GB on a single side
A CD's basic capacity is 746MB, although 650MB is left for the user after error correction overheads are deducted. DVD uses a combination of more precise engineering, higher laser frequency, and improved modulation and error correction techniques, to dramatically improve the capacity of a single disk side.

	Standard CD layout	DVD layout	Improvement Factor	New Capacity
Smaller pit length	0.972 microns	0.4 microns	2.4300	1.82 GB
Narrower track pitch	1.6 microns	0.74 microns	2.1622	3.93 GB
More surface used for storing data	86 sq cms	87.6 sq cms	1.0186	4.00 GB
Better error correction	25% of data area	13% of data area	1.1062	4.42 GB
More efficient channel bit modulation	08:14+3	08:16	1.0625	4.70 GB

UDF
DVDs use the Universal Disk Format (UDF), specified by ISO as a standard for exchanging data. This allows the disk to be read on many different operating systems such as DOS, Windows, Mac and Unix. The filing system supports data, audio and video – or a mix of all three. Some types of files (e.g. video and audio files) are identical on all platforms and these types can be included on a DVD knowing that they are universally readable. Of course, machine specific file types are only readable by the appropriate system. The UDF version used for DVD is MicroUDF and this applies both to read-only and writeable versions. Early versions of Windows did not support UDF. Windows 95 OSR2 supports UDF Bridge (a hybrid of UDF and standard ISO9660 to allow disks to be read by all platforms) while Windows 98 onwards supports UDF.
DVD-ROMs use UDF Bridge while DVD-Video uses UDF format.
MicroUDF supports long filenames (up to 256 characters) and mixed case lettering.
Of course, other files stored on the disk (e.g. application programs, word-processed file, etc.) will still be system specific.

DVD Data Rates

The table above shows how DVD manages to store much more information on the same surface area than a CD. However, this has other implications, primarily on the data transfer rate of a DVD drive in comparison to a CD-ROM drive. The reduced pit length means that a DVD drive spinning at the same speed as a CD drive will read 2.43 times as much data. However, the base (single speed) velocity of a DVD is almost four times the base (single speed) velocity of a CD-ROM drive. These two factors together mean that a single speed DVD transfers data at the same rate as an 8x CD-ROM drive, and a 6x DVD has a data rate similar to a 48x CD-ROM drive. DVD use CLV (see earlier explanation) to maximise storage. So, a 1x speed DVD drive rotates at between 575rpm and 1,475rpm.

A single speed DVD writer takes about an hour to write to a full 4.7GB disk and a 2x model takes half an hour.

Video standards

The main requirements for the DVD-Video format were set out in Hollywood by the Motion Picture Studio Advisory Committee as:

- 135 minutes of video on a single disk, single layer side.
- Choice of 3 or 5 languages (audio tracks) per disk.
- Choice of 4 to 6 subtitles per disk.
- Includes Copy protection.
- Letterbox, widescreen, pan and scan formats.

This specification has been exceeded, with support for eight languages and 32 subtitles and up to nine camera angles, although the playing time is reduced to 133 minutes.

The maximum performance of any element on the DVD is determined by the overall capacity of the disk and the bitrate used for each element. So, for example, if fewer soundtracks were included or the bitrate of the audio tracks was lowered, there would be more space to store video. There are two options for reproducing DVD video:

- Using dedicated hardware to decode the signals and feed them to the monitor (or TV out socket) and to the sound system. This is usually an add-on decoder card.
- Using software to decode the signals, which are then fed to the computer's existing graphics card. This is less expensive but consumes more processor power.

Screen formats

The DVD Book B standard supports a range of screen aspect ratios, from 1.33:1 (the 4/3 standard of normal TVs and monitors) to 2.25:1 (wide screen movies). Early cinema films were produced with a 1.37:1 aspect ratio, known as *"Academy Format"*. When NTSC television was introduced, it set the television screen at a 1.33:1 aspect ratio, rounding off the ratio to whole numbers. The 4:3 ratio then continued in other television standards such as the UK PAL system and eventually was adopted as the computer monitor standard.

Most modern cinema movies are now produced at 1.85:1 and domestic wide-screen TV's display at 1.78:1 (usually advertised as 16:9 sets). The table shows the varieties. The awaited HDTV (high definition television) has a resolution of 1920x1080, which while having a vastly improved screen definition, still follows the 16:9 widescreen format. The widest popular movie ever produced was *'Ben Hur'*, which had a 2.76:1 ratio. Clearly, no movie that was originally produced for cinema distribution will fit exactly into a domestic television or monitor screen. There is a difference between the aspect ratio of the video and the aspect ratio of the screen on which the video is viewed.

Screen standard	Aspect ratio
Standard monitor	1.33:1 (i.e. 4:3)
Old cinema movies	1.37:1
Widescreen television	1.78:1 (i.e. 16:9)
Standard cinema movie	1.85:1
Widescreen cinema movie	2.35:1

When movies are played in DVD players, users can control how they are displayed, including *'squeezing'* the image (everyone looks tall and thin) and *'letterbox viewing'* (all the movie is displayed but the upper and lower portions of the screen are black).

The table shows the effect of displaying a modern 1.85:1 cinema movie on standard monitors (4:3) and widescreen systems (16:9). In some cases, a cinema movie is cropped at each side so that it fits a 16:9 format and provides full screen output. With a Panavision/Cinemascope movie, at 2.35:1, the amount of screen area occupied by the picture (instead of black space) is even less. As examples, *"Good Will Hunting"* was shot in 1.85:1 format while *"The Thin Red Line"* was shot in 2.35:1 format.

Screen	Method	Viewable display
4:3	Pan & scan	40% of image chopped off
4:3	Letterbox	All image viewable, with thick black bars at top and bottom of screen
4:3	Anamorphic	All image viewable, with content greatly squashed vertically
16:9	Pan & scan	25% of image chopped off
16:9	Letterbox	All image viewable, with thin black bars at top and bottom of screen
16:9	Anamorphic	All image viewable, with content very slightly squashed vertically

Disks and players can also make use of *'pan and scan'* technology. As its name might suggest, it allows a viewer to pan and scan around inside a video image that is wider than the screen can display, showing the most important parts of the action at any time. The disk uses a substream of data to indicate which portion of the wider picture to display on a narrower display. Pan and scan is also widely used to broadcast movies on television.

Anamorphic

The labels on many DVD cases describe the video as *"16x9 anamorphic"*, *"enhanced for 16x9 television"* or some other variation on this wording.

Whatever its description, the method ensures the greatest possible quality on 16:9 screens, while still allowing the movie to be viewed on 4:3 screens.

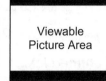

With a non-anamorphic movie, the film is saved in 4:3 format.   To keep the content widescreen, black bars are added to the top and bottom of the screen.   When viewed on a standard TV or monitor, the letterboxed image fills the screen. Since a letterboxed image has black bands at the top and bottom of the screen, the horizontal detail is at maximum but the screen is using less of its lines on viewable information.

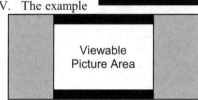

This situation is much worsened when the movie is viewed on a widescreen TV.   The example shown will be familiar to those with widescreen televisions. In this case, not every line contains viewable data – and only a part of each line is used to display the movie. The result is a widescreen movie surrounding by much wasted black space. Of course, the user can adjust the television so that the movie fills the screen but this does provide extra detail. It simply interpolates the image (magnifies the existing data to fill the screen by estimating what the other information would be).

Anamorphic storage works by processing the movie so that the height of the movie is left untouched but the image is squashed vertically (e.g. a football would look like a rugby ball and all the players would look very tall and very thin). With older films, the anamorphic version is processed from the original film. With modern movies, the film can be shot in anamorphic mode by fitting an anamorphic lens to the cameras.

When an anamorphic movie is played through a 4:3 system, the image is letterboxed and looks no different from a non-anamorphic version.

However, when viewed on a widescreen display, the movie fills the screen in the vertical direction and – when the horizontal information is unsquashed – the movie also fills the screen in the horizontal direction.   Since the whole screen is filled with real information (as opposed to the interpolated information of the non-anamorphic version) the quality of the picture is substantially improved.

Anamorphic movies contain flags that a DVD player or a digital television will recognise and handle the screen formatting accordingly.

A 2.35:1 anamorphic movie will still show thin black bars at the top and bottom of the image, since it is wider than a widescreen display.

A huge number of DVD movies, anything from James Bond to Jimi Hendrix, use anamorphic storage.

Some have one side of the disk storing the film in pan & scan format, while the other side store the film in anamorphic format.

OpTex (www.optexint.com) produce an anamorphic attachment for fitting to standard DV camcorders, allowing the production of anamorphic movies by those outside the huge movie corporations.

> **Note:** The above complication only applies to movies that originate in cinema format.   Where other footage (e.g. domestic holiday films or company training films) is used for creating DVD, the movie can be shot in 4:3 or 16:9 format.   The resultant DVD video will then happily display in full screen.

Country codes

The movie industry wants to distribute their films in different parts of the world at different times. So they used their muscle to ensure that DVD players, both hardware and software, had region locking systems.   Every commercial DVD movie disk has a *'country lock'* - a code specific to a region of the world, as shown in the table.

DVD disks will only run in systems that have the same zone code. This results in the cheaper US disks being unable to be played on European DVD drives.

Most DVD drives and software players allow the user to alter the player's region a number of times (typically five times) before the system is locked to the region last selected. In response, *'region-free'* DVD drives are available. These are technically a breach of the DVD specification but are not illegal. These drives do not check the disk's region. Other models, marketed as having *"automatic region detect"* check the disk's region code but do not take action on any information they are supplied by the disk.   Of course, the software playback system also has to handle all regions.   Most software decoders have workarounds where the region can be changed without decrementing the region change counter.   The computer's graphics card has no region coding system fitted, even although it may be used for displaying DVD movie content.

Code	Region
1	USA & Canada
2	Europe, Middle East, S.Africa & Japan
3	South East Asia & Taiwan
4	Latin America & Australia
5	Russia, Africa, India & Pakistan
6	China
7	Reserved
8	Cruise ships, aeroplanes, etc.

Copy protection

DVD movies employ a Content Scrambling System (CSS) in an attempt to prevent illegal copying. The key for unscrambling the video and audio streams should be unique for each disk and the scrambling is performed during the glass mastering process. This CSS method, however, makes DVD videos impossible to use in a Linux system, and so a program called DeCSS has become available to bypass the system. Due to the obvious piracy implications, the DVD Forum tried hard to keep the program out of the public domain, but it has become widespread.

The Macrovision Analogue Protection System (APS) prevents copying to VHS tapes by distorting the composite video output. Producers of DVD movies pay a licence to Macrovision.

Commercial DivX

This is a technology built on DVD and developed by Digital Video Express. On top of the normal encoding in a DVD, DivX was intended to use additional DES encryption for a specific purpose, namely video rental. DivX disks were not to be hired, but purchased. However, they would only allow the video to be played for a certain timespan. After that, any attempt to play the video would cause the DivX system to automatically dial up the vendor to inform them. At this point additional hire time could be purchased, or the disk could be upgraded to unlimited viewing. This aspect of DivX was not popular however, and has made little if any progress.

DivX drops much of the additional functions that DVD provides and performs much like a normal VHS video.

DVD Signal

DVD Video disks consist of a TOC and any number of video tracks. Each track contains up to 9 VOB (Video Object) files, which on a non-ASPI system are all under 1GB in length. These VOB files contain the digital video information, which consists of one MPEG-2 stream at a Variable Bit Rate (VBR), up to 8 audio streams in either Linear PCM uncompressed, Dolby AC-3 or MPEG-2, and up to 32 run-length encoded 4-colour 'subpicture' streams for captions etc.

The video stream is interlaced and at a resolution and frame rate depending on the output type. PAL video is at 720x576 resolution with 25 fps, while NTSC video is at 720x480 resolution with 30 fps. Other resolutions can be used but may not be supported by any given playback device. Like Video CD, DVD is fully capable of employing interactivity in its videos, in fact that is one of its major selling points.

The bitrate of a DVD video stream is typically between 3Mbps and 9Mbps, and most DVD recording software has three or more 'quality levels' as a result.

With the adoption of HDTV (High-Definition TV) in the US, the standard 4.7GB DVD has inadequate storage capacity to hold an entire 90 minute film on one side. While dual-sided or dual-layered disks could alleviate the situation, Sony is developing an entirely new disk, slightly larger than CD and DVD, capable of storing 20GB per side.

Audio standards

DVD supports three 'theatre quality' sound formats - Dolby AC-3 surround sound, MPEG-1 audio and MPEG-2 audio. Europe favours MPEG-2 surround sound, while the USA, Japan and the rest of the world use Dolby AC-3 (5.1). It is possible for a PAL DVD to also include an AC-3 audio track and an NTSC DVD to include an optional MPEG audio track. MPEG-1 is described as '2.0' (i.e. two channel stereo) while AC-3 is '5.1' and MPEG-2 is either '5.1' or '7.1'. The number after the dot indicates whether the sound includes support for a low-frequency effects sub-woofer. The numbers before the dot indicate how many main sound channels are supported. So a 5:1 has a centre sound channel, a channel at all four corners of the sound room, and a sub-woofer.

MPEG-1 samples at 44.1 kHz while MPEG-2 and AC-3 sample at 48 kHz.

Most standalone players have options for audio output. Apart from the analogue output, they might provide digital audio outputs. These may be co-axial or optical outputs. The co-axial connection is a normal RCA socket, perhaps marked as 'S/PDIF'. The optical connection is a snap in socket for an optical cable. Co-axial connections are cheaper but are prone to electrical interference and hum loops. Optical connections are immune to interference and, since there is no electrical connection between the player and the sound system, the possibility of hum loops is eliminated.

DVD-Audio

DVD-Audio, Book C, is not widely marketed yet due to the music industry's search for an unbreakable copy protection system for the disks. Its quality is far superior to audio CD quality, as shown in the table. DVD-Audio also offers a 2-channel mode with a sampling rate of 192KHz.

	CD	DVD-Audio
Resolution	16-bit	24-bit
Sampling rate	44.1KHz	96KHz
Channels	2	5

Recordable DVD

Like CD-ROM, there is more than one option when considering production of DVDs. Pressing of DVDs is similarly expensive unless large numbers are pressed, and so there are DVD-R and DVD-RAM drives available to create single disks or small runs.

DVD-R

Book D of the DVD specification is DVD recordable, more commonly called DVD-R.   This is a write-once system that creates a DVD that many household and computer DVD players can read.   However, it is not re-writeable, limiting its usefulness as a backup medium.

Like CD-R, DVD-R uses a laser beam to permanently transform a dye recording layer.

The DVD-R format supports incremental writing (see earlier explanation) although the DVD can only be read in a DVD recording drive until the disk is finalised.   A finalised disk can then be read in a DVD player.

In fact, there are two kinds of DVD writers and two types of DVD-R media:

DVD-R for General (DVD-R(G))	This is the format designed for consumer products. As such, it is unable to make bit-for-bit copies of DVDs. It is produced in a 4.7GB format.
DVD-R for Authoring (DVD-R(A))	This format is designed for professional use and is available in 3.95GB or 4.7GB sizes.

The DVD-R(G) is the type that is generally advertised and sold through computer shops, magazines, etc. and is simply referred to as DVD-R.

A DVD-R(G) writer cannot write to a DVD-R(A) disk and vice versa. The production of two systems is regarded as an attempt to prevent unauthorised duplication of commercial DVD disks. The DVD-R(A) system is much more expensive than a comparable DVD-R(G) system. Disks created by either type of writer can be read by most players. Players make no distinction between the two types of media.

DVD-R is technically able to write to both sides of a dual sided DVD, though dual-sided media is rare. Alternatively, a "DVD+R9" drive is one that is able to write to dual-layered discs, giving 8.5GB of space. However, there are as yet no dual-layered, dual-sided media available to store the maximum 17GB that the DVD technology can accommodate.

DVD-RAM

Book E specifies DVD-RAM principles. It uses magneto-optical rewriteable technology and is available in the older type cartridge-based and the new type which allows the disk to be removed from the cartridge after writing. DVD-RAM is based on the original agreed specifications of the DVD Forum, the major manufacturers.

DVD-RAM can use one of two media types. The DVD-RAM specification version 1.0 allows only 2.6GB per side, while the newer version 2.0 specification allows 4.7GB per side, equal to a mass-produced DVD 5. This makes it useful for creating DVD masters. Some drives are able to read and write to both types of DVD-RAM.

DVD-RAM disks, once removed from their cartridge, can only be played on a few models of standard DVD player but mostly have to be used on other DVD-RAM drives. Double-sided DVD-RAM disks have to be turned over manually to access both sides.

Despite the format's poor compatibility with other drives, it has great advantages as a backup medium.

Due to its use of magneto-optical technology it provides:

- Longer shelf life, around 30 years compared to 10 years for DVD-RW and DVD+RW.
- Vastly more rewrites. The disk can be re-written to more than 100,000 times.

The main producers of this type of writer are Pioneer, Hitachi and Toshiba.

DVD-RW

The Forum also produced a rewriteable standard, known as DVD-RW.

DVD-RW is a read/write system that operates on a Phase Change system similar to CD-RW disks. The disk surface is of an alloy material that can change back and forth from a crystalline to a non-crystalline (amorphous) structure.

Its development was delayed many times, and the initial aim of a 2.6GB DVD-RW was changed to the currently available 4.7GB version.

The main producers of this type of writer are Pioneer, Yamaha, Panasonic, Mitsui and Ricoh.

The disk can be read by most domestic DVD players and computer DVD drives, and can be re-written to around 10,000 times.

DVD+RW

Sony and Philips broke with the Forum specifications and introduced own format called 'DVD+RW'.

It was developed by Sony and Panasonic outside of the DVD Forum as a rival to DVD-RW. Initially both companies believed 2.6GB was too little, and aimed at 3GB rewriteable disks, but this too has been increased to 4.7GB per side. It also suffered from many delays in production, but the companies involved have more of a stake in previous CD technologies and as a result DVD+RW is likely to be more backwards compatible than DVD-RW. It uses a similar technique to DVD-RW in as much as it writes by creating crystalline/amorphous areas on the disk surface.

The main producers of this type of writer are Philips, Sony, Ricoh and Hewlett Packard.

The disk can be read by most domestic DVD players and by most computer DVD drives, and can be re-written to up to 10,000 times.

There are many other DVD 'standards' in use or in development, such as the 8cm mini-DVDs used in new digital camcorders or the 15GB single-sided disks under development. Even after years of DVDs being on sale, there is still a confusing mass of options, even though DVD-R has finally emerged as the most widely used 'standard'. Sony has decided to produce DVD-RW systems for consumer products and DVD+RW for computer systems, while other manufacturers are concentrating on manufacturing writers that can handle multiple formats.

The table shows some of the main features of each type of format.

	DVD-R	DVD+R9	DVD-RW	DVD+RW	DVD-RAM
Types available	Single sided Double sided	Single sided Double sided Dual layered	Single sided Double sided	Single sided Double sided Dual layered	Single sided Double sided
No of rewrites	Once only	Once only	1,000	100,000	1,000
Data transfer rate (typical)	Up to 16x (177.28Mb/s)	2.4x (26.59Mb/s)	2x (22.16Mb/s)	2.4x (26.59Mb/s)	1.4x (15.52Mb/s) 4x (44.32Mb/s)
Play on domestic DVD player	Yes	Few	Nearly all	Some	Nearly all
Play on computer DVD-ROM drive	Yes	Few	Nearly all	Some	Nearly all

Compatibilities

The range of formats, writers and players leads to problems of compatibility – i.e. a disk from one system not working on another system.

Some very old DVD-ROM drives cannot even read CD-R disks and only read pressed CDs. All newer drives can usually read all formats except DVD-RAM.

However, the system used for re-writeables make them incompatible with each other. For example, DVD+RW can't be read by a DVD-RW systems and vice versa.

The table shows the compatibly between systems (ie whether a disk recorded in one type of drive will be readable in another type of drive).

	DVD-R	DVD-RW	DVD+RW	DVD-RAM
Pressed DVD-ROM	Yes	Yes	Yes	Yes
DVD-R	Yes	Yes	Yes	Yes
DVD+R9	Few	Few	Few	Few
DVD-RW	Yes	Yes	Mostly	Mostly
DVD+RW	Mostly	Mostly	Yes	Mostly
DVD-RAM	No	No	No	Yes

Of course, standard CD drives cannot read DVD disks of any type.

DVD recording drives generally write in their native format, although many DVD-RW writers and some DVD-RAM writers can also write to DVD-R disks and most are also capable of writing to CD-R disks. The DVD+RW writers are currently not designed to burn DVD-R disks (although the fact that DVD-RW disks are more expensive than DVD-R disks may have more than a little to do with this decision). Newer multi-drives are produced that can handle DVD-RAM, DVD-R and DVD-RW, along with CD-R and CD-RW.

DVD Recording Software

DVD recording is still in its infancy compared to CD-R recording, and both the hardware and software involved are currently rather expensive. Due to the fact that DVD drives are far outnumbered by CD-ROM drives in the installed PC base, few producers will use the format for anything other than video at the moment. DVD creation software, then, is also geared towards video. As such, most software will offer capabilities such as video editing, titling, looping, menus and so on. On the technical side, the video stream still has to match the MPEG-2 specification, and multiplexing is offered by many products to ease the burden on the user in that regard.

Creating a DVD

While commercial movies make use of the full range of facilities available in the DVD format, there is a huge growth in DVD writing for archiving and smaller-scale video productions (eg advertising material, training material or storing home movies).

While an ISO DVD can be used to store 4.7GB of raw data for use on a PC, this is essentially the same process as burning a CDR. So this section is concerned with authoring and creating a DVD video disc. The CD burning program Nero has a counterpart DVD and VCD authoring package known as NeroVision. Note, however, that in order to use this package to author SVCDs or DVDs, the MPEG-2 plugin must also be purchased.

Authoring a professional quality DVD video disc is an involved process, but the basic steps for creating a relatively simple DVD are as follows:

- Gather video, audio and graphics assets.
- Import and arrange the assets.
- Configure the menus and sub-menus.
- Write the project.

Importing Assets

There are three types of assets which NeroVision accepts: video, graphics, and audio. In each case, NeroVision is able to use formats that are not native to DVD discs, converting them into the appropriate format just before writing the project. For example, it is acceptable to import WMA audio and DivX video files into NeroVision, even though DVDs only work with PCM, AC-3, and MPEG-2 audio and video streams.

Nonetheless, it may be advisable to convert to MPEG-2 video and PCM audio using a program such as VirtualDub, before importing into NeroVision. This method will provide the author more control over detailed video quality settings as well as providing access to a wider range of transformation effects. Furthermore, some of the more dubious video types such as XviD are not always reliable, and should be converted beforehand so that the output can be confirmed as suitable. It may also be useful to use the bitrate calculator to determine the optimum bit rate for the movie clips to be stored on a DVD.

NeroVision starts by asking the user what type of project to create: VCD, SVCD, MiniDVD, or DVD Video. Each of these work in a similar fashion, NeroVision simply using different storage capacities and video types for each form of project.

Once the type of project is selected (in this case, DVD), NeroVision will move on to the *'Content'* page.

This page has several options:

Capture Video
This opens a window from which NeroVision can capture video from a video capture device such as a DV camera or video card with a TV-Input. The bar at the bottom of the content window shows how much space on a 4.7GB DVD is consumed by the assets.

Add Video Files
Video assets can also be added from an existing file: many major formats are supported including AVI, ASF, MPEG and VOB.

Make New Movie
The *'Make New Movie'* option is the same as the *'Edit movie'* option explained below, except that it starts with an empty timeline.

Make New Slide Show
This opens the Slide Show window, where the user can import graphics and turn them into a video slideshow, as explained later.

Import DVD-VR
NeroVision can import titles from a DVD-VR disc – this is a type of disc that can be edited after creation, to add or replace menus and content.

Edit Movie
If a video asset is selected, the user can edit it with this option. This is done either by selecting the clip and clicking *'Edit movie'*, or by double-clicking on a clip.

Edit Slide Show
If a slide show asset is selected, the user can edit it with this option. This essentially takes the user back to the same window used to create the slide show.

Create Chapters
If a video asset is selected, the user can create *'chapters'* that will be used in a sub-menu once the project advances to the menu stage. The chapters window is explained later.

Making Slide Shows

This option takes the user to the Slide Show editing window, shown opposite. On the top left is the preview box where the user can see what the slide show will look like. To the right of that are the media tab and the transitions tab (shown). The media tab keeps track of the available pictures and audio that can be dragged into the timeline below. The transitions tab allows access to wipes, fades and other transition effects, that can be dragged into the smaller boxes between the pictures on the timeline.

Below these boxes is the timeline itself, which shows the pictures in the slide show, and any transitions between the pictures. There is also an audio tab where the user can place audio files, which play at the same time as the slide show. Finally, below that are a few extra options that

allow the user to delete, crop or rotate pictures, save them, or change the duration for which each picture displays.

Editing Movies

The editor allows multiple video files to be concatenated in a storyboard style, and use transitions between scenes. It also provides text effects, and filtering the colours of the video, using a timeline view. However, NeroVision is not a professional video editing package and its capabilities are limited.

As the screenshot opposite shows, it is similar to the Slide Show editing window, with video clips replacing pictures on the storyboard. The preview box also has buttons that allow the user to take snapshots from the video; record audio; split one video clip into two items for storyboard purposes; and cut a range video from the clip.

The box to the right now has more tabs. There is still a media tab, but it now shows

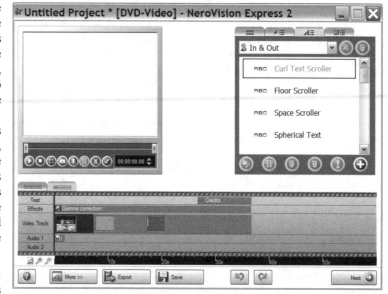

video and audio instead of pictures and audio. There is also still a transition tab, which performs an identical function. However, there are now also a Color Filter tab, and a Text Effects tab.

The Color Filter tab allows access to a few colorisation effects, namely Color Filter, Gamma Correction, and Multiply Pixel. These effects can be applied to any time range along the video timeline. The Text Effects tab allows the user to have moving text appear on screen overlaid onto any part of the video, in various different ways such as scrolling, flying, or rotating text.

One important difference between editing slide shows and editing movies is the timeline view, as shown in the example. The timeline view <u>must</u> be used to place colour filters or text effects, or to add audio overlays.

Only one colour effect and one text effect can be present at any one part of the timeline, but there can be two audio clips played on top of any given part of the video. The example shows the entire video undergoing gamma correction, and text effects being used to display credits at the end. There is also a short audio clip overlaid onto the start of the video.

Creating Chapters

Video assets can also have chapters defined, using the 'Create Chapters' option. This opens up a video viewing dialog box, where the user can either drag the slider to the desired points in the video and select 'Add Chapter' to manually create chapter points; or the Auto Detect Chapters button can be used to create chapters by detecting changes of scene.

Configuring Menus

Once all the assets are in order, pressing the 'Next' button will take the user to the Menus window. If there are no clips that have chapters defined, then there will be only one menu. However, if there are clips with chapters, each clip will have its own sub-menu.

All menus in NeroVision work the same way. An even number of menu options appear on each screen, and if there are more options, arrow buttons are used to move back and forward between each screen full of options. Sub-menus work the same way, except that they also have a button to return to the main menu. While this limits the author's control over the way the DVD plays, it is easier for beginning users and is often sufficient for typical applications of DVD video.

The options for each menu are as follows:

Layout: this allows the user to choose the number of options on each screen, as well as whether each option has a text title or is just a picture. Up to 12 options can appear on each screen.

Background: Allows the user to select a background colour, picture, or video clip to display behind the menu options. If a picture is selected, then certain effects can be applied, though these are basic in comparison to those provided by a full graphics package. This popup menu also allows the user to select an audio clip to repeat while the menu is displayed.

Buttons: This option pops up a range of different types of button frames in which to display the picture for each button. It also has a check-box which, when checked, uses the contents of each video clip as the picture for each button, rather than a static image.

Font: Allows the user to alter the font settings for the title and other text on the menu.

Header/Footer Text: Allows the user to change the text in the menu's header and footer areas.

Shadow: When selected, which it is as default, this option gives all the text and buttons a shadow, and its opacity and distance from the buttons and text can be changed here.

Automatization: If the background is a video clip, or the buttons are animated, this option allows the user to set how long the animation plays for before cycling back to the start. This popup option is also used to make the DVD perform a certain activity, such as moving to the next menu page or playing the first clip, after a certain time has passed with no user activity.

Interaction colours: This allows the user to change the colours that are used to indicate when menu options are highlighted or activated during playing of the DVD.

Writing the project

Once the menu is set up, clicking the 'Next' button will take the user to the preview window, where the final appearance of the DVD can be inspected before proceeding by pressing the 'Next' button again.

This will take the user to the Burn window.

Here, again, there are several options:

Burn To... : This option selects which output device (including Nero's Image Recorder) is to be used to burn the DVD.

Write to Hard Disk Folder: This option selects that the DVD contents should be generated and saved to a folder on the disk for writing to DVD at a later stage.

Volume Name: This allows the user to select what volume name will be given to the DVD. This is the name shown by Explorer when the disc is inserted.

Recording Settings: This gives access to the basic DVD recording settings, such as recording speed, and whether to simulate recording or determine maximum speed at burn time.

Details: This button will show or hide the details of the project, including video resolution and bit rate, number of menus, and so on.

Burn/Write: Press this button to begin burning or saving the project. Once the burn or write is complete, the user is given three options: Burn the Project Again, Save Project, or Start New Project.

Web Site Creation

There is a spectacular expansion in the number of web sites on the Internet.   Many are personal sites but there is also a rapid growth of commercial sites.   Until a few years ago, only the largest companies tended to have web sites. Now, most small companies have their own site.

Web site uses

It is estimated that over 80 million EU citizens and over 130 million American citizens are on the Internet.   Reaching that amount of people by conventional means (e.g. TV adverts, newspapers, leaflets, circulars, catalogues, etc) is a very expensive business.   The creation of private or commercial web sites opens up new and improved forms of communication across the globe.   The variety of existing sites is immense but the most common categories are: e-commerce (promoting products or services, on-line stores).

- Public information (e.g. Inland Revenue, weather, etc).
- Private sites promoting ideas (e.g. politics, religion, music, art).
- Leisure (e.g. sports, hobbies, entertainment, radio stations).
- Reference (e.g. publications, dictionaries).
- Education (on-line learning).
- Support for products (e.g. on-line documentation, FAQs, software updates, drivers).

This chapter covers the essential stages in web site creation:

- Web site design.
- Gathering the resources.
- Implementation of the site pages.
- Uploading to the server.
- Publicising the site.

Web sites and multimedia

The production of multimedia presentations and the creation of web sites share many common areas. They both use text, graphics, audio and video in sets of screens that allow the absorption of information in a manner controlled by the viewer.   They both use similar equipment (still cameras, video cameras, video capture cards, scanners) and the raw material for integration often uses the same file formats (graphic, video and sound formats).   They differ in how they integrate and package these resources.   More importantly, they differ greatly on how they <u>deliver</u> their final product. Most multimedia, due to the large size of the files, is delivered on CD-ROM.

However, in some cases even web documents can contain an impressive amount of multimedia.   In particular, web pages can be supplied on CD-ROM, or provided via an Intranet.   An Intranet is essentially a local network that is based on the same principles as the Internet in general: it uses TCP/IP, and typically provides resources such as http and ftp servers, but only to those users within the Intranet.

HTML pages which are accessed via an Intranet or are provided on a CD-ROM are considerably less restricted in their use of multimedia components, than HTML pages provided over the Internet. Despite the increasing availability of high-speed broadband, large media files on the Internet still restrict that site's audience, and as such, even the slowest modem speeds should still be taken into account in many cases.   Factors such as the processor's speed, and RAM size, are insignificant compared to the bottleneck of downloading the media from the Internet in the first place.

Download problems

The single greatest problem with the Internet is the speed of access to web pages.   In part, this is due to the popularity of the medium.   The congestion on the Internet results in times when transfer rates fall well below the capability of users' modems; sometimes data transfer rates fall to zero.   Even during a quiet(ish) period on the Net, the speed at which users can download pages is governed by the speed of their equipment, and many users are still tied to using slower analogue modems.

This table shows the best possible page download times for a range of modems and different file sizes.

Modem speed (in bits /sec)	Max theoretical transfer rate (in kilobytes/sec)	Fastest theoretical download time for a 40k web page	Fastest theoretical download time for a 400k web page
14.4kbps	1.31KB	30 secs	300 secs
28.8kbps	2.62KB	15 secs	150 secs
33.6kbps	3.05KB	13 secs	130 secs
56kbps	5.09KB	7.9 secs	79 secs
ISDN	11.64kB	2.5 secs	25 secs

These figures take into account the transmission overheads but are still optimistic, as few users achieve an average transfer rate that is close to the modem's maximum figure.   Downloading of large files is usually acceptable when using ftp, since users are storing the file contents and can carry on with another computer activity.   This is not the case with web browsing, as users expect to see page contents appear within a reasonable time.

The consequence for web site designers is that they have to design for the lowest reasonable modem speed.   What constitutes the 'lowest reasonable speed' depends on the audience being targeted, but typically, designing for 28.8k modems will ensure reasonable quality while still being accessible to the vast majority of viewers.   If a new, all-featured, site only performed adequately for users with ISDN or ADSL lines, then the site would have a very limited appeal.   This then is the starting point for web site design.   Site builders do not have a free hand; they have to design with these severe restrictions in mind.

Site components

The main elements of a web site are:

Web Server

This is the computer connected to the Internet that stores the organisation's web pages.   The server may be the property of a single organisation and only store the single web site.   The majority of servers act as the host for many different users.   The users may rent out space on the server or, in the case of many ISPs, a certain amount of web space may be provided to users as part of their normal rental agreement.   Extra web space can usually be rented for an extra fee.

Web Site

Strictly speaking, the server location is termed the 'web site' but it is now customary to refer to each user's set of web pages as a web site.   The diagram shows a web server that is the host for two separate web sites.   A web site is the property of the person or organisation that owns and maintains the collection of files.   Passwords are used to prevent unauthorised access and tampering with web site contents.

Web Page

This is a single page on the site.   It may consist of a single text file, or may be made up of several files, each occupying parts of the screen, combined with other files storing graphics, sound or video.   In either case, the user viewing the page sees it as a single screen display.

Home Page

Each site has a Home Page, which acts as a starting point, displaying the site's contents and providing links to other site pages.   The Home Page may also display a welcome message and have an attractive format to entice viewers further into the site.

Technical characteristics

The main characteristics of web sites are:

Cross-platform

The script for every single HTML web page on the entire Internet is stored in plain ASCII text and can therefore be read by every computer attached to the Internet.   This means that a script written using a PC can be read by the browser software sitting on a Macintosh, a UNIX system, etc.   This maximises the potential readership of sites and allows for easy interchange of documents between different hardware platforms.

Hyperlinking

The main benefit of web browsing is that users can navigate within sites and between sites by clicking on a piece of text or a graphic icon.   Users are presented with page contents that include underlined words or phrases or icons.   These highlighted areas are the 'hyperlinks' and they link information in one document with information in another part of the document - or an entirely different document.   The other documents may reside anywhere on the Internet.   So, clicking on a hyperlink area (the highlighted text or icon) takes the user to another retrieved document - the one pointed to by the hyperlink.   This other document may consist of further text with further links, or it may even contain a video clip, an audio clip, a small Java program, etc.

This is a powerful tool and the site must be designed to take maximum advantage of these facilities.

Dynamic

The page can display contents that vary and this can be implemented in two ways:

- The contents of pages can be automatically altered as an organisation's prices or specifications change, with each viewer seeing the altered contents.
- The web page can be structured so that the same URL will return different content to different users, depending on a variety of factors such as geographical location (e.g. displaying prices in pounds instead of dollars), time of day (e.g. the TV programme schedules) and reader profiles (e.g. using previously gathered data to review arcade games for younger users and car road tests for older users).

Interactive

On the Internet, the user is not necessarily a passive viewer but can use the site for two-way communication.   Sites may provide order forms, voting slips, comments boxes, questions, etc to take input from site viewers.   (See the chapter on developing web sites).

Intelligent

The system knows where the user has been!   It displays hypertext in two colours - one for links that a user has visited and another colour for unvisited links.

'Cookies' can also be used to store information on a user's previous usage, to guide that user's future usage of the site.   Cookies are files that are stored on the user's own local machine and can be accessed by the remote site when the user logs into that site.

Proactive

Traditional web access to information has been through browsing the millions of pages and *'pulling'* out the content that was required.   Since the web is vast and the content is constantly changing, a great deal of time is wasted through browsing and pulling.   An alternative, known as *'Push Technology'* has emerged.   This software allows users to specify the type of content that they prefer (e.g. news, share prices, sport).   The software then automatically finds the required information and places it on the users hard disk for off-line browsing at the user's convenience.   Because this process occurs at regular intervals, the user is kept up to date with their subject area.

Multimedia

The original web page carried little more than text.   Now, the basic page can deliver a wide variety of file formats.   Graphics, sound, animations and video are now commonplace.   Files created in other packages (e.g. Paintshop graphics, Director movies, Premiere videos, Voyetra MIDI music, etc) are easily integrated into web sites.   The introduction of the JavaScript programming language into the Internet also provides platform-independent applets (little programs) that are downloaded from the server and run on the local computer. The one piece of code plays the same game or runs the same animation on PCs, UNIX boxes and Macintoshes.

Design

Like software and multimedia projects, the impact of the final web site depends upon the amount of preparation that goes into the design.   For all but the smallest of sites, a systematic approach to both content and design pays dividends.

There are two chapters in this book devoted to Design, and most of that applies to web sites as much as any other medium. For example, a test specification should be drawn up before beginning to code the web documents, and the site should be tested according to that scheme once it is complete. However, there are a few differences in design regarding web sites. For example, assessing user needs is an integral part of the design process. For HTML pages displayed through a kiosk or on an Intranet, the user base is relatively easy to define. However, for web pages on the Internet, any Internet user could access the material. Designers should recognise this fact, and make sure that material made available for anyone to view is suitable for everyone. This includes not only ensuring that the material is suitable for all ages, but is accessible to as many users as possible, for example to any blind users who may wish to gain access to the information.

In cases of sensitive information, of course, the web site owners should also install secure systems to restrict access, as a splash page containing a warning is not good enough for such cases.

Other important factors in designing web content include:

- Hardware and software constraints. Designing a web page with, for example, high quality video, or requiring an obscure plugin, will put off many users. Even a relatively plain web page with a few graphics may not be fully readable to text-only browsers or mobile phone web browsers. See 'browser differences' below.
- The design environment. The exact software used to develop the web pages can often have a major impact on its design. Different packages offer different features. While a new web team might have the luxury of deciding which software to purchase and use, in many cases the software is already in place. In such a situation the page design must take into consideration the level of support that the software provides for any of the more exotic web interface techniques.
- Page design. While other types of multimedia often have a comparatively free hand in design, web pages typically follow a similar pattern. Although there are several options, such as using framesets, or having the page consist mainly of embedded Flash files, these should be considered at the design stage before beginning to accumulate media files for the project. Also, read the sections on usability and accessibility in the chapters on design.

- Visual cues. Such details as font face and size, indentation, and page placement of text can be very useful in lengthy text pages, but only if a standard format is used. For example, if important words are emphasised inconsistently, by being in italic on one paragraph, and in bold in another paragraph, this defeats the purpose of using such cues. Using style sheets (explained later) makes this easier to implement, but the style of cues still has to be decided, preferably at the design stage.
- Publication factors. Although every web space provider will allow the designer to make use of graphics and most other media types, there may be other considerations. The size of the web site may become an issue if large media files are used, and if server-side scripting or processing is to be used this must be agreed with the web space provider.

Browser Differences

The implementation of web pages should take into account the varying hardware and software in use by viewers of the site. Recent statistics suggest that Internet Explorer is used for around 95% of web usage, with Netscape accounting for 3%, and other browsers such as Opera and Mozilla making up the remainder.

This means that the web developer might very well decide to make a page intended for viewing in Internet Explorer, accepting that it might be less accessible to a small minority of web users. However, even within that majority held by IE, there are different versions in use. The oldest version of IE which is still in widespread use is version 5.0.

Differences between browsers includes a wide array of minor issues such as the precise rendering of pixels in indents, the way colours are used in certain objects, and other relatively minor layout issues which can nevertheless combine to ruin the visual appeal of a page, particularly in complex pages. The only real solution to this is to test the page thoroughly in every browser in which the design team anticipates the page being viewed by users.

However, some of the differences are more substantial. Most importantly for sites that intend to use the most up-to-date technology, IE 5.0 only partially supports XML, previous versions do not support it, and Netscape versions prior to 6.0 do not support it either. The table below documents some important differences between the major browsers in use.

	IE 4.01	IE 5.0	IE 5.5	IE 6.0	Netscape 4.7	Netscape 6.0	Netscape 7.0
XML	N	partial	Y	Y	N	Y	Y
Javascript version	1.2	1.2	1.2	1.3	1.2	1.3	1.3
VBScript	Y	Y	Y	Y	N	N	N
ActiveX	Y	Y	Y	Y	N	N	N

The differences in web browser capabilities can be accepted, and the site designed with flexibility in mind so that the differences between the page viewed on differing browsers are not major enough to cause concern. This also means refraining from using any tags, script items, or other objects that are supported only by one type of browser.

Alternatively, the differences can be overcome by making two (or more) versions of the web site, with one version optimised for one browser, and the other version optimised for another. In the past this most often meant one version for IE, and one for Netscape. However, this implies that the site has some way of sending users to on version of the site or another, based on which browser they are using. This can be done in one of three ways:

- By asking the user. The site can contain in its 'splash' page, links to the different versions of the site. This imposes the choice on the user, and leaves open the possibility that the wrong version may be picked by inexperienced users.
- By using client-side scripting to detect the browser. The script can then either load the appropriate page, or inform the user that the site requires a certain browser. Both JavaScript and VBScript can be used to perform this task. This technique is one method of 'browser awareness', and an example of its operation can be seen in the next chapter.
- By using server-side programming to detect the browser. Every request for a web page includes details of the browser type and version, as well as other information including desktop resolution and operating system in use. This information can be used to direct the user to the appropriate page, or even to automatically generate code to suit the browser.

Design characteristics

An effective web site is the result of effective design and this is characterised by two factors:

- Content   - what the site will contain and how it its pitched.
- Presentation   - how the contents will be displayed (see the chapter on 'Interface Design').

Content

Users don't log in to a site to marvel at the overall presentation. They only stay, and return, if the content is valuable to them.   Soon, millions of students and hobbyists will have the ability to create reasonably advanced web pages. What will distinguish one site from another is the impact made by the page contents.   In that respect, it is identical to writing for any publication.   The site designer must <u>understand</u> the site content.   A thorough appreciation of the overall site flavour, down to the detail on each page is necessary to structure the contents to the best advantage.   If the creator is not the site owner, the site contents must be fully discussed prior to design planning.

Presentation structures

A web site consists of many linked pages. The design of the page contents is accompanied by the design of the structure of the site. The isssue of structures is discussed in the chapter on *'Project Design'*.

Presentation

The contents are the main purpose for creating the site but the presentation of the site's pages has a great impact on drawing users into browsing its contents.   Most users decide their impression of a site within the first 10 seconds of viewing.   This highlights two factors:
- The site should be aesthetically pleasing.
- Pages should not take too long to download.

The following design characteristics should be studied before the final page contents and their presentation are decided.

Universality

The site has to be viewable by the maximum readership.   A decision must be reached on the balance between implementing the features of the newest HTML standards and latest browsers - and the effect of viewing numbers. More functionality is offered by newer standards but, since not all viewers have browsers meeting these standards, this reduces the numbers capable of viewing the site.   As time goes by more viewers will update their software - but by that time, even newer features will have been added!

Regard should be paid to the needs of the over 5 million people in the UK who are registered as disabled.   For example, visually-impaired surfers use special screen readers and these cannot cope with frames or buttons that use graphics instead of text links.

Page Size

Even today, pages will occasionally be viewed on Macs with browsers with screens of 465 pixels wide and PC's with 640x480 screens.   What looks good when designed on a 1024x768 screen may not look so good on these. Furthermore, users often view web pages in a window that is not maximised, so even the most high-resolution monitor might use a browser window of less than 640x480 pixels.

Scanability

Web site authors can learn from newspaper publishers. They know that readers don't read a page from top to bottom. They scan the page, looking first at eye-catching components such as headlines, photographs and lists.   They only look at text after this initial scan.   For best results:
- Keep the most important points at the top of the page - like newspapers.
- Use headings and subheadings.
- Use bulleted lists.
- Use link menus as this improves scanability.

Simplicity

KISS - keep it simple, stupid!   Don't overdo the number of elements (lines, text, graphics, frames, and headings) on a page. A fussy page is confusing and lacks clear navigation.

Style

Many sites revolve around the creator's flair or personality. Some of the best sites are not the most polished, but are sometimes those showing the most vitality/originality.

Readability

The many tips for maximising readability include:
- Use *'white space'*.   These are not necessarily white, but are clear screen areas designed to rest the eye - and focus the eye on important objects.
- The text content of links should be explicit (e.g. not *'important'* or *'file57'*).
- If links are embedded within a sentence, they should be part of the text, not just stuck in
  e.g. do not use -   *"click here to read about my new video camera"*
  instead use -   *"My video camera provides the raw material for the ..."*
- It is OK to use links within the main body text but don't use whole sentences as links.
- Use lines to split the page into discrete areas by topic.
- Above all, spellcheck and grammar check text content
- Use a consistent layout throughout the pages. Use the same size of heading fonts, same method of navigation, same frame sizes, etc.
- Use margins, frames, tables and lists to break blocks of text into manageable chunks.

Colours

Colour monitors' screens are covered in red, green and blue phosphor dots. Each dot can be lit to varying intensities to produce different colours (see the chapter on technology for more details).

Maximum colours

24-bit

A 24-bit graphics card can vary the intensity of each dot to 256 different levels. This produces 256 x 256 x 256 = 16,777,216 different colours. It uses 256 different values for each colour and needs three bytes (i.e. 24-bits) to store the colour of a single dot on the screen. 24-bit graphics are high quality but result in large file sizes, a problem on the Internet.

8-bit

The approach used by GIF and other low colour range images, is to use a pre-defined set of colour values, stored in a table. Each colour has a colour number or *'index'*. This table is called a *'CLUT'* (Colour Look-Up Table) and it stores a maximum of 256 values and these values are used to set the proportions of red, green and blue to be used in each colour. 256 values (i.e. 0 to 255) can be stored in a single byte, hence the name *'8-bit'*. Of course, an image may not use all of the colours in the table or it may use a different set of colour combinations. The range of colours currently stored in the table is called the *'palette'*. If an image contains colours not in the table, the extra colours are obtained by *'dithering'*. The browser produces a pattern consisting of some of the available colours. The result approximates to the wanted colour and often produces unwanted *'hatching'* or *'dotty'* effects.

It is important to know that two GIF images may have different colours within their palettes. One image may be a scanned photograph of a seascape. This palette will be made up mainly of shades of blue. Another image may be of a wood and have a palette mainly of green colours. In each case, when the GIF image is saved, the palette details are saved inside the file. When an application views the image, it reads the palette and uses it to set up the CLUT. If the two images are displayed on the screen at the same time, more colours require to be displayed than can be stored in the colour table and large parts of the image are dithered. That explains why some images appear very strange when loaded.

Conclusions

Leave 24-bit images to kiosk and CD use, or for images designed to be downloaded rather than displayed on-line. Larger palettes on the Internet are often a waste of capacity (they need more web site disk space), time (they take longer to download) and quality (colours will be dithered on some systems). Many designers use 8-bit images for the Internet.

With the increasing use of broadband and other fast Internet technologies, this may become less of a problem in the future – but designers will still have to consider the many millions who do not use fast connections.

Browser-safe colours

The Netscape Navigator and Internet Explorer browsers use the same colour table and this stores six levels for each colour, i.e. 6 red x 6 green x 6 blue = 216 different colours. On an 8-bit colour system, all other colours not in this 216 colour table are dithered.

The six levels for each colour are shown in the table.

Hex	Decimal	Percentage
00	0	0%
33	51	20%
66	102	40%
99	153	60%
CC	204	80%
FF	255	100%

The percentage value shows the relative saturation while the decimal value expresses the RGB level.
HTML uses the hex values for each colour. So, for example, 000000 has all three colours turned off to produce black while FFFFFF has each colour at full saturation, producing white.

PCs and Macintosh computers can both use these 216 colours in their system palettes. However, of the standard Windows palette of 16 colours, only eight appear in the 216-colour palette.

Conclusions

Wherever possible, use the standard 216-colour table to minimise dithering.
Convert existing GIF files to this table's palette, using a graphics package such as Paintshop. This technique works best with clipart, graphs and other non-photographic images. Since photographs have a wide range of colours and many colours in the same range (e.g. lots of blues or lots of greens), converting to 216 colours will degrade the quality of the final display. The 216-colour palette may not already exist in a graphics package but all packages allow for the importing of new palettes. The palette can be downloaded from the Internet and stored in the graphics package. Search the web for *'216 colours'* or use the graphic file offered in:

        http://www.onr.com/user/lights/netcol.html

The site provides a graphics file that contains the palette.
The issue of designing with colour is covered in the chapter on *'Interface Design'*.

Gathering resources

After the design phase is complete, the developer should concentrate on making sure that all of the required resources are available before beginning to actually create the web site. The resources required can be split into two categories: the equipment (both hardware and software) required to develop the web documents; and the media assets to be included in the web site.

Hardware and software resources

While a perfectly acceptable web site can be created armed with only a text editor and knowledge of HTML, a range of hardware and software tools can speed up and broaden a web site's development.

The hardware tools are

- Scanners
- Audio recording equipment
- Digital still cameras
- Digital video cameras

This equipment is used to help gather media for the document. For example, video clips can be acquired through a digital video camera; photographic images can be gathered using the scanner or digital stills camera; and even text can be gathered for the web pages by scanning and using OCR on physical documents.

The software tools include:

- HTML editors
- HTML syntax checkers
- HTML generators
- Site performance testers

These resources are used to generate and validate the HTML documents that are used in the project.

HTML editors/generators

The most basic editing tool is an ASCII editor such as Notepad or DOS EDIT. The author requires knowledge of the entire scripting language and layout, as there is no in-built assistance.

The next step up is an add-on to an existing word-processing package, such as Word.

These can be as simple as a set of macros that provide on-screen buttons to embed tags into the document (e.g. GT_HTML.DOT) or can offer further facilities such as an add-on browser (e.g. Internet Assistant for Word).   Since they are within a word-processing package, all the package's facilities, such as spell checking and text formatting, are available to the author.

The current trend is to use software packages that are dedicated to the production of web pages and entire web sites. These packages use two approaches:

- Text-based HTML editors.
- WYSIWYG-based HTML generators.

Text editors

An example of a text-based editor is shown in the illustration.   The main work area is a text screen and the script entries are placed in this text area.   The cursor is placed where the item is to be added and the desired icon or menu option is selected.

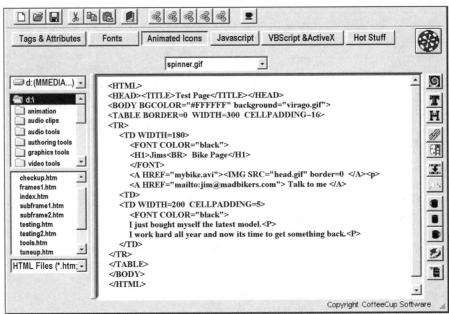

This method speeds up page development but the effect of the script is not seen until it is viewed from the computer's browser (called up via an on-screen icon).   This method involves an amount of trial-and-error - changing the script and viewing the result are separate operations.   These packages are continually increasingly their features and the example package shown, *'Coffee Cup'*, also allows simple integration of graphics and Java applets into the script. These editors are popular choices with writers with some previous HTML knowledge, who use them to get greater control over the site.

The drawback with these packages is that the writer is continually switching between the edit window and the viewing window.   To overcome this, other packages, such as Hippie 97, display both windows on screen at the same time. Writers can edit their entries and view the script and the web page at the same time.

Graphics editors

These are the most popular packages, as the main work area is the web page rather than the HTML script. The writer can concentrate on the design and the package converts the screen layout into an HTML script.   The script can still be edited directly for more complex work.   All the elements such as text, tables, images and buttons can be dragged from menus and dropped into the page editor (i.e. the design screen).

There are facilities for both beginners and experienced authors.

- For novices, the packages provide *'templates'*. These are pre-designed layouts for both personal and business pages.   Once loaded into the editor, a template is then edited to personalise the content. Templates offer comprehensive features such as *'Whats New'*, Table of Contents, Feedback forms and search forms. Beginners can also use *'Wizards'*, which create a layout that results from answers to questions to the author.

- Advanced authors benefit from the simplification of tasks (e.g. resizing table widths or frame sizes by dragging with the mouse, or creating image map links simply by drawing an outline using the mouse cursor).

The packages also integrate some of the graphic functions of other packages, such as providing a clipart library, a catalogue of image thumbnails, or image editing and animation facilities.

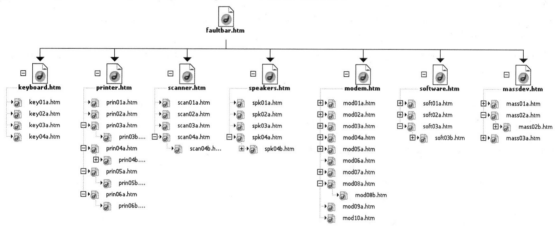

The illustration shows the Macromedia Dreamweaver package being used to display a site map. The panel shows some of the contents of the fault-finding system from the Dumbreck web site.   Dreamweaver can also show the resources that are included on each web page, including internal links, external links and graphics files.

Site management

As a site expands, there are increasing problems of managing the project, resulting in unfinished pages going unnoticed or inadequate navigation (e.g. pages with no links, links pointing to non-existent pages, etc).   The best editors provide not only page creation tools, but tools for managing the overall site. This could include the graphical display of all pages and links, so that the author sees the overall structure. The package may also allow the author to create a *'To Do'* list.   The author creates the basic structure and the To Do list reminds him/her of the tasks still to be completed.

Site management tools could also include improved uploading facilities and database tools.

Validation checkers

These facilities may be built in to editors and are also available as separate utilities.   They check the page documents prior to them being uploaded.   They report on any syntax errors (e.g. missing tags) and check for any browser versions that cannot handle all the commands in the page scripts. Examples are the freeware Xenu and Spyglass validators.

Site performance testers

This software reports on the time taken to load pages and the number of links that currently point to a page.   These facilities can be obtained on-line from tester sites on the Internet.

Asset Management

Once the web developers have all the required hardware and software in place, the gathering of assets can take place. These assets include:

- Graphics, video, sound, music, and other media
- Document templates
- Any files that are to be made available for download
- Stylesheets or other means of maintaining consistency between web pages. (see the next chapter for details)

These assets are discussed in more detail in the following pages. However, just as important as the collection of assets, is organising them in a logical and efficient manner. It has been said that creative professionals spend around 3% of their time simply looking for media they know they have, and even then they find it less than two thirds of the time.

'*Digital Asset Management*' (DAM) is the process used to organise media to make them easier to locate, use, and re-use. There are a variety of DAM providers on the market, many of them providing web space to store media, but the actual location of the files is less important than what is done with them. In a well-designed DAM system, the files will be named according to an agreed convention; the files will follow a rigid structure, and those files will be backed up on a regular basis.

A consistent file naming convention is desirable; for example if web designers use graphics called 'image244.jpg', this name is meaningless unless there is some other document available explaining how the numbers are arrived at. Names like 'flower2.jpg' and 'downloadpage.html' are more descriptive, but can easily result in overly long or confusing filenames, and possibly even duplicate filenames.

A more useful system is one whereby the filenames are arranged according to categories, for example the download section might have files called 'download_index.html' and 'download_feedback.html'. Another common example is to have two sets of images, one of thumbnails and the other being the full image. These files might be named 'flower_thumb.gif' and 'flower_large.gif', with the same rule applying to other images.

The other major factor in asset management is arranging the files into a directory structure, on a centralised resource such as a file server. Note that the directory structure used to store assets need not necessarily be the same as the directory structure that is finally created on the web site. Indeed, it might be useful to have all media files of a specific type within a single folder or sub-folder, in order to quickly edit, compare, or create new media from existing items.

For example, a college could well have different styles for different campuses. Each would have their own folder, and within that, sub-folders for document templates, images, and other media. The images might further be split into 'style-related' images such as buttons and rulers, and 'content-related' images such as staff pictures.

As can be seen, the exact structure and naming of the assets will depend on the project. Most third-party DAM providers use a database of media files, containing information such as resolution, date of creation, author, and so on. For smaller companies an in-house asset management system can be just as effective, however.

Finally, note that it is often useful to have a 'blank' copy of assets wherever possible. In other words, items such as buttons, headings and so on, should have a corresponding file, with no text on it, so that new buttons and headings can be created if the need arises.

Graphics

Graphics play an important, even primary, role in making a site more attractive.   They can also be used to make navigation easier (i.e. by using navigation icons) and can impart information (e.g. displaying photographs, maps, graphs, etc). Nevertheless, there are a few rules on the use of graphics.

- Do not place too many images on one page, as this is both distracting for the viewer, as well as producing long download times.   There are exceptions where the user expects/wants to wait - e.g. to view goods or property, fanzine sites, etc. In general, the purpose of every image should be questioned with unnecessary graphics being ruthlessly eliminated.
- Don't let the page background overpower the content.   The background image must not obscure the foreground text or dominate the page.
- Use the <ALT> attribute on all <IMG> tags. This provides a text alternative for graphic images and is useful for browsers set to read pages in text-only mode.   It also ensures the maximum readership of the site.
- Use thumbnail graphics (i.e. miniatures) on the page, with links to downloading the larger version.   This speeds up the page download. Users can see the draft of the graphics and decide whether it is worth the extra time to download the larger version.
- Use graphics for bullets.   This looks better than standard bullets. Keep the same graphic (e.g. a red ball) for all other page bullets.   The graphic will be loaded into the local PC's browser cache and this reduces subsequent download times.
- Reuse other images in the same way.   The download time overhead only happens once.

- Use image libraries. Graphic files are installed on many web servers. These can be used for the server's web sites, reducing the space used by each site. Since the server also provides more effective caching of its own graphics, this results in speedier access.
- Scanned images should be scanned at the average of 72dpi. Monitors range from about 70dpi to 100dpi. Scanning at greater resolutions increases file space and provides no extra resolution quality.

Graphic Types
The most common graphics formats are GIF and JPEG. They both use compression to minimise file size and download times.

JPEG should be used for photographic images. These are in 24-bit colour but offer increased levels of compression with decreased picture quality.

GIFs should be used for non-photographic images (e.g. clipart, logos, and banners). These files can be reduced to 8-colour or even B&W (although B&W images save little space and are used mainly for aesthetic reasons). The big advantage of GIFs is that they can be organised in a variety of ways (transparent images, animated images and interlaced images - see later).

Document templates

In the same way that it is useful to keep blank copies of web page buttons, a blank copy of the HTML document for a web page is often useful as well. Such 'blank' HTML pages are called 'templates'. It is important to achieve consistency of web pages – it does not look professional to have the front page using entirely different background images and buttons from every other page. Although in some cases two or more styles may be appropriate (for large organisations with different departments, or to showcase your web development work), even then there will typically be several folders full of material, so standardisation is important.

```
<!DOCTYPE HTML PUBLIC "-//W3C//DTD HTML 3.2//EN">
<html>

<head>
<title>Product page</title>
</head>

<body bgcolor="#FFFFEE" link="#990000" vlink="#660000" alink="#FF0000">
<table border="0" width="600" cellspacing="0" cellpadding="0">
 <tr>
  <td width="35%">Product name:</td>
  <td></td>
 </tr>
 <tr>
  <td>Price:</td>
  <td></td>
 </tr>
 <tr>
  <td>Number in stock:</td>
  <td></td>
 </tr>
</table>
</body>
</html>
```

One method of doing this is to use stylesheets, as explained in the next chapter. This is a technical method, which is not accessible to all web users, and there are still some areas that stylesheets do not cover. Indeed, even when using stylesheets, a template can make use of style items easier. For any of these circumstances a template is useful. At its simplest, a template contains just the basic tags, namely the DOCTYPE, HTML, HEAD and BODY tags, as well as links to the relevant style sheets or background images. However, items such as lists, tables, forms and frames are likely to contain the same tags in one page as the next, and a template can be created to make their integration simpler.

For example, if one part of the site contains several pages, each of which has a table showing various statistics about products, then a template could be prepared, such as the one shown in the illustration.

This template could then be filled out for each page, including the name, price and number in stock for each item. Using a template in this manner means that creating new pages will involve less work, and will more closely match the style of other, similar pages, since layout-related items such as width of table columns can be set within the template. This can easily be combined with stylesheets, to provide even greater consistency while being able to update the entire site's style by changing just one file.

HTML implementation

When the design is complete and all the resources (text, graphics, etc) are gathered, the elements can be combined in the set of web pages to comprise the web site.   These are implemented using HTML and are given the extension .HTM with the home page usually being called *'index.htm'*.

The HyperText Markup Language is the language used for all web pages, although some other languages build round an HTML framework.   An HTML script is written in plain ASCII, using any plain text editor (e.g. NotePad or EDIT) or word processor with the document saved a plain text file.   Since ASCII characters are readable by all types of computer (UNIX, PC, Mac, etc) on the Internet, it forms the foundation of a platform-free language.   One script is used for all machines, with each translating the script into its own machine-specific tasks.

A web page is simply a text file (known as a *'script'*) containing a list of commands.   The script lines are used to display text and graphics, check whether the user has clicked on a particular object and jump to other parts of the script (or even other scripts).   In these respects, an HTML page script is similar to a DOS batch file or the script for a program written in interpreted Basic.

However, the script may also contain information about what font style to use for text, which pieces of text are to be checked for user input and so on.   This information is embedded in the HTML file as additional sets of ASCII characters.   These are called *'tags'* and are similar to the codes in Microsoft Word that turn italics or bold face off and on.   With Word, these tags are normally hidden from the user; with HTML, the tags appear as part of the ASCII script.   As long as all browsers know that the tag <I> turns on italics and </I> turns off italics, they can all make sense of the script file.   How each machine displays and prints italics is nothing to do with the web page writer - the translation is up to the user's browser and operating system.   Similarly, HTML may describe a piece of text as having a certain 'header' size, rather than as 24-point Arial.   Each machine will decide what font size and style it will use as a header.   This makes the entire HTML language completely machine-independent and explains its popularity as a means of exchanging information between different computer systems.

Apart from all the text to be displayed on the screen, the HTML script file contains:

- Tags which tell the browser how to display the various parts of the text (font size, underlining, etc).
- Tags which instruct the browser to fetch an image and place it on a particular area of the screen.
- Hyperlinks which take the user to another part of the document or to another HTML document.

There are many applications that are dedicated to simplifying the process.   These vary from add-ons to Microsoft Word through to full-blown design packages.   These packages still produce an HTML ASCII file as their final products.

Note

HTML pages using simple commands can be read by all browsers.   If the latest HTML innovation or add-ons for animations, audio, video, etc are used, then only browsers equipped with these facilities will be able to make use of all the site's features.   Various brands of browser, and even different versions of the same brand, may produce different screen results while executing the same HTML command.   Due to constant changes and additions, no browser software faithfully implements every available command.

Basic structure

The illustration shows the minimum layout of an HTML script.   Note that all the tags start with the '<' (i.e. the less than symbol) and end with the '>' (i.e. the greater than symbol).   Repeating a tag reverses the earlier tag's effects, if the second tag is prefaced with a forward slash character.

```
<HTML>
<HEAD>
<TITLE>
    title text goes here
</TITLE>
</HEAD>
<BODY>
    main script goes here
    ...
    ...
</BODY>
</HTML>
```

The effects of some tags need to be cancelled (e.g. turning on and off italics around a word or phrase).   Other tags, such as drawing a line, need only appear once.   Tags are not case sensitive; they can be entered in upper or lower case, although most writers use upper case for easier recognition.

The tags used in this basic script are:

- The 'HTML' tags are placed at the beginning and end of all HTML documents to tell browsers that the information enclosed is the valid section for translation.
- The 'HEAD' tag contains the title of the web page, as it will appear in the browser's title bar.
- The words placed between the 'TITLE' tags are those that are used when the page is added to a user's bookmark.   It is also the text that is examined and displayed as the header in search engine results.
- The HEAD section can also contain 'META' tags to hold key words to help identify the site to search engines.
- Material placed between the two 'BODY' tags influences the contents displayed in the user's browser window.

Example script

This is a sample of a basic HTML script and its output, as seen by a browser.

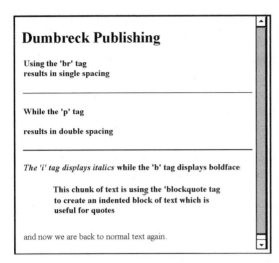

```
<HTML>
<HEAD>
<TITLE>A sample script</TITLE>
</HEAD>
<BODY BGCOLOR="#00FFFF" TEXT="BLUE">
<H1>Dumbreck Publishing</H1>
Using the 'br' tag<BR>
results in
single spacing
<HR>
While the 'p' tag<P>
results in double spacing
<HR>
<I>The 'i' tag displays italics</I>
<B>while the 'b' tag displays boldface</B>
<BLOCKQUOTE>This chunk of text is using the
'blockquote' tag to create an indented block of text which
is useful for quotes
</BLOCKQUOTE>
and now we are back to the normal text again.
</BODY>
</HTML>
```

Most tags also provide additional refinements. These are known as the tag's *'attributes'* and they may provide control over an object's size, colour and screen position. The inclusion of attributes is optional, although non-inclusion usually results in the adoption of the current or default values. For example, objects may be positioned on the left margin by default, while an attribute may be included in a tag to make a particular object right justified.

The various tags used in the above example are:

<I>   All text between this tag and a </I> tag is displayed in italics.

<B>   All text between this tag and a </B> tag is displayed in boldface.

BGCOLOR   This, along with 'TEXT' are optional attributes within the <BODY> tag.
The BGCOLOR attribute sets the colour of the screen background and the TEXT attribute sets the colour of the all the text in the document (unless overruled).
Colours values can be specified in two ways:

1. By naming the colour - e.g. TEXT="BLUE" or BGCOLOR="YELLOW". This is the simplest method when one of the sixteen colour names understood by browsers is required (see later for the full list). The default text colour is black and the default background colour is white.

2. When subtle colours, without any given name are required, values are set by giving the hex value of the amount of red, green and blue in the mix. In the example above, the red value is 00, while the green and blue values are both FF. This is entered as BGCOLOUR="#00FFFF" and results in a cyan background. To obtain blue text, the text attribute could have been specified as "TEXT=#00FF00" - i.e. red fully off, blue fully on and green fully off. The hash symbol '#' should be included to ensure that all browsers recognise the values as hexadecimal amounts.
    Software utilities such as RGB and RGB2WEB allow the writer to move sliders to mix the colours. When the desired colour is viewed in the colour box, the decimal and hex values for that colour are displayed. The values can be noted and included in the page script or, in some utilities, the values can be copied straight from the utility and pasted directly into the page script.

    Provides the equivalent of a carriage return in word processing. The remaining text is displayed on the next line.

<P>   The P tag is seen as the start of a new paragraph and an extra line of white space is inserted.
It provides the equivalent of two carriage returns.

<BLOCKQUOTE>   Any text enclosed between this tag and the </BLOCKQUOTE> tag is treated as a quote and is indented from both sides of the page. The <BR> tag can also be used between these tags.

<HR>   Draws a horizontal line, called the *'rule'*, across the page and is used to separate out or emphasise sections of text. Without any attributes (i.e. used by itself as in the above example) it displays a line that is the width of the browser window.

Optional attributes for the <HR> tag are:

ALIGN=	Use LEFT, RIGHT or CENTER to position the rule on the screen.
NOSHADE	Draws the rule as a solid block. The default is a 3-D shaded rule.
SIZE=	Sets the height of the rule in pixels.
WIDTH=	Sets the rule width in pixels or as a percentage of the window width eg WIDTH=50%

As many of the attributes as required can be used together as in this example:

<HR ALIGN=CENTER NOSHADE SIZE=15   WIDTH=300>

Text formatting

Note that there is no set width to a line of text. Browsers word wrap the text into as many lines as its screen allows. This, in turn, depends on the resolution of the monitor and font size used.   Lower resolution screens and larger fonts result in a paragraph of text spreading over more screen lines.

Also note that in the earlier example, separate script lines were used for the words *"results in"* and *"single spacing"* but the final output displayed it on the same line.   That is because normal carriage returns entered by an ASCII editor are ignored by browsers.   Browsers only respond to specific tag commands to move to a new line (apart from the word wrapping mentioned earlier).

Adding extra spaces between words or lines, for formatting and indentation purposes, are also ignored.   All words are assembled into one giant paragraph unless formatting tags are used.

Font formats

Other font formats are <U> which turns on underlined text and <S> which turns on strikethrough text (eg ~~strikethrough~~).   Another tag called <TT> for *'teletype text'* is used to switch into a non-proportional font such as Courier. It is used to display numeric tables, as all columns can be guaranteed to align vertically. It can also be used to give a different appearance to programme listings of Pascal, C++, etc.

Other formatting tags are <SUP> which displays in superscript and <SUB> which displays in subscript.

The <SMALL> tag will display the content in a smaller than normal font until it is switched off with the </SMALL> tag. Similarly, the <BIG> tag displays the content in a larger than normal font.   The actual size of the BIG and SMALL fonts will depend on the body font chosen by the user.

Heading tags

HTML provides a set of heading tags. These are <H1> through to <H6> and are used to provide headings and sub-headings to improve the document's formatting. All text enclosed by the <H1> and </H1> tags is displayed in the largest font size, with <H6> displaying the smallest font size.   As the example shows, cancelling a heading tag also results in a paragraph break.

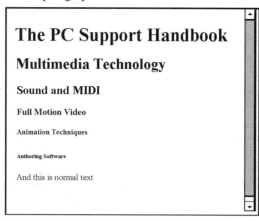

```
<HTML>
<HEAD>
<TITLE>Example heading sizes</TITLE>
</HEAD>
<BODY BGCOLOR="WHITE" TEXT="BLACK">
<H1>The PC Support Handbook</H1>
<H2>Multimedia Technology</H2>
<H3>Sound and MIDI</H3>
<H4>Full Motion Video</H4>
<H5>Animation Techniques</H5>
<H6>Authoring Software</H6>
<P>
And this is normal text
</BODY>
</HTML>
```

Headings should not be used to replace the <B> tag to emphasise parts of the text.   Many search tools use the headings of a page to extract important information from a site.   The tools assume that if the writer found the text to be significant enough to be used as a heading, then it is important enough for search purposes. While a subject heading is a good choice for extraction, an individual word or phrase - emphasised with a heading tag - devalues the site search if it not of any significance.   For example the phrase *"this should **NOT** be tried at home"* should use the <B> tag to embolden the word *'NOT'*. If the word was emphasised using a heading tag, search engines would place an unwarranted significance to the word for search results.

Font faces

The viewer is able to set the typestyle that the browser uses to display web pages. This is set from the *'Fonts'* button on the *'Internet options'* choice in Internet Explorer's *'Tools'* menu.   Users can choose from Times New Roman, Arial, Verdana, Georgia, etc.   The webs site designer, however, may prefer that the viewer see the pages with a particular font. The pages, for example, may have been designed to look best with a sans serif font such as Arial or Verdana. There are a number of ways to influence what the user sees on his/screen and these are discussed below.

FACE

The FONT tag has a FACE attribute that specifies what font or style should be displayed. At it simplest, the lines
        <FONT FACE="serif">   or   <FONT FACE="sans-serif">
can be included in the script.   This ensures that the viewer will see the main class of type, but does not specifies the actual font to be used.   The line
        <FONT FACE="Verdana, Arial, Helvetica">
specifies that the Verdana font should be used as a first option. If the font is not present on the user's computer, the Arial font should be used, followed by Helvetica as the third option. If none of the fonts are installed on the user's machine, the default font will be used.

This is a very simple way of specifying fonts but it has two major drawbacks:

- Not every browser supports this attribute.
- Different computer systems use different names for their fonts (one system might have a Times font, while another has a Times Roman or a Times New Roman font).

Although the method is simple, it does not guarantee the required results for all those viewing the site.

Embedding Fonts

Bitstream have introduced a scheme to store their own TrueDoc fonts on their site.   The designer creates links to their site at truedoc.com and these fonts can be displayed on a users web page.   This requires a little JavaScript and either the <FONT FACE= > tag using Cascading Style Sheets.   The user does not require to download these fonts, as Navigator 4 onwards, and Explorer with a free Bitstream Active X control installed, can read the font elements from the TrueDoc site and display them.   This allows designers to choose fonts in the knowledge that the user will see them the way the designer planed.   Microsoft, of course, has developed a competing standard known as *'TrueType font embedding'*.

Cascading Style Sheets

See the next chapter for details.

Graphic Text

There may be times when no existing font will do for a screen.   For example, the letters of a heading may be required to be constructed from real world objects such as straws, pencils or even human bodies. Alternatively, a special font shape may be required to create the mood for the web site.   For example, an oil company may wish the letters of the heading to look like drops of oil.   Since none of these shapes will appear in any existing font, the only way to ensure that the user sees the text in the required way is to create the words as a graphic file.   This results in a graphics file which, although not too large for use as a heading, could not be used as the entire body text.   If the same type of text is required to appear in different headings throughout the web site, a graphic image can be created for each character that appears, so that these can be re-used throughout the pages.

Flash

Macromedia Flash (see the next chapter) can embed any font into a Flash screen, which can then be displayed on any viewer's computer.   Since the Flash file contains vector data, only the descriptions of character shapes are sent and therefore the viewers computer can reproduce it.   The Flash screen can have rollovers, sounds, animations, fades, etc. and can also have links that jump to other Flash files.   This means that an entire web site could be created without the use of a single installed font.   The problems with this method are that the Flash files are not searched by search engines and are not readable by text readers.   Additionally, older browsers need a plug-in of around 118kB to be downloaded and installed in order to read Flash files and this is likely to put many viewers off.

Colours

Internet Explorer and Netscape recognise the following sixteen colour names:

BLACK	GREEN	MAROON	LIME
WHITE	RED	OLIVE	TEAL
GRAY	BLUE	NAVY	AQUA
SILVER	YELLOW	PURPLE	FUCHSIA

These colour values can be used to set the colour of the screen background, the main text, the borders and shading of objects and the various hyperlink states (e.g. unexplored or explored).

An alternative that is accepted by all browsers is using hex numbers for the RGB values.

To display white text on a black background use either:
        <BODY BGCOLOR="BLACK" TEXT="WHITE"> or   <BODY BGCOLOR="#000000" TEXT="#FFFFFF">
The text of unexplored links is blue by default.   This can be changed with LINK="colour"
        <BODY BGCOLOR="BLACK" TEXT="WHITE" LINK="YELLOW">
The text of explored links is purple/red by default. This can be changed with VLINK="colour"
        <BODY BGCOLOR="BLACK" TEXT="WHITE" VLINK="LIME>
The <BODY TEXT=colour> tag changes the colour of the default text on a page.   To change the colour of a particular paragraph, sentence, word or even a single letter, the <FONT> tag can be used with a COLOR attribute as in this example:

        Do <FONT COLOR="RED"> NOT </FONT> try this at home

The word 'Do' is displayed in the default text colour while the word 'NOT' is displayed in red.   When the browser reads the </FONT> it again displays all text in the original default colour.   Again, the colour values can be entered as one of the given sixteen text values or can be entered as hex numbers.

Escape characters

There are times when the page has to display characters that are already used for formatting commands, such as & and > and <. Using them inside a normal text line may produce unexpected results in some browsers. In addition, some characters are not available in the standard ASCII set and can't be directly typed in from the keyboard.

HTML provides escape sequences to overcome these problems. All escape characters begin with an ampersand character and are either followed by a text sequence or by a numeric sequence.

The range of text escape sequences includes:

Sequence	Displayed character	Sequence	Displayed character
&gt	>	&amp	&
&lt	<	&quot	"

The numeric sequence places a hash symbol between the ampersand and the number and the range includes:

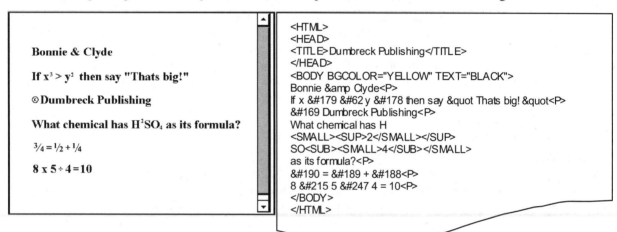

Sequence	Displayed character	Sequence	Displayed character
&#153	™	&#179	^{3}
&#169	©	&#188	¼
&#174	®	&#189	½
&#176	°	&#190	¾
&#178	^{2}	&#247	÷

Creating lists

Most visitors to a web site dislike having to scroll through long paragraphs of text, trying to extract the main points. Often, the information can be displayed more effectively as a list of main points.

HTML supports three types of lists and these are shown in the example below.

Unordered list

This is used when numbering the items has no relevance.   The items appear as a bulleted list as shown in the example. The <UL> and </UL> tags indicate that the enclosed items are list items.   Each individual list item has a <LI> tag. The general layout is:

```
<UL>
<LI> first item to display
<LI> second item
<LI> third item
</UL>
```

The <UL> tag has a number of options, although the final effect may depend upon the browser used.

Use	Explanation	Example
TYPE="DISC"	The bullets are filled circles (this is the default)	●
TYPE="SQUARE"	The bullets are square	■
TYPE="CIRCLE"	The bullets are unfilled circles	O

So, for example   <UL TYPE="SQUARE">   displays an unordered list with square bullets.

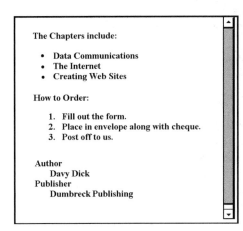

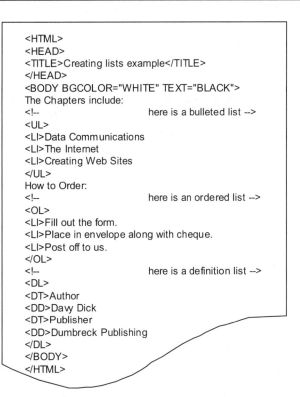

```
<HTML>
<HEAD>
<TITLE>Creating lists example</TITLE>
</HEAD>
<BODY BGCOLOR="WHITE" TEXT="BLACK">
The Chapters include:
<!--                      here is a bulleted list -->
<UL>
<LI>Data Communications
<LI>The Internet
<LI>Creating Web Sites
</UL>
How to Order:
<!--                      here is an ordered list -->
<OL>
<LI>Fill out the form.
<LI>Place in envelope along with cheque.
<LI>Post off to us.
</OL>
<!--                      here is a definition list -->
<DL>
<DT>Author
<DD>Davy Dick
<DT>Publisher
<DD>Dumbreck Publishing
</DL>
</BODY>
</HTML>
```

Ordered list

This is used when numbering the items is significant, such a set of instructions.   The items appear as a bulleted list as shown in the example. The general layout is:

```
<OL>
<LI> first item to display
<LI> second item
<LI> third item
</OL>
```

The <OL> tag has a number of attribute options:

Use	Explanation	Example
TYPE="1"	Standard Arabic numerals will number the list	1, 2, 3, 4, 5, 6, 7
TYPE="A"	Upper case letters will number the list	A, B, C, D, E, F
TYPE="a"	Lower case letters will number the list	a, b, c, d, e, f
TYPE="I"	Upper case Roman numerals will number the list	I, II, III, IV, V, VI, VII
TYPE="i"	Lower case Roman numerals will number the list	i, ii, iii, iv, v, vi, vii
START=	Alters the default starting point for numbering	See below

So,   <OL TYPE="A" START=G">   displays an ordered list with the items listed as G, H, I, J, etc.
While   <OL TYPE="1" START="10">   displays an ordered list numbered as 10, 11, 12, 13, 14, etc.

Definition list

Definition lists, sometimes called *'glossary lists'*, produce a list of terms and their descriptions.
The general layout is:
```
        <DL>
        <DT>  first term
        <DD> first definition
        <DT> second term
        <DD> second definition
        </DL>
```
The <DT> tag places the text in the left of the screen and the following <DD> tag indents the next line.

Nesting lists

Lists can be nested - one list is embedded within another list.   The example also shows the <BR> tag being used within a list to move to a new line without inserting another bullet.

Comments

The script on the previous page inserted comments using the <!-- *comment* --> tag.   Comments make the script easier to understand but their content is ignored by browsers and is not displayed.

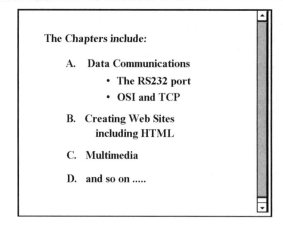

```
<HTML>
<HEAD>
<TITLE>Nested lists example</TITLE>
</HEAD>
<BODY BGCOLOR="WHITE" TEXT="BLUE">
The Chapters include:
<OL TYPE = "A" >
<LI> Data Communications
<UL>
    <LI> The RS232 port
    <LI> OSI and TCP
</UL>
<LI> Creating Web Sites
<BR>
including HTML
<LI> Multimedia
<LI> and so on .....
</OL>
</BODY>
</HTML>
```

Aligning objects

By default, text and other objects such as graphics, tables etc, are aligned down the left of the screen.
An individual heading or paragraph can be positioned using the ALIGN attribute. For example:

          `<H2 ALIGN=CENTER> blah blah blah </H2>`   aligns the text in the centre of the screen
          `<H2 ALIGN=RIGHT> blah blah blah </H2>`   aligns the text to the right edge of the screen
          `<H2 ALIGN=LEFT> blah blah blah </H2>`   aligns the text to the left edge of the screen

With this method, each item has its own individual ALIGN attribute.   Where a larger section of items share the same alignment, the entire section is enclosed by a set of <DIV> tags as in this example:

          `<DIV ALIGN=CENTER>`
          `<H1> My Name </H1>`
          `<H2> My address </H2>`
          `</DIV>`

The <DIV> tag has the advantage that it can enclose all kinds of objects such as paragraphs of text, headings, images, tables, etc.   When a <DIV> tag is used it alters that section's alignment, but the software remembers the previous alignment.   When the </DIV> tag is reached, the alignment reverts to this previous value.   To ensure that the script will work with all browser versions, always cancel a <DIV> tag before issuing another <DIV> tag.

Order of tags

Tags may be *'nested'* - i.e. a new tag or set of tags may be placed within an existing set of tags. To ensure that the script produces the expected results in all browsers, cancellation tags should be placed in reverse order to the order of declaring them.

So,   `<BLOCKQUOTE><I><B> blah blah blah </B></I><BLOCKQUOTE>` is correct while
               `<BLOCKQUOTE><I><B> blah blah blah </BLOCKQUOTE></I></B>` is bad practice.

While some browsers may be more tolerant than others, failure to observe this rule may result in page formatting not looking the way that was anticipated.

Navigating the web site

So far, this chapter has considered:
- Web site contents.
- Design structures.
- Formatting of web page text.

The completed site consists of a collection of web pages held together by a set of *'hyperlinks'*.   The links are another set of HTML tags and they are used to:
- Take the user to another part of the same web page
- Take the user to another web page in the same web site
- Take the user to another web site altogether.

The basis of all web navigation is the *'anchor tag'* or *'link tag'*.   The format of a link tag is:

          `<A HREF="where to jump"> Text for the hyperlink  </A>`

The tag comprises several sections:

\<A HREF="where to jump"\>	The 'A' indicates that it is an anchor tag - i.e. treat the tag as a link. The 'HREF' indicates that is a hyperlink reference (other options can be placed here as can be seen later). The text part indicates what document or part of the document to jump to. This may point to another document using either: • The URL (full hostname and filename) of a document on the WWW. • The name of another document inside the same web site. It can also point to a 'label' within the currently displayed document.
Text for the hyperlink	The text that appears underlined on the screen waiting to be clicked.
\</A\>	The closing tag to indicate the end of the link definition.

Example link tags are:

    <A HREF="order.htm"> Ordering Information</A>
    <A HREF="http://www.dumbreck.demon.co.uk/index.html"> Dumbreck Publishing </A>
    <A HREF="#mboard"> Testing the motherboard </A>

Jumping within a web page

This is commonly used with large linear web pages such as FAQ pages and other technical pages. The link tag points to a particular section of the document that is specially labelled. The label is embedded in the document and is known as the *'anchor'* with its own anchor tag. Labels can be spread throughout the document, allowing jumping both up and down through the document. This technique is similar to the GOTO command used in DOS batch files and some programming languages. The link tag has a hash symbol before the name of the label to indicate that what follows is a label and not a URL. So, "#Chapter1" points to an anchor within the document. The format of the anchor tag is:

    <A NAME="anchor name"> The text to be displayed at the anchor point </A>

Note: In the example, all the text is displayed on a single screen and clicking the hyperlinks has no apparent effect. To test this page, the text sections have to be expanded so that the document requires several pages to display.

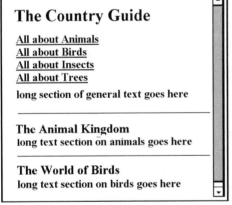

```
<HTML>
<HEAD> <TITLE>Dumbreck Publishing</TITLE> </HEAD>
<BODY BGCOLOR="WHITE" TEXT="BLACK">
<H2>The Country Guide</H2>
<A HREF="#Chapter1">All about Animals</A> <BR>
<A HREF="#Chapter2">All about Birds    </A> <BR>
<A HREF="#Chapter3">All about Insects </A> <BR>
<A HREF="#Chapter4">All about Trees   </A> <BR>
long section of general text goes here    <BR><HR>
<B><A NAME = "Chapter1"> The Animal Kingdom</A></B><BR>
long text section on animals goes here    <BR><HR>
<B><A NAME = "Chapter2"> The World of Birds</A><BR></B>
long text section on birds goes here <BR>
the other chapters go in here <BR>
</BODY>
</HTML>
```

Jumping to another page

A web site usually consists of many pages and the user is encouraged to jump between the pages by clicking the hypertext links.

Consider the following hypertext link:

    <A HREF="order.htm"> Ordering Information</A>

The words *'Ordering Information'* will appear on the screen as the hypertext link. Clicking on that text makes the browser load the web page called *'order.htm'*. This assumes that the file called *'order.htm'* is in the same directory as the web page that is pointing to it. This is the most common case for small to medium web sites. It also simplifies the command since only the file name need be supplied.

Where the site's files are held in a number of directories, relative paths may be specified as shown.

HREF="finance/order.htm"	The web page can be found in the directory called *'finance'* and the 'finance' directory is a sub-directory of the current directory.
HREF="book/finance/order.htm"	The web page can be found in the directory called *'finance'* which is a sub-directory of the *'book'* directory which, in turn, is a sub-directory of the current directory.
HREF="../order.htm"	The web page can be found in the directory above the current directory.

HREF="../../order.htm"	The web page can be found in the directory two levels above the current directory.
HREF="/d|/mysite/order.htm"	The web can be found in the *'mysite'* directory of the D: drive. Note that a vertical bar replaces the semi-colon normally found after a drive letter.

Keep all the site's resources in the same directory - or use relative paths. This simplifies site maintenance, since the site can be moved to different disk directories without changing all the link references.

Note

While tags are not case sensitive, the directory and file functions of some operating systems are case sensitive. So, for example, entering *'Order.htm'* or *'ORDER.HTM'* will result in the file not being found.

```
The Country Guide

All about Animals
All about Birds
All about Insects
All about Trees

long section of general text goes here
```

```
<HTML>
<HEAD>
<TITLE>Dumbreck Publishing</TITLE>
</HEAD>
<BODY BGCOLOR="WHITE" TEXT="BLACK">
<H2>The Country Guide</H2>
<A HREF="animals.htm">All about Animals </A> <BR>
<A HREF="birds.htm">All about Birds        </A> <BR>
<A HREF="insects.htm">All about Insects   </A> <BR>
<A HREF="trees.htm">All about Trees      </A> <BR>
long section of general text goes here       <BR>  <HR>
 </BODY>
</HTML>
```

This is the earlier example altered from one large web document into a set of linked web pages.   Clicking a hypertext link now loads the new web page instead of jumping to another part of the same document.   The list of hypertext links at the top of the document is called a *'link menu'*.

Jumping to an anchor in another page

In the above example, a link loads a new web page and the user sees the top of that web page.   It is possible to link not just to the top of the page but to any anchor within that new page.   The opening tag has to contain both the name of the new page and the name of the anchor as in this example:

<A HREF="birds.htm#robins"> All about robins </A>

Jumping to another site

The link can take the user to any page on any site on the World Wide Web, just by placing the URL in the tag.   This example takes the user to Dumbreck's home page:

<A HREF="http://www.dumbreck.demon.co.uk/index.html"> Dumbreck Publishing </A>

Jumping to another site

The link can take the user to any page on any site on the World Wide Web, just by placing the URL in the tag.   This example takes the user to Dumbreck's home page:

<A HREF="http://www.dumbreck.demon.co.uk/index.html"> Dumbreck Publishing </A>

Graphic images

Graphics can make a huge impact on the effectiveness of a web page.

This section looks at *'Inline Graphics'* which are images that are loaded along with the web page (*'External Graphics'* are only loaded when the user asks for it, usually by clicking a link).

The image tag allows a GIF or JPEG image to be displayed on the web page.

The tag's basic format is:

<IMG SRC="filename">

A number of additional attributes provide for additional formatting of the image.   These are:

ALIGN=	Places the next line of text next to the TOP, MIDDLE or BOTTOM of the image. The first example below shows the result of using MIDDLE. Only one line of the text appears in the middle, with the remaining lines appearing under the graphic. The graphic, by default, is placed at the left margin of the page. If ALIGN=LEFT is used, as in the second example, the graphics is still on the left but the text flows down its right-hand side. Similarly, ALIGN=RIGHT places the graphic on the right margin.

BORDER=	Enlarges the border round the image, if required. The number entered is in pixels.
ALT=	Display a piece of text when the mouse hovers over the image. This is useful when users turn off the facility for viewing graphic images, as they can still get a description of the content.

An example image tag is:

<IMG SRC="world.gif" ALIGN=MIDDLE BORDER=10 ALT="World Map">

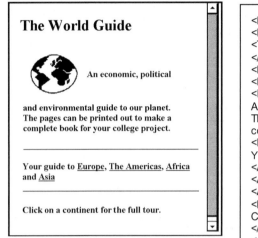

```
<HTML>
<HEAD>
<TITLE>Dumbreck Publishing</TITLE>
</HEAD>
<BODY BGCOLOR="WHITE" TEXT="BLACK">
<H2>The World Guide</H2>
<IMG SRC="world.gif" ALIGN=MIDDLE ALT="World Map">
An economic, political and environmental guide to our planet.<BR>
The pages can be printed out to make a complete book for your
college project.<BR>
<HR>
Your guide to <A HREF="europe.htm">Europe</A>,
<A HREF="americas.htm">The Americas </A>,
<A HREF="africa.htm">Africa </A> and
<A HREF="asia.htm">Asia </A><BR>
<HR>
Click on a continent for the full tour.
</BODY>
</HTML>
```

Changing the ALIGN setting to LEFT produces the result shown in the next illustration.

CLEAR

In the example on the right, the first two sentences were both aligned down the side of the graphic image.

Inserting a <P> or a <BR> after the first sentence will still leave the second sentence aligned down the graphic.

If the second sentence is required to appear below the graphic, the effects of the ALIGN=LEFT attribute can be cancelled by using the <BR CLEAR=LEFT> or <P CLEAR=LEFT> tag.   After this tag, the formatting of text resorts to normal.

Similarly, a <BR CLEAR=RIGHT> tag is used to cancel the effects of a previous ALIGN=RIGHT.

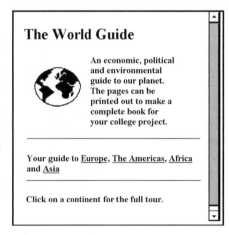

Using a graphic as a hyperlink

Many hyperlinks display underlined text that can be clicked to activate the link. It is also possible to use a graphic image as the hyperlink object, where they are often known as *'Hotspots'*.

If an <IMG> tag is embedded inside a link tag, that graphic image becomes a clickable hotspot link.
In this example

<A HREF="worlddb.htm" > <IMG SRC="world.gif"> </A>

the graphic tag has simply replaced the hyperlink text.   When run, the globe graphic appears with a box outline round it to indicate that it is a clickable object.   The width of this outline is set, in pixels, with the BORDER attribute.

When viewers look at a web page, it is common for many of them fail to appreciate that some of the graphics are hyperlink objects. To avoid this, images can be created in the shape of a text button, as in the second part of the example. In this case, its use is more obvious and the box outline is removed by setting the BORDER value to zero.

The third part of the above example shows graphics images in the shape of direction arrows (i.e. navigation icons). These, and UP and DOWN arrows, are very useful for linear structures.

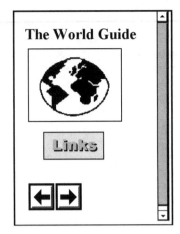

```
<HTML>
<HEAD>
<TITLE>Dumbreck Publishing</TITLE>
</HEAD>
<BODY BGCOLOR="WHITE" TEXT="BLACK">
<H2>The World Guide</H2>
<A HREF="worlddb.htm"> <IMG SRC="world.gif" BORDER= 1 ALT="World
Database"> </A>
<BR CLEAR=ALL><BR>
<A HREF="others.htm">  <IMG SRC="l_btn.gif" BORDER= 0 ALT="World Links">
</A>
<HR>
<A HREF="back.htm"> <IMG SRC="left.gif"  ALT="Previous Page"> </A>
<A HREF="next.htm"> <IMG SRC="right.gif" ALT="Next Page">    </A>
</BODY>
</HTML>
```

Labels can be attached to each, to explain their functions, if this is required:

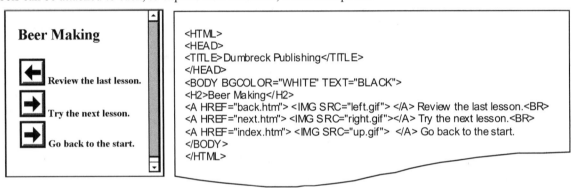

```
<HTML>
<HEAD>
<TITLE>Dumbreck Publishing</TITLE>
</HEAD>
<BODY BGCOLOR="WHITE" TEXT="BLACK">
<H2>Beer Making</H2>
<A HREF="back.htm"> <IMG SRC="left.gif"> </A> Review the last lesson.<BR>
<A HREF="next.htm"> <IMG SRC="right.gif"></A> Try the next lesson.<BR>
<A HREF="index.htm"> <IMG SRC="up.gif">  </A> Go back to the start.
</BODY>
</HTML>
```

This example shows how a graphic can be placed in the middle of a sentence if required.   The script entry for this is:

    Read the section on tool handling<A HREF="back.htm"> <IMG SRC="tools2.gif"> </A> before you start.

Height/Width

The <IMG> tag has HEIGHT and WIDTH attributes and these have two uses.

- If the size of the image is known (most graphic editing packages such as Paint Shop Pro or Photoshop provide this information) its dimensions can be included in the <IMG> tag.
  This reduces display times in some browsers as they load each image and identify their dimensions before displaying the text. If the files' dimensions are supplied to the browser, it can make space for them and allow the user to read the text while the graphics are loading.
- If the HEIGHT and WIDTH dimensions are different from the actual dimensions of the graphic, the browser will scale the graphic display proportionately. The displayed image can be smaller or larger than the original. However, too much enlargement will make the image look too 'blocky' while shrinking an image is wasteful (create a smaller original version as it downloads faster).

Example use:

    <IMG SRC="file.gif" HEIGHT=250 WIDTH=200>

Backgrounds

The background can be a solid colour using BGCOLOR="value" or can consist of a graphic file.   A graphic background is introduced using the BACKGROUND attribute in the <BODY> tag.

    <BODY BACKGROUND="virago.gif">

A single large graphic designed to cover the entire background is too large and takes too long to download.   The browser overcomes this by taking a smaller file and 'tiling' it.   With tiling, the image is repeated vertically and horizontally to fill the screen. This saves the overheads of using large files. The example in the illustration shows the effect.

In this case, the background image has only been tiled into the right hand frame as the BACKGROUND attribute has been inserted into the <TD> tag (explained later).

<TD WIDTH=200 BACKGROUND="virago.gif">

The graphic used has white space round the picture's edges and there is no visible 'join'. Where a pattern is used as a background, the design will require seamless joins on edges - i.e. the edges of the pattern should be designed to create a continuous pattern when tiles are butted together as a background.

A useful method is to create one narrow but wide strip of a pattern. This will cover the width of the screen and will be repeated down the screen. This graphic file will be of small size and will be quick to download.

Marquees

Internet Explorer introduced a moving band of text that scrolls across the screen. The default is to continually scroll from the right, disappearing off the left side and reappearing on the right side.

<MARQUEE>your message goes here </MARQUEE>

Its attributes are:

BEHAVIOR	The default value is SCROLL. A value of SLIDE causes the text to move to the opposite margin and stop. A value of ALTERNATE causes the text to 'bounce' between the left and right margins.
DIRECTION	The default value is RIGHT but a value of LEFT causes the text to appear from the left and move rightwards.
LOOP	Sets the number of times the marquee scrolls. A value of INFINITE causes the marquee to repeat continuously.
BGCOLOR	Sets the background colour of the marquee.
SCROLLAMOUNT	Sets the number of pixels that the marquee is moved with each step.
SCROLLDELAY	Sets the time, in milliseconds, between each step of the marquee's animation.

High values of SCROLLAMOUNT and small values of SCROLLDELAY result in marquees that are too fast to read while low SCROLLAMOUNT and high SCROLLDELAY values result in jerky animations.

Additionally, the font formatting <H> tags can be added to set the size of the scrolling text.
Example of use:

<H2> <MARQUEE BEHAVIOR=ALTERNATE SCROLLAMOUNT=2 SCROLLDELAY=3
LOOP=5 BGCOLOR="RED"> Bargain Offers Today </MARQUEE> </H2>

External graphics

Inline graphics load as part of the web page. This consumes downloading time even when the user is only idly browsing. On the other hand, users are reluctant to switch off the display of graphics since many hyperlinks are made from graphic images. The most user-friendly approach is to allow larger sized graphics to be loaded only upon the specific request of the user. These are termed 'external graphics' since they are not part of the normal web page. External graphics can be called up by clicking on a hyperlink. This can be a conventional hyperlink or, more helpfully, can be a thumbnail (i.e. a miniature version of the graphic). This allows users to click for more detail if they want. For example, a web site for an estate agent wishes to entice users to view as many pages as possible. Users can browse through many properties and only call up large graphic files for the properties that interest them.

<P>This <A HREF="kitchen.gif"> luxury kitchen </A> has to be seen to be believed<P>

This line of script uses a hyperlink to load and display the graphic if the user clicks it.

<A HREF="bigkitchen.gif"><IMG SRC="littlekitchen.gif"></A>

This line of script shows a thumbnail view of the graphic. Clicking on the thumbnail view loads and displays the file storing the larger version.

Interlaced GIFs

A normal file is 'non-interlaced' - the image is drawn one line at a time until the entire graphic is visible. It can be frustrating for the user to wait until there is enough of the file displayed before appreciating the graphic's contents. The header inside a GIF can be set to display in this normal non-interlaced mode or display in interlaced mode. In interlaced mode, the picture is built up in a couple of passes. On the first pass, alternate lines of the graphic are displayed with the other lines being filled in the next pass. The user then sees most of the picture and can decide whether to wait for the rest or jump to another page.

Transparent GIFs

When a graphic file is loaded, its display area occupies a rectangle on the screen. An example is shown opposite. The white background area around the logo spoils the look of the page. The white area can be made transparent, allowing the screen content underneath to be seen. This is known as a 'transparent GIF' and it stores all the colours of the image, with one colour nominated as the transparent colour. Anywhere the transparent colour exists in the image, no pixels are displayed and the underlying screen content shows through.

To create a transparent GIFs with image editing software:
- Select the required transparent colour, ensuring that the colour does not already appear in the foreground part of the image. Use the colour selector to find out the palette index number.
- Ensuring that the entire background is painted to that colour.
- In Paint Shop Pro, use the Colors/Set Color Transparency options to set the transparency value to the palette index number noted earlier.
- In PhotoShop, export the image as a GIF89a image, selecting the colours (more than one colour can be transparent) from the displayed colour palette.

Multimedia

There are many facilities that are not yet built into browsers.   Browsers are either configured to use the computer's existing facilities (sound card, video drivers, etc) or use browser add-ons such as Shockwave, Real Audio, etc. However, even the standard browsers are capable of handling basic multimedia formats such as AU and WAV audio files and MPEG, AVI and MOV video files.

Sound

The <A> tag is capable of playing a sound file.
For example,
            <A HREF="message.wav"> A word from our sponsors> </A>
displays a hypertext link that plays the message.wav file when clicked.

Internet Explorer inline sounds play automatically when the page is loaded, using the <BGSOUND> tag.
            <BGSOUND SRC="message.wav">   or   <BGSOUND SRC="sun.mid">
BGSOUND has a LOOP attribute that sets the number of times the file is played.   If the value is set to INFINITE, the file plays continuously until the page is exited.
This setting should be used carefully as continuous messages or music can be very annoying for users.
AU, MID and WAV files can be used with either of the two methods above.

The equivalent command for Netscape browsers is <EMBED SRC="message.wav">

Video

The <A> tag is also capable of playing a video file.   For example,
            <A HREF="heaven.mov"> The winning goal> </A>
displays a hypertext link that plays the heaven.mov file when clicked.   AVI, MPG and MOV files can be used with this method. Like inline sounds, inline AVI videos can play automatically when the page is loaded using the Internet Explorer DYNSRC attribute in the <IMG> tag.
            <IMG DYNSRC="heaven.mov">

The LOOP attribute sets the number of times the file is played.   If the value is set to INFINITE, the file plays continuously, although this value would not normally be used.   The SRC="file" is used to display a static graphic for browsers that do not support DYNSRC.

The START attribute determines how the video file is activated.   If it is given the value of FILEOPEN, it plays as soon as the page is loaded.   If the value is MOUSEOVER, it does not play until the mouse passes over the blank playing screen.   The CONTROLS attribute adds the stop/start button and position slider.
The above script shows both methods, with the left-hand video screen being the result of using DYNSRC.

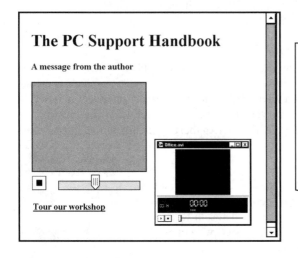

```
<HTML>
<HEAD><TITLE>Dumbreck Publishing</TITLE></HEAD>
<BODY BGCOLOR="#FFFFFF" FONT="BLACK">
<H2>The PC Support Handbook</H2>
<P>A message from the author<P>
<IMG DYNSRC="davy.avi" SRC="dave.gif"
        START=MOUSEOVER CONTROLS> <P>
<A HREF="office.avi" >Tour our workshop </A><P>
</BODY>
</HTML>
```

Creating tables

The <TABLE> tag allows sets of data to be laid out in a structured and readable way.

Its general format is:

```
<TABLE>                                           <TABLE>
<CAPTION> Caption for the table </CAPTION>        <CAPTION> Caption for the table </CAPTION>
   <TR>                                              <TR>
      <TH> Heading</TH>                                <TH> Heading for the first column </TH>
      <TD> Data for cell </TD>                         <TH> Heading for the second column </TH>
      <TD> Data for cell </TD>                         ....
   </TR>                                              </TR>
   <TR>                                              <TR>
      <TH> Heading</TH>                                <TD> Data </TD>
      <TD> Data  </TD>                                 <TD> Data </TD>
      <TD> Data </TD>                                  <TD> Data </TD>
   </TR>                                               <TD> Data </TD>
      ....                                             ....
      ....                                          </TR>
</TABLE>                                          </TABLE>
```

Tables are defined row by row.   The definition on the left is used when the headings are to appear down the first column of the table (as in the example below).   The other definition is used when the headings are to appear at the top of each column.   Headings are displayed in a bold typeface.

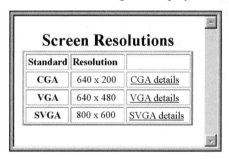

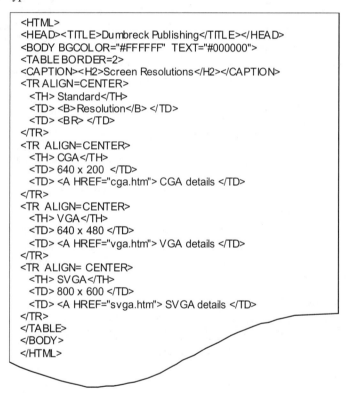

```
<HTML>
<HEAD><TITLE>Dumbreck Publishing</TITLE></HEAD>
<BODY BGCOLOR="#FFFFFF"  TEXT="#000000">
<TABLE BORDER=2>
<CAPTION><H2>Screen Resolutions</H2></CAPTION>
<TR ALIGN=CENTER>
   <TH> Standard</TH>
   <TD> <B>Resolution</B> </TD>
   <TD> <BR> </TD>
</TR>
<TR  ALIGN=CENTER>
   <TH> CGA </TH>
   <TD> 640 x 200  </TD>
   <TD> <A HREF="cga.htm"> CGA details </TD>
</TR>
<TR  ALIGN=CENTER>
   <TH> VGA</TH>
   <TD> 640 x 480 </TD>
   <TD> <A HREF="vga.htm"> VGA details </TD>
</TR>
<TR  ALIGN= CENTER>
   <TH> SVGA</TH>
   <TD> 800 x 600 </TD>
   <TD> <A HREF="svga.htm"> SVGA details </TD>
</TR>
</TABLE>
</BODY>
</HTML>
```

The other main components are:

The optional <CAPTION> tag displays a centred heading for the table.

The text between the optional <TH> and </TH> tags specifies the contents of the heading for the table.

The <TR> and </TR> tags enclose the definition of a row and these sets would be repeated for each row required in the table.

The <TD> and </TD> tags enclose the data that will appear in a cell in the row.   A set of these is required for each cell definition.

The contents of a cell can be text, a graphic image or a hyperlink.

In the example, the cell in the top right corner is empty and this is achieved by:

    <TD>
</TD>.

Formatting tables

The default positions for table components are:

	Vertical position	Horizontal position
ENTIRE TABLE	Defined by the script	At left of screen
HEADING CELLS	Centred	Centred
DATA CELLS	Centred	Left of cell

The table described so far leaves all table and cell formatting to the browser. A range of alterations can be made to the basic table definition to create more interest or to provide for irregular table shapes.

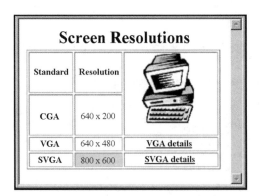

```
<HTML>
<HEAD><TITLE>Dumbreck Publishing</TITLE></HEAD>
<BODY BGCOLOR="#FFFFFF" TEXT="#000000">
<TABLE BORDER=1 WIDTH=100% >
<CAPTION><H2>Screen Resolutions</H2></CAPTION>
<TR ALIGN=CENTER>
   <TH WIDTH=25%> Standard</TH>
   <TD WIDTH=25%> <B>Resolution</B> </TD>
   <TD  ROWSPAN=2  WIDTH=50%  >  <IMG  SRC="monitor.gif">
</TD>
</TR>
<TR ALIGN=CENTER>
   <TH> CGA </TH>
   <TD> 640 x 200  </TD>
</TR>
<TR ALIGN=CENTER>
   <TH> VGA</TH>
   <TD > 640 x 480 </TD>
   <TD COLSPAN=2> <A HREF=vga.htm"> VGA details </TD>
</TR>
<TR ALIGN=CENTER>
   <TH> SVGA</TH>
   <TD BGCOLOR="#DDDDDD" > 800 x 600 </TD>
   <TD  ALIGN=CENTER>    <A  HREF=svga.htm"> SVGA  details
</TD>
</TR>
</TABLE></CENTER>
</BODY>
</HTML>
```

This example shows the result of a number of these extra attributes and they are described below.

Border

The BORDER attribute determines the width of the border round each cell. A zero border values suppresses box drawing and is used to improve general screen formatting as described later.

The BORDERCOLOR attribute sets the colour around a particular cell as below:

```
 <TH BORDERCOLOR="RED"> VGA</TH>
```

The background colour of a cell can be set using the BGCOLOR attribute in the <TD> tag,

e.g.
```
<TD BGCOLOR="#DDDDDD" > cell data </TD>
```

Table alignment

By default, tables are displayed on the left of the screen, with text appearing above and below the table.   As in the case of graph images discussed earlier, ALIGN=LEFT and ALIGN=RIGHT alters the default positioning.   To place the table in the centre of the screen, the tag <CENTER> is placed before the <TABLE> tag and </CENTER> is placed after the </TABLE> tag.

Cell alignment

The ALIGN attributes of LEFT, RIGHT and CENTER, along with VALIGN, are used to place the cell's contents in the required position within the cell. The CELLPADDING attribute is placed in the <TABLE> tag and determines the spacing between the cell walls and the text.
The value is specified in pixels, e.g.
```
        <TABLE CELLPADDING= 6>
```
The CELLSPACING attribute determines the width of the space between the cells, e.g.
```
        <TABLE CELLSPACING=5>
```

The VALIGN attribute can be set to equal TOP, MIDDLE or BOTTOM, to position the cell contents in the vertical direction.

Table widths

The WIDTH attribute is added to the <TABLE> tag to specify how wide the table will appear on the screen. The value can be set in pixels or as a percentage of the screen.   Using pixel values displays a table that does not alter its width when the user's screen is resized.   The percentage value ensures that the table width grows or shrinks depending on the screen resolution of the viewer's browser.

Column widths

The width of each column can be individually set using the WIDTH attribute in either the <TH> or <TD> tag.   Again, it can be specified as a fixed amount of pixels or a percentage of the screen width.
In the above example, the first two columns always occupy a quarter of the screen each, with the third column occupying the remainder of the screen width.   The column widths shrink or expand as the user's screen is resized but the columns always maintain the same ratio with respect to each other and to the overall screen width.

Merging cells

Many tables do not use a layout where there is a symmetrical matrix of cells (e.g. 5x5 or 8x7).

The examples on the next page show tables where cells have been merged - i.e. the data 'spans' more than a single cell. The first example shows a piece of data spanning the entire top row of cells. The third example shows an entire column of cells being spanned by a single data item. The middle example shows the first column being split into two separate vertical areas: the first data item spans the two upper rows of that column, while the second data item spans the two bottom rows.

Projected Sales		
	UK	USA
2002	8000	12000
2003	9000	18000

Male	Deaths	Injuries
	23	267
Female	Deaths	Injuries
	18	120

1998	750	
1999	1100	Web Site
2000	2100	
2001	5000	

To achieve the first effect, the COLSPAN or ROWSPAN attribute is embedded in the <TD> tag. So, if the data has to span the three cells, the value is set to three - e.g. <TD COLSPAN=3> or <TD ROWSPAN=3>.

The scripts for the above three layouts are:

```
<table border=1>
<tr>
<td       colspan=3>Projected
Sales</td>
</tr>
<td> </td><td>UK</td>
<td>USA</td></tr>
<tr><td>2002</td>
<td>8000</td>
<td>12000</td></tr>
<tr><td>2003</td>
<td>9000</td><td>18000</td
></tr>
</table>
```

```
<table border=1>
<tr><td
rowspan=2>Male</td>
<td>Deaths</td>
<td>Injuries</td></tr>
<tr><td>23</td>
<td>267</td></tr>
<tr><td
rowspan=2>Female</td>
<td>Deaths</td>
<td>Injuries</td></tr>
<tr><td>18</td>
<td>120</td></tr>
</table>
```

```
<table border=1>
<tr><td>1998</td><td>750</td>
<td rowspan=4>
<a  href="www.somesite.com">Web
Site
</td></tr>
<tr><td>1999</td><td>1100</td>
</tr>
<tr><td>2000</td><td>2100</td>
</tr>
<tr><td>2001</td><td>5000</td>
</tr>
</table>
```

Screen layouts

Tables are also commonly used to create screen layouts. The example layout shown is widely used. The data is laid out in two columns. The left column displays a page headline, a graphic and a set of menu hyperlinks. The right column displays the main text. When the user clicks a hyperlink, the new page is in the same style, with the same content in the left column. So, as the user navigates round the site, there is a constant unchanging menu on the left.

```
<HTML>
<HEAD><TITLE>Example Frame</TITLE></HEAD>
<BODY BGCOLOR="#FFFFFF">
<TABLE BORDER=1 WIDTH=300 CELLPADDING=16>
<TR>
  <TD WIDTH=150>
  <FONT COLOR="RED">
  <H2>Leeds <BR>Bikers Club</H2>
  </FONT>
  <IMG SRC="verago.gif"><P>
  <A HREF="ourbikes.avi">Watch our video</A><P>
  <A HREF="mailto:jake@leedsbikers.com">Ask for more
details</A>
  </TD>
<TD WIDTH=200 CELLPADDING=5>
  <FONT COLOR="OLIVE">
  Leeds Bikers Club is always looking for new members.<P>
  We meet every Thursday at 7,30pm,
  In the car park of the old mill.<P>
  Come along, bring your mates and try us out!
</TD>
</TR>
</TABLE>
</BODY>
</HTML>
```

The size of each column is set with the WIDTH attribute. CELLPADDING is used to create a space between the two columns. However, this also pushes the data down from the top of the column.

An alternative is to insert a third column between the existing columns and adjust its width to the desired margin.

The lower example shows the same script with the BORDER value set to 1.

Graphic images

To insert a graphic image into a table cell, alter the TD (Table Data) tag to

<TD> <IMG SRC="filename.htm"></TD>

Frames

Frames are supported on all browsers from Netscape 2 and Internet Explorer 3 onwards.

The 'Leeds Bikers Page' example used a table to create two distinct window areas and the 'World Guide' site could be re-written using tables to create the display shown.

The aim was to display a menu of links on the left edge of the screen. Clicking a link alters the display on the right while the left column always displays the menu.

With tables, the whole screen is redrawn and the menu column is redrawn every time the right column displays new contents. The contents of each left column are identical for all pages yet have to be re-displayed after each hyperlink jump.

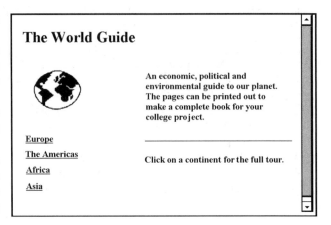

A more efficient way is to create distinct window areas called 'frames'. Frames still produce the same visual display as before but the left frame's contents would not be refreshed when the right frame was redrawn. In the example, clicking a hyperlink only changes the contents of the right hand frame.

This technique can be extended so that several different frames are present on the screen at the same time. For example, long documents may have a menu of links at the top of the document and a duplicate copy at the bottom of the document. For a user who is somewhere in the middle of a document, there is no menu or help in sight. With frames, a permanent menu can be placed at the bottom of the screen. The user can scroll the larger window's contents but the menu remains on screen at all times. Alternatively, a top frame can be used as a window to permanently display the web site banner and logo.

How frames work

The 'frame document' is an HTML page that defines the size and position of each frame on the screen. The frame document does not contain any normal screen data such as text or graphics; it purely defines the screen layout. The screen data is supplied from other HTML pages whose contents fill the screen frames. Each frame is given a name and this name is used to link frames and files.

In the example, there are three frames called 'Main', 'Menu' and 'Banner'. Hyperlinks are used to load different files into the 'Main' or even 'Menu' frames as the user navigates the site.

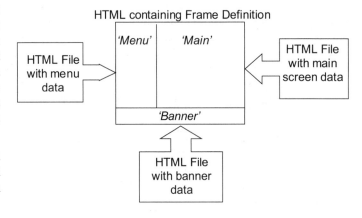

Defining frames

The basic format of a frame document is:

```
<HTML>
<HEAD><TITLE>Dumbreck Publishing</TITLE></HEAD>
<FRAMESET
    The frame definition .....
</FRAMESET>
</HTML>
```

The usual <BODY> tags are replaced by <FRAMESET> tags. These tags enclose the definition of the rows and columns that comprise the screen layout.

A basic layout may simply consist of only two columns or it may simply consist of two rows.
On the other hand, the layout may consist of a variety of frame combinations comprising both row and column shaped frames.
Like tables, dimensions can be expressed either in pixel amounts or in percentages of the screen size.

Simple frame definitions are:

<table>
<tr><td><u>Two-column layout</u></td><td><u>Two-row layout</u></td></tr>
</table>

```
<HTML>                                              <HTML>
<HEAD><TITLE>Dumbreck Publishing</TITLE></HEAD>     <HEAD><TITLE>Dumbreck Publishing</TITLE></HEAD>
<FRAMESET COLS="30%,70%">                           <FRAMESET ROWS="50%,50%">
   <FRAME   NAME="frame1"   SRC= "f1.htm" >            <FRAME   NAME="frame1"   SRC= "f1.htm" >
   <FRAME   NAME="frame2 "  SRC= "f2.htm" >            <FRAME   NAME="frame2 "  SRC= "f2.htm" >
</FRAMESET>                                         </FRAMESET>
</HTML>                                             </HTML>
```

The FRAME tag provides specific information on each frame that will be displayed.

The NAME attribute provides each frame with a unique label for linking purposes (see later).

The SRC= attribute specifies what web page will load into the frame when the frame document is first loaded. Of course, the frame contents can subsequently be changed as will be outlined shortly.

If a two-column definition were used for *'The World Guide'* it would produce the displays shown.

 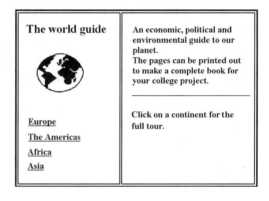

The right-hand screen is similar to the *'Leeds Bikers Page'* example using a table shown on a previous page.

The left hand screen is the result of the user resizing the screen area and clearly shows that the display consists of two separate frame areas.

Complex definitions

More complex definitions are achieved by nesting a FRAMESET specification with another FRAMESET specification. Example scripts for splitting rows and columns are shown below, along with the screen displays that are achieved.

```
<HTML>
<HEAD><TITLE>Dumbreck Publishing</TITLE></HEAD>
<FRAMESET ROWS="90%,10%">
       <FRAMESET COLS="90%,90%">
               <FRAME SRC= "f1.htm" >
               <FRAME  SRC= "f2.htm" >
       </FRAMESET>
       <FRAME  SRC= "f3.htm" >
</FRAMESET>
</HTML>
```

```
<HTML>
<HEAD><TITLE>Dumbreck Publishing</TITLE></HEAD>
<FRAMESET COLS="40%,70%">
       <FRAME NAME="MENU" SRC= "f1.htm" >
       <FRAMESET ROWS="90%,90%">
               <FRAME  NAME="MAIN" SRC= "f2.htm" >
               <FRAME  NAME="BANNER" SRC= "f3.htm" >
       </FRAMESET>
</FRAMESET>
</HTML>
```

Notes

- The script lines are only indented for clarity. The browser ignores the spaces.
- Percentage values for ROWS and COLS don't necessarily add up to 100%. In the example, both column widths are set to 90%. Netscape and Internet Explorer add up the column percentages and distribute them proportionate to the screen. So, in the example, each column is allocated half of the users screen window width. Specifications of 40% and 120% would result in the first column occupying a quarter of the screen.

- NAMEs have been added to the FRAME definition in the second example.
- In these examples, the MAIN area's contents alter every time a new page is selected from the menu.   The BANNER area would probably only be loaded once and remain on-screen at all times.
- The MENU area, like the BANNER area, may never be updated.   Alternatively, it may be used to display sub-menus.   The left display shows the opening menu frame. Clicking on the DISK hyperlink loads the page shown on the right into the MENU frame.   Clicking any disk hyperlink option loads the matching data file into the MAIN frame.   When the user clicks on the Main Menu hyperlink, the original page shown on the left is loaded into the MENU frame once again.

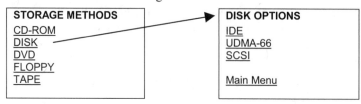

Attributes

The attributes available for FRAMESET definition are:

FRAMEBORDER   Setting the value to zero stops the display of the 3D border round frames.   However, the space allocated for the border displays on the screen as a grey band.

FRAMESPACING   Setting the value to zero makes each frame butt on to the next frame, with no gaps.

Example:

<FRAMESET FRAMEBORDER="NO" FRAMESPACING=0>

Results in no borders being displayed around any frames and the screen appearing as a single display. Earlier versions of Explorer may need FRAMEBORDER to be set to zero instead of "NO".

The attributes available for FRAME definition are:

NORESIZE   The default, as with most Windows applications, allows the user to grab a window border and resize it.   The NORESIZE attribute prevents the user from altering frame sizes.

MARGINHEIGHT   Sets the margin, in pixels, above and below the document.

MARGINWIDTH   Sets the margin, in pixels, between the document and the sides of the frame.

SCROLLING   Controls the user's ability to scroll through a frame's document, and has three settings:

NO: The user cannot scroll through the document.   This should be used with caution. If the screen is small size and the user cannot resize the window, then some screen content will be prevented from displaying.

YES: Vertical and horizontal scrollbars are also displayed in the frame, even when the document is too small to need scrolling facilities.

AUTO: The scrollbars are only displayed if the document is too large for the size of the frame window.

Example:

<FRAME MARGINWIDTH=10 MARGINHEIGHT=15 NAME="MAIN" SRC="file5.htm">

results in a 15 pixel margin above and below the document and 10 pixels of space between the document and the frame's vertical sides.   By default, scrolling facilities are automatically triggered by large documents and the user is allowed to alter frame sizes by dragging them with the mouse.

Noframes

If a browser does not support frames, it won't recognise the frame script and will display a blank page.

To maximise the number of viewers to the site, a non-frame version of the site can be set up.   This uses the Netscape NOFRAMES attribute as shown below.

```
<HTML>
<HEAD><TITLE>Dumbreck Publishing</TITLE></HEAD>
<FRAMESET >
    The frame definition .....
<NOFRAMES>
      The same contents (e.g. text, graphics, and links) without using frames
</FRAMESET>
</HTML>
```

Browsers that can handle frames simply ignore the NOFRAMES section. As users upgrade to more modern browsers, the need for this technique will diminish.

Floating frames

Many sites now use the technique of *'floating frames'*, also known as *'inline frames'*.   With normal sites, a window may be split into different areas (usually frames) but only one window is viewable at any one time.   Users click hyperlinks to change the whole page or parts of the page.

With floating frames, clicking a hyperlink brings up another window that pops up within the existing window. It may also load up another copy of the browser to view the new contents. Closing a floating frame reveals the entire contents of the previous window (without having to be reloaded first).
The basic format of a floating frame is

```
<HTML>
<HEAD><TITLE>Dumbreck Publishing</TITLE></HEAD>
<BODY >
      Content, if any for the main screen .....
      <IFRAME  SRC="filename.htm">  </IFRAME>
</BODY>
</HTML>
```

Several IFRAME definitions can be inserted with the <BODY> tags, if required.

The attributes for IFRAME are:

WIDTH	Sets the width of the floating frame window (in pixels or as a percentage).
HEIGHT	Sets the height of the floating frame window.
ALIGN	By default, floating frames are displayed on the left of the screen, with text appearing above and below the table. ALIGN=LEFT and ALIGN=RIGHT alters the default positioning, as explained earlier for graphics and tables. CLEAR also has the same effect as explained earlier.
FRAMEBORDER	If set to zero, it inhibits the display of borders round the frame.
HSPACE	Sets the horizontal margin in pixels between the frame and other screen contents.
VSPACE	Sets the vertical margin between the frame and other screen contents.
SCROLLING	Same as the earlier definition given for FRAMESET attributes.
NAME	Attaches a label to the frame for linking purposes (see next section).

In addition, the attributes TOPMARGIN and LEFTMARGIN can be inserted into the <BODY> tag. TOPMARGIN sets the space, in pixels, between the top of the page and start of the display of the page contents. LEFTMARGIN sets the space between the left-hand side of the screen and the start of the display of the page contents.

Example:

```
<IFRAME NAME="prices" SRC="filename.htm" WIDTH=300  HEIGHT=300
      FRAMEBORDER=1 HSPACE=5 VSPACE=5 > </IFRAME>
```

This results in a floating frame called *'prices'* with the contents of the *'filename.htm'* displayed in a 300 pixel by 300 pixel window.   The frame displays its border and has a 5 pixel spacing between it and other screen content.   By default, the scrolling facility automatically initiates when required and the window is left aligned.

Linking frames

The use of frames allows one frame's contents to loaded and displayed without altering the other frames on the screen. Since each frame has been given a unique name, the data that is loaded can be directed ('*targetted*') towards that named frame. Since only a part of the screen is being updated, the transition is smoother.   More importantly, less of the screen being updated means that less data has to be downloaded. This results in smaller files being fetched and navigation is therefore faster.

```
<HTML>
<HEAD><TITLE>Dumbreck Publishing</TITLE>
</HEAD>
<FRAMESET COLS ="*,*">
   <FRAME  NAME="MENU"  SRC="f1.htm">
   <FRAME  NAME="MAIN"  SRC="f2.htm">
</FRAMESET>
</HTML>
```

The first script shown creates a screen with two column frame areas. The first column is called MENU and has the contents of file *'f1.htm'* displayed in it.   The second column is called MAIN and initially displays the contents of the *'f2.htm'* file. It produces a screen similar to that shown in the illustration.

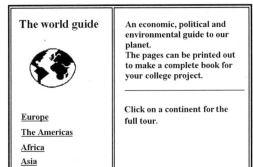

The world guide	An economic, political and environmental guide to our planet.
	The pages can be printed out to make a complete book for your college project.
Europe	Click on a continent for the full tour.
The Americas	
Africa	
Asia	

The contents of the f1.htm file are shown below.   The HREF tags have a TARGET= attribute added to them.   This points to the name of the frame to be updated with the file being loaded.

The example file has four hyperlinks.   If the first link is clicked, it loads the *'europe.htm'* file. Since its target is the MAIN frame, the file's contents are displayed in that frame (i.e. the second column).

The left column's contents remain unaltered while a click on any of the hyperlinks in the menu results in the contents of the second frame being altered.

```
<HTML>
<HEAD>
<TITLE>Dumbreck Publishing</TITLE></HEAD>
<BODY BGCOLOR="#FFFFFF" FONT="BLACK">
<H2>The World Guide</H2>
<IMG SRC="world.gif" ALIGN = MIDDLE ALT="World Map"> <P>
<A HREF="europe.htm"    TARGET="MAIN" >Europe</A><P>
<A HREF="americas.htm" TARGET="MAIN" >The Americas </A><P>
<A HREF="africa.htm"      TARGET="MAIN" >Africa</A><P>
<A HREF="asia.htm"        TARGET="MAIN" >Asia </A><P>
</BODY>
<.HTML>
```

In the example, the one frame was the common target for all updating.   In this case the TARGET= attribute can be removed from each HREF line and be replaced by the single line:
    <BASE TARGET="MAIN">
This line is inserted between the <HEAD> tags.   Where different frames are being updated, this method cannot be used.

The technique of targeted frames can be used to refine the menu system shown earlier.   In the example on the right, the top-left corner box permanently displays a main menu.   Clicking on a menu option displays its corresponding sub-menu options in the lower-left corner box. Clicking on any sub-menu option then displays its contents in the main screen area.   This way, the main menu and sub-menu are visible at all times.

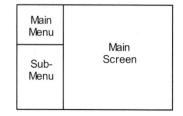

It is possible to make a single click update two frames simultaneously, but this involves the use of JavaScript.

MAILTO

This is a very simple single line of script that allows a user to send an e-mail to the site owner while still inside the site.   The user does not have to leave the browser and enter his/her e-mail program to send the message.   The format is
        <A HREF ="MAILTO: address"> hyperlink message</A>
A typical example is
        <A HREF= MAILTO:sales@dumbreck.demon.co.uk> Send us your comments </A>
When the hyperlink is clicked, the user is asked to provide a subject name for the e-mail and to provide the main text of the message.   When the user completes the details, the software sends the message and returns the user to the previously loaded web page.   An example of its use was seen in the *'Leeds Bikers Club'* site earlier.

Maximising promotion

The later section discusses the methods to promote the completed site by contacting the press, Internet directories, newsgroups, etc.   But the site can be augmented to maximise its drawing power to users, even before it is uploaded on to the server.

Search engines

Every day, large numbers of Internet users employ search facilities to find sites relating to their needs. Many software packages, called *'search engines'*, are available to aid these searches.   The most famous are Alta Vista and Google, with others including HotBot, UK Plus and Excite.

Search engines use software packages known as *'spiders'* or *'robots'* to search the Internet for new sites and alterations to existing sites.   These packages all note the content of web pages to compile indexes for user searches.   The way that each package uses the information will vary with some giving greater emphasis to a particular feature than others.

Keywords

Keywords are the words that most distinguish the site's contents and the ones mostly likely to be used by someone searching the Internet for the site. Do not rely solely on keywords such as *'computer'*, *'car'* and *'employment'* as these are used by many existing sites and produce hundreds of thousands of matches for users of search engines.   Use descriptive words such as *'fragmentation'*, *'Mercedes'* and *'welder'*.

<TITLE>

The text enclosed by the <TITLE> tags is not displayed on the screen but is the common starting point for text gathered by search engines.   Therefore, the text should be as descriptive as possible, using keywords.   This text is also used when a user decides to add the page as a bookmark in his/her browser.

So, *"Great Bargains for All"* is useless while *"Printer Supplies"* is much more meaningful.

Page text

When analysing page content, search engines assume that writers place their most important information at the top of a page. Accordingly, search engines give greater weight to words at the top of the page.   A web page, therefore should have a significant statement at the top of each page.

<META> tags

The <META> tag allows the site's description and ass~~r~~
can be automatically picked up by many of the se~~r~~
<HEAD> tags and have the following formats:

<META NAME="description" C
<META NAME="keywords"

Repeatedly inserting a single word in the k~~e~~
search engines penalise this abuse by ignori~~ng~~
sites whose main file uses frames. A page
informs the spiders about the page's purpose.

```
<HTML>
<HEAD>
<TITLE>The PC Support Handboo
<META name="description" conten
<META name="keywords" content=
software & data, operating systems &
pc configuration, batch files, compute
computer viruses, pc support, upgrading,
web site creation, local area networks, multir
</HEAD>
```

ALT attributes

Some search engines use ALT attribute text in their calculations. So AL~~T~~
helpful to users who have turned off their *'load images'* option.

<NOFRAMES> tags

Placing a site description between the <NOFRAMES> and </NOFRAMES> tags allows ~~u~~
ones not supporting frames) to view the page. The text is also included in search results.

Sponsored Links

Although META tags still have a place in web site promotion, there are now many more ways to gain a ~~l~~
the search engine rankings. In fact, there are consultants whose entire job is to maximise the search engine ~~r~~
a company's web site!

Directory services such as Yahoo! are based on 'suggestions' that web sites be placed into appropriate categori~~es~~
While these suggestions used to be free, they are now typically on a paid basis. However, the Open Directory project
(www.dmoz.org) currently still provides free directory registration, and is used by other sites such as Google and
Lycos.

Furthermore, search engines such as Google allow contributors to pay for better search results. 'Sponsored Links'
relating to specific keywords appear before regular search results on these search engines.

This takes one of two forms: up-front sponsorship, where the money for a sponsored link over a given time period is
paid before the link is placed; and Pay-Per-Click advertising. Pay-Per-Click, as the name suggests, is a system where
the web site owner is charged a small amount for every web surfer that enters their site through the search engine's
link. Although these methods obviously add to the total cost of running the web site, they can be remarkably cost-
effective in promoting some web sites.

Publishing the finished web site

Once a set of web pages has been built, they need to be accessible in some way to the users of the information. This
can be made possible in several ways:

- In a CD-ROM, DVD or other physical media format distribution.
- On a Kiosk.
- Publishing on an Intranet
- Publishing on the Internet

When published on a CD or in a kiosk, HTML files are really little different from any other media files, and the details
in the *'Authoring'* chapter are appropriate. However, HTML and other web documents are intended for use online,
and publishing web pages generally means acquiring a web server and uploading the files onto that server for
consumption.

Web Servers

Large organisations may decide that it is cost-effective to establish their own web server at their own site, incurring
the expense of establishing, preparing and maintaining a permanent server connection to the Internet. Most
organisations and individuals choose to use space on an existing web server. In most cases, an ISP (Internet Service
Provider) provides a fixed amount (perhaps 50MB) of disk space as part of the standard user's rental.

at an extra cost.

ifferent capabilities, and these should be considered along with the cost of the
vider to use. For example:

provided varies. Some free providers offer only a few megabytes, and at the other
er 250MB of space or more.

well as security. To look into this in detail might involve looking at the server
to selecting a web server for in-house use.

vary. Since the data is stored on the provider's servers, they use the provider's internet
is generally much faster than customers' lines.

res may be included, such as DNS name registration, CGI scripting, SSL security, logging,
upport.

ganisation decides to set up and manage the web server themselves, there are of course many
der.

Web Server

quired for a web server is different from that of a typical PC. It needs only basic graphics and sound,
peripherals. The web server needs a reasonably powerful processor, but need not be top of the line.
irements are plenty of memory (to cache common data, improving server performance), a large amount
, and of course the best Internet connection that can be afforded. Note, however, that a very fast Internet
implies that a lot of users will access the server; and the greater the load on the server, the better the
ion of all hardware components should be.

web site with text and images only, and with a limited expected audience, might find a relatively slow fixed
ch as ISDN sufficient. For most cases though, a higher speed solution is desirable, such as DSL or even a
d line. For an Intranet web page server, of course, a local network can be used, which typically provide
ellent speeds anyway.

least as important as the hardware though, is the server software. The software choices that must be made include
he Operating System, as well as the web server software, though the two are in many ways linked. One consideration
when selecting the operating system and the web serving software is its *'portability'*. The API functions used by the
server software may vary, and some software may run only on certain operating systems. Most famously, IIS runs
only on Windows systems, while Apache runs on both Windows and Unix-like systems. Even an entirely Windows-
based IT department might need to consider the portability of the software between one version of Windows and
another.

Windows servers

The main advantage of a Windows based server is its ease of use. Windows systems have two main choices in web
serving software: Apache and Microsoft IIS. Microsoft systems may also use Access, the most widely used database
package, and integrate it into web serving software through query systems such as MySQL.

Linux and Unix servers

Although Linux can be a more daunting prospect to an average PC user, it offers some advantages. For example, it is
inherently more robust and considerably more secure than Windows, although it is by no means foolproof in that
regard. The cost of running Linux software is very low, indeed in some cases it can even be completely free.
However, Linux also has disadvantages, the user-unfriendly interface is just one of those. The number of good, well-
supported web server packages that run on Linux is very limited, with Apache being the only such software of real
note.

Every web server application on Unix-like systems is referred to as a HTTPd (HTTP daemon), from the most basic
NCSA httpd to the latest version of Apache. In many cases the name httpd has carried over into Windows server
applications as well.

Furthermore, Linux is not truly the same as Unix. On PCs, Linux is far more common than actual Unix. However, for
servers, other Unix variants are perhaps better suited, such as FreeBSD, due to their greater efficiency at handling
common protocols.

Configuring the web server

Installation of a web server program is relatively simple. For example, Red Hat Linux typically installs with Apache
built in, while IIS can be installed at the same time as Windows XP. Then, all that needs to be done is to enable the
services. In Unix this can be done by simply typing 'httpd' to start the daemon; on Windows the IIS service is enabled
by default if the service is installed. Both systems use a set of default values so that beginning users need not be
familiar with all aspects of web serving software.

Both Apache and IIS are modular systems, that is to say that they consist of a number of components, and components
may be added or removed from the setup. For example, many web servers also run FTP via a different port. Each
port can be allocated to any one process, so that one server can, potentially, handle many different services such as
http, ftp, email, or even Gopher. The services need only be installed, started up, and given a separate port number

each. Most services have been allocated a 'well-known' port number which is the standard port used for such services. For example, most http servers operate on port 80, while most ftp services are on port 21.

Other services include SSL, PHP, SMTP, and so on, all of which can be handled either by modules that come bundled with the software, or by add-on modules that are purchased separately.

Both Apache and IIS have a default configuration, and for basic web sites this is often sufficient. The http port is set to the standard http port 80; and the default web page directory will be /var/www/html (for Apache) or C:\Inetpub\wwwroot (for IIS). The HTML and other web documents should be placed in this directory and subdirectories.

In depth configuration differs greatly, however. Apache is a command-line system, with a text file (httpd.conf) that contains setup information. IIS is a GUI-operated system, with user-friendly windowed setup options, accessed via the '*Internet Information Services*' icon of the '*Computer Management*' tool. This tool can be used to set up multiple web sites on one computer, as well as an SMTP mail server.

The dialog box for setting up an IIS web site is shown on the right, with the default settings. This example shows a server that is set up for use on an internal network, hence the use of the reserved IP address 10.0.0.10. The standard port of 80 is selected, with no secure SSL port.

The '*Home Directory*' tab can be used to change the location of the files, either on the local hard drive, a remote hard drive, or a redirected location (see later in this chapter for details of aliases and redirection). The '*Documents*' tab can be used to set a default document, in this example the default document would be the file that is displayed if the user simply surfed to http://10.0.0.10.

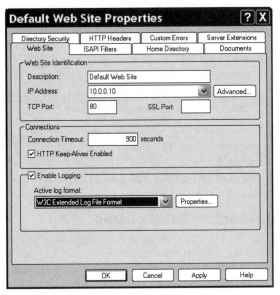

Other server related software

Aside from the Operating System and the Web Server software, there are many other packages that may be relevant to the web serving system. For example:

- However the web pages are to be accessed, it may be useful to test the server with a '*loading application*', or '*performance analysis*' software. Such a program simulates accesses of the server by hundreds or thousands of users at a time, to ensure that the system is capable of dealing with peak access rates and responding to all of them within an acceptable time frame. This application typically runs on the server system, often integrated into the server application itself, and monitors the execution of the web software, producing reports on its performance.

- Validation of web pages may not be necessary, but is desirable to ensure the greatest compatibility with the largest number of browsers. The W3C offers online web page validation testing at   http://validator.w3.org/ However, they only offer validation of HTML and CSS code, not XML, VRML or any other markup language. Furthermore, using a validator on the server is not only more convenient, but allows it to test an entire site instead of one page at a time.

- Security systems are important to any professional web site. This may vary from an SSL application to provide secure connections to users, to a full-fledged Intrusion Detection System (IDS) to help prevent hackers from altering the web site's code.

- Client-side scripting software can provide greater functionality for the web site. There are few web server packages that include support for client side scripting by default, so it is generally installed separately.

Organising Web pages

When all of the files are ready to be made into a web site, the last step before transferring the files onto the server is organising them into an appropriate structure. This is different from, although related to, the organisation of files performed during asset management. If the assets have been managed appropriately, then they will already have been named according to an appropriate naming convention.

However, the directory structure decided upon during asset management may or may not be appropriate for the final publication. The actual directory structure used matters little to the end user, so the structure chosen should be that which is the most efficient for administration of the site, which often means a directory structure that is based on the structure of the pages themselves.

For a very small site of just a handful of pages and images, this might mean having all files in one folder. In a medium-sized web site, it should be split into sub-folders, with each page in each sub-folder being within the same general area of the site. It may even be desirable for each page to have its own sub-directory containing the images and other files used by that page, if the pages of the site each contain many media files.

For large sites, however, more complex structures must be found, often with the pages being spread between multiple servers. A sophisticated Document Asset Management system can help to an extent, making sure that logos and page layouts are consistent between sections of the site where appropriate. However, additional methods are often required, including aliases, and redirection techniques.

Aliases and Redirection

In addition to the normal structure of the web site, aliases can add more flexibility as well as distributing some of the server load between two or more servers. An alias is a facility whereby a server 'links' a specific path to another location. This location could be a different directory on the same server, or the server may retrieve the data from another port, or another server.

The following are examples of using aliases:

URL requested	File sent by server
http://www.myserver.com/	C:\Inetpub\wwwroot\index.htm
http://www.myserver.com/personnel/logo_lg.gif	C:\Inetpub\wwwroot\logos\logo_lg.gif
http://www.myserver.com/downloads/list.zip	linked to C:\downloads\list.zip on another computer which is connected by LAN

An alternative to using aliases is redirection. Using this method, the browser queries a server, which replies with data informing the browser of a new location to go to, to find the file it has requested. This allows the main server to 'point at' different servers for different files, or update its redirection information so that a server can be replaced at a moment's notice.

Uploading Web pages

When the site contents are written and tested, they have to be published. If the web server is stored locally, this is simply a matter of copying the files into the appropriate directories on the server's hard disk. However, if the server space is rented from an ISP, the files must be copied from the local hard disk to the remote server's disk system.

The transfer is known as 'uploading' and the stages of the process are:

- Packaging the elements in a suitable uploading format.
- Testing the site before uploading.
- Transferring the files.
- Testing the final server version.

Format

Each server provider has different conditions and these should be checked before completing the site. Better still, check the conditions out before even starting the site design.

The issues to be considered are:

- The name of the server sub-directory allocated for the new site. This may be already created by the provider. In this case, providing the correct password at the ftp logon automatically directs uploading to the allocated directory.
- Avoid using absolute pathnames for graphic images, since the paths used to store them on the server disk will be different and the files will not be accessible. Using relative pathnames avoids this problem, as does having all the sites files stored in a single directory.
- The most common name for the main site file is expected to be index.htm, but some expect default.htm or other name. The required main filename will be supplied by the ISP.
- Some providers support CGI scripting and offer image libraries and usage counters.
- The final site must fit within the maximum space allocated by the provider.

Pre-testing

Test all the links within the site to ensure that all the pages in structure function as expected. Equally important, test the site with different browsers before uploading. Some activities are peculiar to Netscape or Explorer and newer versions of the same browser support extra features not found in older versions. To maximise the site's readership, a balance has to be struck between the utilising the latest technological innovations and the ability of users to view the pages.

Errors detected at this stage should be recorded, and where possible, rectified. However, there are occasionally errors that only manifest themselves once the web site 'goes live', ie. once the site is published on the Internet/Intranet. If time and budget permits, the site can be pre-tested on an internal network, which can bring out even more errors before committing the site to full publication.

In such a test, the web developers should use loading software to simulate peak demand for the service, as well as checking individual pages for errors at the same time, since important errors have occurred in the past as a result of overloaded servers. The loading should be set higher than it is expected to rise once the site goes live, to allow for possible expansion.

Transferring

The site is uploaded using an FTP session.   When the FTP application is run, it produces a screen similar to that below.

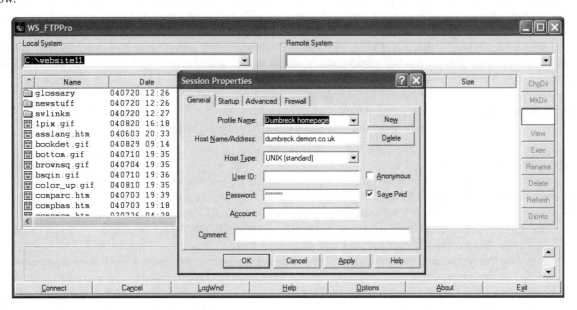

The details to be set up for an upload session are:

Profile Name:

A number of different profiles can be set up; one for uploading to the host server, others for downloading from particular sites, and so on.   The upload details can be saved as a profile and this can be called up each time the site needs to be updated.   The example entry is *'Support Web Site'* but this can be any name as it is purely for local use; it is not sent to the host server.

Host Details:

These are supplied by the server provider.   The example uses a UNIX server and initially connects to the home pages area of the demon site.

User Details:

The user ID and the user password will have previously been agreed with the provider.

Initial Directories:

The Local Initial Directory is the directory on the hard drive that stores the web site files.

The Remote Initial Directory is the directory used for storing the files on the remote server.   This is usually left blank, as the correct password usually automatically directs uploading to the allocated directory.

Clicking *'OK'* and *'Connect'* produces the following results:

- The local computer connects to the remote site.
- The remote server returns a message to the local system. This appears at the bottom of the ftp screen.
- The left window displays all the files in the local disk's web site directory.
- The right window displays the receiving directory on the remote server.   This directory will be empty.   On subsequent visits to update the site's contents, the complete set of site files is displayed in this window.

Between the two window columns are two buttons. One displays an arrow going from the local window to the remote window (i.e. from the local site to the remote server). The other arrow points from the server to the local computer. These buttons are used to copy files between the two computers.

Below the windows is a set of radio buttons. These allow the files to be transferred in ASCII or Binary mode. To upload the entire site:

- Set the transfer mode to ASCII.
- Highlight the HTML files in the local window.
- Click the right-pointing arrow to upload the text files.
- Set the transfer mode to Binary.
- Highlight the non-text files (e.g. graphics, audio, video, executables).
- Click the right-pointing arrow to upload these files.

As an alternate, some ftp packages allow a drag-and-drop method where files are highlighted by the mouse and *'dropped'* into the server window. In either case, the files will appear in the right window. This means that the entire population of Internet users can access them.

Web site security issues

Every computer should be secure, but with computers that are attached to the Internet 24 hours a day, data availability, security and integrity are an even greater concern. In many cases, the information on a web site is available to all viewers, so there can be no unauthorised viewing. However, in other cases there may be confidential information such as customer details stored on the site; and if a site makes its money by selling online material then access to this material should be similarly restricted. The SSL protocol (discussed in the '*Developing Websites*' chapter) and other such protocols can help provide a secure connection to ensure that only authorised persons are able to download the material. The main potential security problems for a web server include:

- Web site defacement (i.e. unauthorised changes to text or images on a web site).
- Unauthorised access to confidential data.
- A '*Denial of Service*' attack, reducing your site's efficiency or even bringing it offline.
- Viruses and similar malicious programs.

Denial of Service

This is a process whereby malicious hackers deliberately reduce an Internet business system's functionality to the point where that service is effectively denied to all legitimate users. There are a number of ways this can be done:

- Exploiting a flaw in the TCP/IP protocol. For example the well-known *"Ping of Death"* method involves sending IP packets that exceed the maximum length given in the TCP/IP specification. This will cause some systems without appropriate patches to crash, hang or reboot.
- Flooding the system with unwanted data. For example, systems may be clogged by sending large numbers of "Ping" requests (a simple and normally useful function to determine if a remote system is available), preventing or slowing legitimate communications. The notorious "*Smurf*" attack is one of these methods. Software to protect against this kind of attack is also usually available.
- Distributed Denial of Service (DDOS) attacks. This usually involves forcing large numbers of unwitting users into accessing a website at the same time, thus overloading it. This is most commonly accomplished by introducing viruses into user systems worldwide. Firewalls can help prevent this to some degree but are not foolproof.

More mundane DoS attacks could include using up system resources for purposes other than those for which they were designed, or sending many fake requests for goods. Many of these attacks are '*asymmetric*', meaning that a small, old computer with relatively slow hardware can potentially crash a much more sophisticated system. The best way to counter such attacks is to make sure the operating system and software is up to date with the latest patches, and security software such as router filters are implemented.

Providing Security

Ultimately, the best defence against unauthorised access, is to keep up-to-date with both security patches, and breaking news regarding security issues. Furthermore, although several tools can be useful in helping improve the security of a website, there is no such thing as an 'unhackable' site. The best that can be hoped for is that a site is difficult enough to hack, relative to the importance of its contents, that it will deter any hacker from spending enough effort to do so. The following list shows some of the most effective types of security systems currently available:

- A '*firewall*' (also discussed in the '*Developing Websites*' chapter) is a basic form of security, but for reasons explained below it is not always used to protect web servers. If it is practical to use it, however, a firewall is a reasonable start to securing a web site. An alternative, but similar, method is to use a '*proxy*' server.
- Proxy servers are servers that connect multiple systems to the Internet, or public Intranet. They are often mentioned in the same breath as firewalls, but proxies do not necessarily have the same security features built in. One feature that all proxy servers share, however, is that of disguising IP addresses. A message sent from a system in the private network to the public network or Internet, will pass through the proxy server, and will be edited so that it appears to come from a different IP address. In such a way, nobody outside the network will know the true IP addresses of the client machines, reducing the possibility of security breach by malicious outsiders.
- SSL can provide security against a few of the hackers' tools, such as '*CGI worms*'. This is a limited form of security however and should not be relied on.
- Intrusion Detection Systems (IDS) are available to look for the telltale signs of an attempted '*hack*'. These can be complex systems and in some cases are very expensive. Some of these systems are software-based, while others are hardware-based, being essentially a '*smart*' rack-mounted networking device similar in appearance to a network hub.
- If a full-fledged IDS system is too expensive, a relatively simple monitoring system may be sufficient. This software will monitor access to the web site, allowing the web maintainers to detect when their ports are being scanned by repetitive access attempts, which is one of the basic hackers' tools.
- Encryption software can be invaluable in some situations. This is a system whereby data is encoded using special '*keys*' so that even if the data is illegally accessed by unauthorised users, they will be unable to view the data since they will not have a key to decrypt the files. Encryption is covered in more detail later.

- The local security of the web server is also important. There is little point in having advanced security hardware and software if a disgruntled employee can easily walk into the server room and deface a web site! Physically securing the room in which the system is located is one part of preventing this sort of activity; the counterpart is to use a secure login system so that only employees who are part of the web administration team have access to the server.
- A good virus detection system is essential in a web server - If the web page contains a virus, all of the users of that page are put at risk, which could result in disastrously bad publicity if users catch a virus from a web site.

The integrity of data consists of other aspects as well as security. The concept of '*Data Assurance*' applies to web servers in a slightly different manner to that which it applies to office PCs, as shown below:

- Availability. The availability of web pages is a prime concern in most cases, since their function is to provide information to users at any time. Firewalls (systems designed to regulate data flowing in and out of a local network) can often interfere with the operation of a web site, especially if it uses any protocols other than simple http. For this reason, web servers are often placed in an area known as the De-Militarized Zone (DMZ), which is unregulated. Such a server must not be used for development, and no confidential information should be stored here without adequate security.
- Confidentiality. This may not apply to all websites, but any server that deals with e-commerce, for example, will require that information on customers be kept confidential. Only users with proper authorisation should be able to view or alter such records.
- Accuracy. The data on the web site should be kept up to date and error free. For a web site, this includes validation of web pages, including any third-party web pages that are included within the site's contents.
- Authenticity. In many cases it is important to ensure that messages and data have not been tampered with, and also that it genuinely comes from the specified party. Cookies can be used to identify users of a website, while secure systems like SSL can be used to provide a more thorough certification of authenticity.

Security Breaches

As has already been stated, no system is entirely safe from such problems as hackers, viruses or denial of service attacks. Every system which is available to more than one user has the potential to be breached. When the breach occurs, it is important to take responsibility for the breach, in order that lessons can be learned, and security tightened to prevent a similar problem occurring all over again. A well-informed management team should realise that security breaches are inevitable on any highly visible system.

Nonetheless, it is usually important to have the web server back up and running in the minimum amount of time. The simplest, but most expensive way to do this, is to have a 'mirror' of the web server available to take over as soon as the main web server fails or is taken down.

Whether a mirror is available or not, however, it is even more important to web servers than ordinary PCs, to make sure that data is backed up, and virus-free. If the web page is not backed up on a regular basis, for example by burning the web contents to CD-R every Friday, then any crash or malicious attack on the server could cause major losses in data availability. And for e-commerce sites, loss of availability means loss of income.

Encryption

Normal traffic on the Internet is carried in plain ASCII format. This is too insecure for organisations wishing to transmit confidential information over the Internet. One answer is to encrypt the message – encode it in such a way that it can only be decoded with the correct password. Simple password protection is offered by packages such as Word, WinZip and Acrobat. The designer places a password on the file and supplies the password to the authorised end user, who can then decrypt the file and use it normally.

Obviously, this imposes a burden on the end user, of decrypting the data. This may put off potential customers, especially if the product's intended audience is the general public rather than technically aware computer users. Companies considering any form of encryption must weight the potential loss of sales due to this extra burden, against the security benefits provided.

Placing a password on a Word document or ZIP file is insufficient to a determined hacker, however. Such systems rely on a complex algorithm to verify that the password supplied is genuine. However, every such algorithm can be broken; with modern processor speeds it is quite possible to use a '*brute force*' method – simply try millions of possible passwords per second until the correct password is found.

'*Public Key*' encryption methods provide better security than a regular password algorithm. This method applies a *'key'* (a mathematical algorithm) to scramble the contents before transmission. The receiving end can unscramble the message and recover the information, assuming that it also uses the same algorithm. Incoming traffic security is implemented using *'public'* and *'private'* keys. An organisation can hand out copies of the public key to all parties likely to send them data. The public key allows users to encrypt messages; they cannot be used to decrypt messages. The private key is held by the receiving organisation and this key can successfully decrypt all incoming messages. This is the basis of the popular encryption program called PGP (Pretty Good Privacy).

PGP should be distinguished from the algorithms it uses. PGP is a piece of software that provides public key encryption, but the actual encryption follows algorithms developed by other groups. PGP previously used an algorithm known as *'RSA'* (Rivest/Shamir/ Adleman, the creators of the algorithm), but now uses *'ElGamal'*, based on the DSS (Digital Signature Standard) algorithm, which is believed to be more secure.

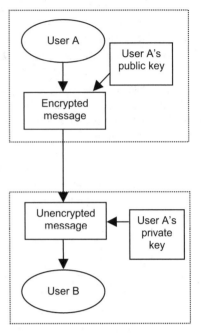

Both RSA and DSS use *'asymmetric keys'*, meaning that the public and private keys are different. (Internal networks can sometimes rely on symmetric key systems, such as DES, if all users can be trusted with the keys)

The actual size of the asymmetric key is relatively small, but even a small key can provide powerful encryption. Even a 512-bit key size could hold any of 10^{150} prime numbers, and modern encryption uses keys typically from 1024 to 4096 bits in size. It has already been proven that an intruder with access to enough computers could realistically break a small size key such as 512 bits, and with processing power increasing each year, users should consider how long they want their information to be secure before choosing a key size. There is a trade-off to be considered, between the speed of decryption of messages by legitimate personnel, and the need for security.

An alternative is to use *'Digital Signatures'* in each document. A public/private key system, similar to that used in PGP and such security systems, can be used to create a signature that is almost impossible to forge. The private key is used in conjunction with a *'message digest'* that is created by performing a hashing operation on the message itself, so the signature cannot be created without the key. This can be used in conjunction with *'digital certificates'* that hold public keys and information on the user of the public keys to prove the signature really is from the person it claims to be from.

Access to web documents

As part of the security of a web site, it is important to ensure that only authorised personnel are able to upload and download files to and from the web server. Even a well-meaning employee could easily disrupt the web site's operation with a poorly written document, or even by mistakenly deleting pages from the site.

If the site is held on space rented from a web service provider, then the password ftp account to the server should only be given to appropriate personnel involved in maintaining the web pages. However, if the web server is internal to an organisation, then maintaining secure access to that server is the responsibility of the IT personnel. IIS, for example, allows users to remotely maintain their web pages. In such a case, the server managers have the option of using an SSL interface to the FrontPage web design software, to ensure that only the appropriate personnel have access to their own parts of the web site.

Final testing

After the site is uploaded, it should be tested. This should be in line with the test specification developed during the design phase, and involves accessing the site as a normal user by entering the site address in the browser. The main page of the site should appear and each link should be tested, to see whether the expected pages appear and the text and graphics are displayed as expected. Test the site with the *'display graphics'* option disabled to ensure that <ALT> tags work.

Test the site with different browsers, to ensure that the site appearance is satisfactory on a range of browser packages. Test the site with different versions of the same browser. For example, an older browser may not have the facility for displaying frames and this checks whether the <NOFRAMES> text works. If possible, the site should also be tested on different platforms. Many Internet users are not PC users and the site may not appear on other machines in quite the way that was planned.

If the site contains JavaScript, or uses any other programming techniques, these will require more thorough testing. They are effectively small applications in their own right, and the techniques that are used to test full blown applications should also be applied to such applets if the site is to be reliable.

Again, bugs must be recorded and reported to the project manager. At this stage, correction of errors becomes more costly, and the project manager must decide whether to invest time and money into correcting any serious errors.

The documentation of errors recorded and/or rectified at the pre-publishing and post-publishing tests can be useful in helping to avoid similar errors in future. As such, an evaluation of the design and implementation of the web site can be of later use. Again, this is part of the normal design process as outlined in other chapters of this book.

Advertising the site

At this stage, the site is available to the wider Internet and has been designed to respond to search engines. Traffic from search engines, however, only generates a minority of the visits to sites. There is much more that can be done to promote the site. The amount of time and money invested in publicising the site depends upon the nature of the site. Individuals and organisations will build a promotion strategy from the techniques listed below. Hobby sites may decide to generate extra hits using cost-free methods such as obtaining directory entries or hosting regular site events. Commercial sites may decide to embark on a range of advertising methods. Charities and special interest groups may decide upon publicity in the media. There is no 'correct' way to promote a site. Site owners will choose the mix of activities that produces the best results for their particular product/message.

Target Audience

The potential audience for the web site does not reflect all of society. Some countries have very low numbers on the Internet, while richer countries such as the USA have large numbers of Net users. There are far more young people on the Net than there are older users. Within each country, Net usage is largely concentrated in the more affluent and professional sections of the population. Net users are still predominantly male, although female participation is growing rapidly. The potential audience, therefore, is what actually exists and not what a site would wish to exist. The site's expectations have to reflect this reality. Sites for the unemployed, travelling people, pensioners, etc can expect fewer hits than sites for youth culture, consumer products, holidays, etc.

Newspapers/Magazines/Radio

It is worth contacting newspapers (both national and local), relevant magazines and radio stations about the launch of a new site. This method only produces results if the site itself is newsworthy in some way (e.g. a charity site, a topical site, covering a niche market, etc). Coverage is free and widespread but may not be targeting the desired audience. This may work better for launching a helpline than launching a specialist site.

Press Releases

In addition to the printed press, sites can be publicised through on-line press releases. Several sites provide on-line daily or weekly information on new sites. Press releases should be short and sharp, using small paragraphs, if they are to be considered for inclusion. Organisations may consider using an on-line distribution service. This is a commercial company that already has the knowledge and contacts and will process press releases for a fee. Their experience can be a benefit as targeting is the key - not just maximising hits.

Site Reviews

There are two types of reviews for web sites - *'Guides'* and *'Cool Sites'*. A *'Guide'* provides a review of a selected number of sites and provides a site rating. The *'Cool Site'* usually reviews and recommends a different site each day. These both provide a high volume of extra traffic for a short time.

Magazine Adverts

The impact of paid advertising depends on the nature of the site and ensuring that the advertising matches the target group. There will be fewer hits from groups who normally do not own/use a computer and advertising costs may determine whether to proceed. On the other hand, adverts placed in magazines for computer users, electronic technicians, educationalists, government users and the IT industry can expect a better return.

Directories

These sites use categories to direct viewers, via menu options, to their chosen topics. They are often described as the *'Yellow Pages'* of the Internet. The menus have many categories and sub-categories. Inclusion on the directory, therefore, specifically targets those requiring the new site's information/ product. Directory providers provide forms for site registration and these gather details on the URL, directory category (e.g. sport, travel, computers) and key details of the site contents. Not all sites are automatically accepted by a directory provider. Yahoo, for example, rejects a third of all submissions. The most popular directories are Yahoo, Ask Jeeves, Lycos, Webcrawler and Infoseek.

In addition to directory services, most directory sites also provide search engine facilities.

Since most Internet purchases are made by users first initiating a search for their products, search engines play a huge part in influencing purchasing. As a result, major search engines such as Google, Lycos and Alta Vista provide a *"paid for placement"* service, where a fee is charged for ensuring that a particular web site appears high up in a user's search rankings. The ranking does not depend on the web site's design – only on the web site owner's willingness to pay. This is good news for those pushing the further commercialisation of the Internet and bad news for independent users.

Newsgroups

There are over 30,000 newsgroups on the Internet and those with topics relevant to the site's contents can be selected for mailing. This is a sensitive area, as some newsgroups do not allow advertising. A posting to a newsgroup should not consist solely of the advert but should bring in the advert as part of a general contribution or answer to another's query. So *"buy my product"* is counterproductive while *"...I hope that answers your question. For more details see my web site ....."* is acceptable.

Posting to newsgroups is a useful method, in as much as the audience reached have all chosen to read in the newsgroup topic and are therefore potentially more receptive to the new site's message. On the other hand, abuse of the newsgroup through blatant adverts and repeated postings will produce a hostile reaction.

Links from other web sites

Other web sites may promote similar interests or products and have an interest in providing links between sites.   An academic or hobby site may be very happy to provide a one-way link to the new site.   Their link may point to the main page or directly to a page that contains their specific interest.   Other sites may swap links, with both sites providing links to the other site.   The hits arising from web links is almost as high as that from search engines.

There is no special procedure for attracting links: an e-mail request to the other sites soon produces their responses.

Banner campaigns

Many sites are run by enthusiastic, and knowledgeable, amateurs.   If they have a costly server, they often are keen to get financial sponsors for their sites.   This can be a cost-effective method of advertising for commercial sites, as many sites attract large numbers of viewers.   Usually, the sponsorship results in advertising banners being placed on the other's site.   For larger companies, the extra expense of having a banner on a larger commercial site may be more attractive.   The cost of advertising on popular directories and search engines is greater than on smaller non-commercial sites.

The site owners can be e-mailed for more information.   Be aware that fewer than 1% of users seeing a banner actually click on it to jump to the new site (known as *'clickthrough'*).   The impact of a banner depends on some crucial factors such as professional banner design, the use of animation, the use of bright colours and banner content appropriate to the user being targeted.

Electronic Newsletters

These aim to draw users into regular contact with the site, by inviting them to sign up to an e-mailing list for a regular newsletter.   The list is used to send regular e-mails outlining site changes, special offers, events, etc.   Before proceeding, there should be clear procedures that allow users to unsubscribe.

Site Events

These are designed to encourage users to pay regular visits to the site.   Events will depend on the nature of the site but could be competitions, games, surveys, on-line interviews with celebrities or experts, pre-recorder audio broadcasts, 'issue of the month', FAQ series.   These are all time-consuming as they require regular updating of the site contents but they make the site more attractive for repeat visits.

Where the site is updated regularly, say so as *"Last updated ......"* messages encourages viewing.

Measuring Results

One simple measure of a site's success is the extra sales/donations/members/enquiries that are generated.

Then again, a site's purpose might be as an information provider.   Sites providing tax or weather information, music charts, train or TV timetables and so on are intended mainly to provide one-way traffic.   For these sites, the best measure of success is the *'hit rate'* - the number of times pages have been viewed.   These figures can be gathered using *'counters'*.   Counters can provide information on the origins of traffic, the total visits to the site and the number of hits on particular pages.   The ISP can be checked for these services.   The hit rate for sites is used in the same way as viewing figures for TV channels.   Increased viewers results in increased fees for advertising on these sites.   This provides an incentive for sites to inflate their visitors' figures.   Reputable sites can pay a fee to non-profit agencies for *'web auditing'*.   These agencies monitor the site, its procedures and its results and pronounce on the accuracy of the figures.

Web page Maintenance

Even when the web site is in place, it is rarely static. Most web pages have new content added on a regular or irregular basis. New content must be regulated and the integrity of the site maintained, to avoid a site that looks disjointed, and may even contain invalid links.

Using a good Asset Management system can help in this regard, making sure that new pages have the same 'look and feel' as existing pages, by using existing style sheets and blank button images. However, it is good practice for those involved in maintaining a web site to keep a 'mirror' of those parts for which they are responsible. This allows the user to ensure that it fits seamlessly into the existing web structure, before uploading it to the server.

Some types of pages require further maintenance. For example, some sites run 'forums' where users may post messages, but these messages should be moderated by the web site authors to prevent any dubious material from being published. These messages may also require feedback from official representatives, which the web administrator may or may not be qualified to provide.

Of course, there are other ways in which user feedback can shape the contents of the web site. A 'feedback' page is a common sight on commercial web pages, where the user can fill out a form giving their opinion on the web site or the products that are available through it. In the latter case, all that the web site maintenance personnel can do is pass on the feedback to the relevant people in the organisation. In the former case, however, the user's comments should be considered carefully by the web site management team, and changes made to the site if it is felt to be appropriate. The user should always be informed that his feedback has been taken into account, and a human response is always appreciated more than an automatically generated reply.

However, all new pages, regardless of the reason for the pages to be added, should be subjected to the same Data Assurance checks as other pages, such as validation of the page's code, and security if necessary.

Developing Web Sites

The previous chapter looked at the steps and the approaches needed for creating a basic web site. It allowed a useful site to be built and provided all the facilities such as graphics, sounds, video and some limited interactivity.

This chapter, read along with the chapters on JavaScript and Flash, takes site design to new levels of user interaction. It looks at three interlinked areas:

- Site enhancements.
- Web programming.
- Commercial web sites.

Site enhancements

The extensions covered in this chapter are designed to either add extra functionality to the site, or enhance page content.

These are:

- Cascading Style Sheets
- Image maps
- Streaming

Cascading Style sheets

While HTML is a powerful tool, its major drawback from the start has been its lack of control. Under standard HTML, it is impossible to set a standard style for the various types of content in all web pages within a site. Approaches involving lengthy, complicated scripts tend to work only under certain circumstances, and are difficult to maintain. Some HTML creation software has capabilities built in for version management, but this may involve extra expense, and is really a workaround rather than a solution.

An alternative is to use Cascading Style Sheets (CSS). This allows page styles (including fonts, background images, borders and so on) to be specified for various classes of objects on the web pages. These definitions cascade down through the various types – for example a font that falls into two categories as described in the Style Sheet will have the settings from both, with the type that is defined last in the Style Sheet having precedence wherever there may be a conflict in style.

CSS is supported to varying degrees by Internet Explorer 3 and onwards, as well as Netscape Navigator 4 onwards. Browsers that do not support CSS will ignore the style part and continue to read the rest of the file, meaning that the HTML page will still display (albeit somewhat less attractively) on an old machine.

Inline Styles

The simplest way to use CSS is simply as an attribute of any text tag. For example the <H1> tag, the <P> tag, the <A> tag and so on can all use style definitions built in to the tag. This can give some greater control, and is useful to over-ride previously defined styles, but misses out on a lot of the power of CSS if it is the sole method used. A simple inline style might look as follows:

```
<P STYLE="color: red">Red text</P>
```

Style Blocks

One way of using style sheets is to specify them inside the web page. In this method, the style sheet is placed inside the HEAD portion of the page source. The Style Sheet is specified within a <STYLE> tag.

Unfortunately, older browsers do not recognise the <STYLE> tag, and so will instead display the source text within that tag instead of using it as a style.

Therefore, in order to preserve backwards compatibility, the contents of the <STYLE> tag should also be within an HTML comment block, so that older browsers are told to ignore it if they cannot handle CSS. The comment block begins with '<!==' and ends with '-->', and so the general structure of such an HTML file is as shown.

```
<HTML>
<HEAD>
<TITLE>Page title</TITLE>
<STYLE>
<!--
Style Sheet definitions
-->
</STYLE>
</HEAD>
<BODY>Page text</BODY>
</HTML>
```

Linked Style Sheets

However, style sheets can be even more useful when they are used outwith a web page's source. If a CSS sheet is stored separately, then each page on an entire site can use a single stylesheet. In this way, the style of all web pages will be the same, presenting a more consistent web site. Also, it means that changes of style require just one file to be updated rather than every single web page. Finally, having a linked style sheet can slightly reduce the size of individual HTML files.

An HTML file can link to a style sheet using the <LINK> tag, as shown. The HREF attribute is a URL to find the linked file, just like in an anchor, while the REL attribute indicates the relation of the link – in this case, a style sheet.

The TYPE attribute indicates the type of style sheet; there are a very few types of style sheets other than CSS, and they are not widely supported.

In this case, the browser will expect to see a CSS style sheet called "style.css" in the same directory as the HTML page. This external style sheet is an ASCII text file containing style definitions exactly as they would appear within the <STYLE> tags if they were inside the web page itself (see below).

```
<HTML>
<HEAD>
<TITLE>Page title</TITLE>
<LINK HREF="style.css" REL=stylesheet
TYPE=text/css>
</HEAD>
<BODY>Page text</BODY>
</HTMl >
```

Alternatively, external style sheets can be imported into style blocks within a web page. This is done within the style block, using the '@import' statement, followed by the URL. To do this, though, the browser needs to know what kind of Stylesheet it is, so the <STYLE> tag itself should contain this information as an attribute.

The import statement could look as follows:

```
<STYLE TYPE="text/css">
@import URL("style.css");
</STYLE>
```

Note

For both methods of using external style sheets, it is possible to use multiple links or imports, as well as style blocks, and even inline styles – this is the cascading aspect of CSS. If a type selector is defined multiple times, then the most recent values for any properties that are specified over-ride previous values. However, any properties that are left undefined in more recent style definitions retain their previous values.

For example, it is possible to have an external style sheet, an internal style block, and an inline style, all with properties applying to the <P> tag. The external sheet might make it indented and define a font face and font size, while the style block specifies an indent and a colour. The inline style might make the font bold and change the font face. In such a case, the resulting text will have the style block's indentation and colour, the inline style's bold weight and font face, and the style sheet's font size.

Fonts in Style Sheets

While <FONT> tags specify a single font that must be used if available, CSS allows the web page designer to suggest a group of fonts, and allow the browser to choose which of those fonts to use, or even override them entirely.

In addition, CSS stylesheets provide greater control over font types. This is achieved by having a number of 'selectors' defined in the stylesheet, followed in braces by the style that should be applied to the selector when used within the web page. The most common kind of selector is a 'type selector', which simply applies a style to all text of a given type. For example, to embolden all text that is specified as being of Header 1 (H1) type, the following style definition might be used:

```
<STYLE>
H1 {font-weight: bold}
</STYLE>
```

Any text within an <H1> tag will now be bold. The details within the braces (the '{' and '}' symbols) are the 'properties' of the selector. If the selector is to have multiple properties defined then these should be separated by a semi-colon (;).

Furthermore, note that each definition is separated from its value by a colon (:). Some browsers will allow web pages to use an equal sign (=) instead of a colon, but this is contrary to the CSS standard and is not supported by all browsers. Consequently, it is recommended that designers use a colon.

Additionally, a property set can be applied to more than one type selector by separating the type selectors with a comma. For example if you wish H1, H2 and H3 text to be both bold and italicised, the following style definition will do that:

```
<STYLE>
H1, H2, H3 {font-weight: bold; font-style: italic}
</STYLE>
```

Some properties are able to specify several sub-properties within them. For example, the 'font' property can be used to contain the font-style, font-size, and font-family properties, in that order. If the properties are accessed individually then they can be put in any order. A font definition can thus be done in one of two ways:

```
<STYLE>
P {font-size: 50px; font-family: sans-serif; font-style: italic}
</STYLE>
```

or

```
<STYLE>
 P {font: italic 50px sans-serif}
</STYLE>
```

For type selectors that apply to text, there are a number of possible properties.
The most common and widely supported options are as follows:

Property	Usage
font-family	Defines the set of fonts that may be used. They should be separated by a comma, and the browser is allowed to use any font from the list that it has available. This includes Windows fonts, but there are also a number of generic fonts that indicate only a general type, most notably 'serif', 'sans-serif' and 'monospace'.
font-style	The style of font to use. eg: 'normal', 'italic' or 'oblique'.
font-size	The size of the font. As well as a size value, it can be specified as 'small', 'medium', 'large' and other such values.
font-weight	The weight (boldness) of the font. For example 'lighter', 'normal' or 'bold'.
color	The colour of the font. Like most HTML colour attributes, it can be defined as a string-value (eg 'red') or as RGB values from zero to 255, such as 'rgb(255,0,0)'
text-decoration	This property can specify 'underline', 'overline', or 'line-through' for text decoration.
text-indent	Indents are very hard to handle in basic HTML; this style sheet attribute makes it much easier.
text-align	Specifies the alignment of the text, using the keywords 'left', 'right', 'center' or 'justify'.
letter-spacing	The spacing between each letter in the text. Spacing can be set to zero or even negative values.

Where a size is specified (such as in font-size, or text-indent for example), the default measurement is in pixels but it can also be specified in points (eg. '20pt'), inches (eg. '1in'), millimetres (eg. '15mm') and other measurements.

Other options in Style Sheets

Style sheets are not all about fonts and text. Web site style includes background images, tables, borders and so on. The following properties can apply to almost any object in a CSS sheet.

Property	Usage
border	This property places a border round an object. The designer can specify the size of the border, and the border style and colour. For example {border: 3px double RGB(0,0,255)} would produce a 3 pixel blue double border. Other keywords include 'solid', 'dotted', and 'dashed'. Individual edges of the border can be specified using the properties 'border-top', 'border-left', 'border-bottom' and 'border-right'.
position	By choosing 'absolute' for the position, the exact position of the object within the window can be specified via the 'top' and 'left' properties. The 'relative' option for position specifies a location relative to the current location on the web page.
width, height	These are separate properties, and they can be used to specify how much space (in percentage or absolute terms) in the window they should occupy.
float	This property can accept the values 'none', 'left' or 'right', specifying whether an object is to be placed 'floating' on the left or right side of the window with text wrapping around.

Furthermore, there are some useful properties that can only be applied to certain HTML tags.
For example:

Property	Usage
background	This property applies to the BODY tag. It allows the designer to specify a colour, an image, whether the image is to repeat if it does not fill the window, whether it should scroll along with the page or stay fixed behind the page contents, and where the image should be positioned.
list-style	For the various types of lists, this property can set the style of bullet, images to be used as bullets, and the positioning of bullets.

The above lists are far from exhaustive, but the designer should be wary that CSS compatibility is sketchy at the best of times. While major properties such as font-styles and colour are relatively safe, the more in-depth CSS is used the more the web page will need to be tested on other browser platforms to ensure readability.

Both *'background'* and *'list-style'* properties are made up of other properties, in the same way as the *'font'* property discussed earlier. A style sheet that makes use of these properties might contain the following definitions:

```
BODY {background: url(santa.jpg) no-repeat top right}
LI {list-style: url(bullet.gif) inside}
```

Class Selectors

The type selector can be a powerful tool for ensuring consistency in a web site. However, CSS also provides greater flexibility than standard HTML, by allowing *'class selectors'*. Like type selectors, these are used to cascade style properties down onto objects shown in the browser window.

However, while types apply to all instances of an object type, classes are more like sub-types that can be chosen within the body text. Each class is attached to a type, by placing a period between the type and the class. If no type is specified, then the class is not associated with any single tag, and can be used with whichever tags are desired.

For example, the style sheet in the example script defines the 'sans' class of <P> tagged text as being displayed in sans serif font, and the 'big' class as being a generic class with adjusted font size. Note that in order to use two classes with one object, the classes must be enclosed in quotes, which are not necessary when only a single class is needed. Since the link is an <A> tag, it may not use the 'P.sans' class, but can use the generic '.big' class.

```
<HTML>
<HEAD>
<TITLE>Page title</TITLE>
<STYLE>
P.sans {font-family: sans-serif}
.big {font-size: 25px}
</STYLE>
</HEAD>
<BODY>
<P CLASS="big sans">This text is 25 pixel high Sans Serif</P>
<P CLASS=big>This text is 25 pixel high default font</P>
<P CLASS=sans>This text is default size sans serif</P>
<A HREF="link.htm" CLASS=big> This is a link which has been made 25 pixels high.</A>
</BODY>
</HTML>
```

Further CSS functions

In addition to type selectors and class selectors, there are a few other selectors. The ID selector is indicated in the style sheet by its preface of a '#' character. ID selectors should be unique, so using an ID selector with more than one object in any given web page is not recommended. There are more forms of selectors but they are rarely used.

Furthermore, CSS can use 'pseudo-elements' and 'pseudo-classes'. Currently, the only pseudo-elements that are defined apply to the <A> tag, and the only pseudo-classes defined apply to text classes.

The pseudo-elements are 'link', 'active' and 'visited'. Since they apply only to anchors, they allow an anchor to apply different styles depending on whether the link within is inactive, active, or has been previously visited. This includes changing colour, font size etc.

Similarly, the pseudo-classes are 'first-letter' and 'first-line'. As the name suggests, these classes can be used to alter only the style of the first letter and first line of the text respectively.

Image maps

An image can be turned into a link simply by putting it within an anchor tag. However, if it is a complex image representing multiple items, the designer may wish to link to more than one URL with a single image. If the graphical areas to be used as links are all rectangular, then it is possible to divide the image up into several boxes (usually placed in the cells of a frame), some or all of which will point to different URLs. However, this is a fussy process, and it is easy to produce a result that does not look as good on some browsers as it does on others. Furthermore, it is impossible to faithfully reproduce an area that is not rectangular as an area to be used as a link.

With an image map, the image is not cut up into chunks in this way; rather, it is a single image, and where the user's mouse is inside the image when he/she clicks the button determines which link to use. For example an image map showing demographic regions of the UK could link to a page of population figures for each region.

There are two methods of implementing image maps: server-side image maps and client-side image maps. Both of these use geometric shapes to define areas on the image map. Each geometric area corresponds to a portion of the image displayed, and mathematical routines can work out from the mouse x and y co-ordinates which region the pointer lies over when the mouse button is clicked.

The table shows the considerations when choosing between client-side and server-side image maps.

Client-side image map	Server-side image map
No special map script is required on the server.	The server needs to have scripting software to handle the mapping service.
When the mouse hovers over a region in the image, the appropriate link is displayed.	Wherever the mouse is in the image, only the x and y co-ordinates are displayed.
Area processing is carried out by the browser, instantly deciding on the URL to download.	Area processing is carried out by the server, resulting in delays.
Only implemented on newer browsers.	Implemented on most browsers.
For very complex maps, can significantly increase the HTML file size and thus download time.	The map is stored on the server, and so does not need to be downloaded at all.

Although both client-side and server-side image maps have advantages and disadvantages, to most private users client-side mapping may be the only option as they are unlikely to have the rights to install mapping software on their web server.

Creating an image map

The steps in creating an image map can be broken down as follows:

- If the image map is to be a server-side image, check that the server is capable of handling image maps and which standard it uses. If it does not handle image maps then additional CGI software will need to be installed to do so (see section on CGI later).

- Create a suitable image. Some images, complex digitised pictures in particular, do not lend themselves easily to geometric image mapping with its distinct areas. Suitable material for image maps might include: demographic maps, computer-generated art, or a photo-retouched image of a car engine for a tutorial on how to fix cars.

- Generate the image map. While this can be done by hand, it is unlikely that any desired image map will be simplistic enough for this to be feasible. There are a number of software packages available, such as Macromedia's Fireworks, which can be used as an interface to generate image maps.

- Create the HTML page. The image tag requires a special attribute in order to turn the image into an image map. If it is a client-side image map then the image map itself must either be included in a tag in the HTML or linked to as an exterior file.

Client-side image maps

A client-side image map consists of two parts: the image, and the map. The image is just a normal <IMG> tag, pointing at a URL to download an image from. However, it also contains the USEMAP attribute, which points to a map containing the areas and URLs to link to. This map can be an external file, or it can be within the HTML file. If it is a map defined within the same HTML page, then it can be referenced by a '#' character, followed by the name defined within the appropriate map definition.

The <MAP> tag itself has a NAME attribute that defines the name as referred to by the image tag. Between the <MAP> and the </MAP>, lie the area definitions.

These are <AREA> tags, which have several attributes, as follows:

ALT	As with the ALT tag in a normal image, this tells the browser what to display if it is incapable of displaying graphics or the graphics have been turned off.
SHAPE	This attribute can be either 'RECT' for rectangles, 'POLY' for irregular polygons, or 'CIRCLE' for circles.
COORDS	These are the co-ordinates that define the dimensions of the shape. They are relative to the top left corner of the image.
HREF	Just as the HREF in an anchor tag points to a URL to use when the content within is clicked upon, the same attribute in an area tag defines a URL to use when the user clicks within the area defined in that tag.

The most important part is the SHAPE attribute, because it defines how the shape is represented on the image map. For example, a 'RECT' shape has two pairs of co-ordinates, corresponding to the two diagonally opposite corners of the rectangle. The 'CIRCLE' shape has three co-ordinates, defining the x and y co-ordinates of the centre of the circle and then the radius of the circle. Finally, the 'POLY' shape can have any number of co-ordinate pairs, each representing a point along the polygon. The polygon is always a filled shape, so the last point is automatically joined to the first point.

The following example shows a simple web page using a very basic image map. Note that the 'default' shape is listed last: areas defined first take precedence over areas defined later when it comes to capturing the mouse x and y co-ordinates and converting them into a URL. In this way the designer can ensure that every point on the image map will result in a URL of some kind.

```
<HTML>
<BODY>
<IMG SRC="image.gif" USEMAP="#imagemap">

<MAP NAME="imagemap">
<AREA SHAPE="CIRCLE" COORDS="113,115,81" HREF="circle.htm" ALT="This is the circle">
<AREA SHAPE="POLY" COORDS="305,45,399,193,214,193" HREF="triangle.htm" ALT="This is the triangle">
<AREA SHAPE="RECT" COORDS="431,44,612,191" HREF="rect.htm" ALT="This is the rectangle">
<AREA SHAPE="RECT" COORDS="0,0,700,200" HREF="default.htm" ALT="This is the region outside the
shapes">
</MAP>

</BODY>
</HTML>
```

Server-side image maps

An image map on a server is usually a file with a .map extension, which is a text file containing the same types of geometric instructions on which areas should link to which URLs. However, the syntax is different when compared with client-side image maps, and indeed different server systems have different syntaxes. What's more, a complex CGI script is needed on the web server to handle the image map processing, although in many cases this script comes with the web server software. However, the web page itself is much simpler; the image map is simply an <IMG> object embedded in a normal anchor tag. The anchor points to the CGI script that handles the mapping, while the image tag only needs to add an ISMAP attribute. So, the image map portion of the web page might look as follows:

Meanwhile, the map file on the server will look similar to a map definition within a client-side <MAP> tag. For example, in the NCSA image map standard, the options included are *'circle'*, *'poly'*, *'rect'*, *'point'* and *'default'*. However, the syntax of that standard means that the .map file for the previous example would look as follows:

```
<A HREF="www.website.com/cgi-bin/imagemap/maps/uk-demo.map">
<IMG SRC="ukmap.gif" ISMAP>
</A>
```

```
default default.htm
circle circle.htm 113,115,81
poly triangle.htm 305,45,399,193,214,193
rect rect.htm 431,44,612,191
```

Using plugins in a web page

The *'Animation and Flash'* chapter looks at creating a Flash animation file for embedding in a web page. There are many other plugins that can be included in a web page, for example:

- Plugins for playing video clips, such as Quicktime or RealPlayer. See the *"Digital Video"* chapter for a discussion of the various video file types.
- Document reading plugins, such as Acrobat or DejaVu. Acrobat is the most common and well-supported document format on the web, although many believe that DejaVu offers greater document security.
- Graphics plugins for more modern file formats such as SVG and MNG. Although these offer more advanced features than GIF or JPEG, the requirement to use a plugin should be carefully considered before using such media.

Unfortunately, there are two tags that can be used to embed objects in web pages. One of these is the proprietary tag introduced by Netscape, <EMBED>, and the other is the *'official'* object embedding tag, <OBJECT>. Both can be used to integrate any external object into a web page via the use of a plugin.

Professional web page editing packages such as Dreamweaver include tools to make these tags up automatically, so the user need not worry about their precise contents. However, as with most things in web design, it helps to understand the underlying principles of the technology when preparing the media and the web pages themselves.

The EMBED Tag

EMBED is the simpler of the two object embedding tags. It can have several attributes that are common to many tags, such as NAME, ALIGN, HEIGHT, ALT, BORDER etc. However, the most important attributes relating to the EMBED tag are the following:

- SRC. This tag is a URL pointing to the source media file, and is the only required attribute.
- TYPE. This is the MIME type of the object being embedded. In the absence of a TYPE attribute the browser must try to determine from the file's extension which plugin to use.
- PLUGINURL. This attribute contains a URL that points to a Java Archive (JAR) file containing the appropriate plugin to play the source file, in case the user does not currently have the plugin installed. This allows the browser to download and install the plugin ready to view the file.
- PLUGINSPAGE. Like PLUGINURL, this is a URL pointing to a site where the plugin can be found. The difference is that this attribute does not point to an automated plugin installation, and relies on manual installation.

The EMBED tag is not part of the official HTML specification, and so it is comparatively poorly documented. For example, it is not clear whether it must be closed by a </EMBED> tag, and most browsers will happily accept the <EMBED> tag without an accompanying </EMBED>. Also, there is an associated <NOEMBED> tag, which is used to specify alternative content to be used if the browser does not support object embedding. In modern PC browsers this is not an issue, so this tag is often left out, even though it is bad practice to do so.

This is an example of the EMBED tag in use:

```
<EMBED SRC="movies/intro.swf" HEIGHT="640" WIDTH="480"
TYPE="application/x-shockwave-flash"
PLUGINSPAGE="http://www.macromedia.com/go/getflashplayer">

  <NOEMBED>
  Welcome to our web space.
  </NOEMBED>

</EMBED>
```

If the browser is able to use the EMBED tag, it will do so, and ignore anything inside the NOEMBED tag, and vice versa. Finally, note that the EMBED tag can contain attributes that are not recognised by the browser. If this is the case, they are assumed to be parameters, which are passed on to the object being embedded. This allows for standard objects that display different content depending on the way in which they are embedded.

The OBJECT tag

This tag was created by Microsoft, and formally became part of the HTML language in HTML version 4.0. It is more flexible than EMBED, but can also be more confusing. Like EMBED, it can contain a number of standard attributes, including ALIGN, HEIGHT, WIDTH and so on. The most important attributes, though, are as follows:

DATA	This tag is mostly used by Java applets, where it indicates a base URL from which to locate any data files that are required by the applet.
CLASSID	This may be a URL, but more often it is simply a numerical identifier that refers to a file type as stored in the Windows Registry. This allows the browser to determine the type of object and use the appropriate plugin.
TYPE	Like EMBED, the OBJECT tag has an attribute to indicate the MIME type of the object.
CODEBASE	This specifies a URL from which the browser can find the appropriate plugin to use the media file specified in the SRC attribute.

The OBJECT tag can also pass parameters to the plugin, just like the EMBED tag, but it is done in a different way. Instead of cluttering up the actual OBJECT tag itself with unrecognised attributes, the parameters are passed by using the <PARAM> tag in between the opening and closing of the OBJECT tag. For example:

```
<OBJECT       classid="clsid:D27CDB6E-AE6D-11cf-96B8-444553540000"
        codebase="http://download.macromedia.com/pub/shockwave/cabs/flas
        h/swflash.cab#version=6,0,40,0" WIDTH="640" HEIGHT="480">

  <PARAM NAME=movie VALUE="movies/intro.swf">
  <PARAM NAME=bgcolor VALUE=#FFFFFF>

  Welcome to our web space.

</OBJECT>
```

Again, this example will display the message "Welcome to our web space" instead of the file "intro.swf" if the browser does not support the OBJECT tag. Please note that the SRC attribute is not a part of the HTML specification for the OBJECT tag, although most browsers will accept this method of specifying the source data file anyway.

Streaming

Downloading audio or video files from the Internet is all very well, but with very large files it is desirable to be able to show such media instantly. This is achieved by 'streaming'. Streaming is used almost exclusively for audio and video data, although there are streaming systems available for VR and even email.

Streaming generally requires special server software or at least a modification to the MIME types on the server software in order to supply the streamed data. However, there are some types of streaming (Such as VivoActive) which 'embed' the streamed file into an object in an HTML page, almost as an image would be.

Additionally, the server requires a new Internet protocol to handle the real-time transmissions, for example RTP (Real-time Transport Protocol), which is now a recognised standard.

On the client's side, the system needs to have software or plug-ins that are capable of understanding the particular streamed file format that is supplied. The software will generally download a few seconds of data into a buffer before beginning to play back the streamed data. If the buffer is used up before the next part of the data stream is downloaded then the software must pause while it continues to download. This means that the data rate of streamed files must match the user's modem speed if it is to avoid jerky or stalled playback in streamed data.

Most server streaming software works using UDP (User Datagram Protocol) rather than TCP/IP (Transfer Control Protocol / Internet Protocol). This is because UDP is capable of higher transmission speeds, at the cost of some reliability. Because streamed data normally consists of error-tolerant data such as video or audio, the shortcomings of UDP are rarely a concern. The main problem with UDP streaming is that most corporate firewalls do not allow UDP traffic, precisely because of its lack of control.

How streaming works

Servers, whether UNIX or NT, operate on the Internet (or an internal intranet) through *'ports'*. In the early days of the Internet, almost every computer on the system was UNIX based, and had a large number of actual physical ports, each of which handled different types of information. For example, email often went through port 21. In today's world of ADSL and ISDN lines, there need not be more than one physical port, but the scheme is still useful logically. Streaming data can use one of those ports, or it can be accessed directly if access is given to a file streamed via HTTP. The URL which points to streamed data need not specify a filename in the URL, but instead may supply a port number or folder path after the server name. The server can usually be configured either to use ports, or to supply streamed data to anyone who tries to access a specified folder name.

Streaming data is not always supplied via the HTTP transfer protocol. If a URL is included in a web page that directly leads to, say, a RealAudio file, then the default action of the browser will be to download the file and either save it or activate a helper application to view it. In order to prevent this, *'pointer files'* (or *'meta files'*) are often used. These are small text files with a different file extension to differentiate them from the actual streaming data files. The pointer file is normally nothing more than one or more lines of text, each of which indicating the URL to receive streaming data. This means that more than one stream can be started by a single link, although they are shown consecutively rather than concurrently.

When the browser is sent to a pointer file, it will notice the file extension and, assuming an appropriate plug-in is installed, will start up the helper application. The application, however, will be passed the text file rather than the actual data stream.

From the pointer file, the application knows where to read streaming data from, and can go about doing so properly.

Streaming can be done in one of a number of ways:
- Live streaming.
- Tape-delayed, or *'almost live'* streaming.
- File streaming.
- Pseudo-streaming, or *'progressive downloading'*.

Live streaming

Because the output is software-controlled, it is possible to send dynamic data, rather than being restricted to the files stored on the server. In this way it is possible to stream data as it is generated. Streaming uncompressed data is not a realistic option, so the server's software or hardware must carry out compression in real-time. This can require expensive compression hardware for MPEG videos.

The software on the server has to be constantly fed with the data to be streamed, and it will encode the data to the appropriate format and provide it to whoever accesses the specified port, or folder name.

Almost-live streaming

Because of the burden of compression, many so-called *'live'* systems are actually delayed by a set time period while the data is compressed. This is the basis of *'almost-live'* streaming methods. Since the data is still dynamic, and is supplied in the same manner as live streams, it appears no different to the user, unless the time delay can somehow be detected. (for example, calling a friend's mobile phone and watching him answer it on web-cam 3 seconds after you hear his voice on the phone)

File streaming

Perhaps the most common form of streaming, file streaming (also called streaming *'on-demand'*) involves transmission of a pre-encoded file. This completely removes the burden of real-time compression. It also gives the supplier the option to provide many versions of the same streamed file that are each encoded at varying data rates to cater for faster and slower client hardware.

Pseudo-streaming

This method involves downloading a file normally, but having software on the client PC use the data as it is downloaded. Often, the pseudo-streamed files can be optimised to make things easier for the client software – for example *'fast-start'* movies that contain extra header information to facilitate viewing the parts of the movie that has downloaded so far. In this way, for example, the viewer can display some parts of an MPEG movie after just 15 percent of the file has been downloaded.

Since pseudo-streaming is exactly the same as a simple download as far as the server is concerned, the server does not require any additional software to be installed.

Streaming Audio formats

The uses for streaming audio include Internet radio broadcasts, commercial music distribution, and samples of audio available elsewhere.

The most common streaming audio formats include:

- Liquid Audio is a commercial system designed specifically for online distribution of music. The client software has built in capabilities to handle purchase of CDs, and download of music samples as well as streaming.
- RealAudio was among the first streaming audio formats, and along with its partner RealVideo, now accounts for the majority of streaming content on the web. While offering superb compression rates, the sound quality is not the best. However, with streaming, it is important that enough data is received that the stream can be played back without stalling, and RealAudio performs that function well. The file has an RM extension and a pointer file in a RealAudio system is a .RAM file, which specifies the internet location of the stream, and also the protocol to use if other than HTTP. On the back of this technology, Real has introduced RealOne, which sees the company as an information provider as well as the provider of the player. The RealOne player, which is basically a combination of RealPlayer and RealJukebox, is available as a free download. However, for a monthly subscription, users gain access to streamed radio stations and sports, news and entertainment services.
- Shockwave Audio files can be created using Director and played on a computer with a Shockwave plug-in.
- MP3 is not a format that was originally intended for streaming audio. However, at lower bit-rates MP3 offers decent quality sound that is still capable of streaming on basic modems. The pointer file for MP3 streaming is an .M3U file, which is nothing more than a collection of locations where the MP3 files reside, or servers and ports configured for streaming. The Audioactive player by Telos Systems is one example of client software that handles M3U and MP3 files.

Streaming Video formats

Streaming video is useful for product demonstrations, entertainment, or video conferencing.

The most common video streaming format include:

- Vivo videos play through a browser plug-in. While Vivo movies gain very good compression, it is at the expense of frame rates and video quality in general. However, Vivo does have one important advantage - it is possibly the easiest form of video streaming around. It operates via HTTP, meaning that the .VIV file will be embedded in an HTML page – requiring no additional server software, and no editing of MIME types on the server at all. It is a so-called *'server-less'* system.
- HTTP also uses the TCP/IP transmission checking that UDP streaming lacks, and can operate through most firewalls. On the down side, because it is HTTP based, there is no control over how many users are allowed access to the file at one time, possibly leading to network congestion. Vivo is owned by RealNetworks.
- VDO is a client/server streaming video method, meaning that both the client and server must install additional software. The VDOLive software, despite its name, can handle on-demand streaming as well, depending on the type of software installed on the server. VDO is in fact a type of AVI compression. This system can use .VDO pointer files, or can be embedded in HTML files and streamed using HTTP streaming.
- RealVideo, part of the RealMedia system along with RealAudio and other software, is a client/server system capable of normal streaming or HTTP streaming, and can handle on-demand or live streaming. It uses .RAM pointer files to point to .RM media files.
- Microsoft's ASF files can be interactive, and have other functions as well as having a choice of codecs. The pointer files used are .ASX files, which bear a remarkable resemblance to .INI files. Microsoft NetShow is the server software, which can handle live broadcasts as well as on-demand streaming.
- StreamWorks is Xing Technology's MPEG streaming platform. It is aimed at high-end systems with very fast transfer rates and works well on intranets, ISDN links and ADSL links - but not so well on the plain old telephone Internet where 56k modems and even some 28.8k modems are common.
- QuickTime's format also offers streaming, with viewing on their free QuickTime player.
- MPEG-4 files have the advantage of storing all elements of a stream as discrete objects. This allows the data sent to a user to reflect their user's system. For example, it may send the full contents to users with high bandwidth connections while sending partial contents to low bandwidth users such as those with slow modems or with mobile browsers). Despite these potential advantages, the quality of MPEG-4 files has still to reach the quality of the rival systems.

Scalability

While most users may have a 56k modem, some still have 28.8k modems, and others have access to faster digital links. A good streaming server will be able to detect the speed of the client, and cater for it by providing an appropriately sized and compressed video stream. This capability is known as *'scalability'*. Some software can perform this on the fly, downscaling files for use when access is slower; but in many cases the only option is to save several files at varying compression rates to cater for the wider audience.

Embedding streamed data in HTML pages

At its worst, streaming can be a complex system, where files have to be encoded on the fly, ports have to be arranged, MIME types set up on the server, and software has to be installed and configured. At its simplest, however, anyone can set up a simple streaming system on an ordinary web server. Vivo videos, for example, can be put on the web server easily, and the only concern is whether the end user will have a Vivo player.

With RealAudio and RealVideo, a little more work is involved, as well as access to a streaming server.

The following general steps apply to RealMedia, but equally apply to most other forms of client/server streaming.

- Ensure that the correct protocols are installed and set up correctly. The web designers should have already decided on a protocol to use for streaming, for example UDP or RTSP.

- Install the streaming software on the server. In the case of RealMedia this software is called RealServer, and is able to handle either live or on-demand streams through TCP/IP, UDP or HTTP. Configure a port on the server to provide the streamed data, if necessary.

- Capture and encode the streamed data, or set up hardware and software to provide live input and encoding. Again, it should already have been decided to which speed(s) of connection the streaming server will cater to.

- Add the streaming file format's MIME type to the server software.

- Create a web page that links to the pointer file, or embed the object directly into a web page. It is advisable that the web page containing the streaming also contains details of the format of the stream so that appropriate plug-ins can be downloaded and installed at the client end.

Bandwidth costs

Being a provider of streamed services incurs running costs. If streamed files are required on server space that is rented from an ISP, there will be charges for the extra bandwidth that will arise from providing these services. Even if the ISP does not have to provide extra server services, the web site's bandwidth usage is certain to rise as many separate users access the site for fairly lengthy downloads.

Where specialised video streaming is provided, these are usually charged on the basis of the number of simultaneous streams that will be available (e.g. allowing 5, 20 or 400 users to download streamed data at the same time). There is also a limit to the total monthly data transfer from the site.

These extra running costs currently limit the uptake of streaming on web sites.

Push technology

While there are 'server-less' systems that have no special software installed on the server in order to perform streaming, there are also 'client-less' systems in operation. Conversely, this means that the client does not install software in order to read streamed data.

This works because the server 'pushes' the software down from the server to the client as the stream is requested. The most common way of doing this is using Java. A user can click on a link, and a Java applet will download and run. This Java applet will then proceed to stream the data from the source. For example, as explained in the Authoring Systems chapter, Director is able to save files as Java applets.

This method involves an extra burden on the client; that of downloading the applet before streaming will even begin. However, it means that the client need not install any software, and this in turn means that the producers need not be concerned with which format to use, and how many users have installed a client for that format.

Virtual Reality on the web

The 'page metaphor' employed by HTML has proven successful, but there are some who believe that certain functions would be better served by a 3D metaphor, where the user can actually 'move around' a web presence and find links represented by objects. A simple but common example is an online 3D model of a building that is in development or up for sale, which the viewer can rotate, and 'fly through' to get a better idea of the object than simple 2D images can provide.

Virtual Reality Modeling Language (VRML) is another markup language in the SGML family, and it is concerned with describing 3D objects for display as 'virtual reality' environments. Like HTML, VRML is simply a text file describing objects, so it is not specific to one type of computer or even one browser.

However, standard HTML browsers are not able to display VRML, and the device-independence comes at the cost of being displayed slightly differently from one VR browser to the next, just as HTML is displayed differently from one browser to the next.

Also like HTML, VRML has been through several versions. Version 1.0 was the original, and the last version was VRML 2.0. After that, the XML language has been used to define VR, which will result in the X3D standard, although it is currently still in development.

VRML can incorporate textured objects, video files, sounds, Java applets and JavaScript programming, but not every feature is supported by every browser. There are as yet only a few fledgling X3D browsers available, and there are only a limited number of VRML 2.0 browsers, of which the most widely known is Cosmo Player. Cosmo is freely downloadable, and acts as a plugin to Explorer and/or Navigator.

A VRML world is a file with the extension .WRL, and it can be included in a web site in one of two ways. The simplest is to simply provide a link to the WRL file, and allow explorer to load up the plugin to display the file in the full window. Alternatively, the EMBED tag can be used to include a WRL file inside an HTML page. The following shows an example of how this is done:

<EMBED SRC="musem.wrl" WIDTH="320" HEIGHT="200" BORDER="0">

Web programming

As the last chapter showed, perfectly useful web sites can be created with just the use of HTML.

However, to produce the extra functionality and looks, developers look to new and emerging technologies. This might be in the form of animations or audio and video streaming. Or it might be through the use of programming languages, many designed especially for web use. Web programming is considered as having two realms of activity - those involved with the clients (i.e. those who browse the web site contents) and those involved with servers (those who provide the web site contents).

Client side programming

This concentrates mainly on how the browser presents information (i.e. layout, style, animation, etc).

Client side programming means that all the program code is run at browser end. This has always been the case, for example, with HTML, but this has now been joined with a range of additional programs such as Java applets, JavaScript, Active X components, VBScript, APIs, DHTML, XML, and plug-ins.

Because they run purely within the viewer's own computer, they have the following advantages:

- They do not require a special server setup.
- They perform quickly once they are downloaded.

On the other hand, they have the following disadvantages:

- The browser has to download the code in order to run it, resulting in slower page downloads.
- The code may contain commands that only work on certain browsers, or browser versions.
- There may be browser compatibility issues with some client-side software. Most notably, Active X and VBScript only work on the Windows platforms and only with Internet Explorer.

Server side programming

This concentrates mainly on what information is communicated between the server and browser. It can involve CGI scripts, Perl scripts, Server Side Includes, Active Server Pages, etc. In this case, the program code is run at the server end and can be used to store, process and package information for display at the browser end. This supports, for example, databases and on-line purchasing.

Consider the operations required when a user is choosing holiday options at a travel agent's web site. The user completes a selection of criteria (e.g. dates, places, preferences, number travelling, etc). This information is sent to the server and is used to consult a database containing flight information, hotel vacancies, etc. The server then constructs a web page that displays the various holiday options that meet the users criteria, complete with costs. The server has carried out user requests, consulted databases, carried out calculations and prepared an individual web page just for that viewer. And all this has taken place within the server end.

Server side programming provides benefits such as:

- Processing takes place at server end, so program speed is not dependent on the age of the computer used for browsing.
- A huge range of facilities (search engines, database handling, maintaining site statistics, etc) are available.

The disadvantages are:

- It relies on what facilities are allowed by an ISP. Internet providers are reluctant to allow user programs that might introduce delays or system crashes and they often place limitations on what languages are allowed.
- Many facilities will only be available through an extra payment to the ISP.
- The program performance is dependent on how busy an ISP is at any time.

Scripting

Web programming is achieved by writing a script. This is a text file that contains a list of all the instructions that the server or browser has to carry out. The computer software (i.e. server software or browser software) reads each instruction in turn and carries out the instruction. The same script can be read by a PC, a Mac or a Linux system, as long as the software contains an interpreter that understands the script language. The script is therefore independent of any hardware platform.

Of course, there are many different languages, each using different instructions in their scripts. While JavaScript is so popular that it is built in to all browsers (e.g. Explorer, Netscape, Opera, etc.), other languages have to be downloaded and installed as browser plug-ins. Similarly, language interpreters have to be installed on the server end and this has to be worked out with the ISP (unless the server is owned).

CGI scripts

CGI (Common Gateway Interface) scripts are the most common method of running programs on a server, based on the input from the user's web browser. The scripts are triggered by the input from a browser.

CGI is not a specific language - it is more a specification for transferring information between a server and a CGI program.

There are a variety of modes that can be achieved by running a CGI script:

- It can be information passed from the user to the server (e.g. completing a form, or clicking a link).
- It can be information passed from the server to the browser (e.g. counter hits, time of day).
- It can be a two-way interchange of information (e.g. ask for a database search, get user-specific pages as a reply).

How CGI scripts work

The diagram shows the normal chain of activities that are involved in initiating and processing a CGI script. The steps are:

- The user's browser points to a URL. This could be from filling in a form or just from clicking an image or piece of hypertext.
- The URL is passed to the ISP ('A' in the diagram). The URL may be accompanied by user data (e.g. when sending in a form) or may not have any data attached (e.g. when calling for the current date or time).

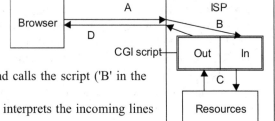

- The ISP recognises that the URL is for a CGI script and calls the script ('B' in the diagram).
- The CGI script, drawn with double line in the diagram, interprets the incoming lines of script ('In' in the diagram).
- This usually involves accessing other resources ('C' in the diagram). The resources could be system data (e.g. the time), user's data (e.g. the user's hit counter or bandwidth statistics), databases, or other applications.
- The requested resources are taken by the CGI script and any processing that may be required is carried out (e.g. calculating prices) before the data is formatted into browser pages (see 'Out' in diagram).
- These pages are sent back to the browser ('D' in the diagram).

The user initiates the call to the CGI script and all the subsequent processing takes place within the server.   The final output is in the form of a web page that is sent back to the browser for viewing.

The scripts contain plain ASCII text and can be in any programming language such as C, Perl, Pascal, Delphi, or Visual Basic. The choice of language is not decisive. What is important is the interface between the server and the script. If the syntax and methods are known, then any programming language can be used to write the CGI scripts.

In practice, however, Perl (Practical Extraction and Reporting Language) is by far the most common language used for CGI scripting and it is available free. Many Unix servers use Perl interpreters. The CGI script is a text file and this is passed to the interpreter, which translates each script line and carries it out.   In most cases, servers keep the CGI scripts in a folder called CGI-BIN or BIN. Libraries of Perl and C scripts are available free on the Internet.

The two most commonly used CGI scripts are those for handling browser forms and for providing traffic counters.

Counters

The one thing that occupies the minds of most web site administrators is the success of the site. Commercial sites can measure their success in terms of sales, numbers added to mailing lists and so on.

Sites promoting charities, hobbies, clubs, etc. may measure their success in terms of new members, the growth in the newsletter circulation, donations, etc.   Sites that provide information (e.g. news, weather, travel, TV schedules, etc.) are designed for one-way traffic and there is little or no information going from viewers to the web site. One measure that most sites pay great attention to is the 'hit rate'.   At its simplest, this counts the number of times a web site has been accessed in a given period.

There is huge interest in viewing figures among the commercial portals and directory services, as increasing viewing figures results in increased advertising revenue.

The simplest counting system requires a small text file to be stored on the web site, often called 'count.txt'.   This is a simple ASCII text file that can be read by any word processor.   For example, it may contain the contents "2753" and these are made up of four text characters.   A counter CGI script sits on the ISP's site and is activated by a call to its URL.   It reads the site's count file, converts it from text into an integer number, adds one to the number, converts it back into a text representation, and stores it back in the site.   This piece of text can then be sent to the browser and the user can see a caption saying something like *"Total visitors since February 2002 : 2754"*.   The number has to be stored as text so that it can be easily incorporated into the HTML page that is sent to the browser.

Most counter scripts compose the individual characters of the hit rate into graphics characters. In the example, the graphic image of the number two is followed by the graphic image of the number seven, followed by five's image and four's image. This is composited into a single image that is sent to the browser for display. The web page that requests a hit counter update will be something like:

```
<img src="/cgi-bin/count">
```

This is a demon counter script.

A script from Tripod is very similar, with <img src=/bin/counter>

The HTML line uses a 'display graphic' tag and this calls the CGI script URL to obtain the graphic. The web site developer can leave the line above as it is, and this results in the site's visitors seeing the hit count. If the count is only for the site administrator's use, the output can be hidden from the visitors' view. In the case of Demon's script, adding sh=F to the script sets the sh (show) attribute to F (FALSE) disables the screen display of the count.

```
<img src="/cgi-bin/count sh=F">
```

Sources of counters

If the ISP provides a counter script, this is the easiest and best option. It is easiest because it saves writing a CGI script for the job. It is also the best option, as using a third party's counter involves giving up some of the privacy of visitors to the third party.

If the ISP makes no provision for counters or the storage of user CGI scripts, the developer can use counters provided by third parties. These are 'free', in the sense that there is no charge for the service. These third parties often provide comprehensive information about site usage. The downside, of course, is that all the information that it has gathered on visitors to the site can also be used by the third party for targeted e-mail.

Examples of third party counters are

www.gostats.com -   this provides lots of usage statistics but demands a largish advert on the web page.

www.thecounter.com - this also provides lots of statistics, and has options for the web display (counter hits can be displayed with third party logo, logo on its own, or no display).

Counter accuracy

Image counters are unreliable. They can be used as a general indication of the site's usage but have the limitation listed below:

- If a viewer sets the browser not to display graphic images, the HTML line containing the IMG tag is ignored and the CGI script is not called. A viewer has visited the site, but the counter has not been incremented.
- If a viewer hits the *'refresh'* or *'reload'* option on their browser, the counter script is called again and a an extra visitor may be recorded on some counters.
- The viewer may get the graphic image from cache, due to a previous visit. The counter script is not called and the visit is not recorded.
- A viewer may enter directly into a lower part of the web site's structure. This may be the result of a link from another site, or the result of a search. If the counter script is on the main page, the visit is not recorded.
- If the web site has a single counter script, sitting in the main page, the script may be called every time the viewer returns to the main page.
- If the same counter call code is placed on every page of the web site, then every page that is accessed counts as a hit. This gives a figure for the total usage of the site, but does not indicate how the site was used. For example, a hit count of 1000 may be 1000 people accessing the main page or just 20 people each accessing 50 pages.

The approaches for overcoming these problems include:

- Use an ISP that allows user-defined CGI scripts.
- Use an ISP that provides a counter CGI script (or even full viewer statistics).
- Use a counter script that maintains a list of recent URLs that accessed the counter and ignores refreshes and revisits.
- Use a third party counter if extra statistics are required (e.g. usage by day/hour, how many resulted from search engines).
- Use a third party supplier who allows multiple counters to be installed. This provides details on hits on individual web pages (e.g. how many viewers read the help page or the glossary page).
- With a single counter, place it on a 'splash page'. This is an opening introductory page that links to the main page. The site provides no links back to the splash page. This means that the counter is only incremented when the visitor first accesses the site.
- With a single counter, place in the frameset page. Again, a visitor only accesses this page once, with all subsequent navigation changes taking place within the frame areas.

Where the counter contents are hidden from visitors, there are two ways that the web site administrator can access the contents of the *'count.txt'* file to view the hit rate:

- Use FTP to access the ISP, and view the file.
- Create a page on the web site that displays the counter contents. The page has no links from anywhere on the site and the address is only known to the administrator. To prevent the administrator incrementing the counter every time he/she looks at the page, the script can often have an added attribute to prevent unwanted incrementing of the hit counter.

For example, in Demon the script is changed to:

`<img src="/cgi-bin/count incr=F">`

Forms

Forms are the standard method of getting information from a browser to a server. Forms are constructed from lines of HTML and are used to call a CGI script at the server end. The CGI script then carries out the processing of the data passed to it. Forms can sit anywhere on a web site, on any web page. They can be placed on a separate web page or can be part of a web page.

A form can contain a single entry (e.g. What is your favourite girl band?), have relatively few entries (e.g. name and address for joining a newsletter mailing list) or can contain many entries (e.g. filling in questionnaires or for entering data for on-line credit card purchases).

The illustration shows the variety of options for entering data into a Form. The script for this web page is described on the following pages.

Radio Buttons

The first two questions use radio buttons to extract a user response. Only a single answer is expected (i.e. the book cannot be expensive and cheap at the same time). A radio button method ensures that only one response can be entered. If a second button is selected, the previous button becomes unselected.

Multiple selections

The third question allows more than one box to be checked, so the user can check none, some, or all of them.

Selection from a list

The fourth question provides a drop-down menu from which a user can select a single choice.

Text entry

There are a variety of ways that a user can enter text into a form. The simplest way is to provide a single box, allowing a single line of text to be entered. The box may initially be empty or may contain an initial value. Providing an initial value is useful when the response for a field is often the same for different users (e.g. a field requesting a delivery address for goods may supply an initial value of *'Same as Invoice Address'*).

A text entry box can also be designed, as in the illustration, to allow multiple lines to be entered. While most other entry boxes are specific, this box allows the user more freedom to enter data in their own words.

Reader Survey

Please fill in the questions and mail to us
Your feedback will help us make the book even better!

Do you rate the book's price as
O Too expensive   O Just about right   O Good value for money

How do you rate the book's contents?
O Poor   O Average   O Excellent

Which of the following chapters do you use most?
☐ Audio
☐ Video
☐ Graphics
☐ Design
☐ Web Sites

What course are you using the book for?
['A' Levels ▼]

Any complaints, comments, suggestions?

[Send to us]   [Oops ! Clear the form]

Implementing Forms

The script for a form is described in the following pages. The script is placed between <FORM> and </FORM> tags and the script can contain fields for entering information and normal text for headings, explanations and notes. All the rules on fonts and alignment apply within the form's script area in the same way as any other part of the HTML script.

The CGI script will be sent a number of items of information from a form and has to be able to distinguish between one item and the next. Therefore, every data entry field on the form has to be given its own name. The form is then submitted to the CGI script as a named item with the value given to it by the user.

For example, if fields were called *'name'* and *'age'*, the values would be sent to the script as
        Name=Davy   and   age=21
These are referred to as *'name/value pairs'*.

Text entry options
The simplest entry method for a form is
        What is your Post Code ? <INPUT NAME="postcode">
The first part is the text that will appear on the screen.   The INPUT tag places a text entry box on the screen next to the text. The developer gives the field a name (*'postcode'* in our example).

        What is your Post Code ? [   ]

When the user types information into the box, it is associated with the *'postcode'* field for sending to the CGI script.

In the above example, the default entry box is far too long, since a Post Code only requires a maximum of eight characters, including the middle space.   The SIZE attribute can be added to specify the size of the text box, as in the following line of code:
        What is your Post Code ? <INPUT NAME="postcode" SIZE=8>
This produces a smaller box but still allows the user to type in more than eight characters.

To limit the characters accepted in a box, the attribute MAXLENGTH can be used, as below:
        What is your Post Code ? <INPUT NAME="postcode" SIZE=8 MAXLENGTH=8>

An initial content can be placed into a text box, using the VALUE tag, as in this example:
        Address for delivery <INPUT NAME="deladdress" VALUE="Same as the Invoice Address">
The screen display would look as in the illustration.

        Address for delivery [Same as the Invoice Address]

Where large sections of text input is expected from the user, the TEXTAREA tag is used.   It has ROWS and COLS attributes that define the size of the text box. The results can be seen in the earlier *'Reader Survey'* illustration.   The tag's format is:
        Any suggestions:
        <TEXTAREA name="comments" rows=5 cols=60></TEXTAREA>

The INPUT tag also supports a PASSWORD attribute, as in this example:
        Enter your personal ID number <INPUT TYPE=password NAME="ID">
The text entered at the keyboard appears in the box as a row of asterisks, preventing anyone from looking over the user's shoulder to note the ID.   The data entered into the field is sent to the CGI script as the original text typed at the keyboard.

Multiple selections
The INPUT tag allows the user to enter text for sending to the CGI script. The use of the TYPE attribute allows the user to select from pre-written options. The form can be displayed with a set of check boxes. This allows the user to select multiple options from a displayed list.
The following code was used to create the checkboxes in the earlier *'Reader Survey'* illustration:
        Which of the following chapters do you use most?
        <INPUT TYPE="checkbox" NAME="audio"   VALUE="ON"> Audio
        <INPUT TYPE="checkbox" NAME="video"   VALUE="ON"> Video
        <INPUT TYPE="checkbox" NAME="graphics" VALUE="ON"> Graphics
        <INPUT TYPE="checkbox" NAME="design"   VALUE="ON"> Design
        <INPUT TYPE="checkbox" NAME="websites" VALUE="ON"> Web Sites<p>

The INPUT tag is using a TYPE attribute.   If this attribute is not included in an INPUT tag it is assumed to be the same as entering 'TYPE="text"' (i.e. the input is assumed to be text).

The above code uses TYPE="checkbox" and this and each field has a NAME and a VALUE that depends upon whether the box is checked.   In the example, VALUE="ON" is used, so checking the first box results in audio=ON being sent to the CGI script.   In fact, the default value that is given to a checked field is 'ON', but other values could be substituted.

If required, some of the boxes could be displayed checked by default. This could be employed where users often choose these boxes from the list.
An example of use is:
        Click any other facilities you require
        <INPUT TYPE="checkbox" NAME="catalogue"   CHECKED> Catalogue
        <INPUT TYPE="checkbox" NAME="newsletter"   CHECKED> Newsletter

Radio Buttons

Radio buttons display a range of options to the user.   The user can only choose one option and so only one name/value pair is used. This means that all the radio buttons are given the same name.
The syntax for this code is:

```
How do you rate the book's contents?<br>
<INPUT TYPE="radio" NAME="content" VALUE="poor">      Poor
<INPUT TYPE="radio" NAME="content" VALUE="average">   Average
<INPUT TYPE="radio" NAME="content" VALUE="good">      Excellent
```

Again, the CHECKED attribute can be added, so that one option is initially selected.

Selecting from a list

Where a long set of options is to be chosen from, the screen may look cluttered with too many checkboxes or radio buttons. As an alternative, the SELECT tag allows a drop-down menu to be created, to save screen space.
The syntax is as shown in this example:

```
What course are you using the book for?<br>
<SELECT NAME="course" SIZE="1">
        <OPTION>  'A' Levels
        <OPTION>  C&G
        <OPTION>  HNC
        <OPTION>  HND
        <OPTION>  BSc
        <OPTION>  MSc
</SELECT>
```

The field has a single NAME and, when the user chooses from the menu, that particular entry after the OPTION attribute is associated with the NAME as the name/value pair for sending to the CGI script.
The MULTIPLE attribute allows the user to select more than one option from the list, but that results in several values being associated with the NAME and this should only be used where the CGI script supports this method.
The SIZE attribute specifies how many lines of options are seen when the page is first displayed. The Up and Down arrow at the edge of the box allow the user to browse through the options.

Submitting the Form

When the user has completed the entries on the form, it can be submitted to the server by clicking on a 'submit' button. The basic syntax to produce this button is:

```
<INPUT TYPE="submit ">
```

This produces an on-screen button with the words 'Submit Query' on it.

The text in the button can be changed by specifying a new value for it, as in the following example script code:

```
<INPUT TYPE="submit" VALUE="Click to send">
```

If the user wishes to clear the entries and start over before submitting the form, the line:

```
<INPUT TYPE="reset">
```

clears all existing data from the forms' fields.   The default text in this button is 'Reset' and this can also be altered by using the VALUE attribute, as in the example below:

```
<INPUT TYPE="reset"  VALUE="Oops ! Clear the form">
```

The user sends the form to the server with the ACTION attribute of the FORM tag. This dictates what action will be taken when the submit button is pressed.   In the example below, the action is to send the form's data to the CGI script that is stored in the URL given in quotes.

```
<FORM ACTION="/cgi-bin/mailform"  METHOD="POST">
```

The example line is for a form running with Demon. Demon stores a cgi script called 'mailform'.   This is Demon's own script and its purpose is to receive the input from the form's fields and send them as an e-mail to the web site owner.   The CGI script may well have another name with another ISP.
The ACTION attribute points to the URL where the script is stored (in this case the cgi-bin folder of the server).
The URL address could equally have been entered in full as

```
http://demon.co.uk/cgi-bin/mailform
```

The METHOD attribute determines the manner in which data is sent to the URL pointed to by the ACTION attribute. It can either have the value 'GET' or 'POST'.
If the GET attribute is used, the user entries are attached to the end of the CGI script's URL (a process known as 'URL encoding').
For the 'Reader Survey' example, the final URL might be:

```
http://demon.co.uk/cgi-bin/mailform?value=good&content=fair&audio=ON&video=ON&....
```

A question mark separates the script URL from the data and each field's name/value pair is separated by an ampersand(&).   This operates more quickly than the processing of POST data, but the reliable length of a URL is only 255 characters.

The POST method is the preferred method as the data is sent separately and has no limit to its size.

The complete script for producing the web page form shown in the earlier *'Reader Survey'* example is:

```
<HTML>
<HEAD><TITLE>Survey Form</TITLE></HEAD>
<BODY BGCOLOR="cyan"><FONT FACE="ARIAL,HELVETICA" SIZE="5">
<center><B>Reader Survey<br></font>
<font size=4>Please fill in the questions and mail to us<br>
Your feedback will help us make the book even better!</B></center></FONT><P>

<FORM ACTION="/cgi-bin/mailform"  METHOD="POST">

<hr width=250 align=center><p><b>

Do you rate the book's price as<br>
<INPUT TYPE="radio" NAME="value" VALUE="poor">     Too expensive
<INPUT TYPE="radio" NAME="value" VALUE="average"> Just about right
<INPUT TYPE="radio" NAME="value" VALUE="good">     Good value for money<br>
<p>

How do you rate the book's contents?<br>
<INPUT TYPE="radio" NAME="content" VALUE="poor">     Poor
<INPUT TYPE="radio" NAME="content" VALUE="average">  Average
<INPUT TYPE="radio" NAME="content" VALUE="good">     Excellent
<p>

Which of the following chapters do you use most?<br>
<INPUT TYPE="checkbox" NAME="audio"    VALUE="ON"> Audio    <br>
<INPUT TYPE="checkbox" NAME="video"    VALUE="ON"> Video    <br>
<INPUT TYPE="checkbox" NAME="graphics"  VALUE="ON"> Graphics <br>
<INPUT TYPE="checkbox" NAME="design"    VALUE="ON"> Design   <br>
<INPUT TYPE="checkbox" NAME="websites"  VALUE="ON"> Web Sites<p>

What course are you using the book for?<br>
<SELECT NAME="course" SIZE="1">
   <OPTION>  'A' Levels
   <OPTION>  C&G
   <OPTION>  HNC
   <OPTION>  HND
   <OPTION>  BSc
   <OPTION>  MSc
</SELECT><p>

Any complaints, comments, suggestions?</b><br>
<TEXTAREA name="comments" rows=5 cols=60></TEXTAREA>
<p align=center>


<INPUT TYPE="submit" VALUE="Send to us">
<INPUT TYPE="reset"  VALUE="Oops ! Clear the form"></center><P>

</FORM>
</BODY>
</HTML>
```

ISINDEX

Forms are a flexible method of creating parameters for a CGI script. However, there is an older method, which is still occasionally seen in use, known as ISINDEX. The ISINDEX tag is normally found within the <HEAD> portion of an HTML file, and simply informs the browser that it should ask the user for a search query. This typically takes the form of a popup dialog box, and the queries that are typed by the user are sent to the CGI script using URL encoding, as mentioned above. This method is now obsolescent, however.

Creating Scripts

In the above cases, Forms and Counters, the CGI scripts were pre-written and the HTML code was used to interface to the scripts. This is a common approach to scripting. There are many scripts that can be downloaded and used, either untouched or after slight modification.   However, for specialist applications, or for more complex requirements, the ability to write scripts is very useful. There is a separate chapter in this book on writing in

JavaScript, the language most used for client-end scripts.

For server-end scripts, a range of languages is available. They have differences but they can all access the server's filing system, interface with databases and create dynamic pages.

Perl

This language has many advantages. It is an open source language and it has been around for a long time. It is used by many systems administrators and hackers. This means that there is loads of library code out there that can be used or modified. It also means that there are plenty of people who can help in the user groups. The language is fairly easy to learn and is strong on text processing (i.e. generating HTTP headers and the automatic writing of HTML). However, it is weak on graphics handling and security. Perl files have a PL extension (e.g. bigscript.pl) and when the server sees this extension it knows to carry out instructions in the file to construct an HTML page based on these instructions. The constructed page is then sent to the user's browser.

The Perl files are stored on the server but can be created and tested on a standalone PC before being uploaded to the server. This requires that the computer have a Perl interpreter installed. ActivePerl is available free from the www.activestate.com
Scripts can be written in any test editor, such as Notepad, and can then be run using the command

    perl bigscript.pl

VisualPerl, also available from activestate.com, provides an windows environment for creating Perl scripts. This package also provides facilities such as:

- Checking of the program's syntax. The line number of an error is reported.
- Viewing the html page that would be created by the script.
- Viewing the script's results as they would be seen on a web browser.

Here is a very small sample Perl server script, just to give the flavour of the language.
The lines on the left are the actual program lines that would be entered, while the right hand column explains their purpose.

#!/usr/bin/perl	This tells a Unix system where to find the Perl interpreter.
$vat=$orders*0.175;	Calculate the VAT (at 17.5%) on the customer's order.
$total=$orders+$VAT;	Add the VAT on to the user's total price.
$datetime=localtime;	Fetch the current time and store it in a variable called $datetime.
Print<<EOF	This is an instruction that all the lines that follow, up to the EOF line, are to be used in the web page that is being constructed.
Content-type: text/html	Sends an HTTP header, to indicate that is a standard web page.
<html>	
<head>	
<title>Small CGI Perl Script	
</title>	
</head>	
<body>	
The time is $datetime<p>	The value stored in $datetime is now substituted for the variable name.
And your total orders including	
VAT comes to $total;	The value stored in $total is now substituted for the variable name.
</body>	
</html>	
EOF	

Although a short program, it has managed to create a page that used a function (getting the date and time from the server's clock), carried out some calculations, stored values and passed information back to a user. Only the lines between the <html> and </html> are used in the page that is sent to the user's browser. For simplicity, this script assumes that the value of the customer's orders is already stored in a variable called $orders and this would probably be fetched from the server's database or from the data supplied in a form sent by the user.

PHP

This is another open source system, from the Apache Software Foundation. It is often used in conjunction with the freeware MySQL database. It is benefiting from growing support and is seen be many as a free alternative to ASP and Microsoft servers. PHP has seen several versions, with the current version being version 4.3. PHP is frequently used alongside MySQL and Apache, on a Linux system, and this configuration is often referred to as a 'LAMP' (Linux/Apache/MySQL/PHP) system. However, PHP is supported just as well by a Windows/IIS/ODBC system.
PHP is a robust system. The support for PHP is impressive, with reported bugs being fixed immediately and new features being added regularly. Fuller details of the language are available on www.php.net.
With Perl scripts, the HTML code was embedded within the Perl script. With a PHP file, the PHP code is embedded within the HTML file. The server system requires that the server have a PHP module installed, to interpret PHP commands.

The script files have the extension PHP (e.g. myscript.php) or PHTML (e.g. myscript.phtml) so that the PHP interpreter can identify the file and carry out the instructions contained in the script. These files often look very similar to HTML files, with added PHP data. This PHP data is enclosed within certain tags, which can take one of several forms. The most common of these is to have the entire PHP code contained within <? and ?> delimiters, just like XML processing directives. Another common method is to enclose larger PHP blocks with script tags, as in the following example:

```
<script language="PHP">
        // This is a PHP comment block.
</script>
```

The interpreter reads every line of HTML code and sends it away to the browser. When it reaches the <?php tag, or the <script> tag, it carries out the PHP commands. When it reaches the ?> tag, or the </script> tag as appropriate, it reverts to sending out the HTML code. It is possible for a PHP file to consist almost entirely of PHP code.

PHP script is a programming language, and it does bear remarkable similarities to the C programming language. For example, PHP script statements (other than those enclosed by '{' and '}' symbols) must end with a semi-colon, and parameters are enclosed in parentheses after each command. The '*Programming*' chapter contains details on many of the basic programming principles, and as such it is recommended that the reader familiarise themselves with these concepts alongside learning the syntax of PHP.

The simplest form of PHP statement is the echo command, such as in the following line:

```
<P>
        echo ("Hello <I>world</I>");
</P>
```

This command has one parameter, which is a string. In PHP, as with many languages, strings are enclosed with quotes. This string can include more HTML tags. In this example, then, the PHP browser will produce the following HTML code to be sent to the client system:

```
<P>
        Hello <I>world</I>
</P>
```

PHP Variables

On its own, of course, the echo function is not very useful. However, when combined with variables it becomes a more powerful tool. In PHP, variables are prefixed with a '$' symbol. As with every other programming language, PHP can perform various activities with variables. The most basic of these are assignment, and comparison.

In assigning a value to a variable, (sometimes called 'initialising') PHP uses a single '=' symbol. For example:

```
$today = "Monday";
```

Note that, although the string is enclosed within double quotes, PHP will accept single quotes instead. However, the typf of quote at the beginning must match the type of quote at the end of the string. This is not simply a cosmetic difference; it affects whether embedded variables will be parsed. In other words, if double quotes are used, you can contain other strings within the current string, as in the following example:

```
$outgoing_message = "It is $today – welcome back!";
```

In the above example, assuming $today contained the value "Monday", the variable $outgoing_message would change to contain "It is Monday – welcome back!". However, had single quotes been used instead of double quotes, it would instead simply contain "It is $today – welcome back!".

Furthermore, if using double quotes, then obviously the string cannot easily contain the double quote character itself. To get around this, an '*escape code*' is used. This is the backslash character ('\'), and allows the developer to include the double quote, among other items, as in the following example:

```
$important_note="The famous quote, \"Do you feel lucky, punk?\" was never actually spoken by
Clint Eastwood."
```

Other escape codes that can be used include the carriage return (\r) and line feed (\n); the tab character (\t), the dollar sign (\$), and of course the backslash itself (\\).

Variable Comparison

When comparing a variable's contents, either to a fixed value or to another variable's contents, PHP uses a double '==' symbol. For example, using an *if* statement, we could write the following script:

```
If($today == "Monday") {
        echo("I hate Mondays!");
}
else {
        echo("Thank goodness it isn't Monday!");
}
```

The equality operator ('==') is not the only type of comparison that is allowed. Types of comparison supported by PHP include those shown to the right.

It should be noted that there are some rules as to the naming of variables.

Comparison	Symbols
Equality	==
Inequality	!=
Greater than	>
Less than	<

Obviously, a variable cannot have the same name as any of the reserved words, or any functions such as echo. It may contain no invalid characters (such as parentheses, or the '+' character, to name just a few), and it may not begin with a numeric character.

As with most programming languages, PHP allows the author to use multiple comparisons at one time, using Boolean AND and OR operators. The following shows an example:

```
If( ($age < 18) or ($credit == 0) ) {
        Echo ("Sorry, you are unable to purchase any items at this time.")
}
```

An example of PHP script

```
<html>
<head>
<title>Small PHP Script
</title>
</head>
<body>
<?php
$title="Learning PHP";          Place the text "Learning PHP" into a variable called $title.
$subtitle="for beginners";      Place the text "for beginners" into a variable called $subtitle.
?>
<h1><?php echo($title) ?></h1>  The value stored in $title is substituted for the variable name.
<p><?php echo($subtitle) ?> </p>  The value stored in $subtitle is substituted for the variable name.

A small script to get started.
</body>
</html>
```

In the example, the first six lines of code are sent unaltered. There are two lines of PHP that place text messages into variables for storage. The <h1> tag is then sent away as standard HTML, before the interpreter sees the echo($title) command. This results in the words "Learning PHP" being sent to the browser. The PHP command is then followed by the simple </h1> and <p> tags being sent. The interpreter is again invoked and converts the echo($subtitle) command into sending "for beginners" to the browser. Finally, it sends out the </p> tag and some normal HTML text before completing the web page.

As can be seen, the PHP code does not have to sit in one place in the file. The code can be placed in many different parts of a large file, as long as each is enclosed by the <?php and ?> tags.

One advantage of PHP is that the script lines can be added to existing HTML files. This allows new features to be added to existing web sites without having to re-write scripts from the beginning. All the existing links, graphics, etc. can remain in the script and the new facilities such as database extracts and other e-commerce functions can be added as amendments to the existing scripts.

As the language is developing, there are not yet a great number of utilities to make coding PHP scripts easier (e.g. the editing and checking mentioned for Perl) but this will improve over time.

Variable types

PHP determines the type of variable by the value it is assigned. For example, all of the variables used so far have been of the *'string'* type; in other words, they have all contained strings of text. Other variable types are available, such as integer; floating-point number; and array. If a variable's first assignment is to a string, as the examples so far have been, then the variable is considered to be a string type. However, if the variable is initially assigned an integer value, PHP considers it to be an integer variable, as in the following example:

```
$age = 18;
```

This will create a variable called 'age' and make it an integer type with value 18. This method is known as 'loose typing', and allows PHP to create space for variables on the fly. However, PHP is also able to reserve space for use as variables later in the script. This is done by using the 'var' keyword, as shown:

```
Var $username;
```

The different variable types can have different operations performed on their contents. All variables can be assigned a value, but integer values can, for example, be altered using addition ('+'), subtraction ('-'), multiplication ('*') and division ('/').

String variables have other operations. For example, one string can be concatenated onto another using the dot ('.') character, as in this example:

Echo ("You have chosen ".$option.", is this correct?");

Variable tests
PHP provides various functions which examine the contents (or otherwise!) of variables:

Function	Description
empty($var)	Returns TRUE if 'var' has not been set
is_array($var)	Returns TRUE if 'var' is an array
is_int($var)	Returns TRUE if 'var' is an integer
is_string($var)	Returns TRUE if 'var' is a string
is_float($var)	Returns TRUE if 'var' is a floating point number
Isset($var)	Returns TRUE if 'var' has been set

Note that the empty function is the opposite of the isset function. Also, a variable that has had a value set, can have it unset, by using the unset function as follows:

unset($myvar)

File manipulation in PHP
PHP allows the author to access files on the server's hard disk. Much of the syntax to do this is similar to that used in the C programming language. A file must be opened before it can be read or written to, and it should be closed after the file access is complete.

To open a file, the fopen function is used, which must be supplied with both a filename, and a file opening mode. The file opening mode is either read-only ('r'), read/write ('r+'), write-only ('w'), append ('a') or read/append ('a+') mode, and on UNIX systems it may also be set to binary mode ('b') to distinguish it from an ASCII file.

This function returns an integer which is used as a reference to an open file stream. In other words, it should be assigned to a variable which is used to control access to the file. For example:

$mydata=fopen("list.dat","r+")

Once a file is opened, it can be read from or written to, as long as it has been opened in the appropriate mode. It is entirely legal to open multiple files at once, with their file objects being stored in different variables. In fact, this is a highly desirable function when processing data, as it can be used to open one file for input data, and another file for output data.

Other functions are available to assist in reading and writing data. There are many such functions, and the following is just a list of some of the more common functions, along with a typical example of their usage:

$nextchar=fgetc($mydata)
The fgetc function is used to get a single character from a file. The only parameter is a file pointer, in this case the variable '$mydata'. The function returns a single character, or returns FALSE if the specified filestream at the end of the file.

$lenghthofmyfile=filesize($filename)
filesize reports the total file size of the file in bytes, or FALSE if an error occurs. The parameter to this function is a filename, not a file pointer, so it can be used to determine the size of files that have not been opened.

$nextline=fgets($mydata,80)
This function is used to input a string of characters from a file. It has two parameters: the first is the file pointer, and the second is the number of characters to input. It returns a string containing those characters, or FALSE if an error occurs. Also, it will stop reading characters if it encounters a carriage return, or the end of the file.

$mydatastring=fread($mydata,16)
This function reads binary data from the file, rather than ASCII text. On UNIX systems, the file must be opened using the 'b' option. On Windows systems there is no differentiation between binary and ASCII files.

$position=ftell($mydata)
ftell reports the current position within the file, in bytes, or FALSE if an error occurs.

If(feof($mydata)) {
The feof function returns TRUE if the filestream specified by the file pointer given is at the end of the file. It returns FALSE otherwise.

fseek($mydata,256,SEEK_SET)
This function is used to move the current position within the file, to 'point' to a new position. When a file is first opened, the filestream is considered to be 'at' the start of the file. Reading or writing data moves the current position of the filestream along (i.e. it points to a new, later position). Fseek can be used to move it further, or move it back. It has three attributes; the first is the file pointer, and the second is an integer offset specifying how far to move (which may be negative). The final parameter is optional, with SEEK_SET being the default if no option is

specified. It determines how the seek should operate. SEEK_SET meaning it sets a new file position, SEEK_CUR meaning it adds the offset to the current position to find the new position, and SEEK_END meaning it adds the offset to the end of the file.

fputs($myfile,$output_string)
fwrite($myfile,$output_string,12)

The fputs function and fwrite function perform an identical operation; that of writing multiple bytes to a file if it is opened in write mode. These functions write the entire contents of the string (which is the second parameter to the function) unless a length is specified in the third parameter. In that case, these functions will write no more than that number of characters, though it may write less if it encounters a new line character.

fclose($mydata)

Closes an open file stream. The parameter specifies which file stream to close. Returns TRUE if the file was successfully closed, or FALSE if there was an error.

Using PHP to respond to queries

So far, all of the capabilities of PHP which have been discussed, have not addressed the possibility of interacting with the user who is viewing the web page that will be produced by the PHP server. One of PHP's main strengths is the capability to use CGI as an interface so that users can access databases on the server via a form or other query format. As described earlier, data can be passed by either the GET method or the POST method. PHP can accept data in either format, and will create one of two arrays to store all the name/value pairs. For example, if the GET method is used, and the URL looks like the following:

http://mypage.com/mysite.php?name=david&mood=happy

Then the PHP processor would set up an *'associative'* array named $HTTP_GET_VARS. An associative array is simply an array that uses a string instead of a number to identify each array element. In this case, the array would have two items, one called *'name'* and the other called *'mood'*, with the values "david" and "happy" respectively.

```php
<?php
        echo("Hello again, ".$HTTP_GET_VARS["name"]);
        if($HTTP_GET_VARS["mood"]=="happy" {
                echo("What a nice day it is today.");
        }
        else{
                echo("Rotten weather we've been having lately.");
        }
    ?>
```

The following example shows a small piece of PHP code, which could be used in this case:

This is a simplistic example, of course, but it illustrates how input from an HTML form can be used to shape an HTML document from the server. Variables can easily be copied from $HTTP_GET_VARS into another variable for editing, and PHP has another array called $HTTP_POST_VARS for use where the POST method is used.

More complex scripts could, for example, be combined with file access code or with database access (see below) to provide interactive web access to server file data or database records.

PHP and databases

The other great benefit of using PHP is its ability to access database information. This kind of technology underpins e-commerce for most large organisations and many smaller ones. Here, web surfers can connect to a company's website, and browse their database of products, with pages being designed on the fly by the server to cater to the viewer's tastes.

The core functions of PHP do not include any database capabilities, but there are several options for including extra functions, and many of those include database connectivity functions. However, connecting to a MySQL server, for example, requires different functions than connecting to an ODBC database. PHP can be used to access many types of database, including of course MySQL and ODBC-compliant databases, but also Microsoft SQL servers, Oracle databases, DBM files, and others, and more functions are being added all the time.

To access a database through PHP typically follows these steps:
- Connect to the database.
- Execute a query.
- Print the results to an HTML document.
- Disconnect from the database.

It is important to disconnect properly from the database, so that records are not locked, which could cause problems with future access to the database.

Since there are so many different forms of database available, there are various different functions to access them. The PHP processor must be configured to provide access to the relevant database functions. For example, if the script is to access an ODBC database, the PHP system must have the ODBC functions specifically installed, while if it is to access MySQL, then those functions must be installed. To simplify access to databases, there is another set of functions known as the *'dbx'* functions. These are *'generic'* database functions, but they still require that PHP be configured to include the functions for any database type that is to be accessed.

Connecting to the database

There are two ways to connect to any database: a transient connection, or a persistent connection. A transient connection simply connects to the database for the duration of the PHP script, performs a few brief operations, typically just one query, and then disconnects. A persistent connection, as the name suggests, keep the connection open at the end of the script, so that future scripts do not need to re-open a connection. However, in a CGI script, persistent connections have no effect.

The function used to connect to an ODBC or MySQL database is as follows:

```
$odbc_connection = odbc_connect("Sales Base", $username, $password);
```

The open function for an ODBC database must specify a *'Data Source Name'* (DSN), which in the example above is the database called "Sales Base". This must correspond to the DSN given to a database which is running on an ODBC system.

The connection optionally specifies a username and password, which in the example above are supplied via two string variables. Since the PHP code should never be viewed by the end user if the PHP processor is working properly and the PHP code is properly written, this is not necessarily a security problem. However, poorly coded PHP can cause a security issue in this regard.

Alternatively, the username and password can be supplied by the end user, via GET or POST, so that the exact range of data which is available to the user can be defined according to their user access rights.

The value returned by the function is a *'resource'* object, which is basically an identifier pointing to the appropriate connection, since PHP is capable of having multiple database connections open at any one time. This resource is used to specify the database connection in any queries or other operations which are to be performed using this database. A boolean value of FALSE will be returned instead, if the connection could not be established.

```
$mysql_connection=mysql_connect("localhost:3306",$username,$password);
```

The open function for a MySQL database is slightly different from an ODBC database. The username and password are still optional, but instead of a DSN name, a server name is supplied. The example above shows the default connection, which is to connect to the local host (in other words, the same machine the PHP processor is running on) on port 3306.

Again, the function returns a resource which identifies the database connection, or returns FALSE if the connection could not be established.

Finally, the method to connect to a database using the standard dbx function is as follows:

```
$dbx_connection=dbx_connect(DBX_ODBC,"","Sales Base",$username,$password);
```

This function must be supplied with a "module" parameter, which specifies the type of database in use. In the above example, DBX_ODBC is used, while DBX_MYSQL would be used for a MySQL database. The next parameter is the host name, which in this case is empty since we are connecting to an ODBC database on the same server. The other parameters are the database name, username and password.

Note: it is quite possible that PHP will fail to connect to a database. Since the connect function will return the boolean value of FALSE instead of a connection identifier if this is the case, the connection identifier can be used to determine whether the database was connected, and therefore whether it is safe to continue. The following example shows how this is done, using the die function to exit from PHP processing if the database could not be connected.

```
$dbx_connection = dbx_connect(DBX_ODBC, "", "Sales Base", $username, $password)
    or die("Unable to connect to database; aborting query.");
```

Executing a database query

Although there are other activities that PHP can perform upon a database, for interactive web pages the most widely useful function is a database query that results in one or more full or partial records being displayed in a formatted web page. Unfortunately, there are differences in how the MySQL and ODBC functions approach queries. However, the general method of operation is as follows:

1) Prepare and execute a query (typically in SQL).
2) Retrieve a record from the results of the query.
3) Retrieve the contents of one or more fields from the selected record.
4) Print the contents of the field onto the HTML page, with appropriate formatting, such as in a table.
5) Repeat steps 2-4 until the end of the query results are reached.

The following illustrates the basic syntax for ODBC, MySQL, and the common dbx method of querying.

```
$odbc_query_result=odbc_exec($odbc_connection,"SELECT * FROM sales");
odbc_fetch_row($odbc_query_result);
$invoice_number=odbc_result($odbc_query_result, "inv_no");
```

The first line prepares and executes an SQL query on an ODBC database, in this case it is an SQL statement selecting the entire contents of the 'sales' table of the database. The function returns a results identifier, which in this case is stored in the variable $odbc_query_result. This identifier is then used to retrieve the records which have been identified. The second line of code above, would probably be repeated several times, with one row from the query result being fetched each time, until the end of the query results are reached, when the odbc_fetch_row function will return a boolean value of FALSE.

Finally, the third line indicates the actual reading of data from the database. In this case, the variable $invoice_number will be given the value of the contents of the inv_no field of the current record in the search results.

```
$mysql_query_result=mysql_query("SELECT * FROM sales",$mysql_connection);
$query_data=mysql_fetch_row($mysql_query_result);
$invoice_number=mysql_fetch_row[0];
```

The first line executes an SQL query on the mysql database. However, the second parameter (the MySQL connection identifier) is optional: if it is not specified, PHP will use the last opened MySQL database link.

The second line uses the mysql_fetch_row function, which returns the contents of one row of data from the results of the query. In the example above, this data is placed into the $query_data variable. This function returns the data as an array, so the $query_data variable is therefore an array, containing one record of data. The individual data elements can be accessed as shown in the third line of code above; this line of code assumes that the invoice will be the first piece of data (i.e. field number zero) in the record.

Note that although the name of the function, mysql_fetch_row, is similar to the function odbc_fetch_row for ODBC, the two functions perform the same task in a slightly different way.

```
$query_data=dbx_query($dbx_connection,"SELECT * FROM sales");
$invoice_number=$query_data->data[0,0];
```

The dbx functions have to deal with a variety of different database formats, and dbx very few functions in comparison to those available to a specific database. As such, the functions are rather more complex. The dbx_query function returns a complex object, which consists of several properties. The most important properties are:

- Rows and Cols. These properties allow the programmer to find out how many rows and columns of data are in the result set.

- Info. This property is optional, and is an associative array, associating field names with the data types of the data contained within those fields.

- Data. This property is the most important, as it contains the actual data returned by the query. It is stored as a two-dimensional array, with the dimensions being equal in size to the rows and cols properties explained above.

The second line of code is simply an example of how such data could be accessed in the PHP script. It shows the first row, and the first column (i.e. row zero, column zero) of the data property being accessed. This would correspond to the first field of data in the first record in the result set.

Disconnecting from the database

This is perhaps the simplest phase of PHP's database interaction process. A database which has been opened using the MySQL, ODBC, dbx, or other database mechanism, must be closed using the same mechanism. Fortunately, the syntax for each method is identical:

```
odbc_close($odbc_connection);
mysql_close($mysql_connection);
dbx_close($dbx_connection);
```

This is just the bare bones of the functionality needed to perform database interaction in PHP. However, the script on the right illustrates its use by brining these functions together into one piece of script:

This piece of code will open a connection to an ODBC database using the standard dbx functions; then perform a query on it. The resulting object is then turned into an HTML table by using the *foreach* loop. The foreach loop is similar to a for loop (see the programming chapter) except that it is given an array to loop through. It is intelligent enough to loop through its contents, one item at a time, until it reaches the end of the array. Each time it loops through, it places the contents of that array element into a variable.

```
<?php
$username="ddick";
$password="secret";

$dbx_connection = dbx_connect(DBX_ODBC,
"", "Sales Base", $username, $password)
        or die("Unable to connect to database;
aborting query.");
$query_results=dbx_query($dbx_connection,"S
ELECT * FROM sales");

foreach($query_results->data as $record) {
        echo("<TR>\n");
        foreach($record as field) {

        echo("\t<TD>".field."</TD>\n");
        }
        echo("</TR>\n");
}

dbx_close($dbx_connection);
?>
```

Since the query returns a two-dimensional array, we require two foreach loops, one to loop through the records (the first dimension of the array), and one to loop through the fields within each record (the second dimension of the array). The contents are placed inside <TR> and <TD> tags in the final HTML document by using the echo command.

Once the loops are completed, the dbx connection is closed.

Active Server Pages

Another method of making dynamic web pages is Microsoft's ASP (Active Server Pages) extension for their servers based on their IIS (Internet Information Server) software, sitting on a windows based server such as NT or 2000. Of course, this would mean that ASP facilities could only be used on IIS servers and these are a minority on the web (most servers use the free *'Apache'* web server software). Third party providers supply extensions that attempt to make ASP compatible with other operating systems.

An ASP file is written in plain ASCII text and is saved with the extension .asp (e.g. *'testing.asp'*). The ASP file is essentially a normal HTML file with additional tags used to perform scripting. ASP tags begin with <% and end with %>, and are there only to be interpreted by the server. The end user never sees these tags even if he or she views the page source, assuming of course that the page code is working properly. Those tags are placed around ASPScript code, which is very similar to VBScript (which is very similar to Visual Basic). HTML is parsed sequentially, and so is ASP script, so placement of script code within the HTML document can be very important. Like PHP scripts, the code can be placed in many different parts of a large file, as long as each piece of code is enclosed by the <%> and %> tags. The script code is for use by the server. If the server is asked for a file with the normal HTM extension, it fetches the file from the server's drive and passes it to the user's browser.

However, if the file has an ASP extension, the server carries out these activities:

- It ignores the normal HTML content and only looks at the code between the <% and %> tags.
- It examines each line of ASP code and replaces each line with a new line of standard HTML code. The content of the new line depends upon the command held in the original ASP line. For example, the line may contain a description and price for an item that was stored on the user's computer as a cookie.
- The new HTML file, made up of the ASP's lines plus those in the original file, are sent to the user.

ASP scripting has several built-in objects that it can access. The *'Request'* object gives the ASP script details of the user's request. This includes much more than just any form data that might be used. From this object the ASP script can garner information about cookies, the web server, and the browser that is being used for that request.

ASP scripts normally use the *'Response'* object to create objects in the HTML output, giving options to build up the page in a buffer before sending, or redirect the user to another page. The *'Application'* object allows the script to access application-specific items, such as using application memory space to store variables from one instance of a script to another, while the *'Session'* object is used to maintain information about a persistent connection. This is when user information needs to be retained, and if the user does not access the server within a specified timeout period the session will be removed.

Finally, the *'Server'* object provides additional functionality by allowing ASP scripts to access COM (Common Object Model) objects stored on the server. COM objects allow programmers to simplify their scripts by interfacing with pre-written objects such as ActiveX data objects. Although programmers can write their own objects, they often re-use existing objects. COM objects can thus be used to carry out the majority of the processing, leaving the ASP scripts relatively easy to understand and maintain while providing a wider range of functions.

Although primarily designed for use with Visual Basic, ASP scripts can be written using JavaScript or Perl.

SMIL

The *'Synchronised Multimedia Integration Language'* is not designed as an all-rounder language. It specialises in organises the timing and display of video, audio and graphic elements in a streamed file. This includes specifying screen positions for objects, timing for showing and removing objects and layering of objects. It even allows a web page to have multiple language versions of soundtracks. Files have the extension SMI or SML and can be read by the Real G2 player. There is an excellent tutorial on SMIL at www.helio.org.

Choosing a language

The choice of server side programming language depends upon a number of factors:

- If the scripts are for placing on an organisation's own web server, then any language is available once the interpreter module is installed on the server. However, if the user is renting space from an ISP, there may be limitations of what language is available on that server.
- Consider who will be writing the scripts and who will be maintaining the scripts. This examines the current knowledge and experience of the programmers.
- Consider what present and future support the programmers will need.
- Consider whether the web site's required applications are specialised, or whether they can be met by using existing modules that are readily available (e.g. go to www.hotscripts.com for many thousands of example scripts in PHP, Perl, etc.).
- Consider if cross-platform compatibility is an issue (it possibly is with Visual Basic).

Server Side Includes

When surfing the Internet, users may find that they are downloading a file with an SHTML extension (e.g. payments.shtml). This is a file that uses SSI instructions. Consider a situation of a web site with several hundred pages. Each page may have company telephone number, the director's name, or the copyright message (e.g. © 2002). If the text was embedded into each file, then any changes entails changing the text of hundreds of files. One technique is to use a utility to change all the entries. Another method is use an include statement in each file.
For example, each page may include the following line:

<!--#include file="phonenum.txt"-->

When the server finds a file with an SHTML extension, it replaces the above line with the text found in the phonenum.txt file. All the hundreds of web pages are now using the text in this single file for displaying the phone number on the page. Now, if the telephone number is changed, only one file is amended and all the site's pages will display this new information.
Consider that the same web site may use the same set of navigation buttons on every page. If the site uses frames this is not a problem, since the menu will appear in its own frame and the code appears only once. Adding extra buttons, removing some menu choices or amending menu options only requires the code for that frame to be altered.
However, if the multi-page site is not using frames, then any alteration requires every page to be altered to the new specification. Fortunately, the include command also supports HTML files. So the following line can be placed in each web page during the construction of the site:

<!--#include file="menubar.htm"-->

Each page, when sent to the browser will have the HTML code from the menubar.htm file embedded in the transmitted script. Once again, a single file can be added or altered and will be reflected throughout the web site. Of course, this method is not confined to altering every page on the site. The technique can be used for just one or two pages. It can be used to good effect to separate the coding and the data. This allows a user with only sufficient skills to use Notepad to update a web site. The contents of the text file (e.g. an item's price, stock level, delivery time, etc.) can be modified and uploaded to the server. Access rights can be used to ensure that these workers only have access to the data files, leaving the main web pages secure from alteration.

The above examples only works with servers that support SSI and web designers should check with their ISP to see whether the system is supports.

Note: The purpose of all the languages described is to create web pages at the server end that are then sent to the user's browser. In other words, all the content of the PHP, Perl or whatever script remains on the server – only the <u>results</u> of the processing are sent to the browser. This means that if a user is in Explorer and uses the *"View"* and *"Source"* options to view the contents of a web page, they will never see the internal code lines of a server-end file.

Dynamic web pages

There is a little confusion over the use of terms such as *"dynamic web pages"* and *"DHTML"*.
As a starting point, it is best to recognise that despite the fact that HTML helped bring the Internet to where it is today, designers were always aware of its limitations:

- It did not provide facilities to dynamically change the content of a web page, depending upon the situation (e.g. time of day, content of cookies, content of databases, data supplied by a user).
- It did not provide sufficient control of text formatting.
- It did not provide sufficient control over screen layout.

The first problem is solved by the use of the CGI scripts, PHP programs, etc. already covered in this chapter. Dynamic pages refer to the contents of a page being dependent upon the circumstances of the user who wishes to view the page, e.g. through use of CGI scripts, PHP, and so on.
A regular user of the Amazon web site, for example, will be given suggestions for new books or CDs that are based on their previous purchasing habits (buy lots of books on archaeology and you will be told of new books on that subject each time you enter the site). This means that the same Amazon home page that is seen by all viewers actually has different links for different users.
Similarly, a user who accesses a travel agent's web site will pull up special offers based on the information supplied in a form (dates, countries, maximum cost, etc.).
Web sites are composing a web page especially for each user, with special page data that is dependent on cookies or other stored information – or information supplied by the user.
This leaves the other two problems – poor text formatting and screen layout. These are tackled through using DHTML, as explained next.
Despite the fact that *"dynamic web pages"* and *"Dynamic HTML"* sound identical, there is one important difference:

- Dynamic page content is an activity that is carried on at the server end.
- DHTML, which is covered next, occurs at the client end.

DHTML

DHTML or *'Dynamic HTML'* refers to the coming together of HTML, CSS, JavaScript, VBScript and ActiveX, plus some add-on browser properties and Java applets to provide these main functions:

- The absolute positioning of every object on the web page, using x and y co-ordinates. This can be achieved through CSS, as explained later. Furthermore, the concept of layering, or 'z-indexing', is introduced: this adds a *'depth'* to the web page, so that objects can be placed on top of other objects, perhaps dynamically changing their z co-ordinate at a later stage to make them closer to the front.

- Data binding, which is a method whereby part of the data within an HTML page is downloaded directly from a web database, rather than being part of the original HTML source. Controls on the web page can allow browsing of different records in the database, without changing the HTML content. This is not supported by Netscape's DHTML model. Microsoft's model uses Data Source Objects (DSOs), which contain specifications on how to retrieve and use each data object.

- Data awareness, the counterpart to data binding, which allows an HTML object to be aware of the database on which the data lies, enabling it to be downloaded or even uploaded. Again, only Microsoft's DHTML model handles data awareness.

- The alteration of page content <u>after</u> the page is downloaded. This is carried out through the scripting language, and Microsoft's ActiveX controls give even greater flexibility at lower bandwidth to dynamic content. For example, a table that was created with DHTML can be sent to the browser and the user can decide to sort or filter the table contents – all without having to go back to the data in the server's database.

DHTML is a problem area since the inherent difficulty is worsened by the fact that Netscape and Explorer use different techniques. Microsoft's implementation of DHTML requires the use of ActiveX.

This may result in a web page acting differently when viewed in the different browsers. As always, the struggle between standardisation and the vested interests of the major players makes programmers work much harder. The web site at www.webreview.com produces a chart of the elements of DHTML that work in both Explorer and Netscape.

The Dynamic Object Model

At the heart of DHTML is the Dynamic Object Model (DOM). In this model, every item on a web page is treated as an object, be it an image, a paragraph, an anchor or any such entity. The model is hierarchical, starting with the *'window'* object representing the browser window. This object has several children, such as the *'location'* object which represents the current URL, and the *'document'* object which represents the HTML document currently residing in memory. Each of these objects can then have further children.

Some objects are, in fact, *'collections'*. These are groups of objects of the same type, for example the *'document'* object contains a *'links'* collection (among other things) that refers to all link objects in the document.

Each object can have *'properties'*, which often correspond to HTML attributes and/or CSS properties, which define how the object behaves. Objects also have *'methods'*, which are ways for the web page designer to make use of the code driving the object.

It is this object model that is used by the scripting language to create the dynamic aspect of DHTML. For example a page could be written so that hovering the mouse over one of several text objects will change the contents of an image object elsewhere on the page to display an image appropriate to the item that the mouse is hovering over.

This is handled through *'events'* that are associated with objects and scripting code. When an event (such as hovering the mouse over the object or clicking on it), happens to an object, the browser will check to see if there is code written for such an occasion, and carries out the code. Microsoft's version of DHTML also supports *'bubbling'*, which is where an event which is not handled by one object 'bubbles up' to the parent object within which it is contained.

W3C Document Standards

The HTML language is constantly in development. The body that oversees this development is the World Wide Web Consortium (or 'W3C' for short), and it has produced many web document standards, including several versions of HTML. The basis for HTML, XML, and other markup languages is the Standardised General Markup Language (SGML), which is in turn based on the principles of Generalised Markup (GM). The diagram below shows the relationship between the major Markup Languages specified by the W3C group.

As can be seen, SGML is the foundation on which HTML, XML and ultimately XHTML are all based, and XHTML combines the principles of XML and the functionality of HTML.

SGML is extremely flexible, and is actually used to describe the syntax of HTML. As such, HTML is considered to be an 'application' of SGML. XML, on the other hand, is similar to SGML but has a reduced set of features to make its implementation more reasonable. Therefore XML is often said to be a 'subset' of SGML.

Where HTML uses a standard set of tags, however, XML is capable of creating user-defined tags. Furthermore, rather than just being a document in itself, an XML file can also contain a description of the elements within the document.

At the heart of modern versions of HTML and other markup languages is the 'Document Type Definition'. A DTD is a text file that is written in the SGML language and defines the elements and behaviour of the markup language. Individual web pages should specify a DTD in order that the browser knows how to deal with the contents of the page.

Unfortunately, modern browsers tend to be extremely lax at checking DTDs and their rules, to allow them to view sloppily written web pages.

The DTD relevant to any given web document is specified using the DOCTYPE tag, at the very start of the document.

For example, at the start of an HTML document written using HTML version 4.0, there should be a tag similar to the following:

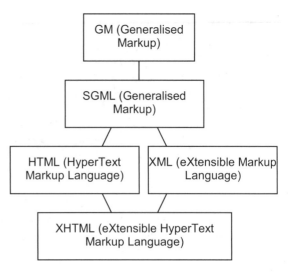

```
<!DOCTYPE HTML PUBLIC "-//W3C//DTD HTML 4.0//EN"
"http://www.w3.org/TR/REC-html40/strict.dtd">
```

This tag informs the browser that the file is an HTML file, and which version of HTML the page is written in. The URL portion does not appear in all DOCTYPE declarations, but when it does appear it points to a DTD file located on the W3C's web site, which contains the SGML specification of the markup language it describes. DTD files are in plain text, like HTML files, but they are a little harder to read since they describe the actual function of the elements.

The following are some of the more common DOCTYPEs:

```
HTML 2.0:      <!DOCTYPE HTML PUBLIC "-//IETF//DTD HTML//EN">

HTML 3.2:      <!DOCTYPE HTML PUBLIC "-//W3C//DTD HTML 3.2 Final//EN">

HTML 4.0:      <!DOCTYPE HTML PUBLIC "-//W3C//DTD HTML 4.0//EN"
                        "http://www.w3.org/TR/REC-html40/strict.dtd">

XHTML 1.0:     <!DOCTYPE HTML PUBLIC "-//W3C//DTD XHTML 1.0 Strict//EN"
                        "http://www.w3.org/TR/xhtml1/DTD/xhtml1-strict.dtd">
```

Markup Structure

At its most basic, a markup document consists of a DTD (Document Template Definition) and the actual document, which is technically referred to as the 'document instance'. The DTD may be included inside the document instance or can be a separate file, allowing for multiple documents fitting the same document template for greater standardisation.

As the name indicates, the DTD defines the 'document type', called a DOCTYPE for short. This DTD describes one or more ELEMENTs, and also describes any 'attributes' that may be used inside any of those elements. These attributes are defined within an ATTLIST tag. For example:

```
<!ELEMENT title (#PCDATA)>
<!ATTLIST title %common.att;>
```

The ELEMENT definition above describes the TITLE tag, which can then be used within the document itself. The ATTLIST refers to the TITLE tag, and specifies that it may use any of the common attributes.

There are a few other items that can be included in a DOCTYPE definition. Those that begin with '<!' and end in '>' are definitions, and those that begin with '<?' and end in '?>' are processing directives, such as directing the browser to use a stylesheet, or include an external entity.

The DOCTYPE describes the basic parts that make up the final document, and the content of each document uses tags that match the ELEMENTs of the DTD. Each ELEMENT can be defined as containing only other ELEMENTS (called 'element content'), or it may contain a mixture of text and ELEMENTS (called 'mixed content'). ELEMENTS may also be defined to be empty. When an empty element is used, it can be written in one of two ways, for example:

```
<separator></separator>
```
or
```
<separator/>
```

This syntax has also been adopted for XHTML, so tags such as BR should now be written as <BR/>.

HTML Version Compatibility

The differences between verions 2.0 and 3.2 of HTML are mainly that of adding new tags and new attributes to existing tags. Versions before HTML 2.0 have no supporting DTD, while version 3.0 was never adopted because it was outdated before it even came into use.

HTML version 4.0 again changed some elements, but more importantly, it allowed for new features such as style sheets, frames, and greater support for multimedia objects. This necessitated that three separate DTDs be used for HTML 4.0 documents: a *'strict'* DTD, a *'transitional'* DTD, and a *'frameset'* DTD. Each of these has different capabilities: Strict is the best for general use; transitional is intended for use where stylesheets may not be implemented by the browser; while the frameset DTD is exclusively for frameset documents.

Of course, HTML 4.0 documents that include frames, style sheets or any other new capabilities are no longer compatible with HTML 3.2. HTML 4.01 was the last HTML version based on SGML; all newer versions will be based on another markup language specification called XML.

The first such version is XHTML, which is so named because it is is based on HTML 4.0 and XML. It reformulates HTML into an XML application, and by following some simple guidelines that are available on the W3C's website, an XHTML 1.0 document is fully backwards compatible with HTML 4.0.

However, some important changes are required for code to be XHTML compliant. Documents <u>must</u> be *"well-formed"*, for example they must not contain tags that overlap; and elements must be properly nested, ie. no tag contents may overlap other tag contents. Also, XHTML is case-sensitive, and as a result all XHTML tags must be in lower case. Another major difference is that all elements must be properly closed; for example paragraph tags, <P>, <u>must</u> be closed with a </P> tag. This rule even applies to empty tags such as BR; in these cases the tag is shown to be empty by ending with '/>' instead of simply '>'. However, in order for this code to be backward compatible, adding a space before the '/>' will allow HTML 4 browsers to recognise the tag. For example, the BR tag would be written <BR />.

Most of the compatibility issues between HTML 4.01 and XHTML 1.0 or 1.1 are imposed by the XHTML standard, and therefore XHTML documents are compatible with HTML 4.01 far more often than vice versa. For example, XHTML attributes may not be minimised, as this illustration shows:

HTML	XHTML
<dl compact>	<dl compact="compact">

Compatibility between documents is important, but perhaps more important is the compatibility between the document and the browser. All major browsers make every attempt to maximise the number of web pages they can display, by being lax about enforcing standards, and by supporting the highest number of proprietary additions to the HTML standards as possible. For example, the infamous <BLINK> tag was introduced by Netscape, and is not part of any HTML standard, yet it is supported by all major browsers.

Browsers that are capable of reading documents written in HTML 4.0 include IE 5.5, Netscape 6.0, Mozilla, and Opera 7. XHTML is supported by IE 6 and Mozilla.

XML

The primary function of XML is to act as a medium for exchanging e-business data. The databases of various companies contain widely differing file structures and will probably even use different names for the same data (e.g. one company may call an item *"cost"* while the other calls it *"price"*). To make one company's database match another is unworkable as no one would want to take on the expense of the change. Besides, there are far too many companies linked to too many other companies to ever achieve a unified database.

This is where XML comes in. It acts a go-between. As long as each company can understand the data in the XML file, they can exchange data between themselves with little effort.

Here is a sample of a small file laid out to XML standards.

```
<?xml version="1.0"?>
<!DOCTYPE booklist>
<booklist>
        <!--XML allows the usual comments to be entered -->
        <book id="PCSH">The PC Support Handbook
                <bookprice currency="GBP"> 29.00</bookprice>
                <bookpages>568</bookpages>
        </book>
        <book id="PCMM">The PC Multimedia Handbook
                <bookprice currency="GBP"> 29.00</bookprice>
                <bookpages>528</bookpages>
        </book>
</booklist>
```

The first line is not essential. It is used to indicate that the file uses a particular version of XML.

The document contains a hierarchy of elements. The root element is the booklist element. It contains two further elements within it – the book elements. Each of these elements, in turn, has a number of nested elements – the bookprice and bookpages elements.

Like HTML, the file is using tags but these are not the standard HTML tags such as <h1> or <font>. The tags were created by the programmer to describe the content of the data, instead of the presentation of the data. One tag indicates that the data describes the quantity of pages, while the bookprice tag indicates that the stored value is a price valued in Great British Pounds.

While a normal browser would simply display the data on the screen, the XML version allows for greater flexibility. For example, the book price could be translated into dollars or Euros before being used.

XML also allows extended linking capabilities through the XLL language. For example, HTML gives designers the ability to link to a portion of another HTML page by using the '#' symbol. XML uses the '|' symbol for a similar function, but this indicates that the rest of the document outwith the specified region is not to be downloaded.

While XML has more powerful facilities than HTML, it has far less browser support, although Explorer 5 and Netscape 6 onwards support XML in most respects.

To guarantee the use of XML with the maximum number of browsers, it can be used on the server only, with stylesheets being used to transform XML content into HTML documents to be sent to the client. In this way the browser need never know that XML was ever involved in generating the web page.

XML Stylesheets

XML does not influence page design in any way - it is entirely concerned with page content. The layout of an XML page is usually left to the use of CSS (see earlier) or XSL (see below). As explained earlier, CSS can change the look of an entire web site simply by altering the single CSS file that is shared by all pages on the site. If the contents of the CSS file can be altered on the fly, then the page can look any way the user wants (e.g. the font size can be enlarged for the visually impaired). The CSS standard can be used without modification to define the appearance of XML content.

XML also has its own stylesheet language, called XSL (XML Stylesheet Language). Like CSS, it can be used on individual tags or applied to an entire document by using an external file. XSL can perform similar functions to CSS, such as text formatting, positioning etc. Of course, the language syntax is different.

For example, XSL is able to match 'templates', in order to convert XML data into HTML content, and can use 'style-rules' to apply style settings such as font size or colour to existing elements. Such processing is done at the client side, and therefore still requires an XML and XSL-capable browser. For maximum compatibility with client machines, the developer may wish to perform the translation from XML to HTML at the server end, providing 'natural' HTML code to the browser.

However, assuming the browser is capable of parsing both XML and XSL, the following code snippets will combine to display formatted data:

test.xml

```
<?xml version="1.0"?>
<?xml-stylesheet href="test.xsl" type="text/xsl"?>
<!DOCTYPE booklist>
<booklist>
        <book id="PCSH">
                <title>The PC Support Handbook</title>
                <bookprice currency="GBP"> 29.00</bookprice>
                <author>David Dick</author>
                <bookpages>768</bookpages>
        </book>
        <book id="PCMM">
                <title>The PC Multimedia Handbook</title>
                <bookprice currency="GBP"> 29.00</bookprice>
                <author>David Dick</author>
                <bookpages>684</bookpages>
        </book>
</booklist>
```

test.xsl

```
<?xml version="1.0"?>
<xsl:stylesheet
xmlns:xsl="http://www.w3.org/TR/WD-xsl">

 <xsl:template match="/">
 <HTML>
 <head>
 </head>
 <BODY>
   <xsl:for-each select="booklist/book">

     <xsl:for-each select="title">
      <xsl:element name="H1">
      <xsl:value-of select="."/>
      </xsl:element>
     </xsl:for-each>

     <xsl:for-each select="author">
      <xsl:element name="H2">
      <xsl:value-of select="."/>
      </xsl:element>
     </xsl:for-each>

   </xsl:for-each>

 </BODY>
 </HTML>
 </xsl:template>
</xsl:stylesheet>
```

The XSL stylesheet here is using the template directive to find the root document element (represented by the '/' character), and replace it with a template. This template can contain other directives, text, tags, and so on. In this case it contains some basic HTML tags, and some more XSL directives, namely the for-each directive.

The for-each directive is used to search for every occurrence of a particular element within the current element. Since the current element is the root document, the first for-each search will return every book in the document.

The other two for-each directives are nested within the first, and as a result they only search for occurrences of the 'title' tag and the 'author' tag within each individual 'book' tag. In this case, since each book has only one title and one author, they will return only one tag each.

Next, inside the for-each directive, is the XSL element directive. This directs the parser to surround the data with a certain tag, in this case the H1 and H2 tags, for title and author, respectively. Finally, the value-of' directive instructs the parser to include the contents of the current tag. In this way, the actual contents of the 'title' and 'author' tags are included in the final document displayed to screen.

This is a simple way to parse XML data sheets and display them as HTML, but even this simple example shows how powerful the languages can be, when combined, to provide selective data from a larger data set.

Using XML as a database

The structure of XML is designed to represent documents of any kind. However, the fact that it can contain self-defined nested elements makes it particularly well suited to database documents. The examples earlier showed how it could be used to store a simple database of book information, and how XSL can be used to determine which information to display, as well as determining the layout of the final displayed page.

However, XML's functionality goes even further than this. Although a DTD can be used to describe the elements in a document, using an XML "*Schema*" takes the concept one stage further. The schema is used to determine not only the structure of elements and attributes, but also their contents. For example, the schema could contain the following:

```
<xs:element name="username">
   <xs:simpleType>
      <xs:restriction base="xs:string">
         <xs:minLength value="6"/>
         <xs:maxLength value="12"/>
      </xs:restriction>
   </xs:simpleType>
</xs:element>
```

This defines an ELEMENT called "username". This is a *'simple'* element, which means it cannot have any attributes and may not contain other elements. The restriction tag informs the XML parser that the element's contents are restricted, and specifies the base type of content, which may be a string, decimal, integer, boolean, date, or time. These base types are, of course, the common data types used in both programming languages and databases.

Finally, inside the restriction tag are some other tags, defining further limitations on what the element may contain. In this the restrictions are that the tag must contain no less than 6 characters, and no more than 12.

As can be seen, this sort of restriction is ideal for databases, where the data entered can then be validated to ensure that it is of the correct type before saving. Additionally, default content can be defined, further lending support to the use of XML in database applications. And another reason for using XML in this way is one of the key features of the design: interconnectivity. In other words, an XML-aware database can create an XML file, DTD and/or schema, describing the database's contents in a way that can easily be interpreted by any other XML-aware database package. At the current time, fully XML and XSD (XML Schema Definition) aware database packages are thin on the ground, but future applications are likely to support its use to an increasing degree.

An introduction to e-commerce

Much of this book is given over to the practical and creative activities of producing multimedia products and web sites. The material examined technologies and techniques that would benefit all web sites, both commercial and non-commercial. Inevitably, however, the pages were full of examples of how the Internet is increasingly becoming an extension of the normal business practices of commercial companies. The idea that the Internet was the *"new economy"* has been shown to be hype from journalists and sellers of web site hardware and software. With a few exceptions, there are no *"new"* products that are only available from the Internet. Activities such as e-banking, purchasing music, books and so on are activities that are also available on many high streets or are available by other means (e.g. phone banking, mail order catalogue shopping). The availability of products and service via the Internet may be a more convenient method for some, but they do not replace traditional outlets.

So, the web is now being approached as a potential tool for reaching additional markets for traditional products.

The growth of products, sales and services via the Internet has been phenomenal. Although, it only represents a small proportion of total sales and services, it is still a huge amount in cash terms. More importantly, the projections are for continued growth and many companies are examining their web sales strategies. In this respect, much of the activities of e-commerce are bound up with the principles of market research, planning, marketing, delivery and support. In other words, it looks at the practical and resource implications of such a move.

Additional to these traditional business concepts, e-commerce introduces the additional problems of engineering, security and confidentiality.

Site designers need to discuss the project with all levels of the company. Although many of the issues below seem to be business issues, they have a huge impact on the design and programming of the site.

New Start-ups

This chapter does not look at new start-ups, business plans, raising venture capital, etc.

Fortunately, there is a wide base of help and support for those seeking to float their own business and the following are just a few of the sites that look at that area.

www.sbgateway.com (Small Business Gateway)	www.bvca.co.uk (for raising venture capital)
www.businessadviceonline.org.uk (run by DTI)	www.ukbi.co.uk (UK Business Incubation Centre)
www.ukonlineforbusiness.gov.uk	www.fsb.org.uk (Federation of Small Businesses)
www.scottish-enterprise.com (Scotland)	www.businessconnect.org.uk (Wales)

For advice on specific aspects of running businesses, these government sites that provide valuable information.

www.hmce.gov.uk	Customs & Excise advice on exporting and on VAT
www.inlandrevenue.gov.uk	Advice on tax affairs
www.dataprotection.gov.uk	Advice on regulating customer databases
www.courtservice.gov.uk	Advice on making claims for debt recovery

Some of the content of these sites is worth a look, even by those operating existing businesses.

Business concerns for e-commerce

The rest of the chapter looks at existing businesses moving to having an Internet presence.

Many of the issues, such as branding and marketing, are similar in traditional selling and in e-commerce but electronic trading requires some different implementation tasks.

Merchandising

The site has to identify its target customers, its product range and its market position. For example, an existing company may have a *"stack 'em high and sell 'em cheap"* approach, reaching for a wide market with a large turnover but small margins. This might be possible if the company already has large stocks in its existing stores. On the other hand, a new company might identify a specialist market (e.g. youth, sports fans) or specialist products (e.g. home-grown produce, arts & crafts, parts for vintage cars, etc.).

Some products are universal.   Books, videos, or CDs, for example, are identifiable products. They are available on any high street.   There is no question about the quality of the goods – the main factors for an e-commerce site are therefore simply price and delivery.   However, items such as clothes are difficult to sense on the Internet – it is hard to appreciate colour, size, material, or quality.   While selling brand names may be easy, selling other clothes poses real problems for Internet traders.

There are many books that go on at great length about merchandising.   While great effort is put into achieving the best image for high street trading, the company has to ensure that handing over the e-commerce design to an agency does not diminish the company's image.   The site usually has to reflect the ethos of the company's main trading effort.

Sales Service

In a high street store, there are plenty of shop assistants to advise customers.   The web site has to provide at least this level of service.   The site should inspire customer confidence. If the company has been trading for many years, the site should clearly say so, as this gives reassurance to wary customers.   For the same reasons, the company's postal address, telephone number and fax number should be displayed on the site.   Customers are wary of purchasing from an 'anonymous' site.

Other confidence boosting measures include assuring customers regarding the confidentiality of their personal and financial details, and clearly stating any conditions of sale, the returns policy, etc.

Customers particularly welcome interactive features on a site. Typical applets are currency converters, weight/length converters and loan calculators.   Applets can also be written especially for a web site. For example, a car spares company may have a parts finder on its site. The user enters details of the car model and year and the applet tells the customer what model of silencer they need to order.

Despite the best efforts to design a site, customers will still have queries about products or services and will judge a company by how they answer the queries.   Firstly, the site can minimise queries by providing an FAQ section on the site. This is in a question-and-answer format and answers all the most frequently asked questions received by the site. If the presence of the FAQ is prominent, customers will read the contents and find most of their questions answered. The time taken to draw up a comprehensive FAQ is more than repaid in the time saved on answering the same queries over and over again.

Where queries are received, a prompt response should be sent, even if this is only an initial automated acknowledgement of the query. The company then has to provide a method that directs the queries to the appropriate department (e.g. sales, returns, and technical support).

The aim of a well-designed sales service is not only to generate a sale – but also to generate repeat business. If the customer had a pleasant and efficient service from a company, they will not only use the site again; they will also recommend the site to their friends and relatives.

Promotions

The issues regarding promoting a web site (advertising, etc) were covered in the previous chapter and this section examines methods of promoting goods.

Promoting goods on a web site is a combination of good business practice and good site design.

The traditional methods of supermarkets apply to most web sites.

These include:

- Quantity discounts (buy a box of six and pay for 5).
- Total amount discounts (spend more than £50 and get a 10% discount).
- Cross-discounting (buying one and getting a different item at a reduced price).
- Short-term promotions (items at the lower price for one week only).
- Stock clearance sales.
- Using a discount on a highly desirable object to draw people to the site.
- Club discounts (join the club and get a discount card).
- Mailshots to existing customers (web sites can e-mail its existing database of customers).

The site designer has to think of how customers want to use a site when designing user interfaces.

Consider, for example, how to sell items that have many variations, such as paint.   Paint comes in hundreds of colours, types and quantities. Having a separate page for every type, colour, etc. would make the site cumbersome and a nightmare to navigate. A better option is to have pages that display all the available colours (like the colour chart that is available in a store).   The order page then contains dropd-down menus for choosing paint type (gloss, emulsion, etc.), colour and tin capacity. The site's back-end program would still has a unique order code for each type/colour/size combination.

Other considerations on site design are:

- Don't force users to register with the site before they can even find the price or description of goods. Users should not have to create passwords and remember questions like *"what's the name of your dog?"*, just to enter a site.   While the information gathered may be useful, it is more likely to result in customers moving to another site.

- If registration is to be used, make it optional. Some users might welcome a future faster or personalised service. But many users want the equivalent of supermarket fast lane (grab an item, pay and get out).
- Don't force customers to download a special plug-in just to use the site.
- Consider providing personalised purchasing recommendations based on previous purchases. This is successfully used by Amazon.
- Provide an option to read the full descriptions for technical goods – some customers value reading the full specification, rather than the advertising hype. It also shows a more professional attitude.
- Use pictures, audio clips, video clips to enhance products. To minimise download times, larger files should only be downloaded on request by the customer.

Transaction Processing

Merchandising, Sales Service and Promotions are all concerned with encouraging users to buy goods or services. Transaction processing is concerned with <u>how</u> these orders are made. As before, the main concerns are ensuring that the site does not place obstacles in the way of orders being placed, and ensuring the easiest and simplest ordering procedures are provided.

For any company serious about selling on the Internet, the site must allow customers to place orders 24/7/365 – 24 hours a day, 7 days a week, for every day of the year. This is essential if the products are to be available for sale to shift workers, insomniacs, overseas customers with different time zones, etc.

A basic web site simply provides information on products and their prices, with sales being struck through conventional telephone calls or paper orders (perhaps forms printed from the web site then faxed). This method is inexpensive but is not convenient to user.

It is preferable that a site offers various payment methods but where online, fax and phone options are provide, almost all completed transactions are online transactions.

Online sales are usually concluded through shopping cart systems, where customers choose goods and add them to their list of purchases (like adding goods in a shopping trolley in a supermarket). When the customer is finished selecting goods, the system takes the customer through various forms which gather the customers address details, credit card details and any other essential information (e.g. the delivery address may be different from the customer's address).

Many customers abandon shopping carts before reaching the end of the ordering process, often because they find the total number of forms off-putting. Therefore, the design of shopping carts should consider the following features:

- The site should clearly explain how orders and personal details are kept secure (e.g. encryption).
- The order pages should clearly display all tax, shipping and other charges.
- The order pages should clearly outline the goods delivery policy. Consideration should be given to providing delivery options (e.g. shipping within 24-hours for an additional charge)
- Delivery details should be explicit (e.g. orders received before 15.00 are despatched the same day). Preferably, the delivery times for each time should appear in the product description. The customer does not want to get to the final checkout page before discovering that a particular item has a 3-week wait for delivery.
- The order pages should only ask the essential details. Do not use order pages to gather lots of customer information that is not relevant to the sale. Use other means (e.g. mailing lists or competitions) to gather this information.
- The order pages should minimise the time a user need spend completing forms. Don't ask customers to enter their date of expiry in a particular format – instead give them drop-down menus for month and year. The shipping address should offer to be the same as the address of the customer placing the order, saving the customer filling in the same details twice.
- Where appropriate, provide on-screen currency converters or weights/measures converters.
- Keep the customer informed of where they are in the ordering process (e.g. *"we now have your delivery details and now need your credit card details. This is the last page"*).
- Where appropriate, use a configurable system. For example, Dell Computers allows customers to choose a system by selecting the components from drop-down lists.
- E-mail an order confirmation to the customer.

Even the largest companies suffer from poor site design. When boo.com collapsed, the analysts declared that the company suffered because its site was over-engineered and too hard to use.

Finally, traders should not deduct from a customer's credit card until the goods are shipped. The web site's software, therefore, should be able to tie in the delivery department's operations with the finance department.

Delivery

Some products are not physical and don't require conventional postal delivery. Software, e-music, graphics libraries, and e-trading, can all be immediately purchased online. Others, such as financial or other professional advice may take a little longer but are still transacted over the Internet. For all other goods, the greatest majority of trading, the items need to be physically transported to the buyer.

A new start-up company has to conclude a bulk shipping agreement with a carrier, so that the delivery times and bulk discounts are known. The deal is usually based on the quantity of packages, weight of packages, delivery area, etc.). If a company ships more goods in a particular year, they can negotiate a lower unit price for the following year.   It is also worth checking whether the carrier provides on-line tracking of parcels, as this allows traders to answer customer queries and monitor the carrier's efficiency.

Consideration should be given to the delivery options that will be provided (e.g. 48-hour, 24-hour at extra charge, international deliveries, optional carriage insurance charges). Consideration should also be given to delivery charges – whether to charge for shipping, charge if order is under a certain amount, only charge for international shipping, etc. Many companies avoid international sales because of the complications in sending goods across national borders. The complications include shipping costs, customs regulations, tax regulations, export documents, licences for certain goods, and bans on trade with certain countries.

Finally, the site should provide feedback to customers, confirming order and delivery details. An informed customer is a happier customer.

Post sales support

One of the biggest sources of dissatisfaction with any company is its after sales service. Waiting in automated telephone queues, unhelpful operators and complicated procedures all aggravate customers and may drive them away from using the site again. Companies and customers both make mistakes and the way that the company overcomes problems decides how they are judged.
The best ways to ensure good post sales support are:

- Providing the fullest information <u>before</u> the customer makes a purchase. This lowers the numbers of misunderstandings. Prevention is better than cure.
- Providing a full FAQ on customer queries and complaints. This could include common mistakes in using equipment or software and known cures for identified problems. On complaints, it could outline the customer's legal rights, facts to be gathered before making a complaint, etc.
- Providing a help desk with staff trained in technical issues, company procedures – and people skills.
- Providing clear procedures for help desk staff.
- Providing a clear returns policy on areas beyond the statutory obligations (e.g. are used, damaged, soiled, old goods accepted for return, who pays the return postage when the trader is not to blame for the return).
- Providing facilities that allow customers to check the current status of order for themselves.
- Providing, where appropriate, software patches, new drivers, etc. on the web site.

Market analysis

A trader wants to operate for many years and wants to maximise the efficiency and profitability of the company. The more information that a company has on its strengths, weaknesses, threats and opportunities, the more it is able to sustain and develop itself.
Gathering and analysing this information is an ongoing task for companies and they have to set up systems that provide this information.   Some of this information will be gathered from trade sources such as trade papers, memberships of trading organisations, commissioned surveys, etc.
However, much valuable information can be gleaned from the way that people use the web site.   Servers produce log files of the traffic through a web site. This data can be processed to produce information on which country visitors come from, which site they linked over from, what pages they visited, etc. There are a number of utilities that make analysing the log files easier.
In addition, counters can be placed on key pages, or all pages, to monitor the amount of hits that each particular page receives.   This shows which pages don't get visited, which don't lead on to shopping cart sales, etc.   These may be problems of site design, page design or simply unattractive product lines.
This information can be used in conjunction with summaries of sales, queries, complaints, returns, etc., to identify issues such as sales trends and which promotions work. This, in turn, provides valuable pointers to how companies should alter their strategies to meet customer needs and maximise sales.

Approaches to creating an e-commerce site

All web sites are resident ('*hosted*') on a computer that is permanently connected to the Internet and uses web server software.   The computer (i.e. web server) can be rented from a supplier or can be owned and run by the company that owns the web site.
These choices have further options as discussed below.

- Use an existing host computer and their software
- Use an existing host computer and buy/develop other software
- Set up own Internet server and buy software
- Set up own Internet server and write the software from scratch

Full solutions

There are many ISPs who are keen to sell a complete e-commerce solution to businesses – at a price. There is a setup charge and a monthly hosting charge, plus extra charges if a company requires special design or programming. For these fees, the company is provided with web storage space and a set amount of bandwidth.

The basic package is a *'virtual hosting'* solution, where the company's web site shares a server with several other subscribers. Of course, each company's files and data are kept separate and secure.

If the subscriber requires more web space or greater bandwidth, there is a *'co-hosting'* solution. Here, the company has its own dedicated server that is located within the ISP's structure and is still maintained by the ISP. As the diagram shows, there is only one web site installed on each server and the provider has a routing system that makes each site appear to be directly connected to the Internet.

Going with an existing Internet solutions provider is usually the cheapest but most restrictive approach.

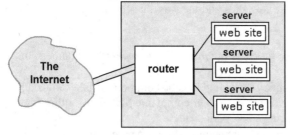

There is no server software to install, since it already exists on the supplier's system. Similarly, unless otherwise negotiated, there is no e-commerce software to install, as it is included in server-based subscription. At it simplest, the company simply supplies product details to fill in the blanks in the ISP's existing e-commerce software.

The full solution approach allows a quick start-up for a small company. There is no hardware or software to buy and there are no worries about security or backups. The site is maintained by making alterations to pages on the local PC and uploading them to the ISP.

However, the use of templates means that many sites have a similar appearance. Also, if a company finds that it develops many new system requirements during its use, the existing software may not be able to accommodate these requirements.

For greater flexibility, a company might rent server space from a provider but decide to use its own e-commerce software in preference to the limited package offered by a solutions provider. This software may be bought from another software supplier or have specially written by a software house. If the company has the expertise, it could also decide to develop its own software.

This option also saves on purchasing Internet hardware and still places the responsibility for the upkeep of the system on the host provider. It has the benefit of allowing the company to choose e-commerce software that most meets their requirements. This method can also be relatively quick to implement and relatively cheap to operate. The e-commerce package will take a little longer to configure compared to filling in supplied templates. However, it is still not likely to meet all future needs, requiring changes or plug-ins.

In both the above cases, the company has to strike a SLA (Service Level Agreements) with the hosting provider. This specifies how long it will take to correct any problems in the event of a hardware or software failure. Of course, an instant response costs more than a less efficient response. The contract usually specifies the guaranteed uptime (e.g. 99%) and the amount of compensation for downtime (usually just a partial refund on the charges).

Local solutions

For large organisations, the option of using its own hardware and software may be preferred. This requires that the company establishes its own server(s), connect to the Internet via a leased line and install the server, security and e-commerce software. It also has to set up maintenance, backup and recovery procedures. This is not a trivial matter and only the largest or more specialist organisations have the broad range of expertise required.

This local solution provides the greatest flexibility, since it can more readily integrate the e-commerce transactions to the company's existing IT resources such as stock control, accounting, e-mail, etc. It also places all the security of the company's data in the company's own hands.

The e-commerce software can be purchased as a tailor-made solution from a software house, or bought as a ready-made solution from a supplier. (choosing an existing system that most closely matches the requirements of the company).

Finally, there is the option of building the site and the e-commerce programming from scratch.

Self-hosting needs time, money, and expertise. However, a home-produced solution can exactly meet the needs of the company. This choice is only an option for a large organisation with a knowledgeable IT department. This is the most expensive and most time-consuming option but can be the best solution for a large organisation. Nevertheless, even some very large organisations prefer the co-hosting option so that it can get on with its main job – that of selling goods or services.

Server considerations

Most servers use the Unix operating system with the free Apache web server software, with Microsoft-based servers (e.g. Windows 2000 plus IIS - Internet Information Server) taking up second place and the rest having only a small market share.   In most cases, either system supports e-commerce software.   If the site is to be designed using Microsoft FrontPage and FrontPage extensions, it is best to use a Microsoft server. If the server is rented from a host supplier, the range of facilities offered should be checked prior to signing an agreement.
This should include:

- Does the server support CGI scripting, Java, JavaScript, PHP, ASP, SSI, streaming, ODBC, Perl, MySQL, etc.
- Does the server have full physical security such as intruder alarms, water detection, fire alarms, backup power, access systems (e.g. swipe cards).
- What reporting facilities does the host provide (e.g. weekly logs or monthly logs).
- How many e-mail addresses would be allocated.
- Does the host support discussion forums, mailing lists, etc.
- How long have they been trading, what is the current customer base, are they financially sound.
- What is their backup policy (e.g. frequency of backups, provision of virus protection).
- Is the supplier a backbone provider, or a reseller of bandwidth from an upstream provider.
- How much of the core capacity of the bandwidth is currently used (i.e. is the supplier working at the edge of its limit).
- If most customers come from the UK, what bandwidth is their line to London Telehouse (the main UK centre). If sales are in Europe, do they have a link to Amsterdam.
- Does provider have its own link to the USA (e.g. to the New York Telehouse). Suppliers with direct links can usually supply a better service but charge higher fees.

It is useful to request examples of existing customers and then check their access times at different times of day.

Home users wishing to experiment with setting up a web server using an old PC might wish to look at the Omnicron OmniHTTPd Web Server software (www.omnicon.ca). The software is free and is compatible with Windows 98, ME, NT and the ActiveState Perl mentioned earlier.

Capacity

The trader's target is that all viewers can navigate throughout the site with minimum delays between pages, to prevent them leaving the site too early.   Therefore, the server has to sufficient bandwidth to meet the expected amount of traffic. If a trader is using its own server, an eye has to be kept on the bandwidth usage, as it should never get above 80% of the system capacity. If the usage regularly exceeds this figure, the connection to the Internet should be upgraded. If the server is provided through an agreement with ISP, the trader should check whether the system bandwidth is dedicated to its server, or shared with other servers. Bursts above the agreed bandwidth are usually tolerated but abuse will lead to demands from the ISP for a new agreement on greater bandwidth provision. Very large increases may also require to be met with extra servers.
The likely arrangements for different company sizes are:

Small company	Single server (either rented or owned)
Medium company	Multiple servers (either rented or owned) probably different servers for databases, streaming, commercial operations, etc.
Large company	Server farms (usually owned)

Finally, a trader may consider having mirror sites in countries where its market is concentrated (e.g. a USA mirror or a German mirror). A mirror site is simply a copy of the UK site sitting on a server on the other country, to ease congestion on the UK site and provide quicker access to overseas customers. Of course, these sites could easily be altered to reflect local customers (e.g. local language and currency).

Getting a domain name

The web site name can be a problem for some companies. Finding an appropriate domain name may be difficult, as many obvious names are already allocated.
The domain name is in three parts, to describe the organisation, its type of activity and the country in which it is (nominally) based.   So, ayrcoll.ac.uk describes Ayr College, which is an academic institution based in the UK.   Some domains, like .gov, .ac, .org, .pro, .coop, .aero and .museum are only allocated on evidence that the applicant fits the particular category (e.g. only colleges, universities, etc. will be granted a .ac domain name). Other domains include:

.org	Charities, professional bodies, trade unions, political parties
.gov, nhs	National government, local government bodies
.co, .com, .biz, .plc, .ltd	Business use
.info, .tv, .name	General use

While .co.uk and .com, are mostly used by commercial companies, there is no restrictions on applying for these domain names.

If the trader is creating a new web site, the domain name arrangements can be included in a total solution package. If a web site already exists, the trader can acquire a domain name along with web diversion, also known as web re-direction or web forwarding. The user thinks he/she is looking at a web site at the new URL but is, in fact, being pointed to the existing URL.

There are a large number of companies, large and small, involved in selling and managing domain names. Nominet (www.nominet.co.uk) is the UK registrar of domain names and it provides a list of over 1,000 sellers and resellers. A search facility on the Nominet site can be used to check whether a domain name is already in use. New.net have challenged the international registry (ICANN) by bringing out an *'unofficial'* set of domains including .mp3, .sport, .travel, .club and .shop. At present, however, these require a special browser plug-in to access them.

There are charges for acquiring and maintaining a domain name. This comprises the registration fee (the one-off fee for setting up the arrangements), the management fee (a monthly fee for web forwarding, e-mail forwarding, etc.) and a NIC fee for the registrar.

If substantial sales are in another country, get a server in that country and get a domain name of that country (e.g. dumbreck.fr or dumbreck.de). Many UK companies choose a .com name as this is perceived by some as being an American or an international domain name. This encourages traffic in those countries, as the site can be in their language, prices are in their currency, etc. It has a 'local' appearance - but note that the site is then subject to laws in that country.

Firewalls

Any computer that is permanently attached to the Internet is in danger of being a target for hackers intent on stealing information or corrupting data. The system is also exposed to virus attack. Systems at risk include web sites, local area networks that are connected to the Internet and individual PCs that have 24-hour connections, such as ADSL or cable modem users. Even individual surfers are vulnerable, while they are connected to the Internet.

There have been many well-reported incidences of breach of security on government and commercial systems. The scope for fraud on a huge scale can be imagined, if all the credit card and confidential details of a company's customers were accessed by hackers.

A degree of protection is provided by fitting a *'firewall'* between the computer system and the Internet.

This allows recognised traffic to pass through while prohibiting all other traffic from gaining access. It should also report any attempt at unauthorised entry. The system is set up so that no one from outside can illegally access a computer that is inside the company. It can filter both incoming and outgoing traffic.

For individuals, a personal firewall is usually implemented in software. These products are available from companies such as Norton (www.symantec.co.uk) and McAfee (www.mcafee.com). A freeware version, for personal use, is available from www.zonelabs.com, as are the ones from www.sygate.com and www.tinysoftware.com. Firewalls can also deal with *'Spyware'*, freeware and shareware programs that include little routines that pass back information that is of use to programmers and advertisers. Spyware works without the knowledge of the user and can be eliminated by a firewall.

For a commercial web site, a firewall can prevent anyone hacking into the site and altering site contents, placing defamatory messages, etc. For a server that handles credit card transactions, it prevents the financial and personal data from being accessed by those outside the company.

It is implemented as hardware, as a combination of hardware and software, or purely in software, although a fully software-based solution is somewhat less secure than a hardware-based solution. The hardware can cost as much as a basic computer and can set itself up automatically or can be configured to the user's needs.

Handling credit card transactions

Despite the growth of Internet commerce, the arrangements for handling credit card transactions are still not clear and straightforward. There are a variety of methods, involving different financial, procedural and hardware/software practices. These vary from farming out the whole operation to another company, to carrying out all operations within the company.

There is much jargon in the world of e-commerce, with term such as PSP (Payment Service Provider), CNP (Customer Not Present), CCP (Credit Card Processor) and so on. Some, like PSP and CNP, are generally more widespread than others. Terms will be explained where appropriate.

E-commerce has two requirements:

- That the transaction be secure
- That an agreed system of payment be used.

A basic web site can allow customers to place order online and provide a telephone number so that the company can phone back for credit card details. This avoids the complications of online transactions but has the big disadvantage of requiring e-mail to be continually monitored 24 hours a day, seven days a week.

In practice, there are two main approaches to collecting money from customers:
- The trader has a merchant account
- The trader uses a bureau, instead of using a merchant account

Example payment systems

The options for traders are given in the table below. Note that the system description is a general description, since each supplier uses its own terminology.

All-in-one system solution	One company hosts the web site and handles all financial transactions. The trader is only involved in sending out goods when informed. The money for the sales are paid into the trader's bank.
All-in-one payment solution	One company manages the merchant account, or bureau account, and handles the credit card transactions. The customer logs in to the supplier's web site to view and select products, but is linked across to the secure web site of the Online Authorising Company for the credit card transaction.
Full in-house solution	The trader has its own secure server, own merchant account and has the necessary hardware and software for handling transactions provided by the merchant account provider. The customer only interfaces with trader (there is no intermediary hardware or software).
Partial in-house solution	The trader has its own secure server and own merchant account but uses another company to process credit cards (a Credit Card Processor).
Non-merchant account	Another company handling all sales arrangements and paying the trader's bank, minus commission. This usually requires a larger start-up fee. A monthly fee and a commission of between 10% and 20% is also payable. There are usually extra fees to add new products. They are officially the vendors of the traders goods, so they keep back a reserve to cover any chargebacks (the money being paid later).
Pay-by-phone solution	The customer uses a premium rate telephone number to make the payment and the trader receives a share of the premium rate income. This avoids any credit card processing.

Merchant Agreement

A company cannot independently carry out secure credit card transactions over the Internet without the use of a *'merchant account'*. For this, the seller of the goods requires the services of a *'merchant bank'*. This is a bank that is able to receive and process credit card transactions. The retailer reaches a *'merchant agreement'* with the bank that allows a merchant account to be set up.   New companies, or small companies moving into credit card transactions, require an agreement to be set up with a bank for credit card transactions. Others already have this facility and wish an account to be set up to cover Internet trading, in addition to its current over-the-counter trading or CNP (Customer Not Present) telephone ordering system.

The bank only concludes an agreement when it is satisfied that the supplier has a sound financial track record and has adequate site security. The agreement will include charges for handling credit card transactions.   This is usually dependent upon the number of transactions, often with a minimum standing charge. So, for example, an online sale might result in paying 2% of the transaction price to the company running the credit card processing and another 5% to the credit card company that is used. The remainder is placed in the merchant account. This is not a large deduction for most companies.   However, companies who deal in large sales of low-priced goods should check that the deductions are purely percentage based, as many have a minimum charge for each transaction. For low-priced goods, the minimum charge might represent a very high proportion of the transaction price, making this form of e-commerce nonviable.

Merchant server

The web site, or at least the credit card sales pages, has to be hosted by a secure server that can handle credit card transactions (known as a *'merchant server'*).   It acts as the link between the customer, the supplier and both their banks.   Apart from the large companies who carry out all trading in-house, every trader uses some form of secure server system.

Bureau services

A PSP (Payment Service Provider) can offer an alternative to merchant accounts. The bureau processes credit card transactions on behalf of a trader. This is a useful option for companies that have newly started up, have no track record and cannot get a merchant account. It is also useful where only moderate sales are anticipated and the mechanics of getting and implementing full merchant operations are thought to be more bother than it is worth. The bureau collects the money and pays it into the trader's normal bank account, after commissions and fees have been deducted.

SSL

The greatest obstacle to e-commerce is the reluctance of buyers to send their credit card details over the Internet. The transactions between the customer and the retailer are routed through many intermediary computers, which threatens the security and privacy of individuals' and companies' bank details. In practice, the data is sent to the server in lots of different packets that might not even take the same route to the server. The server assembles all the packets and reconstructs the message. The chances of anyone capturing all of the message's packets are remote. Nevertheless, public perception and public confidence are the main factors in encouraging commercial transactions.

Security is tackled through systems that encrypt the messages according to electronic locks and keys that are only held by the two parties involved in the transaction. This was first tackled by Netscape who introduced the SSL (Secure Sockets Layer) into their browser. This system is designed to reassure customers that the trader is legitimate and that the transaction is secure. It quickly became the most common encryption standard and is embedded in Netscape and Explorer. To work, the server also needs to be SSL-enabled. The URLs for secured pages on the web site have https:// instead of the usual http:// identifier.

How security is implemented

Security is implemented through the use of digital certificates and through encryption of customer details.

Certificate Authorities (e.g. www.verisign.com) issue digital identity certificates and these are held by ISPs and companies with their own dedicated e-commerce servers. A new company, upon proof of identity and payment of a fee, can acquire a digital identity certificate.

These certificates can then be examined by any browser, to see who is responsible for the secure web page being viewed. Details such as the name and address of certificate's owner are displayed. This confirms that the key belongs to the stated company.

Security is achieved through the use of the server's *'public'* and *'private'* keys. The public key can be used to encrypt data but cannot decrypt data that has already been encrypted with a public key. The private key, however, can decrypt data that has been encrypted by public keys. Thus, there can be many public keys in use but there is only one private key – and that is held securely at the server. Therefore, although many can encrypt data, only the legal holder of the private key can decrypt messages.

The steps in achieving a secure connection are:

- The customer enters a secure web page.
- The browser requests a digital certificate from the server.
- The server provides the browser with the digital certificate, its domain name and a public key. The client end compares the information inside the certificate with the domain name and public key. A match authenticates the server and the browser displays a locked padlock, or a key, on the browser status bar. If the padlock is unlocked, or the key is broken, there is no secure path between browser and server and any data will be sent unencrypted.
- The user can check the certificate and decide whether to proceed.
- The client generates a *'session key'*, an encryption key that is used only for that single transaction. The session key is encrypted using the supplied public key.
- The encrypted session key is sent to the server, where is decrypted using the server's private key. Both sides now have an agreed encryption key. The server sends a message, using the agreed key, to indicate that the session key is understood. Both sides know that the other can communicate.
- When an order is placed, the data is encrypted and sent to the merchant web site where it is decrypted.

Note

If an order form is enclosed in part of an HTML, the padlock symbol will not appear, as the whole page is not seen as being secure. If possible, secure pages should be displayed as standalone pages and not be embedded in a frame. Otherwise, the site has to be programmed to load all the pages in the frame set via https links.

How a transaction is processed

This is a general description of the steps involved in a credit card transaction for a company with its own web site, using a credit card processing organisation.

The visitor to the site indicates a wish to make a purchase. This may be a simple activity, where the site sells a single product. Alternatively, it may be a complex dynamic activity with the buyer using a *'shopping cart'* to choose goods and the web site calculating total costs including taxes and delivery charges. The steps in the transaction process are:

- When the buyer completes the purchase details (type of goods, quantity, name, address, credit card details), these are sent to the merchant server.
- The merchant server requests confirmation to process with the transaction.
- The user clicks the button to confirm.

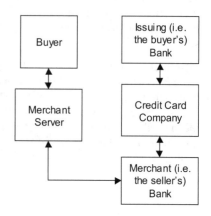

- The merchant server then sends the credit card details to the seller's own merchant bank.
- The merchant bank contacts the buyer's credit card company for a transaction authorisation.
- The credit card company contacts the buyer's bank, to confirm that he/she has sufficient funds to cover the transaction.
- Assuming that the buyer is financially solvent, the credit card company issues a transaction code back through the chain.
- The buyer is informed of the successful transaction and the charges.
- The seller is notified of the order.

Extra code is added to the web site to send the details to the online transaction system.

A large number of software products are available, to enable users to set up on-line stores. These range from hundreds to thousands of pounds, depending upon the facilities required.

Many service companies also provide set up services for suppliers, at an appropriate price.

The setup charges and the charges per transaction mean that suppliers have to have an expectation of reasonable amounts of extra sales to justify the cost of entering the area of credit card transactions.

The supplier's orders are e-mailed on or are stored on a secure area of the server for suppliers to access.

SET

The "Secure Electronic Transaction" system was developed by Visa and MasterCard and has yet to make significant progress as a transaction system. It uses digital certificates with additional information.

Providers and charges

All providers are there to provide a service and to make a profit. This means that the offers should be studied closely and the option should be chosen that best meets the expected sales of the company.

The main elements in the charges are:

- Set-up fee (varies from zero to thousands).
- Monthly/annual charges (varies from zero to three figures).
- Processing charges (varies from 1% to over 10%).
- Fees for additional services.
- Fees for handling different currencies.

The amount of charge for each Internet credit card transaction reduces with volume, which explains the range of figures given in the examples below:

- Secure server collects and pays to an ordinary account – bureau charges 5%-8% of the item price
- Secure server collects and pays to merchant account – Direct Merchant charges – 1%-4% of the item price (this is in addition to the charges levied by the trader's bank).

So, a trader who expects a high turnover might find that a high set-up cost combined with low processing charges is the most economic package. A smaller trader, on the other hand, might be best with a package that charges higher transaction fees but has lower set-up costs.   These calculations have also to take into account the level of monthly charges and whether there is a minimum charge for each transaction.

For companies with cash-flow problems, the frequency of payments from the PSP might be a major factor.

Typical providers of credit card transaction services are:

    www.worldpay.com   www.secpay.com www.kagi.com
    www.datacash.com   www.netbanx.com

Many more can be found from searching the Internet or talking to the bank manager.

The other major factor is the expertise of the trader wanting to get involved in e-commerce.   If the trader's strength lies in traditional marketing, it might have to hand over the e-commerce side to a company that is competent in the e-commerce field.

Other factors in choosing a provider are how any shopping carts, etc. integrate into the system (or does PSP provide its own templates).

Alternatives to credit cards

Many potential customers do not have credit cards and almost all systems are based on collecting money via credit cards.   An option that lets these customers purchase goods or services is the *'pay-by-phone'* system. Everyone is now familiar with premium-rate phone calls. It is used for entering competitions, taking part in television votes, chat lines and many other areas.

This technique can be used to collect money, especially for relatively small sums. When the user indicates an interest in buying goods or services, the browser downloads a dialler applet (a mini-application program).   The applet stops the Internet session and dials a premium-rate number.

This system is limited, since it does not work with ADSL, cable modems or leased lines.   It is only useful for those who are accustomed to using similar services. Other will probably find these schemes too unusual and a bit dubious. Web Redialler from Magenta Systems, and ChargitDIAL operate such schemes and have the task of making the system widely acceptable.

Other methods include Pre-pay cash cards and the Paybox direct debit via mobile phone. Since both require some previous setting up, they will not work for most customers.

Shopping baskets

The web site sells through customers selecting items and providing delivery and financial details. The software to achieve this varies from simple JavaScript programs to giant database-linked programs.
There are three approaches:

- The interfaces are written in-house.
- The templates supplied by a processing company are customised to the trader's requirements.
- Store-building software is purchased and developed to the trader's needs.
- The whole process is handed over to a service provider.

The finished product must integrate with the credit card processing system. If the processing company supplies the templates, or if one company is undertaking the entire order processing, the ordering interface is guaranteed to match the rest of the system.
If interfaces are home-grown, either using a programming language or store-building software, then a prior check should be made with the provider to confirm that the finished product is acceptable to them.
The shopping system has to match the expected turnover. It is easy to run up a five-figure bill, when all that was required was a simple system. The levels of complexity are:

Small inventory – All items fit on one page and can be accommodated with a simple form.
Medium inventory – A shopping basket is organised at client end.
Large inventory – A shopping basket is organised at server end.

With traditional companies, the ordering system has to work with the existing order processing system.

Considerations when choosing a store-builder package include:

- It should provide a large number of template options.
- If required, it should support animated GIFs, Flash animations, audio clips, video clips.
- If required, it should support frames, CSS, JavaScript, XML.
- If required, it should support cookies, hit counters, banners.
- It should be able to import from text files, databases and spreadsheets.
- It should make every customer step ultra-explicit, with clear buttons taking the user to the next stage.
- It should be easy for customers to remove items from the shopping list.
- It should allow customers to search the product catalogue.
- It should always indicate the "cost so far" of the items in the cart, including any tax and shipping charges.
- It should take into account the country in which the buyer is resident.

The product should also support UK VAT rates. UK customers pay VAT on most goods (if in doubt, check with Customs & Excise www.hmce.gov.uk).
Customers in the EU, other than those in the UK, are charged the UK VAT rate. Customers in the EU, who are registered for VAT, are charged the price minus the VAT charge (when proof of their VAT registration is provided). Customers outside the EU are charged the price minus the VAT charge.

Actinet Catalog is the market leader in shopstore creation and it creates output in HTML for the site along with CGI/Perl scripts (this means checking whether the ISP must allow storage of CGI scripts on its site).
The steps in creating a site with Actinet Catalog are:

- Enter the company details.
- Enter the product details (perhaps by importing an existing database).
- Enter the required payment details – COD, invoice with order, credit card
- If credit card,
  - choose to link to a PSP such as WorldPay, NetBanx, etc.
  - choose to use your own local merchant.
- Choose a layout template or create a customised layout
- Preview the site out locally and, if it works, upload it to the ISP./.

Other commonly used storebuilders are EROL, StoreBuilder, ShopFactory, ColdFusion, and ecBuilder.

Programming and JavaScript

This book covers more than one programming language, and as such, this chapter covers the theory and techniques of programming in general, as it can be applied to any of these languages. It also covers the JavaScript language in particular. If the reader is interested in getting started in JavaScript immediately, then the programming methods section can be skipped over, and the reader can begin at the "*JavaScript and Java*" section.

Operating Systems

The *'Computer Technology'* chapter gave an overview of Operating Systems (OS). However, when discussing programming languages, the functionality of the operating system is worth examining in more detail. Very few programs indeed operate entirely at a low level, and instead they rely to varying degrees on functions provided by the OS. For example, Adobe Acrobat is available for both the PC and Macintosh, and the application developers made every effort to make the two packages as similar to one another as possible. Nonetheless, there are still differences, not the least of which is that the Windows version will have a Windows-style interface, using the *'Common Dialog Box'* method to open files.

In such languages, known as *'platform-dependent'* languages, the code which results from the programming process can only run on one type of computer, and quite often only on one operating system for that computer. Recently, however, there has been a surge in *'platform-independent'* languages, the foremost of which has been Sun's Java programming language. These languages rely on a *'Virtual Machine'* that interprets the Java code and converts it to machine code for the machine on which it is running.

Application use of platform functions

The application may make use of functions built in to the platform on which it is running, in a variety of ways. For example:

- Old DOS programs often used interrupt functions such as INT 21h, which would tell DOS to perform a function such as getting keyboard input, or displaying output to the monitor.
- UNIX code written in the C programming language has access to several functions which are not used in other platforms, such as the *'fork'* command and other process-related functions.
- All versions of Windows incorporate an API (Applications Programming Interface) that provides functions to applications, such as common dialog boxes, and access to graphical objects.
- Web based programming languages such as Java and JavaScript may be able to access DirectX objects, common dialogs, and web page elements. Server-side languages such as PHP may also access such facilities as online databases, or files on the server.
- Other application-specific scripting languages will access various elements of the data in that application. For example, the *'Lingo'* scripting language is used within Macromedia Director to manipulate multimedia objects in the Director movie.

The method in which these functions are used varies from one platform to the next and indeed from one programming language to the next. However, certain functions are common to almost all languages and operating systems, such as: opening, editing and closing files; acquiring input from the keyboard; and sending output messages to the monitor.

For any given language, the level to which the functions may be used on another system than that on which it was developed without modification, describes the *'portability'* of the language. For example, if code originally written for use on a UNIX system can be compiled and run on a Windows XP system, then it has a very good level of portability.

As can be seen from the examples above, multimedia and web applications often make use of programming languages. Indeed, this book looks at several multimedia and web-oriented languages, such as Lingo, PHP, and JavaScript. Many of the basics of these languages are similar to one another, so the next several pages will explain the basics concepts of programming in general.

Types of programming language

Programming languages can be classified in different ways. One method of classifying languages is to group them into *'assembled'*, *'interpreted'*, and *'compiled'* languages.

Assembled languages are those which use mnemonic codes to represent each machine code instruction. Since the mnemonics map one-to-one onto machine code commands, the assembler simply converts the mnemonic directly into its machine code equivalent, and assembles any macros that may be used.

Interpreted languages use commands that represent multiple machine code instructions, and the program is stored as a set of such instructions. Due to this setup, an *'interpreter'* is required any time such a program is executed. The interpreter turns each *'source'* command into several machine code instructions, and then executes them.

Compiled languages, like interpreted languages, use commands representing multiple machine code instructions. However, an interpreter is not used. Instead, the programmer uses a *'compiler'* to turn the entire set of source commands (the '*source code*') into assembly code instructions (known as '*object code*'), and these are then stored as an executable binary program file, which can be run at any time without an interpreter or compiler.

In addition, a compiler commonly uses another program, known as a <u>linker</u>. The linker, as its name suggests, is used to link multiple object code files together into one executable. This allows the source code to be developed in modular fashion, with each source file being used to create a single object, and all the objects being drawn together at the time of compiling the program (i.e. at '*compile time*').

Another distinction between languages is the '*level*' at which they operate. Typically, this distinction is between '*Low Level Languages*' and '*High Level Languages*'. This '*level*' represents the amount of abstraction employed. As such, the lowest level of language is machine code itself, followed by assembly language.

Those languages that employ more abstraction are called High Level Languages. This abstraction means the programmer need not worry about the precise contents of CPU registers, low-level control of program flow, and so on, leaving them free to think more about what the program should actually achieve. Languages such as Pascal, Basic, and JavaScript are all considered High Level Languages.

There is another classification, that of 4GL. The 4GL, or Fourth Generation Language, is a term that refers to those languages that work at an even higher level. They typically use built-in routines that carry out a major task in one or two simplified steps. For example, SQL is a 4GL – an SQL programmer can perform a database query in just one command, while a C programmer would likely have to write hundreds of lines of code to perform the same function. 4GLs, however, are very limited in scope, being only able to work with the data they are designed for. SQL, for example, is incapable of being used in any environment other than a database.

Code levels

As explained above, the code in any high-level language which is entered by the programmer is the '*source*' code, and the code which is then created by the compiler or interpreter is the '*object*' code. It is unusual for the object code to be directly executed without first performing a process called linking, which is explained later in this chapter. Once the object files are linked, the final executable program is produced. In a typical system, the object code does not consists entirely machine-readable instructions – it also includes procedure names, variable names and other such details, so that the object can be linked to any other object that knows the correct procedures and/or variables to use.

In fact, for a few programming languages, the object code is not directly executable at all. The most widely used language in this category is Java, which uses the term '*byte code*' instead of object code, to indicate the fact that the compiled Java must be again interpreted into local machine instructions. Despite this, in the majority of cases 'object code' is synonymous with 'machine code', the actual numeric instructions that are interpreted by the processor as instructions to carry out.

History of programming languages

Although there are almost countless numbers of programming languages which have been developed over the years, a few stand out as having a major impact on computing:

In 1957, the programming language FORTRAN (FORmula TRANslation) was developed, and is widely considered to be the first compiled programming language. FORTRAN went through several versions, but is no longer in widespread use. Nonetheless, concepts developed by IBM for FORTRAN have been present in programming languages ever since – such as 'if' and 'do' statements.

BASIC (Beginners All-purpose Symbolic Instruction Code) was another early programming landmark. Developed as an interpreted language in the 1960's in Dartmouth College for non-programmers, BASIC has been adapted for various systems and is still around in the form of Visual BASIC. In this form, it is still the single most widely used programming language today, despite its simplicity and, according to some, its tendency to instil bad habits (such as poorly structured code) in programmers.

Pascal, a compiled language developed in 1971 by Niklaus Wirth, was for a long time one of the most popular languages, especially in academic circles, because it was developed as a teaching language. It was one of the most well-known proponents of such features as '*strong typing*' to encourage good programming practices.

In 1972, shortly after Pascal was developed, another compiled language became as popular outside of academia as Pascal did within. Although it was intended to be strongly typed, the C programming language was primarily developed for creating efficient code in a High Level Language, and as a result it did contain some features that could undermine the concept of strong typing. Also, one of its primary goals was portability; and although its portability is highly questionable today, at the time of its introduction it was more portable than most widely used languages.

In 1983, Bjarne Stroustrup introduced the C language to the concept of 'Object-Oriented Programming' (OOP). The resulting language used the same general syntax as C, but introduced new capabilities relating to objects and their attributes. This language, called C++, is now in widespread use, as Visual C++ and other packages, although its complexity often puts off new programmers.

Between 1990 and 1995, the Java programming language was developed, and was eventually introduced by Sun Microsystems. It was intended to be truly platform independent, yet powerful enough to write entire large-scale applications. To do this, it required a Virtual Machine to be written for any computer system on which the Java code was to run. However, once a VM is created, the Java code is truly portable, being able to run on literally any computer system. This made it ideally suited to small pieces of code known as '*applets*' to run on web pages, where the audience may be using a wide variety of hardware and operating systems.

This gives Java its unusual status of requiring both a compiler and an interpreter. The source code is compiled into an intermediate state known as 'byte code', which cannot be directly executed but must be interpreted by the VM.

JavaScript is a loosely-typed (see later), interpreted language which is based on Java, but is far less comprehensive. It is used to create dynamic web pages, and as such any JavaScript code must be embedded within an HTML document.

Features of programming languages

The syntax of different programming languages is the most striking difference to the casual viewer. After all, a program which uses a very different syntax will have completely different function names, possibly a different program structure, will use different symbols to represent different features, and may even arrange the parts of the source code in a different order.

However, there are more profound differences between languages, which only become apparent after the initial difference in syntax is overcome.

These differences include the following:

Strong Typing

A '*strongly typed*' language is one that will not allow the programmer to 'mix' variables of different types without an explicit conversion. For example, you may not add the integer number 32, and the string variable '12' together, unless you first convert the string '12' into the integer number 12. A '*loosely typed*' language, however, will allow this, either by converting the string without having been told to do so, or by mixing data types, often with disastrous results.

A strongly typed language also checks that parameters passed into procedures or functions are of the correct type, and will not compile the program if the types do not match. Again, an explicit type conversion can overcome this.

Static and Dynamic Typing

Strong typing should not be confused with '*static typing*' and '*dynamic typing*'. A statically typed language requires that variables must be declared to be a certain type <u>before</u> the variable is used. In a dynamically typed language, the variables may be used without being declared, and the compiler or interpreter will automatically assign the variable a type depending on the context. Dynamic typing is useful on small programs, but for large projects, static typing is generally considered to be more useful.

Note, however, that even in a dynamically typed language, even though there is no *requirement* to declare variable types before their use, it is still *optional*, so it is quite legal and is in fact good practice to declare variables even in a dynamically typed language.

Procedural languages

The 'conventional' programming model is that of the procedural language. This model relies on two main concepts: modularity, and scope. The '*modular*' aspect of procedural languages is reflected in the splitting of programs into one or more 'units', any one of which may call on any other unit to perform a task. For example, the source code for a small e-commerce program might have a main program unit, and several sub-programs to perform tasks such as browsing stock, ordering items, and paying invoices. These subprograms would typically come in the form of 'procedures', hence the origin of the term 'procedural language'.

The division of tasks into procedures allows several benefits over 'monolithic' program design (where all code is contained in a single code section). The main benefit is that it is more readable, and is therefore easier to maintain, expand and debug. The next great benefit of modularity is the ability to separate units of code from the main source code file, meaning that they can be developed and maintained independently of one another, perhaps even by completely different groups of programmers. The units can also then be designed with flexibility in mind, so that some units can be useful in other projects as well. This is known as 'code re-use' and is highly desirable as it greatly reduces development time.

The second major component of a procedural language is the concept of '*scope*'. This goes hand-in-hand with the idea of modularity, in that scope defines which variables are available to certain modules. See the section on 'variables' later for more information on scope.

Although the concept of modularity is present in more recent programming models, the general structure of procedural driven programming is losing popularity to event driven or object oriented programming styles.

Event Driven languages

Procedural languages suffer from one major limitation: the flow of program execution at any given point in the program is restricted to the options which are written into the source code. To provide a higher degree of user control over the finished application, an '*event driven*' programming model can be used instead. While event driven languages maintain the concepts of modularity and scope, they also introduce '*events*'. An event is, as the name suggests, simply an occurrence that can be used as a trigger for a certain piece of code to begin executing. Any code activated by an event is known as an '*event handler*'.

A common event type is to detect when the user clicks on a button. A typical application might have several buttons, and each of these buttons is associated with an event which is triggered when the button is clicked. Each event might trigger a separate event handler, or several events might trigger the same event handler but with different parameters. For example there may be a 'save' button, a 'save as' button, and a 'save and quit' button. Clicking on 'save' might trigger the SaveFile event. Clicking 'save as' might trigger the SaveFileAs event, while clicking the 'save and quit' button might trigger the SaveAndQuit event.

It is even possible for event handlers to trigger other events during their processing, which can sometimes be a source of problems and requires programmers to put a degree of care into the timing of events as well as simply the flow of program execution.

Object Orientation

An *'Object Oriented Programming'* language uses data constructs called *'objects'*, which each have a set of *'attributes'*. Each object in the code typically represents one coherent set of information relating to one item. For example, in C++ we might introduce a 'book' object, which would contain such attributes as 'full_title', 'author', and 'price'.

The object can also have code associated with it. Each function or procedure associated with the object is known as one of its *'methods'*, and is used to operate only on that type of object. For example the 'book' object might have methods such as 'order_book' or 'contact_publisher'.

However, an object on its own cannot be used. Instead, we need to create one or more *'instances'* of that object. Each instance is a separate object, given attributes and methods as appropriate to the object type. For example, we could declare an instance of the 'book' object, calling that instance 'Multimedia_handbook', or an array of objects, perhaps called 'books_in_stock'.

Object oriented languages include several other related concepts. One of these in *'encapsulation'*, which is the concept that no object can rely on the internal operation or data of another object. If an object has need of data from another object, it must use one of that object's methods to retrieve that data. This allows the object to supply only data that should be necessary to other objects, reducing the interdependency of code produced.

Another concept in object orientation is *'polymorphism'*, which is the idea that a method can be implemented differently from one object to another. For example, imagine two objects, 'card_game' and 'music_album', both of which have a 'play' method. When the card_game=>play method is used, it will let the user play a card game. When the music_album=>play method is used, however, it will play music for the user, even though the name of the method is identical.

Furthermore, most object-oriented languages include the concept of *'inheritance'*, where an object can be considered to be a *'child'* of another object, and will inherit it's *'parents'* attributes and methods, as well as adding some of its own. For example, we could define an 'imported_book' object, which is a child of the 'book' object, but adds attributes such as 'shipping_cost' and 'overseas_shipping_address'.

How objects work in practice is looked at later in this chapter.

Programming concepts

Although high level programming languages are different, there is a range of factors that they all have in common. The following sections illustrate some of the more important programming concepts that are to be found in programming languages.

Variables

All high level computer languages store and use values, whether they are numbers, characters, or true/false logical values. Sometimes these values are *"constants"* - there are always 7 days in a week, π is always 3.142, and so on.

A variable, on the other hand, is a store whose contents can be altered. A variable has a name and a value. For example, we could create a string variable called name and give it the value *"Davy"*. We could have given it any other value such as *"Sammy"*, *"3CP0"* or *"1.25"*.

Each variable has a certain *'type'*. The type of variable determines what kind of data it may store. Again, the types supported by various languages differs, but the following illustrates some data types which are available in virtually all programming languages:

Integers	Whole numbers, such as 12 or 15,000. Typically, integers are 16-bit numbers which range from -32767 to $+32768$. However, in some languages there are 'signed' and 'unsigned' integers, with unsigned integers having a range from 0 to 65535.
Floating Point	Also called *'real'* numbers, these are numbers that incorporate a decimal point. For example, 1.5, or 3.141. In many languages these are split into *'single precision'* and *'double precision'* types, with double precision providing greater precision to several decimal places. Floating point numbers also allow a much larger range of values than integers, but are not always 100% accurate at storing such large numbers.
Boolean	This is a single binary logical value of either TRUE or FALSE, named after Charles Boole who developed this logic system. A Boolean value can be used, for example, to represent whether a tick-box has been checked.

Array An array is a collection of variables of the same type. Each variable is *'indexed'*, usually by number, starting with zero. For example, if an array called sales contained 15 integer variables, the 5th integer would typically be accessed by typing sales[4].

String A string is a shorthand way of saying 'an array of characters'. And that is precisely what a string is: several ASCII characters linked together to form a string of text. For example a string variable could contain the string "hello world" or "42".

In some languages, the string starts with an 8-bit integer describing how long the string is. However, it has become more normal now to use *'zero-terminated'* strings; i.e. the end of a string is indicated by a NULL value, a process which is often transparent even to the programmer.

In addition to its *type*, each variable also has a *scope*. The scope of the variable defines which parts of the program code can access the variable's contents. Generally, there are three types of scope for any variable:

- **Global** A Global variable is one which is defined at the start of the main program. It is available for any part of the code to access.
- **Local** A local variable is one which is defined at the start of a subprogram. It is considered to be 'local' to that subprogram, and can only be accessed from within that subprogram. Local variables only exist for the duration of the subprogram – their memory is deallocated once the subprogram completes execution, and their contents are lost.
- **Static** This is a local variable whose contents are not lost when the subprogram completes execution. In this way, the subprogram may maintain information from one procedure call to the next. This is useful for certain functions, but it is a design decision whether to use static variables, or global variables for such information.

Operators

A variable is not much use if its contents cannot be changed. *'Operators'* are the symbols that are used to assign, compare and alter the contents of variables. The types of operator that can be used vary depending on the type of variable that is being used. The *'assignment'* operator, which is used to give a variable its value in the first place, is typically the '=' character, although some languages used ':=' instead.

Some common operators are listed below:

Operator	Typical Symbols	Meaning
Equality	==	Tests two variables to see if their contents are the same. In some languages, using '=' instead of '==' can have unpredictable and undesirable results.
Inequality	!= or <>	Tests two variables to see if their contents are different.
Greater Than	>	Tests the first variable to see if its contents are greater, numerically, than the contents of the second variable. Typically only applies to integers and floating point numbers.
Less Than	<	Tests the first variable to see if its contents are less, numerically, than the contents of the second variable. Typically only applies to integers and floating point numbers.
Addition	+	Adds the contents of two variables, typically integers or floating point numbers. For example: **results = var1+var2;**
Subtraction	-	Subtracts the contents of one variable from another, typically integers or floating point numbers. For example: **results = var1-var2;**
Multiplication	*	Multiplies the contents of two variables, typically integers or floating point numbers. For example: **results = var1*var2;**
Division	/	Divides the contents of one variable from another, typically integers or floating point numbers. For example: **results = var1/var2;**

In addition, each language must decide on an order of *'operator precedence'*. In any complex mathematical calculation, this will determine which parts of the calculation are carried out first. For example, consider this statement:

    results = var1+var2*var3

Should the program add var1 and var2, and *then* multiply by var3, or should it multiply var2 by var3 and *then* add the result on to var1? This question is answered by the precedence of the operators. Although languages use different operators, and may have slightly different orders of precedence, it is a rule that multiplicative (i.e. multiply or divide) operators are carried out before additive (i.e. add or subtract) operators.

So, in the example above, var2 would be multiplied by var3, *before* adding to var1. If this is not the desired effect, then the programmer must use brackets to force the compiler to perform the addition first, as in the following example:

    results = (var1+var2)*var3

Subprograms

The way in which functions, procedures, variables and other contents of the source code are structured. For example, any *'strongly typed'* language requires variables to be defined before they can be used. In most such cases, there is a *'variable declaration block'*, where all variable types are declared, at the top of each block of code.

The program structure also defines how *'subprograms'* may be used. A *'subprogram'* may be one of three types:

- **Macros** A macro is simply a single mnemonic line which the compiler or interpreter substitutes with a block of code, almost as if a 'copy and paste' had been performed. As such, they are not truly subprograms, but are included here because they do affect the structure of the code.
- **Functions** A function is a subprogram which performs a specific task, and then *'returns'* a single value. For example, the confirm() method in the JavaScript programming language is a function which displays a dialog box with 'OK' and 'Cancel' buttons, and returns the boolean value TRUE if 'OK' is pressed, and FALSE if 'Cancel' is pressed.
- **Procedures** A procedure is a subprogram that does not return a single value. Instead it carries out its tasks, possibly altering the contents of the parameters (see below), and then returns to the program that called the procedure.

Procedures and Functions have to be *'declared'* prior to their use. For example, say we wished to create a function called 'find_next_prime' in JavaScript, which returns an integer value, this might be declared as follows:

```
function find_next_prime() {
          .....
          return next_prime;
}
```

This shows a functions which is used to calculate the next prime number in a sequence. (It is assumed that the code to actually do this is found in the area marked '......') Once the correct number is found, it is passed back to the controlling program via the return command.

There are the differences in syntax between different programming languages. For example, while Pascal explicitly states whether a subprogram is a function or a procedure, JavaScript uses only functions, which can be treated as procedures simply by failing to return a value. In some languages this would be an error, but in JavaScript this is normal practice. However, the programmer must be careful not to use a function with no return value as if it was a function that *did* have a return value, since this will have unpredictable results.

However, a procedure or a function that is only able to use the same variables as the main program, is limited in its usefulness. In order to make functions and procedures more useful in eliminating redundant code, subprograms can be sent the contents of any particular variables, through *parameters*, as explained later.

Pre-defined routines

It is a basic principle of programming that programmers should not 're-invent the wheel'. In other words, existing code should be used as much as possible so that new code does not have to be developed, because using existing code cuts down on development and testing of code. Re-use of code can come in several forms:

- A few lines of code cut-and-pasted from one routine to the other.
- A procedure or function that is copied from another program or a library of routines, and re-used with few or no modifications.
- Use of pre-defined routines.

Pre-defined routines include those which are built in to the programming language, as well as those which come as part of the libraries of routines that come with the language. These provide a wide range of basic functions, such as mathematical calculations, basic input and output, or simple text processing. Some of these are fundamental to proper operation of a program, while others are simply aids to productivity.

However, take care when using pre-defined libraries; including just one routine from a library might force the linker to link the entire library into the project, resulting in the program being considerably larger than it needs to be. If size or efficiency are major concerns, this might play an important part in deciding whether to use pre-defined routines.

Parameters

A parameter is simply a variable that is accepted by a function or procedure. The subprogram specifies a parameter name, and can refer to whichever variable has been accepted by that parameter name for the duration of the subprogram. This means that the code which calls the subprogram can pass any variable of the same type as a parameter, which is useful in reducing redundancy (see later). For example:

```
set_title("hello world!");
```

This line of code passes a string as a parameter. In this case, the string is a constant value specified as part of the code, but it could just as easily be any other string variable. For example, the declaration of the subprogram might be as follows:

```
function set_title(new_title) {
          ......
}
```

This declares a function called set_title, and informs the interpreter that the function accepts a single parameter, called new_title. If this function were called by the line of code shown earlier, then any references to new_title within the function would in fact refer to the text "hello world!". If, however, the function was called with some other text as the parameter contents, then it would refer to that text instead. In this way, using parameters can make a function more generic.

Again, there are differences in syntax as to how the parameters are passed. JavaScript is loosely typed, and is therefore able to set the type of parameters accepted according to the data they contain. Other languages quite often require the programmer to specify the type of variables to be accepted as parameters. For example, the same parameters in Pascal might be passed into the procedure as follows:

```
procedure set_title(new_title: string);
begin
......
```

The new_title parameter in the declaration above is known as a '*formal parameter*', while the actual value which is passed into the procedure ("Hello world!") is known as the '*actual parameter*'. When the processor is executing code inside the set_title procedure, it can refer to the "Hello world!" string by the variable name of new_title.

The parameters passed can be used in one of two ways: pass-by-value, or pass-by-reference.

A parameter that is <u>passed by value</u> is compiled such that the actual parameter's contents are copied into a temporary memory storage area, until the end of the subprogram. The subprogram is free to do as it pleases with the contents of this temporary variable, and it will not affect the actual variable in the main program.

A parameter that is <u>passed by reference</u>, however, does not create a temporary copy. Instead, the subprogram is merely told where in memory to find the original copy. Therefore, any changes made to the contents of that variable within the subprogram, will affect the variable in the main program as well.

Passing by value is useful for situations where the subprogram will create data based on input variables, but might have to change the contents of those variables in order to do so. Passing by reference is more useful in situations where the parameter's contents are intended to be changed as a result of the subprogram's operations.

Parameter passing and use of subprograms have several benefits:
- More readable code. The code can be split into 'chunks', with each chunk (a procedure or function) performing a specified task. The smaller chunk of code is easier to read and understand.
- The main program is also smaller and easier to understand, since most of the functions are performed in subprograms.
- Easier debugging. Errors can sometimes easily be tracked down to a specific subprogram, which could save the programmer hours of work stepping through a very large main program.
- However, the most important benefit is that of streamlining the code, and eliminating redundancy, by using parameters and generic subprograms.

Note however, that it is important to name functions and procedures appropriately. If a procedure is simply named "procedure_x", then the program which calls the procedure does not gain the benefit of being easy to read, since the intention of the procedure being called will not be immediately obvious.

Streamlining code and eliminating redundancy

Consider the following JavaScript program that converts two numbers from Celsius to Fahrenheit:

```
first_celsius = 12;
second_celsius = 20;
first_fahrenheit = first_celsius*9;
first_fahrenheit = first_fahrenheit/5;
first_fahrenheit = first_fahrenheit+32;
second_fahrenheit = second_celsius*9;
second_fahrenheit = second_fahrenheit/5;
second_fahrenheit = second_fahrenheit+32;
```

As can be seen, this program performs several arithmetic operations to complete each conversion. This example only converts two Celsius measurements; if a large number of conversions were required this program would quickly become even more unwieldy. Procedures can be used to streamline this piece of code.

The following procedure could be written to perform the conversion on any integer parameter:

```
int convert_to_fahrenheit(int celsius_input) {
        int fahrenheit_output;
        fahrenheit_output = celsius_input*9;
        fahrenheit_output = fahrenheit_output/5;
        fahrenheit_output = fahrenheit_output+32;
        return(fahrenheit_output);
}
```

This function accepts a single integer parameter called celsius_input. It copies the contents of this variable into another variable called fahrenheit_output, which exists only for the duration of this function. This value is then converted arithmetically, and the result is returned out of the function. Thus, the main program can make use of this function as follows:

```
first_celsius = 12;
second_celsius = 20;
first_fahrenheit = convert_to_fahrenheit(first_celsius);
second_fahrenheit = convert_to_fahrenheit(second_celsius);
```

This demonstrates the advantages of using subprograms and parameters. This code is easier to read and understand, since the function does all the arithmetic work, and we are left simply with two lines of code which use an appropriately named function to do the conversion.

The code is also smaller. Furthermore, if even more conversions were to be carried out, they would require just one function call each, instead of three lines of code. This method of eliminating redundancy by performing operations on generic parameters is known as '*modular design*'.

Program Structure

Being able to turn a single line of high level language source code into machine code is an important part of every programming language, but a single line of code cannot achieve very much. Every programming language therefore has several '*control constructs*' that allow the programmer to determine the flow of processing when the program executes. These control constructs fall into three categories:

- **Sequence** The normal operation of a program is that after one command executes, the next command begins. If no other constructs are used, the program will be executed, one command after another, from start to finish, in order.
- **Selection** This construct offers multiple paths through the code, and uses some form of comparison operator in order to select which path to take. The simplest and most common type of selection is an 'if' statement.
- **Iteration** This construct is used to make the program 'loop' round, performing one command or a group of commands continually, until a certain comparison is resolved. The simplest form of iteration is based on a countdown – the 'for' statement can be used to iterate the commands contained within, a fixed number of times, for example.

The constructs which are available from one programming language to the next do vary, as does the syntax of those constructs. However, the following illustrates the general methods employed by the most common structures:

Selection structures		

If..then..else	The if statement evaluates an expression, and <u>only</u> carries out the code within if that expression evaluates to TRUE. It may also have an else part, which is only carried out if the expression evaluates to FALSE. In many languages the 'then' word is omitted.	`if(yourage<18) {`
		`        alert("You are too young!");`
		`}`
		`else {`
		`        alert("You may watch this movie.");`
		`}`

Case..select	This statement evaluates an expression, and then chooses one piece of code to carry out, depending on the result of that evaluation. Some languages call this a 'switch' statement instead, and most provide for a 'default' selection if no other match is found.	`switch(yourage) {`
		`        Case <18: alert("Too Young!");`
		`        Case 18: alert("Just old enough!");`
		`        Case >18: alert("Old enough.");`
		`}`

Iteration structures		

For..to	This type of iteration repeats the code, normally a number of times based on a single constant or variable. The syntax of a for loop varies widely, and is not always immediately obvious. The example shows a for loop that is designed to iterate 10 times.	`for(count=0; count<10; count=count+1) {`
		`        alert("the for loop is continuing");`
		`}`

Repeat..until	This structure is used to repeat a certain piece of code over and over, until a certain expression evaluates to TRUE. The repeat statement evaluates this statement at the end of the structure, so it must carry out the code at least once. Some languages use a 'do...while' construct instead; do not confuse this with a 'while...do' construct!	`count=0;`
		`do {`
		`        alert("the repeat loop continues");`
		`        count=count+1;`
		`}`
		`while (count<10);`

While..do	This structure repeats the code within, as long as the expression evaluates to TRUE. If the expression is not TRUE to begin with, then the code within is never executed.	count=0;
		while(count<10) {
		    alert("while loop is continuing...");
		    count=count+1;
		
		}

Commenting

Every high level programming language promotes commenting. Commenting is simply the activity of including a non-executable piece of text in the source code, to describe the code further. In other words, the comment is a piece of text in the source code which is ignored by the compiler.

Comments come in two forms:

      Block comments, which include several lines of comments in a single block; and

      Inline comments, which include a single line of comments, possibly after a line of code.

The comments are separated from the actual code by using a specific symbol at the beginning and end of the comment. In some languages, inline comments use a different symbol than block comments, and do not require a terminating symbol. The following table shows some comments in various languages:

Comment type	Comment example
Typical block comment	/* This is a block comment in JavaScript, PHP, C, C++ and some other languages */ { This is a block comment in Pascal }
Typical inline comment	// These are inline comments in PHP, // JavaScript, C++ and some other languages

Both types of comments are useful for a variety of purposes:

- Documenting the accompanying code. Inline comments can be used to describe what each line of code does, especially useful when the code is optimised and may be difficult to read.
- Documenting subprograms. A block comment can describe the parameters, functions, and return values of each subprogram, making it easier for other programmers to utilise the procedure.
- Version management. Although comments are far from the best way to do this, (it would be up to the programmer to keep the comments up to date) it is better than no version management at all.

Consider the conversion between Celsius and Fahrenheit. It could be written in JavaScript as a single line:

    FH_temp=(C_temp*5/9)+32;

This line performs the conversion in one line. However, in order to do this, the line of code becomes much more dense, making it more difficult to understand. An inline comment could therefore be added to inform the reader as to the line's exact purpose:

    FH_temp=(C_temp*5/9)+32; /* Convert from Celsius to Fahrenheit */

This makes the source code easier to understand.

Working with files

Most programming languages allow the author to access files on the hard disk. In every programming language, the procedure for doing this involves three generic steps: opening the file, performing the read and/or write operations; and closing the file. If a file is not closed before the termination of the program, it can have unpredictable results, ranging from the file becoming unavailable to other programs, to possible corruption of data within the file.

There are several types of file operation that can be performed once a file has been opened, including:

- Reading data from the file.
- Writing data to the file. This generally implies that the file is empty or is to be over-written; if this is not the case, see 'appending', below.
- 'Seeking' to a new location within the file. Read and write operations move in serial fashion, from one byte of data to the next. The seek operation allows the programmer to move 'place' backwards and forwards within the file so that data can be read or written in direct fashion instead.
- Appending data to the end of the file. In other words, adding new data, and making the file larger in the process.

Typically, the file opening phase is performed by a function built into the programming language, and at this point, in most languages, the programmer must specify in which 'mode' to open the file: read, write, or append. Obviously, a file opened in read mode cannot be saved to, and although some languages allow the programmer to read from files opened in write mode, this depends on the methods used and the details of the language itself.

Program Development

Computer programs do not materialise out of thin air - a program should not be written unless it has an identifiable objective. A programming project which is not properly analysed and designed is likely to become subject to various problems, including failing to address the problem appropriately; running over time and/or over budget; not matching user expectations; and of course 'feature creep'.

The *'Project Design'* chapter of this book, although aimed at multimedia projects, also contains several elements that apply to software design. The development of a program should follow a well-defined development procedure. Some examples of such procedures include:

- The Software Development Life Cycle model.
- The Prototyping Model
- The Spiral Model.
- The Rapid Application Development model.

The *'Software Development Life Cycle'* is effectively simply the waterfall method, as described in the *'Project Design'* chapter, but applied to software development. The SDLC is the basic method of software development, and consists of Analysis, Design, Coding, Testing, and Maintenance of the project.

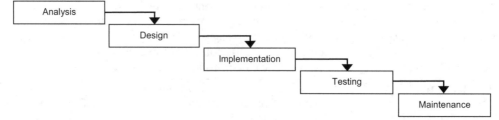

The exact steps into the model vary. For example, *'implementation'* may be called *'coding'* or *'developing'*, or the *'testing'* phase may be broken into multiple test types. Some models do not include a maintenance phase, while others include an Evaluation or Distribution phase instead.

In all cases, however, the first phase should begin with a Feasibility Study, and contain a Requirements Analysis as well as a Task Analysis, as in any other type of project. However, the design, implementation (coding), and testing of a software project use different methods than those for a multimedia project, as explained later.

More refined Life Cycle models based on this one, tend to emphasise that one phase will rarely finish entirely before the next phase begins, without any need to return to previous phases. Such models will allow the developers to freely return to earlier phases to make changes where necessary, while still attempting to follow the model where reasonably possible.

The *'Prototyping Model'* is largely an adaptation of the SDLC to include prototyping techniques. See the *'Project Design'* chapter for an explanation of Prototyping. The prototyping model is particularly useful on certain programming projects where the finished product includes a large amount of user interaction. In such a case, the use of large number of prototypes allow the user many chances to influence the final interface of the product. Prototyping is also useful where the product requirements are ambiguous.

The *'Spiral model'* is a software development model which 'loops round' in multiple passes through four *'task regions'*, as shown in the diagram below. The development begins at the centre of the spiral, and begins looping outward, in most cases creating prototypes as appropriate, until a number of *'passes'* round the spiral have been completed. The number of passes required varies. Some projects will specify a set number of prototypes before an *'operational prototype'* is produced, which is the last prototype before the product is complete. Other projects are more pliable, using the planning phase to decide whether to create a prototype, an operational prototype, or the final product in the upcoming spiral loop.

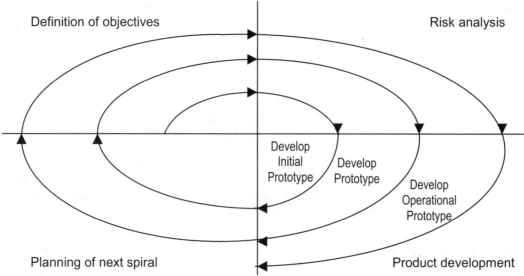

Using a spiral model makes it very difficult to create *'milestones'* in the project, making it less suitable for rigid contracts. Nonetheless, the spiral model can accommodate most phases of the waterfall model into the various parts of its spiral.

The '*Rapid Application Development*' (RAD) model is similar to the basic Life Cycle, but stresses fast production of code. This relies on software specifically designed for RAD or at least for quick code generation in general, and also places even greater importance on re-useable components. For example, Visual Basic or Visual C++ provide plenty of visual and automated tools to produce code quickly.

Software Design Phase

An unwritten rule of programming is *that "90% of the code takes 10% of the time, and 10% of the code takes 90% of the time"*. In other words, just a few badly-designed lines of code can result in a huge amount of work testing and debugging. For this reason, the Design Phase is often considered the most important of all phases in the Life Cycle, since it aims to produce code that requires as little debugging as possible.

Furthermore, the Design Phase must make such decisions as:

- Which programming language to use?
- What kinds of data structures will suit this project best?
- How will the program inputs will be acquired and validated?
- What kind of data will be output by the program?
- What naming convention should be applied to variables and subprograms?
- Should the code fragments be produced as '*monolithic*' code, or discrete object files?
- Will the project be expanded at a later date, and how can this expansion be made as painless as possible?
- How will the project interact with existing hardware and software?

In addition, the design phase actually comprises two different designs: the '*system design*', and the '*software design*'. The system design involves looking at the requirements for hardware and software that must be met before the development of code can begin. The software design is the actual preparation of a design document that will explain how to create a product that meets the requirements as specified in the Analysis Phase.

There are various approaches to Software Design, all of which attempt to create a '*logical design*', which should be easily translated into the '*physical design*' that will constitute the source code of the project. The following is a brief description of the most common approaches to Software Design.

Top-down design

In a top-down design method, the main program is considered to be an abstract '*task*'. This task is then broken down into '*sub-tasks*', which are slightly more specific. These sub-tasks are then hierarchically broken down further into even more specific sub-tasks, until the individual task elements become well enough defined. At this stage, the tasks become small and concrete enough that they can be implemented and understood easily.

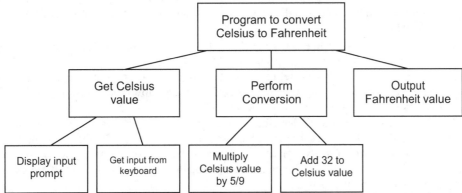

While this systematic '*breaking down*' of tasks goes on, it builds up a picture of a hierarchy of tasks.

For example, the diagram shows a comparatively small project being 'broken down' from an abstract task into several concrete sub-tasks. Each level of tasks on this chart can be easily turned into lines of source code. The '*higher up*' task blocks are created first, and can use '*stubs*' as placeholders for the subprograms it relies upon until they are completed.

A 'stub' is an extremely basic subprogram, which does none or almost none of the processing or Input/Output which the final subprogram is expected to perform. If the subprogram is relied on to provide data, then it will instead create 'fake' data from a few extremely simple lines of code. The stub program will be fleshed out at a later stage in program development, filling in the processing which was missing from the stub when it was first created.

Since stubs contain almost no code, and usually do not require any debugging since none of the code in a stub will appear in the final program, they are extremely quick to create. This allows higher-up parts of the task to use stubs as quick placeholders for functions so that the designer can concentrate on one task at a time instead of getting bogged down in sub-tasks.

However, on a larger scale, breaking down major projects into smaller areas allows these sub-tasks to be allocated to individual programmers or groups of programmers.

Bottom-up design

Over the years, the traditional top-down method of design has been criticised for its reliance on stub procedures. If, for example, one part of the program relies on the output of another part, then the code cannot be tested until every part is finished, leading to what is sometimes called the '*big bang method*' of testing, which is often seen as cumbersome. One reaction to the top-down philosophy is that of bottom-up programming, which as the name suggests, promotes program development from the lower levels first. In order to do this, the design still has to be broken down into small pieces; the difference is that the lowest parts of the hierarchy are created first.

Bottom-up design is more often called '*bottom-up programming*', because the design is essentially the same as a top-down design. The main difference is that the design is easily modified <u>during the coding</u> to incorporate additional sub-tasks into the design where it is found that a certain task needs to be broken down further than originally envisioned. Bottom-up design also often occurs alongside coding, since the bottom-up philosophy tries to specify sub-tasks in sufficient depth that coding can begin while the next sub-task is still being designed. This can have drawbacks, of course, such as ill-defined interfaces between subprograms. As a result, many projects combine aspects of top-down design and bottom-up design.

Test-driven design

It is often said that testing is the most important phase of the project. *"Test, test, and test again"* is the maxim of many a programmer. This has been reflected in the relatively recent design philosophy of '*test-driven design*'. This concept aims the entire design process at creating code that is easy to test properly. Not only is a comprehensive design document drawn up before the implementation begins, but the test driven method explicitly states that code is to be tested as it is written.

The general structure of activity under a test-driven design is as follows:

1) Consider a way to test the code.
2) Write enough code to fail the test, and no more.
3) Observe the code executing and failing the test.
4) Fix the code so that it should pass that test.
5) Observe the code executing. If it does not pass, return to step 4.
6) If you can think of another test, return to step 1.

This is the basic concept behind test-driven design, and follows a philosophy that getting working code is the only goal of programming at the end of the day. The pieces of code must still be tested when linked together in the final project, of course, but it makes the dreaded debugging a far less frightening prospect.

Design Methodologies

Choosing top-down or bottom-up design methods is fine for the 'broad design' of the project. However, the 'logical design' of the program still needs to be laid out, indicating where loops or decisions must be made. There are several formally defined methods of doing this:

- The simplest design methodology is pseudo code. At its simplest, this method is almost completely informal, yet can still be useful in converting a design into code.

- Charting methods can be invaluable in defining the flow of data and program execution in a project. There are a wide variety of charting methods, including Data Flow Diagrams, Entity-Relationship diagrams, Finite State Machines, and Nassi-Scheiderman Charts.

- The term '*formal methods*' specifically describes a group of languages such as 'Z Notation' or 'Vienna Development Method' which are based at least partly in mathetics. These methods use in-depth logic which, if carried out fully and correctly, can at least theoretically 'prove' that the code will function as it should. However, formal methods can be complex and difficult to learn, and as a result are mainly used on critical projects such as military software.

Pseudocode

This type of design notation is intended to create a detailed design of code that can be turned into actual program code with relative ease. To do so, pseudocode uses logical constructs such as loops and selections, but does so in a manner which is not specific to any programming language. The exact notation varies from one implementation of pseudocode to another, since after all it is not necessary to have a single "pseudocode language" as it will only be converted into code anyway. However, pseudocode is still easily recognisable since it tries to be both readable and concrete in order to fulfil its purpose. For example, the following shows a piece of pseudocode, and the corresponding program code in the JavaScript language:

```
Project countdown:                          function countdown() {
    For each number from 10 down to 1            int number;
        Print number                             for(number=10;number>0;number=number-1) {
    End for                                           document.write("<BR>"+number);
End project                                       }
                                             }
```

As can be seen, pseudocode follows the logic of the final program design closely, but is not language-specific and is also much more readable than final program code.

Flowcharting

Another popular but basic method for software design is the flowchart. As its name suggests, this method uses a chart to track the flow of program execution via the various possible routes through the program. Although there are a great variety of extensions to the standard, some of which are more widely used than others, the basic set of symbols consists of the following four:

	Terminal	This symbol denotes either the start or the end of the program. In a normal procedural language, there is only one start terminal, but there may be many end terminals, each one being the result of a different 'route' through the program.
	Process	The core of any program consists of the processing commands. These include calculations, logical operations, or any other commands that result in use of data in some way.
	Input / Output	This symbol is used to indicate an operation that results in any form of data input or output. Depending on the symbols used, this may or may not include saving or loading data to and from disk.
	Decision	This Represents a structure that can result in two or more potential paths of flow through the program. The basic decision consists of just two choices, typically 'Yes' and 'No', or 'True' and 'False'. However, the decision symbol can also be used to represent larger numbers of choices.

The flow of program execution is indicated by arrows, generally from the terminal at the top to the terminals towards the bottom of the diagram. If the program execution flows straight from top to bottom, using only inputs, processes and outputs, then this represents the basic sequential programming structure.

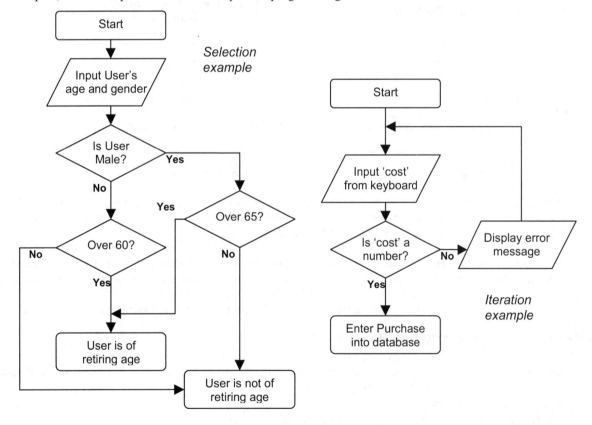

In order to represent the selection or iteration structures, the Decision icon must be employed. For example, the above diagrams are basic flowcharts illustrating the use of selection, in the first diagram, and iteration, in the second diagram.

Since most programs are too complex to represent fully with a single flowchart, it is not unusual for charts to be made at different levels of abstraction. For example, there may be one overall 'main' flowchart, with some processes in the chart being explained further in their own flowchart on another page.

Nassi-Schneiderman charts

A more in-depth charting method is the Nassi-Schneiderman method, which was created by Ike Nassi and Ben Schneiderman. It is a form of graphical flowchart that shows the different possibilities of flow of program execution through any task. It includes chart objects to represent various types of loops, decisions, and concurrent processes. The basic 'building block' of a Nassi-Schneiderman chart is a 'process', which is simply one or more lines of sequential executable code that performs a single activity. The process is drawn as a simple rectangle, and other constructs contain processes.

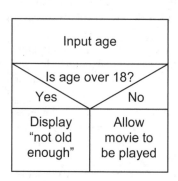

A simple 'if' construct

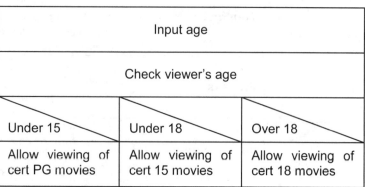

A basic 'case' construct

The two main types of selection are the 'if' and 'case' constructs. The two diagrams above show how these selection methods are represented within a Nassi-Schneiderman chart. The selection objects indicate the decision criteria, and the text beneath each diagonal line indicates the possible routes which may be taken depending on that criteria. Since the 'if' statement only has two possible outcomes, it splits into two possible processes, only one of which will be carried out in any given execution of the task. The 'case' or 'select' statement has multiple outcomes but operates in a similar fashion.

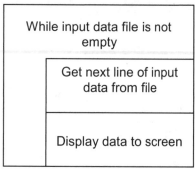

A 'while' loop   **A 'while' loop**

The two loops above indicate two of the more common iteration methods in programming languages. The 'L'-shape of the loop itself illustrates that the while loop tests its criteria before entering the code within, unlike the while loop which carries out the code and then tests the criteria at the end of the loop.

Selection and iteration constructs in Nassi-Schneiderman charts can contain other selections and iterations within, as well as simple processes. However, too many nested loops or decisions can make these charts unwieldy. Therefore, the chart is best when combined with some other design method that will reduce the complexity of the task to a manageable level. For example, top-down design could be used to break the task into sub-tasks, and then Nassi-Schneiderman charts could be created for each sub-task to make it easier to create code for each part of the project.

Software Implementation Phase

This phase is tied closely to the Software Design phase, in that it should produce the code that performs the functions which were specified in that previous phase. Since the programming language should have been decided on by this stage, the implementation phase consists mainly of the following tasks:

- Converting the design into code.
- Streamlining and optimising the code where applicable.
- Ensuring that the code follows any organisational or other standards which have been decided upon.
- Linking the various different code fragments into a cohesive whole.

This stage should also include some basic testing, a process sometimes called 'test as you go', which generally consists of unit testing (see the Testing phase for more details). The code should not be <u>fully</u> tested in the Implementation Phase but in the Testing Phase; however, there is no point collecting the procedures and functions together into a major program if those components may not even compile properly!

Coding the design

A project which has undergone rigorous and well-defined formal design procedures should convert relatively easily into source code. If there are ambiguities, then it may be best to return to the Design Phase, temporarily, to iron out these problems, rather than to simply write code as the programmer thinks best. Such ad-hoc programming may be suitable for very small or personal projects, but in a large software development project it is important that the details are laid out properly in the design to avoid incompatibilities between one area of the project, and another.

The exact process of turning a design into source code varies depending on the design methodology used. For example, in a top-down design, a single 'branch' may be allocated to one programmer or one group of programmers, who would design a procedure to carry out the task.

In all forms of implementation, however, documentation is <u>vital</u>. Every subprogram which is written should be accompanied by, at the very minimum, a block comment that describes the subprogram's input parameters, output parameters, return value (if present), general function, and any changes the function will make to global variables or file contents. Ideally, if time and money permitted, every line of code should be documented, the subprogram's functions should be fully documented in hardcopy, and every subprogram should be generalised as much as possible to increase the chances of re-using the subprogram elsewhere.

One school of thought is that documentation is "like sex – when its good, its great, and when its bad, its still better than none at all." However, bad documentation can give project managers a false sense of security – imagine if one programmer left their job, and another programmer had to work on his code, which was sparsely documented using shorthand, bad grammar, and assuming the reader knows something about the code already. This is little if any better than working with undocumented code, but with the added pressure that the programmer is expected to be able to understand it quickly 'because it has been documented'.

Another school of thought holds that documentation should be used only where it is not possible to write code that is self-explanatory. Writing self-explanatory code is difficult, but can be achieved partly by choosing variable and subprogram names that make sense and describe their contents; and also partly by sacrificing some optimisation (see below) by using operations that are simpler and easier to follow rather than more powerful.

Streamlining and optimising

As mentioned above, the code should be made as easy as possible to re-use elsewhere in the program. For example, the celsius conversion sub-program could easily be used anywhere in any program, as long as it was written in such a way that it did not change the input parameter, and performed the calculation on an input variable instead of a global variable. This streamlines the code from the programmer's point of view.

However, optimising, rather than streamlining the code can often be more beneficial to the end user. Optimisation means 'tweaking' the code so that it improves the program's performance when running. Optimisation can be carried out on individual pieces of code, particularly loops. A loop, such as "repeat..until" or "for..next", can take considerable time to carry out, if their contents are not well considered.

For example, a single screen message containing an update on the progress of the program will have a negligible performance impact. However, consider if the screen is to be updated after every one or two lines of code in a loop that may be executed several hundred, several thousand, or even millions of times. Suddenly the screen updates will be taking up far more processor time than the code itself, and the system will grind almost to a halt while the loop carries out.

This is an extreme example, of course, but illustrates the point that writing efficient code is far more important inside a loop than in any other part of the program. Things that may make no difference at all to the programs performance otherwise, may have a small impact on its efficiency if placed within a loop. For example:

- Floating point calculations take more time than integer operations. Use integers where reasonably possible, even if it means modifying the code a little.
- Similarly, some operations take longer than others. Multiplying an integer by 2, takes more time than doing a bitwise 'roll' one bit to the left, which generally produces the same result.
- Allocating memory is slow compared to general operations. Where possible, allocate memory before the loop begins, and deallocate it afterwards.
- Input and Output are slow. Minimise screen display and other outputs, and use buffers for IO where this can be done.
- Subprograms called from within a loop can be particularly troublesome. A procedure call requires several stack operations, and the subprogram itself should be fully optimised as well.

Organisational standards

Once again, a very small project may be able to get away without implementing any organisational standards whatsoever. However, the larger the project, and the more people working on it, the more important such standards become. These standards include:

- Naming of variables. How long should variable names be? Are they case sensitive? Should the type of variable be indicated in the variable name itself? (eg. NAME_SZ for a zero-terminated string) Should the scope (global and local) of variables be similarly indicated in their names? The design team must take care not to have duplicate variable names, even if one variable is global and the other is local.

- Naming of subprograms. How long should the names of functions and procedures be? Are they case sensitive? What should the name tell the programmer about the subprogram? The design team must take care not to have duplicate subprogram names, as well.

- Format of comments in the code. Should inline comments be tabulated for ease of reading? Should subprograms be prefaced by a comment block? Should large code chunks such as loops be prefaced by a comment block?

- Format of documentation. Should the code be documented fully within the comments of the code, in a separate text file, or even in hardcopy? What information should it contain? And what level of detail is required?

- Indentation. Although strictly speaking the level of indentation of source code is merely a formatting issue, it is so important to the readability (and therefore, maintenance and debugging) of code that it is worth mentioning separately.

A common technique is to indent the contents of any routine by two spaces, with the contents of any loop or decision being indented by a further two spaces. For example, the following piece of JavaScript code has its general contents indented. The contents of individual paths of the 'if' statement are further indented:

```
<script>
  browser=navigator.appName;
  version=navigator.appVersion;
  versionnumber=(version.indexOf("5."));
    if (browser=="Microsoft Internet Explorer" && versionnumber>0)
      location.href="iepage.htm";
    else
      location.href="nspage.htm"
</script>
```

This form of indentation aids readability since the viewer can easily see which pieces of code are contained within certain subsections of the code simply by how far they are indented from the left.

Linking code fragments

Individual subprograms are no use on their own. They must be linked together into a cohesive whole, before being compiled into a final product. This is known as 'linking'. Typically, linking of code refers to the process of compiling discrete code units into object code, and then combining these object codes into an executable file, a process which is performed by specific linking software.

However, it is also possible to 'include' code from one source file into another. This method means that the compiler itself, essentially 'cuts and pastes' the source code from one file into another, before compiling it all into one object file, typically an executable in itself. This is sometimes known as creating a 'monolithic' code block.

As mentioned earlier, it is another design decision as to whether the code should be designed to be monolithic or whether modular object code files should be created and linked together.

Testing Phase

A simple maxim of programming is "test, test, and test again." It is a fact that, from a quality assurance point of view, there can never be too much testing. Even major software houses, who can afford extensive testing on their products, cannot be guaranteed to produce applications which are error-free.

Partly for this reason, testing should not be confined to the Test Phase. Individual pieces of code should be tested before they are linked together. And in the real world, time constraints can sometimes mean that pressure to get a project completed may override the need to perform adequate testing, meaning that testing must continue even after the project is completed, with testing continuing late into the Maintenance Phase.

Testing normally takes several forms, including: Unit Testing, Component Testing, Integration Testing, Acceptance Testing, and possibly other types of testing.

Unit testing

As the name suggests, unit testing is any testing which is performed on an individual unit of code. Typically, this means one subprogram, perhaps created by an individual programmer or a small team. Unit tests are generally designed and carried out by the same people who created the unit, and is often carried out as part of the Implementation phase rather than the Testing phase. Since each unit test functions independently of other units, they need not be carried out in any particular order, instead simply testing each unit as it the coding reaches completion.

What constitutes a 'unit' depends on the project. It typically refers to a function or procedure that performs an end-level task as defined during the Design phase. In an object-oriented language, it might well include object classes and methods.

Most analysts agree that unit testing is the least effective type of testing; it reveals fewer faults than higher levels of testing. However, the faults that are found at this stage tend to be more fundamental, and of course if the same faults are found during component or integration testing, tracing the fault to the correct unit would be time consuming and prone to further errors.

Component testing

Unit testing is useful, but some units rely on data returned from other units. Replacing these function calls with 'stubs' that return static data allows unit tests to be carried out, but is much less valuable than testing the unit with real data as will be created in the final program. Meanwhile, some units cannot be fully tested when not used within a realistic context: again, a 'driver' function call allows the testing to be carried out but is not a thorough test. Both of these problems can be overcome, to some degree, by '*component testing*'.

Also called "Integration Unit testing", this form of test involves linking a limited number of units together to test that they interact properly. A component can occasionally consist of just one unit, when that unit recursively calls itself. However, in most cases, component testing involves at least two units, which are compiled and linked together. In this case, the primary purpose is to detect faults in the interface between two units.

A strategy known as '*incremental testing*' uses component tests extensively. This philosophy takes individual units and combines them into components for testing. Once the first component tests are complete, the components are again linked to other components, to create larger components. This continues, with components getting gradually larger with each increment in the testing level, until all the major components are tested and integration testing can begin.

Integration testing

This is the testing of the application as a whole, once all of the components have been compiled, and linked together. It is sometimes split into "*Application Integration testing*", and "*System Integration testing*".

Application Integration testing, as its name suggests, is the testing of the entire application after all components have been integrated. System Integration Testing, on the other hands, tests the application once it has been placed into the correct environment. For example, a package might go through System Testing once it has been installed on a range of hardware and operating systems, using a range of database types.

Acceptance testing

Often the final level of testing, acceptance testing involves consulting with the end user to see that the system performs in a manner acceptable to them. Acceptance testing is most relevant to systems which are designed to customer specification, since a formal Acceptance Test Plan can be created to make it easier to determine whether the product meets the customer's requirements.

The Acceptance Test varies widely, of course, but in general terms it should encompass exposure to as many situations and events as possible within a reasonable timeframe. The Acceptance Test Plan can

However, a product which is general purpose or otherwise for consumption by the general public, cannot have a well-specified Acceptance Test Plan since there is no single customer to accept the product. Instead, in such a case, testing is typically split into two stages:

Alpha Testing – the stage at which tests are carried out in-house. Alpha tests are best carried out by people who are not familiar with the code, since those who work too closely in creating the project may find their test strategies implicitly skewed towards their expectations. The Alpha test stage is designed to remove the worst bugs before the product enters Beta Testing, and often consists of all tests from Unit Testing up to System Integration Testing.

Beta Testing – This stage is where the product is passed on to typical customers to use normally. This 'normal use' varies widely from one user to the next, of course, and therefore will reveal even more faults in the project. The Beta Test stage is intended to reveal the more common faults that typical users will come across, so that they can be corrected before the product goes to market.

There is often a blurring of the line between Beta Testing and user Acceptance Testing, but Beta Testing tends to be more informal, with reported defects being dealt with as and when it is deemed important. Formal Acceptance Testing, however, is more strict, particularly if a well-written Acceptance Test Plan has been used. Defects can be classified according to priority, and the Acceptance Test Plan should be written with this in mind. The most severe defects could well merit a return to earlier stages of the development process, other important defects would be required to be fixed before formal acceptance, and lesser defects might be acceptable in the short term depending on the contents of the Plan.

Types of errors

Programming is almost as much of an art as it is a science. There are often dozens, even hundreds of ways to do even the simplest operation. Combine even a few simple operations together into a procedure, and you will see that there are a wide variety of mistakes that could be made even in a small subprogram, some of which are more important than others. Errors can be divided into two types: '*Syntax errors*' and '*Logic errors*'.

Syntax errors (or 'compiler errors') are the simplest type of error to find and fix. By definition, a syntax error will be spotted by the compiler, and the compilation will halt, with an error that tells the project team exactly which line the fault is on. Since the compilation typically takes place before even Alpha Testing begins, it will generally be the programmer himself who spots syntax errors.

Such errors can typically be corrected relatively easily. They may be a simple typing mistake, but more commonly they result in a misunderstanding of the structure or parameters of a keyword or subprogram. Proper documentation, either of the language itself or of the subprogram being accessed, should make fixing these faults relatively painless **Logic errors**, on the other hand, can sometimes be devilishly hard to even find, never mind correct. A logic error, as the name suggests, indicates that, somewhere along the line, the wrong type of operation has been applied to some data, and this resulted in a fault. Finding out exactly where the fault lies and fixing it is known as '*debugging*' and is almost guaranteed to take more time and cause more frustration than the initial testing which found the fault in the first place.

Testing methods

However, before any debugging can be done, the program has to be tested in order to find the faults in the first place. Two traditional methods of testing are known as '*black box testing*', and '*white box testing*'.

Black Box Testing – This method envisions the object being tested as if it was contained within a black box. Thus, the testers see the inputs that enter the system, and the outputs that are produced, but have no knowledge of what is going on inside the box. In order for this to happen, of course, the coders must not be involved in black box testing. Black box testing concentrates on making sure that any given set of input data will result in the correct output. This is also sometimes called '*functional testing*'.

White Box Testing – Also called 'clear box' testing or '*structural testing*', this type of testing is considered to be the opposite of black box testing; that is, the testers know at least something about what the system is doing internally. This has the disadvantage that knowing the code might subconsciously predispose the tester, who might well also have coded the unit, to use certain data or even to assume that some defects are in fact normal. However, it also has the advantage that any defects that *are* detected can be dealt with more easily since the tester knows more about what went wrong.

Testing Techniques

Once the style of testing has been decided, and a unit, component or system has been selected to test, the procedure of the tests must be determined. Tests may be done in one of several ways:

- Automated testing. Although some automated test tools do exist, testing a program with another program is obviously far from foolproof. However, it does have the great advantage of being able to run large numbers of tests with a huge range of test data, perhaps by being left to perform tests overnight or even over a weekend.

- Manual testing. Tests are devised and carried out by hand. Appropriate test data must be selected, and the program is painstakingly tested by human beings. Manual tests are slow, but in many situations can reveal faults that would not be found in an automated process. In addition, although automated tests can keep logs, it is possible that human viewing of the process might uncover additional information about the defect that will help in debugging.

- Regression testing. This type of test is only required when an existing program has been altered, even during the maintenance phase. The object is tested again using the same data as previous tests where this is reasonable, to check that the changes have not had a negative impact on the object's current functionality or reliability.

- Performance testing. Although a program may be reliable, it could still be too slow to be used, particularly if it is to be used on a daily basis by large numbers of users. Performance tests include "*stress testing*" using abnormal situations, and "*load testing*" to ensure that the system can cope with unusually high levels of usage.

- Formal testing. If the program has been designed using a formal design technique, then a 'proof' can be formulated. Since this is a lengthy process, proofs typically are applied only to critical sub-sections of the entire code. Formal methods can in theory 'prove' that a certain piece of code is free of defects, but only if it is applied strictly and the formal proof itself should also be checked.

Selecting test data

Once it has been decided what to test and how, the next step is creating actual test situations. In most cases, this involves generating test data to use as inputs to the object being tested. Test data can be chosen at random; indeed in some cases it may be useful to provide a number of random tests, and this is relatively easy to implement in an automatic testing procedure such as a test script. However, it is typically more beneficial to also create test data that most closely matches the kind of real input that is to be expected once the application is installed.

More importantly, however, the test data should be designed to expose any flaws in the code. To do this, the test data should be aimed at causing the faults to occur so that they can be tracked down and removed. This means selecting data using a few relatively simple methods. Test input should be selected with several inputs that are valid, several that fall within each type of invalid input, and those that lie 'on the boundaries'.

Boundary testing and validation

One of the most common type of programming mistakes is the '*fencepost*' error. Such an error involves missing out the last element in a range, or using a slightly incorrect comparison operator (such as "greater than" instead of "greater than or equal to"). This results in the input validation failing in such a way that it either accepts a value that is invalid by one; or fails to accept a valid input that is right on the boundary of the range of valid inputs.

For this reason, testing should include input data that falls on or near the edge of what constitutes acceptable input, in order to root out such faults. Typically, this means testing the following input values:

1)   Inputs which are exactly at each boundary, but is acceptable input.
2)   Inputs which are the smallest discrete number away from each boundary, and are not acceptable input.

For example, a database program that keeps track of data on employees might be intended to allow only data input where the age of the employee is between 18 and 65. The boundary test method would try to enter 17, 18, 65 and 66 as input data, to see which will be accepted and rejected.

Debugging

Finding defects in the code is an important part of the development process. However, once a defect is found, it should be corrected. The process of locating the fault that causes a program defect, and then correcting it, is known as 'debugging'. There are a number of methods that are commonly employed during the debugging process:

- Debugging tools. A reliable debugging tool is immensely useful – it typically allows the programmer to 'step through' each line of code, showing the contents of variables as selected by the programmer. Test data that causes the defect to manifest are entered, and the code followed, keeping an eye on the contents of important variables, until the offending line(s) is/are isolated, and can be modified so that the 'bug' is removed.

- Printlining. This is a common and simple method used often when debugging tools are unavailable or unwieldy. It involves inserting lines of code, usually before and/or after the area of code estimated to contain the fault. These lines are used to print data to screen, either displaying the contents of variables or merely to indicate that a certain selection or iteration has been followed. This is a primitive but effective way of tracing execution and following data contents without using a debugging tool.

- Logging. When printlining or stepping through a program would cause disruption in irs normal operation, the data that would otherwise be printed to screen can instead be output into a file, or into a separate 'logging window' to perform the same function.

- Comment out. Also called 'remming out' (from the 'rem' or remark statement), this is based on the concept of 'divide and conquer'. By temporarily stopping certain lines of code from running, the functionality of the program can be reduced, narrowing down the area of code that actually runs so that the precise location of the bug can be determined.

- Keeping records. If a bug is intermittent, it may be impossible to track it down using the methods described above. Keeping a record of when the fault occurs, and under what circumstances, can yield enough information to indicate the bug's location.

As can be seen, the most important part of debugging is locating the bug. Once a piece of faulty code is located, the way to fix the code will be different from one bug to the next, so there are no hard and fast rules that can be applied to that part of the process.

Maintenance Phase

The final phase of a project, after its acceptance, is its delivery. In an ideal world, this would consist simply of packaging the product and distributing it, as you would any media product. However, unlike media products, no program is bug-free so in the real world so it would be irresponsible of any software house to distribute a product without planning to support and maintain it.

Even the installation of the product may not be as simple as providing an installation CD. Especially in bespoke applications, consideration must be given to existing data, which may need to be converted into a format that can be recognised by the new system.

There are three types of maintenance which should be used on any program:

1)   Corrective maintenance, also called system maintenance.
2)   Adaptive maintenance.
3)   Perfective maintenance.

Corrective maintenance

This type of maintenance involves collecting feedback from users, and correcting any errors in the product that have not yet been discovered. Some cynical users have coined the term 'Gamma testing' to imply that some vendors do not perform adequate alpha and beta testing, leaving end users to do the testing for them. This point has some validity; paying customers should not be expected to participate to any great extent in the testing of the package. The corrective maintenance of the product should be exactly that – correction of a complete product that has a few unexpected and hopefully minor glitches, not development of an as-yet incomplete product.

It has been estimated that corrective maintenance takes an average of around 20% of maintenance time. If a project uses a significant amount of time on corrective maintenance, then it is obvious that the project has been poorly developed, most likely due to faulty requirements analysis, poor design methods, or simply insufficient testing. By this stage it is almost certainly too late to go back and fix mistakes in previous phases, but the team should at least learn from its mistakes. Thought should be given to preparing a project brief outlining where development problems arose, so that future projects do not suffer from similar problems.

Corrective maintenance is generally 'reactive' – in other words, the maintainers react to a reported defect. However, some software houses also use '*preventative maintenance*'. This is a more 'pro-active' approach that looks at defects reported so far, in an attempt to predict possible defects that may occur in the future, so that users do not experience those defects.

Adaptive maintenance

This form of maintenance is essentially modification of an otherwise acceptable program, to accommodate changes in the environment in which it is running. This essentially consists of two types of adaptation: adapting to changes in the system on which the program runs; and changes in the way in which the user wishes to use the program.

Porting code from one operating system or platform to another is an extreme form of adaptive maintenance. More common adaptations include modifications in code to fit changes in hardware; changes in operating systems that have had Service Packs applied; changes in software interfaces such as new database connectivity; or changes in data format such as the restructuring of post codes in a certain area.

However, changes in user requirements are more difficult. Not every project is designed to take into account the possibility of changing user needs, but a project which fails to adapt to changing requirements is a project which is going to have a diminishing user base. Nonetheless, only a certain amount of adaptation should be considered reasonable, otherwise it may be more efficient to create an entirely new project.

Adaptations in this fashion include changes to the functions provided by the program; adding new functions required by users; removing functions that have become superfluous or obsolete; or extending the capabilities of the program with regards to input or output.

Again, adaptive maintenance has been estimated to take 20% of the maintenance time.

Perfective maintenance

Perfective maintenance covers all forms of maintenance that are intended to improve on an already delivered product. Changes to the functionality of the software should rarely be made unless it is in response to user feedback, in which case it would fall under adaptive maintenance rather than perfective maintenance.

Instead, perfective maintenance tends to concentrate on how that functionality is delivered. For example, a common form of perfective maintenance is modification to code to improve its reliability, or optimisation of existing code, to make it run faster. Other perfective maintenance include additional documentation, such as FAQs, additional troubleshooting documentation, and so on.

Perfective maintenance is estimated to take up 60% of all maintenance time.

Maintenance procedure

The maintenance of a program should follow a well-defined method, in the same way as the development process in general. Ad-hoc updates and bug fixes are acceptable on very small projects but not in a large or professional software product. The steps involved in maintenance vary from one organisation to the next, but a typical implementation might involve the following steps:

1) Change Management
2) Impact Analysis
3) Design changes
4) Code changes
5) Testing
6) System Release

It is important that the testing stage includes integration testing as well as unit testing. If the unit which has changed passes its tests, that does not necessarily imply that its inputs and outputs are unaffected. Those inputs from or outputs to other modules in the system could cause a 'run-on' effect that will only be spotted during full testing of the system as a whole.

Also, it is equally important to remember to change the documentation to reflect the changes made. The maintenance procedure includes an analysis that should determine whether new, additional documentation is required, but even if it is not, the existing documentation may well need to be updated or else it risks becoming incorrect.

Change management

This stage is actually ongoing throughout the maintenance of the product. It is the stage which identifies and analyses requests to modify the existing program. A good change management program involves logging change requests, and keeping track of progress regarding the changes throughout the maintenance procedure.

Change requests can be prioritised into '*severity codes*' from 1 to 4:

Severity Code	Description
1 (Critical)	Total system failure, or failure of significant components for a large number of users. A workaround is not acceptable; the problem must be addressed.
2 (High)	Similar to a Critical Severity Code, but for situations where a workaround could be accepted at least in the short term.
3 (Medium)	Failure of a small number of components for a small number of users.
4 (Low)	Failure of a very small number of components, for only a handful of users.

Severity codes may be tied up with a minimum response and resolution time in a '*Service Level Agreement*' between the software provider and the client organisation. For example, an SLA might specify that critical failures demand a response within an hour, and resolution in no more than 24 hours, while a Low Severity problem might allow one business day for response, and 90 calendar days for resolution.

Impact Analysis

Before the change process begins, the analyst(s) involved in the change request should carry out an '*Impact Analysis*'. This is simply an assessment of the time, resources, and budget required to implement the change. Resource requirements include personnel required to implement the change, hardware required, office space, support staff and so on.

It should take into account all the systems that will be affected, not just the module in which the change is expected to take place. For example, will more documentation be required? Will other software still interface correctly with the module? Will users need to be retrained to use the system once the changes are implemented?

If these questions are not addressed in the Cost/Schedule Impact Analysis (CSIA) document, then the change will almost certainly introduce defects in the altered software or in the system as a whole, some of which may not be immediately obvious. This can easily lead to subtle errors that are difficult to debug.

Also, a cost/benefits analysis is not out of the question, especially on larger projects, to ensure that the maintenance procedure will be worthwhile. Costs can be deduced based on Software Metrics, but in order to do this the coding team must produce these metrics during initial development of the product and any maintenance thereafter. Software Metrics include keeping track of the number of Lines Of Code (LOC), lines of comments, number of variables, and in object oriented designs the number of objects, classes and methods involved in common tasks. Another important metric is the productivity rate of the programmers, which will of course vary depending on the complexity of the task. The Impact Analysis stage sometimes also includes 'system release planning' – the scheduling of the change itself, as well as training and documentation to implement the changes at the user's site. Furthermore, impact analysis should consider the possibility that introducing the changes may also introduce new defects. It has been estimated that as often as 50% of changes made in maintenance introduce new defects, even during corrective maintenance designed to eliminate existing defects.

User Documentation

As explained previously, documentation of code is essential during project development and maintenance. However, the programmers are not the only ones who require documentation. The end user cannot be expected to know the ins and outs of an application he has never even seen before. Unless the software contract includes training in the package, then the various forms of documentation supplied with the package may well be the only reference material the end user has access to.

The user documentation can be split into two types:

- Online documentation. This includes any Help system the application may have built in, as well as computerised versions of the paper-based manuals and guides. These have the benefit of the ability to cross-reference and link topics to one another, or run searches for specific words. Online documentation may be kept on CD-ROM or DVD, or it may be installed onto the hard disk for reference; there may even be additional documentation available from the manufacturer's website.

- Printed manuals. Although it may increase the cost of a product, most users prefer to have a paper-based manual. This method saves the user from having to switch between the application and its documentation on-screen, and paper manuals have a number of other minor but distinctive advantages over a screen-based equivalent. Printed documentation is not necessarily always in book format; it can also be found as keyboard overlays, CD or DVD case inserts, and other 'handy' reference formats.

In both cases, the documentation supplied with a product should ideally cover several categories:

- Getting Started guide. This, as its name suggests, is partly a walk-through of basic functions, similar to those found in a 'tutorial guide' (see below), but is also partly an introduction to the most basic concepts used in the package. For example, a 'getting started' guide to a word processing package might explain how to open a new file, edit it, save and close it, while also describing the concepts of 'pages', 'paragraphs' and 'fonts' in very general terms.

- Tutorial Guides. These are step-by-step "How-to" instructions for performing certain tasks. For example, a web page editing package might come complete with several tutorials, including "How to create a table" or "Interfacing with CGI scripts".

- Installation Guide. Even though installation packages are continually being made more user-friendly and tend to follow the same pattern, there are still differences from one package to the next, and installation problems may crop up from time to time. A well-written installation guide should reduce or eliminate these problems.
- Reference manual. This is an index of commands, functions, or other capabilities of the application, along with precise information of the function's requirements, inputs, outputs, and effects. When a user already knows which function to use, the reference manual is useful in finding out more detailed information on how to use that function.
- Troubleshooting guide. No system is perfect, and no user is perfect either. Problems will occur, and the troubleshooting guide should be written in such a way that the most common problems can be diagnosed and effectively resolved by the end user himself or herself, as far as is possible. Typically, the troubleshooting guide also contains information on how to obtain further help if the common problems contained within the guide are not of use.

JavaScript and Java

You will have used JavaScript many times when browsing on the Internet. Most times when you see animated buttons, scrolling text, shopping carts, etc., your browser will have been running a piece of JavaScript that it found on a web page.

Java and JavaScript are not identical terms. Although they are both programming languages, JavaScript is used exclusively on the web, whereas Java is also used to create powerful software programs.

Java

Java is a full-blown programming language, capable of producing software for handling major processing tasks. The code is written and then compiled into a code file that can be run:

- As a stand-alone application, not necessarily connected with web sites, for larger projects.
- Within an HTML page as an *"applet"*. If a web page has <applet> and </applet> tags, then the script for controlling the Java applet code is embedded between these tags. The actual applet code is stored on the web site as a *separate* file, with the extension *"class"* (e.g. demo.class or gfx.class).

JavaScript

JavaScript is a simple programming language that has many uses and has become popular on web sites. By learning this language, web designers make web sites more useful and decorative.

Netscape Communications invented JavaScript under the name *'Livescript'*, along with Netscape 2. JavaScript became popular and a 1.1 version was first released with Netscape 3.

JavaScript is heavily influenced by other languages (C, Perl) but is not the same as Java.

While Java uses a separated, compiled block of computer code, lines of JavaScript are embedded into a normal web page.

What it is used for

Using JavaScript, it is possible to:

- Customise HTML documents on the fly (e.g. adding current date and time).
- Write event handlers for elements on a page (e.g. rollover buttons).
- Validate data at the client side (e.g. checking that a form is only submitted when all fields have been entered).
- Perform other client-side computations (e.g. passwords, calculators).
- Detect what browser is being used and take the viewer to pages designed to work with that browser.

This chapter looks at JavaScript, since it is the language targeted at the greatest number of browsers and the basic statements are understood by both Internet Explorer and Netscape.

Browser Incompatibilities

Before proceeding any further, it is as well to look at some of the problems in implementing scripting for the greatest number of possible users. As in many other areas, Microsoft developed alternatives to existing accepted methods. In this case, they released a similar version of JavaScript, referred to as JScript, for Internet Explorer. The two languages have many similar instructions but have a number of differences that result in Internet Explorer not supporting all of JavaScript's commands (known as *'statements'*), while the added features in Jscript are not understood by Netscape and other browsers.

In addition, various versions of browsers support different versions of JavaScript. Furthermore, Microsoft's Internet Explorer browser is written to support both VBScript (based on Visual Basic) and ActiveX controls. For details of scripting capabilities of browsers, see the *'Web Site Creation'* chapter. Most of the differences in scripting lies in the different Document Object Models used by the major browsers.

For example, both IE and Netscape handle 'layers' as part of their DHTML support. However, each layer in Netscape is considered to be a child of the basic 'document' object. In IE, however, they are children of the 'all' object, which is in turn a child of the 'document' object. This small and subtle difference is enough to stop a javascript based page from working at all under any browser other than the one it is designed for.

The W3C has also introduced its own Document Object Model (DOM) for HTML pages, which differs from the models previously used by IE or Netscape. For this reason, it is best to detect the browser type (explained later in this chapter) and use code which is relevant to the browser in use. The most recent browsers support both the W3C DOM, which is somewhat complex in its implementation, but for compatibility also support either the Netscape DOM or Explorer DOM.

Aside from browser specific objects, there are also differences between the different versions of JavaScript. Fortunately, it is relatively easy to separate the code for different versions of JavaScript, simply by defining which version of script is in use, for example:

```
<SCRIPT language="JavaScript1.1">
        or
<SCRIPT language="JavaScript1.3">
```

Making a page work on all major browsers implies, of course, that the programmer will take note of the differences between how the various browsers handle JavaScript, which is no easy task, especially if older browsers are also to be supported. This means ensuring that all objects and methods are compatible with the major browsers' object models, and that there are no 'quirks' which interfere with the program's operation. Although research into the browsers' object models can indicate where problems may occur, it is often simpler and more effective to write the code and test it in various browsers to see if inconsistencies occur.

Some script incompatibilities can be overcome by using pointers to objects. For example, as previously mentioned, layers are 'children' of different objects under Netscape and IE. A layer called 'layer1' would be accessed as 'document.all.layer1' under IE, but as 'document.layer1' under Netscape. In order to avoid problems, code could be written to determine which browser was in use, and then an object created, perhaps named 'layer1pointer'. This object would point to the 'document.all.layer1' object if it is determined that IE is in use, but would point to the 'document.layer1' object if Netscape was in use.

Embedding JavaScript

JavaScript is only used at the client end (i.e. by the person reading the web page). There are no changes or additions used at the server end. The explanation of client-side programming was explained in the previous chapter.

There are three ways to embed JavaScript in an HTML page:
- Statements that are immediately executed when they are reached. These appear in the main body of the web page.
- Functions/sub-routines that are stored by the script interpreter until they are specifically called from another part of the script. These appear within the <head> and </head> tags.
- Event-handling statements, that are only executed under specific conditions (such as a mouse movement). These appear within an HTML tag.

In addition, a script can be stored as a separate file, with a .js extension (e.g. calc.js or display.js) and be called from within the HTML page.

A browser works its way through an HTML page from beginning to end. When it reaches a <script> tag, it sends the following lines to its JavaScript interpreter for carrying out. When it reaches the </script> tag, it reverts to normal browser HTML processing.

There is no limit to the number of script files that can be included in an HTML page.

All JavaScript (except the event handlers covered later) is enclosed by <script> and /script> tags, as in the example. Each statement should be terminated by a semicolon. While it may be omitted, it is good practice to include it. If you want to place more statement on a line, you have to separate them with a semicolon.

This example script simply writes a single word on the screen.

Left as it is, browsers will assume that the language being used for the script is JavaScript. Since this method can be used for other languages (e.g. <script language="VBScript">), it is common practice to declare that you are using JavaScript, even if it is not strictly necessary.

```
<script>
document.write("Dumbreck");
</script>
```

```
<script language="JavaScript">
document.write("Dumbreck");
</script>
```

If you want to include some of the latest features that appear in the newer versions of JavaScript, then older versions of browsers will not understand them and will produce unwanted screen output. The JavaScript version can be included in the script declaration, as shown.

In this case, version 1.3 is specified. This means that all browsers up to Explorer 4 and Netscape 4 will ignore the script. It prevents unsightly screen

```
<script language="JavaScript 1.3">
document.write("Dumbreck");
</script>
```

output, but prevents the script lines from being run. This may be satisfactory for non-essential scripts (such as flying text) but is a problem for important scripts such as shopping carts. Fortunately, this is a diminishing problem, as more users upgrade their browsers.

The document.write function is the most used of all JavaScript functions and displays the contents that are stored within its brackets.

```
<html>
<head></head>
<body>
This site was last updated on
<script language="JavaScript">
// displays the date and time
document.write("document.lastModified");
</script>
</body>
</html>
```

This next example shows a small but useful piece of script. This displays the date and time that the web page was last modified. For web sites that are regularly maintained, this lets the user know that the web site is worth visiting from time to time.

It also introduces the idea of adding comments to your scripts. Any text on the line after the // symbols is ignored by the browser and is not acted upon or displayed.

This allows the writer to add comments that explain what that part of the script is doing. This becomes more important with large scripts, as it easy to forget what each section does.

If there is a need to write a long explanation, this will need several lines of the script. In this case place /* and */ around the comment, as shown in this example.

```
<script >
/* This method allows comments
that go over several
lines of the script */
document.write("Dumbreck");
</script>
```

If a browser does not support JavaScript (rare nowadays) or has JavaScript turned off, it will display all the lines between the <script> tags on the screen. To prevent this, the script is usually enclosed in normal HTML comments, as shown.

If the browser is not handling JavaScript, it thinks all the lines between <!-- and --> are comments and does not attempt to display them, while still working with JavaScript-aware browsers.

```
<script language="JavaScript">
<!--
document.write("Dumbreck");
-->
</script>
```

Functions

A function is a section of script that carries out a particular set of activities. Some functions are pre-defined (i.e. they are already written), while others can be created by the user. The document.write function is an example of a pre-defined function and more of these will be examined later.

User-defined functions are in two parts:
- The function code, usually embedded between the <head> tags.
- The instruction that calls the function, embedded among the rest of the HTML code between the <body> tags.

```
<HTML >
<HEAD>
<script>
    function hi()
{
        document.write("hello");
}
</script>
</HEAD>
<BODY>

<script>
hi();
</script>

</BODY>
</HTML>
```

The example script shows a function called *"hi"*. Since it is only a demonstration, it does not do very much; it simply displays the word *"hello"*. But this does not happen immediately. Further down in the script, there is a line hi(). When this is reached, it calls the function and the message is only displayed at that point.

Note that the statement(s) that make up the function are contained within a set of curly braces { }. This lets the browser interpreter know when the set of statements (known as a *"block"*) starts and ends.

Passing parameters

Both the function and the instruction that calls the function have a set of brackets after them. In the example, there is nothing between the brackets.

```
<HTML >
<HEAD>
<script>
    function hi(name)
    { document.write("hello ", name); }
</script>
</HEAD>
<BODY>

<script>
hi("Davy");
</script>

</BODY>
</HTML>
```

If we wish, we can place something between the brackets and these contents can be passed back or forwards. The content between the brackets is called a *"parameter"* and the process of moving information is called *"parameter passing"*.

The example shows the earlier script modified to allow a value to be passed from the called instruction into the function.

In this case, a piece of text is being passed (we can tell because of the quotation marks around the letters).

When the line hi("Davy") is reached, the function called hi is called and the parameter (i.e. the word Davy) is passed to the function.

At the function end, Davy is placed in the storage area called name.

The function uses document.write to display the list of values (in this case the text *"hello"* followed by the contents of the store called name). Since name holds the value Davy, the hi function displays *"Hello Davy"* on the screen.

Note that a comma is used to separate different items in a list.

This example shows that there can be two or more parameters in the list that is passed.

Two items are passed to the function, with a comma separating the parameters.
The function is written to accept two incoming parameters. These are stored in variables called name1 and name2.
The function then displays three items – the first parameter, the piece of text, and the second parameter.

```
<HTML >
<HEAD>
<script>
  function getsquare(num)
  {    return num * num;    }
</script>
</HEAD>
<BODY>

<script>
  document.write(" 3 squared is ",getsquare(3));
</script>

</BODY>
</HTML>
```

```
<HTML >
<HEAD>
<script>
    function hi(name1, name2)
    {  document.write(name1, " loves ", name2); }
</script>
</HEAD>
<BODY>

<script>
hi("Davy","Margaret");
</script>

</BODY>
</HTML>
```

This next example shows that a parameter can be passed from a function back to the calling instruction. In fact, values are passed in both directions in this example.

The getsquare(3) instruction passes the value of 3 to the function.
The function then squares the value by multiplying by itself.
It then returns that value back to the calling instruction.
The document.write instruction then displays *"3 squared is 9"* on the screen.

External scripts
It is possible to save a large or self-contained block of JavaScript as a totally separate file and call it up from within an HTML page.   This is useful for writing blocks of script that can be used with many different web pages (e.g. calculating/ verifying dates, complex graphics routines, etc).
It allows the module to be called from any of the site's pages, with the following benefits:
- The code does not need to be embedded within each page, so the overall site size is smaller.
- If the code needs to modified, there is only one file needing altered, instead of having to find and edit every page that contains that section of code.   It removes the inconsistencies that would be caused if a page were overlooked and not modified, or if pages were modified slightly differently.

The external file is simply called by placing the following instruction in the HTML page:

```
<script src="sell.js"></script>
```

Variables in JavaScript
There are four main types of data used in JavaScript:

Numbers	Integers (whole numbers such as 5 or 127) or Floating-Point (decimals such as 5.1 or 0.127). Negative numbers are also supported (-5, -12.5, etc.)
Strings	One or more characters from the printable character set (letters, numbers, punctuation).
Boolean	Whether a condition is True or False.
Array	A group of data where individual items are accessed by their position in the group.

Other types are:

Null	The lack of data. Nothing is stored in the variable. This may be a perfectly acceptable situation (e.g. a form field requesting occupation details may be allowed to be left empty).
Undefined	The lack of data where there should be a value (e.g. a from may require that a post code be entered). An undefined value may also be the result of an error in the script.
NaN	Not a Number. The result of an error in a mathematical operation.

It is important to realise that variable names in JavaScript are case-sensitive. This means, for example, that Name and name are treated as two different variables.

Declaring Variables

JavaScript is "loosely typed". That is, variables do not need to have their type defined before use. However, defining variable types before use can make the code easier to understand, and is generally recommended.

JavaScript uses the var keyword to set up variables.

The following example shows three variables being set and being given initial values.

A fourth variable – quantity – is set up during the function declaration.

The getamount(3) statement send the value of 3 to the variable quantity.

The values are used in a calculation and the result is place in the total variable.

The return total statement sends the final value back to the calling statement, where it is displayed with document.write.

```
<HTML >
<HEAD>
<script>
  function getamount(quantity)
{
   var total = 0;
   var postage = 3;
   var itemcost = 20;
   total = itemcost * quantity + postage;
   return total;
}
</script>
</HEAD>
<BODY>
<script>
   document.write("Order total is ",getamount(3));
</script>
</BODY>
</HTML>
```

Objects

A variable, as we have seen, provides a way of storing data. A variable has a name and usually stores a single value (e.g. age, height, or weight). A variable can also store a collection of the same type of data. For example, variables such as name, address or town store a collection of alphanumeric characters. A database may stores hundreds, thousands or even millions of entries in an array (see later) but each entry is of the same type (e.g. a collection of ages or prices).

For more complex descriptions, JavaScript supports a limited object-based approach.

> **Note** Programmers please note that JavaScript is not a full object-oriented language like Java.
> It does not support classes, inheritance, abstraction, etc.

Consider how much different data is required to describe a person. They have descriptions such as name, age, sex, height, colour of eyes/hair/skin and so on. All of these attributes could be saved as individual variables.

The object-based approach regards the person as an *"object"* and his/her attributes as *"properties"*. So, for example an object called Davy could have properties such as:

> Davy.age
> Davy.height

An added advantage of objects is that they can not only store values; they can also store *"methods"*. A method is a function that is associated with an object.

We have already used a method in the previous example.

> document.write

document is the object and write is the method. Other methods associated with document are open, close and clear. Since document refers to the current web page, it also has many properties such as bgColor, fgColor and linkColor.

The properties of an object can be individually accessed or manipulated.

For example, the lines:

> document.bgColor="blue";
> document.fgColor="white";

set the page to display white text on a blue background. These statements will override the background and foreground colours initially set up within the <BODY> tags.

Some properties, such as document.lastModified are read-only.

As stated, an object can store a collection of related data.

Consider the Date object. As expected it contains data on year, month, day, hour, minute and even seconds. Individual elements can be accessed using *'get'* methods. For example:

> mymonth=birthday.getMonth();

will return the value of the month from the object birthday into the variable mymonth.

Apart from accessing individual elements of an object, the entire object can be manipulated. For example:

> mybirthday=madonnabirthday;

results in mybirthday storing the exact same set of properties and methods as stored in the madonnabirthday object – with only a single instruction.

The Date object is covered more fully later.

The window object has properties such as width and height and methods such as status (which places data in the status bar) and alert (which displays a dialog box). The window object is also covered later.

Once an object class has been defined, it is possible to create extra instances (independent occurrences of objects) of it using new as in these examples:

```
mybirthday = new Date()
xmasday = new Date()
lastpaymentdate = new Date()
```

New object classes can be defined by first creating a function, as in this example;

```
<script>
function book(title, price, quantity)    {
    this.title=title;
    this.price=price;
    this.quantity=quantity;      }
```

An instance of the object can then be created and initialised with the line:

```
pcbook= new book("Support Handbook", 29, 100);
```

Individual items are accessed by naming the instance and the name of the required property:

```
window.status=(pcbook.title);
```

Making calculations

Many scripts make use of mathematical formulas, with shopping carts being the most common example. When using a formula the equals sign separates the result from the calculations. The previous example used:

```
total = itemcost * quantity + postage;
```

Here, the itemcost is multiplied by the quantity, the postage is added to the result and the final figure is placed in the variable called total.

JavaScript uses the arithmetic symbols shown in the table.
The addition, subtraction and division symbols are just as used in school.   The multiplication symbol is an asterisk.

You may not have encountered incrementing before. This simply means adding one to a number.   So if a variable called total held the value of 7, a statement

Total++

would result total storing the new value of 8.
Similarly, a number can be decremented by 1 by placing two minus signs after it.

+	Addition
-	Subtraction
*	Multiplication
/	Division
++	Incrementation
--	Decrementation

This is a slight modification of the calling script shown in the last example (see previous page).
The single line in the original:

```
document.write("Order total is ",getamount(3));
```

has been replaced with the three statements shown.

```
<script>
    fig=3;
    amount=getamount(fig);
    document.write("Order total is ", amount);
</script>
```

In the original, the value 3 was directly sent to the function. In this example, the value is first placed in a variable fig. The parameter being sent to the function is now a variable rather than a direct value.   The value that is returned by the function is placed in another variable amount and it is this variable that is displayed. This example shows that variables can be used as parameters. This method has the added advantage that the values stored in fig and amount remain available for use in any further formulas.

Maths methods

JavaScript has a Math object that is accompanied by a wide variety of methods. A mathematical function is called with this format:

```
result=Math.round(inputvalue)
```

There are many available methods and the more common ones are shown in the table. The examples assume a variable called num currently storing a value of 1.6.

	Value stored in answer
answer=Math.round(num);	2
answer=Math.floor)num);	1
answer=Math.ceil(num);	2
answer=Math.sqrt(num);	1.2649

ROUND

We often round numbers in our head. We see a price in shop marked as £9.99 and mentally note that we need a £10 note to buy it.   However, if we see a price of £9.11 we think of it as £9.
In other words, rounding is a convenient way to get approximations quickly.   After all, it is much easier to calculate the total cost for 19 items if we assume the price to be £10 instead of £9.99.   Every *"estimate"* or *"ball-park figure"* is a rounding of a value to the nearest whole number.
If the input value is .5 or more, then the value is rounded up to the next highest integer (e.g. 3.7 becomes 4), while values less than .5 are rounded down to the integer part only (e.g. 3.3 becomes 3).

FLOOR

This is used to take a number down to the nearest whole number – it produces an integer value. This is has its uses. For example we don't tell people that our age is 37.26; we stay at 37 years until we reach the next integer value (38).

CEIL

Rounding is not useful for calculating the materials for a project. For example, if a paint job needs 5.1 litres of paint, there is no point in rounding down to 5 litres, as there would not be enough paint to finish the job. Assuming paint was supplied in 1-litre pots, the job would require 6 pots. CEIL always returns a value rounded up to the next integer value.

ABS

This is the absolute value of a number. So, values of 1.6 and –1.6 would both produce a result of 1.6. Many stores pay the postage for both goods supplied and for goods returned. If goods supplied is a positive value and goods returned is a negative value, the total postage costs would be inaccurate unless the returns variable was converted into a positive value, as in this example.

The example produces a postage cost of 60. Without the abs, the figure would be calculated thus:

    10 * 4 + -5 * 4

which produces an answer of 20.

```
<HTML >
<HEAD>
</HEAD>
<BODY>
<script>
    sales=10;
    returns=-5;
    postage =sales*4 + Math.abs(returns)*4;
    window.alert(postage);
</script>
</BODY>
</HTML>
```

Event handlers

An event handler is a piece of script that remains inactive until triggered by some event.
The format of the statement is

                event=activity

In other words

                "when this event occurs, do this activity".

The event could be moving the mouse over a button, clicking a button, opening a web page, etc.

This is one the simplest examples of an event handler

        `<a href="test.htm" onMouseOver="alert('hi');" > test page </a>`

The `<a>` tag places a hyperlink on the screen as usual but has `onmouseover="alert('hi');"` added to the line. onMouseOver is the event and `"alert('hi');"` is the activity. When the mouse moves over the text of the hyperlink, an alert box pops up with a message. Notice that this type of JavaScript does not require to be enclosed by `<script>` tags and is embedded amongst the rest of the HTML code.

The above technique is widely used on menu pages, where buttons change colour/shape/size when a mouse is placed over them. This is referred to as *"button rollovers".*

There are two approaches to button rollovers. The first approach is the most common and requires two images for each button. One image displays the button in its normal state, while the other image displays the button's changes when the mouse hovers over it. The button usually changes colour or appears to have been depressed.

The rollover uses two event handlers. The onMouseOver handler displays the image that is seen when the mouse hovers over the link. The onMouseOut handler restores the image to its normal state.

Since these activities only display images after mouse movements, there is still a need to display the button when the page is first loaded. That is the purpose of the `<img src="image1.gif" name="r">` line.

```
<HTML >
<HEAD>
</HEAD>
<BODY>

<a href="nextpage.htm"
onMouseOver="r.src='image2.gif'"
onMouseOut= "r.src='image1.gif'">
<img src="image1.gif" name="r">
</a>

</BODY>
</HTML>
```

The image is given a name, in this case simply *"r"*, and this allows the event handlers to change the displayed image using the r.src= part of the statement.

Pre-fetching

The problem with the last script was the delay between the user hovering over the button and the time needed to fetch the replacement graphic file. Where a menu has many buttons, there will be a delay every time each button is first hovered over. The solution lies in pre-fetching the images into the cache where they can be speedily accessed when required.

This can be achieved in HTML using the line:

        `<img src= "filename" width="0" height="0">`

This line is placed early in the page, or may even be loaded in a previous page. The graphic is loaded while the user is reading the page contents and is invisible on the screen since its dimensions are set to zero.

Pre-fetching can also be carried out in JavaScript as shown opposite. The first two lines of script fetch the images and store them. onMouseOver is used to point to the new button image and onMouseOut is used to point back to the original image.

Another method is to use a function to carry out the swapping of the images. This is shown in this next example script.

```
<HTML >
<HEAD>
<script>
{
buttin=new Image;   buttin.src="buttonin.gif";
buttout= new Image; buttout.src="buttonout.gif";
}
function swap(oldimage, newimage)
{
eval('document.images[oldimage].src='+newimage + '.src');
}
</script>
</HEAD>
<BODY>

<a href="nextpage.htm"
onMouseOver="swap('button', 'buttin')"
onMouseOut= "swap('button', 'buttout')">
<img src="buttonout.gif" name="button">
</a>

</BODY>
</HTML>
```

```
<HTML >
<HEAD>
<script>
{
   buttin=new Image;   buttin.src="buttonin.gif";
   buttout= new Image; buttout.src="buttonout.gif";
}
</script>
</HEAD>
<BODY>

<a href="nextpage.htm"
onMouseOver="document.button.src=buttin.src"
onMouseOut= "document.button.src=buttout.src">
<img src="buttonout.gif" name="button">
</a>

</BODY>
</HTML>
```

The function's job is to replace the existing image with the new image. This works with any two images, so the function can be used with all the buttons on a page.

The eval function evaluates the contents between its brackets. In this case, there are three items joined by plus signs. This evaluates as:

> document.images[button].src=buttin.src

and this ensures that the button image used is the buttin image, when called by onMouseOver.
OnMouseOut calls the eval function to ensure that the buttout image is used as the button image's source.
Yet another method involves storing images in arrays and this is covered later.

Single-graphic rollovers

The alternative button-handling method is a compromise between using a text hyperlink (quick to load but not very pretty) and the previous method (prettiest but requires two graphics to be loaded).
This method requires only a single button graphic. The example shows a graphic that is 180x30 pixels.
When the mouse is moved over the button, the graphic is stretched to 250x30 pixels. When the mouse is moved away, the button restores to its previous width.
While not have the full impact of using two buttons, it provides user feedback while only requiring a single graphic image to be downloaded.

```
<HTML >
<HEAD></HEAD>
<BODY>

<a href="nextpage.htm"
onMouseOver="rb.width=250; rb.height=30"
onMouseOut=  "rb.width=180; rb.height=30">
<img src="buttonout.gif" name="rb"
    width=180 height=30 border=0>

</BODY>
</HTML>
```

Finally, this example script alters the content of the browser's status bar (the one that normally shows a URL when you hover over a hyperlink).

> <a href="orderpage.htm"
> onMouseOver="window.status='Only Visa and MasterCard accepted'; return true"
> onMouseOut="window.status=' ';" > Paying by credit card </a>

It uses onMouseOver to place a message in the status bar and uses onMouseOut to remove the message when the mouse is moved away from the link.   return true is necessary to prevent the message from being immediately replaced by the URL.

Two other commonly used event handlers are:

onLoad

This instruction is inserted in the <BODY> tag as shown:

> <BODY onLoad="alert('This page is only suitable for those over 18 years')">

The activity that onLoad initiates waits until the entire web page contents (text, graphics, etc.) are fully downloaded. In this example, the handler displays a warning message on the screen regarding the page's suitability for adult viewing.

onClick
This activity is only initiated when the mouse is clicked.

```
<a href="creditcard.htm" onClick="alert('Only Visa and MasterCard accepted');" > Paying by credit card </a>
```

In this example, clicking a hyperlink brings up additional important information before taking the user to the new page.

Linking via JavaScript
JavaScript is capable of changing the current URL being viewed, so that a new web page is displayed. In other words, this performs much the same function as an anchor tag, but allows the programmer to use the flexibility of JavaScript to achieve hyperlinks in a variety of ways.

The simple example on the right is the most basic method of using JavaScript to achieve hyperlinks. It simply uses a DIV tag to define an area of text, and then uses the onClick event to send the user to the 'enter.htm' page if any of that text is clicked upon. It changes the current page by setting the 'location' of the current window to 'enter.htm'.

```
<DIV onClick="window.self.location='enter.htm' ">
Enter the site here
</DIV>
```

However, this method has its drawbacks. Java links are not integrated into the browser, so this type of link will not be obvious to the user. Even though the user can click on the text to enter the page, the pointer does not change to a hand when the mouse hovers over the text, as it would a conventional hyperlink. The programmer must make it obvious that the text is a link in some other way.

Alternatively, the second method can be used, as shown. This uses the anchor tag, <A>, to define the text area to be used as a hyperlink, just as in a conventional link. This informs the browser that the text is a link, so that

```
<A HREF=""  onClick="document.location.href='enter.htm' ">
Enter the site here
</A>
```

the mouse pointer changes in the normal way. Additionally, this uses a slightly different method of changing the current page: that of setting the HREF of the current document location. This has the same effect as setting 'window.self.location'.

However, this method has the down side that the popup window that normally displays the URL that the link leads to, will display incorrect information. A better approach would be to use DIV, but include an onMouseOver event that in some way makes it plain that the text is in fact a link. This, however, is considerably more complicated.

Furthermore, JavaScript is not restricted to running when events like onClick or onLoad occur. JavaScript may be activated by any HREF which is triggered, by simply prefixing the JavaScript line with the "JavaScript:" tag. The simplest example of the "JavaScript URL" is a single line of code such as the following:

```
<A HREF="JavaScript:document.location.href='newpage.htm';">Click here to resize the window</A>
```

This performs exactly the same function as a simple HREF pointing to a new page. However, the HREF can just as easily activate a different piece of JavaScript, such as calling up a procedure defined elsewhere. The main difference between using HREF, and using the onClick event, is that HREF JavaScript functions will be activated even when the browser has JavaScript event handling turned off.

Decision-making
JavaScript, like all programming languages, includes facilities to test and compare values and to take action depending upon the results.

For this, it uses the if statement. It should be thought of in the form:

> if (condition) *then* action

In other words, if a certain test is true, then carry out the designated activity. The then is only shown to aid understanding; it is not entered into the script. The test for the condition is always enclosed in brackets.

A few pages back, there was a script to calculate an order's total cost. The formula always added on £3 for postage. Using the if statement, the example shows an alteration where postage is only added if an order's basic total is less than £50. If the basic total is £50 or more the activity is not carried out (i.e. the £3 postage charge is not added to the total).

```
function getamount(quantity)
{
    var total = 0;
    var postage = 3;
    var itemcost = 20;
    total = itemcost * quantity;
    if (total <50) total=total+3;
    return total;
}
```

If you want there to be two or more actions, then they should be enclosed in a set of curly braces.

There is an extension to the if statement that provides one action if the test is true and another action if it is found to be false. This is in the form:

> If (condition) *then* action1 *else* action2

Suppose the function was to add £3 for orders under £50 and add £1.50 for orders of $50 or more.

The statement in the example could be changed to:

> if (total <50) total=total+3; else total=total+1.5;

The table shows the conditional tests that are available.

==	Is equal to
!=	Is not equal to
<	Is less than
>	Is greater than
<=	Is less than or equal to
>=	Is greater than or equal to

Browser detection

Since there are problems in producing JavaScript that runs on all versions of all browsers, you may wish to provide two versions of some web pages – one designed using Netscape-specific code and one using Explorer-specific code.

For this technique to work, a web page has to detect what browser is being used, so that the user is directed to the appropriate next page.

```
<script>
browser=navigator.appName;
if (browser=="Microsoft Internet Explorer")
   location.href="iepage.htm";
else
   location.href="nspage.htm"
</script>
```

The example shows how the script can tell whether a user is browsing with Explorer or not. navigator.appName returns a text message that contains the name of the browser in use. The if test then decides which web page the user will be taken to. Note that two equal signs are used when comparing values.

If a particular browser version is required, the version=navigator.appVersion line can be added. This returns a long string that contains, amongst other details, the version number of the browser software.

In the example, indexOf searches through the text stored in version looking for the character *"6."* If it is present, it returns a number that indicates how far along the text it was found. If it is not found it returns the value-1.

The line

```
<script>
browser=navigator.appName;
version=navigator.appVersion;
versionnumber=(version.indexOf("6."));
if (browser=="Microsoft Internet Explorer" && versionnumber>0)
   location.href="iepage.htm";
else
   location.href="nspage.htm"
</script>
```

```
        if (browser=="Microsoft Internet Explorer" && versionnumber>0)
```

requires that two conditions be true. The browser must be Explorer AND the version number must be 6.

The && symbols are used to indicate that BOTH conditions must be tested to be true before calling iepage.htm.

Simple animation using JavaScript

As can be seen from the previous examples, it is possible to change the source image used in IMG tags in a web page using JavaScript. Using this method, it is possible to perform a number of other tasks. For example, basic animation is reasonably simple.

The example on the right shows some very basic animation, simply swapping two images at a time interval of half a second each time. It works by creating two 'image' objects, and setting them to contain two different GIF images. The <BODY> tag contains an onLoad event, which carries out the javascript contained within, once the body of the HTML file is loaded.

So, once the HTML file loads, it runs the 'animate' function, once only. This function simply uses an 'if' statement to swap the contents of the first image in the HTML document between image1.gif and image2.gif. Then, the setTimeout command is used to make the

```
<HTML>
<HEAD><SCRIPT>
var img1 = new Image( 250, 50 );
img1.src = "image1.gif";

var img2 = new Image( 250, 50 );
img2.src = "image2.gif";

function animate() {
  if (document.images[0].src == img1.src)
    document.images[0].src = img2.src;
  else
    document.images[0].src = img1.src;
    setTimeout("animate();", 500);
}
</SCRIPT></HEAD>
<BODY onLoad="animate();">
   <IMG src="" width=250 height=50>
</BODY>
</HTML>
```

JavaScript interpreter wait for half a second, before running the 'animate' function again. This creates a cycle, continually running the 'animate' function and swapping the two images, until a new page is loaded.

For this sort of simplistic animation, a GIF89a image would probably be more efficient. However, the example merely shows the basic methods involved in image manipulation – JavaScript offers infinitely more flexibility than an animated graphic can provide. For example, it is not too difficult to add code so that more than two images are used, or so that the images vary depending on where the mouse is, or which buttons are clicked, thus adding the sort of interactivity that is impossible using a simple GIF image.

NOSCRIPT

The page also needs to know whether a user has JavaScript turned off. The page may simply be using JavaScript for fancy animated graphics or button rollovers. More importantly, it may require scripts to test that forms have been filled in correctly or that shopping cart calculations are carried out.

Consider, for example, a page with a link to a JavaScript-powered shopping cart page. The shopping cart page should only be entered by those who have JavaScript enabled. Others should be given a message that they require to enable JavaScript before proceeding to the shopping cart page.

This page can be added to the web site. The calling page now links to this intermediate page, rather than directly to the shopping cart page.

```
<HTML>
<HEAD>
</HEAD>
<BODY>
<script>
<!—
    window.location="cart.htm"
-->
</script>
<noscript>
  Your browser has to be JavaScript
  enabled to use the shopping cart page.
</noscript>
</BODY>
</HTML>
```

If the user has JavaScript enabled, then he/she is taken immediately to the shopping cart page.
If JavaScript is not enabled, the page's script is ignored, as it is enclosed in comments and the user is shown the warning message.

Logical expressions

The earlier example used && to link two conditions that both had to be tested true for the whole test to prove true:

if (browser=="Microsoft Internet Explorer" && versionnumber>0)

If required, this can be extended to require even more conditions to be true:

If (test1 && test2 && test3 && test4) …

Similarly, we can have two or more conditions within the brackets, where only <u>one</u> has to be tested true for the whole test to prove true. This is known as an OR logical operator.

Consider a web site that only supplies goods to the UK and Ireland. The site uses a form to take orders. A field in a form, called country in this example, stores the name of the country where the buyer lives.

The script shown ensures that the user is in a position to successfully place an order.

The first line checks for either a country value of *"UK"* or of *"Eire"*.
If country contains either of these values then the overall test condition is true and the variable check is set to true.
If country does not store either of these values, the check variable is set to false.
Note the use of *"true"* and *"false"*; these are known as Boolean values. A Boolean value has only two possible values – that of true or false.

```
if (country=="UK" || country=="Eire")
    check=true;
  else
    check=false;
if (check==true)
  window.location="proceed.htm";
  else
    alert("Sorry, we only supply to the UK and Ireland");
```

The fifth line examines the contents of the check variable.
If it is found to store a value of true, the user is taken to the next page.
If the value is found to be false, the user is shown a warning message.

Complex cases

More complex test conditions can be set up, as long as each separate set of tests are enclosed in their own set of brackets.
So, for example:

((test1 && test2) || (test3 && test4))

is one big test condition that only requires one of the two inner test conditions to be true for the whole test to prove true.

On the other hand:

((test1 || test2) && (test3 || test4))

requires that both test prove true before the overall test is true.

The table shows the result for various test inputs on the above formula.

Test1	Test2	Test3	Test4	Overall Result
true	true	true	true	true
true	true	true	false	true
true	true	false	true	true
true	true	false	false	false
true	false	true	true	true
true	false	true	false	true
true	false	false	true	true
true	false	false	false	false
false	true	true	true	true
false	true	true	false	true
false	true	false	true	true
false	true	false	false	false
false	false	true	true	false
false	false	true	false	false
false	false	false	true	false
false	false	false	false	false

Date & time

JavaScript can handle dates and times in a variety of ways. It provides methods to set up and give initial values to objects that hold dates and times, it provides methods to alter the object's contents at any time – and it provides methods to read the contents at any time.

The formats available for initialising dates are:

now=new Date();	now is set to the current date and time
birthday=new Date("April 28, 1977 09:30:00");	birthday is set to 9.30am on 28th April 1977
anniversary=new Date(1977, 3, 28);	Anniversary is set 28th April 1977
holiday=new Date(1977, 3, 28, 9, 30, 0);	holiday is set to 9.30am on 28th April 1977

Note that in the last two examples the month value is set to 3 for April. This is because month values start from zero. Jan=0, Feb=1, Mar=2, etc.

The methods for altering date/time values are:

setFullYear()	Set the value of the year stored
setMonth()	Set the month value (0 to 11)
setDate()	Set the day of the month (1 to 31)
setHours()	Set the hour (0 to 23)
setMinutes()	Set the minute (0 to 59)
setSeconds()	Set the second (0 to 59)

The methods for reading date/time values are:

getYear()	Fetch the value of the year
getMonth()	Fetch the value of the month (0 to 11)
getDate()	Fetch the day of the month (1 to 31)
getDay()	Fetch the day of the week (0 to 6)
getHours()	Fetch the value of the year

Just like month values, the day of the week value starts from zero. Sunday=0, Monday=1, etc.

This script places the current date on a web page.
A new Date object is created and the current date is placed in the timenow variable.
The day, month and year elements are extracted and displayed with document.write. Note that 1 is added to the thismonth variable to display the correct month (since month values start at zero). A way of displaying the name of the day of the week (Monday, Tuesday, etc) is covered later.

```
<script>
timenow=new Date();
thisday=timenow.getDate();
thismonth=timenow.getMonth()+1;
thisyear=timenow.getYear();
document.write(thisday + " / " + thismonth + " / " +thisyear);
</script>
```

Many web pages display a greeting such as *"Good Morning"* or *"Good Evening"*. This script shows how this is achieved.
The getHours method extracts the current hour of the day.
The if .. else tests decide which message is displayed. Note that there is an if .. then statement inside another if .. then statement.
This is known as *"nesting"*.

```
<script>
now=new Date();
if (now.getHours()<12) document.write("Good Morning");
else
 if (now.getHours()<17) document.write("Good Afternoon");
  else
    document.write("Good Evening");
</script>
```

This script demonstrates how calculations can be made on dates.
The variable now stores the current date.
The variable Xmas is set up to store the date for Xmas 2002.
The daysleft variable subtracts the current date from the date of Xmas. Since the answer is returned as the number of milliseconds between each date, it has to be divided by 1000

```
<script>
now=new Date()
Xmas=new Date("Dec 25 2002 00:00:00");
daysleft=(Xmas-now)/1000/60/60/24;
daysleft=Math.floor(daysleft);
window.status=daysleft + ' shopping days to Xmas';
</script>
```

to get the answer in seconds. It is divided by 60 two times, to get the answer in hours and is finally divided by 24 to get the answer in days.

The previous script used the current date and a future date. This script uses the current date and an earlier date.
The earlier date (i.e. someone's birthday) is subtracted from the current date and the program displays how many days the individual has lived since being born.

Strings

The earlier section on variables explained one type was known as a *"string"* and this contained one or more characters from the printable character set (letters, numbers, punctuation).
If we declare a variable as

Myname="Davy Dick"

```
<script>
now=new Date();
age=new Date("Apr 8 1984 00:00:00");
days=(now-age)/1000/60/60/24;
days=Math.floor(days);
window.status='I am ' +days +' days old';
</script>
```

We have created a string object whose current contents are a string of nine characters (the space is counted as a character).   The first character is said to have an index of zero. In the example string, the index values rise from 0 to 8. Being an object, it has a variety of methods (built-in functions) that can be used to manipulate the contents of the string.

Assuming a string called myname, with the contents *"Davy Dick"*, the table shows some of the more common methods and their results.

posn=myname.indexOf("ck");	posn is given the value of 7
letter=myname.charAt(6);	letter is given the value of i
size=myname.length;	9 (any spaces are counted in the total)
newname=myname.substring(6,8);	newname is given the value ic
myname=myname.toUpperCase();	myname is given the value DAVY DICK
myname=myname.toLowerCase();	myname is given the value davy dick
myname=myname.fontcolor("ff0000");	Displays the text in the chosen colour (red in this example)
myname=myname.fontsize("6");	Displays the text in the designated font size (1 to 7)
letter=letter.bold();	Displays the text in bold
letter=letter.italics();	Displays the text in italics
myname.link("rollover.htm");	Displays a hyperlink with a jump to the designated page or URL

indexOf() returns the position in the string of the value enclosed in the brackets. Remember that the first character has an index value of zero.

charAt() returns the letter that is found in the string at the position given in the brackets. Again the first character in the string has an index value of zero.

length simply returns the total number of characters in the string, including any spaces.

substring() returns a subset of the string whose contents depends on the values sent as parameters (i.e. the figures given in the brackets).   The method returns a string whose first character is given by the first parameter and whose last character is given by the second parameter minus one.   In the example above, the parameters were 6 and 8. This will fetch the characters from positions 6 and 7 in the original string.

The upperCase and lowerCase methods return a string whose characters have all been converted to upper case characters or lower case characters respectively.

The next four methods are used to format text before it is displayed.
The fontcolor() method has the equivalent effect of placing <FONT COLOR="red"> and </FONT> tags around the text, while still remaining within the <script> tags.
Similarly, the bold and italics methods format the text in the way that <B> and <I> tags would within standard HTML.

The link method produces the same effect as the normal hyperlink tags <A HREF="something.htm">link text </A> while remaining within the <script> section.

Concatenation
Concatenation is simply the joining of individual strings.
The example show strings called forename and surname.   They can be concatenated with the line:
        Myname=forename + surname'
But this would result in a new string myname with the contents *"DavyDick"*. The solution is to add another string, containing a single blank space.
The example also shows the <BR> tag being inserted into the string to create a line break and producing a final result of:
        My name is
        Davy Dick

Arrays

Variables are handy for storing single pieces of data. When a collection of similar items has to be stored, it becomes very unwieldy.   Imagine setting up 100 different variables to store 100 prices, along with another 100 variables to store 100 product descriptions – then another 100 variables to store stock levels … and so on.

```
<script>
forename="Davy";
surname="Dick";
myname="My name is <br>" + forename + " " + surname;
document.write(myname);
</script>
```

This is where arrays simplify matters.

An array is a group of items of the same type. You are allowed to have an array of numbers, an array of strings and an array of objects – but all the items in the array must be of the same type. You cannot have an array that stores numbers and strings at the same time.

A string is simply an array of characters, with each individual character being accessed by its index number (how far along the string). An array works in the same way, except that it can access larger items (e.g. the fifth name, the eighteenth address or the hundredth price).

Consider how an array can be used to save the high scores in a game.
The array would be created with the instruction:

        score = new Array(10);

This assumes that we want to store the top ten highest scores. The number in the bracket determines how many elements the array will be able to store.

The contents of each item can be set by stating how far down the list it is stored.   Like strings, the index value commences at 1 instead of zero.
So, the instruction

        score[2]=1775;

places 1775 into the third element of the array.
The example also shows the values of individual elements being printed out.
The total of the three top scores can be added thus:

        bigthree = score[0] + score[1] + score[2];

```
<script>
score = new Array(5);
score[0]=2450;
score[1]=1985;
score[2]=1775;
score[3]=1650;
score[4]=1500;
document.write(score[0]," ",score[1]," ",score[2]);
</script>
```

This is a big improvement on using huge collections of individual variables, all with different variable names, but is not really suitable for handling large databases where better approaches are available.

The section on dates used a script to display the current date on a web page, in the format

        13/10/02

This script can be modified as shown so that it displays thus:

        Saturday 13/10/02

A text array of 7 elements is created and each element is filled with the names of each day of the week.
dow=timenow.getDay();   fetches   the current   day   of   the   week   and weekday=dayofweek[dow];   extracts the corresponding day name from the array.

Using   the   same   technique,   the   script could be altered to include an array of month names so that the web page would display:

        Saturday 13 October 02

Statements such as

        dayofweek[4]="Thursday";

can be used to set the value of individual elements, as shown in the example.

```
<script>
dayofweek=new Array(7);
dayofweek[0]="Sunday";
dayofweek[1]="Monday";
dayofweek[2]="Tuesday";
dayofweek[3]="Wednesday";
dayofweek[4]="Thursday";
dayofweek[5]="Friday";
dayofweek[6]="Saturday";

timenow=new Date();
dow=timenow.getDay();
thisday=timenow.getDate();
thismonth=timenow.getMonth()+1;
thisyear=timenow.getYear();
weekday=dayofweek[dow];
document.write(weekday + " " + thisday + " / " + thismonth + " / " +thisyear);
</script>
```

The entire array can be initialised with values with a single instruction:

        dayofweek = new Array("Sunday","Monday","Tuesday","Wednesday","Thursday","Friday","Saturday");

This replaces the list of single statements.

Flow control

Earlier in the chapter, the if .. else structure was examined. It showed that not every line of a script need be acted upon.
Depending upon the result of the test, either the code after the if was carried out or the code after the else was carried out. At no time would both pieces of code be run one after the other.
Instead of selectively processing statements, there are times when the same instruction may need to be repeated over and over again. This is called "looping" and can be achieved in JavaScript using the for keyword.

        for (loop=0; loop <7; loop++)

The for keyword has three parameters each with a setting of a variable (loop in the example).

```
<script>
dayofweek = new Array("Sunday","Monday","Tuesday",
"Wednesday","Thursday","Friday","Saturday");
for (loop=0; loop <7; loop++)
{
document.write(dayofweek[loop], "<br>");
}
</script>
```

The first value sets the starting index. In the example, this is set to zero, so the starting point is the first element in the list. The second value sets when the loop should cease. As long as the condition is met (in this case loop having a value less than 7), the looping process will continue. As soon as the condition is no longer true (in this case when loop reaches a value of 7), the loop will be exited. The third value controls the stepping amount and this is usually in steps of 1.

Each time the second condition is found to be true, the statements within the curly braces are carried out.

In the example, the statements are carried out seven times, starting with loop=0 up to loop=6. On each occasion, the loop value is used as an index for the dayofweek array. This displays the corresponding day of the week, followed by a line break. The result of running the script is to display:

> Sunday
> Monday
> Tuesday
> Wednesday
> etc

This technique can be used to display sets of data. If a web site stored book information in four different arrays, then they could all be displayed in a single statement:

> document.write(title[loop], "   ", author[loop], "   ", publisher[loop], "   ", price[loop], "<br>");

This next script uses two arrays and an if statement.

A swimming pool offers swimming lessons at different times on different days of the week. The for loop cycles through every item in the arrays but only displays the dayofweek contents when the timeofday contents is found to store *"Afternoon"*.

```
<script>
dayofweek = new Array ("Sunday","Monday","Tuesday","Wednesday","
Thursday", "Friday", "Saturday");
timeofday= new Array("Afternoon", "Morning", "Afternoon", "Evening",
"Afternoon", "Morning", "Afternoon");
for (loop=0; loop <7; loop++)
{
if (timeofday[loop]=="Afternoon")document.write(dayofweek[loop], "<br>");
}
</script>
```

while loops

Another type of control loop is the *"while"* loop.

Its format is:

While (condition is true)
  { carry out the instruction between these curly brackets }

The script in this example stores a list of student test scores in descending order. The script is being used to list all student scores that were greater than 20.

While the value fetched from the array is greater than 20, the value is displayed on the screen. When a value of 20 or less is reached, the loop is exited and control passes to the next instruction outwith the loop.

Again, the script could be amended to display the names of students along with their test scores.

```
<script>
scores = new Array(100,88,67,45,32,28,24,18,12,9);
index=0;
while (scores[index] > 20)
{
document.write(scores[index], "<br>");
index++;
}
</script>
```

All that is needed is the creation of an array of student names and the amendment of the document.write line to read:

> document.write(studentname[index], " ", scores[index], "<br>");

Forms

In an earlier chapter, we looked at creating and using forms for posting as e-mails. In this chapter, we look at using forms to get user input into a JavaScript program. We also look at using JavaScript to verify whether a user has completed the fields in the form before allowing it to be submitted.

This following script is an expansion of the previous script that displayed a list of student test scores.

In the previous version, the test value was fixed at 20, as the value was embedded in the program.

This version uses a form with a single field, allowing the user to decide what test value to use.

When run, it displays the following:

Input the Pass mark		Show results

The user enters a value in the text box and clicks the *"Show Results"* button. This initiates a call to the display function, which uses the user's input in the while loop test condition.

```
<HTML>
<HEAD>

<script>
function display()
{
  scores = new Array(100,88,67,45,32,28,24,18,12,9);
  index=0;
  testvalue=getinput.userinput.value;
  while (scores[index] >= testvalue)
    {
      document.write(scores[index], "<br>");
      index++;
    }
}
</script>

</head><body>
<form name="getinput">
Input the Pass mark <input name="userinput">
<input   type="button"   value="Show   results"
onClick="display();">
</form>

</BODY>
</HTML>
```

Many of the previous examples used fixed values within the script. These can now also be re-written to replace the fixed value with a value input by the user.

Form validation

A previous chapter looked at creating and posting forms. The examples assumed that the user would always make sensible entries. JavaScript allows the contents of forms to be tested before they are posted.

The example shown is for a simple three field form that uses JavaScript to ensure that the form is not submitted if any of the fields have been left empty.

If a field is left empty, the user is given an error message indicating the problem.

When the three fields are given contents, clicking the *'submit'* button posts the form.

The script for creating this web page is shown on the following page.

The three entry boxes are created in the manner discussed previously.

The extra features are:

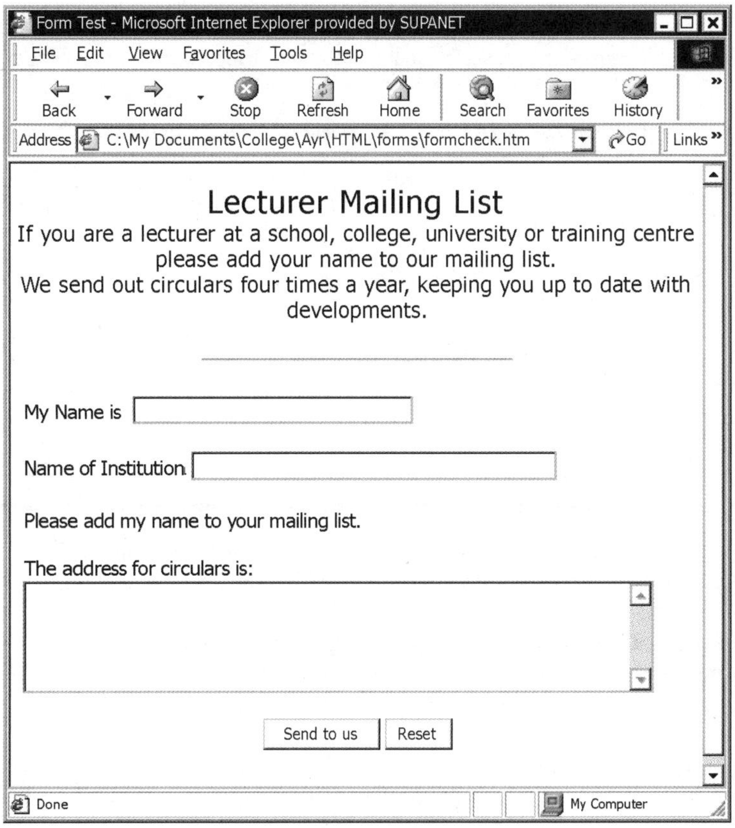

The form has to be given a name. This is not required with a form that is purely HTML-based, but is required by JavaScript.

The form is named during the FORM declaration as shown in this line of code:

```
<FORM NAME="maillist" ACTION="/cgi-
    bin/mailform" METHOD="POST"
    onSubmit="return fieldcheck();">
```

In the example, the form has been given the name *'maillist'*. The other addition is the last few words in the line. The onSubmit event is triggered when the submit button is pressed. It calls a function called fieldcheck that is written in JavaScript. While onSubmit is a command taken from the JavaScript language, fieldcheck is not a pre-written function. This means that it can be given any name (except those already used by the Javascript language).

The function is intended to return a value that is either *'true'* or *'false'*. It should return the value *'true'* if all the fields are found to contain some content; otherwise it should return the value *'false'*. The form will only be posted when the onSubmit call gets a return that is *'true'*.

The function used in the example appears at the top of the HTML page and its lines of code are wrapped in the <SCRIPT LANGUAGE="JavaScript"> and </SCRIPT> tags. Every function has to have a name so that it can be called from within the HTML script (fieldcheck in the example).

The function's code lines are surrounded by braces, as shown below.

```
{
    if (document.maillist.name.value.length < 1)
      {alert ("The name box must have an entry.");
       return false;}
    return true;
}
```

This set of code takes the form:
  If something is found to be the case
    tell the user
    and send the value 'false' back
  Otherwise send the value 'true' back

The *'something'* that is being tested in the example is how many characters are found to be in the form's name field. The document that is being tested is the name field used in the maillist form. One of the values that this field possesses is the length of the text contained in it. If this length is less than one character (i.e. the field is empty) then the results of the test trigger the error message and the return of the *'false'* value. If the field contains characters, its length is greater than zero, no error message is given and the *'true'* value is returned. This results in the form being posted.

The complete script for displaying the *'Lecturer Mailing List'* page, complete with all field validations is:

```
<HTML>
<SCRIPT LANGUAGE=" JavaScript">
function fieldcheck()
{
  if (document.maillist.name.value.length < 1)
    {alert ("The name box must have an entry.");
     return false;}
  if (document.maillist.institution.value.length<1)
    {alert("The name of the institution must be entered.");
     return false;}
  if (document.maillist.address.value.length <1)
    {alert("The address must be entered.");
     return false;}
  return true;
}
</SCRIPT>
<HEAD><TITLE>Form Test</TITLE></HEAD>
<BODY BGCOLOR="white"><FONT FACE="ARIAL,HELVETICA" SIZE="5">
<center><B>Lecturer Mailing List<br></font>
<font size=4>If you are a lecturer at a school, college, university or training centre<br>
please add your name to out mailing list.<br>
We send out circulars four times a year, keeping you up to date with
developments</B></center></FONT><P>

<FORM NAME="maillist" ACTION="/cgi-bin/mailform" METHOD="POST" onSubmit="return fieldcheck();">
<hr width=250 align=center><p><b>
My Name is          <INPUT TYPE=text NAME=name SIZE=30><p>
Name of Institution    <INPUT TYPE=text NAME=institution SIZE=40><p>
Please add my name to your mailing list.<p>
The address for circulars is<br>
            <TEXTAREA name="address" rows=5 cols=60></TEXTAREA><br>
<p align=center>

<INPUT TYPE="submit" VALUE="Send to us">
<INPUT TYPE="reset" ></center><P>

</FORM>
</BODY>
</HTML>
```

The script checks that each field is completed before allowing the form to be posted.
Of course, this does not necessarily mean that the user has entered meaningful information.

Consider the earlier script for displaying student test scores. The user is supposed to enter a value between 1 and 100 as a test value. However, the user may enter one of a number of erroneous entries;

- A value of zero
- A value exceeding 100
- A negative value
- A piece of text instead of a number

The function used in the previous example can be modified as shown in this script.
The line

          if (testvalue>0 && testvalue<101)

contains two test conditions that check for all the possible entry errors listed above.

```
function display()
{
  scores = new Array(100,88,67,45,32,28,24,18,12,9);
  index=0;
  testvalue=getinput.userinput.value;
  if (testvalue>0 && testvalue<101)
  {
    while (scores[index] >= testvalue)
    {
      document.write(scores[index], "<br>");
      index++;
    }
  }
  else {window.alert("error message goes here");}
}
```

Both conditions have to be tested true to display the list of results; otherwise the user is presented with an error message

If the testvalue entered is zero or less, the overall condition fails. Similarly if the testvalue is greater than 100, the overall condition fails. Finally, if the user enters a string instead of a number, the testvalue>0 check fails. Since a string cannot be compared to an integer, the test returns a false value and the overall test fails.

Other validation tests that might be performed include:

- Checking that text is of an appropriate length. Certain input text, such as post codes or national insurance numbers, must be of a certain length to be valid. For the example of a post code, some script similar to the checks above can be used, to ensure that the item's length is at least 5 characters and at most 7 characters.
- Checking the content of text data. Again, using the example of a post code, Javascript can be used to check that the code consists of one or two alphabetic characters, followed by one or two numeric characters, and so on, as this is how post codes work. This involves further complexity but means a more robust result.

Printing a web form

A web site may provide a facility to print out a web page by clicking on a button. This may be for printing an FAQ, a copy of a order or whatever.

The addition of these lines of code add that facility to a page:

```
<FORM>
    <input type="button" name="Printme" value="Print this order" onClick="window.print()">
</FORM>
```

Creating a shopping cart

Most commercial web sites have a shopping cart of some sort. This may range from a simple system up to an extremely large database system.

At the lower end of the market, it may simply consist of a form into which the user enters information – and then prints the form out for posting or faxing.

At the upper end, the form will be linked to a secure system for encrypting the data before it is posted.

The code on the next two pages produces the miniature shopping cart displayed here.

For ease of understanding, the HTML and the JavaScript sections are shown and discussed separately, although there is no reason why both sections could not appear in a single HTML file.

The user can only enter data into the three *"Quantity"* fields, with the other fields being updated by JavaScript functions.

When the data is complete, the user can click on the *"Submit"* button to print out the form.

Clicking on the *"Clear all items"* button resets all the *"Quantity"* fields back to zero.

The script will automatically calculate a 25% discount for items purchased in groups of five or more.

The script will also add on a £2.50 postage charge on orders that total less than £50.

The HTML
The HTML section creates a pretty standard form layout (if necessary, re-read the chapter that explains forms in more detail).

The additional features are:

The fourth line introduces the code stored in the external JavaScript file.

The READONLY attributes ensure that the user cannot enter data into these fields.

The onChange method is used to calculate and display a cost amount into a field, when the user enters data into a *"Quantity"* field and moves to another field. onChange detects this movement and calls the totalcost function.

The fifth last line prints out the screen contents when the *"Submit"* button is clicked.

```html
<HTML>
<HEAD>
  <TITLE>Dumbreck Publishing Order Form</TITLE>
  <SCRIPT src="cart1.js">
  </SCRIPT>
</HEAD>
<BODY>
  <center>
  <h2>On-line Order Form</h2>
  <p></p>
  <h4> Order 5 or more of any item and get a 25% discount on that item</h4>
  <p></p>
  <FORM NAME="itemsform" ACTION="mailto:sales@company.com" ENCTYPE="text/plain">
   <TABLE BORDER="2">
    <TR>
       <TD><b>Item</b></TD>
       <TD><b>Quantity</b></TD>
       <TD><b>Unit Price</b></TD>
       <TD><b>Total Cost</b></TD>
    </TR>
    <TR>
      <TD>First Item</TD>
      <TD><INPUT TYPE="TEXT" NAME="num1" VALUE="0" SIZE="10"
          onChange="this.form.overalltotal.value=totalcost();"
      </input></td>
       <TD><INPUT TYPE="TEXT" NAME="price1" VALUE="£20.00" READONLY SIZE="10"></INPUT></TD>
       <TD><INPUT TYPE="TEXT" NAME="total1" VALUE="£0.00" READONLY SIZE="10"></INPUT></TD>
    </TR>
    <TR>
      <TD>Second Item</TD>
      <TD><INPUT TYPE="TEXT" NAME="num2" VALUE="0" SIZE="10"
         onChange="this.form.overalltotal.value=totalcost();"
         onClick="this.select()"></INPUT></TD>
     <TD><INPUT TYPE="TEXT" NAME="price2" VALUE="£10.00" READONLY SIZE="10"></INPUT></TD>
     <TD><INPUT TYPE="TEXT" NAME="total2" VALUE="£0.00" READONLY SIZE="10"></INPUT></TD>
    </TR>
    <TR>
      <TD>Third Item</TD>
      <TD><INPUT TYPE="TEXT" NAME="num3" VALUE="0" SIZE="10"
         onChange="this.form.overalltotal.value=totalcost();"
         onClick="this.select()"></INPUT></TD>
       <TD><INPUT TYPE="TEXT" NAME="price3" VALUE="£24.00" READONLY SIZE="10"></INPUT></TD>
       <TD><INPUT TYPE="TEXT" NAME="total3" VALUE="£0.00" READONLY SIZE="10"></INPUT></TD>
    </TR>
    <TR>
      <TD colspan="3">Postage and Packing</TD>
      <TD><INPUT TYPE="TEXT" NAME="PPtotal" VALUE="£0.00" READONLY SIZE="10"></INPUT></TD>
    </TR>
    <TR>
      <TD colspan=3><b>Total</b></td>
      <TD><INPUT TYPE="TEXT" NAME="overalltotal" VALUE="£0.00" READONLY SIZE="10"></INPUT></td>
    </TR>
   </TABLE>
   <p></p>
   <input type="button" name="clear" value="Clear all items" onClick="clearitems()">
   <input type="button" name="submit" value="Submit" onClick="document.print()">
  </FORM>
 </center>
</BODY>
</HTML>
```

The JavaScript
The contents of each section of the external JavaScript code is explained below.

This function is called when the user clicks the *"Clear all items"* button. It sets all the quantity fields and cost fields back to zero.

```
function clearitems() {
    document.itemsform.num1.value=0
    document.itemsform.num2.value=0
    document.itemsform.num3.value=0
    document.itemsform.PPtotal.value=0
    document.itemsform.overalltotal.value=0
}
```

This function has four sections.
The first three look at each quantity field and calculate the cost for each item. The last line of each of these sections also updates the overall cost of the purchase.

The conditional statement:
```
if (isNaN(number) || number <1)
    number=0;
```
protects the calculation from being corrupted by incorrect user entries.

If the user enters a zero or a negative number, or if text is entered in the quantity field, the number for the calculation is set to zero. In this way, only positive numbers are accepted for the cost calculations.

```
function totalcost() {
var total=0
number=document.itemsform.num1.value
if (isNaN(number) || number <1) number=0;
if (number>4) price=15.00;
    else price=20.00
document.itemsform.price1.value=currency(price)
document.itemsform.total1.value=currency(price*number)
total=total+price*number

number=document.itemsform.num2.value
if (isNaN(number) || number<1) number=0;
if (number>4) price=7.50;
    else price=10.00
document.itemsform.price2.value=currency(price)
document.itemsform.MMtotal.value=currency(price*number)
total=total+price*number

number=document.itemsform.num3.value
if (isNaN(number) || number <1) number=0;
if (number>4) price=18.00;
    else price=24.00
document.itemsform.price3.value=currency(price)
document.itemsform.total3.value=currency(price*number)
total=total+price*number
```

The fourth section checks the total cost of the goods and either sets the PPtotal (postage cost) contents to zero or £2.50.

```
if(total<50)
    { document.itemsform.PPtotal.value=currency(2.5)
      total=total+2.5   }
    else document.itemsform.PPtotal.value=currency(0);
return(currency(total))
}
```

This last function is used for formatting the output to the READONLY fields.
It is a good example of parameter passing.

```
function currency(inputnum) {
    var outputstring=""
    outputstring="£"+inputnum
    if(outputstring.charAt(outputstring.length-2)==".")
        { outputstring=outputstring+"0";   return(outputstring)  }
    if(outputstring.charAt(outputstring.length-3)!=".")
        { outputstring=outputstring+".00"; return(outputstring)  }
}
```

The four sections of the totalcost function calculate the price for a particular item. Item one and item 3 always have prices that are integer values (i.e. 20, 15, 24 and 18) while item 3 and the postage may contain floating point values (i.e. 7.50 and 2.50).
If we use the formula price * number for integer values, the answer will be an integer value. For example, three of item 1 will have an answer stored as 60 – not £60.00 as we would wish to display it in the form's field. Similarly, five lots of item 2 will produce an answer that is stored as 37.5 instead of £37.50.

Consider the value of 37.5 being passed into the currency function as a numeric value.
The function creates a string that concatenates the pound symbol and the value that is passed in. At this point the outputstring variable stores "£37.5". The string's length is tested as being four characters. The charAt(outputstring.length-2) method looks along the string to position 2 (i.e. 4-2). This finds the "." character (remember that the string index starts at zero). This means that there is only one character after the period, so a zero character is added to the string.
The second test detects times when there is no period in the string, as when the parameter is an integer (e.g. as in the case of sending 60 to the function). In this case both a period and two zeroes are added to the string.
The function always returns strings for display in the form's fields that have a pound sign, a pounds value and a decimal value.

Using Combo Boxes for web navigation

The '*combo box*' (or '*list box*'), as explained in the "*Developing websites*" chapter, is used to present the user with a drop-down box to select one of several options. This is commonly combined with JavaScript code, in order to provide a drop-down list of pages on a web site that the user may travel to. The example shows a simple version of this kind of navigation control.

The select form tag is used, as normal, and some JavaScript code is associated with the onChange event for the combo box. This event is triggered whenever the

```
<FORM name="myForm">
   <SELECT name="jumpto" onChange="document.location.href =
document.myForm.jumpto.options[document.myForm.jumpto.selectedIndex].value">
      <OPTION value="audio.htm">
      Audio data
      </OPTION>
      <OPTION value="video.htm">
      Video data
      </OPTION>
   </SELECT>
</FORM>
```

```
Audio data  ▼
Audio data
Video data
```

user selects an object from the list, typically by dropping down the list box and clicking on an item within. Therefore, whenever the user selects an object from the list, the JavaScript code executes. In this case, the example includes some scripting that will take the value associated with the selected option (either "audio.htm" or "video.htm") and use that as the new document HREF location. The user will then be presented with a drop-down list that looks like the one shown, and whenever one of the options is chosen the browser will be directed to an appropriate HTML page.

Other form input types

Text boxes and single selection boxes are not the only types of input in an HTML form; there are also multiple selection boxes, checkboxes, radio buttons, and others. JavaScript is able to access and even manipulate the contents of any form object. The example shows the use of the three input types mentioned, to create a simple 'quiz' in JavaScript.

This quiz features three sections, one in the form of a multiple selection list box; one in the form of a set of radio buttons; and one split into several checkboxes. The user is prompted to answer the questions by selecting options from the various input objects.

The "submit" button at the bottom of the page will, when clicked, trigger the 'check' JavaScript function. This function uses properties of the form objects to determine which answers have been chosen by the user, and assign a score for each answer which is correct. Finally, an 'alert' dialog box displays the user's score out of 8.

To find out which list items are selected, the script uses the 'selected' attribute of each member of the array which makes up the SELECT object named 'q1'. If a more modular approach were to be applied, this checking could be done within a loop.

Next, the radio buttons and check boxes are examined. Both objects have a 'checked' attribute. The difference is that the set of radio boxes make up a single object, so each item is part of an array named 'q2'. Each item of the array can be examined, and again, a loop could be of use if a more generic version of this quiz were to be developed.

```
<HTML><HEAD>
<SCRIPT language="JavaScript">
function check() {
   var score=0;
   if(document.myForm.q1[0].selected==false) score=score+1;
   if(document.myForm.q1[1].selected==true) score=score+1;
   if(document.myForm.q1[2].selected==true) score=score+1;
   if(document.myForm.q1[3].selected==false) score=score+1;
   if(document.myForm.q2[1].checked==true) score=score+1;
   if(document.myForm.q3a.checked==true) score=score+1;
   if(document.myForm.q3b.checked==true) score=score+1;
   if(document.myForm.q3c.checked==false) score=score+1;
   alert("Out of 8, you scored: "+score);
}
</SCRIPT></HEAD>

<BODY>
<H1>Animal Quiz</H1>

<FORM name=myForm>
   (Q1) Which of the following are mammals?<BR><BR>
   <SELECT name="q1" multiple>
      <option value="a">(A) Eel</option>
      <option value="b">(B) Dolphin</option>
      <option value="c">(C) Whale</option>
      <option value="d">(D) Squid</option>
   </SELECT>
   <BR><BR>(Q2) One of these is not a bird.  Which is it?<BR><BR>
   <INPUT TYPE="radio" NAME="q2">(A) Hawk</INPUT>
   <INPUT TYPE="radio" NAME="q2">(B) Bat</INPUT>
   <INPUT TYPE="radio" NAME="q2">(C) Penguin</INPUT>
   <BR><BR>(Q3) Tick the boxes next to each true statement from the
following:<BR><BR>
   <INPUT TYPE="checkbox" NAME="q3a">The largest single living organism
in the world is an underground fungus in North America.<BR></INPUT>
   <INPUT TYPE="checkbox" NAME="q3b">The oyster changes gender several
times within its lifetime.<BR></INPUT>
   <INPUT TYPE="checkbox" NAME="q3c">The duck's quack does not
echo.<BR></INPUT>
   <INPUT TYPE="submit" VALUE="Check your answers" onClick="check();">
   <INPUT TYPE="reset" VALUE="Clear the answers">
</FORM>

</BODY>
</HTML>
```

Windows

Anyone browsing through web sites will soon be presented with pop-up windows, advertising products and inviting them to visit another site. To most users, this technique is very annoying but there are times when extra Windows can be put to good use:

- Displaying a currency converter
- Displaying a calendar
- Displaying a help page
- Displaying a copyright notice

In the first three cases, the pop-up window is requested by the user, while the copyright notice might be inserted by the designer so that the user cannot avoid being shown the information.

The syntax for creating a new window is:

Window2=window.open("windowcontent.htm", "windowname", "width=300, height=200, toolbar=no status=no");

Window is an object and window.open is a method for creating a new window object. The method uses three parameters:

- The URL that will be loaded into the new window.
- The name of the window for future reference.
- The list of window features, such as size and window bars. Window features, such as the display of toolbars, status bars, menubars, scrollbars can be displayed by making their values equal "yes" or "1". The features can be hidden by making the values "no" or "0". The "resizable" feature controls whether the user can resize the new window.

A new window will automatically appear, if the script line shown above is used.

The example below shows how a new window can be called up from clicking a button.

```
<form name="calc">
<input type="button" value="Click here for currency calculator"
    onClick="NewOne=window.open('calc.htm','CalcWindow', 'toolbar=0,status=0,width=400, height=300');">
</form>
```

The windowname.close method is used to close a window.
In the example the instruction would be:

    CalcWindow.close()

```
<script>
    popup=window.open('message.htm','WinName', 'width=400, height=300');
    ID=window.setTimeout("popup.close()", 5000);
</script>
```

Windows can be resized by JavaScript code, using the window.resizeTo function. This function has two parameters; one for the window's new width, and one for its new height, both of which are integers. For example, the following line could be used:

    CalcWindow.resizeTo(640,480);

This method is specific to the browser, however. In Explorer, the width and height parameters specify the size of the entire window, while in Navigator they specify the size of the inner window, which displays the actual HTML page. And of course, in some browsers, the method is not supported at all.

In Navigator, the attributes top.outerWidth and top.outerHeight can be used to specify the outer size of the window. As such, it is possible to write the code in such a way that an appropriate window size is achieved in both Navigator and Explorer, using an if statement to supply one set of parameters if the browser is detected as Explorer, and another set of parameters otherwise.

Using timeouts

Normally, when a pop-up window is opened, the user has to click to close it. JavaScript provides a timeout facility that can be used to display a pop-up window for a fixed period of time. This can be useful for short messages such as *"Sale closes at end of the month!"* or *"Our products page has been expanded!"*. The example opens a pop-up window and displays the message stored in message.htm.

The setTimeout method has two parameters:

- The activity to be carried out
- The time to wait before the activity is carried out (measured in milliseconds).

In this case, the message is displayed and, after five seconds the pop-up window is automatically removed. The ID value is only used if there is a need to cancel a timeout with a clearTimeout(ID) statement. The ID identifies a particular timeout, allowing several timeouts to operating at the same time.

Dialog boxes

JavaScript provides three methods of providing dialog boxes.

Alert

This simply places a message in a pop-up window and has been used in previous examples.
Its syntax is

        alert("message");

Although this creates a pop-up window with a message, it is not nearly as flexible as using the window object and methods.

Confirm

This method produces a text message and an *"OK"* and *"Cancel"* buttons. If the *"OK"* button is clicked, a true condition is returned, while clicking *"Cancel"* returns a false condition.

The example shows a script intended to be embedded in a larger web page.

The HTML section uses a button with the inscription of *"Download"*; this is probably part of a menu of various buttons.

If the user clicks this button, he/she is shown this pop-up window:

```
<HTML>
<HEAD>
</head><body>

<script>
function choice(temp)
{
if (temp==true)
  location.href="download.htm"
else
  location.href="#.htm"
}
</script>

<form name="testo">
<input type="button" value="Download"
    onClick="temp=window.confirm('Users download this
utility at their own risk. \n Do you still want to continue?');
choice(temp); ">
</form>
</HTML>
```

If the user clicks the *"OK"* button, he/she is directed to the download web page.
If the *"Cancel"* button is clicked, the *"#.htm"* link keeps the user in the current web page.

Note the use of \n to flow the text on to a new line. This is one of JavaScript's special characters. Others are:

        \t (for a tab)
        \f (for form feed)
        \b (for a backspace).

Prompt

An earlier script input a pass mark via a field entry in a form.
Another method uses the window.prompt method, as shown in this modified version of the earlier script.

window.prompt opens a pop-up window and displays an appropriate message (e.g. *"Enter the required pass mark"*).

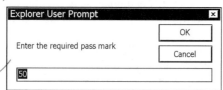

```
<HTML>
<HEAD></HEAD>

<script>
  scores = new Array(100,88,67,45,32,28,24,18,12,9);
  index=0;
  testvalue=window.prompt("Enter pass mark", 50);
  if (testvalue>0 && testvalue<101)
  {
     while (scores[index] >= testvalue)
     {
        document.write(scores[index], "<br>");
        index++;
     }
  }
  else {window.alert("error message goes here");}
</script>
<BODY></BODY>
</HTML>
```

When the user types in an entry, hitting the Return key or clicking the *"OK"* button returns the value into the variable.
Entering a non-numeric entry results in a null value being returned.

Note that the example used two parameters – one contained the message and the other contained the value of 50. This second parameter is known as the *"default value"* and it results in the dialog box being opened with the value of 50 already entered. The entry is highlighted so that it can be overwritten simply by typing in a new figure. If the suggested figure is the one that is wanted, the user need only click on the *"OK"* button. This technique is a useful where a particular value is most often used.

This works with both numeric and text entries. For text entries, the default value might a message such as *"Enter your full name here"* or *"Enter all eight characters in the product code"*.
The use of a default value is optional. If it is not required, then only the first parameter need be included.

Frames

Before tackling this section on how JavaScript handles frames, be sure to understand the material on frames in the earlier chapter.

When a window contains two or more frames, JavaScript treats a frame as a separate object. This allows individual frames to be manipulated by JavaScript.

This HTML page creates the screen display illustrated below. It creates two rows, with the first row being split into two columns.

So, four frame objects are involved here:

- The window that contains the three frames. This is known as the *"parent"* window.
- The three frame objects called categories, subcats and products.

```
<HTML>
<HEAD></HEAD>
<FRAMESET rows="15%, 85%">
   <FRAMESET cols="33%,67%">
     <FRAME NAME="categories" SRC="categories.htm">
     <FRAME NAME="subcats"    SRC="empty.htm">
   </FRAMESET>
   <FRAME NAME="products" SRC="empty.htm" >
</FRAMESET>
</HTML>
```

Normal HTML updates a frame's contents using the target tag as in this example;

```
<A HREF="urlhere.htm" target="framename">Link text goes herel </A>
```

In any web page, window refers to the current page. When a page contains frames, window refers to the current frame. So, to change the content of the frame, the script simply alters the location of the frame (i.e. it loads the current frame with the contents of the provided URL.

```
<A HREF="#" onClick="window.location='audio.htm'"> Link text goes here </A>
```

To alter the contents of any other frame, the link provides the frame information as parent.framename to indicate that the particular frame is held located within the parent window.

```
<A HREF="#" onClick="parent.subcats.location='classical.htm'"> Link text goes here </A>
```

Updating two frames simultaneously

A common use of JavaScript with frames is achieving the updating of two different frames with a single click of a button or hyperlink, something that HTML alone does not support.

The illustration shows an interface for a store selling a range of consumer products. The description and price of each item is to be displayed in the large bottom frame. However, there are too many different categories of goods to place on the top menu.

Therefore the top part of the display is split into two different frames. The left frame displays the main stock categories (CDs, DVDs, etc.).

```
<HTML>
<BODY>
<FONT face="VERDANA,ARIAL, HELVETICA" size="3">
<img src="bar.gif" height=4, width=150>
        <A HREF="#" onClick="window.self.location='audio.htm';
        parent.subcats.location='audiocats.htm'"> Audio CDs </A>
<br>
<img src="bar.gif" height=4, width=30>
<A HREF="#" onClick="window.self.location='video.htm';
parent.subcats.location='videocats.htm'"> Video CDs </A>
<br>
<img src="bar.gif" height=4, width=30>
<A HREF="#" onClick="window.self.location='dvd.htm';
        parent.subcats.location='dvdcats.htm'">   DVDs </A>
<br>
<img src="bar.gif" height=4, width=30>
<A HREF="#" onClick="window.self.location='games.htm';
        parent.subcats.location='gamescats.htm'"> Computer Games </A>
</BODY>
</HTML>
```

Clicking on one of these categories carries out two tasks:

- The content of the left frame is changed, with the category chosen being displayed on the right-hand margin of the frame.
- The content of the right-hand frame is also altered to show a list of sub-categories (Musicals, Comedies, etc.)

If the *"Audio CDs"* link was clicked, the link would be moved to the right-hand margin, the *"Video Tapes"* link would move back to the left margin and the right frame would display sub-categories of music (e.g. Rock, Classical, Country, etc.).

The two frames are updated by the single link by including two instructions in the onClick statement:

```
<A HREF="#" onClick="window.self.location='audio.htm'; parent.subcats.location='audiocats.htm'"> Audio
CDs </A>
```

The Status Bar

JavaScript is able to manipulate the contents of the status bar, which can be useful to provide additional feedback to the viewer. At its simplest, a short string of text can be placed in the Status Bar using the defaultStatus variable.

However, longer strings of text may not fit into the status bar. Indeed, even a relatively short text string will not fit in the status bar if the browser window is small. For this reason, and also for effect, scrolling text in the status bar has become commonplace.

The script shown illustrates a simple program for scrolling text in the status bar.

As can be seen, the defaultStatus object simply stores a text string that is displayed by the browser in the Status bar at any time when there is no other data that must be displayed there.

```
<HTML>
<HEAD>
<SCRIPT language="JavaScript">
scrolltext = "Here is the scrolling text. ";
position = 0;

function scroll(){
    window.defaultStatus=scrolltext.substring(position,scrolltext.length)   +
scrolltext.substring(0,position);
    position=position+1;
    if (position==scrolltext.length)
       position=0 ;
    setTimeout("scroll()", 100);
}
</SCRIPT>
</HEAD>
<BODY onLoad="scroll();" >
Page contents go here.
</BODY>
</HTML>
```

This example uses the onLoad event in the BODY tag to call the scroll function as soon as the page loads.

This scroll function sets the defaultStatus contents and then uses the setTimeout function to call itself recursively even 100 milliseconds. In other words, after every 100 milliseconds, this procedure will run again.

The contents of the string which is to be placed in the status bar is animated by using a pointer variable which we have called 'position'. This points to the current scroll position within the string, and therefore with each iteration of the scroll function it increments by one, until it is equal to the length of the string, at which point it resets to zero.

This pointer, therefore, is used to create the scrolling text. We use two 'substring' methods, one to copy the latter portion of the original text, starting from the pointer position; and the other to copy the starting portion of the text, up to the pointer position. In this way, the length of the string always remains the same, but at every call of the scroll function, its contents move one space to the left.

Changing fonts with JavaScript

Although each section of text may have its own font settings, these are not directly accessible in JavaScript. If we wish to change the appearance of a section of text, we must enclose that section in a set of DIV tags. These allow the JavaScript to access the object as a child of document.all (in IE) or simply a child of the document object (in Netscape).

The DIV object can then be manipulated, and one of the options is to edit the HTML text within the DIV tags, using the innerHTML method. To do this, we need to set up appropriate text to place within the DIV tags.

For example, the <BLINK> tag in HTML is said to be the most annoying feature of web pages, and is not even standard HTML. A common replacement that is less distracting is to have text that gradually changes colour.

The following example shows a very basic colour changing script.

It works by using the '*setInterval*' command to make the browser run the 'change' function every 500 milliseconds.

In this function, we set two variables: changing_text, and newcolour.

The changing_text variable is set the first time the function runs, by checking if it is undefined, and if so, setting it to contain the same text as is initially found within the DIV tags. The newcolour variable is then set by using the switch command; it checks the current contents of newcolour, and based on its contents, it moves along to the next colour name in succession. Thus, newcolour is set each time the function runs, while changing_text is set only once.

Now that we know what colour to use, and the text that is to be placed within the DIV tags, we need to generate a string of text to replace the current contents of the DIV section. This is done by concatenating several strings to make up a piece of HTML containing the colour, and the changing text.

In this example, the contents of the DIV tag will cycle between the following:

```
<FONT COLOR="blue">This section will change colour.</FONT>
<FONT COLOR="green">This section will change colour.</FONT>
<FONT COLOR="red">This section will change colour.</FONT>
<FONT COLOR="black">This section will change colour.</FONT>
```

A similar approach can be taken to change font face, size, or other formatting features, however in most cases changing the font face or size will alter the appearance of the rest of the page. It should be considered carefully whether the effect is important enough to distract the user in this way.

This script works only in Internet Explorer and browsers using the same compatible Document Object Model. It will not work on Netscape Navigator, because the script accesses a document object; namely

document.all.changethis

which refers to the DIV tag. Although later versions of Netscape can understand the DIV tag, such objects are accessed differently; in this case it would be referred to simply as document.changethis.

It is possible, of course, to implement browser detection and use the appropriate reference according to which browser is in use.

```
<HTML>
<HEAD>
<SCRIPT language="JavaScript">
var changing_text;
var newcolour="black";

function change() {
  if (changing_text==undefined)
    changing_text=document.all.changethis.innerHTML;
  switch(newcolour) {
    case "black" :
      newcolour="blue"; break;
    case "blue" :
      newcolour="green"; break;
    case "green" :
      newcolour="red"; break;
    case "red" :
      newcolour="black"; break;
  }
  outputHTML='<FONT COLOR="' + newcolour + '">';
  outputHTML=outputHTML + changing_text + '</FONT>';
  document.all.changethis.innerHTML=outputHTML;
}

setInterval("change()",500);

</SCRIPT>
</HEAD>
<BODY>

This section will remain in the default colour.

<DIV ID="changethis">This section will change colour.</DIV>

</BODY>
</HTML>
```

Working with Image Maps

An HTML image map, like virtually all HTML objects, can also be used with JavaScript. Each image map area can have the same events as most other objects: onMouseOver, onMouseOut, onClick, and so on.

One common use of these functions is to have an image map alongside some kind of text output, which changes as the user moves the pointer from one part of the map to another. This allows the web developers to give more detailed information than is normally found in an ALT tag, and is more visible to the user, since they do not have to wait for the tooltip to pop up.

```
<HTML>
<HEAD></HEAD>
<BODY>
<FORM NAME="myform">
<IMG WIDTH=160 HEIGHT=140 SRC="image.gif" BORDER="0" ISMAP USEMAP="#my_image_map">
<MAP NAME="my_image_map">
  <AREA NAME="topleft" HREF="audio.htm" onMouseOver="document.myform.infobox.value= 'A page about audio
compression and audio formats. Also includes some downloadable sound samples';" COORDS="20,20,70,60">
  <AREA NAME="topright" HREF="video.htm" onMouseOver="document.myform.infobox.value= 'A page about video
compression and video formats. Also includes some downloadable video clips';" COORDS="90,20,140,60">
  <AREA NAME="bottomleft" HREF="animation.htm" onMouseOver="document.myform.infobox.value= 'A page about
animation methods and formats. Includes some downloadable animated GIFs.';" COORDS="20,80,70,120">
  <AREA NAME="bottomright" HREF="scipting.htm" onMouseOver="document.myform.infobox.value= 'A page about using
scripting in web pages. You can find some sample scripts here.';" COORDS="90,80,140,120">
</MAP>
  <TEXTAREA rows="10" cols="20" name="infobox" readonly="readonly"></TEXTAREA>
</FORM>
</BODY>
</HTML>
```

The example script shows how to do this. It uses a GIF image with four clickable areas as an image map, and includes a TEXTAREA object called 'infobox' that is set to 'readonly'. In other words, the user may not alter the contents of the text box; it is used purely as an output text box by the script.

When the user moves the mouse pointer over one of the map areas, the onMouseOver event is triggered, and the inline script changes the contents of 'infobox' to contain some text relevant to that area of the map. The illustration shows the resulting web page, as the user moves the mouse over the bottom left box in the image map.

Working with embedded objects

Javascript can access embedded objects, such as sounds and video files. This is done through the 'embeds' object, which is a child of the 'document' object. This object is an array, in which each array member refers to an embedded object in the document. For example, if the document contains three embedded objects, they can be referred to by using 'document.embeds[0]', 'document.embeds[1]', and 'document.embeds[2]'.   To find out how many embedded objects are in the current document, the method 'document.embeds.length' is used, which returns an integer number.

Each embedded object is associated with a plugin (assuming of course that the appropriate plugin is installed). Some of these plugins provide methods to manipulate the playback of the embedded object. For example, Netscape Navigator comes with LiveConnect, a set of basic plugins including LiveAudio, a plugin for various types of audio file. On a Navigator system (but not on an Explorer system!), the functions provided allow Javascript to control the audio playback. For example, imagine an audio file embedded as follows in an HTML file:

```
<EMBED SRC="sound.wav" AUTOSTART="false" name="myaudio"></EMBED>
```

If this were the first embedded object within the document, then the following functions could be used within JavaScript to start, pause, and stop the sound playing:

```
document.embeds[0].play();
document.embeds[0].pause();
document.embeds[0].stop();
```

The embeds array can also be accessed by name; for example 'document.embeds["myaudio"].stop();'

Animation & Flash

Animation, from the Latin *"anima"* meaning *"soul"*, is the computer modelling of movement.

At their simplest, animations use movement to draw the user's attention to the screen content. At their best, they use animation to explain processes that would be difficult to effectively get across with words alone. CD-ROM encyclopaedias are full of good examples of the effective use of animation - to demonstrate the workings of the petrol engine, the workings of the human ear, and so on.

Animation arises from a collection of graphic images being displayed on the screen one after the other in quick succession. The eye possesses a persistence of vision such that, if the images are updated quickly enough, the viewer does not detect the sequence as a set of different pictures. In this way, animation creates the illusion of movement. This is the technique used to show movies in the film theatre or on television. Ideally, an animation should display at 25 or 30 frames per second, although .

The animation software aids the designer to create animations quickly and with less pain and then exports the finished product in a format that can be used by other packages. Examples of output are SWF, AVI, MOV, and animated GIF formats.

Animation packages use two different approaches:

2D

These animations are drawn in two dimensions - width and height. There is no attempt to represent the third dimension - depth. They are used for simple animations such as animated logos and flying text. They are also used for more complex constructions, such as cartoons and animated sequences.

There is often no need to use more than two dimensions; indeed, trying to produce depth can sometimes make the presentation more obscure rather than clearer. An animation showing the stops that an aircraft would make on a route between Birmingham and Auckland only requires a 2D animation. Similarly, an animation demonstrating a computer's memory management or a sort algorithm in software engineering is best shown in 2D. In addition, of course, the public expects to see traditional cartoons displayed in two dimensions. Application software for creating 2D animations include Macromedia Flash, Microsoft GIF Animator, Alchemy GIF Construction Set and Paint Shop Pro Animation Shop. These are aimed mainly at animations for web use, although they could be used in other multimedia applications. Macromedia Director also incorporates animation facilities, as do many authoring packages.

There are two techniques used in 2D animation.

Cel-based

The cel-based animation works on the same principle as the early film animators (e.g. early Disney) who painted a separate clear acetate sheet for every frame in the animation. This is the technique used in GIF Animator, GIF Construction Set and Animation Shop. The individual frames are created with a painting package and these packages compile them into an animated GIF (type 89a).

Morphing

The morphing method uses the power of the computer to create many of the frames of the animation. The designer draws two key frames and the software creates the intermediate frames, a process known as *'tweening'*. Animation authoring packages such as Flash use a *'path following'* technique, where the application is instructed to create frames that move an object over a path drawn by the user.

Macromedia Flash uses a vector-based morphing approach and can output finished animations as animated GIFs, AVIs, QuickTime movies or even executable files (EXE files).

3D

Three-dimensional animations add the additional dimension of depth. At their simplest, they create animated logos that revolve, spin etc. At their most complex, they are complete 3D cartoons, such as Toy Story, Antz, Monsters Inc and Final Fantasy - or they are objects merged into real-world movies (such as Jurassic Park, The Hulk and Tomb Raider). The objects may represent real-world or fictional characters, or they may represent inanimate objects (such the background in a flyby or walkthrough).

Since the objects are in three dimensions, they have curved and undulating surfaces, producing shadows as they move. The objects' surfaces have textures that have to be rendered. The texture may be skin, fur, scales, cloth, grass, wood, glass, leaves, and so on. As the object is moved, the texture of the object alters and the shadows are altered. This is a very complex operation compared to most 2D productions.

With 2D, the object can simply be dragged a little way across the screen between each frame.

With 3D, every frame contains masses of new detail that have to be calculated and stored. This process, known as *'rendering'* can take a very long time. Of course, once calculated and stored, the animation plays back smoothly at normal speed.

Animation software aimed mostly at simple animations for the web include Cool3D and Simply 3D.
Powerful animation packages include LightWave 3D, Strata Studio Pro, 3D Studio, Bryce 3D and Poser.

- Poser specialises in producing moving human and animal figures and has libraries of faces, hands, hair, etc. Figures can be assembled and organised to walk or run across the screen.

Bryce 3D specialises in creating landscapes where the user controls the map contours and the object surfaces. The illustration was created in a matter of seconds. Of course, creating and animating multiple objects takes a lot longer.

Types of animation

From a web designer's point of view, there are two types of animation.

- Those that work with HTML/standard browsers (such as GIF89A, DHTML and AVI on Windows).
- Those that need a plug-in (an add-on that is installed on the browser) to handle a file's specific format. Examples are Shockwave, Flash, QuickTime and Java. Modern computers tend to be delivered with the most common plug-ins already installed. Otherwise, they can be downloaded from the Internet or found on a CD distributed with a computer magazine. Once installed, the plug-in provides the added functionality to the browser software.

From an application developer's point of view, there are also two types of animation.

- Those that work as standalone projects (e.g. EXE files, AVI animations).
- Those that need the playback computer to have supportive software (e.g. Flash player, QuickTime player, PowerPoint player, Visual Basic or Java run-time modules).

In addition, the developer has to consider *'cross-platform'* issues. Some formats only run on specific operating systems (e.g. EXE files work on Windows-based PCs) while others (e.g. Flash files) run on a range of platforms. Both QuickTime and AVIs can be run on Windows, Mac and Unix platforms. If the animation is created using dHTML, the fact that around 11% of users have JavaScript disabled has to be taken into account.

Animation formats

A range of different animation file formats is available. These range from constructing a sequence from a collection of high-resolution, full-coloured photographic images, to a sequence of relatively simple vector graphics with many of the frames being constructed by the software during playback. They all use differing techniques and have differing characteristics, such as their picture quality, file size, performance, features and degree of user interaction.
The main formats are:

- Animated GIFs (GIF89a)
- Flash
- Shockwave
- QuickTime
- AVI
- DHTML and scripting

Animated GIFs

Early GIF files could only store a single graphic image. Although GIF89a files have exactly the same file extension as static images, it is really a collection of bitmap graphics images embedded in a single file. The file header contains specific playback information. If the viewing software cannot handle animated GIFs, it still reads and displays the first picture in the sequence. Otherwise, it plays back the file as a sequence of pictures at a pre-determined rate, and usually loops to play continuously. Animated GIFs, using GIF89a files, was the first popular animation format to be used on the Web and remains very popular today.
Many applications to create GIF89a animations are available. These range from the freeware *'GIF Builder'*, through shareware packages such as *'GIF Construction Set'* and *'GIF Movie Gear'*, to commercial packages such as Paint Shop Pro's *'Animation Shop'*, *'Image Ready'*, *'Poser'* and Ulead's *'GIF Animator'*.

Advantages

- Creation software is easy, and cheap, to obtain.
- Creation software is easy to use.
- Supported by almost all browsers. Even those tiny number of browsers that do not support animated GIFs still display the first frame as a still instead.
- No browser plug-ins are required.
- HTML code for displaying an animated GI is exactly the same as an ordinary GIF.
- It supports transparent animations.

- Individual frames can be captured from a videotape or video file and compiled into an animation. Hence, a small animation can be created that displays real-world content (e.g. someone winking or waving a hand).
- Supports looping of the animation, so that a short sequence can be continually repeated giving the impression of a longer animation (e.g. the movement of a swing or a clock's pendulum).

Disadvantages

- File sizes can become very large. Since each frame is an independent bitmap image, a long animation becomes too large for most practical uses.
- The screen size of the animation is usually small, as large images increase the file size dramatically. So, unlike Flash for example, a GIF89a file would never be used for a full-screen animation.
- Animations are pretty basic. If a sequence runs at 25 frames per second, it needs 25 different images and this results in large file sizes. While reducing the frame rate requires fewer images per second, it results in very jerky animations.
- Larger files result in longer download times.
- No support for incorporating sound.
- No support for incorporating user interaction (e.g. user can't control the speed of playback, pause, or stop). Once loaded, the animation just sits on the screen and plays.

Animated GIFs are found almost exclusively on Web pages, where are used for banner advertising, eye-catching features or animations of simple concepts. However, they can be used in other ways. For example, they can be incorporated into web pages that are then compiled into executable files (e.g. using the 'HTML2EXE' program). They can also be used in PowerPoint slides (from PowerPoint version 2000 onwards). They can even be imported into 'Flash', where a pre-existing animation can be used to save building a fresh animation within Flash; the extra file size might be a price worth paying to save on development time.

Over the years, developers have used different techniques to minimise the size of animated GIF files, such as image optimisation and compression. Another approach is to look at how the animation is made up. For example, if an animation only has movement in the top right corner, then the image can be broken into smaller sub-images and placed in a table. In that way, most of the scene is only stored once (as static images), while the top right area that displays the movement is made into an animated GIF (of much smaller size since it does have to include all the static detail in every frame).

Despite developers' best efforts, animated GIFs are not really suitable for handling complex animations or long smooth-flowing animations. Consequently, most animation packages use vector-based systems rather than bitmap based systems.

Flash

Flash was initially introduced as a vector-based application, intended to add small items of animated 2D content to web pages (animated adverts, icons, rollover buttons, etc). Over the years, it has developed tremendously with improved features such as powerful scripting facilities (ActionScript), the ability to handle video files, and so on. Its uses have been expanded to include creating walkthroughs, games, kiosks and full applications. With animated GIFs, each frame displayed a separate bitmap image. With Flash animations, each frame is constructed from a set of instructions for drawing lines and shapes. Each frame has slightly different values for the drawings so they result in objects that are slightly altered in shape and position from how they appeared in the previous frame.

In addition, Flash supports 'tweening' which involves defining the screen locations of an object at two keyframes that are spaced some frames apart, and letting the software work out the location of the object for each frame in between.

Advantages

- Since Flash uses vector graphics and tweening, it produces smaller file sizes. For example, the 'moon landing' animations shown later in this chapter produce a file size of 4188 bytes for an animated GIF, compared to just 623 bytes for an equivalent created in Flash. For larger screen resolutions, there are even greater savings.
- Smaller files result in less transmission bandwidth and produce smooth flowing animations.
- Flash animations, being vector-based, offer 'scalability'. Flash objects can be scaled to fit any web page, without the pixelation suffered by a scaled-up bitmap. The same file can be used to fill any area of the screen, from a tiny postage stamp area up to full screen.
- It allows developers to easily specify the screen position of all the elements in the frame, providing much more control over interface and general page layout than with HTML.
- It allows developers to have precise control over the movements of multiple objects in animations, allowing complicated and detailed animations to be produced.
- It can create rollover buttons, etc. without worrying about Java applets or JavaScript compatibility.
- Bitmaps can be incorporated and animated, if required.
- It can incorporate sound, including WAV and MP3, with control over fading.

- It can incorporate real-world video clips, including AVI, MOV, MPG, WMV and DVI. In earlier versions of Flash, an add-on such as *'Flix'* was required but modern versions fully support embedded video clips.
- It supports extensive user interactivity. The ActionScript scripting language for Flash allows the developer to create navigable menus, user entry forms, message handling, file handling, control over screen content and animation, etc. It is possible to create an entire application or an entire web site using only Flash and its scripting facilities. For experienced programmers, it offers the features expected in an advanced object-oriented programming language.
- It provides a range of output formats for the completed project. Apart from its own native Flash format (i.e. a .swf file), it can produce QuickTime movies or Windows or Mac executable files.
- Flash files can also be incorporated into Director projects or into PowerPoint slides, or can be called from HTML within a web page.
- Flash files are platform-independent, running happily under the operating systems of Windows, Macs, Linux, PDAs, etc. This cross platform ability is based on each system having its own player plug-in. Flash players are provided with most browser software, or can be downloaded from the Macromedia website.

Disadvantages

- Since a Flash file has all its objects, including text, embedded within it, it is difficult to provide accessibility. For example, text readers for the blind and partially-sighted cannot easily extract the screen text, the text on buttons, etc., from a Flash file.
- Similarly, the lack of access to the text embedded in a Flash file means that the page contents may not be readily scanned by some search engines, to rank web pages.
- On the other hand, Flash files are not fully secure. Determined hackers can use programs to extract objects such as graphics, audio clips and even ActionScript coding from a .swf file
- Playing Flash animations is CPU intensive. With GIF animations, each frame's contents was already stored as a separate image. With Flash animations, each frame is constructed from its vector instructions, just prior to displaying it on screen. This consumes a great deal of computational power, particularly if the animation is very complex. This limitation must be borne in mind if the finished product is to be displayed on computers of all ages.
- Playback of Flash files requires the computer to have a Flash player plug-in. This is not usually a problem, as about 95% of computer users already have the Player installed. Like all add-ons, the Player is updated as facilities are added to the Flash development software and the user is prompted to download newer versions as they arise.
- Their ease of construction can lead to animation and effects for their own sake, distracting and annoying users. In addition, animations are not appropriate in every circumstance (e.g. a flashing banner is hardly appropriate for a funeral undertaker or a respected professional site).
- Some complicated animations on web site splash pages take far too long to download, driving users away from the site.

As can be seen, the advantages easily outweigh the disadvantages and this explains why Flash has become such a widely used tool for both web and multimedia applications.

Applications that are also capable of producing Flash output files are Adobe Illustrator, LiveMotion and CorelDRAW.

Of course, while Flash can import and embed real-world video, it is still essentially for a 2D vector format.

Shockwave

The authoring package *'Director'* is produced by Macromedia, the same company who market Flash. Director was initially aimed at the creation of larger projects designed for CD-ROM and kiosk applications, as the Internet market was only just developing at that time. It was intended for applications such as product marketing, simulations, education, etc. and is the tool used for creating the front ends of many of the CDs that are given away with computer magazines. Like Flash, it is a 2D vector-based system, although it was initially focussed on bitmap graphics. Each new version of the program makes the software more suitable for web applications, without losing its ability to produce serious output for other media formats.

As explained in the chapter on Authoring Systems, the output of a Director movie can be packaged as a Shockwave file for use on web sites. The user's computer requires a Shockwave browser plug-in to play the interactive material.

Advantages

- It shares many of the advantages that were listed previously for Flash, including vector graphics, tweening, smaller file sizes, faster download times, control over screen layout, high levels of user interactivity, the ability to incorporate a range of different media file types (audio, video, Flash files, etc.). See the section on Flash for more details.

- It is widely used for presenting more complex animations, more computational scripts and the highest quality files.
- Apart from the Shockwave format, Director can output material in other formats including free-standing executables, MOVs and AVIs.
- Like Flash, Shockwave files can handle the movement of multiple objects. In addition, however, Director (from version 8.5 onwards) can create Shockwave files that control the movement of 3D objects.
- It uses its own scripting language called *'Lingo'*, which is credited with being more powerful and faster than ActionScript.
- Like Flash, it supports a form of streaming, allowing a movie to begin playing before all its content is downloaded. The scripting language can control the point at which sufficient content has downloaded to start the playback process.

Disadvantages
- One of the more expensive 2D animation authoring packages.
- These files have a .dcr extension (e.g. *'project.dcr'*) and the browser needs a Shockwave plug-in to view them. Although over 200 million users have the Shockwave player installed, this is not a large majority of the total web population. To view Shockwave content, the other users have to download and install the plug-in from the Macromedia website. Players are available for Windows and Macs, with Linux players being available from third-party developers.
- Developers creating Shockwave for web pages have to consider whether a user will go to the trouble of installing the player, just to view a single item on the web. If that item is something that the users value greatly (e.g. an animation of an industrial process or a walkthrough of an intended new housing development) they would go to the trouble of installing the plug-in. However, if the animation is just for a fancy menu system, users will probably move away to another site.
- Shockwave files tend to load more slowly than Flash files.
- Confusingly, the .swf file extension stands for *'ShockWave Flash'* format, although almost all swf files contain Flash material instead of the Director content that may be implied by the use the word ShockWave.

While Flash was initially designed purely for web animation, Director was initially designed for CD-ROM, kiosk and multimedia applications. As both products have developed over different versions, they have continually overlapped each other in their functions. Some have speculated that they may eventually merge into a single product that combines the best features of both, although Macromedia denies this.

QuickTime

This format was initially developed for Macintosh systems and although widely regarded as a medium for real-world video content, it is also useful for animated content. While QuickTime Pro offers some control over movies, QuickTime animations are often produced from other authoring packages such as Director, Flash, Image Ready, etc. QuickTime files have a .MOV extension (e.g. *'project.mov'*) and display a sequence of still images, similar to an animated GIF.

Advantages
- MOV files can be used in many projects - on the web, within multimedia apps, on CD-ROMs, etc.
- Compression can be applied to MOV files, to lower their file size.
- QuickTime Pro allows the developer to create a number of different outputs, at different compression/quality levels, to suit the connection speeds of different users. This is intended to provide smooth playback to users, whatever their connection speed.
- Like Flash, it supports a form of streaming, allowing a movie to begin playing before all its content is downloaded. This helps make large animation files appear less of a problem to users.
- MOV files can incorporate audio.
- From version 4, QuickTime can handle Flash files.

Disadvantages
- Larger file size than purely vector-based formats.
- Can have longer download times.
- Can produce low quality results where users have slow Internet connections.
- Less in-built user interaction
- No in-built support for scripting.
- Does not support transparency.
- Older browsers / PCs may require a plug-in.
- There is no Unix player for MOV files.

AVI

AVI (Audio-Video Interleave) files were, for many years, the only Microsoft Windows standard format for video files. Like QuickTime, it was used mainly for real-world content, although AVIs can easily store and display animated content. AVI animations are different from Flash and Shockwave formats in the sense that the Macromedia formats are mostly produced using their own application software (i.e. Flash or Director). While other software may be able to output to these formats, most developers use the Macromedia products. Microsoft markets a package called *'Softimage'* for its NT platforms but most AVI animations are created with other applications such as such as Animation Shop, Director, etc. Flash does not directly output to an AVI but the freeware package *'SWF2AVI'* can convert Flash format files into AVIs.

Advantages
- AVIs are supported on all versions of Windows.
- AVI files can be incorporated into many different applications, such as Flash, Director, PowerPoint, etc.
- AVI files can be used in many projects - on the web, within multimedia apps, on CD-ROMs, etc.
- Compression can be applied to AVI files, to lower their file size.
- AVI files can incorporate audio.

Disadvantages
- Larger file size than purely vector-based formats.
- Can have longer download times, as a result of larger file sizes.
- No in-built user interaction or scripting. All animations are created in an application that exports to AVI as a final output format.
- Mac users need to install an AVI player, available from a third-party source.

Dynamic HTML and scripting

With applications such as Flash and Director, the developer concentrates on the look and the effect of the animation and does not need to know *how* the animation is carried out. An alternative approach is for the developer to use scripts that control the movement of screen objects. Instead of having a separate image for each frame of an animation, the script can contain instructions regarding the screen position of an object for each frame. Unlike GIF89a files, there is no set of individual frame images. For example, a ten second animation at 25 fps would need 250 separate screen images for a GIF89a file. In scripting, the image of an object is stored only once. The only other storage overhead is the positional instructions that are stored in the scripts.

Dynamic HTML, or dHTML, is the term used to describe screen content that alters after a web page is downloaded. JavaScript is commonly used to provide a simple form of dynamic content – the screen button that changes colour or position when a mouse is hovered over it.

Internet browsers have a DOM (document object model) that controls how a web page is displayed. The lines of script interact with the DOM to alter some of its characteristics (e.g. the colour of a line of text).

With DHTML, the viewer downloads a web page that contains the usual HTML elements and additional lines of script. With JavaScript, these lines are embedded within the lines of the HTML script (see the chapter on JavaScript).

A more powerful approach uses *'Java applets'*. These are mini-programs that are downloaded as separate files (e.g. *'logo.class'* or *'graphics.class'*) along with a web page. Its script code is compiled and utilises the browser's *'virtual machine'*, which is a plug-in that interfaces the Java programming code to the computer's operating system. These applets can use bitmap images or can draw simple vector lines and shapes.

Advantages
- All browsers support JavaScript.
- The Java Virtual Machine is available for Windows, Macs and Unix, allowing a single applet to be run on multiple platforms.
- Smaller file sizes compared to animated GIFs.
- Faster download times than animated GIFs.
- Incorporates user interaction.
- Can play audio files.
- Supports scripting (see more on the chapter on programming/JavaScript).
- Dreamweaver can produce the necessary code, to save hand coding of instructions.

Disadvantages
- Only useful for web applications (the full Java programming language can be used for creating larger standalone applications).
- DHTML limited to moving bitmaps around the screen.
- Users must have the Java Virtual Machine installed to run applets.
- Users must have JavaScript enabled in their browsers to display JavaScript activity.
- Steep learning curve to understanding programming concepts, script language and/or Dreamweaver.
- JavaScript has limited scripting abilities, compared to rival scripting languages.

Animation Shop

Animation Shop is supplied with Paint Shop Pro and works in a very similar way to all other simple animated GIF software, such as Microsoft GIF Animator or GIF Construction Set.

A set of graphic images is created with a drawing or painting package.   Small changes are made in each successive image. In the example, the digger is slowed edged forward while the digger arm is lowered.

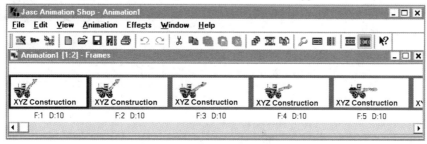

The illustration shows the interface of Animation Shop.   The *'Animation Wizard'* is accessed from the *'File'* drop-down menu and its dialog box prompts for the names of the image files to be added.   The files are added in the sequence that the animation will run and the user controls the delay between displaying each image.   The package also provides for transitions to be added between frames. This provides effects such as wipes, dissolves and fades and these are covered in detail in the chapter on digital video. Every transition adds extra frames to the animation and increases the file size.

The package also provides a *'Banner Wizard'* that allows the creation of moving text effects. Text can be entered and be made to wave like a flag, move like a marquee, and so on. The two wizards help to produce animations quickly, but the user can ignore the wizards and build the design from scratch.

GIF animations consist of a set of graphic images (or *'frames'*), which can be created with any drawing or painting package.   Each successive frame is slightly different from the previous frame, and the images are displayed in succession to give the illusion of movement.

The GIF89a format contains a number of optimisation options that can be used to reduce the size of animations created.   For example, if little changes from one frame to the next, the second frame can make extensive use of

transparency, and browsers will understand that to mean that the transparent areas do not change in that frame. This saves having to store the contents of the unchanged area in each frame.

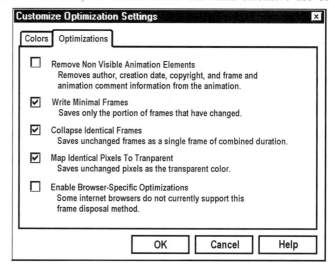

There are other similar options, and in Animation Shop these can be customised when saving the animation, by clicking *'Customize'* after giving a filename. The Customize Optimisations dialog box appears, and the *'Optimizations'* tab contains the options shown in the illustration.

In addition to this, animated GIFs often save a little space by requiring only one CLUT table for their palette.   When using all of these optimisations a GIF89a can be surprisingly compact. The animation created on the next page consists of eight frames each of approximately 1.6kB each, but the resulting animation is under 5kB.

Using Animation Shop

Animation Shop provides an *'Animation wizard'* that allows the user to import a string of existing images into animation frames, and a *'Banner wizard'* to create typical banner animations out of text supplied by the user. Animations can also be created from scratch, using some very simple built-in image editing tools.   Fortunately, Animation Shop is linked to Paint Shop Pro, so images can be exported and edited using that package's superior tools, and the animation can be automatically updated without the need to constantly save and load images.

Most simple web animations consist of simple low-colour images generated using computer graphics packages, and/or some simple text, perhaps moving or blinking. However, it is entirely possible to create animations from photographic quality images, or even a series of stills taken from a full video clip. When dealing with these more detailed images, though, it should be remembered that GIF compression generally results in both a lower number of colours (256 colours instead of up to 16 million colours) and a worse compression ratio than a series of JPEG images. Also, editing photographic images is usually a longer and more difficult process than creating a simple animation from scratch, although the results may look better.

Creating a simple GIF animation

In this example, an animation is being created that shows a basic interpretation of a rocket landing on a lunar surface.   The rocket is to move diagonally from the top corner of the screen down on to the surface.

The initial image to be created is the basic moonscape, with the rocket appearing in the top left corner.

In Animation Shop, clicking the *'File'* menu and selecting the *'New'* option, displays the dialog box shown in the illustration. Since this image is to be a landscape, it should be wider than it is tall. A width of 250 pixels and a height of 100 pixels are appropriate. An opaque background is suited to this type of animation, as we do not want any interference from background images.

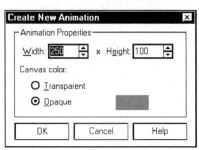

Among the basic painting tools provided in Animation Shop are:

- Paintbrush, which is useful for irregular shapes such as the moonscape.
- Shape, which can draw outlined or filled shapes such as a ellipse for the body of the rocket.
- Line, which can be used repeatedly in order to create irregular but straight objects.
- Fill, which can then fill in the shape created by the lines with any chosen colour.

It may be useful to zoom in, by clicking on the magnifying glass icon, in order to draw objects more precisely.

Adding new frames

A GIF89a file with a single frame is nothing more than an image file. In order to turn it into an animation, more frames must be added. This can be done in several different ways. A new blank frame can be inserted by clicking *Animation / Insert Frames / Empty*. Alternatively, it is possible to create frames out of image files on disk, by clicking *Animation / Insert Frames / From File*. Animation Shop can import a wide range of both graphic and animation file formats, including GIF, JPEG, BMP, IFF, Flick, AVI etc.

However, the most useful method in many circumstances is to copy existing frames, and paste them into new frames. From there, minor changes can be made, thus saving the work of creating a whole new frame from scratch. For example, the second frame of the animation should display the rocket slightly to the left and slightly lower than its position in the first frame.

Of course, more frames still need to be added before the animation becomes useful. Animation Shop can be used to create many new frames out of the existing frame containing the shooting star. These frames can then be edited in Paint Shop Pro by clicking *File / Export Frames to Paint Shop Pro*. Here the rocket can be selected using the selection tool, and moved into new positions as appropriate to each frame.

Arranging the animation

Animation shop can display several frames at one time, as shown below. This allows editing to continue, while giving the designer some idea of how the animation might look when completed. Alternatively, the animation can be viewed as it might appear on a web page, simply by clicking *View / Animation*.

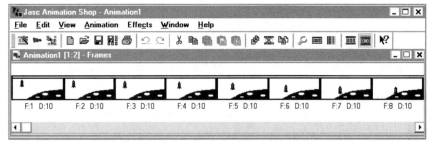

Animated models

One area where animated GIFs can play a significant role is in *'stop-frame animation'*. The most popular example of this art form is the series of *'Wallace & Gromett'* movies.   A series of photographic stills are shot, with the position of the screen objects being changed between shots.   This technique requires lots of planning and even more patience. The completed collection of stills can be converted into an animated GIF for web use, or further converted into an AVI for use in other multimedia applications.

Using a GIF89a animation in a web site

Animation Shop's provides a number of format options when saving a file, including GIF89a. The GIF animation can be referenced in a web site in the same way as any normal image, simply by using the <IMG> tag. If the browser is not capable of displaying animated GIFs, then it will simply display the first frame of the GIF.

The HTML source below will generate the web page shown.

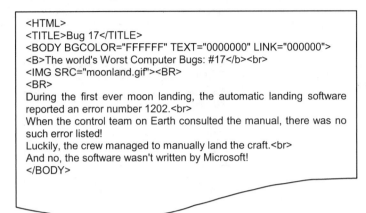

Using Flash

Although Flash is primarily designed for vector images, it also handles sounds and bitmap images.
It can use scripting language to provide navigation, create menu structures, control animations, check user input, make calculations, etc. All of these can be combined into an output suitable for a web site.

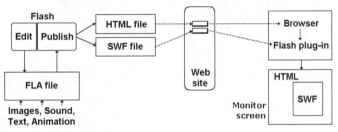

The steps in the process are:

- The designer opens the application.
- Various images, text, etc. are added to a project (a *'movie'*).
- The Flash timeline is used to place activities and animations in a chosen sequence.
- When complete, the project is saved as a FLA file. This file is not uploaded to the web site; it is retained so that it can be returned to for later changes and additions. It is the *'master'* file for the project.
- The designer then publishes the finished project. This uses the material in the FLA file to create two other files- the HTML file that describes and calls up the Flash file, and the Flash (SWF) file itself.
- Both files are uploaded to the web site.
- When a user downloads the HTML page, its code is reader by the normal web browser software (e.g. Explorer or Netscape). This results in the SWF file being downloaded and displayed by the Flash plug-in. The screen outputs of both files are displayed on the user's screen. Sometimes, the HTML file only exists to call the SWF and has no screen output of its own. A web site designed purely in Flash stills needs a small HTML file to initially load it. In other cases, the main web page is made up of screen content displayed by HTML script lines, while the SWF file makes up a small, animated part of the screen (e.g. an animated icon or a moving banner).

The Flash Interface

When the Flash application is opened, it will look similar to the illustration shown (the exact contents will depend on which menus and panels are active at the time).
The main features are:

Work Area

This is the area where objects can be placed, either for temporary parking or for assisting smooth animation. In the illustration, it is the plain white area surrounding by the rulers and sliders.

Stage

This area shows the contents of a single frame. In the illustration, it is the dark central containing the page content.
Objects can be placed on the Work Area and objects on the Stage can overlap into the Work Area – but only the content within the boundaries of the Stage will appear in the final Flash file.

This is useful when animating objects. An object can be placed in the Work Area and animated on to the Stage. For example, a plane can enter the Stage from the left, fly across the screen and move off the Stage into the right hand side of the Work Area. The plane does not suddenly appear on the left edge and suddenly disappear when it reaches the right edge.

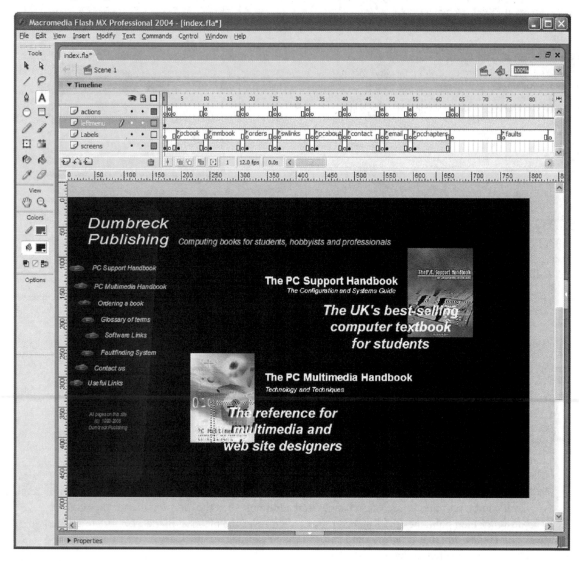

Timeline

Flash movies are a series of frames, with each frame containing some change of scene.   In a simple animation, the movie is run by displaying the contents of each slot in the timeline, one after another. Each slot in the timeline represents one second and the movie can be set to work through the animation at a particular rate (set as fps – frames per second).

Below each time slot is the slot's assets - the screen content that will be displayed during that time slot, along with any sounds that will be played or buttons or scripts that will be activated.

Playback Head

In the illustration, there is a box around frame 1 and this box is known as the playback head. It has a vertical pointer that extends down into the layers of assets, so that the assets for each time slot can be quickly identified. Dragging the playback head across the timeline displays the screen content of each timeslot in rapid succession on to the Stage, and is a quick way to get the feel of an animation.

As normal on Windows applications, Flash has a top tool bar with drop-down menus for common file operations, such as Open, Save and Print. It also provides drop-down menus for most of the package's functions, many of which will be covered in this chapter.

The illustration shows the main graphics tool bar positioned on the left of the screen.

The Windows drop-down menu has an option for Panels.   This allows the display of a number of on-screen panels that provide user-control over text styles, colours, object positioning and alignment, etc. that provide powerful tools for accurate layout and effects.

Other tools will be examined throughout these pages. The examples use Flash MX but all the activities discussed are available in earlier versions, although the menu options will vary slightly.

Layers

To the left of the timeline, Flash displays the movie's layers. Layers use the same technique as explained in the chapter on computer graphics. Flash allows multiple layers in one movie and each layer can have its own screen content. The order of the layers determines which screen content appears on top when the file is displayed. Any content in the top layer appears in front of any screen content in the second layer – and so on.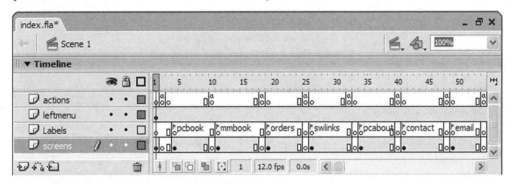

The example shows the bottom layer containing text, the second bottom layer containing a filled rectangle, the second top layer containing a filled circle and the top layer containing a filled triangle.

Layers have a number of uses:

- They allow the separation of objects, so that the problems of interaction between drawn objects (see later) is eliminated.
- They allow for the independent manipulation of objects on each layer, without worrying about interfering with other objects (e.g. deleting an object one layer cannot accidentally delete an object on any other layer).
- They are great for producing 3D effects during animation (e.g. a man walks in front of a car but behind a tree).
- They allow the movie's screen content, audio content, scripts, etc. to exist in their own layers, allowing easy identification of the elements of the movie (all scripts will be found in the scrip layer, and so on).
- They can be labelled to assist easy identification of each layer's purpose.

The example in the illustration shows a movie with four layers.

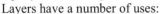

The top layer contains all the movie's scripts (these are called '*actions*' and they handle the interactivity of the movie). The next layer contains a menu that appears on the left of the screen (see the previous page). This menu is continued across the layer for the entire timeline, as the menu is to always be visible. The next layer only contains labels. These are used to identify each area of activity on the timeline. The final layer contains all the other content that will appear on the screen for that movie.

Along each layer in the timeline, symbols are displayed to represent key features.

The black dots along the timeline indicate keyframes, while the outlined dots indicate empty keyframes. The small letter 'a' indicates an action, while a red flag indicates a text label. If the movie contained any animation '*tweens*' they would be represented by an arrow going from the first frame of the tween to the last frame of the tween. It would be good practice to always leave the first frame in a timeline empty, so that it is easy to add more frames at a later time.

The following operations can be carried out on layers:

Inserting a layer	A new layer can be inserted by clicking the plus sign positioned on the left immediately below the layers, or by highlighting a layer, right-clicking and selecting '*Insert Layer*'.
Deleting a layer	Right-click on the layer and choose '*Delete Layer*'.
Renaming a layer	The layer can be renamed by double-clicking on the current layer name and entering a new name.
Hiding/showing a layer	Each layer has a couple of dots and a box symbol. These line up in columns under the eye symbol, the padlock symbol and a square symbol.
	If the dot in the eye column in clicked, a red cross is placed over the dot and the screen content for that layer is hidden (not displayed on the work area). Clicking again reveals the layers contents and the red cross is removed.
Locking a layer	Clicking a dot in the padlock column locks the layer, preventing any alteration to the layer's contents until the layer is unlocked again (by clicking the same dot).

Moving a layer's order   Click on a layer and drag it to its new position. Dragging upwards means that the screen content of the frame will appear closer to the foreground, while dragging a layer to a lower position results in its screen contents being placed further in the background of the final screen display.

Properties

A Flash movie contains many individual objects and any one of these can be individually altered in size, colour, etc.

If the 'Properties' option is chosen from the 'Window' menu, a panel called the *'Property Inspector'* is opened up. This sits below the Stage area and provides information on the current object that is highlighted. For example, clicking on the Stage itself displays properties such as the size of the Stage and its background colour. Similarly, clicking on an object displays information on its dimensions, its position on the stage, etc.

The Property inspector allows these settings to be altered, providing detailed control over all the objects used in a project.

Starting a new movie

A new movie is created by selecting *'New'* from the *'File'* menu.

This produces the dialog box shown.

The *'Templates'* tab offers a selection of ready-made templates to speed up project development. These cover online ads, slide shows, quizzes, forms, etc.

The *'General'* tab offers options to create various scripting files, with the first option being the one to create a new Flash movie.

Selecting *'Flash Document'* and clicking *'OK'* opens the main screen with a default stage area.

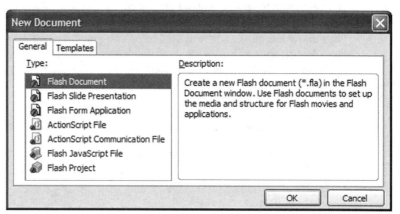

Selecting *'Modify'* from the top menu, followed by *'Document'* from the drop down menu displays the options box shown.

The *'Frame Rate'* box controls how many frames appear on the timeline for each second of the animation. 12fps is the minimum accepted rate for web animations and would create 12 time slots (frames) in the timeline for each second of time. So each frame would display its contents for one-twelfth of a second. 25fps is the likely rate for creating CD projects.

The *'Background Color'*, as expected, sets the background colour for the movie.

The *'Dimensions'* set the movie's screen size and the default value is 550x400 pixels.

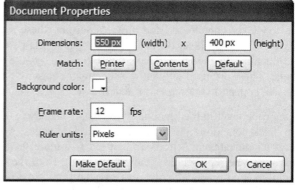

Scalability

Everyone has experienced the problems of web site *'scalability'*. A web page that was designed to fit exactly into a SVGA screen overflows the screen boundaries of anyone viewing on a VGA screen, requiring the user to scroll both horizontally and vertically to view the page contents. On the other hand, if the user has a 1024x768 or 1280x1024 screen, the web site will not fill the screen and will sit in the top left corner of the screen. A possible HTML solution lies in using tables with width values expressed in percentages. This ensures that the content of a site will always spread across the entire area of a screen, no matter how high the monitor resolution may be. The downside to this technique is that the actual text and images do not expand or shrink – they simply become closer or further apart from each other.

Flash offers an improved solution to the problem of scalability, by designing a site where the screen contents expand or contracts to fill the entire screen – no matter what resolution the user's monitor happens to be.

As long as the design sets the original screen dimensions to allow space for the browser's own tool and bars, the web page will comfortably fit in all screen resolutions. The only downside is where a user decides to drag the browser window into a ratio that is not 4:3. For example, if the user drags the browser screen to a long narrow window, Flash will compress the content in the vertical direction, affecting readability severely.

To maintain the movie's aspect ratio for most browsers, a resolution of 778 x 434 pixels, with height and width ratios set at 100% is recommended.

Drawing Tools

Flash has basic drawing facilities and designers often prefer to use a third-party drawing package for creating specialist graphics that are then imported into Flash.

For run-of-the-mill drawing tasks, Flash provides the normal drawing tools that resemble the options provided in other drawing packages -

- Line Tool (for drawing straight lines).
- Pencil Tool (for freehand drawing – with additional Smooth and Straighten options).
- Dropper Tool (for selecting a colour from the screen).
- Pen Tool (for drawing bezier curves).
- Basic squares, rectangles (that can have rounded corners) and circles/ellipses. These shapes can have outlines or no outlines.
- Has line width, line style and fill options.
- Supports Layers.
- Can rotate, stretch, and skew.

Drawing Problems

- If you draw an object with an outline and a fill, you have to double click before dragging the object – otherwise you only drag the fill and leave the outline behind!
- If you draw an object (say a rectangle) and then draw another object (say a circle) such that they overlap, dragging the foreground object 'knocks out' a piece of the object underneath (the part that it overlaps, as shown in the example in the illustration).

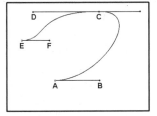

You can use the arrow tool to drag a rectangle round a number of objects then use the Modify/Group options to group them together. This can protect an object from having sections knocked out or from other accidental alteration during development. The objects can be individually accessed again by using the Modify/Ungroup options. Converting an object into a symbol (see later) also protects the object.

Alternatively, placing each element on its own layer prevents unwanted interactions.

Transparency

An object can have its level of transparency set. This is known as its *'alpha'* setting and 100% is completely opaque (i.e. there is no transparency) while 0% is completely transparent (i.e. the object is invisible). Levels in between set the level of transparency. This effect produces very pleasing results (e.g. a face displaying through clouds) or can be used in animations for fading in or out an object.

The steps for setting an object's transparency are:

- Select an object on the stage.
- Choose *'Alpha'* from the *'Color'* menu in the Properties dialog box.
- Set the desired alpha level using the slider.

Remember to have objects in the correct layer order, so that the semi-transparent object is in front of the object that is to show through.

Bezier curves

These steps describe an example of drawing bezier curves:

- Select the Pen tool.
- Move the mouse to the first point on the stage where the curve is to be drawn ('A' in the example).
- Hold the mouse button down and drag in the direction that the curve will take ('B' in the example).
- Release the mouse button.
- Move the mouse to the next point on the stage where the curve is to be drawn ('C' in the example).
- Hold the mouse button down and drag in the opposite direction ('D' in the example).
- Add more points as required ('E' and 'F' in the example).
- 'A', 'C' and 'E' are known as the anchor points, while 'B', 'D' and 'F' are known as tangent handles.
- Select the Subselection tool(the white arrow icon in the Toolbox).
- Using this tool to drag anchor points changes the main points that the curves must pass through.
- Using this tool to drag tangent handles changes the shape of the curve between the anchor points.
- If the last anchor selected is at the same co-ordinates as the first anchor, the enclosed area can be flood filled.

Importing Graphics

The designer will often wish to incorporate clip art and photographic images into a web site. These are brought in using the *'Import'* option from the *'File'* menu. Flash can handle a wide range of graphic file formats including wmf, gif, jpg, bmp, png, pic and ai.

When a file is selected from the menu, it is recorded as an entry in the Flash Library. The Library is accessed via the *'Library'* option of the *'Window'* menu. The entry can be selected in the Library and dragged on to the stage for inclusion in the movie. The Flash Library is covered more fully later.

Importing bitmaps can be compressed to reduce the movie size. Highlight the bitmap image in the Library, right-click and choose *'Properties'* from the menu. This displays the dialog box shown in the illustration and this offers three possible compression methods:

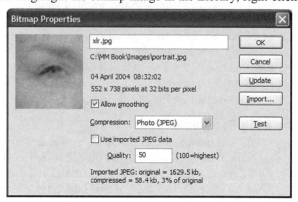

- If the *'Lossless'* option is chosen, there is no loss of image quality but huge savings in movie size are sacrificed.
- If the *'Use imported JPEG data'* box is checked, all images are compressed to the global value set in *'Publish Settings'* (more of this later).
- If the box is unchecked, a *'Quality'* box opens up, allowing a value of 1 to 100 to be set – which applies to that image only and is unaffected by any global settings.

Flash has a bitmap tracing tool that is reached through the *'Trace Bitmap'* option on the *'Bitmap'* sub-menu of the *'Modify'* menu. It converts a bitmap image into a vector image in the hope of reducing the file size. However, it often results in a much larger file than that of using the original bitmap, particularly when using photographic images. With less complex clip art images, it may be worth experimenting.

Entering text

Text is entered in a very similar manner to that used in word processing and drawing packages:

- Click on the Text tool (the capital 'A' in the graphics tool bar).
- In the Properties dialog box, enter the typeface, font size, colour, alignment, etc. Make sure that *'Static Text'* is also selected.
- Click on the stage at the left-most point where the text should begin and enter the text from the keyboard.
- Once entered, the text can be dragged to any new position, if required.

Drop shadow

Many sites use drop shadows for their main text and this is achieved by the following steps in older versions of Flash:

- Enter the text into the frame as described above.
- Copy the text to the clipboard, by highlighting the text and choosing *'Copy'* from the *'Edit'* menu.
- Open a new layer in the movie.
- Paste the text into the new layer, using the *'Paste'* option in the *'Edit'* menu.
- Drag the new layer below the existing layer, so that it becomes the background image.
- Offset the new text to slightly below and slightly to the left of the original, to create a shadow effect.
- Set this shadow text to a dark grey colour.
- Convert the background text to a symbol and Set its alpha value to say 40% or 50%.

With current versions of Flash, the process is a little simpler.

- Select the item of text.
- Click the right mouse button.
- Select *'Effects'* from the *'Timeline Effects'* sub-menu.
- Select *'Drop Shadow'* from the *'Effects'* sub-menu.
- Select the required background colour, offset and alpha level.
- Click the *'OK'* button.

Object Placement

The *'Properties'* dialog box provides information on the exact position and size of an object and allows these to be altered.   It allows the adjustment of an object's exact vertical and horizontal size (handy for ensuring buttons are all the same dimensions) and exact horizontal and vertical position (handy for precision placements of buttons, etc.).

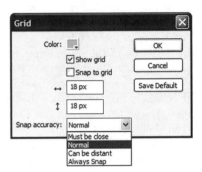

Selecting a group of objects allows the *'Align'* options to set them all to the same height or the same width (handy for ensuring that a number of objects are exactly the same). It can also set all the objects to align themselves to the same horizontal or vertical axis. The *'Align'* options are found in the *'Modify'* drop-down menu.

Like many other drawing packages, Flash can display a grid on the screen. The grid is only visible during editing and is not included in the final movie. The grid aids object creation and placement.

The grid options are reached through the *'View'* menu and the *'Edit Grid'* option displays the dialog box shown in the illustration.

Checking the *'Show Grid'* box displays the grid on the stage.

The resolution of the grid, both horizontally and vertically, can be altered by typing in new values in the boxes.

Checking the *'Snap to Grid'* box results in objects that are added to the stage being automatically aligned to the nearest grid points – dependent on the option chosen in the *'Snap accuracy'* menu. For example, choosing the *'Must be close'* option means that an object dropped on to the stage mid-way between two grid lines will not result in it being aligned to the grid.

Snapping to the grid is a useful tool for rapid development of pages.   For example, a set of menu buttons can be quickly and accurately placed and aligned on the stage by dragging each instance from the Library and dropping it approximately in its correct position.

Note

When copying an object from one frame to another, use the Edit/Paste In Place option rather than just Paste. Using *'Copy'*, then *'Paste in Place'* will paste an object into another frame or scene in the exact same screen position as the original.

Resizing an object

Flash provides a number of tools that alter the size of an object.

Where an accurate final size is not important, the following steps will resize an object:

- Select the object.
- Choose *'Scale'* from the *'Transform'* option on the *'Modify'* menu, or click on the Scale icon in the tool options.
- Drag one of the corners to increase or decrease the object size without altering the ratio between height and width. Drag a side to increase the width without altering the height. Drag a top or bottom to increase the height without altering the width.

This allows a quick dragging method of resizing,

For more precise object sizing, the dialog entries in the Property Inspector can be altered, as explained earlier.

Rotating/Skewing an object

The Rotate and Skew effects shown are created by selecting the object and choosing *'Rotate and Screw'* from the *'Transform'* option on the *'Modify'* menu, or by clicking on the Rotate and Screw icon in the tool options.

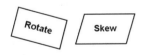

Handles will appear in the corners and on the sides of the object. The object is rotated by grabbing a corner handle and dragging to a new position. The object is skewed by grabbing on a handle on a side and dragging.

A group can also be scaled and rotated (see below) but cannot have its colour outline or fill altered.

For precision scaling, rotation and skewing of a current object, or group of objects, the *'Transform'* option should be selected in the *'Design Panels'* sub-menu of *'Window'*.

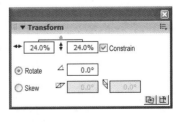

The two upper boxes allow the object to be stretched horizontally and vertically. If the *'Constrain'* box is checked, the percentage change applies to both dimensions (e.g. if 70% is entered in any of the boxes, the other box is automatically set to 70% too). If the box is unchecked, the two dimensions can be set independently of each other (e.g. one can be set to 90% and the other to 60%).

The dialog box also provides precise control over the degree of rotation and skewing of objects.

When the settings have been entered, clicking the *'Copy and apply transform'* button (the leftmost of the two buttons) creates a copy of the original object with all the changes implemented.

Special effects

Flash MX provides a range of tools to manipulate screen objects.

Selecting and right-clicking on an object displays a menu from which *'Timeline Effects'* can be selected.

The *'Effects'* sub-menu provides the Drop Shadow tool already discussed, along with Blur and Explode effects.

The *'Transform/Transition'* sub-menu provides the *'Transform'* dialog box shown in the illustration. The developer can use these tools to have accurate control of movement (including acceleration, deceleration and rotation), size, colour and transparency of screen objects.

The *'Transition'* sub-menu provides tools for creating fades (in and out) and wipes.

If the *'Alpha'* slider is set to 0%. the object will gradually fade away when the movie is played, since the object in the first frame will an alpha value of 100%.

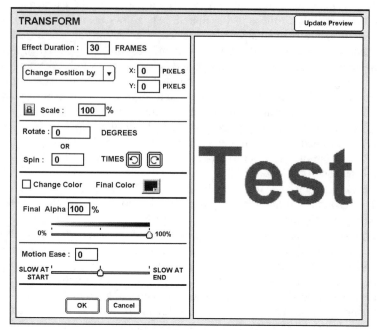

Fading up an item is the reverse of the above process, with the first item in the animation having an alpha value of 0% and the final frame using a value of 100%. If two extra keyframes are added, the first can be 0%, the middle can be 100% and the last can be 0%. This provides a pulsing image if the animation is looped (handy for a pulsing *please wait* message for example).

Fading objects in and out of screens can be very effective, if the effect is not overused.

Rescaling a Movie

Flash allows the stage size of a movie to be altered at any time. The stage can be altered so that the ratio of height to width is maintained, or simply altered to fit a new size (even if the new size does not maintain the aspect ratio). There are a number of reasons why a movie might be rescaled, including:

- A movie designed for use on a web site cannot have the same aspect ratio as a monitor, since the browser tools and bars will occupy some of the screen. If such a movie is later to be used on a CD or kiosk application, the aspect ratio needs to be altered, otherwise the display will be letterboxed with black horizontal bars above and below the movie.

- As explained later, a movie can be displayed inside another movie (e.g. a movie displays a scene of a house. The TV set in the corner displays different movies when an on-screen control is used).

The steps for rescaling a movie are:

- Click anywhere on the Stage area, avoiding selecting any on-screen objects.
- Click on the *'Size'* button in the Properties Inspector.
- A *'Document Properties'* dialog box will appear.
- The *'Ruler Units'* can be set to measure in pixels, inches, millimetres, etc. and the required settings can be entered in the *'width'* and *'height'* boxes, before clicking the *'OK'* button.

Movie construction

Flash provides a number of ways to construct movie projects, depending upon the level of complexity of the total project.

Single timeline

A movie can be constructed using a single timeline and this is often used for small animations, like the ones that are common on many web sites. Examples are a waving flag, a letter being posted, a sliding banner, and so on. All the action can be accommodated on a single timeline and this method is the preferred method for a first attempt at a movie.

Layers

The benefits of layers were covered earlier and beginners quickly learn to use them to advantage for more complex movies (e.g. movies that use multiple objects, animations, sounds and scripting).

Scenes

We are accustomed to watching films made up from multiple scenes, with each scene containing a distinctive piece of footage. Flash can provide a similar approach, where its movie is divided into separate scenes. Each scene can be examined, amended and added to independently of the other scenes in the movie. Selecting a particular scene shows only its layers and contents on the timeline and on the stage. When finished, another scene

can be selected and worked on. However, many desig
example) to using multiple scenes, finding scenes harde·

Movie Clips and Levels

The most powerful tool that Flash offers is the use of
explained further later and has many uses. For exam
other sub-movies to display product descriptions, ·
clips' can be positioned in an empty area of the ·
They can even be moved around the screen, cha·
A movie clip is designed the same way as any o·
a free-standing file, it is designed to run as par·

You can extend the length of an an...
add extra frames into the sequence
You can also add extra points to
This splits the animation into
and then vertically, instead o
could be dragged to a p
point. This would resu
horizontally between be
vertical movement
Alternatively, you c
an animated seque
the object to a n

Testing th
An animati
timeline d
very dif
If you
disp
an

Animation in Flash

As explained earlier, computer animation c·
the impression of movement.
Flash animations are used for creating simulations, ea·
covered in other books, magazines, web site tutorials – and ·
covers only the basics of animations, to make room for Flash issu·
navigation systems, forms, audio and the use of movie clips.

Like other animation applications, Flash uses frames on a timeline. Animation ·
define important points in the animation along the timeline. At each keyframe, th·
modified. Note that the existence of a keyframe in one layer at any point in the timeline ·
that there is a similar keyframe in any other layer at that same point in the timeline. An·
appearance of continuous motion. One solution is to make every frame a keyframe, and modify the c·
frame by hand. This may be the only way to deal with very intricate animations, but bloats the final file size.

The real power of Flash animations is in using *'tweening'*. This involves defining the screen locations of an object a·
two keyframes that are spaced some frames apart, and letting Flash work out the location of the object for each frame
in between.

The example in the illustration is the Flash equivalent of the animated GIF discussed earlier.

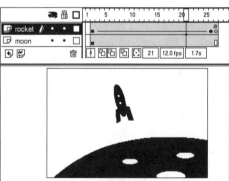

The stage size has been set to 250 x 100 pixels. Frame 1 has been
left empty and so the animation starts at frame 2.
An extra layer has been added to the movie, to separate the two
objects that are used in the animation.
The *'moon'* layer contains the drawing of the lunar surface and the
contents stretch to frame 27 so that the moon surface appears in
every frame of the movie.
The *'rocket'* layer contains the image of the spacecraft and it appears
in the work area just outside the stage area in frame 1. It then
moves diagonally downwards and inwards, to land on the lunar
surface in frame 26.
The rocket layer appears in front of the moon layer and this will
result in the spacecraft landing on the viewer's side of the horizon.
If the rocket layer is dragged below the moon layer, the rocket will land beyond the moon's horizon. The general
process is explained below.

Simple animation

The steps for a simple animation are:

- Move to the frame on the timeline where the animation is to start.
- Create an item to animate (it can be a piece of text, an imported graphic image, or a drawing made using
  the Flash drawing tools).
- Convert the item into a graphic symbol, as only symbols can be animated. With the object selected,
  choose *'Convert to Symbol'* from the *'Modify'* menu. Or select the object and hit the F8 key. Or, simply
  drag the object into the Library. From the dialog box that appears, select the *'Graphic'* option, name the
  object and click *'OK'*.
- Insert a keyframe further along the timeline (the number of added frames depending on length of
  animation time required). Move to furthest frame of the animation and either press F6 or choose
  Insert/Timeline/Keyframe.
- A grey block fills the timeline between the first and last frame of the sequence.
- Click anywhere in this grey block and choose Insert/Timeline/Create Motion Tween. A dotted line will
  appear between the chosen start and end frames.
- Click on the last frame of the sequence and reposition the item in its final stopping place on the screen.

...mation by highlighting the animation strip and pressing f5 as often as required to
– these push the end keyframe further along the timeline.

the animation by going to the desired frame and pressing f6 to add a new keyframe.
two separate tweens. So, for example, the rocket could be made to travel horizontally
diagonally. If the animation were split by adding a keyframe to frame 16, the rocket
sition above the final landing
in two animation movements –
ame 1 and frame 16 followed by a
ween frame 16 and frame 27.

an reposition a symbol in the middle of
nce by selecting that frame and dragging

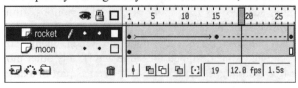

w screen position – Flash automatically adds a new keyframe and splits the tween in two.

animation

n can be viewed and checked at any time during its construction. Dragging the playback head along the
splays the changing screen contents. This gives an impression of the animation but is bit jerky since it is
icult to drag the pointer at an even pace across the timeline.

choose the *'Test Movie'* option from the *'Control'* menu, or simply hit the Ctrl and Enter keys, the screen will
ay the animation smoothly at the frame rate that you set. Alternatively, pressing the Enter key will display the
mation from the current selected frame right through to the end.

o step back and forward through an animation, Flash provides a *'Controller'* as shown
in the illustration.   This pop-up window can be used to play an animation, or display
each frame by stepping through the sequence. It is found within the *'Toolbars'* option
of the *'Window'* menu.

Path Animation

The steps outlined for a simple animation produced an object that moved in one or more straight lines. Of course, not
all objects move in straight lines. Consider a bird circling overhead, the arc of a child's swing, the curve of a
bouncing ball, etc. Such complex movements could be achieved using a large number of straight line movements to
smooth out the animation, with the object being slightly moved for each keyframe. This is a cumbersome, fiddly and
space wasting method.

Flash overcomes this problem by providing a facility for an object to follow a non-linear path such as a curve, spiral
or circle.   The animation still uses a tweening technique. Drawing tools are used to draw a path on a special layer
called the *'motion guide'* layer.   An object can then be linked directly to the start and end of this path. When the
movie is run, the object moves round the stage following the path.

The path is only visible during the editing process and is not seen in the finished movie. Smoothing tools can be used
to iron out any parts of the path that suffer from the user's lack of smooth control of the mouse (a stylus and tablet is a
very useful peripheral for designers who use path animations frequently).

Path animation provides a much more natural movement for some objects, as well as providing a quick and space-
saving way to create complex animation paths.

The steps for creating a path animation are:

- Move to the frame on the timeline where the animation is to start.
- Create an object to animate (it can be a piece of text, an imported graphic image, or a drawing made using the Flash drawing tools).
- Convert the object into a graphic symbol. Choose the *'Convert to a Symbol'* option from the *'Modify'* menu, then choose the Graphic option in the dialog box that appears.
- Insert a keyframe further along the timeline (the number of added frames depending on length of animation time required). Move to last frame of the animation and either press f6 or use Insert/Timeline/Keyframe.
- Create a tween by selecting the block on the timeline that encompasses the animation and then choosing the *'Create Motion Tween'* option from the *'Timeline'* option of the *'Insert'* menu.
- Choose the *'Timeline'* option of *'Motion Guide'* from the *'Insert'* menu, or click the motion guide icon that sits below the layers. A new motion guide layer is added to the timeline.
- Highlight the Motion Guide layer.
- Use the pencil tool to draw the path to be followed.
- Move to the first frame in the sequence (the layer in the timeline that stores the object).
- Move the object so that its centre point sits at the start of the path that has been drawn.
- Move to the last frame in the sequence (the layer in the timeline that stores the object) and ensure that the centre of the object is placed at the end of the drawn path.

Shape Tweening

Shape tweening is an animation that does not necessarily move an object. It is a type of morphing. The object has one shape one its first frame and a different shape on its final frame – and tweening is used to draw all the frames that make the first shape change into the second shape. Shape tweening cannot be used on a symbol or a group. It can provide some very attractive text effects.

The steps are:

- Move to the frame on the timeline where the animation is to start.
- Create an object to animate (it can be a piece of text, or a drawing made using the Flash drawing tools).
- Select the object and then choose the *'Break Apart'* option from the *'Modify'* menu. This creates pieces that are easier to morph.
- If the object is a piece of text, use the *'Break Apart'* option twice. The first time, the text is broken into individual letters; the second time breaks the letters into parts that are easier to morph.
- Select the keyframe in the timeline that stores the object.
- In the Properties dialog box, change the *'Tween'* option to *'Shape'*.
- Insert a keyframe further along the timeline (the number of added frames depending on length of animation time required). Move to where the last frame of the animation is to be and either press f6 or Insert/Timeline/Keyframe.
- In this keyframe, create the new item into which the original item will morph.

Apart from changing shape, this technique can be used to change an object's colour. Instead of changing the object in the last frame, the original content can be left in and have its colour changed.

Reversing an animation

If you need to reverse the motion of a sequence, highlight the frames of the animation on the timeline and choose *'Reverse Frames'* from the *'Timeline'* sub-menu of *'Modify'*.

Some motions are in to two phases, the second phase being a mirror image of the first phase (e.g. the pendulum on a clock, someone sawing wood, etc). For complex movements, mirroring can save a lot of time, effort and file storage. After creating the first animation, copy it and paste it into the next free frame. Hold down Ctrl key and drag the mouse along the second animation in the timeline, then use the Reverse Frames to convert the second animation into a mirror image of the first.

Onion skins

Flash has facilities for *'onion skinning'*, which displays all keyframes simultaneously at varying levels of opacity. This technique is useful to trace the motion of objects through each frame of the animation, as it shows where an animation may benefit from an acceleration or deceleration of motion, or The onion skin icons are located on the left just below the layers.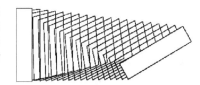

Grouping items

Complex shapes can created by using a collection of simpler shapes. So, for example, a drawing of a car may be constructed from circles, rectangles and filled bezier curves. When completed, the developer wishes to use this collection as a single object. Any changes in movement, size, transparency, etc. should be applied to all the elements in the drawing.

This is achieved by creating a *'group'* from the collection of elements. Using the Selection tool, a rectangle is dragged over all the required elements. The *'Group'* option is selected from the *'Modify'* menu and the group can then be converted to a symbol for animation.

Flash Libraries

Flash provides three types of library for storing source material:

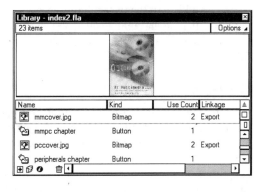

- The normal library, simply known as the *'Library'*, that is stored along with an individual FLA file.   This stores details of the objects used in that particular movie. This library is only available when the FLA file is opened.
- The *'Common Libraries'* is a set of objects that is available for access, whichever FLA file happens to be open. This is covered later.
- The *'Shared Library'* is a special FLA file that allows multiple movies in a project to share the same resources, avoiding the wasteful duplication of having to store objects in each movie. This is also covered later.

The standard Flash Library is an area that stores all the movie's objects such as symbols, clipart, sound files and other movies. They can be organised into folders (e.g. one for sound files, one for symbols, etc). Every time an object is imported into a movie, it is added into the library.

The example shows a library of 23 items. When an item is highlighted, it is displayed in the top window. The list also shows how often an item has been used in the movie. The *'Linkage'* column shows that the two jpeg images are defined to be shared by other movies.

Symbols and Instances

A symbol is a graphic, a button, or a movie. Creating a symbol means that the object's definition information is stored once only in the library and yet can be used many times in a project. The alternative would be to have definition information for each occurrence of the object.

The symbol can be dragged from the library on to the stage and this occurrence of the symbol is known as an *'instance'*. Every instance of the object that appears in the Flash file thus takes up very little space since the object is already defined in the library. You can also copy and paste an instance.

You can modify the Library symbol by selecting any instance of it on the stage, right-clicking and selecting the *'Edit in Place'* option. Alternatively the symbol can be selected in Library list and the image of the symbol that appears at the top of the Library panel can be double-clicked. Either way, the Properties of the symbol are displayed and can be altered.

Any changes made to the object in the library will reflect in all instances, both previous and new. So, for example, if you have a blue button image in the library, multiple copies can be dragged on to the stage. If you then edit the library copy to change the colour to red, all the copies on the stage, in every frame where they appear, are automatically changed to red.

An instance, however, can be independently scaled, rotated, skewed and this has no effect on the Library symbol or on any other instance. However, if the initial properties of a symbol (e.g. colour fill, size or text content) are changed within an instance (by selecting it, right-clicking and choosing the *'Edit'* option) this alters these properties in the Library symbol and in all other instances of the symbol.

Creating a simple button

The button is the heart of all navigation systems and these are the steps for creating a simple button:
- Create a rectangle.
- Select it.
- Convert it to a symbol; choose the *'Button'* option and name the button.
- Double-click on the rectangle.
- The timeline displays Up, Over, Down, and Hit.
- Ensure that the button hit area is big enough.

This is enough to create a button for general navigation use. Since visitors to web sites are accustomed to rollover effects on buttons, you can either use pre-drawn buttons from the Flash common library or create your own as shown next.

Rollover Buttons

The steps for creating a button with a rollover effect are:
- Create a rectangle and select it.
- Convert it to a symbol; choose the *'Button'* option and name the button.
- Double click the button on the stage. The timeline changes to display Up, Over, Down and Hit. Only the Up state has a frame.
- Click the layer under the word *'Over'* and select Insert/Timeline/Keyframe. Change the colour of the rectangle to that required when the mouse hovers over the button.
- Click the layer under the word *'Down'* and select Insert/Timeline/Keyframe. Change the colour of the rectangle to that required when the mouse button is pressed.
- Add text to the rectangle.
- Click on the right-arrow icon just above the Timeline, to return to the normal timeline.

This produces a button that changes colour when the mouse rolls over it and changes to a third colour when it is clicked.

Scripting

In earlier versions of Flash, its built-in scripting language *"ActionScript"* was a separate scripting language. From Flash 5 onwards, it is still called ActionScript, but it is now almost entirely the full ECMA standard JavaScript syntax and statements. Without scripting, a movie would simply run through each frame on the timeline from the first frame to the last frame. ActionScript provides all sorts of control over the way that the user interacts with its movies. Scripting can be used to start and stop activities, jump around different sections of the movie, check user responses, interact with other files (other movies or text files) and much more.

Since ActionScript handles almost the entire instruction set of JavaScript, the chapter on JavaScript should be read if you want to include complex calculations and logic decisions into your movie.

Flash can use scripting to create user-defined functions and supports the common controls such as if..then, do.. while and for.. next. It also supports objects such as Date and Math – and adds extra objects such as MovieClip.

Scripts are added to either frames or to buttons. Frame scripts are run as soon as that frame is reached in the timeline. These might be used to play a sound clip, load variables, loop back to repeat a sequence, etc. The simplest example of a frame script is stop() which prevents the program from moving along the timeline (usually to provide the user with a menu of options).

Scripts attached to buttons are mostly used for navigation purposes, to take the user to another part of the timeline, to load another movie, or control the way a movie is run.

Flash MX uses a menu-based scripting environment, where you can only choose from lists of valid commands and cannot freely edit the script. Earlier versions had an additional *'Expert Mode'*, where the developer could enter code directly from the keyboard.

To attach an action to a button (or a frame), choose Window/Development Panels/Actions from the menu and select the button (or frame). This produces the dialog box shown in the illustration. The main screen displays the code as it is built up.

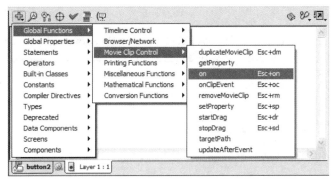

Clicking the large + icon displays a list of suitable script commands, many being part of subsets of commands.

In the example, selecting *'on'* results in a scrollable list of further options. If the option 'release' is selected it results in the following line of code in the Actions script panel:

        on (release) {   }

The on (release) part means that some activity will happen when the user of the completed project clicks on the button and releases the mouse. The activity that will happen is entered between the curly braces - i.e. the *'{'* and the *'}'*. The additional script lines are added by pressing the + icon once again and choosing the required options.

Navigation

Navigation is at the heart of a web site, CD menu system, CAL package or kiosk application. A typical Flash movie has many different screens and animations, and these are spread over many different frames.

To make life easier during development, and specially during later updating and modifications (which might be months later), it is better that the different sections of the movie are given names. Using labels for groups of frames makes them much easier to identify and makes navigation more understandable.

For example, an instruction

        goto("email")

is more understandable than

        goto(23)

Adding labels

In the interests of clarity, it best that a layer be added to the timeline that only stores label information (see the earlier illustration showing layers). When the layer is created and given the name *'labels'*, the mouse can highlight any keyframe section on that layer. The *'Frame'* dialog box in the *'Properties'* panel will initially displays the contents *"<Frame Label>"* and any text label name can be typed in the box to replace it.

The main navigation commands in ActionScript are explained below.

gotoAndPlay

As the name suggests, this instruction moves the playback head to a particular frame with the playback continuing from that point. The frame to jump to is provided between brackets, as in these examples:

        on (release) {   on (release) {
           gotoAndPlay (7);   gotoAndPlay ("email");
        }   }

In this example, the script jumps control to the seventh frame (or the frame labelled *'email'*) on the timeline and Flash carries on working through the frames from that point.

This instruction can be used to move the playback head backwards as well as forwards. So, if an animation ran from frame 2 to frame 20, the animation could be created as a continuous loop by placing the following action on frame 20:

```
on (release) {
    gotoAndPlay (2);
}
```

This script choice is entered by pressing the + icon followed by selecting it via Global Functions/Timeline Control.

gotoAndStop

This instruction moves the playback head to the nominated frame but Flash does not carry on to any further frames. This method is used when the user needs to read instructions, choose from many options, etc. Flow will continue when a button on that frame is pressed to initiate another action. This new action takes the user to another frame, either using a goto() command - or a play() command when wishing to move to the next frame.
An example is:

```
on (release) {
    gotoAndStop ("details");
}
```

getURL

This instruction is the equivalent of the HTML <A HREF="xxx.htm"> command.   It can be used as a hyperlink to:

- Replace the SWF file in the browser with an HTML page that is in the same folder as the SWF file:
```
on(release){
    getURL("tutorials.htm")
}
```

- Replace the SWF file with in the browser with any other web page in the world:
```
on(release){
    getURL("http://www.dumbreck.demon.co.uk/index.htm")
}
```

- Keep the SWF page in the browser and open another web page in a new window:
```
on(release){
    getURL("tutorials.htm","_blank")
}
```

This script choice is entered by pressing the + icon followed by selecting it via Global Functions/Browser/Network.

Navigating blocks of frames

The essence of a web site or CD-based project is its hyperlinking – the ability to jump around the material, going from any point to any point at any time.

However, there are occasions when the viewer is expected to review pages in a consecutive manner, with the proviso that he/she can step back a page to review what was previously displayed. The material only makes sense if it is read in a particular order. Examples are academic works, Hansard (parliamentary proceedings), law court proceedings, financial reports, and some educational works (e.g. the 15 steps to replacing a car battery).   In these cases, the viewer is not the usual casual browser with a short attention span; this block of text is being studied by the serious viewer who is prepared to put in the effort to work through the material.

Flash provides navigation instructions that move the playback head a single frame forward or backwards, without the need to specify the actual frame number or frame label.   This has benefits in the above examples of linear viewing.

Consider placing the text of a novel or an academic work on a web site, with the text spreading over many pages. Jumping to specific frame numbers would pose a problem if you later added extra frames at the start of the movie, as every goto() instruction would need updated.

Similarly, adding or deleting frames of text would alter all frame numbers, requiring extensive updating of scripts.

This updating would be avoided if every single frame had a label. Since each frame had its own label, the frames could be added and deleted without any need for altering any existing script lines.

A simpler method is to label the first frame of the block of text frames, so that the start of the text is easily accessed. From then on, each page would have two buttons – a *"next page"* and *"previous page"* button. They would have the following scripts attached to them:

```
on (release) {              on (release) {
    nextFrame ();               prevFrame ();
}                           }
```

The same approach is used to jump between scenes in a movie that are intended to be viewed consecutively:

```
on (release) {              on (release) {
    nextScene ();               prevScene ();
}                           }
```

Movie Explorer

This facility is opened by choosing the *'Movie Explorer'* option in the *'Other Panels'* drop-down menu *of 'Window'*.

The Movie Explorer option provides a hierarchical view of the entire project (a tree view), similar to a Dreamweaver site map, or even Windows Explorer. This allows the entire project to be seen or individual sections to be examined in detail.

The *'Show'* icons decide what details will be included in the display. The options are:

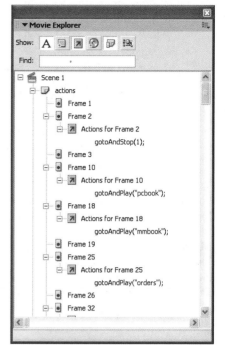

- Display text.
- Display buttons, movies, clips and vector graphics.
- Display ActionScripts.
- Display video, sound and bitmap images.
- Display frames and layers.

If all the icons are clicked, all the elements of the project are displayed. Selectively choosing icons displays only those areas that are of current interest to the developer.

Elements can now be found more easily – just look in the list rather than examining the timeline.

Elements can also be altered (e.g. a script file) without having to consult the timeline.

Entering a word into the *'Find'* dialog box can display all frames that contain that item of text or are called by that name (depending on what *'Show'* options are active).

Handling Text

This section looks at how Flash:

- Uses fonts.
- Displays text on the screen.
- Uses script to update screen text.

Fonts

Flash offers two approaches to using fonts in movies.

- Fonts can be embedded. The font definitions are included inside the final movie.
- The movie can use the fonts installed on the computer of the person viewing the file. Flash calls these *'device fonts'*.

Embedded Fonts

Using embedded fonts ensures that the pages are always seen the way the designer intended, even if the user's computer does not have the font on his/her own computer. This allows distinctive or specialist fonts to be used (in accordance with copyright, of course) but has an overhead in terms of extra file size. Embedded fonts are always anti-aliased, which is useful for displaying large font sizes.

Device Fonts

Device fonts are available in three styles and substitute the following fonts found on the user's computer.

	Windows	Mac
_sans	Arial	Helvetica
_serif	Times New Roman	Times
_typewriter	Courier New	Courier

In other words, if your movie has a piece of text that is declared as being _sans, then a Windows browser will display the text using the Arial font, while a Macintosh browser will display the text using the Helvetica font.

Device fonts do not include any font definition data in the file, thus saving on file size. This method is useful for scrolling text and produces clearer displays at small font sizes. However, it displays a little more jagged at large point sizes, since device fonts may scale but won't anti-alias. Also, different platforms may display the text slightly differently, since Flash uses the fonts found on the user's own computer.

Fonts can be shared between different movies, to minimise the amount of time spent downloading. This technique is explained later.

Creating a text field

Flash handles three different types of screen text:

- Text that does not interact with the rest of the movie (e.g. a page heading). This is Static Text.
- Text that can be altered as the program runs. This is Dynamic Text.
- Text that is entered by the user (e.g. in a form). This is Input Text.

The initial steps for creating a text field are:

- Click on text icon in the toolbar (the one with the capital 'A').
- Move mouse pointer to area of the screen where the text will display.
- Drag open a text box.
- Enter text into the box.
- Highlight the text and click on the 'Text' menu to view the drop-down options.   These allow the font size, style, colour, alignment, etc to be set.   Designers regard 12point as the smallest font size for acceptable viewing.
- Choose *'Options'* from the *'Text'* menu. This opens a dialog box as shown in the following illustrations.
- Choose Static, Dynamic or Input from the drop-down menu.
- Choose any other options, as required.   These options depend on the type of text chosen and all three variations are shown in the illustrations.

Leaving the *'Selectable'* icon unchecked prevents users from highlighting text in the Flash Player and copying and pasting it into other applications. This is available in the Static and Dynamic options.

Static Text Fields

The default for this type is to embed fonts and to anti-alias the text display.   To save on file size, Flash only embeds the letters used in the field. This approach is useful for small pieces of text (e.g. headings and animated text). The field can be changed to use device fonts.

Since the field is never referenced in any script (the contents are not used for input or output), a static text field does not provide a facility to name the field.

Dynamic Text Fields

The default is not to anti-alias. The contents of this type of field can be altered by ActionScript commands and the field can be configured to display large amounts of text. This requires choosing the *'Multiline'* (with word wrap). The *'Render Text as HTML'* icon is to the right of the *'Selectable'* icon. When checked, it allows the display field to display HTML formatting commands (i.e. – a, b, i, p, u, align, font face, font color, and font size) that are included in the output sent to the field. Since the field displays output text, it has to be named so that data can be placed in it. The field name is typed over the *'<Instance Name>'* entry.

It is common to use dynamic text fields for displaying small font sizes, to minimise the fuzziness caused by anti-aliased embedded fonts.

Input Text Fields

The default is not to anti-alias. Like dynamic text, it has multiline, word wrap and HTML options. It does not have a *'Selectable'* option, since the field is initially displayed blank awaiting user input. Instead, it has an option, *'Max chars'*, for setting the maximum number of characters that will be allowed to be entered by the user into that field.

Since the field accepts input data, it has to be named so that data can be fetched and used. The field name is typed over the *'<Instance Name>'* entry and the name of the variable that will hold the inputted data is entered in the *'Var'* box.

Dynamic and Input fields can still have anti-aliased text by embedding the entire font, capitals, lowercase, numbers, punctuation – or characters of your own choosing. These options appear in a separate dialog box that is called up by clicking the *'Character'* button.

Dynamic or Input fields with fonts not embedded behave in the same way as Static fields with Device Fonts enabled.

Basic input and output

Since each dynamic text field has its own name, a field's contents can be altered by a simple ActionScript command such as:

```
on(release){
   outscreen="hello";
}
```

This assumes that the field name is outscreen. In this example, clicking a button changes a block of text on the screen. This would be useful, for example, on a commercial web site, where a menu of buttons is used to display descriptions of different products. Of course, the amount of text would be substantially greater than the example. Each button in the menu would have its own similar script.

If the *'Render Text as HTML'* icon was checked, the text file can include some formatting tags, including <B> and <I>. So, for example, a text file might have the following contents:

```
desc1="<b>Dumbreck Publishing </b>  Publishers of <i>quality</i> textbooks";
```

At one time, Flash content was embedded in HTML code. Now we can embed HTML code in Flash movies. Such is progress!

For a very basic example of using both input and dynamic fields, consider the following steps to create a calculator that takes the cost of an item before VAT and displays the final cost once VAT is added.   The calculation is carried out and the result displayed when the user enters the initial cost in the input field and presses a button.

- Create an input text field and enter 'cost' in the Var box.
- Create a dynamic text field and enter 'netcost' in the Var box.
- Create a button and attach the following ActionScript code to it:

```
on(release){
   netcost=cost*1.175;
}
```

This simple example shows the use of variables and a huge range of mathematical and conditional operators are available in Flash. This allows input from multiple fields to be subjected to complex calculations.

Scrolling text fields

Where large amounts of text are being dynamically pulled up and displayed on the screen, the screen area allocated for displaying the text may not be large enough to display all the text contents. This is overcome in Flash, as in other Windows applications, by vertically scrolling the text within a text window.

The following method works with all versions of Flash and assumes that there is a multiline dynamic text field called contents. The dynamic text field uses an up button and a down button, so that the viewer can control the scrolling of the text.

The following action is attached to the display area's *'Up'* button:

```
on (release) {
contents.scroll= contents.scroll-1;
}
```

and the following action is attached to the *'Down'* button:

```
on (release) {
contents.scroll= contents.scroll+1 ;
}
```

This is only a basic scrolling system, as each user click of the button only scrolls the text by a single line at a time. Space does not permit expanding this system, as it requires some elaborate use of ActionScript.

In modern versions of Flash, the dynamic text field can simply be selected and *'scrollable'* selected from the drop-down menu that appears when the field is right-clicked. The user can then scroll the text in the field by using the up and down arrow keys on the keyboard.

Message boxes

Many applications have user-friendly message boxes that pop-up if you hover over a button or an icon.   The following action can be added to a button to provide this facility:

```
on (rollover){
   message="helpful message"
}
on (rollout){
   message=""
}
on (release){
   gotoAndPlay(3)
}
```

It assumes that a dynamic text field called message exists and initially displays no contents.

The action attached to the button has three elements. The on(release){gotoAndPlay(3)} instruction acts as the button's hyperlink, moving the playback head when the button is pressed and released.

The on (rollover){message="helpful message"} instruction displays a text message on the screen when the user hovers the mouse pointer over the button.

When the mouse is moved away from the button, the on (rollout){message=""} instruction clears the text message from the screen.

This system provides additional information to a user about the consequences of pressing that button.

Note

Always allow some extra screen space for a dynamic text field, as this will help accommodate any differences that might be visible when fonts are displayed on different platforms.

Movie Clips

Flash provides Movie Clips and this is the most significant way to create fully interactive screens and menus. A simple project, such as a animated banner, only requires a single movie with a single timeline.

It is also possible to have all the content for a large complex project in a single movie, using multiple layers, scenes, etc. – accompanied by a long timeline with lots of labels.   While this would work, it creates extra problems during construction and again during amendments and additions. This is because the structure and content of the movie is not easily identified.

Flash allows complex projects to be undertaken by displaying two or more swf files on the screen at the same time.

Levels

Running multiple movies is achieved by using *'Levels'.*   The main movie, the one called up by the HTML file, is loaded in to the basic level – known as level 0.

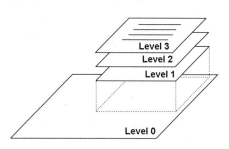

The movie on level 0 can have a script that calls up another swf file and displays it on a higher level, say level 1. If required, it can also call and display another swf movie and display it on a higher level, say level 2.

It is also possible for the movie on level 1 or to display yet another movie, say on level 3.

Only one movie can be placed on a single level. Loading a movie into a level will unload any movie already in that level.

Content displayed on level 1 will be superimposed over any content on level 0, and so on.

The illustration shows a simple example of a menu of level 0, with three buttons. The menu occupies the left side of the screen, leaving the right side empty. Clicking button 1 displays the 1.swf movie on the right side of the screen. Alternatively, clicking button 2 or button 3 displays the 2.swf or 3.swf movies on the screen.

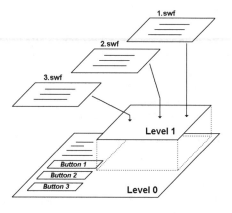

Movie scripts

The movie on level 0 is loaded, as normal, from the HTML file.

The other movies are controlled using the LoadMovieNum instruction attached to a button or a frame script. It loads a new file in the existing Flash window using an instruction such as:

```
on (release) {
    loadMovieNum ("mov2.swf", 2);
}
```

This action loads the movie called mov2.swf into level 2.

```
loadMovieNum("xxx.swf",0)
```

loads a new movie to replace the existing movie in the main screen.

```
unloadMovieNum(x)
```

removes the movie clip that is currently displayed on level x.

```
unloadMovieNum(0)
```

removes the main movie (which calls the movie clips) resulting in a blank screen on the Flash player.

Each movie clip is effectively a mini movie, with its own timeline and ability to handle text, graphics, sounds, animations, script, etc.   Once a movie clip is brought into play, it will run its own timeline independent of the main screen's (i.e. Level 0) timeline.   Or, scripting can be used to control a movie clip or to pass information back and forward between the movie clip and the main movie (e.g. to change size, colour or position).

Note

The first movie loaded in to level 0 sets the background colour for the entire project. If, say, the first movie had a background colour of blue, replacing the movie with another movie with a red background does not result in a red background being displayed. And this is true of all other movies loaded into level 0. If you require the background colour to change, draw a solid rectangle of colour (that covers the entire work area) in the new movie.

Forms

Creating data entry forms using HTML and JavaScript has already been covered but they can also be created using only Flash. This allows forms to be built in to movies.

Simple Form Example

This is an example of a small form that allows users to be added to a company's mailing list.

It has three fields that the user enters personal details before clicking the *'Submit'* button to e-mail the details to the company.

Name				Submit
Address				Clear
Post Code				

The steps for creating this form are:

- Create three input text fields – these can be single line or multiline (e.g. for a large address).
- Give the variables names of name, address and postcode.
- Provide a text label for each input field.
- Create two buttons, one for the actions associated with the *'Submit'* button and one for actions associated with the *'Clear'* button.
- Attach the following action script to the *'Clear'* button.

```
on (release) {
    name="";
    address="";
    postcode="";
}
```

- Attach the following action script to the *'Submit'* button.

```
on (release) {
    subject="Add_me_to_your_mail_list";
    body = "Name:"+name+"Address:"+address+"Post_Code:"+postcode;
    getURL ("mailto:sales@dumbreck.demon.co.uk","","GET");
}
```

The ActionScript associated with the *'Clear'* button ensures that any values for the variables are overwritten by null values. So, if a user makes a mistake in entering the data, the entries can be cleared away by the click of the button and the text boxes on the screen will be restored to empty.

The ActionScript associated with the *'Submit'* button sets up the contents of a typical mail form.

Typical components are *'recipient'*, *'cc'*, *'subject'* and *'body'*. This example does not require a *'cc'* entry, as there will be no carbon copies (duplicates sent to additional URLs). The *'subject'* content is pre-filled with the contents *"Add_me_to_your_mail_list"*. Underscores are used between words to make the received e-mail more readable (see later). The recipient details are embedded in the getURL instruction. Substitute your own URL for the dumbreck URL used in the example.

The body of the message is assembled into a single message by concatenating (stringing together) each of the variables. Each variable is preceded by a piece of text that acts as a label for the data. Thus the string *'Name:'* has the variable name added by the use of a plus sign.   The final value of the body variable is the accumulation of all the labels and variable values.   This is transmitted as a single string in the final e-mail message.

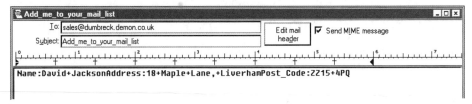

The illustration shows the message as it will be displayed by a typical e-mail program (the example uses Demon's *'Turnpike'* program).

Note the message comprises a single string of characters that has to be unravelled at the receiving end.

Any spaces, as used between words, is replaced in the message by + signs.

The form can be improved in a number of ways:

- By including extra ActionScript to validate field entries (in this case to ensure that no fields are left empty). Other examples of validation would be checking that a numeric field contained only numeric characters or contained sensible values (e.g. preventing users from ordering –500 items).
- By fully integrating the form with the server's cgi scripts. This is not covered since it depends on what facilities are allowed by the ISP and the method of linking to scripts in the server's cgi-bin folder.
- By selecting the input text field to be type *'password'* instead of *'single line'* or *'multiline'*. When the movie runs, any user data entered in this field is displayed on the screen as a set of asterisks. This is useful in preventing others from seeing the content being entered. To use the input content for checking the user password for security clearance requires additional scripting.

- By making the text that the user enters appear in a distinctive font, through choosing an appropriate embedded font as the style for the text input.

Publishing a movie

The FLA file can be viewed at any time using the Controller or by pressing the Ctrl-Enter keys.

By choosing *File / Save*, Macromedia Flash saves the animation as a .FLA file. This file can be loaded back into Flash and edited, but in this format it cannot be viewed except through the Flash editor. To create a standalone application the FLA file has to be *'published'*. Choosing *File / Publish* creates either a standalone program or a condensed file that plays through a web browser add-on.

Publish Settings

In order to publish the file, choose *'Publish Settings'* from the *'File'* menu. This produces a dialog box with several tabs.

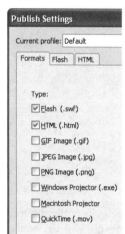

The illustration shows the options in the *'Formats'* tab.

For non-web use (e.g. CDs or kiosk applications) the movie can be converted into a standalone EXE program. This will run in Windows without the need for any other add-on.

Another option is create a movie in QuickTime MOV format. This can then be viewed with the QuickTime viewer or it can be imported into other multimedia authoring applications that can embed MOV files. QuickTime supports Flash, so a MOV (bitmap video) can be brought into Flash, vector animation and control buttons can be added and the combined result published back as a MOV.

For web sites, the default is to create an SWF file (that contains the movie) and an HTML file (that contains instructions to the browser on how to handle the SWF file). If creating a Movie Clip, there is no need to create an HTML file, as the clip will only be called by another movie.

You can check as many of the boxes as required. For example, the FLA file can create an EXE, a MOV, an SWF and an HTML file as a single operation.

The Flash tab options are shown in the illustration.

The JPEG Quality slider sets the degree of compression for all images in the movie, apart from those that have been individually set.

Similarly, the Audio Stream settings will apply to all sound clips in the file, apart from those that have been individually set.

Checking the *'Generate size report'* box creates a text file called *"xxx report.txt"* where *xxx* is the name of the movie being published. This report can be read by any text editor, including Notepad or WordPad. The report lists the number of bytes in the file taken up by each frame, by the text, by graphic images, by symbols and by any embedded fonts.

The HTML tab sets the instructions on movie size and alignment that will appear in the HTML file.

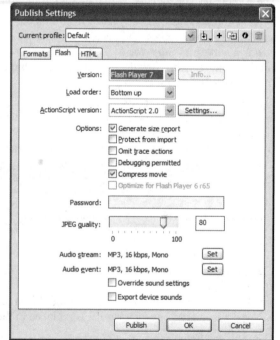

Web publishing

The default settings create an HTML file and an SWF file. The resulting HTML file contains little more than some skeleton HTML tags, and an embedded object. This embedded object includes details that the browser needs to know, such as the filename to load, and where to get the plug-in for the object if it is not already installed. It also defines the height and width occupied by the object. Like images, embedded object sizes can be expressed in pixels or in percentages of the viewable window. In this way a Flash object can be re-sized to fill an entire web page simply by changing the WIDTH and HEIGHT attributes to 100%.

The object tags are recognised by Explorer while the EMBED tags are recognised by Netscape.

classid informs Explorer browsers to load its Active-X plug-in.

pluginspage provides a link to the Shockwave download site for Netscape users who do not have the Flash Player installed.

```
<html>
<head>
<title>index</title>
</head>
<body bgcolor="#000033">
<!-- url's used in the movie-->
<!-- text used in the movie-->
<object classid="clsid:d27cdb6e-ae6d-11cf-96b8-444553540000"
 codebase="http://download.macromedia.com/pub/shockwave/cabs/flash/swflash.cab#version=7,0,0,0" width="550"
height="400" id="varstest" align="middle">
<param name="allowScriptAccess" value="sameDomain" />
<param name="movie" value="index.swf" />
<param name="quality" value="high" />
<param name="bgcolor" value="#ffffff" />
<embed src="index.swf" quality="high" bgcolor="#ffffff" width="550" height="400" name="varstest" align="middle"
allowScriptAccess="sameDomain" type="application/x-shockwave-flash
pluginspage="http://www.macromedia.com/go/getflashplayer" />
</object>
</body>
</html>
```

The rest of the material for the web page, if any, is added between the </OBJECT> and </BODY> tags, and both files can be uploaded to the web site server.

Download performance

If you press Ctrl-Enter to preview a movie, the *'Bandwidth Profiler'* option from the *'View'* menu can be selected. This produces a graph similar to that shown in the illustration. It shows the expected download performance of the movie for a given connection (e.g. 28kbps, 56kbps, and so on).

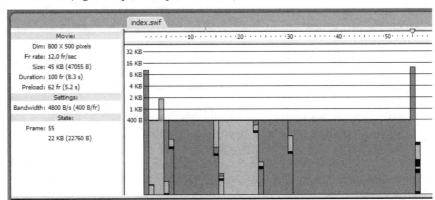

If *'Download settings'* is chosen from the *'View'* menu, a drop-down menu allows the selection of the modem speed for the test.

This utility shows each frame as a block, the size of the block reflecting the size of the frame content.

The left panel reports on the movie's size and likely download time for the nominated connection speed.

Clicking on any block displays that frame's contents in a lower window and updates the left panel with the frame number and the size of that particular frame's contents.

Blocks that extend above the red line are ones that may stop playback until the entire frame is loaded. The first frame is usually large, as it has to store the symbols that are used in the movie.

To prevent users from moving away from your web site, it is best to keep the initial download (i.e. the opening page) to no more than about 40k.

Preloaders

If too much content is placed in the first frame of a movie, there will be a delay while the user waits for screen output. This problem may also occur on other sections of the movie, if the user clicks to move to a frame with significant content (as reported by the bandwidth profiler). The danger is that the viewer gets tired of looking at an unchanging screen and goes somewhere else.

This problem is reduced if users are kept informed of what is happening, perhaps with a download bar reporting on progress on fetching the requested page. Alternatively, the screen may display some fairly plain text content that keeps the viewer reading while the rest of the movie downloads.

It is common to see a small, fairly plain opening screen with a *"movie loading ..."* message or a simple animation at the start of a Flash movie. This is called a *'preloader'* and it is used to smooth out the effects of these peaks identified in the movie identified by the bandwidth profiler.

The simplest preloader is placing a *"movie loading...."* message in frame 1, with frame 2 having a gotoAndPlay(1) action. This would constantly loop to display the message.   An alternative is to display a simple (i.e. small size) animation while the main movie loads.

Now, frame 1 is given one of the following actions:

```
if(_FramesLoaded =10) {
        gotoAndPlay (3);
}
```

In the above examples, the movie has many frames but when the tenth frame is found to be loaded, the script jumps the flow out of the loop to the third frame (where the main movie frames begin).

```
if(_FramesLoaded =_totalframes) {
        gotoAndPlay (3);
}
```

In this example, the entire movie has to be downloaded before the movie will play. This technique can also prevent an action on the main movie being triggered before all of the content is downloaded (e.g. a large sound file). When used to preload a website's opening screen, it is a good idea that the preloader display the size of the file being downloaded and its likely download time for a few common modem speeds, to keep the user informed.

Preloaders can be used anywhere in a movie. For instance, the user can be presented with a frame that displays text. The program flow is paused while the user reads the text; meanwhile, the next frames are being pre-loaded.
Symbols can also be pre-loaded for later use (see later).

Audio

Flash can directly import WAV and MP3 audio files. Most audio editing should be carried out with a dedicated audio editing software package, as it can process the audio more fully (e.g. trimming, adding echo and effects).
WAV files can be imported and optionally converted to MP3s. Right-click on the WAV filename in the library list and select *'Export Settings'* to access the Sound Settings dialog as shown in the illustration.   Select MP3 from the *'Compression'* drop-down list and select the target bit rate.

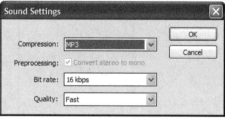

This utility supports 8kbps to 160kbps providing compression ratios from 1.1% to 22.7%
The default settings use the compression options used in the *'Publish Settings'* dialog box. However, you may often wish to apply different compression ratios to audio files (e.g. a speech clip can usually handle greater compression without noticeable deterioration).   In addition, most speech clips can be presented quite happily in mono, so a speech clip can have the *'Convert Stereo to Mono'* check box ticked. This, in turn, allows the bit rate to be halved while providing the same quality of output (albeit in mono).

Other options are *'Raw'* and *'ADPCM'*.   The *'Raw'* setting results in no compression being applied, although the sampling rate can still be lowered and the clip can be converted to mono.
The *'ADPCM'* setting also allows changes to the sampling rate and mono conversion and while it gives less compression, it is often used for short audio clips (such as button clicks) that are required to be synced to events. It may also be useful for speech clips but MP3 is a preferred method for handling music clips.

To incorporate an MP3 sound:
- Import the sound file.
- Create a new layer and keyframe on the timeline. Don't start a sound clip on the same frame as the start of an animation. Doing so produces a shaky start to the animation since the sound file takes time to initialise.
- Drag the file on to the stage from the library.
- Right-click on a frame in the sound layer and choose *'Sound'* from the *'Panels'* option in the drop-down menu.
- Set up any simple effects such as fades and loops.

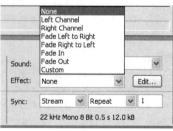

The *'Repeat'* box accepts a numeric entry that controls how often the sound clip will be repeated. So, for example, if you wanted a cock to crow three times a value of three is entered.
Looping allows repetitive sounds such as musical backgrounds, or engine noise, to play for long periods while only using short source clips.

Video

Flash can import a range of different video formats (AVI, MOV, MPG, WMV and DVI). When a video file is imported, the developer is offered the choice to *'Import the entire video'* or to *'Edit the video first'*.

If the entire video is imported, the video bit rate can be set via the *'Compression profile'* option.

The *'Advanced settings'* option produces the dialog box shown in the illustration. The tools include *'Scale'* (handy for producing a small picture-in-picture effect), *'Crop'* (handy for trimming off edges of the picture, such as sub-titles), along with colour correct-ion tools such as brightness, contrast and gamma.

Choosing the *'Edit the video first'* option displays a window that allows the developer to preview the clip and trim the clip, down to the level of an individual frame.

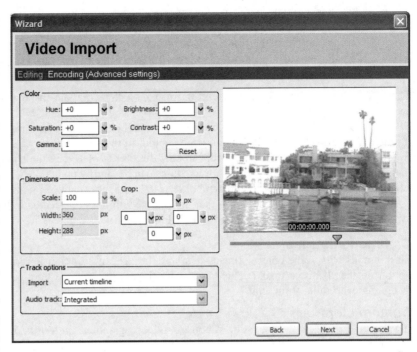

Once imported, a video clip can be manipulated like any other object and can be rotated, skewed, animated, etc.

Note
Older versions of Flash do not have any facility to import video files for use in projects.   However, Flix is an application that converts most video formats (MOV, AVI, MPG, WMV, ASF, etc.) into swf format for inclusion in Flash projects. The tabs allow the setting of image dimensions, frame rate, bit rate, compression, etc.

Full details of the package are available on its web site at **www.wildform.com**.

Asset Sharing

A large Flash project will be constructed from multiple movies. If each movie used the same graphics and sound clips and each embedded the same fonts, there would be a lot of wasted download time.   A leaner faster project would be created if the movies could share one set of resources between them. That would result in only storing a graphic file, a sound file or a font definition file once. Flash uses a number of asset sharing techniques as outlined below.

Shared Libraries
Shared libraries allow many movies to access commonly used artwork and objects. This is useful when creating a project that uses multiple movies. It can also be used to great effect for asset management in collaborative projects, where the libraries are easily accessed by different designers over a local area network.

Shared libraries are particularly useful for sharing complex graphics, digitised photographs, etc. as any changes to the content are reflected across project files.

A shared library file is just a Flash (.swf) movie that is solely used to store the shared symbols.

The steps for creating a shared library are:

- Open the movie that contains the elements that are to be shared.
- Make sure that each item is converted to a symbol.
- For each item, select its entry in the Library and right-click.
- In the drop-down menu that appears, choose the *'Linkage'* option. This displays the dialog box shown.
- Check the *'Export for runtime sharing'* box and the *'Export in first frame'* box.
- Give the symbol a unique name (use a single word and have no spaces).
- Since the final project will have movies stored in different folders, enter the URL where the shared library is being stored.
- When finished, click the *'OK'* button.

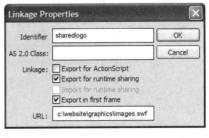

The steps for using a symbol from a shared library are:
- Open a new movie and leave it open.
- Open the movie that contains the shared library, using the *'Open External Library'* option from the *'Import'* option of the *'File'* menu.
- The new movie now has access to two libraries – its own library and the shared library.
- Any symbol can now be dragged from the shared library on to the work area of any frame in the movie.

There are substantial benefits where a set of images (such as graphics used as menu buttons, or product photographs) are used on many movies in a project.

The technique also ensures that all instances of a symbol, e.g. the portrait of the company director, will be updated throughout a project by simply changing the content in the shared library. So, when the director collects his seven-figure golden handshake, the picture of the new director is placed in the shared library and all movies use this new image. Similarly, images of products or locations can be simply updated.

Changing the properties of a shared symbol (e.g. colour or text caption) will certainly be reflected in all swf files that use that symbol. Be aware, however, that the change will not be reflected in the fla files. You have to re-import the symbol from the shared library into a fla file's library in order to update it.

Common Libraries

Flash comes with some objects already available in a set of common libraries, accessed through the *'Other Panels'* option on the *'Window'* menu. This has a collection of pre-defined buttons, forms, etc., savings the beginner from designing everything from scratch.

Custom Libraries

If a designer regularly uses a set of in-house produced graphics, buttons and so on across many projects, it would be useful to have those items accessible from the Common Libraries. This involves creating a custom library as follows:
- Create a new Flash file.
- Open existing fla files and copy the desired elements into the new document's stage.
- Save the file on to the hard disk, in the Libraries folder of the Flash folder (usually found in the Program Files/Macromedia folders).

The custom library will now be listed along with the others in the Common Libraries list, allowing the items to be easily and quickly accessed for other projects.

Shared Fonts

The Shared Library principle can be extended to allow fonts to be shared between movies. Since fonts can consume huge amounts of file size, this is a very useful facility. It works in a very similar way to that outlined above.
The steps are:
- Create a new movie file.
- Open the Library window, click on *'Options'* symbol 🗏 and choose *'New Font'* from the drop-down window that appears.
- In the dialog box that appears, select a font from the drop-down list and give it a name. Check boxes allow italics and bold versions to included, if required. When the *'OK'* button is pressed, the font appears as a symbol in the Library.

The steps for making the font shareable are identical to those shown above for setting up other Shared Library objects.

The steps for using a shared font are;
- Open the movie that contains the shared library, using the *'Open External Library'* option from the *'Import'* option of the *'File'* menu.
- This will display the Library window, listing all the fonts that can be used in other movies.
- Do not close this window, but open the movie that is to use a shared font. This should result in the new movie being displayed – while the shared library window is still displayed.
- Open the library of the new movie. Two libraries should now be displayed on the screen.
- A font can now be dragged from the shared library in to the library of the new movie. The font is now included in the list of fonts shown in the Properties inspector.   A shared font is identified in the list by having an asterisk after its name.
- Text can now be added to the new movie and be formatted to the new font's style via the Properties panel.

Shared Code

If multiple movies share some sections of common code, the code can be created as a separate text file and called up by movies when they are being published.

The external script file can be created in any ASCII text editor, including Notepad and WordPad. The completed code is then saved with an .as extension (e.g. 'bigcode.as') and the file is stored in the same folder as the movies that will use it.

Any action that could be included in a movie can now be replaced by a script line that says:
        #include "bigcode.as"
When the movie is published, it replaces that line of code with the code contained in the external file.

This reduces the size of individual movie files and also any changes to the code will be reflected in all movies that use the code. There is no danger of code in one movie being changed and that in another movie being left unaltered – as long as any changes to an external file are followed by re-publishing the movies that use that file.

This is different from shared library objects, where the objects are fetched during playback time.

With shared code, the script lines are fetched during the time of publication.

Optimisation

When Flash projects are output as standalone executables, or as a QuickTime movie, the computer's playback system can usually cope with all but the most complicated and media-rich content. For web use, however, the limitations of the internet connection often results in poorer performance than was hoped. If the contents in each frame are large, they cannot be downloaded fast enough to keep up the illusion of continuous animation. Developers, therefore, have to ensure that the content is imported and manipulated in such a way as to create the smallest file size possible, while still maintaining the quality of the production. As explained earlier, using the Bandwidth Profiler shows the frames that cause most of the problem and these can be isolated and tackled.

While most of the problems come from importing large bitmapped images and sound files, savings are achievable by the optimum use of the Flash application itself. Since a project assembles all its images and sounds prior to importing them, optimisation should start with these source files.

Optimising sound

The aim is to have audio files that achieve their purpose in the most compact way. In some cases, high-quality audio is essential, while there is often a trade-off between quality and size. Optimisation issues include:

- Keep audio clips as short as practically possible.
- Crop any silences present at the beginning and the end of an audio clip.
- For non-streaming audio, use mp3 files, as they are already significantly compressed.
- Lower the sampling rate and/or the bit depth, where possible, to reduce the file size.
- Use mono instead of stereo, where possible.
- Use audio editing software to perform fades, rather than using Flash audio effects.

The above activities are carried out on audio files prior to them being imported in Flash.

Within Flash, additional savings can be made:

- Using looping of short sound clips to create the impression of a longer sound (e.g. applause, water running, car engine, etc.).
- Use pre-loading techniques (see later).
- Use the same sound at different keyframes but applying different effects (volume, fades, in and out points), so that the one audio clip does more than one job.

Optimising bitmap images

Bitmap image data is stored in the first keyframe in which it appears. Subsequent frames fetch the information from this symbol reference and these frames only store any changes (e.g. position, rotation, scaling, etc.). However, the general rule is to avoid using bitmaps where possible, as they are much larger than vector images. Of course, this is not always possible, as real-world images are sometimes required to display products, photographs, etc.

Optimisation issues prior to importing include:

- Don't use graphics with resolutions higher than 72dpi as user's monitors cannot display any higher quality. If necessary, resample the image down to 72dpi.
- Crop or rescale the image prior to importing.
- Avoid blurry or highly detailed backgrounds in images, as they result in poorer compression.
- Use compressed formats such as JPEG.

Within Flash:

- Don't import a large image and then scale it down, as this produces a small image that still has the file size of the original large image.
- Convert the bitmap image into a symbol, especially if it appears in several keyframes.
- Check if the 'Trace Bitmap' tool can convert the raster image into a smaller vector image (more likely with simpler bitmaps).

Optimising vector images

Flash is mainly aimed at handling vector images and each symbol's values (e.g. line co-ordinates, curve details, colour details, fill details, etc.) are stored in the first keyframe in which they appear. As with bitmap images, subsequent frames fetch the information from this symbol reference and these frames only store any changes (e.g. position, rotation, scaling, etc).

Optimisation issues here include:

- Lines created with the Pen or Pencil tool use fewer bytes than the Brush tool.
- Dotted/dashed/ragged lines use more bytes than continuous lines.
- Filling an area with a solid colour uses fewer bytes than using a gradient fill. Gradients also slow playback.
- Group screen elements, where possible, so Flash can refer to one object instead of many separate objects.
- Using alpha transparency can slow playback.
- Use one layer for objects that remain on screen during the entire animation sequence and another layer for objects that change during the animation. This simplifies development and usually also minimises the number of keyframes that are needed.
- Use the colour adjustments in the Properties inspector to change the colour of an instance of an object, rather than creating a new symbol.
- Minimise the number of separate lines that are required to draw a shape. Many hand-drawn lines suffer from a little hand wobble which makes the straight lines less straight than they ought to be, and curves not quite rounded enough. Use the Selection tool to select the line(s), right-click and choose the *'Straighten'* option, to straighten a kinky line and the *'Smooth'* option to refine a curve. These steps can be repeated if necessary.
- Alternatively use the *'Optimise Curves'* tool for reducing the number of lines used to describe a curve. This tool is found in the *'Shape'* sub-menu of the *'Modify'* menu.   The slider sets the degree of smoothing. If the *'Use multiple passes'* box is checked, the process is repeated until no further optimisation can be achieved. If the *'Show totals message'* box is checked, an alert box reports on the success of the optimisation (e.g. reporting that 123 lines have been reduced to 81).

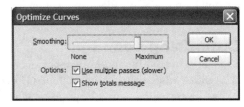

- Try using the *'Optimaze'* tool, available as a separate application. This software works on SWF files (not FLA files) and optimises the vector drawing elements within the file.

Optimising animation

The way that objects are used within Flash also affects the overall file size and the following steps help to minimise file sizes:

- Use symbols for every object, especially those that appear more than once in an animation.
- Reuse symbols, changing some properties, rather than creating extra symbols.
- Use tweened animations in preference to a series of keyframes, to reduce file size.
- Try to avoid tweening too many objects at the same time. This applies to animation and colour tweening and is even more of a problem with shape tweening.
- When an object tweens right off the stage, remove it immediately from the timeline.
- When an object fades away completely, remove it from the timeline.
- If streaming, don't put too many elements in the first few frames of the movie.
- Use Shared Libraries where a project consists of multiple movies.
- Try not to animate bitmaps. They are best used as backgrounds or static elements.
- Preload symbols to iron out bandwidth demands. Every symbol for a frame has to be downloaded before the frame is displayed. If a particular frame introduces many new symbols, the flow could be affected, especially with low-speed modems. If a new layer is created to sit behind the background layer, its contents will never be visible. Symbols can now be loaded into this layer during quiet times (e.g. while the user is reading instructions, looking at menu options, watching another animation, etc.). The symbols are then available later in the animation, thus smoothing out bandwidth surges.

Optimising text and fonts

For many projects, a limited number of different typefaces are desirable, as too many typefaces cheapen the overall look.   From a Flash point of view, having restrictions on the use of fonts also contributes to minimising file sizes. This is because Flash embeds font information inside the SWF file. However, specifying device fonts results in the user's computer using its own fonts instead of embedding fonts.   Although this reduces file sizes, it produces less font options and the final screen display may vary from user to user (depending on the fonts they have available).

- Use as few different font faces and font styles (italics, bold, etc.) as possible.
- Try to use device fonts instead of embedded fonts.
- Use shared fonts (see earlier). Linking to existing font definitions instead of embedding the same font definitions over again saves bytes.
- If embedding a font, specify only the characters needed, using the *'Character'* option in the Properties panel. This prevents saving definitions for characters that won't be used in the project.
- Text should not be broken apart unless for shape tweening purposes.

Using Dreamweaver

The *'Creating* Web *Sites'* chapter made mention of graphical web page editing tools. This chapter looks in more detail at one of the leading tools of this type, Macromedia's Dreamweaver. Like most software applications, Dreamweaver has gone through several versions, and the version that is used in this chapter is Dreamweaver MX 2004.

Dreamweaver provides access to all the major functions of plain HTML, as well as additional capabilities including JavaScript, site management, and even database connectivity. All of this is available through a single user-friendly graphical interface, linking with a variety of software ranging from browsers used to test the code, up to multimedia and database software.

Dreamweaver's basic interface is shown in this illustration.

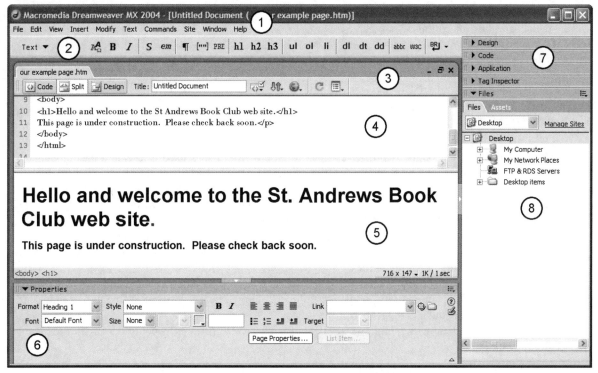

The diagram shows the various parts of the Dreamweaver interface, as follows:
1) The Menu toolbar, similar to the menu bar in any other Windows application.
2) The 'Insert' toolbar, containing the most common functions.
3) The 'Document' toolbar, allowing quick access to various view and document options.
4) The Code view, showing the raw HTML code for the page being edited.
5) The Design view, showing how the web page is expected to look in a browser.
6) The Properties Inspector. This panel is used to change settings of any selected tags.
7) The other panels, each of which contains several tabs allowing access to various options.
8) An opened panel, showing the *'File'* details.

This illustration shows Dreamweaver in *'Split'* view, which allows the developer to view both the HTML code and the page design on one split-screen window. The amount of screen space devoted to both views can be altered by clicking on the bar separating them, and dragging it to increase or decrease the size of the views.

Alternatively, Dreamweaver can be used exclusively in design view or code view (although working entirely in code view loses some of the benefits of a graphical editor). The designer can enter text directly into either view, and in code view can also manually edit the tags and/or script code contained on the page when necessary.

Dreamweaver includes a number of panels, and three toolbars. The panels are collapsed and enlarged by clicking on the panel title or the arrowhead to its left.. They are closed by right-clicking on a panel and choosing *'Close panel group'*. All panels can be hidden by choosing *'Hide panels'* from the *'View'* menu, or by pressing the F4 key. Clicking the F4 key once more brings the panels back on screen.

The toolbars are not collapsible. Instead, choosing *'Toolbars'* from the *'View'* menu shows a drop-down list of the three toolbars. Individual toolbars can be checked to display them, or unchecked to hide them. In the example, the *'Standard'* toolbar is hidden.

Starting Dreamweaver

The first step in developing a web page, like developing any other type of file, is to load an existing file, or create a new one. Although loading a single existing file and editing its contents is quite possible, Dreamweaver provides much greater functionality and integration to those sites that require management of multiple pages, and this is covered later. However, individual HTML files still need to be created, unless they are to simply be copied from an existing location.

Using *'New'* from the *'File'* menu brings the dialog box shown in the illustration. This allows one of several types of file to be created. However, the capabilities for editing files other than HTML have differing levels of support, in some cases being no better than a simple text editor.

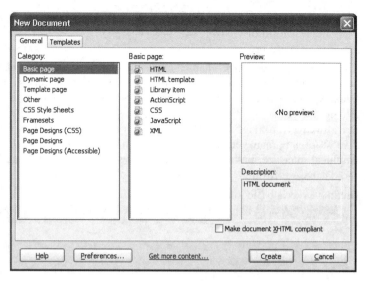

As can be seen from the illustration, Dreamweaver is able to create several *'Basic Page'* types, as well as a range of other file types.

The basic page types include:

- HTML files. The basic component of web sites.
- HTML templates. This is a Dreamweaver-specific type of file that is used to create a base document around which HTML files can be created. This is covered in more detail later.
- Library Items. These are short pieces of HTML code used by Dreamweaver to use repeated instances of a certain item, such as a common piece of text, or an image that will be used on several pages. The library is also explained in more detail later in this chapter.
- ActionScript. Very similar to JavaScript, this is the scripting language used with *'Flash'* animations.
- Cascading StyleSheets (CSS). Dreamweaver includes several methods of integrating CSS styles, including direct editing of CSS data files.
- JavaScript. Dreamweaver also includes a graphical interface to include certain predefined JavaScript capabilities to perform common functions like rollovers. However, the designer is free to write his own script directly by creating a new JavaScript file.
- XML. Although Dreamweaver allows the user to edit XML files its capabilities in this area are extremely basic.

The other types of file that can be created include:

- Dynamic Pages. These include various server-side scripting file types, such as PHP, ColdFusion, and ASP. Dreamweaver includes some functions to help create dynamic pages, but the majority of the code must be written by hand.
- Template Pages. This option allows the designer to create various types of template, including HTML templates, PHP templates, and ASP templates. The same rules apply to all forms of template, with only the type of content differing.
- Other. This section includes a wide range of files, from CSS and JavaScript up to such unusual file types as WML, EDML and C-Sharp. Most of the latter types of files have only extremely basic support in Dreamweaver.
- CSS Style Sheets. This allows access to a variety of pre-defined Style Sheets, which the designer can use 'as-is' or, more likely, build upon. When creating a new stylesheet the dialog box uses the preview box on the right hand side of the dialog box, showing an example of text and tables formatted using those styles. The basic styles include settings for different fonts, colour schemes, link effects and so on, though of course the designer can add to these or edit them as they see fit. CSS in Dreamweaver is covered in more detail later in this chapter.
- Framesets. This group contains a number of frameset layouts. Each frameset defined here has two or three frames, and the preview box shows how these frames are laid out on any site that uses this frameset.
- Page Designs. This comes in three forms; normal CSS Page Designs, Page Designs, and Accessible Page Designs, the latter of which simply contains modified versions from the normal Page Designs re-written to use accessible techniques. In all cases, though, page designs are essentially just suggested layouts that can be used in a typical website to save development time on simple projects.

The user can create a new web page add any stage by choosing *'New'* from the *'File'* menu.

Basic web editing

Once an HTML file has been created, or an existing web page loaded, the designer can begin to add or alter content. The simplest form of content that can be included in a web page is text. Dreamweaver tries to present an interface similar to a word processing package in order to edit web page text. For example, users of Microsoft Word will find some of the shortcuts to be familiar – Ctrl-B to turn the selected text bold, and Ctrl-I for italics.

Designers can begin typing text into the Design view as soon as an HTML file is opened. When editing in this manner, because of some of the unusual properties of HTML, some differences are to be expected between using Dreamweaver and a typical word processor.

For example, HTML can use two different codes to represent the end of a paragraph. The recommended method is to enclose each paragraph with <P> tags, so when the user presses the enter key, Dreamweaver automatically does so. However, the user may not wish to take this approach – text can be separated by using <BR> tags. Dreamweaver allows the user to do so, without having to manually insert the <BR> tags into the code view, by pressing 'shift-enter'. Furthermore, 'ctrl-enter' can also be used to move the editing cursor to the end of the current paragraph, which can be useful for precise placement of images or other objects outside of paragraphs.

Note, however, that the tab key has no effect in the design view of Dreamweaver, since HTML sees all whitespace characters (space characters, tabs, and line feed characters) as just one space between objects. To insert more whitespace that will actually appear on a web browser, we need to use a 'non-breaking space' (see below).

'Insert' toolbar options

The Insert toolbar, as shown on the opening page, has a down-pointing arrow next to the word *'Text'*. Clicking this arrow produces a drop-down menu of options. One option is *'Show as tabs'*. If this is clicked on, the Insert toolbar is displayed as a set of tabs (see the illustration below). Clicking the downward pointing arrow in the top right corner of the toolbar produces a drop-down menu which has an option called *'Show as Menu'*. Clicking this option returns to the view of the Insert toolbar as shown on the first page of this chapter.

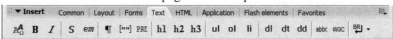

Inserting special characters

To insert non-standard characters or special codes, the down-pointing icon on the rightmost edge of the Insert toolbar should be clicked. This produces a drop-down menu offering access to the following codes:

Line break (the <BR> tag); Non-breaking space; opening quotes; closing quotes; the 'em-dash'; the Pound sign; the Euro symbol; the Yen symbol; the copyright symbol; the registration symbol; the trademark symbol.

The final button gives access to a dialog box containing a larger number of special characters such as those containing umlauts and so on. Clicking any option adds that symbol into the code/screen.

In earlier versions of MX, these were accessed from a separate (now defunct) *'Characters'* tab of the Inset panel.

Inserting and editing text formats

Entering the content is important, but to present a professional image even the most basic web page can benefit from formatting such as changing font faces, italicising and so on. This can be done in one of two ways: firstly, the tags can be inserted using the *'Text'* options of the *'Insert'* Panel, and then typing or pasting the content inside the tags.

Alternatively, the content can be entered into the Design view, and formatting can be applied to existing text by selecting portions to be formatted, and choosing options from the *'Properties'* Panel or the *'Text'* tab of the *'Insert'* panel.

Again, from left to right, the *'Text'* panel is used to insert the following tags:

- The Font tag, for setting font face, size, and colour. This tag cannot be applied to any already existing text that may be selected in the Code or Design windows.; if these settings are to be changed, use the *'Properties'* Panel instead. This option only affects text that is entered *after* this selection.
- Bold and Italic text tags.
- Strong, and emphasised text. In most browsers these are treated the same way as bold and italics.
- Paragraph marks, Block Quotes, and Pre-formatted text. Block quotes are typically treated as indented text by most browsers, while pre-formatted text is displayed in a fixed-size font.
- The three heading types, H1, H2 and H3.
- The three list tags, unordered list (UL), ordered list (OL) and list items (LI).
- The three definition list tags, definition list (DL), definition term (DT) and definition description (DD).
- The abbreviation (abbr) and acronym (W3C) tags, which are used to display a tooltip giving the text's full description whenever the mouse floats over that portion of text.

The *'Properties'* Panel can be used to provide access to these same capabilities and a few more besides. However, the Properties Panel can only be used on an object that is *already* in the web page, and has either been selected or is at the point where the cursor is currently located. The contents of the Properties panel varies depending on the object selected, and the illustration on the next page shows this Panel's contents when a paragraph containing some heading text is selected.

The top row of options is used to select the following settings:
- General format. This can include paragraph, any of the six headings (H1, H2, etc...), or Preformatted.
- The CSS style, if applied (see below).
- Bold and Italic styles.
- Left, Center, and Right alignment, and text justification.
- A combo box allowing the designer to specify a hyperlink associated with the selected object (e.g. making a piece of text into a hyperlink). The link can be typed or selected from the dropdown menu of recently-used links.
- A *'Point to File'* button, in the shape of a target icon, to specify links. The designer can click on the target icon and drag to a file found in the Site Panel (explained later) to link to a page within the same web site.
- Browse for a file to link to. This icon will open a dialog box where the designer can either type in a URL, or browse for a file.

The second row of options includes the following:
- The font face. Some common font lists are included in the drop-down box.
- The font size. A value that is entered in the *'Size'* box can be declared to be the value in pixels, points, inches, centimetres, etc.
- Font colour. The font colour can be specified either by clicking on the small colour box and selecting a colour, or by clicking within the larger box and typing in a six-digit colour code.
- Unordered list, and ordered list.
  Once a list has been created, the *'List Item'* button (greyed out in the screenshot above) becomes active and can be used to change list settings such as the list type (Bulleted, numbered, directory list or menu list); the Style (Roman Numerals, Numeric, Alphabetic etc); and so on.
- Indent and outdent. The *'indent'* in Dreamweaver is simply the <BLOCKQUOTE> tag, since the major browsers all treat this tag as being indented. Block quote can be nested; so that text can be indented to various levels. All the *'outdent'* button does is remove blockquote tags so that the text is indented less.
- A link target frame. The dialog box can be provided with the name of a frame into which the linked document (the one named in the dialog box above the Link dialog box) will be loaded. This is most useful for framesets, where a link will open a page in a different frame, referred to as the 'target'. Do not confuse this with the target button; they perform different actions.

Note: the user selections for a piece of text may be encapsulated into a CSS definition that appears in the HTML code, as in the example below:

```
.style21 {
    font-size: 18px;
    color: #cc0033;
    font-family: Verdana, Arial, Helvetica, sans-serif;
}
```

Additionally, the user is able to select an area of text, and then change its settings by right clicking on the selected text. This will bring up a popup menu, from which the user can access paragraph formats, lists, font alignment, font face, font style, and font size settings. Finally, the same options are available from the *'Text'* menu.
MX 2004 adds an additional button called 'Page Properties'.

Previewing the page

Once a page has been created, there are a few ways to view the finished product. While the page content is displayed in the Design View when editing the page, this is not quite the same as will be viewed by the end user on a browser such as Internet Explorer. The designer can, of course, save the web page, load up Explorer or any other browser, but it is all too easy to forget to update the file or make some other small error. To eliminate such problems, Dreamweaver has an integrated *'Preview in browser'* function.

When Dreamweaver is installed, it will attempt to detect all the web browsers installed in the machine, and set up accordingly. However, if an unusual browser is installed it is simple to set up Dreamweaver to include that browser in its list of preview capabilities. Simply click *File ⟹ Preview in Browser ⟹ Edit Browser List*, and the Preferences dialog box will pop up, allowing the user to add, remove, or modify entries in the list of browsers.
This list contains one *'primary browser'* and one *'secondary browser'*. The file being edited can be previewed in the primary browser by pressing F12; or in the secondary browser by pressing Ctrl-F12. Other entries in the browser list can only be accessed by clicking *File ⟹ Preview in Browser* and selecting that browser.

CSS Styles

Although the Properties panel and Insert panel can easily be used to modify the font properties of any section of text, Dreamweaver includes support for CSS Stylesheets to simplify formatting of text and facilitate coherent styles across documents. See the chapter on *'Developing Websites'* for more details on CSS.

Styles can be applied to text that is in the Design view or Code view windows by the following steps:

- Highlight the text to be formatted.
- Click the downward-pointing arrow in the *'Style'* box of the *'Properties'* toolbar.
- Click on the chosen style to be applied from the drop-down list that appears.

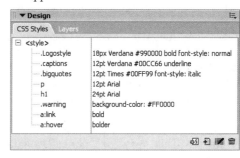

Dreamweaver provides some sample stylesheet definitions and many users might them sufficient for their needs. However, Dreamweaver also allows developers to create their own styles with their own user-defined names. When a style is added to the stylesheet, that style becomes available in the *'Properties'* list of style options. The drop-down list may also contain style definitions that are contained in stylesheets linked to the HTML file.

When a style is chosen from the drop-down list, the selected text is formatted to that style, and all the style's details (size, colour, etc.) are also displayed in the Properties panel.

CSS styles come in three types:

- Redefined tags.
- Class styles.
- Selectors.

Redefined tags are existing tags, such as <H1> or <B>, that are given altered formatting details. In this way, all text that falls within that tag have the appropriate formatting applied. In the example, the <P> tag has been redefined so that all text within paragraphs will be 12 point Arial font. Similarly, all <H1> headings will be in 24 point Arial.

Class styles are identifiers that can be used within a variety of tags to access a wider range of styles. In the example above, .warning indicates a class style that could be used as follows:

<P class="warning">Note: this site contains flashing lights that are unsuitable for viewers with photo-sensitive epilepsy.</P>

In the example above, the <P> tag is used, along with the .warning class style. This means that the P tag style (which in this example is 12 point Arial) is applied, *as well as* the .warning class style (in this example, black text on a red background).

Finally, the selector styles are used to apply a wide-ranging selection syntax that include element styles, child element styles, descendent element styles, and many other options. The user can type in any selector style, but Dreamweaver includes the four most commonly used selectors – the anchor styles. These are: a:link (the style applied to an unvisited link); a:visited (the style applied to a visited link); a:hover (the style applied to a link as the mouse hovers over it); and a:active (the style applied to a link which is active in another window).

The example above includes an a:link and an a:hover selector, which are set in such a way that a link will appear in bold until the mouse hovers over it, at which point it will become even bolder, drawing attention to the fact that the text is a link to another page.

Adding a style

There are several ways to add a new style using the integrated CSS Styles tab. The designer can click on the *'New CSS Style'* icon (the second icon on the bottom of the CSS Styles tab), or select *Text* ⟹ *CSS Styles* ⟹ *New* from the menu. This will present the user with the dialog shown opposite.

The user must select which type of class to create: a class style, tag redefinition, or CSS Selector. Depending on the selection made, the *'Name'* combo box must contain either a class name, tag name, or selector syntax, respectively.

A class style must begin with a dot, and cannot contain any spaces or punctuation characters. In the case of a redefined tag, the name must be of the tag that is to be redefined – the drop down box allows the user to select any of the standard tags. Finally, for CSS Selectors, the anchor selectors (a:link, a:visited etc) are available from the drop down menu.

Finally, the user must decide where to include the style definition – in the current document (*'This document only'*) or in a separate CSS Stylesheet. If the style is to be included in a

separate stylesheet, then the HTML file should already include a link to that Stylesheet. All of the linked stylesheets (although there is typically only one) will appear in the drop down dialog box. If no stylesheets are linked to the HTML document, then Dreamweaver will automatically pop up a dialog to create a new stylesheet in which the style will be defined – and that stylesheet will automatically be linked to the current HTML document.

Once the user is happy with the CSS Style definition, clicking *'OK'* will bring up the dialog box in which the actual style contents can be defined, as shown in the illustration. As can be seen, there is a wide range of options which can be included in any style. So many, in fact, that the Style Definition dialog box has to be split into eight sections: Type, Background, Block, Box, Border, List, Positioning and Extensions.

The illustration shows the options in the *'Type'* section.

This includes the basic text options such as:

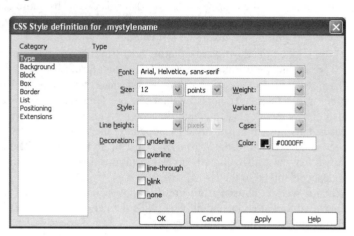

Font This is the font face used. As is normal for HTML, this defines a set of fonts in an attempt to be less system-specific.

Size The font size can be measured in pixels, points, inches, centimetres, and various other measurements.

Weight This indicates the thickness of the characters, and can be set to 'normal', 'bold', 'bolder', lighter', or a range of numbers. (Normal text is equivalent to a weight value of 400.)

Style This may be 'normal', 'italic' or 'oblique'.

Variant This sets the text to 'normal' or 'small-caps', which makes all the lower case characters use capitals but at a smaller size.

Line Height May be set to 'normal' or a value measured in pixels, points or other measurements, including percent of text size ('%'). This is the leading of the paragraph – for example, double line spacing can be achieved by entering a line height of 200%.

Case Can be used to force the text to be 'capitalized', 'uppercase', 'lowercase' or 'none' (no change of case).

Decoration Includes such additional typeface modifications as underline, overline, and line-through (sometimes referred to as *'strikethrough'*).

Color Like other colour selection options in Dreamweaver, the user may either click on the left-hand box and select a colour visually, or type in a colour in the right-hand box in HTML colour format, such as #FF0000 for red.

The other sections of the CSS Style Definition dialog box include the following options:

Background Options

Background Colour As usual, the colour can be selected or entered manually.

Background Image This can be set to 'none' (for no background image) or a URL. The URL can be absolute (e.g. www.mysite.com/myimage.gif) or relative (e.g. Images/firstimage.gif).

Repeat This indicates whether the image should be used once only ('no-repeat'), should repeat in both directions ('repeat') or should repeat in just one direction ('repeat-x' or 'repeat-y')

Attachment This indicates whether the image used as a background should be fixed in place on the screen while the rest of the page scrolls ('fixed'), or the image scrolls along with the rest of the page ('scroll').

Horizontal position and Vertical position These specify how the background image should be placed under the selected object. It may be centred, or aligned with the left, right, top, or bottom edges of the object.

Block Options

Word Spacing and Letter Spacing These specify the spacing between words and letters, respectively. Like other such values, they may be specified in points, pixels, or other values, although the default is 'ems'. Most browsers will not allow words or letters to overlap due to insufficient spacing.

Vertical Alignment This sets the position of the text on the y-axis. 'Baseline' indicates the normal alignment, while 'sub' and 'super' are used for subscript and superscript text. Other options include 'Top', 'Middle', 'Bottom', 'text-top' and 'text-bottom'.

Text Align This may be set to 'left' for left alignment, 'right' for right alignment, 'center', or 'justify'.

Text Indent This indicates the indent level of the text, as usual measured in points, pixels, or other measurements.

Whitespace This tells the browser how to handle whitespace. 'Normal' setting treats all whitespace text as a single space character. 'Pre' has the same effect as the <PRE> tag, treating the text as pre-formatted. The 'nowrap' option tells the browser not to wrap the text onto the next line until a
 (line break) tag is encountered. This may mean that text pushes the cell boundaries making it larger than it would otherwise be; or it may mean that some text is lost because it would stretch past the boundary.

Display This option determines how the object is displayed. 'None' means the object is <u>not</u> displayed at all. 'Block', the default setting, treats the element as a block of text, with line breaks before and after. 'In-line' is the opposite of block, with no page breaks. Other options include 'list-item', 'run-in', 'compact', 'marker', 'table', etc.

Box Options

Width and Height These set the width and height of the element. For example, if the width was set to '100 pixels' then any text within would wrap around before becoming any larger than 100 pixels.

Float This attribute makes text 'float' on either the left or right side of the page; other text will wrap around the element. For example the text which was going to go in a footnote could instead be floating on the right hand side of the page alongside the text it refers to.

Clear This attribute makes the element display clear of any floating layers. For example, if the footnote mentioned in the example above referred only to one paragraph, the next paragraph could have the clear attribute set, to make sure that it does not accidentally appear alongside the footnote as well. The browser will insert empty space to make the element clear of the floating object.

Padding Indicates the distance between the element and any element inside which it appears. It can be set so that a single padding value is used for all sides, or they can be set individually.

Margin Indicates the distance between the element and all other elements. This differs from 'padding' in that several elements can appear within one other element. For example, several paragraphs may appear within the body of a web page. If one is set to have 20 pixels of padding, that padding will apply to the border of the page only. If it is set to have 20 pixels of margin, it will apply that distance to the page, and also to the other paragraphs.

Border Options

Style The border style relates to the appearance of the box that surrounds the object. Any setting other than 'none' or a blank entry indicates a border around the object, which may be solid, dotted, dashed, double, grooved, ridged, inset, or outset. The last four options are "3D-effect" borders. It is possible to apply a different style to each side of the border.

Width This sets the width of the border. It is most usually measured in pixels, though there are a range of measurements to choose from. Like the style, the width of each border can be set separately.

Color This sets the colour of the border, and like the style and width, each border can be set separately.

List Options

Type For list objects, this specifies the type of list. Several bullet points can be selected: disc (a solid circle), circle (a hollow circle), or square. Other options apply to ordered lists, and may be 'decimal', 'lower-roman' (lower case Roman numerals), 'upper-roman' (upper case Roman numerals), 'lower-alpha' (lower case alphabetical), and upper-alpha (upper case alphabetical). If 'none' is selected then the object will not be displayed as part of the list.

Bullet image If none of the types listed above are suitable, an image file can be supplied to use as a bullet instead.

Position This should be used in conjunction with a text indent. It determines whether the indent applies to the text, or to the bullet point. 'inside' means the indent applies to the bullet point, while 'outside' means it applies to the text. If 'outside' is chosen without an indent, most browsers will not display the bullet because it falls outside the displayed area.

Positioning Options

Type The type of position can be 'absolute', 'relative' or 'static'. Static positioning is the default, but any setting of positioning options means the element will be treated as a layer (see later). Absolute positioning means the element is positioned exactly as specified by the 'Placement' attributes of the same dialog. Relative positioning means the element is positioned using the measurements in the 'Placement' attributes, but relative to its default position.

Visibility This determines the element's display setting. It may be 'inherit' (the default), in which the element has the same visibility as the parent element; 'visible', or 'hidden'.

Width and Height These specify the dimensions of the element. Most browsers will not reduce the width or height of an element to less than that which is necessary to display its contents, unless an 'overflow' option is selected to overrule the default behaviour.

Z-Index The 'Z-Index' of a layer determines whether it is displayed as 'on top of' or 'underneath' any other layers, if any overlap occurs. The higher Z-Index objects will be displayed 'on top' of any layer with a lower Z-Index. If two layers' Z-Index is the same, then the object which occurred last in order in the HTML file will be 'on top'.

Overflow This option decides what happens if the object exceeds the size of the layer specified by its 'width' and 'height' attributes. 'Visible' (the default setting) means that the rest of the layer will be visible even though it exceeds the layer's size. 'Hidden' means that any excess will not be visible. 'scroll' means that vertical and horizontal scrollbars will be used to allow viewing of the contents of the layer, while 'auto' will use either vertical, horizontal, or both scrollbars as necessary.

Placement This indicates the placement of the layer, from the top, bottom, left and/or right sides of the page. This is typically used in conjunction with the 'type' attribute to determine the exact location of the layer.

Clip This attribute is used to 'cut' parts out of the layer. The clipping from the top, bottom, left and right indicate a region which is not visible. This is not generally very useful unless used in conjunction with scripting, when it can be used to introduce special effects such as wipes and reveals of layers.

Extensions Options

Page Break   This is used to force a page break in the print out only. It has no effect on normal web viewing, but if it is set to have a page break before and/or after an element, then when printing (or in print preview) any browser which supports these options will add page breaks. This splits the web page printout over pages as decided by the page designer, so that with some care it can be made 'printer-friendly'.

Cursor   This option is used to change the appearance of the mouse pointer when it floats over any element in this style. The options include a hand, a crosshair, a text-editing bar, an hourglass, and so on.

Filter   This applies an IE-specific filter to the elements in this style, such as blurring, drop shadows, flipping and so on. Some of these filters require user editing of variables.

Working with styles

Once a style has been created, it is not set in stone. The designer can change any style settings, using the dialogs described above. There are two methods of accessing these edit dialogs.

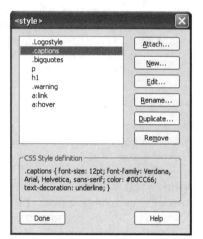

One method is:

- Click on the *'Text'* option in the main menu.
- Select *'CSS Styles'* from the drop-down menu.
- Select *'Manage Styles'*.

This will bring up the Style Sheet Editor dialog box, as illustrated.

The dialog lists the style definitions within the HTML file or Stylesheet being edited. The designer may select a style and edit, duplicate or remove it from here. The box underneath shows the code for each style as it is selected.

An alternative is to select the html file or stylesheet in the CSS Styles tab, and click *'Edit Style Sheet Definition'*, the third button at the bottom of the panel (the one to the left of the dustbin icon).

The designer may also link to stylesheets in separate files, or add a new style to the HTML file or stylesheet currently being edited.

A style can be removed without entering this dialog however, simply by selecting the style on the CSS Style tab and click on the *'Delete CSS Style'* button, the fourth button at the bottom of the panel.

The first button at the bottom of this panel, *'Attach Style Sheet'*, performs the same function as the *'Link'* button from the editing dialog shown above.

Inline Styles

Styles can be defined in an external stylesheet, or in a style definition block within the HTML file. However, it is sometimes useful to define styles for just a single element. Dreamweaver allows the user to edit the attributes of any

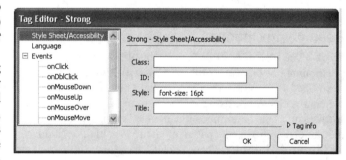

tag. Simply select the entire tag (it may be easier to do this from the Code View than the Design View) and right click on the selection, choosing *'Edit Tag'*.

As shown in the illustration, this opens the Tag Editor dialog box. This allows the user to directly edit any tag's attributes, from several groups listed in the box on the left-hand side. In terms of styles, however, the *'Style Sheet/Accessibility'* option is the relevant group of attributes. The example shows the 'strong' tag, which has the style 'font-size: 16pt' applied. The problem with using this method is that there is no visual interface; the user must be familiar with the CSS code for the style he or she wants.

External Stylesheets

Dreamweaver can use the Link option to attach a stylesheet to an HTML file, or to import its contents into that HTML file. If the stylesheet is to be used as a linked stylesheet, however, it is best that the stylesheet is part of the Site (explained later) to make management of files easier.

Any HTML file can have one or more CSS stylesheets linked to it. However, the order of precedence should be borne in mind. Links that appear earlier in the HTML document are of the lowest precedence, with later linked stylesheets being of higher precedence. Styles defined within the HTML document itself are higher still, but the highest precedence is given to inline style definitions within the tag itself.

If an external stylesheet is linked to an HTML file, then it will simply appear in the CSS Styles tab alongside the HTML file. The designer can then apply, add, edit, or remove style definitions from either the HTML file or the CSS stylesheet.

Sites and assets

Dreamweaver can be used to edit a single HTML file, but it is much more powerful when used as a tool for developing an entire site. The designer can create one or more sites in the *'Site Definition'* panel.

The steps for creating a site definition are:

- Choose *'Manage Sites...'* from the *'Site'* menu. A dialog box then displays all existing site definitions (When Dreamweaver is run for the first time started up, the list will be empty).
- Click the *'New'* button.
- Choose *'Site'* from the drop-down menu.
- Choose either the *'Basic'* or *'Advanced'* site design tab.

'Basic' Tab options

The Basic site design is essentially a wizard that will guide the designer through the process of setting up a site. It will ask for several details:

- A name for the site. This can be any name chosen by the designer.
- Whether the site will use any server technology, such as PHP.
- How to develop files for the final publication: editing locally and then uploading, or directly editing them on the remote site either via network connection or FTP.
- A location to store the site on the local machine.
- How to upload the locally edited files to the server, if this option has been selected; or the location and settings of the network connection or FTP site, if that option was selected.

'Advanced' Tab options

The Advanced tab provides greater control over site settings, as shown in the illustration.

It splits the site settings into several groups along the left-hand side. The example shows the settings in the *'Local Info'* group for a web site which is to be developed.

The Local Info includes a Site Name and folder, and the tickbox indicates that the site list that appears in Dreamweaver should refresh itself automatically – if this is not ticked, the user must manually refresh for changes to take effect.

The *'Default images folder'* specifies another folder, which is where the graphics (GIFs, JPEGs etc) will be stored locally. Both the Local Root folder and the Default Image folder can be selected by typing a folder in or by browsing after clicking on the folder icon.

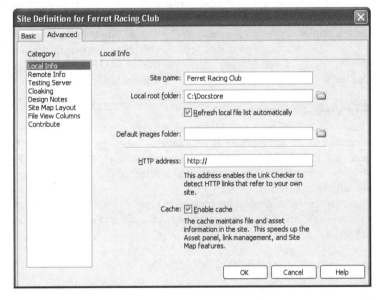

The *'HTTP Address'* indicates the final address that will be used by the web site. It is only necessary for verifying links where absolute URLs have been used.

Finally, the *'Cache'* option decides whether Dreamweaver should maintain an area of local cache.

Remote Info

This group of settings differs depending on what method of remote access is employed. In all cases (except where no remote access is used) two settings are provided: whether to automatically upload files remotely when they are saved locally; and whether to enable *'File check in and check out'*. Check in/check out is a facility used when group access to a web site is necessary, to alert other users to files which have been changed or which are being worked on.

None   No remote access is provided. The user is assumed to take care of any implementation details.

FTP   The files are uploaded to the site by File Transfer Protocol. This will bring up FTP settings including the FTP host DNS name, the directory on the host server to upload files, the login and password used, and other FTP related settings.

Local/Network   The files are uploaded to a server located in a different folder on the local machine, or in a folder on another system on the LAN. The settings necessary include the folder (which may be typed in or browsed), and whether to refresh the remote file list automatically.

RDS   Remote Development Services is a method used alongside Macromedia ColdFusion.

SourceSafe   This is a Microsoft web development platform with which Dreamweaver is able to interface.

WebDAV   The Web Distributed Authoring & Versioning protocol is implemented by some servers such as IIS and Apache, and Dreamweaver is able to upload using this protocol so long as the server also supports it.

Testing Server

This group of settings is used to specify the settings for testing active pages such as PHP scripts. It consists of these settings:

Server Model This specifies the types of active server which is used: ASP JavaScript, for example, or PHP/MySQL.

Access This determines the access method to the active server, in similar vein to the access to the site server, although the only methods allowed are 'none', 'FTP' or 'Local/Network'.

Cloaking and Design Notes

Cloaking is used to exclude certain folders or file types from upload to the remote server. This can be useful to reduce bandwidth costs when changes are expected to be regular and of minor importance. For example, a site with many large graphics might, during development, undergo many large file changes every day, and depending on the connection type it may be costly to upload all of these files after every change. The *'Cloak files ending with'* option is used to exclude certain file types from the uploading process.

The Design Notes, as the window says, are used to store additional design-related information on the files in the project.

Site Map Layout

This group includes several options mainly concerned with the layout of the site map as displayed in Dreamweaver:

Home Page If this is not specified, then the default home page *'index.htm'* or *'index.html'* is used. Otherwise, this specifies the home page of the site.

Number of columns and column width Specifies the number and width of columns displayed when the site map is shown.

Icon Labels Determines whether to display pages in the site as File Names or Page Titles on the site map. Each page will appear with an icon, alongside which will appear either the filename of the HTML file for the page, or the title of the HTML page as specified in its contents.

Options Determines whether to display hidden files, and/or dependent files such as images.

File View Columns

This group of settings is used to determine which columns are displayed in the File view window when the Site tab is expanded to fill the screen. It lists several headings, each of which can have certain options. The built-in column headings include Name (which cannot be hidden), Notes, Size, Type, Modified, Checked Out By. All of these options except Name can be hidden by unticking the 'Show' box, and the contents of the columns can be aligned to the left, right, or center.

Users can create new columns by clicking the '+' box. For these *'Personal'* columns, there are additional options: the column name, the design note with which the column is associated, and whether the column is shared with other users of this site.

Working with Sites

Once one or more sites are created, Dreamweaver will display them in the *'Files'* tab of the *'Files'* panel, as shown in the illustration. Although the designer may have several sites on his hard disk, Dreamweaver can only work with one site at a time, and it is that site whose contents are displayed in a tree format, including such files as HTML files, CSS Stylesheets, images, templates, and so on.

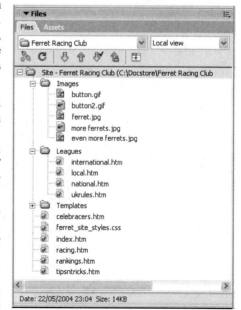

The example shows a site that has been set up such that Images and Template files are stored in separate folders. The Site tab is currently in *'Local View'*, showing the files and folders in the local copy of the site. The drop down box which currently says *'Local View'* can be changed to *'Remote View'* to see the contents of the remote site; *'Testing Server'* to see the files involved in active server testing; or *'Map View'* to show a visual map of the site's layout.

The Local View is useful during development in many ways. It allows the designer to see at a glance which files are included in the project, and most files can be double-clicked to load them into Dreamweaver for editing.

Since all of these files and folders are stored normally, it is quite feasible for users to add, remove or edit files that are in the local site, using explorer or any other software. However, to do so means losing out on some of the integrated features of Dreamweaver.

For example, right-clicking on any line in the Local View of the Site tab will bring up a popup menu including such options as: creating and editing files; performing file 'Get' and 'Put' operations; previewing, cloaking, and checking in/out of files.

More ways to access such functions are provided in the small menu and toolbar inside the Site tab as shown on the previous page. From left to right, the icons shown in the illustration on the previous page perform the following tasks:

Connect/Disconnect from remote host   This icon is used to create or dissolve a connection from the local and remote locations. If the *'remote'* site is on the local machine or network, this option is greyed out.

Refresh   It should only be necessary to refresh the Local View if automatic refreshes are disabled. However, on Remote View or Testing View, it may be useful to refresh before getting or putting files.

Get Files   The *'Get'* command will retrieve a file from the remote site. Both Get and Put commands require that the site be set up to upload files to a remote site of some kind. If the user selects a file or folder in the Remote View and clicks *'Get'*, that file or folder will be copied. If the user selects a file or folder in the Local View, then Dreamweaver will attempt to get the remote version of that file or folder, assuming it exists on the remote site.

Put Files   Similar to *'Get'*, the *'Put'* command works in the opposite direction, copying files from the local site to the remote site.

Check Out Files   The check out system allows multiple developers to work on the site safely, without over-writing each others' work. This is explained in more detail later in this section.

Check In Files   Just as Put is the opposite of Get, Check In is of course the opposite of Check Out. Once a file has been edited, it should be checked in, to allow other users to access the file.

Expand/Collapse   This icon will swap the Site tab between its normal place on the side bar, and a full window view. The full window view is the only way to see additional columns of detail on files in the Local and Remote View; it is also much easier to display a large site in Map View, as shown in the illustration.

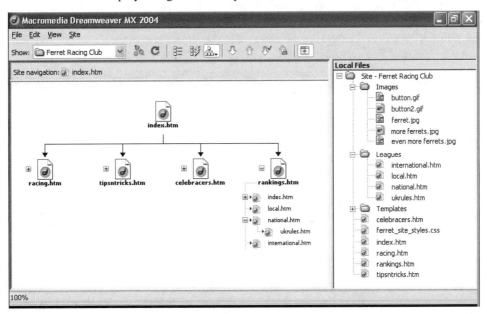

This shows the *'Map View'* of the Site tab in expanded more. The Map View is used to show the links between files in a graphical manner. In expanded view, this graphic takes the form of a horizontal 'tree' structure as shown, but in collapsed view, since there is less space, it displays a vertical structure instead.

The illustration shows the structure of a site called 'Ferret Racing Club'. The file 'index.htm' is the home page of this site, so the Map View defaults to having that file at the top (the 'root') of the tree structure. The lines emanating from the root of the structure indicate files to which there are links within that HTML file. In other words, in the example shown, index.htm contains links to four other HTML files: racing.htm, tipsntricks.htm, celebracers.htm and rankings.htm.

In turn, these files also contain links. Since a structure like this can quickly become unwieldy, all of these 'second level' and deeper links are shown using smaller icons, and in a vertical arrangement. For example, the file 'rankings.htm' in the example above, contains links to four other HTML files. One of those links is a link back to the home page.

Apart from the links from the root page, other links can be expanded or collapsed using the '+' and '-' buttons respectively. For example, the 'racing.htm' page has a '+' icon next to it: this indicates that the page contains links, but that they are not currently displayed in the Map View; clicking the '+' will show them. Since the 'rankings.htm' file has links which *have* been expanded, it has a '-' icon next to it, which can be clicked to remove those links from display in the Map View.

Note that it is quite possible for recursive links to be found in a site. The example shows a page with a link back to the index. Since the index contains a link to the file, the site map can potentially go on forever.

As mentioned previously, the Site Map View starts with the home page at the root of the tree structure. However, the user may right-click on the icon of any other page, and select *'View As Root'*, to make that page become the new root of the structure.   The Site Map will re-arrange itself to show links emanating from that page instead.   To revert back to displaying the index page, click on the words *'index.htm'* in the panel as shown.

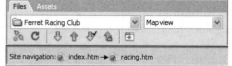

Creating and working with links in Dreamweaver is explained fully in the next section of this chapter.   However, the Site Map View contains a useful graphical way to create links.   When the user selects a page on the map, a target icon appears next to the page icon.   The user may click on the target icon, and drag it to any other HTML file either on the site map or in the Local Files.   This will create the appropriate tag at the end of the body of the first HTML file, to make a link to the second file.   This method can be used to quickly create the appropriate site structure, with the content being added later.
Note: Broken links are indicated by the filename being in red text.

Using Checkin and Checkout

The file checking system is used by Dreamweaver to track changes to files on the site.   In order for it to be effective, all of the site users must use Dreamweaver for uploading and downloading files to and from the remote site, and should use Dreamweaver for editing of files wherever possible.   If any designers use other tools to edit the web pages, they will not be aware of the checking out mechanism, and this could make the whole checking out process ineffective.

The system works on the basis that files on the remote site are those that are being served by the web server, and that those on the local site are merely copies of the actual served files.   When a file is to be edited, a copy is taken from ('checked out of') the remote site to the local site, until editing is complete, at which point the file is copied back up to ('checked in to') the remote site.

The illustration below shows the state of the Ferret Racing Club web site.   The Site tab has been expanded to fill the window, but it is in File View this time, showing the contents of the remote site in the left hand pane, and the contents of the local site in the right hand pane.   Note the speech bubble icon indicating that index.html contains Notes.

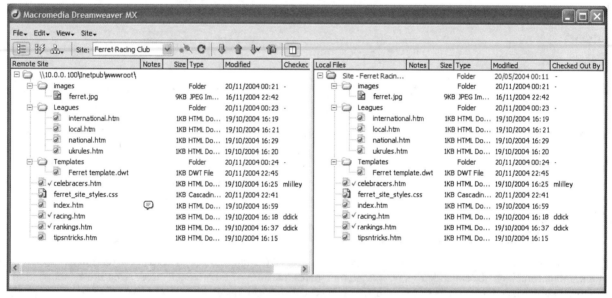

In this case, the remote site has been set to Local/Network, since the web site is stored on a computer attached via a LAN.   The address for this site is 10.0.0.100 (a local LAN IP address) and the folder name is \Inetpub\wwwroot (a common IIS web site folder name).

The example shows that three files have been checked out for editing: "celebracers.htm" has been checked out by user 'mlilley', while "racing.htm" and "rankings.htm" have been checked out by user ddick.   All of the files which are checked out have a tick next to them in both the Remote Site pane and the Local Site pane: a green tick for files checked out by the local user, or a red tick for files checked out by any other user.   A green tick indicates that the user may freely edit the local copy.

Those files that have not been checked out fall into two categories: new local files which have not yet been uploaded to the server; and local copies of files which have not been checked out for editing.   New local files are, of course, free for editing, and have no tick or lock icon next to them, to indicate they may be edited.   However, the moment any file, new or otherwise is checked in to the server, Dreamweaver makes the local copy of that file read-only.   This is to stop users from editing local copies of files without checking them out first.   In this way, so long as all the web site developers obey the rules, no file can be edited by two users at once.   Read-only files are indicated by a small lock icon next the filename.

However, in some circumstances it may be necessary to over-ride another user's lock on a checked out file, perhaps due to an emergency, or simply because the user who checked out the file forgot to check it back in. In such a case, simply try to check out the file in the normal manner, and click 'Yes' when asked whether to over-ride the other user's lock.

Files are 'checked out' from the remote server while any given designer works on them. Checking out a file involves copying the file from the remote site to the local site, and preventing other users from altering it. Dreamweaver knows which files have been checked out because it places a '.LCK' file on the remote server to indicate a file which is locked. In this way, other users working with Dreamweaver will recognise the LCK file, and prevent the user from editing files which have been checked out by other users.

A file which has been edited and then checked in can no longer be edited. This is indicated in Dreamweaver by placing a small 'lock' icon next to the file, indicating that it cannot be edited by the current user until it is checked out again. The check-in process consists of putting the file on the remote server, and removing the file lock so that other users may edit the file.

Creating links

Editing a single HTML file is useful, but links are necessary for a web page of any size.

Dreamweaver allows the designer to create links from the main view window in many ways:

- When editing an HTML file in Code View, the user can enter the A (anchor) tag manually.
- The link icons on the '*Common*' tab of the Insert Panel (as shown on the right) allow the user to link to URLs, use 'mailto' links, or create local anchors. These icons are explained below.
- In the Design View, the user may select some text and place it within an anchor tag. One way to do this is to use the Properties Panel which is normally found at the bottom of the window, as explained earlier in the chapter. It contains a combo box in which a link can be typed or selected, and a '*Point to File*' icon which can also be used for the same purpose. Simply clicking on the Point to File icon, and dragging to a file in the Site tab, will create a link.
- In Design View, the user can select some text to turn into a link, and then right-click on it, choosing "*Make Link*". A dialog box will then appear that allows the user to type in a URL or locate a file in the local copy of the site. This dialog box is explained later.

The Link Icons

As mentioned above, the Insert Panel contains three icons which deal with links.

The '*Hyperlink*' icon will bring up a dialog box similar to that shown on the right. From here the user has access to several options:

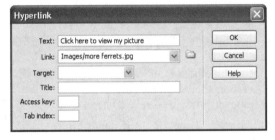

Text – This is the text which will appear in the web page and be treated as a hyperlink.

Link – This is the URL that the link will follow. The folder icon next to this box is used to browse for the file to which the user wishes to create a link.

Target – Like the target option in the Properties Panel, this option is used to specify a target frame in a site which uses a frameset.

Title – The title attribute performs various functions. It may be read aloud by accessible browsers; in some circumstances it pops up as a tooltip similar to the ALT tag; and so on.

Access Key – The function of this attribute varies. On most windows browsers, pressing ALT and the key given as the access key, will invoke that object. In the case of a link, for example, with access key "B", pressing ALT-B will activate that link.

Tab Index – This indicates the place the link takes in the 'tabbing order'. Every link and form item is given a place in the tabbing order – if the designer specifies a tab index for each item this will determine the order; otherwise the browser will determine the order itself, typically going by the order they appear in the page source. The user may use the 'tab' key on the keyboard to move from one link or form item to the next, within the page.

Make Links

As can be seen, the Make Link dialog box allows the designer to create a link either to a file, or a data source. A data source is typically an online database, and in order to link to it, the site must be set up to use a dynamic document type, and have a testing server set up.

For files, the dialog box can be used to browse for a file in the normal manner. There are additional attributes, however:

- The '*URL*' box will change to reflect the link URL which will be used, including any parameters. However, it can also be used to type in an absolute URL such as www.microsoft.com.
- The '*Relative to*' drop-down box allows the user to choose whether links specified relate to the current document, or to the root of the site. For example, if a file in the 'Leagues' folder was to link to another file called 'test.htm' in that folder, and 'Relative to' was set to "Document", then the URL would simply read 'test.htm'. However, if the 'Relative to' was set to "Site Root", the URL would instead read "/Leagues/test.htm".
- Finally, the '*Parameters*' button is used to add HTTP parameters to the URL. This is useful for CGI scripts and other active sites.

As explained elsewhere, HTML parameters are expressed in pairs of names and values. For example, a web page used to send emails to the site administrator might link to a CGI script called 'feedback.cgi'. The page might ask for feedback on the quality of the website, offering choices such as 'poor', 'fair' or 'good'. It would be possible to send this as a parameter, by linking to the URL 'feedback.cgi?quality=good', for example. The Parameters button can be used to introduce these pairs of values.

Link Validation

Although the validation of links on the server can be tested manually, or the page can be run through a third-party validation procedure, Dreamweaver includes some integrated validation:

- To validate the links in a single HTML page, load that page and click *File* ⟹ *Check Page* ⟹ *Check Links*, or if the link checker tab is already visible, clicking the green '*Check Links*' icon.
- To validate all links within several HTML files at once, select the files or folders in the Local View of the Site Tab. Then right-click on them, and select *Check Links* ⟹ *Selected Files/Folders*.
- To validate all links within all HTML pages in a site, right click anywhere within the Local View of the Site tab, and select *Check Links* ⟹ *Entire Current Site*.

In each case, the result will be displayed in the Results Panel, which will generally appear at the bottom of the window. The illustration shows an example of the kind of results that will be displayed here.

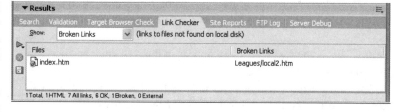

The Results Panel is used for various types of feedback, including Search results, Code Validation, FTP Logs and Link Checking, each of which is accessed by a tab.

The Link Checker tab is further split into three types, which can be chosen through the '*Show*' drop-down box. These three options show different types of link problems:

Broken Links

Dreamweaver can detect links to local files that are incorrect or missing. In such a case, it will indicate which file the link is contained within, and which file the link tries to point to. The example above shows that 'index.html' has a link to file 'local2.htm' which either does not exist, or is not in the location specified.

External Links.

Dreamweaver is not able to verify links to pages or files that are not part of the same site. These '*external links*' are displayed here so that the user is aware of them and can check them manually if desired.

Orphaned Files.

The opposite of a broken link is a file that has no links pointing to it. The typical web surfer will be unable to reach this file at all, which is of course a problem in nearly all cases.

Code Validation

Other than links, Dreamweaver is also able to check the general usage of tags within an HTML page, to verify that there are no errors such as overlapping tags or unclosed sets of tags. Page validation can be performed by *File* ⟹ *Check Page* ⟹ *Validate Markup*, or, if the validation tab is already visible, clicking the green 'Validate' icon. This allows checking of the current page, the entire site, or a selected range of files.

The Validation process finds three main types of errors:

- Nesting errors. These are indicated by an icon of two pieces of paper. They represent a problem where tags overlap so that they are not properly nested. Many browsers will still display the contents as the designer intended, despite the code technically being wrong.
- Warnings. These typically indicate potential problems which could cause trouble in certain browsers.
- Errors. These represent actual faults in the coding of the document, such as unclosed tags, where even a lax browser would be unable to accurately depict the page as the designer intended.

However, as with programming languages, there is often a 'domino effect' where one error, possibly a relatively minor error, could cause worse faults later in the code. A simple nesting error can result in a slew of warnings and errors. The nesting error has 'knocked' the code validation process out of sync, causing it to see additional errors where there are no other errors. This is common and unavoidable, so it is always good practice to fix the 'faults' one at a time rather than try to correct the entire page in one operation.

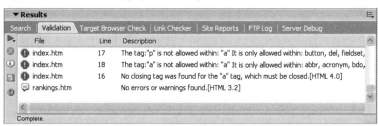

Using images

Other than HTML files, the most commonly used type of file in a web page is a graphic image. Dreamweaver has integrated support for JPEG, GIF and PNG image types. Although it will only show the first frame of an animated GIF, this does not affect the fact that the GIF will still be animated when it is uploaded to the site and viewed by the end user.

Images appear in web pages in one of two ways:

- The page background, as part of the BODY tag.
- As an image within a page, using the IMG tag.

Background images

To set a background image for the whole document, click *Modify* $\Rightarrow$ *Page Properties*, and either type in the image location in the *'Background Image'* box, or click Browse and select the file for the background.

However, through the use of CSS Stylesheets, any region of text may have a background image or a background colour. Simply create or edit a style of any kind, click on the *'Background'* section, and select the image. This can be used either to redefine existing tags (for example, so that all headings have a sparkly background image), or to define a class that can be applied to any tag type.

Dreamweaver also includes a *'tracing background'* option. This is similar to the normal background used in a BODY tag, but will not appear in the final web page. Instead, it will show the background image in Dreamweaver only, allowing the user to *'trace'* objects over it. The tracing image is accessed by choosing *'Page Properties'* from the *'Modify'* menu and selecting *'Tracing Image'* from the Category list. The background image is selected and the slider dragged to the required degree of transparency (the greater the level of transparency,

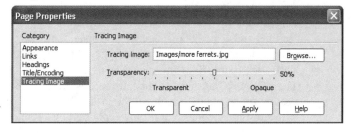

the fainter the image will appear to be in Dreamweaver).

When the 'OK' button is clicked, a line of code similar to that below is inserted into the script code.

```
<body tracingsrc="Images/more ferrets.jpg" tracingopacity="50">
```

Images within a document

Dreamweaver can easily include images in any HTML document, either by fully specifying the image tag, or by simply inserting an image placeholder that does not yet point to an image, but is intended for later use. The *'Common'* tab of the Insert Panel has an icon, shown in the illustration to the right, to perform these functions. Alternatively, the user may click on *Insert* $\Rightarrow$ *Image*, or *Insert* $\Rightarrow$ *Image Objects Image* $\Rightarrow$ *Placeholder*, respectively.

Both options will bring up a dialog box to specify the relevant options. For example, inserting an image will bring up the same dialog box as used to specify links, except that it has a *'preview'* capability instead of a parameters button. Also like links, the image source may be specified as a file, or a data source. The Insert Image icon will insert an IMG tag, with SRC, WIDTH and HEIGHT attributes to match the selected file.

For an image placeholder, the dialog box will contain the following options:

Name	This specifies a name for the image, which may be used by scripting languages.
Width and Height	Since no image file will be specified, Dreamweaver will be unable to automatically insert width and height values. The user should supply them. The default value is 32 pixels.
Color	This indicates the background colour of the image placeholder.
Alternate text	This specifies the contents of the ALT tag for the placeholder.

In both cases, Dreamweaver will create an IMG tag with the appropriate attributes, and display the image (or image placeholder) in the Design View. The image in Design View will have draggable boxes at the sides and corners to resize the image, but unless the image is held in its own layer, it is only possible to resize the image on the right or bottom sides of the image. This is because the left and top sides of the image are placed by the browser depending on its location in the HTML code.

By clicking on the image in the Design View, or clicking inside the IMG tag in Code View, the Properties Panel will change to show the properties of the image, as shown in the illustration.

The panel is split into two sections: a basic properties section on top, and an additional properties section underneath. The small arrow icon in the bottom right corner of the Panel is used to expand or collapse the additional properties section as needed.

The basic properties includes the following sections:

- A thumbnail of the image, along with its size in kilobytes and a small box (blank in the example above) used to give a name to the image where necessary.
- The Width (W) and Height (H) of the image tag.
- The image source (Src) and any link that the image uses. Both of these can be 'targeted' in the same way as text links, by clicking the small target icon and dragging to the desired file. Alternatively the folder icon can be clicked to browse for a file.
- The contents of the ALT tag for the image.
- An *'Edit'* button, used to launch an external graphic editor. This will only work if Dreamweaver has been told which program to use as an external editor, by clicking *Edit* $\Rightarrow$ *Preferences* and selecting the *'File Types/Editors'* section, and specifying a program to link to .jpeg, gif, and any other image types used.
- Tools for cropping the image, adjusting its brightness and contrast and sharpening the image.

The additional properties box contains the following sections:

- An image map name, and icons to select the image map tools. Image maps in Dreamweaver are explained in more detail later in this chapter.
- Vertical and Horizontal spacing. ('V Space' and 'H Space') These are used to put space between the image and the other objects on the page. It is measured in pixels.
- The target frame, if the image is used as a link within a frameset.
- The LOWSRC attribute. This attribute is used to specify a low-resolution, low-colour, or low-detail version of the image, which will be loaded before the actual image is loaded. This is useful for viewers with slow connections, but is only supported by a few of the most modern browsers.
- The size of border that surrounds the image, measured in pixels.
- Three icons to set the alignment of the paragraph in which the image (left aligned, centred, or right aligned) is located. Do not confuse this with the image alignment, as described next.
- The alignment of the image with text or other elements following it.
  The options include:
  - Default: Sets the alignment to the browser default, which is usually 'baseline'.
  - Baseline or Bottom: Aligns the bottom (or 'baseline') of the image with the bottom of the text and/or other elements in the paragraph.
  - Top: The top of the image is aligned with the top of other elements in the paragraph.
  - Middle: The middle of the image is aligned with the baseline of other elements in the paragraph.
  - Left: The image is aligned to the left, with all text flowing on the right.
  - Right: The image is aligned to the right, with all text flowing on the left.
  - Absolute Middle: The middle of the image is aligned with the middle of other elements.

Image Maps

Once an image has been inserted into an HTML file, Dreamweaver is able to turn it into an image map by using four tools to create and edit *'hotspots'*. As explained in other chapters, a hotspot is a section of the image that is linked to a particular URL. These hotspots may be rectangular, circular, or irregular in shape.

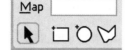

The top part of the image map toolset is simply the name of the map. If the designer does not specify a name, Dreamweaver will simply call the first image map 'Map', the second image map 'Map2' and so on. However, a more descriptive name is sometimes helpful.

The bottom row contains some graphical tools for creating hotspots:

- The Pointer tool. This is used to perform a variety of editing functions on existing hotspots, as explained later.
- The Rectangular hotspot tool. This tool creates a new hotspot, by clicking and dragging within the image area.
- The Circular hotspot tool. Also used by clicking and dragging, the circular tool creates the circular hotspot *within* the area dragged, rather than *around* the area dragged as some graphical editors do.
- The Polygon hotspot tool. This creates an irregularly shaped hotspot, by repeatedly clicking on points in the image. Each click creates a new node in the polygonal shape.

Hotspots are indicated by Dreamweaver placing a translucent shape over the image, matching the hotspot's shape. Each hotspot should be associated with a link. As soon as a hotspot is created or selected by clicking on it with the Pointer tool, the Properties Panel displays the properties of the hotspot. This consists of the Link (which, as usual, can be created by dragging the *'target'* icon to the desired file), the target frame, and the ALT attribute. All three of these can also be changed by right-clicking on the hotspot with the Pointer tool and selecting *'Link'*, *'Target'* or *'Alt'* respectively.

The Pointer tool can also be used to:

- Select hotspots. This is done by a single click on the hotspot.
- Move a whole hotspot, by clicking on it and dragging to the new location.
- Resize a rectangular or circular hotspot. To do this, first click on the hotspot – resize boxes will appear at the sides and (in the case of rectangles) the corners. These resize boxes can be clicked and dragged to resize the hotspot.
- Change the points in a Polygonal hotspot. First, select the Polygonal hotspot – each point will be shown by a small box. Clicking on any of these boxes and dragging, will change the location of that node in the polygon.
- Re-arrange the order of hotspots. Clicking on a hotspot, and then right-clicking will allow the user to *'Bring To Front'* or *'Send to Back'* any of the hotspots. If there are any overlapping areas between hotspots then the order in which they appear will determine which hotspot is used when any given pixel within the overlapped area is clicked.

Tables

Tables are among the most versatile and useful aspects of web pages, and Dreamweaver can create and work with tables in a number of ways. The basic method for inserting a table is to click *Insert* $\Rightarrow$ *Table*, press Ctrl+Alt+T on the keyboard, or click the Insert Table icon on the *'Common'*, *'Layout'* or *'Tables'* tabs in the Insert Panel, as shown on the right.

All of these will bring up the same dialog box, which will configure the table being inserted.

This includes: the number of rows and columns in the table; the Cell Padding separating cells from their contents; the Cell Spacing separating each cell from its neighbours, the total table Width, and the table Border size. All measurements are in pixels, except table Width which may be measured in pixels or as a percentage of the size of the element in which the table is contained. (typically the HTML page width)

When the designer clicks *'OK'* the table is created at the point where the cursor is currently located within the document. Once a table is inserted, it can be modified in many ways, but most of them require the user to select a cell, row, column, or entire table before they can be carried out.

The illustration shows a table that has been created in Dreamweaver, with 3 rows and 3 columns, 10 pixels of cell Spacing, and a 1-pixel border.

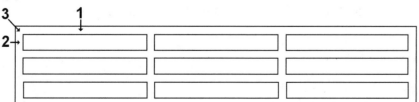

Click on the point indicated in order to select:

1) Clicking here, at the top of a column, would select that column. In this example it would select the three leftmost cells.
2) Clicking here, to the left of a row, would select that row, in this case the three topmost cells.
3) Clicking on the corner of the table will select the entire table.

Alternatively, the user may create a table manually in Code View. When creating a table this way, additional buttons in the '*Table*' tab of the Insert Panel become available. All each of these buttons do, however, is add one of the TABLE, TR, TH, TD or CAPTION tags, along with a closing tag to match.

Modifying a table

There are many ways a table's dimensions and appearance can be altered in Dreamweaver, depending on whether a cell, row, column, or table has been selected. When the whole table is selected, the Properties Panel changes to reflect the table properties, as illustrated below. As normal, the Panel is split into two sections that can be collapsed into one by clicking the small arrow in the bottom-right of the Panel.

The top section of the table Properties Panel gives access to settings such as the Table ID, number of rows and columns, width and height of the table, and other settings, most of which are the same settings as shown when creating a new table.

Note that increasing the number of rows or columns in the table from the Properties Panel will add rows or columns on the end of existing rows or columns; reducing the rows or columns will likewise remove them from the end of the current set of rows or columns. To remove a row or column other than those at the bottom or right hand side of the table, the user must first select or move the cursor inside the row(s) or column(s). Then, right-click on it and select *Table* $\Rightarrow$ *Delete Column* or *Delete Row* as appropriate. These commands can also be accessed from the *Modify* $\Rightarrow$ *Table* menu.

Similarly, if a row or column is to be added other than at the right hand side or bottom of the table, the user must select or click on a row or column and choose the *Insert Row* or *Insert Column* option from the same menu. The *Insert Rows or Columns* option allows more control, by selecting whether to insert rows or columns, and whether the item is to be inserted before or after the current selection. It also allows multiple rows or columns to be inserted.

The expanded Properties for the Table include the following options:

- Clear Column Widths. The top-left icon of this group will remove the WIDTH attribute from all columns. This will force the browser to decide the width of the columns based on their contents. As a result, empty columns may become very small with this command.
- Convert Table Width to Pixels. This will turn all WIDTH attributes into their equivalent measurement in pixels if they are currently in percentages. This, of course, depends on the current size of the window in which the Design View is displayed.
- Convert Table Width to Percent. This top-right icon of the group is the opposite of converting to pixels, and turns all WIDTH attributes into their equivalent percentage values.
- Clear Row Height; Convert Table Height to Pixels; Convert Table Height to Percent. The lower three icons perform a similar function to that of the table width buttons, with regard to cell height instead of width.
- Background colour. Chosen in the usual way.
- Background Image. Like other files, this can be chosen by typing a URL or filename, or using the target or browse buttons.
- Brdr Color. This option sets the colour of the border in the table.

One of the simplest alterations that can be made to a table is to change the width or height of a row or column. Although this can be done from the Properties Panel of the row or column (as explained later), it can also be done visually by moving the mouse to any border (except the leftmost and topmost borders of the table, which cannot be moved), clicking and dragging that border. Dreamweaver will alter the width or height values so that they match the size selected by the mouse.

The illustration shows the screen as the user begins to change the width of the second and third columns by moving the border between them. If the user dragged that border to the right, it would increase the width of column 2 and 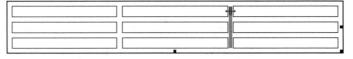 decrease the width of column 3; if dragged to the right it would be vice versa.

Cell Spanning and Splitting

Another useful technique in tables is spanning, such as in the example shown, where the top right cell spans both two columns and two rows. Dreamweaver can implement cell spanning and merging in the following ways:

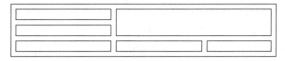

- Select multiple cells, by clicking inside one cell and dragging the mouse to another cell. The border of the selected cells will change colour. Then, from the *'Modify'* menu select *'Table'*, followed by *'Merge cells'*. Alternatively, click on the merge cells icon. The cells will then be merged, and their contents will all be merged into one cell. Depending on the current layout of the table and which cells are to be merged, this may or may not employ spanning in the HTML code.
- Select a single cell and, from Modify's *'Table'* sub-menu, select *'Increase Row Span'* or *'Increase Column Span'*. If a cell already has spanning, this will increase its row or column span by one. If a cell does not yet have spanning, this command will cause the cell to span two rows or two columns.

The opposite, of course, is to turn one cell into several cells, known as *'Splitting'*. Splitting can be used to reduce or remove the cell spanning of any given cell, or it can be used to turn a single non-spanned cell into two cells. In both cases, clicking *'Split Cell'* from Modify's *'Table'* submenu will bring up a dialog box, from which the user can decide whether to split the cell vertically (*'Split cell into columns'*) or horizontally (*'Split cell into rows'*).

Alternatively, the user may click on the split cell icon.

The user may also select how many rows or columns the cell should be split into. If this results in more rows or columns than are currently in the table, then it will make other cells span so that the structure of the table remains the same. For example, if the top-left cell in a 3x3 table is split into two rows, it would change the table to look like the illustration to the right.

Cell formatting

The contents of an individual row, column or cell can be individually formatted in Dreamweaver. Whenever a row, column or cell is selected, the basic section of the Properties Panel shows the common text attributes, as explained earlier. However, the expanded section of the Panel shows attributes specific to table contents, as shown below.

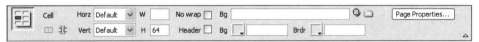

The picture on the left indicates the item that has been selected, be it a cell, row or column.

The other properties include:

- Icons that can be used to merge or split cells, as explained above. These icons are only active when the context is correct; e.g. you cannot use the merge button unless two or more adjacent cells are selected.
- Horizontal and Vertical alignment of the contents of the cell, row or column.
- Width (W) and Height (H) of the column. These default to pixel measurements, but they can also be percentages, for example by typing 25% in the Width box.
- No Wrap. This option is used to prevent any line of text inside the cell from wrapping round if it would pass the right-hand edge of the cell. If *'No Wrap'* is selected and the text is so large that it would normally wrap, then the extra text will simply not be displayed.
- Header. A header cell is formatted by the browser to make it stand out, typically by emboldening and centering the text. It is in most cases a cosmetic concern but it is good practice to use table headers where they are relevant.
- Background image or colour, selected as normal.
- Brdr. This selects a border colour for the individual cell, row or column.

Using layout tables

Throughout the discussion of tables so far, it has been assumed that Dreamweaver is in *'Standard View'*. However, there is also a *'Layout View'*, which is used to graphically insert cells and sub-tables. The user can switch between Standard View and Layout View by clicking the button of the same name in the *'Layout'* section of the Insert Panel as shown in the illustration. When Layout View is active, the two icons shown on the right of the illustration become available. These are *'Draw Layout Table'* and *'Draw Layout Cell'* respectively.

Drawing a Layout Table simply means using the mouse to create a table in Layout View. This is done by selecting the *'Draw Layout Table'* button, and clicking and dragging either in the blank portion at the end of the HTML document, or within an existing table. Note however that, due to the way HTML works, the start of the table will 'jump' to the end of the document. This will result in a very basic table being created, with just one cell.

Drawing a Layout Cell is similar. However, as the name suggests, a Layout Cell is a cell *within* a Layout Table. If a Layout Cell is drawn in a valid area (i.e. an area that does not contain any other content) that is *not* part of a Layout Table, Dreamweaver will automatically create a Layout Table and place the Cell inside it.

A Layout table is essentially the same as an ordinary table. However, it contains some Dreamweaver-specific comments, which it uses to indicate, which cells are part of the layout. This is because Layout Tables are intended not simply for storing pieces of data for display as a table, but for using that table to put content in the correct place on the page.

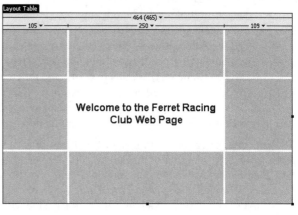

For example, a basic use of Layout tables would be a splash page that contains some text or images in a smallish rectangle in the center of the page. This could be achieved easily in Dreamweaver by clicking *'Draw Layout Cell'* and clicking and dragging in the page to create a small cell. Dreamweaver will automatically insert a table that will fill the remainder of the page, as in the example shown.

Only the central cell, however, has contents that can be edited. This is because Dreamweaver recognises that cell as a *'Layout Cell'* and all non-layout cells are there merely to take up the space in between layout cells.

As such, Dreamweaver can use a 'spacer image' – a single-pixel, transparent image which should have no effect on the appearance of the page – to make sure that browsers are forced to use the correct table size. Alternatively, columns may be set to 'autostretch', meaning that the width of the column will depend on the width of the contents. Only one column may be autostretched.

Frames

The chapter on *'Web Site Creation'* covered the principles and usage of frames. Each frame of a frameset can have its contents changed without altering the contents of any other frames in the set. This makes frames a popular choice for some designers who can (for example) have a logo in one frame, a site menu in another frame and the main site contents in a third frame.

Dreamweaver provides a collection of pre-defined frame definitions.

Clicking the *'Frame'* button on the *'Layout'* options of the Insert panel produces a drop-down menu as shown in the illustration.

The first four are the basic frame options: Left, Right, Top, and Bottom. The others create a page that is split into three frames.

Creating frames

The steps for creating a new pre-defined frameset are:
- Select *'New'* from the *'File'* menu.
- Select *'Framesets'* from the dialog box that appears.
- Select the required frameset from the displayed list and click the *'Create'* button.

Alternatively:
- Select *'New'* from the *'File'* menu.
- Select *'Basic Page'*, followed by *'HTML'* and *'Create'*.
- Click the *'Frame'* button on the *'Layout'* options of the Insert panel and choose a frame layout from the drop-down menu (see above illustration).

Dreamweaver can also turn an existing document into a frame within a frameset. This is achieved by clicking the *'Frame'* button on the *'Layout'* options of the Insert panel and choosing a frame layout from the drop-down menu).

When the frame definitions icons are displayed, as in the above illustration, the darker portion (in blue) is the frame that will be taken up by the currently selected HTML file, while the white areas indicate new empty documents which Dreamweaver will create to fill the new frames. For example, if a page had an image and a caption, these would be placed in the frame area that is darkened in the icon.

Editing the frameset

Once the frameset is created, it is available for editing.

In Code View, the size and layout of the frames can be directly edited, by overwriting the default values by the required values. The changes are then reflected in the frame layout displayed in the Design View.

The outlines of the frame boundaries are displayed in the Design View and these outlines can be dragged to the required screen positions. The code is automatically updated to reflect these new positions. In most circumstances this will resize the frames which share that border. However, dragging a frame border can also be used to remove a frame, by dragging the border to the edge of the page; or can be used to create a new frame, by dragging a border which is at the edge of the page, into the page.

Clicking on the <frameset> definition in the Code View brings up the Properties panel for the entire frameset, as shown in the illustration.

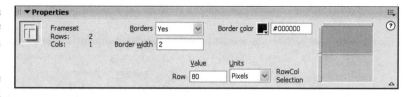

When editing the frameset, the Properties Panel will show information on the number of rows and columns in the frameset, and will allow the following options to be edited:

Borders: This can be set to *'Yes'* (Frames have borders), *'No'* (Frames do not have borders) or *'Default'* (The browser decides whether to use borders or not).

Border Width Indicates the width, in pixels, of frame borders. If frames have a border, this will be displayed in the Design View.

Border Color Selected in the usual way, by clicking on the box or entering a value.

Column or Row sizes Depending on whether the frameset is split into rows or columns, the diagram to the right will show how the frameset is split. This example shows a frameset which is split into 2 rows and 1 column, and the topmost row is currently selected. The value below therefore shows the size of that column, in this case the frame is 80 pixels tall.

Column and Row sizes may be measured in pixels or percentages. However, there is a third option: *'Relative'*. Only one row and/or one column should be set to relative, or the results will be unpredictable. This is because Relative means that the row or column's width/height is determined by filling in the extra space which is not part of any other row or column, making the frame fill the available space.

Editing frames

Each frame is an HTML file in itself, and can be edited, opened, saved etc in the normal way.

A frame can be selected, either by alt-clicking on it in the Design View, or by clicking on the <FRAME> tag in the Code View.

Either way, the frame's Properties Panel will show the properties for that individual frame, as shown in the illustration. This Panel gives access to the following options:

- Frame name. The example calls the frame 'rightframe'. This is the name that will be used if any links are used to send the target URL to this frame.
- Src. This is the initial source URL for the contents of this frame. It can be typed, targeted, or browsed.
- Scroll. This sets whether the frame is scrollable. It can be set to 'Yes', 'No', 'Auto' (use scrollbars only if the content would not fit the frame) or 'Default' (allow the browser to determine whether to use scrollbars).
- No Resize. This defined whether the frame size may be changed by the viewer.
- Borders and Border Color. Defines whether the frame has a border, and what color that border should be. Note that frames which share a border and have different settings may act unpredictably in various browsers, and that in nested framesets, the frame border settings of the parent frameset takes precedence.
- Margin Width and Height. These define a margin between the frame border and its contents, measured in pixels.

Where there are many frames in a frameset, or a frameset has a complex layout, the *'Frames'* panel can be used to quickly jump between frames. If this Panel is not visible, it can be called up by clicking the *;Frames' option from the '.Window' menu.*

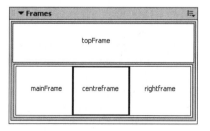

The panel shows the current layout of the frameset, and allows the designer to click in any frame to begin editing that frame. Clicking a frame brings up that frame in the Code View and Design View. The example to the right shows the Panel's appearance when editing the frame called 'centreframe' in a nested frameset.

Linking content to frames

A hyperlink in one frame is used to place an HTML file's contents into another frame. Most commonly, a menu in one frame has options to change the contents of a main frame. The process is in three parts : create a hyperlink, decide what content should be called up by the hyperlink, and decide which frame should be used to display this content.

The steps for creating a link to a frame are:
- In the Design View, enter the hyperlink text or graphic.
- Highlight the text or object in the Design View, to display the Properties Inspector.
- The *'Link'* box is used to enter the HTML page to be placed into the target frame. This box can have its contents typed in, or the file can be selected from the drop-down list, or the *'Point to File'* icon can be dragged to the required file in the *'Files'* panel.
- The *'Target'* box is used to specify which frame the HTML content should be placed in. All frames created by the user for that frameset will appear in the drop-down list and the required frame is selected.

The drop-down list also contains some default choices. These are:

_blank This places the new HTML content in a new browser window, on top of the frameset window.
_parent This places the new HTML content in the parent frameset of the frame the link appears in, replacing the entire existing frameset.
_self This places the new HTML content in the current frame, replacing the existing frame content.
_top This places the new HTML content in the current browser window, replacing *all* existing frames and their contents.

Using forms

The purpose and uses of forms is covered in the chapter on *'Web Site Creation'*.
Dreamweaver creates forms quickly and simply, using the *'Forms'* section of the Insert Panel as shown below.

The leftmost icon in this group is *'Insert Form'*, which is the same as selecting the *'Form'* option from the *'Insert'* menu. This creates an empty form for objects to be placed in.
If the user clicks 'Insert Form' in Design View, default properties (as shown in the Properties Panel) will be applied and an orange dashed line will indicate the contents of the form. If it is clicked in Code View, the properties dialog box will pop up before the form is created.
The Properties of a form include the form name, and other attributes. The *'Action'* typically indicates a CGI script to which the form sends its information to be processed, while the *'method'* used is either the GET or POST method (or the browsers default method of the two). The target frame and encoding method can also be specified. Encoding method is normally *'application/x-www-form-urlencoded'* for textual form data, or *'multipart/form-data'* for a form that contains a File Field indicating a file to upload.

The other icons in this tab, from left to right, are as follows:
- Text Field. This object has properties including the object name, its width and maximum length (both in characters), its type (single line, multiple line, or *'password'*, which does not show data entered on the screen), and its *'initial value'*, which provides its initial contents when the page loads.
- Hidden Field. A form object that will not appear on the web page. It is often used as a temporary storage place for text, or other functions related to scripting. Its only properties are its name and the *'value'* or contents of the field. Hidden fields are shown in Dreamweaver, however, with an icon indicating its presence.
- Text Area. This is basically the same as clicking *'Text Field'* and selecting *'Multiple Line'* in the Properties Panel.
- Checkbox. The properties for this item are simply an object name and value, and an initial state that is either Checked or Unchecked, indicating whether the box has a tick when the page loads.
- Radio Button. Inserts one radio button. Multiple radio buttons may be grouped together simply by giving them the same object name. Other properties include the value assigned to the radio button when each button is checked; and the initial state of each button. Only one button should be checked initially.
- Radio Group. This button brings up a dialog box which gives a faster way to create a number of radio buttons all grouped under one name. Use the '+' and '-' buttons to set the number of buttons, the arrow keys to change the order in which they appear, and click on the *'Label'* or *'Value'* for any button to set those properties. This method can group the radio buttons together within a TABLE, or simply separate each button by a BR line break. Each button will already have a Label, as explained below.
- List/Menu. The Properties Panel allows the designer to set the object name, and select whether the item is a Menu (a drop down selection) or a List (a multi-line selection). The user may also set the height of

a List, and whether multiple selections are allowed. The '*List Values*' button is where the options available in the List or Menu are entered (name of each item and the value returned for each item). Finally, the '*Initialy selected*' list allows the user to choose which option is selected when the page is first displayed.

- Jump Menu. This inserts a combination of a drop-down list, and a JavaScript behaviour to perform one of the more common web navigation interfaces: a drop-down menu of pages to send the browser to. The user must give each option a name and a URL (which must be a local file or left blank for a menu heading), and a target frame (if using a frameset). The whole Jump Menu must also be given a name, and has two other options: '*Insert Go button after menu*', which uses a button labeled 'Go' to jump to pages rather than simply selecting them from the menu; and '*Select first Item After URL Change*' will make sure the first item is initially selected, which is useful if the menu has a heading.

- Image Field. Used to insert an image inside a form.

- File Field. This is a text box and a '*Browse*' button, which are used together to specify a file on the local machine. Its properties include the object name, and its Width and maximum number of Characters.

- Button. The button properties include name, label (the text which appears on the button), and its type: either a '*Submit form*' button, '*Reset form*' button, or '*None*'. (in other words, a general purpose button)

- Label. Any form object may have a label, which is simply a piece of text that appears alongside the object. It is most useful for checkboxes and radio buttons, which usually need some explanation of their purpose. Clicking the label has the same effect as clicking the item to which it is linked.

- Fieldset. A fieldset is an object, which in most browsers has a border around it, and is used to contain other elements in a form. It should also contain a LEGEND tag, which is displayed as part of the border around the fieldset.

Layers

A '*layer*' is basically a section of an HTML document that contains other elements and can be positioned anywhere in the page. The style section earlier explained that any item could be given '*absolute*' positioning on the page – any items that have absolute positioning automatically become a layer. However, it is sometimes difficult or even impossible to achieve the desired effect with layers that have been defined through a stylesheet, since the item's positioning properties are set in the stylesheet rather than while editing the HTML in which it appears.

The more common way to use layers is to employ tags that cause the browsers to create layers. Unfortunately the development of layering technology in browsers was rather haphazard. There are, in fact, four different tags that can be used to create layers: DIV, SPAN, LAYER and ILAYER. Of these, DIV and SPAN are the most widely supported, and DIV is the default tag used to create layers in Dreamweaver.

A new layer can be created by clicking the '*Draw Layer*' icon on the Layout option of the Insert Panel as shown to the right, or by selecting '*Layer*' from the '*Layout Objects*' sub-menu of the '*Insert*' menu.

The user can then draw a layer onto the Design View by clicking and dragging. The resulting layer will be indicated by a thin black line, with small black resize boxes on the edges and corners. Click and drag these to change the dimensions of the layer. To move the layer, click and drag either the thin edge line, or the black and white box in the top left corner.

Layers can contain almost any other elements, except for Layout tables. This allows for easy and precise positioning of such items as buttons, footnotes, text in columns, and so on. Of course, it requires a browser that supports the type of layering used.

When a layer is selected, the Properties Panel, as illustrated, can be used to change the layer's options. These are largely the same options as found in the '*Positioning Options*' of the '*Style*' section: dimensions (in pixels/px; percent/%, inches/in, or centimetres/cm); Z-index; Visibility; Background image and/or colour; Overflow and Clipping.

Layers and Tables

Another way to work with tables is to convert an existing table into layers, or vice versa. Clicking *Modify* $\Rightarrow$ *Convert* $\Rightarrow$ *Layers to Tables* will convert a selected group of layers into a table, after setting options for the conversion in a dialog box. Dreamweaver will create a table of the appropriate number of rows and columns so that the spaces in between layers will be turned into empty table cells; and spanning may be employed to make the cell sizes match the layer sizes as much as possible. Similarly, a table can be converted into a layer by clicking *Modify* $\Rightarrow$ *Convert* $\Rightarrow$ *Tables to Layers*.

When an HTML file contains layers, the '*Layers*' tab of the '*Design*' panel may be useful. If it is not visible, it can be shown by clicking the '*Layers*' option in the '*Window*' menu.

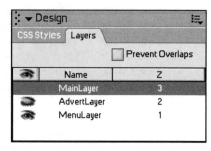

The Layers tab is simply a list of all layers in the current HTML file. The first column indicates the visibility of the layer: if blank it means the layers visibility is set to 'default'; a closed eye means 'invisible' and an open eye means 'visible'. Clicking here will cycle the visibility of the layer through these three options. The other columns list the name of each layer, and its Z-Index. The Z-Index can be changed by single-clicking here and entering a number; the name can be changed by double-clicking and typing in a new name.

Dragging and dropping a layer in the Layers tab will also change the Z-index to rearrange the layers on the screen. Holding down the CTRL key while dragging a layer in the tab will move the layer to become '*nested*' within the layer on which it is dropped.

Nested Layers

A layer may be '*nested*' by placing it *inside* another layer. If the user is currently editing a layer or its contents, then clicking *Insert* $\Rightarrow$ *Layer* will produce a nested layer inside that one. When drawing a layer inside another layer, it may or may not become a nested layer, depending on the setting of the '*Nest when Created within a layer*' option in the Layers section of the preference (see *Edit* $\Rightarrow$ *Preferences* $\Rightarrow$ *Layers*).

Nested layers have some benefits: all the layers nested within another layer will move together as the 'parent' layer is moved, keeping all the layers in line with one another. Visibility of the child layers can also be inherited from the parent, so that making one layer invisible will make all its sub-layers invisible as well.

The Layers tab will show nested layers in a tree-like structure vaguely similar to the Windows Explorer folder view. Dragging one layer inside the nested area of another layer will move it to become a child of that layer. Similarly, nested layers can be moved out of their nest by dragging them either to another nest or to the main layers area.

Templates

As explained toward the start of this chapter, the user may create a new HTML file from a '*template*'. A template is simply an HTML file with additional comments that Dreamweaver recognises as information about how a document created using that template can be edited. For example, a template could be created such that certain sections can be edited, others can not, and some may be optional while others can repeat several times. This allows designers to create a 'master' page that can be used by developers to create pages for a site, in the knowledge that all the pages conform to the same design. It also means that developers of individual pages cannot overwrite sections of a page that the designers wishes to appear on all pages.

There are two ways to create a template:

- Click *File* $\Rightarrow$ *New*, and select '*HTML Template*'.
- Create or edit a regular HTML document, and select *File* $\Rightarrow$ *Save as Template*.

Once a template has been created, the designers may create new HTML files based on that template, by clicking *File* $\Rightarrow$ *New*, and clicking the '*Templates*' tab. This will display all the sites which Dreamweaver has been set up to use, and clicking on any site will display the templates available for that site, as well as a preview of the template contents and its description. Clicking the '*Create*' button creates a new HTML file based on that template.

One of the main benefits of using a template is that Dreamweaver will link files with the templates on which they were based. This means that if the designer returns to alter the appearance or contents of the template, all of the files based on that template will be updated to reflect the changes. So, for example, changes to the company motto can easily be propagated to all template-based web pages by changing the templates and allowing the files to be updated. Of course the updated files will still need to be uploaded afresh to the web server.

Editing a template

Since a template is basically an HTML file, all of the usual HTML tags are available in a template. Clicking the '*Template*' icon in the '*Common*' options of the Insert Panel displays a drop-down menu of the extra functions that apply only to template files. These are:

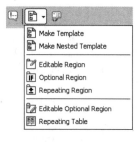

- Make Template. This is the same as clicking *File* $\Rightarrow$ *Save as Template*.
- Make Nested Template. It is possible to have templates based on other templates.
- Editable Region. When a file is based on a template, the editable regions are the only areas in which the user may enter or change the contents.
- Optional Region. The optional region requires an '*expression*' to be defined, which determines whether the region will be displayed in any given file based on that template. The simplest version, which is the default method used, is to base the optional regions on a variable set in the HTML file. So, for example, 'OptionalRegion1' may display if the variable 'ShowOption1' is set, which can be decided for each file

based on that template by clicking *Modify* $\Rightarrow$ *Template Properties* and changing the variables. The optional region is not editable; if the user is expected to edit the contents, then an Editable region must be placed inside it.

- Repeating Region. This defines a section which will repeat one or more times. Repeating Regions, like Optional Regions are not editable but can contain Editable Regions. When a file is based on a template with a repeating region, that region will be shown with four buttons – '+' (add anew copy of the region), '-' (remove the current copy of the region), and arrows to re-arrange the order of the copies.
- Editable Optional Region. This is essentially an optional region that contains an Editable Region, since that is a commonly used combination.
- Repeating Table. Another commonly used combination is a table containing a row that can repeat one or more times, with each cell containing an Editable Region. That is exactly what this icon does.

The example shows a relatively simple template for keeping track of changes to code during software development. The first two editable regions are simply to keep note of the author and the software which the page refers to. The table below is a Repeating Table, so that the author can make multiple entries in the development record for that piece of software.

JavaScript in Dreamweaver

Dreamweaver can work with JavaScript in a variety of ways. As mentioned earlier, it is quite feasible to use Dreamweaver to create and format the HTML, while creating the script by hand or in conjunction with other development tools. However, this need not be necessary: the 'Script' tab of the Insert Panel allows the designer to insert hand-crafted JavaScript into the body of the document, and of course the Code View allows the user to edit the text of any script directly.

Alternatively, for some of the more common and less in-depth applications of JavaScript, there are several functions built in, including:

- Jump Menus, as mentioned in the 'Forms' section of this chapter, are based on JavaScript.
- Rollover Images. This will open a dialog box that allows the user to specify two images, one for when the mouse is hovering over the button, and one for when the mouse is not over the button. This will be controlled by several JavaScript functions that Dreamweaver will automatically insert into the header of the document. The dialog also allows alternate text, link settings to be specified, and has the option to preload the rollover image for speed.
- Navigation Bars. This will also open a dialog box for setting up images used as links. The navigation bar is more complex, though, containing several buttons, each of which can have up to four images; one for when the button is pressed 'down', one for when it is 'up', one for when the mouse hovers over, and one for hovering over while it is 'down'. The buttons can be arranged vertically or horizontally, and there is the option to preload the images for speed.

Rollover images and navigation bars can be inserted by clicking *Insert* $\Rightarrow$ *Image Objects* $\Rightarrow$ *Rollover Image* or *Navigation Bar*.

Element Behaviours

The '*Tag Inspector*' panel contains a '*Behaviors*' tab which can be used to help develop JavaScript for the page. If the panel is not visible, it can be brought onscreen by choosing '*Tag Inspector*' from the '*Window*' menu. The contents of this panel vary depending on where the cursor is located at any time. For example, if a rollover button is selected, the behaviours tab will show the scripts that have been associated with that button's events, as shown in the example illustration. The onMouseOut event, for example, has been associated with the Swap Image Restore action.

Dreamweaver includes a variety of 'actions' by default. An action is either a custom piece of JavaScript code or, as in the case shown, an integrated Dreamweaver action, which consists of JavaScript code, a description, and other settings.

To associate an action with an event, an element must first be selected. The actions that are available will vary depending on the type of element which is selected. For example, an Image can be swapped on mouse out or mouse over, while the body of the HTML page can be associated with PreLoading of images or playing of sounds. Each action has a different set of attributes which will be displayed in a dialog box to set up as soon as the action is selected. Double-clicking an entry in the Behaviours tab will allow editing of these attributes after they have been saved.

Project Testing

No projects work correctly first time. That is not a criticism of the team members or the team leaders. It is a result of the huge complexity arising from the size and scope of these projects. It is not an issue that only affects multimedia projects. All software suffers from the same problem (just how many bug fixes have Microsoft and others issued for their products?). The challenge is to recognise the inevitability of problems and to budget time and resources to tackle them.

Of course, prevention is better than cure and the organisation's culture should be one of minimising problems during the development process. A small design fault is easily fixed at the design stage. If it is missed and is allowed to shape the implementation of the project, it will be much more costly to put right at that later stage. The target of *'get it right first time'* minimises problems, reduces the hassle factor and saves a lot of money. Of course, extra money has to be spent on the testing but this is repaid many times over in the savings on bug fixing.

> Lubarsky's Law of
> Cybernetic Entomology
> *"There is always
> one more bug."*

What can go wrong

To the question *'what can go wrong?'* there is only one answer - *'anything!'*

The problems are in three main categories:

Design flaws These cover any mistakes made prior to commencing the implementation of the project. As such, they cover any shortcomings in the original specification. They could be learning issues (e.g. using the wrong criteria for self-assessment), navigation issues (e.g. poor module linkages), usability or accessibility issues, or simple omissions (e.g. forgetting to tell teams to use a particular font or colour).

Content errors These cover any mistakes made on the actual screens of the project. Typical problems might include incorrect statements, misspellings, grammatical mistakes, poor quality images or video, or deviations from the design document criteria.

Programming errors These cover any mistakes in the logic and operational flow of the project. Typical problems might include links that don't work, incorrect file handling, mistakes in calculations and running totals, and system crashes.

Errors can range from the very serious (e.g. security breaches or shopping cart faults), through serious (e.g. loss of a major function or missing pages) to less serious (e.g. page layout problems or misspelled words). Of course, every error is a problem and needs to be addressed.

Project testing

The testing stages are vital to ensure that the product meets the client's needs and to maintain the reputation of the company. Testing is the process of locating errors or shortcomings in the project, with the aim of eliminating them before the project is distributed.

Some of the tests cover errors in content and screen design - although a tightly worded design document should limit these types of problems.

Much of the testing concerns the detection of flaws in the functions of the project, mainly navigation errors, errors when passing information between modules and other errors (such as search engines, database activities, file handling, etc).

And, of course, there can be problems, even when the project meets the specification. Flaws in the specification may result in an unsatisfactory final product, or the client may wish to alter the specification.

Multimedia companies put in place procedures to minimise the disruption to a project's completion and these centre round two types of check:

Evaluation

Evaluation checks that the project performs according to the users' requirements. Validation tests ensure that the project has been built to the original specification and has not moved away from the client's original intention. These tests are on content, presentation and style, testing whether it addresses the agreed client group, and such issues.

Testing

These verification tests ensure that the project functions perform correctly. This tests that all buttons work correctly, all navigation tools take the user to the intended destination, self-assessed tests provide correct marks, all video and audio clips play correctly, etc. Functionality testing covers internal screen functions and navigation between screens and this is covered later.

Some checks may be subjective, requiring a judgement to be made (e.g. deciding whether the tone/mood of a project or the use of text content is satisfactory). The aim, however should be to have as much of the checking done on a purely objective basis. This means devising testing methods that make each check result in a pass or fail (e.g. *"Do all images have ALT tags"* or *"Does each page have the company logo?"*).

Testing, Usability and Accessibility
This chapter looks at four distinct, but linked, issues:

Evaluation	Checking how close the project relates to the original specification (purpose, content, mood, etc.).
Testing	Checking the technical implementation (e.g. scripting errors, broken links, browser inconsistencies, etc.)
Usability	Checking how easy the project is to use (e.g. ease of navigation, finding information, carrying out data entry activities, etc.).
Accessibility	Checking whether people with sight, hearing, mobility or cognitive difficulties can still access the same information as other users.

Although they are looked at separately, there is some overlap between these issues. For example:
- A project can be free of any programming errors or content errors and still be unusable.
- A project can be accessible and still not be usable.
- A project can be usable for fully empowered users, but be inaccessible to others.
- A project can be usable and accessible but still contain errors (e.g. miscalculating shopping carts).

Evaluation and testing
As previously mentioned, the project should be constantly evaluated – i.e. *prior* to its commencement, *during* its implementation and *after* its completion.
The checks that are carried out before the project's completion are:

Design evaluation
This is designed to reach clarification and agreement with the client on the requirements specification and design document. The intention is to have agreement on a detailed set of specifications that the client will sign off as acceptable as the basis for the project implementation. Increasing the specific details in these specifications reduces the scope for future controversy, a problem known as *'feature creep'*. If the client wishes to change the project at a later date, they can be clearly identified as alterations to the agreed specifications and will have to be paid for by the client.
Before meetings the clients, the organisation's own experts would carry out their own design evaluation, This aims to correct problems and to sharpen the terms of the specification. This may take the form of a *'cognitive walkthrough'*, where the goals and sub-goals (and the actions necessary to meet these goals) of each task are compared against psychological criteria. This aims to identify the required cognitive processes and uncover any learning problems. Another approach is *'heuristic evaluation'*, where tasks are compared to usability criteria such as checking whether the system is predictable, consistent, contains task-oriented dialogue, provides feedback, does not produce memory overload, etc.

Concurrent testing
This approach recognises the need for continuous assessment by those developing the project's modules. The policy of *'Test early, Test often'* aims to identify and rectify errors during the development of each module. Bear in mind that a module may contain programming script (e.g. for file handling, database operations, mathematical calculations, etc.) that has an effect on other modules in the project. Correcting errors at this stage is more efficient and prevents a possible knock-on effect in other modules.

Unit testing
Often carried out by the programmer who created the screen or module (set of interlinked screens). This promotes *'quality at source'* - the programmer finds his/her own faults faster and clears them up quicker than an outside tester. The down side is that the programmer can often overlook the same fault, due to his/her familiarity with the work. It is almost universally true that everyone prefers programming to testing. This means that organisations have to create a climate that ensures that testing is carried out adequately.

Integration testing
When the project is complete, all the screens and elements of the project are linked together. Integration checks that all the links work and that no errors have been introduced by the passing of information between modules. This test is also required when new functionality is introduced to a project. While integration testing ensures that the new works correctly, the introduction of the new code may have affected the operation of other modules in the project. To detect this, developers carry out *'regression testing'*, which examines the effects of new functions on existing functions.

Alpha and beta versions

In the commercial world, software developers produce two main testing stages. The *'alpha'* product is an early implementation of the product and is expected to contain lots of errors. It is intended for internal circulation only, so that these errors can be detected an eliminated. The testers are very thorough and very strict, so that the worst problems are eliminated before it goes out for more general testing. Once the alpha testing has eliminated the worst of the bugs, the *'beta'* version is provided to a selected audience outside the company, to people who have not been involved in its production. It is supplied on the basis that it will contain some errors and these new testers have not been party to any of the previous discussions and come to the product with a fresh eye. Since they do not have any preconceptions, they will detect problems that were overlooked by the company testers. The feedback from the beta stage is crucial in curing these problems, thus producing as reliable and useful a product as possible.

Acceptance testing

When the project is finished its internal debugging stages, it is ready to be presented to the client. The aim is to get the client's agreement for a final sign-off. This allows the project to be installed or distributed. As mentioned before, it is vital to get the client's sign-off for the design stage at an earlier time, so that acceptance tests concentrate on the search for operational errors. If not, the client may start raising issues and requesting amendments to design issues (usually requiring substantial extra work). The larger the number of client representatives at the acceptance testing, the more chance there is of new demands emerging. Acceptance testing requires that the two parties have previously agreed on the tests to be carried out.

Concurrent testing and unit testing is carried out in-house - within the organisation's own staff, while acceptance testing is carried out with the representative(s) of the client.

Testing methods

There is a range of tests that should be carried out and these are listed below, mainly as a set of questions with yes/no (i.e. pass/fail) answers.

Internal screen tests

These tests are designed to check that the screen layout and all internal functions (i.e. those that carry out activities within the screen but do not take the user to another screen) work correctly.
Typical tests are:

- Are all the required screen elements included in the page?
- Does the page contain unnecessary distracting animations or superfluous graphics?
- Does the page title match the page contents?
- Do all page elements use a common consistent layout and presentation (e.g. the title page, the 'Home' button, etc. is always in the same place and always uses the same font, colour, design)?
- Do all the typestyles, font sizes, colours and positions match those specified in the design document?
- Does the background, button design and hyperlink colours match those in the design document?
- Has all body text been spell checked and grammar checked?
- Has the text been proofread? Remember, spellchecking is not sufficient. There may still be errors such as typos (e.g. *'pot'* instead of *'top'*) wrong use of words (e.g. complimentary/complementary, affect/effect, its/it's, etc.), incorrect punctuation that alters the meaning of a sentence, or incorrect numbers (e.g. telephone numbers, numbers in tables, etc.).
- Has the text used in buttons, headings, ALT tags, captions in videos, etc. been checked?
- Are all sounds and images satisfactory (e.g. quality, content, context, compression).
- If a web page, is the page size acceptable, or would it create problems with download times?

Compatibility testing

These tests are designed to check that the project's pages display satisfactorily in a variety of different user environments. The finished project, whether a website or a standalone application, will be viewed by users with different operating systems, different browsers, different plug-ins and computers with different amounts of computing power, memory, disk performance, etc.

- Do the pages display correctly with different operating systems?
- Do the pages display correctly with different browsers, including different versions of the same browser?
- Do the pages display correctly on different platforms (e.g. Windows, Mac, Unix)? In particular, look for the variations in fonts that are supported by different platforms.
- Do the pages still perform satisfactorily if a computer does not have a particular plug-in installed?
- Do the pages still perform satisfactorily if a computer does not have Java or JavaScript supported and enabled?
- Do the pages still display satisfactorily on computers whose monitors only support 256 colours?
- Do the pages still display satisfactorily on monitors with differing screen resolutions?

The issue of accessibility is also relevant here but is covered separately later.

The differences in implementing HTML and display rendering may make it impossible to create a project that is viewed identically on every computer. However, the finished product should still look satisfactory under differing systems. Fortunately, Dreamweaver can test a page or an entire website for compatibility with different browsers.

Functional tests

While screen tests and compatibility tests mainly look at static elements of pages, functional tests check that all interactive elements on a page function correctly.

- Are all user functions present?
- Do all functions work (e.g. shopping cart, forms, chat services, site search facilities, printing of pages or documents)?
- Do all users controls (e.g. mouse, keyboard, touch screen) function correctly?
- Do button rollovers roll over?
- Do image map components change when the pointer hovers over them?
- Does a long text window scroll?
- Are non-functioning controls greyed out or hidden? Do they still function despite being greyed?
- Do the buttons that start video clips, animations, or audio clips fetch and run these components?
- Do the user's media controls (e.g. volume control, video pause button) function as intended?
- Do Flash animations or animated GIFs perform satisfactorily?
- Do alert boxes and pop-up windows appear as required?
- Do forms accept input, validate input and process input as required?

The last item on the above list is actually a huge potential problem area for large dynamic projects. As soon as a project allows users to input data, there is scope for all kinds of data errors. Examples are:

- Leaving a data entry field blank.
- Entering text into a field designed to take a numeric entry.
- Entering numbers into a text field.
- Entering numbers that are errors (e.g. an age of –7 or an order quantity of –3).
- Entering real numbers in an integer-only field (e.g. entering 5.7 in a quantity box).
- Entering numbers that are unreasonable (e.g. allowing a customer to order 10m yachts).
- Entering text that is unreasonable (e.g. entering 500 characters for a surname).
- Entering data with leading or trailing spaces.
- Entering the wrong case in case-sensitive fields (e.g. entering *"Davy Dick"* in a field that only accepts lower case characters).

Of course, the developer should have written code that checks for such mistakes and the purpose of the tests is to see whether the code exists and is effective.

Bear in mind, that some of the incorrect data that is entered may be due to insufficient help to the user in the data entry page, or poorly labelled fields (issues of usability are covered later).

For details on testing scripts, see the chapter on programming.

Navigation tests

These are designed to check that all controls that move the user around the project act in the way laid down in the navigation map.

The likely navigation elements in a project are:

Next screen	Previous screen
Next topic	Previous topic
Return to home screen	Exit
Return to top of this sub-menu	Move to new project area

The most common problems are:

Broken links

This occurs where a page contains a link that points to another page that is not present. It has either forgotten to be written, is stored in the wrong folder, or has been overlooked when packaging the product.

Orphaned pages

These are pages that are included in the product (e.g. sitting on a website or stored on a disk) but do not have any links that point to them. They have either been discarded from the project but not deleted, or other pages has omitted the links to them.

Incorrect links

The link does take the user to the expected page. For example, a button says *'Contact Us'* but the link is to a page on product prices.

Broken links and orphaned pages can be checked manually but tools exist to carry out this task in a quicker and more efficient way, reporting on any link discrepancies found. Site validation tools can detect these errors and some authoring packages also provide a site map that shows the links between pages. A link testing ability is built into Dreamweaver.

The checks for each link are:
- Is the required link present?
- Is the link clearly identifiable and clearly labelled?
- Does the link work?
- Does the link point to the correct page?
- Do all links to the same page use the same description?
- Does every page have a link?
- Are there any pages that do not have a link?

Once the project's navigation system is tested and found to be fully operational, further link checks are only required when changes are made to the project. However, many websites include a list of links to other websites of a similar nature. These are external links and these need to be checked on a regular basis, as the other sites may close, change their address, etc. Again, a link management tool can detect and report on broken external links.

Finally, ensure that graphic images are not used as the main, or only, navigation method. This slows down browsing for users, who have to wait for all the buttons to download before making navigation choices. It also breaks a major accessibility requirement (see later).

It is also useful to obtain software for analysing web server logs, as they can produce information on problems such as missing images, broken links and CGI script errors.

Validation testing

HTML code, particularly when hand-coded, is prone to containing errors, code that is not cross-browser or cross-platform compatible, or code that is not up to the highest specifications. Visual inspection of code, or looking for the results of errors by running the code, is time-consuming and difficult. Fortunately, popular authoring packages such as Dreamweaver, GoLive and FrontPage have built-in code validation facilities. For those hand-coding, freeware and shareware tools are downloadable from the Internet.

HTML validation checks the code against the DTD (Document Type Definition) for a given HTML version. If it passes the check, it should be fully compatible with browsers that support that level of HTML. If the site passes tests against all HTML specifications, it should also be compatible with all robots, spiders and automatic indexing tools.

Developers are aware that while browsers are tolerant of minor deviations from the specification, validation checkers are very strict in their tests. This means that many tests result in a list of infringements and the report might need some interpretation, to separate out serious problems from trivial issues. An example of a trivial error is forgetting to use a </B>, </I> or other such tag to close a piece of text or a statement. While nearly all browsers will handle the error, it will still be be reported as an error by most validators.

Some developers test their work with several validators, to compensate for any differences in emphasis between different validation tools.

Code validation is not confined to HTML. Flash developers can validate Actionscript scripts using the *'Check Syntax'* button in the Actions window, while Director developers can test Lingo statements or JavaScript scripts in Director's *'Message'* window.

Performance testing

Pages can pass all the above tests and still produce a product that runs too slowly for users. A project that is packed with graphics, audio and video clips places great burdens on getting all the data to the user in time to prevent glitches. This used to be a problem with poorly specified computers, but now most computers have enough power to handle these multimedia demands. Only the oldest machines struggle to handle large video clips, for example.

Most performance problems lie with websites, as the speed of most users' connections is not sufficient for smooth-running, high-quality, media-rich content. Although the number of users with ADSL connections is on the increase, most have much slower modem speeds.

- Does the project run satisfactorily on the poorest medium?
- Are any single pages too large?
- Has HTML been optimised (e.g. removing superfluous tags inserted by WYSIWYG editors, removing redundant spaces in the code)?
- Have graphic images been optimised (compressed, reduced colour depth, no more than 72dpi, trimmed, made progressive download)?
- Do all images have WIDTH and HEIGHT attributes (to allow the other page elements to be rendered while the images are downloading)?
- Do all images have ALT and TITLE attributes (to display a description while the images are downloading)?
- Are images being reused (to save time by fetching from cache rather than a fresh download)?
- Are elements being pre-fetched (to smooth out peaks in data flow)?
- Has streaming being used, where appropriate?

Flash has a *'Bandwidth Profiler'* that displays the strains on the communication system for different pages at different transfer speeds.

Usability testing

Usability is the measure of how well users can work with an interface to achieve their ends.
It is defined in ISO9241 as

> *"the effectiveness, efficiency and satisfaction with which specified users achieve specified*
> *goals in particular environments"*

In the real world, usability is about how easy or difficult it is to operate a remote control for a video recorder, a PDA, a mobile phone, etc. without the use of a manual.

In a multimedia/web project, it seeks to measure:

Effectiveness	Did users achieve what they set out to do?
Efficiency	Were the tasks easy/intuitive or difficult?
Satisfaction	Did users find the results rewarding/pleasurable?

The tests covered in the chapter so far would result in a project that worked from a purely functional point of view. All the features would be present, all functions would operate without error, and so on. While this is highly necessary, it does not look at the three issues above. A project can have all the necessary content and fully working navigation and scripts, but still be difficult to use. For example, if it takes ten menu clicks to reach an important feature, it is unlikely that most users will ever get that far.

Additionally, failures in certain tests (e.g. through navigation errors or scripting errors) have a direct impact on usability, as they can make certain tasks difficult or impossible.

It is also important to bear in mind that usability can also be influenced by the knowledge and/or experience of the target audience. A web site designed for chemists would be less usable by the normal browsing public, with poor effectiveness leading to low efficiency and resulting in low user satisfaction. On the other hand, a web site giving basic prescription drug information would be efficient for chemists to use, but would produce low effectiveness and satisfaction ratings.

Tests employ usability guidelines that are based on principles of information design, HCI (human-computer interaction), ergonomics, graphic design, and cognitive psychology. While the visual aspects are important, it is estimated that over 80% of usability improvements come from examining consistency and task focus.

Project usability can be considered at two levels:

Project level	Covering issues such as information architecture, navigation, overall mood, house style, etc.
Page level	Covering issues such as use of headlines, page-level functions (e.g. forms), page elements, etc.

Benefits to users

Research claims that web site users only find the information they need about 60% of the time. Put another way, most sites are so badly designed that many users cannot even find the pages that the developers placed there for them to access! Clearly, usability improvements would greatly reduce wasted time for users, along with lowered frustration and negative feelings towards these sites.

Usability testing should ensure that users are provided with a project that is:

Easy to understand	User is provided with all necessary instructions (e.g. clearly labelled buttons and links, online help, contextual help, and error messages).
	User is kept aware of progress in the system (e.g. messages such as *"You are now in step 3 of 5 in the ordering process"*).
	User can use knowledge of similar systems (e.g. *'Home'* button, *'Print'* button, *'Back'* button).
	User can easily remember interface tasks for re-use on another occasion.
Easy to use	User is presented with clear navigation choices and feedback throughout the project (e.g. breadcrumb trails, site maps, and titled pages).
	User is able to recover from entering errors (e.g. error messages, examples of usage).
	User does not have to wait for screen data or suffer glitches in audio or video performance.
	User can find required pages with minimum effort.
Easy to control	User is able to alter typeface, font size, window size, etc.
	User can skip animations, or replay sections, turn audio off and on, etc.

Making the project more usable benefits the user through a more efficient and pleasurable experience.

End-users can also make considerable savings from using a project that has its usability well tested and well developed.

Consider, for example, a bank, a call centre, or other such high throughput organisation. A project interface with high usability might reduce throughput time by 30 seconds per transaction, compared to one with low usability. When this saving is multiplied by the number of transactions carried out every day by thousands of operators, the financial savings can be very substantial. In fact the savings per year greatly outstrip the initial added cost of building in good usability.

Benefits to clients

Usability, while primarily aimed at the end-user of the project, has significant impact on the client's performance. After all, if users cannot find the items that interest them they cannot buy the goods/ingest the knowledge/support the ideas, etc. that are being promoted by the client.

Research claims that around 50% of potential web site users are lost due to users being unable to find the items that are in a site. Also worrying, 40% of users do not return to a site if they had a bad experience on their first visit. Signs of poor user experience can be identified in traffic and activity logs.

This is not just a website issue. If a multimedia-based CD/DVD is badly organised, users will not spend a lot of time exploring its contents. This makes usability extremely important for clients.

Usability testing should ensure that clients are provided with a project that:

Increases usage	Users exploring deeper into the project pages, viewing more data.
Increases sales	Fewer abandoned items in shopping carts. More repeat visits.
Increases user loyalty	More pleasurable and satisfying visits. Greater brand identification.

These positive responses from increased usability meet the client's expectations more fully.

Benefits to developers

Research claims that most projects overrun their budgets, with the main factors being unforeseen usability problems. Additionally, by far the largest proportion of maintenance costs is caused by unforeseen, or unmet, user requirements. Early and repeated usability testing should ensure that developers create a project that has:

Reduced development time	Problems are spotted earlier, before they cause major rewrites. The finished product comes to the market earlier.
Reduced development cost	Reducing wasted effort means reducing production costs.
Reduced customer support	Usable programs require less training and less technical support.
Increased awareness	Developers learn lessons that can be carried into future projects.

So, building usability into products does not just benefit users; it has direct benefits for both clients and for developers. Usability, therefore, is not simply something to consider if there is spare time – it is an essential feature of project design and implementation.

When to test

Usability testing is the method that determines many of the initial design decisions. Usability testing is also used during the implementation process, to ensure that the design functions according to the project specification. These tests are carried out with end-users or people who are representative of target end users.

Usability testing is also carried out by developers during the implementation phases (e.g. during unit testing), and also prior to final user testing. Expert advice may be sought from specialists in the field, who are often equipped with their own testing laboratories. Alternatively, individual developers in the team may be sufficiently expert to carry out these tests.

Testing should occur:

- During the design phase (e.g. with prototypes).
- During implementation (both end-user and expert tests).
- Prior to product release.
- After product release (e.g. examining traffic and page usage logs, obtaining user feedback).
- After maintenance (e.g. making alterations, adding new features).

In other words, usability testing is an on-going process for any project.

Testing in-house

This section looks at what developers should examine when carrying out their usability checks.

Content tests

The key feature of any project is its content, since that is the primary reason that the target audience uses the project. Some of the checks are entirely objective (e.g. using an acronym without explaining its meaning), while others are more subjective to a degree (e.g. deciding if the correct mood has been set).

Typical content tests are:

- Is the purpose of the project instantly recognisable?
- Is the purpose of each page instantly recognisable?
- Does the mood/tone of the project reflect the intended target audience?
- Does the intellectual/experience level of the project match that of the intended target audience?
- Is all critical information present?
- Is information arranged so that simple concepts lead to more complex concepts (usually through links to pages containing greater detail)?
- Does each paragraph contain a unique concept or unique piece of information?
- Do individual pages contain too much information (see 'Interface Design' chapter on 'chunking')?

- Are sentences and paragraphs kept simple?
- Are headings and sub-headings used to summarise page contents?
- Are page contents easily scanned (e.g. freedom from clutter or distracting media, using bulleted lists, highlighted keywords)?
- If pages are written by different developers, has a common house style been used?
- Do pages use abbreviations and acronyms, without explaining their meaning?
- Do pages use unfamiliar words or concepts, without sufficient explanation?
- Are terms used consistently across different pages (e.g. an item is not called a *'computer'* on one page, a *'system'* on another page, and *'hardware'* on yet another page)?
- Do pages use jargon, slang or *'in jokes'*?
- Are all pages checked for correct spelling, grammar, correct word usage, capitalisation and punctuation?
- Could long textual explanations be supplemented by graphs, tables, diagrams? Note that *replacing* text with images leads to poor accessibility (see later).
- Are pages too dependent on images to pass information?

Navigation tests

General link tests have been described earlier, covering broken links, orphaned pages, etc. The tests below are considered more from a usability point of view, rather a basic functional point of view.

- Does the project have a clear information structure, organised to meet user needs?
- Do pages adequately explain their content and purpose?
- Are key pages buried down too many levels, making important material difficult/slow to find?
- Are users shown clear navigation information (e.g. breadcrumb trails, site maps, titled pages, status messages such as *"You are now in step 3 of 5 in the ordering process"*)?
- Are users shown clear navigation choices (e.g. clear and meaningful labels for buttons and links)?
- Are navigation tools located on a familiar screen position, consistently throughout the project's pages?
- Do links on different pages, pointing to the same resource, use the same link description?
- Does the navigation structure match the information structure (e.g. providing vertical links, horizontal links and lateral links where required)?
- Does each page contain a link to the home page?
- Do all pages allow an easy exit link (e.g. to abandon a shopping cart or a long registration procedure)?
- Are any pages *'self-referential'* (containing links that point to themselves)?
- Do pages use standard link colours?
- Do any pages rely solely on buttons where the text is embedded in the button's graphic image (aside from accessibility violations, there are many Internet users who browse with graphics turned off)?
- Do long page download times slow user navigation (e.g. links that use graphic text images cannot be followed until the image is downloaded for viewing)?
- If a website uses frames, does it also use NOFRAMES with all the same content and navigation facilities?

Screen tests

If the main project content is correct and is organised and accessed correctly, the next tests look at the way the information is presented on individual screens.

- Is similar information organised and displayed in a similar way (e.g. avoiding showing sales figures for England as text, Scottish results as a table, and Welsh results as a bar graph)?
- Do all pages conform to the house style (e.g. structure, layout, fonts, colours for headings, etc.)?
- Does the screen presentation match the mood/feel of the project content?
- Do the pages display without scrolling (especially when there are navigation links or transaction buttons at the bottom of a page)?
- Are relative sizes used for tables and frames?
- Is the same/similar background used for all pages?
- Are backgrounds plain or using subdued patterns?
- Is there sufficient contrast between the background colour(s) and the colour of the foreground elements (e.g. using black text on a light coloured background)?
- Do pages have underlined text and underlined links on the same screen?
- Is some text coloured blue, so that users confuse this normal screen text with blue-underlined link text?
- Are some long passages of text displayed in bold or all capitals?
- Do pages only use shadows on text with large font sizes, if at all?
- Do page elements use web-safe colours?
- Do pages use colour coding as a primary method of conveying information, breaking accessibility requirements?
- Is most text left-aligned, avoiding constantly mixing centred and left-aligned text?
- Do all table have headers and summaries?

Functional tests

If a project has the correct content, the correct navigation and the correct screen presentation, the next checks should be on the functionality that is built in behind the scene.

- Do all functions carry out their required tasks accurately and safely (e.g. calculations, searches, file handling, etc.)?
- Do all functions with user input include error-trapping (e.g. incorrect data entered by users, such as requesting an airline ticket for 30th February)?
- Do functions provide easy recovery in the event of error?
- Do functions carry out their tasks in a reasonable time?
- Does the user require security (e.g. password entry)?
- Does the user require privacy?
- Does the project suffer from glitches in audio or video performance?

The chapter on programming looks at testing lines of script.

User support tests

By this stage, the project has proven stability and many desirable features but has still not considered the relationship between the user and the project interface. These tests look at help and feedback to users.

- Are there 'Help' pages or windows, for explaining difficult or awkward activities?
- Do 'Help' pages provide the full steps for an activity?
- Do 'Help' pages provide examples of usage?
- Do data entry fields explain any restrictions (e.g. "do not enter any spaces between characters in the Post Code")?
- Does the project provide the user with a facility for searching the pages, where required?
- Does the project provide supportive material (e.g. a dictionary of abbreviations and acronyms)?
- Does the project always provide feedback, where necessary (e.g. a link changes colour when hovered over, a 'click' is produced when a button is pressed, messages such as "your order has been successfully processed")?
- Does the project produce error messages when the user mishandles the system (e.g. incorrect data being entered, no disk in a drive, etc.)?
- Do error messages clearly explain what has gone wrong, and show how the difficulty can be solved?
- Do page contents prevent cognitive overload (e.g. too many items on a page, too many links/buttons on a page)?
- Do users have to remember information from one page, in order to fully use another page?
- Does the project include a method for users to contact the author/publisher/distributor/webmaster?
- Where material requires a plug-in, is there an alternative (e.g. a document being in both PDF and HTML format, providing a static image alternative where the user has no Flash or ShockWave plug-in, etc.)?
- Where a project has a necessary data transfer delay, does the project keep the user informed (e.g. displaying a download 'Progress Bar' or displaying a message such as "Downloading the questions. Please wait ...")?
- Do pages provide shortcuts for expert or regular users (e.g. remembering a delivery address, entering the product code from a printed catalogue)?
- Does the project inform the user of the freshness of the information (e.g. a copyright date on a CD/DVD or a 'last updated' message on a website)?

User control tests

These last tests examine how much control the user has over how the project is presented.

- Can users skip viewing long introductory pages?
- Can users control video clips and animations (e.g. play, pause, stop, rewind)?
- Can users control audio content (e.g. play, pause, mute, stop)?
- Can users set their own typefaces and font sizes?
- Can users control the window size?
- Will allowing users some control reduce the site's operations or usability?
- Can users decide whether to allow plug-ins to be downloaded?
- Can users turn off displaying the project's graphics?

Testing with users

Up to now, usability testing has used a checklist approach. This is a very useful way to check usability, as the lists reflect years of shared previous experiences. These checks are easily carried out at any time during development and the checklists can be used both by developers and usability experts.

However, they cannot cover every eventuality. One problem with developers testing their own work is that they approach the task with pre-conceived ideas. They already have a global view of how a particular project is constructed, and know all the content and all the available functions. It can be difficult for them to see the project from an inexperienced user's point of view. As a result, they can misread the overall look and feel of the project, omit facilities that others may find important, and fail to appreciate users' abilities and experience. Testing from checklists, while very important, is only part of the process.

If an organisation does not have the time or the expertise to carry out exhaustive usability testing, the services of experts can be called in. These may be experts in usability, experts in the subject area of the project, or preferably both. They can carry out checklist tests, or can carry out tests with people who are representative of the target audience for the project. If an organisation has sufficient resources and experience, it can carry out checklist testing or user testing in-house.

If usability is the measure of how useful and satisfying the project is to a user, there is only one group of people who can make that judgement with certainty – the users themselves. After all, the project is not created for developers or for clients; it is created for end users (the target audience). The best way to find out user reactions is to present the project to them, let them use it, and note their reactions. The purpose of the testing is to shape the early development of the project, as well as in later testing. The tests examine user goals, user challenges, user limitations, user responses – all from the point of view of the target user group. These tests often reveal that users carry out operations in ways that were not anticipated, or look for features that the developers never expected.

To make meaningful decisions, user tests must produce data that can be analysed. This data will be:

Objective   Data that measures performance (e.g. time to perform tasks, number of errors)

Subjective   Data that measures attitudes and preferences (e.g. ease of learning, ease of use, satisfaction with results)

When considering objective results, developers often adopt the attitude that *'there is no such thing as a user error'*. In other words, if there is a problem with the use of the system, the system is the problem, not the user. Of course, this is not strictly true, since there will always be users who will enter incorrect data regardless of how much help they receive (through ignorance or through maliciousness). The purpose of this attitude, however, is to make designers and developers aware of their responsibility in ensuring the project is as user-friendly and as error-free as possible.

Similarly, when considering subjective results, *'the user is always right'*. In other words, if most users find the project difficult or unrewarding, then the project *is* difficult and unrewarding – no matter what the views of the developers.

The results are analysed to detect problem areas in the design, so that developers can improve the content, the interface, the functionality and the presentation before the project is released.

When to test

Since testing aims to detect and eliminate problems with design and implementation, it follows that usability testing should occur during the development of the project. Early tests shape the direction of the design, while subsequent tests ensure that the additions and alterations during implementation do not affect the project's usability.

It is widely accepted that several small tests (with fewer users) are more effective than one large test at the end of the project's development. After all, the earlier defects are detected, the more money and time is saved.

Testing with only a handful of users at a project's early stage is more effective than testing 100 users at the end of its implementation.

Even after a project is released, continual informal methods can maintain user feedback and help future releases of the project, or other projects. Developers commonly place feedback forms on web sites. They also examine the site's usage logs to detect which pages are never accessed, etc.

Who to test

Full validation testing using test laboratories usually involve 8 to 12 users and this mostly occurs towards the end of the project development.

For periodic checks throughout the development, a smaller group of 3 to 5 users is normally tested. It has been found that using three users for three tests uncovers more top-level problems than using nine users for a single test. As few as two users could uncover around 50% of these problems, while five users could uncover around 80%.

Small groups are surprisingly effective at detecting top-level problems such as opening pages, main menus, information architecture, navigation, etc. Small groups are less effective at detecting problems at a page level, since they will not normally navigate through all the pages in a project. Testing with small groups is easier to organise and much easier to document. Repeating the tests with different people each time detects fresh problems.

The users should have no connection with the development of the project and there should be no detailed prior discussion with the testers about the project content and functionality. That way, they approach the test with a completely open and fresh frame of mind.

If possible, the group of users should reflect the intended client audience. A project for children should be tested by children, while a project for scientists should be tested by scientists. Where a project is targeted at a general audience, the test group could include users with differing experience and expertise. Where the test group does not match the ideal requirements, this should be taken into consideration when analysing the test results.

Where to test

The point of testing is to document user activity and reactions. Therefore, there must be some method of accurately logging both objective and subjective results. Testing can be carried out in both formal and informal locations. These can include a professional laboratory, the developer's own location, the end users' work place, or even at home.

Laboratory tests

A test laboratory has the advantage of providing all necessary facilities such as computers with different operating systems and different browser versions, two-way mirrors, audio and video recording equipment, etc. The other important advantage is the availability of experts that are skilled in handling and observing users.

Users' activities may be observed, without distraction, behind a two-way mirror. In some cases, they may use computers to log user activity (such as which pages were visited, how long users spent on particular pages, how users coped with tasks, used help facilities, etc.).

The disadvantage of this system is the *'goldfish bowl'* environment. Users are out of their natural environment and cannot be guaranteed to act naturally. For example, they often act in a way that they think is expected of them. Also, when questioned, they give the answers they think the observer wants to hear. Users in laboratory environments often overlook things that they would have otherwise spotted. To counteract this, testers often compile sets of tasks that they ask the users to perform, to supplement their own activities. While this interrupts the users' free flow of action, it does ensure that the vital parts of the project are tested.

Since laboratory testing is detailed and expensive, it is usually employed at the end of project implementations, where it provides final validation and valuable lessons for future projects.

Tests at developers

Where projects are on a tighter budget, or where an organisation already has developers with sufficient expertise, testing can be conducted on the premises where the project is being implemented. This is a useful method where the users are not connected with the client initiating the project (e.g. where a project is for general commercial release).

Users are tested in an office environment although they are now openly observed and recorded (no two-way mirrors). A tripod-mounted camcorder records users' actions and also records a later interview with the users.

Tests in the field

These are conducted under more natural conditions, such as in the users' workplace or the users' homes. These tests are cheap to run, and often detect shortcomings not found in other tests. They are, however, more difficult to observe and note-taking often replaces video recording.

What to test

At the early design stage, users would be shown rough sketches (*'mock-ups'*) of the project. They would also be shown examples of other comparable products, either previous products or products from a competitor. This way, users are less inhibited about making comments and valuable information can be gathered at this early development stage. At the next stage, users can be shown prototype projects (see the chapters on project design). Since prototypes do not contain distractions such as images, animations, etc. users can concentrate on the main content and navigation and this provides more useful feedback. As the implementation progresses, the project that is shown to users is progressively more content-rich and more functional.

An implementation evaluation takes place after a runnable system has been produced and is a user-centred activity. Its task is to identify user perceptions, user satisfaction and user problems. It focuses on the project's tasks rather than its features and requires participants that match as closely as possible the customers who will use the final project.

Test preparations

Preparation is the key to getting the maximum benefit from a usability test. Letting users loose on the project and *"going with the flow"* is far better than no testing at all. However, a worked out strategy for testing is much more effective in extracting the greatest amount of meaningful feedback. If testing is a combination of observation and questioning, then the testers should know what they are meant to observe and what questions they are meant to ask. As mentioned earlier, testing encompasses two approaches and preparations for both objective and subjective testing are covered below.

Objective testing

A commonly used technique is the GQM (Goal-Question-Metric) method. This has three parts:

Goal	Decide on the goals of the test.
Question	For each goal, decide what question needs to be answered.
Metrics	For each question, decide how success will be measured.

Examples of goals might be testing how the operations of a shopping cart system perform, or testing whether a search facility is efficient.

Examples of the questions that flow from these goals might be how many users can successfully complete a purchase process (for a shopping cart goal) and how many users can successfully find information from the search facility

Examples of metrics might be deciding that 90% of users must complete a successful transaction and that 70% must complete a search that uses two pieces of search data.

Other tests may measure the time taken to carry out tasks, the error rate for user activities, etc.

The aim of this method is to produce users test results that meet a declared standard of quality and performance. Testing user experience against these metrics produce pass or fail usability results. Tests are objective, since they don't depend on anyone's view of the project. They are task-oriented and the results are measurable.

This method has many advantages:

- It forces testers to clarify exactly what is expected from a usability test.
- It provides clear tasks for users.
- It allows the project to be tested in comparison to other products.
- It ensures that specific pages are tested, that might otherwise not have been visited by the user.
- It allows checks on whether changes or additions have altered previously measured results.
- It provides clear and easily understood results.

This method is particularly useful for testing specific functions and project performance. It need not replace the need for user observation to detect other features of the project. For example, 70% of users might complete a complex search successfully. However, users may have taken 15 minutes to achieve a search, had 8 unsuccessful attempts, referred to the help pages three times, etc. Of course, if the goals had been more tightly specified, these factors would have appeared in the goals, questions and metrics.

Subjective testing

Subjective testing measures user attitudes and preferences (e.g. ease of learning, ease of use, satisfaction with results). It is best to avoid asking loose open-ended questions such as *"Did you like using the project?"* as they do not focus on the detailed information that is required.

Examples of focussed questions are:

"Who do you think the project is aimed at?"
"On a scale of 1 to 10, how useful was the project for you?"
"What features did you like the most? And why?"
"What features did you dislike the most? And why?"
"Which parts did you find it hard to understand? And why?"
"Was it easy to find what you wanted? If not, why?"
"Was there anything you couldn't do with the project"
"Was there anything you thought was missing from the project?"
"Was there anything you would remove from the project? And why?"
"Did you find the content too simple, too complicated, or about right?"
"Of the two projects you looked at which one was best? And why?"

Of course, the questions will vary, depending on what is being tested but the aim is always to encourage the user to provide details of their experiences.

Some answers are specific (e.g. users did not understand the purpose of a particular button). For less specific areas, like ease of use, users should be asked to quantify their feelings on a scale of 1 to 10. This makes users concentrate on their answers and also provides quantitative replies that can be analysed more easily later. An alternative to a point scoring system is to ask users to choose which adjective best describes a feature (e.g. confusing, explicit, useful, boring, etc). The choice of adjectives for each feature depends on its nature, some being content related and some being function related. These questions are usually asked at the end of a testing session, normally in the form of a questionnaire that users complete.

Running a usability test

Prepare users

While not revealing too much about the project being tested, users need some introduction regarding what is expected of them. They need to be assured that their contribution is important and that their views or performance will not be challenged or criticised in any way.

Above all, users have to realise that their most valuable contribution is to keep observers informed about their actions and thoughts as they work through the project. Users must be encouraged to speak out loud as they work, so that their thoughts can be recorded by camcorder or by or observers. They should report their reactions to each new page they access, and declare what they intend to navigate to next, and what they expect to find in the new page. They should be encouraged to voice concerns and questions, while realising that most questions will not be answered during the test.

Observe users

It is important the users carry out testing with the minimum of interruption. They should not be coaxed or guided into a particular action or view. They should not be given hints about using particular functions or about which pages to navigate. In general, they should be left alone. In a laboratory test, they are observed from behind a two-way mirror, to prevent unnecessary interaction. In other test environments, the observer remains in the room with the user(s), although this can sometimes affect user behaviour. In limited situations, users may be given help when it is requested.

The users' spoken thoughts and their physical actions are recorded on videotape and as written notes.

Typical observations are which buttons were clicked, which pages were viewed, which routes were taken to navigate to particular pages, which pieces of data entered is recorded. Other factors that are recorded are the time taken to make choices or to carry out a sequence of operations, the number of errors, the number of re-tries, etc.

Testing may be a mixture of objective testing and subjective testing. The videotape and the written notes record the users' performance on tasks, while the users' verbal contributions provide an insight into areas of confusion or lack of knowledge.

While users should generally be allowed to carry out their appraisal without interruption, there are occasions when testers may ask questions during a test session. For example, if a user spends a long time staring at a particular screen, the tester should ask what the user is thinking, what activity is planned next, or if there is some problem with the page.

Testers have to concentrate on what is happening, to accurately record it. While noting users' favourable reactions to parts of the project, they have to spot any shortcomings that are impacting on the users' easy and efficient use of the project.

Apart from the notes written during the test, it is common for testers to write some main conclusions and recommendations at the end of the test session.

Tools for testing

Various software tools are available for testing website projects. These analyse the lines of code and compare them to the agreed standards for usability or accessibility. Breaches in these standards are then reported for developers to examine and use to correct shortcomings. These are extremely useful tools but they don't replace the need for user testing, since they can't cover issues such as user satisfaction, etc. They cover objective issues only. So, they are not designed to cover spell checking, grammar checking, appropriate use of words and headings, attractive and helpful layout, etc.

In their given area, these tools are very efficient and find problems quickly and without error, compared to manual checking.

Some of these tools are off-line (i.e. the software is purchased and installed on the developer's computer) and others are on-line (i.e. the check facility is offered by a particular website).

The best-known usability checker is LIFT, available on-line (www.usablenet.com) and as a plug-in for Dreamweaver.

Page issues

status	test name	priority	guideline	issues
⚠	Non spacer IMG with valid ALT	1	508(a) WCAG(1.1)	9
⚠	Spacer IMG with valid ALT	1	508(a) WCAG(1.1)	2
⚠	OBJECT with valid CONTENT	1	508(a) WCAG(1.1)	1
?	Scripts are accessible	1	508(l) WCAG(6.3)	14
?	Non spacer IMG needs LONGDESC	1	508(a) WCAG(1.1)	10
?	SCRIPT with valid NOSCRIPT	1	508(a) WCAG(1.1)	3
?	Multimedia with equivalent audio description	1	508(b) WCAG(1.3)	2
?	Multimedia with synchronized alternative	1	508(b) WCAG(1.4)	2
?	Avoid causing the screen to flicker	1	508(j) WCAG(7.1)	2
?	Clarify natural language usage	1	WCAG(4.1)	1
?	Use clear language for site's content	1	WCAG(14.1)	1
?	Colors are visible	1	508(c) WCAG(2.2)	1
?	Non spacer IMG with equivalent ALT	1	508(a) WCAG(1.1)	1
?	Text only equivalent page may be needed	1	508(k) WCAG(6.2)	1

It checks to W3C guidelines and the illustration shows an extract from a LIFT report on part of a website.

Each item on the list is reported in detail, explaining the problem, its effects and suggesting solutions. LIFT also covers some accessibility issues. The illustration shows that LIFT has detected pages that use image files without using ALT text, and an animation that might cause screen flickering. The report prioritises shortcomings, with priority 1 needing immediate attention.

Test results

The most important part of the whole process is using the test findings to validate the project and discover the problems found by users. Some problems will have become very obvious during the testing (e.g. nobody understood what the *'Go Ahead'* button was for). Others will only become clear after compiling of the results of the user questionnaire (e.g. how many found the project interesting or fun).

The steps for rationalising all the test evidence are:

- Examine the videotapes, and record any details that were overlooked by the test observers.
- Play back the audio tapes and document the findings, both from user comments and user replies to questions from the tester.
- Combine all the results from the users' questionnaires.
- Extract the relevant facts from the testers' observation sheets (e.g. number of keystrokes, number of errors, etc.).
- Extract the key findings of the testers' written notes.
- If appropriate, print out the report of running the project through usability software.
- If appropriate, extract the findings of the usability experts.
- If appropriate, extract the findings from any focus group meetings or seminars.

With all this information now available, testers and developers would sit down together and identify the main problems and prioritise them.

This would lead to a list of recommendations for project improvements to be carried out by the development team. These improvements may be targeted at all areas of a project, covering style, content, labelling, navigation, functionality, etc.

Accessibility

Accessibility, at its simplest, is ensuring that a project provides the same information and services to every user – regardless of any physical, sensory, cognitive, environmental or technological barriers.

When the UK Disability Rights Commission (www.drc-gb.org) examined web sites, it reported that

"most websites are inaccessible to many disabled people and fail to satisfy even the most basic standards for accessibility recommended by the World Wide Web Consortium".

Clearly, there is a big gap between the requirements of a sizeable proportion of our citizens and the output from web publishers. Accessibility is lost if some users are unable, due to a particular personal barrier, to comprehend a site's content or use its functions. This prevents sections of the community from carrying out home banking, internet shopping, online searches, browsing, etc.

Note

Many of the points concern issues that could be raised in other chapters (e.g. Design, Animation, JavaScript, etc.). Bringing them all together under a common heading helps to focus developers' attention to accessibility as an important issue, and not just a footnote in various chapters. For new developers, accessibility is an important design issue. For those maintaining existing projects, it's a retrofitting process that involves understanding accessibility problems and how projects can be amended to provide accessibility.

Those affected

Most people think of blindness when naming a condition that inhibits others from fully using the Internet. While sight impairment is the largest group (there are 2 million visually impaired people in the UK), the table below lists the main categories of people affected by poor accessibility.

Complete blindness	Users can't read normal screen text content without a screen reader. They can't read text in buttons or images, and can't understand page content when graphic images or video is used as sole method of imparting information.
Low vision	Users can't see normal screen content without using a screen magnifier. They have problems with screens that have small text, have poor contrast, etc.
Colour blindness	Users' perception suffers from reduced screen contrast, and they can't distinguish when colour coded information is used. While only 0.5% of female viewers suffer from colour blindness, the figure is 8% of all males.
Seizure problems	Users are prone to seizures when the screen displays flashing contents.
Cognitive problems	Users have problems comprehending complex layouts and complex contents.
Deafness	Users can't comprehend page content when audio is used as the sole method of imparting information. There are 9m people in the UK with hearing difficulties.
Mobility problems	Users may not be able to use a keyboard, or have limited hand movement (e.g. difficulties in clicking the mouse on small icons). Some users have only partial use of their hands, caused by arthritis, muscular dystrophy, paralysis, injuries, etc. Users with no hand movement employ devices such as mouth sticks, head pointers or infrared devices.

To this list must be added:
- People with temporary disabilities.
- People with environmental problems (e.g. extreme lighting, noise, slow data transfer).
- People with text-only or low-resolution devices such as PDAs and web telephones.
- People with graphics turned off.
- People with JavaScript turned off.
- People without supportive plug-ins (e.g. Flash, ShockWave, codecs, etc.).
- People with specific operating systems, browser versions, etc.
- People with sound turned off.

As can be seen, a large number of people suffer problems of accessibility. Similar problems affect other countries (e.g. the American Bureau of Census estimates that as many as 54 million persons in the United States have one or more disabilities).

In the past, these areas were mostly ignored. Many regarded it as unnecessary extra work. Others avoided them through ignorance of the facts or through ignorance of how to tackle them. However, the government's 1995 Disability Discrimination Act *requires* information providers to make their services accessible. Many regard it as only a matter of time before a site owner is taken to court to demonstrate that is illegal to design a site such that it is not accessible to a full range of users.

Accessibility for everyone, including people with disabilities, should be regarded as a human right. There is certainly a strong moral or humanitarian case for creating accessible products. However, if the moral case, or the legal case, does not move clients, there is also a strong commercial case for ensuring accessibility. Nine million aurally impaired, two million visually impaired, plus countless others from the categories listed above add up to a sizeable chunk of the potential market for projects one that should not be ignored by those with a message or a product to promote.

Usability and accessibility

Usability and accessibility are closely linked, but separate issues.

If a project has been *thoroughly* tested for full usability, it should also provide full accessibility, since there cannot be full usability without full accessibility. For example, an otherwise extremely usable project is flawed if it does not provide for deaf users (or blind users, or any other group of users).

On the other hand, full accessibility does not imply full usability. A project can allow full access to all groups and still not be fully usable (e.g. poor navigation links, missing pages, sloppy scripting, etc.).

Consequently, there are separate tests for accessibility. Indeed, accessibility for one group does not imply accessibility for another group. For example, providing a soundtrack for blind users will not help deaf users.

An accessible project allows *all* users to understand *all* content, navigate *all* pages, and use *all* functions.

While the aim is also to give every user the *same experience*, this is not always achievable. A text description of a famous piece of music cannot compare with the listening experience. Similarly, text is a poor substitute for an image of the Mona Lisa or a video clip of someone's new baby. From a creative point of view, blind users can never use a set of drawing tools, with fine control over mouse movements, etc.

However, that is not to say that developers should not strive to provide all users with a similar experience.

Assistive Technology

Most users interface with projects using a monitor, a mouse, a keyboard and a set of loudspeakers. However, these items are inadequate for sections of users. Blind users can't see monitor screens, deaf users can't hear loudspeaker output, and physically disabled users may not be able to use the mouse or the keyboard.

Assistive technology is any hardware or software add-on that allows page content to be fully viewed and used by people with disabilities. Since these disabilities differ, a range of different assistive technologies is used.

The most common assistive technologies are:

Screen Readers	These programs convert page text into synthesised speech. They have several disadvantages – they cannot translate graphic images, video clips, and animations. They have difficulty handling complex screen layouts, multiple frames, using tables for layout, etc. They rely heavily on pages providing descriptive alternatives for navigation links. They also speak in a 'robotic' synthesised voice. However, they have the huge advantage of opening up vast new sources of material for blind users who previously had to rely on audiocassettes or Braille sheets. Examples of screen readers are JAWS, Window Eyes, outSPOKEN, and the IBM HomePage Reader.
Braille Display	This hardware is often described as a *'Dynamic Braille Display'* as it produces a line of Braille that can change on an ongoing basis. The device reads the page text and produces raised dot patterns to represent letters and numbers. These are read by blind readers touching the patterns with their fingertips. Most displays use between twelve and twenty cells patterns per line, with six dots being used per pattern. They have exactly the same

disadvantages and advantages as screen readers.

Examples of Braille Displays are those from Freedom Scientific, Dolphin and the Alva Access Group.

Screen Magnifiers   These programs take a portion of a page and magnify it to fill the entire monitor screen. This allows users with low vision to more easily see page contents. To view the entire page, users have to use both vertical and horizontal scrolling. Additionally, enlarging graphic images results in 'pixelated' displays.

Examples of screen magnifiers are ZoomText and MAGic.

Keyboard and Mouse Alternatives   These hardware devices allow user access to those who cannot handle the keyboard or mouse. They include head pointing devices, eye trackers, touch screens, joysticks, switches, etc. They have problems coping with navigation that requires precise pointer positioning (e.g. tiny sphere images used as links, imagemaps, etc.)

Another alternative is voice recognition (e.g. Dragon Naturally Speaking and IBM ViaVoice), where voice commands are accepted within projects.

Add-on software is sometimes referred to as 'user agents'. These provide an alternative means for users to access information – if the developers have allowed their use. In other words, developers do not need to write code that sends screen output to a loudspeaker, etc.: they only have to ensure that such devices can understand the pages. For example, ensuring that all information is available in text format, so that screen readers can do their work.

These are design issues, covering layout, screen elements, navigation and so on.

Accessibility testing checks to what extent a project's content, interface, navigation and functions accommodate users with disabilities.

Testing issues

The UK has the 1995 Disability Discrimination Act. The United States has 'Section 508', which was an amendment to the Workforce Rehabilitation Act. Amongst others, it requires that programs developed or purchased by the Federal Government be accessible to people with disabilities. Their legislation is more specific and acts as very useful guidelines for all project developers. A full set of 508 standards was developed by their Access Board and a very useful accessibility checklist was developed by a non-profit body known as WebAIM (Web Accessibility In Mind). This checklist can be found at www.webaim.org/standards/508/checklist

The rest of this chapter examines all the issues that affect accessibility. It does not take a checklist approach, as the issues are probably less publicised than others. Magazines and books tend to concentrate on the 'arty' and 'gimmicky' aspects of project creation. Accessibility issues need to be *understood* before they can be tested and the following pages attempt to fill in some of the gaps left by other publications.

Information alternatives

Providing alternative, and equivalent, content is the single biggest step towards providing accessibility. It provides additional ways of communicating information.

The information needs of each group depends on their situation and is summarised below:

Blind users   Since screen readers can only handle text, so every visual non-text element (e.g. images, animations, video) should have a text-based equivalent. Users will not see the original elements but need to be informed of their existence and their content.

Deaf users   Since they can't hear any audio content, all sound elements (e.g. prompts, error beeps, voiceovers) should have a text-based equivalent. Users will not hear the sounds but need to be informed of their existence and their content.

Users with mobility problems   Those who can't use a mouse should be offered keyboard control. Those who can't use a keyboard should be able to use the project with other input devices.

Users with cognitive problems   Those who experience problems comprehending complex layouts and complex contents should have the screen content simplified and easily understood.

Note: Other users (those with low vision, colour blindness, or potential seizure problems) are not usually helped by providing alternative content. They are helped by the thoughtful use of screen content (see later).

Text equivalents

In most cases, equivalent content means providing a text alternative for every non-text element on a page. This includes graphic images, sound clips, animations, video clips, charts, diagrams, graphs, and tables. Graphic images include text that is contained within an image, such as a logo or a navigation button, symbols, image maps, animated GIFs, bullets, photographic images and decorative graphics.

Since none of the above can be detected by a blind user, the text must adequately describe the information that they contain. If the content is light, no more than about eight words, it may be provided using the HTML ALT tag (see later). Graphical browsers, the most common type in use, display ALT text without any word-wrapping and this can result in messy displays for sighted users who have graphics turned off.

If the content is wordy, it can be included in the body of the page, or use the HTML longdesc tag. This tag is not yet widely supported, although it can be interpreted by the IBM HomePage Reader.

An example of using longdesc is:

```
<IMG src="prestwick.gif" alt="The first Golf Open Championship was held in Prestwick" longdesc="golfhistory.htm">
```

The long description is stored in a separate HTML file and a user agent that supports the tag will load the supportive file and display its text as a caption on the image.

If an element requires a large amount of explanation (e.g. a video clip), it can be placed on a separate page with a link to it placed on the original page (e.g. the page containing the video clip). These are usually called *'d-links'* or description links, since they place a link with the single letter *'D'* next to the image. Clicking the *'D'* loads the content from the supportive page with the extra content.

In all other cases, the text description of a link must adequately describe the nature of the destination page. As with on-screen text, ALT text has to be proof-read.

Note

Providing text equivalents produces three potential output formats for each page element – on-screen text, synthesised speech and Braille output. The user can choose the format, employing a user agent to access the last two formats.

ALT tags for images

HTML allows an image on a page to have text associated with it, using the ALT tag. Normally, this text is displayed when a user hovers the mouse over an image, or when the user has graphics turned off. Screen readers take this text and convert it into synthesised speech or Braille output, allowing blind users to extract meaning from a graphic image. This is very useful in general, and vital when graphic buttons are used as navigation links.

Decide what content is essential and what is decorative. Don't add text descriptions for decorative images and give meaningful descriptions to essential images.

Essential images

Essential images should be given tag content that has real meaning.

This first example adds very little information:

```
<IMG SRC="hotel.gif" ALT="picture of hotel">
```

while this second example provides much more meaning for blind users, while not needlessly distracting sighted users:

```
<IMG SRC="hotel.gif" ALT="The Outrigger Hotel sits right on Bondi Beach">
```

If an image contains complex information, such as a chart, diagram or graph, it text should not be placed in an ALT tag. Instead, it should be stored in a longdesc tag, or stored in a separate file that is called up by a D-link (see earlier).

Decorative images

Many images are purely decorative; they add no extra information to a page. These include clip art, list bullets, fancy divider lines, and spacer GIFs. If these elements are not given an ALT tag, screen readers will say the word *'IMAGE'*. To prevent this unwanted and confusing report, the ALT value can be set as empty (given a null value) i.e. ALT="". Screen readers ignore this empty tag and produce no audio output.

Bullet point images

Since small images are often used for bullet points in lists, it is common to inform the user that the following text is part of a list, using alt= "Item:" In no case, should bullets be described as alt="golden ball bullet image" or similar. Avoid long text descriptions for bullets, as a page may contain many bullet points and the description will be read out aloud over and over.

Text within images

Embedding text in an image, sometimes called *'Text-GIFs'*, is a common way to produce fancy text effects that are independent of the fonts installed on a user's browser. From an accessibility point of view, they must be accompanied by text descriptions so that blind users can understand their content.

If the organisation's name is already displayed as text, the logo should be regarded as a decorative image (see below). If the name only appears in the logo image, it would be acceptable to repeat the name as ALT text.

Navigation images

Where Text GIFs are used as navigation links, it is absolutely essential that they have text descriptions attached to them (through the ALT tag). If an image link contains the word *'Prices'* users immediately know its purpose. Similarly, the text description need only say *'Prices'*, with a description such as *'Link to the Prices Page'* being unnecessary.

Some navigation systems use text to explain each link and the text is preceded by a clickable icon such as an arrow or a sphere. If the text is itself a clickable link, the icon can be given a null description. If the icon is the only clickable part (i.e. the text is not a clickable link), the icon image could be given a clear navigation description. Better still, however, would be to re-design the link so that the text was clickable and the icon was ignored. This is a much better method for those with mobility problems, as the text link presents a much bigger target.

Text tags for multimedia

Audio

An audio clip should be accompanied by a *'transcript'*. A transcript contains the word-for-word content of the clip, along with a description of any non-verbal content (e.g. explosions, applause, telephone ringing, etc.).

An additional side benefit of providing a transcript is that the content of the audio clip now becomes available for searching and indexing.

Video

Producing a text equivalent for a video clip is even more detailed, as it has to contain all the audio content, as described above, along with descriptions of the visual content. The visual content does not only include scenic information (e.g. descriptions of the location and the main characters). Viewers receive a lot of information from body language, facial expressions, etc. and these must also be included in the descriptions.

In other cases where the audio content is time dependent (e.g. a voiceover accompanying an animation), the text description should be displayed in stages. This ensures that the text explanation is synchronised with the screen activity. Captioning of video for deaf users is covered later.

In addition, every Java applet, Flash file, plug-in, etc. should be provided with an ALT description.

ALT tags and search engines

In addition to benefiting users with disabilities, text equivalents also helps all users find pages more quickly, since search robots can use the text when indexing the pages. Search engines, such as Google, can index an accessible site to a greater degree than a non-accessible site. This is because the accessible site has much more textual information to index. Text is not hidden away in graphic images and pages have more ALT text describing buttons, images, etc.

Text-only pages

The creation of a text-only version of a project is not desirable. Its existence can make its users feel excluded from the *'main'* scene. From a developer's point of view, it is extra work to create and extra work to maintain along with changes in the primary version. Despite this, some see text-only versions as way out of planning a fully-accessible product, or an escape from retrofitting an existing project with full accessibility.

In the great majority of cases, projects should not include a text-only version. However, in cases where it is impossible to include full accessibility, a text-only version should be created (as a last resort).

The requirements for text-only pages are that they:

- Are fully accessible (i.e. alternatives are provided for components, such as scripts or plug-ins, that are not directly accessible).
- Provide the equivalent information and/or functionality.
- Have their content updated whenever the primary content changes.
- Are immediately and obviously accessible from the project's main page.

Once a text-only web page is created, the HTML code on the main page adds the following line into the <head> section of the primary page.

```
<link title="text-version" rel="accessible" href="text_page.html" media="aural, Braille,tty">
```

Both pages contain the same information, but when a user accesses the main page with a user agent installed (e.g. screen reader, Braille device), the text-only version is automatically loaded and processed by the user agent.

Note

Creating text-only pages only helps those with visual disabilities. It does not provide any added accessibility to other groups of users, such as those with hearing, cognitive or mobility problems.

The BBC provide a tool that automatically removes graphical content (images, animations, video, formatting) and creates text-only equivalent of pages. It is called *'Betsie'* (BBC Education Text to Speech Internet Enhancer) and is available for download as a PHP script from www.bbc.co.uk/education/betsie/index.html.

Non-text equivalents

Text equivalents are required for blind users who need screen readers to translate text to synthesised speech. Of course, other users have other specialised needs.

Video

Deaf users, for example, can watch the visual content of a movie clip but don't receive the sound content. A partial solution lies in providing subtitles (a word-for-word text representation of the spoken content). An improvement is to provide a full caption, which adds descriptions of non-verbal content such as sound effects. The captions must be synchronised with the movie action. Subtitles and captions are both generally superimposed along the bottom of the video clip.

Another possible technique is to add a secondary video clip to a page to accompany the main video clip. This can contain someone using sign language to report on the audio content.

Audio

There is no need to produce an audio equivalent for every screen element. While this may be useful for blind users, it can be a very time-consuming task and produces no real improvement over using screen readers. Audio descriptions are more natural than synthesised speech but produce much larger files and their contents are not available to search engines.

Deaf users can extract much information from just listening to a video clip. However, they can't appreciate details like location, descriptions of actors, etc. This can be achieved by using 'video descriptions'. This entails editing the audio track to include such information as "three soldiers climb out of the upturned car". Useful comments are inserted at appropriate points in the audio track of the video. This technique is useful for creating *talking books* from video clips but would interrupt the synchronisation of audio and video tracks for mainstream users, unless they are carefully inserted during natural pauses in the audio track.

Text

Users with cognitive difficulties have problems dealing with large amounts of text and get more information from non-text equivalents such as pictures, icons, audio, and video.

PDFs

Adobe Acrobat, from version 5.0 onwards, allows screen readers to access PDF file contents, where the content is text-based. PDF files that are simply scanned images of text save the text as graphics and cannot be used by screen readers, unless the contents are processed by OCR (optical character recognition).

Improved screen readability

Everyone benefits from screens that are easily read and improving readability plays a significant role in increasing accessibility, particularly for users with colour blindness or low vision.

Colour contrast

One of the first things that users notice about a page is its overall layout and use of colour. There are a few simple rules that ensure the maximum readability.

- Use a background that is either a plain single colour, or has a faint pattern. Do not use backgrounds that have pronounced patterns or images.
- Ensure that the colours used for foreground page elements have sufficient contrast with the background colour. Dark text on a dark background, or light text on a light background, makes for reading difficulties for all users and causes severe problems for low vision users. Note that it is the contrast that is important, not the selection of colours. In other words, very light blue text on a very dark blue background might be acceptable.
- Ensure that colour combinations do not cause problems for users with colour blindness (see later).
- Ensure that the colour scheme can be altered by the user (e.g. via browser settings). Some low vision users prefer a black-on-white scheme while others prefer a yellow-on-black scheme. Be aware, for example, that forcing a word to be highlighted in blue (e.g. using <font colour>) will result in it being invisible if the user decides to use a blue background.

The aim is to ensure that all the screen elements are discernible by all users. If in doubt print out a page on a monochrome printer and see whether everything appears distinct. Alternatively, screen capture a page, paste it into a drawing package such as Paint Shop Pro or PhotoShop, convert it to greyscale and look at the results.

Colour coding

Projects often use colour coding to highlight information. For example, a website may use a blue background for all product pages, a yellow background for all shopping basket pages, and so on. Within a single page, it may use blue buttons for a particular set of links, and red buttons for another set of links. Another common use is to colour required fields in a form red. While these may help mainstream users, they cause problems for users who are blind, colour-blind or have low vision.

That is not to say that colour coding can't be used to aid mainstream users. It means that colour coding should not be used as the *only* way to highlight information. The same information can be displayed using page titles, sub-headings, using bold text, icons with text labels, etc. That way, the project can be understood and navigated by both sighted users and users with sight impairments.

Colour blindness

This term covers users who have difficulty distinguishing between certain colour combinations, through to users who see certain colours, usually greens and reds, as shades of grey. Red-green combinations are most troublesome, followed by yellow-blue combinations and orange-yellow combinations.

Fonts

Users with low vision can make web pages more readable by changing the default size of the displayed font, or changing the type used for displaying text.

Developers should not force the look of a particular screen on users, by preventing the typeface and font size from being altered by the user.

For this reason, absolute font tags are frowned upon while relative tags, such as <BIG> and <SMALL>, can help users. Similarly, headers, such as H1 or H2, should not be used for highlighting text. They should be used to create sections and subsections on the page and thereby inform users about the document's structure.

Formatting

Most users open a page and can immediately understand its main purpose and main content. This is because they can see the entire page contents on screen. Users with screen readers only know of a page's content piece by piece, as each piece of text is spoken aloud to them.

There are a number of steps that can improve accessibility:

- Write clearly and concisely.
- Reduce the number of words on the page to the minimum necessary.
- Divide large blocks of text into smaller blocks (e.g. using ordered lists).
- Place the most important information in headings, subheadings, and at the beginning of paragraphs and lists. Do not use header tags to emphasise words.
- Use header tags to produce page structure, as tags such as <H1> and <H2> are processed by screen readers. This allows the user to instruct the screen reader to jump to the next heading, if the content in the current heading is not of interest.
- Use semantic tags (e.g. <STRONG> and <EM>) instead of format tags (e.g. <B> and <I>). Screen readers will emphasise words with semantic tags when reading text out loud.
- Use style sheets to control presentation.

Other layout issues

Most projects use graphics to make the pages look pretty, when graphics should really be added to make the pages more *understandable*. While some eye candy is acceptable, images are really intended to pass information. Developers should consider the contribution of each graphic element before including it in a page.

A useful check of a web page is to view with the browser set not to display graphics. If the page looks wrong, it will be even worse for screen readers.

Flashing

Many people suffer from photosensitive epilepsy. This means that they can suffer a seizure if exposed to flashing lights or rapid changes in light intensity, as with strobe lighting. Seizure can triggered by lights that flash at frequencies from 2Hz (2 flashes per second) up to 55Hz (55 flashes per second), with peak sensitivity occurring around 20Hz. Others who are not prone to seizures can still experience nausea when exposed to flashing lights within that frequency range. Most users, although not physically affected, still find the effects annoying.

Developers must ensure that the screen content does not include any element that produces a flash or flicker effect within the problem range. This includes animated GIFs (banner ads often use flashing effects to attract attention), animations, video content, or any content influenced by applets or plug-ins. It also includes use of the HTML BLINK or MARQUEE commands. Animated text and buttons are also problem areas for assistive technology

Improved navigation options

The essential features of good navigation are that users can quickly identify navigation choices, can understand what each link leads to, and can easily select a navigation option. These same factors also hold true for accessible sites. While all users benefit from good navigation procedures, they are even more important for users with mobility, cognition and sight barriers.

Screen readers inform the users of a link, by changing pitch/voice, or by saying the word *'link'* before reading out the link text. Developers should design pages so that navigation options are easily accessible.

This means:

- Providing a site overview, with a text-based site map or table of contents (this would benefit all users).
- Providing additional plain text links in addition to any graphic buttons (usually situated along the bottom of the page).
- Providing clear descriptions of the target page for each link. The descriptions should be understandable without the aid of other text or graphics, since screen readers may create a list of all links on a page.
- Providing link descriptions that are no longer than 10 words.
- Providing spacers between text links. If links are positioned next to each other, the screen reader will interpret them as a single link and read out their texts as a single text. A blank space is not suitable as a spacer. Instead, use the bar character '|' or square brackets, surrounded by spaces.

Screen layout

Mainstream users understand a web page's organisation at a single glance, recognising which parts are the main content, which parts are navigation options, which parts are advertising, etc. However, users with screen readers don't have that visual overview and can have great difficulty in appreciating a page's structure. They rely on the screen reader to get the information to them.

Screen readers process page content using *'linearisation'*. This means that the reader works its way through the contents in a linear fashion, processing each line at a time. Unfortunately, many web sites use tables to create layouts and this upsets the entire reading process.

Consider the typical layout example below:

Title/logo text	
Navigation link 1 Navigation link 2 Navigation link 3 Navigation link 4 Navigation Link 5	Main content text

Like many web sites, it places its navigation links in a panel on the left-hand side of the screen.

When a screen reader meets a table, it processes the first cell of the first row, followed by any further cells in the first row, before doing the same with the second row, then the third row, and so on.

In the example, linearisation produces the following audio output:

Title/logo text
Navigation link 1
Navigation link 2
Navigation link 3
Navigation link 4
Navigation link 5
Main content text

The user has to listen to all other content before being presented with the main page content. The user is told of further navigation choices before even hearing what the page is about.

Simply placing the menu bar on the right side allows users to hear the content before making navigation choices.

Title/logo text	
Main content text	Navigation link 1 Navigation link 2 Navigation link 3 Navigation link 4 Navigation Link 5

Since many users are unaccustomed to having a right-side menu bar, the layout could repeat the link options as text links along the bottom of the page.

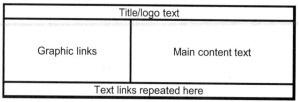

If the graphic buttons are given null ALT values, they will be ignored by screen readers, which will only read the text links. This allows mainstream users to use their normal mouse-controlled buttons, while other users only hear the text links.

Skipping navigation links

Another method, one used by sites such as CNN and IBM, is to place a link at the beginning of the page. This will be the first item to be read out loud by a screen reader. This link offers to take users straight to the page's main content, skipping over logos and navigation buttons. This allows right-side menu bars to remain, satisfying mainstream users. The main content needs to be identified with an anchor such as <A name=Main>.

The link text may be visible on screen, or it may use tiny text or text that is the same colour as the background (this way it is read by screen readers but does not disturb mainstream users). It is also possible to use a 1-pixel GIF image with an ALT description. Any of these links would use the <A href="#Main"> command to jump to the content section.

Order of links

Users with mobility problems may not be able to accurately position the mouse cursor over a navigation button or link. Users with vision impairments can't see where the mouse cursor is positioned. It is therefore important that users can move between important screen elements without using the mouse. The solution lies in using the keyboard's *'Tab'* key to move between selected screen elements such as links and the fields of forms. The order in which the elements are visited is set using the TABINDEX attribute, as in this example:

```
<a href="orders.html" tabindex="3">
```

In this example, the link to the orders page is the third element to be visited on the page.

Some links are embedded within a sentence and mainstream users can immediately identify the link in the sentence. So that screen readers can report on link contents as early as possible, it is a good idea to *'front load'* the link in the sentence.

For example:

The *Bermuda Triangle has been a much-discussed topic for many years*
is better than

A much-discussed topic for many years has been the Bermuda Triangle

Image maps

Image maps can be a quick and convenient way to navigate. For example, a geographical map of the USA can show each of the individual states and any one of these complex shapes can be clicked on to jump to a page about that state. This can be useful for mainstream users, but image maps are not accessible for users with low vision or poor hand co-ordination. In addition, not all screen readers can handle image maps.

Firstly, each active region of the image map should have an ALT description attached (i.e. to each AREA tag). Some screen readers can then create a list of links from the ALT descriptions.

An additional step is to provide additional text links, allowing users to Tab to these links. These text links may be situated close to the map, as an A-Z index, or may be located along the bottom of the page. An A-Z index is also useful for mainstream users (why hunt the map trying to find South Carolina when it is easier just to click on its name in the index?). Developers should avoid using server-side image maps, as they work by sending mouse co-ordinates from the user to the server. The requirement to use a mouse makes this system inaccessible.

Data presentation

Tables for layout

Although designed for displaying sets of data, tables are most often used on web sites for setting up screen layouts. With the table border set to zero, the table structure is not visible on the screen. This has encouraged developers to create elaborate and complex table structures to achieve accurate screen positioning of text and objects. This has caused real problems for screen readers (see the earlier explanation of *'linearisation'*).

This does not necessarily mean that tables should not be used for layout purposes (although some argue that tables should only be used for their original purpose). Developers, however, must recognise the accessibility problems that could occur and design screen layout tables accordingly.

- Use the simplest possible table layout.
- Do not introduce any unnecessary rows and columns.
- Avoid spanned rows and columns, and tables nested inside tables
- Do not use any structural markup (e.g. <TH>) to achieve screen formatting. Its use in layout tables may result in screen reader treating the content as a data table.
- Include structural elements that produce headers, lists, etc., so that the page makes sense after linearisation.
- Check whether the contents of the table make sense when linearised; if not, provide an equivalent alternative.
- Use proportional sizing, rather than absolute sizing.

When all user agents support style sheet positioning, using tables for layout purposes should be replaced by the use of style sheets.

Tables for data

Data tables are used to display sets of data in grid layouts. The columns and rows of data are laid out and have their contents described with header and/or row titles.

As mentioned earlier, when a screen reader meets a table, it processes the first cell of the first row, followed by any further cells in the first row, before doing the same with the second row, then the third row, and so on.

Manufacturer	Iiyama	Sony	Philips
Product	20" TFT	42" Plasma	19" CRT
Price	490.95	4543.22	135.85

In the above example, linearisation produces the following audio output:

"Table with four columns and three rows. Manufacturer. Iiyama. Sony. Philips. Product. 20" TFT. 42" Plasma. 19" CRT. Price. 490.95. 4542.22. 135.85"

Clearly, even with this small table, the contents are very difficult to understand. With a little extra thought, the same information can be presented in this table layout:

Manufacturer	Product	Price
Iiyama	20" TFT	490.95
Sony	42" Plasma	4543.22
Philips	19" CRT	135.85

The audio output is now much more understandable:

"Table with three columns and four rows. Manufacturer. Product. Price. Iiyama. 20" TFT. 490.95. Sony. 42" Plasma 4542.22. Philips. 19" CRT. 135.85"

Screen readers can be put into a *'table reading mode'* where the user can navigate through data cells in the grid and have the contents of individual cells read out. To achieve this, the table should be properly coded in HTML with row and column headers (<TD> and <TH>). This is required to indicate which headings are associated with which data cells.

Adding a caption at the top of a table provides an overview of its contents and hence aids accessibility. Users can choose to examine the table contents or ignore them.

The caption tag is placed in the HTML code immediately after the table tag:

```
<table .........>
<caption> Prices for screen displays</caption>
```

Additionally, a summary may be added to a table. Unlike the caption, it does not display on the screen but is used by screen readers to provide a description of the table contents.

```
<TABLE summary="Prices for screen displays">
```

The rules for data table accessibility are:

- Use the simplest possible table layout.
- Do not introduce any unnecessary rows and columns.
- Avoid spanned rows and columns, and tables nested inside tables (e.g. the widely used *'JAWS'* screen reader cannot handle spanned rows very well).
- Use proportional sizing, rather than absolute sizing.

Forms

Just like the tables above, linearisation of a form can produce incomprehensible results on a screen reader if the form is not laid out in an accessible manner.

The form below is easily understood by mainstream users but it is not reasonable to expect users with screen readers to remember the order for all eight items.

Forename	Surname	DOB	Tel No	House No	Street Name	Town	Post Code

In the example below, the set of prompts and input fields have been changed from a vertical to a horizontal format. This makes the form much more understandable by screen readers while not sacrificing any clarity for mainstream users.

```
Forename    _____
Surname     _____
DOB         _____
Tel No      _____
House No    _____
Street Name _____
Town        _____
Post Code   _____
```

The aim is to clearly associate each prompt with its input text field. The above example achieved this by situating the prompt label next to the field (usually on the left of the field). It is also possible to display the prompt *inside* the text entry field, as in this example:

```
Type your Post Code here
```

This can be of benefit to all users and the HTML code for it is:

```
<INPUT type="text" ... value="Type your Post Code here">
```

Yet another approach is to place a '*' character inside the text field. This is known as a 'placeholder', as users can use their browsers search facility to take them directly to form fields without tabbing.

If the form contains radio buttons or check boxes, their small size causes problems for users with mobility problems. To increase the area that can be clicked on, the radio button or check box can have the text prompt attached to it programmatically. This means that when users click on the text prompt (a larger area) it has the same effect as clicking on the radio button or check box.

An example is:

```
<form>
<input type="radio" name="sex" id="male">
<label for="male">Male</label>

<input type="radio" name="sex" id="female">
```

There are rare occasions when the form layout is too complex to be met by any of the above techniques. In these cases, the site should provide an alternative form that is fully text based and accessible, including the provision of a helpline phone number or email address where users can get assistance.

Frames

Frames allow the screen to be split into separate areas, each being fed with information from different HTML files. This is commonly used to display company logos, etc. in one frame, navigation links in another frame, and the main content in yet another frame. Mainstream users can see all the three contents, known as a *'frameset'*, as being a single cohesive screen of information.

Screen readers interpret the situation differently. The *'Jaws'* reader informs the user that the page contains a frameset and then reads out the contents of each frame. It also provides a keyboard shortcut to jump between frames. The IBM *'Home Page Reader'* reports on the frames that are present and allows the user to choose which frame to read (handy for skipping over logos, banner advertising and other unwanted frame content).

Although frames can be a nuisance for screen readers, they do not necessarily produce accessibility problems. As long as each frame is given meaningful <TITLE> tag information, users can quickly identify frame purpose and contents. Another way is to use the title attribute in the frames defined in the frameset of the main page that defines the overall frame structure, as in the example below:

```
<FRAMESET>
        <FRAME src="banner.htm"  name="banner" title="banner">
        <FRAME src="navbar.htm"  name="navigation" title="navigation">
        <FRAME src="content.htm" name="content" title="content">
</FRAMESET>
```

The Lynx text browser uses the name attribute to describe a frame, while the IBM Home Page Reader uses the information in the <TITLE> tags of the individual frame pages of the frameset.

The descriptions used in the example give clear navigational information to users, while descriptions that relate to the page layout (e.g. 'top bar', left bar', etc.) provide poor accessibility.

For those users whose software cannot read frames, developers should consider providing a <NOFRAMES> section at the end of each frameset. This section should contain meaningful content and should have links that allow the user to access the individual HTML files of the frameset, outside of the frames environment.

Finally, developers should not program frame targets that create a new window on the screen.

Mobility issues

Most applications are designed for mouse control and this is a very useful method for mainstream users. However, users with limited or no hand movement are unable to use the mouse and could be locked out of using a project. Users with no hand movement need special devices to move a pointer around the screen. Users with limited hand movement can move a mouse but cannot maintain accurate pointer positioning.

Methods for providing accessibility to users with mobility problems are based on:

- Converting delicate, precise operations into more manageable activities.
- Converting small navigation targets into larger targets.
- Supplementing mouse activities, allowing a keyboard or other input device to carry out the same operations.

Simplifying navigation

Those with limited hand movement may prefer to use a mouse but find that buttons, icons, image map areas, etc. are simply too small to allow them adequate mouse control.

Making all active screen links larger involves:

- Making small icons larger – or, better still, providing text alternatives.
- Providing text alternatives for image maps.
- Ensuring that no applets require a mouse to carry out their activities.

Providing text alternatives benefits both mouse users (who are offered larger link targets) and keyboard users (who can Tab between links).

Mouse alternatives

Users with no hand movement can use aids such as blow-suck tubes, head wands and mouth sticks. These devices carry out the functions of a standard keyboard, so projects must ensure that every operation (with only a few exceptions such as drawing and painting) that can be achieved with a mouse can also be achieved through keyboard activities. Projects that accept keyboard input can almost always also accept devices that emulate keyboards.

Fortunately, users with limited hand movement can mostly use a keyboard with much less effort and difficulty than with a mouse.

Access Keys

These are sometimes also called *'accelerator keys'*, as mainstream users can use them as shortcuts. Elements, such as text entry fields, can be directly made the focus of attention, by pressing some *'Alt plus other key'* combination.

| City | | Alt-C |
| Post Code | | Alt-P |

This example above was created using the HTML code below:

```
<label for="city" accesskey="c"></label>
<label for="postcode" accesskey="P"></label>
City <input type="text" name="city" id="city">Alt-C<br>
Post Code <input type="text" name="PC" id="postcode">Alt-P
```

Each field has been provided with a label and also instructions on which key combination to use. This technique can also be used to jump to links. Typing the appropriate key combination highlights the selected link, and pressing the Enter key activates the link.

Cognitive issues

Users with cognitive impairments have adequate vision, hearing and manual dexterity. Unlike other user groups already mentioned, cognitive impairments cover a wide range of limitations. These can range from attention difficulties, retention difficulties, reading disorders and learning disorders – through to strokes, Downs Syndrome or Alzheimer's Disease. Some, like dyslexia, are fairly common while other, such as brain injury result in very specific problems.

Since the problem areas are wide, accessibility concentrates on reducing the general cognitive load involved in using the overall project and its individual pages. This covers issues such as reducing the amount of information to be retained, simplifying content, simplifying tasks, and simplifying navigation.

Methods for providing accessibility to users with cognitive problems are based on:

- Using clear and simple language.
- Summarising longer passages of text.
- Grouping similar elements on the page.
- Using a consistent layout across pages.
- Using a simple navigation system.
- Using recognisable graphics and icons to illustrate the text.

Most of these issues are really usability issues, but usability shortcomings impact most on those with cognitive difficulties.

Developers should understand that providing supportive graphics need not detract from the experience of users with low or no vision. The additional graphics help users with cognitive difficulties understand page content more easily. The images' tags can be null values, so that they are not processed by screen readers. As long as visually impaired users are provided with adequate textual material, they can ignore the supportive graphics. Bear in mind that if the images are so useful that they ought to be shared by all, then they are not really supportive material but essential material.

Scripting issues

JavaScript is the most common scripting language used on client-side programming. There are two common uses for client-side scripting:

- To create visual effects (e.g. flashing colours), or an aid to navigability (e.g. rollovers to indicate which button is currently the focus of attention or areas of a table that change background colour as the mouse moves over them).
- To alter the screen information (e.g. error-detection, shopping cart calculations).

In the first case, the project would work equally well whether the scripting was turned on or off. The added functionality does not really add anything to the page's information content. Therefore, their inclusion, or otherwise, does not affect the accessibility of the page. These scripts do not significantly influence accessibility, as long as screen readers are able to ignore the scripts.

In the second case, the scripts directly alter screen information. If this altered information cannot be detected and processed by screen readers, then users with vision difficulties will not receive the information. As a result, accessibility is reduced. In these situations, equivalent information must be made available, or an alternative page that offers accessibility must be provided.

Some script commands, such as document.write, are understood by screen readers. In most cases, however, screen readers and other assistive technology is still trying to develop sufficiently to handle scripts that alter screen information. In the meantime, developers can restrict scripts to those that are known to be compatible with existing assistive technology, or can include <NOSCRIPT> tags.

Scripts that don't work with assistive technology (e.g. scripts that only work with a mouse) should be avoided.

To see how a page looks and performs with scripting turned off, JavaScript can be turned off in Explorer by choosing:

Tools / Internet Options / 'Security' tab / 'Internet' icon/ 'Custom Level' button

Scroll down to the scripting section and set the radio button to Disable Active Scripting.

Style sheets

Documents should have two properties – content and presentation. The content is produced by HTML statements and the layout and presentation are controlled by CSS (Cascading Style Sheets).

It is vital, from an accessibility point of view, that pages are constructed in a way that allows them to be read and understood – even with CSS turned off. Some readers/browsers do not recognise style sheets and the presentation information contained in them is ignored.

The roles of HTML and CSS in accessibility are:
- Use HTML for structural elements such as heading and lists. Assistive technology needs these structural elements to help navigate the content. Using CSS achieves the same visual appearance but is not processed by screen readers.
- Use the HTML <STRONG> and <EM> tags to emphasis words. These can be processed by screen readers, while CSS equivalents are ignored.
- Use style sheets for layout. The layout commands are ignored by readers and browsers that are not capable of handling CSS.
- Use style sheets for colour, indentation and other formatting.
- Use style sheets for controlling font styles and sizes, instead of the old HTML <FONT> tag.
- Use style sheets to indent text, instead of the HTML <BLOCKQUOTE> or <LIST> tags.
- Allow style sheets to be replaced by user's style sheets. Users with low vision, often wish to use their own style sheet (e.g. large font sizes, yellow text on a black background)

Flash

Web pages that are coded in HTML allow screen readers to look at the code lines in a sequential fashion.

Flash, on the other hand, often operates in a parallel fashion, with different elements being operable at the same time (e.g. an animation playing, accepting user input to a form, validating input). Flash files often have animated content and the screen text is embedded in the file and may not be readily available for external processing by assistive devices. These features cause severe accessibility problems and, if a web site is entirely Flash based, it could be totally inaccessible.

Fortunately, both Macromedia and the developers of assistive technologies are actively pursuing how to access Flash content in a meaningful way.

Flash Player 6 onwards makes text content, input text fields and text in buttons available to screen readers.

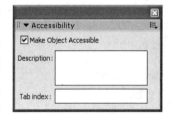

Flash MX allows these objects to have a written description added to them using the 'name' property and these descriptions are available to screen readers. Static text is available to screen readers by default, although it can be converted to an 'instance' (like the input text fields and text in buttons) to allow further accessibility options to be applied to it. Developers can also declare that objects are not presented to screen readers, to prevent confusing the readers (see the illustration).

Of course, the text content is not the only content of a Flash file and the remainder of the content needs to be described to users with low or no vision.
- Use meaningful descriptions for the 'names' of buttons and input text fields (the name of a block of static text is automatically assigned the actual text content of the block).
- Provide textual alternatives. Flash MX provides an ActionScript method called 'Accessibility.isActive()'. This checks to see if an assistive device is in use and returns true (if installed) or false (if not installed). If the check returns a false value, the script can call up a standard HTML file with equivalent material.
- Provide full textual equivalents for all graphical information.
- Any navigation options within Flash should be available to those without Flash players or readers that can't understand Flash files. A very common problem is web sites that use Flash as a full-screen opening page. Although they provide a 'skip intro' link, that link is within Flash and therefore not available to users who can't read Flash content. Ideally, the Flash content should be inset to a standard HTML page that has conventional text links that take users into the main site.
- Ensure that all navigation, selection and activation options can also be implemented using the keyboard.

Tools and testing

Many of the general tests and usability tests apply to accessibility and these should be tested first. However, even projects that have been previously tested and brought into use may not have been tested for accessibility. Indeed, many sites need to be retrofitted with accessibility features.

Some accessibility tests are simple.

Firstly, turn off displaying graphics.

The steps for Internet Explorer are:
- From the 'Tools' menu, select 'Internet Options', followed by clicking the 'Advanced' tab.
- In the 'Accessibility' options, check the 'Always expand alt text for images' box.
- In the 'Multimedia' options check the 'Show image download placeholders' and uncheck the 'Show pictures' box.

If web pages are now viewed, the graphics are not displayed and the ALT text appears in the placeholder instead. This lets developers see whether the page content is still understandable.

Other checks include:

- Turn off sounds – is any information or meaning lost?
- Turn off style sheets – is any information or meaning lost ?
- Turn off scripts – is any information or meaning lost?
- Ignore the mouse. Can the pages still be used with only keyboard operations? Can the Tab key move focus from link to link?
- Change the fonts and colours – are pages still readable?
- Resize the browser window – are pages still readable?
- View the pages in greyscale or black and white – is any information or meaning lost? Is it possible to detect which links are visited and which are unvisited?
- Do labels have meaningful descriptions?
- Are ALT descriptions meaningful?

Tools for testing

Lynx

This is a text-only browser that is commonly used by those with low vision. It is a free (public domain) application that can be downloaded from http://lynx.browser.org/

The application can be installed and used to test web sites, seeing pages exactly as seen by low vision users. Page content is displayed a line at a time, with all the text in tables being linearised. Graphics are ignored and replaced by the ALT text descriptions.

To test a single page, a Lynx simulator can be found at www.delorie.com/web/lynxview.html   This is a free service, accepting a URL and returning a Lynx view of that page.

IBM Home Page Reader

A free 30-day trial of this screen reader can be found at www.ibm.com/able/hpr.html This allows developers to listen to how pages sound in this talking browser.

Vischeck

This free online tool simulates viewing a web page through the eyes of a colour-blind user. It can be found at www.vischeck.com.

Bobby

This program checks web pages for accessibility compliance. Securing a *'Bobby Approved'* icon demonstrates that the site meets all accessibility criteria that can be tested by an automatic tester (since it can't check for issues such as colour contrasts, appropriate use of labels, etc.).

The program is available online, at www.cast.org/bobby where it will test single pages (with a limit of 1 page per minute). It can also be purchased and installed for offline use, to check multiple pages and entire sites.

It offers some user selection and returns a report that includes recommendations.

LIFT

This program, mentioned already for usability testing, also carries out accessibility validation, reporting any deficiencies and making suggestions for cures.

Final thoughts on testing

If projects are subject to such prolonged testing, why are they still distributed containing errors?

The project undergoes concurrent testing, unit testing, integration testing, usability testing and acceptance testing, yet errors still manage to pass through the testing procedures. A certain amount is inevitable, while other factors are predictable. Developers are often pressurised to produce quantity and quality can suffer as a result. Early release dates leave little room for adequate testing. There may also be intense pressure to release a product before the competition complete theirs. The only way to ensure the best quality product is to factor sufficient testing resources into the project budget.

> *"The totality of features and characteristics of a software product that bear on its ability to satisfy stated or implied needs"*
>
> The ISO 9126 definition of quality for software products.

User instructions

Once the project has been thoroughly tested,

The candidate should produce user instructions and technical advice on how to run the application. This could be done by, for example, on paper documentation or on an insert in a jewel case for a CD or DVD, or a help file on computer or on the Web.

Index

Also available from the same author

The Computing Reference for Students

The PC Support Handbook is one of the UK's most popular computing textbooks for students training in computing, IT and PC Support.

It is handy book size (245mm x 190mm) and contains 776 pages of explanations, tables and diagrams.

The twenty-one chapters cover:

- Computer Basics
- Numbering Systems
- Memory
- System Selection
- Configuring Windows
- Computer Security
- The Internet

- Software and Data
- Computer Architecture
- Discs & Drives
- Hardware Installation
- PC Support
- Data Communications
- Web Site Creation

- Operating Systems
- Display Technology
- Computer Peripherals
- PC Configuration
- Fault Finding
- Local Area Networks
- Multimedia

The book costs £29 per copy. Where five or more copies are purchased, the price is reduced to £20 per copy. There is no extra charge for post and packing.

Dumbreck Publishing
8A Woodland Avenue, Kirkintilloch, Glasgow, G66 1AS
Tel/Fax: 0141-775-2889
E-mail: sales@dumbreck.demon.co.uk

Check out our web site
www.pchandbooks.com

Glossary

Software links

Faultfinding System

How to contact us

Useful links

Get familiar with computing terms. Quickly look up the meaning of acronyms (from AGP to ZIF)

Reviews of the software packages that help you get the best out of our books. All programs are freeware or shareware.

An expert system that guides you through the steps to identify your computer problem.

All comments and suggestions are welcomed. Or fill in our short user survey.

Links to other web sites with related content. These sites contain technical information, tutorials, etc.